CORPUS DICTIONARY

OF

WESTERN CHURCHES

CORPUS DICTIONARIES

In preparation:

Corpus Dictionary of Religion

Corpus Dictionary of Eastern Christianity

CORPUS DICTIONARY
OF
WESTERN CHURCHES

Edited by

T. C. O'Brien, Ph.D., S.T.D.

CORPUS PUBLICATIONS: Washington/Cleveland

CORPUS INSTRUMENTORUM

EDITORIAL OFFICES
1330 Massachusetts Avenue, N.W., Washington, D.C. 20005

SALES & DISTRIBUTION
2231 West 110th Street, Cleveland, Ohio 44102

Copyright © 1970 by Corpus Instrumentorum, Inc.

Library of Congress Catalog Card Number: 78–99501
FIRST PRINTING 1970
Printed in the United States of America

To Sir Oliver and Lady Crosthwaite-Eyre.

Amicis fidis in fidei pignus.

PREFACE

The *Corpus Dictionary of Western Churches* is a reference volume on the Churches that have developed throughout the history of Western Christianity. Special attention is given to North American Churches in the Western tradition that are of either historical or contemporary significance, particularly those reported in the National Council of Churches' *Yearbook of American Churches* (1969). The *Dictionary* designates these religious bodies as Churches in the common, descriptive sense that they are bodies of Christians with distinctive beliefs, practices, and some form of organization. The description is without prejudice to specific ecclesiological viewpoints, whereby, for example, one Church regards itself exclusively as the true Church; another, as a branch of the one comprehensive Church; another, as an imperfect reflection of the true, invisible Church. Christians do not agree on the nature of the Church; all, however, observe that the church life characteristic of Christianity manifests diversity. The *Dictionary* is designed to provide information on that diversity.

Concise information on the Churches as part of the historical and cultural pattern of the Western world is itself useful. Such information, however, also serves a specifically Christian purpose: the ideal "That all may be one." Discord among Christians, whose convictions clash and whose paths diverge, is a painful stumbling block to the ideal of Christian unity (See Vat II Ecum, Introduction). But Christians who long for the realization of the ideal seek to talk and to listen to one another with mutual respect based on a true recognition and awareness of one another's traditions and beliefs. The majority of contributors to this *Dictionary* belong to the Churches and traditions about which they write. The Christian reader is offered an understanding of Churches other than his own and of his own in relation to others. The volume represents and seeks to further the *civilis conversatio* among Christians. To Roman Catholic readers the volume also offers a way to fulfill the ecumenical recommendations of Vatican Council II: "We must come to understand the outlook of our separated brethren. Study is absolutely required for this, and should be pursued with fidelity to truth and in a spirit of good will" (Vat II Ecum 9).

The Churches form the core of this work, and all other entries have been included as subsidiary to the aim of presenting the history and life of the Churches and their relationships to one another. Subsidiary material includes founding or formative events in church history; confessional documents; terms of doctrine, worship, polity, and practice; theological themes as they divide or unite the Churches; and personalities. The approximately 2,300 entries have been chosen to highlight the unity and diversity that mark the specifically ecclesial or institutional aspect of church life. The coverage of all the Churches, including the Roman Catholic, has been shaped to this context. Biographies have been selected on the same basis. The aim has been conciseness: clear, generally brief articles for ready reference. Bibliographies have been provided wherever possible; titles indicated refer the reader to fuller treatment of the subject and to more detailed bibliographies. The desire to provide a work of ready reference has dictated the compressed dictionary format. Entries are arranged alphabetically in word-by-word order. Inversions have been kept to a minimum; where they have been included, for example, in the titles of the various confessions of faith, there is also a cross reference under the uninverted form.

The Churches are given under their official titles, and generally in uninverted form. Internal cross references have served the objective of conciseness in dealing with any entry, while at the same time indicating to the reader supplementary material. Internal cross references are indicated in three ways: first, by the asterisk (*) preceding a term or name occurring naturally in the flow of the text; second, by the use of small capitals in parentheses inserted in the text after a word or sentence to which the cross-referenced term especially applies; and, third, by the use of an asterisk and small capitals at the end of an entry, when the cross-referenced term is allied to the whole entry. Finally, available statistics have been included simply to suggest the size or influence of the various Churches.

As editor responsible for the volume, I wish to express my thanks to the many collaborators who enabled me to complete the task. In keeping with editorial policy, articles are unsigned. But I wish to acknowledge what a great privilege it has been to receive from the contributors work of such high quality, and what a delight it has been to experience the willingness and friendly cooperation of these Christian colleagues. The assistance of Dr. Tracy Early, Father Thomas Gilby, Professor Norman Maring, Dr. Frederick Maser, Dr. Jaroslav Pelikan, and Professor John Woolverton has been extraordinary. I wish also to express my warmest appreciation to the staff of Corpus Instrumentorum, Inc. The whole manuscript of the *Dictionary* has been read with eminent care and unfailingly helpful criticism by Paul K. Meagher, O.P., editor-in-chief of the Corpus religious dictionary program. In the early days of preparation Dr. Josephine Riss Fang, and in the final crucial stages, Sister M. Claudia, I.H.M., assisted by Mrs. Sue Santiago and Miss Brenda Chavious, have borne the considerable burden of checking title forms, verifying cross references, and bibliographical material. The styling and copy editing of Mrs. Mary N. Eldridge have contributed incalculably to the quality of the work. The secretarial tasks involved, and especially final typing of the manuscript, have been carried out by a cooperative and able staff. In addition to the actual contributors the work owes its completion to the information and recommendations so generously given by historians, archivists, general secretaries of the various Churches, and by the deans of seminaries and colleges.

THOMAS C. O'BRIEN

Feast of Pentecost
May 25, 1969

LIST OF CONTRIBUTORS

AHERNE, Sister Consuelo Maria, S.S.J., Ph.D., Professor of History, Chestnut Hill College, Philadelphia, Pa.

ALLISON, The Rev. C. FitzSimons, Ph.D., Professor of Church History, Protestant Episcopal Seminary in Virginia, Alexandria, Va.

BARRETT, The Rev. David B., Ph.D., Secretary of Research, Unit of Research, Church of the Province of East Africa, Nairobi, Kenya.

BAYNE, The Rt. Rev. Stephen F., Jr., S.T.M., First Vice President, Executive Council of the Episcopal Church, New York, N.Y.

BEAUREGARD. Erving Edward, M.A., Associate Professor of History, University of Dayton, Dayton, Ohio.

BOCK, Paul, S.T.M., Ph.D., Associate Professor of Religion, Heidelberg College, Tiffin, Ohio.

CALDER, The Rev. Ralph F. G., Overseas Appointment Bureau, Christian Education Movement, London, England.

CARTHY, Margaret, Ph.D., Assistant Director, General Education Program, University of Maryland, College Park, Md.

CEROKE, The Rev. Christian P., O.Carm., S.T.D., Professor of Scripture, Catholic University of America, Washington, D.C.

CHANDLER, The Rev. Douglas, D.D., Professor of Church History, Wesley Theological Seminary, Washington, D.C.

CLARK, The Rev. Bayard Stockton, B.D., Special Assistant to Head of Adult Education Programming, Dept. of Health, Education and Welfare, Washington, D.C.

CODDINGTON, Mrs. Dorothy, New York, N.Y.

COLBERT, Edward P., Ph.D., Department of History, East Illinois University, Charleston, Ill.

CORBISHLEY, The Rev. Thomas, S.J., M.A., Superior of Farm Street Church, London, England.

CORE, The Rev. Arthur, B.D., Ph.D., Professor of Church History, United Theological Seminary, Dayton, Ohio.

COSTELLOE, The Rev. Martin Joseph, S.J., Ph.D., Professor of Classical Languages and Chairman of the Department, Creighton University, Omaha, Neb.

DAMBORIENA, The Rev. Prudencio, S.J., Ph.D., Professor of Church History, St. Louis University, St. Louis, Mo.

DELETTER, The Rev. Prudent, S.J., Ph.D., S.T.D., Professor of Dogmatic Theology, St. Mary's College, Kurseong, India.

DENNIS, The Rev. George T., S.J., Sc.Eccl.Or.D., Associate Professor of History, Loyola University of Los Angeles, Cal.

DONLON, The Rev. Stephen Edward, S.J., M.A., S.T.D., Loyola University, Chicago, Ill.

DURBIN, Paul T., Ph.D., Professor of Philosophy, University of Delaware, Newark, Del.

EARLY, Tracy, Ph.D., Office of Information and Public Relations, World Council of Churches, New York, N.Y.

EENIGENBURG, The Rev. Elton M., Ph.D., Department of Christian Ethics and Philosophy of Religion, Western Theological Seminary, Holland, Mich.

ENO, The Rev. Robert B., S.S., S.T.L., Professor of Patrology, St. Mary's Seminary, Baltimore, Md.

FANG, Josephine Riss, Ph.D., Acquisitions Librarian, Boston College Libraries, Chestnut Hill, Mass.

FLOOD, The Rev. James J., S.T.D., Professor of Sacramental Theology, St. Charles Borromeo Seminary, Philadelphia, Pa.

GALLIN, Sister Mary Alice, O.S.U., Ph.D., Professor of History and Chairman of the Department, College of New Rochelle, New Rochelle, N.Y.

GARCIA, The Rev. Manuel, O.P., S.T.D., Professor of Fundamental Theology, Pontifical University of St. Thomas Aquinas, Rome, Italy.

GARDNER, The Rev. Marvin A., Jr., B.A., B.C., Church of the Ascension, Mt. Vernon, N.Y.

GILBY, Very Rev. Thomas, O.P., S.T.M., General Editor, New English translation of the *Summa Theologiae,* Blackfriars, Cambridge, England.

GODBEY, John C., B.D.. Ph.D., Assistant Professor of Church History, Meadville Theological Seminary, Chicago, Ill.

GRAHAM, The Rev. Holt H., T.D., Professor of New Testament, Protestant Episcopal Theological Seminary in Virginia, Alexandria, Va.

HAYDEN, Michael J., Ph.D., Professor of History, University of Saskatchewan, Saskatoon, Sask., Canada.

HEANEY, The Rev. John J., S.J., S.T.D., Professor of Theology, Fordham University, Bronx, N.Y.

HINNEBUSCH, The Rev. William A., O.P., Ph.D., Professor of Church History. Pontifical Faculty of Theology, College of the Immaculate Conception, Washington, D.C.

HOFFMAN, The Rev. John C., Ph.D., S.T.D., Professor of Theology, University of Windsor, Windsor, Ont., Canada.

HOLBROOK, The Rev. Clyde A., B.D., Ph.D., Chairman, Department of Religion, Oberlin College, Oberlin, Ohio.

HUGHES, The Rev. John Jay, Ph.D., Münster, Germany.

JELLY, The Rev. Michael, O.P., S.T.L., Dominican House of Studies, Washington, D.C.

JOHNSON, Edgar B., General Secretary, Church of the Nazarene International Headquarters, Kansas City, Mo.

KAVANAUGH, The Rev. Kieran, O.C.D., S.T.L., Professor of Spiritual Theology, Our Lady of Mt. Carmel College, Washington, D.C.

KOLLAR, The Rev. Nathan, O.Carm., S.T.D., Professor of Liturgy, Whitefriars Hall, Washington. D.C.

KRAHN, The Rev. Cornelius, M.A., Th.D., Mennonite Historical Library, Bethel College, North Newton, Kans.

LATIMER, The Rev. Canon Ralph R., General Secretary, Anglican Church of Canada, Toronto, Ont., Canada.

LYNCH, Cyprian J., O.F.M., M.A., Professor of History, St. Bernardine of Siena College, Loudonville, N.Y.

MCFADDEN, Thomas, Ph.D., Professor of Theology, Loyola College, Baltimore, Md.

MACKENZIE, The Rev. John Anderson Ross, Ph.D., Professor of Church History, Union Theological Seminary, Richmond, Va.

MACMASTER, Richard K., Ph.D., Assistant Professor, Western Carolina University, Cullowhee, N.C.

MACOSKEY, Robert A., B.D., Ph.D., Professor of Christian History, Crozer Theological Seminary, Chester, Pa.

MCSHANE, The Rev. Edward Daniel, S.J., S.T.L., Hist.Eccl.D., Professor of Church History, Alma College, Los Gatos, Cal.

MAHONEY, The Rev. William B., O.P., Ph.D., Aquinas Institute of Philosophy and Theology, River Forest, Ill.

MALONE, The Rev. Edward Francis, M.M., S.T.D., Professor of Dogmatic Theology and Dean, Maryknoll Seminary, Maryknoll, N.Y.

MANROSS, The Rev. William W., S.T.D,. Ph.D.. Professor of Church History and Librarian, Philadelphia Divinity School, Philadelphia, Pa.

MANTEUFEL, Thomas, Ph.D., Concordia Historical Institute, St. Louis, Mo.

MARAS, Raymond J., Ph.D., Associate Professor, Modern European History, University of Dayton, Dayton, Ohio.

MARING, The Rev. Norman H., Th.B., Ph.D., Professor of Church History, Eastern Baptist Theological Seminary, Philadelphia, Pa.

MARTHALER, The Rev. Berard L., O.F.M.C., M.A., S.T.D., Chairman, Department of Religious Education, Catholic University of America, Washington, D.C.

MASER, The Rev. Frederick E., D.D., LL.D., Director of Public Relations, Philadelphia Conference, United Methodist Church, Philadelphia, Pa.

MATZERATH, The Rev. Roger, S.A., S.T.D., Director, Graymoor Ecumenical Institute, Garrison, N.Y.

MITCHELL, Mr. Glenford E., Secretary, National Spiritual Assembly of the Bahá'ís of the United States, Wilmette, Ill.

MORRISON, John L., Ph.D., Chairman and Professor of the Department of History, Mount Saint Mary's College, Emmitsburg, Md.

MOST, The Rev. William George, Ph.D., Professor of Latin and Greek, Loras College, Dubuque, Ia.

MUELLER, Brother William, F.S.C., M.A., Instructor in Theology, De La Salle College, Washington, D.C.

MÜLLER, The Rev. Liguori, O.F.M., Ph.D., Siena College, Loudonville, N.Y.

NELSON, The Rev. John Oliver, Ph.D., Director, Kirkridge, Bangor, Pa.

NUGENT, Donald G., Ph.D., Professor, Department of History, University of Kentucky, Lexington, Ky.

O'CONNOR, Lady Patrick, M.A., London, England.

OLIN, John C., Ph.D., Associate Professor, Department of Modern European History, Fordham University, Bronx, N.Y.

O'NEILL, The Rev. Colman E., O.P., Ph.D., S.T.M., Universitäts Professor, Fribourg, Switzerland.

OSBORN, The Rev. Ronald E., B.D., Ph.D., Dean, Christian Theological Seminary, Indianapolis, Ind., Past General Minister and President, Christian Churches (Disciples of Christ) International Convention.

PALMER, The Rev. Paul F., S.J., S.T.D., Professor of Theology, Fordham University, Bronx, N.Y.

PARKER, Dorothy Mills, Washington correspondent, *The Living Church*, Washington, D.C.

PENN, Donald R., Ph.D., Professor of History and Chairman of the Department, Georgetown University, Washington, D.C.

PELIKAN, The Rev. Jaroslav, Ph.D., Titus Street Professor of Ecclesiastical History, Yale University, New Haven, Conn.

PETTIT, The Rev. Walton S., B.D., Richmond, Va.

PRESTON, Robert M., Ph.D., Professor, Dept. of History, Mount Saint Mary's College, Emmitsburg, Md.

REID, The Rev. John Patrick, O.P., S.T.L., M.A., Professor of Philosophy, Providence College, Providence, R.I.

RIGHTOR, The Rev. Henry H., LL.B., D.D., Associate Professor, Pastoral Theology, Protestant Episcopal Theological Seminary in Virginia, Alexandria, Va.

RODGERS, The Rev. John H., Jr., Th.D., Associate Professor of Systematic Theology, Protestant Episcopal Theological Seminary in Virginia, Alexandria, Va.

RONK, Albert T., D.D., Professor of History, Ashland Theological Seminary, Archivist and Historian, Brethren in Christ, Ashland College, Ashland, Ohio.

RUSSELL, The Rev. Robert Philip, O.S.A., Ph.D., Chairman, Department of Philosophy, Villanova University, Villanova, Pa.

SCHEPERS, The Rev. Maurice Bonaventure, O.P., S.T.D., Professor of Theology, La Salle College, Philadelphia, Pa.

SHEERIN, The Rev. Francis L., S.J., M.A,, S.T.D., Professor of Dogmatic Theology and Patrology, Alma College, Los Gatos, Cal.

SHEPHERD, The Rev. Massey Hamilton, Jr., Ph.D., S.T.D., D.D., Professor of Liturgics, Church Divinity School of the Pacific, Berkeley, Cal.

SHORT, Howard E., Ph.D., Editor, *The Christian*, St. Louis, Mo.

SKARDON, Alvin Wilson, Jr., Ph.D., Assistant Professor of History, Youngstown University, Youngstown, Ohio.

SMYLIE, The Rev. James H., Th.D., Professor of American Church History, Union Theological Seminary, Richmond, Va.

STANKIEWICZ, Wladyslaw J., Ph.D., Professor, Department of Political Science, University of British Columbia, Vancouver, B.C., Canada.

STEIN, The Rev. James K., Ph.D., Th.D., Associate Professor of Church History, Evangelical Theological Seminary, Naperville, Ill.

STEVENSON, The Rev. Dwight E., D.D., Professor of Homiletics, Lexington Theological Seminary, Lexington, Ky.

SUELFLOW, The Rev. August R., Ph.D., S.T.M., D.D., Director, Department of Archives and History, Concordia Historical Institute, St. Louis, Mo.

SUELZER, Mary Josephine, S.P., Ph.D., former Academic Dean, St.-Mary-of-the-Woods College, Ind.

TOLLES, Frederick B., Ph.D., Litt.D., Director, Friends Historical Library of Swarthmore College, Swarthmore, Pa.

TYLENDA, The Rev. Joseph, S.J., S.T.D., Professor of Theology, Woodstock College, Woodstock, Md.

VOLL, The Rev. Urban, O.P., S.T.D., S.T.M., Professor of Moral Theology, Pontifical Faculty of the Immaculate Conception, Washington, D.C.

WEINLICK, The Rev. John R., B.D., Ph.D., Dean, Moravian Theological Seminary, Bethlehem, Pa.

WEIS, The Rev. Earl A., S.J., Editor, *Catholic Theological Encyclopedia*, Corpus Instrumentorum, Washington, D.C.

WHALEN, The Rev. John P., S.T.D., Managing Editor, Corpus Instrumentorum, Washington, D.C.

WHALEN, William Joseph, M.S., University Editor and Assistant Professor of English, Purdue University, West Lafayette, Ind.

WILLKE, Jean, Ph.D., Associate Professor of History, Trinity College, Washington, D.C.

WOOLVERTON, The Rev. John F., B.D., Ph.D., Professor of Church History, Virginia Theological Seminary, Alexandria, Va.

WRATHER, Miss Eva Jean, B.A., Disciples of Christ Historical Society, Nashville, Tenn.

ZEENDER, John K., Ph.D., Professor of History, Catholic University of America, Washington, D.C.

LIST OF ABBREVIATIONS

COMMON ABBREVIATIONS

abp.	archbishop	*ibid.*	*ibidem*, in the same place
A.D.	*Anno Domini*	*idem*	the same
A.M.	*Artium magister*, Master of Arts; usually M.A.	i.e.	*id est*, that is
		introd.	introduction
Ap	Apocalypse or Rev (Revelation)	isl., isls.	island; islands
art.; arts.	article; articles	It.	Italy; Italian (in giving It. form of a word)
ARV	American Standard Revised Version		
AV	Authorized Version (King James)	JB	Jerusalem Bible
b.	born	J.C.D.	*Juris Canonici Doctor*, Doctor of Canon Law
B.A.	Bachelor of Arts		
B.C.	Before Christ	Jr.	junior
BCP	*Book of Common Prayer*	Lat.	Latin (in giving Lat. form of a word)
B.D.	Bachelor of Divinity	lib.	*liber*, book
bibliog.	bibliography; bibliographer; biblio-graphical	LL	Late Latin
		loc. cit.	*loco citato*, in the place cited
bk., bks.	book; books	LXX	Septuagint Version
Bl.	Blessed	M.A.	Master of Arts
bp., bps.	bishop; bishops	ME	Middle English
B.S.	Bachelor of Science	MHG	Middle High German
c.	*circa*; *circum*, about (e.g., *c.*750.)	Mme.	Madame
c.; cc.	canon; canons	Msgr.	Monsignor
card.	cardinal	MS; MSS	manuscript; manuscripts
CCD	Confraternity of Christian Doctrine Version	N	North; northern
		n.; nn.	note; notes
cent.	century; centuries	N.A.	North America
cf.	confer; compare	n.d.	no date of publication
ch.	chapter; chapters	NE	northeast
C of E	Church of England	NT	New Testament
col., cols.	column; columns	NW	northwest
d.	died	OE	Old English
D.D.	Doctor of Divinity	OHG	Old High German
DV	Douay-Challoner Version	Ont.	Ontario
E	East; eastern	*op. cit.*	*opere citato*, in the work cited
ed., eds.	editor; editors; edition; editions; editorial; edited by	OT	Old Testament
		p.; pp.	page; pages
e.g.	*exempli gratia*, for example	pa.	paper; paperback
Eng.	England; English (in giving Eng. form of a word)	par.; pars.	paragraph; paragraphs
		passim	throughout the work; here and there
ep., epp.	*epistola*; *epistolae*, letter; letters	Ph.D.	Doctor of Philosophy
esp.	especially	pl.	plural
et al.	*et alii*, and others	pt., pts.	part; parts
etc.	*et cetera*, and so forth	q.v.	*quod vide*, which see
fasc.	fascicle	RC	Roman Catholic
ff.	following (pages)	repr.	reprint; reprinted
fl.	*floruit*, flourished; lived	rev.	revision; revised; revised by
fol.	folio	Rev.	Reverend
Fr.	France; French; Father (title)	RSV	Revised Standard Version
Ger.	Germany; German (in giving Ger. form of a word)	Rt. Rev.	Right Reverend
		RV	Revised Version
Gr.	Greece; Greek (in giving Gr. form of a word)	S	South; southern
		SE	southeast

sec.	section; sections	theol.	theology; theologian; theological (in citations)
sic	thus; so		
Sr.	Sister (title); senior	tr.	translation; translator; translated by
SS.	Saints		
S.S.L.	Licentiate in Sacred Scripture	univ.	university
St.	Saint	U.S.	United States
S.T.B.	Bachelor of Sacred Theology	v.	volume; volumes
S.T.D.	Doctor of Sacred Theology	*v.*	versus, against (in legal citations)
S.T.L.	Licentiate in Sacred Theology	Ven.	Venerable
S.T.M.	Master of Sacred Theology	vs.	versus, against
s.v.	*sub verbo*; *sub voce*, under the word or heading	Vulg	Vulgate
		W	West; western
SW	southwest	wks.	works

TITLES OF REFERENCE BOOKS

AAS   *Acta Apostolicae Sedis.* Rome 1909–

ACW   *Ancient Christian Writers: The Works of the Fathers in Translation,* ed. J. Quasten et al. Westminster, Md.-London 1946–

AFH   *Archivum Franciscanum historicum.* Quaracchi-Florence 1909–

AFP   *Archivum Fratrum Praedicatorum.* Rome 1931–

Altaner   B. Altaner, *Patrology,* tr. Hilda Graef from 5th German ed. New York 1960.

ASS   *Acta Sanctae Sedis.* Rome 1865–1908.

Bihlmeyer-Tüchle   K. Bihlmeyer and H. Tüchle, *Church History.* 3 v. Westminster, Md. 1958-66 v. 1 *Christian Antiquity,* tr. V. Mills, 1958; v. 2 *The Middle Ages,* tr. V. Mills and F. Muller, 1963; v. 3 *Modern and Recent Times,* tr. V. Mills and F. Muller, 1966.

Bréhier HistPhil   E. Bréhier, *History of Philosophy,* tr. J. Thomas and W. Baskin. 5 v. Chicago 1963–67.

Butler   A. Butler, *The Lives of the Saints,* rev. ed. H. Thurston and D. Attwater. 4 v. New York 1956.

Catholicisme   *Catholicisme. Hier, aujourd'hui et demain,* ed. G. Jacquemet. 7 v. Paris 1947–

CCL   *Corpus Christianorum.* Series latina. Turnhout, Belgium 1953–

CE   *The Catholic Encyclopedia,* ed. C. G. Herbermann et al. 16 v. New York 1907–14. Suppl. 1922.

CIC   *Codex iuris canonici.* Rome 1918. Reprint Graz 1955.

Copleston   F. C. Copleston, *History of Philosophy.* Westminster, Md. 1946– . v. 1 Greece & Rome, 1946, 2d ed. 1950; v. 2 Medieval Philosophy, Augustine to Scotus, 1950; v. 3 Ockham to Suárez, 1953; v. 4 Descartes to Leibniz, 1958; v. 5 Hobbes to Hume, 1959; v. 6 Wolff to Kant, 1960; v. 7 Fichte to Nietzsche, 1963; v. 8 Bentham to Russell, 1966.

CSEL   *Corpus scriptorum Christianorum orientalium.* Paris-Louvain 1903–

CTS   *Catholic Theological Society of America. Proceedings.* New York 1946–

D   H. Denzinger, *Enchiridion symbolorum,* ed. A. Schönmetzer. 32d ed. Freiburg 1963.

DACL   *Dictionnaire d'archéologie chrétienne et de liturgie,* ed. F. Cabrol and H. Leclercq. 15 v. Paris 1907–53.

Dansette   A. Dansette, *Religious History of Modern France,* tr. J. Dingle. 2 v. New York 1961.

DDC   *Dictionnaire de droit canonique,* ed. R. Naz. 7 v. Paris 1935–65.

DE   *Dizionario ecclesiastico,* ed. A. Mercati and A. Pelzer. 3 v. Turin 1954–58.

De Vaux AncIsr   R. de Vaux, *Ancient Israel, Its Life and Institutions,* tr. J. McHugh. New York 1961.

DHGE   *Dictionnaire d'histoire et de géographie ecclésiastiques,* ed. A. Baudrillart et al. Paris 1912–

DictEngCath J. Gillow, *A Literary and Biographical History or Bibliographical Dictionary of the English Catholics from 1534 to the Present Time.* 5 v. London-New York 1885–1902. Reprint N.Y. 1961.

DictLetFranç G. Grente et al., *Dictionnaire des lettres françaises.* v. 1 Le XVIIᵉ siècle; v. 2 Le XVIIIᵉ siècle. Paris 1954–60.

DNB, DNBSuppl. *The Dictionary of National Biography from the Earliest Times to 1900.* 63 v. London 1885–1900; reprinted, with corrections, in 21 v. 1908–09, 1921–22, 1938; suppl. 1901–

DNBConc *The Concise Dictionary of National Biography.* 2 v. Oxford 1961. v. 1, From the Beginnings to 1900; v. 2, 1901–1950.

DSAM *Dictionnaire de spiritualité ascétique et mystique. Doctrine et histoire,* ed. M. Viller et al. Paris 1932–

DTC *Dictionnaire de théologie catholique,* ed. A. Vacant et al. 15 v. Paris 1903–50. Tables générales 1951–

EC *Enciclopedia cattolica,* ed. P. Paschini et al. 12 v. Rome 1949–54.

ECQ *The Eastern Churches Quarterly.* Ramsgate 1936–

EDB *Encyclopedic Dictionary of the Bible,* tr. and adap. L. Hartman from A. Van den Born's *Bijbels Woordenboek.* New York 1963.

EncLuthCh *The Encyclopedia of the Lutheran Church,* ed. J. Bodensieck. 3 v. Minneapolis 1965.

EncModChrMiss *Encyclopedia of Modern Christian Missions,* ed. B. L. Goddard. Camden, N.J. 1967.

EncPhil *The Encyclopedia of Philosophy.* 8 v. New York 1966.

EncRelKnow *The New Schaff-Herzog Encyclopedia of Religious Knowledge,* ed. S. M. Jackson. 13 v. Grand Rapids, Mich. 1951–54.

EncRelKnowSuppl *Twentieth Century Encyclopedia of Religious Knowledge,* ed. L. A. Loetscher. 2 v. Grand Rapids, Mich. 1955.

EphemThLov *Ephemerides theologicae Lovanienses.* Bruges 1924–

FathCh *The Fathers of the Church: A New Translation,* ed. R. J. Deferrari et al. New York 1947–60; Washington, 1961–

Fliche-Martin A. Fliche and V. Martin, eds., *Histoire de l'église depuis les origines jusqu'à nos jours.* Paris 1935–

Gilson HCP E. H. Gilson, *History of Christian Philosophy in the Middle Ages.* New York 1955.

Gründler J. Gründler, *Lexikon der christlichen Kirchen und Sekten.* 2 v. Vienna 1961.

Hastings ERE J. Hastings, ed., *Encyclopedia of Religion and Ethics.* 13 v. Edinburgh 1908–27.

HistAmMeth *The History of American Methodism,* ed. E. S. Bucke et al. 3 v. New York 1964.

Hughes HC P. Hughes, *A History of the Church.* 3 v. New York 1947–49; v. 1–2 2d ed. 1949; v. 3 1947.

Hughes RE P. Hughes, *The Reformation in England.* 5th ed. 3 v. in 1. New York 1963.

Jedin-Baus K. Baus, *From the Apostolic Community to Constantine,* with a "General Introduction to Church History" by H. Jedin, tr. from 3d rev. Ger. ed. New York 1965. (v. 1 of *Handbook of Church History,* ed. H. Jedin and J. Dolan).

Jedin Trent H. Jedin, *History of the Council of Trent,* tr. E. Graf. v. 1–2 St. Louis 1957–60. *Geschichte des Konzils von Trient.* 2 v. Freiburg 1949–57; v. 1, 2d ed. 1951.

Kittel TD G. Kittel, *Theological Dictionary of the New Testament.* 8 v. planned. Grand Rapids, Mich. 1964–

LACT *Library of Anglo-Catholic Theology.* 97 v. Oxford 1841–63.

Latourette CRA K. S. Latourette, *Christianity in a Revolutionary Age: A History of Christianity in the Nineteenth and Twentieth Centuries.* 5 v. New York 1958–62.

Léonard HistProt É. Léonard, *History of Protestantism,* ed. H. H. Rowley, tr. M. H. Reid, v. 1 1968.

LibCC *Library of Christian Classics.* Philadelphia 1953–

LTK   *Lexikon für Theologie und Kirche,*
ed M. Buchberger. 10 v. and Ergänzung-
band. Freiburg. New ed. by J. Hofer and
K. Rahner, 1957–66. Suppl. 1966, Vatican II.

LW   *Luther's Works,* ed. J. Pelikan and
W. Hansen. 57 v. planned. St. Louis-
Philadelphia 1957–

Mayer RB   Ed. F. E. Mayer, *The Religious
Bodies of America.* 4th ed. rev. A. C.
Piepkorn. St. Louis 1961.

MedRenSt   *Medieval and Renaissance Studies.* London 1949–

MennEnc   *The Mennonite Encyclopedia.* 4
v. Hillsboro, Kans.-Scottdale, Pa. 1955–
59.

MGH   *Monumenta Germaniae Historicae.*
Berlin 1826–

NCE   *The New Catholic Encyclopedia.* 15
v. New York 1967.

OED   *The Oxford English Dictionary,* ed.
J. A. H. Murray et al. 13 v. New York
1933.

Olmstead   C. E. Olmstead, *History of Religion in the United States.* Englewood
Cliffs, N.J. 1960.

Pastor   L. Pastor, *The History of the Popes
from the Close of the Middle Ages.* 40 v.
London-St. Louis 1938–61.

PG   *Patrologia Graeca,* ed. J. P. Migne. 161
v. Paris 1857–66.

PL   *Patrologia Latina,* ed. J. P. Migne. 217
v., indexes 4 v. Paris 1878–90.

Quasten   J. Quasten, *Patrology.* 3 v. Westminster, Md. 1950–61.

RechTAM   *Recherches de théologie an-
cienne et médiévale.* Louvain 1929–

RGG   *Die Religion in Geschichte und Gegenwart.* 3d ed. 6 v. Tübingen 1957–63;
Index 1965.

Schaff Creeds P. Schaff, *The Creeds of
Christendom.* 3 v. 6th ed. Reprint. Grand
Rapids 1966.

Smith-Jamison   J. W. Smith and A. L. Jami-
son, eds., *Religion in American Life.* 4 v.
Princeton, N.J. 1961–63. v. 4 is *A Critical
Bibliography of Religion in America,* by
N. R. Burr. 2 v. 1961.

SPCK   Society for Promoting Christian
Knowledge. Publications. London 1698–

SSL   *Spicilegium sacrum Lovaniense.* Louvain 1922–

ThAq ST (Eng-Lat)   Thomas Aquinas, *Summa theologiae,* ed. T. Gilby et al. 60
v. planned. New York 1965–. Bilingual:
Latin and English.

TL   *Theological Library,* ed. A. M. Henry,
tr. W. Storey et al. 6 v. Chicago 1954–58.
v. 1 Introd. to Theology, 1954; v. 2 God
and His Creation, 1955; v. 3 Man and
His Happiness, 1956; v. 4 Virtues and
the States of Life, 1956; v. 5 The Historical and Mystical Christ, 1958; v. 6
Christ and His Sacraments, 1958.

Vorgrimler Vat II   *Commentary on the
Documents of Vatican II,* ed. H. Vor-
grimler, tr. L. Adolphus, K. Smyth, R.
Strachan. 5 v. New York 1967–

WCH   *World Christian Handbook, 1968,*
H. Wakelin Coxhill, Sir Kenneth Grubb,
eds. Nashville-New York 1968.

BOOKS OF THE BIBLE

Acts	Acts of the Apostles	Dan	Daniel
Am	Amos	Dt	Deuteronomy
Ap	Apocalypse or Rev (Revelation)	Ec	Ecclesiastes
Bar	Baruch	Eph	Ephesians
1–2 Chr	1 and 2 Chronicles [1 and 2 Parali-	Est	Esther
	pomenon in LXX (Septuagint) and	Ex	Exodus
	Vulgate]	Ezek	Ezekiel
Col	Colossians	Ezra	Ezra (Esdras B in LXX; 1 Esdras in
1–2 Cor	1 and 2 Corinthians		Vulgate)

Gal	Galatians	Nah	Nahum
Gen	Genesis	Neh	Nehemiah (2 Esdras in LXX and Vulgate)
Hab	Habakkuk		
Hag	Haggai	Num	Numbers
Heb	Hebrews	Ob	Obadiah
Hos	Hosea	1–2 Pet	1 and 2 Peter
Is	Isaiah	Phil	Philippians
Jas	James	Philem	Philemon
Jdt	Judith	Pr	Proverbs
Jer	Jeremiah	Ps	Psalms
Jg	Judges	Rev	Revelation
Jl	Joel	Rom	Romans
Jn	John	Ru	Ruth
1–3 Jn	1, 2, and 3 John	1–2 Sam	1 and 2 Samuel (1–2 Kings in LXX and Vulgate)
Job	Job		
Jon	Jonah	Sir	Sirach (Ecclesiasticus in LXX and Vulgate)
Jos	Joshua		
Jude	Jude	S of S	Song of Solomon
1–2 Kg	1 and 2 Kings	1–2 Th	1 and 2 Thessalonians
Lam	Lamentations	1–2 Tim	1 and 2 Timothy
Lev	Leviticus	Tit	Titus
Lk	Luke	Tob	Tobia
1–2 Macc	1 and 2 Maccabees	Wis	Wisdom
Mal	Malachi	Zech	Zechariah
Mic	Micah	Zeph	Zephaniah
Mk	Mark		
Mt	Matthew		

DOCUMENTS OF VATICAN COUNCIL II

Vat II ApostLaity   Decree on the Apostolate of the Laity (*Apostolicam actuositatem*)

Vat II BpPastOff   Decree on the Bishops' Pastoral Office in the Church (*Christus Dominus*)

Vat II ChrEduc   Declaration of Christian Education (*Gravissimum educationis*)

Vat II ChModWorld   Pastoral Constitution on the Church in the Modern World (*Gaudium et spes*)

Vat II ConstCh   Dogmatic Constitution on the Church (*Lumen gentum*)

Vat II DivRev   Dogmatic Constitution on Divine Revelation (*Dei Verbum*)

Vat II EastCath   Decree on Eastern Catholic Churches (*Orientalium ecclesiarum*)

Vat II Ecum   Decree on Ecumenism (*Unitatis redintegratio*)

Vat II MinLifePriests   Decree on the Ministry and Life of Priests (*Presbyterorum ordinis*)

Vat II MissAct   Decree on the Church's Missionary Activity (*Ad gentes*)

Vat II NonChrRel   Declaration on the Relationship of the Church to Non-Christian Religions (*Nostra aetate*)

Vat II PriestForm   Decree on Priestly Formation (*Optatam totius*)

Vat II RelFreed   Declaration on Religious Freedom (*Dignitatis humanae*)

Vat II RenRelLife   Decree on the Appropriate Renewal of the Religious Life(*Perfectae caritatis*)

Vat II SacLit   Constitution on the Sacred Liturgy (*Sacrosanctum Concilium*)

Vat II SocComm   Decree on the Instruments of Social Communication (*Inter mirifica*)

CORPUS DICTIONARY

OF

WESTERN CHURCHES

A

ABBADIE, JACQUES (Abadie; c.1654–1727), French *Reformed apologist. A. was pastor of the Huguenot refugees in Berlin, 1680–88, then of the Savoy Church in London, 1690–99; he was dean of Killaloe, Ireland, 1699–1726. His most important apologetic treatise, *Traité de la vérité de la religion chrétienne* (3v., 1684–89; Eng. tr., 2v., 1694), was a defense of Christian teaching based on principles of reason and was popular in France. Other apologetic works were written to support Reformed against RC teaching, but in a temperate tone. He also wrote a moral treatise, *L'Art de se connaître soi-même* (1682; Eng. tr. and abridgement, 1694). See DHGE 1:19–22; DNB 1:1–3.

ABBOT, GEORGE (1562–1633), Abp. of Canterbury. After his academic career had led him to the vice-chancellorship of the Univ. of Oxford, A. won royal favor by his defense of hereditary monarchy (1606). His reputation was increased by his success in inducing Scotland to accept the idea of *episcopacy, which prepared the way for the union of the Scottish and English Churches. He was appointed bp. of Lichfield and Coventry (1609), was transferred later in the same year to London, and became abp. of Canterbury in 1611. From early life his convictions were markedly *Puritan and anti-Roman, and this put him in opposition to high churchmen generally (whose influence was growing while that of the Puritans was declining), and particularly to W. *Laud, whom he antagonized by an accusation of "popish" sympathies. He was among those chosen to prepare the Authorized Version of the Bible. See life by P. A. Welsby (1962); DNB 1 (1885), 5–20.

ABBOTT, LYMAN (1835–1922), Congregational preacher and editor. Before being ordained (1860), he had practiced law. He served as pastor in Terre Haute, Ind. (1860–

65), New York City (1865–69), and in Brooklyn, where he succeeded (1887) Henry Ward *Beecher as pastor of the Plymouth Church and won acclaim for his clear, practical sermons. With Beecher he edited the *Christian Union* (1876; named *Outlook* in 1893). His sermons and writings reflected and popularized 19th-cent. *liberal theology, with emphasis on social reform and adaptation of evolutionary theory to Christian ideas. His works included *Christianity and Social Problems* (1896), *The Evolution of Christianity* (1892), and *Theology of an Evolutionist* (1897). See J. V. Brown, *L. A.: Christian Evolutionist* (1953).

ABECEDENARIANS, a name that in its religious reference refers to a part of the Anabaptist movement in Wittenberg c.1522. The *Zwickau Prophets, particularly N. *Storch, proclaimed that the sole rule of faith is interior illumination by the Holy Spirit. The Bible is a dead letter; all human learning, esp. theology, is to be despised; the ABCs are the most learning that anyone should have. In keeping with these ideas, *Karlstadt renounced the doctorate, gave up teaching for a time, and became a manual laborer.

ABRAHAMITES (Bohemia), an 18th-cent. sect, also called Israelites. They were mostly peasants of Jewish and Protestant background in the vicinity of Pardubice near Prague. Their name came from their claim to be followers of the patriarch Abraham. While denying all Christian teachings, they made use of baptism and Christian wedding services to avoid legal reprisals. Their whole scripture was the Lord's Prayer and the Ten Commandments. When, after the Edict of 1780, they did not identify themselves as either Protestant or Catholic, the Emperor Joseph II expelled them and the sect soon scattered and disappeared. See E. Winter, *Der Jose-phinismus und seine Geschichte* (1943); A. Molnar, RGG 1:72–73.

ACCEPTANTS, members of the clergy in France and the Netherlands who, during the controversies over *Jansenism, accepted the bull *Unigenitus* (1713) of Clement XI. The bull was a condemnation of 101 propositions (D 2401–2501) from P. *Quesnel's *Nouveau testament avec des réflexions morales sur chaque verset.* Acceptance of the bull was imposed by Louis XIV on the Sorbonne and on parliament in 1714. A majority of the clergy accepted it, but were opposed by a strong minority. At the heart of the bitter controversy that ensued was the issue of the pope's personal infallibility; in accord with the second of the four *Gallican Articles, the minority appealed to a general council in 1717 (see APPELLANTS). During these conflicts the Schism of *Utrecht took place (1723). The Acceptants achieved a victory in 1730, when adherence to the bull *Unigenitus* was made obligatory by royal decree; still, resistance to the bull lingered for many decades. See bibliog. for Jansenism.

ACT OF SUPREMACY, in England the law enacted by Parliament in 1534 under *Henry VIII, renewed (it had been repealed by Mary Tudor) and revised in 1559 under Elizabeth I, constituting the reigning sovereign earthly head of the Church of England. The Elizabethan version declared the monarch to be the supreme governor, "as well in all spiritual or ecclesiastical things or causes as temporal." All ecclesiastical jurisdiction for the visitation, reformation, and correction of the ecclesiastical state and persons, and of all manner of errors, heresies, schisms, etc., was forever united and annexed to the crown. The Elizabethan act also renewed the 1534 Annates Statute of Henry, which had put all appointments of bishops in the royal hands (see CONGÉ D'É-LIRE). An oath acknowledging the royal supremacy and rejecting all foreign powers was imposed on all ecclesiastics, public offi-

cials, and candidates for holy orders and academic degrees. The effect of the act was to end communion with Rome and to make the C of E a *national Church. See Hughes RE 1:247–281; 2:21–35.

ACTS OF UNIFORMITY. Successive revisions of the Book of Common Prayer were accompanied by Acts of Uniformity requiring conformity to its prescribed rites. The first such Act was adopted in 1549, making the new Prayer Book mandatory in all religious services. Intended to replace the varied former uses with a single order of worship, it was prepared by *Cranmer and other bishops and theologians. Its distinctive features were the use of the vernacular, communion in both kinds, and transformation of the Mass into a Communion service. Severe penalties were prescribed for any priest refusing to use the Prayer Book, or for anyone ridiculing the new rites, with life imprisonment being imposed for a third conviction. The second Act of Uniformity was passed in 1552, accompanying the revised Prayer Book, which reflected Cranmer's changed views of the Eucharist. Expressing a Zwinglian interpretation of the Lord's Supper, it also omitted the requirement of wearing ecclesiastical vestments in services of worship. The provisions and penalties of the 1549 Act were declared to be still in force, and a section was added providing similar punishments for persons attending religious services in which any forms other than those of the Prayer Book were used. Since the Prayer Book and the Act of Uniformity were revoked during Mary's reign, a third Act of Uniformity was passed in 1559, at the accession of Elizabeth I. In accord with her desire for a *via media*, the Prayer Book was modified to make it more widely acceptable. References to the body and blood of Christ were added, the *Black Rubric denying the Real Presence was omitted, and wearing alb and cope was required. The early Stuarts enacted no new Acts of Uniformity during their reigns, but by special proclamations and rigorous enforcement, they tried to achieve religious uniformity. After the suspension of the Act of Uniformity during the Civil Wars and the Cromwellian era, Charles II was faced with the settlement of the religious problem. Presbyterians desired a comprehensive Church that would include them; Independents, Baptists, and Quakers wanted freedom of worship. Parliament settled the question by the Act of Uniformity of 1662, accompanied by a modified Book of Common Prayer. More elaborate than its predecessors, the new Act required the clergy publicly to declare their "unfeigned assent and consent" to use the Prayer Book. Teachers in the universities, as well as private tutors, were also to subscribe a similar declaration. The earlier Acts of Uniformity were stated to be still in effect. This Act resulted in ejection of about 2,000 clergy from their churches and in making *Dissenters of Presbyterians. Heavy penalties for nonconformity and strict enforcement of the Act failed to achieve religious uniformity, however, and in 1689 the *Toleration Act exempted Protestant Dissenters from its requirements. The Acts of Uniformity were important both to the establishment of the C of E as the national Church, and to the difficult progress toward religious toleration of Nonconformists. See H. Gee and W. H. Hardy, *Documents Illustrative of English Church History* (1921); R. S. Bosher, *Making of the Restoration Settlement* (1951); A. G. Dickens, *English Reformation* (1964). *BOOK OF COMMON PRAYER.

ADAMITES, a Christian sect of the 2d cent. mentioned by Epiphanius (PG 41:953) and Augustine (PL 42:31). Its members attended their religious assemblies in the nude. They may perhaps be identified with the Carpocratians described by Clement of Alexandria (PG 8:1112–13), a group that practiced sexual promiscuity and community of wives. Sects with similar beliefs and practices appeared in later times in The Netherlands, France, and Bohemia (see PICARDIANS). See G. Bareille, DTC 1:391–392; H. Grundmann, RGG 1:91–92.

ADIAPHORA (Gr., indifferent things), a term first used in Reformation times among Protestants to signify certain Catholic doctrines and practices that could, it was claimed, be admitted or rejected without prejudice to Protestant belief (see INTERIMS). In later Protestant controversy the term was used in reference to worldly pleasures (alleged to be neither good nor evil in themselves) in which a Christian could legitimately indulge. In both cases there were those who denied that the adiaphora were truly matters of indifference. *ADIAPHORISTS.

ADIAPHORISTS, Melanchthon's followers in the 16th-cent. controversy in Germany precipitated by a compromise attempted in the Augsburg *Interim (1548) as interpreted in Melanchthon's modification of it known as the Leipzig Interim (1548). According to Melanchthon a number of Catholic ceremonies and rites were "adiaphora," i.e., morally indifferent in themselves, and could be admitted without sacrifice of Protestant principles for the sake of peace. M. *Flacius Illyricus opposed this, declaring that such concessions would bring a return of "popery." The controversy was brought to an unsatisfactory close with Article 10 of the *Formula of Concord (1577), which stated that ordinarily anything not explicitly covered in the Scriptures was a matter for individual churches to decide, but that in times of persecution no such concessions should be made. The term was also applied to a party in a 17th-cent. controversy between Pietists (see PIETISM) and their adversaries. Anton Reiser (1628–86) declared the opera to be anti-Christian, and Pietists generally took the position that amusements and the arts were not compatible with the dignity of a Christian and ought to be condemned. Their opponents held that such things were indifferent in themselves. F. D. E. *Schleiermacher proposed a compromise that many found satisfactory: he denied the concept of indifference but declared that ordinary pleasures were part of the whole of human life and as such were not only permissible to a Christian but could very well be a matter of duty. See A. Baudrillart, DTC 1:396–398; Schaff Creeds 1:298–302.

ADLER, FELIX (1851–1933), founder of the Society for *Ethical Culture. He was born in Alzey, Germany, the son of a rabbi who came with his family to the U.S. when A. was six. After graduation from Columbia in 1870, A. studied at Berlin and Heidelberg preparing for the rabbinate; but through his study, particularly of Kant and biblical criticism, he came to reject traditional religion. He became professor of Hebrew and Oriental literature at Cornell in 1874, but in 1876 resigned to found the New York Society for Ethical Culture, a movement of ethical humanism. From 1903 till his death he was professor of political and social ethics at Columbia, while continuing to play a leading role in the society and various movements of social reform. See D. Muzzey, *Ethics as a Religion* (1951).

ADMONITION TO PARLIAMENT, a document of the English Puritans (1572), demanding esp. abolition of *episcopacy .

ADONAI SHOMO, an American communal sect founded in 1861 in Petersham, Mass., by Frederick Howland, a former Quaker. The Hebrew name means "the Lord is here." Howland taught millenarianism, the personal inspiration of every believer, and that true followers of Christ participate in eternal life here and now. Members of his community worshiped on Saturdays by a special offering of the Lord's Prayer. The group, which at no time numbered more than 150, disbanded in 1896. See T. Horgan, NCE 4:80.

ADOPTING ACT, a provision in 1729 by Presbyterian clergy at Philadelphia that every entering clergyman or candidate for the ministry should declare the *Westminster Confession and the *Westminster Catechisms to be "in all the essential and necessary articles, good forms of sound words and systems of Christian doctrine." To counter tendencies within Presbyterianism toward Arianism and Unitarianism, clergy of Scottish and Irish origin had been advocating subscription to the Confession as a requisite for membership in the *presbytery and *synod. Those, like Jonathan *Dickinson, with origins in England and New England resisted such a measure as being contrary to Scripture and even to the spirit of the Confession. The Adopting Act was a compromise. A clergyman who could not accept some point in the Confession or Catechisms was obliged to state his scruples to the presbytery or synod for a decision as to whether the matter was so essential or necessary as to warrant exclusion from the ministry. The act made American Presbyterianism a confessional body permitting a broad liberty in interpretation of doctrine. Tension, explicit in the compromise, has also been a cause of disruption throughout the history of the denomination. See E. A. Smith, *Presbyterian Ministry in American Culture: A Study in Changing Concepts, 1700–1900* (1962).

ADOPTIONISM (Adoptianism), the teaching that Jesus is the Son of the Father by adoption, not naturally. The term has been used to designate Monarchianism, Nestorianism, and the 12th-cent. teaching of the Abelardian school that the humanity of Jesus had no substantial entity of its own (D 750). As an explicit doctrine Adoptionism refers to the Christology of certain Spanish bps. in the 8th and 9th centuries. As human, Jesus was son of God by adoption, in virtue of exceptional grace; as divine, he was naturally the son of God. Elipandus of Toledo, who well knew the difference between person and nature, is quoted as saying that Christ is adoptive in humanity and not at all adoptive in divinity (PL 96:918); but he avoided saying that Christ was an adopted person. A favored term of Elipandus for the Redeemer is *Dei* *simul et hominis filius* (at once the son of God and of man). He may have been led into his difficult position by his earlier condemnation of *Migetius's statement that the second person of the Trinity is that made from the seed of David according to the flesh and not that begotten by the Father. His stand may also have been influenced by his having to deal with Moors and Mozarabs under Moslem and Nestorian influence. His fellow bps. supported him, and the Mozarabic liturgy did refer to the Redeemer as *homo adoptivus,* although probably in a metaphorical sense.

The works of *Felix of Urgel, ally of Elipandus, are lost, and his position is given in his adversaries' texts. Brought to account by both Charlemagne and Pope Adrian I (D 595, 610–611), Felix died (818) in the custody of Bp. Agobard of Lyons, who proceeded to refute Adoptionist views discovered among Felix's papers. Alcuin in a long disputation pointed out to Felix that the issue came down to a need to say that concrete human nature was "assumed" by the Word and not "adopted." Spanish Adoptionists were regarded as a threat not only by Alcuin, who with Benedict of Aniane waged an intensive campaign to keep monks on the Spanish frontier orthodox, but also by the papacy, in supporting the Carolingians against Felix and in the Council of Frankfurt (794; D 612, 615), and by Albar of Córdoba, who c.850 charged that Elipandus had afflicted Mozarab Spain with the evil. See É. Amann, *Histoire de l'Église* 6:129–152. Fliche-Martin 6:129–152; ThAq ST 3, 23.4.

ADVENT CHRISTIAN CHURCH, a Church formed in 1860 by adherents of the *Adventism of W. *Miller and previously named Advent Christian Association and Advent Christian Conference. Those who organized the Church were led by Jonathan Cummings (1785–1867), a follower of Miller, who preached that Christ's second coming would be in 1853 or 1854. At the foundation of the Church, particular stress was laid upon *conditional immortality as taught by

Charles F. Hudson and George Storrs. While accepting Adventism, the Church differs from *Seventh-day Adventists by Sunday observance, by disregarding OT prohibitions on unclean foods, and by rejecting the prophetic gifts of Ellen G. *White. The Church is *congregational in polity; five regional conferences and other church agencies are coordinated in the Advent Christian General Conference of America. In 1967 there were about 30,000 members in 418 churches in the U.S. and Canada. Missionary work was begun in 1891 and continues in India, Japan, Malaysia, Mexico, the Philippines, and Nigeria, with 1,767 members in 55 mission churches. The Church supports two colleges, Aurora in Ill. and Berkshire Christian College in Lenox, Massachusetts. In 1964 the Life and Advent Union merged with the Advent Christian Church.

ADVENT OF THE LORD, see SECOND COMING.

ADVENTISM, the belief that Christ's second coming, or advent, is at hand to inaugurate the millennium in which the wicked will be annihilated and the kingdom of the saints established. In this generic sense, *chiliasm, *apocalypticism, or *millenarianism, as seen in the Montanists, Anabaptists, Fifth Monarchy Man, Jehovah's Witnesses, and many other bodies, are forms of adventism. The term has a particular historical connection, however, with the Adventist groups arising in the 19th cent., esp. as the result of the preaching of W. *Miller. Concentrating on the books of Daniel and of Revelation, Miller not only announced the nearness of the millennium, but computed the exact date (see TIME SETTING). Christians from various Churches accepted his ideas, but many abandoned Adventism when his predictions went unfulfilled. From those who remained unshaken the various Adventist Churches were formed. See E. Clark, *Small Sects in America* (1949). *ADVENT CHRISTIAN

CHURCH; *CHURCH OF GOD (ABRAHAMIC FAITH); *LIFE AND ADVENT UNION; *PRIMITIVE ADVENT CHRISTIAN CHURCH; *SEVENTH-DAY ADVENTISTS.

ADVERTISEMENTS, BOOK OF, see BOOK OF ADVERTISEMENTS.

ADVOWSON, in English law a proprietary, often hereditary, right of presenting a cleric for an ecclesiastical benefice. The advowson is the form that the feudal institution called *advocatio* or *advocatia* took in England, where the *advocatus ecclesiae* signified one enjoying this right. The Statutes of Provisors of 1351 resisted papal interference with advowson. The right was acquired originally by one who built, or was patron of, a church or abbey; then advowson became attached to the manor on which the establishment stood. Thus, in current law an advowson is either appendant, attached to an estate, or in gross, detached and possessed by itself. A presentative advowson is one in which presentation is submitted to a bishop for approbation of the presentee; a collative advowson is one exercised by the bishop himself. See R. Laprat, DHGE 5:1220–41.

AFFAIRE DES PLACARDS, L', in the history of French Protestantism, the name given to the events of the night of Oct. 17–18, 1534, when the Huguenot Reformers in Paris and other cities put up printed posters attacking the Mass. In offensive language, the handbills also attacked all, including Lutherans, who taught the Real Presence. Since a poster was even affixed to the bedchamber of Francis I at Amboise, the incident, which erupted in a period of relative calm and revealed Huguenot power and boldness, marked a change in the King's moderate policy toward the Reformers. A period of severe repression followed until the Declaration of Coucy (July 16, 1535). See A. Bailly, *La Réforme en France*

jusqu'à l'Édit de Nantes (1960), 121–133; Léonard HistProt 1:233.

AFFIRMATION, AN, see AUBURN AFFIRMATION.

AFRICAN CHRISTIANITY (Contemporary), one of the most massive and variegated responses to the Christian faith in the history of Christian missions. After the extinction of the Church in North Africa by the year A.D. 1000, RC missions began south of the Sahara early in the 16th cent.; Protestant missions began three centuries later. After 1800 almost every variety of European and North American Christianity was introduced somewhere onto the African scene and left its imprint. By the year 1900 missioners had begun work with about 400 of the 750 tribes south of the Sahara and had translated the NT into about 100 vernacular tongues. The Christian population in sub-Saharan Africa grew from virtually zero in 1800 to about 65 million in 1967: about 30 million Catholics in 300 dioceses, about 22 million Protestants in 600 national Churches or missions, 6 million Orthodox (almost entirely in Ethiopia), and 7 million adherents of the *African Independent Church Movement (AICM). Also by 1967 the majority of these dioceses and Churches had come under strong African leadership. National and international *Bible societies, again with predominantly African leadership, had brought about one of the greatest intellectual achievements of Christian missions in all times, namely the translation of the Holy Scriptures, in whole or in part, into 395 languages in sub-Saharan Africa. In almost all of these translations a traditional African religious vocabulary has been used to express Christian concepts. Despite strong African leadership, Christianity has still been regarded by many in Africa as a foreign religion, heavily influenced by Western ecclesiastical traditions and patterns, with Western denominational rivalry imposed on the African response to the gospel. But in many areas the Church has now entered the third or fourth generation of its existence, and strong indigenous expressions of Christianity are beginning to emerge. These may be reviewed under four heads as follows.

Renewal and Revival Movements within the Churches. Within the RC and Protestant Churches in Africa about 1,000 popular religious movements of renewal, revival, protest, or dissidence had crystallized sufficiently to possess distinct names and membership by 1967. Most of these movements were begun on African initiative, or in a few cases under missionary leadership with strong African backing, e.g., the *Jamaa* (Family) movement within the RC Church in Katanga, Congo-Kinshasa, which was begun after World War II among the Luba tribe, under the inspiration of the Belgian missionary Placide Tempels, and by 1967 had about 20,000 adult members throughout the Congo. Other such renewal movements have been the East African Revival, or *Balokole* (Saved Ones), mainly within the Anglican Church, which had spread to about 70 east African tribes. A similar movement in Madagascar is the *Fifohazana* (Those Who Have Woken Up) Revival, which has affected some 100,000 members of the Lutheran and other Protestant Churches. All such renewal movements have spread spontaneously, usually on lay initiative. A considerable number of renewal movements have sprung up within the RC Church since the liberal reforms of Vatican II. Lay leaders have become bolder, to the point where clashes with the clergy occur. In central Africa the canonization of the Uganda martyrs by Paul VI in 1964 touched off a wave of enthusiastic movements, not among the Ganda themselves but among tribes in adjoining territories. In the Tanzanian Dioceses of Bukoba and Rulenge arose the movement called *Banyakaroli* (Followers of Charles; named after the Ganda protomartyr Charles Lwanga, who was murdered in 1885). Under the zealous leadership of a RC lay prophet of the Haya tribe, Bernardo, the *Banyakaroli* went about preaching in

blood-red *kanzus* (cassocks) and traveled to distant dioceses to conduct lay retreats. By 1967 they were in serious difficulties with the hierarchy. In the Congolese Dioceses of Kabinda and Luluabourg, a similar movement, Bena Nzambi wa BaMartyre ya Baganda (Children of God of the Uganda Martyrs), had actually broken off and become a separatist body by 1966. But in 1967 the vast majority of such RC movements were still inside the Church.

Beginning with the first feeble stirrings of reaction in the early days of Christian missions, such movements within the Churches have gradually increased with each succeeding decade until by 1967 they had reached astonishing proportions. Exact enumeration of the total of all such movements over the whole period is clearly impossible; the records do not exist, and in any case the phenomena themselves were only barely discernible and often short-lived. But even if a majority of them were very small, sometimes a grouping of only 10 or 20 church members, a rough assessment yields some startling figures. To begin with, there are the 5,000 separatist Churches in the AICM, virtually all of which were at one time movements within the mission Churches. Next, for every successful attempt to form a separatist body there have been several that fell short of schism; hence, it is possible that at least an additional 5,000 attempts at forming dissident movements have failed. Then there has been the mass of similar movements, large or small, that have not attempted to secede but have been able to exist as renewal movements within the Churches. Therefore, about 10 to 20 thousand distinct groupings of renewal or dissidence, successful or frustrated, have arisen within the Churches in Africa during the last 2 centuries of the missionary era. By 1967 all such existing movements still within the Churches probably embraced several million persons in the Protestant, RC, and Orthodox communities across the continent. The ensemble represents a vast reservoir of religious unrest and a fertile field for indigenous reformers intent on creating a truly African

Christianity, having a spirit that is conformed to nationalist aspirations and native culture.

Leader Figures. A large number of charismatic leader figures have been thrust up by such movements within the Churches. Many have been seers, visionaries, or prophets, coexisting in varying degrees of tension with foreign missionaries and African church leaders. Others have been renowned healers; still others have been pioneer missionaries to unevangelized areas, such as John Tsizehena, a Malagasy Anglican youth who evangelized and became bp. of the Northern Church of Madagascar. In addition, countless African musicians, male and female, have supplied traditional African tunes with Christian words, e.g., in Tanzania Christians of the Wagogo tribe sing whole chapters of the Gogo Bible to Gogo music in their evangelistic work. Other leaders have been preachers of great power, employing traditional African techniques of public speaking—question and answer, responsive singing, dialogue preaching, dual staccato preaching (one preacher speaking rapidly for a few minutes, then the second taking over without a pause, then the first, etc.), and even preaching out of doors to huge crowds while running up and down long avenues.

The African Independent Church Movement (AICM). This phenomenon, unprecedented for size and importance in the entire history of the expansion of Christianity, is dealt with in the article African Independent Church Movement.

Complex of New Religious Forms. In movements both within the historical churches and in the AICM, there are at least 200 varying new emphases in Christian belief and practice, representing a genuinely African response to the Christian faith. All center around the basic African concept of the people of God as a community and the legitimacy of Christianizing African traditional concepts and practices. They represent a creative response on the part of African Christianity to the turmoil and disruption that followed the breakdown of traditional patterns of life as a result of contact with the Western world. A selection of these new forms or emphases is given below, divided for convenience into nine categories.

Community Structure. Under this heading are included small face-to-face communities, based often on traditional social structure, characterized by fellowship, agape, and philadelphia; communal life; communities of love; prominence of women; strong lay leadership; the desacralization of politics.

Land and Property. Included are centers of religious innovation called holy villages or renewal centers; houses of prayer; prayer plots; holy places for vigils; open-air worship sites; communal ownership of land and agricultural or commercial enterprises; "The Lord's Acre" plots for church crops; and a stress on philanthropic funds, burial societies, and mutual-help societies.

Laws and taboos. These include sabbatarianism; tithing and fasting; personal austerity; prohibition of tobacco, alcohol, and pork; often a rejection of European medicine; a marked legalism in church affairs; spiritual vagrancy or fluidity of membership; experimental membership; occasional dual or plural membership (in mission and separatist Churches); and random borrowing from various historical denominations.

Religious concepts. Among these concepts are a supernatural view of life; the divinity of the Holy Spirit; God as the Living God, the God of Power, the God of Miracles, the God of the Impossible, the God of the Ancestors; theories of mythological eras in church history; and a claimed indigenous or African theology.

Religious leadership. A wide range of leadership is seen: corporate leadership; decisions made by the group rather than by individuals; prophets and prophetesses; healers, faith healing; titled officials; differentiated leadership systems; evangelists; judges; dialogue preaching; lay involvement; mothers-in-God; traditions of prophets' miracles; new holy books; stress on spiritual gifts, pneumatic phenomena, trances, visions, and dreams; and revelation on sacred mountains. Polygamists are accepted as members but not as officials.

Religious symbolism. Included under this heading are symbolic colors revealed in dreams; blue and white as sacred colors; new forms of dress, e.g., white robes for all participants, and uniforms; symbolic letters or embroidery; monograms; large red crosses; special headwear; beards, shaven heads; removal of shoes; indigenous craftmanship; carrying of holy staffs, banners, or flags as symbols of pilgrimage; and the use of candles and candelabra in revelation.

Magical concepts. The reality of magic is recognized but all its forms are opposed, whether benevolent or malevolent. Also noted are destruction of all fetishes and rejection of charms and nostrums.

Rituals. Various forms of ritual are: special greetings with prayer and ritual; ritual postures during prayer; blessing of medicines; blessing of newly bought articles; ritual dancing; anointing with oils; foot-washing; use of holy water; purification rites; communal weeping for sins; ringing of handbells; exorcism of devils; millennial release from sorcery; and mass confession of witches.

Worship. The following practices are observed: sealing of doors and windows during worship; indigenous liturgies; praying bands; mass *glossolalia; multilingual praying ensemble; religious grunting, hic-coughing, or humming; religious joy and ecstasy; long prayers; testimonies; stress on the name of Jesus; drums or flutes in worship; use of megaphones, hand clapping, rhythmic movement, and antiphonal responses; annual conventions or festivals; processions; incessant religious itineration; vernacular hymns; indigenous tunes in worship; and the use of vernacular names of endearment for Jesus.

Although many of these features have occurred in other eras and areas of the Christian world mission, their intensity and proliferation in Africa accentuate both the African genius for religion and religious creativity and also the rapidity with which Christianity is becoming rooted in African culture and society. See C. P. Groves, *Planting of Christianity in Africa* (1958), v.4; D. B. Barrett, *Schism and Renewal in Africa* (1968).

AFRICAN INDEPENDENT CHURCH MOVEMENT. Widespread Christian missionary activity in sub-Saharan Africa began around the year 1800, and since 1819 schisms and other religious movements have grown in number each decade. By 1967 there were 5,100 distinct bodies among 290 different tribes in 33 African nations and colonies (and Madagascar), with an estimated total of 6,900,000 adherents (total nominal community). By 1967 more than 100 new bodies, with at least 300,000 new adherents, were emerging each year. An average of seven hitherto uninvolved tribes became part of the movement each year as well. In ecumenical circles the emergence of these Churches is designated as the African Independent Church Movement (AICM), though in fact the vast majority of these bodies do not know of each other's existence and are in no sense a consciously organized movement. Of the more than 1,500 books, reports, and articles in 20 languages written on the AICM, most deal with a single body or area, but a handful attempt an overall description and analysis of the whole movement. A wide range of terminology is used: some of the classifications are favorable, e.g., spiritual movements, renewals, revivals; others indicate characteristics, e.g., charismatic, prophetic, separatist, schismatic; others are derogatory, e.g., syncretistic, neopagan, non-Christian.

Geographical and Historical Scope. The AICM is spread across the whole of sub-Saharan Africa, but with particularly large concentrations in the Union of South Africa (3,000), Nigeria (500), Congo-Kinshasa (500), Ghana (200), and Kenya (160). In the sub-Saharan regions, western, central, and eastern Africa each has a total of about 1 million adherents, while southern Africa has well over 3 million. In northern Africa, almost entirely Muslim in religion, there are about 12,000 adherents of separatist bodies. The first of these independent church movements occurred in 1819 in western Africa, where in 1967 about 800 separatist ecclesiastical bodies existed, each with its own distinct name and organization. In northern Africa the first schism took place in 1869; subsequently seven bodies in Egypt have separated from Protestant missions. Since 1872 southern Africa has produced at least 3,200 such secessions, the greatest proliferation being among the Zulu of South Africa. In central Africa about 570 movements have arisen since 1888, almost all in French-speaking territories; in Congo-Kinshasa alone, 200 bodies have emerged since independence in 1960. The last region to become involved was eastern Africa in 1894; although it had in 1967 the smallest number of groups (350), these groups included dynamic religious leaders and were growing as rapidly as anywhere else on the continent. At least 90% of all the 5,000 secessions over the last century and a half still existed in 1967 as organized bodies with gradually increasing memberships. The Berlin Conference for the partitioning of Africa (1885) marked an upsurge of the AICM; since then expansion has been at a remarkably even rate. Some 10% of all bodies formed since the start have rejoined their parent Church, been suppressed, or have otherwise disbanded. The average size of a body is only 1,370 adherents, but many have more than 50,000 members, and the largest (Église de Jésus-Christ sur la terre par le prophète Simon Kimbangu, or ÉJCSK, in Congo-Kinshasa) has about 200,000 adult members.

A Single Phenomenon. The AICM may give a preliminary impression of a mass of disparate and unrelated movements, with causes as numerous and different as are the prophets who lead them. Observers have naturally tended to emphasize local causes, which vary widely from case to case—personal friction, racial incidents, ambition, missionary paternalism, political and economic crises. Closer analysis, however, has revealed a correlation between separatism and the following elements, less visible but common to all tribes involved: a strong traditional African society, e.g., polygamous structure and ancestral cult; strong colonial impact, e.g., high literacy and the presence of white settlers; strong missionary impact, e.g., high missionary concentration and vernacular translations of the Scriptures. The correlation suggests that the underlying cause of the whole AICM is the clash of African culture with colonial and missionary cultures. A further common feature is the diffusion, unparalleled in previous Christian expansion, of the vernacular Scriptures in a total of 411 African languages. One may speak, therefore, of the AICM as a single phenomenon; and one unique in history. Granted the spectrum of types, ranging from the ultraorthodox to the definitely syncretistic, almost all these bodies are nevertheless characterized by a clear acceptance, often under new and original African forms, of the centrality of the historical Jesus as Lord. In varying degrees there are in virtually every movement: a central confession of Christ as *Kyrios* (using the traditional vernacular term for chiefship); a marked resurgence of traditional African custom and world view; and a strong affirmation of their right to be both fully Christian and fully African, independent of foreign pressures. All over the continent the African Churches, working quite spontaneously and in the main independently, seem to be engaged in an attempt to synthesize the apostolic kerygma with genuinely African insight, based on ideas derived from the vernacular translations of the Bible. Beyond the tragic spectacle of schism after schism, therefore, a renewal of Christianity, truly indigenous in form, is emerging.

Civil and Ecumenical Status. There are three developments in recent years that indicate a fundamental shift in the relations between the AICM on the one hand and governments and ecumenical Christianity on the other. First, determined efforts have recently been made by the independent Churches to secure government recognition through application to register as legitimate societies. In the case of most of the larger bodies, this has already been successful. In Kenya, Nigeria, and Congo-Kinshasa, particularly, there were so many applications during 1960–67 that the movement as a whole is being treated with a new and marked respect. Further, a similar determination is being shown to win ecumenical recognition and to work toward Christian unity. Here a definite strategy—almost certainly unorganized and spontaneous—seems to be in process. In the first place, importunate applications for membership have been made in increasing numbers since 1955 to national Christian councils across the continent; but in only a handful of cases, notably in Kenya, Cameroon, and Rhodesia, has this membership been granted. When such efforts prove fruitless, bodies have bypassed national councils and applied directly to the major ecumenical bodies. Here, their reception has been equally cautious; by 1966 the All-Africa Conference of Churches had accepted into membership only four of the many applying bodies—the African Church (Nigeria), the African Brotherhood Church (Kenya), the African Methodist Church (Rhodesia), and the Église Protestante Africaine Baptiste (Congo). Among the applications received by the World Council of Churches in 1966 were those of the Église Harriste (Ivory Coast) and of the ÉJCSK. (The latter's application was approved by the World Council's Central Committee in 1969, and membership becomes final in Feb. 1970).

The next step of the separatist bodies has been to form federations with assistance from liberal elements in the historical Churches. The happiest examples of this today are the African Independent Churches Association (AICA) and the Assembly of Zionist and Apostolic Churches, both in South Africa, which receive assistance (particularly with theological education) from the Christian Institute of Southern Africa and the Christian Council of South Africa. But, lastly, if all such ecumenical feelers are rebuffed, the separatist Churches have shown that they can organize powerful rival Christian councils: the East African United Churches in 1967 organized 40 constituent members, and COS-SÉUJCA (Conseil Supérieur des Sacrificateurs pour les Églises-Unies de Jésus-Christ en Afrique), from Luluabourg, claims to act on behalf of about 50 bodies.

Membership statistics for 17 of the largest Churches of the AICM are listed in order of size in the following table. "Adherents" is the term used for the total nominal community of a body, including adult members, fringe members, and children.

Body and Nation	Date Founded	Adherents
Église de Jesus-Christ sur la terre par le prophète Simon Kimbangu, *Congo-Kinshasa*	1921	500,000
Zion Christian Church, *South Africa*	1914	200,000
Church of Christ, *South Africa*	1910	200,000
Society of the One Almighty God, *Uganda*	1914	110,000
Lumpa Church, *Zambia*	1954	100,000
Divine Healer's Church, *Ghana*	1954	100,000
Christ Apostolic Church, *Nigeria*	1931	94,000
Église Déimatiste, *Ivory Coast*	1923	90,000
Church of Christ in Africa, *Kenya*	1957	75,000
Mai Chaza Church, *Rhodesia*	1952	70,000
Église Harriste, *Ivory Coast*	1913	68,000
Apostolic Revelation Society, *Ghana*	1939	60,000
Legio Maria, *Kenya*	1963	60,000
African Israel Church Nineveh, *Kenya*	1942	60,000
Église du Réveil, *Madagascar*	1955	50,000
Eternal Sacred Order of the Cherubim and Seraphim, *Nigeria*	1925	50,000
African Apostolic Church of Johane Maranke, *Rhodesia*	1932	50,000

SOURCE: D. B. Barrett, *Schism and Renewal in Africa: An Analysis of Six Thousand Contemporary Religious Movements* (1968).

NOTE: The date of these estimates is the period 1964–67, except for the Lumpa Church and Église Déimatiste (1958) and the Society of the One Almighty God (1921).

Missionary Character. One final development of major significance for the evangelization of Africa is that independency has now taken on a distinctively missionary character. In at least 16 nations separatist Churches are growing faster than their Protestant or RC counterparts. In western Africa, where the historical Churches are making little headway in the Muslim north, separatist congregations have been established in most of the major Muslim towns and cities. Elsewhere in Africa, numerous bodies have commenced missionary work far distant from their home areas, e.g., the ÉJCSK has work in southwest Africa, the African Apostolic Church of Johane Maranke (Rhodesia) has spread as far west as Luluabourg and Kinshasa, and Zionists have moved from South Africa to all adjoining nations including Mozambique. The major concern behind this development of expansion seems to be genuine evangelization rather than mere proselytizing.

Significance. From many points of view the AICM is a phenomenon unique in the entire history of Christian missions. There is first the immense number of schisms and adherents involved (one-fifth of the entire Christian community in Africa); second, a remarkably uniform spread across a third of Africa's tribes in the last 100 years; and third, for the first time in history the paradoxical coexistence of four elements—strong animistic traditional societies, mass movements into the historical Churches, formidable missionary assaults of traditional religion and society, and the widespread provision of vernacular Scriptures, which have been interpreted as vindicating much of the traditional African way of life. The AICM has therefore a significance equal to the encounter of the post-apostolic Church with the Gnostic movement in the 2d cent., the East-West schism, and the fragmentation of Christendom in Europe during the Reformation. In most cases AICM bodies attempt to Christianize traditional African customs, and this has inevitably led to charges of *syncretism. An ecumenical assessment of their theological character, however, would have to acknowledge that, although in many respects they fall short of recognized Christian orthodoxy, their almost universal claim to confess Jesus as Lord, Savior, and God establishes them as genuine Christian Churches. See R. C. Mitchell and H. W. Turner, *Bibliography of Modern African Religious Movements* (1966); D. B. Barrett, *Schism and Renewal in Africa: An Analysis of Six Thousand Contemporary Religious Movements* (1968); H. W. Coxill, et al., *World Christian Handbook 1968* (1967), 227–228. *LEGIO MARIA; *AFRICAN CHRISTIANITY; *ANCESTOR CULT.

AFRICAN METHODIST EPISCOPAL CHURCH, a denomination founded in the 1790s by members of the Methodist *Society of Philadelphia who seceded from their congregation because of racial discrimination. One of their number, Richard Allen, erected a separate place of worship for them on his own ground at his own expense. For a few years it was served by pastors ordained by an Anglican bishop. In 1799, however, Francis *Asbury, bp. of the mother Church, after futile attempts to win back the Negroes made Allen their bishop. In 1816 the new Church invited Negro Methodists of Baltimore and other cities, who were likewise on the verge of seceding from their congregations, to attend a *general conference with a view to forming a connection. The new Church grew rapidly in the North and was soon sending missionaries to Liberia (1824) and to Haiti (1827). After the Civil War it added numerous southern Negro congregations to its membership. It now conducts institutions of higher education in seven states and Liberia. Two seminaries supply its preachers, and it publishes five periodicals. Since the late 1920s the African Methodist Episcopal (AME) Church has been plagued with internal dissension, esp. over the issue of episcopacy. It has also suffered from litigation with former members. Since its doctrines and form of worship are similar to those of the other African church bodies in the U.S., a merger with the Christian Methodist Episcopal Church and the AME Zion Church seemed imminent early in the 20th cent. but interest waned. In 1969, however, plans were being made for such a union in 1972. The *Consultation on Church Union also includes these three Churches. The AME is the largest of the Negro Methodist bodies in the U.S.; in 1951 its census reported 5,878 churches and 1,166,301 members. See HistAmMeth 3:581–583.

AFRICAN METHODIST EPISCOPAL ZION CHURCH, denomination founded in 1796 by members of the John Street Methodist Episcopal Church of New York City in protest against racial discrimination. The first place of worship of the new Church was built in 1800 and named Zion; but only in 1848 was the word added to the church title to distinguish it from the other *African Methodist Episcopal (AME) Church. The Church was originally supplied with unordained pastors by the Methodist Episcopal Church. The first ordained minister was assigned in 1821. The AME Zion Church is the second largest of the African Methodist bodies in the U.S. Its 1965 census reported 4,583 churches and 1,-100,000 members. It conducts missions in Liberia, the Bahamas, Ghana, Nigeria, and South America. Its chief college is Livingstone in N.C., with which Hood Theological Seminary is connected. It publishes three periodicals besides other literature. A member of the World Council of Churches, it participates also in the *Consultation on Church Union. In 1969 negotiations for a 1972 union with the African Methodist Episcopal Church and the Christian Methodist Episcopal Church were progressing. See HistAmMeth, 3:585–586.

AFRICAN ORTHODOX CHURCH, a body founded by George Alexander McGuire in 1921 for the purpose of providing Negroes with an Episcopalian type of Church. Valuing *apostolic succession, McGuire had himself consecrated bishop by J. R. *Vilatte. The Church continues to stress historic sacraments and rituals; its teaching is a blend of Western and Eastern creeds, and its liturgy, a mixture of Anglican, Greek, and Roman forms. In 1957 it had 6,000 members, with 24 churches in the U.S., Canada, Latin America, and the Union of South Africa.

AFRICAN UNION First Colored Methodist Protestant Church, Inc., a Church that traces its history to 1805, but in its present form was organized in 1866 by the merger of the African Union Church and the First Colored Methodist Protestant Church. Both had separated from the Methodist Episcopal Church. The Church is Methodist in doctrine; but its polity excludes *episcopacy. Membership in 1969 was 8,000; headquarters are in Wilmington, Delaware.

AGAPEMONE, CHURCH OF THE, see CHURCH OF THE AGAPEMONE.

AGENDA, in its primary sense, liturgical uses or the books prescribing them. The Council of Carthage (390) applied the term to the entire eucharistic service; some early African liturgies limit it to the anaphora. Throughout the Middle Ages the word designated the liturgical practices and books proper to particular places; after the Reformation the term fell into disuse among Roman Catholics. Among the German Lutherans the word has always signified the prescribed forms of service and the service book itself (see CHURCH ORDER). In another sense the 17th-cent. English theologians distinguished between *agenda*, matters of religious practice, and *credenda*, essentials of belief. See EncRelKnow 1:84–86.

AGGIORNAMENTO (Ital., updating), a term popularized by Pope John XXIII. The word is now used to indicate the attempt to modernize the RC Church's teachings and practices so that contemporary men will better understand and accept them. It is an ongoing process that has only begun to take shape; yet certain distinctive trends have gradually emerged, indicating the probable trend of Catholic thought in the immediate future.

Theology before Vatican II was largely characterized by a systematic approach that highly valued the integration of reality into a comprehensive world-view based on a comparatively few, solid theological principles. Now, proponents of desystematization argue that contemporary reality is too rich and manifold to be limited by any current or past world-view. Desystematization, they think, enlarges the possibility of genuine and meaningful progress, since the development of doctrinal and moral thought would not be left exclusively to the explicitation of formerly implicit principles. Newer principles could be deduced from the knowledge available today. Desystematization is a reaction to the extreme forms of systematic theology that tended to reject new thought and the new stirrings of the Spirit in the Church. Still, desystematization itself has the endemic danger of becoming not only iconoclastic but also anarchic.

A second trend is the stress laid on personal, usually at the expense of legal, natural, or institutional, values. Allied to the philosophic position loosely termed personalism, exponents of this movement severely condemn the encroachment of man-made restrictions upon the rights and dignity of human persons. They oppose various political, economic, social, educative, and religious systems that have been tolerated in the past because of ignorance or necessity. There are differences of opinion as to what institutional stresses can be abandoned or lessened, and also as to whether evolution or revolution, a gradual and nonviolent or a quick and violent change, offers the better method of establishing the primacy of personal values.

The coming of age of the layman is still another recognizable trend. In an updated Church he should no longer be taken as a passive, voiceless, spiritually incompetent follower. He should be accorded his right to be heard both in theology and in church affairs. The new emphasis on the role of the laity in the life of the Church gives the movement toward *aggiornamento* a "secular," as opposed to a more "sacred," direction.

Aggiornamento also stresses *ecumenism. Vatican II officially designated non-Catholic Christian bodies as separated Churches and communions. There is no longer talk of reunion with Rome, with its connotation of the return of prodigal sons to an unerring father. This is now replaced by emphasis on the common Christian search for the activity of the Spirit with each tradition contributing, according to its capacity, insights gained since the scandalous divisions of Christianity, with the hope that eventually the mutual mistakes of the past will cease to influence the present and the future.

There are many other features to be observed in this movement. In addition to its original denotation of updating, it is acquiring the humbling connotation of "catching up with" the knowledge of reality (esp. regarding human existence and behavior) already available from nontheological sources. RC theology takes all this seriously and is at the present time suffering some of the crises and the inevitable uncertainties of a new movement.

AGLIPAY, GREGORIO (1860–1940), first bp. of the *Philippine Independent Church, sometimes popularly called the Aglipayan Church. He was ordained an RC priest in 1889. During the Philippine Revolution (1898) against Spanish rule, the Filipino rebel leaders made him a military vicar general in order to take over government of the RC Church. He was excommunicated (1899) by the abp. of Manila and became a guerilla fighter. After the U.S. took over the Philippines, the nationalist leader, Isabelo de los Reyes, Sr. (1864–1938), set up the Philippine Independent Church (1902), and A. was elected supreme bishop. He received consecration from 12 priests, but never from a bishop. Until his death he remained head of his Church, which dwindled in numbers after an initial success. In 1935 he ran unsuccessfully for president of the Philippines. See P. S. de Achútegui and M. A. Bernad, *Religious Revolution in the Philippines: The Life and Church of Gregorio Aglipay* (2v., 1960–66).

AGLIPAYANS, members of the *Philippine Independent Church, popularly named for Gregorio *Aglipay.

AGNOSTICISM, in general, not knowing about religious truth; more specifically, not having rational certitude about it. Absence of certitude may range from having no more than a merely opinionative judgment to a condition of doubt, either just negative or more positive, but not proceeding so far as to reject religious truth. The term does not come from the Latin but from the Greek, *agignosko*; the alpha is privative. The fact should be noted to avoid the solecism of Cecil Rhodes, who, when asked about his religious belief replied simply, "I can only reply, *Agnosco*. I don't know."

Agnosticism should always be defined in a given system of reference: it may be about the so-called natural truths of religion: the existence and nature of God, the immortality of the soul, the moral law. Thus as a rationalist, a man may be skeptical about them and yet be an ardent Christian. Or agnosticism may concern specifically Christian truths of faith, at various stages or periods of articulation: thus a believer may be agnostic about an institutional Church, a Presbyterian about episcopacy, an Anglican about the pope, or a Roman Catholic about a current usage concerning indulgences. Agnosticism has several styles. The reverent agnosticism that hesitates before anthropomorphism or cocksureness about divine things is nobly represented by Moses Maimonides, and indeed by the *theologia negativa* of a high

mystical tradition in Christianity. Then there is the wistful agnosticism of earnest thinkers who would like to believe but cannot honestly bring themselves to do so; they were prominent in the Victorian era, when the term first came to be widely used. Finally there is the complacent agnosticism of those who do not bother or do not care to make the effort required to find out about eternal truths. Culpability enters, if at all, only with these last; it may be assessed in accordance with the rules governing the influence of ignorance on moral responsibility, as when one is too lazy to discover what is important or fears to discover it lest it prove awkward. See H. de Lubac, *Drama of Atheistic Humanism* (1949); J. Collins, *God in Modern Philosophy* (1959).

AGONISTICI, roving bands of Donatist terrorists more commonly known as *Circumcellions. The name is derived from the Greek word *agon*, used to designate a martyr's contest. They also called themselves *milites Christi*. See Optatus, *De schism. Donat.* 3.4; Augustine, *Enarr. in Psalm.* 132.6. *DONATISTS.

AGRICOLA, JOHANN *(c.*1494–1566), German Reformer whose family name was Schneider (Schnitter), known also as Magister Islebius. A native of Eisleben, A. studied under Martin Luther at Wittenberg. He preached Lutheran doctrine in Frankfurt and Eisleben and in 1536 taught theology in Wittenberg. He came into bitter conflict with Luther by maintaining that the believer was freed from observance of the law of God (see ANTINOMIANISM). The *Formula of Concord rejected this view in its articles (5 and 6) on *law and gospel.

ALBANENSES, one of the larger 13th-cent. bodies of *Cathari in Italy. Adherents were numerous in Lombardy, especially in the vicinity of Verona. The founders probably migrated from Albania, which may account for the name. The Albanenses professed absolute dualism, insisting on the eternal coexistence and complete equality of the principles of good and evil. Christ, they held, had a human body in appearance only. See S. Runciman, *Medieval Manichee* (1961), 126–127.

ALBIGENSES, the *Cathari in S France named from the city of Albi, one of their centers, by the Council of Tours (1169). In spite of repeated condemnations by church councils (Reims, 1148; Verona, 1184), the Albigenses continued to increase, especially in Languedoc and Provence. Among the contributing factors were the protection of an indulgent nobility, the laxity and negligence of an effete clergy, and the common people's admiration for the rigorous asceticism practiced by the *perfecti*, as the full-fledged devotees called themselves. The Albigenses taught a literal Manichaean dualism. Two equal and coeternal principles competed for control of the universe: the principle of good, which created the spiritual world, and the principle of evil, which created the material world. Human souls were created good, but some of them were enticed to rebellion by the evil principle and were punished by being imprisoned in material bodies. Christ, who had a human body in appearance only, was a perfect spirit, who could not die or rise and was not divine. He came only as a teacher to announce a salvation that consisted in total liberation of the soul from matter. This liberation was to be accomplished through asceticism or *consolamentum*, a ceremony by which one was admitted to the ranks of the *perfecti*. If the soul were not completely purified at death, it would be imprisoned in yet another body.

Albigensian dogmatic teachings were a denial of the most fundamental Christian beliefs. They were bitterly against the Church, for its corrupting NT teaching and for using material things in its rituals. Their moral precepts, if carried out on any large scale, would have completely disrupted the Christian social order. The *perfecti* were obliged to abandon their spouses, while ordinary believers were allowed almost complete sexual liberty. Sacred suicide, called *endura*, was advocated as the highest act of virtue. Oaths, military service, capital punishment, and even self-defense were proscribed. The profession of faith of Lateran Council IV was against their teachings (D 800–802).

By the beginning of the 13th cent. the Albigenses had become a threat to the very existence of the Church in S France. Innocent III at first attempted to convert the heretics by sending Cistercian and later Dominican preachers into the infected area, but sermons and disputations proved generally ineffective. When the Papal Legate Peter of Castelnau was murdered in 1208, the Pope decided that the use of force was justified and launched a crusade against the recalcitrant Albigenses. During the next 10 years the army led by Simon de Montfort forced the surrender of the most important heretical strongholds, employing in the process methods that were cruel even by medieval standards. Fighting continued until 1229, but its purpose became political the incorporation of Languedoc into France. Once deprived of baronial protection, the Albigenses found it necessary to flee or go underground. Their final extirpation was accomplished by the Inquisition established by Gregory IX in 1233. By the end of the 14th cent. their power was completely broken. See M. Lignières, *L'Hérésie albigeoise et la croisade* (1964); E. G. A. Holmes, *Albigensian or Catharist Heresy* (1925); S. Runciman, *Medieval Manichee* (1961), 116–170; H. Söderberg, *La religion des Cathares: Études sur le gnosticisme de la basse antiquité et de moyen-âge* (1949); H. J. Warner, *Albigensian Heresy* (2v., 1922–28); G. W. Davis, ed., *Inquisition at Albi, 1299–1300* (1948).

ALBRIGHT, JACOB (Albrecht; 1759–1808), evangelical preacher and church founder. Born at Fox Mountain, Pa., of immigrant parents from the German Palatinate, A. received little schooling; he was confirmed into the local Lutheran church. After service in the Continental Army, he married, settled, and prospered at Reamstown, Lancaster Co., Pennsylvania. The impression left by itinerant revivalists, and the sudden death of several of his children, moved him to reflect on his own spiritual condition. Following a conversion experience in 1791, he united with a nearby Methodist *class and was later licensed as a lay preacher. He began in 1796 to preach the gospel of personal salvation and pious Christian living to his spiritually slumbering neighbors, moving some to antagonism, others to conversion. By 1800 three small classes totaling 20 persons had been organized. In 1803 he experienced a lay ordination by representatives of these classes. His adherents became known as Albright People, or Albright Brethren, or German Methodists. His plan for a German branch of Methodism was not accepted by Methodist bishops; but in 1807 at the first annual conference with his lay preachers A. adopted an organization patterned after the Methodist Episcopal Church; this was the beginning of the Evangelical Church. *EVANGELICAL UNITED BRETHREN.

ALBRIGHT BRETHREN (Albright People), see ALBRIGHT, JACOB.

ALCHEMIST HERETICS. John XXII's condemnation of alchemists in 1317 seems directed against the fraudulent pretensions of many practitioners of the art rather than against any clearly identifiable doctrinal eccentricity inherent in their teachings. Still the esoteric jargon and the flights of mystical allegory in which alchemists commonly indulged exposed many of them to the charge of heresy. The 14th cent. saw many clerics brought to trial for the practice of alchemy and other occult arts. The inquisitor Nicholas Emeric (d. 1399) prosecuted many alchemists as heretics. The 15th-cent. *Adamites in Bohemia found a place for alchemy in their thinking and inspired the

painter Hieronymus Bosch to take an interest in the art. See J. E. Grennen, NCE 1:268–270.

ALDERSGATE, a name prominent in the history of *Methodism. At a religious meeting in Aldersgate Street, London, on May 24, 1738, J. *Wesley felt his heart strangely warmed as he experienced a vivid faith and assurance that Christ had taken away his sins and given him peace. Wesley's Aldersgate experience is regarded as the beginning of the Methodist Churches. See F. J. McConnell, *John Wesley* (1939), 57–67.

ALETHIANS, see SHAKERS.

ALEXANDER, ARCHIBALD (1772–1851), American Presbyterian theologian, founder of Princeton Theological Seminary. Born at Lexington, Va., he studied at Washington College, Chestertown, Md., and was ordained in 1794. From 1796 to 1807 A. served as president of Hampden–Sydney College, the first Presbyterian college in Virginia. In 1807, as *moderator of the *General Assembly, Alexander strove to convince Presbyterians of the need for a theological seminary. In 1812 Princeton Theological Seminary was authorized and he became its first professor, remaining there until his death. He was one of the principal *Old School Presbyterian theologians, basing his courses on Turretine (see TURRETINI) and other Calvinist theologians. A.'s *Brief Outline of the Evidences of the Christian Religion* (1825) was a standard apologetic work. He defended verbal inspiration and inerrancy of Scripture in his *Canon of the Old and New Testaments* (1826). In *Thoughts on Religious Experience* (1841) he defended a moderate Calvinism against the *revivalism of the New School. See J. W. Alexander, *Life of A. A.* (1854); H. T. Kerr, *Sons of the Prophets* (1963). *PRINCETON THEOLOGY.

ALIEN IMMERSION, among Baptists, signifies a baptism correctly performed, but by a minister authorized in a different denomination, hence an "alien." Such a baptism is recognized by more liberal Baptist groups; conservatives reject it as invalid, but differ as to which ministers are to be considered alien.

ALLIANCE OF THE REFORMED CHURCHES throughout the World Holding the Presbyterian Order, formed in 1875, one of the strongest of several ecumenical denominational organizations dating from that era. The Alliance involves over 65 constituent church bodies, from more than 45 countries, representing over 40 million adherents. The General Council, a delegated body that has the responsibility for governing the Alliance, has held meetings since the first one in Edinburgh (1877). It has always been federative and advisory, existing to promote the common interests of the member bodies. It has no power to obligate or to interfere in the internal affairs of a member body. With headquarters in Geneva, the general secretary coordinates the work of the Alliance in various geographical areas under area secretaries. At the General Council meetings considerable attention has been given to theological discussion, problems of religious liberty, and ecumenical relations. During World War II the organization did much to continue fellowship among Christians on both sides of the conflict. While the Alliance covers a wide range of national and linguistic differences, its greatest support has come from Europe and North America. In 1959 it held a historic meeting in São Paulo, Brazil, on "The Servant Lord and His Servant People," at which time it noted the existence of strong Churches holding *Reformed doctrine and the Presbyterian system in Hispanic America and other parts of the world. In 1954 the Alliance revised its constitution. In 1968 final plans were made for the *International Congregational Council to merge with the Alliance of Reformed Churches, Representatives of the Alliance and the RC Church engaged in formal discussions in 1969 on issues of common interest. See *Report of Proceedings* (1877–).

ALUMBRADOS, name for the adherents of a form of religious *illuminism in 16th-cent. Spain. Their history is obscured by polemical charges against them. The name was apparently first applied (1492) to a group led by Antonio de Pastrana, religious of Ocaña, who was accused of immorality. The divine mission he professed was a renewal of pure contemplation that merges the human being in the divine essence and makes him incapable of sin. In 1529 a secret community of Alumbrados was uncovered at Toledo, grouped around Fray Alcazar and Isabel de la Cruz. Claiming visions and uttering prophecies, they followed strange practices of piety, and undertook spectacular mortifications. After similar incidents throughout Spain, involving fraudulent miracles, levitations, and stigmata, the Alumbrados were proscribed by the Inquisition (1568, 1574, 1623). Not all Alumbrados went to extremes; many, however, were credulous regarding the marvelous and were eager to make the extraordinary the normal in the life of prayer. Many theologians reacted with an extreme intellectualism. Thus the *Sinner's Guide* and the *Treatise on Prayer and Meditation* by Louis of Granada were put on the Index. Teresa of Avila, John of the Cross, and Ignatius of Loyola all came under suspicion because of the anti-illuminism of the period. See T. K. Connolly, NCE 1:356; J. Vincke, LTK 1:407.

AMALRIC OF BÈNE (Amalricus, Amaury, Amauri de Chartres; d. 1206 or 1207), inspirer of the Amalricians. Professor of logic and theology at the Univ. of Paris, A. apparently followed the teaching of John Scotus Erigena. In 1209 clerics and laymen calling themselves Amalricians were discovered in Paris teaching pantheism, proclaiming the age of the incarnation of the Holy Spirit in every man, and that those who were so deified were like Christ incapable of sinning. A.'s teaching was condemned by a synod in Paris in 1210 and by Lateran Council IV in 1215 (D 808). The errors of the Amalricians seem to have occasioned a proscription of Aristotle's writings on natural philosophy in 1215. See Bihlmeyer-Tüchle 2:306; Gilson HCP 240–241, 654.

AMALRICIANS, a name for those who, in the early 13th cent., followed the pantheistic and antinomian teachings of *Amalric of Bène.

AMANA CHURCH SOCIETY, one of the oldest and most successful American communal bodies. It originated under the influence of *Pietism in western Germany when Johann Rock and Eberhard Grüber organized the Community of True Inspiration in 1714. Calling for a return to pure Christianity and a life of simplicity, members held that God deals directly with man through inspiration and revelation. After initial success, the group declined until 1817, when it was revived by Christian Metz and Barbara Heineman, who again claimed the charism of inspiration. Difficulties with the German government over their pacificism and opposition to oaths led the group in 1842 to immigrate to the U.S.; near Buffalo, N.Y., they adopted a pure communist form of living in order to pursue more effectively their ideal of Christian simplicity. When additional land and greater isolation became desirable, they migrated in 1854 to Iowa, where they founded the town of Amana and several adjacent villages. Communal forms were followed until 1932, when the members voted a reorganization of community life. All property and control of temporal affairs was vested in a joint stock corporation, the Amana Society, which today farms the original 25,000 acres and also manages a variety of business enterprises. The Amana Church Society, governed by elected elders, handles all ecclesiastical matters.

The doctrine of the society is basically that of the evangelical tradition, along with the distinguishing belief that God "even now operates audibly through the instruments of true inspiration." There is no paid ministry and services consist mainly of prayer, testimony, and readings from the works of the inspired. Baptism by water is rejected in favor of the concept of baptism as a purely spiritual occurrence. The rite of confirmation is observed at the age of 15. The Lord's Supper with *footwashing is celebrated rarely. Older regulations governing simplicity of dress, house, and amusements have been relaxed, as has been the ban on participation in warfare. In 1967 there were 761 members in the 7 congregations.

AMERICAN BAPTIST ASSOCIATION, fundamentalist body with historical and theological antecedents in *Landmarkism. As early as 1850, Landmarkists posed a threat to cooperation at the denominational level among Southern Baptists: they rejected a move to transfer control of the mission enterprise from local churches to denominational boards and formed a separate missionary program. The continuing drift of the Southern Baptist Convention away from an ecclesiology based on the *local church toward associations of churches resulted in the organization of the American Baptist Association at Texarkana, Tex., in 1902. The heaviest population of these churches is to be found in the SW; in 1968 there were 3,247 churches with 731,-000 members. Because of the strong emphasis on the autonomy of the local church, the denomination receives the name Church Equality Baptists.

AMERICAN BAPTIST CONVENTION, a large denomination, organized in 1907 as the Northern Baptist Convention. Although defending congregational polity and local church autonomy, prerevolutionary Baptists formed themselves into voluntary *associations to develop fellowship, mutual concern, and more effective service.

The most formal of these was the Philadelphia Association, founded in 1707 and composed of 25 churches scattered from N.Y. to Virginia. As a result of an inspiring report of missionary opportunities in Burma, several associations of churches met at Philadelphia in 1814 to organize in what was soon called the Triennial Convention. Its activities expanded rapidly and resulted in the formation of additional boards with special interest in home missions and Christian education. All the Baptists in the U.S. continued to work harmoniously until 1845, when regional passions surrounding the question of slavery led to separate organizations in the North and the South (see SOUTHERN BAPTIST CONVENTION). Instead of an over-all denominational organization in the North, a multiplicity of agencies conducted missionary, educational, and social work, until need for better coordination led to the formation of the Northern Baptist Convention (1907). The name was changed in 1950 to the American Baptist Convention. Several reorganizational steps were taken after 1950, resulting in 1961 in doubling the size of the general council of the denomination to include all executive ministers of state conventions, heads of agencies, and staff persons. The heads of each separate society became associate general secretaries of the Convention. National offices were moved from New York City to Valley Forge, Pennsylvania.

In 1968 the Convention reported a membership of 1,538,988, in 6,063 churches. While adhering to traditional Baptist teaching and polity, the Convention is theologically more progressive than some other Baptist groups; it accepts *open communion and participates in ecumenical endeavors. Missionary work, increasingly ecumenical and cooperative, is done in 12 foreign and 11 home mission fields. Among the most active Protestant denominations in the field of higher education, the Convention founded, and still maintains ties with, 22 colleges, 11 junior colleges, 4 preparatory schools, and 8 seminaries. Among the great universities historically connected with it are Brown Univ., Bucknell Univ., and the

Univ. of Chicago. See O. K. and M. M. Armstrong, *Indomitable Baptists* (1967).

AMERICAN BIBLE CHURCHES, name used by local churches belonging to the *American Evangelical Christian Churches.

AMERICAN BIBLE SOCIETY (ABS), an organization founded in New York City in 1816 for the purpose of distributing faithful translations of the Scriptures, in all languages, at low cost or free, throughout the world. ABS works in 150 countries and distributes Scripture translations in more than 1,300 languages and dialects. Most translations are made by missionaries in the field, working with Christian nationals. ABS also supplies Bibles for the blind, in Braille and on "Talking Bible" records. To avoid theological controversy or competition with commercial publishers, its Bibles are limited to the text alone, without notes or comments. Since its inception ABS has distributed more than 800 million complete or partial Bibles, with an annual average, in the 1960s, of 43 million.

AMERICAN BOARD of Commissioners For Foreign Missions (ABCFM), the first missionary society in the U.S. to send missionaries overseas. The ABCFM was formed in 1810 by a group of Congregationalists who had experienced a call to the missions while students at Williams College at a famous "haystack meeting" in 1807. It was incorporated legally in Mass. 2 years later. From the beginning the policy was not narrowly denominational; the board served not only the Congregational but also *Reformed (1826–66) and Presbyterian Churches (1812–70). Even after these arrangements were terminated, the ABCFM continued to sponsor Christian missionaries of many denominations. First missionaries, among them L. *Rice and A. *Judson, were sent to India in 1812. The field was extended throughout the Near East, the Far East, and Africa. From 1868 onward three Woman's Board of Missions worked in conjunction with ABCFM, and were amalgamated with it in 1927. Various mergers of the Congregational Churches have resulted in the ABCFM's becoming part of the United Church Board for World Ministries, formed in 1961, one of the instrumentalities of the *United Church of Christ.

AMERICAN CATHOLIC CHURCH (Syro-Antiochean), a Church combining Old Catholic and Roman Catholic elements in its doctrine, worship, and discipline, but which is completely independent. Syro-Antiochean in the title refers to the episcopal succession of its bishops, which derives through J. R. *Vilatte from the Syrian Jacobite Church. The history of this Church is traced back to the body established by Vilatte in 1885 in Wisconsin; but its present organization dates from 1915. Briefly (1925–26) it was in communion with the North American Old Catholic Church and the Polish National Catholic Church. E. L. Petersen, primate from 1940, compiled its present liturgy. Headquarters are in Miami, Fla.; in 1969 Archbishop H. F. Wilkie was president; membership was 450.

AMERICAN CATHOLIC CHURCH, Archdiocese of New York, a Church with Old Catholic and Roman Catholic doctrines and ritual, but not belonging to either communion. J. F. A. Lashley established it in 1927, and received episcopal consecration that derived through J. R. *Vilatte from the Syrian Jacobite Church (see EPISCOPI VAGANTES). Membership in 1969 was 8,347, with 20 churches, all in the New York City area.

AMERICAN COUNCIL OF CHRISTIAN CHURCHES (ACCC), a body made up of 15 conservative fundamentalist Churches. The founder and until 1968 the dominant personality was Carl McIntire (b. 1906). It was organized in 1941 to provide a means of cooperative effort by Churches whose members felt that the Federal Council of Churches (now National Council of Churches) gave too wide a latitude to theological liberals and economic socialists. There are no official figures available on ACCC membership. The *Southern Methodist Church and the *Bible Presbyterian Church (Collingswood Synod) are among the member Churches. Headquarters are maintained in New York City. In 1968 Dr. McIntire's influence was challenged, and a strain in relations with his *International Council of Christian Churches developed. The ACCC should not be confused with the *National Association of Evangelicals, which represents a wider spectrum than the politically conservative American Council of Christian Churches, with its right-wing activism.

AMERICAN ETHICAL UNION, a federation of societies belonging to the *Ethical Culture movement. Established in 1889, it was in 1968 made up of about 30 societies, with a total membership of about 7,000.

AMERICAN EVANGELICAL CHRISTIAN CHURCHES (American Bible Churches), an association of *local churches formed in 1944 with the aim of compromising the differences between pure *Calvinism and *Arminianism. Member churches, which are autonomous, are usually known as American Bible Churches. *Community Churches are also affiliated. Ministerial applicants subscribe to: (1) the Bible as the written word of God; (2) the virgin birth; (3) the deity of Christ; (4) salvation through Christ's atonement; (5) the guidance of life through prayer; (6) Christ's second coming; and (7) the establishment of the kingdom of God on earth.

AMERICAN EVANGELICAL LUTHERAN CHURCH, one of four Churches that in 1962 entered the union forming the *Lutheran Church in America. It had been established for Danish immigrants in the Midwest in 1872; the name Danish Evangelical Lutheran Church in America, which was adopted in 1874, was changed in 1954 to American Evangelical Lutheran Church. See EncLuthCh 2:1367–68.

AMERICAN LUTHERAN CHURCH, one of the three principal bodies of the Lutheran Church in North America, the others being the Lutheran Church in America and the Lutheran Church—Missouri Synod. The American Lutheran Church was created in 1961. It brought together four groups that had previously been distinct bodies, although they were involved together in many forms of cooperation and fellowship: the American Lutheran Church (formed in 1930 from the Iowa, Ohio, and Buffalo Synods), the Evangelical Lutheran Church (a body uniting various synodical groups of Norwegian background), the *United Evangelical Lutheran Church (a Danish-American body), and the *Lutheran Free Church (a Norwegian-American group). Geographically, the American Lutheran Church is strongest in the Midwest and upper Midwest, with considerable representation also in the Pacific Northwest. Theologically, it combines a variety of emphases within the Lutheran tradition, including both orthodox and pietist theologies in its heritage (see ORTHODOXY; PIETISM). This combination has tended to cast it in a mediating role between the Lutheran Church in America and the Lutheran Church—Missouri Synod. With both it had established full fellowship of pulpit and altar by 1969. It has been neither as vigorous in its ecumenical role as the former of these synods nor as aloof from other, non-Lutheran groups as the latter. Characteristic of the American Lutheran Church has been a strong interest in the Christian world mission. From its Pietist roots in both Germany (esp. as represented by the work of Wilhelm *Löhe) and Scandinavia it has inherited the general concern for evangelization and a specific interest in certain fields of mission work, including Africa. In the U.S., too, the Pietist heritage has stimulated a greater attention to the evangelistic task of the Church than has sometimes characterized Lutheranism. The headquarters of the American Lutheran Church are in Minneapolis, Minnesota. Its seminaries are: Luther Seminary, Saint Paul, Minnesota; Wartburg Seminary, Dubuque, Iowa; and Capital Seminary, Columbus, Ohio. Its total membership of baptized and confirmed Lutherans is approximately one-third of the eight million total of American Lutheranism as a whole, numbering (1969) 2,575,506 baptized souls. See F. Meuser et al., EncLuthCh 1:44–59.

AMERICAN MILLENNIAL ASSOCIATION, an organization formed in 1858 at Boston, Mass., to propagate the teachings of the *Evangelical Adventists.

AMERICAN PRAYER BOOK, the authorized liturgical book of the Protestant Episcopal Church. The Anglican churches in the American colonies used the BCP in its Jacobean (1604) and Caroline (1662) editions. After the Revolution a revision of the BCP was adopted as the norm of liturgical worship by the first *General Convention of the Protestant Episcopal Church in 1789. In addition to necessary alterations in the prayers for civil rulers, the principal change made in this first American Prayer Book was the form of holy communion, derived from the 1764 Liturgy of the Scottish Episcopalian *nonjurors, who had consecrated the first American bp. in 1784, Samuel *Seabury of Connecticut. The rite, in distinction to the BCP form, included in the consecration of the Eucharist an oblation of the elements and an invocation of the Holy Spirit. Major revisions were completed in 1892 and in 1928, with enrichments from ancient and modern sources, and with more flexible rubrical adaptations for varied occasions of public worship. The General Convention of 1967 authorized a new revision, now in process, with trial use of proposed forms prepared by the Standing Liturgical Commission. The trial revisions have met with a very mixed reaction from members of the Church.

Canon law of the Episcopal Church requires all public services to conform to the text of a standard book in the charge of an official custodian. Alterations may be made only by vote of two successive general conventions, which meet triennially. Diocesan bps. may authorize forms for special occasions not provided by the Prayer Book. See E. L. Parsons and B. H. Jones, *American Prayer Book, Its Origins and Principles* (1937); M. H. Shepherd, Jr., *Oxford American Prayer Book Commentary* (1950).

AMERICAN PROTECTIVE ASSOCIATION (APA), an organization founded to oppose the RC Church and its parochial schools. The APA was established on March 13, 1887, in Clinton, Iowa, by Henry F. Bowers and seven other men. It carried on the tradition of *nativism and Know-Nothingism and sought to limit the growth of Roman Catholicism in the U.S. by restricting immigration. APA activities centered in the mid-western states; membership grew when it was announced that Abp. F. Satolli would arrive in 1892 as first apostolic delegate to the U.S. By 1896 the APA claimed 1 million members and achieved a measure of influence in Republican politics. It had recognized chapters in 24 states, published more than 70 periodicals, and sponsored lectures by former priests and former nuns warning against the Roman menace. Some Protestants, such as Washington *Gladden, branded the APA as bigoted and un-American. W. J. H. Traynor, editor of the *American Patriot,* succeeded Bowers as president of the APA in 1894. Political errors led to a rapid decline after 1900, but the organization lingered on until 1911. See D. L. Kinzer, *Episode in Anti-Catholicism: The American Protective Association* (1964).

AMERICAN RESCUE WORKERS, an organization that developed by separation from the *Salvation Army. Maj. Thomas E. Moore was appointed commander of the American Salvation Army forces by William *Booth a few months after the first Salvationists landed in the U.S. in 1880. Under Moore's direction the work expanded rapidly (1881–84), and beginnings were made in Canada. Following Booth's directions, Moore held all property in his own name and was responsible only to Booth. He sought to incorporate the Salvation Army as a religious body to own property in its own right and to make it more democratic in its polity. Moore was dismissed and in 1885 organized his following under the name Salvation Army in America, and under the direction of five trustees. In 1889 a second split led to reunion of one group with the British parent body; the other remained loyal to Moore (who died in 1898 as pastor of a Baptist church in Kansas). In 1913 the Moore group changed its name to American Rescue Workers. In 1968 it directed 99 stations with 338 evangelists and 31,140 members. Its beliefs, type of organization, and fields of dedication are indistinguishable from those of the Salvation Army.

AMERICAN TRACT SOCIETY, an organization founded in New York City in 1825 for the dissemination of Protestant literature. The society was interdenominational, and received strong financial support. It published and distributed not only "tracts," or leaflets, but also Sunday school literature and volumes of Protestant devotion, history, and biography. It was the publisher for temperance movements and *Bible societies, and helped in the evangelization of immigrants and of settlers in places where there was no church.

AMERICAN UNITARIAN ASSOCIATION, denomination formed in 1825, incorporated in 1847, and since 1961 part of the *Unitarian Universalist Association.

AMERICANISM, a term associated with the debate within Roman Catholicism in the U.S. in the late 19th cent. concerning the extent to which traditional RC practices should be adapted to the American milieu. In the effort to relate Roman Catholicism to American society, the open-minded approach of some bps., e.g., James Gibbons, John Ireland, and John J. Keane, was viewed with suspicion by the more conservative members of the Church led by Abp. Michael A. Corrigan of N.Y., who feared that such efforts threatened the integrity of RC doctrine. Controversy between the two groups over parochial schools and the language question (whether, as a protection to faith, to preserve the native language and customs of the immigrants or to Americanize them as quickly as possible) was further exacerbated by such incidents as the participation of Gibbons, Keane, and others in the Parliament of Religions held in conjunction with the Chicago Columbian Exposition (1893); differences of opinion with regard to Catholic membership in the Knights of Labor and other societies; and debate over the single tax proposal of Henry George. When a French translation of W. Elliott's *Life of Father Hecker* led to an exaggerated interpretation of the author's ascetical principles and apologetical practices, the issues of Americanism were hotly debated in France, where the progressives and conservatives were already at odds over the *ralliement*, a movement inspired by the Pope for Catholic acceptance and participation in the French Republic.

In his apostolic letter *Testem benevolentiae* addressed to Gibbons (Jan. 22, 1899), Leo XIII referred to the controversy aroused by the *Life of Father Hecker*, esp. in the interpretations given in European reviews, and he condemned as false doctrines certain new ideas concerning the manner of leading a Christian life. Based on the principle that the Church should relax its ancient rigor and develop more effective ways of attracting converts, the condemned errors maintained that in an era of liberty external guidance was less necessary in the search for Christian perfection; that the natural virtues were better suited to modern times than the supernatural; that the active virtues were more important than such "passive" virtues as humility and obedience; and that religious vows were opposed to the spirit of the present time and that religious life was of little use to the Church.

In his letter, the Pope did not say that anyone held the condemned propositions, and he made it clear that he exempted those laudable political and social qualities of the American people that were also sometimes called Americanism. In the U.S., the more conservative prelates thanked the Pope for saving the American Church from the danger of heresy, while the followers of Gibbons maintained that no American Catholic held the condemned doctrines and that the errors that had acquired the name of Americanism were caricatures of the real ideas of Father Hecker and of American Catholicism as it actually existed. The papal condemnation tended to accentuate the generally conservative cast of American Catholicism, and the subsequent censure of *modernism (1907) contributed further to the theological silence characteristic of the RC Church in the U.S. in the succeeding decades. See T. T. McAvoy, *Americanist Heresy in Roman Catholicism* (1963); R. D. Cross, *Emergence of Liberal Catholicism in America* (1958); A. M. Greeley, *Catholic Experience* (1967), 150–215.

AMERICANS UNITED for Separation of Church and State, a shorter form of title used by *Protestants and Other Americans United for Separation of Church and State (POAU).

AMILLENARIANISM (Amillennialism), the studied disbelief in millenarianist doctrine, whether of the premillenarian or postmillenarian variety. Those characterized as amillenarianists generally base their position on the claim that the scriptural passages on which millenarianists rely, esp. Rev ch. 20, are figurative and allegorical and hence cannot reasonably be taken in a literal sense. *MILLENARIANISM.

AMIS DE L'HOMME (Friends of Man), a sect founded in Switzerland by Alexandre Freytag (1870–1947). It is sometimes called the Army of the Eternal, and sometimes also the Church of the Kingdom of God. Freytag was a disciple of C. T. *Russell from about 1898 and in 1916 was a prominent member of the coterie of Bible Students at Geneva. Disappointed with the unfulfillment of prophecies credited among the Bible Students, he began to develop a doctrine of his own. He published three books: *Divine Revelation* (1918); *Message to Humanity* (1922); and *Life Eternal* (1923). More than a million copies of his writings have been sold. He claimed to be the messenger announced in Mal 3.1 and the faithful servant of Mt 24.45. Denying the immortality of the soul, he taught that eternal life is something man could enjoy here on earth if only he could free himself from the sin of egoism, the one sin to which all evils and sickness are reducible. The achievement of pure altruism was therefore to be the cardinal objective of believers. This positive aspect of their doctrine and the benevolent activities in which it is expressed throw a friendlier light on the Amis than their somber millennial inheritance would cause one to expect. But like the Bible Students and the Jehovah's Witnesses, they hold other religions, and esp. the Roman Catholic, in abomination. Their methods of spreading their message have much in common with those of the Jehovah's Witnesses. With imperturbably courteous persistence they go methodically from door to door with their literature. After Freytag's death there was a division among his followers. One segment, led by M. Ruffner, carried on with headquarters at Cartigny in Switzerland, and some French groups have been faithful to this allegiance. Most of the French groups, however, accepted the leadership of Bernard Sayerce, who was already head of the movement in France during Freytag's lifetime. He claimed that Freytag had destined him to succeed to leadership of all the Amis. Headquarters of this segment are in Paris. There are Amis groups in Belgium, Germany, and Italy. See H. C. Chéry, *L'Offensive des sectes* (1961), 198–232.

AMISH MENNONITES, those Mennonites, commonly called simply the Amish, named after J. *Ammann. They separated from the main body of Mennonites in Switzerland and Alsace (1693–97). The main issue was a desire for strict enforcement of *Meidung*, i.e., the avoidance or "shunning" of the excommunicated, and for a more rigid separation from worldly ways. This practice of nonconformity remains their main characteristic; their basic beliefs are Mennonite. There are no longer any Amish in Europe; most migrated to N.A.; the rest rejoined the main body of Mennonites. In the 18th cent. migration to Pa. took place, and there Amish customs and language still reflect the "Pennsylvania Dutch" culture developed by German-speaking Lutherans, Mennonites, Moravians, Reformed, and others. The Amish also have most consistently retained the cultural features that sprang up around Anabaptist-Mennonite beliefs in Switzerland. The Amish continued not only in Pa. but also in Ohio, Ind., Ill., Iowa, Neb., and Kans. and in the Province of Ontario, Canada. As they moved westward, they lost some of their rigidity and adjusted more readily to their environment.

The *Old Order Amish are the most conservative group, and because of their disapproval of a gradual acculturation, numerous splinter groups arose. The Central Conference of Mennonites, or Stuckey Amish, belong to the General Conference Mennonite Church. The Egli Amish separated in 1864 under the influence of a revival movement, which led to the founding of the Defenseless Mennonites, later called the Evangelical Mennonite Church. The "New Amish" (Neutäufer) started in Ohio in 1846; they also came under the influence of revivalism and formed the majority in the organization of the Apostolic Christian Church. A separation in 1927 led to the formation of the Beachy Amish Mennonite Churches. In general, there has been a tendency for separating Amish groups to join one of the larger Mennonite conferences. See J. A. Hostetler, *Annotated Bibliography on the Amish* (1951); MennEnc 1:93–98.

AMMANN, JAKOB (fl. 17th cent.), founder of the *Amish Mennonites. He was a Mennonite elder in the Canton of Bern, Switzerland, when in 1693 he excommunicated all the other elders of Switzerland. His grievance was their refusal to impose *Meidung*, or *avoidance of the excommunicated. The action caused the separation of his followers, the Amish, as a distinct body of Mennonites. His conservatism extended to other practices, e.g., simple uniformity in dress, that remain typical of the Amish. He also introduced *footwashing into the Swiss Mennonite congregations. He resided in Alsace, possibly as elder of a congregation, probably from 1694 to 1708, but little else is known of him. See MennEnc 1:98–99.

AMOSITES, named for Amos of Wodnian, a small party among the *Bohemian Brethren who maintained, against the majority decision, that for Christians to support civil law or authority was contrary to the gospel.

AMSDORF, NIKOLAUS VON (1483–1565), German Lutheran theologian. While a professor at Wittenberg (1511–24), A. became a close friend and disciple of Martin Luther, assisted him in translating the Bible, and later supervised the Jena edition (1555–58) of Luther's works. Luther and the elector of Saxony named A. bp. of Naumburg-Zeitz (1542–47), but the Imperialists expelled him during the Schmalkaldic War. A. urged the high Lutheran party to separate from *Melanchthon (1557) and fought ceaselessly for Luther's teachings, though in doing so he was maneuvered into the extreme position of declaring that *good works are actually detrimental to salvation, a teaching repudiated by Article IV of the *Formula of Concord (1577). See P. Brun-

ner, *Nikolaus Von Amsdorf als Bischof von Naumburg* (1961); A. Kawerau, EncRelKnow 1:159. *SYNERGISTIC CONTROVERSY; *MAJORISTIC CONTROVERSY.

AMSTERDAM ASSEMBLY, first general assembly of the *World Council of Churches (WCC), Aug. 22–Sept. 4, 1948. It had as its theme "Man's Disorder and God's Design," and was attended by 351 delegates from 44 countries and 147 Churches, plus alternates, consultants, observers, and visitors. Membership was based on the formula, later revised: "The World Council of Churches is a fellowship of churches which accept the Lord Jesus Christ as God and Saviour." The WCC was formally constituted Aug. 23. The Assembly adopted a constitution, designated Geneva as headquarters, and elected W. A. Visser 't Hooft general secretary. The following were to serve jointly as presidents: Pastor M. Boegner (Reformed, France), Abp. G. Fisher (Anglican, England), Prof. T. C. Chao (Anglican, China), Bp. G. B. *Oxnam (Methodist, U.S.), Abp. S. Germanos (Orthodox, Greece), and Abp. E. Eidem (Lutheran, Sweden). See W. A. Visser 't Hooft, ed., *Man's Disorder and God's Design* (5v., 1949).

AMYRALDISM, interpretation of the doctrine of predestination named for M. *Amyraut (1596–1684). Described as "hypothetic universalism," the theory includes these points: God wills all men to be saved provided they believe; man has the power, but in practice, because of *total depravity, not the will to fulfill this provision; only those are unconditionally chosen to be saved who by grace are the elect. Amyraldism was rejected in the *Helvetic Consensus Formula (1675). See Schaff Creeds 1:480–483.

AMYRAUT, MOÏSE (1596–1684), French Calvinist theologian, proponent of a theory on *predestination called after him Amyraldism. From 1633 he was a professor at the theological academy in Saumur, and was a respected representative of the *Reformed Church in France. In an era of sharp conflict A.'s works were notably pacific and moderate. See R. Stauffer, *M. A.: Un Précurseur français de l'oecuménisme* (1962).

ANABAPTISTS (rebaptizers; Gr. *ana*, again), diverse Reformation groups named from the practice of repeating baptism. The more essential, subjectivist content of the Anabaptist religious message was similar to teachings of such medieval groups as the *Beghards, *Brothers and Sisters of the Free Spirit, *Waldenses, and *Taborites, but no historical connection has been proved. The Anabaptists were inspired by the extreme interpretations of Reformation doctrine developed in Germany and in Switzerland. In both places religious ideas became intermingled with socio-political currents, and Anabaptists became the object of ferocious persecution by civil and ecclesiastical authority, both Protestant and Catholic, and were slaughtered by the thousands. The Anabaptists of German origin were revolutionaries, prominent among them the *Zwickau Prophets, N. *Storch, and T. *Münzer. The *apocalypticism of Münzer was brought to Holland by M. *Hoffmann; persecution there led to the flight of *John of Leiden, and Jan *Matthys and to the establishment of the theocratic kingdom of Münster. This episode of religious and moral extravagance, ending in bloodshed, put an end to the revolutionary side of the Anabaptist movement (1555).

In Switzerland leaders of the *Swiss Brethren (see GREBEL, C.; BLAUROCK, G.; HUBMAIER, B.; MANZ, F.), breaking with H. *Zwingli *c.*1520, stressed more the Anabaptist religious vision and practiced passive nonresistance toward secular authority. The central religious message of such Anabaptists was that saving faith is essentially a freely accepted inner experience of Christ and that the rule of faith is no external authority, not even the Bible, but the inspiration of the Holy Spirit given to the individual believer. One consequence was that baptism is meaningful only as the adult's outward profession of personal faith. (See BELIEVER'S BAPTISM; INFANT BAPTISM.) Another was the social equality of all believers and their freedom from any subjection to, or involvement with, civil authority.

The Anabaptist religious message was taken up by *Menno Simons, and J. *Huter and continues among *Mennonites and *Hutterian Brethren. Emphasis on inner experience influenced H. *Niclaes (see FAMILISTS), S. *Franck, and C. *Schwenkfeld (see SCHWENKFELDERS). Further, the religious ideals of the Anabaptists affected subsequent religious history in Holland and England and so in the United States. This influence included rejection of rigid Calvinism (see ARMINIANISM; EPISCOPIUS, S.), and opposition to an *established Church, stress on inner religious experience, human brotherhood and equality, nonviolence and pacifism. Such ideas helped form the religious milieu in which the Religious Society of Friends and the Baptists came into being. See R. S. Armour, *Anabaptist Baptism* (1966); H. S. Bender, *Anabaptist Vision* (Pa., 1955); F. Blanke, *Brothers in Christ* (tr. J. Nordenhang, pa., 1961); G. W. Forell, NCE I:459–460; H. J. Hillerbrand, ed., *Bibliography of Anabaptism 1520–1630* (1962); MennEnc I:113–116, 532–534; and the series of Anabaptist sources published by Herald Press, Mennonite Publishing House, Scottsdale, Pennsylvania.

ANCESTOR CULT (Africa), veneration for family ancestors, also called currently "remembrance of the living dead." South of the Sahara Desert, the ancestor cult is still important in the religion of 70% of the 700 African tribes on the continent; but it is completely absent from the remaining 30%. As an expression of family and clan continuity and solidarity, the recently deceased ancestors (especially illustrious persons or those who died with a grievance) are regarded as still inhabiting the family land. They exercise absolute control over the living; all life exists under their surveillance. They are treated with fear and reverence; they are venerated and, occasionally, worshiped. Special shrines may be built for them or masks worn for them to speak through.

In contemporary Africa the ancestor cult is still a force to be reckoned with. Among the Bantu peoples in particular, it represents the hierarchical social system carried over into the spirit world; it validates the traditional political structure; it ensures fertility, health, prosperity, and the continuity of past and future in family life; and it is a sanction for the respect of living elders. To attack it, therefore, as Protestant and RC missionaries almost without exception have done, was to attack something basic in tribal and family structure.

In reaction to this attack, the *African Independent Church Movement across the continent has reasserted the ancestor cult to some extent. Some bodies actually mention the ancestors in their name: Dini ya Msambwa (Religion of the Ancestors) in Kenya, Église de Nos Ancêtres in the Congo (Kinshasa), and Calici ca Mokolo (Church of the Ancestors) in Malawi. In South-West Africa, the Herero Church combines ancestral worship with the holy communion service. Hence, although most similar bodies across Africa hold the basic doctrines of Christian faith, they have attempted to Christianize, with varying success, this deep-rooted belief of traditional societies in their solidarity with the ancestors.

ANDERSON, LARS (Laurentius, Lorenz Andreae; *c.*1480–1522), Swedish theologian and Reformer. After study at Rostock, Leipzig, and Greifswald, A. became a canon at Strägnäs and secretary to Bp. Mattias. He was converted to Lutheranism by Olavus Petri whom he helped to introduce the Reformation into Sweden. When the Swedish estates chose Gustavus Vasa as king, A. was appointed chancellor (1523). He had a major part in the proceedings of the Council of Örebro (1529), which gave political status to the new Church, but for opposing Vasa's later attempt to give the Swedish Church a presbyterian polity he was convicted of treason and sentenced to death along with Olavus Petri. The penalty, however, was commuted to a heavy fine and deprivation of office; A. spent the rest of his life in retirement. See J. Wordsworth, *National Church of Sweden* (1911).

ANDREÄ, JAKOB (1528–90), German Lutheran theologian. He was also called by the German name *Schmidlin* and the Latin *Faber* from the fact that his father was a blacksmith. Ordained in 1546, A. helped introduce the Lutheran reform teachings and *church order in many places in Germany. He was counselor of Duke Christopher of Württemberg at the Diets of Regensburg (1557) and Augsburg (1559); attended several theological colloquies with *Reformed theologians; and was made (1561) professor of theology and chancellor at the Univ. of Tübingen. From 1568 onward he worked to rescue Lutheranism from the divisions caused by disputes between Gnesiolutherans and Crypto-Calvinists. Six sermons that he preached in 1572 on these controversies began a process of conciliation culminated by the *Formula of Concord (1577). One of its co-authors and signers, he wrote the *Epitome* to the Formula. See A. Piepkorn, EncLuthCh 1:73–74.

ANDREWES, LANCELOT (1555–1626), Anglican bp., theologian, preacher. Educated at Pembroke Hall, Cambridge, A. was elected to a fellowship there (1576), took orders (1580), and as a prebendary of St. Paul's (from 1589) came to prominence as a preacher. Twice he refused offers of a bishopric, but was finally persuaded by King James I, who esteemed him greatly, to accept appointment to the See of Chichester (1605). He later was transferred to Ely (1609), and thence to Winchester (1613). A. was one of the translators of the Authorized Version of the Bible; the Pentateuch and historical books of the OT are in large part his work. His exposure to Puritan influence during his Cambridge days in no way shook his fundamental conservatism. Although firmly antipapal and an able defender of the English Church against the attack of Robert Bellarmine, A. was in many respects (e.g., in his view of the Eucharist) theologically nearer to the traditional Catholic than to the Protestant position. This appeared also in his attachment to older liturgical forms. He had a marked aversion to Calvinism and is regarded as a representative of distinctively Anglican theology, upon which he had a strong formative influence. His literary fame rests primarily upon his sermons, which are perhaps too intricate and erudite for modern taste, but are yet rewarding in the delicacy and power of their language and in the rich meaning A. never fails to extract from his texts. In his personal life he was ascetical and saintly. His *Preces privatae* (*Manual of Private Devotions*), a collection of prayers composed for his own use, is a classic of devotional literature. Works: II v., ed. J. P. Wilson and J. Bliss (LACT, 1841–54). See R. W. Church, "Lancelot Andrewes," in A. Barry, ed., *Masters of English Theology* (1877); T. S. Eliot, *For L. A.* (1928).

ANGELIC BRETHREN (Ger. Engelsbrüder), a spiritualistic group called also Gichtelians, after the founder Johann Georg Gichtel (1638–1710). He was a lawyer, who claimed to have visions and mystical dreams. He came in conflict with the Lutheran Church over his mysticism and agitation for church reform and was expelled from Regensburg as a heretic. After a period of wandering, he settled in Amsterdam. Deeply impressed by the writings of J. *Boehme, he edited their first complete edition (1682). The Angelic Brethren were not members of any Church, but held their own gatherings of silent worship and of testimony to their own visionary experiences. The name connotes their imitation of angels by the renunciation of marriage (Mt 22.30) and devotion to quiet contemplation; they also practiced voluntary poverty. Small communities in The Netherlands, Germany, and Russia survived into the 20th century. See Gründler 1:454; M. Schmidt, RGG 2:1568–69.

ANGELUS CLARENUS (Peter of Fossombrone; *c.*1245–1337), a leader of the Franciscan *Spirituals in Italy. Born Peter at Fossombrone, he entered the Friars Minor in 1270. He was a cleric but not a priest, and gained fame as a preacher, moralist, and translator of the Greek Fathers. Opposing all mitigations of the Franciscan rule in regard to poverty, he held that neither pope, nor council, nor general chapter could change it because, like the Scriptures, it was inspired. He was imprisoned (1275) for his intransigent advocacy of Spiritual doctrines. After his release (1289) he joined a group of like-minded friars who were going as missionaries to Armenia. Peter took the name Angelus, and the group became known as *Celestines in 1294, when Celestine V granted them immunity from the jurisdiction of the Franciscan minister general. When the immunity was revoked by Boniface VIII, the group retired to the Island of Trixonia in the Gulf of Corinth. At the death of Liberatus of Macerata (1307) A. assumed leadership of the fugitive company, which thereafter was known as *Clareni. In 1311 he was summoned to Avignon to answer charges of heresy but was protected by Card. Colonna. After the bull of John XXII, *Sancta Romana* (1317), A. was excommunicated and imprisoned, but he succeeded in getting his freedom through a letter of appeal to the Pope.

Returning to Italy, he reorganized his followers and proclaimed them the true Friars Minor and the authentic Church of Christ. After a period of security until 1334, A. had to flee to Basilicata, farther south in Italy, and there he died. His most influential writing was *Historia septem tribulationum*. A. has been accused of *Joachimism, but C. Pesaro and others have attempted to establish his great sanctity. See L. Bernardini, *Frate Angelo da Chiarino* *alla luce della storia* (1964); V. Doucet, "Angelus Clarenus ad Alvarum Pelagium," AFH 39 (1946), 63–200; D. Douie, *Nature and Effects of the Heresy of the Fraticelli* (1932), 49–80; L. Oliger, *Expositio Regulae Fratrum Minorum auctore Angelo Clareno* (1912), ix–lxxvii; C. Pesaro, *Il Clareno* (1921); L. von Auw, *Angelo Clareno et les Spirituels franciscains* (1952).

ANGLICAN CHURCH, the *Church of England; also used commonly of any of the Churches of the *Anglican Communion.

ANGLICAN CHURCH OF CANADA, since 1893 an autocephalous Church of the *Anglican Communion. Third largest of Canadian religious bodies, it has 1,300,000 members in its 28 dioceses, grouped in four ecclesiastical provinces. The Church shares a common origin with the Protestant Episcopal Church in the U.S. Prior to the American Revolution, political considerations both in England and in the colonies prevented the establishment of the episcopate in N.A., and Anglican jurisdiction was loosely vested in the bp. of London. With the coming of independence to the U.S. the C of E in the remaining provinces of British N.A. began developing its own separate tradition. The emigration of the continuing loyalists from the U.S. following the Revolution added strength to the scattered Anglican population, esp. in Ontario and Nova Scotia. In 1787 Charles Inglis (1734–1816), sometime rector of Trinity parish in New York City, was consecrated bp. of Nova Scotia, the first Anglican bp. appointed outside the British Isles. Aided by the British missionary societies, the Anglican Church moved westward with the nation. The confederation of four civil provinces to form the Dominion of Canada (1867), and the later addition of other provinces, stimulated parallel action by the Anglican ecclesiastical provinces; in 1893 a national general synod was established and Canada's first primate elected.

The Church remained the Church of England in Canada until 1955, when the title Anglican Church of Canada was adopted, the first use of "Anglican" in such a manner.

Growth in Canadian national unity and self-awareness in the 19th and 20th cents. has been echoed in the life of the Anglican Church. Relations with the Episcopal Church in the U.S. became increasingly strong in the mid-20th cent., culminating in the establishment of the Regional Council of North America in 1968. The Anglican Church of Canada (ACC) has in the past maintained strong ties with the C of E and continues to uphold the faith and order of that Church; it uses in its worship the *Book of Common Prayer, revised in 1918 and again in 1959. Negotiations for organic union with the *United Church of Canada (UCC), on the basis of the *Lambeth Quadrilateral, are being actively pursued. In 1943 the General Synod extended an invitation to other Churches of Canada to explore the subject of Church union; the UCC responded.

In 1965 *The Principles of Union Between the Anglican Church of Canada and the United Church of Canada*, a document prepared by the ACC Committee on Christian Unity and the Church Universal, was formally approved by the General Synod of the ACC and the General Council of the UCC. The General Commission, consisting of 20 persons from each Church, was appointed to implement the *Principles*. A joint office for church union is maintained in Toronto, with an executive commissioner from each Church representing the General Commission. The General Commission has set as its goal the presentation of a basis of union not later than 1972. In June 1967, the Presbyterian Church in Canada agreed to send observers to the meetings of the General Commission. In Dec. 1967, the General Commission invited the Canadian Catholic Conference of Bishops, the Lutheran Church in Canada, and the Canadian Conference of Baptists in Canada to send observer-consultants to its meetings. See P. Carrington, *Anglican*

Church in Canada (1963); *idem, Christian Unity and the Anglican Communion* (1965).

ANGLICAN COMMUNION, "a fellowship, within the One Holy Catholic and Apostolic Church, of those duly constituted Dioceses, Provinces, or Regional Churches in communion with the See of Canterbury" (1930 Lambeth Conference, Resolution 49). The definition adds that these Churches "uphold and propagate the Catholic and Apostolic faith and order as it is generally set forth in the Book of Common Prayer"; "are particular or national churches, and, as such, promote within each of their territories a national expression of Christian faith, life and worship"; and "are bound together not by a central legislative and executive authority, but by mutual loyalty sustained through the common counsel of the Bishops in conference." The name seems to have been used first in 1851. "Anglican" refers not to language or culture but to common ancestry in the Church of England.

In this fellowship 21 churches are included. Four are in the British Isles—the Church of England, the Church in Wales, the Church of Ireland, and the Episcopal Church in Scotland. Next oldest in separate existence are the Protestant Episcopal Church in the U.S. and the Anglican Church of Canada. Following (in the Lambeth order of seniority) are the Church of India, Pakistan, Burma, and Ceylon; the Church of England in Australia; and the Churches of the Provinces of New Zealand, of South Africa, and of the West Indies. Founded by Anglican missionary effort are Nippon Sei Ko Kai (Holy Catholic Church of Japan) and Chung-Hua Sheng Kung Hui (Holy Catholic Church of China). More recently organized Churches are those of the Provinces of West Africa and Central Africa, the Archbishopric in Jerusalem, the Province of East Africa, and the Church of Uganda, Rwanda, and Burundi. The first autocephalous Church in Latin America is the Igréja Episcopal do Brasil. There are also 11 extraprovincial dioceses under the abp. of Canterbury; and finally the Iglésia Episcopal de Cuba, an extra-provincial diocese under its own metropolitan council. About 46 million Christians are included (1969) in the membership of the various Churches, gathered in 364 dioceses in 35 ecclesiastical provinces.

The unity of the Anglican Communion is neither constitutional nor confessional. The prayer books of the various Churches differ increasingly as revision and liturgical development continue; nevertheless, there is still unity in the central matters of faith and order among the Churches, and the lack of a "central legislative and executive authority" has thrown correspondingly greater weight on various voluntary and informal but significant inter-Anglican agencies and gatherings. The *Lambeth Conference is the oldest and most important of these. Second only to it is the Anglican, Congress, a decennial gathering of bishops, priests, and lay people from all Anglican dioceses, last held in 1963 in Toronto. The abp. of Canterbury holds a preeminent position of honor among the Anglican metropolitans and in many ways plays a patriarchal role. Administrative liaison is supplied by the Anglican executive officer, who is responsible for the coordination of many practical matters. See G. W. C. Wand, *Anglicanism in History and Today* (1962); H. G. G. Herklots, *Church of England and the American Episcopal Church* (1966); *idem., Frontiers of the Church* (1961); S. Neill, *Anglicanism* (1958).

ANGLICAN ORDERS, as a point of dispute, orders in the C of E derived from Matthew Parker, Abp. of Canterbury. He was consecrated Dec. 17, 1549, by two bps. who had been consecrated with the rite of the Roman Pontifical under Henry VIII and two others consecrated with the Edwardine Ordinal under Edward VI. This Ordinal was also used at Parker's consecration; all four consecrators joined in the imposition of hands and in uttering the essential form. A further link connecting Anglican orders with the Latin hierarchy is provided by M. de Dominis, a former abp. of

Spalato (Split, Yugo.), who came to England in 1616 and who, like Parker, appears in the table of consecration of all Anglican bps. today. The "Nag's Head Fable," first published in 1604 and asserting that Parker's only consecration was a mock ceremony in a Cheapside tavern, lived on for 3 centuries despite numerous refutations. This and all other attempts to dispute the historical succession of Anglican orders were passed over in silence when their invalidity was reaffirmed in the bull *Apostolicae curae* (1896). The unbroken historical succession of these orders is now admitted by all competent authorities. Beginning in the 1930s the constituent Churches of the *Anglican Communion have entered into intercommunion with the Old Catholic and Polish National Catholic Churches, the orders of which are recognized as valid by the Holy See. The mutual participation of bps. of each of these Churches in the episcopal consecrations of the other Churches has introduced a new valid line of succession into Anglican orders. In 1960 the Holy See took practical cognizance of this changed situation by granting to a converted Anglican priest in the U.S. a matrimonial dispensation from the diriment impediment of the major orders he had received from Anglican bps. of the above succession. On Jan. 27, 1968, Bp. Joseph Höffner of Münster, Germany, gave conditional ordination as deacon and priest to J. J. Hughes, a former priest of the Protestant Episcopal Church, in view of the Old Catholic succession of the Anglican bps. from whom he had previously received the same orders.

Rejection of purely Anglican orders in *Apostolicae curae* is based upon defects of intention and form in the 16th century. (The bull avoids a direct judgment about the validity of the expanded forms of ordination in use among Anglicans since 1662.) In 1956 F. Clark classified no less than seven different interpretations of the intention by those seeking to show why it was rightly condemned. Clark himself presents the most thorough and scholarly reasoning on why the intention was declared invalid; yet the authorities he cites do not, when read in context, support him.

Of greater weight is the papal argument from defect of form. This asserts that the English Reformers rejected the sacrifice of the Mass and drew up their new ordination rites to express this rejection, carefully eliminating from the elements retained from the old rites all references to any priestly power of offering sacrifice in the Mass. These rites were therefore incapable, it is argued, of passing on what opponents of Anglican orders invariably call "the sacrificing priesthood."

Defenders of Anglican orders admit the English Reformers' rejection of eucharistic sacrifice but point out that valid orders can be conveyed and received by those whose theology of orders is heretical. They assert that the denial of the sacrifice of the Mass must be judged in the light of mistaken ideas about eucharistic sacrifice said to have been current in the 16th century. Opponents reply that the ideas of eucharistic sacrifice prevalent on the eve of the Reformation were sound and orthodox and that the English Reformers deliberately rejected this body of traditional teaching. The counter-reply asserts that the vast multiplication of Masses in the late medieval period had produced a highly questionable theology: the idea of a limited value of every Mass with the quantitative conception of grace that this implied, and the widespread idea that each Mass added something to Calvary. They maintain that the Reformers' protest, though exaggerated, was thus occasioned by real theological abuses that are rejected by RC theologians today. The controversy involves a fundamental judgment about the nature of the Reformation and remains unsettled.

Critics of *Apostolicae curae* also argue that it reflects a narrow and polemically colored theology of the ministry that is not fairly representative of the full RC tradition. Contemporary attempts to break the impasse also include the development of radically new ideas about the nature of *apostolic succession, which, if accepted, could open the way to the recognition not only of Anglican orders but of Protestant ministries having no claim to intact historical succession. See F. Clark, *Anglican Or-*

ders and Defect of Intention (1956); *idem.,*
Eucharistic Sacrifice and the Reformation
(2d ed., 1967); J. J. Hughes, *Absolutely Null*
and Utterly Void (1968), with bibliog.;
idem., Stewards of the Lord (1969).

ANGLICAN ORDINALS, the four formularies for conferring orders in the C of E,
important in the history and nature of Anglicanism. The Ordinals have been printed
with the *Book of Common Prayer, although not properly a part of it. The four
Ordinals appeared respectively in 1550,
1552, 1559, and 1662; the last remains in use.
The 1550 Ordinal, the work of T. *Cranmer
and other bishops and theologians, was
modeled on the Pontifical of the Sarum rite.
M. *Bucer's revision of the ordination formula and exhortation to ordinands reflected a pastoral rather than a sacrificial
acceptance of the priesthood. The 1552 Ordinal omitted the ceremony of handing the
chalice with the bread to the ordinand. The
1559 Ordinal contained only minor revisions. The formula was: "Receive the Holy
Ghost. Whose sins thou dost forgive they
are forgiven; whose sins thou dost retain
they are retained. And be thou a faithful
dispenser of the Word of God and of His
Holy Sacraments. In the name of the Father and of the Son and of the Holy Ghost.
Amen." The significant modifications in
the 1662 Ordinal were the insistence in the
preface on the requirement for episcopal
consecration or ordination prior to acceptance as a lawful bishop, priest, or deacon;
the revision of the formula of ordination,
i.e., with the laying on of hands the bishop
was to say, "Receive the Holy Ghost for
the office and work of a priest in the Church
of God, now committed to thee by the imposition of our hands. Whose sins thou dost
forgive they are forgiven; whose sins thou
dost retain they are retained. And be thou
a faithful dispenser of the Word of God and
His Holy Sacraments. In the Name of the
Father and of the Son and of the Holy
Ghost. Amen." The Ordinal printed in the
American Prayer Book substantially conforms in preface and in the actual text to
that of 1662. There is, however, an alternate

form, which omits mention of the forgiveness of sins. See J. J. Hughes, *Absolutely*
Null and Utterly Void (1968), with bibliog.;
J. A. Hardon, *Spirit and Origins of Ameri-*
can Protestantism (1968), 191–200; bibliog.
for Book of Common Prayer. *ANGLICAN
ORDERS.

ANGLICAN ORTHODOX CHURCH, a
Church formed in 1963 by a group, led by
James Parker Dees (1915–   ), that separated
from the Protestant Episcopal Church.
Dees, formerly an Episcopalian priest in
Statesville, N.C., is presiding bp. (1969),
having been consecrated by two bps., one
Ukrainian Orthodox, the other Old Catholic, in 1964; thus the Church possesses the
*historic episcopate and *apostolic succes-
sion. Doctrinally and liturgically the Anglican Orthodox Church is conservative and
evangelical. Biblical inerrancy and a fundamentalist acceptance of Christian teaching,
as well as the Reformation understanding
of salvation by faith alone, are stressed. The
historic creeds, the *Thirty-Nine Articles,
and the *Book of Common Prayer are accepted as *doctrinal standards to be strictly
followed. High church tendencies are rejected, esp. *sacerdotalism, the doctrine of
the Real Presence, and veneration of the
Virgin Mary. The Church also strongly advocates political and social conservatism,
protesting church involvement in liberal
policies in regard to international issues
and race relations. The separation from the
Episcopal Church was in fact a protest
against doctrinal liberalism and participation in the *National Council of Churches,
which the Anglican Orthodox Church regards as left-wing. Headquarters are in
Statesville; parishes are in Wash., Va.,
Calif., Miss., Fla., N.C., S.C., and Ohio;
there is an affiliated diocese in South India,
its bishop consecrated by Bp. Dees in 1966.

ANGLICANISM, the tradition and practice
of the *Anglican Communion, that worldwide body of Christians in communion
with the abp. of Canterbury. National
Churches, which are found in six conti-

nents, possess a wide range of autonomy. The bps. gather each decade in England for their *Lambeth Conferences; the resolutions, though not binding, are significant expressions of the opinions of the Anglican episcopate. The hierarchy possesses a minimum of coercive authority; Anglicans are bound together, most importantly, through their use of the *Book of Common Prayer (BCP), variously amended and revised through the centuries. *Lex orandi, lex credendi* is a most important principle of Anglicanism and places great weight upon worship and its forms, which still largely follow those of T. *Cranmer (1489–1556). The distinctive formularies and the basis for the historical claims of Anglicanism are to be found in the reign of Elizabeth I (1558–1603) and not that of Henry VIII or Edward VI. Elizabeth's decisions, along with those of Parliament and *Convocations in regard to the ecclesiastical settlement, are to be seen in the BCP of 1559, which largely follows Cranmer's second Book of 1552, and in the *Thirty-Nine Articles, issued in the same year as the closing of the Council of *Trent. The BCP and the Articles, together with the careful retention of continuity with the medieval Church through ordination and polity, form the basis for the Anglican claim to be "truly Catholic and truly Reformed."

The writings of John *Jewel (1522–71) have been traditionally regarded as indicating the Anglican posture toward Roman Catholicism. On the critical differences in doctrine and practice he appealed to Scripture, the first four general councils, and the Fathers of the first 6 centuries of undivided Christendom. He sought to prove that the necessary reformation could not be accomplished by the Council of Trent and that national Churches have a right to legislate through provincial synods. John *Whitgift (1530–1604) and Richard *Hooker (1554–1600) provide in their writings the lines between Anglicanism and the demands of the Puritans in regard to ceremonials, polity, and doctrine. Hooker's *The Laws of Ecclesiastical Polity* generally has been accepted as the most central and balanced view of

the distinctive Anglican positions, esp. in regard to his appeal to Scripture, reason, and tradition in questions of authority. Hooker's three headings conveniently schematize the often perplexing spectrum of emphases within historical Anglicanism. Though each of the three basic emphases accepts the judgment of Scripture as primary, the evangelicals' emphasis upon Scripture leads them esp. to put strong weight upon preaching, the doctrines of the Fall, justification, and atonement and to stress *kerygmatic theology. Charles *Simeon (1759–1836) is an example of this emphasis within Anglicanism.

Those whose emphasis is upon reason are referred to as latitudinarian, liberal, or modernist. Their appeal is most frequently to toleration and freedom, with stress upon apologetics, historical and biblical criticism, and the atonement as exemplary, not substitutionary. Abp. John *Tillotson (1630–94) is an example of this emphasis.

The emphasis upon tradition has produced men of deep commitment to institutional continuity, polity, liturgy, and conformity, with stress upon the doctrines of the Church, sacraments, and the incarnation. Abp. William *Laud (1573–1645) has always been regarded as personifying much of this heritage. More central figures illustrating the nature of Anglicanism, in addition to Cranmer and Hooker, are John Donne (1571 or 72–1631), Frederick Denison *Maurice (1805–72), and Abp. William *Temple (1881–1944). See, besides works of figures mentioned above, E. J. Bicknell, *Theological Introduction to the Thirty-Nine Articles* (3d ed., 1955); *Doctrine in the Church of England: The Report of the Commission on Christian Doctrine Appointed by the Archbishops of Canterbury and York in 1922* (1938); P. E. More, F. L. Cross, *Anglicanism* (1951); S. Neill, *Anglicanism* (pa., 1958). *CHURCH OF ENGLAND; *PROTESTANT EPISCOPAL CHURCH.

ANGLO-CATHOLIC CONGRESSES, rallies held in London in 1920, '23, '27, '30, '33, and again in '48, to further the cause of

Catholicism within the *Anglican Communion. They were often stirring occasions in the best tradition of meetings at the Albert Hall. In 1934 the Congresses were united with the *English Church Union to form the *Church Union. See *Reports*, esp. 1920 and 1933.

ANGLO-CATHOLICISM, the group or movement within Anglicanism seeking to stress the continuity of the *Anglican Communion with the pre-Reformation Church and to move toward the closest possible agreement in faith and practice with the RC and Orthodox Churches. This use of the name dates only from the *Oxford movement, and did not become popular until the late 19th century. In rare earlier usage, now obsolete, it referred simply to the C of E or the Anglican Communion (as in the 1865 appeal by the metropolitan of the ecclesiastical province of Canada, which led to the first *Lambeth Conference, in which he described the Canadian bps. as "representatives of the Anglo-Catholic branch of the Christian Church").

Anglo-Catholicism (like the earlier *high-church or *low-church groups) is a spirit, a school of thought, a movement, sometimes a party, but never an organized Church in itself. It sees its role as that of recalling the Anglican Churches to fresh awareness of their Catholic nature, as witnessed by apostolic order, sacramental life, creedal continuity, and the like. Its roots lie in the Oxford movement (sometimes called *Tractarianism or the Catholic Revival), the explosive awakening within the C of E, starting in 1833 in the famous sermon of John *Keble on "National Apostasy." The immediate occasion was the plan of Parliament to abolish 10 Anglican dioceses in Ireland. But the burden of the Oxford movement was rediscovery, not merely protest— a vigorous restatement of the essentially Catholic character of the C of E. The early years of the movement were intense and often divisive. Among the first leaders some, John Henry *Newman among them, became Roman Catholics; this increased

the sharpness of the conflict. In later years, as ceremonial enrichment became characteristic of the movement, there was often bitter hostility on the *ritualism issue. The more lasting monuments of Anglo-Catholicism, however, are two—a strong and adventurous ecumenical spirit and a powerful renewal of concern for the Church's social witness. The 20th-cent. *Faith and Order movement, for example, was to owe much of its inspiration to Anglo-Catholic leadership, both in England and elsewhere. On the social side the influence of the Anglo-Catholic Summer School of Sociology during the 1920s and 30s was notable in developing relevant and virile Anglican witness in social and political affairs (see CHRISTIAN SOCIALISM).

ANNALES ECCLESIASTICI, the 12-v. church history published (1588–1607) by Baronius as a RC reply to the *Magdeburg Centuries*, a Lutheran history. *BARONIUS, CAESAR, VEN.

ANNUAL CONFERENCE (Methodist), the administrative body for the churches in a particular district, as well as the group of churches in that district. *CONFERENCE (METHODIST).

ANOINTING OF THE SICK, a sacrament in the RC Church, sometimes called extreme unction, conferred by a priest on Christians when they are seriously ill. The scriptural basis for this anointing is Jas 5.14–16. Elders of the Church anoint the sick man "with oil in the name of the Lord. And the prayer of faith will save the sick man, and the Lord will raise him up again; and if he has committed any sins, he will be forgiven. . . . pray for one another, and this will cure you." The person involved is not dying (as in Jn 4.46–54, 11.1–44) but seriously ill. Prayers inspired by faith, here of the community and not just of the elders or the sick man, effect (in the future tense) "saving," "raising up," and "forgiving sins"—the first two referring to a restoration of bodily health, only the third referring to a spiritual healing from grave sin. (Lev 14.10–20 similarly associates the anointing of lepers with their being both cured and forgiven.) Jesus was famed for "curing all kinds of diseases and sickness" (Mt 9.35) and gave this power to his Apostles (Mt 10.1; Mk 6.7–13; Lk 9.1). Mark observes that they "anointed many sick people with oil and cured them" (6.13). None of these texts intimate the formal institution of a sacrament of anointing by Christ; at best they describe the mentality and practices by which Christ and the Apostles would have expressed his divine power, effected the sanctifying of a person during a critical period in his life, and formalized the anointing of the sick into an effective ritual sign.

The history of the anointing as a sacrament (apart from earlier, hurried, ambiguous statements or allusions in other writers) begins with the first clear, authentic statement of Innocent I (d. 417) to Decentius (*Ep.* 25.8; PL 20:559–560): he associates the sacrament with the Epistle of James, says that the chrism employed in its administration is blessed by the bishop, that priests and bishops are the legitimate ministers, that it is a complement of penance. Comparable in importance is the ritual in the *Apostolic Tradition* of Hippolytus (5; B. Botte, ed., *La Tradition apostolique de S. Hyppolyte* [1963], 18–19) for the blessing of oil for the sick, implying the prevalence and solemnity of the anointing. St. Augustine (d. 430) included the ritual of Jas 5.14–16 in his *Speculum* (PL 34:1036) as a practice of the Christian life. He personally often visited the sick and "laid his hands on them" (Possidius, *Vita S. Aug.* 27; PL 32:56). Bede the Venerable (d. 735) in his commentary on James describes the rite and affirms the antiquity of the anointing (*Super divi Jacobi epistolam* 5; PL 93:39–40).

The 12th-cent. schoolmen's philosophizing on the data of Scripture and tradition produced two different emphases: one on the bodily cure (Hugh of St. Victor [d. 1141], William of Auxerre [d. 1231]); the other on the forgiveness of sin for the dying (Peter Lombard [d. 1160], who popularized the name extreme unction, St. Thomas Aquinas [d. 1274], and St. Bonaventure [d. 1274]). The latter emphasis on the supernatural effects and on the imminence of death was to be underlined by the Council of Trent (1545–63) in its definition (D 1698). But a shift from sacrament of the dying to sacrament of the sick is evidenced by the apostolic letter of Pius XI of Feb. 2, 1923 (AAS 15 [1923], 73–75), and by Vat II SacLit (73–75). The peculiar function of this sacrament is to help cure the recipient, who is sick, and to help him bear his illness so that it can become, despite the physical evil that it remains, a spiritual benefit—strengthening his confidence in God, helping him accept his weakness with humble dependence on others, his mortality, and sinfulness. Secondarily, it forgives the sins for which he is contrite and which he has not been able to confess in penance.

The Eastern Orthodox Churches (except the Nestorians) consider this anointing to be a sacrament. Protestant Churches do not. However, the Anglicans provide for an anointing rite in the BCP; such a rite is also to be found in the Scottish and American Prayer Books (1929). See J. P. McClain, NCE 1:568–575; P. Palmer, "Purpose of Anointing the Sick: A Reappraisal," TS 19 (1958), 309–344; K. Rahner, *Church and the Sacraments* (1963).

ANTHROPOSOPHY, a form of *theosophy developed by Rudolf *Steiner in several books published between 1902 and 1925. The central idea of Steiner's system is to see the history of mankind's evolutionary development in its relation to the Christ-Event. Steiner broke with the Hinduism of Annie *Besant and the Theosophical Society and in 1912 founded the Anthroposophical Society. Anthroposophy is based on man's spiritual origin and his historic evolution. Steiner posited a stage of prehistory, which he identified as Lemuria, in which mind evolved and man gained self-consciousness under the influence of Ahrimanic spirits. At a later stage, which he called Atlantis, man became aware of the material universe through the inspiration of Luciferic spirits.

Both of these early stages saw the rise of a higher consciousness through oracles and mystery centers. Man progressed through the evolutionary stages represented by the Indian, Persian, Assyrian-Babylonian, Egyptian, and Greco-Roman civilizations, which culminated in the Christ-Event. Christ wrought for all mankind what the mysteries had done for individuals; he gave them a knowledge of their true higher self. In Steiner's view, the cosmic centrality of the Christ-Event is crucial. He held the divinity of Christ and believed that Gnosticism had erred in failing to give equal recognition to his humanity. Steiner saw the future of man as requiring a threefold social order in a delicate balance of his economic, judicial, and religious character. The role of Anthroposophy is to assist man to attain the needed Higher Knowledge, or direct perception of reality as spiritual fact, which was unperceived at the conscious level. This Higher Knowledge is also threefold. It consists of Imagination, by which we perceive material realities, Inspiration, by which awareness of the spiritual or astral world and of reincarnation is attained, and finally Intuition, by which we have direct knowledge of the Higher Worlds. Sources on Steiner's theories are his *Christianity As Mystical Fact* (1902), *Knowledge of the Higher Worlds* (1904), and *An Outline of Occult Science* (1909).

ANTI-BURGHERS, in Scotland members of the Associate Presbytery in the *Seceder Tradition who rejected the oath imposed by law in 1747 on each burgess of certain cities, that he "professed and allowed within his heart the true religion presently professed within the realm and authorized by the law thereof." The Burghers, accepting the oath, and the Anti-Burghers were reunited in 1820 with the formation of the *United Secession Church.

ANTICLERICALISM, a spirit opposed to Catholic domination of the state. The word became current in the late 19th cent., but the attitude was concretely expressed earlier during the French Revolution, when the RC Church was deprived of its privileges until the Concordat of 1801 and the Congress of Vienna. Following the Napoleonic era, as liberal ideologies stirred uprisings against conservative regimes, the Church was closely allied with reactionary monarchies, arranging concordats that supported clerical control of culture. Where the RC Church was the only Church allowed, liberals often became anticlerical. Germany's *Kulturkampf had its counterpart in France and Belgium, and strong anticlerical movements developed in Spain, Portugal, Italy, and Latin America. Anticlericalism is also used in a more general sense for opposition to the domination of church life by the clergy, or to according them any privileged status in the Church or in society. See J. H. Nichols, *History of Christianity, 1650–1950: Secularization of the West* (1956). *LAICISM.

ANTICREEDALISM, opposition to any *creed, as a rule of faith. In principle, Protestants have always regarded creeds and *confessions of faith as standards subordinate to Scripture; in practice the historical Churches often treated them almost as infallible (see CONFESSIONALISM). Anabaptists, Friends, Baptists, and Seventh-day Adventists excluded creeds. The rejection of creedal formulas was a strong constitutive element in the foundation of many Churches with roots in revivalism—the Christian Churches, the Holiness Churches, Pentecostal Churches (see INDEPENDENT CHURCHES). Under the influence of the *Enlightenment in the 18th cent. and of *liberal theology and the *Social Gospel in the 19th, there was a widespread skepticism with regard to creeds. The theological temper of the 20th cent., with its distrust of the constructs of human thought, has led to a growing tendency toward extreme latitude in the interpretation of creedal statements.

ANTIDENOMINATIONALISM, literally opposition to *denominationalism, but in common usage, mainly resistance to any centralized form of church polity or organization. Antidenominationalism reflects a desire to emphasize the autonomy of the local *congregation with regard to belief, government, and mission. It has been a principal influence in the history of the Christian Churches, the Baptists, Pentecostalism, and the Independent Churches.

ANTIMISSION BAPTISTS, a designation for *Primitive Baptists, because since the early 19th cent. they have resisted the establishment of any organization to promote home or foreign missions. Such agencies, they maintain, lack any basis in the NT.

ANTIMISSIONARY MOVEMENT, a hostile reaction that arose in some Protestant Churches in the first half of the 19th cent. to the formation of national missionary societies (see MISSIONS). This resistance, which was strongest during the years 1820–40, has been peculiarly associated with certain Baptist groups (see ANTIMISSION BAPTISTS), but in fact it cut across denominational boundaries and appeared in other bodies as well. Most of the opposition stemmed from a distrust of national organizations that were springing up at the time to coordinate activities of different church groups in many areas. Such organizations, it was feared, might lead to the breakdown of the distinctive beliefs and practices of particular Churches, impose an orthodoxy, and perhaps even issue in a kind of union of Church and State. But other objections were also raised. Some condemned the reliance upon human organizations to do the work of God. Others, of more liberal bent, saw no urgency in missionary work because they could not conceive a loving God capable of holding heathens to account for their ignorance. In addition to this, there was heated protest from rural areas and from the frontier at the idea of paying missionaries to do God's work. The opposition abated after the 1840s, but it has lingered on in some Baptist groups in the South. See B. H. Carroll, *Genesis of American Anti-*

Missionism (1902); W. W. Sweet, *Religion on the American Frontier: The Baptists* (1931).

ANTINOMIANISM (Gr. *anti*, against, *nomos*, law), the theory that human actions are not subject to moral law or that actions usually considered sinful are not so for true Christians. Luther used the term in opposing J. Agricola, but the idea has been recurrent in Christian history, although with varying bases; it has often been expressed in sexual license. The teaching that grace frees man from the bondage of the law was distorted into the antinomianism reproved by St. Paul (1 Cor 6.12–20; Eph 4.19). Opposition between the God of the Jews and the God of the Christians or between the OT and NT was held as grounds for licentiousness among the Gnostics (Carpocratians, Adamites, Cainites, Ophites) and the rejection of all law by *Marcion (see G. Bareille, 1398–98). The theory that marriage and the body are evil led to the practice of sexual abuses among the Manichaeans, ancient and medieval (*Albigenses, *Cathari, *Waldenses). Perfectionism and reliance on inner experience and personal inspiration included antinomianism in theory and sometimes in practice among the *Brothers and Sisters of the Free Spirit, *Beghards, *Anabaptists, *Familists, *Seekers, and *Ranters. The Antinomian Controversy (1527–60) in which Luther was involved arose from an extreme interpretation of his teaching on faith without works, and grace vs. law (see LAW AND GOSPEL); the controversy dragged on until 1577 and the *Formula of Concord (art. 4–6; cf. D 1536, 1570). The Calvinist theology of the divine decree of election was interpreted by some in Puritan England, and in the 19th cent. by certain of the *Plymouth Brethren, to mean that the actions of the elect could not possibly be sinful. The Antinomian Controversy in colonial New England concerned the spiritual teaching of Anne *Hutchinson. In modern times some view existentialist ethics, situation ethics, and moral relativism as forms of antinomianism because they either reject or diminish the normative force of moral law. See G. Bareille, DTC 1:1391–99; J. Fletcher, *Situation Ethics* (1966); R. Knox, *Enthusiasm* (1950); J. L. Witte, LTK 1:646–647; Bihlmeyer-Tüchle 3:71.

ANTIPAEDOBAPTISTS (Antipedobaptists; Gr. *pais*, child, *baptizein*, baptize), those who oppose *infant baptism. The name was first applied to British Baptists by William Wall in his *History of Infant Baptism* (1705). Eventually it became a more general designation for all those who reject infant baptism in favor of *believer's baptism.

ANTIREMONSTRANTS, strict Calvinist opponents of *Arminianism; also called *Contra-Remonstrants.

ANTISECTARIANISM, a spirit that deplores party divisions among Christians, as opposed to *sectarianism in its narrow sense. Today greater awareness of what Christians share, and of the need for unity, foster antisectarianism. As sectarianism is used to designate *denominationalism, antisectarianism also connotes opposition to any centralized form of church polity or organization. *ANTIDENOMINATIONALISM.

ANTITRINITARIANISM, any interpretation of Christian belief that rejects the doctrine of the Trinity. Its more important ancient forms were Modalism and Arianism. In the era of the Reformation *Socinianism was antitrinitarian; *Unitarianism is one modern form of antitrinitarianism, and the Jehovah's Witnesses strongly reject the Trinity as "the devil's doctrine." The interpretations given to trinitarian doctrine by Mormons and Christian Scientists bear little resemblance to the traditional Christian meaning. Apart from official teachings of religious bodies, such theological trends as rationalism and *liberal theology have diminished serious belief in the Trinity in many of the Churches. Once the divinity of Christ is rejected, there is little meaning left in the doctrine of a triune God.

ANTOINISM, the cult founded by Louis Antoine (1846–1912), a Belgian laborer who, after his retirement at Jemeppes-sur-Meuse, started conducting spiritistic séances and from that advanced to faith healing. He attracted followers who came to accept him as the "Healer," the "Father." Being only semiliterate, he did not personally put his doctrine in writing, but words uttered by him in trance-like states were taken down by his followers and gathered in a collection known as *The Teachings of the Father*; this became the gospel of the cult. At Antoine's "disincarnation" in 1912, leadership of the cult was assumed by his wife (the "Mother") and held until she in turn was "disincarnated" in 1940. Antoinism denied being a religion, declaring its followers free to worship as they pleased. Nevertheless it propounded a doctrine, a mixture of spiritism, *theosophy, and vague mysticism that was presented as a new revelation. Antoinism does not deny the reality of physical evil, but calls for faith (in its understanding of the term) to remedy the disease of the soul upon which all bodily affliction depends. Antoinism survived World War II and in the late 1950s had several thousand adherents. The cult's claim to a greater membership is regarded as greatly exaggerated. See H. C. Chéry, *L'Offensive des sectes* (1961), 256–267.

ANTONIANS, a small sect in the Swiss cantons of Aargau and Zurich, named for the founder Anton Unternährer (1759–1824). He was a Catholic who turned preacher, proclaiming a doctrine of absolute *antinomianism as the way to God; he died in prison for his denunciation of civil authority. Antonians no longer oppose authority, and they interpret love to mean brotherly love, not the sexual liberty advocated by their founder.

ANXIOUS BENCH (Anxious Seat; Mourner's Bench), a feature of the revivalistic new measures practiced by C. G. *Finney. It was a pew at the front of the room where those who were repentant and eager to turn to God were invited for guidance from the preacher.

APELLITES, a sect founded by a disciple of *Marcion, Apelles, who lived in Rome in the 2d century. Apelles was closely associated with a female visionary, Philumene, whose revelations he recorded. In opposition to Marcion's theory of a God of the OT and a God of the NT, Apelles maintained that there was only one divine principle, the God of the NT who revealed himself in Jesus, and who lived and died in a real body formed of cosmic matter. In his *Syllogisms* he rejected the OT more strongly than had Marcion. He maintained moreover that all that was necessary for salvation was hope in Jesus crucified and good works. See G. Bareille, DTC 1:1455–57; Bihlmeyer-Tüchle 1:153.

APOCALYPTICISM, a term with two meanings: (1) A type of literature, prominent in Judaism from *c.*250 B.C. and in the 1st cent. of Christianity. Couched in symbolic language, using such elements as visions, figures, numerology, the invention of grotesque animals, and pseudonymity, this type of literature portrayed the evil of present days, but judgment and better days to come. The Book of Daniel in the OT was the first great apocalyptic work; Revelation (the Apocalypse) in the NT is of the same genre. Other examples are the Books of Enoch, Baruch, I and II Esdras, the Shepherd of Hermas, and the Apocalypse of Peter. (2) An attitude equivalent or akin to *millenarianism. Apocalypticism in this sense has been a perennial basis for the formation of new Christian bodies. It is characterized by appeal to apocalyptic literature, expectation of Christ's second coming and the righting of grievances, and insistence on penitence and poverty. The *Montanists in the early Church; the *Fraticelli inspired by *Joachimism in the Middle Ages; the *Taborites in the 15th cent.; the Münster *Anabaptists in the left-wing Reformation; and in modern times *Seventhday Adventists and *Jehovah's Witnesses exemplify apocalypticism.

APOCATASTASIS (Gr., restoration or reestablishment), in Christian theological history, the term denoting the doctrine of a final restoration of the whole creation (including fallen angels, men, and demons) to harmony with God. The Greek word *apokatastasis* appears in Act 3.21, in the phrase "till the time for the universal restoration." Clement of Alexandria, Origen, and Gregory of Nyssa were early advocates of the doctrine. The fifth ecumenical council at Constantinople (A.D. 553) implicitly condemned the doctrine in its condemnation of Origen (D 433), whose restorationism had been explicitly condemned at the Synod of Constantinople in 543 (D 409, 411). John Scotus Erigena affirmed the doctrine. In the Reformation era some Anabaptists proposed it, and their teaching was condemned by Article 17 of the *Augsburg Confession. In the 17th cent. Jane Lead and Johann W. Petersen of the *Philadelphians proclaimed the apocatastasis; in the 18th cent. the Pietists J. A. Bengel and F. C. Oetinger cautiously considered it. F. *Schleiermacher (*The Christian Faith*, Appendix: "On eternal Damnation") and his followers gave the doctrine wider influence. Karl *Barth clearly admitted the possibility of an apocatastasis (*Church Dogmatics* 2.-2:295). In the U.S. the Universalists (see UNITARIAN-UNIVERSALIST ASSOCIATION) have been its chief advocates. See R. Eddy, *Universalism in America* (2 v., 1884–86); D. P. Walker, *Decline of Hell* (1964); G. Müller, "The Idea of an *Apokatastasis Ton Panton* (Universal Salvation) in European theology from Schleiermacher to Barth," *Annual Journal of the Universalist Historical Society*, 6 (1966), 47–64. *RESTORATIONISM.

APOLOGY OF THE AUGSBURG CON-FESSION, one of the confessional documents of Lutheranism, included in the Book of Concord. After the presentation of the *Augsburg Confession to the imperial Diet on June 25, 1530, three RC theologians, J. *Eck, J. *Faber, and J. *Cochlaeus, were asked to prepare a response. This they did in the *Confutatio,* a rebuttal, which on Aug. 3 was read to the assembly. The Lutherans were obliged to respond in turn. They did so in the Apology of the Augsburg Confession. Philipp *Melanchthon, chief author of the Augsburg Confession, also undertook its defense, and a first draft was ready on Sept. 22, 1530. When this was rejected, Melanchthon undertook a more ample defense, which was published in the spring of 1531 and forms the present text of the Apology. Both the irenic language (even and esp. on the Eucharist) and the polemical sharpness of the Augsburg Confession appear in the Apology, which thus forms an authoritative commentary on the Confession itself. See T. G. Tappert, ed., *Book of Concord: The Confessions of the Evangelical Lutheran Church* (1959).

APOLOGY OF THE TRUE CHRISTIAN DIVINITY, statement of Quaker belief by Robert *Barclay. He published it first in Latin, *Theologiae verae Christianae apologia* (1676), then in English, *Apology of the True Christian Divinity as the Same is Set Forth and Preached by the People Called in Scorn "Quakers"* (1678). While the Society of Friends in principle has never adhered to a *confession of faith, the *Apology* has been recognized as an authentic declaration of beliefs, although modern Quakers regard it with reservations. Barclay was a theologian, and the *Apology* is written in a scholastic style. It consists of 15 propositions on the following: (1) the need for true knowledge of God; (2) the need of inner revelation as source of faith; (3) the Scriptures; (4) the Fall; (5) redemption by Christ, the true light; (6) the saving and spiritual light by which every man is enlightened; (7) justification, Christ formed within us; (8) perfection; (9) perseverance and the possibility of falling from grace; (10) the ministry, based on God's gift, not a human commission; (11) spiritual worship; (12) spiritual baptism, and the rejection of *infant baptism; (13) spiritual sharing in the body and blood of Christ; (14) civil magistrates and religious matters; (15) hat-doffing and similar salutation, and worldly recreations. The doctrine of the *Apology* on the *Inner Light became particularly celebrated. See L. Eeg-Olafson, *Conception of the Inner Light in Robert Barclay's Theology* (1954); D. Freiday, *Barclay's Apology in Modern English* (1967).

APOSTASY (Gr., revolt), the renunciation of a previous loyalty, ordinarily religious. Like its antonym, *conversion, it is a complex human reality involving a change in the principle(s) that control the synthesis and direction of life. In fact what may be objectively apostasy both from moral and canonical considerations may psychologically and subjectively appear as a conversion in its primordial sense of a change *from* something to something else. Nevertheless the pejorative connotation of such "de-conversion" remains strong, since reasons for it are quite often of a somewhat weak value from an objective and critical perspective. In its theological sense, apostasy represents a departure from God in varying degrees according as the apostate was previously united with God by faith and profession alone, by the living of faith in obedient love, or by some special connection, e.g., vows or sacred orders. Thus RC canon law deals with apostates from the religious life and sacred orders as well as those who are apostates in the complete sense, i.e., from the faith. Such disbelief does not entail a transfer to a non-Christian religion or even transfer to another Christian Church; apostasy is essentially a departure. (ThAq ST 2a2ae, 12.1).

APOSTLES' CREED, a *creed, authorship of which was for centuries attributed to the Apostles, and which enjoys a high degree of authority in Churches of the West. References to a *Symbolum Apostolorum* occur from the 4th cent., and Rufinus of Aquileia, writing in 404, relates that the Apostles composed a creed. The first known written version of the Apostles' Creed as we have it is in the *Scàrapsus* by Priminius of Reichenau, written between 710 and 724. Rufinus wrote of the creed in use at Aquileia (S. Italy), which differed only slightly from the ancient *Roman Creed. This formulary achieved stability only by the 4th cent., but in substance it can be clearly traced to *c.*190 in both Greek and Latin texts. The legend of apostolic authorship does reflect the witness by Justin Martyr, Irenaeus, and Tertullian to a "rule of faith" handed down by the Apostles. Actual creedal formularies were devised for candidates for baptism, as, e.g., the *Apostolic Tradition* of Hippolytus (*c.*170–*c.*236) indicates. The creeds were passed down orally in the era of persecution. The Apostles' Creed slightly amplifies the Roman Creed, and is in fact a link with the faith of the primitive Church.

Many authorities see the emphasis of this creed upon Jesus Christ as an elaboration of St. Peter's confession in Mt 16.16; and its arrangement according to the Three Divine Persons as the development of the baptismal formula in Mt 18.19. The articles of the Apostles' Creed are simple statements, admitting of ready substantiation in Scripture. Criticism or difficulties blocking its acceptance are those inherent in the Bible itself and in the whole Christian message. Early in the Middle Ages this creed became part of the baptismal ritual, of daily liturgical offices, and even of private prayers. At the time of the Reformation, it was accepted as a *doctrinal standard by the main Protestant traditions; it continues to be used widely in worship. It remains the principal *ecumenical creed in the West, because of its widespread acceptance, and because, as the *Lambeth Conference of 1920 and the *Lausanne Conference (1929) of *Faith and Order suggested, it provides a possible basis for agreement among Christians. See D 10–36; J. N. D. Kelly, *Early Christian Creeds* (2d ed., 1960).

APOSTOLIC CHRISTIAN CHURCH (Nazarean), a small denomination originating in the Midwest *c.*1850 with the revivalist preaching of S. H. Froelich. A minister of the Reformed Church in Switzerland, he was obliged to emigrate because of opposition to his preaching of repentance and conversion. Before coming to the U.S. he had established communities in several European countries. The Apostolic Christian Church was formed chiefly from German-speaking Swiss immigrants to whom Froelich preached. Half of the membership (2,347 in 1966) is in Ill., the rest, in scattered congregations throughout the northern half of the United States. This Church particularly stresses the doctrine of *entire sanctification. *Conscientious objection and the refusal of oaths are also taught, since many of the early members of the Church had been Mennonites. While there is a fellowship of association among the approximately 50 local churches, polity is strongly *congregational.

APOSTOLIC CHRISTIAN CHURCHES OF AMERICA, a loosely organized group of *Holiness Churches. The first congregations were begun among Swiss and German immigrants by the Swiss preacher Benedict Weyeneth *c.*1847. The central doctrine is *entire sanctification; *conscientious objection is also taught and strictly practiced. There were (1968) 8,740 members in 72 churches, three-quarters of them in Illinois. Polity is strongly *congregational. Ministers are unsalaried.

APOSTOLIC FAITH, a title adopted by many early groups in *Pentecostalism. C. F. *Parham (1873–1929) used the title to connote a return to the apostolic Pentecostal experience. It remains the name of those local assemblies that directly descend from Parham's work. He was strongly opposed to any organization above the local church, and member bodies of the Apostolic Faith Movement are loosely affiliated with the church at Baxter Springs, Kansas. Another body, called The Apostolic Faith, was organized in Portland, Ore., in 1907 by Mrs. Florence L. Crawford. These two groups are unrelated, but both adhere strictly to the early, characteristic teachings of Pentecostalism, and to a "faith policy" in regard to finances (see FAITH MISSION). The Portland group, though numbering less than 5,000 members, sends throughout the world and without charge religious literature printed in more than 70 languages. See J. T. Nichol, *Pentecostalism* (1966).

APOSTOLIC LUTHERAN CHURCH OF AMERICA, the name adopted in 1962 by the Finnish Apostolic Lutheran Church of America. The latter name was taken in 1929 by one of several groups of Apostolic Lutherans in the U.S. who were of Finnish background. The Finns had brought to the U.S. the revivalistic tradition of Lars Levi *Laestadius. The first immigrants joined the Scandinavian Evangelical Lutheran Congregation in Mich., but in 1871 separated under the lay preacher Solomon Korteniemi, and were registered as the Solomon Korteniemi Lutheran Society. In 1879 the name was changed to the Apostolic Lutheran Congregation to distinguish it from nonrevivalistic, Evangelical Lutheran groups. The Apostolic Lutheran Church of America (latest statistics available, 1961, about 7,000 members) traces its history to the Korteniemi group. There are, however, other small groups of Apostolic Lutherans. They share the practice of closed fellowship within the group, simplicity of dress and manner, emphasis on the autonomy of the local church, deemphasis of theology, and the practice of confession and absolution. See A. K. E. Holmio, EncLuthCh 1:97.

APOSTOLIC OVERCOMING HOLY CHURCH OF GOD, a Pentecostal body organized in 1919 as the Ethiopian Overcoming Holy Church of God; the present name was adopted in 1927. The founder and still (1968) head is Bp. W. T. Phillips, who left the Methodist Episcopal Church and

the Apostolic Faith Mission in order to give freer expression to his own Pentecostal experience. Church services are highly emotional and ecstatic. There are local churches in 14 states, and missions in the West Indies and Africa. Headquarters, Mobile, Ala.; last reported (1956) membership 75,000. See J. T. Nichol, *Pentecostalism* (1966), 130–131.

APOSTOLIC SUCCESSION, in RC teaching, the relationship of the bishops of the Church to the Apostles, to whom Christ gave the commission summarized in Mt 28.18–20. The development of a theory of apostolic succession was preceded by its acceptance in practice. In the 2d cent., Gnostic claims to a secret doctrinal tradition provided the first occasion for conscious reflection on the existing practice. The historians Papias and Hegesippus argued that the doctrinal agreement of all local churches having an uninterrupted line of bishops going back to the Apostles authenticated their teaching against Gnostic claims. Similar agreements were given by Irenaeus (*Adv. haer.* 3.3.1) and Tertullian, who first used the expression *ordo episcoporum* (*Adv. Marc.* 4.5.2). The position that only a minister incorporated into the apostolic succession through valid ordination can validly administer certain sacraments was developed by medieval scholastics, reflecting on the existing practice of the Church. They also developed a distinction between "material" apostolic succession (valid reception of the sacrament of orders) and "formal" apostolic succession (valid orders, plus communion with the college of bishops under the pope, successor of Peter and center of the unity of the episcopal college). RC theologians have considered the relationship of bishops belonging to the material apostolic succession but separated from the bishops in communion with the pope to be analogous to the relationship of non-Roman Christians to the RC Church. Both cases present a host of questions that are controverted in RC theology.

The older view of apostolic succession emphasized the uninterrupted chain of episcopal consecrations, which in theory permits every bishop (and through him the clergy he has ordained) to trace his commission back to one of the Apostles. Since Vatican Council II apostolic succession has been viewed more in terms of incorporation into a collegial body, the original members of which were the Apostles (Vat II ConstCh, 21). Although the bishops are collectively the successors of the Apostles (*ibid.*, 20), the Apostles had a unique status because of their special personal relationship with Christ, the one foundation of the Church (see 1 Cor 3.11). The Apostles were appointed to build up the Church on the foundation Christ had laid (see Eph 2.2.; Rev 21.14; Mt 16.18). They passed on their commission to others, who came to be called bishops. The Pastoral Epistles teach that the bishop's first task is to transmit faithfully to others the apostolic teaching, thus maintaining the *local church in the foundation laid down by its apostolic founder (see 2 Tim 1.6 and 13; 2.2; 1 Tim 3.2; Tit 1.9).

The 16th-century Reformers fought not so much for or against apostolic succession as such as for the true Church, which, according to the *Augsburg Confession, was to be found only where God's word was rightly preached. Luther taught that the only true bishops were those who succeeded the Apostles not locally or historically but in teaching the apostolic gospel. In his *Institutes of the Christian Religion* (4.7.23) Calvin recognized apostolic succession in theory but said that it was necessary to abandon it in practice because the bishops had erred from the truth. Anglicanism has preserved an intact historical succession with the pre-Reformation hierarchy and insists on the necessity of the *historic episcopate, while refusing to impose any doctrine about this episcopate or to condemn the ministries of Protestant Churches that, because of historical circumstances, lack episcopacy. Though contemporary Anglican teaching about apostolic succession often approximates the RC doctrine

(while denying the papal primacy and infallibility as defined at Vatican Council I), more Protestant views enjoy equal rights in Anglicanism. In practice Anglican insistence on episcopacy has proved a major barrier to reunion with Protestant Churches.

The question of the ministry is a crucial dogmatic difficulty in contemporary ecumenical discussion (see CONSULTATION ON CHURCH UNION), but a certain reconciliation of views is discernible since Vatican Council II. RC theologians are striving to soften the rigid juridical positions of the past, and many Protestants show a certain awareness of the value of apostolic succession and episcopacy in constituting and guarding doctrinal and sacramental unity. See Y. Congar and D. Depuy, eds., *L'Épiscopat et l'église universelle* (1962); H. Küng, *Structures of the Church* (1965); *idem, The Church* (1968); K. Rahner and J. Ratzinger, *Episcopate and Primacy* (tr. K. Barker, 1962); K. E. Kirk, ed., *Apostolic Ministry* (1957); A. Ehrhardt, *Apostolic Ministry* (1958).

APOSTOLICAE CURAE, the bull issued by Leo XIII on Sept. 13, 1896, which confirmed the existing RC practice of treating the orders of convert Anglican clergy as invalid by declaring that "ordinations carried out according to the Anglican rite have been and are absolutely null and utterly void." The document was occasioned by a reunion campaign started in the 1890s (with astonishing initial success) by the Anglican Lord *Halifax and the Abbé *Portal, and aimed at initiating a theological dialogue between their two Churches. An eight-man papal commission was set up in the spring of 1896 to investigate Anglican orders. In 1910 Cardinal Merry del Val, who had been secretary of the commission, stated in a private letter that at the end of the secret proceedings the case for validity had been lost by one vote. Heavy pressure for a negative verdict was brought on the Holy See by F. A. (later Cardinal) Gasquet acting on behalf of Cardinal Vaughan and the English

RC hierarchy. On July 16, 1896, the cardinals of the Holy Office in the presence of Leo XIII unanimously passed the negative verdict subsequently promulgated in *Apostolicae curae*. The Secretary of State, Cardinal Rampolla, who had been friendly to the Anglicans in the preceding reunion campaign, absented himself from this meeting. The bull was drafted by 31-year-old Merry del Val. Beginning at Vatican II demands have been raised by RC theologians that the case be reopened. See J. J. Hughes, *Absolutely Null and Utterly Void* (1968). *ANGLICAN ORDERS.

APOSTOLICI (Apostolics), a name used by the following groups: (1) Apostolici was an alternate name for the Apotactics, a 3d–4th-cent. communal group in the East. (2) The Apostolici in 12th-cent. France and the Rhineland were obscurely connected with eastern Manichaeism. Members often outwardly conformed to the Church, but their aim was antihierarchical; in the Rhineland they apparently attracted many followers, including clerics. St. Bernard of Clairvaux preached and wrote against the Rhineland Apostolici (PL 183:1088–1102). The Apostolici practiced vegetarianism and celibate cohabitation but without a marriage contract; they rejected oaths, veneration of saints, prayers for the dead, and infant baptism. Some claimed that the power of Eucharistic consecration was shared by all and was to be exercised at every meal. See E. W. McDonnell, NCE 1:698–699; S. Runciman, *Medieval Manichee* (1961), 119–20. (3) The Apostolici of the 13th and 14th cents. were adherents of a lay evangelical movement begun at Parma by Gerard *Segarelli as a return to the apostolic life of poverty, penance, and preaching. The founder's attacks on the clergy and the institutional Church stirred rebellion against ecclesiastical authority. Members adopted a distinctive garb but followed no rule and took no vows, being bound together by what Segarelli called interior obedience. Their way of life combined mendicancy, vagabondage, and idleness. Their doctrinal views seem to have been somewhat imprecise until Fra *Dolcino assumed leadership in 1300. A man of considerable talent and a degree of education, he gave the movement a semblance of organization and a doctrine combining *Joachimism and his own form of *millenarianism. The sect was condemned by a number of popes and councils, and in 1305 Nicholas V finally summoned a crusade to extirpate it. Fra Dolcino was captured and later executed. Small pockets of these Apostolici lingered on into the 15th cent. but exercised no significant influence. See E. Anagnine, *Dolcino e il movimento ereticale all'inizio del trecento* (1964); E. W. McDonnell, NCE 1:698–699; J. M. Vidal, DHGE 3:1038–48.

APOSTOLICITY, the abstract nominal form of the adjective "apostolic," one of the four terms used by the Nicene Creed in qualification of the Church. RC theologians have commonly taken the designation as applicable to the Church by reason of its origin, its mission, its doctrine, and its continuity in ministerial succession. As applied to origin it means that the Church is identical with the Church established by the Apostles. In reference to mission, it signifies that like—and through—the Apostles the Church is commissioned by divine mandate to proclaim the person and doctrines of Christ until the end of time. It is apostolic in doctrine because it preserves the deposit of revealed doctrine committed to the Apostles. Its ministerial succession is apostolic because the lineage of the *historic episcopate reaches back in uninterrupted sequence to the Apostles. RC apologetics, which counts apostolicity among the four distinguishing notes or marks of the Church, has developed these themes extensively. It cannot be claimed, however, that apostolicity has proved to be an easily applicable test of the true Church. The scarcity of documentary evidence relating to the primitive Church, and the ambiguity of much that has survived, make the continuity of doctrine, practice, and institutions difficult to prove or disprove. The fact of the historical continuity of the episcopate is perhaps easier to deal with, but this lies outside the concept of apostolicity as understood by many Protestant theologians.

While in Anglicanism the historic episcopate is regarded as essential to the Church, the Protestant Churches long rather ignored apostolicity. Calvin acknowledged the possibility of apostolic succession but abandoned it because in fact the bishops had erred (*Institutes of the Christian Religion*, 4.7.23). The Lutheran view became general, that apostolicity meant fidelity to the witness of the Apostles to the true gospel, not a historical or local succession to them. The rejection of a teaching authority or ministerial priesthood includes a rejection of apostolicity as continuity in a special office of the Church. Generally, apostolicity as "lineal descence," in the words of the *Scots Confession (Art. 18), has had no relevance in Protestantism. Rather it was regarded as one of the claims of Rome from which the Church must be purged. Apostolicity, however, is professed by the historical Protestant Churches. (To Quakers and others who have replaced the historical dimension of Christian faith with inner spiritual experience, this fidelity is not essential.) The desire to keep the preaching of the gospel true to the teaching and witness of the Apostles was one of the motivations of the Reformation. The ideal of restoring the Church to the life of the apostolic Church has motivated the foundation of new Churches. Protestant Churches, as well, share in the acceptance of apostolicity as signifying the Church's continuance of the mission and witness of the Apostles. See G. Thils, *Les Notes de l'Église dans l'apologétique depuis la Réforme* (1937); *idem*, NCE 1:699–700; J. Pelikan, *Riddle of Roman Catholicism* (1959).

APPELLANTS, a term with two historical usages: (1) the secular priests in England who in 1599 appealed to Rome against the pro-Jesuit policies of George Blackwell, who had been given the title archpriest and been put in charge of RC priests in England; (2) members of the French clergy who, in their resistance to the bull *Unigenitus*, appealed (1717) to a general council. Pope Clement XI's condemnation of 101 propositions from a work of P. *Quesnel (D 2401–2501) was opposed (1714) by a strong minority; a bitter controversy with a flood of polemical literature against the *Acceptants of the bull ensued. The minority held that by censuring what was really true Catholic doctrine, the Pope had demonstrated that he was not personally infallible. The Appellants acquired their name by reason of the formal public act of appeal made at the Sorbonne by four bps. to a general council (March 5, 1717), an act conforming to the spirit of the *Gallican Articles. Excommunication by Clement in 1718 of the 12 bps., 3,000 priests, and countless laymen numbered among the Appellants had little effect since they had strong support in Parlement and from the regent, Philip of Orléans. He eventually turned against them, used force to make them submit, and in 1730 made acceptance of *Unigenitus* mandatory. Not all Appellants were Jansenists, but many did join the *Schism of Utrecht, and Jansenists in France never relinquished their opposition to *Unigenitus*. See bibliog. for Jansenism.

AQUARIAN MINISTRY, a *New Thought sect established in 1918 by George Brownell at Santa Barbara, California. It had strong affinities with occultism and astrology, while its principal stress was on the ability of the human mind to attain health and prosperity by affirmative thinking and placing itself in tune with the rhythms of the universe. The name was selected to be an indication of the new dispensation under which the human mind could attain fulfillment. Its membership and influence have been slight.

AQUEI (Hydrotheitae), a group referred to without name by Augustine (*Haer.* 75), relying on Filaster (*Haer.* 96). Augustine states that they believed water was un-created and co-eternal with God. The name Aquei (Lat. *aqua*, water) was invented by Danaeus in his edition of Augustine's *De haeresibus* (1576; PL 12:1203). The author of *Praedestinatus* (c.75) calls the same group Hydrotheitae (Gr., *hydor*, water; *theos*, God).

ARCHDEACON, originally a deacon chosen by the bp. to assist in liturgical and administrative functions in the diocese. The office is known to have existed from the 3d cent.; the title, from the 4th. Often the archdeacon in practice had right of succession to the see. Growth and abuse of the power of the office led to its curtailment after the 12th cent., and after the Council of Trent the title became largely honorary in the RC Church. In the C of E and some other Anglican Churches, however, the office and title continue. The archdeacon must be a priest ordained for at least 6 years; he supervises the discipline and tem-poralities of a fixed territory (archdea-conry), may also induct both vicars and *churchwardens into their offices, and ex-amines and presents candidates for ordina-tion. See A. Amanieu, DDC 1:948–1004; G. W. O. Addleshaw, *Beginnings of the Paro-chial System* (1953). *ARCHPRIEST.

ARCHDIOCESE, see DIOCESE.

ARCHPRIEST, a title applied in several senses: (1) From the 4th or 5th cent. it desig-nated a priest (presbyter) chosen to assist the bp. directly, and esp. by substituting for him in specifically priestly functions (see ARCHDEACON). There were cathedral or ur-ban archpriests and from the 4th cent. rural archpriests, similar to the present-day rural deans or vicars forane (see CIC. c. 217). Rural archpriests were important to the de-velopment of the parish system. The title survives as honorific, attached to some principal churches in France and Italy. In

the Eastern Churches the office in some cases carries with it territorial jurisdiction. (2) The superior over secular priests in Eng-land, 1598–1621, was called archpriest. (3) By custom, an older priest assisting one newly ordained at his first Mass was sometimes unofficially designated as archpriest. See A. Amanieu, DDC 1:1004–26; G. N. O. Addle-shaw, *Beginnings of the Parochial System* (1953).

ARMINIAN, characterized by adherence to *Arminianism, as this is either a specific theological system or simply a doctrinal emphasis on human cooperation with grace.

ARMINIANISM, primarily the theological system inspired by J. *Arminius, and by extension any similar theological position. Historical Arminianism belongs to 17th-cent. Holland, where it was condemned by the Synod of *Dort (1618–19) and given sys-tematic formulation by S. *Episcopius. Its basic, anti-Calvinist tenets were contained in the "Remonstrance" (1610; see REMON-STRANTS): (1) predestination is conditioned by God's foreknowledge of man's belief; (2) Christ died for all and all can benefit by his atonement; (3) although fallen and in need of grace, man cooperates in his regenera-tion; (4) grace is not irresistible; (5) grace can be lost and hence final perseverance is not assured. The Remonstrant Church sur-vived persecution and continues to exist in Holland. There in the 18th cent. Arminian-ism became associated with Socinianism and other rationalist tendencies.

In its wider use, designating a theologi-cal viewpoint, the term Arminianism ap-plies first of all to an emphasis on the free-dom to accept grace. The latitudinarians of 17th-cent. England were anti-Calvinist and were called "Arminians," but had no close link with Dutch Arminianism. The theol-ogy of John *Wesley was Arminian, not because of his opposition to Calvinism, but because of his *perfectionism. Arminianism is taken as an anthropocentric theological emphasis in the accepted classification of *Reformed Churches into "Calvinist" and "Arminian." Arminianism characterizes all Wesleyan Methodist groups, the Holiness Churches, the United Brethren, the Evangelical Alliance, and the Salvation Army; the Mennonites and the General Baptists, while older than historic Arminianism, also classify their own theology as Arminian. Finally, simply on the basis of their being liberal, rationalist, or "enlightened," many other theological trends have been labelled Arminian. This was the broader sense Arminianism had in Jonathan *Edwards's polemics; and in which it was a prominent feature of the *Great Awakening, a part of *revivalism, and a formative element in American Universalism and Unitarianism. Often singled out as characteristic of American Protestant theology, Arminianism has had a broad influence upon the history of Protestantism in America. See A. W. Harrison, *Arminianism* (1937); Mayer RB 199–200, 283-342; G. O. McCulloh, ed., *Man's Faith and Freedom* (1962); Smith-Jamison 1:242–251; Schaff Creeds 1:509–519.

ARMINIUS, JACOBUS (Jakob He[a]rmandszoon, or He[a]rmann, etc.; 1560–1609), Dutch theologian for whom *Arminianism is named. A. studied at Marburg, Leiden, Geneva, Basel, Padua, and Rome. He was ordained as a pastor at Amsterdam in 1588. His theological training was in Calvinist orthodoxy; but his mind was formed also by humanist learning, the philosophy of Peter Ramus, and esp. at Leiden by liberalizing attitudes toward religious and political freedom. Designated in 1589 to debate against D. V. *Coornheert's denial of the orthodox Calvinist doctrine on predestination, A. came instead to reject it himself. His subsequent life was one of controversy, esp. with F. *Gomarus, who contested his appointment to the faculty of Leiden in 1603. A. was charged with *Socinianism and *Pelagianism; political considerations added acrimony to the debates.

But A. gradually clarified his own criticisms of strict Calvinism and his defense of human freedom under grace and achieved renown as a theologian of moderation. His works (Eng. tr. J. Nichols and W. R. Bagnall, 3v., 1956) were not a systematized exposition of Arminianism, but were patterned to the exchanges of controversy. Nor were his efforts to modify the *Belgic Confession or the *Heidelberg Catechism successful. Nevertheless, the liberal and humane theological trend he inspired had a considerable influence upon the subsequent history of Protestantism. See Bihlmeyer-Tüchle 3:202; A. W. Harrison, *Beginnings of Arminianism to the Synod of Dort* (1926); *idem, Arminianism* (1937); G. O. McCulloh, ed., *Man's Faith and Freedom* (1962).

ARNAULD FAMILY (Arnaut; Arnault), French family distinguished for its near monopoly of the Jansenist movement (see JANSENISM). The father, Antoine II (1560–1619), further enhanced the established family name in the practice of law and left a legacy of anti-Jesuitism, in his *Plaidoyer . . . contre les Jesuites* (1594–95), for the 10 of his 20 children who reached maturity. The six girls entered the Cistercian convent of *Port-Royal. Catherine (1588–1651), the eldest, entered after a marriage that gave Antoine and Isaac Le Maistre as theologians for the Jansenist cause. Two sisters, Anne (1594–1653) and Madeleine (1607–49), were relatively undistinguished, but Marie Claire (1607–42) had her brief moment of importance by opposing the Abbé de *Saint-Cyran, imperiling family as well as conventual unity. Jeanne, Mère Agnès (1593–1672), is overshadowed by her sister Jacqueline, Mère Angélique, but she wrote, besides valuable source material for history, a mystical work, *Le Chapelet secret du Saint Sacrement* (1627), which played its part in the controversies. Among the brothers it was Antoine, the 20th child, who became "le Grand Arnauld."

The temper of the Arnaulds, despite their theological and ascetic preoccupations, was legalistic. While they concerned themselves with the grand issues of predestination and grace, they did so in a legalistic manner. Moreover, they delighted in controversy and perhaps injured their cause by their implacable hatred for Jesuits. Their endless legal debate and devices, such as Antoine's distinction between law and fact, and their "respectful silence" in the face of papal decisions did much to discredit their claims of evangelical simplicity.

Mère Angélique (Jacqueline; 1591–1661). She had succession to the abbacy of Port-Royal assured her at the age of 7, although she was close to 11 when she assumed office. At first she drifted with the relaxed discipline of the convent, but she was converted at 16 and began a series of ruthless reforms that extended even beyond Port-Royal. A brief contact with St. Francis de Sales, to which she ever afterward made reference, almost led to her joining the Visitandines, but in 1622 she was back at Port-Royal with her mother and four sisters. In 1625, at the age of 34, she moved the entire convent to the influential Faubourg Saint-Jacques in Paris. Although she was replaced by her sister Agnès as abbess in 1630, she retained her great influence. She was in her 40s when she came under the influence of Saint-Cyran, under whom the community became Jansenist in principle and practice. She was abbess again, 1642–54, and died shortly after signing the formulary of 1661 at the age of 70. Her three volumes of memoirs, conferences, and writings are still extant.

Antoine (1612–94). His father died when Antoine was only 7; through his mother and his Port-Royal sisters, he came under the influence of Saint-Cyran. After studying law he entered the Sorbonne, where his bachelor's thesis on the doctrine of grace (1635) was a brilliant success. While still prominent in intellectual circles of Paris, he received sacred orders and entered into even closer association with the Port-Royal circle of Jansenism. Under the direction of Saint-Cyran he wrote *De la fréquente communion* (1643), which stressed the need for careful preparation for communion and which, according to St. Vincent de Paul, kept at least 10,000 people from the sacrament. Antoine was the real popularizer of Jansenism, for he went beyond the teachings on predestination and grace to elaborate practical conclusions on sacraments, not only the Eucharist but particularly penance, for which he demanded perfect contrition. While a brilliant theologian, he injured his cause by his bitter polemics. The Jesuits protested so vigorously that Antoine was stripped of his titles (1656) by the Sorbonne even though he sought the support of the Dominicans and of *Pascal, who defended him magnificently in the first of the *Provincial Letters. In reply to Alexander VII's *Ad sanctam beati Petri sedem*, published in France in 1657, and condemning five propositions attributed to C. *Jansen's *Augustinus*, A. formulated the distinction between *droit* and *fait*. Accepting the pope's right to condemn heresy, he denied the fact that the five propositions condemned were present in *Augustinus*. Although A. was reinstated at the Sorbonne by Louis XIV in 1669, he imposed exile in Holland on himself from 1679. He wrote against the Calvinists, against Malebranche, on *Gallicanism, on various biblical subjects, as well as on philosophy, science, and mathematics. While less radical than the original Jansenists in his teaching, he was the main source for the diffusion of Jansenist principles. See J. Q. C. Mackrell, NCE 1:840–843; bibliog. for Jansenism.

ARNDT, JOHANN (Arnd; 1555–1621), German Lutheran theologian and ascetical writer. After studying theology at Wittenburg, Strassburg, and Basel, A. became pastor at Badeborn in 1538 but was deposed in 1590 by Duke John George for opposing the order to remove pictures from churches and to omit exorcism rites from baptism. He served churches in Quedlinburg, Brunswick, and Eisleben. In 1611 he was made superintendent for Lüneburg through the good offices of Johann *Gerhard, whom he had befriended. A.'s chief works, *Vier Bücher vom wahren Christentum* (4v.,

1606–09) and *Paradiesgartlein aller christlichen Tugenden* (1612), were inspired by St. Bernard, Tauler, and Thomas à Kempis and were widely used as devotional reading. They stress the theme of Christ working in the heart of the believer. Through P. *Spener and *Pietism, his influence on Lutheran theology, hymnody, and devotional life extended into the 19th century. See I. Ludolphy, EncLuthCh 1:105–106.

ARNOLD OF BRESCIA (d. 1155), medieval reformer. A., who had studied at Paris under Peter Abelard, was ordained in Brescia and became a canon regular and prior of his monastery. A man of extreme austerity, he denounced clerical licentiousness and simony and became a leader of the populace against the political power of the bishop. He denied the right of Church or clergy to own property, urging the people not to receive the sacraments from priests who owned property. He was condemned at Lateran Council II (1139). Exiled from Italy, he took refuge in Paris; in 1141 he was condemned again, with Abelard, at the Council of Sens. He was banished from France, passed through Switzerland and Bohemia, and was reconciled for a time with Pope Eugene III in 1145 at Verona. In Rome he led a revolt of the populace against papal temporal power; after 9 years as virtual ruler of Rome, he was condemned and executed. The Council of Verona (1184), in condemning lay groups challenging clerical power, listed Arnoldists (D 760), but it is doubtful that A. ever actually formed a sect. See J. A. Brundage, NCE 1:844; Hughes HC 2:233–234.

ARNOLD, EBERHARD (1883–1935), the founder of the Society of Brothers (Bruderhof). Born at Königsberg July 26, 1883, he attended the Univ. of Breslau. As executive of the Student Christian Movement in Germany, scholar of the NT, and follower of Christophe F. Blumhardt, he drew together in 1920 a Society of Brothers, first on a farm in Sannerz, then on a large farm-estate in

the Rhoen hills. His ideal was the Sermon on the Mount: agape, nonviolence, common possession. He later found Hutterite settlements in the Dakotas to be like those of the Society, and he briefly joined one of these communes. A prolific writer in German, he is best known in English translation for *Salt and Light* (1967), which gives most of the principles of the Bruderhof. He died in Darmstadt in 1935; his influence is ably carried on by members of his family.

ARNOLD, GOTTFRIED (1666–1714), German Lutheran writer on mysticism. After studying theology at Wittenberg (1685–89), A. came in contact with the Pietist P. *Spener and experienced a conversion. For the most part, until his marriage in 1701, he devoted himself to writing. In *Die erster Liebe* (1696) and his chief work, important for the wealth of sources it quotes, *Unparteriensche Kirche—und Ketzerhistorie* (1699–1700), he maintained that the Church had fallen away from the early ideals and that those mystics who had been classified as heretics were alone representatives of true Christianity. In 1702 he accepted a pastorate, and his later works, mostly devotional, avoided earlier extremes. His novel views on the Church and Christian history impressed many literary figures of the *Enlightenment. Some of his hymns came into popular use. See R. Fischer, NCE 1:845.

ARNOLDISTS, see ARNOLD OF BRESCIA.

ARTICLES DECLARATORY (Church of Scotland), the statement setting forth the distinctive claims of the *Church of Scotland as a *national Church. The "Articles Declaratory of the Constitution of the Church of Scotland in Matters Spiritual" were recognized by Parliament in 1921 and enacted by the General Assembly of the Church in 1926. The Church declares itself to be part of the Holy Catholic or Universal Church, adheres to the Scottish Reformation, and receives the word of God as its supreme rule of faith and life (Art. 1). Its principal subordinate standard is the *Westminster Confession; its *polity is presbyterian; its system and principles of worship, orders, and discipline are in accordance with the *Westminster Standards (Art. 2). This Church is in historical continuity with the Church of Scotland that was reformed in 1560 and acknowledges its distinctive call and duty to bring the ordinances of religion to the people in every parish through a territorial ministry (Art. 3). It receives from its Divine King and Head the right and power, subject to no civil authority, to legislate and to adjudicate finally in all matters of doctrine, worship, government, and discipline (Art. 4). It has the right to frame or modify its subordinate doctrinal standards, "always in agreement with the Word of God" (Art. 5). It acknowledges the divine appointment and authority of the civil magistrate within his own sphere, and the duty of the nation to render homage to God (Art. 6). It recognizes the obligation to seek and promote union with other Churches (Art. 7) and claims the right to interpret, modify, or add to its Declaratory Articles, subject to the conditions of the first article (Art. 8). See J. R. Fleming, *History of the Church in Scotland, 1875–1929* (1933), 310–312, text.

ARTICLES OF PERTH, see PERTH, ARTICLES OF.

ASBURY, FRANCIS (1745–1816), second bp. of the Methodist Episcopal Church, the first ordained in the United States. A native of Handsworth, Staffordshire, England, A. left school at 12 to serve as an apprentice. Hearing Methodist preaching at Wednesbury, he was converted at the age of 14 and later became an itinerant preacher under John *Wesley. He answered Wesley's call for service in America and preached his first American sermon at Philadelphia, Oct. 28, 1771. A. traveled extensively among the Methodist *societies in America, enforcing Methodist discipline and securing allegiance to John Wesley. In 1772 Wesley appointed him "General Assistant in America." During the Revolutionary War most of Wesley's itinerants returned to England; A. remained in America, although he was forced into hiding for suspected English sympathies. The Methodist societies in the Colonies had been regarded as part of the Church of England. Since their own preachers were not ordained, and many Anglican ministers had fled, after the Revolution the societies asked Wesley to provide for their having the sacraments. Wesley ordained Thomas *Coke in England as general superintendent (bp.) of American Methodism, sending him with two others to the U.S. to ordain Asbury. Asbury, however, desired appointment by election, and the Methodist preachers elected him at Lovely Lane Chapel, Baltimore (1784). There he was ordained general superintendent, and the Methodist Episcopal Church in America was organized. During his administration he traveled widely, kept a *Journal*, now invaluable to historians, wrote hundreds of letters, and preached constantly. There were about 1,200 Methodists when he came to America; 214,000 at his death. See L. C. Rudolph, *F. A.* (1966); E. T. Clark, ed., *Journal and Letters of F. A.* (1958); F. E. Maser, *Dramatic Story of Early American Methodism* (1965), 62–65, 78–83, 93–94.

ASSEMBLIES OF GOD, the largest Pentecostal body in the U.S.; 1968 membership, 576,058 in 8,506 churches; headquarters, Springfield, Mo. The name and organization date from a "General Council of Pentecostal (Spirit Baptized) Saints from local Churches of God in Christ, Assemblies of God and various Apostolic Faith Missions and Churches, and Full Gospel Pentecostal Missions and Assemblies of like faith in the U.S.A., Canada, and Foreign lands" (K. Kendrick, 84), held in April 1914 at Hot Springs, Arkansas. The aim was to overcome the lack of organization characteristic of early Pentecostalism and to express doctrines in which Pentecostals were agreed. In a "Statement of Fundamental Truths" issued in a subsequent general council (St. Louis, 1916) the Assemblies affirmed the teachings of Pentecostalism and of *fundamentalism, including an emphasis on *premillenarianism. The Assemblies reject *sacramentalism and *infant baptism; affirm separation from the world and *entire sanctification, but as gradual, not instantaneous. Polity combines *presbyterian and *congregational elements. The local church retains autonomy and the power to accept or reject policies of higher bodies. Supreme legislative and executive power resides in the General Council; the working administrative body is the General Presbytery, composed of 16 presbyters. Local churches are united in district councils for their region. The denomination, at least in the U.S., is making an effort to work out a systematic body of doctrine; this theological reflection is still at its beginning but promises to bear fruit. In the U.S., also, worship services and those in which *glossolalia and *divine healing take place have become more restrained than in early Pentecostalism. There are signs that the Assemblies might become a link between conservative Pentecostals and other Christian Churches. The Assemblies have more than 900 missions in 75 lands; the *Assembléias de Deus* in Brazil is the largest of all Pentecostal denominations, with a total membership (1968) exceeding 1½ million, and a phenomenal 230% rate of growth each decade. See C. Brumback, *Suddenly from Heaven* (1961); K. Kendrick, *Promise Fulfilled: A History of the American Pentecostal Movement* (1961); J. T. Nichol, *Pentecostalism* (1966).

ASSEMBLY, GENERAL, see GENERAL ASSEMBLY (PRESBYTERIAN).

ASSOCIATE PRESBYTERIAN CHURCH OF NORTH AMERICA, a small body of Presbyterians numbering about four congregations and 650 members (1968), which derives from the *Seceder Tradition in Scotland. The denomination accepts the *Westminster Confession and the *Westminster Catechisms interpreted by what it calls "Associate Testimony." It encourages solemn *covenanting, *closed communion, psalm singing, and opposes membership in secret societies. In 1858 those who held these views refused to enter into a union of Presbyterians that became the United Presbyterian Church of North America (now part of the United Presbyterian Church in the U.S.A.).

ASSOCIATE REFORMED PRESBYTERIAN CHURCH (General Synod), a body of Presbyterians organized in 1821 in order to perpetuate distinctive characteristics of Scottish covenanters. The body accepts the *Westminster Confession and *Westminster Catechisms as *doctrinal standards; it is organized after the Presbyterian system that includes an annual meeting of the General Synod. Its headquarters are in Due West, S.C.; Erskine College and Erskine Theological Seminary are located in Due West; and the publication *Associate Reformed Presbyterian* is published there. While many of its members and leaders have been absorbed by other Presbyterian bodies, the denomination in 1968 still numbered about 140 congregations, with 27,500 members.

ASSOCIATION (Baptist), an agency of Baptist *polity. Recognizing both the right of every congregation to be self-governing and the obligation of each church to the others, Baptists have expressed their sense of interdependence through associations. An early English association (1625) expressed the "associational principle" thus: "There is the same relation between particular churches . . . as there is betwixt particular members of one church, for the churches do all make up but one body or church in general under Christ their head." The Philadelphia Association, organized in 1707, illustrated the purposes of such a body. It sought to promote doctrinal unity, helped to provide a suitable ministry, offered assistance in settling disputes, occasionally sent representatives on missions to the South, and after the advent of the foreign missions movement raised funds to help W. *Carey's mission in India. The Association never had juridical power over churches, but it could exclude uncooperative members. By the mid-20th cent. the functions of the Association had largely been taken over by other agencies, and its usefulness was being questioned. See N. H. Maring and W. S. Hudson, *Baptist Manual of Polity and Practice* (rev. ed., 1966).

ASSOCIATION FOR THE PROMOTION of the Unity of Christendom, a society founded Sept. 8, 1857, in London to unite Anglicans, Orthodox, and Roman Catholics in daily prayer for the restoration of visible unity to Christendom. The climate was prepared in an irenical pamphlet, "On the Future Unity of Christendom," by a lay RC convert from Anglicanism, A. Lisle Phillips (1809–78; in the latter part of his life he took the name A. Phillips De Lisle), who in 1838 had founded the Association of Universal Prayer for the Conversion of England. He and the architect A. W. Pugin (1812–52) were the RC leaders in the project, joining with the Anglicans, Bp. A. P. Forbes (1817–75) and F. G. Lee (1832–1902), who converted to Catholicism near the end of his life. Members of the Association recite each day the Lord's Prayer followed by a designated prayer for unity. By 1864 the Association had over 5,000 Anglican, 1,000 Catholic, and 300 Orthodox members. In that year, allegedly through the intervention of the future Cardinal H. E. Manning (1808–92), it was condemned by Rome. The RC members were required to withdraw, bringing the Association to an end in its original form, though it continued to function in some ways. Its publication, the *Union Review*, begun in 1863, continued until 1875. For a connection between the Association and the current *Week of Prayer for Christian Unity, see R. Rouse and S. C. Neill, eds., *History of the Ecumenical Movement 1517–1948* (2d ed., 1967), 348. See also H. R. T. Brandreth, *Dr. Lee of Lambeth* (1951).

ASSURANCE OF SALVATION, the Christian's certitude that because his life is based on faith, he is saved from sin and numbered among the elect. Luther's strong emphasis on faith as the sole principle of salvation gave prominence to this assurance. By faith the true believer is comforted with the conviction that God is faithful to his promises; the assurance is absolute. Calvinism grounded such assurance in the sovereign absoluteness of divine *election. RC teaching in the Council of Trent denied the possibility of an absolute certitude of one's salvation (D 1566). Both RC and classical Protestant views recognize that salvation does remain an object of hope, and that certitude of salvation is modified by the believer's capacity to fall away or be unfaithful to God's love.

John *Wesley stressed the idea of assurance as a conscious factor in Christian living. In his understanding, assurance is the experience of being able to live without voluntary sin (SEE CHRISTIAN PERFECTION). The idea was developed in the U.S. in *revivalism and the *Holiness movement, and assurance in this sense is a characteristic teaching of many of the Churches originating in these movements. *ENTIRE SANCTIFICATION; *PERFECTIONISM.

ATHANASIAN CREED, a creed, called also the *Quicumque vult* from the initial words of the Latin text, thought until the 17th cent. to have been composed by St. Athanasius. In 40 rhythmic statements it clearly, if not gracefully, expresses the belief in the Trinity and the incarnation that is necessary for salvation. The author remains a mystery, but the name of St. Ambrose among others has been suggested. The formulary is not Athanasian in content or style; it was composed between 434 and 542, and was possibly a compilation from many sources. Written in Latin, it was later translated into Greek (earliest Gr. MSS are of the 14th cent.); its use seems to have begun in Arles in the 6th cent. and spread. From the 9th cent. it appeared in the liturgy. Its former frequent recitation in the Roman liturgy at Prime on Sundays ceased when that canonical hour was suppressed by Vatican Council II in 1963 (Vat II SacLit 89). The Athanasian Creed, retained by the great Reformers, was esp. esteemed by Martin Luther. Acknowledged in the Anglican *Thirty-Nine Articles, it retains its place, in spite of some opposition in the C of E, as part of Morning Prayer in the Book of Common Prayer on certain days. The Protestant Episcopal Church, however, in its adaptation of the Articles and the BCP dropped this creed. In the East it is not one of the doctrinal standards, but from the 17th cent. it has been part of the Russian liturgy. See G. Owens, NCE 1:995–996.

ATHEISM, CHRISTIAN, see CHRISTIAN ATHEISM.

ATONEMENT, LIMITED, see LIMITED ATONEMENT.

AUBURN AFFIRMATION (1924), a document whose full title is *An Affirmation Designed to Safeguard the Unity and Liberty of the Presbyterian Church in the United States of America.* Signed by almost 1,300 Presbyterian ministers, the document, drafted primarily by church leaders of the Synod of New York, protested loyalty to evangelical Christianity and adherence to the *Westminster Confession during the height of the fundamentalist-modernist controversy. The *Affirmation* held, however, that the constitutional system of the Presbyterian Church allowed clergymen to hold differing theories concerning the interpretation of Christian faith and that the General Assembly of the denomination acted unconstitutionally in 1910 in defining "essential and necessary" doctrines, thus amending the *doctrinal standards without the concurrence of two-thirds of the pres-

byteries. The *Affirmation* was sent to every minister in the denomination and aroused great interest. It indicated that many men who were not fundamentalists were evangelical believers. A special commission appointed in 1925 to study the causes of unrest in the Church confirmed the constitutional contention of the Affirmationists about the organization of the denomination. With the adoption of the commission's report, the General Assembly attempted to preserve liberty of its members and unity of the denomination amid the theological ferment of the period. See L. A. Loetscher, *Broadening Church* (1954).

AUCTOREM FIDEI, a bull of Pius VI (Aug. 28, 1794) condemning the acts of the diocesan Synod of *Pistoia (1786), after thorough study by a papal commission. Impelled by Scipione de' Ricci, Bp. of Pistoia-Prato, the synod had enacted Gallican-Jansenist reforms subsequently rejected by the assembled bishops of Tuscany, but its decrees were widely disseminated. *Auctorem Fidei* censures verbatim, each in a carefully specified sense and with an individual theological note, 85 propositions on the Church, the hierarchy, grace, sacraments, worship, and religious orders (see D 2600–2700). Suppressed in several countries, the bull nevertheless ultimately disabled *Jansenism and *Gallicanism. See J. Carreyre, DTC 12.2:2202–30; Pastor 39:127–156.

AUFKLÄRUNG, see ENLIGHTENMENT.

AUGSBURG, RELIGIOUS PEACE OF, an agreement aimed at "a continual, firm, unconditional peace" between Lutherans and Catholics reached by the Emperor Ferdinand I and the German electors at Augsburg, Sept. 25, 1555. The treaty marked the establishment of *territorialism in the sanctioning of the principle *cuius regio eius religio.* It was a victory for Lutheranism to the extent that Lutheran Churches were granted civil recognition equal to that of the Roman Church, and the right to all properties taken over before the Treaty of Passau (1552). For Catholicism it was at least acceptable because it ensured protection in the states of Catholic princes and provided against further losses of property in sees whose bishops might become Protestants. The agreement regulated the religious situation until the Peace of Westphalia (1648) concluding the Thirty Years' War, a conflict intensified by the concession of tolerance by the Peace of Augsburg to Lutherans alone among Protestants. See Léonard HistProt 1:285–286.

AUGSBURG CONFESSION (*Confessio Augustana*), the chief particular Lutheran *confession of faith, presented to the imperial Diet held at Augsburg on June 25, 1530, and published in 1531. The principal issue before the Diet was the continuing threat of the Turks, but the religious questions that divided Roman Catholics and Protestants were also urgent. The spokesmen for the Lutheran cause, under the leadership of the elector of Saxony, wanted to set forth a defense of the Reformation as they had been carrying it out in their lands. To this end they commissioned Philipp Melanchthon (Martin Luther was under the ban of the Empire and could not appear at Augsburg) to draw up a statement of Lutheran doctrine—both the doctrines that Lutherans shared with Roman Catholics and those distinctively Lutheran. Basing his composition on earlier formulations of Lutheran teaching (most notably the so-called *Schwabach Articles and *Torgau Articles) and employing J. *Jonas, G. *Spalatin, and J. *Agricola as consultants, Melanchthon summarized the principal articles of Luther's positive position as well as the "abuses which have been corrected." Luther gave his approval to the document.

The Augsburg Confession consists of 28 articles. The First Part (1–21) is on the chief articles of faith. On God, original sin, and the person of Christ, Articles 1–3 affirm fidelity to the orthodox Catholic tradition.

Article 4 states the Lutheran doctrine of justification, which is followed by articles on the office of the ministry (5) and "the new obedience" (6). Articles 7–15 deal with the doctrine of the Church and of the sacraments, including the matter of ecclesiastical order and rites. Article 16 treats of civil government. The remaining articles of the First Part take up certain controverted questions: the return of Christ as judge (17); free will (18); the cause of sin (19); the relation of faith and good works (20); and the cult of saints (21). The "corrected abuses" enumerated in the Second Part (22–28) include reception of both kinds in the Eucharist, the marriage of priests, the Mass, confession, the distinction of foods, monastic vows, and the power of bishops.

Despite the sharpness of some of its polemics, the Augsburg Confession strove wherever possible to stress the common ground with Roman Catholicism and to state its own position irenically. It was subscribed by seven German princes and two free cities and was intended as a confession of the entire Lutheran community, not just of its theologians. The accepted text of the confession is the so-called *Invariata, prepared for the *Book of Concord (1580). The other confessions in the Book of Concord are taken by Lutherans to be explanations of the Augsburg Confession, just as it in turn claims to be an explanation of the Catholic creeds. See T. G. Tappert, ed., *Book of Concord: The Confessions of the Evangelical Lutheran Church* (1959); E. Schlink, *Theology of the Lutheran Confessions* (tr. P. F. Koehneke and H. J. A. Bowman, 1961). *APOLOGY OF THE AUGSBURG CONFESSION; *VARIATA.

AUGSBURG INTERIM, see INTERIMS.

AUGUSTANA EVANGELICAL LUTHERAN CHURCH (AELC), one of the four church bodies that merged in 1962 to form the *Lutheran Church in America. It was founded in Wisconsin in 1860 by 36 Swedish and 13 Norwegian congregations.

The title, which refers to the unaltered *Augsburg Confession (Confessio Augustana)* indicates the confessional conservatism to which the Church was committed. In 1870 the Norwegians withdrew to form a synod of their own. At the time of the merger in 1962, AELC membership numbered more than 500,000. See G. E. Arden, EncLuthCh 2:1368–73.

AUGUSTINE, ST.

AUGUSTINE, ST. (354–430), bp. of Hippo, Father of the Church, the single most influential theologian in the history of the Church in the West.

Life. Born of a Christian mother, Monica, and a pagan father, Patricius, at Tagaste in the African province of Numidia, A., while pursuing rhetorical studies in Carthage (371–374), underwent an intellectual and moral crisis. A reading of Cicero's *Hortensius* awakened in him a burning desire for wisdom, which led him on a long and tortuous search for truth. He first turned to the Scriptures but was quickly repelled by the inelegance of their style and language. He next joined the Manichaean sect, to which he was powerfully attracted both by its professed rationalism and its facile dualistic solution to the problem of evil, remaining in it in the lower rank of "hearer" (*auditor*) for nearly 9 years. About this same time he formed a concubinary relationship from which was born a son, Adeodatus, who later figured as interlocutor in A.'s short dialogue, *The Teacher*. While professor of rhetoric in Carthage (376–383), serious doubts on basic Manichaean teachings led to a progressive alienation from the sect that culminated in his disappointing encounter with Faustus, the most celebrated representative of the sect at that time. A new and more dangerous intellectual crisis arose during Augustine's brief sojourn in Rome (383–384) when, discouraged by his failure to discover truth, he began to adhere somewhat to the philosophy of the New Academy, which denied the possibility of human certitude. He left for Milan late in 384, having successfully competed for the municipal chair of rhetoric in that city, where he was soon joined by Monica. Two influences there gradually prepared the way for his return to the Catholic faith. First, the Sunday preaching of Ambrose, to which he was attracted by professional curiosity, introduced him to an allegorical interpretation of the Scriptures and to an exposition of Catholic teaching that belied many of the doctrines advanced by the Manichaeans. Second, his first acquaintance with the spiritualistic philosophy of neoplatonism, represented by Plotinus and Porphyry, helped to free his mind from the residue of Manichaean materialism and from the skepticism of the New Academy. Augustine's intellectual conversion to the Catholic faith was largely inspired by his abiding belief in a Divine Providence that could not fail to provide a sure way of salvation and by the growing conviction that the unique authority and prestige enjoyed by the Church pointed to it as a divinely appointed instrument to achieve this purpose. His moral and final conversion, which was delayed some time by the burden of sensuality and worldly ambition, reached its dramatic climax in the summer of 386; in response to a mysterious voice, he read a passage from St. Paul (Rom 13.13–14), which led to his decision to dedicate himself completely to the love and service of God (see *Conf.* 8.12.30).

in order to prepare for baptism, A. withdrew to the villa Cassiciacum near Milan (probably the present-day Cassago in Brianza). His first Christian writings, composed in dialogue form, belong to this period and represent his first efforts to construct a Christian philosophy, namely, a kind of rational inquiry inspired and guided by revealed truth. Early the following year (387) he was enrolled as a candidate for baptism, and during the Easter Vigil (April 24–25) he received the sacrament from the hands of Ambrose, together with his friend Alypius and Adeodatus. While awaiting embarkation to Africa at the Roman port of Ostia, Monica was seized with a fatal illness. The ecstatic experience shared by mother and son during Monica's last days is described by A. in his *Confessions* (9.10–11). After Monica's death he spent a year in Rome, making an extensive study of the numerous monastic communities. Soon after his return to Tagaste in Africa he set up his first monastery, a kind of lay institute devoted to study, prayer, and above all to the strict practice of the common life. During a visit to the basilica in Hippo in 391, where the aged Bp. Valerius was pleading for the services of a priest, A. was presented by the people for ordination, which he accepted, though reluctantly, as a manifestation of God's will. At A.'s request, Valerius provided a portion of the church property for a monastery, where he continued to live in community. The new foundation, and later the episcopal residence, became a center of ecclesiastical training that provided numerous clergy for the Church in N Africa, including some 10 bishops. In 396 A. was consecrated auxiliary bp. to Valerius, whom he succeeded within the year as bp. of Hippo.

A.'s remaining 34 years were filled with activity, both pastoral and polemical. Like other bps. of that day, he spent considerable time hearing and adjudicating cases of litigation, civil and religious. Despite delicate health, he was an indefatigable preacher, not only in Hippo but also in Carthage and other cities to which he was frequently invited. Even as a priest he played a conspicuous role in councils and synods of the African Church. At the invitation of bps. assembled in plenary council in 393, he pronounced a discourse on the Creed, later published under the title *Faith and the Creed*. He figured prominently as bp. at the councils held at Carthage between 397 and 419, and at the Council of Milevis in 416. As a pioneer of monasticism in Africa and author of a religious rule still widely used by male and female institutes, he has had a lasting influence upon the history of spirituality in the West. A.'s polemical efforts, which occupied nearly all of his ecclesiastical career, were the occasion for a vast theological literature that has decisively affected the thought and life of the Church down to the present time. Of the church

Fathers and Doctors, he is the one most frequently cited in the documents of Vatican Council II; in the important *Dogmatic Constitution on the Church* he figures no fewer than 25 times.

A. was successively engaged in three main controversies, which roughly cover the following periods: Manichaeism (388–405). Donatism (394–411), and Pelagianism (412–430). During his second sojourn in Rome as a layman A. undertook a refutation of Manichaeism in a work entitled *The Catholic and Manichaean Ways of Life*. In Africa he successfully engaged in public debate with the foremost Manichaean spokesmen. His reply to one of them, *Contra Secundinum*, A. himself regarded as the most effective of his anti-Manichaean treatises. It was mainly through A.'s polemical efforts and influence that the Donatist schism, which had seriously threatened the Church in Africa for nearly a century, was finally terminated. Although he at first urged and pursued a policy of leniency and persuasion, later, because of increasing atrocities perpetrated by the Donatists, he invoked the repressive measures enacted against the schismatics by the imperial laws. In the course of this polemic he had occasion to articulate important points of doctrine on the nature of the Church and on the objective efficacy of the sacraments against tenets that had given rise to the Donatist schism. Toward the end of this controversy A. was confronted with a "new heresy" propagated by the "enemies of God's grace." In essence, Pelagianism was a kind of Christian Stoicism that exaggerated human freedom and moral self-sufficiency while denying original sin and any strict need for grace. By A.'s personal influence and numerous writings in defense of grace, Pelagianism was condemned by three African councils whose action was confirmed by Pope Zosimus in 418. The error reappeared during Augustine's last years in a form later known as Semi-Pelagianism. In two complimentary works, *The Gift of Perseverance* and *The Predestination of the Saints*, he defended the gratuitousness of grace with special reference to the "beginning of faith" (*initium fidei*) and to final perseverence.

Works and Teachings. Augustine's writings have, with few exceptions, been preserved in their entirety. They include more than 100 books, in addition to some 240 letters and more than 500 sermons. His books, which include such masterpieces as the *Confessions, The Trinity,* and *The City of God,* cover a wide range of topics, philosophic, apologetic, moral, and exegetical. His dogmatic works comprise in large part the numerous polemical treatises directed against Manichaeism, Donatism, and Pelagianism. The doctrinal synthesis achieved by A. is neither a theological nor philosophical system, strictly speaking. It is more properly described as a Christian wisdom whose content and spirit have variously exercised a profound influence upon the intellectual history of the West for more than 1,500 years. In its essence, authentic Augustinianism aims at a progressive comprehension of revealed truth by reason illuminated by faith and with the resources of philosophic principles and method at its disposal (*fides quaerens intellectum*). Faith and reason thus cooperate as two distinct but inseparable sources of knowledge. The following doctrines are characteristic of this Augustinian dialectic:

The Primacy of Faith. The priority of faith is emphatically affirmed even in A.'s earliest works, where the respective roles of faith and reason are assessed with respect to the pursuit of truth (see *C. Acad.* 3.20.48; *De Ord.* 1.5.16). For A., the final and supreme authority is Christ, whereas for reason, his express preference is the philosophy of Platonism insofar as this is not at variance with revealed truth. From the primacy accorded to faith God becomes at once the principal source of knowledge and the central object of human inquiry. Accordingly, God is comprehensively viewed as the cause of being, the source of truth, and the ultimate norm of moral life (see *De Civ. Dei* 8.4).

God and the Soul. The theocentric character of Augustinian speculation readily explains his concentration on the soul and why the soul and God comprise the two principal objects of human inquiry (see *Solil.* 1.15.27). Since the soul's spiritual nature brings it into closer proximity with God, its progress in knowing God is largely determined and measured by its advance in self-knowledge. This so-called "metaphysics of internal experience" imparts to Augustinianism its distinctive mark of "interiority," which in turn makes possible A.'s exploration of the triune God through the analogous manifestations that appear within the life and activities of the soul. In contrast to the Greek theologians who sought to discover "vestiges" of the Trinity in physical nature, A. turns rather to the divine image of the soul in his effort to unfold in human language the inscrutable mystery of God's inner life. The soul as "image" is not only the most authentic reflection of the triune God but is also the cornerstone of A.'s theology of the spiritual life. Actually, religious perfection consists essentially in the progressive restoration of the soul's image, defiled by sin, to its true and proper condition. The method of interiority is further reflected in A.'s epistemology, where the basic certitudes spring from the indisputable evidence of the thinking subject and from changeless and necessary truths within the soul. The quest for certitude is, in effect, the search for God, since to discover an order of changeless truth transcending the mind itself is to perceive an absolutely unchanging reality reducible to God himself.

Augustinian Illumination. Although it manifests biblical and neoplatonic influences, A.'s explanation of the origin of intellectual knowledge cannot, at least in its final and definitive expression, be reduced to any of the classical epistemologies of Greek philosophy. For A., the source of such knowledge must be sought within the soul, whose spiritual nature brings it into a habitual and connatural relationship with the higher world of intelligible reality illumined by the participated light of God's uncreated light. And since the perception of truth is essentially realized by the inner activity of the mind, the senses can do no more than prompt (*admonere*) the soul to turn its attention to the truth within. As a logical corollary to this epistemological doctrine, A. draws the significant pedagogical conclusion that learning is essentially autodidactic. Teachers exercise a role analogous to that played by the senses since they merely direct the pupil to discover for himself the truth that is present within.

Seminal Reasons. A.'s notion of seminal reasons, adopted in part from Platonic and Stoic sources, was devised in an attempt to harmonize the revealed doctrine of the uniqueness of God's creative act with the successive appearance of new forms of life. His theory, sometimes referred to as "virtual creation," reveals a tendency already observed in his explanation of intellectual knowledge to exalt divine causality by minimizing the dynamic quality of secondary causes operating in nature. According to A.'s view, while all things were created at once, some came into being in their actual state while the rest were virtually created, namely, produced in a seminal or potential state. See G. Bonner, *St. Augustine of Hippo* (1963); E. Portalié, *Guide to the Thought of Saint Augustine* (tr. R. J. Bastian, 1960). For a listing of the more important Latin editions of A.'s works, see NCE 1:1049–51; H. Marrou, *St. A. and His Influence through the Ages* (tr. P. Hepburne-Scott, 1957).

AUGUSTINIANISM, a school of philosophical and theological thought claiming fidelity to the doctrine of St. Augustine of Hippo. For the 8 centuries following his death in 430, the authority and influence of St. Augustine were predominantly theological in nature. Nevertheless, in the development and formulation of his theology, based mainly upon Scripture and ecclesiastical tradition, he had consciously appropriated and assimilated much of the prevailing philosophy of his time. This was the neoplatonic philosophy of Plotinus and Porphyry, which may already have been modified by Christian influence by the mid-4th century.

Medieval Augustinianism. Medieval Augustinianism began to appear soon after the 13th-cent. introduction of Aristotelian metaphysics into the Univ. of Paris. As an intellectual movement, it was mainly a reaction against the "new learning," which was viewed as a serious threat to Catholic orthodoxy. To the traditional mind this was an attempt to replace the Christian wisdom of Augustine with the pagan wisdom of Aristotle. To meet this challenge, a new doctrinal synthesis emerged that, while remaining Augustinian in its theological content, appropriated a number of philosophical notions ascribed to St. Augustine, though several of these were derived from a neoplatonism influenced by Avicenna and Avicebron. Because of its dubious authenticity, some historians have preferred to describe the movement as either a pre-Thomistic school or as an eclectic-Aristotelianism.

The principal doctrinal tenets of this school were: (1) There is no autonomous philosophy independent and separate from theology. (2) The will enjoys a primacy over intellect, with the resulting voluntarist view that beatific vision is formally constituted by man's highest affective power rather than through an act of intellectual contemplation. (3) The soul knows itself directly and is really identified with its various powers or faculties. (4) Every created reality, spiritual as well as corporeal, is ultimately constituted of matter and form, with the result that the soul, being a complete substance, is individuated by its own spiritual matter. (5) To achieve its higher forms of knowledge, including God, the soul requires a special divine "illumination." (6) Within the structure of every composite reality there are several substantial forms hierarchically ordered, including the form of corporeity, identified with light. (7) The notion of "seminal reasons," or of a "virtual creation," to describe the causal or potential mode of being imparted at creation to living things that appear progressively in the course of time. (8) The absolute impossibility of an eternally existing world.

Proponents of this doctrine pertained for the most part to the Franciscan Order, though several, including Peter of Tarentaise (later Innocent V) and Richard Fishacre belonged to the earlier Dominican school. Notable among the Franciscan representatives of this movement were: Alexander of Hales, John Peckham, Bonaventure, Roger Marston, Matthew of Aquasparta, William de la Mare, and Richard Middleton. The famous condemnation issued by Abp. Tempier at Paris in 1277, which included several Thomistic doctrines, provided the Augustinian traditionalists with a decisive but short-lived victory. Within a few years, largely owing to the basic eclecticism of the period, the main body of Augustinianism was gradually absorbed into the mainstream of the new scholastic movements, both Thomistic and non-Thomistic. See F. Van Steenberghen, *Aristotle in the West* (tr. L. Johnston, 1955).

Augustinianism and Grace: Reformation Era. In their theology of grace the Augustinians of the period continue the tradition of their early school, particularly the tendencies introduced into it in the 14th cent. by Gregory of Rimini (d. 1358). These include a greater preoccupation with the problem of grace and a wider use of the writings and authority of St. Augustine. The new doctrinal controversies of the 16th cent. concerning original sin, *concupiscence, and justification occasioned a more thorough and detailed study of the Saint's anti-Pelagian works in an effort to present his teachings on grace in terms suitable to meet the challenges posed by Luther and the new theology. The principal exponent and defender of the Augustinian school at the Council of Trent was Girolamo *Seripando, who also served for a time as papal legate. His teaching on grace, as related to baptism and justification, is deeply rooted in a notion of concupiscence inherited from Gregory of Rimini. Concupiscence is viewed as sinful not only as a result and penalty of original sin, as well as a source of personal sin, but also because its persistence, even after baptism, renders it impossible for man to accomplish the full and perfect observance of God's law. Augustine is invoked to support the view that man cannot fully observe the commandment forbidding evil desires since concupiscence remains in active opposition to the precept; he can, at best, only fulfill the injunction not to follow these evil desires. Since, according to the Augustinians, such a condition is necessarily displeasing to God, they tried unsuccessfully to have removed from the final form of Trent's decree on justification the statement that "God finds nothing hateful in the reborn." Like Seripando, they were convinced that this notion of concupiscence, as well as the related doctrine of *"double justice," were Pauline and Augustinian in origin. The double justice theory had already been proposed as a doctrinal compromise to reconcile RC and Lutheran teaching on justification, though Luther himself found it unacceptable. As viewed by Seripando, the justice effected in man, enabling him to perform good works, remains incomplete owing to concupiscence and must be further complemented by a second justice, the justice of Christ, in order to merit eternal life. This application of Christ's justice is made possible by man's incorporation into the Mystical Body through a previous grace that enables him to believe and trust in Christ the head. The culminating and decisive role of this twofold justice can be seen in the following steps traced out by Seripando in the process of justification: (1) the first grace, or call to the faith; (2) a second grace, which enables man to accept the first and to turn from sin through penance; (3) the remission of sin by incorporation into the Mystical Body by acts of faith and trust in Christ its head; (4) infusion of charity and gifts of the Holy Spirit enabling man to keep the commandments; (5) application of the justice of Christ to complement the justice of his members, which remains incomplete by reason of concupiscence.

The central doctrine of concupiscence, which underlies the doctrine of justification, was to play an equally important role in the explanation of efficacious grace by the Augustinian theologians of the 17th and

18th centuries. See H. Jedin, *Papal Legate to the Council of Trent: Cardinal Seripando* (tr. F. C. Eckhoff, 1947).

Augustinianism and Grace: 17th and 18th Centuries. The Augustinian theologians of this later school, also known as *Augustinenses* and the school of H. Noris, endeavor to present an authentic and timely statement of Augustine's teachings on grace in order to rehabilitate his authority against interpretations that resulted in the condemnation of the doctrines of Calvin, Baius, and Jansen. Accordingly, Augustinians of this period are principally preoccupied with such questions as the original state of justice, predestination, and the necessity and nature of efficacious grace vis-à-vis man's free will. Basic to the development of their theology of grace is the notion already defended by the early school and inspired by St. Augustine's doctrine of the soul as "image," that man's spiritual nature is naturally ordered toward beatific vision. Hence, these later theologians emphatically deny the possibility of a purely natural state for man and at the same time endeavor to safeguard the gratuity of the supernatural order by introducing a distinction current at the time between God's "absolute" and "ordered" power, the latter being his power as directed by his essential attributes of wisdom and goodness. Consequently, not only sanctifying grace, but also such preternatural endowments as knowledge, immortality and integrity, were owing to man because of a certain fittingness on the part of the Creator. Because of the quasi-natural character of these latter, the Fall entailed both the loss of grace and an impairment to full natural human integrity. Hence the special necessity for a "medicinal" grace to remedy this impairment, and the further conclusion that concupiscence results from original sin alone and constitutes its material element.

The Augustinian teaching on the divine economy of grace is thus based upon a strictly concrete and historical view of man considered in the successive states of innocence and sin. Even before the Fall man needed and received a grace that conferred upon his will the "power" (*posse*) to do good but that did not guarantee either the consent of the will (*velle*) or the consummation of the good work (*perficere*). Characterized as "indifferent" (*gratia versatilis*), such a grace, sufficient for man in his innocent condition, was one that man could either accept or resist, so that in the performance of good the will played the principal role. Because of his fallen state this grace is no longer sufficient and there is required an efficacious grace (*gratia efficax*), which, though leaving freedom intact, infallibly produces its effect.

The same historical view of man likewise underlies the Augustinian theology of predestination. Predestination before the Fall, as well as reprobation, resulted from God's foreknowledge of man's future merits (*post praevisa merita*), while, in consequence of Adam's sin, predestination to grace and glory is absolutely gratuitous on the part of God, prior to, and independent of any foreknowledge of man's merits (*ante praevisa merita*). Reprobation, understood in a negative sense, is the direct result of original sin and embraces those who, in accordance with the "just judgment of God," comprise the so-called *massa perditionis*. While acknowledging God's salvific will, these theologians think it at least probable that sufficient grace is not given to all, citing in support of this view infants who die unbaptized and adults who have no knowledge of Christian revelation. In explaining the nature of efficacious grace, these later Augustinian theologians adduce what is perhaps the most celebrated and controversial point of doctrine in their entire theology, namely, the *delectatio victrix*, which the early school of Giles of Rome (d. 1316) had appropriated from St. Augustine without further development. As outlined by Noris, the will of man in his fallen condition is drawn by two opposed forces of attraction, concupiscence (*cupiditas mali*) and grace (*cupiditas boni*), and inevitably yields to the stronger attraction. Only when grace exercises the stronger attraction and effectively overcomes the contrary delight of concupiscence is such grace efficacious, though in accepting this grace, as G. L. Berti insists, the will is acting with complete freedom (*liberrima voluntate*). Grace remains "inefficacious" when the power conferred is insufficient to overcome the attraction of concupiscence and leaves the will in a "weak" and "feeble" state, as Augustine had pointed out in one of his later anti-Pelagian works (see *De Grat. et lib. arb.*, 17). Augustinians acknowledge no essential difference between these two kinds of grace; grace becomes efficacious by reference to the relative intensity of the present evil attraction and to the moral condition of the recipient. Consequently, one and the same grace may prove efficacious for some but inefficacious for others. See W. Bocxe, *Introduction to the Teaching of the Italian Augustinians of the 18th Century on the Nature of Actual Grace* (1958).

Recent Augustinianism. Although contemporary Augustinianism is represented by no particular school or system, theological or philosophical, its influence is apparent both in the nature of the problems posed and in the various approaches adopted toward a solution. Contemporary thought shares with Augustine its concern for problems that arise in exploring the mysterious complexity of the human person or in describing man's destiny in its fuller existential dimensions. In particular, current spiritualistic and existential movements show a marked preference for the spirit and form of dialectic initiated by Augustine. In France and Italy the Augustinian "metaphysics of internal experience" is the point of departure for the several forms of the "philosophy of the spirit" represented by Lavelle, Sciacca, and Carlini. Augustine's impact upon the existential movement can be traced back to its origin with S. *Kierkegaard, who credited Augustine with having discovered the "dialectic of existence" to solve the mystery of human existence by assigning a priority to faith over reason. The Augustinian primacy of faith is stressed even further by Karl Jaspers, who regarded Augustine as the founder of true philosophy. Since, according to the German philosopher, reason cannot reach beyond mere phenomena, faith alone can grasp reality, including not only God's existence but even one's personal identity. Finally, the prominent role given to the teachings of Augustine in Vatican Council II, where he is cited more frequently than any other Father or Doctor of the Church, suggests not only a fuller exploration of his theology but also new possibilities for fruitful dialogue between Catholics and those Protestant communities that historically have revered his authority. See J. Guitton, *Modernity of St. Augustine* (tr. A. V. Littendale, 1959).

AUGUSTINUS, Cornelius *Jansen's treatise on grace, source work for *Jansenism, published posthumously and secretly at Louvain, July 14, 1640. It was written in Latin in three books. Book I is a historical introduction on the persistence of *Pelagianism. Book II depicts man as angelic before his Fall, demonic afterward. Book III concludes that fallen man is radically evil and capable only of sin; redemption reaches only a predestined few. Jansen denies sufficient grace; he admits freedom of will only as freedom from coercion. This he claimed as St. Augustine's definitive teaching; he documents his propositions with isolated texts of Augustine, some used earlier by Luther and Calvin. Jesuits and some others saw this as moderated Calvinism, reviving *Baianism, which had been condemned by Pius V and Gregory XIII. Like Cardinal Richelieu, they sought papal condemnation of *Augustinus*. Urban VIII complied on March 6, 1642, with *In eminenti*, not published until June 19, 1643. See F. Mourret, *History of the Catholic Church* (tr. N. Thompson, 8v., 1931–57), 6:384–389; H. Daniel-Rops, *Church in the Seventeenth Century* (tr. J. J. Buckingham, 1963), 339–346; Pastor 29:62–130.

AULÉN, GUSTAF (1879–   ), bp. of Strangnas, Swedish Lutheran theologian, professor at the Univ. of Lund. With Anders *Nygren, A. was a leader of the *Motiv-

forschung (see *MOTIF RESEARCH) school, which stressed the essential truth of Christian doctrine rather than the form of presentation. The school also emphasized the connection between the early Christian Fathers and the Reformation. A.'s important works are *Den allmänneliga kristna tron* (1923; Eng. tr., *The Faith of the Christian Church*, 1954); *Den kristna gudsbilden* (1927); and the Olaus Petri lectures of 1930, *Den kristna försoningstanken* (abridged Eng. version by A. G. Hebert, *Christus Victor*, 1931).

AUTO-DA-FÉ (Portuguese, act of faith),the public ceremony wherein the decisions of the Spanish Inquisition were proclaimed. The elaborate event included a procession, a sermon, and a reading of the decisions of the Inquisition, followed by recantations, reconciliations, and the handing over of the obdurate to the secular arm. Popular usage often erroneously connects *auto-da-fé* with the execution of heretics. The first *auto* was held in Seville in 1481; the last, in Mexico in 1850. See H. Kamen, *Spanish Inquisition* (1965); R. I. Burns, NCE I:1116. *INQUISITION, SPANISH.

AVOIDANCE, also called shunning, the Mennonite practice of ostracizing those who have been placed under the *ban. The Swiss Anabaptists did not observe avoidance. Obbe *Philips introduced the practice among Dutch Anabaptists *c.*1533, and *Menno Simons continued it. There was continuous difficulty with the problem of applying the penalty without harshness, and with the question of marital avoidance when one spouse was excommunicated. The zeal of Jakob *Ammann to observe shunning was the cause of the separate existence of the Amish. Only the Old Order Amish and a few other conservative groups still enforce this form of discipline. Shunning has been referred to colloquially in the U.S. as an Amish mite, from the German word for it, *Meidung.* See MennEnc I:200–201.

AZUSA STREET REVIVAL, a main source from which *Pentecostalism spread. The Revival was begun in April 1906 by W. J. Seymour, a Holiness preacher who had been introduced to Pentecostal doctrine by C. F. *Parham. Sessions were held in a former Methodist Church on Azusa Street in Los Angeles, California. Those who there received *baptism with the Holy Spirit directly or indirectly influenced the establishment and spread of the Assemblies of God, Apostolic Faith (Portland, Ore.), Christian Churches of N.A., Church of God (Cleveland, Tenn.), Pentecostal Holiness Church, the Church of God in Christ, and other bodies. The Revival also had its effect on the spread of the Pentecostal movement to Europe and South America. See J. T. Nichol, *Pentecostalism* (1966), 32–37.

B

BABYLONIAN CAPTIVITY, the deportation of the Jews to Babylonia (598 and 587 B.C.) and their retention there until Babylon fell to the Persians under Cyrus (538 B.C.). In Christian times the term has had two celebrated metaphorical applications. It was used: (1) by Petrarch and others in referring to the residence of the popes at Avignon (1309–77); and (2) by Martin *Luther in his treatise *A Prelude Concerning the Babylonish Captivity of the Church* (1520). Luther's reference was to the bondage in which he declared the Church had been kept by Roman teaching on the sacraments, transubstantiation, and the sacrificial character of the Mass and by withdrawal of the chalice from the laity.

BACKUS, ISAAC (1724–1806), Baptist pastor, revivalist, and advocate of religious liberty. Reared a Congregationalist, he experienced conversion during the *Great Awakening, joined those who accepted revivalist conversion, called the Separate, or New Light Congregationalists, and soon became a minister. Protesting payment of taxes to support the standing order, he advocated religious freedom. In 1756 he joined the Baptists and traveled over 15,000 miles as a preacher throughout New England. From 1770 he was the Baptist leader in a campaign to disestablish the Congregational Church in Massachusetts, and for this purpose organized the Warren Association in Warren, Rhode Island, with two other ministers. Although influenced by *Enlightenment ideas, his appeal for religious liberty was based primarily on religious grounds. Besides tracts on religious freedom and numerous polemical works, he wrote a three-volume *History of New England, with Particular Reference to the . . . Baptists* (1777), valuable as a source work and as a vindication of religious liberty. See W. G. McLoughlin, *I. B. and the American Pietist Tradition* (1967).

BAGNOLENSES, one of the principal branches of the *Cathari in Italy in the 13th century. The name probably derives from Bagnola, a town near Mantua, where many of the adherents resided. They taught a mitigated form of dualism according to which the evil principle did not create the material universe but fashioned it from the four primordial elements. They also held that Christ had not a real, but a phantom, human body. See A. Dondaine, ed., *Un Traité néo-manichéen du XIIIe siècle: Liber de duobus principiis* (1939); I. da Milano, EC 2:689–690; A. Borst, *Die Katharer* (1953), 101, 237.

BAHÁ'Í FAITH, less correctly Bahá'ísm, a belief that recognizes the unity of God and his prophets, teaches that divine revelation is continuous and progressive, and that the founders of all past religions, though different in the non-essential aspects of their teachings, proclaim the same spiritual truth. The Bahá'í Faith is named after Bahá'Ulláh (Glory of God), whom his followers in more than 300 countries and territories believe to be the most recent in a succession of divine educators such as Moses, Christ, and Mohammed. The central principle of this faith is the oneness of mankind. It teaches the necessity and inevitability of an organic change in the structure of present-day society, and the removal of all forms of provincialism and prejudice, recommending the reconstruction and demilitarization of the whole civilized world, anticipating a consummation of human evolution, the coming of age of the entire human race, and attainment to a permanent and universal peace. This pivotal theme revolves around the belief that the fundamental purpose of religion is to promote harmony and conjoins with the principles of an unfettered search after truth, of equal opportunity, rights, and privileges of both sexes. Compulsory education and abolition of extremes of wealth and poverty are advocated; work performed in the spirit of service is regarded as worship.

The Bahá'í Faith grew out of Babism in Persia, a religion founded in 1844 by Mırza Alı Muhammad of Shıraz (1819–50). Taking the name al-Bāb (the gateway), he proclaimed his twofold mission as an independent prophet and herald of "One greater than Himself." Al-Bāb was imprisoned and finally killed, as were thousands of his followers In 1863 while an exile in Baghdad, Mırza Husayn 'Alı Nūrı (1817–92) announced that he was the one of whom al-Bāb had spoken. He subsequently wrote, under the title Baha'Ullāh, more than 100 books and letters in which he enunciated the spiritual and social principles of the new faith and urged the leaders of mankind to establish a world government by mutual agreement.

Baha'Ullāh appointed his son, 'Abd-al-Bahā (servant of the glory; 1844–1921), interpreter and exemplar of his teachings. 'Abd-al-Bahā visited the U.S. in 1912 and laid the cornerstone for the Bahá'í house of worship in Wilmette, Illinois. He appointed his grandson, Shoghi Effendi (1896–1957), guardian of the Bahá'í Faith. In his *Book of Laws* Baha'Ullāh provided for administrative insitutions, at the head of which is the Universal House of Justice. This supreme body was established in 1963 and has its headquarters in Haifa, Israel. See Shogi Effendi, *The World Order of Baha'u'llāh* (1965).

BAIANISM, the system Michael *Baius, proposed in his treatises on man, his nature and Fall, and grace (1563–66). Condemned in the 79 propositions that state the main erroneous points (see D 1901–79), it has been called an "Augustinism gone astray" (see H. de Lubac, *Augustinisme et théologie moderne,* 1965). Baius wished mainly to explain two points, as Augustine had done: (1) the corruption of man's fallen nature; and (2) his need of divine grace. He took as his starting point the nature of man, who is meant to seek God by keeping the commandments and for that purpose was given the gifts of the original state: grace, the Spirit, subordination of his lower to his higher powers. These gifts belong to his "natural" state, not as resulting from his nature but as required for man to be able to live as he should and keep the law of God. The original state and the gifts involved are natural in this sense (D 1901–07, 1909, 1911, 1978). By keeping the commandments man merits life eternal by a natural merit, as his due for his efforts (D 1904–07, 1911–15). This thorough naturalism, or *Pelagianism is the reversal of Augustine's teaching. It confuses nature as historical native state of man (Augustine) and as opposed to supernatural. It reverses the perspective of nature and grace: to Augustine's mind nature is meant for grace; according to Baius grace is at the service of nature and man has a claim to all the gifts needed to keep the law.

The original situation was ruined by the Fall. Original sin means the loss of natural justice; it is a corruption of man's nature. Man no longer understands the things of God. He loves the world instead of God. *Concupiscence dominates (D 1948–50). Unless helped by grace (i.e., a passing help for good actions), fallen man sins in all that he does voluntarily (D 1925, 1927, 1928, 1939, 1946). Sin is what does not conform to the law, even when committed under the compulsion of concupiscence (D 1940, 1946). What man does without love for God, he does for love of self and the world (D 1938). Thus the naturalism of the original state, combined with Baius's legalism, leads to an idea of man's fallen state that, while conforming in some aspects with the letter of St. Augustine's writings, reveals a contrary spirit, esp. regarding love and grace. In Baianism love of God and grace are not inner transformations of man but are passing helps to fulfill the commandments and are unnecessary for meriting life eternal. Righteousness is mere conformity of man's actions with the prescriptions of the law, not an infused gift, or *habitus* (D 1942, 1969). Nor is freedom required for sin or for merit (D 1967). Concupiscence, though not free, is sin (D 1974–75), but in the just it no longer dominates. Every sin is mortal (D 1920). Springing from love of self instead of love of God, it adheres to an evil end.

Against this background appears the inherent ambiguity of Baianism, Augustinian in wording, anti-Augustinian in spirit. Baius's basic naturalism, the starting point of his system, is foreign to Augustine. He distorts the reading of Augustine's teaching on the Fall and its reparation, on grace and charity, by the legalism that pervades his views on justice and merit, sin and freedom. The condemnation of Baianism on the nature of man and grace settled in RC doctrine the points of faith on man's gratuitous call to the supernatural and life eternal, his fall from it through sin, and his restoration by the grace of Christ. See X. Le Bachelet, DTC 2:38–III.

BAIUS, MICHAEL (Michel de Bay; 1513–89), the Walloon theologian, best known in theology for the 79 propositions condemned by Pope Pius V in 1567 and listed in D 1901–79 as "errors of Michel de Bay about the nature of man and grace." Born at Meslin l'Évêque (Hainaut), he studied philosophy (1533–36) and theology (1536–41) at the Univ. of Louvain. From 1544 to 1551 he taught philosophy there and meanwhile gained his licentiate (1545) and master's degree in theology (1550). In the following year he became professor of theology and remained so till his death, being also from 1575 dean at St. Peter's and vice-chancellor of the university. B. inaugurated a new method in the study of theology, at the time when the Council of Trent was in session. He anticipated by nearly 4 centuries the "return to the sources" that characterizes contemporary theology. For him, this meant Scripture seen through the eyes of Augustine. A healthy desire for a theology closer to life inspired the new venture, but its antischolastic Augustinism was not without danger of deviation (see H. de Lubac, *Augustinisme et théologie moderne* [1965], ch. I). Friction arose between Baius and J. Hessels, the new team, and their older colleagues at the university, R. Tapper and J. Ravesteyn. In 1560 the Sorbonne condemned 18 propositions of Baius, who made ready for a reply, and the conflict came into the open. Pope Pius IV imposed silence; the Council of Trent was to decide the question. Baius and Hessels actually went to the Council, May 1563, but avoided a discussion.

Meanwhile Baius started publishing, a first tome appearing in 1563 with three tracts: *De libero arbitrio, De iustitia et iustificatione,* and *De sacrificio*. A second volume followed in 1564–65: *De meritis, De primi hominis iustitia, De virtutibus impiorum, De sacramentis,* and *De forma baptismi*. From these and other unpublished writings of Baius, Ravesteyn drew 28 propositions that, together with many more, were condemned by the Universities of Alcalà and Salamanca (1565), for the Netherlands at the time were under the King of Spain. In a new edition of his first volume Baius included additional tracts, *De peccato originis, De charitate, De indulgentiis,* and *De oratione pro defunctis* (1566). The Louvain faculty turned to Rome for a judgment. After 40 more propositions taken from the new volume had been condemned by Alcalà, a papal commission, at the request of Philip II, took up the case. Of the 120 propositions condemned in Spain, 76 were condemned also by Pius V's bull *Ex omnibus afflictionibus* (1567). Baius submitted to the condemnation at once; after a futile attempt at obtaining a revision of the judgment, he abjured the propositions in the sense meant in the bull. His attitude, however, was not unambiguous. New propositions of his provoked new trouble. Pope Gregory XIII confirmed the condemnation of Pius V, and Baius again submitted, declaring that several of the condemned propositions were found in his works in the sense meant in the condemnation. To put an end to the continuing uneasiness, a summary of the doctrine contrary to the condemned propositions was drawn up and accepted by the Louvain faculty as an obligatory guide (1565). B. died, as he had remained throughout his troubled career as a theologian, a Catholic at heart. His firm conviction that his teaching was not different from that of St. Augustine (which to his mind could not be wrong), and the ambiguity left by the punctuation in Pius V's bull, the so-called *comma pianum,* may explain B.'s hesitancy about submission. See P. J. Donnelly, NCE 2:19–21; P. Smulders, LTK 1:1198–99. *BAIANISM.

BALFOUR, ARTHUR JAMES (1848–1930), British statesman and philosopher. Educated at Eton and Trinity College, Cambridge, B. took an active part in political life, holding at different times from 1891 until 1922 positions of importance, including that of prime minister (1902–05). He is remembered for issuing as foreign secretary the so-called Balfour Declaration (1917), which was a qualified pledge of support to the Zionist cause. His interest in religion found expression in his *Defence of Philosophic Doubt* (1879), a work showing the need of a solution through the non-rational (i.e., religious faith) to the problems left unsolved by the philosophical and natural sciences. He took a stand against both naturalistic positivism and the sort of idealism that would identify man with God, or see in man a necessary manifestation of God. Further development of his thought is to be found in his *Foundations of Belief* (1895) and in his Gifford Lectures, *Theism and Humanism* (1915) and *Theism and Thought* (1923). See biog. by his niece, Blanche E. C. Dugdale (2v., 1936).

BALLOU, HOSEA (1771–1852), Universalist minister. Born in Richmond, N.H., he was converted from Calvinism to *Universalism by influences deriving from Caleb Rich and by biblical study. His own views were soon clearly distinguishable from the Relly-Murray interpretation of Universalism. The influence of *Reason the Only Oracle of Man,* by the deist Ethan Allen, is discernible in B.'s major work, *A Treatise on Atonement* (1805); some of his concepts derive from *Thoughts on the Divine Goodness* by

Ferdinand Oliver Petitpierre. B.'s *Treatise on Atonement* is the first systematic statement of Universalist teaching; he argues that sin is finite, rejects the doctrine of the Trinity, and interprets atonement as reconciliation, a "renewal of love." Later, embroiled in controversy with the Restorationists (see RESTORATIONISM), he rejected the doctrine of punishment after death. Ballou was the dominant figure in the growth of American Universalism. See R. Eddy, *Universalism in America* (2v., 1884–86); E. Cassara, *H. B.* (1961).

BALLOU, HOSEA (1796–1861), Universalist minister; grandnephew of the preceding. Born in Guilford, Vt., the son of a Baptist, B. became a Universalist. He served Universalist pastorates in Stafford, Conn., and in Roxbury and Medford, Massachusetts. His major work was *The Ancient History of Universalism* (1829). See R. Eddy, *Universalism in America* (2v., 1884–86).

BAMPTON LECTURES, an annual series of lectures established under terms of the will of J. Bampton (d. 1751) to be delivered in the university church, St. Mary's, Oxford, in exposition and defense of the Christian faith. The first series was given in 1780; since 1895 the lectures have been given biennially, a change made necessary by depreciation in the value of the fund. The lectureship is restricted to Anglican M.A.s of Oxford or Cambridge. The lectures, always published after delivery, constitute on the whole an important collection of apologetical literature, and individual series over the years have provided notable stimulus to scholarship and theological debate.

BAN (Ger. *Bann*), the term for the form of excommunication practiced particularly by Mennonites. There are two kinds of ban: exclusion from communion (*kleiner Bann*) and complete exclusion from membership in the Church (*grosser Bann*). The prominence of the ban in Mennonite history rests upon the teaching that the Church must be kept visibly pure; only by discipline of those who have failed to live up to the decision involved in *believer's baptism can this purity be assured. The ban was one of the points of disagreement between the Swiss Anabaptists and Zwingli; its importance to church life was declared in the *Schleitheim Confession (1527) and later in the *Dordrecht Confession (1627). Early Anabaptist leaders stressed the need first to admonish scandalous sinners, then to apply the ban. Repeatedly in Anabaptist and Mennonite history stricter or milder interpretation of the ban, and particularly the complete *avoidance or shunning of the banned, became a cause of division (see AMISH; AMMANN JAKOB). The ban is still recognized as essential to church discipline by modern Mennonites, although not all enforce it. See MennEnc 1:219–223.

BÁÑEZ, DOMINGO (1528–1604), Spanish Dominican theologian, for whom the system of grace called *Báñezianism is named. Born at Valladolid, at the age of 15 he began his philosophical studies at Salamanca, and 3 years later he joined the Dominican convent of San Esteban there. He studied theology under Bartolomé de Medina and Melchior Cano. From 1552 until his death he taught theology in various places: 1552–61 in the Dominican convent at Salamanca; 1561–66 at the newly founded university in Avila; 1567–70 at Alcalá; 1570–73 he was Durandus professor at Salamanca; and after the death of Medina (1581) he held for 20 years the "Chair of Prime" at the university. Báñez was one of the great commentators on the *Summa Theologiae* of St. Thomas Aquinas and a profuse writer. Of his scholastic commentaries, the following were published in modern times through the care of V. Beltrán de Heredia: *In 1am-2ae* v.1 (*De fine ultimo et de actibus humanis*), v.2 (*De vitiis et peccatis*), v.3 (*De Gratia Dei*), 1942-1948; *In 3am partem* v.1 (*De Verbo incarnato*), v.2 (*De sacramentis*), 1951, 1953. B's theological writings would themselves have given him a place in the history of theology, even apart from his system of grace. Like the other Spanish theologians of the 16th- and 17th-cent. scholastic revival, B. was highly systematic, essentialist and conceptualist in approach rather than biblical or existential. This makes his profound speculative thought of more historical than vital interest to post-Vatican II theology. While at Avila, B. became the spiritual director of St. Teresa and remained so until her death in 1582. He was the defender of her reform as well as of her writings. His influence, it is said, explains the Thomistic cast of mind underlying her spirituality. For Teresa, B. was a learned, firm, and understanding director. See W. J. Hill, NCE 2:48–50.

BÁÑEZIANISM, the name given to the system of grace (or explanation of the cooperation between divine grace and free will) constructed by Domingo *Báñez. The historical occasion for its origin was in the controversies on grace between Jesuits and Dominicans in Spain, and particularly over L. *Molina's *Corcordia liberi arbitrii cum gratiae donis, divina praescientia, providentia, praedestinatione, et reprobatione* (Lisbon, 1588), which was censured by Báñez for the Inquisition. After Molina's self-defense, the book was approved. When the controversy following on this was delated to Rome, Molina denounced Báñez to the Inquisition in Castile. Báñez replied by publishing (1595), in collaboration with P. Herrera and D. Alvarez, an *Apologia* against certain assertions of Molina, and 2 years later a *Libellus supplex* to Clement VIII. Báñez himself did not take any part in the *Congregatio de auxiliis held in Rome (1598–1607). The problem that both Molinism and Báñezianism seek to solve is this: how do efficacious grace and human free consent go together? Both agree that for a salutary or supernatural act God grants prevenient actual grace intended to be sufficient to bring about man's free consent. They also agree that, when the free consent follows in fact, the grace received is a greater gift of God than was sufficient grace. The point of disagreement regards the difference between a sufficient grace that will remain purely sufficient (i.e., to which man will not freely consent) and one that will become efficacious in fact (i.e., to which man will freely consent). Molina says that there is no objective difference between the two; the difference exists only between a purely sufficient grace and a grace efficacious in the actual event.

Báñez maintains that sufficient grace, or prevenient grace given to arouse the free consent, does not actually bring about this consent unless there is added an efficacious grace, different from merely sufficient prevenient grace. He says so because of his view on God's physical premotion of all free acts, by which in a mysterious manner and without prejudice to human freedom God brings about man's free consent. Truly efficacious grace is a physical premotion that of its inner nature produces a free consent. It is on God's part a physical predetermination of man's free act on which the free consent infallibly, or of the very nature of efficacious grace, follows as a free consent. This paradox is not a contradiction, because there can be no opposition between the causality of the First Cause and the act of the secondary free cause, since both the act and its freedom are given being, or created, by God. The concept of efficacious grace as physical premotion and physical predetermination is linked with the idea of predestination *ante praevisa merita*, i.e., independent of the foreknowledge of merit and of man's free consent. In fact, God's decree by which he predestines a man for salvation through free cooperation with grace is purely gratuitous and in no way dependent on man, though it does not take effect without man's free cooperation. Báñezianism stresses God's supreme dominion over everything created and the mystery that envelops man's free consent to efficacious grace. Freedom itself appears as a mysterious gift insofar as a divine physical predetermination and physical premotion, which of their nature entail man's free consent, do not destroy but rather constitute that freedom. In fact,

created freedom does not mean independence from the Creator and First Cause that gives it being but only from created coercion or necessity. See M. J. Farrelly, *Predestination, Grace and Free Will* (1964).

BAPTISM, the Christian rite of initiation by washing. Both its Christian beginnings and its connection with non-Christian ritual washings (both Jewish and pagan) are obscure. There is in the NT no account of the institution of baptism by Jesus Christ; rather, each time it is referred to it is already taken for granted as a constituent element of Christian faith and life. Christ's words to Nicodemus, "Unless one is born of water and of the Spirit, he cannot enter the kingdom of God" (Jn 3.5), seem to presuppose baptism. Similarly, the command to "make disciples of all nations, baptizing them in the name of the Father and of the Son and of the Holy Spirit" (Mt 28.19) does not seem to be an act of instituting baptism but a commission to employ it in the world mission of the Church. Necessary to a valid baptism, according to most theologians, are the use of water (whether by immersion or by sprinkling is a matter of controversy), the invocation of the Holy Trinity (although some passages in the NT do seem to speak of a baptism in the name of Christ only), and the intention that this action be the baptism of the Church (although the validity of the baptism does not depend upon the state of grace of the officiant).

Baptism is usually said to confer three benefits: the remission of sins, the infusion of grace, and incorporation into the Church. When it was administered as part of the process by which one renounced paganism and embraced Christianity, the remission it granted was ordinarily related to the actual sins that the candidate had committed before his conversion. Baptism and repentance are therefore linked in the NT as a break with the sinful past and a renunciation of the dominion of sin. With the advent of *infant baptism as the general practice of the Church the remission was understood to include *original sin as well.

Indeed, the practice of infant baptism provided St. Cyprian and above all St. Augustine with powerful evidence for the doctrine of original sin; for if baptism did effect remission, this could not apply to actual sins in the case of an infant but had to apply to what he had inherited. As a means for the infusion of divine grace, baptism has the special importance of emphasizing and documenting the priority of the divine initiative in the establishment of the new relation between God and man. The grace of God is not earned or seized or won but is received when God, through his selected channel, pours it into the baptized. This baptismal grace, once received, marks the baptized unalterably. He may prove unfaithful to it, but he cannot remove it; and if he falls away from the faith and then returns, baptism is not repeated. By remitting sins and infusing grace, baptism becomes the initiation of the new Christian into the community of faith. It is therefore the most fundamental of all the sacraments, for upon it all the others depend, each of them adding its special spiritual endowment to the grace already given in baptism. The solemn repetition of one's baptismal vows, particularly in its modern liturgical form, is a profound reminder of the meaning of baptism.

As has already been indicated, both the mode and the subject of baptism have been issues of doctrinal controversy. There seems to be little question that the primitive Christian practice was a baptism by immersion, usually in flowing water. From this some Protestant groups have concluded that any other method of washing is a violation of the divinely prescribed pattern and therefore not a proper baptism. The same groups have also repudiated the practice of infant baptism as inconsistent with the personal faith and explicit commitment to Christian discipleship that baptism demands. The defenders of the traditional practice have contended that the mode of baptism is an indifferent matter, so long as water and the name of the Trinity are used. The baptism of infants is justified by its apologists either on the grounds that infants can have true faith even though they can neither understand nor express it, or on the grounds that baptism is the initial step of a relationship to Christ and to the Church, of which *Christian nurture, confirmation, and the deepening commitment of the believer are the continuation. Even its defenders are increasingly careful to avoid the magical connotations that have sometimes appeared in the theology of infant baptism, stressing its place in the life of the Church. See G. W. Lampe, *Seal of the Spirit* (1951); K. Barth, *Church Doctrine of Baptism* (1948); J. Jeremias, *Infant Baptism in the First Four Centuries* (1960); ThAq ST 3, 66–71.

BAPTISM FOR THE DEAD, a rite practiced by the ancient *Marcionites and in modern times by the Mormons and by the New Apostolic Church; they base the practice on 1 Cor 15.29. The exact sense of the passage in St. Paul has been disputed from antiquity, but with the above-mentioned exceptions commentators agree in denying that St. Paul meant to teach that baptism could be effectively administered on behalf of the dead. Mormons consider that baptism by water is necessary, but that all pre-Mormon administrations since the 5th cent. were invalid. Consequently dead ancestors are baptized with water by proxy. The proxy must be a Mormon of good standing, worthy to enter the inner chambers of the temple where the rite is performed. See B. M. Foschini, NCE 2:68, bibliog. *LATTER–DAY SAINTS, CHURCH OF JESUS CHRIST OF.

BAPTISM OF BELIEF, see BELIEVER'S BAPTISM.

BAPTISM WITH THE HOLY SPIRIT (Second Baptism; Spirit Baptism), in Holiness and Pentecostal teaching, the reception, distinct from *justification or *conversion, of Christ's Holy Spirit, usually manifested by some outward sign; the experience of the first Pentecost renewed for the recipient.

*Holiness Churches teach it as the means through which *entire sanctification is bestowed. In *Pentecostalism, baptism with the Spirit is central, an instantaneous, ecstatic experience, transcending mere purification from sin and conferring the Holy Spirit himself. Furthermore, it is necessarily accompanied by *glossolalia, and often by other charismatic gifts. Citing Joel 2.23 and many NT texts (e.g., Acts 1.4–8; 10.46; 12.16–18; 19.1–7; 1 Cor 12.14), Pentecostals insist that a continuous experience of Pentecost is essential in the ordinary life of the Church and of the Christian. Even as the first disciples, all must await, but can confidently expect, this baptism as by fire. The purpose of Spirit baptism is considered to be the endowment of the recipient with new understanding, courage, and patience both for his own Christian life and for his share in evangelism. Among Pentecostals the pattern for "receiving the blessing" usually has consisted in a fervent sermon of the minister recounting other "breakthroughs" of the Spirit; the coming forward of the seeker; his cries, trembling, rhythmic movements and trance; the muttering of unintelligible sounds; the imposition of hands by the pastor and elders; and the shouts of joy for the blessing received. Recently among more sophisticated groups such sessions have taken place in a more sedate atmosphere and with less emotionalism. Baptism by the Holy Spirit is connected with Pentecostal *dispensationalism, i.e., the present is the dispensation of the Holy Spirit (the passage on the *latter rain in Joel 2.23 is so interpreted). The experience of baptism with fire is the connotation of "Fire Baptized" in Pentecostal terminology. See Mayer RB 315–320; J. T. Nichol, *Pentecostalism* (1966), 8–15 and bibliog.; N. Bloch-Hoell, *Pentecostal Movement* (1964); P. Damboriena, *Tongues as of Fire* (1969).

BAPTIST FEDERATION OF CANADA, a federation of three regional bodies representing more than 137,000 Baptists. Although the Federation includes most of the Baptists in Canada, there are several other Baptist bodies in the country based on language, ethnic traditions, or in some cases a particular doctrinal emphasis. Although Baptist work in Canada can be traced back to 1761, the Wolfville Baptist Church, Nova Scotia, is considered the mother church of the Canadian Baptists, having been founded in 1778 and being today the oldest Baptist church in continuous use in Canada. During the 18th cent. in the Maritime Provinces revivals were led with great success by Joseph Alline, who, though not a Baptist, greatly influenced the Baptist work. Partly because of his preaching and partly because of a general reaction against the New England Congregationalists, the Anglicans, and the Roman Catholics, the Baptists grew with surprising rapidity. Following the American Revolution, Baptist missionaries from N.Y., Mass. and Vt. established churches in what today are Ontario and Quebec. Work in western Canada did not begin until 1870, when the Baptist Missionary Convention of Canada sent Alexander MacDonald to Manitoba. A church was organized in Winnipeg in 1875, and by 1876 ten churches, with a membership of 400, had been established. After several unsuccessful attempts at union, these three major regional bodies, the Baptists of the Maritimes, of Central Canada, and of Western Canada, united the 1943–44 to form the Baptist Federation of Canada.

BAPTIST GENERAL CONFERENCE, a group of Swedish Baptist Churches that began to dissociate from the *American Baptist Convention after 1944. Grounds for the separation were the Convention's resistance to a creedal test imposed on denominational leaders, and its participation in the *National Council of Churches. The Baptist General Conference stresses theological conservatism and denominational autonomy. It maintains missions in Assam, Brazil, Burma, Ethiopia, Japan, and the Philippines; it also supports Bethel College and Seminary, St. Paul, Minnesota. In 1968 there were 91,206 members in 573 churches.

BAPTIST MISSIONARY SOCIETY (BMS), the first modern Protestant missionary society, established in 1792 in Kettering, England, through the efforts of William *Carey. He was its first missionary, going in 1793 to India, the first great field for the Society, where it sponsored schools and translations of the Bible. Africa, esp. the Congo, China, the East and West Indies, and South America have all had missionaries from the Society. Since 1901 a Medical Missionary Auxiliary has been part of its program. The Society now supports about 3,000 workers in the mission fields. See EncModChrMiss, 67–70.

BAPTIST WORLD ALLIANCE, a fraternal association uniting Baptist *conventions around the world, established in 1905 in London, with John Clifford as first president. The stated purpose of the Alliance is "more fully to show the essential oneness of Baptist people in the Lord Jesus Christ, to impart inspiration to the brotherhood, and to promote the spirit of fellowship, service and cooperation among its members; but this Alliance may in no way interfere with the independence of the churches or assume the administrative functions of existing organizations." Maintaining headquarters in Washington, D.C., it has an executive secretary and a small staff; an executive committee meets annually to discuss common interests and make necessary decisions. The Alliance gathers information, publishes the *Baptist World*, provides aid in emergencies, and resettles displaced persons. Where religious rights have been denied Baptists, it may use its good offices to seek remedies. It also serves as a means of communication and help for scattered Baptists. See F. T. Lord, *Baptist World Fellowship* (1955).

BAPTISTS, those many autonomous Christian bodies that, while exhibiting great diversity, share a similar congregational *polity and the doctrine of *believer's baptism. The largest Protestant denomination

in the U.S., the Baptists have a history of outstanding preachers and scholars and of emphasis upon personal religious experience, religious freedom, and the separation of *Church and State.

History. Claims of a continuous Baptist history from the 1st cent., or of links with the *Anabaptists, are not supported by historical evidence. The Baptists were a natural development from English Congregationalism. They shared the *gathered-church theory of the Congregationalists: each local congregation has everything necessary to make it a Church, having, under the headship of Christ, power to elect its own officers, determine membership, and carry out discipline. Baptists, however, maintained that the *visible Church must reflect the invisible Church and so restrict its membership to persons old enough to give credible testimony of conversion; thus infants were ineligible for baptism. Baptists emerged at three distinct points from Congregational backgrounds. The first was in Holland in 1609, when a band of *Separatists, refugees from England, with their pastor, John *Smyth, concluded that *infant baptism had no scriptural warrant. They formed a new church, Smyth baptizing himself and the others. He soon felt uneasy about his "se-baptism," and the Church became divided; the minority chose Thomas *Helwys pastor and returned to England in 1612. They became the *General Baptists, since, having been influenced by *Arminianism in The Netherlands, they asserted that the atonement of Christ had been for all men. A second Baptist group began around 1638, when several members withdrew from a congregation in London and adopted believer's baptism. Retaining a more consistent *Calvinism, they stressed *predestination and *limited atonement; hence they were called *Particular Baptists. A third emergence of Baptists occurred in America when Roger *Williams helped reorganize the Church at Providence, R.I., on the basis of believer's baptism.

In England during the Civil Wars and the *Commonwealth, Baptists increased in numbers. The repressive legislation of the

*Restoration did not halt their growth, although some suffered imprisonment. Granted freedom to worship by the *Toleration Act of 1689, the General Baptists declined because of inroads of *Unitarianism, lack of capable leadership, and an unprogressive spirit; Particular Baptists experienced a century of stagnation resulting from a hyper-Calvinism as expressed in the works of their leading theologian, John Gill (1697-1771). The formation in the late 18th cent. of a New Connexion of General Baptists, and a theological renewal led by Andrew Fuller (1754-1815), led to vigorous evangelism and foreign missionary activity. The 19th cent. witnessed a marked increase in Baptist membership, which reached a peak of about 400,000.

In the U.S. the *Great Awakening gave an impetus to Baptist expansion, and after 1740 their ranks in New England were augmented by the aggressive evangelism of the Separate Congregationalists, hundreds of whom became Baptists. From New England Shubael *Stearns and Daniel *Marshall moved to Sandy Creek, N.C., which became the center for a phenomenal growth (see REGULAR BAPTISTS; SEPARATE BAPTISTS). Spreading into all the neighboring states, these revivalistic Baptists laid the foundations for present Baptist strength in the South. In Pa. and N.J. Baptist work began in 1688, and the Philadelphia Baptist Association was formed in 1707. Numerically small prior to the American Revolution, the Association exerted considerable influence upon the shape of Baptist faith and practice in America. At the beginning of the 19th cent. Baptists had risen to first place among the denominations in America, and although overtaken by the Methodists by 1860, they subsequently regained the lead. In the *Yearbook of American Churches* (1969), 27 Baptist bodies are listed, of which the *Southern Baptist Convention is the largest *(c.*11 million), followed by the *National Baptist Convention, U.S.A., Inc. (5,500,000), the *National Baptist Convention of America (2,668,000), and the *American Baptist Convention (1,500,000).

Emphasis on local autonomy, strong individualistic tendencies, and the lack of common confessional standards have contributed to the fragmentation of Baptists. In the 18th cent. the *Free Will Baptists broke away because of their Arminianism. In contrast, a strong predestinarian group protested against missionary organizations, Bible societies, and *revivalism, and organized separately as the *Primitive Baptists. Northern and Southern Baptists divided over slavery and polity in 1845. The Landmarkists, with an extreme emphasis upon the independence of local churches and a claim that Baptists are the only true Church, formed about 1850. Negro Baptists organized in 1895 but divided into the National Baptist Convention, U.S.A., Inc. (1915), the National Baptist Convention of America (1916), and the *Progressive National Baptist Convention, Inc. (1961). Some Baptist bodies have their basis in ethnic backgrounds, such as the *North American Baptist General Conference (German) and *Baptist General Conference (Swedish). The *General Association of Regular Baptists (1933) and the *Conservative Baptist Association (1947) resulted from the fundamentalist-modernist controversy. Lack of a magisterium opened the way to diverse theological developments. Although Baptists originally had *confessions of faith, which served as standards (see NEW HAMPSHIRE CONFESSION; ORTHODOX CREED), these have largely disappeared and it is commonly asserted that Baptists have never had creeds. Partly in reaction against the *liberal theology of their divinity school at the Univ. of Chicago, several more conservative seminaries were organized. Baptists furnished leaders for the *Social Gospel movement (Walter Rauschenbusch, Leighton Williams) and also leaders of the fundamentalists (W. B. Riley, T. T. Shields, J. R. Straton, C. L. Laws). The pluralism of the American Baptist Convention is evident in the persons of William Hamilton, Martin Luther King, Jr., Carl F. H. Henry, and Billy Graham.

Practice. Baptist services of worship have always tended toward informality with emphasis upon preaching. Prior to the 19th cent. they objected to the observance of Christmas and Easter. Their places of worship, called auditoriums, were unadorned except for the Bible, pulpit, baptistery, and Lord's Table. Now, however, there is greater variety, and one may find churches with sanctuaries, crosses, pictures, candles, stained-glass windows, vested choirs, a gowned minister, and even Lenten services in some Baptist churches of the North. Typical emphasis upon simplicity and relatively informal conduct of the service of worship still remains. While always maintaining a congregational polity, Baptists early formed *associations to express their interdependence. The surge of activism in the early 19th cent. led to the formation of societies, esp. to promote and support foreign missions: the Triennial Convention (1814), the American Baptist Publication Society (1824), the American Baptist Home Mission Society (1832), and the American and Foreign Bible Society (1837). State *conventions first were formed in the 1820s in both North and South; larger, more comprehensive, organizations began with the formation of the Southern Baptist Convention (1845), the National Baptist Convention, U.S.A. (1895), and the Northern Baptist Convention (1907). All of these organizations depend upon voluntary cooperation from churches, as no association or convention has legal power over an autonomous local church; these larger organizations exist as means for voluntary cooperation in larger tasks. There is no organic connection between the organizations on these different levels, but they cooperate in varying degrees to carry out the programs instituted by their respective national agencies.

Baptists early took an interest in ministerial education, founding Brown Univ. (1764), Colby College (1813), Colgate Univ. (1820), and George Washington Univ. (1821). A great many other academies and colleges sprang up in nearly all states. There are today more than 100 Baptist junior colleges, colleges, and theological seminaries in the United States. While many shared the interest in education, there has always been a tension between the emphasis upon spiritual qualifications and educational preparation of a minister. Consequently, educational standards vary greatly. The American Baptist Convention has adopted minimum standards that require both college and seminary degrees, and most Churches respect these criteria; but a church may ignore such rules and ordain a person of no formal education.

From England the U.S. Baptist missionaries spread their principles around the world, so that Baptists are found in more than 100 lands. In 1968 the aggregate membership was 28,000,000, six-sevenths of which was in the United States. Most Baptist bodies belong to the *Baptist World Alliance, and some have regional organizations, such as the European Baptist Federation and the North American Baptist Fellowship. Several American groups help to support the Baptist Joint Committee on Public Affairs in Washington, D.C., which seeks primarily to keep in touch with legislation affecting Church-State relations. Baptists vary as to their attitudes toward the *ecumenical movement. The American Baptist Convention, the National Baptist Convention, the *Seventh-Day Baptists, and the Baptist Union of Great Britain and Ireland are members of the *World Council of Churches as well as of their own national councils, but Southern Baptists and most others remain aloof. No official observer was sent by the Baptist World Alliance to Vatican II, although many Baptists favored such representation. The American Baptist Convention, through its Commission on Christian Unity, has had consultations with Roman Catholics, some of its seminaries have working relations with RC seminaries, and numerous individual theologians are involved in Protestant-Catholic dialogue. See O. K. and M. M. Armstrong, *Indomitable Baptists* (1967); R. G. Torbet, *History of the Baptists* (rev. ed., 1963); N. H. Maring and W. S. Hudson, *Baptist Manual of Polity and Practice* (rev. ed., 1966); E. C. Starr, ed., *Baptist Bibliography* (6v., 1947–58).

BARCLAY, JOHN (1734–98), minister of the Church of Scotland and founder of the *Bereans, or Barclayites. The son of a Perthshire farmer, B. was educated at St. Andrews Univ., where he was strongly influenced by Archibald Campbell (1691–1756), professor of church history. Subsequently B. became assistant minister, first at Errol (1759–63) and later at Fettercairn (1763–72) under Antony Dow. Censured by his presbytery for his work *Rejoice Evermore, or Christ All in All* (1766) in which he taught that every believer receives direct revelation, he was denied the vacant charge on Dow's death in 1772. B. became minister to a small congregation of followers in Edinburgh; having obtained ordination in Newcastle (1773), he returned to form his Church in Edinburgh, the Berean Assembly, which took its name from Acts 17.10–14. He later (1776) established the Bereans in Fettercairn, London, and Bristol. He published several works on the Bible.

BARCLAY, ROBERT (1648–90), theologian of the Religious Society of Friends. Born in Morayshire, Scotland, and educated at the Scottish Catholic College in Paris, B. followed his father in becoming a Quaker (1667). B.'s reputation as a foremost theologian of the movement was established by a work first published in Latin, *Theologiae verae Christianae apologia* (1676), and later in English, *Apology of the True Christian Divinity as the Same is Set Forth and Preached by the People Called in Scorn "Quakers"* (1678). The work is a corpus of 15 propositions, developed in scholastic style, with arguments drawn from Scripture and the Fathers. Largely a polemic against Calvinist theology, the *Apology* stands as a Quaker classic, esp. for its second proposition, "Concerning immediate revelation," on the doctrine of the *Inner Light. The work is still highly, but not uncritically, esteemed by modern Quakers. While, like his co-religionists, often imprisoned, eventually B., through the favor of the Duke of York (later James II) was able to assist William *Penn in establishing the Quakers in

Pennsylvania. B. never came to America. His other writings include a *Catechism and Confession of Faith* (1673), *The Anarchy of Ranters* (1676), and *The Possibility and Necessity of Inward and Immediate Revelation* (1686). See L. Eeg-Olofsson, *Conception of the Inner Light in R. B.'s Theology* (1954); D. Freiday, *Barclay's Apology in Modern English* (1967); Mayer RB, 415–421, with bibliog.; E. Russell, *History of Quakerism* (1942). *APOLOGY OF THE TRUE CHRISTIAN DIVINITY.

BARCLAY, ROBERT (1833–76; sometimes "Junior" to distinguish him from the preceding), English Quaker, historian. B.'s *Inner Life of Religious Societies of the Commonwealth* (1876) is rich in information on the array of religious sects arising during that period of religious ferment. See R. Knox, *Enthusiasm* (1950), 169–175; DNB Conc 1:59.

BARCLAYITES, a name given to the *Bereans, whose leader was John *Barclay.

BARMEN DECLARATION (1934), a German Protestant manifesto. The so-called *German Christians came to power with Hitler in 1933, and were helped by Nazi power in electing Ludwig Müller imperial bp. of the newly combined German Evangelical Church. Increasingly this Church was used politically. Church youth were lured into the Hitler youth movement; faithful pastors were intimidated. Martin *Niemöller formed an antiestablishment Pastors' Union. He was also influential in calling the first Synod of the *Confessing Church, at Barmen in May, 1934. Karl *Barth was the leader in the formulation of the starkly worded Declaration; it spoke more clearly than any previous Christian formulation in asserting independence of the Church from state authority—a position strange to many European Lutherans, Calvinists, and Roman Catholics. It firmly upheld Jesus Christ as the one Word of

God that men are to hear, trust, and obey; no other source of revelation is valid. Six "evangelical truths" are lifted up, each as a sharp annotation of a verse of Scripture: Jn 14.16; 1 Cor 1.30; Eph 4.15–16; Mt 20.25–26; 1 Pet 2.17; and Mt 28.20. Introductory passages of the Declaration are directly circumstantial, and yet, as theologian Emil *Brunner noted, and as has been shown by later "adoption" of the Declaration by at least one communion (United Presbyterian Church in the U.S.A., 1966), this is a historic pronouncement on Christian authority, with importance far beyond the 1934 German crisis. It is a classic refusal of "false doctrine, as though the Church in human arrogance could place the Word and work of the Lord in the service of any arbitrarily chosen desires, purposes, and plans." For text, see *The Book of Confessions* (United Presbyterian Church in the U.S.A., 1967).

BARNETT, SAMUEL AUGUSTUS (1844–1913), Anglican cleric, social reformer. He studied law and modern history at Oxford, and was ordained deacon in 1867. He was vicar of St. Jude's, Whitechapel, a parish in the London slums (1873–94). He pioneered the social settlement movement in London, starting a university extension program in his parish. His wife, Henrietta Octavia (married in 1873), aided him in his work and collaborated on his important book *Practicable Socialism* (1888). Other works include *Religion and Politics* (1911) and *The Service of God* (1897). See life in two volumes by Henrietta Octavia Barnett (1919).

BARONIUS, CAESAR, VEN. (1538–1607), Italian Oratorian, cardinal, and church historian. B. was the disciple of St. Philip Neri, whom he succeeded (1593) as superior of the Oratory. Under Philip's direction he undertook a reply to the *Magdeburg Centuries*, a Lutheran ecclesiastical history and apology for the Reformation. B.'s monumental, 12-volume *Annales ecclesiastici*, published in Rome, 1598–1607, is a work of a lifetime of research in the Vatican Archives and other rich Italian libraries. B. began the research when he was 20; 30 years passed before the appearance of the first volume. He attempted a point-by-point refutation of the Lutheran historians, his main thesis being that the Church remained fundamentally uncorrupted through the Middle Ages. He had completed the work only as far as 1198 at the time of his death; it was brought forward to the 16th cent. by Odorico Rinaldi (1594–1671). Like the *Magdeburg Centuries*, the *Annales* was partisan and contained many errors even though B. was meticulous in his research. The manuscript and its revisions were done in his own hand. The work is valuable today principally as a compilation of documentary sources. B. was also Vatican librarian, reviser of the Roman Martyrology, and in 1605 was nearly elected pope. He was declared venerable by Benedict XV in 1745. See J. Wahl, NCE 2:105–106, bibliog.

BAROQUE THEOLOGY, RC and Protestant scholasticism that emerged from the Reformation period and shared in the exuberant humanism characteristic of art and thought until the *Enlightenment of the 18th century. Mirroring the experience of the freedom of faith in a loving God, it was progressive in its openness to new opinion. Rejecting the divisive and debasing elements of a humanism separated from the Christian gospel, it also emphasized continuity with the early Church. This traditionalist concern spurred the production of patristic and biblical studies and brought a revival of scholastic theology. As a theological methodology it often reduced itself to historicism. The theological enterprise became interpretation of the evidence of the past. Since the new science rejected this limited methodology, theology resisted its discoveries and was unable to incorporate them into any contemporary synthesis. The rise of empirical science and its resultant secularization prepared the demise of baroque theology. See Y. Congar, *History of Theology* (tr. H. Guthrie, 1968), 144–179.

BARROW, HENRY (Borrowe; *c*.1550–93), English Congregationalist. Educated at Cambridge, he was converted *c*.1580 from a libertine life to Puritanism. He was arrested by order of Abp. Whitgift in 1586, and while in prison wrote in defense of separatism and congregational independence: *A True Description of Visible Congregation of the Saints . . .* (1589) and *A Brief Discovery of the False Church* (1590). In 1590 he was charged with circulating seditious books and in 1593 was hanged at Tyburn. B. has been mentioned in connection with the *Marprelate Tracts, but there is little evidence to support their attribution to him. See F. J. Powicke, *H. Barrowe, Separatist, and the Exiled Church in Amsterdam* (1900). *CONGREGATIONALISM.

BARTH, KARL (1886–1968), the foremost Protestant theologian of modern times. Born at Basel, Switzerland, he was the son of a *Reformed Church pastor. After his education at Berlin, Tübingen, and Marburg, he was ordained by his father at Bern (1908). B. began his career as a pastor, and became prominent for his socialist political views. In 1919 he published his *Römerbriefe* (*Epistle to the Romans*, Eng. tr. E. C. Hoskyns, 1933), which revolutionized theological thinking. The publication led to his appointment (1921) as professor of Reformed theology at the Univ. of Göttingen in Germany. He was subsequently professor at the Univ. of Münster (1925–30) and of Bonn (1930–33). In 1932 he published the first part of volume one of his masterwork, *Church Dogmatics*, which by 1962, when he discontinued the work, had become a 6-million-word work in 12 volumes. In 1933, when the Nazis established the puppet *German Christian churches, B. began his opposition to the Third Reich. In 1934 he was the chief author of a resounding protest, the *Barmen Declaration. He was expelled from Germany in 1935, and became professor at the University of Basel. He continued his resistance to Nazism, which he regarded as essentially an anti-Christian heresy. Besides his theological labors, he took an active part in the postwar world's efforts to assist Churches living under Communist regimes. He retired from teaching in 1962.

In his theology Barth spoke from the Calvinist tradition; consequently the themes "Word of God" and "Predestination" are dominant in his thought. His approach, however, was prompted by a strong reaction against Protestant liberalism, esp. as represented by F. *Schleiermacher. B. found fault with this 19th-cent. theologian's analysis of man's religious motivation, the actualizing of which leads to some sort of established union between man and God. The *Kirchliche Dogmatik* (*Church Dogmatics*, G. W. Bromiley, T. F. Torrance, eds., 1936–62) is based on certain principles that reveal the viewpoint of the system and trend. One key principle may be expressed as the futility of religion, i.e., of any attempt on the part of man to reach or "attain" God, who is, according to B., "altogether other" (*totaliter aliter*). The position includes the rejection on B.'s part of the analogy of being, i.e., the use of man's own ideas and own language to think and speak of God. A famous passage in the introduction to the *Dogmatics* designates such use of analogy as the anti-Christ, and as sufficient motive to reject Roman Catholicism out of hand. The principal correlative to this negation is B.'s affirmation of the possibility of God's reaching man through his Word. For theological discourse, this implies the use of the "analogy of faith," i.e., man's employing the knowledge communicated in God's Word to understand reality (himself included), which remains quite opaque in itself. Thus, for example, B. stated outright that any valid knowledge or understanding we have of man as such is attained through our knowing the Man, Jesus Christ, who is God's Word about man —a word both of judgment and of justification.

B.'s system of theological discourse, moreover, is committed to "consequent Christology" (discourse centered on Jesus Christ), which reduces all the particulars of theology to the Christological mystery. Perhaps the best example of this is B.'s reinterpretation of Calvin's doctrine of *double predestination. He professes to accept this doctrine as part of the Reformed tradition. For him, however, the first instance of double predestination is the simultaneous rejection and acceptance of the justification of Jesus Christ on the part of God the Father. This is the paradigm of the human situation and the sole means through which man can really understand his own situation. The example serves to bring out another characteristic, B.'s use of the dialectical method. For him this means that the simultaneous affirmation and negation of a given theological point is necessary on account of the inherent ambiguity of all these matters as far as the human mind is concerned (see DIALECTICAL THEOLOGY). "Consequent Christology" is employed in the organization of the *Dogmatics* to the effect that, although the work appears to be organized on trinitarian lines (Doctrine of Creation—the Father; Doctrine of Reconciliation—the Son; and Doctrine of Redemption—the Spirit), in reality each section emphasizes the role of Christ—in creation, as the work of the word of God; in reconciliation, as the work quite proper to Jesus; and in redemption, as the work accomplished by the Spirit of Jesus. B.'s teaching is opposed to the position and style of the *Bultmann school. The debate as it centers on the mystery of the resurrection reveals that B. held that the resurrection of Jesus is a historical event upon which Christian faith and Christian theology are founded. This event is, in fact, the ultimate break-through on God's part into the domain of man, i.e., the world, which man quite wrongly considers to be his own. It might be inferred that Barth's position is fundamentally antihumanist. This is quite true, insofar as humanism means either an implicit form of "religion" understood in the liberal sense of man's initiating a relationship with God, or the construction of an idol to human excellence and perfection.

B.'s influence on Protestantism (and mediately on RC thought, too) seems to have been a strong affirmation of divine transcendence set forth at the onset of the technological revolution. Whether or not the affirmation has been (or will be) given the hearing it deserves is a moot question. See J. Hamer, *K.B.* (tr. D. M. Maruca, 1962); H. Hartwell, *Theology of K. B.: An Introduction* (1965).

BASEL, CONFESSIONS OF, two Reformation *confessions of faith. (1) The First Confession of Basel (*Confessio fidei Basileensis prior*) was written in first draft in 1531 by J. *Oecolampadius, and in final form by O. *Myconius in 1532; it was adopted officially by Basel in 1534. Accepted as well by the city of Mülhausen in Alsace, it is also called the Mülhausen Confession (*Confessio Mulhusana*). The 12 articles of the document express teachings of both *Luther and *Zwingli. (2) The Second Confession of Basel (. . . *posterior*) is a title sometimes given to the First *Helvetic Confession. See Schaff Creeds 1:385–388.

BASEL, COUNCIL OF, council summoned by Pope Martin V (1417–31) to meet in Basel in 1431 in compliance with the decree *Frequens* issued (1417) by the Council of Constance. Martin died before the Council convened, and it was left to his successor, Eugene IV (1431–47), to deal with it. The Council of Basel developed in two stages, both dominated by antipapal sentiment. In the years 1431–37 Eugene IV grudgingly extended his approbation. When Eugene transferred the Council to Ferrara in Sept. 1437 (and later to Florence), the most adamant conciliarists refused to move. During the period 1437–49 Basel continued in open defiance of the Pope, even electing a pope of its own, Felix V (1439–49). Attendance at Basel was never very large, and bishops were in a minority throughout. The Council's most notable achievement was negative: it illustrated the failure of extreme conciliarism. The Council's negotiations (1433) with the Hussites led eventually to the agreement known as the *Compactata. See J. Gill, *Constance et Bâle-Florence* (1965); *idem, Eugenius IV: Pope of Chris-*

tian Union (1961); *idem,* NCE 2:141–142. *CONCILIARISM.

BAXTER, RICHARD (1615–91), Puritan writer. B. was self-educated in theology, devoting special attention to scholastic theology and the teachings of *Nonconformists. He was ordained in 1638 in the C of E, but within two years had rejected *episcopacy. In parochial work at Kidderminster (1641) and in the Parliamentary army he strove for moderation of religious differences. In keeping with his convictions he rejected the bishopric of Hereford (1660) and was henceforth barred from ecclesiastical preferment. His revisions of the *Book of Common Prayer to make it more acceptable to Puritans were rejected at the *Savoy Conference (1661). After the *Act of Uniformity of 1662, he left the C of E and suffered harassment until the *Declaration of Indulgence in 1687. His more than 200 writings express his piety, pastoral concern, and desire for religious tolerance; *The Saints' Everlasting Rest* (1650) is a classic of devotional literature. B. also composed several well-known hymns. See H. Martin, *Puritanism and R. B.* (1954); G. Nuttall, *R. B.* (1965); W. Orme, ed., *The Practical Works of . . . R. B.* (23v., 1830).

BAY PEOPLE, those *Puritans who came from England between 1630 and 1640 to establish the Massachusetts Bay Colony. They were distinguished from the *Plymouth People, who had come from The Netherlands in 1620 to settle at Plymouth. The two groups united to make Congregationalism the established form of religion in the Mass. colony.

BEA, AUGUSTIN (1881–1968), Jesuit priest, later cardinal; biblicist and ecumenist. Born in Riedböhringen, Germany, near the Black Forest, he entered the Society of Jesus, 1902; did seminary studies at Valkenburg, Holland, and was ordained in 1912; and pursued higher studies in Oriental

philology at the Univ. of Berlin. He was named provincial of German Jesuits, 1921, and subsequently professor at the Pontifical Gregorian University, Rome. From 1928 he was professor for OT at the Pontifical Biblical Institute, Rome; during his tenure there B. was rector 1930–49 and editor of the scholarly journal *Biblica,* 1931–51, to which he contributed numerous studies. In 1959 John XXIII appointed B. to the college of cardinals to head the *Secretariat for Promoting Christian Unity. B's success in organizing the Secretariat and making it a focal point for Christian unity won him international esteem. See R. A. F. MacKenzie, "Augustin Bea (1881–1968)," *Biblica* 49 (1968), 453–456.

BEACHY AMISH Mennonite Churches, named for Bishop Moses M. Beachy of Salisbury, Pa. (d. 1946), leader of a separation from the Old Order Amish Churches. The division, which began in 1923 and culminated in separation in 1927, was based upon Beachy's mild attitude toward the *ban. These Churches now differ from the Old Amish by their use of meeting houses for worship, evangelistic preaching, and Sunday schools, and by a progressive adaptation to modern life. There are about 4,000 members in Pa., Ohio, Ind., Va., and Iowa. See MennEnc 1:254.

BEATIANS (Ger. Beatianer), the followers of a Lutheran preacher, Johann Saliger (Seliger, Ger. for *beatus).* The founder taught that bread and wine were really changed into the body and blood of Christ in the Holy Eucharist and that original sin is identical with human nature and therefore Christ did not have a human nature specifically like that of other men. Congregations of Beatians existed at Lübeck and Rostock only from 1569 to *c.*1600. See K. Algermissen, LTK 2:84.

BECKER, PETER (1687–1758), leader of the German·Baptist Brethren (see BRETHREN

CHURCHES). B. was a weaver; listed as an *Anabaptist at Dudelsheim, Germany, in 1714, later the same year he became associated with the Brethren in the Palatinate. Because of refusal to conform to the state Church, he migrated with others first to Krefeld in the lower Rhineland (1715), then to Germantown, Pa. (1719). There he organized the first congregation of Brethren in the New World and was its minister until his death.

BECON, THOMAS *(c.*1513–67), Protestant divine, who wrote also under the name of Thomas Basille. A Norfolk man, educated at St. John's College, Cambridge, and a "diligent hearer" of Hugh Latimer, he was in trouble as a Protestant under Henry VIII. With the accession of Edward VI he enjoyed the favor of Cranmer and the Protector Somerset. On the accession of Mary he was imprisoned and ejected from his living; he repaired to Strassburg and Frankfurt. On that of Elizabeth he was installed as canon of Canterbury. A Lutheran, moderate in tone to begin with, he became more of a Zwinglian and, it is said, rather coarser. See D. S. Bailey, *Thomas Becon and the Reformation of the Church of England* (1952).

BEECHER, HENRY WARD (1813–87), editor, social reformer, and preacher. After graduation from Amherst (1834) and Lane Theological Seminary (1837), where his father, Lyman *Beecher, was president, he held small pastorates until being called (1847) to Plymouth Church in Brooklyn. His eloquence made him the most celebrated preacher of his era; he abandoned Calvinistic orthodoxy for a warm, humane, and liberalist presentation of Christianity, and for the cause of liberalism withdrew from the Congregational Church. He supported and dramatically crusaded for the abolition of slavery and later for woman's suffrage. He won early literary fame by his *Seven Lectures to Young Men* (1844), was a constant contributor to periodicals, found-

ing editor (1870) of the non-denominational *Christian Union* (afterwards called the *Outlook*); he also wrote a *Life of Jesus Christ* (1871) and, in support of Darwinism, *Evolution and Religion* (1885). During the difficult days of an unsuccessful law suit for adultery brought against him, he inaugurated the Lyman Beecher Lectures on preaching at the Yale school of divinity, which had vast influence on American preaching. Biographies were written by Lyman *Abbott (1903) and P. Hibben (1927).

BEECHER, LYMAN (1775–1863), American Congregationalist minister. He was the son of a minister and studied at Yale, where he was greatly influenced by Timothy *Dwight. In 1799 he was ordained as pastor of a church at Easthampton, Long Island, remaining there until 1810, when he was called to Litchfield, Connecticut. B. was active in promoting *revivalism and home missions. He was a founder of the *American Bible Society and is credited with beginning the temperance movement in New England with the foundation in 1825 of the American Temperance Society. His theological views were akin to those of his friend Nathaniel W. *Taylor, who taught a moderate Calvinism that permitted man to open himself to divine grace by choosing to accept Christ. This revitalized Congregationalism gave to Conn. a *Second Great Awakening and regained ground lost to the Unitarians. In 1826 B. accepted a call to found a new Congregational Church in Boston, and there opposed the Unitarian W. E. *Channing. B. was active in promoting Lane Theological Seminary in Cincinnati as a center of home missionary effort on the frontier and became its first president in 1832. He was simultaneously called to the Second Presbyterian Church in Cincinnati under the *Plan of Union, but his liberal views led to his presentment in 1835 before the *presbytery. The charges were dismissed but the incident contributed to the détente in 1837 between Presbyterians and Congregationalists. B.'s appeals for home missions included warnings that Roman Catholics were prepared to fill any vacuum left by Protestants in the West and may have fed the anti-Catholicism of the period. He left Cincinnati in 1850 and spent his last years in the Brooklyn home of his famous son, Henry Ward *Beecher. His best-known work is *A Plea for the West* (1835). See W. W. Sweet, *Religion on the American Frontier: The Congregationalists* (1939).

BEGHARDS, an association of laymen that arose in the Low Countries at the end of the 12th cent. as a companion organization to the female *Beguines. Beghards lived a common life, renounced private property, and practiced continence, but they did not take vows. Most of them were employed in the textile industry and exercised considerable influence in forming the religious opinions of the lower classes. They were repeatedly reprimanded by church authorities during the 13th and 14th cents. for their involvement in heresy (D 891–899). They disappeared at the time of the French Revolution. See bibliog. for Beguines.

BEGUINAGE, see BEGUINES.

BEGUINES, properly a designation for several lay sisterhoods originating in the Low Countries in the 12th cent. as expressions of the contemporary religious fervor of lay urban society. In medieval documents, however, the term was frequently used of the *Apostolici, *Brothers and Sisters of the Free Spirit, *Spirituals, *Fraticelli, or of heretics of every sort. The etymology of the term is the subject of considerable debate. Some suggest that it derives from the name of the Belgian priest Lambert le Bégue, who around 1170 contributed his considerable fortune for the construction at Liège of a center for the care of crusaders' widows. Similar but independent foundations were made in Belgium before the end of the century by Bl. Yvette of Huy and Bl. Mary Oignies. The movement spread quickly from the Low Countries to Switzerland, Germany, and France. Members of the Beguines were virgins and widows who agreed to observe continence and obedience, engage in works of charity, and live a semiconventual life. They were not religious in the traditional canonical sense and were free to leave the community at will. They did not take vows and retained ownership of their own property. They observed no common rule, had no motherhouse, and were subject to no superior-general. They were not affiliated with any of the established religious orders and were not under the direction of any special ecclesiastical official. Since each foundation was completely autonomous, there was wide divergence in their religious practices and observances. Most of the Beguines, however, wore a gray habit and a distinctive Flemish headdress.

A beguinage was a city within a city. Surrounded by a wall and sometimes by a moat, it contained a church, hospital, perhaps a school, a guesthouse, and several separate cottages in which the pious ladies lived either singly or in two's or three's. They maintained their own households and might have servants. Those who had no income supported themselves, usually as weavers or lace-makers. All devoted part of their time to charitable activities, especially teaching, nursing, and caring for the poor. The services they rendered earned them the esteem of all classes in society. By the end of the 13th cent. there was scarcely a city in the Low Countries that did not have at least one beguinage. At one time the foundation at Ghent had more than 1,000 members. The use of the name Beguines for heretics came about because the beguinages became influential centers for the propagation of a type of popular mysticism that clearly tended toward *illuminism. This tendency was held in check during their early history, when most of the Beguines came from upper-class families and possessed some degree of education. But with the passage of time needy unmarried women seeking security became the majority. Other factors that rendered the Beguines vulnerable to heresy were their loose organizational structure and their almost total lack of hierarchical supervision. Not all the charges of heresy and immorality that were lodged against the Beguines can be taken at face value. Many of their foundations certainly were infected with the *antinomianism of the Brothers and Sisters of the Free Spirit and the *Joachimism of the Spirituals and the Fraticelli; but others, especially those in the Low Countries, never strayed far from orthodoxy and were stoutly defended against accusations of heresy by bishops, princes, and the people. When Lateran Council IV (1215) ordered independent religious houses to affiliate with one of the established religious orders, Bp. Jacques de Vitry induced Honorius III to exempt several beguinages from the decree. When the Council of Lyons II (1274) reenacted this law, many groups of Beguines associated themselves with the Franciscan, Dominican, or Augustinian Third Orders. The Council of Vienne (1311–12; D 891–899) accused the Beguines of actively propagating a number of errors on the nature of Christian living, and ordered their suppression. But in 1321 John XXII allowed those beguinages that accepted reform to continue in existence.

In the course of the Reformation beguinages located in areas of Europe where Protestantism became the official religion were suppressed. During the course of the Napoleonic Wars most of the Beguines' foundations in France disappeared. Today there are 13 beguinages still in existence, 11 in Belgium and 2 in Holland. See E. W. McDonnell, *Beguines and Beghards in Medieval Culture* (1954); D. Philips, *Beguines in Medieval Strasbourg. A Study of the Social Aspects of Beguine Life* (1941).

BEHMENISTS, in 17th- and 18th-cent. England, Christians devoted to the writings of J. *Boehme. Many of them became members of the Religious Society of Friends.

BEISSEL, JOHANN CONRAD (1690–1766), German-born mystic, sabbatarian, celibate; founder of the *Ephrata Community. Orphaned at 8, apprenticed to a baker-musician, he became a master baker and an expert creative musician. At Heidelberg, he was converted from a dissolute life to pietistic fervor. Fleeing persecution, he migrated to Pennsylvania, where, lacking opportunity to ply his trade, he apprenticed to learn weaving from Peter *Becker, minister of the *German Baptists of Germantown. Before joining this group, he retired to the wilderness and lived as a hermit. In 1724, he affiliated with the Brethren and served as minister. Controversy over his mysticism and sabbatarianism resulted in his withdrawal; he founded the Ephrata Society in 1728. B.'s musical creations were in seven-part harmony, written to imitate the music of heaven.

BEKENNENDE KIRCHE, see CONFESSING CHURCH.

BELGIC CONFESSION, the *Reformed *confession of faith, first published in 1561 by Guy de *Brès. The document was written in French, then translated into Dutch, German, and Latin. The synod at Antwerp that organized the Reformed Church in the Low Countries in 1566 adopted this confessional standard in a revised form, approved by Geneva, and this text was accepted at the Synod of *Dort (1619). A clear statement of *Calvinism, the Confession ranks next to the *Gallican Confession of 1559, which it closely resembles, as a doctrinal standard for Reformed Churches. The contents are divided into 37 articles; art. 36, on the relations of civil powers to the Church, has presented a continuing problem of interpretation. See L. Verduin, EncRelKnow-Suppl 1:121–122; Schaff Creeds 1:502–508 and 3:383–436.

BELIEVER'S BAPTISM, the practice of administering baptism only to persons old enough to make responsible decisions and personally profess faith in Jesus Christ.

Conflicting convictions as to the proper subjects of baptism constitute a major barrier among Christians. The fact that most Christian Churches administer baptism to infants raises the question as to when and why this practice became so prevalent and why so many Christians object to it. Scholars have combed the documents of the early Church, but there is no indisputable reference to *infant baptism prior to Tertullian early in the 3d century. Many interpreters, however, have inferred such a practice from incidents in which Jesus blessed children (Mk 10.13–16 and parallels); from the statements regarding Lydia, who "was baptized and her household" (Acts 16.15); and from presumptive evidence growing out of the strong corporate sense of the Jewish family. The NT and other early documents indicate a close connection of repentance, faith, and instruction with the rite of baptism. Moreover, as late as the 4th cent. Gregory of Nazianzus, Gregory of Nyssa, and Basil of Caesarea were not baptized until adulthood. By the 5th cent. infant baptism had become almost universal, and not until the 16th cent. did the issue again become controversial. In contrast to the other main Reformation traditions, the *Anabaptists rejected infant baptism and administered the rite only to those who made a conscious profession of faith. The practice provoked hostile reactions, and many Anabaptists were martyred. In the 17th cent. the Baptists emerged from the *Independent wing of Puritanism specifically over this issue, for Baptists repudiated infant baptism as both unscriptural and inconsistent with the concept of the *gathered church. A vigorous polemic between Baptists and other Protestants in England and the U.S. continued into the 19th century. A lecture (1943) of Karl *Barth denying any NT basis for infant baptism (see *Teaching of the Church Regarding Baptism* [tr. E. A. Payne, 1959]; *Church Dogmatics* [v.4, 1961]) and the fact that a large number of baptized persons never become confirmed or attend church services, have provoked debate about baptism by Protestant and RC theologians. Although some see in believer's baptism too much emphasis upon the element of human decision, others see it as uniting the objective redemptive activity of God in Christ with the personal response of the individual believer. Coming in faith and repentance, he acknowledges the initiative of God's gracious forgiveness, accepts the Lordship of Christ over his life, and by the power of the Holy Spirit is regenerated and incorporated into the Church of Jesus Christ. See D. Moody, *Baptism: Foundation for Christian Unity* (1967); A. Gilmore, ed., *Christian Baptism* (1959); R. S. Armour, *Anabaptist Baptism* (1967).

BELIEVERS' CHURCHES, a designation sometimes used for those bodies that accept only *believer's baptism and reject *infant baptism.

BEREAN FUNDAMENTAL CHURCH, a body founded in 1934 at Denver, Colorado. It emphasizes conservative Protestant doctrines and in 1968 had a membership of 1,982, with 37 churches. Headquarters are in North Platte, Nebraska.

BEREANS, the followers of John *Barclay (1734–98), known also as Barclayites. The name is derived from the community mentioned in Acts 17:10–14. Berean assemblies were formed in Edinburgh, Fettercairn, London, and Bristol. Barclay and his followers held the chief Calvinist doctrines, esp. the study of the Scriptures, which for the believer enlightened by the Holy Spirit were full of the knowledge of Christ. They stressed the believer's assurance of salvation and regarded unbelief as the unforgivable sin. Natural theology was repudiated as impossible. After Barclay's death, Bereans tended to merge with Congregationalists, and the group had disappeared by the end of the 19th century.

BERETTINI, a name applied to the 12th-cent. *Humiliati, because their garb was of an undyed grey wool, called *beretto* in Italian.

BERNEUCHEN CIRCLE, a Lutheran liturgical movement named after yearly conferences of theologians and laymen held, since 1923, at a German estate, from which later, in 1931, the Michaelsbruderschaft originated. With the participation of such prominent theologians as Wilhelm Stählin, Karl Bernhard Ritter, and L. Heitmann, the movement has effected a renewal and promotion of liturgical practices. From the Berneuchen "Spiritual Weeks" of prayer new orders or rituals for the liturgy have been developed. See M. H. Shepherd, Jr., NCE 8:905–906, bibliog.

BESANT, ANNIE (b. Wood; 1847–1933), Anglo-Irish theosophist and political and social reformer. She married an Anglican clergyman, F. Besant, but they were later legally separated (1873). She lost custody of her children in 1879 because she was an atheist. She promoted such causes as free thought, birth control (she was tried for promoting immorality but acquitted), Fabian socialism, workers' strikes, and free education. Converted (1889) to *theosophy by Mme. H. P. Blavatsky (1851–91), B. became the most influential theosophist, heading the Theosophical Society, 1907–33. Settling in India, she founded Central Hindu College, organized the India Home Rule League, and was elected (1917) president of the India National Congress. Of her numerous theosophical writings, *Esoteric Christianity* (1901) esp. helped to inspire the foundation of the *Liberal Catholic Church. See A. H. Nethercot, *First Five Lives of A. B.* (1960); *idem, Last Four Lives of A.B.* (1963).

BETHEL BAPTIST ASSEMBLY, INC., the name under which a denomination numbering 6,925 members in 27 churches chose to incorporate in 1960. It was founded at Evansville, Ind., in May 1934 under the name Evangelistic Missionary Alliance.

BEUCKELSZOON, JAN, see JOHN OF LEIDEN.

BEVERIDGE, WILLIAM (1638–1708), Anglican bp. of St. Asaph in Wales; theologian. B. was born in Barrow, Leicester, and studied at St. John's College, Cambridge. His ecclesiastical career seems to have suffered from his sympathetic attitude toward the *nonjurors, and he was not made a bp. until 1704. B.'s works include a collection of Greek canons, the *Eunodikón* (1672), and his masterwork, *Exposition of the Thirty-Nine Articles* (1710). His writings evidence a partiality toward Calvinist predestinationism. Several collections, all incomplete, of B's works have appeared: T. Gregory (2v., 1720); T. H. Horne (9v., 1824); J. Bliss (LACT 12v., 1843–48). See DNB 4 (1885), 447.

BEZA, THEODORE (De Besze; 1519–1605), Genevan Reformer. Born at Vézelay in Burgundy, France, and educated a humanist, he wished to become a classical scholar, but at his father's insistence he studied law for a time at Orléans (1535–39). He abandoned this career, however, and went to Paris, where he composed in Latin his *Poemata Juvenilia*. The poetry reflected his dissolute way of life. During an illness in 1548 he abandoned Catholicism and was converted to the teachings of Calvin. He was appointed professor of Greek at Lausanne, and in 1558 moved to Geneva to teach Greek. When Calvin died (1564), Beza succeeded him, combining the office of Moderator of the Company of Pastors with work as preacher and teacher. While at Lausanne, he had tried to win toleration for the *Waldenses of Piedmont and the *Huguenots of France. In Geneva, he continued his efforts on behalf of French Protestants, attending two futile conferences (Poissy and St. Germain), and then helping to raise men and money to support Condé in the French *Wars of Religion. Through correspondence and personal contacts, he influenced *Reformed Protestants in various countries, arguing their right to revolt against a ruler who denies religious liberty. Among his polemical works, one of the most notable was his defense (1554) of the burning of M. *Servetus against the criticisms of S. *Castellio. He arranged several Psalms in French verse, publishing them with others written by Marot. He also published a celebrated Greek text of the NT along with an annotated Latin translation (1565); in 1582 a second edition, which included the codex of the Gospels he had discovered in 1562, the *Codex Bezae*, was published. Several theological treatises also came from his pen (*Tractationes theologicae*, 1570–82); he gave *double predestination great emphasis. See P. F. Geisendorf, *Théodore de Bèze* (1949).

BIBELFREUNDE (Friends of the Bible), a small religious group influenced by *Pietism. Originating in Württemberg, Ger., *c.* 1857, they were extinct by the end of the 19th century. Their name derives from an emphasis on the Bible as the only acceptable devotional reading. They practiced public fasting and on Sundays marital continence.

BIBLE, AUTHORITY OF, the quality, conceded to be inherent in Sacred Scripture as the word of God, that makes it a secure norm of religious faith and practice. For centuries before the time of Christ, but at a period difficult to fix precisely, the books of the OT were accepted by the Jews as authored by the spirit of God. Jesus and the Apostles conformed to this Jewish viewpoint on Israel's sacred books (see Mk 12.36; Jn 10.35), and the early Christian Church conceived of its own sacred literature in the same manner. Because it was believed that the human authors of this religious literature, produced within and for the Jewish and Christian communities, were in a special sense divinely illumined for this purpose, this literature was accepted as the norm of faith. Thus the binding authority of Scripture derived from its divine authorship.

The unique authority of the Bible was taken for granted until the 19th cent., when it was placed in question by the discoveries of various modern sciences, such as astronomy, biology, and ancient history. Some Christians, however, undeterred by the impact of scientific knowledge upon the understanding of the Bible, continue to remain fundamentalist, i.e., they accept biblical statements, independently of their cultural and historical contexts, as formulations of literal truth. The scientific viewpoints on the origin and age of the earth, the universe, and man, as well as discrepancies between archeological findings and biblical data, have required a revision of the traditional concept of the authority of the Bible. Although the principle of the authoritative character of Scripture for faith remains intact, the understanding of the meaning of this principle as underlying truth in the Bible has undergone a considerable evolution. It is now recognized that prior to the 19th cent. sufficient attention was not paid to the role and limitations of the spirit-inspired human authors of the biblical books. Their points of view and modes of expressing their ideas were necessarily limited by the culture and audiences of their own time. Consequently, modern biblical scholarship recognizes the presence even of "myth" in Scripture, i.e., a non-scientific way of perceiving and expressing reality universal in antiquity, and no longer expects of Scripture the kind of accuracy in the understanding of material reality, including history, demanded by modern man. Indeed, to expect this level of truth in Scripture would require a divine illumination that would be an undesirable paternalism derogating from human intellectual striving to discover the meaning of the universe for man's natural life (see Gen 1.26).

The modern discovery of the limitation on the authority of Scripture that restricts its message to man's understanding of his relationship to God and to his neighbor under God brings into full and clear focus the profoundly religious nature of Scripture. In a way that will forever escape complete scientific analysis, the Bible records the privileged moments in human history, initiated by God himself, when man has most directly confronted his creator. Man learns from the Bible to comprehend himself as alienated from God through his own willful caprices, but as yet pursued by the divine love, inviting, guiding, and directing him to overcome this alienation through faith in the divine power, goodness, and mercy, so as to take his place in a renewed community of mankind in the house of his Father (see Hos 11.1–4; Jn 14.2–3).

The Protestant Reformers of the 16th cent. made the authority of Scripture the supreme norm for the life and faith of the Church. Roman Catholicism has consistently maintained that Scripture is not its own interpreter: since the Bible, as the literature of an ancient time, is subject to misunderstanding and misrepresentation, the Church has the role of safeguarding and teaching the authentic biblical meaning. Each of these positions possesses its own elements of truth. Modern critical scholarship into the origin and meaning of the Bible has resulted in considerable unanimity of interpretation between Protestant and Catholic biblical scholars. But the relationship between the authority of the Church and the authority of Scripture continues to be a point of divergence. See J. Levie, *Bible, Word of God in Words of Men* (tr. S. H. Treman, 1961); C. H. Dodd, *Authority of the Bible* (1928). *ANABAPTISTS; *INNER LIGHT; *INFALLIBILITY; *TRADITION; *FUNDAMENTALISM.

BIBLE CHRISTIANS, Methodist denomination in England formed in 1815 by William O'Bryan (1778–1868), hence also called Bryanites. He was a Wesleyan Methodist preacher; the separation resulted from a dispute over his preaching within the jurisdiction of others. By 1819 his *society

counted 8 chapels and 2,389 members. Women preachers and laymen had an important place; missionaries were sent to Canada, the U.S., and Australia. O'Bryan left the group after being pressured to relinquish control to the *conference in 1827. Bible Christians united with the Methodist New Connexion and the United Methodist Free Churches in 1907, forming the United Methodist Church. This in turn joined with the Wesleyan Methodist and the Primitive Methodist Churches in 1932 to form the reunited Methodist Church in England. See W. J. Townsend et al., eds., *New History of Methodism* (2v., 1909), 1:502–514; W. S. F. Pickering, ed., *Anglican-Methodist Relations* (1961).

BIBLE PRESBYTERIAN CHURCH, see REFORMED PRESBYTERIAN CHURCH, EVANGELICAL SYNOD.

BIBLE PRESBYTERIAN CHURCH (Collingswood Synod), one segment of the fundamentalist movement within the Presbyterian tradition; organized in its present form in 1955 by the Rev. Carl McIntire. As a student at Princeton Theological Seminary, McIntire (b. 1906) was greatly influenced by J. Gresham *Machen. In 1929, when Machen left Princeton to found Westminster Seminary, McIntire joined him; he obtained his degree from Westminster in 1931. McIntire was active in the formation of the fundamentalist-oriented Independent Board of Presbyterian Foreign Missions. The 1936 *General Assembly abolished the board and censured McIntire for contravening the discipline of the Church and disrupting its peace. McIntire united with Machen in founding the Orthodox Presbyterian Church in 1936 but separated from it the following year to found the Bible Presbyterian Church. The Bible Presbyterian Church, largely dominated by McIntire's personality, developed a tradition of politically conservative activism, while its parent body, essentially a bulwark of orthodox Calvinism, did not enter the socio-economic sphere. The Bible Presbyterian Church was the moving force in the formation of the *American Council of Christian Churches (1941) and the *International Council of Christian Churches (1948). The belief that the Bible Presbyterian Church was too deeply involved in political conservatism led to the secession of the larger number of its congregations from the above-mentioned councils in 1955 and its subsequent reorganization.

McIntire and his followers formed the Bible Presbyterian Church (Collingswood Synod), known at first as the Bible Presbyterian Association. The larger body retained the Bible Presbyterian name until 1961, when it became the Evangelical Presbyterian Church. (It is now part of the Reformed Presbyterian Church, Evangelical Synod.) The McIntire group maintains Shelton College, Cape May, N.J.; Highland College, Pasadena, Calif.; and Faith Theological Seminary, Elkins Park, Pennsylvania. The Church is associated with the Twentieth Century Reformation Hour radio broadcasts. Headquarters are at Collingswood, N.J.; no official figures are available on membership.

BIBLE PROTESTANT CHURCH, a fellowship of independent local churches, which adopted this corporate name in 1940. The Bible Protestant Church considers itself to be the continuing Eastern Conference (formed in 1914) of the Methodist Protestant Church. One-third of the membership of this conference dissented against the union in 1939 of the Methodist Protestant Church with the Methodist Episcopal Church and the Methodist Episcopal Church South (see METHODIST CHURCH). The basis for the dissent and the doctrinal position maintained in the Bible Protestant Church has been its fundamentalism. Some features of Methodist polity are retained, but congregational independence is dominant. The Church is a founding member of the *American Council of Christian Churches. Membership in 1968 was about 2,600, in 43 churches.

BIBLE SCHOOLS, schools originating in the late 19th-cent. movement to equip laymen to serve better as Sunday school teachers and in personal evangelism. D. L. *Moody founded the Moody Bible Institute at Chicago in 1886, and the Nyack Missionary Training Institute grew out of classes begun in 1882 by A. B. Simpson. The original purpose was supplemented soon by an aim to provide a short course of preparation for pastors and missionaries. As *liberal theology spread, Bible schools and institutes sprang up in many larger cities, intent upon counteracting *modernism. Many of these schools adopted the *Scofield Reference Bible with its *dispensationalism, emphasizing biblical prophecies and the expectation of the imminent second coming of Christ. Conditioned to be suspicious of the major denominations, their graduates tended to be separatistic, serving *independent Churches and mission boards or loosely organized denominations like the Baptists. Since World War II there has been expansion of such schools, but desire for recognition by accrediting bodies has led to changes in curriculum to make more room for liberal arts. In 1947 the Accrediting Association of Bible Colleges was organized to set standards for this type of school. Several schools changed their names from Bible Institute or Bible School to Bible College, and some of them have raised standards sufficiently to be recognized by the regular regional accrediting associations. For example, Barrington College (R.I.), Philadelphia College of the Bible, and Nyack Missionary College (N.Y.) have made such transitions and received regular accreditation.

BIBLE SOCIETIES, nonprofit organizations for printing and distributing copies of the Bible. The *Society for the Promotion of Christian Knowledge, founded in London (1698), included among its objects the provision of Bibles for poor people. The *British and Foreign Bible Society was established in 1804, with members of the C of E and *Nonconformists cooperating. Its sole purpose was printing and distributing Bibles, and membership was open to all who paid the necessary fee; local societies were started throughout the British Isles. Auxiliary societies were also organized in British colonies, and agencies were developed to reach eastern Europe and Asia. The Canstein Bible Institute was founded at Halle, Germany (1710), to make the Scriptures available to the poor, and during the 19th cent. numerous Bible societies were constituted in Germany, the Netherlands, France, Russia, and Switzerland, most of them formed by Protestants. In the U.S. the first Bible society began in Philadelphia in 1808. In 1816 many local groups consolidated to organize the *American Bible Society, an interdenominational organization. In 1932 the British and Foreign Bible Society and the American Bible Society began to integrate their work in various lands. In 1946 the *United Bible Societies was established, bringing together many of the larger national societies. The Bible today is translated into more than one thousand languages and dialects, and inexpensive editions of the Bible, or portions of it, are available in most parts of the world.

BIBLE WAY CHURCHES of Our Lord Jesus Christ, World Wide, Inc., a Pentecostal body formed in 1957, when 70 churches broke off from the Church of Our Lord Jesus Christ of the Apostolic Faith. While retaining the doctrine of the original group, the Bible Way Churches established a less authoritarian organization. In 1968 membership totaled 25,000, with 343 churches.

BIBLICISM, the approach to the understanding of the Bible that combines *fundamentalism and *literalism and insists that the very thought and language of biblical times are the normative source for Christian faith and for its expression. To some extent, traces of biblicism are found in all eras when the Bible enjoys a special vogue

in Christian thought and life. The most persistent feature of biblicism is *millenarianism, an interpretation that accepts biblical reflections on the end-time (e.g., Rev; Mk 13.24–27) as literal historical descriptions of events to come, especially the second coming of Jesus. The high-water mark of biblicism in theological circles was reached in the works of Cocceius (1603–69), a Dutch scholar, and of J. A. Bengel (1687–1752), a German scholar. Although modern biblical scholarship has abandoned the approach of biblicism, popular understanding of the Bible remains noticeably affected by it.

BICKERTONITES, members of a Mormon body, established in 1862 under the leadership of W. Bickerton. They prefer to refer to themselves as the Bickerton Organization. The Church is designated as *Church of Jesus Christ (Bickertonites).

BIGOTRY, an exaggerated and irrational devotion to one's own creed, party, etc., with a corresponding intolerance of those who hold opposing views. The term is esp. applied where the intolerance is extended to the point of denying personal rights to members of groups different from one's own. Bigotry may derive from race, political allegiance, or other interest, but it is esp. identified with religious intolerance, perhaps because religious zealots have often been prominent in attempting to enforce religious dogma through use of the secular power, both in punishing heretics and in restricting secular privileges to those who subscribe to the officially approved religion. In contemporary usage the term is often used for those who prejudge political candidates or others on the basis of religious creed, or who restrict their personal friendships to those of their own group. Bigotry is generally based on creed or group affiliation and is to be distinguished from Pharisaism, which is an assumption of personal moral superiority and separation from those considered morally inferior. From the standpoint of Christian morality bigotry is an offense against love, and results from a confusion whereby devotion to God is confused with devotion to a particular religious group.

BILLING, EINAR (1871–1939), Swedish Lutheran bp. of Västeras (1930–39) and theologian. While not directly influential outside of Sweden, B. was responsible for a new theological vigor in his own country. Professor at the University of Uppsala (1908–20), he gave new insights into Luther studies, and emphasized Reformation ideas of the Church as the agency of forgiveness. From his research on the Bible he explained revelation as a continuous interpretation of human history, with God's words and deeds having an ever-present application and invitation.

BINITARIANISM, a classification used esp. in England for the belief or doctrine that the Godhead exists in two persons only, the Father and the Son. Thus the Pneumatomachi (Macedonians), who rejected the divinity of the Holy Spirit, were teaching a form of Binitarianism.

BIRÓ, MÁTYÁS DÉVAI (*c.*1500–*c.*1545), Hungarian Reformer. He has sometimes been referred to as Dévai, from his birthplace, Déva in Transylvania. He was a Franciscan, a chaplain of a Hungarian noble, when he became attracted to Reformation teaching. He was a student at Wittenberg, 1529–30, esteemed by Luther, in whose home he lived. Returning to Hungary, he preached Luther's doctrines in several Magyar regions, and was called the "Hungarian Luther." After 1541 he apparently changed from Lutheranism to Calvinism, esp. in Eucharistic teaching; Luther attacked him as a *sacramentarian in a letter of 1544. B. published (1537) one treatise attacking the doctrine of Purgatory; his *Orthographia Ungarica* was published posthumously (1549).

BISHOP, an ecclesiastical title and office, the meaning of which varies among Christian confessions. This difference of understanding constitutes one of the major obstacles to ecumenical progress. Neither the Lutheran nor the *Reformed traditions acknowledge the office of bishop as the term is understood in the RC, Orthodox, and Anglican Churches. They have only ministers (of the word, of baptism, and of the Lord's Supper). In some confessions in certain countries the title "bishop" has survived in consequence of special historical circumstances, but the meaning attached to the office is without hieratic significance. Thus in northern Lutheran countries— Sweden, Norway, Denmark, and Finland— the Churches have bishops. In Sweden they are officers of the official state Church who are nominated by the king from three candidates elected by the pastors. Their function is to serve as presidents of cathedral chapters and as administrators of the churches. They ordain and visit. Lutheran bishops in Iceland and Lithuania have a similar role. The Reformed Church in Hungary has bishops at the head of ecclesiastical districts, but their rank is not higher than that of pastors. The Czechoslovak National Church and the Evangelical Lutheran Church of Slovakia also have bishops. In the U.S. several Evangelical Churches have bishops, in imitation perhaps of the Episcopal Church. The Evangelical Church of Germany had no bishops, apart from a short-lived (1524–87) episcopacy in East Prussia, which succeeded formerly RC sees, and with the exception also of certain court clergymen or general superintendents who were granted the title by king or emperor. After 1918, discussions of restoration of the title to leaders of ecclesiastical provinces led to the appointment of territorial superintendents with the title "bishop" in some places, e.g., Bavaria, Hannover, Hamburg. The Anglican Communion holds the order of bishop as the highest of the three orders of the ministry. Ordination by a bishop is essential to all who enter the ministry, although this raises the thorny question of apostolic succession, about which some are disposed to take a broader view.

The Methodist Churches in the U.S. in their concept of the bishop are nearer to the evangelical than to the Anglican position; the order of bishop is not considered to be a sacrament any more than that of deacon or of elder. Bishops are superintendents of districts and form the Council of Bishops. More traditional in its concept is the small Old Catholic Communion formed after Vatican Council I. It has branches in Holland, Germany, Switzerland, Austria, the Philippines, and the U.S., all members of the *Union of Utrecht. These consider themselves national Churches under validly ordained bishops.

In the RC Church, bishops are considered to be, by divine institution, the successors of the Apostles. They hold the place of the Twelve, not, of course, as founders of the Church and witnesses of the resurrection, but as heads of local churches and jointly responsible for the Church's mission as the universal sacrament of salvation (Vat II ConstCh). Their function is threefold: prophetic (or teaching); sanctifying, through sacrifice and sacraments; and pastoral, as leaders of the people. A priest is joined to the college of bishops by episcopal ordination, the sacramental nature of which was definitely stated by Vatican Council II, although this had previously been subject to some doubt. All bishops, whether residential and in charge of a local church or diocese, or not (as in the cases of titular, auxiliary, coadjutor, or retired bishops), are thus members of the college of bishops jointly responsible for the world mission of the Church. The college of bishops, gathered in ecumenical council with and under the pope (or in communion with him in their dispersion throughout the world) constitute the supreme doctrinal and jurisdictional authority in the Church, authority being understood, in the mind of Vatican Council II, as service to the people of God. See S. E. Donlon and A. Rock, NCE 2:588–591; A. Adam et al., RGG 1:1300–11; G. Weigel, *Churches in North America* (1961); K. Rahner, *Bishops: Their Status and Function* (tr. E. Quinn, 1964). *APOSTOLIC SUCCESSION.

BISHOPS' BOOK, a work of the English Reformation, entitled the *Institution of a Christian Man* (1537), prepared by a commission of English bps. and scholars. Based on the *Ten Articles of 1536, it was a series of popular instructions to be read in churches, on the Apostles' Creed, the seven sacraments, the Ten Commandments, the Lord's Prayer, and Ave Maria, with two supplementary statements on justification and purgatory. King Henry VIII gave it no official approval but allowed its publication and use for 3 years. It probably represents the best statement of the "reformed Catholicism" of the C of E following the break with the papacy and King Henry's openness to alliance with the Lutheran princes of Germany. See C. Lloyd, *Formularies of Faith Put Forth by Authority during the Reign of Henry VIII* (1856 ed.); for King Henry's corrections and Abp. Cranmer's comments, see *Works of Thomas Cranmer* (1846), 2:83–114.

BLACK CHRISTIANITY, a mid-20th-cent. movement among black Christians, esp. those in predominantly white Churches of the U.S., to develop a form of Christianity expressive of black thought and responsive to the special needs of the black community. It has developed as a conscious reaction to patterns of life in white Churches that are considered racist and harmful to Negro life. In some ways, black Christianity has existed since the days of slavery, when Negro preachers often addressed congregations of converted slaves in a distinctive style of oratory and the congregations sang spirituals. Following the Civil War, Negroes generally separated from white congregations to form their own churches, which were organized into separate denominations, mostly Baptist and Methodist. Those denominations have continued to exist, under black leadership and often related to schools and other institutions. The predominantly white RC and Protestant Churches have had some Negro membership, and, with growing emphasis on integration, the number of blacks has increased. Negroes in integrated denominations, increasingly have felt, however, that whites have structured church institutions and developed theological teaching in ways that have maintained white dominance and black subordination. Negro churchmen, furthermore, have participated in the growing emphasis on black self-consciousness in the Negro community and the increasing determination to protest all-white domination or inferences of white superiority. As a part of this black self-consciousness, some Negroes have come to speak of a black Christ, black theology, and black ethics. They refer to Jesus as a "revolutionary black leader" and condemn white Churches for trying to make him white. The proponents of black Christianity charge that white Christians have perverted the Christian message of brotherhood, and that white Churches therefore do not represent true Christianity. Consequently, not only must black Christianity speak to the special needs and experiences of the Negro community, but it also has a mission to renew the white Churches. Black caucuses have been organized in Protestant and RC Churches to promote such goals.

Black Christianity is in some ways akin to what happened throughout history in all cultures as Christianity became indigenous. It portrays Jesus and his mother as black, just as artists in many countries and centuries have drawn biblical characters to resemble people of their own community. Black Christianity in the U.S. follows this pattern, but with more assertiveness and self-conscious opposition to the pattern of the dominant elements of American Churches. Major features of black Christianity have been its positive evaluation of the distinctive features of the Negro Churches and its assertion that traditional white standards in homiletics, music, liturgy, and other elements of church life cannot be used to judge Negro Christians. As in the Negro community at large, some advocates of black Christianity favor withdrawal from the white community into all-black institutions, whereas others favor integration and a struggle for greater black influence within the predominantly white Churches. Some favor temporary separation to build Negro strength so that integration can be accomplished on a more equal basis in the future. Participants generally feel that the movement is essential if the Church is to be of service to the black community in its current efforts to change the structures of American society, and they identify strongly with what is called the black revolution. They see a need for increasing the Negro's pride in his distinctive appearance, way of life, African ancestry, and inherent worth. Apart from such a movement, they feel, blacks will abandon the Church as irrelevant.

Black Christianity has been strongly ecumenical, emphasizing the common interests of Negro members of all Churches. The National Committee of Black Churchmen (originally named "of Negro Churchmen") was organized in 1967 to promote the movement. Critics point out the danger of perverting the biblical message by interpreting it so largely in the light of the interests of one ethnic group. But there has been general recognition that the failure of white Churches to give full acceptance to Negro Christians has made necessary some movement for change.

BLACK JEWS, a name commonly given to the members of the *Church of God and Saints of Christ, founded in 1897 by W. S. *Crowdy, combining Pentecostal elements with black nationalism and Jewish practices. In 1968 it claimed some 200 churches and 38,000 members.

BLACK RUBRIC, a name used since the 19th cent. for a "Declaration on Kneeling" in the *Book of Common Prayer (BCP) of the Church of England. Inserted without authorization into the 1552 BCP, it stated that kneeling for holy communion did not imply any "real or essential presence of Christ's natural body and blood" in the Holy Eucharist. Dropped from the 1559 BCP of Elizabeth I, the declaration was resumed in the 1662 revision with the significant alteration of "real and essential" to "corporal presence." The declaration was printed not in red but in black to indicate that it was not properly a rubric but an explanation. The convention is not retained in current two-colored editions of the BCP. The Black Rubric has never appeared in the *American Prayer Book. See bibliog. for Book of Common Prayer.

BLAIR, JAMES (1655–1743), first commissary for the C of E in Virginia; founding president of William and Mary College. B. was a Scotsman and an Anglican priest who went (1685) as rector to Henrico Co. in the Virginia colony at the request of Bp. Compton of London. Four years later he was appointed commissary for Virginia, i.e., Compton's delegate over the Church for all nonepiscopal functions. The office was designed to reform the deplorable condition of the colonial Church, esp. the standard of living, discipline, and training of the clergy. Through B.'s able efforts a measure of success was achieved, and most of the vacant parishes were supplied with rectors. William and Mary College was chartered in 1693. See Olmstead 51–52.

BLANDRATA, GIORGIO (Biandrata; 1515–c.1590), Italian Unitarian. Because of antitrinitarian views, B., a physician, had to flee from the Inquisition in Italy in 1556. In Geneva he came into conflict with Calvin over the Trinity, and went to Poland. There he became a leader in the Minor Church. As court physician in Transylvania, he won over Franz *Dávid to Unitarianism. He was a friend and correspondent of Faustus Sozzini (see SOCINUS). See E. M. Wilbur, *History of Unitarianism* (2v., repr., 1965). *SOCINIANISM.

BLAUROCK, GEORG (Görg; fl. 16th cent.), Swiss Anabaptist, former monk, and for a time a follower of *Zwingli at Zurich. He joined with C. *Grebel and others, however, to form the Swiss Brethren. In token of their insistence upon a free and inner belief, he had Grebel rebaptize him; then he did the same for the rest of those present at a meeting of the brethren in Jan. 1525. B. was a powerful preacher and a leader of the Anabaptists in Switzerland and southern Germany after Grebel's early death. See R. M. Jones, *Studies in Mystical Religion* (1923), 374, 378; bibliog. for Anabaptists.

BLAVATSKY, HELENA PETROVNA (1831–91), founder of modern *theosophy. B. was born in Russia of a German family named Hahn. She married (1848) the elderly Gen. N. P. Blavatsky, but they soon separated. She traveled widely, spending, she claimed, several years in Tibet, where she received the occult tradition. H. P. B. (as theosophists call her) and H. S. Olcott founded the Theosophical Society (1875) in New York City. In *Isis Unveiled* (1877) and *The Secret Doctrine* (1888), B. asserted she had brought together and restated for the West some of the ancient teachings that had appeared through the centuries at different times and places. B. and Olcott went to India (1879), where they reorganized the Theosophical Society, with headquarters in Adyar. She gained a large following, among others, Annie *Besant. While theosophists revere her, honoring her death date (May 8) as White Lotus Day, others have looked on many of her claims as fraudulent. See A. L. Cleather, *H. P. B.* (1922); J. Symonds, *Madame B.* (1959).

BLONDEL, DAVID (1591–1655), Protestant historian. Educated at Geneva, B. was pastor at Houdan near Paris from 1614 until 1650, when he accepted the chair of history at l'École Illustre in Amsterdam. At Paris he was influential in protecting the rights of French Protestants. An erudite and thorough historian, he published many works. His *Pseudo Isidorus et Turcianus vapulantes* (1628; against a book by the Spanish Jesuit Francisco Torres) disproved the authenticity of the False Decretals. This was put on the Index in 1661 for its antipapal slant, and in 1759 for the same reason, as were all of B.'s other historico-theological writings. Among these, to the displeasure of some Protestants, were two exploding the myth of Pope Joan, *Familier éclaircissement de la question si une femme a été assise au siège papal* (1647) and *De Joanna Papissa* (1657). See A. Lambert, DDC 2:936.

BOARD FOR HOMELAND MINISTRIES, an agency for evangelical works of the United Church of Christ. The benevolent and mission boards of American Congregationalism grew in a variety of ways from local societies and state organizations. The need for coordination led to the first national Congregational convention in 1852 and in 1893 to the formation of the Congregational Home Missionary Society. In 1925 all related organizations were united in the Board of Home Missions. This and other boards of the Congregational Churches retained a very large measure of autonomy. After 1935, however, their financial appeal was made jointly through the state conferences, with home missions to receive 36% of the funds. When the United Church of Christ was formed in 1957, the title was changed to Board for Homeland Ministries. Its basic task is evangelism in all its modern forms: Christian education, church extension, higher education, health and welfare, race and neighborhood concerns, the further education of ministers in service, and publishing.

BOEHM, MARTIN (1785–1812), a prominent figure in the beginnings of the United Brethren in Christ. Born into a Mennonite home, of Swiss ancestry, B., after a conversion experience (1758), began an itinerant, revivalistic ministry that eventually led to his expulsion from the Mennonite commu-nion. His sermon in 1767 at Long's barn near Lancaster, Pa., occasioned Philip *Otterbein's comment, "We are brethren." From his farm home, B. continued his preaching ministry and joined Otterbein in supervising the society called the United Brethren in Christ. *EVANGELICAL UNITED BRETHREN CHURCH.

BOEHME, JAKOB (1575–1624), German mystic and speculative thinker. A shoemaker and a prosperous merchant, although having only an elementary education, B. dealt with profound questions in original ways. The archaic language of his works, much of it derived from Paracelsus, and their unsystematic form have received varied reactions: W. *Law called him "the blessed Jacob"; John *Wesley characterized his work as "sublime nonsense, inimitable bombast." Nevertheless, B.'s ideas were to influence such philosophers as Schelling, Kierkegaard, Nietzsche, Bergson, and some modern existentialists. B. sought to resolve the problem of God's connection with the disunity apparent in nature and human life. Influenced esp. by a pastor at Görlitz in Silesia, he had a mystical experience in 1600, which was the source of his subsequent views. He always maintained that he wrote of what had been inwardly revealed to him. B.'s teaching, esp. his concern for the reality and value of nature, differed strikingly from the medieval mystical tradition. His first book, *Aurora* (1612), dealt with God in nature and the mystery of God's relationship to evil in the world and in men. Opposed by a local clergyman, he ceased publishing, 1612–19, but thereafter produced numerous works. His mature views were articulated *c.* 1622–23 in *The Way to Christ, On the Election of Grace, On the Great Mystery,* and *On Christ's Testaments.* All his works dealt with the basic problem of the unity of the Yes and No, of good and evil. To the theogonic, metaphysical, and cosmological aspects of the problem, he proposed as the answer the indwelling Logos by which man was regenerated and the cosmos was to be made new. See R. M. Jones, *Spiritual Reformers in the 16th and 17th Centuries* (pa., 1959), 151–234; J. J. Stoudt, *Sunrise to Eternity: A Study of Jacob Boehme's Life* (1957). *BEHMENISTS.

BOGOMILS (Slavic *Bogomili*), a movement and sect that originated in medieval Bulgaria on dualistic Manichaean foundations and later spread under different names and forms throughout the Balkans, Asia Minor, Russia, and western Europe. The earliest evidence of the movement appears in the second half of the 9th century. Its founder is said to have been an Orthodox priest from Macedonia by the name of Bogomil, a Slavic translation of the Greek *theophilos*, beloved of God. The theological tenets of the movement are known only from indirect sources, the apologetical writings and official documents emanating from the Orthodox and Catholic Churches (late 10th cent., e.g., *Treatise on the Bogomils* by the Bulgarian priest Cosmas; early 12th cent., Euthymios Zygabenos, *Panoplia dogmatica*). Its theological outlook appears to have been dualistic, admitting the existence and eternal conflict of God and Satan, a conflict affecting the whole universe and manifest in it, with spiritual things, such as the soul of man, expressing and fostering the power of God and material things building up the kingdom of Satan. From this follows the rejection by the Bogomils of church ritual and organization. They manifested the same attitude toward organized feudal society, arms, wars, married life, property, and material work. This points to the influence of known heretical movements of the Christian East, such as Messalianism (rejection of work for prayer), Manichaeism, and Paulicianism. There is definite historical evidence of contacts with and influence from the last of these; a large number of Paulicians were deported in the 10th cent. by the Byzantines from Armenia to eastern Bulgaria, an area which soon became one of the most active centers of Bogomilism. In partial disagreement with the Paulician interpretation of the conflict between God and Satan as a sort of eternal balance of power, the Bogomils generally stressed hope in the final victory of God and the deliverance of the spiritual world from the servitude of the material world through Christ.

The Bogomil movement soon spread in every direction from the two major Bulgarian centers of Thrace and Macedonia. The first to be affected was the Byzantine Empire, which occupied all of Bulgaria at the beginning of the 11th century. The Bogomils seem to have been well established in the major centers of the Empire, where they were known also as "Phoundaites" (scrip bearers). In 1111 one of their leaders, Basil, was tried and burnt at the stake in Constantinople. By the end of the 12th cent. they had appeared in Serbia, Bosnia, and Dalmatia. Bogomilism also spread to Russia, where adherents were known as *strigolnitzi*, to northern Italy and southern France, where they were known by such names as *Cathari, *Patarines, *Albigenses, Bulgarians, or Buggars. These manifested not only a definite theological, ecclesiastical, and social resemblance to the older Bulgarian sect, but there is also evidence of a missionary and organizational dependence of these Western groups on Bogomil centers in Bulgaria. Some Western sources even mention a common head of the dualist sects of Europe, a sort of Bogomil pope, residing in Bulgaria. Bogomilism encountered not only the expected opposition of the established Churches of East and West but also the full might of the secular power, which saw in Bogomilism a disruptive influence on society. Crusades and pogroms, together with the unrelenting missionary work of the Church as well as of Islam, finally brought the movement to an end. The sect did, however, find refuge in Bosnia, where it flourished as the national religion from the early 13th to the mid-15th century. There under Turkish rule the Bogomils became Moslems, and in the 17th cent. the last remnants of the group in Bulgaria were converted to Roman Catholicism. See D. Obolensky, *Bogomils: A Study in Balkan Neo-Manichaeism* (1948); A.

Borst, *Die Katharer* (1953); D. Angelov et al., *Bogomilstvoto v Bulgarija, Vizantija i Zapadna Evropa v Izvori* (1967).

BOHEMIAN BRETHREN, the common name for the Unitas Fratrum (Unity of Brethren), which was organized in 1457 and flourished in Bohemia, Moravia, and Poland until the Thirty Years' War. Of the factions arising after the death of Jan *Hus (1415), only the *Utraquists, founders of a national church, survived the civil wars ending in 1434 (see TABORITES). Finally, Hussites of a later generation, inspired by *Peter of Chelcić toward more thorough-going reform, left the Utraquists to form a new body. The Bohemian King himself allowed them to settle on crown lands in the village of Kunwald, though later he tried to suppress them. They stressed the Bible as the only source of doctrine, simplicity in worship, communion in both kinds and avoidance of human explanation of the sacrament, and godly living as evidence of saving faith. Having among them former Utraquist priests, they delayed establishing their own ministry until 1467, when one of their leaders was ordained at the hands of the Waldenses. Subsequently, they adopted the three orders: bishop, presbyter, and deacon. Though persecuted as an illegal sect, they grew to number 400 churches and 200,000 members by the time of Luther. First-generation austerity gave way to liberalization by the early 16th century. They were renowned for piety, use of Scripture, hymn singing, and their schools. Their first hymnal appeared in 1501. After the Thirty Years' War the Brethren became an underground Church in Bohemia and Moravia. In Poland they kept identity within the Reformed Church. J. *Comenius, one of their bishops, was their leader during this trying period. Surviving Brethren were incorporated into the Renewed Moravian Church, beginning in 1722. See E. de Schweinitz, *History of the Unitas Fratrum* (1885); P. Brock, *Unity of Czech Brethren* (1957); A. W. Schattschneider, *Through Five Hundred Years* (1956).

BOHEMIAN CONFESSIONS, doctrinal statements of the *Bohemian Brethren issued in 1535 and 1573. (1) The Confession of 1535 was, among a series of Bohemian statements of faith dating from 1467, the first fully Protestant doctrinal expression by the Brethren. It was written in Latin, signed by Brethren noblemen, and presented as a proof of orthodoxy to King Ferdinand in 1535. The document has a long, apologetic preface and 20 articles of faith closely resembling the *Augsburg Confession. It states that formerly the Brethren had rebaptized converts, but that they had dropped the practice; they feared being confused with Anabaptists. Their doctrine of the Lord's Supper, though stated vaguely, shows accommodation to the Lutheran view. At their request and expense, Luther published a slightly amended version with a favorable preface in 1538. (2) The second Bohemian Confession, printed by the Brethren in Wittenberg in March 1573, was, with some variations, essentially the document presented jointly by Protestants in Bohemia to Emperor Maximilian in 1575. It sought to reconcile the positions of Utraquists, Lutherans, Calvinists, and Bohemian Brethren. Substantially conformed to the 1535 Confession, it showed the influence of Melanchthon's views on the Eucharist. It served as the doctrinal statement of the charter granted to Protestants by King Rudolph in 1608, recognizing them as having equal rights with Roman Catholics. See Schaff Creeds 1:576–580; E. de Schweinitz, *History of the Unitas Fratrum* (1885).

BONHOEFFER, DIETRICH (1906–45), German theologian, executed by Nazi captors April 8, 1945, at Flossenbürg. A Lutheran, he began his university study at Tübingen, then traveled; at Rome the rich Roman liturgy and its monastic setting inspired a lifelong fascination. At 19 he studied theology in Berlin with Adolf *Harnack, though his first thesis, *Sanctorum communio*, strongly reflected the thought of Karl *Barth. After teaching briefly in

Berlin, he spent the 1930–31 academic year at Union Theological Seminary in New York, wondering at American church life as "Protestantism without Reformation." Back in Germany, his resistance to Nazi power led him to broadcast in 1933 a direct attack on the *führer*-principle and, later, Nazi anti-Semitism. An 18-month London pastorate allowed him to arouse international sympathy for the resistance Church and to visit Anglican monastic communities, which inspired his later work, *Life Together* (Eng. tr., 1954). He took a leading part in framing the 1934 *Barmen Declaration, which became the banner of the *Confessing Church. He taught (1935–37) at the Confessing Church seminary at Finkenwalde on the Baltic, a center of resistance until the Nazis closed it, arresting 27 students. Weeks later *The Cost of Discipleship* (2d rev. ed., Eng. tr., 1960; pa., 1963), the most widely read of his books, appeared. He held secret meetings and, after a brief American visit, began a perilous double life as a privileged Army Intelligence courier and a theological insurgent. In 1942 he offered to an Anglican bp. in Sweden a peace plan involving Hitler's arrest; it was refused.

Imprisoned in 1943, he kept writing, and came to accept the plan to assassinate Hitler that failed in 1944. His self-questioning *Letters and Papers from Prison* (Eng. tr., *Prisoner for God*, 1954; pa., 1962) and some work on his *Ethics* (ed. E. Bethge, Eng. tr., 1955) are from this period. Then he was moved to concentration camps, Buchenwald, Schoenberg, finally Flossenbürg, where he was executed just as the liberating Allies approached. His last act was to lead a worship service with men of many nations. His thinking and example have stirred large currents of commitment and Christian political witness. He saw the Church limiting itself to certain segments of life and demanded that it lay claim to the whole of things and summon men not to be religious but to be fully human. In theology he shared Barth's rejection of *liberal theology, yet from Harnack he developed the idea of a theology for "a world come of age." In ethics he stressed a disciplined obedience to Christ, but in "holy worldliness." B.'s idea of the world, however, is expressed in his *Ethics*: "In Jesus Christ the reality of God entered the reality of this world.... God and the world are comprised in this name [Jesus Christ]. In Him all things consist (Col 1.17). Henceforward one can speak neither of God nor of the world without speaking of Jesus Christ." Hotly condemning "cheap grace," his Christology used existentialist philosophy to restate traditional doctrine. The 1,128-page work *Dietrich Bonhoeffer: Theologie, Christ, Zeitgenosse* (1967), by his close friend Eberhard Bethge, is the largest resource. See M. Bosanquet, *Life and Death of D. B.* (1969); R. Marle, *Bonhoeffer: The Man and His Work* (1968); M. Marty, *Place of Bonhoeffer* (1962).

BONI HOMINES, a name popularly given to the *Perfecti among the *Albigenses, Brothers and Sisters of the Free Spirit, and other medieval sects. The term was also employed to designate members of four religious orders: Order of Grandmont (12th cent.), Canons of Villar de Frades (13th cent.), Friars of the Sack (13th cent.), and Minims (15th cent.).

BONN AGREEMENT, a document issued at a formal Anglican–Old Catholic meeting held at Bonn, July 3, 1931, and chaired by A. C. Headlam, Bp. of Gloucester. The Agreement was based on dogmatic unity, mutual recognition, and independent cooperation. It was accepted by all Anglican, European Old Catholic, and Polish National Catholic Churches.

BONN REUNION CONFERENCES, meetings to effect Christian reunion. Presided over by I. von *Döllinger, the first two were private meetings of Orthodox, Anglican, and Protestant theologians invited by Old Catholic leaders; these gatherings constituted an important ecumenical dialogue of the 19th century. The first conference (1874) witnessed harmony on several points. The larger, second conference (1875) discussed only the *filioque* question, accepting St. John Damascene's formula. Although Döllinger's hope for more conferences was not realized, the way was paved for later ecumenical initiatives. See C. B. Moss, *Old Catholic Movement* (1966).

BONOSUS OF NAÏSSUS (d. *c.*400), bp. of Naïssus in Illyricum. According to a letter attributed to Pope Siricius but belonging to St. Ambrose, B. denied the perpetual virginity of Mary and maintained that after bearing Jesus she had other children. Condemned by Anysius and the bps. of Illyricum, who had been directed by the Council of Capua (391) to investigate his orthodoxy, B. continued to exercise his episcopal office. Later a question was raised about the validity of the orders he had conferred. Pope Innocent I settled the matter by declaring that new ordinations were not necessary for those whom Bonosus had ordained before his condemnation but that those ordained after were to be deposed from their office. Followers of B., called Bonosians, survived as a sect in Spain and Gaul until the 7th century. See A. Amore, EC 2:1891.

BOOK OF ADVERTISEMENTS, instructions for the C of E on the order of services and the apparel of officiants, issued in 1566 by Abp. M. *Parker, under order of Elizabeth I. Intended to achieve uniformity, the regulations, esp. those regarding ceremonial and the use of the surplice in celebrating holy communion, were defied by Puritans intent on ridding the Church of all traces of Roman Catholicism. See V. J. K. Brook, *Life of Archbishop Parker* (1962).

BOOK OF COMMON ORDER (Church of Scotland), title of three official books of worship. (1) The first, by John *Knox, called also Knox's Liturgy, was one of the major documents of the Scottish Reformation. In Frankfurt Knox had prepared a first draft, which expressed the simplified form of service he favored. When he moved to Geneva, he drew up the Order of Geneva, which he brought to Scotland in 1559, and which, as the Book of Common Order, received official sanction in 1564. Intended to be a guide for ministers, the Book, though rugged and sometimes verbose, strongly expresses the biblical character of Scottish worship. It remained in general use until 1637, when the unsuccessful attempt to introduce the liturgy of W. *Laud occurred; part of the resistance of the Church of Scotland included adoption of the Puritan *Westminster Directory for Public Worship in 1643 in place of Knox's book. (2) The "Euchologion or a Book of Common Order" (1867) was published, after a period of liturgical aridity, by the Church Service Society to replace the Westminster Directory. The work helped to restore form and dignity to worship in the national Church. (3) The Book of Common Order (1940) was issued by the *General Assembly of the Church, and remains to the present the accepted and authoritative standard of worship in Scotland. These books have had an influence evident in the various editions of the Book of Common Worship prepared for Presbyterian Churches in the United States. See S. W. Sprott and T. Leishman, eds., *John Knox's Liturgy* (1868); W. D. Maxwell, *History of Worship in the Church of Scotland* (1955); J. Melton, *Presbyterian Worship in America* (1967).

BOOK OF COMMON ORDER (United Church of Canada), a book of worship officially accepted in 1932. A replacement for an older, provisional work, which simply combined the best material from the service books of the three communions joined in the United Church of Canada, the Book of Common Order (BCO) contains distinctive modifications in keeping with the liturgical movements of the time of its adoption. In 1968 the General Council replaced it with the Service Book (SB), which reflects yet further liturgical studies emphasizing the unity of word and sacrament, and the actional and corporate character of public worship. The BCO's content is that found in most service books of the *Reformed tradition. Orders for the Lord's Supper, baptism, and the general conduct of public worship are accompanied by a wide selection of prayers and Scripture lessons appropriate for the various seasons of the liturgical year. Other special services practiced in congregational life are given as well, including confirmation, marriage, and burial of the dead, together with those found in an Ordinal, such as ordination and induction.

The SB, being intended more specifically for regular worship, does not contain the services from the Ordinal but has a greatly expanded selection of materials for public worship and a more comprehensive lectionary, which provides prophecy, epistle, and gospel for each Sunday of a 3-year cycle. An abbreviated, companion "service book for the use of the people" is also planned, containing the basic services, prayers, and readings from the SB, to enable a greater congregational participation in the act of worship. In accepting the Book of Common Order, the intention of the United Church of Canada is to provide a resource for the enrichment of public worship but not to inhibit the leading of the Spirit or the minister's need to respond to specific situations. In actuality, the BCO has been widely used, esp. in the conduct of the sacraments and special services.

BOOK OF COMMON PRAYER (BCP), the authorized liturgical book of the C of E, used also by other Churches of the Anglican Communion. The full title is *Book of Common Prayer and Administration of the Sacraments and Other Rites and Ceremonies of the Church*—"common prayer" signifying public divine service (see OED 2:694). The First Prayer Book of Edward VI, which had been preceded by earlier vernacular texts, was imposed by Parliament in the Act of Uniformity of 1549. T. *Cranmer's supervision of this edition gave the BCP its beauty and aptness of language. A first revision (The Second Prayer Book of Edward VI) issued under the Act of Uniformity of 1552 was suppressed by Mary Tudor's Act of Repeal (1553) reinstating the Latin liturgy; but the Act of Uniformity of 1559 under Elizabeth I brought back the BCP of 1552 slightly modified. This was proscribed and supplanted by the *Westminster Directory for Public Worship, 1645–60. After the Savoy Conference (1661) on Puritan objections, another Act of Uniformity (1662) by Parliament prescribed the revision prepared by *Convocations; except for optional shortened services allowed in 1872 and new lectionaries of 1871 and 1922, this remains the current BCP. In 1928 the House of Commons rejected a revision that had been in process since 1904 (see REVISED PRAYER BOOK).

Among the non-English adaptations of the BCP, that in use by the Protestant Episcopal Church in the U.S. was established by a general convention in 1789 and modified in 1892 and 1928; since 1967 a further revision has been in process (see AMERICAN PRAYER BOOK). In content (morning and evening prayer services, Psalter, communion service, rites for the sacraments and Ordinal) the BCP derives from the Breviary, Missal, ritual, and pontifical. Cranmer's main sources were the Sarum liturgical texts and the Quignon Breviary for the 30-day distribution of the Psalter. The BCP of 1662 employed the Authorized or King James Version, except for Psalms. Parts of the revision rejected in 1928 are incorporated by some editions and designated "Alternative Orders"; these as well as the supplements used by other Anglican Churches supply rites and ceremonies not in the basic BCP.

Doctrine, of course, has dictated the origins and revisions of the BCP. The 1549 version already obscured the sacrificial aspect of the Holy Eucharist. The 1552 revision, influenced especially by *Peter Martyr Vermigli and M. *Bucer, removed any reference to sacrifice and rejected the "real and essential presence . . . of Christ's natural flesh and blood" (see BLACK RUBRIC) in its order for communion. Some slight concessions to Puritan belief (see MILLENARY PETITION) were reflected in the 1662 revision, but the Black Rubric was so modified as to reject only a "corporal presence of Christ's natural flesh and blood." The 20th-cent. revision was rejected because, while it did not satisfy Anglo-Catholics, it still ran counter to Protestant attitudes toward the Real Presence, the sacraments, and ritual. Modern adaptation of the BCP is an issue beset with a diversity of views, literary, liturgical, and doctrinal. Trial use of new orders for holy communion (Series 1 and Series 2) is now being made (1969). See F. E. Brightman, *English Rite* (2v., 1915); P. Brooks, *Thomas Cranmer's Doctrine of the Eucharist* (1965); on the 1662 BCP, G. J. Cuming, ed., *BCP: Durham Book, C of E* (1961); C. W. Dugmore, *Mass and the English Reformers* (1958); Hughes RE 2:105–113; F. Proctor and W. H. Frere, *New History of the BCP* (1951); E. C. Ratcliff, *Book of Common Prayer of the Churche of England* (1549 and 1552 texts, 1949); *idem, BCP 1549–1661* (1949); M. H. Shepherd, *Reform of Liturgical Worship* (1961); J. W. Suter and G. J. Cleaveland, *American BCP* (1949); B. Wigan, ed., *Liturgy in English* (1962); W. K. Lowther Clarke, *Prayer Book of 1928 Reconsidered* (1943). *ANGLICANISM.

BOOK OF COMMON WORSHIP (Church of South India), the book of worship containing approved orders for use in the Church of South India (CSI). It contains orders for baptism, confirmation, communion, marriage, burial, and ordination, together with lectionaries and other worship materials. The service for ordination was used at the inauguration of CSI in 1947, but other parts of the book were prepared from time to time subsequently and published separately, first in English and later in Indian languages. After a revision of all materials in 1961 by the Synod Liturgy Committee, the book was authorized by the Synod in 1962 and published in 1963. It is considered a notable product of the ecumenical movement, prepared by a Church composed of varied traditions and making use of material from a wide range of sources, ancient and modern. It reflects much of the work of the liturgical renewal movement. Scripture passages are taken mostly from the RSV. Although the book is officially authorized, used for diocesan and synodical occasions, and generally accepted, its use is not mandatory for local congregations. The Constitution of the CSI states: "No forms of worship which before the Union have been in use in any of the uniting churches shall be forbidden in the Church of South India, nor shall any wonted forms be changed or new forms introduced into the worship of any congregation without the agreement of the pastor and the congregation." See T. Garrett, *Worship in the Church of South India* (1958).

BOOK OF CONCORD *(Konkordienbuch; Liber Concordiae),* the assembled confessions of the Lutheran Church, published in 1580 at Dresden; first authentic Latin ed., Leipzig, 1584. The confessions are: the Catholic creeds (Apostles', Nicene, and Athanasian); the *Augsburg Confession; the *Apology of the Augsburg Confession; the *Schmalkaldic Articles; the *Treatise Concerning the Power and Primacy of the Pope*; the *Small Catechism* and the *Large Catechism* of Luther; the *Formula of Concord. Taken together, the confessions in the Book of Concord constitute the doctrinal standard by which Lutheranism defines itself, the norm to which Lutheran Churches and clergymen are pledged, and the official interpretation of the Lutheran relation both to the RC tradition and to other Churches. There has never been, however, unanimous acceptance by all the Lutheran bodies of the complete content of the Book of Concord. See T. G. Tappert, ed., *Confessions of the Evangelical Lutheran Church* (1959); F. Bente, *Historical Introduction to the Book of Concord* (1965).

BOOK OF CONFESSIONS (United Presbyterian Church in the U.S.A.), the volume of *confessions of faith adopted in 1967. The confessions included are: the Nicene and the Apostles' Creed, Scots Confession, Heidelberg Catechism, Second Helvetic Confession, Westminster Confession and Shorter Catechism, Barmen Declaration, and the new *Confession of 1967. Officers of the Church promise to perform their duties under the instruction and guidance of this volume of confessions.

BOOK OF CONGREGATIONAL WORSHIP, a guide for worship. A feature of early Congregationalism was its dislike of fixed liturgy as denying the freedom both of the worshiper and the Holy Spirit. In the second half of the 19th and into the 20th cent., however, a movement for the better ordering of worship was made by Thomas Binney, John Hunter, W. E. Orchard, and others. It led to the publication by the Congregational Union of England and Wales in 1916 of the *Congregational Hymnary* and in 1920 of *A Book of Congregational Worship.* The latter was designed for use by minister and congregation and consisted of 10 orders of service and suggestions for the sacraments and other occasions. Apart from some infelicities, its weakness was that it sought to combine conflicting theories of worship and was not animated by any clear principles. The Book was not very widely used, but was the first of its kind, and it was followed by better and more popular productions. *BOOK OF SERVICES AND PRAYERS.

BOOK OF DISCIPLINE, see DISCIPLINE; DISCIPLINE (METHODIST); DISCIPLINE, BOOK OF (PRESBYTERIAN).

BOOK OF MORMON, one of the sources of divine revelation for Mormons. The book was first published in 1830 by Joseph *Smith, Jr. In 1823 he claimed that a heavenly personage, the Angel Moroni, son of Mormon, led him to the discovery of a set of golden plates on Mount Cumorah, near Palmyra, N.Y., where Moroni had buried them more than 1,000 years before; with the plates were a set of spectacles, the Urim and Thummim, to be used for deciphering the Reformed Egyptian characters inscribed upon the plates. The Book of Mormon is Smith's translation of Moroni's history of the series of extinct races that had inhabited America from 600 B.C. to A.D. 400. To one of these races, the Nephites, Jesus appeared after the ascension and established his Church. The Mormon Church was founded as the restoration of the Church Jesus had established according to this record, and for Mormons the Book has always been accepted as containing sacred revelation from God. Non-Mormon critics have questioned both the existence of the original golden plates and the veracity of the Book of Mormon. The many anachronisms it contains point to a discrepancy of 12 to 15 hundred years from its alleged time of composition. See F. M. Brodie, *No Man Knows My History: The Life Story of Joseph Smith* (1945); Mayer RB 456–457; E. C. McGavin, *How We Got the Book of Mormon* (1961); T. F. O'Dea, *Mormons* (1957). *LATTER-DAY SAINTS, CHURCH OF JESUS CHRIST OF.

BOOK OF RITUAL (Evangelical United Brethren Church), authorized by the General Conference of 1954 and first published the following year, an attempt to enhance the corporate worship of the denomination, which had emerged from revivalistic, *free-church American Protestantism. Many of the rituals included in this Book had previously been a part of the denomination's *Discipline.* Both the longer and shorter services of holy communion are adaptations of the holy communion service used by the Methodist Church, and were a tie with historic Protestant worship forms through the Anglican Book of Common Prayer. A major departure is the change of the words of administration of the bread (and cup) from reading, "The body (blood) of our Lord Jesus Christ," to "The Lord Jesus Christ, who gave his body (blood) for thee, preserve thy soul unto everlasting life." In addition to a ritual for infant baptism there also appears one entitled "The Dedication of Infants."

BOOK OF SERVICES AND PRAYERS, a manual of worship for the Congregational Union of England and Wales. This book, compiled by a committee appointed by the Church, was published in 1959. Its use by ministers was not required, but it came into wider general usage than any previous publication. It was designed and intended not as a book of common prayer but as a guide for ministers and lay preachers in the ordering and conduct of worship. The first part consists of orders of service for public worship, for the sacraments, and for a variety of special occasions. The second part consists of a wide selection of prayers, many specially composed. The third part consists of scripture sentences and a lectionary. A useful book, it represents a contribution to the better ordering of Congregational services. No original understanding of the nature of worship by modern man, however, nor any attempt to move beyond the religiously conventional is evidenced by the Book.

BOOK OF SPORTS, popular name for a declaration (1618) on Sunday recreation by James I of England. It stated that after divine service on Sundays, "no lawful recreation should be barred to his good people, which should not tend to breach the laws of his kingdom and the canons of his church." Dancing, archery, vaulting, and May-day games were among the sports permitted, contrary to Puritan sabbatarianism. Ordered to be read in the churches, the declaration was, nevertheless, largely disregarded. It was republished by Charles I in 1633, and its reading was staunchly enforced by Abp. W. *Laud to the great dismay and indignation of the Puritans. Parlia-

ment in 1643 ordered that all copies of the declaration be gathered up and burned. See C. Hill, *Society and Puritanism in Pre-Revolutionary England* (1964); L. A. Govett, *The King's Book of Sports* (1890). *SABBATARIANS.

BOOK OF WORSHIP (Methodist), a liturgical manual of the Methodist Church. The history of the Methodist Hymnal reveals a growing interest in liturgy that culminated in the adoption of *The Book of Worship for Church and Home* by the *General Conference of 1944. It won wide acceptance, and in order to meet a still growing need the General Conference of 1956 ordered a revision that was published in 1960. The book is divided into five parts: (1) General Services of the Church (orders of worship, orders for baptism, holy communion, marriage, ordinations, and other services); (2) aids for the Ordering of Worship (the Christian year, prayers, and other aids); (3) the Acts of Praise (Psalter, canticles, and other acts of praise); (4) the Occasional Offices of the Church (consecrating a church, licensing persons to preach, and similar offices); (5) services in the Methodist tradition (morning prayer from John Wesley's Sunday service, Love Feast, *Aldersgate Sunday, and other services). See HistAmMeth 3:562; N. B. Harmon, *Understanding the Methodist Church* (1955).

BOOK OF WORSHIP (Swedenborgian), properly the *Liturgy or Book of Worship for the Use of the New Church Signified by the New Jerusalem*, was adopted by the *General Convention of the New Jerusalem in the U.S.A. in 1834, revised somewhat in 1854, and again revised by a committee appointed in 1911 to prepare a liturgy that would be acceptable to all Swedenborgian groups. The Book of Worship provides for a worship service similar to Morning Prayer and Sermon in an Episcopal Church, with scriptural selections chosen to stress that the Lord in his divine humanity is to be worshiped. There are liturgical services for the celebration of baptism, the holy supper, marriage, and funerals, as well as the Articles of Faith adopted by the New Church General Conference in England, and a hymnal.

BOOTH FAMILY, a 19th-cent. family, of partly Jewish origin; some of its members were the founders of the Salvation Army; later, others established the Volunteers of America.

William (1829–1912). Born in poverty at Nottingham, Eng., and receiving little formal education, B. experienced a conversion at 15 and in 1846 was licensed as a street preacher by the New Wesleyan Connexion, a Methodist body. His thought was greatly influenced by Charles G. *Finney's *Lectures on Revivals.* Public preaching by B.'s wife led to his expulsion by the Methodists in 1861, and he founded the Christian Revival Association in London in 1865 as a nondenominational Bible Christian Church, later called the Christian Mission. In 1878 he adopted the name Salvation Army and wrote *Articles of War* based on the British Army *Field Pocket Book* for his evangelists. In his lifetime he held title to all Salvation Army property and had full authority over all its members; he held the title General of the World Wide Salvation Army (1934–39). His evangelism was directed to the need of repentance for sin and the experience of *sanctification. He launched a successful crusade against white slavery in 1885 with journalist W. T. Stead and in 1890 startled British readers with his appeal for slum dwellers, *In Darkest England,* also written with W. T. Stead. He pioneered in social work for alcoholics and the unemployed. See R. Collier, *General Next to God* (1965).

Catherine (Mumford; 1829–90). Wife of William and "Mother of the Salvation Army," she married William in 1855 and shared in his evangelical preaching and in the formation of the Salvation Army. She devoted herself not only to preaching but also to alleviating the sufferings of destitute women and children.

Evangeline Corry (1865–1950). Daughter of William, under her command from 1904, the Salvation Army made great progress in the United States. She wrote many Salvationist hymns.

Ballington (1857–1940). Son of William and Catherine, with his wife he commanded the Salvation Army in the U.S. (1887–96) but separated to form the Volunteers of America, of which he was general-in-chief and president.

Maud Ballington (Charlesworth; 1865–1948). Wife of Ballington, with her husband she was first a Salvation Army leader. After his death (1940) she commanded the Volunteers of America. She was deeply dedicated to the rehabilitation of prisoners and was one of the founders of the Parent-Teachers Association.

BORDELUMIANS (Ger. Bordelumsche Rotte), a pietistic-enthusiastic sect that appeared in 1737 in Bordelum near Flensburg, N Silesia, under the leadership of a tinker, Ernst Fischer, and two Protestant theology students, Franz Borsenius (Barsvenius; d. 1743) and David Andreas Bähr. Members regarded themselves as saints, but their rejection of the authority of Church and State, as well as their advocacy of community of wives and property, led to their official suppression by King Christian VI of Denmark (1739) and to their eventual disappearance. See M. Schmidt, RGG 1:1366; P. Tschackert, EncRelKnow 2:234.

BORELISTS (Boreelists), a branch of *Collegiants at Amsterdam (c.1645), named for one of their leaders, Adam Borel (Boreel; 1603–67). He was a Hebraist and humanist, imbued with the mystical writings of S. *Franck, S. *Castellio, and D. V. *Coornheert. The Collegiants at Amsterdam followed Borel's counsel to reject all established forms of Christianity as distortions and to rely on interior revelation for a pure understanding of Holy Scripture. See R. M. Jones, *Spiritual Reformers in the 16th and 17th Centuries* (pa., 1959), 117–120.

BOURIGNON, ANTOINETTE (1616–80), self-styled visionary and prophetess. A. was born at Lille, France. From youth she claimed to be guided by visions and inner inspiration to a mission of religious reform. She was frequently suspect to the authorities and spent many hours in law courts. While she had collected circles of followers at Lille, Ghent, and Malines, she enjoyed her finest successes at Amsterdam from 1667 to her death. Although she denied the divinity of Jesus Christ, B. always counted herself a Catholic, bent on reforming the whole Church. Some have labelled her a quietist, but her writings, edited by P. *Poiret (19v., 1679–84), are a mélange drawn from many, often contradictory, religious traditions. They are distinctive chiefly as evidence of her utter reliance on her own inner experience. Decrees of the Holy Office proscribing B.'s writings were issued in 1669, 1687, and 1757. "Bourignonism" had a surprisingly strong impact in Scotland. See R. Knox, *Enthusiasm* (1950), 352–355; A. MacEwen, *A. B., Quietist* (1910); P. Pourrat, DSAM 1:1915–17.

BOURNE, HUGH (1772–1852), founder of the Camp-Meeting Methodists in England, who in 1811 joined the *Clowesites, forming the Primitive Methodist Church. Converted by reading Methodist literature, he joined a Methodist *society, began preaching in 1801, and in 1808 was expelled for supporting camp-meetings, which were forbidden by Wesleyan Methodists. In 1810 B. formed the Camp-Meeting Methodists. He was general superintendent of the Primitive Methodist Church, 1814–19, and visited the Primitive Methodists in the U.S. and Canada. See J. Ritson, *Romance of Primitive Methodism* (1909); W. J. Townsend et al., eds., *New History of Methodism* (2v., 1909) 1:56ff.

BOWNE, BORDEN PARKER (1847–1910), Methodist philosopher of "personalistic-idealism." His career was spent as professor of philosophy and theology at Boston Univ.

(1876–1910). Relying on reason as the sole criterion of truth, B. sought to develop a system free of theological, philosophical, or scientific dogmatism. In his system, also called "personalism," person, thinking-self, is the ultimate reality. Person is either the creator, God, or the created person, man. Nature has its reality in relation to man's knowing and willing, and as the expression of God's rational willing. Man relates himself to God through his ethical response to the world as manifestation of God's will. B.'s philosophic system influenced Methodist theology esp. through the liberal theologians E. S. *Brightman and A. C. *Knudson. His works include *Metaphysics* (1898) and *Personalism* (1908). See F. J. McConnell, *B. P. B.* (1929), bibliog.; P. A. Bertocci, EncPhil 1:356–357.

BRADFORD, WILLIAM (*c.*1590–1657), Pilgrim father and governor of Plymouth Colony. At the age of 16 he joined the Church formed by Puritan *Separatists at Scrooby, England. After a brief imprisonment, he went into exile with the group in Leiden, where he became learned in Calvinist theology. He came with the Pilgrims to Plymouth, and was a signer of the *Mayflower Compact; he was chosen governor (1621), and held the office for 30 years. His *History of Plymouth Plantation* (not published in full until 1856) is the primary source for all knowledge of the Plymouth Colony (modern ed. S. E. Morrison, 1952). B. showed some degree of religious toleration, a rare quality among the Puritans of New England. See B. Smith, *Bradford of Plymouth* (1951).

BRANCH THEORY, the view that although the Church is in internal *schism, with its main segments not in communion with one another, nevertheless those segments, retaining the historic *apostolic succession and holding to the faith of the undivided Church continue as living branches of the Church. In this form, the theory became popular in 19th-cent. England, following the *Oxford movement. Three branches were usually identified, Roman, Orthodox, and Anglican. In some broader usages of the theory, particularly in the U.S., the *historic episcopate disappeared as a criterion, and the number of branches was multiplied to include most or all of the major Christian divisions. The theory commands little contemporary respect save, perhaps, as a simple historical diagram of the successive divisions in the Church's life. With ecumenical attention increasingly focused on the given unity of Christians in baptism and in the saving acts of God, and with the development of common ecumenical action and even united Churches, the theory seems to explain little and justify even less. It may be said, however, that the idea served, at a critical time, to remind Christians both of the continuing, organic nature of the Church's life manifested in its historic institutions and also of the very givenness itself of unity in Christ as a reality which in some way overcomes the breaches in the visible Church.

BRAY, THOMAS (1656–1730), Anglican priest, founder of the *Society for Promoting Christian Knowledge (SPCK) and the *Society for the Propagation of the Gospel (SPG). While rector of Sheldon in Warwickshire, B. was made commissary of the bp. of London for the American colonies to develop support for the C of E there. The experience of planning this work prompted him to establish the SPCK (1698); he went to Md. in 1699, but decided he could contribute most to his mission by working in England. He established the SPG in 1701. His efforts to have a bp. appointed for the Church in New England were unsuccessful. Many free parochial libraries in England were part of the legacy of his labors. See life by E. L. Pennington (1934). *PROTESTANT EPISCOPAL CHURCH.

BREDA, DECLARATION OF, see DECLARATION OF BREDA.

BRENT, CHARLES HENRY (1862–1929), Protestant Episcopal bishop, leader in the *ecumenical movement. Born in Newcastle, Ont., and graduated (1884) from Trinity College in Toronto, he was ordained in 1886 and served in parishes in Buffalo, N.Y., and Boston, Massachusetts. He was bp. of the Philippines (1901–18) and served on many local and international commissions to end the opium traffic. He was elected bp. of western New York in 1918. As a missionary bp. he attended the *Edinburgh Conference of 1910. Impressed with its promise for Christian unity, he influenced the *General Convention of the Protestant Episcopal Church to set in motion the program that led to the *Lausanne Conference (1927). This first world conference of *Faith and Order met under his presidency. It was B.'s hope that the Churches could find areas of basic doctrinal unity, while maintaining the variety of their own proper traditions. See A. C. Zabriskie, *Bishop Brent, Crusader for Christian Unity* (1948); F. W. Kates, *C. H. B.* (1948).

BRÈS, GUY DE (Guido de Bray; 1522–67), Calvinist preacher in the Low Countries. A Belgian artisan born at Mons, B. first embraced Lutheranism, c.1548. He became an itinerant student and preacher and, after a stay at Geneva and Lausanne, changed over to Calvinism. He had a prominent role in the establishment of the *Reformed Church in the Low Countries, as pastor and preacher at Sedan, Antwerp, and Valenciennes. The last was then under Spanish rule, and B. was accused of conspiracy and hanged. He was the author of the *Belgic Confession (1561), and of two polemical works, one against Catholics and the other against Anabaptists. See W. F. Dankbaar, RGG 1:1401–02; J. Dedieu, DHGE 10:545–546; Schaff Creeds 1:504.

BRETHREN CHURCH (Ashland, Ohio), one of the Brethren Churches, organized at Dayton, Ohio, in 1883 by expellees and separatists from the Fraternity of German Baptists (named the Church of the Brethren in 1908). The principals were called progressive because they advocated before and practiced after their expulsion: evangelistic meetings; Sunday schools; prayer-meetings; a paid ministry; an educated clergy; freedom in dress; and a congregational polity. The Brethren Church holds the German Baptist doctrinal heritage: *trine immersion, threefold communion of *footwashing, Lord's Supper, and Eucharist; anointing the sick with oil; and nonconformity. Different leanings theologically, ranging from liberal to conservative, from Calvinistic to Arminian, plagued the Church as the 20th cent. advanced. Controversy in the 1930s, concerned with theological hair-splitting, institutional control, and personalities reached a climax in 1939 that led to the formation of two separate organizations—the Ashland, Ohio, group and the National Fellowship of Brethren Churches, designated as the Grace Group. Principals in both groups agree that much of the discord and divisive contention was due to definition and interpretation. The Brethren Church, with headquarters in Ashland, Ohio, maintains a college, seminary, and publishing company in that city.

BRETHREN CHURCH (Grace Group), the *National Fellowship of Brethren Churches, so designated to distinguish it from the Brethren Church (Ashland, Ohio), from which it separated in 1939.

BRETHREN CHURCHES, those bodies springing from the German Baptist Brethren movement originating in the Rhenish Palatinate of Germany in 1708. The founding group, separatists from the state Churches (principally *Reformed), were Pietists and Anabaptists. Persecution drove them from their homes to the lower Rhine and Lowlands, and thence to Pennsylvania. The migration was complete by 1735. They referred to themselves as Baptist Brethren but in Germany were dubbed Dompelaars, and in America Tunkers, Dunkers, and Dunkards. They adopted the legal name Fraternity of German Baptists in 1836. Dis-

tinguishing features in doctrine and practice are: baptism by *trine immersion; a threefold holy communion of *footwashing, Lord's Supper, and Eucharist (love feast); anointing the sick with oil; *nonconformity to the world; *nonresistance; and refusal to swear an oath. This last conflicted with the Pennsylvania oath of allegiance during the Revolutionary War and scattered many of them westward to the wilderness; they became the backbone of many new settlements. A schism arose among the Baptist Brethren in Pa. as early as 1728, led by Johann Conrad *Beissel, advocating extreme mysticism, celibacy, and sabbatarianism. The schismatic group divided the Church, and set up the *Ephrata Community. The Baptist Brethren grew in numbers rapidly after the Revolution. Controversy as to methods of witness and *church order (1850–80) divided the membership into three discordant elements—ultra-conservative, progressive, and middle-ground conservative. The matters in dispute included evangelistic meetings, Sunday schools, prayer-meetings, paid ministry, high schools, personal dress, and ecclesiastical authority. In 1881, an estimated 4,500 ultra-conservatives seceded and organized as Old German Baptist Brethren because the Church would not disown the progressive element. In 1882, reacting, the main body expelled the progressive leader, Henry R. Holsinger, and his sympathizers; these progressives—4,000–6,000 strong—formed the Brethren Church. No dissent concerned theology, rites, or biblical doctrine; all elements in the new relationships held to the basic doctrine. All three Brethren groups continued: the Old Order Brethren, ultra-conservative; the Fraternity of German Baptists (name changed to The Church of the Brethren in 1908), becoming more progressive; and the Brethren Church, theologically conservative. Theological disagreement in the Brethren Church during the 1930s about *Arminianism, and a clash of leadership, divided the Church into the Ashland, Ohio, group and the National Fellowship of Brethren Churches, or Grace group.

BRETHREN IN CHRIST, a denomination, formerly known as River Brethren, that developed as a distinct Church in Lancaster Co., Pa., about 1778, among German-speaking settlers of Anabaptist and Pietist background. They were originally known as River Brethren (or Brotherhood by the River) because they were groups of fervent Christians living in communities near the Susquehanna River. Jacob Engle (1753–1832) was recognized as the first overseer of the Brethren in their organization into districts in the 1780s; he visited congregations in Ontario, Canada, in 1789. The Brethren refused to take oaths or bear arms and were strict pacifists. They adopted a distinctive garb and frowned on anything that would detract from a religious simplicity. Until late in the 19th cent., Brethren worshiped in barns and private homes. Doctrines include fundamental articles of Christian belief, with emphasis on justification from past sins and sanctification as purifying the heart. They baptize by immersion and combine an agape meal with the service of the Lord's Supper. The Brethren divided in 1843 and again in 1855 over the issue of building churches and otherwise departing from traditional ways. These divisions led to the formation of the Old Order, or Yorker, Brethren and the United Zion Church. Brethren congregations became numerous in south-central Pa. and were transplanted to the Midwest U.S. by settlers from that section. In 1968 there were 159 congregations of the Brethren in Christ, with a combined membership of about 8,600, chiefly in Pa. but also in Ohio, Ind., Ill., Iowa, and Kansas. The Brethren were not legally incorporated as a Church until 1904, but from the first they have been organized into districts, which usually correspond to civil counties, under an elected overseer. Local congregations retain much autonomy under their own elders. The Brethren in Christ support foreign missions in Africa and Asia. The Foreign Mission Board and publishing activities have been centralized at Harrisburg, Pennsylvania. See A. W. Climenhaga, *History of the Brethren in Christ Church* (1942).

BRETHREN OF CHRIST, also, Christ's Brethren, another name for the *Christadelphians, founded by John Thomas (1805–71) in 1848. These names were preferred over "Christian."

BRETHREN OF EARLY CHRISTIANITY, a small communal group in Bright, Ontario, similar in belief and practice to the *Hutterian Brethren. The founder was a Hungarian immigrant, Julius Kubassek (d. 1961). *COMMUNAL MOVEMENTS.

BRETHREN OF THE COMMON LIFE, an association of men intent upon a more perfect interior life, which was organized among the disciples of Gerard Groote (1340–84) at Deventer in the Netherlands. Its members, clerical and lay, took no vows but lived in common; instead of seeking alms, they supported themselves largely by their work as copyists. From Deventer, houses of the Brethren spread to other cities in the Netherlands and in Germany, and everywhere they exerted an important influence by their promotion of the *Devotio Moderna—the new approach to spirituality that had its beginning in the teaching of Groote—of which the Deventer house was a leading center. In some places they established schools, a few of which flourished remarkably and contributed much to the improvement of education in the Low Countries and, through eminent pupils, to the rise of the *New Learning. The Brethren encountered opposition, some of it resulting from the attacks leveled by Groote and his disciples against ecclesiastical abuses, and some from the mendicant orders, which looked with disfavor upon the "uncanonical" type of organization the Brethren had adopted. This opposition impeded the growth of the society, and in many cases the Brethren or those imbued with their spirit sought surer canonical status by becoming canons regular. The religious upheaval of the 16th cent., the rise of new teaching orders, the establishment of diocesan seminaries, and the growth and development of the universities led to the extinction of the Brethren by the end of the 17th century. See W. J. Alberts, NCE 2:788–790; A. Hyma, *Brethren of Common Life* (1950); T. P. Van Zijl, *Gerard Groote, Ascetic and Reformer, 1340–1384* (1963).

BRETHREN OF THE LAW OF CHRIST (Fratres Legis Christi), one of the names for the 15th-cent. *Bohemian Brethren or *Unitas Fratrum. The name connotes their emphasis on practical Christian life (see Gal 6.2).

BRETON HERETICS, a name sometimes given to the fanatical followers of *Éon de l'Étoile. After his condemnation at a provincial council in Reims in 1148, several of his followers were burned, but for pillage and murder rather than for religious doctrine. See N. Cohn, *Pursuit of the Millennium* (1957), 38ff.

BREVIARY, ROMAN, liturgical book of the Roman rite that contains the complete text of the Divine Office. It is the result of the compilation of many liturgical books used in the divine services, e.g., the *collectarium, hymnarium, psalterium,* and *responsoriale.* The earliest MS of the Breviary is dated 1099; this is a large choir book. The portable Breviary, the type most commonly used in modern times, appeared in the 13th century. The present Roman Breviary originated in the curia of Innocent III, was adopted and revised by the Franciscans in 1240, and the friars made it popular throughout Europe. Subsequent accretions called for reform, and the revision demanded by the Council of Trent was published by Pius V in 1568. There have been later revisions, esp. in the 20th century. Vatican Council II declared its desire to carry through the restoration already begun by the Apostolic See and laid down general norms that were to be followed (see Vat II SacLit 83–101). See P. Salmon, *Breviary Through the Centuries* (tr. D. Mary, 1962);

S. J. Van Kijk and J. H. Walker, *Origins of the Modern Roman Liturgy* (1960).

BRIGGS, CHARLES AUGUSTUS (1841–1913), American biblical scholar. After graduating from the Univ. of Virginia, B. for 2 years attended Union Theological Seminary, New York City, then the Univ. of Berlin (1865–70). There he was trained in the methods of higher criticism in biblical studies. Upon his return to the U.S., he was pastor of a Presbyterian church in Roselle, N.J., until his appointment (1874) as professor of Hebrew at Union. In his lectures and writings he opposed the *Princeton theology, and proposed a study of the Bible that was critical but not rationalistic. His inaugural lecture (1890) as professor of biblical theology, however, in which he warned against a literalist view of the Bible, brought a demand for his dismissal by the *General Assembly of the Presbyterian Church. The seminary refused to accede; a few years later it became non-denominational. B. was tried and acquitted of heresy, but the General Assembly withdrew his credentials as a minister in 1893. He received Episcopalian ordination in 1899. As general editor of the *International Critical Commentary on the Holy Scriptures,* he contributed his major work, *Commentary on the Book of Psalms* (1906). He was also active in seeking RC and Protestant reunion. See L. A. Loetsche, *Broadening Church* (1957); B.'s defense against heresy charges was published by Scribner's in 1892.

BRIGHTMAN, EDGAR SHEFFIELD (1884–1953), Methodist philosopher-theologian. He was professor of philosophy at Boston Univ. (1919–53), where he kept prominent the personalist-idealism of B. P. *Bowne. Much of B.'s interest was in religion, esp. in grounding all religious truth in reason. He stressed the revelation of God through the evidence of divine reasonableness and proposed that experience finds God to be finite, because of limits within the divine nature, from the cosmos, and from human freedom. His works include *The Problem of God* (1930), *The Finding of God* (1931), *Is God a Person* (1930). See D. W. Soper, *Major Voices in American Theology* (1954), 194–218; P. A. Bertocci, ed., *Person and Reality* (1958), with bibliog.

BRITISH AND FOREIGN BIBLE SOCIETY, largest of all *Bible societies; established in London, 1804, with Anglicans and members of other communions cooperating. Local societies were started throughout the British Isles, and later in the British colonies. The Society has remained strictly interdenominational in organization and policy and has restricted its activities to the printing and distribution of Bibles.

BRITISH COUNCIL OF CHURCHES, an amalgamation into one organization, 1942–43, of those British agencies that had carried on the work of interdenominational cooperation begun largely by the *Oxford and *Edinburgh Conferences in 1937. The theological basis for the Council is the same as that of the *World Council of Churches, except that it qualifies itself as "a fellowship of churches which accept our Lord Jesus Christ as God and Saviour" in these words: "with the understanding that any body which has hitherto been represented on the Commission [for union] shall continue in membership of the Council, if so willing, even though it does not itself accept this basis." Included, therefore, are 118 members representing the Church of England, of Scotland, of Wales and of Ireland as well as the Salvation Army, the Society of Friends, the Unitarian and Free Churches, five interdenominational organizations, and 20 other agencies. Besides carrying on the work of the amalgamated agencies, the Council has a fourfold purpose: (1) "to facilitate common action by the churches in evangelistic enterprize, in promotion of international friendship, in stimulating a sense of social responsibility, and in guiding the activities of the churches for the welfare of youth; (2) to facilitate such other common action as

may later be determined; (3) to promote co-operation in study and . . . in the studies promoted by the World Council of Churches; (4) to assist the growth of ecumenical consciousness. . . ." See G. K. A. Bell, ed., *Documents of Christian Unity* (Third Series, 1948), 142–145.

BROAD CHURCH, a 19th-cent. phrase, inspired by the older *high-church and *low-church categories, describing a temper of mind within Anglicanism generally opposed to doctrinal definition and sympathetic to the most liberal interpretation of Scripture, creed, rubric, etc. Now little used, the sense of it might be found in "liberal" or (a generation ago) "modernist." In some ways, broad church corresponds in meaning to *latitudinarianism, but the two should not be confused.

BROOK FARM, the best known of the early 19th-cent. U.S. *communal movements inspired by the *perfectionism and *millenarianism of the time. Among the prominent New England writers who participated, many of them *transcendentalists, were George Ripley (1802–80) and William E. Channing (1810–84), founders; Theodore Parker (1810–60), George W. Curtis (1824–92), Nathaniel Hawthorne (1804–64), Charles A. Dana (1819–97), and Margaret Fuller (1810–50), close associates; Orestes Brownson (1803–76) and Isaac Hecker (1819–88), visitors. Brook Farm, near West Roxbury, Mass., was founded in the belief that it was the business of Christianity to overthrow social evils. The community was structured to unite intellectual and manual work in a noncompetitive society. When efforts at farming were unsuccessful in supporting cultural and creative pursuits, the members became dependent upon outside help to supplement the income from their excellent school. In 1844, influenced by the socialism of Charles Fourier (1772–1837), the members converted Brook Farm into a Fourierist phalanx. Thereafter, the school was neglected, and a fire (1846) left the community insolvent; it was disbanded in 1847. The literary organs of the Brook Farm experiment were, successively, the *Dial* (1840–44), the *Phalanx* (1943–45), and the *Harbinger* (1845–49). See L. Swift, *Brook Farm: Its Members, Scholars, and Visitors* (1900); E. R. Curtis, *Season in Utopia* (1961); K. Burton, *Paradise Planters: The Story of Brook Farm* (1939).

BROOKS, PHILLIPS (1835–93), Episcopal bp. of Massachusetts, celebrated preacher. A graduate of Harvard (1855) and Virginia Theological Seminary (1895), B., then rector in Philadelphia, first came to national attention by his eulogy of President Lincoln when the latter's body lay in state. He added to his renown by distinguished service as rector of Trinity Church in Boston from 1869 until his consecration as bp. in 1891. The influence of the Anglican F. D. *Maurice is seen in B.'s positive view of tolerance; believing that denominations should receive those whom Christ does, he showed a *comprehensiveness that found agreement even with the conservative Presbyterian C. *Hodge. B. pursued interest in German theology in a year abroad (1882), and shared Lotze's conviction that truth was not gained solely by the intellectual powers. He searched constantly for ways to bring the power of ideas to bear on the human will to change human behavior. Integrity, personal conviction, and imaginative powers of inspiration through a poetic use of words were among his special gifts. In his theology he was Christocentric and liberal incarnationalist without forensic or penal views of the atonement. He preached about sin, yet proclaimed: "You can never make men see all their sins aright except by seeing rightly the very highest idea and possibility of their existence. Man has been preached to too much on the bad side. . . . the Fall has in it the capacity of Man." He shared the limitations of the optimistic age of *liberal theology. To this he added a humanistic heritage derived from 17th-cent. Anglicans and the idealism of the *Cambridge Platonists. H. *Bushnell's theory of

language and the interrelatedness of reality influenced him. The controversy over his election to the episcopate epitomized the historic tension between *high-church and *broad-church parties that polarized within Anglicanism at the time in consequence of the *Oxford movement, and it points out B.'s own representative role. Among his published lectures were *Lectures on Preaching* (1877), *Influence of Jesus* (1878), and *Lectures on Tolerance* (1887). In 1865–66 he wrote the carol "O Little Town of Bethlehem." See B. S. Clark, "P. B. in Biography," *Historical Magazine of the Protestant Episcopal Church* 31 (1962), 54–57, which compares the biography by R. W. Albright (*Focus on Infinity*, 1961) esp. with that by A. V. G. Allen (3v., 1900).

BROTHERS AND SISTERS OF THE FREE SPIRIT, designation for lay sects arising in the 13th cent. in parts of Germany, the Low Countries, Switzerland, and Italy. Their teaching stemmed from a crude pantheism; their oneness with God meant freedom from all moral restraint (see ANTINOMIANISM) and the rejection of Church and sacraments. The teachings of certain *Beghards and *Beguines that were condemned by the Council of Vienne (1312; D 891–899) were derived from the Brothers and Sisters of the Free Spirit. In spite of the Inquisition, they survived down to the Reformation; some historians attribute to them an influence on the Anabaptists. See Bihlmeyer-Tüchle 2:307–308; R. Knox, *Enthusiasm* (1950), 86–87, 100, 103, 173; R. M. Jones, *Studies in Mystical Religion* (1923), 203–216.

BROWN, WILLIAM ADAMS (1865–1943), Presbyterian clergyman and professor of theology. Educated at Yale, Union Theological Seminary, N.Y., and the Univ. of Berlin, B. taught at Union after his ordination (1893) until his retirement. Under the influence of German liberals and American pragmatists, he became an evangelical-liberal and a mediating voice in the theological debates of the period (see LIBERAL THE-

OLOGY). In 1913 he was severely criticized by the *General Assembly of the Presbyterian Church because some of his writings were regarded as too liberal. He was deeply involved in ministerial education, the work of the Board of Home Missions of the Presbyterian Church in the U.S.A., the development of the Federal Council of Churches, and in early conferences that led to the formation of the World Council of Churches. He was the author of *Essence of Christianity* (1902), the widely used textbook *Christian Theology in Outline* (1906), and the autobiographical *A Teacher and His Times* (1940).

BROWNE, ROBERT (*c.*1550–1633), "father of the Congregationalists." As a student at Cambridge, B. was influenced by T. *Cartwright's presbyterian theories on the Church. Without license or ordination B. formed his own *Nonconformist congregation at Norwich; after a prison term for this, he took his followers to Middelburg in Holland. There he published (1582) *A Book which showeth the Life and Manner of True Christians*, and *A Treatise of Reformation without Tarrying for Any*. Eventually he returned to England, submitted to the C of E, and was ordained. He was put in prison for a civil altercation, and died there. His idea that the local congregation is independent of superior civil or ecclesiastical authority was the inspiration of the Congregationalists (see INDEPENDENTS), who in their early days were often called Brownists. See C. Burrage, *True Story of R. B.* (1906); A. Peel and L. H. Carlson, eds., *Writings of Robert Harrison and R. B.* (Elizabethan Non-Conformist Texts 2; 1953).

BROWNISTS, a name given to early Congregationalists, after Robert *Browne, because of his advocacy in writing and in practice of their form of polity. *CONGREGATIONALISM.

BRUDERHOF, the German designation for the unique and efficient settlements established by *Hutterites to carry out their principle of community of goods. In the 1600s in Moravia and Slovakia, the population of a Bruderhof was about 300; but in 1951 the 96 Bruderhofs of several denominations existing in various parts of the world averaged about 100 persons each. Each Bruderhof consists of a number of houses around a common square, together with farmland, pond, mill, woods, and workshops. The ground floor of a house contains common workrooms, a kitchen, and a dining room, which also serves for the celebration of the Lord's Supper. High, steep roofs allow for two levels of small upper rooms for married couples and their young children. Each household elects a brother to act as steward to make purchases and to organize and direct work on farm and shop. See J. C. Wenger, MennEnc 1:445–448; E. Arnold, *Torches Together* (1964). *SOCIETY OF BROTHERS.

BRUDERSCHAFT "DER KÖNIG KOMMT!" (Ger., Brotherhood "The King Comes!"), a religious body founded by Hermann Kocks (d. 1949) in Duisburg, Ger., in 1946. Doctrines include elements of Pentecostalism as well as *millenarianism. Polity is congregational, and the head of each community is called an "angel." The group exists in northwest Germany.

BRUEGGLERS (Brüggeler Rotte), a pietistic-enthusiastic sect similar to the *Buttlarists and *Bordelumians. They denied the authority of the Church, and held some Gnostic teachings and practiced sexual libertinism. They were founded in 1745 in Brüggelen, Switz., by two brothers, Christian (b. 1710) and Hieronymus Kohler (1714–53), who together with a woman, Elizabeth Kissling, proclaimed themselves the Trinity, the woman being the Holy Spirit. Hieronymus was tried and executed in Bern (1753), and the group was later absorbed by the *Antonians. See M. Schmidt, RGG 1:1446–47; W. Hadorn, EncRelKnow 6:370.

BRUNNER EMIL (1889–1962), Swiss theologian, linked with Karl *Barth as pioneer proponent of *crisis theology. B. taught systematic theology at Zurich from 1924 to 1953. Through his lectures and the rapid translation of his works into English, his influence in the U.S. has been considerable. His extensive involvement in the ecumenical movement proceeded according to his concept of the Church as a noncultic fellowship of believers. B. gave early direction to the Oxford Group movement as a voluntary association based on this concept but abandoned it in 1938, when it changed into *Moral Re-Armament and lost its Christological basis.

B. manifests his debt to S. *Kierkegaard and M. *Buber in his attempt to synthesize the biblical message with an existentialist emphasis on personalism and the impossibility of a merely rational approach to God. Unlike Barth, he admitted a *natural theology, but not as a saving knowledge of God. The notion of revelation is pivotal in his theology: since saving human knowledge of God exists only insofar as God has disclosed himself, the criterion for doctrine is its correspondence to revelation, not any coherence within a theological system. Revelation is a person (Christ) and an event (the incarnation and resurrection); it transcends both dogma and the biblical "cradle" in which Christ is to be found. The word of God in the Bible is only an indirect revelation, not to be identified (as in the theory of verbal inspiration or the notion of revealed doctrine) with the word of God properly speaking. Christ is God's revelation in his continual manifestation to the man of faith. B. stresses that man can be understood only as a being-in-response. Man, as the image of God, is personally related and totally responsible to the holy, loving God. But man is also in revolt against God: he is sinfully irresponsible and must be saved by the effective action of Christ enabling man to achieve integrity through personal communion with God and his fellow men. Works in Eng. tr.: *Divine Imperative* (1937); *Man in Revolt* (1939); *Dogmatics* (3v., 1950–62); *Letter to the Romans* (1959). See C. Kegly, ed., *Theology of E. B.* (1962).

BRYANITES, a nickname for *Bible Christians, a Methodist denomination formed (1815) by William O'Bryan (1778–1868).

BUBER, MARTIN (1878–1965), Jewish religious and social philosopher. B. was born in Vienna and received his doctorate there in 1904. Following this he made an intensive study of Hasidism, which became an important influence in his life. He early became a Zionist, emphasizing however its cultural rather than its political aspects. After some years of editorial work in Vienna and Berlin he moved to Frankfurt (1923), where he taught in the Free Jewish Academy founded by F. Rosenzweig (1886–1929) and at the Univ. of Frankfurt. Forced from the latter position in 1933, he remained active in the German Jewish community until 1938, when he became professor of social philosophy at Hebrew Univ., Jerusalem, a post he held until 1951. Author of many scholarly works and, with Rosenzweig, translator of the Bible into German, he was best known for *I and Thou* (1923), a short book in a poetic, allusive style influenced by Nietzsche. He emphasized the difference between the I-thou relationship and the I-it. His view of personal relationship has influenced numerous Christian theologians, including E. *Brunner and F. *Gogarten, particularly in their views of revelation. See M. Diamond, *M. B.* (1960).

BUCER, MARTIN (Butzer; 1491–1551), leading figure in both the continental and English Reformation. He was born in Alsace, at Schlettstadt, where in 1506 he entered the Dominican Order. At Heidelberg, through Luther's disputation there in 1518, he became convinced of Reformation teaching; in 1521 he received papal dispensation from his religious vows; in Landstuhl he was excommunicated in 1523 for his Lutheran preaching. He became a pastor at Strassburg and worked with W. *Capito to implement the reform in the city. He also promoted the Reformation in Hesse, Ulm, Augsburg and elsewhere. He was one of the first priests to marry (1522); after his first wife's death (1541) he married the widow of Capito. In 1548 at the invitation of T. *Cranmer he went to England and became regius professor of divinity at Cambridge until his death. His bones were disinterred and burned during Mary Tudor's reign; but the remains were reburied at Great St. Mary's Church when Elizabeth I came to the throne.

B.'s attempts to conciliate in the disputes between the Lutheran and the Swiss segments of the Reformation brought him into disrepute with both sides. His church order at Strassburg formed the basis for the one developed at Geneva by John Calvin, who worked with B. at Strassburg, 1538–41. He also contributed to Calvin's theology of predestination. In the disputes over the Real Presence, B. was largely responsible for the conference at Marburg between Luther and Zwingli in 1527 (see MARBURG ARTICLES); he collaborated in the formulation of the *Tetrapolitan Confession (1530); and the *Wittenberg Concord (1536). His own *receptionism concerning the Real Presence attempted to mediate between the Lutheran and Zwinglian interpretations. B. participated as well in several efforts at conciliation between Protestants and Catholics both in Germany and in France. He developed a theory of the Church as an extension of the incarnation and as the true communion of saints, transforming the whole social and political sphere with works of charity and mercy. These views were contained in his chief work, *De regno Christi* (posthumous, 1557). His departure from Germany was based on the conviction that the Augsburg Interim was an interference of the State with the realm of conscience. In England B. was largely responsible both for the ordinal of 1550, which rephrased the ordination formula (see ORDINALS, ANGLICAN), and for the 1552 revision of the *Book of Common Prayer. See H. Eels, *M. B.* (1931); C. Hopf, *M. B. and the English Reformation* (1946).

BUCHMAN, FRANK NATHAN DANIEL (1878–1961), founder of *Moral Re-Armament (MRA). Born at Pennsburg, Pa., B. was an ordained Lutheran minister when he experienced a religious conversion at Keswick, Eng., in 1908. This led him to develop new evangelistic methods aimed at changing the world by changing men. He continued his religious work and study in the U.S. until 1921, when he returned to England. With university members of both Oxford and Cambridge, he formed an organization for personal and world betterment called the First Century Christian Fellowship, later (1929) the Oxford Group, and finally (1938) Moral Re-Armament. B.'s evangelical program had great success, especially among students and members of the upper classes, primarily as a way of personal holiness; at the outbreak of World War II many dissociated themselves from MRA because of disappointment with it as a way to world peace; after the war it enjoyed some resurgence, esp. as an anticommunist crusade. Throughout its history the movement has been guided fundamentally by B.'s principles: adherence to the Four Absolutes—purity, unselfishness, honesty, and love; public confession of sins as a step toward conversion; surrender to the will of Christ and to divine guidance. B. traveled widely promoting his ideas and experienced some opposition from churchmen and university authorities. His views are contained in his work *Remaking the World* (1947). See bibliog. for Moral Re-Armament.

BUCHMANISM, a name, sometimes used disparagingly, for *Moral Re-Armament (MRA), after the founder Frank *Buchman.

BUDÉ, GUILLAUME (1467–1540), French humanist who played an important role in the revival and progress of Greek studies. Proficient in theology, philosophy, mathematics, law, and medicine, he studied Greek under John Lascaris, noted Byzantine émigré humanist, and became one of the world's foremost authorities in the field. Sent by Louis XII as ambassador to Rome for the coronation of Julius II (1502) and again on a mission to Leo X (1515), he directed the Fontainebleau Library, origin of the Bibliothèque Nationale, and obtained from Francis I permission to found the Collège des lecteurs royaux (1530), which later became the Collège de France, for the study of Latin, Greek, and Hebrew. In his *Commentarii linguae graecae* (1529) he urged the study of Greek letters and departed from the scholastic spirit; however, desiring to reconcile the Renaissance spirit with Christianity, he demonstrated this possibility in his *De transitu hellenismi ad christianismum libri III* (1535). He is also author of *Annotationes in XXIV libros Pandectarum* (1508), on Roman law; *De asse et partibus eius* (1514), on Roman money, displaying his ability as philologist, archeologist, and numismatist; and *l'Institution du prince* (1547). Among his correspondents were Thomas More and Erasmus. Although B. had been one of the judges who condemned the humanist Louis de Berquin to be burned as a heretic (1529), he was for a while considered to have Calvinist leanings. After his death, his wife and two sons, Jean and Louis, converted to Calvinism, and as professor of Oriental languages at Geneva, Louis translated into French the Hebrew Psalter (1551). See J. Plattard, *G. B. et les origines de l'humanisme français* (1923).

BUGENHAGEN, JOHANN (1485–1558), a close associate of Martin Luther in the early years of the Reformation. Born at Wollim, Pomerania—thus called Pomeranus or Dr. Pomer—he was a Premonstratensian Canon, who became a well-known humanist, and was attracted to biblical studies by Erasmus. By 1521 he had embraced Lutheranism, taught at the Univ. of Wittenberg, exercised pastoral duties there, and was Luther's confidant and confessor. He was the first Reformation priest to marry (1522), and he officiated at Luther's

own marriage (1525). B. remained an enthusiastic defender of the Lutheran system, encouraged the British to join in the Reformation, and wrote strongly against Zwinglian eucharistic teaching. He helped Luther translate the Bible into German, and was commissioned to organize the Lutheran Church in the N German provinces and in Denmark. His *church orders helped shape the Reformation in those places. In 1537 he crowned King Christian III and his consort as monarchs of Denmark and consecrated seven men as superintendents (i.e., bishops) of the Lutheran Church, disregarding *apostolic succession. At Luther's funeral, he was chosen to preach the eulogy of his master, the man "through whom has Christ now conquered for nearly thirty years." See W. Tillmanns, *The World and the Men around Luther* (1954), 90–94; E. W. Zeeden, *Legacy of Luther* (tr. R. M. Bethell, 1954).

BULLINGER, HEINRICH (1504–75), Swiss reformer. His early education with the *Brethren of the Common Life and his association with the humanists at the Univ. of Cologne led to a distaste for scholasticism, a cultivation of the Fathers of the Church, esp. Augustine, and an interest in the thought of Erasmus and the theological innovations of the Reformers. While pastor of Bremgarten (1529–31) he married a former nun, Anna Adlischwiler, by whom he had 11 children. He was won to Zwinglianism through a sermon by *Zwingli at the Great Minster of Zurich and succeeded him as pastor there in 1531. B. strove particularly to achieve doctrinal concord among the Reformers. He collaborated with Calvin on the *Zurich Consensus (1549). He assisted in the formulation of the First *Helvetic Confession (1536); the Second, adopted in 1566, was his personal testimony of faith, written in 1562. The First was accepted by the Protestant cantons (excepting Strassburg and Constance); the Second won not only the approval of all the Protestant cantons but also acceptance throughout Europe and Great Britain. B. offered generous hospitality to those fleeing from the Huguenot wars in France and from the persecution of Mary Tudor. He had strong links with England; he supported the coup to seat Lady Jane Grey on the throne (1553) and later counseled Elizabeth in her dealings with the Puritans. He is the author of 12,000 letters and more than 150 works, among which are a biography of Zwingli, the *Diarium*, the *Zürcher Chronik*, and the *Decadi.* See G. W. Bromiley, ed. and tr., *Zwingli and Bullinger* (LibCC 24; 1953); O. E. Strasser, RGG 1:1510–11, bibliog.

BULTMANN SCHOOL, the theological movement of the 20th cent. that has its origin in the thought of Rudolf Bultmann, German Protestant exegete of the Univ. of Marburg. The immediate context of Bultmann's work is twofold: (1) the continued search for the "historical Jesus" on the part of Protestant biblical scholars, according to the methods of the 19th-cent. school of higher criticism (with 20th-cent. improvements or modifications); (2) the existentialist philosophy of Martin Heidegger, once a colleague of Bultmann at Marburg, whose system Bultmann has employed in his program of demythologizing the Scriptures, especially the NT. The immediate impetus for Bultmann, however, was the rethinking of Protestant positions just after World War I, which he undertook together with Karl *Barth, from whom he rather quickly dissociated himself.

The program of demythologizing takes as its point of departure the acceptance of modern man's supposed incapacity either to comprehend or to accept the "mythical" categories in which most of the NT is expressed: the cosmogony of a "three-layered" universe (the world, the underworld, and the world of heavenly beings), with man caught in the middle and acted upon or manipulated by demons from the one side and angels (and even God) from the other. Once this sort of cosmogony is put aside, a serious question arises for Bultmann as to the meaning of the Gospels, which witness to the role of Christ in history. Bultmann's exegesis is a rather devas-

tating attack on the Gospels' historicity in the ordinary sense of the word, while he makes use of Heidegger's distinction between what is *historisch* and what is *geschichtlich.* The former term qualifies a reality that takes place objectively in the physical world. The term *geschichtlich* stands for reality that has meaning for man, without regard for whether or not it occurred or exists as a physical entity. For Bultmann the word of the Gospel is *geschichtlich*; and this is verified eminently as regards the event of Jesus' resurrection. This event speaks to man in his peculiar situation in the world, a world in which he has the choice of living either inauthentically, i.e., by lending himself as an instrument of all those brute forces that determine his existence; or authentically, i.e., by faith. Thus the Heideggerian categories of authentic and inauthentic existence for man are transposed into Christian terms. Man may either live by faith or cede to the fear of death and thus deliver himself up to some form of escape. The physically historical event of Jesus' crucifixion is the paradigm of living by faith (authentic existence); and the resurrection-event (Bultmann makes no positive statements as regards its being physically historical) is the sign of the reality of the life into which man passes by facing death with Jesus. Thus it appears that, according to Bultmann, the preaching of the word in the Church is, in substance, a challenge offered to man to take Jesus as a model—but in the context of the modern world.

The influence of Bultmann (so as to constitute a school) upon theologians and Christians at large (German Lutherans in the first instance, but also Protestants and Catholics throughout the world) would be difficult to overestimate, esp. with regard to his perfecting of the "history of traditions" method of exegesis. See J. Macquarrie, *Scope of Demythologizing* (1960).

BUNTING, JABEZ (1779–1858), dominant leader of the Wesleyan Methodist Church during the first half of the 19th century. He was born in Manchester, Eng., educated at Manchester Grammar School, and became a Methodist minister in 1803. Appointed to London, he won acclaim as a preacher and founded the *Eclectic Review*. Elected president of the *conference four times, he greatly strengthened Methodist organization, promoted missionary work as secretary of the Wesleyan Missionary Society 18 years, and supported higher education, becoming first president of Wesleyan Theological Institution, Hoxton, in 1834. A rebellion *c.*1848 against his dominance eventually cost the Church 100,000 members. See T. B. Bunting, *Life of J. B.* (1859); M. Edwards, *After Wesley* (1935); W. J. Townsend et al., eds., *New History of Methodism* (2v., 1909).

BUNYAN, JOHN (1628–98), author of the *Pilgrim's Progress*. B. was born at Elstow near Bedford at a time when Puritanism was at its height. As a child his imagination was affected by sermons. At 16, when about to follow his father in the tinker's trade, he was called up on the Parliamentary side of the Civil War. He married and after an agonizing religious conversion joined a *Nonconformist group. For defying the law against lay preaching he was imprisoned for 12 years. He wrote 60 books, of which five have survived, the most famous being *Grace Abounding to the Chief of Sinners* (1666) and *The Pilgrim's Progress* (1678). See J. Brown, *J. B., His Life, Times and Work* (1883; rev. F. M. Harrison, 1928); O. E. Winslow, *J. B.* (1961); H. Talon, *J. B.: The Man and His Works* (tr. B. Wall, 1951).

BURGHERS, in Scotland members of the Associate Presbytery in the *Seceder Tradition who recognized the oath enjoined by law in 1747 on each burgess in certain cities that he "professed and allowed within his heart the true religion presently professed within the realm and authorized by the law thereof." The Anti-Burghers opposed the oath. The separation between Burghers and Anti-Burghers ended in 1820 with formation of the *United Secession Church.

BURIAL HILL CONFESSION, a Congregational statement of belief. The abandonment of the *Plan of Union (with the Presbyterians) and the end of the Civil War gave a new sense of national unity in mission to Congregationalism in the United States. A national council was formed, and met in Boston in 1865. At a session held at Burial Hill, Plymouth, agreement was reached on a declaration of faith. It was the first declaration by Congregationalists since the *Cambridge Platform (1648). Simple and brief, orthodox in content but exuberant in expression, religious rather than theological, general rather than specific, it had the merit of a generous catholicity. It was, however, comparatively little known or used.

BUSHNELL, HORACE (1802–76), American Congregationalist theologian, "father of *liberal theology" in the United States. Graduated from Yale in 1827, he studied law until he was moved at a revival meeting in 1831 to enter Yale Divinity School. Ordained in 1833 as pastor of the North Congregational Church, Hartford, Conn., B. remained there until 1859, when he resigned to devote all his time to writing. As a preacher, he was Christocentric, and Christ as the vitalizing principle was the keynote of his preaching. He drew on Jonathan *Edwards and on German idealists, esp. F. *Schleiermacher for his theological insights. On the basis of his theory that language is symbolic and imperfect, deriving full meaning from social use, he acknowledged that dogmatic and theological language is inadequate and, in the spirit of charity, hoped that different insights might be combined in comprehensive truth, so as to elevate what was science and opinion to the level of spirit and life. B. stressed the interrelatedness of human beings, esp. in the Church, and the immanence of the supernatural in the natural. His *Discourses on*

Christian Nurture (1847) defended the claim of the children of Christian parents to a share in Christian fellowship, against those who relied on revivals to bring regenerate adults into the Christian family (see CHRISTIAN NURTURE). His *God in Christ* (1849) raised a storm of controversy by acknowledging that the Trinity signified God not in his ultimate being but only in the modes by which he reveals himself as Father, Son and Holy Spirit; B. clarified his concepts in *Christ in Theology* (1851). In *The Vicarious Sacrifice* (1866) and *Forgiveness and Law* (1874), he gave his mature views on the atonement, not as vicarious expiation but as a moral example. B. was the key figure who eased the transition for evangelical Christians from the old to the new theology, by presenting them with a Christocentric theology that relied less on external proofs and rationalizations than on inward testimony and Christian experience. His *Christian Nurture* and other writings helped break down extreme individualism and directly influenced the *Social Gospel of Washington *Gladden and others. See B. M. Cross, *H. B., Minister to a Changing America* (1958).

BUTTLARISTS (Ger., Buttlarsche Rotte), a German group that carried *Pietism to excesses of libertinism. A young woman, Eva von Buttlar (1670–after 1717), left her husband in 1702 and founded a group of *Philadelphians, who were influenced by Jakob *Boehme. In expectation of the coming millennium they rejected the Church, sacraments, and marriage, and practiced unrestrained libertinism. Expelled for moral reasons by local authorities, the group had to move around considerably. Eva declared that she was the heavenly Sophia, and that she and two of her followers, the theologian J. Gottfried Winter and the medical student Georg Appenfeller, were an image of the Trinity. Eva was accused of blasphemy by the civil authorities. She and Appenfeller were married, and temporarily converted to Catholicism. The couple finally settled in Altona, where Eva is said to have died peacefully after a quiet life as a member of the Evangelical Lutheran Church. Her followers apparently disbanded. See M. Schmidt, RGG 1:1555–56; F. W. Dibelius, EncRelKnow 2:321–322.

BUTZER, MARTIN, see BUCER, MARTIN.

C

CAELICOLAE (Lat., heaven-worshipers), the members of a late 4th- and early 5th-cent. cult in N Africa. St. Augustine in 397 or 398 mentions (Ep. 44, PL 33:180) encountering them at Tubursicum, and that they had an elder *(maior)* and a new kind of baptism. In 409 the Emperor Honorius passed a law against them. Whether they were Christians, Jews, or did in fact worship the heavens, is unknown. They did not long survive. See G. Bareille, DTC 2.2088–89.

CAGOTS (also known in med. France by other names, e.g., Gahets, Capots, Crestias, Chrestians, Agots), an outcast people or class in S France who from the 13th cent. until the French Revolution were obliged to live in isolation and were denied ordinary political and social rights. They dwelt chiefly in the countryside; in towns, they were grouped together in ghetto-like areas. The reason for their segregation is unknown. It has been suggested that they were the remains of an unassimilable foreign stock, or that they were the descendants of excommunicated heretics (*Albigenses or perhaps *Beghards); however there is little evidence to support either view. More likely they were the descendants of people isolated because of contagious disease, esp. leprosy. See G. Marsot, *Catholicisme* 2:351–352.

CALIXT, GEORGE (Calixtus, Kallisen; 1586–1655), German Lutheran theologian; professor at the Univ. of Helmstädt, 1614–55. Moved by the horrors resulting from religious division in the Thirty Years' War and by contacts established with Catholics and Reformed Churches, C. devoted his life to the cause of church reunion. To achieve this purpose he proposed that differences between denominations be settled by a minimum of *credenda* (fundamental articles of faith), which would be determined according to the *consensus quinquesaecularis,* i.e., the teachings agreed on during the first 5 Christian centuries. He participated in ecumenical dialogues, notably, the Colloquy of *Thorn (1645). C.'s efforts are now often praised by ecumenists, although with reservations; Lutherans, both in his time (see CALOV, A.) and since, have charged him with a *syncretism ultimately harmful to ecumenism. In his works (e.g., *Epitome theologiae,* 1619; *Apparatus theologicus,* 1698; *Epitome theologiae moralis,* 1634) C. set out as the aim of theology not pure doctrine but Christian living, based on a message more ethical than dogmatic. See J. T. McNeill, *Unitive Protestantism* (rev. ed., 1964); R. Rouse and S. Neill, *History of the Ecumenical Movement* (2d ed., 1967).

CALIXTINES, another name for the 15th-cent. *Utraquists of Bohemia, because of their insistence that at holy communion the chalice (Lat. *calix*) be given to the laity.

CALL, God's gracious relationship toward man by which he summons man to a share in his kingdom and a participation in the redemptive graces of Christ. In Scripture, call generally refers to the summons to a particular task, e.g., the call of Matthew (Mt 9.9); but in its dogmatic use, call is the divine invitation to election and salvation (Rom 8.30). Hence, call is related to predestination in its strict and proper meaning of election to glory. In this sense it is always effectual, so that the "called" and the "elect" are co-extensive. Since the time of Augustine, ecclesiastical writers and theologians refer to a general and external call, which is the divine invitation to the privileges of the kingdom, and which men are free to accept or reject, and a special and internal call, which is the free act of the grace of God in which the divine election is revealed and realized in man. This special call has its origin in God, and Scripture refers to it as a "holy" (2 Tim 1.9) or "heavenly calling" (Heb 3.1). The term is prominent in Protestant dogmatics. It is explained as occurring when an individual, hearing or reading the word, becomes aware that God, through the illumination of the Holy Spirit, efficaciously offers him salvation. Hence, it is a divine pledge of salvation and is dependent upon *election, since God calls to salvation those whom he has elected.

*Reformed theologians distinguish two calls: an external call offered by the preaching of the word and directed to all men, and the internal or special call, the truly proper efficacious call, which, through the activity of the Spirit infallibly inculcates faith in the heart of the elect. This efficaciousness proceeds from the Spirit's power to bring about man's conversion. Lutheran theologians reject this double call as weakening the universality of God's salvific will and appearing to make his external call to the nonelect a nonserious invitation. These theologians hold that the call is given through the gospel, as mediated through word and sacrament. It expresses the earnest will of God to save all, it is adequate and sufficient for conversion if man offers no resistance to the Spirit, and it is universally offered to man. The reason why it may remain ineffectual in certain cases is rooted not in the divine will in denying the Spirit but in the fact that God recognizes man's potentiality to so actuate his selfhood that he may choose to rebuff the gospel. Though the call is at times described as the initial step in the process of salvation, it is not a once-for-all event for the Christian. It may come at any moment in life, but when it does come and gains a response, it never departs; it remains as a continuously present active power so that the Christian is "called" every day of his life. The call does not excuse the recipient from certain conditions; he must respond in faith, embrace the offering of new life, live in repentance unto regeneration, until he matures in sanctity. These conditions do not nullify the basic truth that the call is a purely gratuitous grace of God.

Call may also designate a "call to the ministry," as that movement of God inspiring an individual to the service of the word; or it may designate the "ministerial call," i.e., the invitation on the part of a congregation to a minister to become their resident pastor. In RC terminology a vocation means a call to the religious or priestly life. The call is considered to come from God, not as a direct inspiration, but through the inclinations of grace. A canonical call refers to approval of a candidate for orders by church authorities.

CALOV, ABRAHAM (Calovius, Kalau; 1612–86), German Lutheran polemical theologian. After receiving his doctorate at Rostock (1637), he was a pastor at Danzig; then from 1650 he held various scholastic and ecclesiastical offices while living at Wittenberg. At the Colloquy of *Thorn (1645) he first came in contact with G. *Calixt and thereafter made what he called the *syncretism of Calixt the target of many of his writings. His works, rigorously logical and almost always polemical, assailed not only Calixt but RC, *Reformed, Socinian, and mystical teachings as well. The *Systema locorum theologicorum* (12v., 1655–77) is a monument of orthodox Lutheran scholasticism. See A. C. Piepkorn, EncLuthCh 1:352–353.

CALVARY PENTECOSTAL CHURCH, INC., a body formed in 1931 at Olympia, Wash., by a group of preachers. They sought to set up not a distinct denomination but a simple fellowship in keeping with Pentecostal ecclesiology. Membership (8,000 in 22 churches in 1960) is greatest in the NW United States. Missions are sponsored at home and in India and Brazil. Ministers, men and women, need have no formal training but must feel a divine call before being ordained. A general superintendent, executive board, and annual general conventions conduct church affairs.

CALVIN, JOHN (1509–64), Reformer and theologian, one of the major figures of the Reformation. From him came the most incisive and systematic doctrinal formulation in early Protestantism, and his *Institutes of the Christian Religion*, which first appeared in 1536, is the major Reformation theological work. Calvin's activity centered in Geneva, but his influence dominated *Reformed Protestantism in France, the Netherlands, and Scotland and was very strong in England and in parts of Germany and central Europe. Léonard says that he organized and consolidated Protestantism, and created the "Reformed" man and the modern world.

He was born in France, at Noyon in Picardy, where his father, Gérard Cauvin, or Chauvin (Calvin is a latinized form), was a functionary in the service of the bishop and cathedral chapter. Destined by his father for a career in the Church, he was tonsured (he never received any kind of ordination throughout his life), endowed with ecclesiastical benefices, and sent to Paris at the age of 14 to study at the university. He attended the Collège de la Marche, then the Collège de Montaigu, where he received a Master of Arts degree in 1528. Undoubtedly many of his ideas were formed by his close association with Mathurin Cordier, a humanist scholar, with a cousin, Pierre Robert *Olivétan, already attracted by Lutheran teaching, with the family of Guillaume Cop, the physician of the French King. About the time that C. finished at Montaigu his father directed him to study for the more lucrative profession of law. Accordingly the young scholar went to the Univ. of Orléans (1528–29) and then to the Univ. of Bourges (1529–31), studying with some of the most eminent jurists of his day. In these years he also pursued humanist and literary interests and learned Greek from the scholar Melchior Wolmar, a Lutheran. In 1531 his father died (excommunicated because of a quarrel with the cathedral chapter over the closing of an estate), and C. terminated his studies in law to devote himself wholly to literary scholarship. He returned to Paris, attended the new trilingual college—later called the Collège de France—which Francis I founded, and in 1532 published his first work, a commentary in the humanist tradition on Seneca's *De clementia*.

Classical humanism, however, was not long to remain his chief preoccupation. Sometime in late 1533 or early 1534—the exact time and circumstance are not clear—there occurred what he once referred to as a *conversio subita*; it was not, however, a sudden conversion in a revivalistic sense. This great turning point in his life has been linked with an address his friend Nicholas Cop, rector of the Univ. of Paris, delivered on All Saints' Day, 1533. The address, containing passages from Erasmus and Luther, provoked speedy action by the authorities against Cop and others believed to be implicated. C. (who for a long time was thought to have been the real author of the discourse) fled Paris for a time, returned briefly, then left again. At Angoulême, it appears, he gathered his thoughts and arrived at his decision to break with the old Church and devote himself to the cause of Protestant reform. The Reformation had won its most formidable exponent after Luther. In May 1534 he renounced his benefices at Noyon; he left France late in 1534 or early in 1535, because of the stringent measures against Protestants, and found haven in Protestant Basel. There he entered into contact with other Swiss and Strassburg Reformers, and in March 1536, published the first draft of the *Institutes of the Christian Religion*. Prefaced by a letter to the King of France, Francis I, the *Institutes* was intended as a statement and defense of the beliefs of the persecuted French Protestants. Subsequent editions and enlargements of this magisterial work were published throughout his lifetime, the most important being those of 1539 and 1559. He returned briefly to France in 1536 to settle some family business, and in June set out once again, intending to go to Strassburg, but war between Francis I and Emperor Charles V obliged him to take a long detour, during which he stopped for the night at Geneva. There G. *Farel pleaded with him to remain and help spread the new gospel. C. reluctantly gave in, and Geneva henceforth became the center of his ministry and of his dynamic reform.

When he began this new phase in his own life and in the course of the Reformation, this city of some 13,000 inhabitants was engaged in a struggle to maintain its municipal independence against the efforts of the Duke of Savoy to reestablish control. In the course of that struggle, Protestantism, backed by neighboring Bern, had made its appearance in the city, and Farel and other preachers had won acceptance of their reforms by the municipal authorities. By Nov. 1535 the Mass had been finally suppressed. Geneva had turned from Catholicism largely for political and anticlerical reasons; the task of organizing and establishing the new *church order remained, and it was this task that Calvin now made his own. He soon rose to a position of leadership alongside the elder Farel. In Jan. 1537 they submitted to the city council for approval a set of articles on church government reflecting C.'s ideas and style. In Feb. they added an *Instruction and Confession of Faith according to the use of the Church of Geneva*, based on the *Institutes*; a short time later a confession of faith obligatory for all Genevans was appended (see GENEVAN CATECHISMS). C. planned a strict unity of belief and practice and the close supervision of conduct; he insisted that the ministers of the Church have the right to excommunicate the wayward. In early 1538 the Genevan government came under the control of men hostile to the Calvin-Farel uniformity and discipline, and in April the city council ordered the two to leave Geneva. C.'s banishment was temporary; it lasted from April 1538 to Sept. 1541, during which time C. settled in Strassburg at the invitation of M. *Bucer and took charge of a church for French Protestant refugees. His activities as pastor and theological lecturer kept him very busy. Bucer's influence on his ideas of predestination, the Church, and the ministry was very strong; and C. adapted Bucer's liturgy for use by his own congrega-

tion. In 1540 he married Idelette de Bure (d. 1549).

As division and contention continued among the rival factions at Geneva, C.'s supporters urged his recall from Strassburg. This sentiment gained ground, and in 1540, with the city government now controlled by the pro-Calvin faction, or *Guillermins*, he was officially invited to return. Resisting at first, he finally accepted and in Sept. 1541 reentered the turbulent city that had once cast him out. He remained there the rest of his life, and in this great period of his dominance Geneva became an austere stronghold of Protestant orthodoxy, the model city of a vibrant and aggressive Protestant faith. His new constitution for the Genevan church, the *Ecclesiastical Ordinances* (*Ordonnances ecclésiastiques*), was approved by the city fathers on Nov. 20, 1541, with modifications restricting the autonomy of the Church. The *Ordinances* structured the so-called *theocracy in Geneva and became the basic charter of Calvinist or Presbyterian *polity. They provided for four ministries or offices—pastors, teachers, elders, and deacons—and for a council, or consistory, of pastors and elders to maintain moral discipline and good behavior in the community. Not until 1555 did the consistory, however, gain the long-disputed right to excommunicate. To implement the *Ordinances* C. published a form for worship services, and the second of the Genevan Catechisms. A struggle to achieve conformity and rigid ecclesiastical discipline in the city ensued after 1541, and the conflicts occupied C. till the last years of his life. When Sebastian *Castellio, the college rector, quarreled with C. over certain minor doctrinal points, he was banished (1545). In a more serious encounter, C.'s vehement critic, Jacques Gruet, was beheaded (1547). In flight from France, the antitrinitarian Michael *Servetus stopped at Geneva in Aug. 1553, was arrested on C.'s demand, tried for heresy, and burned alive. During these years C. also faced the opposition of a faction known as Spiritual *Libertines, headed by Aimé Perrin. These opponents of C.'s theocratic system were finally suppressed in 1555, and thereafter his dominance was unchallenged. In the later years refugees from abroad flocked to Geneva as to the fountainhead of reform, and a more concerted effort to evangelize distant lands, particularly C.'s native France, was begun. Calvinism became a revolutionary movement of international scope toward the close of its founder's life. In spite of the sufferings of illness in his final years, he continued tirelessly to direct his Church and proclaim the scriptural word as he so sternly and dogmatically conceived it.

In addition to the *Institutes* C. continuously published theological treatises on main points of his system, and polemical works to meet challenges to his doctrine. He also wrote commentaries on most of the books of the Bible. (Key works, including the 1559 definitive edition of the *Institutes* are in LibCC 20–23.) Both in Latin and French his style was superb, his expressions precise, and his logic formidable. He displayed in his works a vast knowledge of the Fathers. For Protestantism in its second generation he deepened the reliance on the word of God (although his own exegesis was by no means always restrained by the letter of the sacred text); he also created a practical sense of cohesiveness and solid strength. To the Reformed tradition he left its distinguishing themes, the sovereignty of God, predestination, the disciplined Church, the fourfold order of ministry. His was the ideal of Church and State working together to establish God's kingdom on earth; but while he extolled obedience to a godly civil power, he established also the power of the Church and freed it from strictly national limitations. C.'s Reformed man was the active Christian, whom stern Christian virtue fitted for the modern world, the world of business. Much of Western history, esp. in the English-speaking world, from C.'s time to the 20th cent. was shaped by his theology, his political and ecclesiastical theory, and his practical administration. See F. Wendel, *Calvin* (tr. P. Mairet, 1963); J. T. McNeill, *History and Character of Calvinism* (repr., 1968); E. Doumergue, *Jean Calvin* (7v., 1899–1927); J. Calvin and J. Sadoleto, *Reformation Debate* (ed. J. C. Olin, 1966), containing C.'s important and autobiographical "Reply to Sadoleto"; Léonard HistProt 1:292–351, 411–428, bibliog. *CALVINISM; *PRESBYTERIANISM.

CALVINISM, the theological teaching of John *Calvin or, more broadly, the doctrine and way of life of the *Reformed and Presbyterian Churches. Even before Calvin's death the influence of his teachings reached beyond Switzerland. In the Palatinate the Elector Frederick III was so firmly persuaded of the virtues of Calvinism that he adopted and promoted its doctrines in his territories. In France the first national synod (1559) adopted a solidly Calvinist form of discipline and the *Gallican Confession. In the Netherlands the organization of the Reformed Church had increased particularly between 1562, when the *Belgic Confession was published, and 1574, when the first provincial synod was held. Dutch Calvinism was constantly divided from this time, partly over the Church-State issue, but particularly over *Arminianism. The Synod of *Dort (1618–19) rejected this modification of Calvinism on the doctrine of *election and approved a rationalistic expression of Calvinism in the so-called *Five Points of Calvinism. In England Calvinist ideas found acceptance among some leaders of the English Church, and during the reign of Edward VI M. *Bucer (1491–1551) proposed a system of church discipline based on Scripture. From 1570 Thomas *Cartwright (c.1535–1603) advocated Calvinist views at Cambridge with some effect; in 1572 the *Admonition to Parliament* set forth the views of English Presbyterians on the ministry, worship, and polity. In 1643 commissioners from the General Assembly of the Church of Scotland attended the *Westminster Assembly of English divines summoned to advise the Long Parliament on the form of government for a Church united on a Presbyterian basis. The *West-minster Confession follows Calvin's stress on the sovereignty of God and the authority of the Holy Spirit speaking in Scripture, and expressly teaches *double predestination. It also adds to Calvin, however, by its doctrine of two covenants, i.e., of works and of grace (see WESTMINSTER CATECHISMS). Calvinism has persisted in England in the evangelical tradition, though it never took root as strongly as it did in Scotland and later in North America (see CHURCH OF SCOTLAND; UNITED PRESBYTERIAN CHURCH IN THE U.S.A.).

The Theology of Calvinism. Classic Calvinism is marked by certain main themes.

The Sovereign Regulating Will of God. The peculiar dynamism of the Calvinist Reformation came from the dominant stress it laid upon the idea that all things are governed by God's providence. "Not only heaven and earth and the inanimate creatures, but also the plans and intentions of men, are so governed by his providence that they are borne by it straight to their appointed end" (*Institutes of the Christian Religion* 1.6.18). Fundamental to all of Calvin's thought was the conviction that his whole life was mastered by God and that no real freedom was possible until his own will was gathered up into the sovereign will of God. From this conviction Calvin derived his doctrine of election and *predestination, i.e., God's eternal decree "by which he determined with himself what he willed to become of each man. For all are not created in equal condition; rather, eternal life is decreed for some, eternal damnation for "others" (*Inst.* 3.21.5). We may not question this ineluctable will of God: "God has sufficiently just cause for election and reprobation in his own will" (*Comm. on Rom* 9.11). Merits are of no avail, worthiness is disregarded—the goodness of God reigns alone. While it seems evident that Calvin here goes beyond Scripture—despite his stated aim: "Let this be our sacred rule, . . . not to seek to know anything about it except what Scripture teaches us" (*Comm. on Rom* 9.14)—and while it is

notorious that this is the doctrinal core against which all opposition to Calvinism has been directed, it must also be borne in mind, first, that Calvin (in common with all the Reformers) based his doctrine of predestination on Augustine and earlier scholasticism; second, that his doctrine of predestination cannot be isolated from his doctrine of the Church, and both must be understood in their relation to Christ; third, that Calvin intended his teaching to be a consolation for the persecuted of France, a discipline for the undisciplined of Geneva, and also the source of his own encouragement in his "extraordinary battles." What Calvin found in the doctrine of election, in Karl *Barth's words, was "a final word on the whole reality of the Christian life, a word which tells us that the existence and the continuance and the future of that life are wholly and utterly of the free grace of God" (*Church Dogmatics,* 2.2, 86).

If Calvin's doctrine has a weakness, it is that in explaining predestination he points to God rather than to Christ. Election is a secret and absolute decree, independent of and antecedent to the person and work of Christ. Calvin can even say that election precedes grace (*Inst.* 3.22.2, 9). The darker side of the *decretum horribile,* however, came to dominate in much of later Calvinism. The Westminster Confession is typical: "By the decree of God, for the manifestation of his glory, some men and angels are predestinated unto everlasting life, and others foreordained to everlasting death" (Ch. 3). Thomas Boston of Ettrick (1676–1732) could even write: "The godly husband shall say *Amen* to the condemnation of her who lay in his bosom; the godly parents shall say *Hallelujah,* at the passing of the sentence against their ungodly child." (*Man's Fourfold State,* 4.4). Modern Calvinism has moved almost completely away from such expressions and has sought to give the work of Christ a more central place. Barth, for example, has criticized Calvin for failing to understand that the subject of the decision reached at the beginning of all things is the triune God, the Son of God no less than the Father and the Spirit, and therefore he feels it necessary to part with Calvin at this point (*Church Dogmatics*, 2.2, 60 ff., 106 ff.).

Christocentricism. Nevertheless, in common with nearly all early Protestant thought, Calvinism does have a strongly Christocentric character. "We cannot move the smallest distance from Jesus Christ without our salvation vanishing away, since it resides entirely in him" (*Inst.* 2.16.1). In all his teaching Calvin sought to bring the person and work of Christ into the center. The older confessions and catechisms of the Reformation, e.g., the Second *Helvetic Confession and the *Heidelberg Catechism, are markedly more Christological in both content and attitude than, e.g., the later Westminster Confession and Catechisms. The fundamental contention of the earlier documents is that there is one absolute authority for Church and man alike, Jesus Christ, and one covenant of grace that is completely fulfilled in Christ, who is its whole substance. The characteristic emphases of Calvinism—*solus Christus, sola gratia, sola fide,* and *sola scriptura*—are primarily Christological affirmations that the life and faith of the Church have their sole source in the person and work of Christ, and that the doctrine and practice of the Church must be subjected constantly and critically to a radical Christological correction.

Scripture As the Supreme Rule of Faith and Life. In his *Reply* to J. Sadoleto (1477–1547), who raised with Calvin the question of authority, Calvin answered: "There is no other light of truth which could direct our souls into the way of life [than Scripture]." Scripture is the only source of our knowledge of Christ, and we are not to look beyond it for guidance in faith or conduct. As the *Scots Confession (1560) states, Scripture is "sufficient to instruct and make the man of God perfite" (Art. 19). In its essential meaning, i.e., in all things necessary to be believed for salvation, Scripture is clear and certain, but it "seriously affects us," Calvin writes, "only when it is sealed upon our hearts through the Spirit" (*Inst.* 1.8.5). When he speaks of the inward testimony of the Holy Spirit, Calvin means that the Bible is authoritative because it is authenticated by the witness of the Spirit. Though he appears at times to hold a narrow doctrine of verbal inspiration and even speaks of Scripture as "produced by the dictation of the Holy Spirit" (*Inst.* 4.8.6), it is more accurate to say that Calvin related the function of the Holy Spirit in God's "authorship" of Scripture to the Spirit's function in interpreting Scripture to us. The Spirit is bound to Scripture as the medium of his revelation; Scripture and Spirit are two aspects of the same testimony (*Inst.* 1.9.3).

All ecclesiastical traditions must therefore be subservient to Scripture; indeed, on the principle of *quid non iubet, vetat* (i.e., what God does not expressly command in Scripture he forbids), Calvin and many later Calvinists insisted that the only doctrine, worship, and polity allowable are those explicitly laid out in Scripture. Doctrinally, this meant for Calvinism that theology must be grounded on the biblical revelation alone; liturgically, that the use of hymns, responses, and instrumental music is to be excluded from worship, and the Christian Year abandoned; and in polity, that the practice of the ancient Church (which for Calvin meant something like Presbyterianism) was alone permitted. In most Reformed Churches today some of these interpretations have been substantially modified, though the idea that the Church must always listen to the living word of the Spirit in the written words of Scripture has made Calvinism typically critical of any unalterable or irreformable structures of church life, formulations of faith, or forms of worship.

The Church. Following the teaching of the early Fathers, notably Cyprian and Augustine, Calvin did not hesitate to speak of the Church as essential for salvation. "Let us learn even from the simple title 'mother' how useful indeed how necessary it is that we should know her" (*Inst.* 4.1.4). To abandon the Church is to revolt from Christ also. God's covenant of grace has been since the beginning, and there has never been a time when there was not a true

Church of God in the world. There has been a "Kirk in all ages fra Adam" (Scots Confession, Art. 5; cf. Second Helvetic Confession, Ch. 17). This Church is invisible, in a sense, since only God knows his own. "The Church may be called invisible," as the Second Helvetic Confession states, "not that the men composing it are invisible, but because they are known only to God" (Ch. 17). The Church, however, is also visible and discernible, not by what the Scots Confession calls "Antiquitie, Title usurpit, lineal Descence, Place appointed, nor multitude of men approving ane error" (Art. 18), but by "the Word of God purely preached and heard, and the Sacraments administered according to Christ's institution" (*Inst.* 4.1.9). To these "certain marks and tokens" of the Church the Scots Confession added "Ecclesiastical discipline, uprightlie ministred . . . whereby vice is repressed and vertew nurished" (Art. 18). Continuity in the Church is therefore understood within Calvinism not in a static but in a dynamic and Christological way. It is constituted not by *apostolic succession or even by the ministry, but by Jesus Christ himself who calls his Church into being through the ministry, without which the Church cannot exist (cf. Second Helvetic Confession, Ch. 25). Christ is the Word which he himself proclaims—in the daring phrase of the Reformers, *praedicatio verbi divini est verbum divinum*—and the minister of his own sacraments of baptism and the Supper. The means by which Christ calls his Church into being and sustains it is the ministry of word and sacraments. This ministry, however, is distinguished from the *priesthood of all believers. The real continuity of the Church is guaranteed, therefore, only if the ministerial continuity corresponds to doctrinal continuity, and apostolic continuity without reference to doctrine is a "vain pretense." Above all the Church is a community—"the society of all the saints which, spread over the whole world, and existing in all ages, yet bound together by one doctrine, and the one Spirit of Christ, cultivates and observes unity of faith and brotherly concord" (*Reply to Sadoleto*). If, then, as Calvin affirms, the Church is one, holy, catholic, and apostolic, on what grounds did he justify the Reformation? He answered the question by calling the Romanists to contemplate the ruins of the Church surviving among themselves. They were the schismatics; for among them, he observes to Sadoleto, "the light of divine truth had been extinguished, the Word of God buried, the virtue of Christ left in profound oblivion, and the pastoral office subverted." Calvin's view of the Church is marked by what would today be called a strong and comprehensive ecumenism. Because the Church lives in Christ, its unity is not only commanded by him but also given by him, and through the Lord's Supper we are "forged into one body with Christ" (*Inst.* 4.17.2). Though it must be conceded that later Calvinism is notoriously divisive, an ecumenical openness has nevertheless been typical of Calvinism at its best. As J. T. McNeill says, "the idea of catholic unity dominated the church theory of Calvin" (*Unitive Protestantism* [1964], 217). His was an ecumenism not simply of space (i.e., of those Churches now found throughout the world) but also of time. The Church is one with what the Scots Confession calls "the Elect of all ages, of all realmes, nations and tongues," but it also includes "the Elect that be departed, commonlie called the Kirk Triumphant" (Art. 16).

Obedience to God in the Political Order. Church and State, to use the definition of Marc-Édouard Chenevière (*La Pensée politique de Calvin*, 1937), are two complementary institutions, aiding but distinct from one another, each with its own sphere of work and its proper mission. In general, it may be said that Calvinism has exhibited a firm respect for law and order, a deep antipathy toward any kind of political authoritarianism, and a resolute commitment to religious freedom. In particular, the following characteristics may be noted: (1) The duty of the State is to preserve order and promote piety. The magistrate as much as the minister has been called by God to his office, and Christians may therefore legitimately seek political office and express their faith in civil responsibilities. (2) Though Calvin himself favored as the ideal form of government a combination of aristocracy and democracy, one of the distinctive strengths of Calvinism has been its resilience under varying political forms. The democratic and representative character of the Reformed Church in France probably enabled it to survive the early persecutions up to the *Edict of Nantes (1598). (3) Calvin allowed the possibility of passive resistance to tyranny, though only cautiously and as a last resort. In more recent years the role and resistance of the *Confessing Church in Germany under Hitler testify to the vigor of the Calvinist commitment to religious freedom. The *Barmen Declaration (1934), which climaxed the church struggle in Germany, was a notable modern attempt by Lutheran and Reformed Christians to take their stand in the word of God against a hostile ideology. (4) Calvinism has attempted, though with obvious failures, to seek to obey the will of God within the political order. The *theocracy of Geneva and the Puritanism of New England both demonstrate the Calvinist axiom that the life of faith and the political sphere alike are to be regulated by the word of God. At a time when the pulpit still molded public opinion and clergymen were often presidents and leading professors in colleges, John Witherspoon (1723?–94), a Presbyterian minister, president of the College of New Jersey (now Princeton), and the only clerical signer of the Declaration of Independence, taught moral philosophy to numbers of future American statesmen, among them James Madison (1751–1836). Witherspoon's political teaching was based upon the Calvinist emphasis on God's sovereign rule over the whole of life, his confidence in human ability under God, and a suspicion of man's sinfulness that led him to favor a government of checks and balances and a separation of powers. This kind of approach to government has been aptly summarized by a contemporary theologian, Reinhold *Niebuhr, who draws on the broad Calvinist tradition when he says:

"Man's capacity for justice makes democracy possible; but man's inclination to injustice makes democracy necessary" (*The Children of Light and the Children of Darkness* [1960], xi).

Modern Theological Developments. In *The Nature of the Atonement* (1855), John McLeod Campbell attacked, on the one hand, the hyper-Calvinism that subordinated everything to the arbitrary act of God in election and substituted a legal for a filial relationship to God, and, on the other hand, the religious subjectivism that failed to take seriously the saving significance of the human obedience of Christ. The logical determinism that Campbell opposed persisted in the 19th and 20th cents. in the extreme evangelical form of fundamentalism and the radical secular form of positivism (Hegel, Marx, et al.), while subjectivism persisted in the influence of F. *Schleiermacher's pietism and the liberal quest for the historical Jesus. In the 20th cent. three major theologians in the general Reformed tradition have helped to turn Protestant theology in a different direction. In Zurich, where he was professor of systematic theology from 1924, Emil *Brunner opposed the Calvinist orthodoxy and idealistic liberalism of the 19th cent. in his *crisis theology and contributed major works to the new debate—*The Mediator* (Eng. tr., 1934), and *Man in Revolt* (Eng. tr., 1939). Karl Barth, in his *Church Dogmatics*, opposed both hyper-Calvinism and the older liberalism with a Christological concentration of breadth, scope, and balance. Barth forced theologians to contemplate anew the full humanity of Jesus Christ—what Calvin expressively called "the vivifying flesh of Christ"—and insisted that dogmatic theology must be grounded on the reality and norm of the incarnate Word of God; he was also a truly ecumenical theologian who spoke a theological language increasingly understood by Catholic and Protestant alike. In the U.S. the publication of *The Nature and Destiny of Man* (2v., 1941–43) by Reinhold Niebuhr was an attempt to relate Reformation theology to the problems of human existence, and in Niebuhr's works the impact of *neo-orthodoxy has been brought to bear in a distinctive way on U.S. theology and political life. See F. Wendel, *Calvin* (1963); W. Niesel, *Theology of Calvin* (1956); E. A. Dowey, *Knowledge of God in Calvin's Theology* (1952); J. T. McNeill, *History and Character of Calvinism* (repr., 1968); Léonard HistProt 1:420–428, bibliog.

CALVINISTIC METHODIST CHURCH (Presbyterian Church of Wales), a Church that originated through the revivalistic preaching of certain men, who, though associated with John *Wesley, rejected his *Arminianism. H. *Harris, G. *Jones, and others were successful in their preaching in Wales and established many *societies of the Methodist type; in 1743 these were organized as the Welsh Calvinistic Methodists, with George *Whitefield as first (and nominal) moderator. The initial success was followed first by decline, then by a new growth c.1790. Until that time the societies remained within the C of E, but persecution led in 1795 to the first steps toward separation. The Church first ordained its own ministers in 1811; in 1823 a confession of faith, patterned on the *Westminster Confession, was adopted; in 1864 the first general assembly of the Church was held. Total autonomy was formally guaranteed by the Calvinistic Methodist or Presbyterian Church of Wales Act (1933). The polity of the Church is through associations, similar to Methodist *conferences. Membership in 1968 was 187,651, in 1,601 congregations. See W. Williams, *Welsh Calvinistic Methodism* (1872); M. W. Williams, *Creative Fellowship* (1935).

CAMBRIDGE PLATFORM, a 1648 statement of organization for Congregational Churches. In 1646 the General Court of the Massachusetts Colony called a synod of representatives of the Churches of the four confederated New England colonies— Massachusetts Bay, Hartford, New Haven, and Plymouth. Three sessions were held in Cambridge in that year and the next 2 years. At the last session there was adopted *A Platform of Church Discipline*, known historically as the Cambridge Platform. "The Cambridge Platform is the most important monument of New England Congregationalism, because it is the clearest reflection of the system as it lay in the minds of the first generation on our soil after twenty years of practical experience" (W. Walker, *The Creeds and Platforms of Congregationalism*, 1893). It was not a doctrinal confession but a practical plan based on four principles: the autonomy of the *local church; the representative character of the ministry; the covenant relationship of church membership; and the obligation of fellowship and friendly counsel with other churches. *CONGREGATIONALISM; *COVENANT THEOLOGY.

CAMBRIDGE PLATONISTS, a group of philosophical divines, mostly from Emmanuel, a distinctly Protestant college by foundation and tradition. Under the *Commonwealth and the *Restoration they stood rather aloof from the warring ecclesiologies of Puritans and high Anglicans; they advocated policies of tolerance and *comprehensiveness and taught a rational illuminism deriving from neoplatonism, early and medieval, and influenced by Descartes. The judgment of reason, the arbiter of both natural and revealed religion, depended on a man's being *dikaios* and *agathos*, upright and good at heart; it was the light in our world by virtue of God's indwelling in the mind. The group, which seems to have originated with N. Culverwel, included B. *Whichcote, R. *Cudworth, and H. *More. They breathed a spirit of piety and charity, at once gentle and confident, in an atmosphere of general *odium theologicum*, and this spirit is still alive among Anglicans with scientific interests who would set themselves down neither as strong sacramentalists nor as muscular Christians. See J. Tulloch, *Rational Theology and Christian Philosophy in the Seventeenth Century* (2v., 1872); F. J. Powicke, *Cambridge Platonists* (1926).

CAMERARIUS, JOACHIM (Kammermeister; 1500–74), German Lutheran humanist and biographer. C. joined the Erfurt circle of humanists in 1518. In 1521 he went to Wittenberg and became in time *Melanchthon's favorite pupil. After teaching in Nuremburg and Tübingen (1526–41), C. moved to Leipzig, where he reorganized the university. Striving for Lutheran unity, he endeavored to gain acceptance for the *Augsburg Confession and to mediate in the controversies aroused by A. *Osiander's theory on justification. He was the earliest biographer of Melanchthon and the author of many philological, historical, pedagogical, and biographical works. Ludwig Camerarius (1573–1651), a statesman prominent in the Thirty Years' War, was his grandson. See R. H. Fischer, NCE 2:1105; F. Lau, RGG 1:1602.

CAMERON, JOHN (1579–1625), Calvinist theologian. A native of Scotland, educated at the Univ. of Glasgow, C. spent most of his professorial career at the theological academy of Saumur, in France, where he succeeded F. *Gomarus in 1618. C.'s views on predestination and grace influenced the so-called "hypothetic universalism" of M. *Amyraut. *HELVETIC CONSENSUS FORMULA.

CAMERONIANS, those Presbyterians in Scotland named for Robert Cameron (1648–80), who resisted when Charles II began after the Restoration (1660) to impose his authority on the Church and restore *episcopacy. In the Southwest Cameron and others who disassociated themselves from "the unfaithful, silent complying ministers of the times," made public both their *covenanting loyalty and their opposition to royal tyranny, in the Sanquhar Declaration of 1680. Cameron himself was slain by dragoons in that same year, when the "killing times" began. The Cameronians, calling themselves the "Witnessing Remnant of the True Presbyterian Church in Scotland," are best known from 1712 as the Reformed Presbyterian Church. This body was united with the Free Church in 1876. Strongly nationalistic, holding to the divine right of Presbyterianism, and embracing a narrow evangelical faith, the Cameronians left a distinctive mark on later Presbyterianism. See P. Walker, *Six Saints of the Covenant* (repr., 1901), 1:218–365.

CAMISARDS, French Calvinist extremists who revolted against the attempt of Louis XIV to suppress the *Reformed faith. The curtailment of Huguenot worship that followed the revocation of the *Edict of Nantes in 1685 and the growth of *apocalypticism, inspired largely by the writings of Pierre Jurieu, gave rise to a resistance movement in southern France. In the Cévennes and neighboring areas c.1700 a variety of prophets were claiming direct divine inspiration, and their predictions of doom were accompanied by ecstasies, trances, and convulsions. The Camisards broke into open revolt in 1702, assassinating a priest who had imprisoned some Huguenots and fighting with a fanatical ferocity against the RC Church and its priests. Government forces retaliated with similar cruelty until the revolt was suppressed in 1704. A subsequent outbreak in 1709 was quickly put down. Some Camisards fled to England, where they were known as "French prophets," and to Germany. The movement was disavowed and its religious pretensions condemned by many leading French Huguenots, but the spectacle of revolt was used by the government to justify the reinforcement of its severe policy in regard to the Huguenots. Because of the occurrence of *glossolalia and ecstatic experiences among the Camisards, they are sometimes considered among the antecedents of modern Pentecostals. See H. Baird, *Huguenots and the Revocation of the Edict of Nantes* (2v., 1895); A. Ducasse, *La Guerre des Camisards* (1946); R. Knox, *Enthusiasm* (1950) 357–370.

CAMP MEETING, a frontier revivalistic method originating in Logan Co., Ky., c.1800, during the *Second Great Awakening, when Presbyterian and Methodist ministers organized a 4-day sacramental meeting. To accommodate the throngs of people, meetings were held outdoors. Each minister preached, and many people were visibly affected and converted. Soon similar meetings became common. Preachers of every denomination exhorted crowds simultaneously, and conversions were accompanied by emotional stress expressed in shouting, weeping, and various other physical manifestations. The Methodists institutionalized the camp meeting, changing it eventually to an annual inspirational summer conference. See C. A. Johnson, *Frontier Camp Meeting: Religion's Harvest Time* (1955). *REVIVALISM.

CAMPBELL, THOMAS and ALEXANDER, father and son, leaders of an American reform movement that issued in the Christian Churches (Disciples of Christ).

Thomas (1763–1854), father of Alexander, was reared in Co. Down, northern Ireland, as an Anglican. He was converted to Seceder Presbyterianism and educated for its ministry at the Univ. of Glasgow and the Seceder Seminary at Whitburn, Scotland (see SECEDER TRADITION). He established an academy and served a pastorate in Co. Armagh until emigration to western Pa. in 1807. Disciplined by his *synod for anti-Calvinist teachings and for "unfencing" the communion table, he renounced its authority and organized the Christian Association for promoting church unity, writing his now classic ecumenical document *Declaration and Address* (1809), which proclaimed that the Church is "essentially, intentionally, and constitutionally one." He relinquished leadership of the new movement to his son, but continued his ministry, established academies in Pa. and Ky., and assisted his son in editing religious publications. See biographies by his son (1861); W. H. Hanna (1935); L. G. McAllister (1954).

Alexander (1788–1866), son of Thomas, born in Co. Antrim. He renounced communion with Seceder Presbyterians while a student at the Univ. of Glasgow. Joining his father in Pa. in 1809, he became part of the Christian unity movement. He settled on his farm, later called Bethany, in what is now W. Va.; ordained in 1812, he soon assumed leadership in the movement begun by his father. After several years' connection with the Baptist Association, the adherents by 1830 were forced into separate communion. He propagated the principles of the Disciples in lecture tours; in notable debates with the Socialist Robert Owens (1829) and RC Bp. John Purcell (1837); and in 55 volumes published by his Bethany Press, as well as in two monthlies, the *Christian Baptist* (1823–30) and the *Millennial Harbinger* (1830–64). From 1840 he was founder, president, and professor of Bethany College, which provided free education to ministerial students. Inspired by the *Enlightenment and John Locke, the American system and Thomas Jefferson, he advocated a system of church government embracing both local autonomy and organic unity, freedom and order, through democratically delegated authority and elective assemblies. His theology combined high, or Catholic, doctrines of the Church and sacraments with Protestant emphasis on the *priesthood of all believers and acceptance of St. Peter's confession of faith in Mt 16.16 as the only prerequisite for Christian communion. Although he opposed slavery, his stand for tolerance and reason prevented schism among the Disciples on this issue. He fostered advance of the ecumenical movement, from new Bible translations to evangelical alliances, favoring organic rather than federal plans of union and forecasting eventual cooperation between American Protestants and Roman Catholics. See P. Gresham, ed., *Sage of Bethany: A Pioneer in Broadcloth* (1960); E. J. Wrather, *Creative Freedom in Action: A. C. on the Structure of the Church* (1968).

CAMPBELLITES, early members of the Christian Churches (Disciples of Christ) named from their leaders, T. and A. *Campbell. The name has always been unacceptable to the Disciples of Christ themselves.

CANADIAN COUNCIL OF CHURCHES, an organization formed in 1944 as an agency for cooperation among member Churches. It is the authorized counterpart in Canada of the *World Council of Churches, and has the same basis for membership, acceptance of "Our Lord Jesus Christ as God and Saviour." Member bodies are: the Baptist Federation of Canada, Evangelical United Brethren, Presbyterian Church in Canada, Reformed Episcopal Church, United Church of Canada, Salvation Army, and Society of Friends. The Council has no legislative authority over participating bodies but serves as an instrument for their common interests and concern. Biennial meetings are held; an executive council carries on interim administration of the departments of Christian Education, Ecumenical Affairs, Evangelism, Overseas Missions, and Social Relations. Headquarters are in Toronto, Ontario.

CANADIAN LUTHERAN COUNCIL, a cooperative agency of Lutherans in Canada. It was organized in 1952 at Winnipeg, when representatives of Canadian Lutheran Churches adopted a constitution modeled on the National Lutheran Council (U.S.A.). The council grew out of the need for cooperation in ministering to military personnel in World War II. The members of the Canadian Council are: The American Lutheran Church, the Augustana Lutheran Church, the Evangelical Lutheran Church, the Lutheran ·Free Church, the United Evangelical Lutheran Church, and the United Lutheran Church in America. The council has five divisions: Canadian Missions, Public Relations, Welfare, Student Service, and War Service. See W. A. Mehlenbacher, EncLuthCh 1:361–362.

CANONS OF DORT, the five "heads of doctrine" issued by the Synod of Dort (1619) against *Arminianism. A technical and scholastic presentation of Calvinist doctrine on predestination and grace, they became normative for many *Reformed Churches. *DORT, SYNOD OF.

CAPITO, WOLFGANG FABRICIUS (1478–1541), Reformation theologian. Capito is the Latinized form of the family name, Köpfel. When still a Catholic priest, C. was a preacher at Basel and Mainz, where he also became chancellor of the archbishop. He was a friend of Erasmus and entered into correspondence with Luther and Zwingli. C. obtained an ecclesiastical appointment at Strassburg in 1523, but soon became a Reformer. His chief service to the Reformation was the effort to moderate theological differences between Lutherans and Zwinglians, esp. in regard to the Holy Eucharist. Thus he collaborated with M. *Bucer on the *Tetrapolitan Confession (1530) and the Concord of *Wittenberg (1536). He published a *Responsio de Missa* (1537) and *Hexaemeron Dei* (1539). See O. E. Strasser, *La Pensée théologique de W. C.* (1938); R. Stupperich, RGG 1:1613.

CAPPEL, LOUIS (1585–1658), a Calvinist theologian and exegete. Prof. at the theological academy of Saumur from 1613, C. developed a theory opposed to the literal inspiration of Scripture. In his many works he pursued a textual criticism that took into account the Septuagint and other Bible versions and showed that the Massoretic Hebrew text should not be regarded as sacrosanct. Articles 1–3 of the *Helvetic Consensus Formula were directed against his ideas. See Schaff Creeds 1:479–480.

CAPUTIATI, a name applied to several groups because of some special association with the cowl or hood (Lat. *caputium*). Among these were: (1) A lay-confraternity, founded *c.*1182 by the carpenter Durando Chaduiz at Le Puy in the Auvergne. He claimed that in a vision the Blessed Virgin commissioned him to promote peace, thus his followers were also called *Paciferi* (Lat., peace-bearers). They wore a white habit and a hood with an image of the Virgin attached. The confraternity attracted many members to a life of poverty and simplicity. These Caputiati played an important part in overcoming the marauding bands of mercenaries called *routiers* (see COTEREAUX), but their history was brief because they fell out of favor with the nobility. There is no evidence that they held doctrines contrary to the teaching of the Church. (2) A violent, iconoclastic faction of *Lollards, led by an ex-Augustinian, Peter Pateshull, in 1387. They kept their heads covered with the cowl in the presence of the Blessed Sacrament. (3) A group of Spanish Franciscan Observants, led by Juan de Guadalupe and approved by Alexander VI in 1496. They lived an eremitic life and wore a distinctive cowl as part of their habit. See F. Courtney, NCE 3:94; L. Spatling, EC 3:715; F. Vernet, DTC 2:1695-96.

CAREY, WILLIAM (1761-1834), a Baptist missionary, born in Northamptonshire, England. After serving an apprenticeship, he became a shoemaker. Converted at 17, he joined the Baptists at 22 and was ordained 4 years later. Through reading *Captain Cook's Voyages*, geography books, and biographies of John Eliot and David Brainerd, he became concerned about the unsaved millions around the world and helped found the *Baptist Missionary Society (1792). Sent to India by that organization, he became a pioneer missionary who has been called "the father of modern missions." After 6 years, he and several associates founded a missionary colony at Serampore. Here they became self-supporting through operating schools, printing for the government, and Carey's work as professor of Bengali at Fort William College. Having a gift for languages, Carey had learned Greek, Hebrew, Latin, Dutch, and French before leaving England. In India he mastered Bengali, Sanskrit, and Hindustani, as well as a number of dialects. Besides his services in spreading Christianity, his chief contributions were the establishment of Serampore College, translation of the Bible into numerous Indian tongues, publication of grammars and dictionaries in six Indian languages, establishment of the first Indian newspaper, helping to abolish infanticide and suttee (the custom prescribing that a widow must die at the time of her husband's funeral), and encouragement of agricultural improvements through his Horticultural Society. See S. P. Carey, *William Carey, D.D., Fellow of Linnaean Society* (1923).

CARLSTADT, ANDREAS RUDOLF, see KARLSTADT, ANDREAS RUDOLF BODENSTEIN VON.

CAROLINE DIVINES, Anglican theological writers who, esp. in the 17th cent., stressed RC elements in Anglicanism as essentials. They defended episcopacy, ritual, and the doctrine of the Real Presence. Among those so classified were Richard *Hooker, Lancelot *Andrewes, William *Laud, and Jeremy *Taylor, but there were many others. The classification, despite the name, is not restricted to theologians who wrote during the reign of Charles I (1625-49) or of Charles II (1660-85). See G. Albion, NCE 3:133-134, for complete list and for bibliog.

CARPZOV, surname of a German family of theologians and lawyers who served the cause of Lutheranism in the 17th and 18th centuries. (1) Benedikt (1595-1666), professor of law at Leipzig from 1645 until his death. B. was the first to give methodical arrangement to German criminal law and to prepare a complete system of Protestant church law. He was an implacable opponent of G. *Calixt. (2) Johann Benedikt I (1607-57), theologian, brother of the preceding. He served as archdeacon at St. Thomas, Leipzig, and as professor of theology at the university there. His elucidation of the Lutheran confessions gained him the title of father of symbolics. (3) Johann Benedikt II (1639–99), theologian, son of the preceding. Professor of ethics and later of theology at Leipzig, he also worked as pastor and editor. His revision of his father's homiletic manual led him to oppose *Pietism. The bitter enmity in which he held Philipp *Spener was rooted partly in the latter's criticism of the theological training imparted at Leipzig. (4) Samuel Benedikt (1647–1707), court chaplain at Dresden, brother of the preceding. He became court preacher at Dresden as early as 1674. Called to the Kreuzkirche and later made superintendent, he was well disposed toward the Pietists until his brother became leader of the opposition and persuaded him to change his attitude. (5) Johann Gottlob (1679–1767), theologian, son of Johann Benedikt II. Most learned of the Carpzovs, he was pastor at Dresden and professor of Hebrew at Leipzig. He wrote a valuable introduction to OT studies (1714–20), which maintained the verbal inspiration of the Scriptures and opposed the rising rationalist biblical studies. (6) Johann Benedikt V (1720–1803), classical scholar and theologian, grandson of Johann Benedikt II. Professor of Greek at Helmstädt and editor of classical texts, he wrote *Liber doctrinalis theologiae purioris* (1768) to oppose the rationalism of Albrecht Teller. See I. Ludolphy, EncLuthCh 1:370–371.

CARTHAGE, COUNCILS OF, synods held in the city of Carthage, in North Africa. Christian Carthage from the 3d until the 6th cent. held ecclesiastical primacy in North Africa. From the time of the episcopate (248–258) of St. Cyprian, a number of provincial councils were held in Carthage, some of them of more than local importance. Several of the councils convoked by Cyprian dealt with the reconciliation of the *lapsi*; the practice of granting sacramental reconciliation to repentant apostates became universal, but not the view that baptism administered by heretics was invalid. The most important councils of Carthage were those held under Bp. Aurelius (391–429) with the active participation of St. Augustine. Some of them dealt with the *Donatists, esp. on the rebaptism of those who had been baptized by heretics. By far the most important teaching condemned at these councils was *Pelagianism, which denied the Fall, original sin, and the need of grace and therefore called into question a basic Christian truth, men's need of Christ the Redeemer. The 15th (or 16th) Council of Carthage (May 418), at which 214 African bps. met, promulgated 8 (or 9) canons on original sin and grace (D 222–230). Pope Zosimus's encyclical letter to the East (D 231) may not have had the force, generally attributed to it, of raising these canons to the status of infallible decisions; nor perhaps did their approval at the subsequent council of Carthage, 418, in the presence of papal delegates. But in actual fact they have had a decisive influence on the theology of grace. They were resumed and sanctioned at the Second Council of Orange (529) and again, 10 centuries later, at the Council of Trent (D 1511–12, 1551–53). With the Vandal conquest of North Africa (429) the era of the great African councils came to an end. See C. M. Aherne, NCE 3:160–161; P. Fransen, LTK 6:3–4.

CARTWRIGHT, PETER (1785–1872), pioneer Methodist evangelist on the American frontier. His family moved in his childhood to Ky., where he was converted at a Methodist *camp meeting in 1802. He was licensed to preach soon afterward and was commissioned to organize a new circuit in western Kentucky. He was ordained a deacon in 1806 and an elder in 1808. C. was one of the Methodist circuit riders of the frontier country, tirelessly traveling over Ky., Ind., and Ill., holding meetings and establishing new churches; he received over 12,000 into the Methodist Church. A lifelong foe of slavery, he moved in 1824 to Sangamon County, Ill., and served in the state legislature in 1828 and again in 1832. He was influential in the movement to establish public school systems in the young state and was a founder of Illinois Wesleyan University. In his old age he traveled as far as Boston on evangelistic tours. His *Autobiography* (new ed., 1956) inspired Methodists of later generations. See H. H. Grant, *P. C., Pioneer* (1931).

CARTWRIGHT, THOMAS (*c.*1535–1604), leader of the Elizabethan Puritans and the chief exponent of Presbyterianism in England, C. was educated at Cambridge. There in 1567–68 he "preached vehemently against the surplice," and from 1569, when elected Lady Margaret professor of divinity, he sought to reform the existing ecclesiastical *polity of the C of E according to the Geneva model of discipline and government. Should the Church fail to reform itself, he taught, the magistrate must assume the enforcement of godly discipline. The *Admonition to Parliament* (1572), which he supported, and his translation of Walter Travers's *Disciplina ecclesiastica* are important statements of English Puritanism. Despite opposition, exile, and imprisonment, C.'s influence was strong. See A. F. Pearson, *T. C. and Elizabethan Puritanism, 1535–1695* (1925).

CASSANDER, GEORG (*c.*1513–66), Flemish lay theologian, liturgist, and humanist. After becoming a master of arts at Louvain, C. began teaching antiquities at Bruges in 1532. Later he lectured at Ghent. In 1544 he transferred to Cologne for study, but at the request of the Duke of Cleves he went to Duisberg to work toward reconciling the Anabaptists. There he became the first director of the academy founded in 1549. Confident of restoring Christian unity, he labored from 1561 until his death to unite Catholics and Protestants in Ferdinand I's territories, but his efforts pleased neither side. His first anonymous treatise, *De officio pii ac publicae tranquillitatis vere amantis viri in hoc religionis dissidio* (1561), was attacked by Calvin and by both Catholics and Protestants at the Conference of *Poissy (1561). His writings, accepting clerical marriage and communion under both

kinds, were placed on the Lisbon Index in 1581. Another collection of his works, when published posthumously at Paris (1616), were likewise opposed by Rome. C. minimized creedal differences, particularly in the doctrines of original sin, the Lord's Supper, and justification. His hope was to achieve consensus on the doctrines contained in the Apostles' Creed. It is recorded that he retracted his teachings on his deathbed and forbade publication of his last writings; but his friends did not honor his wishes. C. contributed to the primitive science of liturgics by his essay on the liturgy for the celebration of the Lord's Supper (1556) and his *Ordo romanus de officio Missae* (1558). See J. Lecler, *Toleration and the Reformation* (tr. T. L. Westow, 2v., 1960); N. N. Huyghebaert, NCE 3:180.

CASSIAN, JOHN (*c.*360–*c.*435), monk, priest, spiritual writer. After some years in a monastery at Bethlehem, C. studied the religious life in Egypt, was ordained deacon at Constantinople by John Chrysostom (*c.* 400), and some 4 years later came to Rome to enlist the aid of Pope Innocent I for the exiled Chrysostom. Probably in 414 or 415, after ordination to the priesthood, C. went to Marseilles, where he founded two monasteries, one for men and the other for women. The rules of these monasteries are not extant, but their tenor may be deduced from the founder's ascetical writings. The *Institutes* in 12 books set forth external observances (Bks. 1–4) and discuss the eight principal vices opposed to religious perfection and the remedies to overcome them (Bks. 5–12). The *Conferences*, tripartite and consisting of 24 conferences in all, were greatly admired for their edifying content. They were recommended by authorities on the monastic life and enjoyed great popularity as spiritual reading throughout the Middle Ages, despite the fact that C.'s doctrine, esp. in Conferences 3, 5, and 13, was patently Semipelagian (see SEMIPELAGIANISM). C.'s third work, *Against Nestorius on the Incarnation of the Lord*, was written at the request of a Roman archdeacon, later Pope Leo I; C. contended that Nestorianism was derived from Pelagianism. See O. Chadwick, *J. C.: A Study in Primitive Monasticism* (1950); P. Godet, DTC 2.2:1823–29; M. Olphe-Galliarde, DSAM 2:214–276.

CASSIANISTS, a small group in 9th-cent. Spain, teaching an *Adoptionism similar to that of *Migetius.

CASTELLIO, SEBASTIAN (1515–63), a French Reformer. Educated in the humanist tradition, he was a noted classical scholar and champion of religious toleration. Becoming acquainted with Calvin at Strassburg in 1540, he was persuaded the following year to move to Geneva, where he headed the academy there. In 1544, he became alienated from Calvin, who refused his request to be ordained a minister. Although Castellio had volunteered to minister to plague victims when other ministers feared to do so, his ordination was denied because he questioned the inspiration of the Song of Solomon and disagreed with Calvin's interpretation of the phrase "descended into hell" in the Apostles' Creed. Moving to Basel in 1545, he lived in dire poverty until his appointment in 1553 as professor of Greek. He was eventually (1553) appointed professor of Greek. Among his works were a collection of Bible stories in classical Latin and both a Latin and a French translation of the Bible, the Latin in classical, the French in popular style. Advocating toleration of diverse religious opinions, he criticized Calvin's part in the burning of Servetus (1553) in a pseudonymous work, *Concerning Heretics*. This book, one of the earliest and most articulate defenses of religious liberty, evoked rejoinders from Calvin and T. *Beza. See F. Buisson, *S.C., sa vie et son oeuvre* (2v., 1892); R. Bainton, *Studies on the Reformation* (1963); Leonard HistProt 1:430–431, bibliog.

CATAPHRYGIANS (Phrygians), a title used by a number of early ecclesiastical writers, e.g., Eusebius and St. Epiphanius, to designate the *Montanists, a prophetic and chiliastic movement founded by *Montanus in Phrygia in the latter part of the 2d cent. and persisting into the 9th.

CATECHISM (Gr. *katechein*, cause to be heard; hence, instruct orally), the act of instructing in Christian doctrine, but esp. a book presenting such instruction, usually in question-and-answer form. The first use of the term to mean a book was probably by Lutheran authors *c.*1528, but instruction given in the early Church to catechumens in preparation for baptism is reflected in many writings (e.g., the *Didache*, Irenaeus' *Epideixis*, Tertullian's exposition of the Lord's Prayer). St. Augustine's *De catechezandis rudibus* and *Enchiridion* shaped catechetical instruction in the West, esp. as to the organization of material under the headings of the Creed, the Our Father, and the Commandments; by the 13th cent. sections on the sacraments and the Hail Mary were added. The *Disputatio puerorum per interrogationes et responsiones*, attributed to Alcuin, and the *Catechesis Weissenbergensis* were 9th-cent. catechisms for the clergy and literate laity. Throughout the Middle Ages there were manuals for parish priests to use in imparting instruction to the illiterate by oral repetition. St. Thomas Aquinas's *Compendium theologiae* (1272–73) and his instructions on the Creed, the Our Father, the Hail Mary, and the Commandments may be regarded as adult catechisms. John *Wycliffe prepared expositions of the Creed, the Commandments, and the Lord's Prayer for use in the family. In 1420 J. Gerson wrote *L'ABC des simples gens*; the *Cathecyzon* (*c.* 1510) by J. *Colet was the attempt of a humanist at a more Bible-centered catechism in contrast to medieval compilations on Christian conduct and sins.

The era of the Reformation formed the catechetical tradition that prevailed until recent times. On the Protestant side, the catechisms of the Hussites (1426–36) and of the Moravian Brethren (*c.*1502) influenced

Martin Luther. In 1529 he published his *Smaller Catechism*, a classical text in Lutheranism, and a year later his *Larger Catechism* (see CATECHISMS, LUTHER'S). John Calvin's first catechism (1536) was too ponderous for children, and 5 years later he prepared a second (see GENEVAN CATECHISMS). But in the *Reformed tradition, the *Heidelberg Catechism (1562) is preeminent. In Presbyterianism the *Westminster Catechisms (1648), esp. the Shorter Catechism, famous for its beauty and preciseness, had lasting and widespread influence. These catechisms not only were works of instruction, they also became accepted as official *confessions of faith (see RACOVIAN CATECHISM). The Anglican *Book of Common Prayer has always included a catechism, which originally was printed in the section on confirmation. Methodist catechisms grew out of a 39-page pamphlet by John *Wesley, *Instructions for the Young*. Baptist catechisms date from as early as 1653. In all languages and in most Protestant traditions there appeared not only the classic catechisms but also adaptations reflecting theological currents, thus the catechisms of *Pietism and the 19-cent. rationalist catechisms. Those Churches which were anticreedal resisted the use of catechisms.

In the RC post-Reformation period the work of St. Peter Canisius became classic. He published a catechism, *Summa doctrinae christianae*, in three forms (1555; 1556; 1558 or 1559); the third, of intermediate length and level, was translated into German and other languages and was widely accepted. The *Catechism of the Council of Trent, or Roman Catechism (1566), was more a theological guide for pastors, and was considered to have special authority. From the Tridentine era into the 20th cent. catechisms usually followed the traditional order of Creed, Lord's Prayer, Commandments, and sacraments. Contents were capsulized theological formularies and were strongly apologetic. Esp. in the 19th cent. a quasi-authoritative status was achieved in England by the "Penny Catechism" (*Catechism of Christian Doctrine*, 1898) and in the U.S. by the Baltimore Catechism (*Catechism of the Third Plenary Council of Baltimore*, 1885).

Contemporary conception and use of the catechism in RC and Protestant Churches is a radical departure from the past. This is very evident in comparing RC education texts before and after Vatican Council II. A realization of the need for a formational approach has led many Christian educators to question the suitability of a formal catechism for classroom use. They see a need for Christian nurture to be expressed in terms of the personal love of Christ for every man and for this nurture to be conveyed in a person-oriented methodology. They are wary of a verbal indoctrination that would disregard the element of mystery in faith. Examples of this approach may be seen in the Protestant works of Randolf Crump Miller and Wesner Fallaw and in the RC *New Catechism* and *Fundamentals and Programs of a New Catechesis* issued by the Higher Institute of Catechetics in Nijmegen, Holland. There is current emphasis also on the development of ecumenically directed formats. Some of the efforts to reorganize and reformulate catechetical material have aroused vigorous controversy. See G. S. Sloyan, *Speaking of Religious Education* (1968); *idem*, NCE 3:225–231; R. C. Miller, *Education for Christian Living* (2d ed., 1963); G. E. Carter, *Modern Challenge to Religious Education* (ed. W. J. Reedy, 1961).

CATECHISM OF THE COUNCIL OF TRENT, a summary statement of doctrinal matters concerned principally with the creed, the sacraments, the commandments, and the Lord's Prayer. It is also called the Roman Catechism in view of the fact that it was issued at Rome in 1566 by the order of Pope Pius V. It is designed for the use of parish priests and teachers and not specifically for the laity or for catechetical instruction to the young. It was projected early in the Council of Trent (1546) but was not completed until 1564, after the close of the council. It was published originally in

Latin, and since has been translated into many languages. It was used widely in seminaries and had a semiauthoritative standing because of its auspices and connection with the Council of Trent. The theological reasoning involved in the doctrinal expositions contained in the Catechism is based largely on Thomistic theology, and its contents are expositional and pedagogic rather than polemic. See J. A. McHugh and C. J. Callan, *Catechism of the Council of Trent* (1947).

CATECHISMS, CALVIN'S, see GENEVAN CATECHISMS.

CATECHISMS, LUTHER'S, the chief statements of the Lutheran doctrine for laymen and part of the *Book of Concord (the collection of Lutheran confessions). During the autumn of 1528 Luther had participated in a visitation of the parishes of Saxony. He found there a shocking ignorance of the fundamentals of Christian teaching, not only among the common people, but even among the clergy. To remedy this condition, he wrote two catechisms, both in 1529. They were written in German, then translated into Latin. The *Small Catechism* (*Kleine Catechismus*), or *Enchiridion*, is intended for use by the laity as an introduction to the essentials of Christianity; there is probably no summary of Christian doctrine more representative of Luther and Lutheranism than this. The *German Catechism*, or *Large Catechism* (*Grosser Catechismus*), was addressed to the clergy, as a kind of epitome of doctrinal and moral theology. It was based on several series of sermons delivered by Luther during 1528 and 1529. The plan of both Catechisms follows three points: the Ten Commandments, the Creed, and the Lord's Prayer. Taken together, the two works show the concern of the Lutheran Reformation for an authentic renewal of the teaching of the Church in accord with the meaning of Scripture and in response to the need of the laity for the "doctrine of the gospel." See T. G. Tappert, ed., *Book of Concord* (1959); J. M. Lender, tr., *Luther's Large Catechism* (1967). There are many individual editions of the *Small Catechism* in English and other languages.

CATHARI (Gr. *katharoi,* the pure or perfect ones), a name properly applied to full-fledged members (Perfecti) of several neo-Manichaean sects that appeared in western Europe during the 12th cent. but generally employed as a collective designation for the sects themselves. Catharism, the most widely diffused of all medieval heresies, was not only anticlerical and antisacramental, but also anti-Christian and antisocial. Its creed combined elements of Manichaeism, Docetism, Monarchianism, Gnosticism, and Hinduism. Doctrinal unity was lacking among the various Cathar groups, but all of them professed some form of dualism. They affirmed two mutually opposed principles: one spiritual, which was the plenitude of all goodness; and the other material, which was the source of all wickedness. Some, such as the *Albanenses and *Albigenses, professed absolute dualism, holding that the two principles were equal and coeternal. Others, such as the *Concorezzenses, held that the material principle was a lesser being that did not create but only formed the world out of preexisting matter. All the Cathari, however, affirmed that the two principles were engaged in perpetual warfare, that the earth was their battleground, and that man's primary concern must be to free himself from servitude to matter. Because matter was evil, Christ could not have had a true human body, have died, or have risen from the dead; because human procreation resulted in the union of spirit with matter, marriage was essentially evil; and because sacred suicide, called *endura,* liberated man's spirit from matter, it was the highest act of virtue.

The dualism of the Cathari was derived from the Eastern *Bogomils and Paulicians, and was probably introduced into western Europe by merchants, pilgrims, and returning crusaders. By the beginning of the 13th cent. numerous Cathar sects were established in southern France, northern Italy, northeastern Spain, and the Rhineland. Each was headed by a bishop and included two classes of adherents—Perfecti and believers, or hearers. Initiation of the Perfecti was a ceremony called *consolamentum*, consisting of imposition of hands and the book of the Gospels on the head of the recipient. Thereafter, one so initiated was obliged to a life of poverty, continence, asceticism, and preaching. Believers' only obligations were to tender reverence (the *melioramentum*) to the Perfecti, to support them, to attend their sermons, to refrain from oaths and military service, and to receive the *consolamentum* before death. Beyond this, they were held to no fixed moral code and usually lived accordingly. Suppression of the Cathari proved extremely difficult. Their final extirpation was accomplished by vigorous activity of the *Inquisition and the Albigensian Crusade. By the opening of the 15th cent. all traces of Catharism had almost completely disappeared. See A. Borst, *Die Katharer* (1953); L. Cristiani, *Heresies and Heretics* (1959), 61–65; H. Daniel-Rops, *Cathedral and Crusade* (1957), 527–552; S. Runciman, *Medieval Manichee* (1961), 116–170; F. **Vernet**, DTC 2:1987–99.

CATHOLIC APOSTOLIC CHURCH, a body established in England as a mission to announce to all the Churches Christ's second coming and the restoration of the primitive Church. The early members came from a prayer circle at the home of Henry Drummond (1786–1860), banker and member of Parliament. E. *Irving, by his preaching of *premillenarianism and of the renewal of the charismatic gifts of the early Church, exercised great influence, and the members of the Church, against their preference, are often designated Irvingites. The Church acknowledged the rule of the twelve Apostles as the sole authority in the true Church; accordingly, by the "outpouring of the Holy Spirit" twelve apostles (Irving not among them) were chosen by 1835,

and the first community was established. Other offices were angel (bishop), prophet, evangelist, pastor, and teacher (see Eph 4.11). Besides premillenarianism and features similar to those of modern *Pentecostalism, the doctrines of the Church included the Apostles', Athanasian, and Nicene Creeds. The Church recognized seven sacraments as signs of interior grace; the Eucharist was celebrated as a sacrifice; and auricular confession was required for mortal sins. Confirmation was known as sealing, the reception of the fullness of the Holy Spirit by those of mature age. RC devotions, esp. to the Blessed Virgin Mary, vestments, and ceremonials were adopted.

The spread of the new Church began with a missionary tour, lasting 1,260 days, by the original twelve apostles to many countries; only in Germany, where some RC priests joined them, did they win many converts. A congregation was formed in the U.S. in 1848. It was the belief of the Church that the apostles would live until the second coming of Christ, and when they began to die, a schism in Germany about appointing successors led in 1863 to the formation of the *New Apostolic Church. By 1901 the last apostle had died; there have consequently been no new ordinations or administration of confirmation. Only a few priests survive, the liturgy is much curtailed, and the Church has dwindled to about 50,000 members, half of them in Germany. See P. E. Shaw, *Catholic Apostolic Church, Sometimes Called Irvingites* (1946). *PENTECOSTALISM.

CATHOLIC EMANCIPATION, in 19th-cent. England, the movement, in the words of the culminating Roman Catholic Relief Act of 1829, "for the relief of his majesty's roman catholic subjects" (10 George IV, c.7). Catholics looked for support less to the Tories than to the Whigs, who by their history and *hauteur* were more tolerant of nonconformity to the Establishment, as long as it did not menace the security of property or evoke vulgar enthusiasm. The way for emancipation was opened by the

Quebec Act, 1774, which, to the anger of Protestants both at home and in the American colonies, accorded the French Canadians nearly all the privileges they had enjoyed under the Bourbons. The clergy and people of French Canada showed their gratitude by the stand they took in the American War of Independence. The lesson did not pass unnoticed. Roman Catholics in Great Britain and Ireland existed under civil disabilities and penalties of the penal laws dating back to the 16th cent., many of them draconian, and indeed savage measures, which, though no longer enforced, still hung over them like a threat. The first concession was the abolition of penalties for religious observance (1778); it was greeted by outbreaks of mob fury in Edinburgh and Glasgow, and by the Gordon Riots in London, the worst disturbance the capital had known for 4 centuries. Further steps followed in Ireland, which then had its own parliament; Catholic ecclesiastics were granted legal protection and security of property rights (1783); successive acts admitted Catholics to the professions (1791) and to the franchise (1793) and established the Royal College of Maynooth (1795). Moves to extend these benefits to England and Scotland were actively promoted, leading to something of a rift between clergy and laity, or at least between those ecclesiastical leaders who were suspicious of state nomination and veto and those of the gentry who were prepared to be statutorily designated as "protesting catholic dissenters."

The atmosphere was eased by the influx of thousands of French priests, *emigrés* from the French Revolution, who received much sympathy and support and who gave much edification (as, later, Pius VII was warmly regarded for his sufferings under Napoleon); the cause was espoused by the eloquence of Edmund Burke and Henry Grattan; and some hopes were cherished because of the Prince of Wales's morganatic marriage to a devout Catholic, Maria Fitzherbert. Further relief, however, was postponed by George III's scruples about his coronation oath to maintain the Anglican Establishment unimpaired. Yet support was growing, even from such Tories as George Canning. Also Jacobitism had been dead for 50 years as a political cause, and the House of Stuart had become extinct with the Cardinal of York early in the 19th century. Thus no difficulty remained about swearing allegiance to the Hanoverian succession. Liberalism was in the air that was breathed on both sides of the House.

But it was because of one man that the windows were flung open. Daniel O'Connell, the newly elected member for Clare (1828), one of the most powerful political influences of the time, and a foremost figure in the Catholic Association, organized to gain civil liberties for Catholics; he faced the Tory government of the Duke of Wellington and Sir Robert Peel with the imminent prospect of a solid bloc of Irish Catholic members of Parliament prepared to disrupt the Union if necessary. Both men made a clean break with their past commitments—Wellington with characteristic common sense and pragmatism; Peel with a more tortured conscience, the first of the two great switches for which that honorable man was charged with apostasy by supporters; he resigned his seat for Oxford University and was not reelected. In 1829 the bill was passed; oaths to which no Catholic could subscribe were abolished for membership in the legislature and for public offices, though denial of the temporal power of the papacy within the United Kingdom was still required, and some petty restrictions were inserted as a sop to bigotry.

When the shouting was over, men might well wonder what all the fuss had been about. Grievances still remained in Ireland, but they arose chiefly from injustices inevitable when an ascendancy class is largely alien in religion and culture; they were not to be settled until the next century, and then on purely political grounds. For the rest, obsolescent discrimination against Catholics on points of detail was removed by later acts (1844, 1871, and finally in 1926). Now Catholics are restrained only from the

Crown, the offices of Lord Chancellor and Keeper of the Seal, and a few university posts. See D. Gwynn, *Struggle for Catholic Emancipation, 1750–1829* (1928); *idem, Hundred Years of Catholic Emancipation* (1929).

CATHOLIC RELIEF ACTS, see CATHOLIC EMANCIPATION.

CATHOLICISM, the universal community formed by the teaching, worship, and practice of the Catholic Church, usually understood of the RC Church, which tightens the meaning of the term to intercommunion within a common obedience and discipline. Unlike *catholicity, which refers to a quality, Catholicism refers to a system. After the disruption of East and West, the name *Orthodox was assumed by the Greeks, the name Catholics by the Latins; after the Reformation those who remained in communion with Rome kept the name, and Catholicism was contrasted with Protestantism, Lutheranism, Calvinism, and so forth. This is also its ordinary, noncontroversial usage in England, though Roman Catholic is the designation known to English law, and the C of E has never renounced the title of Catholic and claims to be a branch of the universal Church. The term is then given the comprehensive sense of transcending diverse communions, hence *Anglo-Catholicism. Good manners and a sense of the occasion and knowing when not to be a stickler for words will dictate whether one centers Catholicism on Rome or leaves it with a more diffuse meaning.

CATHOLICITY (Gr. *katholikos,* the quality or the characteristic of universality). Though not of scriptural origin, the adjective "Catholic" has been considered properly descriptive of the Church as a whole since the time of Ignatius of Antioch (d. *c.* 110); by the 3d cent. it was commonly accepted as part of the Church's title; from the 4th cent. it has been incorporated in the principal creeds. In its earliest use it designated the whole Church spread throughout the world as distinguished from the *local church, and esp. from heretical and (later) schismatic sects. In this sense it meant in effect much the same as orthodox. In controversy with the *Donatists, St. Augustine insisted that the Donatist sect, confined to a small portion of Africa, could not possibly qualify as the true Church. In later theology a wide interpretation was given to the word and numerous ways were pointed out in which universality could be attributed to the Church, which was Catholic, e.g., by geographical diffusion; by the temporal dimension of its mission; by its inclusion of men of all nations, types, and walks of life; by its possession of revelation in its full integrity and of all the means necessary to salvation. At the time of the Reformation, defenders of the Roman faith were quick to point out that the bodies separating themselves from communion with Rome sacrificed the catholicity in which the Church had always set great store. Appropriating to themselves the description of Catholic, they reproached the Protestants, as St. Augustine had the Donatists, for separating themselves from the unity of the Catholic faith. Some Protestant bodies dropped the word Catholic from their versions of the creeds, substituting "Christian" in its place. But the majority claimed a *de iure* catholicity. The *Augsburg Confession (Art. 22) distinguishes between the Catholic Church and the Roman Church. The Second *Helvetic Confession, the *Scots Confession, and the *Westminster Confession make the same distinction implicitly; catholicity refers to the universality of the Church, and its fidelity to the true gospel. The Reformation is understood to be precisely the recovery of orthodoxy from the distortions of Rome. The Church as Catholic, however, was not emphasized in subsequent Protestant history. Yet the idea perdures in all references to the Church universal, realized in many forms and locations and present wherever the gospel is rightly preached and the sacraments rightly administered.

Anglicans see the note of catholicity verified in their Church by reason of a *comprehensiveness large enough to embrace conflicting interpretations of the faith. In post-Tridentine RC theology the notion of catholicity was stressed and developed for polemical purposes as a note or mark by which the true Church can be recognized. Among modernists there were those who found value in catholicity understood in the Anglican sense of comprehensiveness (see MODERNISM). In more contemporary RC theology there has been a tendency to see catholicity as implying the legitimate and indeed necessary diversity of thought and practice within the latitude permitted by the unity of faith. From this point of view, the idea of catholicity is complementary to that of unity. This notion has been fruitful in the modern development of the theology of the missions, and it underlies the currently popular concept of missionary adaptation. In current ecumenical discussion, e.g., in the Consultation on Church Union, the catholicity of the Church refers to the elements of the ancient Church that survived in the Reformation, esp. the creeds, the historic episcopate, the priesthood, and the sacraments. See H. Thurston, CE 3:449–452; G. Thils, "La Notion de catholicité de l'église à l'époque moderne," EphemThLov 13 (1936), 5–73; *idem*, NCE 3:339–340; G. H. Tavard, *Quest for Catholicity: A Study in Anglicanism* (1964); D. T. Jenkins, *Nature of Catholicity* (1942); J. Pelikan, *Riddle of Roman Catholicism* (1959). *UNITY OF THE CHURCH.

CELESTIAL MARRIAGE, a belief of the Church of Jesus Christ of Latter-day Saints concerning matrimony. According to the *Doctrines and Covenants of Joseph *Smith, Jr., marriage may be either temporal or eternal. The latter is called celestial because it will continue in heaven. The belief is connected with Mormon stress on the importance of marriage to man's salvation and eternal happiness. Only a Mormon man and woman worthy to enter the inner chambers of the temple, where the ceremony is performed, may enter into a celestial marriage.

CELESTINES, a congregation within the Benedictine Order founded by Peter of Morrone (Celestine V) about 1240. He became a monk in 1235 and soon after retired into the wilderness around Monte Morrone in Abruzzi, where he lived a very austere life in imitation of St. John the Baptist. He was soon joined by a number of companions and in 1264 Urban IV approved their way of life, which incorporated Cistercian severity, Franciscan poverty, and some of the organizational features of the mendicant orders. In the 15th cent. the order had about 150 houses, mostly in Italy and France. The Celestines ceased to exist as an order under the suppressions of anticlerical governments in the late 18th and early 19th centuries. The *Clareni, a group of Franciscan *Spirituals authorized as a separate community by Celestine V, are also referred to as Poor Hermits of the Lord Celestine, as Celestines, or as Franciscan Celestines. See J. Duhr, DSAM 2:377–385.

CELESTIUS (Caelestius; d. 429), a principal exponent of *Pelagianism. C. probably was born in Italy; after being educated as a lawyer, he became a monk. He first met *Pelagius *c*.405 during the latter's sojourn in Rome. When the city fell (410), the two went to Africa, where C. propagated Pelagius's doctrine with intemperate zeal, and was condemned in 411 for denying original sin and criticizing *infant baptism. Later he was ordained at Ephesus. In 416 he transferred to Constantinople; but the local bp. had him removed almost at once, and Pope Innocent I excommunicated him along with Pelagius in 417. The following year C. turned up in Rome, presented the new pope, Zosimus, with a complete account of his beliefs, and succeeded in gaining his favor. Renewed investigation, however, and the condemnations of the Council of *Carthage XVI (418; see D 222–230) made Zosimus confirm Innocent's excommunications (see D 231). C. thereupon went into hiding for several years and then proceeded to Rome once more. The Council of Ephesus (431) condemned him along with Pelagius, but by that time C. had probably died. In propagating Pelagianism C. played a larger role than Pelagius himself; and the judgments against the teaching were in the first place directed against him. See G. Bardy, *Catholicisme* 2:753.

CELIBACY, the condition of life without marriage that is undertaken by clerics upon the reception of major orders in accordance with the discipline of the Church. Scriptural basis for the practice is claimed in the example and teaching of Christ, who spoke of leaving one's wife for his sake (Mk 10.29) or for the kingdom of God (Lk 18.29), thus indicating a special value to be found in virginity, as can be seen also in eschatological perspective in the statement that in the resurrection there will be no marriage (Mt 22.30). The calling to this state, however, was a special grace and vocation (Mt 19.11–12). Paul, although he wished all men to be in the same state as himself, also presented this as an individual charism (1 Cor 7.7).

Development of the Law of Celibacy. From the early days of the Church the inner affinity of religious celibacy and evangelical office made itself manifest. Many clerics chose to be unmarried or discontinued marital relationships after ordination. The earliest statutes, like that of Elvira (306), were not universal. The attempt to prescribe clerical celibacy as a law for the universal Church at Council of Nicaea I (325) did not succeed, but the council did forbid marriage after receiving higher orders according to what it described as the "ancient tradition of the Church." The situation in patristic times was complicated by the currency of a dualistic trend of thought, such as was manifest, e.g., in Encratism, which attacked the goodness of the married state and hence threatened to distort the authentic NT ideal of celibacy. In the East, the Trullan synod (692) enforced

the rule that still prevails in principle in the Eastern Churches: married bishops had to separate from their wives; priests and deacons could marry only before ordination. In the West, the Church moved gradually toward the canonical obligation of clerical celibacy through the combined efforts of popes and regional councils. In practice, much of the legislation centered about the enforcement of continence for the married clergy. The rule of celibacy was a main point of the reform of Gregory VII (d. 1085), which was carried out without benefit of new legislation. The notion that the obligation to celibacy arises from a vow implicit in the reception of orders seems to have originated with this pontiff. A decisive step was taken when Lateran Council II (1139) declared that marriages of subdeacons, deacons, and priests after ordination were not only unlawful but invalid. Thenceforth, for the Latin Church, only those who freely accepted strict celibacy "for the sake of the kingdom of God" were to be admitted to higher office in the Church, and celibacy was established by law in terms that have remained substantially unchanged in the Roman Catholic Church down to the present time.

Notwithstanding the fact that clerical celibacy was clearly a canonical obligation after Lateran II, the general observance of the law throughout the West was neither easily nor speedily secured. But consistent pressure and the application of severe penalties against priests practicing concubinage—after Lateran II all married priests could be so classified—brought about a fairly high level of compliance by the mid-13th century. There were scandalous exceptions, chiefly among the unbeneficed clergy, yet they were recognized almost everywhere as scandalous and exceptional.

From the Reformation to Vatican Council II. In the 2 centuries that preceded the Reformation an accumulation of troubles and disasters—among which were the Great Western Schism, the Black Death, the Hundred Years' War—led to a great decline in the morality of the clergy. In the face of this situation either of two courses could appeal to men seriously intent upon reform: mandatory celibacy could be abolished entirely, or a mighty effort could be made to bring about its general observance. The Protestant Reformers chose the first course; the Counter-Reformation the latter. Luther at first made no quarrel with priestly celibacy, but in 1523 he condemned the practice as a human institution. In this he was followed by the other Reformers. Thus obligatory celibacy was repudiated by the *Augsburg Confession, the First and the Second *Helvetic Confession, the *Thirty-Nine Articles, and other confessional formulas. This decision was in part at least a consequence of the rejection of the Mass and much of the sacramental system of the old Church, a position that required them to take a new and largely desacralized view of the priestly office. The Council of Trent voiced the Counter-Reformation's insistence on the observance of celibacy. It reaffirmed the stand taken by Lateran II, but in so doing rejected the opinion of some extremists that marriage and the priestly office were incompatible by divine law. The council declared that the invalidating prohibition of marriage for clerics in major orders was based either on ecclesiastical law or on the vow implicit in the reception of orders, thus leaving open to dispute the question of the ultimate source of the obligation (see D 1809). More important perhaps in the long run for the future of celibacy in the RC Church than the council's reaffirmation of the position of Lateran II was its insistence upon the establishment of seminaries wherein candidates for the priesthood could receive proper training for their priestly work and an effective spiritual formation to prepare them for the obligations they would undertake. Gradually the seminaries did their work, and little by little the scandal of incontinence was overcome until at length it could be said that the clergy as a whole throughout the world were observing the law of celibacy with substantial fidelity.

Nevertheless, it cannot be reasonably claimed that RC priests have all been of one mind about the value and reasonableness of the obligation under which they live. No doubt some have accepted, or have continued in its observance, with some degree of unwillingness, but the actual prevalence of such sentiment down to recent times is difficult to estimate. That some disaffection existed is clear enough. Groups withdrawing from communion with Rome (e.g., the Old Catholics, the national Czechoslovak Church), have invariably repudiated celibacy as a requirement for their clergy. Individual priests defecting from clerical ranks quite commonly have done so with a view to marriage. But until recently defection statistics have been closely guarded secrets, and open discussion and writing in favor of the abrogation of celibacy were discouraged by ecclesiastical authority. Still there is evidence of recurrent agitation against celibacy to be gathered from official documents in which church authority has sought to quell opposition to the law. In the early 19th cent. an association was formed in Germany to advocate a change in the law, and Gregory XVI denounced the move in his encyclical *Mirari vos* (1832); 14 years later Pius IX defended the law in his *Qui pluribus;* Pius X in *Pascendi* (1907) noted with disfavor the attempt of modernists to question the right of the Church to impose the obligation; Benedict XV in a consistorial allocution (1920) declared that the Church would not mitigate its discipline on this point. Under Pius XI a decree of the Congregation of the Sacraments required that every candidate for the priesthood take an oath in writing to attest that he was assuming the obligation freely and with full knowledge of what he was doing, and the same Pope made a point of celibacy in his *Ad catholici sacerdotii* (1935). Despite the efforts of the Holy See, agitation continued. It was apparent in the German reform program *Der Katholizismus der Zukunft* published anonymously in 1940, and it has gained force and come much more into the open since that time.

Current Discussions. No discussion of the problem of celibacy as a whole was permitted at Vatican Council II. After the council, however, those eager to press forward with the work of reform have included celibacy among the established institutions and practices they think should be questioned. In the new climate of dialogue, ecclesiastical authority, esp. at local and regional levels, has been hesitant—or perhaps unable—to stifle discussion. In any case, the pastoral problems raised by the scarcity of vocations, coupled with an unprecedented increase in the number of priests giving up their ministry, has caused the celibacy issue to clamor for attention. Other factors contributing to the increasing criticism of celibacy include: the attention concentrated by the debate about contraception on the excellence of the married state and the highlighting of values realized in sexual activity; the readiness of many contemporary personalists to see marriage as necessary to an individual's fulfillment; and the veering of certain theologians toward a less sacralized view of the priestly ministry and a new definition of the role and function of the priest in contemporary society. Moreover, some have probably been encouraged by recent apparent mitigations in the Church's discipline in this matter to think that an ultimate modification of the law is possible. For example, Vatican Council II approved of a restoration of the permanent diaconate, and the norms of its restoration, as published by Pope Paul VI (1967), permit in certain circumstances the reception of married men to that order. Popes Pius XII, John XXIII, and Paul VI have granted dispensations to married ministers converted to Catholicism permitting them to receive Catholic orders without separating from their wives. The Church has also shown greater indulgence in recent times in granting laicized priests permission to marry.

In the face of the widespread and sometimes obstreperous criticism of the law, Paul VI in 1967 published his encyclical *Sacerdotalis celibatus*, in which he reaffirmed the position taken by Lateran II and Trent, pointed to the values of celibacy, considered the objections currently raised against it, and denied that the exceptions admitted in the contemporary practice of the Church represent a weakening of the ideal or a true mitigation of the law itself. The encyclical, however, far from quieting the debate, served rather to intensify it. There was protest and denunciation from those already firm in their opposition. In the U.S. an organization was formed to promote the cause of optional rather than mandatory celibacy for priests. This organization, which took the name National Association for Pastoral Renewal (NAPR), at first operated with some degree of secrecy but later came out into the open, and its membership, advisory board, and activities are now known to the public. Among other things, it has conducted a survey of opinion among RC priests regarding their views on celibacy; it arranged a National Symposium on Clerical Celibacy (Sept. 6–8, 1967), and it has been urging the National Conference of Bishops to make a study of the problem. Organizations of the same type in other countries, notably in Holland, have been engaging in similar activity. See Pope Paul VI, *Encyclical Letter on Priestly Celibacy* (USCC, 1967); for canon law of, J. W. Rehage, NCE 3:481–488; for history of, P. Delehaye, NCE 369–374; E. Vacandard, DTC 2.2:2068–88; H. Thurston, CE 3:481–488; G. H. Frein, *Celibacy: The Necessary Option* (1968); J. Blenkinsopp, *Celibacy, Ministry, Church* (1968).

CENTRAL CONFERENCE (Methodist), a *jurisdictional conference outside the territory of the U.S. *CONFERENCE (METHODIST).

CENTURIATORS OF MAGDEBURG, the authors of *Historia Ecclesiae Christi* (1559–74), which is also called the *Magdeburg Centuries, a Lutheran, apologetical church history divided by centuries. The principal "centuriator" was M. *Flacius Illyricus, who conceived the plan for the work.

CERDO (2d cent.), Gnostic teacher who taught in Rome (*c.* 140) and is known only through the writings of SS. Irenaeus, Epiphanius and Hippolytus. From these sources it seems that C.'s teachings are reflected in those of *Marcion, his disciple. C. did not found a sect. See G. Bareille, DTC 2:2138–39, with patristic texts.

CHAIR OF UNITY OCTAVE, also called the Church Unity Octave, a period of prayer for Christian unity held each year, Jan. 18–25. The Octave, which finds its inspiration in the prayer of Christ for his followers, "That all may be one" (Jn 17.21), was founded (1908) by Lewis Thomas Wattson (1863–1940), an American Episcopalian clergyman. The distinctive purpose of the Octave was the corporate reunion esp. of the Anglican Church with the RC Church, although the intentions for prayer also included other Christians and non-Christians. Originally called the Church Unity Octave, the prayer movement was stimulated by a suggestion in 1907 that a special sermon on Christian unity be preached each year on June 29th, the Feast of SS. Peter and Paul. Wattson replied by launching an 8-day period of prayer for Christian unity from the Feast of St. Peter's Chair in Rome, Jan. 18, to the Conversion of St. Paul, Jan. 25. Among the first results of the Octave was his own reception, together with a small group of Anglican religious (the Franciscan Friars of the Atonement and the Franciscan Sisters of the Atonement), into the RC Church (Oct. 30, 1909). The Church Unity Octave was extended by Benedict XV on Feb. 25, 1916, to the whole Church and enriched with indulgences. At the insistence of Pius XII the name was changed, becoming the Chair of Unity Octave. Born out of a desire for corporate reunion in a period antedating the ecumenical movement, and formed in its most flourishing period by a theology of the Counter-Reformation, the Octave today under the influence of ecumenism has yielded to and combined with the *Week of Prayer for Christian Unity. The contributions of the Octave have been the manifold prayers for unity it stimulated, the view of corporate

reunion that it upheld, and the preparation it gave to the RC world for receiving the ecumenical movement. See D. Gannon, *Father Paul of Graymoor* (1959).

CHANNING, WILLIAM ELLERY (1780–1842), American Unitarian minister. Born in Newport, R.I., of a distinguished family, C. graduated from Harvard in 1798. He was elected regent at Harvard in 1801. After receiving approval to preach, he began his ministry at the Federal Street Congregational Church in Boston in 1803. When Jebidiah Morse attacked the liberal Congregationalists in 1815, accusing them of covertly agreeing with the strictly humanitarian Christology of the English Unitarian Thomas Belsham, C. defended them as "liberal Christians." He emerged into clear leadership of the liberals with his famous sermon, "Unitarian Christianity," which he preached at Baltimore in 1819 for the ordination of Jared Sparks. When younger Unitarian ministers pressed for the organization of a separate denomination, however, C. expressed his disapproval of Unitarianism as a sect. He declined the offer of the presidency of the American Unitarian Association when it was organized in 1825. In later years, he became increasingly an advocate of social reform, with particular opposition to slavery. He and Theodore *Parker are recognized as the two greatest leaders in the development of American Unitarianism.

Basic intellectual influences on his theological development were derived from Francis Hutcheson, Adam Ferguson, Richard Price, and Samuel Hopkins. The influence of John Locke is seen in C.'s emphasis on the rational character of revealed religion. He was convinced of the unique authority of Jesus and of the validity of miracles as "Christian evidences." He distrusted a transcendentalist reliance upon immediate intuition. The concepts of the unipersonality and the moral character of God were crucial in his theology. In Christology, he was an "Arian." He rejected the Chalcedonian interpretation of the Incarnation on scriptural and rational grounds. His optimistic evaluation of human nature is shown in his belief that Christ's life demonstrated that the achievement of moral perfection is possible for other men. There were several editions of his writings, the latest of which was *Works of W. E. C.* (6v., 1903). See J. W. Chadwick, *W. E. C.* (1903); R. L. Patterson, *Philosophy of W. E. C.* (1952); D. P. Edgell, *W. E. C.* (1955); A. W. Brown, *Always Young for Liberty* (1956); S. E. Ahlstrom, ed., *Theology in America* (1967), 193–210.

CHARGE, in Methodism, the local church (station charge) or a group of local churches (circuit charge). It is the basic unit of Methodist organization. *CONFERENCE; *DISTRICT SUPERINTENDENT.

CHAUNCY, surname of two New England clergymen. (1) Charles (1592–1672), Puritan minister, second president of Harvard. After a brief imprisonment (1634) in England for his hard Puritan line on church order, he migrated to the Plymouth Colony (1637). After a parish ministry until 1654, he was chosen to be president of Harvard. He was a stanchly conservative theologian, a scholar, and a respected preacher.

(2) Charles (1705–87), great-grandson of the preceding, spokesman of a rationalist enlightenment in New England. From 1721 until his death he served the First Church of Boston. He strongly opposed the emotionalism in the *Great Awakening, and the ideas of Jonathan *Edwards, e.g., in his *Enthusiasm Describ'd and Caution'd Against* (1742) and *Seasonable Thoughts on the Present State of Religion in New England* (1743). His *Arminianism, *universalism, and rationalist views on the Trinity began the departure from Calvinist doctrine among New England Congregationalists that culminated in the emergence by 1825 of *Unitarianism as a distinct denomination. He also strongly opposed *episcopacy in the American colonies.

CHAUTAUQUA MOVEMENT, a lecture, discussion, and entertainment enterprise popular in the U.S. in the late 19th and early 20th cents., of particular service to communities in which cultural and educational opportunities were limited. The movement, forerunner of later adult education programs, began in 1873 when Methodist minister, and later bishop, John H. Vincent (1832–1920) proposed that the Methodist *camp meeting association include a training course for Sunday school teachers in its summer institute at Chautauqua Lake, New York. Subsequent changes broadened offerings to include courses in the arts, sciences, and humanities, and lengthened the term of the institute. The Chautauqua Literary and Scientific Circle was organized to sponsor local programs to accommodate those who wished to read and study under guidance but who could not attend the institute. Some 80,000 members were enrolled by 1887, and the total increased to more than 100,000 by 1891. For a time (1885–98) the operation was given formal status as Chautauqua University under a charter from the State of New York. However, the more popular programs were the reading circles and the summer assemblies, which after 1880 featured preachers and speakers of national reputation. Until World War I, the circles and assemblies were widely imitated, and spread across the country in various forms. A decline set in and the movement practically disappeared in the postwar years. See J. E. Gould, *Chautauqua Movement* (1961); H. P. Harrison, *Culture under Canvas* (1958); J. H. Vincent, *Chautauqua Movement* (1886).

CHEMNITZ, MARTIN (1522–88), German Lutheran theologian, a co-author of the *Formula of Concord. After studies at several Lutheran centers in Germany, he was librarian for Albert of Prussia (1550); he entered the ministry at Wittenberg (1533), where he also lectured briefly. Throughout the rest of his life he maintained the post of pastor in Braunschweig. His first major contribution to theology was a reply to the teachings of the Council of Trent (*Examen Concilii Tridentini*, 4v., 1565–73). He was called upon to resolve doctrinal disputes besetting the Lutheran churches, and prepared *corpora doctrinae* for several of them. In the Lutheran controversies on ubiquity (see UBIQUITARIANISM) and the person of Christ he contributed ideas reflected in Article 8 of the Formula of Concord. Together with J. *Andreae he was largely responsible for the draft of the whole Formula. In addition C. also was engaged by the authorities in the establishment of church polity and practice. His influence has been recognized as one of standardization of Lutheran doctrinal formulas and church organization. See A. C. Piepkorn, EncLuthCh 1:390–391; E. G. Schwiebert, NCE 3:548–549.

CHICAGO-LAMBETH QUADRILATERAL, a more precise title for the *Lambeth Quadrilateral. The four-point basis for church reunion was approved by the *General Convention of the Protestant Episcopal Church at Chicago in 1886; then by the *Lambeth Conference of 1888.

CHILIASM (Gr. *chilias*, a thousand), the belief, based chiefly on the literal interpretation of Rev ch. 20, that Christ will come to rule visibly upon earth for 1,000 years before the end of the world. It is used as a synonym for *millenarianism, but it is less proper to identify it with any but the premillenarian variety of millenarian thought since chiliasm, insofar as it has a distinctive meaning, expects the personal corporeal reign of Christ upon earth for 1,000 years.

CHORIZANTES, see DANCERS.

CHRIST CATHOLIC CHURCH of America and Europe, an Old Catholic Church containing Eastern and Western rite congregations. Opposing the doctrine of papal infallibility and desiring vernacular liturgy and Polish clergy, certain Polish-Americans established Old Catholic parishes. In 1937 several of these and other independent Catholic and Orthodox congregations, particularly in N.J., formed the Polish Old Catholic Church, electing as bishop J. Zielenka, once American administrator of the *Mariavites. Zielenka's consecrator had received consecration from Old Catholic Abp. J. R. Vilatte (see EPISCOPI VAGANTES). To broaden its appeal the Church took the name Christ Catholic (1959). Zielenka's death (1961) led to selection of Abp. P. A. Zurawetzky, whose episcopal orders derive from independent Orthodox lines. Zurawetzky is also president of the Holy Synod of Orthodox Catholic Churches in America. The Church, with headquarters at Rahway, N.J., has a small but growing membership.

CHRISTADELPHIANS, a sect founded in 1848 by J. Thomas (1805–71), an English physician who settled in the U.S. in 1832. Thomas joined the *Disciples of Christ but severed his connection with that body in 1834 for doctrinal reasons and developed a theology of his own. He refused to describe himself and his followers as Christian, because that term had become corrupted by the connotation of apostasy; in its place he chose the name "Christadelphians," i.e., brethren of Christ. The brethren reject the doctrine of the Trinity and the existence of hell; call for a revival of primitive Christianity; look to the second coming of Jesus Christ to reign for 1,000 years; claim that only baptism by immersion is effective; and teach *conditional immortality, that only those who hold the divine truth as recognized by the Christadelphians will be saved. Like *Jehovah's Witnesses they are opposed to war and military service and indeed seek to dissociate themselves from the activities of the civil community in general; they forbid marriage with nonmembers. Church *polity is congregational, the separate societies (called ecclesias) are only loosely bound together. There are no salaried clergy, but the liturgical and administrative functions usually exercised by ministers are committed to "serving brethren" elected to that office by congregations for a term of 3 years. In 1964 overall membership was estimated to be nearly 16,000 in the U.S. with another 20,000 in Canada, England, Australia, and New Zealand. See R. Roberts, *Dr. Thomas, his Life and Work* (1884); B. R. Wilson, *Sects and Society* (1961); W. J. Whalen, NCE 3:628.

CHRISTENDOM ("Christian" plus the "dom" suffix that signifies dignity or domain), in general the condition or state of being Christian; Christianity; Christians collectively. In its early use it was contrasted with "heathenness" and it came to have a geopolitical meaning, in which sense it means the Christian domain, or the countries professing Christianity. By the late Middle Ages Christendom included the territory of the old Roman Empire, with the addition of Ireland, Scandinavia, the new German lands, the Slav countries, and, in popular feeling, the African regions of Prester John. It was enlarged by later colonialism but diminished in the East by the inroads of Islam. The term has contemporary relevance, it would seem, only in its early and general sense.

CHRISTIAN, a term that as a noun means one who believes in Christ and as an adjective means that which pertains to the historical movement stemming from Christ. According to Acts 11.26 the term was first used at Antioch by outsiders to describe the followers of Christ. It is not the usual designation of the NT, which more commonly uses such terms as brethren (Acts 1.16), believers (Acts 2.44), saints (Acts 9.32), and disciples (Acts 11.26). It appears to have been more widely used by pagans, and according to Tacitus it was in common use by the time of the Neronian persecution *(Annals,* 15.44). In times of persecution the acknowledgment or denial of the name was often crucial. Pagans sometimes confused Christus with *chrēstos,* meaning good or

kind, and used the term *chrestiani.* The apologists answered that although this was a misunderstanding, it was a true indication of the character of Christians (Tertullian, *Apol.* 3 and 5). The term Christian also came early to describe the type of character appropriate to a disciple of Christ. Approaching his martyrdom, Ignatius wrote, "Let me not merely be called Christian but be found one" *(Ad Romanos* 3.2). Thus Christian came to be used as an adjective to describe not only those persons and institutions that claimed a relationship to Christ but more properly those who showed the character considered proper to this relationship, as in references to Christian character, Christian acts, and the like.

In the modern period, with the many divisions of Christianity and the varying attitudes toward Christian doctrine, there has been discussion as to which persons, groups, and movements are properly designated Christian. Some have held that good character is more important than right belief and that a Christian is one who has such traits as humility and kindness, whether or not he accepts Christian doctrine. Unitarians have been divided between those who wish to consider Unitarianism a Christian body, though departing from many points of orthodox doctrine, and those who wish to consider it a body transcending the differences of the various world religions. In the doctrinal conflicts among other Churches the question has been discussed whether their opponents could properly be reckoned Christian, and what were the basic points that were essential to merit that designation. The followers of Alexander *Campbell wished to eliminate denominational differences and be called simply "Christians." In the modern movement toward Christian unity the determination of what constitutes a Christian Church has been a question of considerable importance. The constitution of the *World Council of Churches has determined a definition in these words: "churches which confess the Lord Jesus Christ as God and Savior according to the Scriptures and therefore seek to fulfill together their common calling to the glory of the one God, Father, Son, and Holy Spirit."

CHRISTIAN AND MISSIONARY ALLIANCE, a missionary association that has taken on the characteristics of a Protestant Church in the Holiness tradition. Dr. A. B. Simpson (1843–1919), a Canadian-born Presbyterian clergyman, held several pastorates before embarking on an independent evangelistic career in New York City in 1881. At a convention in 1887 his followers organized twin societies: the Christian Alliance, which concentrated on home missions, and the Evangelical Missionary Alliance, which sent missionaries overseas. In 1897 the two bodies were combined as the Christian and Missionary Alliance. Membership in the 1,200 congregations in the U.S. and Canada totals 70,000. There are almost twice as many members in foreign mission fields. In 1967 the Alliance supported 830 active foreign missionaries and 1,590 pastors, evangelists, and other licensed ministers in North America. This small denomination spends $4 million a year for missions and ranks seventh among U.S. Protestant denominations in foreign mission work. Major mission fields served include India, Guinea, the Ivory Coast, Mali–Upper Volta, Gabon, Vietnam, Cambodia, Laos, Thailand, Colombia, Ecuador, Peru, Chile, Argentina, Hong Kong, Israel, Japan, the Philippines, Indonesia, New Guinea, and several Arab countries. In the U.S. missionaries work among Mexicans, Indians, Negroes, Jews, and mountain people. The Alliance seeks to establish native Churches as soon as possible and to move on to new areas. Missionaries and native workers preach in 180 languages and dialects. The Christian and Missionary Alliance, like other Holiness Churches, teaches the *foursquare gospel (that Jesus Christ is Savior, Sanctifier, Healer, and Coming Lord), the second coming, *baptism with the Holy Spirit, and *divine healing. Local churches are known as "Alliance" churches but are sometimes called Alliance Gospel Tabernacles. Congregations are relatively autonomous but they must adhere to the General Constitution of the Church. There is no creedal statement. The Alliance operates three Bible colleges in the U.S. and one in Canada to prepare missionaries. See L. L. King, EncModChrMiss 133–137; A. B. Simpson, *Fourfold Gospel* (1925); idem, *Wholly Sanctified* (1925).

CHRISTIAN ATHEISM, a concept associated with the *death-of-God thinking of some American Protestants and, more specifically, with the writing of Thomas J. Altizer. The concept has emerged from a disturbing encounter of this thinking and events and forces of contemporary culture. The dissolution of the Christian era is proclaimed, together with a dawning awareness that the totality of human experience points to the death of God. Those who share this conviction are advised to find some meaning in affirming and discerning a profane form of Christ's presence to the world. The Christian atheist, holding fast to Christ even without God, feels cut off from all previous forms of faith. Elements allegedly drawn from Christian tradition include eschatology as orientation of life to an absolute future and devotion to Christ as the Incarnate Word. In the absence of a viable theism, it is difficult to maintain a Christology without radically revising the concepts and propositions of orthodoxy. Altizer makes considerable use of two kinds of material, the history of religions and the insights of visionaries of recent times, and his concern presupposes that the arguments and conclusions of Christian theism are presently bankrupt. The role of negation in speaking of God provided a clue for the extreme pronouncement of God's death. In Christ God empties himself, alienating himself from transcendence and absoluteness. God is dead as the alien other in heavenly isolation, as an enemy to the fullness of man. Man goes forward, with Christ, without God. The theme of Christian atheism has proved to be ephemeral. See T. J. Altizer, *Gospel of Christian Atheism* (1966); T. W. Ogletree, *Death of God*

Controversy (1966), B. Murchland, ed., *Meaning of the Death of God* (1966).

Puerto Rico, Mexico, and Canada. See J. T. Nichol, *Pentecostalism* (1966), 132–133.

CHRISTIAN CATHOLIC CHURCH, a denomination organized in Chicago (1896), then transplanted to Zion City, Ill., in 1901 by John Alexander *Dowie, evangelist and faith healer. Zion City became the center of the Church; the community successfully operated business enterprises and was organized theocratically under Dowie, until his deposition and replacement by Wilbur G. Voliva in 1906. From Dowie the Church has retained *faith healing, *universalism (the belief that punishment for sin is temporary), baptism by *trine immersion, tithing, and a strong opposition to tobacco, liquor, and medical doctors. Since Voliva *millenarianism and biblical fundamentalism, as well as general conformity to other conservative Protestant bodies, have characterized the Church. Zion City has ceased to be exclusively a church community. The Church has congregations in only four other cities but conducts extensive foreign missions.

CHRISTIAN CATHOLIC CHURCH OF SWITZERLAND, see CHRISTKATHOLIKEN.

CHRISTIAN CHURCH OF NORTH AMERICA, GENERAL COUNCIL, Pentecostal body incorporated under its present name at Pittsburgh, Pa., in 1948. The history of this Church goes back to the Pentecostal movement among Italian immigrants in Chicago, beginning in 1907. Autonomous Pentecostal assemblies were established in Calif. and throughout the East and Midwest. Their decentralized association was known as the Unorganized Italian Church of North America. In 1939 "Unorganized" was dropped from the title; in 1942, because the English language was increasingly used in services, the word "Italian" was replaced by "Christian." The autonomy of local churches is stressed. Membership in 1968 was about 8,000; mission activity is conducted in Belgium, Italy, the Philippines,

CHRISTIAN CHURCHES, a title adopted in the name of Christian unity and anti-creedalism. Besides the Christian Churches (Disciples of Christ), the name has been used by another group of Churches, the first of which was originally the Republican Methodist Church, established (1793) in Va. under the leadership of James *O'Kelly in protest against *episcopacy in the Methodist Church. The name was changed to Christian Church a year later, when the Church adopted the Bible as the only creed, Christian living as the only basis for membership, and congregationalism as the form of polity. In 1801 the Baptist minister Abner Jones established in Vt. a Christian Church along the same lines. During the *Great Awakening in Ky., Barton W. *Stone led a group of followers out of the Presbyterian Synod, and soon they also took (1804) the name Christian Church, for the same basic reasons. Stone himself united with the Disciples of Christ, but most of his Christian Churches remained apart. The three lines in this "Christian movement" came to be united on principles representing their original inspiration. Because of their rejection of creeds, they avoided even Trinitarian formulas and doctrines. Most of the Christian Churches joined in the 1931 merger that formed the General Council of Congregational and Christian Churches and later (1957) became part of the *United Church of Christ. Whether in or outside of the mergers, the local congregation remains absolutely autonomous and continues the heritage and name of the Christian Church.

CHRISTIAN CHURCHES, International Council of, see INTERNATIONAL COUNCIL OF CHRISTIAN CHURCHES.

CHRISTIAN CHURCHES (Disciples of Christ), International Convention of, a Protestant body originating in the ministry of Barton W. *Stone and of Thomas and Alexander *Campbell on the American frontier. In 1804 Stone, a Presbyterian minister, and a group of colleagues in Ky. dissolved the Springfield *presbytery, calling their congregations "Christian Churches," and their members, "Christians." They sought freedom and union for all believers on the basis of the Bible alone. In 1809 Thomas Campbell, a Presbyterian of the *Seceder tradition from Ireland, formed the Christian Association of Washington (Pa.). Decrying *sectarianism, he called for biblical "unity, peace and purity" in the Church. His son, Alexander, soon assumed the greater prominence. From 1813 to 1830 they worked within Baptist *associations, promoting a "new Reformation" on the basis of the NT alone and calling themselves Disciples of Christ; they designated their congregations biblically as Churches of Christ. They opposed as unscriptural human creeds and *confessions of faith, authoritarian ecclesiastical government, and sectarian names. Led by Walter *Scott to model their evangelism on Acts, they won thousands of converts. Under A. Campbell's leadership as editor (*The Millennial Harbinger*), debater (against the agnostic Robert D. Owen, the RC Abp. John B. Purcell, and others), and preacher, they presented a rational, biblical, practical interpretation of Christianity, free of theological subtlety and of revivalist emotion. In 1832 a number of Disciples and Christians in Ky. joined hands to signify their union as one people. By the 1840s Campbell was urging cooperation and church organization. In 1849 the first general convention formed the American Christian Missionary Society. In due course other national agencies also came into being (for foreign missions, benevolence, church extension, ministerial relief, temperance). In 1917 the International Convention of Disciples of Christ was formed to review the work of all reporting agencies, to advise them and the congregations on policy, and to provide a means of fellowship and inspiration. In 1934 the agencies formed Unified Promotion, voluntarily accepting a procedure for the allocation of contributed funds. In 1956 the convention changed its name to International Convention of Christian Churches (Disciples of Christ) and in 1967 constituted a delegate assembly elected by the congregations.

Meanwhile the practical problems of coordinating the work of scores of agencies (state and national) led to demands for "restructure." These demands coincided with a growing uneasiness over the concept of agencies as "societies of individuals" and the inherited doctrine that located the Church only in local congregations. *A Provisional Design for the Christian Church (Disciples of Christ)*, adopted in 1968, provides for the Christian Church in the U.S. and Canada with a general assembly composed of voting representatives from congregations and from regions, an interim general board, and an administrative committee; for the Christian Church in regions; and for the Christian Church in autonomous congregations. Power of decision on policy resides in the General Assembly; its chief officer is the General Minister and President. The course just sketched, as well as other sociological and theological factors, resulted in divisions within the movement. Before 1900 resistance grew against "innovations" that some accounted unscriptural—missionary societies, the use of musical instruments in worship, the one-man pastoral system that began to replace the collegial pastorate of the nonsalaried elders. In 1904 the dissidents issued a separate preacher list and the Federal Religious Census of 1906 named *Churches of Christ as a body distinct from Disciples of Christ. After 1900 some Disciples took offense at other tendencies: *open communion (reception of persons from other Churches without requiring immersion), the inroads of *liberal theology, and participation in councils of Churches and other ecumenical enterprises (interpreted by the opponents as an acceptance of *denominationalism). "Independent" or "direct support" missions developed, along with Bible colleges and seminaries "loyal to the plea," separate conventions, and rival publishing enterprises. In 1955 a *Directory of the Ministry of the Undenominational*

Fellowship of Christian Churches and Churches of Christ appeared as a listing distinct both from that of the Churches of Christ mentioned above and from the *Year Book of Christian Churches (Disciples of Christ)*. Some congregations and ministers, however, continue to let their names appear both in the *Directory* and the *Year Book*. In 1967 the former recorded 1,086,000 members for the "undenominational fellowship"; the latter indicated 1,875,400 Disciples in the U.S. and Canada.

The early Disciples undertook to set forth a simple biblical theology. Distinctive elements centered chiefly in the doctrine of conversion and in ecclesiology. As to conversion, the emphasis fell on a rational response in faith to the message of the gospel, with the baptism of the obedient believer by immersion signifying his acceptance of the lordship of Christ. In ecclesiology, Disciples sought to return to the faith and order of the apostolic Church as they found it in the NT, repudiating creeds as tests of faith and fellowship and seeking the union of Christians on the basis of the revealed essentials of the Church. Campbell outlined his views in the *Christian System* (2d ed., 1839), the arguments of which were restated and expanded by lesser authors for three generations. At the beginning of the 20th cent., new approaches in biblical criticism undercut the absolutism that had characterized the mind of Disciples, but a liberal reformulation of their theology emerged, later somewhat tempered under the influence of *neo-orthodoxy. A major reassessment was undertaken by the Panel of Scholars appointed in 1956; their work appeared in three volumes, W. B. Blakemore, ed., *The Renewal of Church: The Panel Reports* (1963).

The worship of Disciples has followed the practices of the liturgically free churches in America, except for the observance of holy communion each Lord's Day. Traditionally the elders presided, with the words of institution and prayers of thanksgiving, but now the minister commonly officiates. The original ministry of the Disciples included elders and deacons ordained to care for the congregations and a general order of evangelists, under no authority and exercising none except that of influence. Elders and deacons generally earned their living at secular callings. The evangelists who planted and guided the congregations gained a meager living from their ministry. With urbanization, congregations began to engage full-time pastors. Under the *Provisional Design* congregations call their ministers with the counsel of the regional minister. Policies as to ordination and ministerial standing are set by the General Assembly and administered by the regions. The polity of the church remains congregational insofar as internal congregational life is concerned but recognizes the Church as existing also in regions and in nations. General offices are in Indianapolis, Indiana. The Disciples of Christ Historical Society maintains an important library and archival collection in Nashville. The Christian Church, by changing its corporate name from "The Christian Churches," reluctantly but unequivocally accepted status as a denomination. The commitment to the unity of Christians continues unabated. The Church holds membership in the National Council of Churches, the World Council, and the Consultation on Church Union. See W. E. Garrison and A. T. DeGroot; *Disciples of Christ: A History* (2d ed., 1958).

CHRISTIAN CONGREGATION, evangelistic association formed in 1887 at Kokomo, Ind., and closely related to the Christian Churches. A union of congregations and individual members, it is noncreedal and nondenominational though organized on a *congregational pattern. It opposes sectarian controversy and seeks fellowship in Christian love. It is strongest in the rural areas of Ind., Ky., and Ohio, in Tex., and in Appalachia. Total membership in 1968 was 44,914, with 251 churches.

CHRISTIAN ENDEAVOR, INTERNATIONAL SOCIETY OF, interdenominational youth movement founded in 1881 by

Francis E. Clark, a Congregationalist pastor in Portland, Maine. Clark organized a group of young people in order to involve them in the work of the Church and to strengthen their religious commitment. The idea spread rapidly, esp. among the evangelical Churches, and in 1885 the United Society of Christian Endeavor was formed. In 1927 the present name was adopted; it designates the union of local societies in the U.S., Canada, and Mexico. Growth outside the U.S. was similarly rapid, and in 1895 national unions of local societies were brought together in the World's Christian Endeavor Union. The movement has been expanded to include all age groups, and presently numbers millions of adherents in thousands of local societies representing 80 denominations in 50 countries. Essential requirements for membership are the confession of Christ, service for Christ, loyalty to the Church, and Christian fellowship. Local societies offer courses in religious training and leadership, sponsor devotional and recreational activities, and provide opportunities for participation in social welfare projects.

CHRISTIAN METHODIST EPISCOPAL CHURCH, a denomination that had its roots in a proposal made in 1866 by the *General Conference of the Methodist Episcopal Church, South, when faced with desertion of its Negro members. The Conference voted to organize black members into "separate missions, churches, charges, districts, and Annual Conferences of their own." It also legislated that, whenever an entire congregation with sole use of a building joined either of the two African Methodist Episcopal Churches then in existence, the congregation be allowed to keep the edifice. When difference arose between the two African Churches, the bps. recommended that a new Negro Church be established. In 1870 delegates met in Jackson, Tenn., to organize a denomination, which they named the Colored Methodist Episcopal Church (changed in 1954 to Christian Methodist Episcopal Church). They

adopted the doctrine and discipline of the Methodist Episcopal Church, South, "after taking out and putting in such things as would be for the highest interest of the Church." Until 1880 the Church received only token support from its parent body, but after that date support increased; and in the 1939 union that formed the *Methodist Church a recommendation was made that in the South the Methodist Church should continue its historical support of the Negro body. From the first, the Christian Methodist Episcopal Church made the establishment of schools of higher education one of its major objectives. It conducts schools in five states and publishes several periodicals. It is a member of the World Council of Churches and of the Consultation on Christian Union. In 1965 membership of the Church totaled 446,718, in 2,598 churches. Plans for union in 1972 with the African Methodist Episcopal Church and the African Methodist Episcopal Church Zion were progressing in 1969. See HistAmMeth 3:385-386.

CHRISTIAN MISSION, the first name given to the *Salvation Army by W. *Booth. With reorganization in 1878, the name was changed.

CHRISTIAN NATION CHURCH, U.S.A., a *Holiness Church incorporated in 1896 as the Christian Nation Church by a group of independent evangelists, describing themselves as "equality evangelists," at Marion, Ohio. In 1961 it was reincorporated under its present title. It teaches justification, *entire sanctification, *divine healing, and the second coming of Christ but rejects the charismatic manifestations of *Pentecostalism. The Church encourages large families. It forbids tobacco, liquor, personal adornment, worldly amusements, social organization, marriage with the unrighteous, and remarriage after divorce. Membership in 1966 was 3,300, with 16 churches and 21 ordained clergy.

CHRISTIAN NURTURE, as a technical term, a theory of religious education. Although owing something to the contributions of such Unitarians as W. E. *Channing and T. *Parker, the origin of the concept is found in H. *Bushnell's *Christian Nurture* (1847). Reacting against the *revivalism of his day, which assumed a dramatic conversion in adulthood to be necessary, he declared that "the child is to grow up a Christian, and never know himself as being otherwise." He believed it wrong to expect a child to grow up as a sinner on the assumption that he could not become converted until he reached maturity. Such a presupposition ignored the family, the Church, and other organic means of God's bestowal of grace. In Bushnell's thought there were, at least implicitly, certain tendencies that became prominent in the latter half of the century: (1) divine immanence; (2) organic development in religion and morals; (3) an emphasis upon the human element in Jesus Christ; and (4) recognition that children have potentialities for good as well as for evil. Under the influence of such Europeans as A. *Ritschl and A. *Harnack, as well as of American educators, these concepts were developed in the 20th cent. into an extremely anthropocentric type of religious education, optimistically seeking to establish a perfect democratic society that was equated with the kingdom of God, leaving little place for divine transcendence. Some reactions against these trends came in the 1940s. See H. S. Smith, *Faith and Nurture* (1941).

CHRISTIAN PERFECTION, a Methodist doctrine, first taught by John *Wesley. He defined it as "loving God with all our heart, mind, soul and strength. This implies no wrong temper, none contrary to love remains in the soul; and that all thoughts, words and actions are governed by pure love" (*A Plain Account of Christian Perfection*, 1777). He stated that Christian perfection is not perfect knowledge, or freedom from certain mistakes, or freedom from infirmities ("inward and outward imperfections that are not of a moral nature"), or freedom from temptation. Rather, he felt it is freedom from known outward sin, since "whosoever is born of God sinneth not," as well as from such inward sins as evil thoughts and tempers. It is inward and outward purity arising from a new, clean heart that completely loves God. The attainment of perfection is by an act of God's grace distinct from and following upon conversion or justification, whereby a believer, by faith, was filled with the Spirit of God and empowered to overcome all sin. In short, whereas justification is a change in man's condition whereby God, through an act of pardon, forgives man his sins, restoring him to divine fellowship, Christian perfection is a change in man's very nature; God "extirpates man's sinful nature," empowering him to overcome all sin and to live a life of perfect love.

The doctrine created a great deal of trouble in many of Wesley's *societies, esp. in London, where T. *Maxfield encouraged Methodists who, claiming such a grace themselves, felt that only those with a similar experience were sufficiently informed spiritually to teach them. Eventually, led by Maxfield, these people split from Wesley, forming independent congregations. The result was that many of the Methodist preachers ceased teaching Christian perfection, fearing a dispute similar to that in London. Wesley himself never claimed to possess "perfect love"; several times he discussed with his brother Charles the advisability of omitting the doctrine from Methodist teaching. He decided against this action, however, continuing to proclaim it and urging his preachers to do the same. He felt that in Christian perfection God had given the Methodists an important doctrine to propagate. Wesley's doctrine was taken up and elaborated in *revivalism, and esp. the *Holiness movement. The interpretation of the Holiness Churches was not accepted by most Methodist bodies (see ENTIRE SANCTIFICATION).

Contemporary Methodists explain Christian perfection as a gradual growth in grace whereby a believer is enabled to live a victorious Christian life. They stress the "going on" to perfection rather than the "attainment" of it, and they use modern terminology, referring to Christian maturity, a personality integrated in God, or spiritual wholeness. See C. W. Williams, *John Wesley's Theology Today* (1960), with bibliog.; F. J. McConnell, *John Wesley* (1939), 191–216; N. B. Harmon, *Understanding the Methodist Church* (rev. ed., 1955), 72–74. *PERFECTIONISM; *CONCUPISCENCE.

CHRISTIAN REFORMED CHURCH, a body formed in 1857 as a result of a departure from the parent *Reformed Church in America. The chief issues of disagreement were doctrine and policy regarding membership in secret societies. After early setbacks, the Church grew through the affiliation of Dutch immigrants and others who were dissatisfied with the alleged liberalism of the parent body. In 1968 membership exceeded 270,000, in more than 600 congregations; headquarters are in Grand Rapids, Michigan. The Christian Reformed Church firmly adheres to the *Heidelberg Catechism, the Canons of *Dort, and the *Belgic Confession as *doctrinal standards. The language of worship is no longer Dutch but English. Government is in the hands of the 32 classes into which local congregations are grouped; there is a general *synod that meets annually and is composed of two ministers and two laymen from each *classis. The Church strongly opposes membership in Masonic or other similar lodges. The parochial schools maintained by this Church have an enrollment exceeded among Protestants only by Lutheran and Seventh-day Adventist schools. The Church also maintains Calvin College and Seminary in Grand Rapids, Mich., two junior colleges, 18 homes for the aged, and a publishing house. It supports about 50 missionaries in Japan, Formosa, Nigeria, and South America, as well as 70 home missionaries for work esp. among Indians and Negroes. See M. M. Schooland, *Children of the Reformation: The Christian Reformed Church, Its Origin and Growth* (1958).

CHRISTIAN SCIENCE, the doctrines of the *Church of Christ Scientist, received from Mary Baker *Eddy, esp. those on the power of spiritual mind to dominate material forces.

CHRISTIAN SOCIALISM, a term that, taken narrowly, refers to the short-lived movement (1848–54) that rose from within the C of E, against the *laissez-faire* doctrine of Bentham and James and J. S. Mill, which combined with capitalism to dispossess the people and produce the squalor of early industrialism. The movement advocated the reform of society by the application of Christian principles. Its effective founder and organizer was J. M. F. Ludlow, a barrister well versed in law, politics, and economics; his fame is overshadowed by F. D. *Maurice and C. *Kingsley. A vigorous campaign was launched, by meetings and periodical publications, and after the scares of Chartism and the revolutions of 1848 encountered great hostility. This did not kill it, however; rather it died from the indifference of the workers themselves, from the counterinterest of the Great Exhibition and the Crimean War, and from the spreading bourgeois mid-Victorian confidence in inevitable material progress. Its monument is the Working Men's College, its legacy the growth of the Cooperative and the Trade Union movements.

The *Tracts on Christian Socialism* (1850), like the *Tracts for the Times*, belong to the confines of a period, but the Christian Socialist movement, like the *Oxford movement, opened out into wider power. The early Tractarians were pre-Disraeli Tories without much concern for social problems as such, but those of the next generation were very alive to them: a comparison between J. H. Newman and H. E. Manning will suggest the difference. One feature of *Anglo-Catholicism has been an involvement with the cause of social reform, which can be traced from the Guild of St. Matthew to the Christian Social Union, and which culminates in the Malvern Declaration (1951). The encyclicals of Leo XIII promoted a like RC concern, of which one expression was the Catholic Social Guild. The movement was even more influential on the Continent; Bishop Ketteler of Mainz and the Comte de Mun, to mention but two names, grounded their policies on well-articulated and classical RC moral doctrines, and were the harbingers of the days when the RC electorate in democratic countries often voted well to the left; in the Austria of Ignaz Seipel it called itself Christian Socialism. In the U.S. the movement was later in starting, and for various reasons has not made a political impact under that name. To go no farther back than Washington *Gladden and W. D. P. Bliss, the evils of economic individualism have been diagnosed and the remedies, the social responsibility of ownership and a more equitable distribution of wealth, have been applied, ever more and more comprehensively.

The movement has differed from the socialism of the first and second International by its stress on the right to private property, and from communism by its order of priorities; the first has tended to scorn it as offering mere palliatives, the second to suppress it or give it the kiss of death. In the 2d half of the 20th cent., however, the dimensions of the debate have changed, religious men of different obediences have converged, and there are not a few who proclaim themselves both Christian and Marxist. See C. Raven, *Christian Socialism* (1921); G. C. Binyon, *Christian Socialist Movement in England* (1931); J. Dombrowski, *Early Days of Christian Socialism in America* (1936).

CHRISTIAN UNION, an association of local churches first organized in Columbus, Ohio, in 1864, by persons seeking a oneness in Christ and a freer form of ecclesiastical organization. While they do not stress any particular system of doctrine, member churches retain the doctrines generally acceptable to all evangelical denominations. They emphasize oneness in Christ; the Bible as their only rule of faith and practice, with each member left free to interpret any disputed theological question; the Lord's Supper; baptism, and in some cases *footwashing. A good life is the sole requisite for membership; preachers are enjoined from using the pulpit for political topics. Polity is *congregational, but local churches are united loosely in council meetings conducted for fellowship and denominational business; a general council meets every third year; a state council, annually. Headquarters are in Excelsior Springs, Mo.; membership in 1965 was 5,281, in 228 churches. Christian Union supports both a home and a foreign mission program.

CHRISTIAN UNITY BAPTIST ASSOCIATION, a body formed in 1934 by those who, advocating *open communion, withdrew from the Regular Baptists in North Carolina. The denomination in 1968 numbered about 650 members, in 11 churches. *Footwashing is practiced regularly as an act of humility.

CHRISTIAN VOLUNTEER FORCE, a fundamentalist body similar to the Salvation Army, founded in Glasgow, Scotland, in 1917 by James Hutchison.

CHRISTIANITY, the historical movement stemming from Jesus Christ and based upon commitment to him. A distinction is sometimes drawn between the historical movement that has existed under the name of Christianity and the ideal that would exist if those who call themselves followers of Christ were true to his spirit and teachings. Thus, on the one hand, much that has gone under the name of Christianity is said not to be true Christianity, whatever the church affiliation of those who have been unfaithful to Christ's teaching may have been. On the other hand, Christians and Christian bodies that have no visible communion with others because of disagreement on points of doctrine tend to look upon each other as heretical or at least as guilty of departing in some respect from Christ's teaching. Yet the persistence even in opposing bodies of a strong commitment to the person of

Christ, fidelity in worship, devotion to the Scriptures, and Christian service is evidence of a rightful sense of the term that transcends many specific differences of belief. Christianity in the ideal sense can be further subdivided, understanding it from the doctrinal standpoint or from the ethical. Although some have placed greater emphasis upon the distinctive Christian teachings and others upon the Christian ideal of ethical behavior, most Christians have held that to some degree the two are properly indivisible. In general usage everyone who affirms a commitment to Christ is considered in some sense a part of historical Christianity.

CHRISTIANS, the name used after 1830 by the followers of Alexander and Thomas *Campbell, to indicate opposition to *denominationalism; they also called themselves Disciples of Christ. *CHRISTIAN CHURCHES (DISCIPLES OF CHRIST), INTERNATIONAL CONVENTION OF.

CHRISTKATHOLIKEN (Christian Catholics), the Old Catholic Church of Switzerland. The decrees of Vatican Council I, mainly for their alleged dogmatic sanction of the *Syllabus of Errors, led many Swiss RC middle class laymen to embrace Old Catholicism. At the first national meeting of Swiss Old Catholics (1872), an address by Breslau Professor Reinkens contributed to the group's rapid spread. At their next national meeting (1873) the Old Catholics declared themselves independent of the Roman hierarchy. In 1875 the constitution of 1874 was adopted by the first National Synod of the Christian Catholic Church of Switzerland. In 1876 the National Synod, comprising 54 clergymen and 108 laymen representing 73,380 persons, elected E. Herzog bishop. Herzog was consecrated by German Old Catholic Bp. Reinkens. Berne became the episcopal seat. In 1968 Christkatholiken numbered 22,000. See C. B. Moss, *Old Catholic Movement* (1966).

CHRISTMAS CONFERENCE, meeting of Methodist preachers in Baltimore, Md., in 1784, which organized the *Methodist Episcopal Church. The conference was called by F. *Asbury and T. *Coke, who had been ordained by John *Wesley as a general superintendent (bishop) of the Methodist work in America. At the Conference, Asbury was ordained a general superintendent, after being elected to the office by the preachers. A *ritual, a *Book of Discipline, and standards of doctrine were also adopted. See HistAmMeth 1:197–240; F. E. Maser, *Dramatic Story of Early American Methodism* (1965), 84–97.

CHRISTO SACRUM (Lat., sacred to Christ), a religious society in existence from 1797 to 1838, founded by Canzius Onder de Winhart, mayor of Delft, Holland. It sought to promote universal Christian love regardless of any church affiliation and stressed belief in the divinity of Christ and salvation through his death as a bond uniting Christians. Although founded as a defense against *deism and not intended as a separate religious group, the society was nevertheless condemned by the *Reformed Church authorities and ceased to exist with the closing of its building in 1838. See J. A. Gerth van Wijk, EncRelKnow 3:48.

CHRIST'S MISSION, INC., an evangelical Protestant association devoted primarily to assisting former RC priests and nuns and to promoting Protestant missionary work among RC laymen. It was founded in 1883 by James A. O'Connor, a RC priest who had left the clergy and established a monthly magazine, the *Converted Catholic*. This periodical, which became *Christian Heritage* in 1958, has been the principal activity of the group and its chief means of reaching potential converts. Christ's Mission, Inc., has aided a number of former RC priests in preparing for the evangelical ministry. In 1960 it formed the Protestant Council on Roman Catholicism at Buck Hill Falls, Pa., under the direction of Stuart

P. Garver. Headquarters are in New York City and Sea Cliff, New York. Changing circumstances have taken away the point of the Christ's Mission polemics, and the association seems to be evolving into a denomination.

CHRIST'S SANCTIFIED HOLY CHURCH, a *Holiness Church formed at West Lake, La., in 1903, when white evangelists brought the doctrine of *entire sanctification "as a distinct experience . . . wrought instantaneously" into a Negro Methodist church. In 1957 it reported 600 members in 30 churches. Headquarters are in Jennings, Louisiana.

CHURCH, etymologically, house of the Lord (from Middle Eng. *chirice*, Old Eng. *cirice*, and ultimately from late Gr. *kyriakon*, of the Lord). Apart from designating a building for worship, usually Christian, the term is variously applied to religious associations. (1) In legal or political usage the Church may refer to the established Church, e.g., in England. In discussion of the relations of Church and State both terms have an abstract meaning, Church referring to religious association and interests of citizens in contrast to State, their civil association and interests. Any specific religious body may be referred to as a Church in the same legal context. (2) The sociology of religion uses various classifications for religious associations. Church is contrasted with sect or mysticism, e.g., by E. *Troeltsch. The bodies classified as Churches are more institutionalized and stress historical origins, confessions of faith, form of government, and use of sacraments and liturgy (see SECT). (3) Christian ecclesiastical use of the term varies with theological presuppositions. There are two main contrasting uses. In RC terms the Church is the Roman Catholic Church, which believes itself to be the one true Church in historical and doctrinal continuity with the Church as Christ founded it. In

this identification the visible institutional Church and the Church of the NT are regarded as one. The language and viewpoint of Vatican Council II, however, opened the way to a less rigid acceptance in recognizing the authentic ecclesial elements in other Christian bodies. While there have been and are minor Protestant groups that have identified themselves as the only true Church, the general Protestant use of the term is more comprehensive. Both historically and doctrinally Protestants refuse to identify the one true Church with any institutional body. The Church is the Church of the gospel; it is the community of believers; it exists wherever the true gospel is preached. Visible forms and institutions, always reformable, vary. The Church is the Church universal and includes the various Churches or denominations. Each specific Christian body may be called a Church, in the sense and to the degree that it is an authentic expression of the Church that Christ intended.

CHURCH (NT), the community of believers in Jesus of Nazareth as the risen, ascended Messiah and Lord (Acts 2.36), who are baptized in his name (Acts 2.38), receive the teaching of the Twelve about him (Acts 2.42), and as members of the community of believers share in the eucharistic table (Acts 2.42). The community of believers was early designated as the *ekklēsia* in Christian preaching to Greek audiences. *Ekklēsia*, meaning an assembly, was used in the LXX translation of the Hebrew Bible to translate the Hebrew *qahal*, also meaning a meeting, gathering, or assembly. The actual assembly, where the baptized and instructed believers in Jesus came together, occurred at the Eucharistic liturgy (Acts 2.42). Since the assembly was unified in its religious ideas and aspirations ("one Lord, one faith, one baptism," Eph 4.5.), the term *ekklēsia*, "church," acquired the meaning in the NT of all those who, whether actually physically gathered together for worship or not, held to the same faith in Christ. They were expected to express this faith on the first day of the week in actual physical assembly to worship through the Eucharistic rite (Acts 20.7). Thus the term *ekklēsia* carries in the NT its own specific connotations with reference to Jesus of Nazareth, to other believers with whom one is in the community of faith, and to a formed sociological reality, an actual grouping of people who share the same concerns over the purpose and shape of life.

The first epistles of St. Paul, 1 and 2 Th (A.D. 50–52), use *ekklēsia* in this sense. Paul writes to "the church of the Thessalonians in God the Father and the Lord Jesus Christ" (1 Th 1.1; 2 Th 1.1), i.e., to those in Thessalonica who profess faith in Jesus as savior and Lord. He envisions them as listening to the reading of his letters on the occasion of the eucharistic gathering. In 1 Th 2.14 he uses the plural *ekklēsiai* to refer to the members of the Christian communities scattered throughout Palestine who were persecuted for their faith: "For you, brethren, have become imitators of the churches of God in Christ Jesus which are in Judea; for you suffered the same things from your own countrymen as they did from the Jews . . . ." The *ekklēsia* is thus a community of believers, who, as individuals, carry their faith with them as persons, and who, whether in actual physical assembly for the Eucharist or not, are viewed as forming a unity through the identity of their religious beliefs and aspirations of conduct. The *ekklēsia* is not a mere aggregate of believers in Jesus of Nazareth. Its determinative element is prophecy, the divine call, entering into history first through Jesus himself (see Mk 1.14–15) and then through the proclamation by the Twelve of his resurrection (Acts 2.14–36). The acceptance of this proclamation and its implications is an act of faith in the word of God (1 Th 1.5–8; 2.13), which carries with it the continuing presence of God in Christ bestowing the gift of salvation (Phil 2.12–13), i.e., the liberation of man from sin and its effects (1 Cor 6.11). From the standpoint of this sanctifying divine presence acting upon believers, the Church is viewed by Paul as destined for a holy and sinless exist-

ence, toward which it takes its first faltering steps within the reality of history (Eph 5.25–27).

In NT times local churches lay under two sources of leadership. The first was an administrative function, held by the *presbyter* (literally, elder) or *episkopos* (literally, overseer; in English, bishop), terms undifferentiated in meaning in the early decades of the history of the NT Church (Acts 14.23; 20.28). One of the primary responsibilities was to conserve the teaching of the Twelve and St. Paul in its authentic meaning (Acts 20.17–35). The second source of leadership was a charismatic endowment, shared by other members of the Church besides the administrative leaders. Charism in this sense was a manifestation of the presence of the Holy Spirit, esp. through prophecy (Acts 11.27–28), teaching (Acts 13.1–2), and preaching (Acts 6.8–10). The NT employs various images to sound the depths of theological meaning in its concept of the Church, e.g., the people of God (its own self-understanding as called to faith), the new creation (the renewal of humanity through the Church), and the body of Christ (the Church's transcendental relationship to God through Christ). See R. Schnackenburg, *Church in the New Testament* (1965); Paul S. Minear, *Images of the Church in the New Testament* (1960).

CHURCH (Theological Interpretations). Throughout the entire history of Western Christianity notions of the Church are proposed as reconstructions or developments of one or another aspect of NT teaching. In the NT documents, moreover, various points of view may be discerned: the Pauline emphasis upon the Church as the body of Christ; Luke's description of the Church as the historical fulfillment of God's plan; the Johannine reflection on the Church as life in Christ; and Matthew's thought concerning the Church as the community of the New Law.

Patristic Era. In the patristic period, several heterodox currents of thought stand as prototypes of later ecclesiological theories. The earliest is the 2d-cent. Marcionite concept of the Church as altogether cut off from the people of God of the Old Covenant. This concept is rooted in the radical opposition alleged by *Marcion between the God of the OT and the God of the New. In the second half of the 2d cent. *Montanist doctrine was exclusivist in another direction, namely that the Church subsists only in a community of holy ones, the elect, who look to the Holy Spirit, rather than to the Lord Jesus, as the principle of their cohesion and activity. *Tertullian professed (*c.*200) this type of "pneumatic ecclesiology." A modification of this position is present in the 4th-cent. *Donatist view, according to which ecclesial ministry is invalid unless the minister is holy. St. Augustine concerned himself esp. with the Donatist contention; and from the polemic he instituted against it comes the strong Catholic tradition concerning the objective value of the exercise of the ministry in the Church, without immediate regard for the minister's holiness. Perhaps more important, however, is Augustine's synthetic development of various NT themes concerning the Church, e.g., in the *City of God.* While not an ecclesiological treatise, this work is an idealistic decription of the Church, with special emphasis upon the idea that the Church is the locus wherein the New Law bears fruit in the obedience of faith.

Medieval Period. The medieval period produced no explicit treatises in ecclesiology. This does not mean, however, that views concerning the Church were not developing. The various spiritualist movements were recrudescences, in one form or another of the Montanist movement. Abbot *Joachim of Fiori (*c.* 1132–1202) set forth a more elaborate theory of the historical transition from the age of the Father (the OT), through that of the Son (the NT up to the time of Joachim), to that of the Holy Spirit (which was then to be inaugurated). Mainly, however, medieval thought on the Church was concerned with an interpretation of its relationship to the civilization engendered by the spread of Christianity.

The close association of Church and State occasioned the theories of the canonists concerning the precedence of the pope over all other powers in the world, and the exercise of the "two swords." A step toward a comprehensive description of the mystery of the Church was made in the period during which the various forms of *conciliarism were put forth. Yet Juan de Torquemada's treatise, *De Ecclesia* (1489), was more an attempt to put to rights the claims of the conciliarists in favor of papal prerogatives than a broad ecclesiology. In the same age, Jan *Hus and his disciples were professing a theory of the Church close to that of the Montanists, though the emphasis was not so much on holiness as on *election as constitutive of the true Church. Thus, for the patristic and medieval descriptive formulas *communio sanctorum* and *communio fidelium,* Hus substituted *communio electorum.*

Reformation. Each wing of the Reformation adopted an ecclesiology peculiar to itself. Luther and his disciples saw the Church as the congregation of saints or believers, among whom the Gospel is purely preached and the sacraments are rightly administered (see *Augsburg Confession, Art. 7). Implicit in this description is a further distinction, namely between the external and the internal Church, the latter of which is the "true" Church. The true Church does not come into being, however, except through the external preaching of the gospel, which may either bear fruit (thus the internal Church) or for practical purposes, i.e., for the Christian life, remain unheeded (external Church). In the *Reformed tradition a broader definition, akin to that of Hus, is given. The Church is comprised of all those who are predestined. The preaching of the gospel and the administration of the sacraments are the normal (though not indispensable) ways in which predestination is realized (see Second *Helvetic Confession, Ch. 17). Nevertheless, the later notion of the invisible Church really has its origin here (see *Westminster Confession, Ch. 25). The Anglican tradition influenced very deeply in the beginning by

Reformed preachers from the Continent, developed according to its own style. The episcopal structure of the Church was maintained (as in the Swedish branch of Lutheranism), though without reference to the primacy of the pope. Finally, in Reformation times the so-called left-wing movements emerged, with quite spiritualized ideas about the Church, reminiscent of Montanism and the more recent theories of Hus. In their ideas of the Church, groups like the Anabaptists were forerunners of the *Nonconformists in Great Britain (Baptists, Methodists, Quakers). RC theologians of the Reformation era, esp. Robert Bellarmine, composed their theology particularly in reaction to theories of the Reformers. Thus they put heavy emphasis on the external aspects of the Church, the Church as a visible, juridic society. Once these lines had been drawn, the only thing that could apparently change the situation would be the introduction of an entirely new way of thinking, which would challenge both Protestant and Catholic.

18th–19th Centuries. In fact, the *Enlightenment was such a challenge. The rationalist movement, insofar as it affected Western Christianity, produced the so-called liberal interpretation of the nature of the Church. In its most extreme form, e.g., in the thought of J. S. Semler (1725–91), the Church was viewed as a free society wherein the values of freedom of conscience and fraternity are realized—and nothing more. The romantic reaction to such a radical view of the Church is exemplified in the thought of F. *Schleiermacher, the father of *liberal theology. Given his interpretation of the nature of the Christian life, i.e., as consisting in the development of "religious feeling," the Church could be nothing more than the association of men who experience this feeling of dependence upon God, after the pattern set by the religious experience of Jesus himself. More orthodox views of the Church prevailed during this post-Reformation period where Protestantism more or less maintained its original thrust. In the U.S., among Baptists, Methodists, and

Presbyterians, the idea of the free covenanting of believing Christians was much in evidence (see COVENANT THEOLOGY). Modern RC ecclesiology also was affected by the rationalist movement, but in a different way. Especially under the influence of the Roman theological school, a negative reaction to the rationalist movement caused an even greater emphasis to be placed upon the role of the magisterial authority in the life of the Church than had previously been the case. This culminated in the definition, at Vatican Council I, of the dogma of papal infallibility.

20th Century. With the beginning of the 20th cent. a new era of ecclesiology seems to have been begun, ushered in by the movement of modern critical biblical research. The liberal view of the Church has been challenged from within Protestantism, with a consequent return to a concern for the structural aspects of the Church, e.g., the authenticity of a duly constituted ministry—though interpretations vary widely, as became evident in the early days of the ecumenical movement (e.g., the first meeting of *Faith and Order in Lausanne, Switzerland, in 1925). Many Protestants, however, have come to recognize the necessity of abandoning the idea of a separation between visible and invisible Church. Thus they maintain, in common with Roman Catholics, the integrity of the body of Christ as a mystery that has both visible and invisible aspects. Similarly, RC reassessments took place and culminated in the deliberations of Vatican Council II. One of the major documents of the Council had to do directly with the mystery of the Church. The dogmatic constitution, *Lumen gentium*, presents a view of the Church that is quite comprehensive and takes into account the ecumenical dialogue. Thus a broader theory of *membership in the Church than has hitherto been developed is presented, with a view toward putting the entire ecumenical movement in the perspective of the mystery of the Church as the people of God, which exists in the form of the mystical body of Christ. *VISIBLE CHURCH.

CHURCH (GENERAL HISTORY). The historical outline presented here concentrates on church history in Western Christendom. The persons, events, and themes indicated are a record of the past and an explanation of what there is both of unity and of diversity in church life in the present.

THE CHURCH TO THE REFORMATION

The history of the Church in the West for 16 centuries is the history of one historical reality. By the 13th cent. that Church had become finally separated from the Church in the East. With the Reformation the external unity of the Church in the West also was shattered, so that the Reformation is the central dividing mark in Western Church history.

Pentecost to the Edict of Milan. The only actual annals or chronicles in this period, until Eusebius of Caesarea (260–340), the father of church history, are the NT Acts of the Apostles. Together with some pastoral and polemical writings, Acts show that Pentecost began a period of phenomenal expansion. The Church became a recognizable entity in the Roman world: early there were *local churches, not only those addressed by Paul, but others in Italy, Gaul, Spain, Germany, the Danubian provinces, North Africa, and Egypt. They were organized either monarchically under the bishop or under a college of presbyters presided over by the bishop. From Clement of Rome, Ignatius, Irenaeus, Tertullian, and in the *rebaptism controversy of Cyprian of Carthage with Pope Stephen I, there is evidence of the See of Rome consciously exercising her primacy as teacher and center of unity. The doctrinal life of the Church manifested itself in the composition of the Gospels and the other NT books. Internally the Judaizing Christians were put down; the need to face the pagan world motivated the apologists, esp. Justin Martyr and Irenaeus. A further test was the first of the perennial appearances of dualism, in the form of Manichaeism. *Tertullian opposed Marcion, who separated the God of law in the OT from the God of love in the NT; but

Tertullian embraced the apocalyptic doctrines of the *Montanists. The first efforts at positive theological elaborations came from Clement of Alexandria and his disciple Origen. The Church, regarded as a force inimical to the interests of Rome, lived in the catacombs as imperial persecutions made this the age of martyrs, who were revered as living with Christ, and whose intercession was sought. With the conversion of Constantine and the Edict of Milan (313) the persecutions ceased and, save for the brief interlude under Julian the Apostate, the Church came into a favored position in the Empire and manifested its presence by the splendid edifices that were built for the worship of God.

The 4th to the 7th Century. Benevolent as it was in fact, Constantine's attitude toward the Church marked the beginning of a caesaropapism, stifling to the Byzantine Church—e.g., in the laws and conduct of Justinian and in the beginnings of the schism between East and West—but also foreshadowing the conflicts between medieval popes and emperors. Nevertheless, from Constantine on the Church flourished. *Monasticism was born, first in the East through Anthony, Athanasius, and Basil, in Ireland through Patrick, and on the Continent through Martin of Tours, Benedict, and Gregory the Great. The monks contributed mightily to the missionary activities which would lead to the conversion of all of western Europe. With the baptism of Clovis (496), Gaul was brought into the Church; the evangelization of England was resumed in 596 by Augustine of Canterbury; gradually the barbarians, some Arian, some pagan, who invaded the empire, became Catholics. The doctrinal life of the Church was no less intense; there was a continuous defense of orthodoxy and a growth in theological thought. In Africa the struggle with the *Donatists, which dragged on for centuries, was complicated by political issues, as were the Christological controversies that led to the first great *ecumenical councils: Nicaea (325) and Constantinople I (381), against Arianism; Ephesus (431), against Nestorianism;

Chalcedon (451), against Monophysitism; Constantinople III (680), against Monothelitism. These centuries are also the era of the Fathers. In the East there were Athanasius, Basil, Gregory of Nazianzus, Gregory of Nyssa, John Chrysostom. In the West Jerome labored to provide a sound text of the Scriptures; Augustine's writings against Manichaeism and Pelagianism set the tone of theological thought in Europe for centuries; Gregory the Great's moral writings had lasting influence on the practice of the Christian life.

Medieval Period (600–1500). In these centuries, the Church passed through cycles of reverses and reform in all phases of its life.

Church Expansion. At the outset expansion met serious setbacks. Beginning about 600 Islam tore away North Africa and most of Asia from the Church and even extended itself into Spain. The Iconoclast emperors in the East beginning with Leo III (717–741) began a process of alienation between the Byzantine patriarchates and Rome, which by the early 13th cent. had become complete schism (see SCHISM, EAST-WEST). Missionary activity continued to effect the conversion of all of Europe: begun earlier by St. Boniface (d. 442) and St. Columba (d. 597), it spread to the Slavs with St. Cyril (d. 869) and Methodius (d. 885); the Magyars and Poles were converted by the 10th cent.; the Scandinavian countries by the 11th; and those east of the Baltic by the 12th or 13th.

Papal Rule. Because of the prestige of Gregory the Great and the absence of civil authority, a process begun in his reign (590–604) lead to the formation of the States of the Church. The pope became a secular ruler, and a problem new in the West, the conflict between pope and princes, had its beginnings. The alliance of the papacy with the Frankish monarchy in the person of Pepin III culminated in the coronation by Pope Leo III of Charlemagne (800) as the first Holy Roman Emperor. Although during the reign of the Carolingians there was notable progress, with their collapse the papacy became a chattel within the feudal

scheme, first of the Roman princes, then of the Germany monarchy. This situation was arrested beginning with the pontificate of Leo IX (1048–54), during which a reforming decree on papal elections was enacted. Church reform, which owed much to the monastic foundation of Cluny (910), reached its peak in the work of the great Hildebrand, Gregory VII (1073–85), and extended not only to the opposition to Emperor Henry IV over lay investiture, but also to all levels of ecclesiastical life. Urban II (1088–99) continued it and gained new moral prestige for the papacy by inaugurating the *Crusades (1095).

By the second half of the 12th cent. the Gregorian reform had begun to lose impetus and the papacy became involved in resisting the absolutism of Frederick Barbarossa (1152–90). A new vigor emerged with the election of Innocent III, whose reign (1198–1216) marked the summit of papal sovereignty, and whose reform was crowned by the work of Lateran Council IV (1215). Under Innocent the Church was institutionalized by the canonists. His policies of centralization and control were not wisely carried out by his successors. The papal right to nominate all bishops, the right of provision, was exploited for financial gain; under Innocent IV (1243–54) heavy papal taxation began. At the Council of Lyons I (1245) he also successfully excommunicated Frederick II, thus achieving a kind of victory of pope over emperor. The extreme expression of papal claims to supremacy came with Boniface VIII's bull *Unam sanctam* (1302) in the disputes with Philip IV of France. There followed immediately, however, the election of the Frenchman Clement V (1305–14) and the beginnings of the *Babylonian captivity of the papacy at Avignon (1309–77). Much antipapal sentiment resulted; it was articulated by *Marsilius of Padua and *William of Ockam and put into practice with England's statutes of *Praemunire and Provisors. No sooner had the Pope returned to Rome than the *Great Western Schism (1378–1417) erupted with the scandal of rival claimants to the papacy. Among the attempts to heal it was the theory of *conciliarism that dominated the Councils of *Pisa (1409), *Constance (1414), and *Basel (1431–49). A degree of reform was achieved under Martin V (1417–31) and Eugene IV (1431–47), who also fashioned a brief reunion with the Greeks at the Council of Florence (1438–40), but *Gallicanism was born in France and everywhere the prestige of the papacy dimmed. In the period of the *Renaissance, the popes presented themselves to the world as unabashedly secular potentates. This had its benefits in the form of papal patronage of the arts, but the worldliness and corruption surrounding the papacy under Innocent VIII (1484–92), Alexander VI (1492–1503), and Julius II (1503–13) cried out for reform.

Christian Life. The 7th through the 12th cent. were a monastic era. Early fervor gave way to a period of decadence, but in 910 Cluny emerged. The strong federation of Cluniac houses had parallels elsewhere (see MONASTICISM). In the 11th cent. the renewal was centered in Citeaux, whose greatest representative, Bernard of Clairvaux (1090–1153), by his writing and preaching powerfully affected Christian devotion, esp. to Mary and to the Passion of Christ. A reform movement of clerics, the Order of Prémontré was founded in 1120. When the older orders failed to meet the needs of the times, in the 13th cent. the two great mendicant orders, the Dominicans and the Franciscans (soon to be followed by others of their type—Carmelites, Augustinians, and Servites), came into being. St. Dominic's ideal was to fulfill the need for doctrinal preaching; St. Francis of Assisi gave the noblest expression to the lay evangelical movements of the time. The bitter years of Avignon and the Western Schism saw also factious rivalries among the mendicants and a decline in their ideals, a decline hastened by the general havoc worked by the Black Death.

Christian life was also deeply affected by *apocalypticism and by the spiritual renewal fostered by groups of laity. The Franciscan *Spirituals, the *Fraticelli (see JOACHIMISM), and the *Flagellants often assailed the institutional Church and its sacraments. Some of the lay movements, e.g., the *Humiliati and the *Waldenses, stressed reform through evangelical poverty; they met with ecclesiastical resistance for their preaching. A more theologically guided poverty movement was inspired by John *Wycliffe (see LOLLARDS), whose ideas were followed by Jan *Hus (see HUSSITES) in Bohemia. The *Brothers and Sisters of the Free Spirit, as well as the *Beghards and *Beguines, concentrated on a spiritual renewal through a more intense, personal, devotional life. At the end of the 14th cent. the *Devotio moderna fostered by the *Brethren of the Common Life was a religious revival in the same spirit of personal prayer and sanctification.

Christian Thought. Such learning as survived in the early centuries of this era was due to the monk-missionaries. Under Charlemagne, however, Alcuin, himself from the cathedral school of York, presided over the Carolingian renaissance. His pupil Rabanus Maurus made Fulda a source of ecclesiastical learning in Germany. Rabanus also was involved in doctrinal disputes with *Gottschalk on predestination and with Paschasius Radbertus on the Eucharist. In the period of the Gregorian reform the cathedral schools, like that at Chartres, flourished. By the end of the 12th cent. these schools had begun to decline, but the seeds of future glory had been planted. St. Anselm (c.1033–1109) had given strong impetus to the intellectualizing of theology; Gratian had composed his Decretals; Peter Lombard (c.1100–60), his *Sentences*; and Peter Abelard (1079–1142), his *Sic et non*. The 13th cent. saw the full flower of *scholasticism, through the translation of the complete text of Aristotle's works, and the emergence of such great universitites as Paris, Oxford, and Bologna. This was the environment of William of Auvergne (c.1180–1249), Alexander of Hales (c.1170–1245), Bonaventure (1221–74), Albert the Great (c.1200–80), Robert Kilwardby (d. 1279), John Peckham (c.1225–92). Thomas Aquinas (c.1225–74) was able to give to the Church his monumental synthesis of Christian thought.

There followed, however, the parceling of theology into schools and the gradual ascendancy of *nominalism, with an adulteration of the understanding of the Christian message. The rationale of the Devotio moderna was a kind of anti-intellectual reaction to the empty rationalism of nominalism. The Renaissance itself paralleled the secularization of the papacy in the tendency to divorce learning and life from the influence of the Church.

PROTESTANTISM

The abuses in doctrine and in life that had festered and spread in the Renaissance Church demanded remedy and reform. The Reformation by its *formal principle, the sole authority of Scripture, and by its *material principle, justification by grace through faith alone, revolutionized Christian history in the West. The external unity of the Church was shattered. Roman Catholicism and Protestantism became two divergent views on man's relationship to God, the sacraments and esp. the Eucharist, the ministry, and the Church, as well as two opposed practices of the Christian life, in devotion, liturgy, and discipline. Both Protestants and Catholics profess the "one, holy, catholic, and apostolic Church"; that profession has a dimension of historical continuity with the Church established by Christ. But with the Reformation, church history becomes an account of historically different Churches. The term Protestant originated from the *protestatio* at the Diet of Speyer (1529) of Lutheran princes against the policies of Charles V. It came to be accepted as a designation for the Churches that had their immediate or remote origins in the Reformation inaugurated by Martin Luther. Protestantism is here used to group such Churches. (See PROTESTANTISM for the presentation of doctrinal themes of agreement and diversity.)

The Various Protestant Traditions. The Reformation, inaugurated by Martin *Luther, immediately gave rise on the Continent to three main traditions. Luther's own doctrines were most faithfully followed by Lutheran or Evangelical Churches, mainly in Germany and in Scandinavia. The reform teachings first of *Zwingli, then of John *Calvin, became the doctrines of the *Reformed Church, mainly in Switzerland, the Rhine Valley, the Netherlands, and among the *Huguenots of France. The radical or left wing of the Reformation was represented by the various groups, often of differing beliefs, in Germany and Switzerland, called *Anabaptists. Their heritage was perpetuated by the Mennonites and similar groups (see REFORMATION). In the British Isles the *Church of England, first under *Henry VIII, then finally under *Elizabeth I, became a national Church. Within *Anglicanism some defend its Protestant character, i.e., adherence to Reformation ideas and to Calvinist influences; others stress its Catholic continuity. Under John *Knox, the *Church of Scotland became a model of Presbyterianism (see REFORMATION). Removed from the mainstream, yet often classified as Protestant, was the small rationalistic and Unitarian movement called *Socinianism.

During the reign of Elizabeth I (1558–1603) the Puritan party arose in the Church of England, protesting against ritual and episcopacy. Puritans who separated from the C of E gave rise to Congregationalism. Also Congregational in their concept of the Church, were the Baptists, named for their practice of *believer's baptism, and originating c.1608. To the *Noncomformist or *free churches in the 17th cent. were joined the Society of Friends (Quakers) founded by George *Fox, whose ideas reflected many of the spiritualizing and experiential emphases of the left-wing Reformation. In the 18th cent. on the Continent the Moravians were a renewal of the pre-Reformation *Unitas Fratrum. In England John Wesley formed the first Methodist societies, at first as circles for a more personalized spiritual life within the C of E (see METHODISM). The Methodist revival became a powerful factor in the development of American Protestantism. Other groups arose in the Protestant background, e.g., the Catholic Apostolic Church, Swedenborgians, Mormons, Adventists, and Jehovah's Witnesses, that do not have an obvious connection with the mainstream of Protestantism (see CHURCH, U.S. HISTORY). Pentecostalism had its remote origins in the Holiness interpretation of Wesley's doctrine (see HOLINESS MOVEMENT). While adhering to many common Protestant teachings, the Pentecostal movement is sometimes classified as a "third force" (i.e., distinct from Catholicism and Protestantism) because of its own specific doctrines.

Doctrinal and Theological Trends. The need to enunciate the essentials of Reformation teaching and the exigencies of controversy arose in the Reformation era itself. The 16th and 17th cents. were an era of *confessions of faith. The Anglican *Thirty-Nine Articles reflected both the Lutheran *Augsburg Confession and the theology of the Reformed tradition. The principal Lutheran confessions were gathered in the *Book of Concord (1580). In theology, Lutheran orthodoxy was marked by a highly scholastic method and form; Johann *Gerhard was its greatest exponent. The Reformed confessions of faith relied on Calvin's *Institutes of the Christian Religion* (see GALLICAN CONFESSIONS; SCOTS CONFESSION; BELGIC CONFESSION; SECOND HELVETIC CONFESSION; HEIDELBERG CATECHISM). Calvinist theological orthodoxy was marked by the development of *covenant theology. The Synod of *Dort reflected this scholastic Calvinism in the canons directed against *Arminianism. The *Westminster Standards were patterned on the mode and content of the canons of Dort. The *Caroline Divines in the C of E emphasized ancient Catholic elements as essentials of Anglicanism.

In reaction to the speculative concern for orthodoxy, *Pietism arose in the 18th cent., with the theologizing of A. *Franck, the devotional writing of P. *Spener, and by its spread affected most of the Protestant Churches. The Pietist influence first on Methodism, then on the revival movement in all the Churches, remained a formative influence on Protestantism; it also largely inspired the missionary expansion. The effect of the *Enlightenment and *deism

was to dilute the faith of many church members, even clergy, into a mere nominal adherence to Christian belief. After the cold rationalism of the Enlightenment came the subjectivism or romanticism of F. *Schleiermacher, the development of emphasis on the socio-historical interpretation of Christianity, and the growth of biblical criticism. These were prominent features of *liberal theology, with its stress on the historical, ethical, and subjective interpretation of the gospel. The work of E. *Troeltsch, A. *Ritschl, and A. *Harnack were particularly formative of the liberal spirit. The liberalism of the 19th cent. was not universally accepted. The strength of conservative, evangelical Protestantism manifested its resistance to liberal theology and led to the fundamentalist-modernist controversies that continue in the 20th century. Both the *Oxford movement and the evangelical reaction to it may be viewed as a conservative concern for the true essentials of the Christian Church. In the post–World War I era, with the confidence of liberal theology shattered, the theological movement called *neo-orthodoxy arose, led by Karl *Barth. It was a reassertion of the doctrines of Reformation teaching and above all of the primacy of the transcendent word of God. The impetus to regain the Christian gospel as a unique divine revelation affected all the major 20th-cent. theologians (see TILLICH, P.; NYGREN, A.; AULÉN, G.; CULLMANN, O.; BULTMANN SCHOOL).

Ecumenical Protestantism. A desire for Church unity was a part of the Reformation. Politics and polemics, however, built walls of separation both between Protestants and Catholics and between Protestants and Protestants. The Reformation principle *cuius regio, eius religio,* and the assumption of the need for unity of religion in the state, also served to harden division and to promote persecution of dissidents. The missionary expansion of Protestantism at first reflected divisions and rivalries. Begun under the Pietist impulse, esp. by the Moravians, the Protestant missionary endeavor widened until nearly all denominations became involved (see MISSIONS). The missionary experience itself was the source of the modern ecumenical movement. By the late 19th cent. Protestant missionaries had extended their work throughout the world, and new Churches had been formed in many countries. The mission societies were often experiments in cooperation, and the realization of missionaries of the need to present Christianity as united led to the Edinburgh meeting in 1910 of the *International Missionary Council. A missionary bishop of the Episcopal Church, Charles *Brent, was its inspirer. Out of this beginning grew *Life and Work, *Faith and Order, and eventually (1948) the *World Council of Churches. Besides the denominational mergers, actual and planned, that have resulted from the ecumenical movement, it has had other broad effects. Among them has been the liturgical movement within Protestantism, a deeper examination of central ecclesiological questions, the Church and its mission, Scripture and tradition, the ministry. These inquiries have not been conducted in denominational isolation or in a polemical spirit. They have profited the Protestant Churches themselves; they have opened the way to Roman Catholic self-evaluation and broadened its Catholic theological perspective. They have created a better appreciation of the dimensions of Christian disunity and a sense of urgency for Christian unity. (The specific Protestant bodies are the subject of special articles.)

ROMAN CATHOLICISM

The term *Roman Catholic was first used disparagingly by the Reformers, but then came to be accepted as an official title. The Roman Catholic Church is the continuing institution and the body of believers who, despite the Reformation, remained in communion with the Pope.

Roman Catholic Reform. What has been ineptly called a "Counter-Reformation" was an inner reform seeking to remedy the same ills that created receptivity to the Reformation. This inner revival had begun first as a renewal of

Christian life before the Reformation, and it continued. In Spain there were reforming bishops, Fernando de Talavera y Mendoza and Francisco Ximenez de Cesneros; and at Salamanca a vigorous resurgence of theology, esp. of *Thomism. In Italy there were St. Philip Neri and the Oratory of Divine Love; the Theatines of St. Cajetan; the Barnabites of Antonio Maria Zaccaria; the Somaschi of St. Jerome Aemiliani; Ursuline nuns were founded by Angela Merici. In 1540 the Jesuits, with their Ignatian spirituality, their complete availability to the Holy See, and their educational system, came into existence. A strict congregation of Benedictines (the Camaldolese) and an austere branch of Franciscans (the Capuchins) were founded and the Augustinians were reformed, esp. under Girolamo *Seripando; Teresa of Avila and John of the Cross established the Discalced Carmelites. When the Church addressed itself to the issues of doctrine and practice raised by the Reformation, the inspiration behind the reform movement within the Church made itself felt. The Council of *Trent (1545–63) succeeded against all odds in enunciating the Church's teaching and in fashioning instruments of practical reform because of the great popes of the period, Paul III (1534–49), Julius III (1550–55), Paul IV (1555–59), Pius IV (1559–65), and the devotion of learned and loyal conciliar fathers. In the same era the sustained purposefulness brought success to new missionary efforts; side by side with Spanish and Portuguese colonizers went the friars of the mendicant orders as well as the Jesuits, to evangelize the New World and the Far East. Here unfortunately persecution and the Chinese Rites controversy, which led to the imposition of European ways on the missionary activity, did much harm to the effort.

After Trent the effort at inner reform continued, esp. under Pius V (1566–72), Gregory XIII (1572–85), and Sixtus V (1585–90). In Germany Catholic recovery was aided enormously by St. Peter Canisius (1521–97) and his catechisms. St. Charles Borromeo (1538–84) in Italy was the personification of Tridentine reform decrees.

St. Robert Bellarmine (1542–1621) led RC apologetics against Reformation thinking. In France there were St. Francis de Sales (1567–1622), De Bérulle (1575–1629), De Condren (1588–1641), Olier (1608–57), St. John Eudes (1601–80), and St. Vincent de Paul (1580–1660). Cardinal Hosius (1504–79) and the Jesuits saved Poland for the Church; in Hungary the leader was Cardinal Pazmany (1570–1637). The ultimately vain disputes of the *Congregatio de auxiliis (1597–1607) were a setback to theological progress. The political upheavals that were part of the Reformation brought on the Thirty Years' War (1618–48), which intensified Catholic-Protestant bitterness and losses to Catholic political power and property.

The Thirty Years' War to the French Revolution: 1648–1709. Two different sets of crises, internal theological quarrels and the attempts of kings to enslave the Church, left it weakened at the eve of the French Revolution. The philosophical developments of the *Enlightenment and the revolutions in scientific thought existed apart from any ecclesiastical auspices. The case of Galileo evidenced the suspicion and hostility of churchmen toward science. The deists and Encyclopedists successfully discredited the Church in the minds of the educated. Meanwhile the intellectual energies of churchmen were expended in controversies occasioned by *Jansenism and *Quietism. The moral rigorism of Jansenism left its influence, perhaps into the 20th century. These movements were also rallying points for Gallicanism and had political consequences. Roman authority was openly challenged at this time by the Bourbon Kings in France. Gallicanism dated back to the days of Avignon; Louis XIV made it a political doctrine amounting to the headship of the monarch over the Church. A German rebellion against Rome received its rationale from Johann Nikolaus von Hontheim (1701–90), under the name Febronius, whose teachings were in fact put into practice by Joseph II under the influence of the Enlightenment. Both *Febronianism and *Josephinism were resisted

by the popes. The same sort of interference, along with the hatred of deists and Jansenists, underlay the outlawing of the Jesuits in Portugal, France, and Spain. To this the Holy See acceded, with Clement XIV (1769–74) officially suppressing them in 1773.

In these years too, however, the Passionists were founded by St. Paul of the Cross (1694–1775), the Redemptorists by St. Alphonsus Liguori (1696–1787), the Brothers of the Christian Schools by St. John Baptist de la Salle (1651–1719); there were also St. Benedict Joseph Labré, St. Leonard of Port-Maurice, and St. Louis Grignion de Monfort. It was also the era of the popularization of the devotion to the Sacred Heart after the apparitions to St. Margaret Mary Alacoque (1647–90), which did much to counteract the teachings of the Jansenists in the devotional life of the Church.

Century of Liberalism: 1789–1870. From the time of the French Revolution the forces of liberalism were most often openly and violently hostile to the Church, the response of the churchmen was usually, but perhaps inevitably, defensive and reactionary.

Assaults on the Church. Through the Revolution the Church lost all its properties in France; the *Civil Constitution of the Clergy stripped the Church of its rights; there were bloody persecutions, a *Constitutional Church, and finally the replacement of Catholicism by the cult of reason. With Napoleon Bonaparte the damage was legally undone through the Concordat published in 1802; but, by the subsequent attachment of the Organic Articles and Napoleon's personal interference, papal power in France was thwarted. In 1809 the Papal States were annexed to the Empire and Pius VII made prisoner. When he was released upon Napoleon's exile in 1814, not only had the Church lost much property, but the universities (Salamanca, Sorbonne, Alcalá, Coimbra, Bologna, Louvain) had been secularized, the faculties of theology abolished, monasteries destroyed or emptied, and many religious orders decimated or weakened.

The so-called restoration of the Church was a struggle against liberalism by popes who could not but identify with the absolutist, monarchist ideas of the *ancien régime*. Not only were they temporal rulers, who had suffered at the hands of the revolutionaries, but the forces of liberalism were anticlerical and predominantly devoted to destroying the Church as an influence in human affairs. Unfortunately, papal resistance put the Church out of touch with the movement of history and the sentiments of mankind, for the liberals alone seemed intent on facing the real political and social ills. Papal opposition to liberalism showed itself in the condemnation of F. Lamennais (1782–1854) by Gregory XVI (1831–46). Pius IX (1846–78) condemned the teachings of rationalism, liberalism, and indifferentism in his *Syllabus of Errors* (1864). He became a victim of some of the forces he sought to oppose in the Risorgimento, and saw Rome itself captured (1870) and papal temporal sovereignty lost by the Law of Guarantees (1871). An exception to the damaging effect on the Church was in Germany. There the prince-bishops finally disappeared from ecclesiastical life. Concordats in Bavaria, Prussia, Hannover, and the Rhineland led, because of papal firmness, to a clear establishment of the papal primacy over the German Church. In 1848 the Congress of Mainz made a move toward promoting Catholic ideas in social-political life, which had its bearing on the foundation of Centrum, a Catholic political party, in 1859. Catholic life and learning flourished with leaders like F. Stolberg (1750–1819), F. Schlegel (1772–1829), J. von Görres (1776–1848), and J. *Möhler (1796–1838).

Inner Life of the Church. Politically perplexed and harassed as the Church was throughout this era, the Church's own life was strengthened. Catholics reacted to the continued mistreatment of the popes with a devotion to the person of the Holy Father that became a characteristic of Catholicism for the next century. In 1814 the Jesuits were restored; during the 19th cent. many new religious orders were founded, e.g., the Salesians; of the older orders, the Domini-

cans were reformed by H. Lacordaire and A. Jandel and the Benedictines revitalized by Dom Guéranger. The ministry of the Church was enriched by the holiness of St. John Vianney, the Curé d'Ars (1786–1859) and St. John Bosco (1815–88). The Society for the Propagation of the Faith was established by Pauline Marie Jaricot (1799–1862). The expansion of the Church took on a new aspect in the great century of immigration to the U.S., Canada, and Australia. The sons and daughters of the immigrants became the source of a new vitality for the Church. Mission activity was increased, often with great suffering, in the Orient and in Africa, notably by the Holy Ghost Fathers, White Fathers, Society for the African Missions, and Scheut Fathers. Finally, on the initiative of Pius IX, two dogmatic pronouncements were made. In 1854 Pius personally proclaimed as dogma the Immaculate Conception of Mary (4 years afterward the apparitions at Lourdes occurred). He also convoked *Vatican Council I (1869). It was attended by a larger body of bishops than had attended any previous council. Before it was suspended (1870), its work included proclamation of papal *infallibility as a dogma and a series of pronouncements on the soundness of reason, the transcendence of faith, and the relationship between the two.

Between the Two Vatican Councils: 1870–1963. The century between the two Vatican Councils was an age of papal leadership. The popes directed the Church in the spheres of politics, social and doctrinal teaching, and practice in an effort to reach where possible, or to confront where necessary an alienated world.

Social Teaching. Leo XIII ended the reactionary attitude toward liberalism by teaching Catholics, e.g., in the encyclical *Immortale Dei* (1885), to exercise their rights and powers as citizens in the secularist states. In the encyclical *Rerum novarum* (1891) he condemned atheistic communism. He dealt with the *Kulturkampf of Bismark; faced anti-Catholic policies of the Third Republic in France; and refused to submit papal sovereignty to the Italian monarchy. The firmness of Pius X against the government of Combes and the *Associations Cultuelles* in France meant material loss to the Church but established freedom from state interference. Benedict XV stanchly refused to take sides during World War I; he strove rather for peace and the alleviation of suffering. Pius XI reestablished the relations of the Holy See with many governments by a series of concordats and solved the Roman Question on papal territorial sovereignty through the Lateran Treaty (1929). He condemned the persecution of the Church in Spain and Mexico; denounced the excesses of state absolutism in Benito Mussolini's Fascist Italy in the encyclical *Non abbiamo bisogno* (1931); and took a stand against the antihuman, anti-Christian ideology and practice of Adolf Hitler's Nazi Germany in *Mit brennender Sorge* (1937). He condemned atheistic communism and the persecution of the Church in Russia in the encyclical *Divini Redemptoris* (1937). To the Catholic faithful he expressed the sacred meaning of their political life with the encyclical establishing the feast of Christ the King (*Quas primas,* 1925). Pius XII had the heartbreaking task of being peacemaker to a world at war. His *Summi pontificatus* (1939) set out a program for peace and for rule by law that he repeated over and over. In his reign he was the implacable enemy of atheistic communism.

The social problems caused by the industrial revolution, urbanization, and the exploitation of the worker by unrestrained capitalism for a century were addressed in the encyclicals *Rerum novarum* (1891) and *Quadragesimo anno* (1931). These were supplemented by the teaching of Pius X and Pius XI in Catholic Action and the encyclicals of Pius XI on Christian marriage (*Casti connubii,* 1930) and education (*Divini illius Magistri,* 1930), in which the rights of the person and the family were defended against the encroachments of the State. A whole Catholic social program of teaching and action was inspired and flourished. Pius XII's addresses on problems of marriage and family life opened the way to investiga-

tions of the urgent questions of the population explosion and birth control.

Doctrinal Life. Leo XIII's *Aeterni Patris* (1879) was more than a revival of Thomistic studies; it was a call to Catholic intellectuals to reenter the world of learning, to follow the example of St. Thomas Aquinas by respect for the autonomy of human intelligence whereby a better service can be rendered also to faith. A great resurgence began in Catholic universities and among Catholic scholars. Pius X defended the same soundness of reason against the religious subjectivism of *modernism. The *Deus scientiarum Dominus* (1931) of Pius XI reorganized seminary studies. Pius XII's *Humani generis* (1950) was more than a restraint on theological extremism; together with the astonishing range of the Pope's addresses over every field of knowledge, it opened up and encouraged Catholic theology and thought. Biblical studies received a strong impetus from the *Providentissimus Deus* (1893) of Leo XIII, which was renewed and extended by the *Spiritus Paraclitus* (1920) of Benedict XV and the *Divino afflante Spiritu* (1943) of Pius XII. Not only was Catholic biblical scholarship encouraged to meet the new rationalist criticism on its own grounds, but a more profound appreciation of the Bible in Catholic theology and life was fostered.

Christian Life. This period was marked also by a deepening of the spiritual life and devotion of the faithful. Leo XIII issued his encyclicals on the rosary and on the Holy Spirit (*Divinum illud munus,* 1897); Pius X by his decrees (1905, 1910) on frequent communion fostered a practice that transformed the spiritual life of Catholics. His reforms of Church music, the breviary, and the calendar in a sense initiated the liturgical movement. He also had canon law codified. The jubilees (1933) proclaimed by Pius XI were marked by numerous canonizations; he also zealously promoted the retreat movement and devotion to the Sacred Heart. In the reign of Pius XII the Holy Year 1950 was climaxed by the proclamation of the dogma of the Assumption; a Marian Year was observed in 1954. Pius

XII's encyclicals, *Mystici corporis Christi* (1943) and *Mediator Dei* (1947), intensified the study and appreciation of the structure of the Church and the meaning of the liturgy in its life. In its worldwide status the Church in the 20th cent. lost free external communication with her members in many countries of Eastern Europe, China, and Cuba. The progress of the missions in Africa was disturbed by the political turmoil in the emerging nations. Latin America suffered a dire shortage of clergy. Neopaganism and atheism created an atmosphere that made for leakage in membership and a dearth of vocations to the priesthood and religious life. But the Church in North America also came of age in the 20th century. Missionary activity expanded, and new stress was laid on the development of a native clergy. In Latin America the Church began to fulfill its responsibilities in the movement for social reform. Catholic scholarship matured and progressed.

Age of Vatican Council II. In the person and pontificate of John XXIII the efforts of his predecessors were in one sense fulfilled, in another transformed. He renewed and adapted the Church's social teaching in *Mater et magistra* (1961) and *Pacem in terris* (1963), later supplemented by Paul VI's *Populorum progressio* (1967). On the political level a modus vivendi was achieved with many of the Communist regimes. The moral prestige of the papacy in the cause of world peace grew; Paul VI addressed the United Nations (1965). But John's *aggiornamento* most of all transformed the doctrinal and practical life of the Church itself. The Church became and will remain for some time a changing Church. In its preparations, deliberations, and aftermath *Vatican Council II brought to the whole Church the full impact of the energies that had built up in theological, biblical, and liturgical studies since Leo XIII. The documents of the Council spread a new consciousness of the nature and internal life of the Church as the People of God. The collegiality of the bishops and the positive development of the place in the Church of the laity diminished in the minds of Catholics the monolithic, centralized image of Church government and communicated a sense of a broader active participation in the life of the Church. A full and responsible engagement in the ecumenical movement was fostered. Practical Christian life was most directly affected by the reformed liturgy, permeated with scriptural readings, and integrated with the preached word of God.

The state of the Church after Vatican II remains one of fluidity. The rethinking of the structure of the Church has brought a desire in many to rid it of all its institutional structures. An *underground Church movement that treats the parochial system as obsolete has developed. The encyclical *Humanae vitae* (1968), reaffirming conservative RC teaching on birth control, provoked many manifestations of an authority crisis that exists on all levels in the Church. The personal cult of the Holy Father that had characterized Catholic life no longer flourishes. Popular devotions, such as the rosary and novenas, long typical of Catholic piety, are not widely cultivated. The priest's obligation of celibacy and the nature of his ministry are debated. The main thrust of theological study has been dominated by the pursuit of biblical themes and by kerygmatic motivation; the scholastic instruments of theology have been abandoned; yet theologians have experienced the need of new philosophical methods, new language, and a new world view for theological development.

CHURCH (U.S. HISTORY). This article is limited to the Western Christian tradition. Church history in the U.S. is the history of two separate, and until the mid-20th cent. usually antagonistic, forms of Christianity, Protestantism and Roman Catholicism.

PROTESTANTISM IN THE U.S.

While the uniqueness of American Protestantism often has been exaggerated, it remains true that religious patterns imported from Great Britain and the Continent have been adapted in the New World through the interaction of its diverse peoples to produce the peculiar ethos of American Protestant Christianity. By the end of the Revolutionary era characteristic traits had begun to develop: *denominationalism, *revivalism, religious *freedom in the setting of *Church-State separation, and *voluntaryism.

Colonial Period. Denominationalism was not planned; with varying degrees of success establishment in the European pattern was attempted in most of the colonies: of the C of E throughout the South; of the *Reformed Church, by the Dutch in New York; of Congregationalism in New England, except for Rhode Island. There, and in Pa., N.J., and early Md., diversity of belief was accepted. Enforcement of uniformity in all the colonies, however, gave way to the need for settlers; toleration had to be granted. Gradually the denominational system, not E. *Troeltsch's church-sect pattern, emerged, with each group accepting others as genuine expressions of Christianity. Revivalism appeared in the *Great Awakening, which began about 1726 in N.J. with T. J. *Frelinghuysen, a Dutch Reformed pastor, and which through G. *Tennent, J. *Edwards, and G. *Whitefield spread throughout the colonies. One important reason was that, in sharp contrast with the European situation, only about a tenth of the colonials were church members. Revivalism became a continuing means of evangelism and fostered both division and cooperation. Tensions developed over the place of emotions in genuine religious experience (thus C. *Chauncy's *Enthusiasm Described and Cautioned Against*, 1742, and J. Edwards' *Treatise Concerning Religious Affections*, 1746). Disagreement also arose over whether education or vital Christian experience was the primary qualification for ministry (thus G. Tennent's *Danger of an Unconverted Ministry*, 1740). Stress on religious experience tended to overshadow doctrinal distinctions, and denominational differences often gave way to a spiritual unity of shared religious feeling. John *Wesley's words were

often quoted: "Is thy heart right, as my heart is with thine? . . . If it be, give me thy hand."

With the winning of independence, most of the state constitutions abolished existing forms of establishment (although vestiges remained in Mass. until 1833) and granted a measure of religious freedom. Religious tests for voting or office holding, retained against Roman Catholics, antitrinitarians, and atheists in some places, were ended by the First Amendment of the U.S. Constitution. Thus, because of the *de facto* existence of diverse denominations, the cooperation fostered by revivalism, the activities of Baptists and Quakers, and the rationalism of the *Enlightenment, the U.S. embarked on the "great experiment," religious freedom. Separation from the State gave to the Churches in the U.S. a fourth, and in some senses their most distinctive, characteristic: voluntaryism. Separating civil and religious functions did not prevent religion from exerting a marked influence on social and political life, even from Revolutionary days. A religious survey made c.1780 shows the following numbers of Protestant Churches: Congregational, 749; Presbyterian, 495; Baptist, 457; Anglican, 406; Lutheran, 240; German Reformed, 201; Quaker, 200; Dutch Reformed, 127. (There were also 56 RC churches.)

From the Revolution to the Civil War. The postwar movement westward beyond the Appalachians challenged the Churches to provide a ministry and church buildings in the West. A new wave of revivalism to reach the unchurched and to combat *deism began in the 1790s and led to new conversions and the establishment of new Churches. Beginning in the East, this *Second Great Awakening motivated college students to become missionaries, pastors to move westward, and laymen to propagate their faith as they joined the westward trek. In the West the revivals were inaugurated with interdenominational sacramental gatherings, which developed into the *camp meeting, esp. among Methodists. A new phase of revivalism began c.1825 with Charles G. *Finney. Instead of the strict Calvinism of the *Westminster Confession, he emphasized individual freedom and responsibility in conversion and developed new measures to elicit decision, e.g., protracted meetings, the *anxious bench, public prayers naming individuals, public prayer by women, emotional music, and moving illustrations in sermons (see OBERLIN THEOLOGY). These means subtly contributed to a change in theology as emphasis shifted from the workings of God's Spirit to human influences. Evangelism and church extension were carried on not only by the new revivalist methods but also by formal organizations for home missions. By the *Plan of Union of 1802 Congregationalists and Presbyterians collaborated to open churches in the western states. Most denominations organized home mission societies, or cooperated in the American Home Mission Society (1826). Baptist preachers and Methodist *circuit riders, both drawn from the ranks of the common man, greatly appealed to the American spirit, and by 1860 these two denominations comprised nearly four-fifths of American Protestants. The first half of the 19th cent. was an era of Protestant optimism, in which the further characteristic of activism emerged. Foreign and home mission agencies, both denominational and interdenominational, were formed, e.g., *American Board of Commissioners for Foreign Missions, 1810; American Bible Society, 1816; American Sunday School Union, 1824 (see SUNDAY SCHOOLS); *American Tract Society, 1825. Under church auspices hundreds of academies and colleges were established, many of which survive. Protestant agencies for social and humanitarian causes multiplied, e.g., American Education Society, 1816; American Colonization Society, 1817; American Temperance Society, 1826; American Anti-Slavery Society, 1833. Religious optimism was also reflected in the numerous utopian communities that sprang up.

Voluntaryism was a source of vitality, yet it also fostered individualism and a proliferation of denominations, strengthened lay control sometimes to the point of anticlericalism, and eroded *confessionalism. Revivalism was criticized by H. *Bushnell in his *Christian Nurture* (1842) and by J. W. *Nevin in *The Anxious Bench* (1843; see MERCERSBURG THEOLOGY). Both deplored the once-for-all dramatic conversion. Many among the newer Lutheran and Reformed immigrants feared an exaggeration of subjective experience as detrimental to the objective elements of salvation, Church, ministry, and the sacraments. The phenomenon of denominationalism became intensified. In New England a rationalistic *Unitarianism led by W. E. *Channing drew many away from Congregationalism. *Universalism appealed chiefly to the rural and less-educated classes. Under the impact of the revivalistic accent on freedom and the *New England theology represented by N. *Taylor and L. *Beecher, *Arminianism undermined rigid Calvinism. Over this issue *Old School and New School Presbyterians divided (c.1837). Among the Baptists, Old School or Primitive Baptists (c.1830) and Landmarkists (1850) split off (see LANDMARKISM), claiming to preserve the true Baptist heritage. A *high-church movement led first by J. H. *Hobart appeared within the Protestant Episcopal Church. Divisions over theology, evangelistic methods, standards for membership, and ministry splintered other denominations; new groups appeared, e.g., Christian Churches, Disciples of Christ, and Latter-day Saints (Mormons). Differences over slavery also moved the major denominations into sectional divisions, many of which remain. At a time when Christian unity had an opportunity to transcend differences, the major bodies failed as a reconciling force to prevent a fratricidal war. Another unfortunate aspect of the era was Protestant support of *nativism.

From the Civil War to World War I. In the postbellum period the Churches sought to help the freedmen establish their own Churches, mission and education societies, and national organizations. The majority of black Americans found special affinity for the Baptists and Methodists, and many black Churches date from this time. Economic changes spurred by the Civil War created the industrial society of the North, and with it the religious and social problems of an urban population, often exploited by capital and victimized by fluctuations of the economy. To reach the masses in the big cities, the methods of revivalism were again employed; D. L. *Moody was the outstanding revivalist of the period, adapting and refining older methods. Home and foreign missions were accelerated, notably by the Student Volunteer movement (1888). The larger denominations organized special ministries to the various ethnic groups among the immigrants. Early social reform movements relied on individual persuasion and charitable organizations; by 1880 a few pioneers (e.g., Washington *Gladden) were becoming aware of the changing nature of ethical problems and the new social mission of the Church. The *Social Gospel movement did not fully penetrate the Christian conscience until the early 20th century. A tract for the times was W. *Rauschenbusch's *Christianity and the Social Crisis* (1907); his *Theology of the Social Gospel* (1917) was a statement of the theological basis for individual and social salvation. Denominations formed departments to educate their membership in social concern and methods of service and established Christian centers, settlement houses, and *institutional churches. The YMCA and YWCA also were founded. The Churches faced a new problem occasioned by *liberal theology. The truth of the Genesis account of creation was challenged by Darwin's *Origin of Species* (1859). Higher criticism of the Bible began to find its way into the seminaries soon after the Civil War and was generally accepted by 1914. The developments in psychology, sociology, and comparative religion offered naturalistic explanations of the origin of religion, without any supernatural reference. Exponents of the adaptation of Christianity to new learning were called progressives or modernists. Evolutionary theory became the source of great Protestant optimism for the continual betterment of the world. World War I came as a blow

to the Social Gospel movement; conferences and conventions still talked of social reform but the drive was gone. Revivalism lost its effectiveness in the North, and many Churches reacted against the theatrics of Billy *Sunday and his imitators. Unrest over the Social Gospel and biblical criticism became fixed in an organized *fundamentalism; while exhibiting various forms, it was essentially a protest against a surrender of what were regarded as essentials of the gospel. The denominations hardest hit by the fundamentalist-modernist controversy of the 1920s were the Northern Baptists and the Presbyterians. Theological factors were added to cultural ones to bring about secessions and new denominations, with liberal or conservative polarizations. The pattern of denominationalism had become more complex with the appearance of the Church of Christ, Scientist (*c.*1875) and the Ethical Culture Movement (*c.*1876); in the 20th cent. Pentecostalism emerged and spread among those who regarded the older Churches as cold and impersonal.

Since 1920. The 1929 economic depression seemed to deepen a religious depression that had already begun. Theological changes introduced in the 1930s, however, were to pave the way for the progress of the *ecumenical movement and the post-World War II religious renewal. *Neo-orthodoxy, a name disavowed by many classified as its spokesmen, was a reaction to liberal theology (see BARTH, K.; TILLICH, P.). R. *Niebuhr's *Moral Man and Immoral Society* (1932), E. *Lewis's *A Christian Manifesto* (1934), and the series "How My Mind Has Changed" in the *Christian Century,* *c.*1940, reflected the departure from liberal theology in the United States. The new mood was marked by recognition of man's capacity for evil and inability to save himself and of salvation history as the core of the Bible; new appreciation developed for a high Christology, the transcendence of God, and the place of the Church. Greater unity and cooperation of the Churches was fostered; it was both evidenced and assisted by the formation of the National Council of Churches of Christ in the U.S.A. (1950) and the World Council of Churches (1948). In 1962 a *Consultation on Church Union began, with the goal of forming a united Church comprising the majority of American Protestants. With Vatican Council II a great change in Protestant-Catholic communication increased on the theological and practical levels. The quickening of interest in religion during the 1950s was regarded by some as ephemeral, by others as a genuine religious renaissance. Involvement of laymen in Christian witness through their work, sociopolitical activity, and participation in public worship increased. Renewal was sought through the mass evangelistic methods of Billy *Graham and through small fellowship groups and programs of Christian social action.

By the 1960s the revival of religion seemed to wane; statistics of church membership evidenced a leveling off or a decline. Confusion and division beset theology, as radical theologians proclaimed the *death of God, critics advocated abandonment of the institutional Church, ethicians proclaimed the new morality. Earlier accent on human sinfulness gave way to stress on man's ability to revitalize the secular city and to transform the changing social environment. The immanence of God and his action in the world independently of the Church became primary themes. At the same time the new evangelicals appeared, seeking to reassert the essentials of fundamentalism without its anti-intellectualism, quarrelsomeness, and narrow base of fellowship. Opposed to the National and World Council of Churches, they formed organizations such as the *National Association of Evangelicals and the Evangelical Theological Society. More rigidly doctrinaire and separated individuals organized the *American Council of Christian Churches.

Thus at the end of the 1960s considerable confusion was apparent in Protestantism, as the theologies of Barth, Bultmann, and Tillich seemed to have lost their appeal, and no clear new direction was in sight. New bases of assurance regarding the reality of the triune God, new means of winning men to Christian discipleship, new approaches to Christian unity, new styles of personal and social ethics, new methods of Christian instruction and nurture, new forms of apologetics to confront a technological society and the world's religions, and new ways of expressing concern for the totality of human life were being sought. It was clearly a period of transition from old and accustomed ways to the development of other forms of structure and belief whereby the Church could fulfill its mission in a pluralistic society. See E. S. Gaustad, *Historical Atlas of Religion in America* (1962); W. S. Hudson, *Religion in America* (1965); H. S. Smith, R. T. Handy, and L. A. Loetscher, *American Christianity: An Historical Interpretation with Representative Documents* (2v., 1960, 1963); S. Ahlstrom, *Theology in America* (1967); Smith-Jamison v. 1; S. E. Mead, *Lively Experiment* (1963).

ROMAN CATHOLICISM IN THE U.S.

The history of Catholicism has been a process of gradual, often painful maturing, self-realization, and Americanization.

Early Missionary Efforts. Starting with Juan Ponce de León's Florida expedition, the Spanish attempted a program of acculturation centered around the mission system. Although criticized by historians under the spell of the "Black Legend," or by those who regretted the destruction of Indian culture, the Spanish missionary effort was basically successful. In California, Junipero Serra founded nine missions (1770–82), including Monterey-Carmel, San Gabriel, San Francisco, Santa Clara, and San Buenaventura. Before that time, 17th-cent. Franciscans had converted some 35,000 Indians in New Mexico and established numerous missions in Florida. In Texas and throughout the Southwest, Spanish clergy developed missions for the Indians, introduced new forms of architecture, and acquired cartographical knowledge of the area. French missionaries worked among the Indians of the Great Lakes and Mississippi Valley. While several Jesuits, including Jean de Brébeuf and

Isaac Jogues, suffered death at the hands of the Indians, the general peace that prevailed after 1649 permitted Jesuits, Recollects, Capuchins, and diocesan priests from New France to extend French influence into the future states of Ill., Mich., and Wis., and down the Mississippi River. Despite the expulsion of the Jesuits (1763), Catholicism had become the dominant religion in the Mississippi basin by the time of the American Revolution.

Catholics in the Colonies. English settlers along the East Coast of the future U.S. were steeped in an anti-Catholic tradition. Legal and social restrictions against the very small Catholic minority therefore abounded throughout the British colonies, with some exceptions in Md., N.Y., and Pennsylvania. Under the first proprietors of Md., the Catholic Lords Baltimore, Catholics controlled the colony and used their power to adopt (1649) an Act Concerning Religion, which guaranteed religious toleration to all but non-Trinitarians. However, the defeat of the Catholics (1654) by Protestant forces resulted in the repeal of the Toleration Act and subjection to Puritan rule. After the Revolution of 1688 in England the Anglican Church became the established Church, and Catholics in Md. experienced disabilities comparable to those in other colonies. The Revolution of 1688 also ended a period of religious liberty for Catholics in New York. Some Catholics had migrated there after the English acquired the colony from the Dutch (1644). The new proprietor, James, Duke of York, appointed (1682) a Catholic governor, Col. Thomas Dongan, whose act of religious toleration lasted only until his overthrow (1688) by the Calvinist Jacob Leister. Five years later, the C of E became the established Church in the colony. Pennsylvania, founded as a "Holy Experiment" in political and religious pluralism, afforded Catholics a unique opportunity to establish churches and other institutions. In 1734, Joseph Gleason, S.J., opened a chapel in Philadelphia, and other Jesuits ministered to Palatinate Catholics in the Conestoga and Lancaster region. Even in areas like Pa., with 1,300 Catholics

in a population of 200,000 (1756), the number of Catholics in British America remained small throughout the colonial period. By 1785 there were but 25,000 Catholics among the American population of 4 million. Nevertheless, as the colonial era ended with the Revolution, the condition of American Catholics markedly improved.

Problems, Conflicts, and Growth. The French Alliance of 1778 brought French clergy and an unofficial moratorium on anti-Catholic propaganda. Catholics outstanding in the service of the new nation included: Charles Carroll, delegate from Md. to the Philadelphia Congress; Daniel Carroll and Thomas FitzSimons, members of Congress; Stephen Moylan, Washington's mustermaster general; and John Barry, one of the founders of the American navy. Many states abolished legal restrictions, providing a more tolerant milieu for Catholics. John Carroll, who had been named superior of the American Catholic missions (1784), was consecrated (1790) first bp. of the American Church. In Carroll's diocese of Baltimore, coextensive with the national boundaries, the lack of clergy was critical. In 1785 there were but 24 priests to serve 25,000 Catholics scattered throughout the United States. Some relief was afforded by the arrival of priest-refugees from the French Revolution; among them were Sulpicians who established St. Mary's Seminary in Baltimore (1791). Carroll also encouraged the creation of other educational facilities. Georgetown Academy and Georgetown Visitation Convent were founded in Washington, D.C., in the 1790s. In 1808 and 1809 Mount St. Mary's Seminary and St. Joseph's School were begun in the town of Emmitsburg, Md.; St. Joseph's was established by Bl. Elizabeth Seton, foundress of the Daughters of Charity, the first native sisterhood.

As Carroll recruited additional clergy from Spain, Ireland, and Germany, priests were often assigned to congregations with a language and culture different from their own. Conflicts developed between pulpit and pew and between clergy and episcopal authority. The focus of the problem was lay trusteeism. In the presence of foreign and refugee clergy, lay trustees began to assume not only control of the purse and of church property, but power over the pastor as well. In Philadelphia, German members of St. Mary's Church established a separate church, Holy Trinity, which remained in schism until 1802. Other lay trustee conflicts erupted in St. Louis, Mo., Baltimore, Md., Norfolk, Va., and Charleston, South Carolina. To the bishops, lay trusteeism was a usurpation of episcopal prerogative and a violation of canonical provisions for episcopal appointment and dismissal of pastors. After the famous Hogan schism in Philadelphia, the issue was presented to the Vatican. Pius VII in *Non sine magna* (1822) upheld the principle of lay trusteeism in temporal matters but condemned the excesses that had occurred in the American system. In the 50 years following *Non sine magna,* the American Catholic population increased from 195,000 to 4,504,000. Natural reproduction and territorial acquisitions in the Mexican War accounted for part of this growth, but immigration was the principal factor. About 2,700,000 Catholic immigrants, more than half of them from Ireland, came to the U.S. at this time, and ecclesiastical jurisdictions multiplied. Beginning in 1808, when Baltimore was made a metropolitan see with suffragan dioceses at Bardstown (later Louisville), Boston, Philadelphia, and New York, some 43 dioceses and 7 archdioceses were created by the time of the Civil War.

Early Parochialism. The presence of enormous numbers of immigrants in the cities, where they chiefly settled, raised questions of urbanology that a century later remained partly unanswered. Poor and socially alienated, the Catholic immigrants had common bonds only with one another and their clergy. As a result, they flocked to ghettos, welcomed clerical dominance, and displayed generally parochial and passive characteristics. Their defensive posture was hardened by outbreaks of anti-Catholic *nativism after the 1820s. At times sophisticated, as in the John Breckinridge–John Hughes debates, and at times biased, as in

the case of Samuel F. B. Morse's *Foreign Conspiracy against the Liberties of the U.S.* (1834) and Rebecca Reed's *The Awful Disclosures of the Hotel Dieu Nunnery of Montreal* (1836), the anti-Catholic movement occasionally assumed violent form, as in the burning (1834) of the Ursuline Convent at Charlestown, Mass., and the riots (1844) in the Kensington section of Philadelphia, where 13 were killed and 50 injured. Nativist attacks strengthened Catholic parochialism, which found expression in the development of a separate school system, unsurpassed in size by any other private school system in the world. With foundations of the system laid by the First Provincial Council (1829), the establishment of parochial schools was made virtually mandatory by the Third Plenary Council of Baltimore (1884). The cost of the system led Bps. J. Hughes and J. Ireland, as well as Catholic groups in Savannah, Ga., and Poughkeepsie, N.Y., to make unsuccessful bids for state aid. As a result, parochial schools have since been maintained without significant assistance from public funds.

Attitudes toward Social Problems. Although the school question set Catholics somewhat apart in society, they displayed considerable conformity to the mainstream of American thought and mores. Catholics tended to shun reform movements, although some Catholic support was given, esp. in the 1830s, to such peripheral concerns as temperance and prison reform. Catholics tended to identify with the Democratic Party and to adopt the most conservative Democratic position on the central issue of the day, Negro slavery. While many Protestant Churches were splitting over slavery, the Catholic Church in the U.S. continued to be united and in general harmony. Abolitionists and antislavery Quakers obtained little if any support for their cause among American Catholics. However, Catholics did respond to the Civil War itself, supplying chaplains, nurses, and soldiers to both the Union and Confederate armies. Like other institutions, the Church suffered heavy physical losses in the wartime devastation of the

South. After the war, the Second Plenary Council of Baltimore (1866) addressed itself to the problem of the emancipated Negro, decreeing that every means be taken for the religious care and instruction of the freedman. Through a combination of racial prejudice, timidity, and inadequacy of resources, the conciliar aims were not enforced, although a few indications of concern for the Negro can be noted—e.g., Bp. John Mary Odin's support for St. Joseph's School in Louisiana; Mother Katharine Drexel's founding of the Sisters of the Blessed Sacrament (1891); and the establishment in the U.S. (1871) of the Josephite Fathers for the Negro apostolate. The number of Catholics continued to increase in the postwar era, trebling between 1870 and 1900. Many Catholics joined the new labor organizations then being formed, forcing the controversial union question upon church leadership. In general the Church supported labor's efforts to improve wages and working conditions through unionization. However, several U.S. and Canadian bps. feared the Knights of Labor and opposed its policy of secrecy, but Cardinal Gibbons, along with Abp. J. Ireland of St. Paul, Minn., Bp. J. J. Keane of Richmond, Va., and Rector Denis J. O'Connell of the North American College in Rome, acted to block any Roman condemnation. They argued, successfully, that any censure of the Knights would be regarded as a rejection of labor's legitimate rights. These same prelates were among those in the vanguard of the movement to relate Catholicism more effectively to the American way of life. Their efforts were frequently opposed by the more conservative bps. led by Abp. Michael Corrigan of New York. The two groups held differing views over such questions as the censoring of the teachings of Henry George, parochial schools, and the assimilation of large numbers of immigrants.

From Americanism to Vatican II. Aided by the Paulist journal, *Catholic World*, which urged greater lay concern with the liturgy and activity of the Church, laymen were becoming more involved in church affairs, notably in diocesan newspaper work. Their resurgence was symbolized by a lay congress, held in Baltimore (1889) and organized by three dynamic lay leaders: Peter L. Foy, William J. Onahan, and Henry F. Brownson. Participants read papers on major issues, chiefly Church-State relations. As the bps. were guiding the lay renaissance, they themselves began to feel the restraining hand of Rome. Despite widespread American opposition, the office of apostolic delegate to the U.S. was established by Leo XIII, and F. Satolli was named to the post (1893). Of even greater moment was Leo XIII's letter *Testem benevolentiae* (1899). The errors condemned in the letter stemmed from a faulty understanding of *Americanism propagated initially by the French edition of W. Elliott's *Life of Father Hecker*. Although the condemned views were never held in the U.S., the effect of the papal letter was to strengthen the hand of the conservative bps. and to dampen enthusiasm for reform among the hierarchy. Thereafter the bishops' efforts were diverted from adjustment to democratic society toward development of the physical plant of the Church and pastoral care of its flock.

One late 19th cent. effort to raise the intellectual tone of American Catholic life was the founding of The Catholic University of America in Washington, D.C.; first proposed at the Second Plenary Council (1866) by Abp. Martin J. Spalding of Baltimore, the idea was not accepted until the eloquent plea of John Lancaster Spalding was delivered at the Third Plenary Council (1884). It gained strong support from Gibbons, Ireland, and Keane, and 5 years later became a reality. Out of the Catholic University came the Catholic equivalent of the Social Gospel movement, formulated by such professors as W. J. Kerby, John A. Ryan, and John O'Grady. But as Catholic efforts concentrated on the amelioration rather than the solution of problems of social injustice, agitation for change continued. A liturgical reform movement began in the 1920s, led by such pioneers as V. Michel, W. Busch, and G. Ellard. A kind of intellectual revolution, reflected in various periodicals and reviews, in the organized striving of a number of different movements, in the foundation and activities of learned societies, was already astir in the 1920s; it expanded during the 1930s, and gained great momentum after World War II. The brick-and-mortar preoccupations of earlier times began to be superseded by a conception of new goals and new standards of excellence and achievement. The role of the laity in the activity of the Church, fostered by Catholic Action and emphasized in different ways by such groups as the Catholic Worker Movement and the Grail, began to grow in importance. All this helped to prepare the Church in the U.S. for Vatican Council II's decrees adapting the Church to the modern world. In post-Vatican II years "new nuns," "new laymen," a vernacular and adapted liturgy, a new ecumenical spirit to replace its antiquated separatism, and a new sense of social responsibility began to find their place within the traditions of the American Catholic Church. This has not taken place without some disturbance and turmoil as Catholics felt their way toward a more common understanding of what was and what was not conformable to their traditions.

The Catholic Church in the U.S. by 1968 had grown to a total of 47,468,333, nearly one-fourth of the total national population. Catholic strength is greatest in the northeastern U.S., where 44.1% of the nation's Catholics reside, and in the north-central states, with 30.6%. See J. T. Ellis, *Guide to American Catholic History* (1959); idem, *Catholics in Colonial America* (1964); M. H. Rice, *American Catholic Opinion in the Slavery Controversy* (1944); J. T. Ellis, *Life of James Cardinal Gibbons, Archbishop of Baltimore* (2v., 1952); T. T. McAvoy, *Great Crisis in American Catholic History 1895–1900* (1957); H. T. Browne, *Catholic Church and the Knights of Labor* (1940); R. Trisco, NCE 14:563–572, s.v. "Vatican Council II"; A. Greeley, *Catholic Experience: A Sociological Interpretation of the History of American Catholicism* (1967).

CHURCH, INVISIBLE AND VISIBLE, see INVISIBLE CHURCH.

CHURCH, NATIONAL, see NATIONAL CHURCH.

CHURCH AND STATE, a problem of relationships varying with different concepts of State and of Church, and with the relative power of each institution to support its claims. Although potential conflicts of interest and loyalty existed from the outset, no formal theory of relations between Church and government was sought until Christianity became the state religion. Even then, theories developed slowly, and not until the later Middle Ages were precise definitions of State and Church (and their relations) formulated. No final solution has been discovered, and probably no model would be universally applicable. Progress has been made toward attaining *religious freedom, while still allowing opportunity for religion to influence values and structures of society. The varied typologies proposed for analyzing Church-State relations (H. Stroup, *Church and State in Confrontation*, 1967) testify to the difficulty of developing an adequate theory. It should be noted that similar problems have arisen relative to older religions and emerging modern governments (see, e.g., D. E. Smith, *India As a Secular State*, 1963; idem, *Religion and Politics in Burma*, 1965).

NT Indications. In reply to a question, Jesus said: "render to Caesar the things that are Caesar's, and to God the things that are God's" (Mk 12.17). This command recognizes that a distinction exists between the two realms, but it does not explain just where the dividing line lies. Paul's admonition to "be subject to the governing authorities" (Rom 13.1–7) acknowledges the Christian's duty to obey political powers on the grounds that God has appointed civil governments to keep evildoers in check. Therefore, he explains, payment of taxes and respect are due them. Elsewhere Christians are urged to pray "for kings and all who are in high positions" (1 Tim 2.2). Peter wrote, "Fear God. Honor the emperor." (1 Pet 2.17), but he implied that deference to rulers had limits when he declared: "We must obey God rather than men" (Acts 5.29). In the Apocalypse, however, the Roman Empire is symbolized as a beast who is opposed to Christ and his disciples (ch. 13), and some think that this represents a position contradictory to that of Paul. The two passages are not necessarily inconsistent, however, since the underlying presupposition carried over from the OT is that human governments are all in God's hands and are his instruments in fulfilling his redemptive purpose. The duty of obedience to civil rulers, therefore, is always qualified by the condition that they are doing their work of restraining evil and seeking peace and safety. When they, like Roman emperors, claim divine prerogatives and demand worship that belongs only to God, they are to be resisted. In such situations, Caesar is claiming what belongs to God.

The Church and the Roman Empire. In spite of these indications regarding Church-State relations, the NT does not formulate a clear theory on the subject. From Nero to Constantine, the Church had no legal right to exist, and there was no need to frame a Church-State theory. Persecution was frequently the lot of Christians, beginning at least as early as the reign of Nero. The final effort to eradicate Christians from the Roman world came under Diocletian and began in 303, but with the Edict of Milan (313), issued by Constantine and Licinius, Christianity became a *religio licita* and was tolerated. Whatever his motives may have been, Constantine progressively offered assistance to Christianity, ordering Sunday observance, giving privileges to the clergy, calling councils, and helping to suppress schisms and heresies. By the late 4th cent. (380), Gratian and Theodosius the Great ordered that Christianity be recognized as the sole religion of the Empire. This new situation created a need for closer definition of the relationships between Church and State, but such

theory developed only gradually. Constantine, in accord with previous custom, regarded himself as the religious leader (*pontifex maximus*) and assumed the power of intervening in church affairs. Gratian gave up that title, but he and his successors continued to regard themselves as responsible for directing church affairs. The establishment of the capital at Constantinople (Byzantium), as well as other factors, led to a different conception of Church-State relations in the East than that which developed in the West. In the Byzantine Empire, caesaropapism became the prevailing theory, but in the West the Church had more freedom from direct control by the civil governments, and the Middle Ages witnessed the tendency for the Church to gain superiority over civil government.

Medieval Ascendancy of the Church. Partly because of ineffective leadership in the western part of the Empire, the bishops of Rome had to take responsibility for judicial affairs, military defense, and other secular interests. When Ambrose of Milan warned Theodosius that even emperors are subject to the Church, he took a step that signaled the direction to be taken in western Europe. It was Pope Gelasius I, however, who first clearly stated the doctrine of the two realms (494), as it was generally conceived in medieval western Europe: "There are . . . two powers by which this world is chiefly ruled: the sacred authority [*auctoritas*] of the Popes and the royal power [*potestas*]. Of these the priestly power is much more important, because it has to render account for the kings of men themselves at the divine tribunal. . . . You know that it behoves you, in matters concerning the reception and reverent administration of the sacraments, to be obedient to the ecclesiastical authority rather than to control it." This text was the subject of endless debate as later canonists analyzed the etymological significance of his use of *auctoritas* and *potestas*, trying to deduce the implications of spiritual supremacy for temporal affairs. Long, involved struggles ensued as the concept of a single society with two aspects, each with its own responsibilities, was worked out. In the West, the Empire existed only in theory after the deposition of Romulus Augustus (476), except for a brief revival under Justinian I. The Teutonic invasions resulted in a series of Germanic kingdoms over which the Byzantine rulers lacked effective control. Freed from direct control of Byzantium, popes increased in prestige and power; the baptism of Clovis, missions to frontier peoples, alliance with Frankish kings, the spurious Donation of Constantine, the genuine Donation of Pepin, and other influences contributed to winning the Germanic tribes to orthodoxy and fellowship with Rome and to establishing the temporal power of the papacy. Having been crowned by Pope Leo III as emperor of the Romans, Charlemagne sought to revive the Empire in the West. He held views tending toward caesaropapism and would have liked to limit the role of the pope to spiritual affairs, but he had no competent heirs to continue his policies. Later popes used the precedent of Charlemagne's coronation to show that emperors received their crowns from the papal office; emperors claimed the right to approve those elected to the papal office. Hence by the 11th cent. the elements of an inevitable struggle were present.

The death of Charlemagne had been followed by decentralized government and the feudal system, which tended to subordinate the Church to secular authorities. Since bishops and abbots were often also vassals of a temporal lord, kings and noblemen often appointed bishops as well as lower clergy, investing them with the insignia of their offices simultaneously with the reception of their homage as vassals. Popes might protest this situation, but not until the 11th cent. was secular control checked and the freedom of the Church ensured. When Gregory VII (Hildebrand), an advocate of reform, challenged the right of Henry IV to appoint a bishop of Milan, the issue was joined in the investiture struggle. In 1075, he issued a decree forbidding lay investiture, following it with the *Dictatus papae*, which asserted the powers of a

pope, including the explicit claim "that he may depose emperors." Although Gregory won a victory at Canossa, the struggle was resumed after Henry returned home, and Gregory died in exile from Rome. The question was tentatively settled by the Concordat of Worms in 1122, which represented a compromise between the proponents of royal theocracy and those of papal theocracy. Bishops in Germany were to be chosen according to canon law and invested with their insignia by an ecclesiastical officer. The king or emperor could be present at the election, and he could accept the homage from the appointee. Since, however, he could refuse to make the chosen person his vassal, he had a virtual veto power over clerical appointments. Similar agreements were made elsewhere, and tensions were somewhat eased; but the theory of papal right to depose kings remained unsettled.

By the reign of Innocent III (1196–1216), the question of relationships between temporal and spiritual authorities appeared to be solved, with the latter being dominant and granting rights to the former. The papal claims were stated in an analogy: "The moon derives her light from the sun, and is in truth inferior to the sun in both size and quality, in position as well as in effect. In the same way the royal power derives its dignity from the pontifical authority." Innocent successully challenged kings and lesser nobility on numerous occasions, using his power of interdict and the right to absolve citizens of allegiance to a disobedient sovereign as proof of his contention that the royal power is subordinate to pontifical authority. His success in forcing John of England to accept a papal appointment to the See of Canterbury was one of the most striking manifestations of his power. The period of Innocent III, however, was the zenith of papal power, and the aspirations of kings to consolidate their powers to form strong national states led to the curtailment of papal influence and prestige. When a century later Boniface VIII ventured to force Philip IV of France and Edward I of England to cease taxing the clergy, he had to compromise with them. When he clashed with Philip over the trial of a clergyman by a civil court, his bull *Unam sanctam* (1302) proclaimed that both temporal and spiritual swords "are in the power of the Church" and "the temporal authority subject to the spiritual power." Moreover, the spiritual power can sit in judgment on earthly powers, but the spiritual power can be judged "only by God not by man." These assertions no longer carried the weight of authority with kings that Innocent III's words had had, and Boniface came to an ignominious end as the prisoner of Philip's soldiers.

Emergence of the Secular State. The Avignon residence of the popes (1309–77) and the *Great Western Schism (1378–1417) further weakened the authority of the papal office, and the decision to vote by nations at the Council of *Constance indicated the growing self-consciousness of national states. Simultaneous with these developments canonists and theologians were proposing theories that challenged the whole concept of the pope's temporal power. *Marsilius of Padua in *Defensor pacis* (1324) argued that power resided with the people and the princes who represented them, and he denied all clerical authority over temporal affairs. Conciliar theorists such as Conrad of Gelnhausen, Henry of Langenstein, John Gerson, and Nicholas of Cusa sought to make popes subject to the corporate community. John *Wycliffe in his *De civili dominio* (1376) stated that ecclesiastical power is rightly held only by those who are in a state of grace, and therefore unworthy clergy (even the popes) may be deposed by temporal rulers. With these trends, the balance of power seemed to be swinging more toward the State.

With the upheaval of the Reformation, the concept of a single society with temporal and religious aspects continued, and a close relationship between Church and State was almost everywhere assumed. Luther sharply distinguished the temporal from the spiritual but considered many ecclesiastical matters (such as administration) nonessentials. So long as they did not interfere with the gospel itself, he permitted princes to exercise episcopal supervision of Church affairs. Thus developed the Erastian territorial system that characterized most of the Lutheran states (see ERASTIAN-ISM). Calvin sought to make clear distinctions between the spheres of Church and civil government, believing that it was the duty of the latter to maintain peace and to protect the Church and to get its instruction from the Scriptures through the pastors. He was not entirely successful in making this system work in Geneva, but the *Reformed Churches generally tended to accept such views and to avoid civil domination. The Church of England began by substituting the king for the pope as the head of the Church, and king and Parliament took responsibility for regulating ecclesiastical government, worship, and discipline. The Catholic theologian Cardinal Bellarmine sought to clarify the position of the national State by denying the "direct power" of the Church over temporal authorities. Since he held that it had an "indirect power," however, his position still allowed for clerical intervention in civil affairs. Only the left-wing of the Reformation, the Anabaptists, insisted that the spheres of Church and State were completely separate; their views seemed so anarchical that they were persecuted by all of the other parties. In England in the 17th cent. left-wing Puritanism (Baptists, some Independents, Quakers) contended for religious liberty, supported by a separation of Church and State; Richard *Hooker was strongly Erastian. With the emergence of a theory of natural rights (e.g., Hobbes, Grotius, Locke), a new view arose that rooted civil government in a social contract rather than in God's appointment (see COLLEGIALISM; TERRITORIALISM), and the secular State began to come into existence. Such a State tended to make the Church subservient to the common good of society, but eventually where it took democratic form it fostered tolerance and expected religion to steer clear of political issues. In various forms, however, attempts at state control of the Church have recurred: in

*Gallicanism; the *Civil Constitution of the Clergy; *Febronianism; *Josephinism; and the *Kulturkampf and 20th cent. totalitarianism, both fascist and communist.

The U.S.: Separation of Church and State. The U.S. was the pioneer in a new system that sought to guarantee religious freedom through separation of Church and State. Although the proprietors who founded colonies usually expected to reproduce institutions with which they were familiar in Europe, including an *established Church, conditions in America were not favorable to this arrangement. During the colonial period there were established Churches in most colonies. In the South (Md., Va., N.C., S.C., and Ga.), as well as in four counties of N.Y., the C of E was established by law, although with varying effectiveness. In New England (Mass., Conn., and N.H.), Congregationalism represented the "Standing Order." In R.I., N.J., Pa., and Del. there was no state Church; Md. had begun without one, but before the end of the century had established the Anglican. In spite of laws regarding church attendance, tithes, etc., it was difficult to enforce provisions for establishment, because the need to attract settlers led to the offer of religious toleration for dissenting groups. By the time of the Revolution, when the new states wrote their constitutions, most of them disestablished their churches. In Va. establishment was abolished only after a 10-year struggle (1786), and Mass. maintained the vestiges of its establishment until 1833.

First Amendment. The U.S. Constitution forbade religious tests for public office, and its First Amendment provided that "Congress shall make no law respecting an establishment of religion, or prohibiting the free exercise thereof." Hence, an experiment began in the U.S. that was regarded as hopelessly utopian by most Europeans. Debates have long been carried on as to the reason for this decision, but the outcome was the result of a number of influences. Baptists such as Isaac *Backus favored separating Church and State in order to protect the freedom of the Church and the individual conscience from the State; the rationalistic deists were more concerned to protect the State from clerical domination; and from a practical standpoint, the pluralistic nature of the population would have made it impossible for all to agree on which Church to establish. The lack of a religious establishment in a state did not keep constitution writers from incorporating clauses that denied the right of atheists to hold office, kept Catholics from voting or holding office, or otherwise required conformity to some religious belief for full citizenship. Nevertheless, for all practical purposes a new experiment in Church-State relationships had been inaugurated.

Throughout much of the 19th cent., it was assumed that the American doctrine of separation of Church and State was perfectly clear, but the 20th cent. has revealed inconsistencies and problems that show that it was never clearly defined. Much debate has centered on the question of the intention of the Founding Fathers in framing the First Amendment. The question is not easily answered, for they did not all mean the same thing. Taken at face value, the Amendment says simply that the federal government cannot establish a religion or deny religious liberty to anyone. The intention of men like Thomas Jefferson is obvious. They considered that government best that governs least, regarded religion as primarily a private affair between an individual and God, and so saw no reason for conflict between government and religion. Others clearly had as their primary concern to keep the federal government from interfering with religious matters in order that each state could handle such questions. Some interpreters contend that the intent was to make a secular nation of the U.S.; others hold that the aim was to make the U.S. a Christian nation, but neutral with respect to particular denominations. If a secular nation had been desired, chaplains would not have been appointed for the Senate and the House of Representatives, as well as for the military services. If the Founding Fathers had wanted to establish Christianity without favoring a denomination, they could have assessed taxes for religion and allowed everyone to designate where he wanted his money to go. Such a proposal was seriously considered in Va. and elsewhere. There was actually no unanimity among those who wrote and voted for the First Amendment, and the quest for the "original intention" is seeking a will-o-the-wisp.

Supreme Court Decisions. Religious issues of a controversial nature arose in the 19th cent., but they were settled in state courts, since the First Amendment left such matters to the states. Today, however, religious disputes have come under the umbrella of federal law. Only since *c.*1940 has this been true, for in that year the Supreme Court decided that the religious liberty clause of the First Amendment applied to the states because it was guaranteed by the Fourteenth Amendment (*Cantwell et al. v. State of Conn.*). Since that time the Supreme Court has dealt with a number of critical religious issues, and has gradually been seeking a working definition of the religious clause of the First Amendment. Whatever the original intention may have been, conditions have changed and have altered the way in which the Amendment must be understood today. The Supreme Court has often been criticized for its decisions, but it has a difficult task to decide what is, or is not, equivalent to "an establishment of religion" in the 20th cent. and to determine where the freedom of an individual (or group) conflicts with the freedom of others or with obligations to the larger good of the community. The role of government has changed, so that the welfare state has taken over functions that once were primarily in the hands of the Churches. The care of the poor, hospitals, homes for the aged, and children's homes involve expense that goes beyond church capabilities; but there is still need for such church institutions, and they can be operated only with government aid. Private colleges render aid through research and other means to their communities as well as to the state and federal governments, and questions of aid are put into a new light. Questions of individual

conscience, laws governing business on Sundays, taxation of church property, religious tests for office-holding, religion in the public schools, and public support for parochial schools have all come before the Supreme Court in recent years for adjudication.

With the rising tide of secularism, no Church-State issues have been of greater importance or evoked more heated arguments than the questions of religion in the public schools and the public support of private schools. Certain decisions have become landmarks, laying down guidelines for the development of a more consistent constitutional approach to the problems. In 1947 (*Everson v. Bd. of Ed.*, N.J.), the bussing of Catholic school children was approved on grounds of the child-benefit theory. The first significant decision regarding religious exercises in the public schools was that of *McCollum v. Bd. of Education* (Ill., 1948). Releasing children from classes during regular hours and using the school building for religious instruction was declared unconstitutional. In *Zorach v. Clauson* (N.Y., 1952), however, it was declared constitutional to release children from school to attend religious classes in a church. The Supreme Court in *Engel v. Vitale* (N.Y., 1962) ruled that a prayer provided by the Board of Regents could not be required of pupils. Furthermore, in the following year a decision on two cases (*Abingdon School District v. Schempp* and *Murray v. Curlett*) concluded that any prayer, Bible reading, or other religious exercise required by public officials was a violation of the freedom of children who did not wish to participate. In 1966 the refusal of the Supreme Court to review a decision of the Maryland high court seemed to sanction the use of public funds for private colleges, but the basis of such support was to be determined by the extent to which such a college could be considered secular or sectarian. Two further significant decisions were handed down in 1968. By a 6–3 vote (*Bd. of Ed. v. Allen*) the Supreme Court upheld a New York law that provided for the loan of textbooks to parochial schools.

At the same session it opened the way for citizens to challenge congressional acts (*Flast v. Gardner*), where questions of "standing" had closed this avenue before. A 1969 decision (*Presbyterian Church, U.S.A. et al. v. Mary Elizabeth Blue Hull Memorial Church et al.*) ruled that civil courts could not intervene in legal disputes that arise from the withdrawal on doctrinal grounds of a local church from a denomination. The court decision both indirectly favored one side in a controversy over church doctrine and directly affected denominational structures.

These are all crucial decisions, and they illustrate the democratic process at work seeking a viable solution to a vexing and ambiguous constitutional amendment; it is clear that the phrase separation of Church and State is not so precise as it once seemed. Many, following a statement of Jefferson in a letter to a Baptist association, have spoken of a "wall of separation" between Church and State. Such absolute separation is almost an impossibility in our complex society, and in a pluralistic society some workable solution must be found. It appears that instead of a single wall, there are two parallel walls between Church and State. On one side of the two are matters that are clearly religious and not subject to civil interference; on the other side are political questions that are not in the province of the Churches. Between the walls, however, is a middle gray area, which the Supreme Court and continuing dialogue between contesting parties must work out in the interests of justice. See C. A. Antieau, et al., *Religion under the State Constitutions* (1965); *idem, Journal of Church and State* (1959–); O. Cullmann, *State in the New Testament* (1956); S. Z. Ehler and J. B. Morrall, *Church and State through the Centuries: A Collection of Historic Documents with Commentaries* (1967); N. Q. King, *Emperor Theodosius and the Establishment of Christianity* (1960); J. J. McGrath, *Church and State in American Law* (1962); M. R. P. McGuire et al., *NCE* 3:726–758; K. F. Morrison, *Two Kingdoms: Ecclesiology in Carolingian Political Thought* (1964); A. P. Stokes and L. Pfeffer, *Church and State in the United States* (rev. ed., 1 v., 1964); B. Tierney, *Foundations of the Conciliar Theory: Contributions of the Medieval Canonists from Gratian to the Great Schism* (1955).

CHURCH ARMY, a volunteer agency in the C of E, organized in 1882 by the Anglican clergyman Wilson Carlile (1847–1942) along the lines of the Salvation Army. The purpose of the Church Army is evangelical; members do welfare work among the poor.

CHURCH ASSEMBLY, formal title, The National Assembly of the Church of England; established by the Enabling Act of Parliament in 1919, and composed of three divisions—the House of Bishops, including all the members of the Upper Houses of the two *Convocations; the House of Clergy, including all the members of the Lower Houses of the Convocations; and the House of Laity, consisting of laymen and women elected by the dioceses of both Convocations for 5-year terms. The Church Assembly is primarily responsible for preparing ecclesiastical measures for consideration by Parliament; it also prepares and administers the central financial budgets of the C of E, and establishes and oversees the Church's main national administrative agencies. It is not authorized to make decisions on theological matters. Meetings are usually held three times a year, in London, under the presidency of the abp. of Canterbury. Annually an official year book is published, which is a useful guide to the organizations and agencies of the Church of England. See G. Mayfield, *Church of England, Its Members and Its Business* (1958).

CHURCH ATTENDANCE, presence at church services. Among Roman Catholics the expression, as commonly used, generally refers to presence at Mass; among Protestants, to presence at Sunday morning worship and communion services; in neither case, to participation in other services held for purposes of worship, study, or church-related activity. Among Catholics church attendance on Sundays (and holy days of obligation) is obligatory under church law; the relevance of this law and its binding force have been questioned since Vatican Council II. Among Protestants it is encouraged, but as a privilege one ought to delight in using rather than as an obligation. Some Protestant denominations require candidates for church membership to make a promise of attendance, but one who neglects to attend incurs no specific penalty. Consistent failure, however, might lead to one's being dropped from the church rolls. The sense of obligation commonly felt by Catholics makes attendance and nonattendance a rough basis for the distinction sometimes drawn between practicing and nonpracticing Catholics. The absence of a sense of obligation among Protestants makes nonattendance less significant in the interpretation of the statistics of church membership. The statistics of the *World Christian Handbook* (1968) distinguish between "Communicants or Full Members," and "Total Christian Community." Actual church attendance is a factor in determining each. See H. W. Coxill et al., eds., *World Christian Handbook 1968* (1967), 57–58. *SUNDAY OBSERVANCE; *STATISTICS OF RELIGIOUS BODIES.

CHURCH EQUALITY BAPTISTS, members of the *American Baptist Association. In the 1924 organization of this body the autonomy and the equality of all local churches were strongly asserted against concentration of authority in *conventions.

CHURCH IN WALES, title of the autocephalous Church of the *Anglican Communion, since 1920, when the four dioceses of the C of E in Wales were disestablished and disendowed; two additional dioceses have subsequently been created. The Church is organized as a single province, but with no fixed metropolitan see, the bishops electing one of their number to serve as metropolitan. Membership of the Church is estimated at 1,300,000. In general the Welsh people accepted the principles of the English Reformation. This was supported by a policy, begun by *Elizabeth I, of appointing Welsh bishops and encouraging the use of the Welsh language. The NT was translated into Welsh in 1567 as was the BCP of 1559, and the entire Bible in 1588. Following the *Restoration, however, the Crown began generally to appoint Englishmen, often nonresidents and in plurality, to major Welsh ecclesiastical posts. By the end of the 18th cent. the position of the *established Church had been drastically eroded among the Welsh; and the 19th cent. saw a rapid growth in the dissenting bodies, notably *Calvinistic Methodists, which ultimately made the disestablishment of the Church inescapable. Since 1920 the Church in Wales has gained markedly both in numbers and in its indigenous character, with wide use of Welsh and a vigorous independence from the C of E in both direction and policies. See S. Neill, *Anglicanism* (pa., 1958).

CHURCH MEETING, a distinctive element of the *congregational polity of Congregationalists and Baptists, the gathering of the entire congregation to consider material or spiritual concerns of the local church. Acknowledging that Christ alone is head of the Church, they seek through prayer and discussion to ascertain the mind of Christ. Unanimity is sought, but when decisions must be reached before all are in agreement, a majority vote may be accepted See D. Jenkins, *Congregationalism: A Restatement* (1954). *GATHERED CHURCH.

CHURCH MERGER, see MERGER.

CHURCH MISSIONARY SOCIETY (CMS), an agency for the Church of England's missions. It was founded in 1799 as the Society for Missions in Africa and the East; the present name was adopted in 1812. Officers, members, and missionaries must belong to the Anglican Communion. Theologically, while upholding the historic creeds, the *Thirty-Nine Articles, and the Book of Common Prayer, the CMS emphasizes the evangelical side of Anglicanism, and the primacy of God's word. Mission work has been sponsored in Africa, the Near East, and the Far East. The CMS has counterparts in other Churches of the Anglican Communion. See EncModChrMiss 161–164.

CHURCH OF CHRIST (Fettingites), a small Mormon Church established at Independence, Mo., by Otto Fetting. An apostle of the tiny Church of Christ (Temple Lot), he claimed to have received a series of visits, starting in 1927, from a heavenly messenger identified as John the Baptist. The messenger gave instructions to Fetting to start building the temple in Independence, Mo., at a site dedicated in 1831 by the Mormon prophet Joseph *Smith, Jr. Fetting relayed these instructions to members of the Church and they began to dig an excavation. But when Fetting received another revelation that all members of the Church of Christ (Temple Lot) were to be rebaptized, the Church disfellowshipped him and about 1,000 of his followers in 1930. In 1968 there were several hundred members of the Fettingite Church. *LATTER-DAY SAINTS, CHURCH OF JESUS CHRIST OF.

CHURCH OF CHRIST (Temple Lot), a small Mormon Church at Independence, Missouri. Although most of the followers of the Mormon prophet Joseph *Smith, Jr., accompanied Brigham *Young from Nauvoo, Ill., to Utah, some stayed in the Midwest. Several congregations around Bloomington, Ill., rejected what they believed to be false teachings in Utah Mormonism, such as polygamy. An early leader of this splinter group was Granville Hedrick, and the dissidents were known as Hedrickites. These people returned to Independence, Mo., in 1867 and began purchase of the

"temple lots," real estate parcels that had been dedicated by Smith in 1831 as the site of the greatest Mormon temple. Although both the Utah Church of Latter-day Saints and the Reorganized Church of Latter Day Saints have tried to obtain possession of this land, it remains the property of the Church of Christ (Temple Lot). This Church accepts the *Book of Mormon and all revelations given to Smith up to Feb. 1834. A general bishopric directs the activities of the Church under supervision of a general conference and a council of apostles. About one-third of the members and their leader, Apostle Otto Fetting, were disfellowshipped in 1930. In 1968 the Temple Lot Church reported 2,800 members, in 24 congregations. *CHURCH OF CHRIST (FETTINGITES).

CHURCH OF CHRIST, SCIENTIST, a religious body founded by Mary Baker *Eddy in 1875 as the Christian Science Association and chartered in 1879 as the Church of Christ, Scientist. In the first edition of *Science and Health* (1875), Mrs. Eddy laid down the fundamental truths that were to guide her followers. There is no such thing as matter. Eternal Mind is the source of all being. The apparent dualism of mind and matter is an error. Our senses are fallible and sense-impression does not convey true knowledge. Disease is caused by mind alone, and the appearance of disease conveyed by the senses is an error of incorrect thinking. The new discovery by the Christian Scientist is of the real meaning of the gospel message that had been obscured by centuries of misunderstanding. Christian Science is the wisdom of the Eternal Mind revealed through Jesus Christ, who taught the power of Mind (i.e., Truth, God) to overcome the illusions of sin, sickness, and death. What is the key to an understanding of God? It is that God, infinite Love, is Mind. He is not material, and his creation, man, is spiritual, governed by Mind, not matter. Every individual has the inherent power from God to think and act rightly. He can love instead of hate, be confident instead of fearful. Hate, fear, prejudice, and sensuality stem from the erring material concept of existence. God did not create these evil characteristics, therefore they can be dispelled through a correct understanding of him. The role of Christ is to make this understanding possible. He is the divine manifestation of God, which comes to the flesh to destroy incarnate error. Since sin is an example of incorrect thinking, Christ's atonement is simply an invitation to correct the erroneous thought. He released men from sickness, sin, and death, and exhorted them not to be afraid, to love one another, to sin no more. When erring human beliefs were routed, God's law was expressed in healthy bodies, love, purity, and justice.

In its earliest form, the Church of Christ, Scientist, was composed of healers who sought to end the illusory conflict of mind and body by dispelling belief in disease and thus to bring health to the sick. The success of these early practitioners, all trained by Mrs. Eddy in her Massachusetts Metaphysical College, brought large numbers of converts to Christian Science, and by 1886 the movement was widespread enough to need a National Christian Science Association with annual conventions. In addition to providing her followers with the doctrinal work *Science and Health*, Mrs. Eddy drew up a legal code to direct and preserve her movement. The *Manual of the Mother Church*, first published in 1875, provided for every detail of church government, worship, and permissible activities. In polity, the Church of Christ, Scientist, is totally centralized. Branch churches depend directly on the Mother Church in Boston, and no local or regional organization is permitted. In turn, the board of directors, who succeeded Mrs. Eddy, have no authority beyond what is already set down in the *Manual of the Mother Church*, so that they merely administer Mrs. Eddy's decisions and may not innovate. Services for worship are centrally prescribed and consist of selections chosen from the Bible and from *Science and Health* and a lesson–sermon prepared for all Christian Science churches by a committee at the Mother Church in Boston. There are no clergy in the usual sense, but each branch church has two readers to perform the service. Only specially trained practitioners take part in the healing ministry. In the U.S. in 1965 there were some 3,300 branch churches. The directors are forbidden to publish membership figures.

CHURCH OF DANIEL'S BAND, a body Methodistic in background and organization, organized at Marine City, Mich., in 1893. The band idea was derived from the old class meeting in Methodism. This Church seeks to revive primitive Wesleyanism, esp. with regard to *Christian perfection. Moral standards are rigid. After larger membership early in the 20th cent., last reported statistics (1951) showed only 200 members in four churches.

CHURCH OF DIVINE SCIENCE, a religious denomination with many similarities to Christian Science, developed from the *New Thought movement. In 1887 Malinda E. Cramer founded the San Francisco Home College of Divine Science, while Nona L. Brooks, Fannie Brooks James, and Emma Curtis Hopkins began a New Thought study group in Pueblo, Col., in the same year. Both groups united in 1889 as an association of kindred spirits. In 1898 they determined to organize churches and ordain ministers and established the Divine Science College at Denver, Colo., for this purpose. In 1899 Nona Brooks was settled as pastor of the First Church of Divine Science in Denver, the mother church of the denomination. The master ideas of the Church of Divine Science can be found in *Truth and Health* by Fannie James and *Divine Science and Healing* by Malinda Cramer, which are the twin founts of its doctrine. They hold that God is everywhere, that God and man are one, that creation is self-manifestation or the emanation of the life and substance of God. Creation, then, is spirit and both spirit and substance are aspects of God. From this starting point, they argue the unreality of disease and the ability of mind to cure the body by bringing it to a harmony with the universe of Spirit. The Church of Divine Science has been associated with the International New Thought Alliance since its formation in 1914.

CHURCH OF ENGLAND, the Church established by law as the national Church of the kingdom (not of Northern Ireland, Scotland, or Wales). The C of E includes some 27½ million baptized members in 43 dioceses, grouped in the two provinces of Canterbury and York. The abp. of Canterbury is primate of all England. Apart from legendary fragments, the earliest witnesses to Christianity in the British Isles are probably references in Tertullian and Origen, which suggests that a permanent Christian presence can be identified by the beginning of the 3d century. The first Christians may well have been soldiers and merchants, and perhaps also slaves brought to work in Britain's tin and lead mines. The attendance of British bps. at the Council of Arles (314) bespeaks a Church already settled and organized, a process in which the Roman garrisons probably played a significant part. But with the withdrawal of the imperial forces and the coming of the Anglo-Saxons, the Church entered a period of confusion and disorder. Much of the Christian community seems to have retreated into Wales and the West and North of England. Tribal life revived, in a renewed isolation from the Continent, and monastic and eremitical communities appeared; with these, Celtic church life developed its unique characteristics that were to play a significant part in later English church history.

A second period of church life began with the Roman mission under Augustine, in 597. This tradition soon began to govern the renewed church life in southern England, while in the North, as at Iona and Lindisfarne, Celtic influences were strong. This resulted in a nourishing cross-fertiliza-

tion of the medieval Church in England, in constitution and polity as well as arts and liturgy. Still sharply isolated from the Continent, pre-Conquest England was a singular laboratory for the development of national unity and characteristics. The coming of the Normans in 1066 added yet another rich element to the amalgam already present, but even this powerful continental impulse did not displace the strongly independent spirit within the Church and among the people of the islands. Never a part of the Holy Roman Empire and always far from the centers of ecclesiastical power, England and its Church notably reflected the growing national spirit that was to find classic expression in the Tudors. Yet the Church remained stanchly loyal to the Roman See, despite the increasing restlessness at papal control of English affairs.

The Reformation in England strongly reflected the kingdom's peculiar tradition and situation (see REFORMATION). All the diverse elements that entered into the explosive continental scene were felt and echoed in England. The essentially conservative Luther and the more radical and intellectual Calvin were heard and studied; and the renewal movement within the RC Church, the so-called *Counter-Reformation, made its mark. The extremist teaching of the Anabaptists was as much part of the English scene as was the humanist tradition identified with Erasmus. Yet, while each of those elements was reflected in aspects of the English Reformation, that movement of renewal still followed its own course and came to its own solution in the reformed Church of England. In coming to that solution, certain forces had major effect: the personal power and ability of both Henry VIII and Elizabeth I; the growing significance of kingship; the ferment of the Renaissance; the influence of printing and the control of it; the new vigor of nationalism; anti-clericalism; the New World; a growing sense of lay responsibility; changes in economic power. The solution was more than a century in its formulation—from the first *Book of Common Prayer (1549) to the *Act of Uniformity (1662)—and reflected the agony of those turbulent years. But the Church that emerged understood itself as in no way a "new" Church but only the reformed and renewed Church which had been part of English life from the first—which, indeed, had played a determining role in the creation of the nation.

The reformed Church exhibited certain particular characteristics. One was an emphasis on continuity (as in the determination to maintain the historic episcopal succession). Another was nationalism; it was a national Church established by law of which the Crown is the supreme governor. The supremacy of Holy Scripture as the test and proof of doctrine was reemphasized. Still another characteristic is sometimes called "inclusiveness" but is perhaps more clearly described as a "nonconfessional" attitude, a will to establish only the most central Christian statements and creeds as essential to the Church's life, and to leave as "opinion" much that in other traditions finds confessional expression (see COMPREHENSIVENESS). During the centuries of separation that followed the Reformation, the C of E has been both strengthened and weakened by those characteristics. The national principle can help the Church serve as the nation's conscience; it can also degenerate into mere privilege and *Erastianism. "Inclusiveness" can become a cloak for formalism and indifference as well as serve the Christian faith well in helping to meet the challenge of scientific discovery and theological restatement. The instruments of continuity can defend the faith; they can also breed indifference to new movements of the spirit. The history of the C of E illustrates both such strengths and weaknesses.

An unexpectedly powerful influence within the history of the Church has been the birth and growth of autocephalous Anglican Churches outside of England. The oldest of these, the *Protestant Episcopal Church in the U.S., was only the first of the now 21 gathered in the *Anglican Communion. Whether originally planted in empire or Commonwealth soil or by missionary expansion elsewhere, each of the young Churches brought to its own people the inheritance of faith and order, of tradition and temperament, found in the mother Church. Each has adapted those gifts to its own setting; each in turn has illuminated in a new way the insights and agreements characteristic of the English Church. Thus, while the C of E retains its strongly national character, it has been able to make a vivid contribution to world Christianity and to the ecumenical dialogue. Perhaps the most marked characteristic of the C of E in its post-Reformation history has been its capacity to retain within its life many of the theological and social tensions that elsewhere often have been destructive to church unity and vitality. In part, this reflects its tradition of "inclusiveness"; in part, it reflects a peculiar strength of national establishment. Perhaps most significantly, it reflects the strong sense of historical continuity that in turn tends to foster a patient temper of mind able to hold in tension forces and ideas often violently at odds with one another. Puritanism, evangelicalism, the Catholic revival (see OXFORD MOVEMENT), the controversy about evolution or the fundamentalist problem all have illustrated critical issues that have threatened to divide Christians yet have been contained within the life of the Church of England. See J. W. C. Wand, *Anglicanism in History and Today* (1962); H. G. G. Herklots, *Church of England and the American Episcopal Church* (1966); *Doctrine in the Church of England: The Report of the Commission on Christian Doctrine Appointed by the Archbishops of Canterbury and York in 1922* (SPCK, 1938). *ANGLICANISM.

CHURCH OF GOD, a designation used by more than 200 separate religious denominations in the U.S., many of them numerically very small, and by many similar religious bodies in other countries. Fundamentally the name Church of God has been used to stress the fact that all of these Churches are gathered by the power of God and claim no historic continuity with the historic Reformation Churches. With a few possible exceptions, these Churches share the view that the Church is an assembly of the regenerate, who are summoned by the Holy Spirit out of every nation and tribe and out of the existing religious denominations as well. Because of this basic view of the Church as the visible form of the invisible community of the elect, these Churches have all relied on the experience of religious conversion, repentance, acceptance of Jesus Christ, and subsequent baptism as the only means of adding new members to their congregations. The revival service and the evangelist are of great importance as a consequence. A firm literal belief in the Bible as the only rule of faith is also a marked characteristic. Emphasis on particular biblical texts may vary, but all denominations agree that the organization and practices of the Church described in the NT provide an adequate picture of the Christian life; therefore, they practice baptism by immersion and footwashing, recognize the several orders of ministers, apostles, deacons, exhorters, evangelists, bishops, and teachers, and frequently accept the speaking with tongues that follows upon *baptism by the Holy Spirit (see GLOSSOLALIA). Strongly committed to the religious revival, these Churches teach that salvation is freely given to those willing to accept it. Signs of a true conversion are essential for membership and for ordination, and a converted ministry is more highly valued than an educated one.

Denominations that call themselves the Church of God arose in three distinct circumstances; the religious revival among German-speaking Pennsylvanians in the 1820s, the *Holiness movement after the American Civil War, and the Pentecostal movement in the early years of the 20th century. John *Winebrenner was closely associated with the revival in south-central Pa. in 1823–25. His converts agreed to form themselves "into a church on the New Testament plan called the Church of God" . . . and "to take the Scriptures of the Old and New Testaments as the only authoritative rule of [their] Christian life and practice." The Winebrenner movement by 1830 was formally organized as the Churches of God in North America (General Eldership). A similar movement toward nondenominational Christianity among the Pennsylvania German Brethren in Christ led to the establishment of the Church of God As Organized by Christ under the leadership of P. J. Kaufman in 1886. The Holiness movement had a marked influence on the Churches of God (General Eldership), as well as on other denominations. Daniel S. Warner, one of its ministers, became convinced of the importance of the second work of grace, or the experience after initial conversion of the cleansing from inner sin by the Holy Spirit. He found many of his colleagues were likewise preaching Holiness. They gathered together in the Holy Alliance Band and later left the Churches of God (General Eldership) to form the Church of God (Anderson, Indiana). Except for its emphasis on Holiness, it holds the same doctrinal position as the older denomination. The Holiness movement inspired the preaching of Richard J. Spurling, Sr., in Monroe Co., Tenn., in 1886. He gathered a small number of followers into a Holiness Church that developed into the Church of God, formed in 1906 at Cleveland, Tennessee. Speaking with tongues as a sign of baptism with the Holy Spirit was recognized in the Church of God at Cleveland, Tenn., and it was a major factor in the Pentecostal movement. Several divisions have split the Cleveland group into the Church of God (Cleveland, Tenn.), the Church of God of Prophecy, the Church of God (Queens Village, N.Y.) and the (Original) Church of God. These divisions have been primarily concerned with the attitude of their members toward Ambrose J. Tomlinson, the first general overseer of the Church of God, and do not reflect real differences on doctrine or polity. Nearly all of the other denominations that use the designation Church of God are also a part of the Pentecostal movement. See W. W. Sweet, *Revivalism in America* (1944); B. Warfield, *Perfectionism* (1958); J. T. Nichol, *Pentecostalism* (1966); H. Tomlinson, *Diary of A. J. Tomlinson* (3v., 1953).

CHURCH OF GOD (Anderson, Indiana), a *Holiness Church, founded in 1878 as a result of the influence of the Holiness Movement on the Churches of God in North America (General Eldership). Many of the characteristics of the parent body, such as reliance on the Scriptures as the only source of faith, worship, and polity, the conscious effort to avoid *sectarianism, the specific use of baptism by immersion, *footwashing and the Lord's Supper celebrated together, and the form of church organization with overseers and a council of elders, have been retained in the younger Church. The principal difference between the two bodies, and the primary cause of their division, was the acceptance of the Holiness revival by the Indiana group. The work of the Holy Spirit in sanctifying the individual and cleansing him from inner sin in a second religious experience following an initial conversion is the central theme that characterizes the Church of God of Anderson, Ind., as part of the Holiness tradition of Methodist origin and gives it its identity as one of the Holiness Churches.

The prime mover in the distinct development of the Church of God in its early days was Daniel S. Warner (1842–95), a graduate of Oberlin College, licensed to preach by the Churches of God in North America in 1867. Warner experienced a second conversion at a Holiness revival in 1877 and formed a Holiness Alliance Band of others who had received the *second blessing. Opposed by the General Eldership, he formed his own congregation at Upper Sandusky, Ohio, in 1878 and was soon joined by others in the North Indiana Eldership who had undergone similar experiences. With three other preachers, Warner formed the independent Church of God at Beaverdam, Ind., in 1881. He had begun editing the *Herald of Gospel Freedom* in 1878, which became the *Gospel Trumpet* in 1881, a major force in the spread of the movement. Warner and his colleagues held revivals throughout Mich., Ohio, and Ind., 1886–91, which gave the Church of God a firm base in this area. The growth of the Church has been most marked in the 20th century. In 1916 there were 202 churches with 7,784 members. By 1926 the figures had tripled to 644 churches with 23,647 members. In 1968 there were 2,276 congregations with 143,725 members. Each congregation is autonomous but united to the central governing body through regional overseers and a council of elders. See A. L. Byers, *Birth of a Reformation* (1921); C. E. Brown, *When the Trumpet Sounded* (1951).

CHURCH OF GOD (Apostolic), a fundamentalist, Pentecostal body, founded at Danville, Ky., in 1897 by Elder Thomas J. Cox as the Christian Faith Band Church. It drew its inspiration from the *Holiness movement, mediated through the Church of God (Anderson, Ind.), with which Elder Cox had been connected, and from *Pentecostalism, manifested in the *second blessing and *glossolalia. Members are admitted on confession of faith and repentance and are baptized by immersion. Services are evangelistic, stressing holiness and *entire sanctification by the Holy Ghost. *Footwashing is held to be a divine ordinance, and the Lord's Supper is celebrated with unleavened bread and unfermented grape juice. The Church adopted its present name at a general convention in 1915 and was incorporated at Paris, Ky., in 1919. Headquarters were transferred to Bluefield, W. Va., by Elder Cox. Its membership has always been very small; it claims only 22 churches at the present time, and has been concentrated in mountain regions of W.Va., N.C., and Ky. since its foundation.

CHURCH OF GOD (Cleveland, Tenn.), a denomination that originated in the early days of Pentecostal movement. It traces its beginning to the revivals at Camp Creek, N.C. (see CHURCH OF GOD). The early holiness and revivalist group was named the Christian Nation; the name Church of God was taken in 1907. In 1909 A. J. Tomlinson was elected general overseer. He administered the Church almost single-handedly, until dissatisfaction with his fiscal policies led in 1923 to his removal from office. The Church gradually recovered from this crisis. A biennial general assembly was made the highest governing body. The Church maintains the usual Pentecostal doctrines, a strict code of conduct for members, and observes *footwashing as an ordinance. Membership in 1966 was about 220,000 in 3,727 congregations. The leader and historian of the Church is Charles W. Conn. See C. W. Conn, *Like a Mighty Army* (1955).

CHURCH OF GOD (Queens Village, N.Y.), one of the Churches that began with the revivals preached at Camp Creek, N.C., in 1896 (see CHURCH OF GOD). This particular branch, sometimes also called Church of God, World Headquarters, was formed by Homer A. Tomlinson in 1943 after his brother Milton had been elected general overseer of the Church of God that had been headed since 1923 by their father, A. J. Tomlinson. Queens Village, N.Y., the home of Homer Tomlinson, became headquarters of congregations that remained loyal to him as his father's personal choice as successor. In doctrine, worship, and polity this Church does not differ from the other Churches of God of the same lineage. Until his death in 1968, however, Homer Tomlinson exercised a highly centralized control. In 1967 there were about 75,000 members, in 1,925 congregations. He made many worldwide evangelistic tours and proclaimed world headquarters for his Church to be at Jaffa Gate in Jerusalem. He also ran for the presidency of the U.S. as head of the Theocratic Party, on a platform of social reform based on biblical texts.

CHURCH OF GOD (Seventh Day), a body that organized separately from the *Church of God (Seventh Day), Denver, Colo., in 1933. The leader of the separation was A. N. Dugger; headquarters were established in Salem, West Virginia. Doctrines and practices remained the same in the new Church.

Church officials are chosen by lot; government is by a 12-member apostolic council. In 1960 there were about 2,000 members, in 7 congregations.

CHURCH OF GOD (Seventh Day), Denver, Colo., an Adventist Church formed in 1865 by a small group that chose the name Church of God (Adventist) rather than Seventh-day Adventists. The dissenters also rejected the visions of Ellen G. *White, whom Seventh-day Adventists revere as a prophetess. The Church of God established headquarters and a publishing house in Stanberry, Mo., in 1900; it later moved its general offices to Denver, Colo., but kept the press in Stanberry. Doctrines include Christ's imminent second coming, and *conditional immortality. The Church observes Saturday as the day of worship and imposes tithing and abstention from pork, alcohol, tobacco, and narcotics. In 1967 there were about 4,000 members, in 91 congregations.

CHURCH OF GOD, Inc. (Original), a body that had its beginning in the preaching of Richard G. Spurling along Coker Creek, Tenn., in 1886 and his formation of the Christian Union. In 1896 this small group moved to Camp Creek, Cherokee Co., N.C., and in 1902 Richard Spurling, Jr., and William F. Bryant organized a Holiness Church at Camp Creek. When the Church of God held its first annual assembly in 1906 and fixed its headquarters at Cleveland, Tenn., Spurling remained behind. A. J. Tomlinson was elected moderator in 1909, and his influence was great. Rapid centralization, creation of a Council of Elders (1916) and a Council of Twelve (1917) and the decision to give Tomlinson full control over local preachers seem to have strained relations with a more conservative element in the Church of God. The division began in 1917, and in 1922 this conservative group was incorporated separately as The (Original) Church of God. In its doctrinal position, The (Original) Church of God accepts the Bible as the rule of faith and rejects all creeds as unscriptural. Repentance, justification, and regeneration are taught in the traditional Protestant sense, as well as sanctification by the Holy Spirit and *glossolalia. The Church practices baptism by immersion, the Lord's Supper and footwashing. In polity The (Original) Church of God is congregational. An annual general convention directs the work of the publishing house and Ridgedale University, a correspondence school. In 1968 there were 75 churches and 18,000 members.

CHURCH OF GOD AND SAINTS OF CHRIST, a body founded by William S. Crowdy in 1897, combining Pentecostalism with black nationalism and Jewish rituals. Crowdy, a cook on the Santa Fe Railway, experienced in a vision the central truth of his preaching: that the Negroes are identical with the Chosen People of the Bible. He formed his first congregation at Lawrence, Kan., where many southern Negroes had migrated in search of land and freedom. His message found adherents among these dispossessed people and later took root in urban areas. Crowdy claimed to be inspired by the Talmud, observed Saturday as the Sabbath, celebrated Passover, and used the Jewish calendar. He moved his headquarters in 1900 to Philadelphia, where he was succeeded by Bp. W. H. Plummer in 1916. Since 1917, headquarters have been at Portsmouth, Virginia. In 1906 there were 48 churches in the movement; in 1916, 92; and in 1926, 112 churches. In 1968 there were an estimated 200 churches with 38,000 members. Services are evangelistic, with the characteristic Pentecostal *revivalism, a stress on Jewish customs, and a downplaying of elements found in other Christian services.

CHURCH OF GOD AS ORGANIZED BY CHRIST, a small body founded in 1886 by P. J. Kaufman, an ex-Mennonite. The Church resists any form or element of *ecclesiasticism or *denominationalism, including creeds, and bases membership upon the call of Christ and an internal baptism. Teachings include *nonresistance, obedience to the law of Christ, and repentance. Baptism, the Lord's Supper, and *footwashing are observed as sacraments. A rigid avoidance of all worldliness in conduct, dress, and entertainment is required.

CHURCH OF GOD BY FAITH, Pentecostal Holiness Church, founded in Jacksonville, Fla., in 1919 by Elder John Bright. It was chartered as a religious body at Alachua, Fla., in 1923. The Church of God by Faith acknowledges belief in one Lord, one faith, and one baptism and in sanctification, *baptism with the Holy Spirit and by fire, and *glossolalia. In 1967 there were some 105 congregations, chiefly in the Deep South, and an estimated 5,300 members.

CHURCH OF GOD GENERAL CONFERENCE (Abrahamic Faith), organized from several small Adventists bodies at a national meeting in Philadelphia in 1888. In 5 years the national organization ceased to function, and was not revived until 1921 in Waterloo, Iowa. The corporate name of the Church of God (Abrahamic Faith) is the Church of God General Conference, Oregon, Illinois. The Church accepts most of the doctrinal positions of the larger Adventist Churches: Christ's imminent second coming and *conditional immortality. Unlike other Adventist bodies, however, this Church is unitarian. The first article of its statement of faith declares "We believe that only one person is God and that He is a literal (corporeal) being—almighty, eternal, immortal, and the Creator of all things." The same statement affirms that Jesus Christ "did not personally pre-exist" and that the "Holy Spirit is not a person but is God's divine power and influence." Ministers for this Church are trained at Oregon Bible College. Mission stations are maintained in India, Nigeria, Mexico, and the Philippines. In 1968 there were 5,800 members, in 118 churches, in the U.S. and 3,700 in other countries. Some local congregations are known as Church of God in Christ Jesus, a name that was used by the founding groups.

CHURCH OF GOD IN CHRIST, the largest Negro Pentecostal body in the United States. Together with C. P. Jones, Elder C. H. *Mason first formed the Church as a Holiness Church in 1897. Mason, after attending the *Azusa Street revival, introduced Pentecostalism and formally organized the Church as Pentecostal in 1907; Jones withdrew in protest. The Church is organized on the NT basis of other Churches of God, accepts *baptism with the Holy Spirit, manifested through *glossolalia, and *divine healing. Practices include baptism by immersion, *footwashing, and the Lord's Supper. During his lifetime Mason was "Chief Apostle," or bishop, as well as elder. The Church differs from other Pentecostal bodies by maintaining an episcopal polity. When formally organized, it counted 10 congregations in Tenn., Miss., Ark., and Oklahoma. In 1948 over 14,000 delegates took part in the dedication of Mason's Tabernacle in Memphis, Tenn., as world headquarters. In 1964 it claimed 4,150 churches and 419,466 members in the U.S., Africa, and the West Indies. See J. T. Nichol, *Pentecostalism* (1966), 102–104.

CHURCH OF GOD IN CHRIST (Mennonite), a Church organized in Ohio (1859) under the leadership of John Holdeman (1832–1900). He led a small group of followers out of the Mennonite Church with the aim of restoring a pure evangelical church life, enforcing traditional Mennonite discipline, *nonresistance, and *nonconformity to worldly manners and dress. The Church won adherents in Kansas, and among Mennonites from Russia in the province of Manitoba, Canada. The Church recognizes the *Dordrecht Confession of Faith; in 1968 there were about 8,000 members. See MennEnc 1:598–599; 2:789 s.v. "Holdeman."

CHURCH OF GOD IN CHRIST, INC. (Pulaski, Va.), a small Pentecostal Church formed at Alldreds, N.C., in 1942, with headquarters later moved to Pulaski, Virginia. The original group, dissatisfied members of the Tomlinson Churches, were joined in 1944 by members of the (Original) Church of God, Inc., who dissented from that body's lenient attitude toward divorce.

CHURCH OF GOD OF PROPHECY, a Church in the line of descent from revivals at Camp Creek, N.C., in 1896 (see CHURCH OF GOD). The Church of God of Prophecy as distinct from other Churches of this lineage began in 1923, when A. J. Tomlinson was removed from office as general overseer of the Church of God (Cleveland, Tenn.). Tomlinson continued his own Church of God; upon his death in 1943 his son Milton A. Tomlinson was elected general overseer. The phrase "of Prophecy" was added to the title in 1953. The Church differs little from other Churches of God of the same background. In polity, however, the general overseer must be elected by the council of elders and the state overseers. Membership in 1966 was about 44,000, in 1,469 churches. Missions are maintained in Sierra Leone and Latin America. See J. T. Nichol, *Pentecostalism* (1966), 138–140.

CHURCH OF ILLUMINATION, religious fellowship formed in Quakertown, Pa., in 1908, which draws its inspiration from the writings of R. Swinburne Clymer (1878–   ). It is allied to the Fellowship of the Rosy Cross, which has also maintained its headquarters at Beverly Hall, Quakertown, Pa., where the Academy and Temple of the Illuminati of the Church of Illumination is located. Formal organization has been limited to 14 congregations, with an estimated 9,000 members and 96 ministers. A Book of Worship issued in 1952 provides a highly ritualistic form of church service. The thought of the Church of Illumination is found in the voluminous writings of Clymer, whose personality has dominated the movement since its inception. Local churches are required to maintain a library of his published works. Besides his books on Rosicrucian and occult subjects, Clymer developed his religious philosophy in *Christisis* (1911), *Illuminated Faith: Christic Interpretations of the Gospel of St. Matthew* (1912), *Mystic Interpretations of the Gospel of St. John* (1913), *The Way to Godhood* (1914), and *Soul Consciousness Is the Way to Christhood* (1925). He preaches a form of Gnosticism with *Rosicrucian and *New Thought influences. Central to his teaching is the idea of progressive divinization. God has created a divine spark in every man. This divine spark is the *Christos.* It is also the unconscious soul, which may be brought into consciousness, then becomes an inexhaustible source of wisdom and power. This process of awakening the unconscious soul is the process of regeneration; by it mortality takes on immortality, and the son of man actually and literally becomes the "son of God." This is the heart of the Christian message as interpreted in the Church of Illumination and is said to be the truth handed down by the priesthood of Melchizedek to that small body of chosen seekers initiated into the mysteries of the divine law.

CHURCH OF IRELAND, official title of the autocephalous Church in both Eire and Northern Ireland that is in full communion with the See of Canterbury and the other Churches of the *Anglican Communion. It is organized in 14 dioceses in two provinces, Armagh and Dublin (not corresponding to the political divisions of the island). Its membership of about 500,000 is heavily concentrated in the North, where 27% of the population is estimated to be Anglican, as against 3% in the Republic. Except for the years 1800–69, when it was united with the C of E, it has been autocephalous. Its origin as a separate body is to be found in the Reformation in Ireland. The ecclesiastical policies of Henry VIII and his successors in England were also generally pursued in Ireland, but were not acceptable to the great majority of the people. The situation was complicated by the fact that the *established Church of Ireland was under powerful English influence, extending even to the refusal to permit the translation of the BCP into Irish, and to the encouragement given by the Crown to Scottish and English Protestants to settle in Ireland, early in the 17th century. A new RC hierarchy was established in 1614, around which the bulk of the Irish people gathered. However, the Church of Ireland continued to be the established Church of the nation until 1869. Anglican life in Ireland is characterized by extreme simplicity in ceremony and liturgy, coupled with a theological tradition strongly orthodox and deeply rooted in the classical sources of Christian doctrine. As in the case of the RC Church in Ireland, the Church of Ireland has played a major role in overseas missionary effort. See W. A. Phillips, ed., *History of the Church of Ireland from the Earliest Times to the Present Day* (3v., 1933, 1939); T. J. Johnston et al., *History of the Church of Ireland* (1953).

CHURCH OF JESUS CHRIST (Bickertonites), a small Mormon Church. Among those Mormons who rejected the leadership of Brigham *Young was Sidney Rigdon, once chief counselor of the Mormon prophet Joseph *Smith, Jr. Rigdon attempted to establish a Church of his own and baptized a number of converts, including William Bickerton. When Rigdon gave up the attempt, Bickerton assumed leadership of the tiny group and organized the Church of Jesus Christ after 1852. He denounced Young for introducing into Mormonism polygamy, *baptism for the dead, plurality of the gods, and secret temple rites. The Bickertonites accept the *Book of Mormon and the prophethood of Smith but reject *Doctrine and Covenants and many beliefs propounded by the much larger Utah Church. They have won converts among Italian-Americans, Indians, and Nigerians. In 1968 there were about 2,500 members in 43 churches in Pa., Ohio, Colo., and Mich., and another 3,500 in

Africa. Headquarters are in Monongahela, Pennsylvania.

CHURCH OF JESUS CHRIST (Cutlerites), a small Mormon Church founded by Alpheus Cutler. A follower of the Mormon prophet Joseph Smith, Jr., and master mason of the Nauvoo temple, Cutler did not follow Brigham *Young and most of the Mormons to Utah. He founded his own splinter Church in 1853 in Fremont County, Iowa, but never attracted many converts. There is a tiny congregation in Clitherall, Minn., and a group in Independence, Mo., that attempts to follow the cooperative United Order proposed by Smith.

CHURCH OF JESUS CHRIST OF LATTER-DAY SAINTS, see LATTER-DAY SAINTS, CHURCH OF JESUS CHRIST OF.

CHURCH OF JESUS CHRIST OF LATTER-DAY SAINTS (STRANGITES), see LATTER-DAY SAINTS (STRANGITES), CHURCH OF JESUS CHRIST OF.

CHURCH OF OUR LORD JESUS CHRIST OF THE APOSTOLIC FAITH, INC., a Pentecostal body founded by R. C. Lawson at Columbus, Ohio, and moved to New York in 1919. It traces its doctrine to the Apostles, Prophets, and esp. Jesus Christ. Special emphasis is given to the premillennial second coming of Christ and *baptism with the Holy Spirit. The Lord's Supper and *footwashing are observed as ordinances. The Bible is the sole norm for faith and practice. In 1954 it had 45,000 members, with 155 churches in 27 states, the West Indies, Africa, and the Philippines. The Church is the parent body of the *Bible Way Churches of Our Lord Jesus Christ, World Wide, Inc.

CHURCH OF SCOTLAND, before the Reformation, the Scottish Church, now the *national Church, adhering to *Presbyterianism. The true founder of the Scottish Church was St. *Ninian (360?–432), a shadowy figure who came to Britain from Rome as a missionary bp. and at Candida Casa (Whithorn) built a church of stone, dedicated to St. Martin of Tours. Ninian was active 397–431 in the area of Galloway, Dumfriesshire, and Cumberland, and there is some archeological evidence of a successful mission among the southern Picts. The best-known figure in the early Scottish Church, however, is St. Columba, an Irish abbot, born in Donegal in 521. The Irish Church differed in certain ways from the Roman, and when Columba came to Scotland in 563 with 12 monks to establish a monastery on Iona, the island became the center from which Celtic Christianity spread to Scotland. In a later period the influence of Iona was extended into Northumbria by Aidan, who founded a settlement on the island of Lindisfarne, but at the Synod of Whitby, 664, the usage of Northumbria was conformed to that of Rome. The Synod marks the beginning of the decline of the Celtic influence, though until the time of Margaret (1070–93) clergy known as Célidé, or Culdees, who represented the Celtic tradition, were active from Iona to St. Andrews. Repeated Norse attacks on Christian centers in the 9th cent. made it impossible for Iona to remain a center of leadership, and increasingly royal and ecclesiastical power gravitated toward the East, where from c.900 St. Andrews became the chief seat of ecclesiastical power. In the reign of Malcolm Canmore (1058–93) Scotland began to emerge from its political and cultural isolation, largely through Margaret, his devout Saxon wife, who exerted a civilizing influence on her husband and helped to introduce the customs of the Catholic Church in which she had been reared, e.g., the date for the beginning of Lent and the abolition of certain "barbarous rites" (the vernacular?) in the Mass. Margaret's reforms represent the final overthrow of Celtic Christianity in Scotland. Her son David became king in 1124, and David's reign must be reckoned the most important of any before the Reformation. He continued Margaret's policies of conforming the Church in Scotland to the Churches of England and the Continent. He also encouraged the introduction of new monastic orders, esp. Canons Regular, Benedictines, and Cistercians. The medieval period gave Scotland the splendor and vitality of its monastic institutions, its universities, its vernacular Scriptures and its sacramental life, yet the defects of the medieval period are also obvious: a general relaxation of discipline, impoverishment of the parish churches, pluralism, the intellectual and moral decline of the clergy, and a decline in church attendance and religious devotion. Many of the abbeys and priories had fallen into the hands of royal bastards or the nobility, and anticlericalism was widespread. Moneys paid in taxation to Rome diminished the authority of the king and the resources of the country.

The Reformation was first introduced to Scotland through Lutheran teachings brought in by merchants trading from the Low Countries; but an act of Parliament prohibited such teachings, and in 1528 Patrick *Hamilton was burned at the stake in St. Andrews for advocating Lutheran views. By 1530 copies of Tyndale's New Testament were being distributed, and a new faith and hope began to stir. The Reformation came to Scotland in 1559–60 with the return of John *Knox from Geneva. By June 1559 the Army of the Congregation (i.e., the Reformers) seized Edinburgh, Mary of Guise was deposed, and with English help, the French were expelled. The Estates of Scotland, meeting in the "Reformation Parliament," in Aug. 1560, abolished the jurisdiction of the pope, forbade the celebration of Mass, and approved the *Scots Confession. The exiled Mary, Queen of Scots, returned in 1561 and for the next 6 years sought to restore her kingdom to its Roman allegiance in face of the outspoken criticisms of Knox. In Dec. 1560 the first *General Assembly met and began to appoint ministers and readers to various parishes. In Jan. 1561 the first *Book of Discipline was submitted to Parliament and in

1564 the *Book of Common Order was confirmed by the General Assembly as the standard of worship in the Reformed Kirk. The Scottish Reformation is characterized by its stress on the primacy of the word of God, the development of popular education and the independence of the Church. The presbyterian polity that emerged from 1575, however, was the creation not of Knox, but of A. *Melville and his followers. Melville's Book of Discipline (1581) asserts against *episcopacy the absolute parity of ministers and against the supremacy of crown or parliament the absolute freedom of the Church. From Melville's time the balance of power shifted constantly between the presbyterian and episcopal parties in the Church of Scotland until 1690, when Presbyterianism was finally established and the *Westminster Confession officially approved.

From 1680 to 1843 the history of the Church of Scotland is one of constant division and secession, largely over the question of patronage or state intrusion (see CAMERONIANS; SECEDER TRADITION; FREE CHURCH OF SCOTLAND). In the latter half of the 19th cent., however, despite the doctrinal and biblical controversies occasioned by the intellectual ferment of the age and symbolized by the heresy trial of W. R. Smith (1846–94), movements toward reconciliation and reunion began to be seen, and in the reunion of the United Free Church with the established Church in 1929 the last major division in Scottish Presbyterianism was healed. The concise statement of the *Articles Declaratory appended to the uniting act of 1929 well expresses the character and enshrines much of the history of the Church of Scotland: "The Church of Scotland is part of the Holy Catholic or Universal Church . . . adheres to the Scottish Reformation; receives the Word of God which is contained in the Scriptures of the Old and New Testaments as its supreme rule of faith and life; and avows the fundamental doctrines of the Catholic faith founded thereupon. The principal subordinate standard of the Church of Scotland is the Westminster Confession of Faith approved by the General Assembly of 1647, containing the sum and substance of the Faith of the Reformed Church. Its government is Presbyterian, and is exercised through Kirk Sessions, Presbyteries, Provincial Synods, and General Assemblies. . . . The Church is in historical continuity with the Church of Scotland which was reformed in 1560. . . . As a national church it acknowledges its distinctive call and duty to bring the ordinances of religion to the people in every parish of Scotland through a territorial ministry. . . . This Church . . . receives from . . . its Divine King and Head, and from Him alone, the right and power subject to no civil authority to legislate, and to adjudicate finally, in all matters of doctrine, worship, government and discipline in the Church." See J. H. S. Burleigh, *Church History of Scotland* (1960); W. D. Simpson, *St. Ninian and the Origins of the Christian Church in Scotland* (1940); A. B. Scott, *Pictish Nation, Its People and Its Church* (1918); J. A. Duke, *History of the Church of Scotland to the Reformation* (1937); J. Knox, *History of the Reformation in Scotland* (ed. W. C. Dickinson, 1949); J. R. Fleming, *History of the Church in Scotland, 1843–1929* (2v., 1927, 1933). *CALVINISM; *PRESBYTERIANISM.

CHURCH OF SOUTH INDIA, a Church formed Sept. 27, 1947, at St. George's Cathedral, Madras, through the union of about one million members of the South India United Church (Congregational and Presbyterian); the South India Province of the Methodist Church; and the South Indian dioceses of the Church of India, Burma, and Ceylon (Anglican). Bp. M. Hollis was elected first moderator of the Synod, the chief governing body. The Church of South India (CSI) is significant for the ecumenical movement as the first union of non-episcopal Churches with a Church holding to the *historic episcopate. It attempts to maintain the contributions of the congregational, presbyterian, and episcopal traditions that it incorporates, though it is not itself the continuation of any one

of them. Since its formation the CSI has negotiated with Baptists and Lutherans, but has so far not achieved union with them. Discussions leading to the formation of the CSI began at a conference in May 1919 at Tranquebar, site of the landing of the first Protestant missionaries to India in 1706. An official joint committee began work in 1920 and issued the Basis of Union and the Constitution in 1941. Unity was achieved basically along the lines of the 1888 *Lambeth Quadrilateral. No difficulty arose over the first three points, but the fourth, historic episcopate, led to extended discussion. It was agreed to accept episcopate, with bishops to be ordained by bishops, but to affirm no theory of its meaning. The five existing Anglican bps. were accepted, and nine additional bishops were ordained, including representatives of each of the uniting Churches. Of the fourteen, six were Indian and eight British.

At the time of union all communicant members of the uniting Churches were accepted as full members of the CSI, and all ministers of the uniting Churches were given full standing without further ordination. A local congregation, however, is not compelled to accept a pastor lacking episcopal ordination, and all ministers entering the CSI after the union are episcopally ordained. The 1955 *Lambeth Conference expressed reservations about the union because of the acceptance of ministers not episcopally ordained but approved a limited form of intercommunion. CSI developments have occasioned extensive discussion in other parts of the world, both among the parent bodies of the Churches involved and among others who see in the CSI plan possibilities for union elsewhere. The CSI has served as an example particularly to other younger Churches seeking unity under somewhat similar circumstances. The drive toward unity in South India was motivated in large measure by the desire to achieve greater missionary effectiveness. Also, with growing nationalism, Indian Christians began to assert greater independence from Churches and mission societies of the West and to seek a form of church life suited to their own needs. See M. Hollis, *Significance of South India* (1966); B. Sundkler, *Church of South India* (1954).

CHURCH OF THE AGAPEMONE, a 19th-cent. English revivalist body founded by Henry James Prince with the help of Samuel Starky. Both were C of E clergymen who together began a revivalist movement in Somerset in the 1840s. Because of their bizarre doctrine they were forbidden to preach. Leaving the C of E, they established their own ministry, claiming to be personifications of the Holy Spirit. In the village of Spaxton, *c.*1850, they founded "Agapemone" (Gr., abode of love), a religious community of men and women holding property in common. Charges brought against them led to a trial that revealed licentious practices. Briefly the sect gained new members when J. H. Smyth-Pigott became its head and opened *(c.*1890) a branch establishment in London called the Ark of the Covenant. The sect disappeared in the early 20th century.

CHURCH OF THE BRETHREN, until 1908 the Fraternity of German Baptists, the continuing parent body among Brethren Churches originating in southwest Germany in 1708. Disputes over methods of witness and *church order in 1881–82 led to divisions: the Old German Baptist Brethren broke off (1881) from the main body in favor of greater conservatism; the Brethren Church separated (1882) in favor of progressivism. The Church of the Brethren is the largest (1968 membership, 191,452) of the Brethren Churches. Local congregations are largely independent, but there is a legislative annual conference and a general brotherhood board for the social and evangelical works of the Church. The Church maintains six colleges and one seminary. It actively participates in the World and National Council of Churches. *BRETHREN CHURCHES.

CHURCH OF THE FULL GOSPEL, INC., an earlier name for the *General Conference of the Evangelical Church, Inc.

CHURCH OF THE GOSPEL, a *Holiness Church founded at Pittsfield, Mass., in 1911. It advocates biblical doctrines of holiness of heart and practices baptism by immersion. In 1965 it had 42 members, 4 churches, and 2 ordained clergy.

CHURCH OF THE LIVING GOD (Motto: Christian Workers for Fellowship), a *Holiness Church founded in 1889 at Wrightsville, Ark., by William Christian, who believed in the truth of "Freemason religion." He wanted his organization to be known as "operative Masonry" with its first three degrees to be *believer's baptism, the Lord's Supper (with water and unleavened bread), and *footwashing; local churches are "temples." The Church is governed by a bishop and a quadrennial general assembly, and is supported by tithes. In 1964 it had 45,320 members, with 276 churches. *HOUSE OF GOD, WHICH IS THE CHURCH OF THE LIVING GOD.

CHURCH OF THE LUTHERAN BRETHREN OF AMERICA, a small Lutheran body organized at Milwaukee, Wis., in 1900 by eight Norwegian pastors and five congregations located in Minn., Wis., N. Dak., Ill., and Iowa. Doctrinally it emphasizes the need and possibility of a personal, conscious experience of conversion and salvation. Children of church age are instructed for 2 years, but they take no vow at their confirmation. Only when there is an individual experience of faith are persons accepted as communicant members. Lay participation and nonliturgical worship are stressed. There are no altars, and the sacraments are reduced to two. The Church has 6,000 members and conducts missions in Africa, Japan, and Formosa. These are supported by contributions far greater than the average per capita offerings of other Lutheran bodies. See A. R. Wentz, *Basic History of Lutheranism in America* (1955).

CHURCH OF THE NAZARENE, a Protestant denomination, specifically committed to the propagation of the doctrine of *entire sanctification as espoused by John *Wesley, the founder of Methodism. It traces its beginning to a meeting at Pilot Point, Tex., in 1908, when sectional *Holiness Churches, namely, the Church of the Nazarene, chiefly centered in Calif., the Association of Pentecostal Churches, chiefly in New England, and the Holiness Church of Christ, chiefly in Okla., Tex. and Ark., met and formed a single organization under the name Pentecostal Church of the Nazarene ("Pentecostal" was dropped in 1919, in repudiation of Pentecostalism, esp. *glossolalia). The Nazarene belief stated briefly is: "That there is one God, the Father, Son and Holy Spirit. That the Old Testament scriptures given by plenary inspiration contain all truth necessary to faith and Christian living. That man is born with a fallen nature and therefore is inclined to evil and that continually. That the atonement through Jesus Christ is for the whole human race, and that whosoever repents and believes on the Lord Jesus Christ is justified and regenerated and saved from the condemnation of sin. That the finally impenitent are hopelessly and eternally lost. That believers are to be sanctified wholly, subsequent to regeneration, by the incoming of the Holy Spirit through faith in the Lord Jesus Christ. That the Holy Spirit bears witness to the new birth and to entire sanctification in the heart of believers. That our Lord will return, the dead will be raised, and the final judgment will take place" (*Nazarene Manual*).

Nazarene services are open to demonstrations of praise, but modern trends are toward more formality. The Church forbids use of liquor and tobacco, as well as worldly amusements. The government of the Church is representative. Local churches are grouped to form districts. Each district is under the jurisdiction of a superintendent elected by the district at its annual assembly, which is composed of lay representatives and ministers from each congregation. Every 4 years the various districts send representatives, in proportion to membership and equally divided between ministers and laymen, to a general assembly, which in turn elects general superintendents and a general board of approximately 40 persons, made up equally of lay and ministerial members, to direct the work of the denomination through its several departments. Each local church elects its own pastor, provides its own facilities, and is free to carry on its particular program of worship and evangelism. However, each congregation supports the broader interests of the Church through annual budgets and operates under the jurisdiction of the district and general superintendency. The Church is composed of approximately 5,000 congregations, with a world membership of nearly 500,000 in 50 countries. The Sunday schools enroll in excess of 1 million. The Church maintains eight liberal arts colleges, a central Bible College, a graduate school of theology in the U.S., and Bible colleges in Canada, the British Isles, and other areas. The Lillenas Publishing Company, music division of the Nazarene Publishing House, is the largest denominational publisher of gospel music in the world. See C. T. Corbeth, *Our Pioneer Nazarenes* (1958); T. C. Smith, *Called unto Holiness* (1962). *NAZARENE MANUAL.

CHURCH OF THE UNITED BRETHREN IN CHRIST, see EVANGELICAL UNITED BRETHREN CHURCH.

CHURCH OF TRUTH UNIVERSAL, a *New Thought sect, founded in 1910 by Albert C. Grier at Spokane, Washington. Its founder was an ordained minister of the Universalist Church and drew most of its early members from his own congregation. His thought was akin to that of the *Fillmores, and the Church of Truth is similar in most respects to the *Unity School of Christianity. Grier's stress on the centrality of Jesus Christ and his message kept the group from uniting with the International New Thought Alliance until 1920, after it issued a statement of beliefs more compatible with traditional Christianity. The group established the University of Metaphysics at Spokane and began the publication of *Truth Magazine* in 1911. Grier later transferred his ministry to Pasadena, Calif., and later to the Church of the Healing Christ in New York City. Erma Wells succeeded him in the direction of the Church of Truth and its activities on the West Coast. Never a large body, its membership had declined very considerably by 1965, and eventual amalgamation with the Unity School has been under consideration.

CHURCH ORDER, norms for church life. In this broad sense the term is virtually interchangeable with "church polity." Some writers (e.g., D. Stevick, *Canon Law: A Handbook*, 1965) distinguish the concepts by defining polity strictly in political terms, as the "arrangement of authority whereby power is distributed and the work of the group is carried out." "Order" is then made to refer to something more basic, inhering in the essential constitution of the Church (74–76). It is difficult, however, to find such a consistent distinction in the general use of these terms. "Church order" was an early term applied to manuals setting forth norms for church life in particular localities. J. Quasten, e.g., refers to the *Didache*, the *Didascalia*, and the *Apostolic Tradition* as church orders (see Quasten 1 and 2), and these documents cover a wide range of subjects, including government, liturgy, and discipline. R. *Hooker chose the term "polity" because it "containeth both government and also whatsoever besides belongeth to the ordering of the Church in public" (*Of the Laws of Ecclesiastical Polity*, 3.1.14). Today each denomination has its own books describing or stating, in normative regulations, its polity.

Church order also has a specific reference, namely, to Reformation Churches, esp. in Germany. The church order (Ger. *Kirchenordnung*) comprised the regulations in each territory, promulgated usually by the secular ruler, regarding worship, sacraments, discipline, and polity. Church orders implemented Reformation theology in practical church life; they remain an important source for Reformation history.

CHURCH POLITY, see POLITY.

CHURCH SESSION (in Scotland, Kirk Session), the lowest court in *Presbyterianism. The session consists of the pastor or minister and the ruling *elders (who in most Presbyterian Churches may be women) of a particular church or congregation. The minister is usually the moderator or chairman of the session. The session is charged generally with maintaining the spiritual government of the church, and for this purpose its powers include the reception, dismissal, and pastoral overseeing of members (discipline over members is a constitutional function now rarely exercised); the instruction, examination, and ordination of ruling elders; the development and supervision of the educational work of the church; and the regulation of times and places of worship (though the conduct of worship is a ministerial not a sessional act). Meetings are held at times approved by the session, usually at least quarterly. Ministers are subject not to the session but to the *presbytery, in which the session is represented by the minister and a representative elder.

CHURCH STATE, see STATE CHURCH.

CHURCH TRIUMPHANT, a communistic body founded in Chicago in 1886 by Cyrus R. Teed and moved by him in 1903 to Estero, Fla., where in 1968 the group still claimed about 5,000 members. It adheres to a doctrine of Koreshanity (from Koresh, the Hebrew form of Cyrus), which Teed attributed to revelation. Included among its beliefs are reincarnation, alchemy, astrology, and the imminent second coming of Christ; but the most distinctive feature is the total rejection of modern science in favor of Teed's "cellular cosmogony." The earth is a hollow ball, 8,000 miles in diameter, with men living on the inner rather than the outer surface. The planets are seven mercury discs moving about within the ball, and the stars are reflections of these discs. Perceiving this brings the key to all the problems of life and death. The existing religious, social, and political order will soon give way to a new dispensation wherein the followers of Koreshanity will build a new capital city from which the saints will rule the world. Teed did not escape accusations of personal corruption and public fraud.

CHURCH UNION, an association in the C of E founded in 1934 under the presidency of Lord *Halifax by the amalgamation of the *English Church Union and the *Anglo-Catholic Congress. Its purpose is "to uphold the doctrine and discipline of the Church and to extend the knowledge of Catholic faith."

CHURCH UNITY OCTAVE, the name from 1908 to 1949 of the annual period of prayer for Christian unity, Jan. 18–25, begun by Lewis Thomas Wattson. In 1949 the name *Chair of Unity Octave was adopted. *WEEK OF PRAYER FOR CHRISTIAN UNITY.

CHURCH WORLD SERVICE (CWS), an organization founded (1946) to integrate the refugee and other overseas relief programs of U.S. Protestant and Orthodox Churches. In 1950 CWS became a department of the National Council of the Churches of Christ in the U.S.A. and in 1964 combined with the Division of Foreign Missions to form the Division of Overseas Ministries. The work of CWS in over 40 countries is channeled mainly through local or regional churches and missions, often in cooperation with other agencies, such as Catholic Relief Services and international and government organizations. Direct aid is supplemented by technical and economic assistance aimed at long-range self-help. See H. E. Fey, *Cooperation in Compassion: The Story of Church World Service* (1966).

CHURCHES OF CHRIST, a group of autonomous local churches, originating in the *Restoration movement. With a membership of 2,350,000 in the U.S., they are particularly strong in the South, esp. in Tenn. and Tex., but are rapidly spreading throughout the North and abroad. The early history of this group is the same as that of the Disciples of Christ, or Christian Churches. Within the Disciples of Christ a conflict in the late 19th cent: between progressives and conservatives led to gradual separation, the conservative group calling themselves Churches of Christ. The separation was officially recognized in 1906, when the U.S. census of religious bodies for the first time listed the Churches of Christ as distinct from the Disciples of Christ. Participants in the Restoration movement of the early 19th cent., calling themselves Disciples or Christians, had the dual goals of Christian unity and the restoration of simple NT Christianity. Congregational in church polity, anticreedal in outlook, they affirmed no creed but Christ and no authority but the Bible. They observed adult baptism by immersion, and the Lord's Supper each Sunday. Essentially the conflict between conservatives and progressives centered on whether changes being made in the movement were compatible with the NT. Conservatives opposed the establishment of a missionary society, believing that no intercongregational organization existed in the 1st cent. (see ANTIMISSIONARY MOVEMENT). They opposed the addition of instrumental music in worship as lacking any NT basis. They also opposed the assumption of pastoral powers by some preachers on the grounds that the early Church was ruled by elders and that preachers were simply preaching elders. They also opposed the practice of *open communion. Some objected to Sunday schools and to individual communion cups. As Disciples moved into the mainstream of Protestantism, they were influenced by *liberal theology, biblical criticism, the *Social Gospel, and the ecumenical movement. All these the conservatives rejected. In general the Churches of Christ believe that the Disciples have accepted many "innovations" whereas they have maintained the original approach of the leaders of the Restoration movement.

Churches of Christ have *a cappella* singing in their services. Local churches are autonomous; they are governed by elders and deacons appointed under NT qualifications. Biblical doctrines stressed include the view that the Father, the Son, and the Holy Ghost are members of the one Godhead; the Incarnation, virgin birth, and bodily resurrection of Christ; the universality of sin after the age of accountability, the only remedy being the vicarious atonement of Christ; the Church as the body and bride of Christ. A vigorous program of evangelism has led to rapid growth in membership. A "Herald of Truth" radio and television program sponsored by a church in Abilene, Tex., is nationwide. A large number of publications are issued. There are 21 colleges, 41 secondary and elementary schools, and 20 homes for the aged sponsored by these churches. Under a planned exodus movement, groups of member families have moved from regions in which the churches were well established to other sections of the U.S. in order to found new churches. The group of families from Midland, Tex., which moved to Somerset Co., N.J., made the move, they said, in order to establish there "a strong nondenominational church patterned after the doctrine of the New Testament." In recent years efforts have been made to expand inner-city missions and to make the church colleges racially inclusive. Missionary expansion has been most extensive since World War II in Europe, Asia, and Africa, where there are more than 450 full-time workers. All of this has been done without benefit of a missionary society or a national headquarters. Unlike the Disciples of Christ, the Churches of Christ are not members of the National or World Council of Churches. They maintain that this form of ecumenicity is a departure from the Restoration movement, which called for unity through return to the faith and practices of the early Church. Participation in the ecumenical movement means acting as a denomination among other denominations and accepting post-NT ecclesiastical developments; Churches of Christ disclaim being a denomination. See E. West, *Search for the Ancient Order* (2v., 1951).

CHURCHES OF CHRIST IN CHRISTIAN UNION, a denomination organized at Marshall, Ohio, in 1909 by a group that separated from the Christian Union Church in defense of the doctrine of *entire sanctification. These churches, about 200 in 14 states, are independent of one another, although linked through a biennial general council and annual state councils. In addition to entire sanctification, the second coming of Christ and healing are stressed. Revivals and camp meetings are important features of church life. In 1952 the Reformed Methodist Church merged with these Churches, to form a Northeast District. Headquarters are in Circleville, Ohio; membership in 1965 was about 7,500.

CHURCHES OF GOD, HOLINESS, a Pentecostal body founded in 1914 by K. H. Burruss. Doctrine includes justification, *entire sanctification, and the gift of the Holy Spirit subsequent to conversion (see BAPTISM WITH THE HOLY SPIRIT). In 1965 the Churches reported 25,600 members, with 32 churches; headquarters are in Atlanta, Georgia.

CHURCHES OF GOD IN NORTH AMERICA (General Eldership), religious bodies that developed from the preaching of Elder John *Winebrenner in central Pa., 1820–60. Expelled from the German Reformed Church in 1825 for his acceptance of camp meetings and revivals, he directed a movement closely parallel to the efforts of Alexander *Campbell. He believed that "it is contrary to Scripture to divide the Church of God into different sects and denominations" and consciously sought to keep his revival movement among Pa. Germans from hardening along sectarian lines. Winebrenner's first congregations were formed "on the New Testament plan" by a mutual covenant "to take the Scriptures of the Old and New Testaments as the only authoritative rule of our Christian life and practice." Each local church was self-governing, with the minister called and ordained by the congregation. The Churches of God relied on camp meetings and revivals to renew their congregations and gain new members. They practiced baptism by immersion, *footwashing, and the Lord's Supper in accordance with Jn 13.4. In 1830 Winebrenner's followers created a system of general and regional elders, modeled on the Methodist *district superintendents. By 1860 the Churches of God had gradually spread through Pa. into the Midwest and West, generally following the movement of Pennsylvanians to new regions. Efforts to develop in urban centers, such as Chicago, proved unsuccessful. The secession (1878) from the North Indiana Eldership of Daniel S. Warner and a number of others, influenced by the *Holiness movement, led to the formation of the *Church of God (Anderson, Ind.). In 1968 there were 376 congregations and 36,995 members, concentrated in Pa. and the Midwest. The General Eldership meets at Harrisburg, Pa., every 3 years; local churches are self-governing.

CHURCHES OF THE NEW JERUSALEM, also called the Swedenborgian or the New Church, religious bodies relying on the writings of Emanuel *Swedenborg for much of their distinctive beliefs and forms of worship. Swedenborg himself had nothing to do with the foundation of a distinct denomination; he conceived of a spiritual association of devotees from all the Churches. The movement toward a distinct New Church began with a group gathered by Robert Hindmarsh in London in 1783 to discuss the thought of Swedenborg; formal organization was in 1815. Swedenborgianism spread rapidly to the U.S., where the

first congregation was formed at Baltimore in 1792. The ideas expressed by Swedenborg in his voluminous writings on theological subjects were in sharp contrast to the Lutheranism he professed in his life. He wrote of his visions of heaven and hell and of the things revealed to him by spirit messengers. His unique communications with the other world made him, in the eyes of those who chose him as the prophet of their New Church, the privileged channel of revelation, the "new Jerusalem" of Rev 3.12; 21.2. His writings on theological subjects and his interpretations of the Bible are held to be directly inspired and inerrant revelation. It was revealed to Swedenborg that his writings would be the basis for the teachings of a new Christian Church. The fundamental doctrine of the Churches of the New Jerusalem is the correspondence of the natural world to spiritual reality. The movement had a significant influence in preparing American and British Christians for acceptance of spiritualism and psychic phenomena.

Through the "science of correspondence" Swedenborg developed a personal interpretation of the Scriptures and traditional Christian teaching. Thus the Trinity is understood as a trinity of attributes of the one divine Person; the Incarnation, as God becoming the Lord Jesus, identifying himself with humanity; the Atonement, as putting man right with the spiritual world. At death man is liberated from the body forever, then as free spirit he makes his choice of living in the heaven of good or the hell of evil. Thus, while Swedenborgians profess Christian truths, observe infant baptism and the Lord's Supper, and have a quasi-episcopal polity, judgment of their Christian orthodoxy depends on how closely any group follows Swedenborg's interpretations. The Churches place great emphasis on spiritual self-realization, leading to philanthropic service. In the U.S. there are two Swedenborgian bodies: the General Convention of the New Jerusalem in the U.S.A. and the General Church of the New Jerusalem. See J. K. Smyth and W. F. Wunsch, *Gist of Swedenborg* (n.d.).

CHURCHWARDEN, a lay officer in the Churches of the *Anglican Communion. Since early medieval times in England, churchwardens (usually two) have been appointed in every parish to take care of the temporalities. Though the *rector has control of the church edifice and its appurtenances, the wardens are responsible for its repair and for providing the furnishings necessary for the performance of divine service. They are also required to maintain order in the church and churchyard, and have the power to arrest offenders. Shortly before the Reformation, and continuing after, they assimilated the originally distinct office of sidesmen (synods men) or questmen, who represented the parish in diocesan synods or visitations and were responsible for presenting offenders against ecclesiastical law to the ordinary. The office, which is elective, exists with some modifications of function in all branches of the Anglican Communion. See R. Burn, *Ecclesiastical Law* (8th ed., 1824), 1:396 and 397–415; J. H. Blund, *Book of Church Law* (1873), 248–278.

CIRCUIT, a term used more often in early Methodism than today, signifying a group of churches served by one minister, sometimes with the help of one or two associates, who traveled among the churches. Geographically a circuit was quite large in early Methodism, sometimes comprising 10 or more churches. The preachers often used horses to travel their circuits and thus were called "circuit riders." With the growth of the churches, single church stations with settled pastors supplanted the circuit stations, although in rural areas and the South and West there still are circuits, not, however, with the large number of churches that characterized early Methodism. See N. B. Harmon, *Understanding the Methodist Church* (1955), 102; *Cyclopaedia of Methodism* (ed. M. Simpson, 1880), 219; *Doctrines and Discipline of the Methodist Church* (1964).

CIRCUMCELLIONS, bands of *Donatist peasants who terrorized Upper Numidia and Mauretania in the 4th and 5th centuries. Their name was derived from the attacks they made upon the settlements about which they roamed (*circum cellas vagantur*; Augustine, *In Psalm.* 132.3). The movement began as a protest against Roman landlords and an attempt to secure the abolition of debts and the liberation of slaves, but it later took on the character of a religious war. The Circumcellions, who looked upon themselves as *Agonistici* (Gr., champions) or *Milites Christi* (Lat., soldiers of Christ), waylaid travelers, sacked towns, burned churches, and committed every kind of excess to shouts of *Deo laudes* ("Praise to God"; Augustine, *Ep.* 108.14). Despite the numerous attempts of Roman authorities to suppress them, they succeeded in gaining new recruits because of their easy code of morality, religious fanaticism, and conviction that one who fell in battle with either pagans or Catholics received a martyr's reward. See Optatus, *De schism. Donat.* 3.4; G. Bareille, DTC 2:2513; W. H. C. Frend, *Donatist Church* (1952).

CIRCUMCISED (*Circumcisi*), name given to the *Passagiani, a 12th-cent. Judaizing sect in Lombardy, because they resumed the rite of circumcision.

CIVIL CONSTITUTION OF THE CLERGY, the law of July 12, 1790, restructuring the Church in France, making it virtually a department of state, effectively severed from Rome. Although matters of dogma were left to Rome, the revolutionary decree, an achievement of the National Constituent Assembly, inspired by *Gallicanism, revoked the privileged status the clergy had enjoyed for centuries and subordinated them to the State. The legal document, which King Louis XVI signed (Aug. 24) unwillingly, together with the clerical loyalty oath decreed on Nov. 27, created a schism and turned a sizable force of nonjuring clergy and faithful against the Revolution.

The new French Church was given the following organization: each of the 83 *départements* (largest political subdivisions in the nation) constituted one religious diocese, all in turn being consolidated regionally into 10 metropolitan sees; only one parish was allotted to towns with a population of less than 6,000; the law abolished benefices, titles, offices, and privileges except those specifically retained in the new Constitution. Bishops were to be elected by majority vote in each departmental assembly; eligibility to bishoprics required 15 years of service in the particular diocese. The newly elected bishop was not to apply to the pope for confirmation; rather, he would be canonically instituted by his senior bishop and take a solemn oath in public to uphold the Constitution of the Clergy, and his episcopal responsibilities to the nation. Curés, usually rectors, eligible after 10 years of service, were elected by majority vote in the district assemblies; an oath was obligatory. Each bishop received the right to choose assistants (*vicaires*), but only from his diocese. In all these elections any tax-paying citizen, Catholic or not, had suffrage. The State fixed and paid the salaries of the clergy, ranging from 50,000 livres for the bp. of Paris to 1200 livres for the curé, and 700 livres for vicars in the smallest towns. Laws regarding clerical residence were quite strict, and infractions were penalized. Pius VI in one brief suspended or excommunicated clergy submitting to the revolutionary regime. Then in the bull *Charitas* (April 13, 1791) he rejected clerical elections and termed the oath sacrilegious and the Constitution heretical and schismatical. The schism in the French Church lasted until the Concordat of 1801. See J. H. Stewart, *Documentary Survey of the French Revolution* (1951); F. Mourret, *History of the Catholic Church* (tr. N. Thompson, 1955), v.7.

CLAPHAM SECT, an appellation by Sydney Smith (1764–1840) that stuck to an informal group of Anglican *evangelicals, who in the late 18th cent. worshiped at Clapham parish church and shared a sense of social responsibility and the conviction that religion should be manifested in good works. They were people of substance and were conservative-minded; many were interrelated through marriage, and they formed a pressure group with an influence out of proportion to its size. The best-known members are Zachary Macaulay and William Wilberforce. It promoted the abolition of Negro slavery and the increase of missionary work and Sunday schools, and founded the *British and Foreign Bible Society and the Society for Bettering the Condition and Increasing the Comfort of the Poor (1794).

CLARENI, a group of Franciscan *Spirituals founded by Liberatus of Macerata and later given brief legal existence by Celestine V. This pope granted them immunity from the authority of the minister general of the Friars Minor in 1294; they are therefore referred to as Poor Hermits of the Lord Celestine, or simply as Celestines. Their autonomy was revoked by Boniface VIII, but they refused to disband. In 1307 *Angelus Clarenus assumed leadership, and it is from him that the group is called Clareni. Even before his death in 1337 they became suspect of *Joachimism and identified with the *Fraticelli. In 1473 several groups of friars known as Clareni were reunited to the Franciscan Order; it is not clear whether the remnant of Angelus's group was among them. See L. Bernardini, *Frate Angelo da Chiarino alla luce della storia* (1964); D. Douie, *Nature and Effects of the Heresy of the Fraticelli* (1932); L. Oliger, "Ange de Cingoli," DHGE 3:17–19.

CLARKE, ADAM (1760 or 1762–1832), Wesleyan preacher, antiquarian, and Oriental and biblical scholar. Born at Moybeg, Londonderry Co., Ireland, he joined a Methodist *society in 1778 and began preaching at once. John *Wesley invited him to Kingswood School in 1782, later using him as a preacher. As a scholar, C. aided the Bible Society in editing Oriental versions of the Scriptures, and was recognized by many learned societies. He was three times president of the Wesleyan Methodist Conference. In 1808 the British government employed him in editing historic state papers. His many writings include *Memorials of the Wesley Family* and his chief work, a labor of 30 years, *Commentary and Critical Notes* on the Bible. See J. W. Etheridge, *Life of the Rev. A. C., LL.D.* (1858); J. Everett, *Life of A. C.* (1849).

CLARKE, SAMUEL (1675–1729), English philosopher and divine. After earning the Doctor of Divinity degree, he received from Queen Anne the rectorship of St. James, Westminster, where he delivered two impressive series of sermons (1704, 1705), on "The Being and Attributes of God and the Evidence of Natural and Revealed Religion," later published together in book form. In 1712 he published his celebrated treatise *Scripture Doctrine of the Trinity*, which, betraying Unitarian and latitudinarian ideas, brought him for a time into conflict with *Convocations. An ardent disciple of Isaac Newton, he tried to use in natural theology a method as nearly mathematical as possible. He ranks among the foremost rationalist theologians of his time. See E. Sprague, EncPhil 2:118–120.

CLARKE, WILLIAM NEWTON (1841–1912), Baptist clergyman and theologian. C., a professor of theology at Colgate from 1890, presented his own theological system in his *Outline of Christian Theology* (1890), which went through many editions and did much to diffuse *liberal theology. He sought to incorporate evolutionary theory and the new biblical criticism. Departing from the rationalistic theologizing of the 19th cent., C. tried to formulate theological concepts on historical and experiential grounds. He explained the authority of the Bible by the universality of its moral teachings; the Church meant simply a collective name for those living practical Christian truths. His other writings include: *What Shall We Think of Christianity?* (1899) and *The Use of Scripture in Theology* (1905). See C. L.

Howe, Jr., "W. N. C.: Systematic Theologian of Theological Liberalism," *Foundations* 6 (1963), 123–135; Smith-Jamison 1:290–294.

CLASS (Methodist), a small subdivision (at first about 12 persons and a leader) within an early Methodist *society. Each member of the society was placed in a class; leaders supervised the lives of the class members, who met each week for prayer and spiritual exhortation. A few Methodist bodies still have class meetings. See HistAmMeth 1; F. E. Maser, *Dramatic Story of Early American Methodism* (1965), 52–55.

CLASSIS, an ecclesiastical governing body for a particular geographical district in *Reformed Churches; Presbyterian denominations employ the term *presbytery for the same body. Classis membership consists of the clergymen and representative *elders of the district. The classis ranks in authority above that of the Reformed consistory (Presbyterian church session) and below that of the particular or regional synod and the general synod (Presbyterian general assembly). The classis serves a judicial function by acting as a court of appeal from the consistory of the local congregation. The classis oversees its congregations and the personal conduct and ministerial labors of each clergyman. It grants licenses to preach, ordains clergymen, and can admonish, suspend, and depose them.

CLAUDIANISTS, a turbulent sect of *Donatists founded by Claudianus, a Donatist bp. of Rome who was banished because of the riots occasioned by his disputes with Pope Damasus. He went to Carthage, where he soon quarreled with the Donatists there. He broke with Parmenian, the Donatist bp., and set up his own rival community. He was later readmitted to the Donatist communion by Primian over the opposition of the church elders. See P. Monceaux, *Histoire littéraire de l'Afrique chrétienne* (1922), 6:112–113.

CLERGY (Gr. *klēros*, lot; see Acts 1.17), those persons who have been set apart from the general body of church members, the laity, by ordination as leaders of the Church. The term traditionally embraces bishops, priests (presbyters, elders), and deacons, though in some Churches, such as those in the *Reformed tradition, the deacons are lay persons. The concept of special persons within the Church who exercise a distinctive function is generally traced to the NT and Jesus' setting apart the 12 Apostles, together with the action of the apostolic Church as recorded in Acts and the outline of requirements for bishops and deacons in 1 Tim ch. 5 and Tit ch. 2. In the Eastern and the RC Churches ordination is considered a sacrament (holy orders), which gives an indelible character to the one ordained. Protestant Churches recognize only baptism and communion as sacraments, though they generally have special rites of ordination. Congregationalists, Baptists, and Quakers, as well as some groups within other Churches, minimize or deny outright the distinction between clergy and laity. The authority and power of the clergy are variously conceived. Administering the sacraments, preaching, and leading in worship are generally considered their responsibilities. The RC clergy govern the Church, but in the Protestant Churches governing power is normally shared by the laity. See R. Dunkerley, ed., *Ministry and the Sacraments* (1937). *ORDINATION; *LAITY.

CLERICALISM, a term originating in the latter half of the 19th cent., and generally used in a pejorative sense, signifying domination of civil government and temporal affairs by the Church. It emerged from opposition to RC influence in France during the Second Empire, being popularized by Gambetta's slogan, *"Le cléricalisme, voilà l'ennemi!"* Although the word was new, the condition it represented had existed during certain periods of history, as from the time of Gregory VII through the papacy of Innocent III. Similar domination by the Church also resulted from some of the concordats arranged between popes and the rulers of national states. Its meaning has been broadened by some to apply to all attempts of Churches to influence social and economic aspects of life. See J. Lecler, *Two Sovereignties: A Study of the Relationship between Church and State* (1952).

CLOSED COMMUNION (Close Communion), restriction by a Church of participation in the Lord's Supper to its own members; the opposite of open communion, the more general practice among Protestant Churches. While the term is not used, closed communion is in fact the law in the RC Church. Closed communion has been particularly associated with Baptist history. Until the 20th cent., most Baptists practiced closed communion, i.e., refused to share in the Lord's Supper with *pedobaptists. Their argument was: Nearly all Christians consider baptism a prerequisite to communion; *infant baptism is not true baptism; therefore, pedobaptists are not baptized and should not partake of the bread and the cup. From the beginning there were some open-communion Baptists, such as John *Bunyan, who defended his practice in *Differences in Judgment about Baptism No Bar to Communion.* The adherents of closed communion, however, constituted the great majority in Great Britain, North America, and elsewhere. Since Baptists acknowledged others to be Christians, and had close relations with Congregationalists and Presbyterians in England, they sometimes felt embarrassed by their positions; it was awkward to refuse to share in the Lord's Supper with people with whom they worshiped and sometimes exchanged pulpits. In England, Robert Hall advocated open communion in *The Terms of Communion* (1815). During the ensuing century, British Baptists retreated from their closed-communion practice. In the U.S., progress toward open communion was slower, but it had clearly begun by 1914. Today most Baptists in the North practice open communion, a minister usually announcing that all Christians are welcome to the Lord's Table. In the *Southern Baptist

Convention there is a diversity of practice; the tendency in the SW is strongly toward closed communion, but in the SE many churches practice open communion. Many smaller fundamentalist Baptist bodies retain closed communion. *Landmarkism interpreted closed communion even more narrowly, restricting participation in the Lord's Supper to members of a particular congregation; but this view has had limited influence outside its ranks. See D. M. Himbury, "Baptist Controversies, 1640–1900," *Christian Baptism* (ed. A. Gilmore, 1959).

CLOWES, WILLIAM (1780–1851), leader of the Clowesites, a group of English Methodists who in 1811 joined the Camp-Meeting Methodists to form the *Primitive Methodist Church. C. was converted in 1805, joined a Methodist *society, but was expelled in June, 1810, for attending camp meetings, which had been proscribed by Wesleyan Methodists. Aided by James Steele, who had also been expelled, he formed the Clowesites. As a revivalist he was particularly successful around Hull. See J. Ritson, *Romance of Primitive Methodism* (1909).

CLOWESITES, the followers of William *Clowes in England, who joined the Camp-Meeting Methodists in 1811 to form the *Primitive Methodist Church.

COCCEIUS, JOHANNES (Coch, Koch; 1603–69), pioneer in biblical theology. Of German birth, he spent the major portion of his professional career in the Netherlands at the Univ. of Leiden. He was an expert in Hebrew and in rabbinic literature. In his masterwork, *Summa doctrinae de foedere et testamento Dei* (1648), he systematized *federal theology. This and some of his other writings are important because they sought to develop theology not on the basis of scholastic Calvinist orthodoxy but on biblical concepts, esp. that of God's cove-

nant. His thought had a marked influence on *Pietism. After his death there was a protracted controversy between his followers and the orthodox *Reformed theologians of Leiden. His collected works were published in 8 volumes at Amsterdam (1673–75).

COCHLAEUS, JOHANNES (Johann Dubeneck; 1479–1552), German humanist, theologian, and polemicist. His first interests were in humanism, both in his studies at Cologne (1504–07) under Ulrich von *Hutten, and as rector of a Latin school in Nuremberg (1510–17). He also studied law at Bologna (1515–17), and theology at Ferrara (1517) and Rome (1517–19), where he was ordained. He was sympathetic with the desire for reform, but Luther refused (1520) to engage in debate with him, and C. launched his series of nearly 200 polemical writings. They are strong in rhetoric, weak in theology; Luther replied to only one of them. With J. *Eck and J. *Faber, C. prepared the *Confutatio* in response to the *Augsburg Confession (1530). He also attended most of the other conferences of the period that sought to reunite Protestants and Catholics. His polemical temper prevented him from being effective. C.'s *Historia Hussitarum Libri XII* (1549) is a source work on the Hussites. For 4 centuries his *Commentaria de actis et scriptis Martini Lutheri* (1549) shaped RC Reformation studies, until abandoned as distorted and naïve. See J. P. Dolan, *History of the Reformation* (pa., 1965), 24–25.

COKE, THOMAS (1747–1814), first bp. of the Methodist Episcopal Church in the United States. C. was born of wealthy parents at Brecon, Wales; educated at Oxford, he was ordained in the C of E and given a parish in Somersetshire. He traveled 20 miles expressly to meet John *Wesley. When he later preached Methodism in his own church, he was dismissed, and he joined Wesley, helping him supervise the Methodist *societies and write the *Deed of Declaration. In 1784 Wesley ordained C.

as general superintendent (bishop) of Methodist work in America, sending him with two other preachers to ordain F. *Asbury. C. met Asbury at Barratt's Chapel, Del.; they arranged that all Methodist preachers should meet in Baltimore in Dec. 1784, when the Methodist Episcopal Church in America was organized and Asbury ordained. C. crossed the Atlantic 18 times, at his own expense, to assist both British and American Methodism. He frequently presided at the Irish Conference as well as at the British Conference and with Asbury in the United States. He encouraged Methodist work in Nova Scotia, and esp. in the West Indies. He died on a missionary journey to India and was buried in the Indian Ocean. See J. W. Etheridge, *Life of the Rev. T. C., D.C.L.* (1860); Hist-AmMeth I. *CHRISTMAS CONFERENCE.

COLET, JOHN (1467–1519), dean of St. Paul's, humanist. Of a wealthy family (his father was twice lord mayor of London), C. studied at Oxford and on the Continent, where he acquired a love for the New Learning. After his return to England he was ordained (1498) and began lecturing on the Epistles of St. Paul at Oxford, using the findings and the method of humanistic scholarship in his critical study of the text. At the same time he undertook a campaign of criticism against the ecclesiastical abuses of the time. In 1504 he was named dean of St. Paul's, in which office he proved himself an able and vigorous administrator. He used a considerable portion of the large fortune inherited from his father in the foundation of St. Paul's School. His outspoken attacks upon the scandals in the Church led to some questioning of his orthodoxy; he was brought up once for trial, but the charges against him were dismissed as frivolous. At Oxford he had become a close friend of *Erasmus, and in London he was the intimate friend and spiritual adviser of Thomas More. He represents the calmer, humanistic, Erasmian stream of Catholic reform that was soon to be overwhelmed by the swifter onrush of the Reformation. The basic account of Colet's life was given by

Erasmus (*Epistolae* 3.335). See E. Hunt, *Dean Colet and his Theology* (1956).

COLLEGIALISM, a concept of Church-State relations, derived from the natural-right theories of H. Grotius (1583–1645) and S. Pufendorf (1632–94). The term itself is attributed to J. Boehmer (d. 1745) of the Univ. of Halle. Both Church and State are *collegia*, voluntary associations created by the members' will to unite; both societies are independent of each other in aim and purpose. Thus the State has no inherent right over ecclesiastical matters (see IUS CIRCA SACRA). Collegialism goes further in separating Church and State than does *territorialism. The concept of the Church that collegialism implies is opposed to *episcopalism; authority in the Church resides equally in "teacher and hearers," not in the body of bishops. See EncRelKnow 3:159–160.

COLLEGIALITY, as used in reference to RC bishops (collegiality of bishops, episcopal collegiality), a term indicating that the episcopal office or function is of its nature corporate, that episcopal consecration aggregates a bishop per se to a body bearing corporate responsibility for the whole Church, although for actual membership in the episcopal college it is necessary that the one so consecrated be "in hierarchical communion with the head of the college [the Roman pontiff] and the members" (Vat II ConstCh 22). In past centuries the emphasis has been strongly placed on the individual role of the bishop as pastor of a single diocese and also upon his subordination to the pope as pastor of the whole Church. In more recent times and during Vatican Council II that emphasis has been balanced by insistence on the bishop's inclusion within the college that succeeds the apostolic college, and consequently on the fact that joined with the pope and the rest of the episcopate each bishop shares in the pastoral direction of the whole Church.

Ultimately this collegial arrangement rests on Christ's free determination in founding and organizing the Church as he saw fit. But in keeping with the teaching of Vatican II (*ibid.* 22–23) it is possible to discern the fitness of such an arrangement. It manifests the catholicity of the Church; it reflects the variety of individual communities within the Church; it ensures that the pastors of individual, local communities cultivate, as members of the college, a concern for the whole Church; it brings out more clearly the virtuality (potentiality, capacity) of each local church so to represent the totality that the whole may realize itself as event (in the eucharistic celebration) in it as a part. If the vitality of each part is such that it could become the whole, it would seem more fitting that its head and center of life should share collegiately in the direction of the whole. See J. Colson, *L'Épiscopat catholique: Collégialité et primauté dans les trois premiers siècles* (Unam Sanctam 43, 1963); C. Journet, *Church of the Word Incarnate* (tr. A. H. C. Downes, v.1, 1955), 1:98–120; K. Rahner, *Bishops: Their Status and Function* (tr. E. Quinn, 1964); K. Rahner and J. Ratzinger, *Episcopate and the Primacy* (tr. K. Barker et al., 1962).

COLLEGIANTS, religious groups in 17th- and 18th-cent. Holland, first at Rynsburg (hence also called Rynsburgers), then at Amsterdam and other Dutch cities, rejecting any institutional Church and stressing personal, mystical experience. They were originally *Remonstrants deprived of their ministers by the Synod of *Dort (1618–19). They began to meet without ministers, calling their gatherings *collegia*. These meetings consisted in Bible reading, prayer, and spontaneous Spirit-prompted addresses (*colloquia prophetica*). The local *collegia* gathered twice a year for general meetings at Rynsburg, where *believer's baptism by immersion was practiced. The Rynsburg Collegiants became more rationalistic in their ideas under the influence of Spinoza; the Amsterdam group (see BORELISTS) were more mystical. The Collegiants had influence upon English Seekers, and esp. upon the Friends. See R. M. Jones, *Spiritual Reformers in the 16th and 17th*

Centuries (pa., 1959), 113–132; MennEnc 1:639–640.

COLLOQUY OF THORN, see THORN, COLLOQUY OF.

COMENIUS, JOHN AMOS (Komenski; 1592–1670), bp. of the *Unitas Fratrum (Unity of the Brethren) and pioneer educational reformer. Born in Moravia of a family belonging to the Unitas Fratrum, he was educated in schools of his Church, and at Herborn and Heidelberg. Returning to Moravia (1614), he combined teaching and writing books on education with pastoral service, having been ordained in 1616. Driven from Moravia by the Thirty Years' War, he headed the Brethren's schools in Lissa, Poland; he brought about pedagogical reforms in Sweden and Hungary. Civil War in England thwarted the plans for universal education he had projected with friends there. As a bp. in exile he helped his Church maintain episcopal succession, which was later transferred by his grandson to the Renewed *Moravian Church. C. spent his last years in Amsterdam, teaching and writing celebrated devotional and pedagogical works. See M. Spinka, *J. A. C.* (1940).

COMMON LIFE, BRETHREN OF THE, see BRETHREN OF THE COMMON LIFE.

COMMON ORDER, BOOK OF, see BOOK OF COMMON ORDER.

COMMON PRAYER, BOOK OF, see BOOK OF COMMON PRAYER.

COMMON WORSHIP, a translation of the Lat. *communicatio in sacris*, referring in RC terminology to participation by members of the Church in worship services of other Churches.

COMMON WORSHIP, BOOK OF, see
BOOK OF COMMON WORSHIP.

COMMONWEALTH, in English history,
the government during the period 1649–60.
The victorious parliamentary army, after
the beheading of Charles I (1649), proclaimed England a commonwealth. Oliver
*Cromwell became Lord Protector in 1653,
and the subsequent period is also called the
Protectorate. The Restoration of the Stuart
monarchy terminated the era. These were
years of great religious difference among
the Puritans, the appearance of many
*Nonconformist bodies (Familists, Seek-
ers, Ranters, Diggers, Levelers, Quakers),
and the growth of the Baptists. See R. Barclay, *Inner Life of the Religious Societies of
the Commonwealth* (1876); W. C. Braithwaite, *Beginnings of Quakerism* (ed. H. J.
Cadbury, 2d ed., 1955), 1–28; R. Knox, *Enthusiasm* (1950), 139–175.

COMMUNAL MOVEMENTS, non-monas-
tic communities motivated by religious or
ethical ideals, which to some extent own
property in common; sometimes called
communistic settlements or intentional
communities. Although found in several
civilizations and religions, the communal
movement most typical in Western society
has generally originated from a deliberate
attempt to revive the structure of the primitive Christian community of Jerusalem,
which "held all things in common" (Acts
2.44; 4.32). After this first apparently unsuccessful experiment, Christian communitarian life, with some exceptions, developed within the monastic context. During the Middle Ages a common life was led
by several lay religious groups such as the
*Beghards and *Beguines and the *Broth-
ers and Sisters of the Free Spirit. In colonial
Spanish America paternalistic communal
societies were established for the Indians,
the Jesuit Reductions in Paraguay being the
best-known example.

In the wars and general disorder following the establishment of Lutheranism in
Germany many peasants joined Anabaptist
and millenarianist groups, some of which,
like the *Hutterian Brethren, practiced
community ownership of property. To
avoid persecution several of these groups
immigrated to America, where the idea of
communal living developed and expanded.
The first significant group was the *Ephrata
Community, established in 1732 in Pennsylvania. But the full flowering of communitarian experiments took place in the
first half of the 19th cent. with *revivalism
and the multiplication of sects. Some secular communities, e.g., New Harmony, Ind.
(1825), and Icaria, Ill. (1849), were founded
but did not long survive. The religious societies were largely millenarianist in inspiration, and their survival depended mainly
on the strength of their leaders. Those still
in existence have had to change their way
of life significantly. The most important of
the 19th-cent. groups were the following:
the *Harmony Society, also known as Rappites after their founder Johann Rapp; the
Separatist or Zoar Community; the Hopedale Community; or Miniature Christian
Republic; the Adonai Shomo; and the
*Oneida Community, which was the most
prosperous. Of the older groups still in existence the best known are the Hutterites
from Germany, the *Doukhobors from
Russia, now in Western Canada, and the
*Shakers in New England.

Most contemporary communal movements have had a rather ephemeral existence. The Catholic Worker Movement,
e.g., gave rise to several short-lived farming
communes. But a number, chiefly pacifist in
outlook and encouraging marriage, have
managed to prosper. Among Catholics the
most flourishing are the Nomadelfia Community in southern Italy (1947) and the
Laborious Order of the Ark founded by
Lanza del Vasto in France (1954). The *Society of Brothers and the *Brethren of
Early Christianity are fundamentalist in
theology, similar to the Hutterites, and engage in profitable farming and manufacture.
Most other Protestant communal movements have become more nondenominational. The more significant ones are the
Zions Order of the Sons of Levi in Missouri, Koinonia Farm in Georgia, the Holy

Apostles Church in Nigeria, and the Riverside Community in New Zealand. The outstanding example of a contemporary secular communal society is furnished by the kibbutzim in Israel, which began in 1909 and have played a major role in the development of that nation.

While religious groups continue to found communal societies, a large number of contemporary communities have been formed without any specifically religious motive in view. They manifest a great variety in their manner of communal life, their organization, and motivation. Some, for example, the Esalin community in California, regard communal living as a vital aid in attaining emotional or psychological maturity. Others have chosen to drop out of contemporary society, rejecting its values, such as monogamy, as meaningless, and have formed so-called "hippie" communities. Many of these, in contrast to earlier communal societies, have decided to remain in the cities, although such groups as the Diggers in California sometimes engage in farming. See R. Brown, NCE 4:29–32.

COMMUNICANT, strictly, one who "communicates," i.e., partakes of holy communion, is in the habit of doing so, or is eligible to do so. The term may distinguish in some Churches those who have been confirmed from those who have not, or connote one who meets minimum church membership standards (e.g., where a Church requires at least annual communion). In a broader sense, communicant is used as a synonym for church member.

COMMUNICATIO IN SACRIS, a RC phrase, for Catholic participation in the worship services of other Churches. Until Vatican Council II this was absolutely forbidden. The Council, however, using the term to mean common worship, recognized its desirability in certain circumstances, for ecumenical reasons; the fact that it signifies unity of belief generally rules out common worship; yet the gaining of a needed grace sometimes commends it. (Vat II Ecum 8). Special recognition of the possibility of *intercommunion with the Eastern Churches was also given by the Council (Vat II East-Cath 26–29).

COMMUNION, a term sometimes used to refer to a Church, denomination, or other religious group, e.g., the Presbyterian communion or the Methodist communion. It is sometimes used in reference to Christian bodies when some question exists concerning whether it is theologically proper to use the term Church. The word recalls the phrase "communion of saints" in the Apostles' Creed. It also suggests a sense of fellowship, particularly as this may center around the service of holy communion, through which Christians are united. The problem of *intercommunion, to bridge the separation of the various Christian communions, has been one of the difficult questions of the ecumenical movement. From one point of view the service of holy communion is the center of the life of the Church, and those who participate in it share a common life. For some, therefore, it would seem to be pretending something that is not yet true if Christians who are not united nonetheless participate in the service together. Others, however, hold that because of a common faith in Christ the members of the various Christian groups already form one communion in the most essential matters, despite their differences, and that this unity is appropriately expressed in common participation in the service of holy communion, even while the doctrinal and organizational differences persist. Some Roman Catholics have acted in accord with this second view, but official approval has been given only in regard to receiving holy communion in the Eastern Churches (see Vat II Ecum 8; EastCath 26–29).

COMMUNION, CLOSED, see CLOSED COMMUNION.

COMMUNION, HOLY, see HOLY COMMUNION.

COMMUNION, OPEN, see OPEN COMMUNION.

COMMUNION UNDER BOTH KINDS, the form of administering holy communion whereby the laity receive both the bread and the wine. It is in contrast to the practice of giving only the bread to the laity, with the wine consumed by the priest. Communion under both kinds, or species, was the normal practice in the Church from the beginning; withdrawal of the cup from the laity began in the 12th century. St. Thomas Aquinas in the 13th supported the new practice, though he allowed communion under both kinds. The older practice continued in Rome as late as the 14th cent., but it was outlawed by the Council of Constance (1415). The change was accompanied by no explicit dogmatic justification, but apparently resulted from a desire for simplified administration. It may also have reflected an increased emphasis on the distinction between clergy and laity. Theologically, however, it was asserted that the laity were not deprived of any spiritual benefit when the cup was withheld from them, since Christ was fully present in any part of either species. The theological defense suggests that emphasis was now on the reception of the physical elements, rather than on the action of participation in a community meal, as had been the case earlier.

In the early 15th cent. the question became a major issue in the *Hussite movement, though it was not emphasized by Jan *Hus himself. Those who advocated communion under both kinds (*sub utraque specie*) became known as *Utraquists, or *Calixtines, from their demand for the cup (*calix*). The creed of the Utraquists was contained in the Four Articles of Prague (1420), of which Article 2 stated, "The sacrament of the most Holy Eucharist shall be freely administered in the two kinds, that is bread and wine, to all the faithful in Christ who are not precluded by mortal sin—according to the word and disposition of Our Savior." The Articles were incorporated in the *Compactata* approved at the Council of Basel in 1436 for the Church of Bohemia. They remained the creed of that Church until 1620, when all non-Roman rites were prohibited. Communion under both kinds became a mark of the Churches of the Reformation, and it has been the practice of Anglican and Protestant Churches subsequently (see *Augsburg Confession, Art. 23; *Thirty-Nine Articles, Art. 30). Restoration of the cup to the laity was a symbol of overcoming the distinction between clergy and laity and an assertion of the *priesthood of all believers. It also reflected the rejection of *transubstantiation.

In recent years the RC Church has made some moves toward restoring communion under both kinds. Liturgical studies generally have placed emphasis on the practice of the earlier centuries of the Church, and that has led to new interpretations of the meaning of the Eucharist. Out of the liturgical movement has come a renewed understanding of it as a meal in which the community shares, a meal comprising both food and drink. The importance of common participation in the liturgical action of the Church, as contrasted with a passive laity receiving the ministrations of the clergy, has been another theme of liturgical renewal. The Constitution on the Liturgy approved by Vatican Council II allowed the cup to the laity in certain cases, such as the first communion of newly baptized adults (Vat II SacLit 55). Such a development has importance not only for RC worship but also for the *ecumenical movement. The difference in RC practice and that of Protestantism and Eastern Orthodoxy has been very readily noticed by the average layman. In principle, it is now possible for all Churches to develop a common practice. Inasmuch as the withholding of the cup from the laity was often seen as a mark of their secondary position in the Church, the change is also valuable in restoring the conception of the Church as a community, or as a family. See J. A. Jungmann, *Mass of the Roman Rite* (tr. F. A. Brunner, 2v., 1951–55), 2:382–386. *EUCHARIST.

COMMUNITY CHURCHES, *local churches, independent of denominational connections, that accept members from any Protestant denomination. They vary in patterns of organization, worship, and membership conditions, but usually have a doctrinal basis broad enough to admit Christians of all persuasions, who, as members of these Churches, may still retain their own denominational loyalties. Community churches originated in villages and rural areas that could not support more than one church, but are common today in newer suburban areas where religious pluralism exists along with a minimizing of denominational distinctions. Although these churches are independent, they sometimes belong to the loose association called the International Council of Community Churches, organized in 1950. This organization has no jurisdiction and serves primarily to provide fellowship and a channel of missionary outreach. In 1950, only about 300 of 3,000 known community churches were associated with this Council. See J. Ruskin Howe, ed., *That They All May Be One* (n.d.); Mayer RB 376–377.

COMMUNITY OF TRUE INSPIRATION, an early name for the *Amana Church Society, because the members of the society believed they were acting directly under divine inspiration.

COMPACTATA, a religious agreement between *Hussites and the Council of *Basel. The Compactata were designed to end the Hussite Wars; they evolved from negotiations that were begun (1433) with Hussite representatives invited to Basel by Eugene IV, and continued at Prague. By the time of Hussite acceptance, which was tied to the political aims of the Emperor Sigismund, at the Diet of Iglau (1436), and ratification by Basel (1437), this Council was at odds with Eugene IV; the Compactata never received papal approval and were annulled by Pius II (1462). A drastic curtailment of the *Four Articles of Prague, they provided that: (1) approved preachers were free, but were obligated to respect ecclesiastical authorities; (2) communion under both kinds was permissible as long as faith in communion under one was safeguarded; (3) the clergy had the right to hold property, but those in vows could not hold temporal office; (4) serious public sins should be punished by lawful authority. See Bihlmeyer-Tüchle 2:442–443; Hughes HC 3:322–325.

COMPANATION (Lat. *cum*, with; *panis*, bread), a term that was sometimes used in Eucharistic discussions as a synonymn for *consubstantiation. *IMPANATION.

COMPARATIVE SYMBOLICS, the branch of theological studies that treats the various Christian creeds and public confessions of faith (symbols); it investigates the origin, nature, and contents of such statements, in comparison with other confessions or symbols. Most Churches regard the so-called *ecumenical creeds as normative in some sense. But individual Churches have also adopted specific creeds and confessions, e.g., the Lutheran *Augsburg Confession; the Reformed *Heidelberg Catechism or *Westminster Confession; the RC decrees of the Council of *Trent. A number of factors complicate the study of comparative symbolics. Some Churches refrain from drawing up any specific creedal statements, either because they hold to the principle of "deeds, not creeds," or because they feel that each individual Christian has the right to interpret the Scriptures on his own. Other Churches have formulated creeds in the past but view them only as the record of past experience and in no way normative for doctrine or practice in the present.

COMPELLE INTRARE (Compel them to enter), the Vulg. text of Lk 14.23, alleged in the Middle Ages as a kind of scriptural charter for the *Inquisition. The authority of St. Augustine was claimed for such an interpretation. But neither Augustine, this text, nor the teaching of the whole NT sanctions the use of force to exact faith from the individual.

COMPREHENSIVENESS, most often used with respect to the Anglican tradition, a word denoting any of three characteristics: (1) the moderation that characterized much of the Reformation in England, a moderation in large part intended to provide a reformed Church within which it would be possible for the people generally to find their place, without compromising any element of essential individual belief; (2) the necessity, if such inclusiveness is to exist, that the reformed Church conserve every essential element of historic Christian faith and order and require conformity to as little of what is nonessential as possible; (3) the characteristic often held before individual Anglicans as an ideal, that their manner of discipleship be such as to open to them as many diverse understandings of God and of the traditions of Christian life as is possible, for the deepening and enriching of their own ministries. See Mayer RB 274; Schaff Creeds 1:598–600; H. R. McAdoo, *Spirit of Anglicanism* (1965). *ANGLICANISM.

CONCILIARISM, the teaching that an *ecumenical council exercises supreme authority over the whole Church; the term was formerly also often used as a catchword for theories asserting that a council is superior to the pope. Historically conciliarism appeared in a variety of forms, some orthodox, some not. The conciliar movement, which peaked at the Council of *Constance (1414–18) and led to the resolution of the *Great Western Schism (1378–1417), was an outgrowth of conciliarism. Though antipapal conciliarism was later condemned because of the ecclesiology it implied, it reappeared both in *Gallicanism and in *Febronianism. Appeal to a general council was also a recurrent theme in the early days of the Reformation in Germany.

Modern authors trace the roots of the conciliar theory to the canon lawyers of the early 13th century. Although in practice canonists generally supported papal claims to a plenitude of power, in theory they discussed curbs and restraints to forestall the abuse of this power if it were to fall into hands of a venal or incompetent pope. To safeguard the Church against such an eventuality, they established the norm that even the pontiff is bound by councils in matters touching the faith and the general state of the Church. These canonists commonly taught that conciliar decisions are to be preferred to the word of the pope alone.

By the start of the 14th cent. various conciliar theories were brought from the academic forum into the political arena. Political theorists, retained to defend the prerogatives claimed by emperors and kings from papal encroachment, elaborated antipapal conciliarism. *Marsilius of Padua (c.1275–1342), in the employ of Louis IV of Bavaria, denied, in his work *Defensor pacis,* the divine origin of the papacy and asserted that supreme authority resides in a council representing laity as well as clergy. During the Western Schism, when the Church was divided by allegiance to rival popes, conciliar theories were put into action. Theologians from all over Europe worked together in the amorphous effort known as the conciliar movement; the leaders were Conrad of Gelnhausen (c.1320–90), Peter d'Ailly (1350–1420), and Jean Gerson (1363–1429) of the Univ. of Paris; Francesco Zabarella (1360–1417) in Italy; and Dietrich of Niem (1340–1418) in Germany. Their aim was to convoke a council that would heal the schism and reform the Church in head and members. Although canon law legislated that only the pope can convoke a council, the conciliarists agreed that the extraordinary situation created by the schism had to be dealt with by extralegal means. Their first attempt, the Council of *Pisa (1409), compounded the confusion by electing a third claimant to the papacy, but their efforts finally bore fruit at the Council of Constance.

Two decrees illustrating the impact of conciliar theory on Constance are: *Sacrosancta* (April 6, 1415; sometimes called *Haec sancta,* from its opening words) and *Frequens* (Oct. 5, 1417). The first contains the classic statement of conciliarism: that being a general council representing the Catholic and militant Church, Constance held its power directly from Christ, and that even the pope must obey the council in matters pertaining to faith. Modern theologians continue to debate whether the *Sacrosancta* carries the weight of a dogmatic definition. Modern historians all agree that the decree *Frequens* was primarily disciplinary. It stipulated that, as councils are an ordinary part of church life, they should be held frequently to ensure continuing reform.

The conciliar movement exhausted itself during the protracted and sterile proceedings of the Council of *Basel (1431–49). Pope Pius II (1458–64) dealt the *coup de grâce* with the bull *Exsecrabilis* (D 1375) in 1460. He denounced appeals from papal authority to a general council. Nonetheless the 16th-cent. Reformers called for a council to vindicate their position. Later the Four *Gallican Articles (1682) cited Constance to the effect that general councils are superior to the pope. In the 18th cent., Febronianism held for conciliar rather than papal primacy. It was largely in response to Gallicanism and Febronianism that Vatican Council I defined papal supremacy and denounced those who would appeal to an ecumenical council as being superior to the Roman Pontiff (D 3063). See B. Tierney, *Foundations of the Conciliar Theory* (1955); E. F. Jacob, *Essays in the Conciliar Epoch* (rev. ed., 1963); H. Küng, *Structures of the Church* (1964); L. M. Örsy, NCE 4:109–113.

CONCORD, BOOK OF, see BOOK OF CONCORD.

CONCORD, FORMULA OF, see FORMULA OF CONCORD.

CONCOREZZENSES (Gerati), a division of the Italian *Cathari in the 13th cent.; the name was probably derived from Concorezzo, a Lombard town. The leader was Gerato. Doctrine, derived from the *Bogomils of Bulgaria, was a mitigated dualism according to which the evil principle was created, not eternal, and inferior to the principle of good. It is estimated that the *Perfecti among them numbered about 1,500 in the year 1250. See A. Dondaine, "La Hiérarchie cathare en Italie," AFP 19 (1949), 280–311; *idem*, ed., *Un Traité néo-manichéen du XIIIe siècle: Liber de duobus principiis* (1939), 64–78; A. Borst, *Die Katharer* (1953), 93–100, 235; F. Vernet, DTC 3:779–781; H. C. Lea, *History of the Inquisition of the Middle Ages* (1888; repr., 1958), 1:98, 107.

CONCUPISCENCE, a term entering theological discussion from the Vulgate *concupiscentia* found esp. in Rom 7.7–24; Gal 5.24; see also 1 Jn 2.15–17. As reflecting these sources, it came to mean the unruly propensity or tendency to sin existing in man from *original sin. In English, except in technical theology, the word has all but lost this meaning. For both Lutheranism and Calvinism, original sin and concupiscence were identified: the abiding propensity to evil in man was held to be a sinful condition, inherited by every man and imputed to him until he was saved by grace. John *Wesley's doctrine of *Christian perfection, and the later doctrine of *entire sanctification concerning deliverance from involuntary, inbred sin, presume that evil tendencies remaining after justification are sinful. The Council of Trent affirmed that the RC Church never understood concupiscence to be sin, except in the sense of being the fruit of original sin and the seed of personal sins. Both *Baianism and *Jansenism asserted the sinfulness of concupiscence. St. Augustine's heated emphasis on concupiscence is exaggerated and lent itself to the interpretation that it is identical with original sin and is the direct source of the transmittal of original sin. St. Thomas Aquinas expressed a view equivalent to that adopted by Trent: Concupiscence, the lack of an original harmony in man's desires with his true destiny, is part of original sin (the "material" element, he calls it); this ceases to be a sinful condition once the absence of the will's right relationship to God (the "formal" element) is rectified through baptism.

Concupiscence has also had a place in the vocabulary of moral theology as a designation for human emotion in general, and the emotion of desire in particular. As part of man's makeup, it is good, not evil; its relationship to his moral choices can be either beneficial or adverse. Because the desire for temporal ends does frequently subvert right moral decisions, concupiscence is often considered as a cause of personal sin. The narrowest use of the term identifies it with lust, e.g., when one of the benefits of matrimony is said to be "the allaying of concupiscence."

CONDITIONAL IMMORTALITY,

the teaching that the human soul is inherently mortal and receives immortality only as a gift of grace or on condition that a person has lived an upright life. The term is often used interchangeably with annihilationism, because the teaching usually concomitant to conditional immortality is that the souls of the wicked are annihilated. Annihilationism strictly speaking, however, presupposes that the soul is immortal; total extinction is a punishment for sin. The doctrine of conditional immortality is ascribed to the 4th-cent. apologist Arnobius the Elder (PL 5:908) and to 16th-cent. *Socinianism. But the idea had its widest circulation in the 19th cent., esp. in the U.S., England, and Germany. In England the chief exponent was E. O. White; in the U.S. Charles F. Hudson's *Debt and Grace* (1857) and *Christ Our Life* (1860) were influential in the adoption of the teaching as a fundamental doctrine of the Advent Christian Church. Some form of conditional immortality is taught by Seventh-day Adventists and by Jehovah's Witnesses. Lateran Council V (1513) condemned those who taught that the soul was mortal (D 1440).

CONFERENCE (Mennonite),

meetings of the representatives of Mennonite congregations, which deal with matters of doctrine, discipline, and church activities. In some Mennonite bodies the conference has authoritative power; in others its function is advisory. Use of the conference dates from the earliest days of Mennonite history. Originally members were the ministers, but in modern times lay representatives have been included. Formal organization and a regular schedule of meetings began in the late 18th and early 19th centuries. The district conference represents the congregations in one region; the general conference, the congregations of a whole Church. See MennEnc 1:669–670.

CONFERENCE (Methodist),

a term with both a geographical and a jurisdictional sense in Methodist *polity. Originally the Conference designated those ministers called together for consultation by John *Wesley; then after his death, the 100 preachers named by him (see DEED OF DECLARATION). In England the Conference is now a body meeting annually in two sessions, one made up of ministers, the other of ministers and lay representatives of the churches. The conference may not alter doctrinal standards, but it controls other church matters.

In the U.S. the *Methodist Church has the following interrelated conferences: (1) Quarterly Conference, the ruling body of the local church. Besides its many obvious functions, it elects the lay representatives to the Annual Conference. (2) Annual Conference, the basic governing unit of the Church. It is composed of ministerial members and lay representatives from each Quarterly Conference; it is presided over by a bishop. Ministerial members vote on ordination of new ministers and their election to the conference; the whole conference votes on constitutional amendments and elects delegates to the Jurisdictional and the General Conferences. Boundaries of an Annual Conference within the U.S. are set by the Jurisdictional Conference; of one outside the U.S., by the Central Conference. (3) Jurisdictional Conference, a regional division of the Church, administering affairs within the United States. It is composed of equal numbers of lay and ministerial delegates elected by the Annual Conferences. The chief work is setting boundaries for Annual Conferences, and electing bishops. Quadrennial meetings, presided over by a bishop, immediately follow the General Conference, which determines the number of members and the boundaries of the Jurisdictional Conference "upon the consent of the majority of the Annual Conferences of each of the Jurisdictional Conferences involved" (Discipline 1964, 23). At the time of the merger of three branches of Methodism into the Methodist Church (1939), six Jurisdictional Conferences (five geographical and one racial), were constituted, all the Negro Annual Conferences being placed in a Central Jurisdiction. The latter is fast disappearing, since later legislation has admitted Negro Conferences to other Annual Conferences within their Jurisdictional Conference. (4) Central Conference, the name given to a Jurisdictional Conference outside the U.S. and its territories. (5) General Conference, the highest legislative body of the Church. Meeting quadrennially, it is made up of equal numbers of lay and ministerial delegates elected by the Annual Conferences. Bishops preside, but are not members. Functions include the revision of the Methodist Ritual, Hymnal, or Discipline, and the establishment of a budget for the whole Church. The General Conference may not alter the *Twenty-Five Articles of Religion, abolish episcopacy, change the General Rules, or appropriate Publishing House funds for any purpose but the support of retired preachers, their widows, and orphans. See N. B. Harmon, *Understanding the Methodist Church* (rev. ed., 1955), 102–114; *Doctrines and Discipline of the Methodist Church* (1964).

CONFERENCE OF HAGENAU, see HA-GENAU, CONFERENCE OF.

CONFERENCE OF RATISBON, see RE-GENSBURG, CONFERENCE OF.

CONFERENCE OF THE EVANGELICAL MENNONITE CHURCH (formerly, De-

fenseless Mennonites), a body founded by Henry Egly (1824–90) among the Amish Mennonites of Ind., Ill., and other states *c.* 1864. The foundation was strongly influenced by emphasis on personally experienced regeneration. Membership in 1968 was about 2,500. Since 1953, the Church has been allied in a joint conference with the Evangelical Mennonite Brethren Church. See MennEnc 2:264–266.

CONFESSING CHURCH (Bekennende Kirche; 1934–45), German anti-Nazi evangelical movement. Even before Adolf Hitler's appointment as chancellor (1933), a *German Christian program, starting in Prussia and Thuringia, had begun to combine doctrinal liberalism, extremist nationalism, and anti-Semitism. As he came to power, Hitler encouraged them, bidding his little "brownshirts" go to church, portraying Jesus as hero and *führer*, seeking a monolithic ecclesiastical structure. A German Evangelical Church was indeed formed by German Christians who claimed that they represented National Socialism in the Churches. Soon disloyal pastors were suspended and church order disrupted. Martin *Niemöller, an important Berlin pastor, resisted this usurpation by forming an independent Pastor's Emergency Federation. A young theologian, Dietrich *Bonhoeffer, broadcast a stirring refusal to accept the Nazi *führer-prinzip* (leader-principle) and anti-Semitism. At Barmen in May 1934, the first synod of the Confessing Church was held, despite threats by political Nazis and the sycophantic German Christians. A resounding Theological *Barmen Declaration rejected the false doctrine that the Church should and could appropriate the characteristics, the tasks, and the dignity of the State, thus itself becoming an organ of the State and claimed that Christian and churchly obedience is owed only to Christ. The national bishop of the German Christians, Ludwig Müller, was rejected.

Redoubled persecution followed. Confessing Church bishops were arrested and variously harassed. But a second synod, at

Dahlem in Oct. 1934, again stood firm. Three uncommitted church bodies now joined, though the government refused to recognize the now considerable body. Before the third synod met, in Augsburg in 1935, Nazi pressure was increased; some church finances were taken over, church courts were disallowed, and a Nazi Ministry of Church Affairs was given new powers. Torn between allegiances, Lutherans withdrew from the Confessing Church into their own council, the Lutherrat, weakening the resistance. The Gestapo now prevented notable pastors from preaching. The state forbade ecumenical contacts abroad. Neimöller was placed under house arrest. When World War II came in 1939, Confessing Church emphases were voiced anew by a Confidential Council of Clergy, which spoke out boldly against euthanasia (1940), secularizing of the Church in Poland (1941), Nazi indignity to Christianity (1942), the taking of church funds, and the crushing of the Jews (1943). The Nazis drafted 45% of the clergy, leaving mostly old and weak pastors. State rituals were timed to coincide with church observances. Paper for Bibles was barred (1940), most church publications were throttled (1941), and missions and chaplaincies were downgraded. Finally, when the war ended (1945), Bp. Theophil Wurm summoned leaders to Treysa to dissolve the German Christian state Church and form a new *Evangelical Church of Germany (EKD). Soon these leaders also created Evangelische Hilfswerk for crucial relief work and drew up the Stuttgart Declaration acknowledging war guilt. The Confessing Church demonstrated heroic resistance to state interference, to denaturing theology, to persecution of Jews, to political acts long regarded by many Lutherans and others as exempt from Christian comment. Its Barmen Declaration ranks among classic statements of Christian freedom and obedience under Christ. See S. Herman, *Rebirth of the German Church* (1946).

CONFESSIO AUGUSTANA, see AUGSBURG CONFESSION.

CONFESSIO GALLICANA, see GALLICAN CONFESSION.

CONFESSIO TETRAPOLITANA, see TETRAPOLITAN CONFESSION.

CONFESSION, a term with several religious uses: (1) self-accusation of sin, whether public in liturgical prayers, or private to a priest, as in the RC sacrament of penance (see CONFESSION, AURICULAR); (2) a Church or denomination, so designated because a *confession of faith has been regarded by many as essential to church life; (3) the tomb of a martyr, e.g., the Confession of St. Peter, in Rome.

CONFESSION, AURICULAR, the practice of confessing one's sins specifically and in private to a priest in order to receive absolution or pardon. Auricular, or private, confession in the RC Church is part of the sacrament of penance and is distinguished from public confession, whether specific or generic. According to the Council of Trent, secret confession (the term auricular is not used) has been practiced in the Church "from the beginning." The Council does not deny that the penitent may confess his sins publicly, for his own humiliation and for the edification of the Church, but states that such confession is not necessary by divine law. Nor is it always prudent (D 1683). More recent historians of penance are in general agreement that public confession was never obligatory in the early Church, although penitents may well have confessed publicly the major sins for which they were doing penance. The reason for private rather than public confession is explained by the 5th-cent. Greek historian Sozomen: "Now in seeking pardon it is necessary to confess the sin; and since from the beginning the bishops decided, as is only right, that it was too much of a burden to announce one's sins as in a theater with the congregation of the Church as witness, they appointed for this purpose a presbyter, a man of the best refinement, a man silent and prudent. To him sinners came and confessed their deeds . . ." (*Eccl. Hist.* 7.16; PG 67:1457). Some local churches in the vicinity of Rome had the practice of reading out the sins for which penitents were performing their penance; this was regarded by Leo the Great as a "defiance of Apostolic rule" (*Letters* 168; PL 54:1210).

Intimately bound up with the question of auricular confession is the necessity of confessing one's serious sins according to number, kind, and the circumstances that may change the nature of the sin. According to Trent such sacramental confession is necessary by divine law (*iure divino*). Trent allows, however, that a confession may be incomplete because of forgetfulness (D 1707). RC theologians offer other reasons besides forgetfulness that excuse a person from making an integral confession of sins, e.g., the physical or moral impossibility of making a complete confession. In such cases, the sins that have been indirectly absolved by the grace of the sacrament are to be confessed in a subsequent confession.

Martin Luther, while rejecting RC doctrine and practice on penance as a sacrament, strongly proposed confession and absolution. Article 4 of the *Augsburg Confession and Part IV of the Smaller Catechism extol private confession and absolution but reject the need for detailed enumeration of sins. Early in Lutheran history, however, auricular confession fell into disuse; there have been some modern efforts to restore it. The *Reformed Churches rejected private confession outright (e.g., Second *Helvetic Confession, c. 14). Both traditions retained general, public confession as preparation for the Lord's Supper, which became the practice generally of all Protestant Churches. In the Anglican Communion, the *Book of Common Prayer includes a general confession as part of the communion service; some Anglo-Catholics observe auricular confession. Within the Old Catholic movement, auricular confession is recognized, but its use is not obligatory. See P. F. Palmer, ed., *Sacraments and Forgiveness* (*Sources of Christian Theology* 2, 1960); C. J. Peter, "Auricular Confession and the Council of

Trent," CTS 22 (1967), 185–200; B. Poschmann, *Penance and the Anointing of the Sick* (rev. ed., tr. F. Courtney, 1964); O. D. Watkins, *History of Penance* (2v., 1920); H. Lindroth, EncLuthCh 1:561–565; E. F. Latko, NCE 4:131–132.

CONFESSION OF AUGSBURG, see AUGS-BURG CONFESSION.

CONFESSION OF BASEL, see BASEL, CONFESSIONS OF.

CONFESSION OF CZENGER, see HUN-GARIAN CONFESSION.

CONFESSION OF DORT, see DORDRECHT CONFESSION OF FAITH.

CONFESSION OF FAITH, an external acknowledgment of belief. Because the Christian faith is ecclesial, it calls for a public acknowledgment of Christ (Mt 10.32–33). The Gospels themselves are confessional literature rather than sheerly objective historical sources. The most ancient and most basic confession of the early Christian community was "Jesus is Lord" (1 Cor 12.3; Acts 2.21–36; Rom 10.9; Phil 2.11). As the expression of faith was elaborated upon, esp. in the liturgy, catechetics, and polemics, it crystallized into Christological, Trinitarian, and ecclesial formulas. The confession of faith is often taken synonymously for creeds, symbols, and professions of faith containing specific and principal beliefs. During the Reformation various communions drew up official doctrinal statements, e.g., the *Augsburg Confession of 1530. Since then the term "confessions" has come to designate the Protestant groups that espouse statements of doctrine, sacramental matters, and polity. The trend is to amend such statements into formulations that are briefer and more contemporary, but binding only to the extent that they are consonant with the Scriptures. See particular confessions of faith under proper titles.

CONFESSION OF LA ROCHELLE, see LA
ROCHELLE, CONFESSION OF.

CONFESSION OF 1967 (United Presbyterian Church in the U.S.A.), part of the
revision of the confessional position of this
Church, and the most important doctrinal
shift in American Presbyterianism since organization in the colonial period. As one of
the results of the union of the Presbyterian
Church in the U.S.A. and the United Presbyterian Church of North America (1958), a
special committee was formed to compose
a contemporary statement of faith for the
new denomination. The conception of the
committee grew. Believing that the living
Church of Jesus Christ has the right and
duty to restate the faith from time to time,
the denomination followed the proper constitutional steps to revise its confessional
position. This invoked a Book of Confessions, including the Nicene Creed, the
Apostles' Creed, the *Scots Confession
(1560), the *Heidelberg Catechism (1563),
the Second *Helvetic Confession (1561), the
*Westminster Confession and *Shorter
Catechism (1647), the Theological Declaration of Barmen (1934), and the Confession
of 1967. This new Confession is notably biblical; it is based upon the theme of reconciliation in 2 Cor 5 (God's Work of Reconciliation, the Ministry of Reconciliation,
and the Fulfillment of reconciliation).
Trinitarian and ethical in its emphasis, the
Confession attempts to suggest what reconciliation means in regard to modern war,
poverty, and race and sex relations. The
Book of Confessions was adopted over-
whelmingly and with a subscription formula; officers of the denomination promise
to perform their duties under the "continuing instruction and guidance" of this
volume of confessions.

CONFESSION OF WÜRTTEMBERG, see
WURTTEMBERG CONFESSION.

CONFESSIONALISM, the position that adherence to a *confession of faith is necessary for church life. In this literal sense any
Church that is confessional, i.e., expresses
its faith in a doctrinal standard, accepts
confessionalism as a principle; it was operative in the establishment of the Lutheran
and *Reformed Churches. The opposite is
*anticreedalism. The pejorative use of
confessionalism connotes an exclusive adherence to a confession, implying the superiority of one Church over all others. The
RC Church is often singled out as most
extremely confessionalist. In theory Protestant ecclesiology is able to justify the coexistence of many confessions of faith thus:
even if Christ established one Church, its
actual existence will find diverse expressions. Practically, however, an exclusive
confessionalism has often manifested itself
and caused divisions. The ecumenical
movement strives to overcome such
confessionalism without advocating *syncretism or indifference to confessions, or
desiring their abolition. Protestant thought
seeks a solution in reemphasis on the witness of Christ in Scripture as the supreme
rule of faith. RC acceptance in Vatican
Council II of the ecclesial character of
other Christian communions has been regarded as a hopeful ecumenical step. But
confessionalism remains one aspect of the
problem of church unity.

CONGÉ D'ÉLIRE (Fr., leave to elect), in
English law, the royal permission to choose
a bishop. The congé d'élire before the Reformation was in effect a compromise in the
disputes between kings and popes over the
right to appoint bishops. From 1214 the
crown granted permission to cathedral
chapters to elect bishops, reserving the
right of confirmation by royal assent. By
the Annates Statute (1534) under Henry
VIII, renewed in the *Act of Supremacy
(1559) under Elizabeth I, the congé d'élire
was changed: cathedral chapters were to
elect to vacant sees candidates nominated
by the crown in "letters missive."

CONGREGATIO DE AUXILIIS (1598–
1607), a commission instituted at Rome by

Pope Clement VIII and continued by Paul V, because of the bitter dispute between Jesuits and Dominicans "on the helps of divine grace." Clement took the dispute into his own hands (1594) because in Spain and Portugal it had upset the academic world and even had become a scandal to the faithful. The controversy, begun at Salamanca in 1582 and having its counterpart at Louvain in 1587, became violent when the Jesuit L. *Molina published his *Liberi arbitrii cum gratiae donis . . . Concordia* (1588). The Dominicans, led by Domingo *Báñez, denounced him to the Spanish Inquisition; the Jesuits made countercharges. The Dominican position, labeled by the Jesuits as a form of Lutheranism or Calvinism, was this: grace is efficacious in itself, not because man cooperates with it; grace causes man's cooperation since it is a physical premotion and predetermination of his will, consistent with God's gratuitous, infallible predestination. The Jesuit position, branded as a new *Pelagianism by the Dominicans, was this: grace, offered equally and sufficiently to all, becomes efficacious because of man's free acceptance; it does not directly move the will, but cooperates with it; yet God's predestination remains gratuitous and infallible because of *scientia media*, the knowledge by which before offering his grace God foresees man's free acceptance. The main agenda for the 120 sessions *De auxiliis* (after 1602 under the personal presidency of the Pope) was the examination of propositions from Molina's *Concordia*. Beginning in 1602 the position of each side was also debated; the principal spokesman for the Dominicans were Diego Álvarez and Tomás de Lemos; for the Jesuits, Gregory of Valencia and Ferdinand de la Bastida.

Under Clement in 1598, 1602, and 1605, and under Paul V in 1606, the commission recommended condemnation of Molina's teaching. Neither Pope acted on the recommendation, however; many universities as well as political friends interceded against a step that would have been damaging to the Jesuits. At the meeting on Aug. 28, 1607, of eight cardinals with Paul there was no clear consensus. He suspended the inquiry, re-serving final judgment, and declared each side free to defend its teaching but not to label the other as heretical (see D 1997). In 1611 both were forbidden to publish on the debated issue, a prohibition renewed in 1625, 1641, and 1654, but which later became a dead letter. Never has a doctrinal point been more thoroughly examined. Yet the *De auxiliis* exhausted eminent theologians not in the cause of theological progress but in a controversy that was fruitless and was an influence in the rise and progress of *Jansenism. The classic histories of the *De auxiliis*, both partisan and polemical, are the version by the Jesuit L. de Meyer, *Historiae controversiarum de divinae gratiae auxiliis* (2d ed., 2v., 1742), and the version by the Dominican J. H. Serry, *Historiae congregationum de auxiliis libri quinque* (2d ed., 1740). See T. Ryan, NCE 4:168–171; L. Bournet, DHGE 5:959–970, with bibliog. *BÁÑEZIANISM; *MOLINISM.

CONGREGATION, those gathered together for worship, as distinguished from minister or preacher; also the local church. In English versions of the Bible the word is used for the collective body of Israel or for a public solemn assembly. It may refer to the entire Church, as in the *Thirty-Nine Articles, which define the Church as "a congregation of faithful men." In reaction to the Anglican term "parish," which implied that all residents of a given area were church members, Congregationalists and Baptists held that the true Church was made up only of genuine Christians and that local assemblies, or "congregations," of such persons constituted the visible church on earth (see GATHERED CHURCH). In the U.S. the tendency toward self-governing local congregations affected nearly all Protestants, and the term is generally synonymous with *local church. In RC usage the administrative departments of the Roman Curia are called Congregations; one type of religious community is called a congregation; the association of several monasteries of one religious order is also called a congregation, e.g., the Benedictine Congregations.

CONGREGATIONAL, related to the form of church polity in which the *local church, or congregation, is autonomous. While Congregationalism is named from this polity, many other Christian bodies, esp. those originating from English *Noncomformists, are congregational. Congregational polity is distinguished from both episcopal and presbyterian forms of government.

CONGREGATIONAL AND CHRISTIAN CHURCHES, GENERAL COUNCIL OF, union of local Christian and Congregational Churches (see CONGREGATIONALISM) effected in 1931; most participants became (1957) part of the United Church of Christ (UCC). The General Council was strictly an association of local churches, not a national Church or denomination. The merger was based upon mutually accepted principles of polity, esp. the autonomy of the local congregation. The association fostered fellowship in missionary and educational work; local churches continued their historic traditions. At the time of the formation of the UCC there were about 1,300,000 members of the Congregational and Christian Churches. (On the local congregations that did not enter the UCC, see CONGREGATIONAL CHRISTIAN CHURCHES, NATIONAL ASSOCIATION OF; CONSERVATIVE CONGREGATIONAL CHRISTIAN CONFERENCE.)

CONGREGATIONAL CHRISTIAN CHURCHES, NATIONAL ASSOCIATION OF, see NATIONAL ASSOCIATION OF CONGREGATIONAL CHRISTIAN CHURCHES.

CONGREGATIONAL CHURCH IN ENGLAND AND WALES, formerly the Congregational Union of England and Wales, an association formed in 1832 to provide a fellowship and an instrument for Congregational churches that had hitherto expressed themselves through local associations or county unions. The early days of the Union were difficult; not all the churches immedi-

ately associated themselves with it, and it had financial problems. The 19th cent., however, provided the right kind of atmosphere for the encouragement of Congregationalism. By the end of the period the denomination had so grown and the Union had won such favor that it was possible to think of a United Congregational Church. Though still a free association of churches, the Union had become a highly organized institution that touched the life of the churches at almost every point. A new constitution was accepted in 1871. In membership the churches reached a peak in the first decade of the 20th cent., when the Council of the Union was formed (1907) and the Central Fund inaugurated (1909). After World War I, the churches were divided into 9 provinces, each with a moderator. Organizations to meet a variety of modern needs were attached to the Union. Gradually it became apparent that the Union was acquiring a new character. The old *independency was no longer sufficient. Salaries of ministers increasingly were being controlled centrally, as were other decisions affecting the local churches. In 1966 it was agreed to reconstitute the Union as the Congregational Church in England and Wales, membership being on a covenant basis. At the same time, the possibility of union with the Presbyterian Church of England was being revived.

CONGREGATIONAL HOLINESS CHURCH, Pentecostal body formed in 1920 by members of the Pentecostal Holiness Church who regarded *divine healing as compatible with the use of medical remedies. The Church strictly maintains a *congregational polity and rigid moral standards. In 1966 it reported approximately 5,000 members. See J. T. Nichol, *Pentecostalism* (1966), 125–126.

CONGREGATIONAL METHODIST CHURCH, a small denomination of about 15,000 members, organized in 1852 by a group in Ga. who withdrew from the Methodist Episcopal Church, South. The separation was caused by a rejection of *episcopacy and *itinerancy and by a desire that each local church should have the right to call its own pastor rather than receive one appointed by a bishop. In 1887 the denomination suffered a sharp decline when two-thirds of its members withdrew to join the Congregational Church. In doctrine the Church remains Methodist. It supports Westminster College and Bible Institute at Tehuacaua, Tex. In 1968 it had 223 churches and 308 ministers. See HistAmMeth 3:594.

CONGREGATIONAL METHODIST CHURCH OF U.S.A. see FIRST CONGREGATIONAL METHODIST CHURCH OF U.S.A.

CONGREGATIONAL SINGING, singing of hymns by assembled worshipers, a feature of most religions, but esp. Christianity. Early Christians, following Jewish tradition, sang Psalms, and there is mention of a hymn sung by Jesus and his disciples in the Upper Room (Mk 14.26). In the early Middle Ages hymn singing underwent considerable development in both the Greek and the Latin Churches. The later Middle Ages saw congregational singing decline, partly because church worship continued to be in Latin and singing was largely restricted to clergy and choirs. Outside the churches folk songs in the vernacular were popular. The Reformation restored congregational singing to a prominent place, making it one of the distinguishing marks of Protestant worship. This development was well under way even before Luther, and much of pre-Reformation change in the Church found its expression in song. Jan *Hus made use of popular song to advance his cause, translating Latin hymns and writing original hymns in Czech. Quick to use the newly invented printing press, the *Bohemian Brethren published a Czech hymnal in 1501. Their first German version appeared in 1531, and their first Polish version, in 1554. With Luther congregational singing came into its own on a national

scale. His use of hymns, many of which he wrote himself, along with his translation of the Bible and his catechisms, played an important part in the establishment of the Reformation. Among Calvinists congregational singing was long restricted to metrical versions of the Psalms, esp. in England and Scotland. Anglican hymnody was slow to develop because of the Anglican Church's retention of pre-Reformation patterns of worship. Not until the time of Isaac Watts (1674–1748), first English hymn writer of note, did hymnody in England catch up with its much earlier development in Germany. By then England began to feel the upsurge of song characteristic of the Wesleyan revival. Back of this revival was German *Pietism, brought to England by the Moravians. Their hymns were one of the first items to attract John *Wesley to them, though it was his brother Charles who became the great hymnist of Methodism. Count *Zinzendorf occupied a similar role in the Renewed *Moravian Church. More enduring were the hymns of the English Moravian James Montgomery (1770–1848).

Prominent in German hymnody, both of the Lutherans and the Moravians, is the chorale tune marked by plain melody, strong harmony, and stately rhythm. Both Pietist and English revival hymns tend to be subjective and individualistic. The 19th-and 20th-cent. equivalent are the so-called Gospel songs. Many of these are the product of American frontier *revivalism. The hymnody of every Church is subject to a winnowing process in which hymns of quality, expressive of the best of Christian thought and feeling, become the great hymns of other Churches. Interdenominational exchange of hymns and their translation into many languages has made all church hymnals significant symbols of ecumenicity.

In the RC Church, although the structure of the Roman rite provided for congregational participation in liturgical song, the actual singing was long left to specially trained choirs, except in religious houses in which the whole community was commonly expected to join in. The retention of the Latin liturgy tended to discourage interest on the part of the people at large, and even the attempt of Pius X to improve ecclesiastical music in the long run retarded the development of any widespread congregational participation in the singing, for efforts were focused on Gregorian chant, which proved too esoteric a medium for general use by ordinary people. Leaders in the liturgical movement continued to call for more active participation on the part of the congregation. Their desire found official voice in Vatican Council II's *Constitution on the Liturgy* (ch. 6) and in the decree *Musicam sacram,* which urged that whenever a sacred action is celebrated with song, the whole body of the faithful should contribute the active participation, which is rightly theirs. The adoption of the vernacular for the liturgy encouraged the hope that these directives could be successfully carried out, but many obstacles remained to be overcome: the traditional reluctance of many Roman Catholics, esp. in the U.S., to sing out in church; the banality of many liturgical songs when translated into the vernacular; the dearth of really good music and suitable hymns; the lack of agreement with regard to standards and taste; and esp. the unwillingness on the part of many to experiment, a reluctance due in some cases to ingrained habit and conservatism but understandable in other cases as a reaction to the extravagance of some experimentation. Against these obstacles some progress has been made, but much remains to be done. See H. B. Marks, *Rise and Growth of English Hymnody* (1948); J. Gelineau, *Voices and Instruments in Christian Worship* (1964); F. J. Guentner, NCE 4:171–173; *idem, Crisis in Church Music?* (1967).

CONGREGATIONAL UNION OF ENGLAND AND WALES, the original name for the *Congregational Church in England and Wales, established in 1832.

CONGREGATIONAL WORSHIP, BOOK OF, see BOOK OF CONGREGATIONAL WORSHIP.

CONGREGATIONALISM, that form of church life maintained and expressed in the independence and autonomy of the local church or congregation. The Church is held to consist essentially in a gathering of covenanted believers under the sole headship of Christ and guided by his Spirit. Independence is freedom from binding creedal statements and from any control, ecclesiastical or civil, over the local church. Defending the rights of the believer's private judgment, those adhering to Congregationalism believe that by their association and fellowship the assembly of believers derives an understanding of matters of belief, worship, and *church order suited to actual experience and need. A congregational form of polity is maintained by Baptists and other denominations; the churches called specifically Congregational have their main history in the U.S. and England.

Congregationalists regard themselves as conforming to the order prevailing in the NT churches. They find their ideal affirmed in the early ecclesiology of both Luther and Calvin and that practiced by the Swiss Anabaptists. In English history, J. *Wycliffe and the *Lollards are regarded as precursors of the "Congregational Way." The first Congregational church is claimed, with some probability, to have been one pastored by Richard Fytz in London as early as 1567. It was Robert *Browne in his *Reformation without Tarrying for Anie* (1581) who became the explicit advocate of *independency. Congregationalists took their place in the 17th cent. alongside Puritans and Separatists in their opposition to the C of E in theological agreement on the basic tenets of Calvinism and in sustaining persecution. By 1609 many, led by Browne and John *Robinson, took refuge in Holland. Under the *Commonwealth, Congregationalism was able to establish itself fully in Eng., although disabilities against all *Nonconformists continued until the 19th cent., and in 1658 the *Savoy Declaration, a modification of the *Westminster Confession, was adopted. Congregational Churches were united in fellowship and formed county associations; and such ties led to the establishment in 1832 of the Congregational Union of England and Wales. Congregationalists led in the formation of the London Missionary Society (1795); the Colonial Missionary Society (1836) led to the spread of Congregationalism to Australia, New Zealand, Canada, and South Africa.

Under the inspiration of John Robinson, Congregationalists left Holland on the *Mayflower* and in 1620 founded the Plymouth Colony in Mass., basing the settlement on the Mayflower Compact. These Plymouth people with the Bay people in 1648 set forth an agreed program of church government in the *Cambridge Platform. The Congregational Churches in the New England colonies became practically established Churches, and traces of establishment lasted into the 19th century. Congregational Churches were formed in the Northwest Territory from 1796 onward by settlers from New England. A *Plan of Union in effect, 1801–52, for cooperation with Presbyterians on the expanding frontier actually worked to the diminution of Congregational influence. In New England itself, doctrinal division (1819–25) led to the loss of a third of the churches there to *Unitarianism. Congregational churches throughout the nation drew together in regional or state associations. A denominational consciousness in keeping with the American pattern increased, and by 1871 the first National Council of Congregational Churches was held in Oberlin, Ohio. The Council continued to function until the merger of Congregational with Christian Churches in 1931 created the General Council of Congregational and Christian Churches. In 1959 a further merger, regarded as a landmark in the ecumenical movement, brought about the *United Church of Christ (see CONGREGATIONAL CHRISTIAN CHURCHES, NATIONAL ASSOCIATION OF; CONSERVATIVE CONGREGATIONAL CHRISTIAN CONFERENCE).

Congregational Churches have been notably active in educational and missionary works. Most of the older colleges in New England, and more than 40 others, as well as 10 theological seminaries, are of Congregational origin. Missionary work began among the Indians from the beginning of the Plymouth Colony. In 1810 the *American Board of Commissioners for Foreign Missions was formed, and 2 years later it sent out the first American foreign missionaries; the Board now forms part of the United Church Board for World Ministries. The American Home Missionary Society, organized in 1862, helped the spread of Congregational churches throughout the West; it still continues as an agency for home missions and other evangelical services. Internationally most Congregational Churches are members of the International Congregational Council, set up in 1948 after a series of occasional meetings dating from 1891. Reckoned as the official "confessional agency," it has represented Congregationalism throughout the world in the ecumenical movement. Douglas *Horton was its official observer at Vatican II. In 1966 decisions were taken that are expected to lead to union with the *Alliance of Reformed Churches in 1970.

The history and life of Congregationalism reflect its nature as primarily a form of church polity. There is considerable emphasis on full lay involvement in the life of the local church and in all forms of association; government is normally by meetings of members. While local churches are not constituted as parts of national or regional Churches, they are normally voluntary participants in regional, national, or international associations. The extent of organization and the degree of surrender of autonomy have increased considerably since 1900. Ministry is ordinarily also functional to the local church, though in ordination the wider fellowship is almost invariably associated and recognition given for a general ministry. Women are ordained.

Because of its independency and non-creedalism, Congregationalism is not characterized by fixed tenets of doctrine. English Congregationalism retained the Savoy Declaration. In the U.S. the changing patterns of American theology have been reflected in, and often shaped by, Congregationalists. The Calvinism of the Westminster Confession and Catechism was the background of the *covenant theology of the theocratic New England colonies, and of the *New England theology of Jonathan *Edwards in the *Great Awakening. Reaction to Calvinism, as well as the inroads of rationalism, set off the split of Congregationalists into Trinitarians and Unitarians. Liberalism became a characteristic of Congregationalists in the 19th and into the 20th cent., but some local churches were strongly evangelical and conservative (see LIBERAL THEOLOGY; BUSHNELL, HORACE; SOCIAL GOSPEL; GLADDEN, WASHINGTON). A renewed consciousness of specifically Christian identity and tenets has grown in contemporary Congregationalism. The emphases of private judgment, independency, and Congregational fellowship remain, but are accompanied by aspiration to a unity with the branches of the Universal Church of Christ (see KANSAS CITY STATEMENT). These elements are apparent in Congregationalist participation in the ecumenical movement and esp. in the United Church of Christ. See G. G. Atkins and F. L. Fagley, *History of American Congregationalism* (1942); M. Starkey, *Congregational Way* (1966).

CONGRUISM, in RC theology, a theory attempting to reconcile the efficaciousness of grace and the freedom of the human will. The Jesuits Francisco de Suárez (1548–1617) and Robert Bellarmine (1542–1621) were principal exponents of congruism. The theory rests its reconciliation on the suitableness, or congruity, of an efficacious grace to the state or condition of the will of the recipient. Mere congruity does not explain the efficacy of grace, since a grace must be congruous even to be sufficient (see GRACE, SUFFICIENT). Congruism explains that grace becomes efficacious from three sources: from the consent a person would give, should a particular grace be offered; from the divine foreknowledge anterior to any divine decree (*scientia media*) of the consent that would be given; and from God's benevolent absolute decree to give the grace. Both congruism and *Molinism agree in explaining the efficacy of grace by elements not inherent in the grace itself and in recourse to *scientia media*. They agree as

well that there is a divine decree that a person shall perform a good action, a decree that is infallibly effective and anterior to the actual consent of the human will. Congruism differs from Molinism by holding that God first decrees absolutely (not on condition of man's accepting grace) that a man shall perform a good act, and therefore decrees the efficacious grace to perform it.

Congruists also hold that in the divine plan God first intends to give the reward of glory to some adults and consequently intends absolutely that they acquire merit. This is the doctrine of formal predestination prior to foreseen merit that distinguishes congruism from Molinism.

Congruists, with all Catholics, admit reprobation of the lost, but unlike Molinists they hold it to be, in the divine plan, negative and prior to divine prevision of man's final state of soul. Some are antelapsarian (Suárez), others postlapsarian (Bellarmine). All, however, conceive reprobation to be a mere nonpredestination, or nonefficacious election to glory. See H. Quillet, DTC 3.1:1120–38.

CONNECTIONAL, referring to a Methodist form of polity, or one similar to it, i.e., one based on a system of *conferences. The term *connexion was used by John *Wesley for the interassociation of Methodist *societies. Conference replaced the term connection as the designation for regional divisions and organizational units in church structure. Connectional polity is more centralized than the *congregational; unlike the *presbyterian it allows for *episcopacy as a function, not a sacred order, in the Church.

CONNEXION (Connection), a term often used by John *Wesley of Methodism itself, or of the interassociation of Methodist *societies. The term is still in use and connotes a form of polity that is not *congregational but connectional, i.e., through the various *conferences. See N. B. Harmon, *Understanding the Methodist Church* (rev. ed., 1961), 14; OED 2:839.

CONSCIENTIARII (Ger. *Gewissener*), a Pietist group founded by Matthias Knutsen (b. 1646), an itinerant theologian who spread his teachings among the students of the Univ. of Jena beginning in 1674. Claiming personal conscience and reason as the sole authority, he rejected Bible, church affiliation, and human immortality. The univ. publicly dissociated itself from Knutsen and his teachings. The Conscientiarii were minor forerunners of the *Enlightenment. See W. Göbell, RGG 2:1557.

CONSCIENTIOUS OBJECTION, the refusal by an individual, because of a sense of duty to his fundamental ethical understanding, to be inducted into the armed forces or to participate in or to support the military activities of his country. Conscientious objection has been part of the history of several Christian Churches (see PACIFISM). Two general types of conscientious objectors exist: the absolute pacifist and the ordinary pacifist, or selective objector. The absolute pacifist maintains that no violence of any type may ever be employed, even if it means that an innocent person may die or suffer untold injuries. The ordinary pacifist distinguishes between international armed conflicts and the suppression of crime and injustice within the framework of an established society. He objects to support of, or participation in, any international conflicts but concedes that a defensive type of violence can be employed to rectify domestic conflicts. In either case, both types of pacifists object to war between nations.

The absolute pacifist may base his objections on religious or nonreligious grounds. The religious pacifist will normally predicate his opposition to warfare on the Sermon on the Mount (Mt 5.3–11) and the Fifth Commandment, "Thou shalt not kill" (Ex 20.13). The nonreligious or ethical pacifist bases his opposition on a personal moral code, derived from an understanding of a fundamental ethical order and, in particular, the meaning of human interrelations. Like the religious pacifist, he would rather suffer even martydom than violate the dictates of his conscience.

The selective objector is opposed to a particular military action because he feels it is immoral or unjustified or because the means employed in effecting it are immoral. Included in this category are military personnel who refuse to obey a command that would force them to participate in an immoral war or to commit a crime against humanity. Vatican II defined the moral position of such personnel when it urged military men to follow their consciences in wartime situations and to refuse to carry out any order they consider to be violations of natural law (Vat II ChModWorld 79). The principles of the selective objector can be either religious or nonreligious or a combination of both. He often cites the just-war doctrine, the Nuremberg principle, or some basic principles derived from an existential philosophy as his criteria for objection. The just-war doctrine is the norm traditionally used by Christians in justifying a country's resort to war. Unless a Christian's conscience is in some measure and in some way assured that the conditions for the just war are met, he would not be justified in participating in such a war. The Nuremberg principle simply claims that every individual is personally responsible for any act that he may commit, even if he is ordered to commit the act. Finally, numerous selective objectors are opposed to contemporary warfare. They might have been willing to engage in some conventional wars in the past, but they feel that only two patterns of warfare will exist in the future: a nuclear missile war between great powers and a counterrevolutionary or imperialist war. They object to both, either because the means of warfare are intrinsically evil or destructive of humanity, or because the end of the war is immoral and not conducive to the welfare of mankind.

As a general rule, the historic Christian Churches have approved of violence or war whenever all the conditions for a just war are fulfilled. The Churches have condoned the suffering of injustice in silence until the point is reached where the injustice becomes so intolerable that one's conscience dictates some form of corrective action. If the Christian does not then act, he assumes partial guilt for the injustice. The

Churches have also taught that the individual cannot participate in any undoubtedly unjust war; further, if the individual is convinced that, because of circumstances peculiar to himself, participation in a military activity would violate his conscience, he should claim conscientious objector status.

Conscientious objection and pacificism were doctrines characteristic of the Swiss Anabaptists and the Mennonites. Frequently they were persecuted and had to migrate because of their refusal to bear arms. From George Fox the Quakers received a similar doctrine and have been leaders in the cause of pacifism. Some of the German Brethren Churches have maintained the same opposition to war. The Jehovah's Witnesses refuse military service, but on the grounds that all political governments are corrupt, and enemies of the kingdom of God. All of these religious strains directly contributed to the U.S. legal recognition of conscientious objection. While in 1968 the World and National Councils of Churches, the American RC bishops, and the major organizations of many denominations have endorsed selective conscientious objection, it is not recognized in law, and many conservative church groups have repudiated it. The RC Church, well aware of the complexities of contemporary societies and international relations and conflicts, has attempted to redefine its moral position on conscientious objection. Vatican II declared: "It seems right that laws make humane provisions for the case of those who for reasons of conscience refuse to bear arms, provided, however, that they accept some other form of service to the human community" (Vat II ChModWorld 79). The National Conference of Catholic Bishops emphasized the place of personal responsibility in decisions about war: "No one is free to evade his personal responsibility by leaving it entirely to others to make moral judgments."

The conscientious objector thus faces a moral dilemma, the consequences of which can be deleterious to his future welfare. But the sincere conscientious objector is aware of these consequences and is willing to suffer them, in order to preserve his conviction and integrity. See P. Ramsey, *War and the Christian Conscience* (1961); R. T. Powers, NCE 4:205.

CONSECRATION, in Holiness and Pentecostal teaching, the act of one who, after justification, dedicates himself to living a perfect Christian life; it is a preparation for *entire sanctification, by which the sinlessness willed in consecration is achieved.

CONSENSUS FORMULA, HELVETIC, see HELVETIC CONSENSUS FORMULA.

CONSENSUS HELVETICUS, see HELVETIC CONSENSUS FORMULA.

CONSENSUS OF GENEVA (*Consensus Genevensis*), a polemical treatise written (1552) by John *Calvin in defense of his doctrine of predestination against Albertus Pighius (*c*.1490–1542) and others. In 1542 Pighius had published a criticism of Luther's and Calvin's doctrine of predestination, maintaining an almost Pelagian view of human freedom. Jerome Bolsec (d. 1584) also declared that Calvin's doctrine of predestination was a denial of God's grace. While alluding to Bolsec, the Consensus was mainly a violent attack on Pighius. Absolute predestination, said Calvin, is the only solid ground for a believer's assurance of salvation. The document was subscribed by the pastors in Geneva; in other cities, however, reaction was largely unfavorable, as many objected to the idea of a divine decree of reprobation. Philipp *Melanchthon, who had changed his views on free will and predestination, was among the critics of the Consensus. Further controversy was stirred by the burning of M. *Servetus (1553) and by Calvin's conflict with Sebastian *Castellio, a former colleague who had become a bitter enemy. While *double predestination came to be accepted by the *Reformed Churches everywhere, the Consensus was not generally used as a doctrinal standard. See Schaff Creeds I:474–477.

CONSENSUS OF SANDOMIERZ, a formula agreed on between Lutherans, Calvinists, and Bohemian Brethren at Sandomierz, Poland (1570), as an attempt at unity. Retaining their identities, the three bodies recognized as true expressions of Christian faith the Augsburg, Bohemian, and Helvetic Confessions. For a brief period the Consensus brought about a federated union with pulpit exchange and *intercommunion. Lutheran participation ended with the *Formula of Concord (1580). See Schaff Creeds 1:586–588.

CONSENSUS QUINQUESAECULARIS (Lat. *quinque*, five, *saeculum*, century; also Quinquecentennial Consensus), a term applied by Georg Doisch (1597–1694) to a conciliatory theory of the Lutheran theologian G. *Calixt. In an attempt to overcome differences among Lutherans, both with each other and with other Churches, Calixt proposed a distinction between fundamental and nonfundamental teachings. The first were those concerning which there was universal agreement during the first 5 centuries, and which are necessary for salvation; all other creeds, including those of the Reformation, were to be regarded as interpretations or extensions of the Apostles' Creed and not necessary for salvation. The theory touched off the Syncretistic Controversy, in which Calixt was attacked, esp. by A. *Calov. Most Lutherans repudiated Calixt's approach to irenics as neither historically nor theologically sound. The *consensus quinquesaecularis* still is discussed in connection with *ecumenism. See J. L. Neve, *Lutherans in the Movement for Church Union* (1921); A. C. Piepkorn, Enc-LuthCh 1:350.

CONSENSUS TIGURINUS, see ZURICH CONSENSUS.

CONSERVATIVE AMISH MENNONITE CHURCH, the name of the *Conservative Mennonite Conference from its formation in 1910 until the adoption of its present name in 1954.

CONSERVATIVE BAPTIST ASSOCIATION OF AMERICA, an agency for cooperation among Baptist Churches adhering to *fundamentalism and the principle of the complete autonomy of the *local church. Member Churches insist upon their separateness from all other ecclesial bodies, Baptist and non-Baptist; they reject *open communion, *alien immersion, and any relationship to the National Council of Churches. The origins of the Association were in the Fundamentalist Fellowship, organized within the American (then the Northern) Baptist Convention in the 1920s; participants in the Association withdrew from the convention in order to promote their conservative theological and ecclesial aims. In 1968 the Association, with headquarters in Arlington, Ill., had some 1,500 churches, with about 300,000 members.

CONSERVATIVE CONGREGATIONAL CHRISTIAN CONFERENCE, an association created in 1948 when the proposed formation of the United Church of Christ was felt to threaten the independent tradition. It was formed to provide fellowship for Churches in the tradition that shared a conservative evangelical theology. For a long time with no more than 20 member Churches, the Conference claimed almost 100 by the end of 1967. With one notable exception in Boston, the churches are small. The governing body is a board of directors, but there are no full-time officers other than a missioner-at-large. Individual missionaries overseas are supported by churches, but there is no organization. The Conference also has an international link with groups of Congregational Churches in Australia, Brazil, and Guyana.

CONSERVATIVE DUNKERS, a name for the members of the Church of the Brethren. *PROGRESSIVE DUNKERS.

CONSERVATIVE MENNONITE CONFERENCE, a body organized at Pigeon, Mich. (1910), as the Conservative Amish Mennonite Church; the present name was adopted in 1954. The organizing members were Amish Mennonites who favored a greater progressivism than the Old Order Amish, esp. in regard to organized church work. This Church has always subscribed to the *Dordrecht Confession of Faith. It has close ties to the Mennonite Church. There are congregations in Pa., Md., Del., N.Y., Va., Ky., Ohio, Ind., Ill., Kans., and Iowa. See MennEnc 1:700–702.

CONSISTORY COURT, in some Presbyterian Churches a church *court corresponding to the *session (in Scotland, kirk session) or, as in French Reformed Churches, to the presbytery.

CONSOLAMENTUM, the Catharist rite of initiation for the *Perfecti. Consolamentum was also received by the ordinary believers at the hour of death. *CATHARI.

CONSTANCE, COUNCIL OF, one of the most important councils in the history of the Church and the papacy, held at Constance in southern Germany. It surpassed all previous councils in duration (Nov. 5, 1414, to April 22, 1418) and rivaled most in the number, if not in the dignity, of prelates attending. The Council's chief task was to end the *Great Western Schism, which began in 1378 with two rival popes and later, after the Council of *Pisa (1409), a third. The Council of Constance also had to adjudicate the doctrinal issues raised by John *Wycliffe and Jan *Hus and to initiate a program of church reform.

Procedures. From the beginning the Council was plagued by procedural problems. In 1413 the Pisan Pope, John XXIII, under pressure from the Emperor, Sigismund, authorized the Council, but early in 1414 he withdrew from Constance. Encouraged by Sigismund and supported by the argumentation of the conciliarists, the Council continued without papal approbation. In the 5th session (April 6, 1415) it passed the controversial decree *Sacrosancta* (called also *Haec sancta*, from its opening words), constituting itself as a general council representing the Catholic Church and holding authority immediately from Christ. The notorious misconduct of John XXIII caused the Council to depose him (May 29). Gregory XII, the Roman pope, formally abdicated on July 4, 1415, after reconvoking Constance as a general council. Efforts to persuade Benedict XIII at Avignon to resign were fruitless, and he too was finally deposed in July 1417. Another procedural problem was presented by the large Italian majority. It was resolved by a decision to vote in blocs; each of the four "nations," the Italian, German, French, and English, was to have one vote. The Spaniards joined the proceedings at the end of 1415 as a fifth "nation."

Doctrinal Issues. From the writings of Wycliffe 24 propositions already censured at the Synod of London in 1382, together with 21 others, were condemned at the 8th session (D 1151–95). At the 15th session, the Bohemian nationalist and reformer Jan Hus heard himself condemned for views similar to Wycliffe's (D 1201–30). The safe conduct granted him by Sigismund apparently was not a guarantee of immunity against trial. Hus was handed over to the secular arm and burned at the stake, July 6, 1415. The execution made Hus a national hero in Bohemia, and inspired the *Hussite movement. In the following session, the Council repudiated a proposition justifying tyrannicide (D 1235).

Reform. The Fathers at Constance, esp. the Germans and the English, were insistent on the need for reform "in head and members." They shared a suspicion that the papacy was unable or unwilling to pursue the cause of reform effectively, and therefore, before proceeding to the election of a pope, the Council promulgated several reform measures (Oct. 5, 1417). The most important was the decree *Frequens*, which sought to establish councils as instruments of reform by stipulating that they were to be convoked frequently and at regular intervals. Constance was not successful as a reform council because the Fathers were more concerned about the head than the members; they attacked the symptoms rather than the causes of corruption.

Schism. The Council's main achievement was to heal the schism that had divided Western Christendom for almost 40 years. After receiving the resignation of Gregory XII and deposing John XXIII and Benedict XIII, the way was clear to elect a pope who would be accepted by all. The choice was Oddo Colonna, a cardinal of the Pisan obedience, who took the name Martin V (1417–31). The abnormal circumstances of the Western Schism raised constitutional and ecclesiological issues that have been much discussed ever since Constance. The broad questions revolve around the very nature of an ecumenical council and its authority vis-à-vis the pope. Specifically it is asked what constituted Constance as a legitimate council: the original convocation by John XXIII, the decree *Sacrosancta*, the convocation by Gregory XII immediately before his resignation, or subsequent approval of its proceedings by Pope Martin V? Much of the debate turns on the force of *Sacrosancta*: whether it is a dogmatic decree defining the nature and function of a council or essentially a practical decision justifying Constance in terms of the extraordinary circumstances created by the Western Schism. There is as well the problem of the extent to which *Sacrosancta* and *Frequens* sanction conciliarism. As much for the dogmatic issues it raises as for its procedures, Constance is unique in the history of councils. See B. Tierney, NCE 4:219–223; A. Franzen and W. Müller, eds., *Das Konzil von Konstanz. Beiträge zu seiner Geschichte und Theologie* (1964); A. Franzen, "Council of Constance: Present State of the Problem," *Concilium*, 7:29–68.

CONSTANTINOPOLITAN CREED, a designation of the Nicene Creed, applied because the acts of the Council of Chalcedon (451) attribute the Nicene Creed to the fathers of Council of Constantinople I (381). *NICENE CREED.

CONSTITUTIONAL CHURCH, the Church formed in France by the *Civil Constitution of the Clergy, July 12, 1790. A loyalty oath to this Constitution imposed on all clergy, Nov. 27, 1790, led to a separation of jurors and nonjurors; and a schism into the Constitutional Church and the "Refractory Church," continuing faithful to Rome, resulted. The organization of the Constitutional Church was worked out in 1791; the hierarchy was formed, Bps. Talleyrand-Périgord and Gobel instituting and consecrating new bps. without papal sanction. The "old" Church, the nonjuring clergy, and most of the French faithful continued, esp. after papal condemnation of the Civil Constitution (1791), to repudiate the Constitutional Church, in spite of persecution. With the fall of Louis XVI, Aug. 1792, the Constitutional Church itself began to suffer. In Sept. the Assembly took away clerical jurisdiction over the registration of vital statistics and legalized civil marriage and divorce. Under the Convention (1792–95) the cult of reason was decreed and the Constitutional Church was disestablished; many of its priests fled or apostatized. With the Directory (1795–99), the abolition of salaries for the clergy deprived them of practically their sole income. The Constitutional Church continued a feeble existence until the Concordat of 1801, at which time it was abolished by Napoleon Bonaparte. See F. M. Anderson, *Constitutions and Other Select Documents Illustrative of the History of France, 1789–1908* (2d ed., 1908); L. Gershoy, *French Revolution and Napoleon* (1964); J. H. Stewart, *Documentary Survey of the French Revolution* (1951).

CONSUBSTANTIATION (Lat. *cum*, with; *substantia*, substance), the teaching that the substance of Christ's body and blood is conjoined to the substance of bread and wine in the *Eucharist; companation occurs, though rarely, as a synonym for consubstantiation. The eucharistic theories of John *Wycliffe included an affirmation of the perdurance of the whole reality of bread and wine. But consubstantiation has been particularly associated with Lutheran eucharistic teaching; the designation, however, has never been regarded as adequate by Lutherans. Lutheranism does reject *transubstantiation, i.e., the change of the substance of the eucharistic elements, and does affirm that the body and blood of Christ are truly distributed and taken with the bread and wine (*Formula of Concord, Art. 7). The Lutheran understanding of body "with the bread," however, is meant simply as a full acceptance of the literal meaning of the words of the sacrament, so strongly affirmed by Luther in his *Confession Concerning the Lord's Supper* (1528) and defended against *Reformed teaching by Lutherans. The mode of Christ's eucharistic presence is simply called a "sacramental union" (*Ibid.*, Art. 7). The term consubstantiation is less than satisfactory to Lutherans because it represents an attempt to philosophize about the manner of the *Real Presence and implies a union of the body and blood of Christ with the bread and wine other than the union existing in actual sacramental use. See H. Sasse, *This Is My Body* (1959). *IMPANATION.

CONSULTATION ON CHURCH UNION, discussions concerning merger among several U.S. denominations. Originally proposed by Eugene Carson Blake in a sermon at Grace Cathedral, San Francisco (1960), during the episcopate of Bp. James Pike, the Consultation on Church Union (COCU) is often called the Blake–Pike Proposal. The United Presbyterian and the Protestant Episcopal Churches invited the Methodist Church and the United Church of Christ to an exploratory meeting at Washington, D.C., in April 1962. By the second meeting, at Oberlin, Ohio (1963), the Evangelical United Brethren and the Disciples of Christ had also become participants, and several other denominations sent observer-consultants. Subsequent meetings have been held annually: Princeton, N.J., 1964; Lexington, Ky., 1965; Dallas, Tex., 1966; Cambridge, Mass., 1967; Dayton, Ohio, 1968, and Atlanta, Ga., 1969. The Dayton and Atlanta meetings included 9 participating Churches; added to those mentioned were the African Methodist Episcopal; African Methodist Episcopal, Zion; Christian Methodist Episcopal; and the Presbyterian Church in the U.S. Underlying this impulse to church union are diverse factors, but also some common assumptions: (1) The Church of Jesus Christ is one, and that oneness ought to become visible to the world. As expressed in a COCU document, "The people of God exist as one people and only one. . . . They have been made so in Christ; and he wills that they make this unity evident." (2) There is an awareness of the need for renewal in the Church. By clarification of convictions concerning the gospel, by linking public worship more closely to mission, and by involving the entire laity in the ministry of the Church, reform and renewal may be furthered. (3) A conviction is growing that a complex, urban society calls for new forms and approaches on the part of the Church, and it is becoming clearer that a reconciling Church must itself be reconciled.

From the outset the aim has been to establish a Church that will be "truly catholic, truly reformed, and truly evangelical." "Catholic" refers to both continuity in time and universality in space; "reformed," to a willingness to be exposed continually to the judgment and correction of the Holy Spirit as he works through Scripture and in history; and "evangelical," to justification by grace through faith and the supremacy of Holy Scripture in doctrine and moral teaching. The Church also is to be confessional, liturgical, sacramental, and episcopal. The meanings of these terms have been explained in *Principles of Church Union*. The delegates at Dayton voted that a plan of union be prepared for consideration not later than 1970. At the 1969 meeting in Atlanta, the outline of a plan of union was unveiled, with the full plan scheduled for presentation in 1970—perhaps with considerable revision. The outline proposed a Church with four geographical levels: parish, district, region, and nation. It would have bishops for district, regional, and national bodies, presbyters serving parishes, and deacons performing specialized ministries. At the national assembly, representatives of three groups—laity, presbyters and deacons, and bishops—would vote separately, with concurrence by each required on matters of faith and order. The ordained ministries would be open to both men and women, and reordination of existing ministries would not be required. Parishes would use several of the current parish buildings of the uniting Churches, though regular Sunday worship would not necessarily be held in all. Some buildings might be designated for special ministries, such as social service projects or community action groups. P. Crow, Jr., of the Christian Church was installed as general secretary of COCU at the meeting. Bp. J. Mathews, United Methodist Church, continued as chairman. No determination had yet been made concerning a statement of belief, how title to property should be held and certain other matters. Participants expressed special concern that minority racial and ethnic groups be included at all levels of the united Church, but no method had been worked out. See *COCU: Principles of Church Union, Guidlines for Structure, A Study Guide* (1967); J. R. Nelson, "Reckless Obedience at Dayton," *Christian Century* 85 (1968), 478–479; J. A. Mackay, *Christian Reality and Appearance* (1969).

CONTRA-REMONSTRANTS (Counter-Remonstrants, Antiremonstrants), Calvinist opponents of the *Remonstrants; they were also called Gomarites (see GOMARUS, F.). In reply to the *Remonstrance* of 1610, setting forth the tenets of *Arminianism, the strict Calvinists sent to a conference held at The Hague in 1611 a *Counter-Remonstrance*, hence the name Contra-Remonstrants. They maintained a rigid *supralapsarianism. The controversy led to the Synod of Dort (1618–19), which the Contra-Remonstrants completely dominated. The Remonstrants were not given a proper hearing and were subjected to repressive measures for some time after Dort. See bibliog. for Arminianism.

CONVENTICLE ACT (1664), in English history an act aimed at enforcing religious uniformity by forbidding religious gatherings. The *Act of Uniformity (1662) had affected *Nonconformist ministers, and the Conventicle Act was directed against dissenting laymen. A special incitement to its passage was fear of political insurrection, as Baptists and Independents had been suspected of involvement in Venner's Plot (1661) against Charles II. Rumors were rife that another conspiracy was afoot. The Act prohibited persons 16 years and older from attending private religious meetings held "in other manner than is allowed in the Liturgy" at which more than five persons besides the householders themselves were present. Heavy penalties were provided for offenses. Originally limited to 3 years, it was reenacted with a few modifications in 1670. It was abolished by the *Toleration Act of 1689. See H. Gee and W. J. Hardy, *Documents Illlstrative of English Church History* (1921); H. W. Clark, *History of English Nonconformity* (2v., 1911–13), v.2.

CONVENTION (Baptist), a state and national organization through which local churches cooperate. In 1821 Baptists began to form state organizations. Opinions varied as to a suitable name; most states adopted the term "convention," but a few described themselves as a general, or union, association. In 1845 Southern Baptists organized separately as the *Southern Baptist Convention, and subsequently other national conventions followed. State and national conventions are not considered to have churchly character and authority, but are instruments by which churches work together. Delegates, or "messengers," usually meet annually, and between meetings permanent officers and agencies carry on the work. See P. Harrison, *Authority and Power in the Free Church Tradition* (1959).

CONVERSION, a term with several Christian uses. (1) Conversion is a turning from sin to God in faith and repentance. Whether this is a work totally of God by his grace or a work in which man also cooperates has been a matter of controversy (see PELAGIANISM; SYNERGISTIC CONTROVERSY; ARMINIANISM). The Arminian emphasis on man's cooperation is a decisive principle in *revivalism, which has conversion as its objective. (2) Conversion may also mean a drawing closer to God, from a routine, insensitive, to a more intense way of living the Christian life. This use of the word is involved in the *conversio a saeculo* (turning from the ways of the world), which is a part of the meaning and history of monasticism. In a similar use the term is applied to turning points in the lives of those who became evangelists or leaders of movements of spiritual renewal in the Churches. John Wesley's own experience of conversion in this sense underlies his doctrine of *Christian perfection, which has given a special nuance to the term conversion. In this reference the term connotes an experiential, often emotional awareness of the saving grace of Christ. The ideal of conversion in this sense is the living of a life free of the domination of inbred sins (see SANCTIFICATION). (3) Conversion also is used to mean change from complete nonbelief in Christ to belief. One may become a Christian from being either an atheist, an agnostic or an adherent of a non-Christian religion. (4) Conversion in a particular RC usage was used until Vatican Council II to mean change from membership in another Christian Church to membership in the Roman Catholic Church. The *Decree on Ecumenism does not use this terminology but speaks of one who becomes a Catholic as "being reconciled" with the Church, and as one who seeks "full Catholic communion" (Vat II Ecum 4). Such phraseology follows the Council's acknowledgment of other Christian Churches as "ecclesial communities," and of all who share in baptism and trinitarian faith as brothers. Thus joining the RC Church from another Christian body is not to be compared to conversion from being a non-Christian to being a Christian. See P. Aubin, *Le Problème de la "conversion"* (1963); W. Barclay, *Turning to God: A Study of Conversion in the Book of Acts and Today* (1964); C. Williams, NCE 4:287–290.

CONVERT, in general, one in whom a change has occurred in ideas, convictions, beliefs, values, or allegiance from a prior attitude of positive opposition or at least indifference to acceptance and adoption. Most often the term is used in reference to religious conversion, and when so used may denote: (1) one who turns away from a life of sin to a life of moral goodness and integrity (the NT concept of *metanoia* can be identified with this view; see Mt 3.2; Lk 1.77; 3.8); (2) one who passes from ignorance or indifference to Christ to acceptance and commitment to him and his way of life (some Protestant communions emphasize "acceptance of God's plan of salvation," which includes repentance, faith in Jesus Christ, and regeneration); or (3) one who accepts new denominational adherence with renunciation of former confessional loyalties. In the last sense the RC Church has conducted a vigorous convert apostolate, which has declined after recent ecumenical involvement. Vatican II, however, noted that ecumenism is not opposed to conversions, since "both proceed from the marvelous ways of God" (Vat II Ecum 4).

CONVOCATIONS OF CANTERBURY AND YORK, provincial gatherings of the clergy of the C of E; often referred to simply as "Convocations." The origin of the Canterbury Convocation is traced to Theodore of Tarsus, Abp. of Canterbury from 668 to 690; York originated in 733. At first they included prelates only; but in 1225 representatives of cathedrals and monastic communities were added, and by the end of the 13th cent. they had reached their present basis of membership. Since the 15th cent. each Convocation has met in two houses—the Upper House of bps. and the Lower House of representatives of the clergy, called "Proctors." In pre-Reformation times Convocations were the bodies through which the clergy taxed themselves and made grants to the Crown. Under Henry VIII their powers were sharply curtailed, but they remained in increasingly stormy existence until 1717, when Whig objection to the independence of the clergy resulted in the royal decision to forbid further meetings of Convocations. In 1851, however, meetings were resumed. Currently they meet two or three times a year, often jointly and, since 1885, in association with a House of Laymen in each province. The Convocations themselves, however, remain clerical in membership. They are concerned mainly with theological and liturgical matters, and increasingly with ecumenical and inter-Church affairs. As the oldest continuing deliberative and legislative religious assemblies in England, they have played a central part in the history of both Church and State. Since the Reformation settlement, their relationship to Parliament has been confused. With the establishment in the C of E of the *Church Assembly, which has many characteristics of a national synod, their situation is still more unclear. They remain, however, the only collective embodiment of the clergy of the C of E capable of sharing, with Parliament, in decisions about such central doctrinal matters as the Book of Common Prayer.

CONVULSIONARIES, Jansenist zealots who opposed the bull *Unigenitus* and whose behavior was marked by bizarre phenomena. After the death (1727) of François de Pâris, a young clergyman noted for rigorous asceticism and firm adherence to the cause of the *Appellants, his grave in the churchyard of St. Médard became the site of supposedly miraculous cures understood to vindicate Jansenist beliefs. With the cures came large crowds and instances of trances, convulsions, *glossolalia, prophecies, and erratic behavior. After the cemetery was closed (1732) by government order, groups continued to meet in private homes, where emphasis shifted from cures to convulsions to endurance of peculiar tortures without physical harm as proof of divine favor. Despite being suspected of indecencies and of subjection to diabolical influence, sects of convulsionaries survived in diminishing numbers to the 18th century. Although condemned by many responsible Jansenists, the convulsionaries divided the hitherto united Jansenist ranks in France. See R. Knox, *Enthusiasm* (1950), ch. 16.

COORNHEERT, DIRCK VOLCKERTS-ZOON (1522–90), Dutch literateur and engraver, who also held political positions at Haarlem and in the States General. His principal work, *Zedekunst dat is Wellevens Kunste* (Art of Living Well, 1582; modern ed., 1942) was one of the first books of ethics written in a modern language. He was under influence of the writings of S. *Franck and S. *Castellio and of the *Theologia germanica; thus his writings stress the religion of inner experience (see INNER LIGHT). He taught that the true Church was invisible, made up of those who believe the simple and clear Scripture teaching; no authoritarian or teaching Church was necessary. Still C. opposed the excessive subjectivism of D. *Joris and H. *Niclaes. His opposition to rigid Calvinism and to religious persecution had a marked influence on J. *Arminius. C. was also one of those whose thought inspired the *Seekers. See H. Bonger, *D. V. C.* (1941); R. M. Jones, *Spiritual Reformers in the Sixteenth and Seventeenth Centuries* (pa., 1959), 104–113; and MennEnc 1:709–710; W. H. Beuken, NCE 4:302.

CORPORATION ACT, the first act of the so-called Clarendon Code, designed to secure loyal supporters of Charles II in local governments. During the Interregnum, Baptists and Independents had been active in military service and public offices, and they were suspected of disloyalty to the *Restoration. In 1661, Parliament passed an "Act for Regulating Corporations" in order to exclude such persons from municipal governments. All mayors, town clerks, and other magistrates were, by March 25, 1663, to take oaths of allegiance and supremacy. Each such person was also to declare that it is unlawful to take arms against the king for any reason, and to abjure the *Solemn League and Covenant. Moreover, everyone holding such office must have taken the sacrament of the Lord's Supper according to the rites of the C of E within a year previous to election or appointment. In 1828 this act was repealed. See H. Gee and W. J. Hardy,

Documents Illustrative of English Church History (1921).

CORPUS CATHOLICORUM, a title with two uses: (1) name of the body of Catholic imperial states of Germany (*Reichsstände*) from c.1700 to 1806, founded as the counterpart of the Protestant *Corpus Evangelicorum*, but never achieving political significance; (2) a society in Bonn, Germany, founded in 1917 by J. Greving (d.1917), and the collection of Reformation writing published under the same name, *Corpus Catholicorum*. A RC counterpart to the Protestant *Corpus Reformatorum*, the collection contains writings of RC theologians and controversialists of the Reformation (1517–63). The series, however, also incorporated the Reformation studies and texts begun in 1905 by J. Greven; and since 1926 issued more popularized accounts of Catholic life and struggles during the Reformation. See H. Jedin, LTK 3:63.

CORPUS DOCTRINAE (pl. *Corpora doctrinae*), name used for a collection of confessions of faith by 16th-cent. German Protestants. In 1560 a private printer in Meissen published the *Corpus doctrinae Philippicum* (or *Misnicum*), a collection of Philipp *Melanchthon's writings. The *territorial churches published numerous other *corpora doctrinae* containing their confessional statements. They were finally replaced by the *Formula of Concord (1577) and the *Book of Concord (1580), which sought to bring confessional unity among all German Lutherans. See E. Wolf, RGG 1:1012–13; G. Kaweran, EncRelKnow 3:273–275.

CORPUS EVANGELICORUM, political union of the Protestant imperial estates (*Reichsstände*) formed under the leadership of the Duke of Saxony after the Peace of Westphalia (1648) to represent Protestant interests in the German Diet (*Reichstag*). The parallel organ, the *Corpus Catholicorum*, did not achieve the same political importance since RC interests were furthered by the Emperor and a large part of the nobility. The *Corpus Evangelicorum* played a role in obtaining tolerance for Protestant minorities, and in the Gregorian Calendar Reform (1699). Both the *Corpus Catholicorum* and the *Corpus Evangelicorum* were discontinued after the collapse of the Holy Roman Empire (1806). See J. Heckel, RGG 1:1873–74; K. Repgen, LTK 3:64–65.

CORPUS REFORMATORUM (CR), the title of a collection of Reformation works written before 1555. Those of Luther were not included because of the existence of the so-called Erlanger edition. The first section of CR began with P. *Melanchthon (ed. K. G. Bretschneider, H. E. Bindseil, v.1–28, 1834–60), but was incomplete and required some 53 supplements. The 2d section, works of John Calvin, is considered superior and complete (ed. W. Baum et al., v. 29–87, 1863–1900). The 3d section, works of H. Zwingli, is also a complete collection (ed. E. Egli et al., v.88–98, 1905–41). Reprints of the Melanchthon and Calvin volumes were issued in 1964.

COTEREAUX, one of the bands of roving mercenaries called *routiers* who pillaged the French countryside during the 12th and 13th centuries. They often robbed and abused clerics and desecrated churches, but more out of desire for plunder than anticlerical conviction. Because Lateran Council III (1179) condemned the Cotereaux together with the *Cathari, it is often erroneously assumed that the two shared beliefs. See F. Vernet, DTC 3:1924–26; H. C. Lea, *History of the Inquisition of the Middle Ages* (1888; repr., 1958), 1: 25–126.

COTTIONS, a sect condemned by Charlemagne in 789. Members wandered about the country as penitents, half naked but loaded down with chains. Little else is known about them.

COTTON, JOHN (1584–1652), leader in Puritan New England. Born in Derby, Eng., educated at Cambridge, where he was imbued with Puritan ideas, C. early adopted *congregational principles but did not experience conversion until 1612. In that year he was called to St. Botolph's Church, Boston (Eng.), and, despite scruples against the *Book of Common Prayer and certain ceremonies, remained there 20 years. By 1633, finding his position untenable, he resolved to emigrate to the Massachusetts Bay Colony. Already 48 years old, he had won a reputation as a scholar and preacher, and had been associated with the leading Puritans of his day. On arrival, he was chosen teacher of the church in new Boston and soon became a popular preacher. In the episodes that led to the expulsion of Roger *Williams and Anne *Hutchinson, he tried to play a mediating role. In politics his theocratic ideas helped to shape New England government. His views on Church and State provided a springboard for Roger Williams's *The Bloudy Tenent of Persecution* (1644), and his rejoinder led to *The Bloody Tenent Yet More Bloody* (1652). During the English Civil Wars, he declined an invitation to the *Westminster Assembly of Divines; and as New England sought to avoid Presbyterian polity, the Synod of 1648 embodied in the *Cambridge Platform ideas from Cotton's *The Keyes of the Kingdom of Heaven* (1644) and *The Way of the Churches of Christ in New England* (1645). See L. Ziff, *Career of John Cotton: Puritanism and the American Experience* (1962); idem, ed., *J. C. on the Churches of New England* (1968).

COUNCIL OF BISHOPS (Methodist), an official body composed of all the bishops of all the Jurisdictional and Central *Conferences. The Council of Bishops was not a traditional constitutional body within Methodism, but was instituted at the Uniting Conference of the three major American Methodist bodies, which formed the *Methodist Church in 1939. It meets at least annually, planning "for the . . . oversight and promotion of the temporal and spiritual interests of the entire church and for carrying into effect the rules, regulations, and responsibilities prescribed and enjoined by the General Conference. . . " (*Discipline*). The Council annually elects a president and chooses the bishop to deliver the episcopal address (state of the Church message) at the General Conference. By a two-thirds vote, it may call a special session of the *General Conference. See *Doctrines and Discipline of the Methodist Church* (1964), index; HistAmMeth 3:463–464.

COUNCIL OF THE TWELVE APOSTLES, in the Church of Jesus Christ of Latter-day Saints (Mormons), the body that, subordinated to the *First Presidency, oversees the Church and ordains its ministers. Members are chosen by the revelation that Mormons believe continually to be given to the Church, esp. through its president.

COUNCILS (Roman Catholic), official church meetings convoked to deliberate doctrinal or disciplinary issues of common concern. The Code of Canon Law, reflecting historical precedent, divides councils geographically: diocesan synods and provincial councils deal with local and regional problems; *ecumenical councils, both in representation and in breadth of concern, are worldwide and exercise supreme authority over the whole Church.

COUNTER-REFORMATION, a name for the spiritual revival, administrative renovation, and political confrontation whereby Roman Catholicism responded to the challenge of the Reformation of the 16th century. The name, coined by the 19th-cent. church historian L. von Ranke, is unsatisfactory insofar as RC reform anteceded the Reformation and was partially independent of it. On the strictly spiritual and ecclesiastical side, the groundwork of Catholic reform was laid by Christian humanists, e.g., Erasmus, and by men of a more ecclesiastical type, e.g., Ximénez de Cisneros (1436–

1517) and the founders of the Oratory of Divine Love—all prior to the Reformation. The movement effectively entered the service of the papacy under Paul III (1534–49). The papacy would thereafter retain the direction of reform, though it was given a more militant turn under Paul IV (1555–59), who earlier inspired the Roman Inquisition (1542). He instituted the Index of Forbidden Books (1558) and an uncompromising if despotic reform of morals. The reorganization of the Roman Curia under Sixtus V in 1588 created the modern papal bureaucracy. The manpower for reform came particularly from such new or reformed religious orders as the Theatines, Capuchins, Oratorians, and above all the Jesuits, founded by St. Ignatius Loyola in 1540. Other key personalities of reform were SS. Charles Borromeo, Theresa of Avila, John of the Cross, Vincent de Paul, and Francis de Sales. Their characteristic piety was sacramental, dynamic, and often mystical. This spirit dominates the Baroque art of the time. The most conspicuous institutional aspect of reform was the Council of *Trent (1545–63). Trent belatedly clarified doctrine and provided the reform decrees that, along with the resurgent papacy, shaped RC history up to the mid-20th century. Conflicting conceptions of a *general council militated against effective Protestant attendance, and Trent's generally anti-Protestant stance confirmed the religious schism.

The phrase "Counter-Reformation" has its most apt application to political history, particularly the Wars of Religion. Here the leading Catholic champion was the Hapsburgs. After the failure of his earlier efforts to conciliate the German Lutherans, the Holy Roman Emperor, Charles V (1519–56), resorted to the Schmalkaldic War (1546–55). This ended in stalemate and the Religious Peace of *Augsburg (1555), which allowed toleration for Lutherans. The Counter-Reformation entered its major phase about 1559, when the son of Charles, Philip II (1556–98) of Spain, and Henry II (1547–59) of France terminated the long Italian wars for a concerted effort to eradicate Protestantism. The last chance for religious reunion in France was the Colloquy of *Poissy (1561), followed by 30 years of religious and civil wars, including the infamous *St. Bartholomew's Day Massacre (1572). Philip of Spain's reign was marked by efforts to subdue the rebellious Netherlands, intervene in France, and settle accounts with England, highlighted by the disastrous Armada, 1588. The final phase of the Counter-Reformation was the largely political Thirty Years' War, terminated by the Peace of *Westphalia in 1648. The Counter-Reformation failed to restore religious unity primarily because it became too identified with Hapsburg power. Henceforth, religion was a diminishing feature in politics and the Protestant-Catholic schism a reluctantly accepted fact. See P. Janelle, *Catholic Reformation* (1949); H. O. Evennett, *Spirit of the Counter Reformation* (1968); H. Daniel-Rops, *Catholic Reformation* (tr. J. Warrington, *History of the Church*, v.5, 1962); E. L. Lamps, NCE 4:384–389; A. G. Dickens, *Counter Reformation* (1969).

COUNTESS OF HUNTINGDON'S CONNEXION, a federation of chapels, having no central ecclesiastical authority, established in England by the Countess of *Huntingdon in the 18th century. After building a large number of chapels and using C of E clergymen as ministers, she began employing unordained Methodist preachers trained in her college at Trevecca, Wales. Invoking the *Toleration Act, she formally established the Countess of Huntingdon's Connexion, ordaining her first ministers in 1783. Presbyterian in policy, Anglican in liturgy and *Calvinistic Methodist in theology, the chapels were independent of each other and many joined other denominations. There are (1968) about 3,500 members, with 37 chapels in England. *CONNEXION.

COURT (Presbyterian), any of the governing bodies in *Presbyterianism; also called a judicatory. *CHURCH SESSION; *PRESBYTERY; *SYNOD; *GENERAL ASSEMBLY.

COVENANT THEOLOGY, not so much a separate system as an idiom used to explain the mystery of the election and perseverance of the saints, within the framework of the Calvinist tradition. While covenant or *federal theology (Lat. *foedus*, covenant) has a wider history in which the writings of H. *Bullinger and J. *Cocceius are particularly prominent, its English and Scottish development are alone considered here. Federalism came into prominence in the era of the Westminster Assembly (1643–49); the *Westminster Confession (c.7) speaks of a covenant of works and a covenant of grace. The covenant idea and covenant thinking greatly influenced theological developments on both sides of the Atlantic among Presbyterians and Congregationalists; the concept of covenant also regulated the interpretation of church order and of the socio-political order, esp. in New England. Prominent in the development of covenant theology were John Preston's *The New Covenant or the Saints Portion* (1629) and James Durham's *Sum of Saving Knowledge* (1650). Covenant terminology was taken from the OT and interpreted through legal and commercial notions of contract. The covenant was a contractual relationship between the Christian and God; at the moment of regeneration the Christian is received into a compact with his creator; the sacraments are given as seals of this covenant. By portraying regeneration as a contract, requiring mutual consent, covenant theology could preserve the doctrine of predestination while urging the unregenerate to accept God's free gift of grace. Because the covenant was binding, it expressed the sureness of salvation. Personal covenanting came to be more strongly emphasized than baptism; the private act of the believer, more than the act of God or Christ. Covenant theology also tended to sharpen the distinction between the *visible Church and the *invisible Church. The true Church was thought to be constituted of those covenanting together to form a congregation, i.e., of those already personally covenanted to God. The *Mayflower Compact and the whole political order in New England were motivated by the covenant idea, and Perry Miller has discussed the influence of covenant thinking on early American history. See P. Miller, *New England Mind* (2v., pa. 1961); idem, *Errand into the Wilderness* (1956); *idem*, "From the Covenant to the Revival," Smith-Jamison 1:322–368.

COVENANTERS, name given to those who followed the old Scottish practice of covenanting, i.e., entering into a "band" to maintain a religious or political cause. The covenants of the 16th cent. were reflected in the *Kings's Confession of 1586. In the 17th cent., the *Scottish National Covenant (1638) was signed amid scenes of enthusiasm in Greyfriars Kirk by persons of all ranks who repudiated "all kinds of papistry" (meaning in particular the form of Anglicanism proposed in Abp. W. *Laud's attempt to impose the Book of Common Prayer on the Scottish Church) as tending to "the subversion and ruin of the true Reformed religion and of our liberties, laws and estates." In 1643, while the *Solemn League and Covenant was being widely signed, the English Parliament summoned the *Westminster Assembly to secure "the nearest conjunction and uniformity in religion" advocated in the Solemn League. The supporters of the Covenants were in turn, however, later crushed by Oliver *Cromwell, and after the Restoration of Charles II a policy of repression was undertaken. The battle of Rullion Green (1666) scattered the Covenanters, whose open-air conventicles were regarded as seedbeds of rebellion; the battle of Bothwell Bridge (1679) was the prelude to fearful persecution, imprisonment, and deportation. The struggle came to an end at the Revolution Settlement (1668). Marked by an evangelical devotion and loyalty to the crown and kingdom of Christ, the Covenanters waged a struggle, fanatical at times, in defense of the spiritual independence that has characterized the history of the Scottish Church. See J. King Hewison, *Covenanters* (2v., 1908). *ASSOCIATED REFORMED PRESBYTERIAN CHURCH (GENERAL SYNOD); *CHURCH OF SCOTLAND; *CAMERONIANS.

COVENANTING, a term with two meanings: (1) the practice begun early in the Scottish Reformation of entering into a "band" to maintain a religious or political cause (see COVENANTERS; SCOTTISH NATIONAL COVENANT; SOLEMN LEAGUE AND COVENANT); (2) the believer's act of entering into the special relation with God that is stressed in covenant theology, or *federal theology.

COX, THOMAS J. (1845–1934), founder of the Church of God (Apostolic). C. served in the Union Army and entered the ministry in 1886. He organized the Christian Faith Band Church at Danville, Ky., in 1897, loosely associated with the Church of God in Indiana. A general convention in 1915 adopted the present name and made Elder Cox its Apostle and General Overseer. He made Bluefield, W.Va., its headquarters.

CRANMER, THOMAS (1489–1556), Abp. of Canterbury at the beginning of the English Reformation. His character was so composed of light and shade that it can scarcely be suggested in a brief account. Yet through his shifts there runs a consistent *Erastianism, and genuine devotion must have infused his noble liturgical style in the Book of Common Prayer of 1549, the *Homilies*, and the *Litany*. Considering the risks he allowed, he must have been blessed with a high survival value, until his pitiable but finally not inglorious end. A Nottinghamshire man, he lost his fellowship at Jesus College, Cambridge, when it was discovered that he kept a secret wife at the Dolphin Inn; but on her death in child-bed he was reinstated. Entering into the household of the Earl of Wiltshire, the father of Anne Boleyn, he was appointed to embassies to Italy and Germany to lobby in favor of Henry VIII's divorce from Catherine of Aragon. Although he had compromised his position by intrigues with the Protestant princes and by marrying the niece of A. *Osiander—he had to keep her well out of sight until the next reign—he was promoted to abp. of Canterbury on the death of Warham and was confirmed by Clement VII (1533). The King knew his man; his marriage to Anne Boleyn was duly pronounced valid, and 3 years later it was duly pronounced invalid. Though active in the desecration of St. Thomas's shrine at Canterbury, C. seems of all the Protestant magnates to have had least to do with the *dissolution of the monasteries. He married Henry to Anne of Cleves, 1540; a few months later he was the chief instrument in procuring the divorce. Selected by the council to convey to the King information about the misconduct of his fifth wife, Catherine Howard, he was commanded to visit her in the Tower, where he held out delusive hopes of mercy. Henry clearly liked "my chaplain," and it cannot have been just for his subservience. He attended the King on his death-bed and celebrated the solemn Requiem Mass (1547).

After the accession of Edward VI he could display a more open Protestantism. Continental Reformers were welcomed, images destroyed, ancient ceremonies abolished. C.'s own theological views, which shifted from Lutheranism towards Zwinglianism, seem to have been both latitudinarian and perplexed, which may help to explain his later recantations; only on the Royal Supremacy was he relatively constant. He was not a persecuting man, by the standards of his times, and was liked by his friends, though he betrayed the Seymours to the Dudleys, and made but a timid gesture to save his colleague Thomas *Cromwell from disgrace. His judgment on whether the Princess Mary should be allowed the practice of the Catholic religion was that "to give license to sin was sin, but to suffer it and wink at it for a time might be borne." Drawn into the rising for Lady Jane Grey (1553), he at first pleaded not guilty but later confessed to the indictment, and was condemned to be executed at Tyburn. Queen Mary's clemency spared his life, but charges of heresy were closing in against him. After long delays, disputations, pleas, and counterpleas, he was publicly degraded at Oxford; despite a series of increasingly submissive recantations, he was sent to the stake two months later. In his final address he repudiated all that he had written out of fear. He put his hand into the flame, and crying out "This hand has offended," very soon was dead. See biographies by A. F. Pollard (1904); F. H. Hutchinson (1951); J. Ridley (1962). *BOOK OF COMMON PRAYER.

CREED (Lat. *credo*, I believe), a summary statement of the principal items of Christian belief, sometimes specifying errors to be rejected. The term is also used to include any *confession of faith, declaration of belief, or the body of church teachings. Several of the creeds, including the Apostles' and Nicene, are constructed according to a three-part formula, referring to the three persons of the Trinity, a pattern thought to have been modeled upon Mt 28.19. The creeds developed from baptismal rituals in the early centuries; the candidate for baptism memorized the basic statement of the Church's belief and declared it at baptism as his own commitment. Official creeds in fixed form began to develop in the 3d and 4th cents., but important affirmations of faith are found earlier, as in the Shema of Dt 6.1–25, as well as in the NT. The most fundamental of the latter is generally held to be "Jesus is Lord" (1 Cor 12.3; Phil 2.11). The creeds are generally regarded as *doctrinal standards in the Churches and as a witness to the world of what Christians stand for. They serve affirmatively as guides to what is basic Christian teaching, and negatively as bulwarks against distortions of the Christian message. Worshiping congregations recite them in unison as an expression of their common faith. Creeds have been opposed by some Christians who regard them as an infringement on individual freedom, and by others who consider the Bible the sole authority for Christian belief. Nonetheless, almost all Christian groups have found it important, even essential, to make some statement expressing their central convictions. See J. Leith, *Creeds of the Churches* (1963); J. N. D. Kelly, *Early Christian Creeds* (3d ed., 1960);

Schaff Creeds; F. X. Murphy, NCE 4:432–438. *APOSTLES' CREED; *ATHANASIAN CREED; *NICENE CREED; *CONFESSION OF FAITH; *CONFESSIONALISM; *ANTICREEDALISM.

CREEDS, ECUMENICAL, see ECUMENICAL CREEDS.

CREGLINGIANS, a short-lived sect at Creglingen in Württemberg in the mid-19th cent.; it also spread to Bavaria, where it was prohibited (1853), and to Rothenberg-ob-der-Tauber. Supposedly influenced by the ideas of the Pietist mystic and enthusiast Johannes Tennhardt (1661–1720), the Creglingians accepted a kind of communistic social teaching, wore their hair long, and did not cover their heads (see 1 Cor 11.4–10). For their denial of Church and State authority they were considered a threat to society. See K. Algermissen, LTK 3:91.

CRISIS THEOLOGY, name given to the earliest phase of the theology of Karl *Barth and those associated with him, esp. Emil *Brunner (see DIALECTICAL THEOLOGY). "Crisis" here may be taken in either of two senses. It may refer to the proximate occasion prompting this theological trend, i.e., the outbreak of World War I and the consequent disillusionment of Barth and his associates with the optimism of *liberal theology, esp. as regards its thought about society and culture. "Crisis" may also refer to the mode in which the Barthians tended to express themselves, i.e., in "critical categories," such as the negation of any power in man to reach God, the absolute necessity of God's grace, and the importance of eschatology.

One of the important features of the theology of crisis was its return to the sources of Reformation thought, bypassing Protestant scholasticism. Barth esp. repudiates, however, the interpretation given the fathers of the Reformation by F. *Schleiermacher and E. *Troeltsch. Barth's comméntary (1919) on the Epistle to the Romans was like the charter of crisis theology. He employed the Pauline polemic against justification by works of the Law to upbraid modern theologians for having fallen into the trap of granting to human nature the capacity of attaining to God and of practicing "religion" effectively.

CROMWELL, OLIVER (1599–1658), English Puritan, military and political leader. He was born in Huntingdonshire of a land-owning family that owed its start to property gained from Henry VIII's *dissolution of the monasteries (see CROMWELL, THOMAS). Influenced by Puritan preachers and teachers, C. experienced a religious conversion c.1628. In the Long Parliament, which opened in 1640, he early became identified with the *Independents and took an active part in the steps that led to the Civil Wars. Impelled by a Puritan conscience and a sense of divine calling, he played an important role in decisive victories at Marston Moor (1644) and Naseby (1645) and eventually gained control of the New Model Army, composed of Baptists, Independents, and various sectaries. After the execution of Charles I, C. and his Independents established England as a Commonwealth. Troubles took him to Ireland (1649), where he subdued the populace by drastic measures, including the massacres at Drogheda and Wexford. In 1651–52, at Dunbar and Worcester, the commander-in-chief put down Scottish forces supporting the Pretender, Charles II. Faced with internal and external crises, C. needed greater power. Convinced that providence had destined him to save his country, he became Lord Protector (1653) and exercised power in an arbitrary but benevolent way. He refused the title of king, however, when it was proffered him in 1657. In religious matters, he ended the attempt to establish Presbyterianism and allowed toleration to *Nonconformists who agreed on essential gospel truths. Even Catholics and others were generally tolerated, as long as they did not disturb the peace. Continuing domestic unrest, financial crises, threats from abroad, and his own poor health plagued him all of his days as Lord Protector. When he died, his son, Richard, proved incapable of forwarding his father's policies, and Charles II was invited to return to the throne. See R. S. Paul, *Lord Protector: Religion and Politics in the Life of O. C.* (1955); C. H. Firth, *O. C. and the Rule of the Puritans in England* (1953); H. Aveling, NCE 4:470–471.

CROMWELL, THOMAS *(c.1458–1540)*, lay political figure prominent in the English Reformation. Born in Putney, he became a mercenary soldier in Italy, an entrepreneur in the Low Countries, moneylender, lawyer, general factotum to Cardinal Wolsey, who employed him as agent in the dissolution of the lesser monasteries and for his foundations at Oxford and Ipswich, and member of Parliament, where he rose steadily as fixer for the King's business. Though included in *Foxe's Book of Martyrs, he was in fact a ruffian whose brutality broke through his smooth and witty address; he was able, unscrupulous, lewd, indifferent to religious values, and looked to the Reformers because they seemed the supporters of absolute power. The only cause to which he was devoted was the single polity under the Royal Supremacy. He arranged for the translation of the *Defensor pacis* of *Marsilius of Padua at his own expense. He belonged to the seamier side of the Renaissance, and was the first English politician to be familiar with Machiavelli; contemptuous of dreamers like Plato, he set himself to consult the inclination of the prince. It was destined to destroy him, but in the meantime he became the second most powerful person in the realm. He was appointed royal secretary in 1534, and under the Act of Supremacy proceeded against Thomas More and John Fisher (whom he succeeded as chancellor of Cambridge University), sent Reynolds and the Charterhouse monks to their death, suppressed the religious houses, persecuted the Princess Mary for her Catholicism, and bullied the clergy. Appointed the king's vice-regent "in spirituals," he exercised a lay tyranny over the Church in England such as had not been seen before and has not been since. His only positive service to the Church for which posterity can be grateful was to order the keeping of parish-registers for every wedding, christening, and burial. He was generally hated, and the chief demand of the Catholic rising in the North was that he should be expelled from the council and condignly punished. His main incursion into foreign policy led to failure and his death. To gain the support of the Protestant party in Germany against a coalition between the Emperor and the King of France, he arranged the marriage of Henry VIII with Anne of Cleves (1540). The threat was never real, and the King, unattracted by the lady, divorced her a few months afterwards. Though C. was created Earl of Essex, the royal rage was smouldering and suddenly burst without warning. Without trial, but by bill of attainder, C. was indicted on charges as devious as his own proceedings and sentenced to the block and a clumsy headsman on Tower Hill. In his final address he repudiated all heresy and declared that he died in the Catholic faith. See A. G. Dickens, *T. C. and the English Reformation* (1960); R. B. Merriman, *Life and Letters of T. C.* (2v., 1902). *DISSOLUTION OF THE MONASTERIES.

CROWDY, WILLIAM S. (d. 1916), founder of the *Church of God and Saints of Christ. Born of slave parents in the South, C. migrated to Okla. and worked as a cook on the Santa Fe Railway. He saw in a vision in 1896 that Jesus Christ and other biblical personages were Negroes. He drew on Judaism and Holiness revivalism as patterns for his Church, formed at Lawrence, Kans. (1897), and dedicated to the belief that Negroes were the Chosen People. In 1900 he transferred his headquarters to Philadelphia. The new movement claimed some 92 congregations at C.'s death in 1916. Appealing to the dispossessed rural migrants, in the wake of the Negro exodus to Kans. and Okla. in the 1890s, the movement later became primarily urban. See E. U. Essien-Udom, *Black Nationalism* (1962); H. Brotz, *Black Jews of Harlem* (1964).

CRUSADE OF THE PASTOUREAUX, see PASTOUREAUX, CRUSADE OF THE.

CRUSADES, medieval military expeditions organized by the Church for the liberation of the Holy Land and the defense of Christianity. Despite some dispute about its origins, the idea of the crusades had its roots in pilgrimages, esp. to the Holy Land, in the use of military force against excommunicates and heretics, and in the efforts of the Church to put an end to warfare between Christians. The actual crusades, however, were occasioned by the Byzantine need of military assistance against the Seljuk Turks in the late 11th century. Pope Gregory VII had planned to lead the vassals of the Holy See to help Byzantium and then go on pilgrimage to Jerusalem. With Pope Urban II this plan was revived. Although the sources are not clear on all details, it seems certain that Emperor Alexius I requested Western military assistance and that he and the Pope hoped to reestablish formal union between the Greek and the Latin Churches (one cannot rightly speak of schism at this date). At Clermont in France, Nov. 27, 1095, Urban II proclaimed the crusade, appealing to the Western knights to cease fighting one another, to aid their Christian brothers in the East, and also to free Jerusalem. This last element impressed itself most on the simple religious imaginations of the warriors and led to an amazing wave of popular enthusiasm. So successful in fact were the Pope's words that the crusade took on a vastly different form than had been intended. The carefully laid plans of Pope and Emperor called for a highly disciplined military expedition. Instead, unruly mobs wandered and pillaged their way to Constantinople. Eventually, however, the better-organized troops led by Western nobles arrived and, after some diplomatic problems, proceeded on their long and laborious march through Asia Minor to Antioch and finally, July 14, 1099, fought their way into Jerusalem. Subsequent crusades were organized to aid the Latin states of Palestine and Syria, but in 1187 the Turks recaptured Jerusalem. Papal efforts to keep the crusading ideal alive met with more and more criticism and skepticism, and the crusades that did take place either accomplished little or proved disastrous.

It is difficult to evaluate the results of the Crusades. For a time they kept the Turks at bay; they greatly stimulated cultural development and trade; they gave rise to the military and hospital orders. Yet those whom they were designed to help, the Eastern Christians, suffered more as a result, esp. in the so-called Fourth Crusade of 1204. This, perhaps more than anything else, solidified the schism between East and West; it was no longer a dispute between theologians and bishops but a resentment and hatred felt by all classes. Yet, although they went about it poorly, most of the crusaders did make enormous sacrifices for what they felt was a sacred obligation, the defense of Christians and the liberation of the Holy Land. It was an enterprise well in harmony with the medieval mentality. See S. Runciman, *History of the Crusades* (3v., 1951–54); K. Setton, ed., *History of the Crusades* (2v., 1955–62); H. E. Mayer, *Bibliographie zur Geschichte der Kreuzzüge* (1960).

CRYPTO-CALVINISM, a censorious name for views originating with P. *Melanchthon, esp. in regard to the *Real Presence (see PHILIPPISM). The Gnesiolutherans saw Melanchthon's position as a dangerous compromise with the Calvinist teaching on the Eucharist—hence as a hidden or secret Calvinism. The bitter conflict among second-generation Lutherans is reflected in the *Formula of Concord, Art. VII, strongly reaffirming Luther's doctrine on the Real Presence. *MAIOR, G.; *FLACIUS ILLYRICUS, M.; *UBIQUITARIANISM..

CUDWORTH, RALPH (1617–88), a Somerset man, fellow of Emmanuel, afterwards Master of Christ's College, Cambridge, and a familiar of the *Cambridge Platonists. He was on good terms with the government of the Lord Protector, but though he was confirmed in his office after the *Restoration, he soon retired from Cambridge. He was a learned Hebrew scholar and the author of biblical and ethical writings; his great book is *True Intellectual System of the Universe, wherein all the reason and philosophy of Atheism is confuted and its impossibility maintained* (1678). Aimed at Hobbes, the great contemporary advocate of materialist philosophy, it states the arguments of the ancient atheists so fairly that, as Dryden said (dedication to the *Aeneid*), "he raised such strong objections against the being of a God and Providence, that many think he hath not answered." In fact he elaborated, if rather antiquatedly to a generation that read Descartes and Spinoza, strong and balanced Platonic and Aristotelian theism, which in part anticipates later theories of the unconscious. See S. J. Passmore, *R. C.* (1951).

CUIUS REGIO, EIUS RELIGIO (a territory's religion [is] that of its prince), the formula approved in the Religious Peace of *Augsburg, whereby princes of the empire were given the right to determine the religion of their subjects. The phrasing is attributed to Joachim Stephani, a canonist of Greifswald. The most important result that flowed from the *ius reformandi,* as the principle came to be called in the 17th cent., was to ensure the permanence of the Reformation. Originally it allowed only the Lutheran and the Catholic religions. Not until the Peace of *Westphalia (1648) was provision made for the *Reformed Churches and for any minorities that had been tolerated in 1624, the normative year. The efficacy of the *ius reformandi* was limited by the so-called ecclesiastical reservation, which decreed that a bp. or abbot going over to the Reformation must surrender his office and possessions. During the deliberations attendant on the Peace of Augsburg the majority of Protestants favored allowing individuals freedom of choice in religion; but during the *Counter-Reformation whole principalities were kept true to the Reformation by law. Theoretically, the *ius reformandi* is still operative; if a Swiss canton, for instance, would vote to change its religion, the principle could be invoked. See J. Heckel, RGG 1:1888–89; H. Rabe, LTK 5:825.

CULLMANN, OSCAR (1902–), biblical theologian, NT exegete, and patristic scholar. Since 1938, he has been professor of NT and ancient church history at the University of Basel. Committed to the ecumenical movement, he was a Protestant observer at the Vatican Council II. C. insists on a strict philological-historical method of exegesis, i.e., an unprejudiced openness to the terminology and thought patterns of the NT authors. The gospel message is not metaphysical speculation but the proclamation of concrete historical events that occurred at a particular time and place. Although C. acknowledges dependence on Schweitzer for his emphasis on eschatology and on Bultmann for form criticism, he rejects the philosophical and theological presuppositions of both Protestant *liberal theology and Heideggerian existentialism. The explanation of salvation history (*Heilsgeschichte*) is pivotal in C.'s thought. In contrast to the Greek understanding of time as cyclical, the Bible presents time as linear and dynamic. The Christian does not escape time or consider it meaningless; time is the arena where God acts to accomplish redemption. The biblical time line can be divided into three sections: the period before creation; the time between creation and the end of the world, during which a succession of redemptively decisive events take place and move toward eventual consummation; and the segment stretching forward eternally from the end of the world. This succession of redemptive acts is called salvation history. Since the Christ event is at the qualitative midpoint of salvation history and is the decisive center of time, the fulfillment of time has already happened, even though this fulfillment is still being accomplished in the present. Salvation has come; only its consummation is awaited.

The study of salvation history enables C. to achieve the main goal of his theological enterprise, the NT idea of Christ. He maintains that the communities responsible for the formation of the NT evolved their Christology primarily in terms of the various Jewish messianic titles. These Christologies must be placed primarily in a Judaic rather than Hellenistic frame of reference. The messianic titles manifest not the nature of Christ but his functions in salvation history. They apply to the earthly work of Jesus (Servant of the Lord), to his future work (Son of Man), to his present work (Lord), or to his pre-existence (Word). Moreover, the working out of this Christology is directly traceable from the self-consciousness of Jesus, which can be known from the NT data, to the post-Resurrection faith and theological reflections of the earliest Christian communities. The Gospels give an accurate picture of Jesus's own self-concept as the source from which the Church could establish the connection between Christ and the total expanse of time and eternity.

In his patristic studies, C. wrote extensively on the Pseudo-Clementine literature of the 3d and 4th cents., the meaning of the Eucharist in primitive Christianity, the earliest Christian confessions of faith, and the relationship between Church and State in the first 2 centuries. Both in patristics and in biblical theology, he raised issues of considerable ecumenical importance. He upheld the practice of *infant baptism but denied the RC notion of the relationship between Scripture and tradition. His study of Peter's role in the Church concluded that Peter's special position and power expired with the apostle's death. See Cullmann's works: *Christology of the New Testament* (tr. S. C. Guthrie and C. A. M. Hall, rev. ed., 1964); *Early Church* (tr. A. J. Higgins, 1959); *Vatican Council Two: The New Direction* (ed. and tr. J. D. Hester et al., 1968); *Peter: Disciple, Apostle, Martyr* (tr. F. V. Filson, 2d rev. ed., 1962).

CULT (Lat. *cultus*, worship), a term denoting either worship or a certain type of religious body. In the first sense cult is the act of worship, a specific set of worship forms, or the veneration of God or the saints under some particular title. As a classification, a cult resembles a *sect. Although these terms are sometimes distinguished, in popular usage and even in the language of many who have a professional interest in the subject, "cult" and "sect" are used interchangeably. For example, E. T. Clark's *The Small Sects in America* (1949) deals with many of the same groups as does Jan K. Van Baalen's *Chaos of the Cults* (1953). Sociologists of religion have tried to arrive at more precise definitions by analysis of belief systems and rituals of such religious groups. J. M. Yinger, e.g., distinguishes the cults by their small size, localization, dependence upon a leader with magnetic personality, and beliefs and rites that deviate widely from the norms of society. Because of its deviant beliefs and the problems of succession following the death of a leader, the cult tends to be of short duration, and unlike the sect it is not apt to become transformed into a *denomination. The focus of a cult, Yinger says, is upon the individual; there is no interest in changing the social order. Pure types of the cult are rare in the U.S., according to Yinger, but examples are some "Muslim" and spiritualist groups among Negroes. See J. M. Yinger, *Religion, Society, and the Individual* (1964).

CUM OCCASIONE, a bull of Innocent X issued May 31, 1653. It condemned five propositions of Cornelius *Jansen, four as heretical (D 2001–05). These predestinarian propositions (a summary of Jansen's *Augustinus* by Nicolas Cornet of the Sorbonne) minimize freedom and merit: saving grace is irresistible and not given to all. An appeal of Bp. Habert of Vabres for papal condemnation, drafted by St. Vincent de Paul, was signed by some 80 French bps.; 11 bishops defended *Jansenism. A congregation of cardinals held 50 meetings (the Pope attended 10) and consulted the universities and leading theologians; condemnation followed. The Jansenists, led by A. *Arnauld, countered by denying that the propositions as stated were attributable to Jansen. See

Pastor 30:239–280; H. Daniel-Rops, *Church in the Seventeenth Century* (tr. J. J. Buckingham (1963), 349–353.

CUMBERLAND METHODIST CHURCH, one of the smallest Methodist denominations in the U.S.; organized in Grundy Co., Tenn., in 1950. The Church. is a splinter group from the Congregational Methodist Church, which it disagreed on minor points of polity and doctrine. It consists of four churches and about 65 members, all in Tenn.; its work is administered by one general board presided over by an elected president rather than a bp., the Church having rejected episcopacy. See HistAmMeth 3:594.

CUMBERLAND PRESBYTERIAN CHURCH, an American frontier body, which emerged from what is now the *United Presbyterian Church in the U.S.A. as a result of controversies concerning the *Westminster Confession and educational standards for the ministry. The division arose first in the Transylvania Presbytery in the Synod of Kentucky. This area was the scene of great revivals that created the demand for more ministers and encouraged attacks on a fatalistic interpretation of predestination (see REVIVALISM). The Presbytery of Cumberland was charged with ordaining clergymen of unsound doctrine and was dissolved. In 1810 ministers Finis Ewing, Samuel King, and Samuel McAdow founded the new denomination. The Westminster Confession of Faith was adopted only "as far as" it was in agreement with Scripture, and it was revised several times without ever committing the denomination to a fully *Arminian position. The *General Assembly has met annually; the leading publication has been the *Cumberland Presbyterian*; there is a Cumberland Presbyterian Center in Memphis, Tennessee. Conversations about reunion with the parent body, which had been carried on from the beginning, had only slight success in 1906; those who insisted upon preservation of independence, continued the Cumberland Presbyterian Church. In 1967 there were 936 congregations, with nearly 90,000 members.

CUMMINS, GEORGE DAVID (1822–76), founder of the Reformed Episcopal Church. Born in Smyrna, Del., C. studied at Dickinson College (A.B., 1841; M.A., 1844) and was licensed to preach in 1842 by the Baltimore Conference of the Methodist Episcopal Church. He entered the Protestant Episcopal Church in 1845 and was ordained the same year. He served as rector of churches in Norfolk and Richmond, Va., Washington, D.C., and Baltimore, Md., before accepting a call to Trinity Church, Chicago, in 1863. Chosen in 1866 as assistant bishop of Kentucky, he strongly opposed the influence of the *Oxford movement in the Episcopal Church. His Society to Promote Evangelical Religion brought him into conflict with the *General Convention in 1868–69. He had the support of the Virginia Theological Seminary faculty and other influential low churchmen, who joined him in promoting an American branch of the *Evangelical Alliance as a counterbalance to the spread of Catholic doctrine and ritual within the Episcopal Church. His insistence on intercommunion with evangelical Protestant Churches and his belittling of Anglican orders led to formal charges against him. In Dec. 1873, with 20 other evangelicals, he established the Reformed Episcopal Church, but few Episcopalians followed him.

CURATE (Lat. *curatus*, charged with, or entrusted with, the care of something), a term originally used to designate a priest to whom the cure (care) of souls was committed, i.e., a priest in charge of a parish. The cognate terms in French, Italian, and Spanish—*curé, curato, cura*—retain this meaning. In the English-speaking world, however, the term as popularly used came to be applied not to the principal priest of a parish but to a clergyman who assists the principal priest in the performance of his parochial duties. From pre-Reformation times the beneficed incumbent of a parish was often unable because of a plurality of benefices, or actual occupation in other matters, or the size of his parish, to perform personally all the offices for which his benefice made him responsible. His duties therefore had to be discharged with the help of a nonbeneficed clergyman whom he employed for that purpose, and it is the latter who came to be called the curate in English. Pluralism has been eradicated, and means other than benefices have been found to provide for the assignment and support of the clergy in their pastoral work, but the term curate continues in Anglican, and to a lesser extent in RC, usage to signify an assistant priest in a parish. In the RC Church in the U.S. a priest appointed to help the pastor of a parish is more commonly called an assistant.

CUTLERITES, see CHURCH OF JESUS CHRIST (CUTLERITES).

CZECH CONFESSIONS, another name for the *Bohemian Confessions of 1535 and 1575.

CZECHOSLOVAK CHURCH (Církev Československá), a *national church. An organization of priests presented to Benedict XV in 1919 a petition that included election of bps., democratization of church government, vernacular liturgy, and freedom from celibacy. When the petition was rejected by the Pope, a few rebelled, were excommunicated, and in 1920 formed the Czechoslovak Church. The first bp., Matthew Pavlek, obtained valid consecration but left the Church after struggling in vain against liberalizing tendencies. Thereafter *apostolic succession was rejected. The Church took on a presbyterian form of government, but with four unconsecrated bps., the bp. of

Prague being patriarch. The first patriarch was Karl Farský, and under him liberal religious thought prevailed: the Scriptures were taken as but one of many witnesses to God's word; the critique of religious truth was man's reason; Christ was Son of God only in an ethical sense; original sin and other Christian dogmas were rejected. The Church did not maintain the numerical strength achieved during its early days when it was closely identified with Czech nationalism. Latest obtainable figures (1955) showed a membership of 950,000. Since 1948 the Church has sought the favor of the Communist regime. See Gründler 1.362–363; Latourette CRA 4:196–197; L. Nemec, *Church and State in Czechoslovakia, Historically, Juridically, and Theologically Documented* (1955), 124–130.

CZENGER, CONFESSION OF, another name for the *Hungarian Confession (1557 or 58), adopted for the *Reformed Church by a synod at Czenger on the NE border of Hungary.

CZERSK1, JOHANN (1815–93), cofounder of the German Catholic movement (*Deutschkatholizismus). Two years after his ordination as a priest, he left the Church and founded in 1844 a reform community of dissatisfied Roman Catholics. In 1846 he joined with Johann *Ronge in organizing the German Catholic movement. Ronge's more rationalistic ideas prevailed, and C. lost his position of leadership. He spent his remaining years as an obscure, itinerant preacher, eventually abandoning Christianity entirely.

D

DANCERS, a fanatical sect that first appeared in the Rhineland and the Low Countries, esp. at Liège, in 1374. The characteristic trait displayed by its devotees was frenzied dancing, interspersed with caterwaulings that resembled a litany. Half naked and bedecked with flowers, the Dancers engaged in their gyrations to the point of exhaustion. They were never treated as heretics but were considered to be possessed; their cure was attempted through exorcism and pilgrimages to the shrine of St. Vitus. The dancing mania was a sporadic phenomenon through the late Middle Ages. See J. F. K. Hecker, *Dancing Mania of the Middle Ages* (tr. B. G. Babington, 1885), M. F. Laughlin, NCE 3:626, s.v. "Chorisantes."

DARBY, JOHN NELSON (1800–82), leading figure in the establishment of the *Plymouth Brethren. D., a grandson of the naval hero Lord Nelson, was graduated from Trinity College, Dublin (1819), and for a time was a lawyer. He was ordained in the Church of Ireland (1825) and served as a curate in Wicklow. Dissatisfied both with the state ties of the established Church and with the divisions among *Nonconformist Churches, he became attracted to those groups of like-minded Christians, calling themselves Brethren, Christians, Believers, or Saints, who sought to restore a simple primitive Christianity. Since the largest center of the movement was Plymouth, England, the adherents became known as Plymouth Brethren. D.'s ideas on *dispensationalism, the presence of Christ in the gathering of the devout, the Brethren's assurance of salvation, and the charismatic ministry of all in their communities made him a leader, so that the Plymouth Brethren were often called Darbyites. After a division among them in 1848 over association with non-Brethren, the name was particularly applied to the Exclusive Brethren as opposed to the Open Brethren. D. made evangelical journeys to continental Europe, the U.S., Canada, the West Indies, Australia, and New Zealand. The 32 volumes of his collected writings were published in London (1867–83). See DNB 5:493–494; O. T. Allis, *Prophecy and the Church* (1945); C. B. Bass, *Backgrounds to Dispensationalism . . .* (1960).

DARBYITES, a popular name for the *Plymouth Brethren because of the prominence of J. N. *Darby in their origins. More particularly the name was applied to the Exclusive Brethren after a division in the movement in 1848.

DAVENPORT, CHRISTOPHER AND JOHN, two brothers prominent in 17th-cent. ecclesiastical and political life.

Christopher (religious name, Franciscus a Sancta Clara; 1598–1680), Franciscan theologian. Born at Coventry, C., with his brother John, studied at Oxford (1613–15) and while there converted to Catholicism. He continued his studies, first at Douai and then at Ypres, where he joined the Franciscans (1617). He studied theology at Salamanca, then taught briefly at Douai before being appointed (1625) to restore the Recollects in England. He served as chaplain for Queen Henrietta Maria before the Civil War. In his devotion to the cause of reunion, he cultivated friendly relations with many Anglicans, one of whom, Jeremy *Taylor, came under suspicion because of the association. C. himself was forced into hiding during the Civil War, using the aliases Francis Hunt and Francis Coventry. With the *Restoration (1660) he again became court chaplain and converted Anne, Duchess of York. He wrote numerous philosophical, historical, theological, and pastoral treatises (collected 2v., Douai, 1665–67). His *Paraphrastica expositio ar-*

ticulorum confessionis Anglicanae, published as an appendix to *Deus, natura, gratia* (1634), sought to show the compatibility of the *Thirty-Nine Articles with RC teaching; it was condemned in Spain but not in Rome. See H. Dauphin, DHGE 14:109–111; DictEngCath 2:24–28.

John (1597–1670), Puritan minister, a founder of New Haven Colony (Conn.). After studying with his brother Christopher at Oxford, J. was ordained in the C of E. While a vicar in London he adopted Puritan views. He left England, going first to Amsterdam (1633) and then to America (1637). With Theophilus Eaton (d. 1658) and others he helped found the colony of New Haven. In 1667 because of religious (see HALFWAY COVENANT) and political disputes J. left New Haven to become minister of the First Church in Boston. His works include *The Power of Congregational Churches Asserted and Vindicated* (1672).

DAVID, CHRISTIAN (1690–1751), evangelist and missionary of the *Moravian Church. Born in Moravia, D. had a deep religious experience at the age of 20, and after a period of uncertainty converted from Catholicism to *Pietism. He combined traveling at his carpenter's trade with evangelism. After meeting Count *Zinzendorf he was instrumental in the Count's opening his estates to Bohemian Brethren refugees and felled the first tree for the building of *Herrnhut in 1722. D. helped build settlements elsewhere in Germany and in Pennsylvania and served briefly as a missionary in Greenland. As a preacher he deeply impressed John *Wesley during the latter's visit to Herrnhut. See G. Hamilton, *History of the Moravian Church* (1967).

DÁVID, FRANZ (1510–79), Transylvanian Unitarian leader. Born in Koloszvár (Cluj), he studied in Wittenberg (1545–48) and returned to Hungary to become rector of a RC school. He became a Lutheran and superintendent of the Hungarian Lutheran Church (1557). After debates with the Calvinist leader, Peter Mélius, D. became a Calvinist and was superintendent of the Hungarian *Reformed Church (1564). Debates within the Reformed Church and D.'s own inquiring mind led him to question the doctrines of the Trinity and the divinity of Christ. With G. *Blandrata, he won many of the nobles over to Unitarianism. At a general synod in 1568, some Reformed ministers separated, under his leadership, forming the nucleus of a Unitarian church, of which he became bishop. His inquiries led him to reject the addressing of prayer to Christ. Since innovations in religion had been forbidden by royal decree, D. was arrested, tried, and died in prison. He is regarded as the founder of the Hungarian Unitarian Church. See E. M. Wilbur, *History of Unitarianism* (2v., repr., 1965), 2:16–80.

DAVIDSON, RANDALL THOMAS (1848–1930), Abp. of Canterbury. The son of Scottish, Presbyterian parents, D. was educated at Trinity College, Oxford. He was resident chaplain to Abp. Tait (1877–82), married Tait's second daughter, and was his biographer (1891). Queen Victoria came to esteem him as a valued counselor and in 1883 appointed him dean of Windsor. He was bishop of Rochester (1891–95), then of Winchester (1895–1903), and was engaged in controversy over use of ritual in the Church of England. He was appointed abp. of Canterbury in 1903. In this office he was conciliatory and fair, striving to preserve the unity and the *comprehensiveness of the Church of England. He resisted disestablishment of the Church in Wales (1920), mediated in conflicts concerning *modernism, presided at the ecumenically important *Lambeth Conference of 1920, and encouraged the *Malines Conversations. He also spoke out for the Church on political and social issues. From 1906 onward he labored in the cause of a revision of the Book of Common Prayer; he was disappointed by the rejections (1927, 1928) of the *Revised Prayer Book. He resigned in 1928, and was elevated to a peerage as Baron Davidson of Lambeth. See G. K. A. Bell, *R. D.* (2v., 1935).

DAVIS, ANDREW JACKSON (1826–1910), Spiritualist leader. Born in Blooming Grove, N.Y., he had only a few months of schooling before he was apprenticed to a shoemaker as a child. In 1843 he met an itinerant lecturer on mesmerism and soon gained fame as a clairvoyant and faith healer. In 1845–47 he gave a series of lectures while in a trance; they were transcribed and published as *Nature's Divine Revelations* (1847). His many books on occult subjects, notably *The Great Harmonia, The Philosophy of Spiritual Intercourse* and *A Stellar Key to the Summer Land*, had a marked influence on the development of Spiritualist thought and provided much of its terminology. The Children's Progressive Lyceum, which he founded at Buffalo, N.Y., in 1863, as a Spiritualist "Sunday school," is regarded as the beginning of Spiritualism as a denomination.

DAWN-BIBLE STUDENTS ASSOCIATION, a body separated from the *Jehovah's Witnesses in 1920, accepting the teachings of Charles Taze *Russell but rejecting those of Joseph Franklin *Rutherford. Headquarters are in East Rutherford, New Jersey.

DE HAERETICO COMBURENDO, an act passed by Parliament in 1401 against the *Lollards. Those accused of heresy were to be tried by ecclesiastical courts and, if convicted, handed over to the civil power for execution by burning. Some see in this act the introduction of the *Inquisition in England. First repealed by Henry VIII and then reenacted by Mary Tudor, the act was finally revoked under Elizabeth I. See Bihlmeyer-Tüchle 2:437; K. B. McFarlane, *John Wycliffe and the Beginnings of English Nonconformity* (1953), 160–183.

DE MOTIONE OECUMENICA (On the Ecumenical Movement), the instruction issued by the RC Congregation of the Holy Office (now Congregation for the Doctrine of the Faith [Dec. 20, 1949]; AAS 42 [1950], 142–147) prescribing that bishops give prudent encouragement and direction to, while shielding the faithful from the dangers arising from, the *ecumenical movement. The document was a response to the growing desire among many persons outside the Church for the reunion of all who believe in Christ. In tone the instruction recalls the defensive documents of the Counter-Reformation period. Its significance, however, lies in the cautious but positive first steps taken toward the opening of a new era of RC participation in the ecumenical movement. *DECREE ON ECUMENISM.

DEACON (Gr. *diakonos*, servant, helper), one of the ranks or orders in the Christian ministry. Its institution has traditionally been traced to the Apostles' choice of seven disciples to see to the service of the poor (Acts 6.1–6). In NT times deacons preached and baptized under the direction of the presbyters, or bishops. The first usage of the term makes it clear that its specifically Christian meaning was well known (Phil 1.1; 1 Tim 3.8). By the end of the 1st cent. the order formed a distinct, hierarchical rank in third place after bishops and priests, as is clearly mentioned by SS. Clement of Rome, Ignatius of Antioch, and Polycarp. In general, deacons assisted at the Eucharist and baptism, led the laity in prayers, chanted the gospel, and received the offerings from the people. Their original office of collecting and distributing alms gave them a certain importance and influence, so that the first deacon, or *archdeacon, often became the bishop's chief administrative officer. Deacons frequently served as counselors of the bishop and as diocesan functionaries and, owing to their experience and prominence, many of them were subsequently elected bishops. This was particularly true in the major sees, such as Rome, where they also functioned as papal legates. The number of Roman deacons was long restricted to seven, a situation regarded as being the origin of the seven cardinal deacons. But during the later Middle Ages the diaconate diminished considerably in importance, so that it generally became merely the final stage in preparing for the priesthood. The RC Church maintained the practice of ordaining as deacons only those who intended to become priests; they were bound by celibacy. Practically, their own function became participation in solemn liturgical ceremonies. Vatican Council II increased the number of these functions. The Council also decreed that the diaconate may be restored as a permanent and separate rank in the Latin Church and that married men may be ordained to this rank (Vat II ConstCh 29). The diaconate is one of the three orders recognized in the Anglican Communion, and is received as a step toward the priesthood. The deacon exercises liturgical functions similar to those of the RC deacon.

The Eastern Churches have retained the diaconate as a permanent and separate order, both in monasteries and among the parish clergy, in which case married men are ordained. The deacon's chief function is an important one, since he leads the prayers of the faithful.

Protestant usage of the term varies. John Calvin in the *Ecclesiastical Ordinances* for Geneva named four orders of ministry: pastors, teachers, elders, and deacons. In the *Reformed and Presbyterian Churches the deacons are laymen who continue the basic functions assigned to them by Calvin, administration of church goods and poor relief, as well as the care of the infirm. In the Lutheran tradition in the U.S. the deacon has similar functions. In Europe Lutheran deacons are full-time church workers caring for spiritual and social works of the Church; an assistant pastor may also be called deacon. In other Churches the deacon is usually a layman, chosen or appointed, sometimes for works of mercy or the temporal concerns of the local church, sometimes to assist the minister in his preaching and spiritual ministra-

tions. See F. S. Weiser, *Serving Love: Chapters in the Early History of the Diaconate in American Lutheranism* (1960).

DEACONESS, a woman officially designated to perform certain functions in the Church. The office apparently existed in apostolic times, although the terminology is not clear (Rom 16.1; 1 Tim 3.11). The term itself does not seem to have come into use until the 4th cent., which also saw a marked increase in the importance of the position, as it is described in the *Didascalia Apostolorum* and the *Apostolic Constitutions*. Apparently they were ordained by the *laying on of hands by the bishop. The deaconess was to devote herself to the care of the sick and the poor, to help instruct women, and keep them in order in church. Her most important function was to assist at the baptism of women, chiefly for the sake of propriety since baptism was generally performed by immersion. When adult baptism grew rarer, the office of deaconess decreased in importance and soon died out, although it lasted somewhat longer in the Eastern Church. The possibility of deaconesses in the RC Church is involved in contemporary discussions about the ordination of women.

In the 19th cent. several Protestant Churches revived the office in a modified form by establishing or approving communities of women who would devote themselves to hospitals and other charitable works. The first such community was founded in 1836 by T. Fliedner, pastor of a Lutheran and Reformed parish in Kaiserswerth, Germany. In their ceremony of dedication the new deaconesses promised to be obedient and faithful to their calling. The restoration of the office spread throughout Europe. The Anglican Church approved the order in 1861, and diocesan institutes modeled on Kaiserswerth were established. The deaconess was ordained by the imposition of hands of the bishop. Four deaconesses from Kaiserswerth in 1849 came to staff what is now the Passavant Hospital, Pittsburgh, Pa.; the first

American motherhouse for deaconesses was established in Philadelphia in 1890. Both of these foundations are Lutheran. Most of the Protestant denominations have adopted the office of deaconess in some form. The largest number, over 700, are in the Methodist Church, but there are many also in the Episcopal Church, the United Church of Christ, and in the United Church of Canada. See J. Forget, DTC 4:685–703; M. Winter, EncLuthCh 1:659–664; F. S. Weiser, *Serving Love: Chapters in the Early History of the Diaconate in American Lutheranism* (1960); idem, *Love's Response: A Story of Lutheran Deaconesses in America* (1962).

DEATH OF GOD, a theme given prominence in modern thought by F. Nietzsche (1844–1900), for whom it was "an attempt at a diagnosis of contemporary civilization, not a metaphysical speculation about ultimate reality" (W. Kaufmann, *Nietzsche* [1956], 78). The concept had been used earlier, e.g., by Hegel; it is even found in primitive myths of dying and rising gods. In Christian theology the death of Christ is, from one standpoint, the death of God; but the doctrine of the Trinity safeguards against any thought that God ceased to exist. The phrase became the theme of a popular movement of *radical theology in the U.S. in the 1960s, particularly through the writings of T. Altizer and W. Hamilton. The concept did not achieve clear definition but seemed to express a conviction that God had ceased to be an effective force in modern life. This cessation was regarded by its advocates as an event of positive value, releasing man from religious and other structures of the past for a new freedom in the future. The idea was combined with a shift of emphasis from worshiping God to following Jesus and from faith to love. It was also connected with views derived from the prison writings of D. *Bonhoeffer (1906–45), including that of the "world come of age." It became almost a slogan for a time through publicity in the popular press but failed to gain significant support among theologians. See T. Altizer and W. Hamilton, *Death of God* (1966).

DECLARATION AND ADDRESS, a document of the Christian Association of Washington, Pa., "agreed upon and ordered to be printed," Sept. 7, 1809, stating the particular beliefs and early practices of the Churches variously known as Disciples of Christ, Christian Churches, the Christian Church, and Churches of Christ. The printed document has 56 pages of some 500 words each. The Declaration proposes "that we form ourselves into a religious association . . . for the sole purpose of promoting simple evangelical Christianity, free from all mixture of human opinions and inventions of men." The Address opens with the assertion that "the church of Christ on earth is essentially, intentionally and constitutionally one." Rejecting creeds as mere human formulas, it states further that "nothing ought to be inculcated upon Christians as articles of faith, nor required of them as terms of communion but what is expressly taught and enjoined upon them in the word of God." An Appendix tries to make it clear that "we have no intention to interfere, either directly or indirectly, with the peace and order of the settled churches . . . or, by endeavouring to erect churches out of churches—to distract and divide congregations." The unity it advocated, at a moment when the leader of the Christian Association, T. *Campbell, had renounced the authority of his *presbytery and the Pennsylvania Synod of the Seceder Presbyterian Church, was not achieved. The Association became the Brush Run Church in 1811. See W. E. Garrison and A. T. De-Groot, *Disciples of Christ: A History* (rev. ed., 1958), 145–161; Mayer RB 381–382; Schaff Creeds 1:931–933.

DECLARATION OF BREDA, the assurances given by King Charles II of England at Breda in Holland, April 4–14, 1660, before the *Restoration; the granting of "liberty to tender consciences" was included.

DECLARATION OF FAITH AND ORDER (Congregational Union of England and Wales), a statement adopted at the second General Meeting of the Congregational Union of England and Wales in 1833. The *Declaration of the Faith, Church Order, and Discipline of the Congregational, or Independent Churches,* which arose from a paper to the constituting Meeting of the Union in 1832 and circulated to the Churches, consisted of seven Preliminary Notes, twenty Principles of Religion, and thirteen Principles of Church Order and Discipline. Churches accepted the Declaration because it was not considered authoritative but simply a statement, for general information, of what was commonly believed and accepted among Congregationalists.

DECLARATION OF RIGHTS (1689), a statement assented to by William III and Mary before their coronation. It guaranteed the continuation of the C of E, the fundamental liberties of Englishmen, and the rights of Parliament. This declaration was presented to William and Mary by a committee of the Convention Parliament, and after their assent had been secured it was enacted as the Bill of Rights in 1689. Beginning with a catalogue of the misdeeds by which James "did endeavour to subvert and extirpate the Protestant religion and the laws and liberties of this kingdom," the Bill denied the right of the King to suspend, dispense, or execute laws without the consent of Parliament. It secured for Englishmen their personal liberties, the independence of the courts, the rights of habeas corpus and of jury trial, freedom of speech, and free elections; it also ensured frequent and regular Parliaments with freedom of debate for members. Provision was made for succession to the throne, first through the heirs of William and Mary; in case they had no issue, through Princess Anne of Denmark and her heirs; if she had no children, through any heirs William might have by future marriage. The Bill declared that any person in communication with the Church of Rome, or who "shall profess the popish religion, or shall marry a papist," should be excluded from the English throne. See H. Gee and W. J. Hardy, *Documents Illustrative of English Church History* (1921); G. Clark, *Later Stuarts, 1660–1714* (2d ed., 1955). *ROYAL DECLARATION.

DECLARATION OF THE FRENCH CLERGY, title of the Four *Gallican Articles, issued under the heading *Déclaration du clergé de France sur la puissance ecclésiastique du 19 Mars 1682.* The Declaration was issued by an assembly of bishops and lower clergy convoked by Louis XIV to assert the liberties of the French Church (in conflict with Rome).

DECLARATION OF THE SOVEREIGN, see ROYAL DECLARATION.

DECLARATION OF UTRECHT, an Old Catholic *doctrinal standard, issued (1889) in Germany by the Utrecht conference of the five bps. of Dutch, German, and Swiss Old Catholic Churches (see UNION OF UTRECHT). It is binding on all bps. and priests. Doctrinal principles are eight: (1) adherence to *Vincent of Lérins's rule of faith, where the threefold test of orthodoxy is *quod ubique, quod semper, quod ab omnibus creditum est:* thus acceptance of the first seven ecumenical councils; (2) rejection of the *infallibility and universal episcopate of the pope, because they contradict the ancient Church's faith, but acceptance of the bishop of Rome as *primus inter pares;* (3) rejection of the dogma of the Immaculate Conception because it is against Scripture and the tradition of the first centuries; (4) rejection of such modern papal pronouncements as *Unigenitus* (1713), *Auctorem fidei* (1794), and the *Syllabus of Errors* (1864); renewal of protests against the Roman Curia's errors and its attacks on *national Churches; (5) rejection of the Council of Trent's disciplinary decrees, and acceptance of its dogmatic decisions only if they harmonize with primitive church teaching. According to Bp. U. Küry, a Swiss Old Catholic, the last is the most significant point since the Dutch Church thereby "ceased to be in any sense Roman Catholic, and placed herself, with other Old Catholic Churches, alongside the Orthodox and Anglican Communions: she opened the way to future reunion of all nonpapal Catholic Churches, which her adherence to Trent had hitherto made impossible"; (6) acceptance of the eucharistic *Real Presence as a commemoration of the crucifixion, but without any mention of *transubstantiation; (7) hope for agreement between Christian Churches; (8) willingness to eliminate ecclesiastical abuses and the worldliness of the hierarchy. See U. Küry, *Die Altkatholische Kirche* (1966); C. B. Moss, *Old Catholic Movement* (1966).

DECLARATIONS OF INDULGENCE, proclamations (1660–88) by which the later Stuarts vainly sought to achieve religious toleration. Efforts to extend religious freedom were complicated by conflicting interests between the C of E and Dissenters, divided opinions among Dissenters, the contest between King and Parliament, and widespread fear of Roman Catholicism. In the Declaration of Breda (1660), Charles II had agreed to "declare a liberty to tender consciences," provided that Parliament enact appropriate laws. In fulfillment of this pledge, he issued a Declaration of Indulgence in 1660 but could not get approval of Commons; a similar Declaration, in 1662, was voided by Parliament. The *Act of Uniformity (1662) dampened hopes of all parties wishing broader tolerance; about 2,000 ministers were ejected from their livings. Charles issued another Declaration of Indulgence (1672) suspending all penal laws against Dissenters and *Recusants. Although many were released from prison and began to worship publicly, Parliament persuaded King Charles to withdraw his dispensation, and persecution was resumed. The opposition to toleration stemmed partly from determination to en-

force religious uniformity and partly from the dilemma that toleration could not easily be granted to Protestants without including Catholics. A primary objection to the 1672 Declaration of Indulgence, however, grew out of the constitutional struggle then in progress between Parliament and the King. Pressure for the withdrawal of religious toleration was a challenge to the royal right to waive penalties prescribed by Parliament.

When James II succeeded to the throne (1685), he was determined that Catholics should have liberty. Unlike his brother, he was a devout Catholic and had the Mass said openly. He expected not only to remove political and religious disabilities but eventually to restore the Catholic faith in England. In 1687, he issued a Declaration of Indulgence. Expressing the wish that "all the people of our dominions were members of the Catholic Church," he declared that "the conscience ought not to be constrained nor people forced in matters of mere religion." The chief provisions of the Declaration were that: (1) the C of E should continue as before "by law established"; (2) penal laws for nonconformity were suspended; (3) private worship of all peaceable persons was permitted; and (4) pardon was granted to all "nonconformists and recusants" convicted for violations of laws regarding religion. James proceeded to appoint Catholics to posts in government, in military service, in the judiciary, and at Oxford. A year later, he reissued the Declaration, ordering bps. to see that it was read in all the churches; seven who refused to obey were imprisoned, tried for libel, and acquitted. The King's high-handed methods had alienated many, and his proceedings against the bps. brought a climax of feeling. When the birth of a son indicated the probable succession of RC rulers, political leaders decided that a dynastic change was needed; this was accomplished by the *Revolution of 1688. See F. Bate, *Declaration of Indulgence, 1672* (1908); H. Gee and W. J. Hardy, *Documents Illustrative of English Church History* (1921); D. Ogg, *England in the Reigns of James II and William III* (1955).

DECLARATORY ACTS (Scotland), two statements, one of the United Presbyterian Church (1879), the other of the Free Church (1892), regarding the *Westminster Confession. Both Acts modified certain articles of the Confession (esp. on atonement, election, human depravity, and the civil magistrate) and recognized liberty of opinion concerning nonessentials of the *Reformed faith. A small group, who thought any departure from the Confession an apostasy, seceded from the Free Church and became the Free Presbyterian Church. The Acts, however, permitted a broader freedom of theological inquiry than before and relieved ministers and officeholders of the Churches from committing themselves to principles inconsistent with liberty of conscience and the right of private judgment. See J. R. Fleming, *History of the Church of Scotland, 1875–1929* (1933), 306–308 (text).

DECLARATORY ARTICLES, see ARTICLES DECLARATORY (CHURCH OF SCOTLAND).

DECREE ON ECUMENISM (*Unitatis redintegratio*), the pastoral document of Vatican Council II that sets forth for all Roman Catholics the guidelines and methods by which they may respond to the grace of the Holy Spirit calling for "restoration of unity among all the followers of Christ" (Vat II Ecum 1). Adopted by a vote of 2,137 to 11 and promulgated Nov. 21, 1964, by Paul VI at the end of the third session, the document is the result of three earlier texts. On Dec. 1, 1962, the General Congregation of the Council decided to combine into a single schema: a document, *On the Unity of the Church*, composed by the Commission for the Eastern Churches; a chapter on ecumenism intended for the schema, *On the Church*; and a draft prepared by the *Secretariat for Promoting Christian Unity on general ecumenical principles. The comparatively short 24 sections or articles of the Decree (an introduction and three chapters) treat Catholic principles on ecumenism, the practice of ecumenism, and Churches and ecclesial communities separated from the Roman Apostolic See.

Recognizing that the present division among Christians "contradicts the will of Christ, scandalizes the world, and damages that most holy cause, the preaching of the Gospel to every creature" (*ibid.*, 1), the Decree notes that among "our separated brethren" a movement for the restoration of unity "fostered by the grace of the Holy Spirit" has increased day by day. The chief advances made by the Decree on Ecumenism are the acceptance of this ecumenical movement and the encouragement given to Catholics to participate in it according to their Catholic principles. The Decree also makes an important contribution to the beginnings of a new *ecclesiology. For the first time in a RC ecclesiastical document, religious bodies tracing their origins from the Reformation are called Churches, with ecclesial gifts and sacred actions capable of giving birth to the life of grace and admission to the community of salvation (*ibid.*, 4). Calling "spiritual ecumenism" the soul of the ecumenical movement, the Decree lays down two objectives for the practice of worship in common (*communicatio in sacris*): to express the unity of the Church, which generally forbids common worship, and to obtain grace, which sometimes commends it (*ibid.*, 8). Among the guidelines offered for Catholic ecumenical activity, the first is to avoid expressions, judgments, and actions that do not represent the condition of our separated brethren with truth and fairness (*ibid.*, 4). Dialogue between experts is encouraged as are cooperative works carried out for the "common good of humanity." It is hoped that, under the attentive guidance of the bishops, these ecumenical activities, together with common prayer and church renewal, will overcome the obstacles preventing "perfect ecclesiastical communion" (*ibid.*, 4). See L. Jaeger, *Stand on Ecumenism: The Council's Decree* (tr. H. Graef, 1965).

DEED OF DECLARATION, a legal instrument created by John *Wesley in 1784 in

England. It was necessitated because the Wesleyan Methodist meeting houses and property were held in trust for Wesley, and for those whom he appointed, as premises to be freely used for preaching. Wesley wanted this provision extended on his death to the yearly conference of Methodist preachers. The term *conference needed legal definition. The Deed explained the words "yearly conference," declaring who are its members and how their succession was to be continued. Wesley chose 100 of his more than 200 preachers, thus creating, for legal purposes, a conference within the conference. With the union of all Methodist bodies in 1932, the legal 100 was retained only as an honorary residue of a few persons. See J. S. Simon, *John Wesley, the Last Phase* (1934), 208–219; L. Tyerman, *Life and Times of the Rev. John Wesley* (3d ed., 1876), 417–426.

DEFENSELESS MENNONITES, a name used by members of both the *Conference of the Evangelical Mennonite Church and of the *Evangelical Mennonite Brethren before adoption of the present titles. "Defenseless" is a reference to the Mennonite doctrine of *nonresistance.

DEISM, a theory of natural religion that, in its modern form, appeared first in the latter half of the 17th cent. in England. The deists were acute, if not profound, thinkers with a philosophy logically persuasive and, to a point, emotionally attractive. Goethe, who witnessed the deist phase of German thought, suggested that in an atmosphere saturated with Newtonian science and the cult of common sense, deism was a perfectly sensible religion to adopt. The English deists, with few exceptions, claimed that their crusades against miracles and priestcraft were undertaken solely for the sake of a pure, natural Christianity. Deism spread during the 18th cent. to Germany, with G. Lessing and H. S. Reimarus, and to France, where it left a lasting impres-

sion and attracted an influential and growing public. Voltaire was the outstanding spokesman and propagandist for a form of deism that, as designed, was intended to replace Christianity.

Deists recognize the existence of a God distinct from the world, possibly even a personal God, but deny that God exercises providential care of man or the universe. It is doubtful that their God is a creator; in any case he has left the world to itself, without intervening further in the course of nature or of human life. Deism requires a God to explain the order and reign of law in the world and, less certainly, the world's origin and continuance. The rationalists and empiricists of the late 17th and 18th cents. who rejected Christianity sought a basis in nature and in reason for belief in a Supreme Being that did not entail faith in traditional religious creeds. Deism is thus a form of rationalism, tinged with skepticism and in revolt against revealed religion. A law of nature is postulated—immanent and immutable—originally implanted by the author of nature, but its actual operation may be studied exhaustively without reference to its author.

Deism, called the "halfway house to atheism," restricts the scope and depth of man's relations to God, in which religion consists. For deism, a religion wholly in harmony with reason must confine itself to the fewest possible truths, all of which must be purely natural. No revelation is required to discover these truths; in any case a positive or revealed religion is impossible for deists, because it would presuppose on the part of the creator the suspension of his own natural laws. The source of the tragic history of so-called "revealed" religion is the uncritical reliance on authority and the absence of universally valid criteria of true religion. The deist demands, as a correlative to his concept of God, a purely "natural religion," freed from the shackles of dogmatic, ecclesiastical, and institutional Christianity. See L. Stephen, *English Thought in the Eighteenth Century* (v.1, 1876); F. E. Manuel, *The Eighteenth Century Confronts the Gods* (1959).

DENK, HANS (Denck; *c.*1495–1527), advocate of a religion of inner experience. D. was a humanist, and associate of J. *Oecolampadius. Through the influence of T. *Münzer in Nuremberg (1523) and then of B. *Hubmaier in Augsburg, D. became a leading preacher of Anabaptist views in Augsburg, Worms, Strassburg, and Basel. D.'s name is not bound simply to that movement, however. He opposed Protestant theories of predestination and RC teaching on the sacraments and the external Church in favor of individual inner mystical experience. Each was free to choose to live by Christ, the indwelling Word. D. published several short treatises that reflect the mysticism of the * *Theologia Germanica,* and he collaborated in translating the prophetic books of the Bible from Hebrew into German. Works: *H. D. Schriften* (ed. G. Baring and W. Fellmann, 1955–60). See A. Coutts, *H. D., c.1495–1527, Humanist and Heretic* (1927); J. F. G. Goeters, RGG 2:82; R. M. Jones, *Spiritual Reformers in the 16th and 17th Centuries* (pa., 1959), 17–30.

DENOMINATION, in a broad sense a synonym for *sect or for any church body composed of local congregations united in belief and government. In the more precise typology of E. *Troeltsch, denomination stands between the "church type" and the "sect type," as a religious group accommodated to the prevailing culture, willingly accepting itself as one among many other denominations, stressing practical cooperation, and minimizing distinctive theological differences. The theological view underlying such a concept was at least implicit in the Reformers' refusal to identify the Church with a particular institution, but the 17th-cent. *Independents gave expression to the idea as a rationale for the existence of Christian unity under diverse doctrinal, organizational, and liturgical forms. The term itself came into use in the 18th-cent. revivals in England and the U.S.; John *Wesley, for example, stated: "From real Christians of whatever denomination I earnestly desire not to be distinguished at all" (*The Character of a Methodist*). Both the underlying idea and denominations themselves are particularly a feature of Christianity in the U.S., because of religious freedom and the separation of Church and State. See J. M. Yinger, *Religion, Individual, and Society* (1957); W. S. Hudson, "Denominationalism as a Basis for Ecumenicity," *Church History* 24 (1955), 32–50; S. Meade, *Lively Experiment* (1963), ch. 7. *VOLUNTARYISM.

DENOMINATIONALISM, a term used in several senses: (1) a synonym for *sectarianism in all its senses; (2) a view of the Church that allows and even favors the coexistence of many differing church bodies (see DENOMINATION); (3) the theory and practice that joins many local churches in one ecclesiastical body, united by belief and government. Denominationalism in the third sense has often been opposed in the U.S. by those stressing *congregational polity or seeking to emphasize *voluntaryism. Such opposition has appeared in the Christian Churches and Independent Churches, in Pentecostalism, and among Baptists, e.g., the General Association of Regular Baptist Churches. *ANTIDENOMINATIONALISM.

DEUTSCH-KATHOLISCHE KIRCHE, see DEUTSCHKATHOLIZISMUS.

DEUTSCHE CHRISTEN, Christians in Germany under the Hitler regime who sought to form a Church conformed to Nazi ideology. *GERMAN CHRISTIANS.

DEUTSCHKATHOLIZISMUS, a German Catholic schismatic movement begun by Johann *Ronge and Johann *Czerski about 1845. Ronge, a priest from Breslau (Wroclaw), was degraded from the priesthood and excommunicated after his attack on the bp. of Trier for fostering veneration of the relic of the holy coat in 1844. After Ronge founded a reformed congregation at Breslau in 1845, he was joined by Czerski, also a degraded priest, in organizing a new body, the Deutsche-Katholische Kirche, which rejected, among other things, papal primacy, celibacy, indulgences, devotion to the saints, veneration of relics, and all the sacraments except baptism and the Lord's Supper. In the climate of liberalism and nationalism hostile to the dogmatic character and *ultramontane tendencies of the RC Church in Germany, Ronge's agitations won a widespread following, but his influence was short-lived. Within several years the new Church numbered 80,000 adherents with several hundred congregations. While ostensibly founded on Scripture, the new Church was heavily rationalistic and soon lost all vestiges of its RC background, as well as many followers who had hoped for genuine reform from within the RC Church. In 1850 most of the German Catholics united with the Protestant Free Congregations, and in 1859 many merged with the Friends of Light, an anti-Christian sect. A few German Catholic Churches retained their original identity and lingered into the 20th century. See G. Maron, RGG 2:112–113.

DÉVAY, MÁTYÁS, see BIRÓ, MÁTYÁS DÉVAI.

DEVOTIO MODERNA (Lat., modern devotion), a school and trend of spirituality that originated in the circle around Gerard Groote (1340–84) and his disciple Florentius Radewijns (1350–1400), founder of the *Brethren of the Common Life and of the Canons Regular of Windesheim; it reached its highest expression in the *Imitation of Christ* of Thomas à Kempis (1380–1471). In addition to Groote, Radewijns, and à Kempis, other prominent authors of the school were Gerlac Peters (1378–1411), Henrik Mande (1360–1431), its greatest mystic, and Johannes Mauburnus (Mombaer, 1460–1501), whose *Rosetum exercitiorum* was practically an encyclopedia of the spiritual-

ity of the Devotio moderna. During the 15th cent. Devotio moderna spread into parts of Germany, France, Spain, and possibly Italy. Called "modern" in contrast to the speculative and scholastic spirituality of the "old" German mysticism of Meister *Eckhart, it eschewed speculation and made little place for learning. The questions posed by the *Imitation of Christ*, I.I: "What does it profit you to talk learnedly of the Trinity . . . ? Of what value is knowledge without the fear of God?" indicate the school's underestimation of culture, knowledge, and purely human values. Marked by a pronounced preference for affective spirituality, Devotio moderna drew inspiration from Cistercian, Carthusian, and Franciscan sources. Christocentric rather than theocentric, it cultivated devotion to the Eucharist, meditation on Christ the man, and the imitation of the virtues of Christ. Accordingly it encouraged devout reading of the Scriptures, circulated copies of the Bible, and promoted translation into the vernacular. This school of spirituality claimed that self-knowledge, the practice of the virtues, and the avoidance of vice lay at the root of perfection. Though not excluding mysticism, it insisted upon self-abnegation and effort of the will: "The more constraint you put upon yourself the more progress you will make; that is certain" (*ibid.*, 1.25). Born during the dark days of the *Great Western Schism, Devotio moderna lacked an appreciation of the Church and the hierarchy. It placed great stress on the inner life of the individual but had less regard for external works and ritual. Intention, reflection, and fervor were primary. To encourage these, it introduced method into meditation and the other exercises of life. Advocating solitude, silence, and retirement from the world, the disciples of this school manifested little concern for the apostolate.

While Devotio moderna itself was anti-intellectual, most of the humanists of northern Europe, notably Erasmus, were affected by its positive spirituality. This explains their preoccupation with religious interests and with reform. The emphases in this form of spirituality were also dispositive for Reformation teachings on the nature of the Christian life. Devotio moderna as a school of spirituality disappeared as the Reformation brought an end to its main centers; many of its teachings, however, were absorbed into Erasmian, Ignatian, Benedictine, Franciscan and Dominican systems of spirituality. See R. R. Post, *De Moderne Devotie* (2d ed., 1950); A. Hyma, *Christian Renaissance* (1925).

DEVOTIONS. In the singular, devotion means primarily the quality or condition of being devoted or given earnestly to God's worship and service, the essence of *religion taken as a virtue. By extension it is sometimes applied, esp. among Roman Catholics, to the sensible experience, generally vaguely pleasurable, that sometimes but not necessarily accompanies fervent prayer; thus, e.g., to pray with devotion may mean to pray with sensible warmth; to pray without devotion, to pray with no sense of warmth, or with a feeling of aridity. In the plural the word is often applied to practices, usually involving prayer or religious reflection, of a kind apt to arouse the quality of earnestness in God's service. Thus a manual of devotions is a book of prayer designed for private as distinguished from formal public or liturgical worship. In a similar sense, among Protestants, organizational meetings at a local church may be preceded by "devotions," i.e., a short period of devout reflection that usually includes a hymn, a Scripture reading, and a prayer. "Popular devotions," in RC usage, is a term covering a wide variety of optional prayers and practices, often peripheral to the central themes of Christian worship, that people find helpful as means of arousing devotion in the primary meaning of the term—e.g., the rosary, the way of the cross, such special services as novenas and triduums, and the invocation of special saints.

DIALECTICAL THEOLOGY, a type of theological thought developed in Germany and Switzerland after World War I; also called *crisis theology. The leading proponent was Karl *Barth; his associates were Emil *Brunner, Rudolf Bultmann, Edward Thurneysen, and Friedrich *Gogarten. They were united in reacting against *liberal theology; in time Barth's associates developed the original viewpoint in ways opposed to his thought. Barth's theology was described by others as "dialectical" because of its form and its content. Theology must develop itself in paradoxical statements—in simultaneous affirmative and negative statements, and in thesis and antithesis—because its content deals at once with God's critical negation of man's world and the divine affirmation contained in the redemptive Word. Barth's own thought proceeded along these lines. Dialectical theology has been criticized for being antihumanist, for suppressing the significance of the Word becoming incarnate; but it was an important influence not only on Protestant *neo-orthodoxy but also on RC theological thought. See J. Macquarrie, *Twentieth Century Religious Thought* (1963); P. Schilling, *Contemporary Continental Theologians* (1966).

DIALOGUE, in general, includes every form of meeting and communication between individuals, groups, and communities to bring about greater understanding and better human relations in an atmosphere of sincerity, integrity, respect for persons, and mutual confidence. Three fundamental types of religious dialogue may be distinguished: (1) encounter on the basis of simple human solidarity, with a view to drawing the participants out of their isolation and mutual mistrust; (2) encounter on the plane of action, which aims at establishing the conditions for collaboration toward fixed objectives, despite doctrinal differences; and (3) encounter on the plane of search for truth with respect to doctrinal questions in which the participants are personally involved. Dialogue differs from instruction, which is ordered essentially toward the doctrinal enlightenment of one of the participants, whereas dialogue consists in mutual give and take. It differs from polemic and controversy insofar as these are ordered principally to the defending of a position and to demonstrating the falsity of an adversary's position. Dialogue is not a simple confrontation because it seeks on both sides a rapprochement and deeper understanding. Finally, dialogue as such does not aim at persuading the other of the value of one's own position. Dialogue of Christians with other Christians of differing traditions, with those of non-Christian religions, and with unbelievers is a unique phenomenon of the present age. See J. Loew, "Personal, Pastoral Contact with The Non-Believer," *Concilium* 23 (1967), 103–110; R. Kwant, *Encounter* (1963). *ECUMENISM.

DIALOGUE, INTERFAITH, see INTER-FAITH DIALOGUE.

DIASPORA (Gk., dispersion), members of any religious body living as a minority, whether in or outside their homeland, and maintaining contact with the central authorities of that body. The earliest use of the word is in the LXX, where it translates several Hebrew expressions. One implies the concept of Judaism as a sowing, a growth, and a longing to be gathered. The Jewish diaspora began with Assyrian and Babylonian deportations (722 and 597 B.C.). By NT times it had become so widespread that Alexandria alone contained a million Jews. Christians took over from Judaism the consciousness of living in a diaspora (see 1 Pet 2.11). The notion faded rapidly, however, when Christianity became the established religion. (Some 20th-cent. thinkers are convinced that Christianity is returning to its original diaspora status.) The term was revived in Germany about 100 years ago to designate Protestants living in RC lands and members of the RC Church living in Protestant lands. At times it applies to immigrant and mission congregations as well. Although the principle *cuius regio eius religio* once established religious unity in German principalities, many fac-

tors gave rise to diaspora conditions: consolidation of Protestant and RC lands, boundary changes, the free passage of artists, students, etc., population shifts, the weakening of the principle of a state Church. The first recorded use of diaspora in the sense of a religious minority was probably that of the High Consistory of the Old Prussian Union in 1852. The term is used esp. in Lutheran literature. See F. Lau, EncLuthCh 1:700–704; B. Schulz and J. P. Michael, LTK 3:343–346.

DIBELIUS, OTTO (1880–1967), German Lutheran bishop. Born of a Prussian family of civil servants and churchmen, D. entered the ministry after a year of advanced study at the Univ. of Edinburgh. His practice of mingling freely with his parishioners and encouraging them to take an active part in the life of the Church set a precedent in Germany. In 1925 he became superintendent of the Kurmark church district, where he continued the policies he had initiated as a pastor. His first important publication as bishop, *The Century of the Church* (1927), urged ministers to lead the Church into all the concerns of public life. He applauded the separation of Church and State that resulted from the fall of the Reich in 1918—a sharp departure from Luther's view of the role of the State. In 1937 he preached against anti-Semitism, for which act he was suspended from office; but his resistance to Nazism continued despite threat of re-arrest. After the collapse of Germany he joined Pastor *Niemöller in 1945 in signing the Stuttgart confession of guilt in the name of the German Protestant Churches. The same year he was appointed bishop of Berlin-Brandenburg. He was the first chairman of the executive council of the Evangelische Kirche in Deutschland (EKD), a federation of confessional Churches that he helped establish in 1948. D.'s devotional and historical writings attained the rank of best sellers, partly because of their conversational style. See O. Dibelius, *In the Service of the Lord: An Autobiography* (tr. M. Ilford, 1964).

DICKINSON, JONATHAN (1688–1747), Presbyterian clergyman and educator. Born in Mass. and educated at Yale, he settled at Elizabethtown (now Elizabeth), N.J., where he preached regularly to six or seven congregations and exerted wide influence on the synod of Philadelphia. While he considered himself a strong Calvinist, he refused to support strict subscription to the *Westminster Confession and was responsible for the compromise in the *Adopting Act of 1729. D. also participated in the *Great Awakening, and, when the "Old Side" Presbyterians opposed the revivalistic spirit and practices of the "New Side" clergymen, he helped form the synod of New York (1745). He assisted in founding the College of New Jersey, now Princeton University. Some of his theological writings, *Sermons and Tracts* (1793) and *True Scripture Doctrine Concerning Some Important Points in Christian Faith* (1841), extended his influence into the 19th century.

DIGGERS, in England, a group of *Levelers, led by G. *Winstanley. In 1649 about 30 Diggers began to cultivate (dig) a tract of common land in Surrey, thus putting into practice the theory of Winstanley that Christianity required social equality through common ownership of land. The Diggers were disbanded by mob violence in 1650 and the movement ceased. See L. H. Berens, *Digger Movement* (1906).

DIOCESE (Gr. *dioikēsis,* administrative unit), a territorial unit of the Church, governed by a bishop ruling in his own name and not as delegate of another. The diocese is an administrative division chiefly in the RC, Anglican, and Old Catholic Churches. Vatican II defines a diocese as "that portion of God's people which is entrusted to a bishop to be shepherded by him with the cooperation of the presbytery" (Vat II BpPastOff 11). While certainly not of divine institution, territorial division of the Church is attested to in the 1st century. An urban Christian community was organized under its bishop, whose authority gradually expanded to cover the rural areas. These communities, or territorial divisions, were at first called simply churches (Gr. *ekklesiai*), then parishes (*paroikiai*). The term diocese, already used in the 4th cent., did not become the exclusive term to designate territorial divisions until the 13th century. In the Eastern Church a diocese meant a much larger administrative unit comprising several provinces, corresponding to usage of the term in civil administration. What is called a diocese in the Western Church, the Eastern Church calls an eparchy. The establishment and the boundaries of a diocese generally follow civil territorial divisions and are usually named after the city in which the bishop resides. The erection, changing of boundaries, and suppression of a diocese belong by right to the highest authority in a particular Church. In the RC Church this has come to be the prerogative of the pope. In the best interests of the faithful Vatican II decreed that an extensive revision of the present diocesan administration and boundaries be undertaken as soon as possible, but this has not yet been put into effect. The Council also laid down norms for such changes (Vat II BpPastOff 22, 23). In the C of E dioceses may be erected only by act of Parliament; in the Protestant Episcopal Church the determination of dioceses belongs to the *General Convention of the Church. In the Eastern Church it is determined by the patriarch (or his equivalent) with his synod. An archdiocese is essentially the same in structure as a diocese, except that its head, an archbishop, enjoys prestige of rank and ceremonial precedence.

DIODATI, GIOVANNI (1576–1649), Swiss Protestant theologian, b. in Geneva of a family of Italian Protestant refugees. He succeeded Theodore *Beza as professor of theology and rector of the academy at Geneva (1618). An uncompromising Calvinist, D. was a co-formulator of the canons of the Synod of *Dort against *Arminianism. His translation of the Bible into Italian (1607) was used by Italian Protestants until the

20th century. He also translated Paolo Sarpi's *Storia del concilio di Trento* (1621) into French. See É. de Budé, *Vie de Jean Diodati* (1869).

DIPPEL, JOHANN KONRAD (1673–1734), Lutheran theologian, alchemist, physician, and chemist, credited with the invention of the dye called "Prussian blue." D. was born at Frankenstein, studied at Giessen, and became in his youth a staunch defender of Lutheran orthodoxy. But, after a time, and through the influence of G. *Arnold, he turned to *Pietism. He began to teach that the Church had betrayed its ideals from Constantinian times, disparaged dogma in favor of piety and practical Christianity, and attacked the institutional Church. These views brought criticism and strong opposition; he wandered from one place to another until he was expelled successively from Germany, Denmark, Holland, and Sweden. In his last years he engaged in bitter polemics against the mysticism of Count *Zinzendorf. D's main works were: *Orthodoxia orthodoxorum* (1697), *Papismus Protestantium vapulans* (1698), and *Vera demonstratio evangelica* (1729).

DIRECTORY OF PUBLIC WORSHIP, see WESTMINSTER DIRECTORY FOR WORSHIP.

DISCIPLES OF CHRIST, one of the names used by the followers of Alexander and Thomas *Campbell after 1830. In the early 20th cent. there was a division, with the conservative element taking the name Churches of Christ; the progressives, Disciples of Christ. The 1956 convention of the latter changed the name to Christian Churches, but Disciples of Christ remains the informal designation. *CHRISTIAN CHURCHES (DISCIPLES OF CHRIST), INTERNATIONAL CONVENTION.

DISCIPLESHIP, derived from the NT "disciple," which is the Anglicized form of the Latin *discipulus*, by which the Vulgate translates *mathētēs* (learner or follower). In modern Protestant usage, the concept of discipleship stresses obedience to Jesus Christ. Instead of interpreting Christian life chiefly in terms of assent to doctrines, religious feelings, or participation in churchly activities, it implies that to be a Christian means to obey Christ in the totality of life. Thus the meaning of discipleship is akin to that underlying Thomas à Kempis's *Imitation of Christ*. Therein the writer explains his understanding of what it means to "follow His [Christ's] teachings and His manner of living" (1.1). The connection between the concept of the *Imitation* and discipleship is suggested by D. *Bonhoeffer in a work entitled in German *Nachfolge* (cf. German title of the *Imitation*, *Nachfolge Christi*), but which in English was translated *The Cost of Discipleship* (tr. R. H. Fuller, 1953). Asserting that "cheap grace" is grace without discipleship, he declared that faith is real only when it is expressed in obedience. Modern hymnals commonly have a section captioned "Discipleship," and parenthetically may note "Christian Life" as a synonym. Pastors often refer to preparatory classes for church membership as "discipleship classes," and publication houses publish discipleship materials for use in such classes.

Historically, there have been various conceptions of normative expressions of Christian life. The contemporary authority crisis has created problems for one who would set forth standards of individual or corporate Christian behavior. The inadequacy of traditional Protestant styles of Christian living has been described by E. Farley in *Requiem For A Lost Piety* (1966). A contemporary approach to Christian life is P. Hessart, *Christian Life* (1967). See F. H. Littell, "Discipline of Discipleship in the Free Church Tradition," *Mennonite Quarterly Review* 35 (1961), 111–119; J. A. Mackay, "Call To Discipleship," *Theology Today* 7 (1950), 217–227.

DISCIPLINE, a term referring to the way the life of Christians is to be ordered, particularly in the community life of the

Church. In that sense it comprises the various elements of law and general procedure that the Churches have developed on the basis of Scripture and historical experience. The term "Discipline" is also used for the summaries of such regulations, published under the title Book of Discipline. The Book of Discipline generally contains the requirements of the particular Church in regard to rights and responsibilities of officers and organizational units within the total church structure; procedures for ordaining clergy and assigning them to their individual places of service; rubrics by which the rites of the Church are to be conducted; acceptance and excommunication of members, and similar matters. Discipline is the Church's attempt to make *discipleship concrete. The Christian faith is viewed as a way of life in which believers are united in communities where they seek to obey the commands of Christ. In the past, it has often been asserted that a precise order of discipline could be derived from the NT, but the possibility of that is increasingly questioned. Emphasis is shifting, therefore, to an effort toward gaining from the NT an understanding of the basic purpose of the Church, with detailed regulations left for determination on the basis of their suitability for fulfilling that purpose.

The *Reformed tradition is noted for a special emphasis on discipline, and is sometimes interpreted as an attempt to make the strictly disciplined life of monastic communities the pattern for the whole Church. John Calvin asserted that the Church should regulate the religious and moral life of its members, and under his leadership the church in Geneva became famous for its strict discipline. Adapting Calvin's Geneva *Ordinances,* John *Knox published rules for reforming the Church in Scotland in First Book of Discipline (1560).

Discipline is often used with particular reference to that aspect of church government that involves correction of members for their failure to fulfill Church requirements. In the RC Church this aspect of discipline is exercised primarily by hierarchical authority, according to a complex system of penalties, e.g., excommunication, prescribed by canon law. In Protestant Churches this responsibility more often rests with the local congregation. In past generations an offender was often required to appear before a meeting of the congregation, which would consider his case and possibly excommunicate him if he were obstinate and did not show contrition. The procedure frequently led to an undue emphasis on minor matters, as well as a spirit of self-righteousness in those judging the conduct of their fellow Christians; general revulsion against such aspects, along with the spirit of a more tolerant age, has led to the virtual end of the practice. Many church leaders are seeking an alternative form of discipline, but none has been widely accepted.

DISCIPLINE (Methodist), a book containing the Constitution, General Rules, Articles of Religion, Government, and Ritual of the Methodist Church, as well as the decisions of the Judicial Council, the Social Creed, and Miscellaneous Resolutions of the *General Conference. The formal title is *Doctrines and Discipline of the Methodist Church.* In 1743 John *Wesley wrote the General Rules for his *societies. Largely rules of conduct, they have been adopted by all Methodist bodies. In 1744 Wesley began calling yearly conferences of his preachers. Periodically he published cumulative summaries of the proceedings called "Large Minutes." When the Methodist Episcopal Church in America was organized in 1784 it adopted: (1) a Discipline based on Wesley's "Large Minutes" of 1780, (2) his Twenty-Four Articles of Religion, and (3) a *Ritual. The Articles of Religion were Wesley's abridgment of the *Thirty-Nine Articles of the Anglican Church. The Americans added a 25th Article: "Of the Rulers of the United States of America (see TWENTY-FIVE ARTICLES OF RELIGION). The Ritual was Wesley's abridgment of the *Book of Common Prayer. In 1808 the Church adopted a Constitution. In time the Discipline was expanded to include these and other elements. With the merger that formed the Methodist Church in 1939, a new Discipline was adopted.

The Discipline may be revised quadrennially by the General Conference, which, among other restrictions, may not alter the General Rules or the Articles of Religion or abolish episcopacy. Methodist respect for the Discipline is seen in the book's "Episcopal Greetings," where it is referred to as "revelation of the Holy Spirit working in and through our people." See J. J. Tigert, *Constitutional History of American Episcopal Methodism* (1916); HistAmMeth 1:213–232; N. B. Harmon, *Organization of the Methodist Church* (2d rev. ed., 1962).

DISCIPLINE, BOOK OF (Presbyterian), the title of two works on *polity. (1) The first, written largely by John *Knox and approved by the General Assembly of the Church of Scotland in 1560, sets forth the "policy and discipline" by which the life of the Scottish nation was to be reformed. The chapters on the ministry, superintendents, and compulsory national education are esp. important, but the recommendations, were never fully implemented, chiefly because the proposed educational system involved loss of revenue by the nobility. (2) A second Book of Discipline (1581), expounds the scheme of church government by which most Presbyterian Churches have been regulated. Written mainly by A. *Melville, the document distinguishes civil from ecclesiastical government and helped create a polity that secured cooperation between Church and State without confusing the jurisdiction proper to each. Church government ordinarily consists in the offices of minister, teacher, elder, and deacon. The powers of *presbytery, *synod, and *general assembly are also defined. See bibliog. for Church of Scotland.

DISESTABLISHMENT, a term referring generally to withdrawal of the legal status of an *established Church and particularly to a movement in England. In the 19th cent., English *Nonconformists won freedom from former disabilities and engaged in efforts to abolish establishment. Congregationalists, such as R. W. Dale and Edward Miall, were foremost in the sustained effort for disestablishment. In 1844, the British Anti-State Church Association (later the Liberation Society) was formed. As other rights were granted, however, opposition to establishment waned. Subsequently, some voices have been raised within the Church of England itself for disestablishment, particularly after the House of Commons rejected (1927–28) the proposed changes in the Book of Common Prayer long desired by many Anglicans (see RE- VISED PRAYER BOOK). More recently, prominent persons, such as Cyril Garbett, Abp. of York, have insisted upon more self-government for the Church, even if it means disestablishment. See H. Davies, *English Free Churches* (1952); C. Garbett, *Church and State in England* (1950).

DISPENSATIONALISM, a system of Bible interpretation set in a framework of a particular type of *premillenarianism. Fundamental to the system is the concept "dispensation," defined as "a period of time during which man is tested in respect to his obedience to some specific revelation of the will of God" (New Scofield Reference Bible [1967], 3). "Dispensation" is an Anglicized form of the Latin equivalent of the Greek word *oikonomia*, which means administration, management, or economy, as of a household or business. The implication of the word for this system is that God has dealt with men at different periods on different terms. Seven dispensations are distinguished: (1) Innocence, during the Edenic covenant in which man was tested by the prohibition of eating of the tree of the knowledge of good and evil; (2) Conscience, after expulsion from the garden, the testing of men by a requirement to avoid all evil known by conscience; (3) Human government, during which men were in submission to laws made by fellowmen, and governments were given the right of capital punishment; (4) Promise, during the Abrahamic covenant, making unconditional promise of blessing through Abraham's seed; (5) Law, when Israel, though remaining under the Abrahamic covenant, was placed under a disciplinary system; (6) Church, the era beginning with the postresurrection outpouring of the Holy Spirit when salvation depends upon belief in the gospel of Jesus Christ; and (7) Kingdom, the millennium, the time when God's promises to Israel will be fulfilled as the faithful are restored to their land under the Davidic monarch, with Christ as King. This millennial kingdom involves only Israel and has nothing to do with the Church. At its close, Satan's final rebellion takes place; he is cast into the lake of fire, and Christ delivers the kingdom to the Father.

While focusing upon eschatology, dispensational premillenarianism involves the meaning and significance of the entire Bible. Its advocates emphasize their consistent literalism, including fulfillment of OT prophecies, a sharp discontinuity between Israel and the Church, and the removal of the Church from earth (pretribulation rapture) before the millennium. To some conservative Christians the entire system seems fantastic, and has been labeled a heresy. Its critics charge that its ideas are novel, its typology fanciful, and its hermeneutical principles arbitrary. Its proponents, however, consider "dispensational truth" the only valid approach to the Bible. Having roots in the *Plymouth Brethren movement, the ideas were given systematic form in the *Scofield Reference Bible first published in 1909 (rev., 1917 and 1967). L. S. Chafer published *Systematic Theology* (8v., 1947), embodying the system, and Dallas Theological Seminary makes dispensationalism pivotal in its curriculum. Many *Bible schools have used the Scofield Bible as a text, and thousands of people have been so indoctrinated in the system as to make them suspicious of all who disagree with them. Hence, dispensationalism has been the source of divisiveness among conservative Christians. For a positive view by a modern scholar, see C. C. Ryrie, *Dispensa-*

tionalism Today (1965). For a critique by a former dispensationalist, see C. B. Bass, *Backgrounds to Dispensationalism* (1960).

DISPUTATION OF LEIPZIG, theological debate, June 27–July 16, 1519, in which J. *Eck opposed first *Karlstadt and then Martin *Luther. A literary exchange between Eck and Karlstadt had already taken place over Luther's *Ninety-Five Theses. Once Luther intervened in the debates (from July 4), Eck, the experienced disputant, made the doctrinal authority of the Church the central issue and drew from Luther an unequivocal agreement with doctrines of Jan *Hus against papal authority. The Disputation marked the end of Luther's earlier hesitations; his direct antipapal assaults, *The Liberty of the Christian Man, To the Christian Nobility of the German Nation,* and *On the Babylonian Captivity of the Church,* all appeared in 1520, as did the bull *Exsurge Domine* excommunicating him. See R. Fife, *Revolt of Martin Luther* (1957), 327–394.

DISSENTERS, a term applied broadly to a variety of English protesters. The name originated during the *Restoration and was first used by the *Westminster Assembly (1643), referring to its *Independent members as "dissenting brethren." The term became common after 1662, when previous *Nonconformists were ejected from the established Church and called Dissenters. Nonconformist and Dissenter soon became interchangeable terms, replacing the earlier Puritan label, and were applied to all Protestants not communicants of the C of E. Logically Catholics should have been included in the appellation, but they were known as Recusants. Congregationalists, Baptists, and Presbyterians comprised the bulk of the Dissenters at first; Friends (Quakers) and Unitarians were small but influential minorities. Methodists, separately organized in 1791, during the 19th cent. became the largest Nonconformist Church. By 1900, the term *free Churches was replacing the designations Dissenter and Nonconformist. See E. Routley, *English Religious Dissent* (1960).

DISSOLUTION OF THE MONASTERIES, the gradual confiscation of the income and property of the English monasteries by Henry VIII. The religious houses had become unpopular both with the *New Learning of the 16th cent. and with Henry himself. Although many monasteries performed invaluable educational and charitable services, others were noted for intellectual lethargy and greed. But Henry's need for money, not the ideal of reform, moved him, though his agent T. *Cromwell, to suppress the monasteries. Two royal commissioners sent on a visitation of the monasteries wrote, in what became known as the "Black Book," a grossly exaggerated report of monastic simony and immorality. The report pointed out that the smaller monasteries were the most guilty, and in 1536 Parliament suppressed all monasteries with revenues below £1,200 a year, giving their incomes to the King. Obviously the incomes of the larger monasteries presented a continual temptation to Henry's greed—a temptation that was for the moment thwarted by the Pilgrimage of Grace, an uprising over the suppression of the smaller monasteries. By 1539, however, the strength of the King was so great that one after the other of the larger monasteries was forced to surrender, the Carthusians holding out the longest and providing a number of martyrs. Eventually even the shrine of St. Thomas at Canterbury was despoiled, and wagonloads of gold, silver, precious stones, and costly vestments were taken to the King. Some of the funds from the suppression were used to establish new sees in England. See Hughes RE 1:36–89; 282–329.

DISTRICT SUPERINTENDENT (Methodist), an important administrative officer in the Methodist Church. He is a minister appointed by the bp. and supervises a number of churches (see CHARGE) within a geographical area or district of the *Annual Conference. The Conference determines the number of districts within its boundaries, and the bp. decides the boundaries of the districts after consultation with his district superintendents. The *Discipline carefully outlines the numerous duties of the district superintendent; chief among them are the duty to travel through his district to preach, to oversee the spiritual and temporal affairs of his churches, and to see that the Discipline is enforced and the program of the General Conference carried out. In the absence of the bp., during the intervals between Annual Conferences, the district superintendent may receive, change, or appoint preachers to the churches. The district superintendents of the Annual Conference make up the bp.'s cabinet. They represent the preachers on the cabinet and advise the bp. concerning preachers' appointments. They also act as a liaison between the bp. and the churches. The district superintendent serves on many important committees of the Conference, and his work, while not necessarily spectacular, is a source of strength to the Methodist organization. See N. B. Harmon, *Understanding the Methodist Church* (1955), 124; *Doctrines and Discipline of the Methodist Church* (1964).

DIVINE HEALING, a cardinal belief and practice in *Pentecostalism. Divine healing differs from the mental or metaphysical healing of *Christian Science, *New Thought, or *Spiritualism. Nor is it like *faith healing, in which a cure may come about simply through the internal belief of the sufferer. Divine healing is rather a gift or charisma (see Acts 4.30) from the power of the Holy Spirit to impart health to others. Healing is practiced through the laying on of hands (Mk 16.18), the observance of the prescriptions in James 5.14–18, and often with the use of anointed handkerchiefs or aprons (see Acts 19.12). With the exception of some extremists, most Pentecostals do not reject medical science; they rather see divine healing as a superior way to health. The basis for viewing healing as part of the *foursquare gospel is that bodily ills are a curse connected with sin, and that as Jesus atoned for all sin, so he delivers from all bodily infirmity. There are two types of Pentecostal healers: those who perform their task quietly, in chapels or private homes, in a ministry that is a blend of prayer, counseling, and the laying on of hands; and those professional healers who travel from city to city or from country to country to give healing sessions, often attended by huge crowds. Among the latter the best known is Oral *Roberts. There has been a great stress upon divine healing since World War II in Pentecostalism; it is also regarded as an essential means in the missionary enterprise. When the practice of divine healing does not effect a cure, some Pentecostal writers ascribe the failure to a lack of faith, or to sin; others, simply to the unsearchable wisdom of divine providence. See N. Bloch-Hoell, *Pentecostal Movement* (1964), 147–151; J. T. Nichol, *Pentecostalism* (1966), 15–17, 221–226; O. Roberts, *My Own Story* (1961).

DIVINE SCIENCE COLLEGE, an organization incorporated in Denver, Col., in 1898 by the first proponents of Divine Science (see CHURCH OF DIVINE SCIENCE). The local association of adherents of Divine Science is also called a Divine Science college and church. These local groups belong to the Divine Science Federation International, organized in 1957 to achieve unity in doctrine and practice.

DOCTRINAL STANDARD, a statement used by a Church as its authoritative understanding of the Christian faith, and as a guide by which it is distinguished from other Churches. Doctrinal standards are sometimes ranked in a hierarchy of importance, but all are generally considered subordinate to revealed truth as originally given in Christ and the Scriptures and are regarded as attempts to outline the funda-

mental truths of revelation. Normally individual members of the Church are expected to accept the standard, and clergy and teachers, to conform their teaching to it. Doctrinal standards acquire political importance where one Church is legally established or in some way favored and assent to its standards is required for those who would enjoy the privileges granted to the *established Church. Among some liberal groups opposition has arisen to any doctrinal standard as an unjust coercion of the individual conscience. Some *free Churches have rejected doctrinal standards, holding that the Bible is the sole and sufficient standard of belief; but they have nonetheless generally adopted covenants, declarations, or other statements defining their understanding of Christian doctrine.

Principal RC doctrinal standards have included creeds—notably the Apostles', the Nicene, and the Athanasian—and the doctrinal decisions of the popes and the *ecumenical councils. Among the Protestant Churches the variety of doctrinal standards is extensive. Doctrinal standards for Lutheranism are found in the *Book of Concord (1580), which contains the three ecumenical creeds, the *Augsburg Confession, Luther's Small Catechism (see CATECHISMS, LUTHER'S), and other confessions. The *Reformed Churches give less emphasis to confessions, but have been guided by such standards as the *Geneva Catechism (1545), the *Gallican Confession (1559), the *Belgic Confession (1561), and the *Heidelberg Catechism (1563). For the Presbyterian tradition stemming from England the *Westminster Confession has been primary. The Anglican standards are the *Book of Common Prayer and the *Thirty-Nine Articles.

In the rise of the ecumenical movement the discussion of doctrinal standards for a united Church has taken place particularly through the *Faith and Order movement, now a part of the *World Council of Churches. The World Council at its founding made an affirmation of faith in Christ as God and Savior the doctrinal standard for admission, but the desire of some Churches for a fuller statement led to a later expansion to include references to the Trinity and the Scriptures. Although some Christians insist that the Church should hold strictly to the doctrinal standards of the past, others consider it necessary to reexamine standards in the light of Scripture or modern knowledge or both. Those emphasizing historical relativity assert that the wording of a standard must be interpreted in the light of the historical period in which it was composed and that the expression of the same essential faith today may require different language.

DOCTRINE IN THE CHURCH OF ENG-LAND, the report in 1938 of a commission, set up in 1922 by the abps. of Canterbury and York, composed of members of the C of E holding moderate catholic, evangelical, and modernist positions. The report was documentary and not meant to be normative—an examination of belief actually held, not an authoritative declaration or a prescription of the limits of doctrinal variation. Its purpose was forgotten by some of its critics, though of course it did reflect contemporary persuasions.

DOCTRINES AND COVENANTS, a book published in 1835 by Joseph *Smith, Jr., at Kirtland, Ohio. It records the divine revelations Smith claimed to have received. The work is a doctrinal source of major importance for the Mormons and is the first expression of their belief in a continuing revelation to their Church in the persons of its leaders. *LATTER-DAY SAINTS, CHURCH OF JESUS CHRIST OF.

DOCTRINES AND DISCIPLINE of the **Methodist Church,** see DISCIPLINE (METHODIST).

DOGMATISM, a term used to discredit as presumptuous any proposal of philosophical or religious truth as certain, absolute, or authoritative. In modern philosophical usage, the term has become widespread since Immanuel Kant claimed that existing systems of thought accepted their presuppositions uncritically. In a religious context, Christians are charged with dogmatism because they accept their tenets as revelation. Among the Churches those espousing authoritative creeds or official teaching have been accused of dogmatism by nonauthoritarian or anticreedal Churches. Contemporary insistence upon the relativeness and inadequacy of all human concepts and language leads to the view that any theology claiming to be a valid formulation of divine revelation is dogmatism.

DOLCINO, FRA (d. 1307), a medieval reformer who assumed leadership of the *Apostolici after the death of Gerard *Segarelli in 1300. D. possessed considerable executive talent and gave the sect some semblance of organization, reducing its doctrines to writing and adding a number of Joachimist concepts and some of his own apocalyptic prophecies (see JOACHIMISM). He prophesied the extermination of the cardinals and the pope and God's choosing a new pope. When the bps. of Novara and Vercelli took action against him, Dolcino and 4,000 followers entrenched themselves in the Italian Alps. In 1305, Pope Clement V summoned a crusade against them because of their raids on the villages to obtain provisions. After 2 years of armed conflict they were finally subdued. Dolcino and his spiritual sister, Marguerite of Trent, were captured and cruelly executed. See E. Anagnine, *Dolcino e il movimento ereticale all'inizio del Trecento* (1964); G. Mollat, NCE 4:957; J. M. Vidal, DHGE 3:1041–44, s.v. "Apostoliques."

DOLET, ÉTIENNE (1504–46), French humanist and printer. D. was important in the French Renaissance for his contribution to Latinity, notably the *Commentarius linguae latinae* (2v., 1535, 1538), and for promotion of the French language through his press. A rationalist from early years, he was three times arrested by the authorities and after the third was burned at Place Maumbert, Paris, as a lapsed heretic. The charges against him included esp. his denial of the immortality of the soul. A heretic in RC eyes, and despised by Calvin as a blasphemer, D. was not a Christian; neither was he an atheist, but rather an early deist and freethinker. See H. Chamard, DictLetFranç 1:232–234; R. C. Christie, *É. D.: Martyr of the Renaissance* (1889); J. Lecler, DHGE 14:575–577.

DÖLLINGER, JOHANNES JOSEF IGNAZ VON (1799–1890), Church historian and controversialist. D. lived mainly in Bavaria. Born in Bamberg, he entered the Univ. of Würzburg at 16, and in 1820, the seminary at Bamberg; he was ordained in 1822. He was professor of church history and canon law at the lyceum in Aschaffenburg (1823–26) and at the Univ. of Munich (1826–72); in 1873 the King appointed him president of the Royal Bavarian Academy of Sciences. Because of his refusal to accept the declaration of Vatican Council I on papal infallibility, D., together with his friend and biographer J. *Friedrich, was excommunicated, April 1871. Though D. was instrumental in organizing the Old Catholic movement (see NUREMBERG DECLARATION), he never formally joined it. He attended Mass in RC churches, but did not receive the sacraments. All attempts to reconcile him with the RC Church were unsuccessful, and he received the last rites from Friedrich, now an Old Catholic priest. Until his open break with Rome, D. was prominent in the Catholic revival of Germany. He corresponded with, and in his travels visited, church leaders in France, Italy, and England. Something of an Anglophile, he admired Wiseman, wrote to Newman, and had a close friendship with his onetime pupil Lord Acton. The prestige he enjoyed among scholars and prelates in Europe and America made him valuable as a collaborator and formidable as an opponent.

His early fame resulted from historical studies; the first to win acclaim was *Die Lehre von der Eucharistie in den drei ersten Jahrhunderten* (1826). Perhaps his greatest opus is the study on the origins and consequences of the Reformation: *Die Reformation, ihre innere Entwicklung und ihre Wirkungen im Umfange des Lutherischen Bekenntnisses* (3v., 1845–48). It was followed by a biography of Luther (1850; Eng. tr., 1853). Running through the last two works is the theme that the Reformation marked a break with the national traditions of the German people. Shortly before 1850 D. began to comment in writing and lectures on Church-State relations. In this period the papacy came more and more under his attention. He argued successfully that St. Hippolytus of Rome was the author of the newly discovered *Philosophoumena*. It was the basis for a study of the Roman Church A.D. 200–250, which D. published as *Hippolytus und Callistus* (1853; Eng. tr., 1876). About the same time he openly inveighed against the proclamation of the dogma of the Immaculate Conception (1854), primarily because of the manner in which it was done. He became increasingly distrustful of ultramontanes and critical of the Roman exercise of power. In 1861 he questioned the historical basis and usefulness of the Papal States in two published lectures: *Kirche und Kirchen, Papsttum und Kirchenstaat* (Eng. tr., 1862). D.'s loyalty to the pope was strained further in 1864, when Pius IX condemned some of his opinions in the *Syllabus of Errors* (cf. proposition 13; D 2913). Besides his numerous other scholarly and critical works, there are his pseudonymous writings. By intention polemical, the two best known were directed against Vatican I and the definition of papal infallibility. Using the pen name Janus, D. wrote a series of articles, later published in book form as *Der Papst und das Konzil* (1869; Eng. tr., 1870 and 1873). Many opposed the definition because they felt it inopportune, but D. opposed the doctrine itself, chiefly on historical grounds. During the council, he kept abreast of the proceedings with the help of well-placed contacts, Lord Acton among them. Under the pseudonym Quirinus, he attacked the conduct of the council, complaining that its leaders discriminated against those bps. who resisted the definition. These attacks appeared first as letters purporting to be from Rome and later in a volume, *Römische Briefe vom Konzil* (1870; Eng. tr., 1870).

All 20th-cent. critics are impressed with D.'s facility for languages, his encyclopedic learning, and the extent of his writings, but also see much of his work as derivative and his theological horizons as limited. His strengths and weaknesses indicate the possibilities and limitations of a purely historical approach to theology and doctrine. See S. Lösch, *D. und Frankreich* (1955), with a list of D.'s writings, including Eng. translations; S. J. Tonsor, "Lord Acton on D.'s Historical Theology," *Journal of the History of Ideas* 20 (1959), 329–352; *idem*, NCE 4:959–960; J. J. Hennesey, *First Council of the Vatican: The American Experience* (1963).

DOMINE (less correctly, Dominie), an informal title for a clergyman in the Netherlands and other countries where the Dutch Reformed Church in its various branches is located. It has been used in this way by other Protestant denominations, and also as a synonym for "minister." The Latin meaning of "lord" or "master" is not implied by the church use. The double connotation of reverence or respect and of affection characterizes it. While the term has been used by many church members into the mid-20th cent., Americans have generally discontinued its use on the ground that it does not fit the modern age.

DONATISTS, members of a predominantly North African schism who broke away from the Church in 312 and received their name from their leader, *Donatus, who was consecrated bishop in 315 and died in exile *c.*355. Despite vigorous efforts on the part of Roman, Vandal, and Byzantine rulers to suppress it, Donatism persisted in North Africa into Moslem times. The immediate cause of the schism was the election of a successor to Mensurius as bp. of Carthage in 311. Without waiting for the arrival of their Numidian confreres, the assembled bps. proceeded to elect Caecilian, Mensurius's archdeacon, as his successor. This offended the absent bps., particularly Secundus, Bp. of Tigisis, a see that had for 40 years enjoyed the right of consecrating the bp. of Carthage. Under the presidency of Secundus 70 bps. met in Carthage and declared the consecration of Caecilian invalid on the grounds that he had been consecrated by Felix of Aptunga, a *traditor*, i.e., one who had handed over the Scriptures to the pagans during Diocletian's persecution. This council then elected Majorinus bishop. The bitter disputes that rose from this schism at Carthage required the intervention of the Emperor; Constantine I asked Pope Miltiades to settle the issues. In a council held at Rome on Oct. 2, 313, the bps. of Italy and Gaul decided in favor of Caecilian. Majorinus appealed the decision to the Emperor. A second council convoked in Arles on Aug. 1, 314, reaffirmed the decision. Another appeal met with no more success. A synod held in Milan on Nov. 10, 316, declared that Caecilian was lawfully elected, validly consecrated, and in just possession of the See of Carthage. In the meantime Majorinus had died. Donatus, his successor, proved an able and energetic leader; in 317 he was banished by Constantius to Gaul or Spain along with other Donatist bps. for encouraging the *Circumcellions, Donatist terrorists, who were plundering the provinces. When Julian the Apostate became emperor in 361, these exiles were allowed to return to Africa, where the schism flourished for another 30 years.

After Parmenian, Donatus's successor, died in 391, the movement was weakened by internal schisms and dissensions. Continued Donatist attacks on the Catholics prompted the bps. assembled in a council at Carthage in 404 to ask Emperor Honorius to include the Donatists in the laws against heretics. On Feb. 12, 405, he issued an edict denouncing the Donatists as heretics for their practice of rebaptism and ordering them to restore the churches taken from the Catholics. When the Donatists petitioned for withdrawal of the edict, the imperial tribune Marcellinus at a large council held at Carthage in June 411, decided in favor of the Catholics. Further imperial decrees were issued against the Donatists in 412, 414, and 428.

The remarkable success of Donatism in the face of vigorous opposition may be attributed to political, social, and religious factors. The Donatists claimed to be the champions of the slaves and oppressed natives in the face of the Roman landlords. Their simple and uncomplicated doctrine, stressing the sanctity and the exclusiveness of their Church, appealed to a fanatical strain in the populace who looked upon themselves as a society of saints, though the Catholics regarded them as cruel and ruthless adversaries. Their errors were combatted by Optatus of Milevis and in particular by St. Augustine. The Donatist controversies led to the clarification of a number of important questions, e.g., the efficacy of the sacraments *ex opere operato*; the nature of the Church, of schism, and of heresy; and the relations between Church and State and of heretics to a Christian state. See W. H. C. Frend, *Donatist Church* (1952); G. Bareille, DTC 4.2:1701–27; A. Pincherle, EC 4:1851–55.

DONATUS (d. *c.*355), bp. of Casae Nigrae in Numidia and later Donatist bp. of Carthage. At the end of the persecution under Diocletian, D. headed the party opposed to the election of Caecilian to succeed Mensurius as bp. of Carthage. Attacking Caecilian and his supporters as *traditores* (see TRADITOR), he, with other Numidian bps., elected Majorinus as metropolitan. This marked the beginning of the Donatist schism (312). The following year D. himself became schismatic bp. of Carthage and head of the party that came to bear his name. He was a man of eloquence and strong personality, accused by St. Augustine of arrogance and impiety. See W. H. C. Frend, *Donatist Church* (1952). *DONATISTS.

DORDRECHT, SYNOD OF, see DORT, SYNOD OF.

DORDRECHT CONFESSION OF FAITH, an Anabaptist formula, accepted by some Mennonite Churches in the United States. The author was Adriaan Corenlisz, of the Flemish Mennonite Church at Dordrecht (Dort) in Holland; the Confession was accepted chiefly as a platform for union and cooperation between Flemish and Frisian Mennonite groups. There are 18 articles, expressing, beside general Christian beliefs, *believer's baptism, *footwashing, *avoidance (i.e., ostracism of the excommunicated), *nonresistance, and the prohibition of oaths. Mennonites traditionally have not imposed creedal formulas on the conscience of the individual; the Dordrecht Confession has been used as a catechetical instrument. Text: J. C. Wenger, *Doctrines of the Mennonites* (1952), 78–86. See J. C. Wenger, MennEnc 2:92–93.

DORT, SYNOD OF (Dordrecht, near Rotterdam), an assembly of the *Reformed Church, convened to deal with *Arminianism, it met in 154 sessions, Nov. 1618–May 1619. The States General of Holland convoked the meeting to settle the long conflict between *Remonstrants and *Contra-Remonstrants; 27 representatives from Reformed Churches of Switzerland, the Palatinate, England, and Scotland attended. In part because of political considerations, the Arminians, represented chiefly by S. *Episcopius, were from the beginning treated as defendants on trial; many weeks passed before they were even admitted to the sessions. Their teaching was condemned, and many of their leaders were imprisoned or banished. Against the Arminians' *Remonstrance*, the five doctrinal chapters of the Synod, called the Canons of Dort, asserted unconditional divine *election and *reprobation; the *limited atonement of Christ; the *total depravity of men; *irresistible grace; and the *assurance of salvation or perseverance of the elect. The Canons of Dort were accepted as a doctrinal standard by the Reformed Church in Holland and by the *Reformed Church in America. They were given recognition, but less formal acceptance, by Reformed Churches elsewhere. See Mayer RB 225–226; Schaff Creeds 1:509–523; 3:550–597. *CALVINISM.

DOUBLE JUSTICE (*duplex justitia*), the notion, first advanced by J. Gropper (1503–59), a RC theologian at Cologne, as an attempt by certain pre-Tridentine and esp. RC theologians to reach a compromise on the doctrine of *justification. As the formula itself suggests, its proponents sought to find a *via media* between *forensic justification and the view that identified the process of justification with the actual forgiveness of sins and the inner renewal of the soul through the infusion of grace. While acknowledging a personal inherent justice (righteousness), defenders of the double-justice theory contended that such justice remains essentially incomplete and therefore insufficient for man to reach eternal life. Accordingly, it must be completed by an imputation of the justice and merits of Christ in virtue of man's incorporation into the mystical body by faith and hope in Christ its head. Defenders of this view, mainly Augustinians, claimed support for their position from St. Paul and from the writings of Augustine, though the doctrine was largely inspired by a notion of *concupiscence that had been introduced into this school in the 14th cent. by Gregory of Rimini (see AUGUSTINIANISM). Thus according to G. Seripando (1492–1563), who championed the double-justice theory at the Council of Trent, concupiscence remains even after baptism as a dynamic source of sin and as a positive hindrance to the complete observance of the commandments. Since such a state is displeasing to God, and therefore somehow sinful, the justice of Christ must be applied to all members of his mystical body to supply what is wanting to their personal justice so that they can reach eternal life. Although the Council of Trent in formulating the decree on justification (D 1520–83) rejected, without condemning, double justice, the doctrine nevertheless occasioned an examination in detail at Trent of the whole question of justification. See Jedin Trent 2:253–261.

DOUBLE PREDESTINATION, the teaching that God predestines some men to certain salvation and reprobates others to damnation (see REPROBATION). There are two forms: *supralapsarianism holds that there is an effective twofold divine plan of salvation and damnation anterior to God's foreknowledge of the Fall; *infralapsarianism, or sublapsarianism, holds that the plan is subsequent to foreknowledge of the Fall. Infralapsarianism is found in St. Augustine, and became the more common teaching of Churches in the Reformed tradition after the Synod of *Dort. Supralapsarianism was made explicit in *Calvinism by Theodore *Beza. In both forms, double predestination implies the positive reprobation of some to damnation. In this sense it is rejected by RC and Lutheran doctrinal standards and by *Arminianism. *PREDESTINATION.

DOUKHOBORS (Dukhbors; Russ., Spirit-wrestlers), members of a communal, mystical movement that originated in 18th-cent. Russia as a protest against the State and the Russian Orthodox Church. Rejecting the doctrine of the Trinity and the authority of the Bible, these peasants, who originally called themselves Christians of the Universal Brotherhood, taught that Christ was simply a man and reappears periodically in chosen men; that the soul is mortal and undergoes metempsychosis; and that those led by the Spirit are incapable of sin (see ANTINOMIANISM). Because of their opposition to government, private property, schools, war, and oaths, Doukhobors were periodically persecuted by the tsars and expelled by the Cossacks from their villages. With the assistance of L. Tolstoy and of English and American Quakers about 7,000 immigrated to W Canada (1898–99). They developed communal farms and became prosperous, but were plagued by a succession of dissolute leaders and by schisms. One of the leaders, Peter Vasilivich Verigin, who claimed that Christ was reincarnated in him, was killed by a time bomb in 1924. Under the leadership of his son about 18,000 Doukhobors, mostly residents of Saskatchewan, seem to have abandoned the original communal ideals and many socially objectionable practices. A radical group in the movement, the 1,500 Sons of Freedom in British Columbia, however, have been charged with 800 acts of violence including bombing, arson, and other acts of destruction; one of their means of protest has been picketing in the nude. See H. B. Hawthorn, ed., *Doukhobors of British Columbia* (1955); S. Holt, *Terror in the Name of God* (1964); G. Woodcock and I. Avakumovic, *Doukhobors* (1968).

DOWIE, JOHN ALEXANDER (1847–1907), evangelist, faith healer, and founder of the *Christian Catholic Church. Taken from Edinburgh, Scotland, to Australia by his parents, D. returned to study at the Univ. of Edinburgh; in 1870 he was ordained as pastor of a Congregational church near Sydney. He became a full-time evangelist in 1878 and in 1888 left Australia to preach in the United States. He established his headquarters at Chicago in 1890. Faith healing, his main concentration, won him followers. As a preacher he was vituperative and slangy in crusading against liquor and tobacco and frankly sensationalist in his approach to evangelism. In 1896 he established the Christian Catholic Church and in 1901 opened Zion City, Ill., for his followers. D. proclaimed himself the Prophet Elijah in 1901, and in 1904 was anointed as the First Apostle. He was deposed as unfit to rule Zion City and the Church in 1906 and devoted his remaining days to lawsuits to recover his property rights.

DOWIEITES, followers of John Alexander *Dowie. *CHRISTIAN CATHOLIC CHURCH.

DU BOSE, WILLIAM PORCHER (1836–1918), American Episcopal theologian. He studied at The Citadel, Charleston, S.C., and the Univ. of Virginia, and after military service in the Civil War was ordained (1866). He accepted a call to the Univ. of the South in Sewanee, Tenn., in 1871 as chaplain and professor of ethics, lecturing on Aristotle. In 1873 he formed the department of theology and in 1894 became its dean. His thought was influenced by both the *Oxford movement and the *Mercersburg theology. He held that the Church is the life incorporate and corporate in Jesus Christ and that the sacraments were acts of God's incorporation of man into Christ, not expressions of faith. He also held that man cannot interpret Scriptures apart from the mind of the Church. His principal works are *The Soteriology of the New Testament* (1899); *The Gospel in the Gospels* (1906), a study of the apostolic faith; *The Gospel According to St. Paul* (1907), which stresses the principle of authority; and *The Reason of Life* (1911). See Smith-Jamison 1:298–303.

DUCK RIVER (AND KINDRED) Associations of Baptists, associations originating (1843) as a protest movement against the antimission sentiment supported by a rigid Calvinism in the Elk River Association of Baptists. Because of their avowal of the mission enterprise, members are sometimes known as Missionary Baptists. Evangelically Calvinistic, they subscribe to the general tenets of Baptists, adding *footwashing as a third *ordinance commanded by Christ. With their work confined largely to Tenn., Ala., Ga., Ky., and Miss., Duck River Baptists numbered about 7,000 members in 69 churches in 1967.

DUNKERS (Dunkards, Tunkers; Ger. *tunken,* dip, immerse), originally a Pennsylvania Dutch nickname for the German Baptist Brethren (see BRETHREN CHURCHES), based on their practice of *trine immersion. *CONSERVATIVE DUNKERS; *OLD ORDER DUNKERS *PROGRESSIVE DUNKERS.

DUTCH REFORMED CHURCH, one of the early names of the *Reformed Church in America. After the American Revolution it was called the Dutch Reformed Church in North America, and also the Reformed Dutch Church in the U.S.A. Incorporated in 1819 as the Reformed Protestant Dutch Church, it adopted the name Reformed Church in America in 1867.

DUVERGIER DE HAURANNE, JEAN, see SAINT-CYRAN, ABBÉ DE.

DWIGHT, TIMOTHY (1752–1817), Congregationalist minister, eighth president of Yale. He was born at Northampton, Mass., the grandson of Jonathan *Edwards. D. graduated from Yale (1769) and entered the ministry 5 years later. He was a chaplain in the Continental Army, pastor at Greenfield Hill, Conn. (1783), and principal of a boys' school there. As president of Yale (1795–1817) he became the leader of the *Second Great Awakening, against the inroads of *deism, teaching and preaching the *New England theology of Edwards, in a revival of evangelical faith. His teaching was published posthumously as *Theology Explained and Defended* (5v., 1818–19). He also wrote the hymn "I Love Thy Kingdom Lord." See life by C. E. Cunningham (1942).

E

EASTER LITANY (Moravian), the liturgical service used by the Moravian Church at its Easter sunrise service. Believing that the Resurrection is the victorious climax of the Christian faith, the Moravians at the time of Count *Zinzendorf thought it appropriate to use Easter as a time to express their fundamental beliefs. Accordingly, they prepared a litany that, in lieu of a formal creed, became their most authoritative statement of faith. It dates from 1749 and was originally composed in German. It is used not as a formula to be subscribed to but as an act of worship. Trinitarian in emphasis, it explicitly acknowledges the activity of each person of the Godhead. It embodies many Pauline texts, the Lord's Prayer, and phrases from the ancient creeds. There is evidence of Lutheran influence, and some of its phrases are direct quotations from Luther's *Catechisms, especially in regard to man's absolute dependence upon God for salvation through Christ. Other emphases are the blood atonement, baptism, the Lord's Supper, eternal life, and fellowship between the Church on earth and the Church triumphant. The Litany begins in the church building and concludes at the cemetery, which Moravians commonly call God's Acre. See Schaff Creeds 3:799–806; W. H. Allen, *Who Are the Moravians?* (1966).

EASTON, BURTON SCOTT (1877–1950), biblical scholar. Born in Conn. and educated at the Univ. of Göttingen, the Univ. of Pa., and the Philadelphia Divinity School, he was ordained to the priesthood in the Protestant Episcopal Church in 1905. E. was professor of NT at Nashotah House in Nashotah, Wis. (1905–11), Western Theological Seminary in Chicago (1911–19), and the General Theological Seminary in New York City (1919–48). His major work, done in the field of NT criticism, is represented by *The Gospel according to St. Luke, A Critical and Exegetical Commentary* (1926); *The Gospel before the Gospels* (1928); *Christ in the Gospels* (1930); *The Purpose of Acts* (1936); *What Jesus Taught* (1938); and a *Commentary on the Pastoral Epistles* (1947). He was for a number of years associate editor of the *Anglican Theological Review* (for his biog. and bibliog. see v.35. pp. 147–161). He was chosen by the Library of Congress to catalogue the Migne edition of the Greek and Latin Fathers.

EBENEZER SOCIETY, the name under which the present *Amana Church Society was incorporated when it was first established near Buffalo, N.Y. (1842).

ECCLESIA (Lat. transliteration of Gr. *ekklēsia*). In secular use *ekklēsia* was a civic assembly, the word derived from *ekkalein*, to call out, summon. In biblical usage, e.g., in LXX, it referred to the assembly called by God out of the world to be his people. The NT writers, e.g., St. Paul, use *ekklēsia* to designate local assemblies of Christians, such as the Church of God gathered at Corinth (1 Cor 1.2). A more universal reference is plain, however, in St. Paul's Christological Epistles (Ephesians, Colossians) as he speaks of Christ as the head of his body which is the *ekklēsia*, the entire assembly of those who believe in him as Lord (Eph 1.22–23). The term *ekklēsia* is also employed in reference to the internal structure of the assembly (Mt 16.18; 18.17). Thus in the NT the word signifies the assembly of the people called and chosen by God, through and in Jesus Christ, in whom the ministry of the assembly exists. The *ekklēsia* is an assembly with an internal order of interdependence, for the sake of its world mission. The term, as well as its biblical meaning, is prominent in current ecumenical dicussion on the nature of the Church. See K. L. Schmidt, Kittel TD 3:501–536. *CHURCH (NT); *ECCLESIOLOGY.

ECCLESIASTICISM, a term normally used in a derogatory sense referring to a supposed excessive devotion to the Church as an institution, to the neglect of the Church's ministry. Those who stress the needs of the world and the obligation of the Church to give both spiritual enrichment and humanitarian service use the term in criticism of churchmen who seem to them concerned primarily with increasing the worldly power of the Church in dominating society. Ecclesiasticism implies a greater regard for an institution than for persons, specifically that institution through which the churchman gains his own power and honor. Critics of ecclesiasticism have interpreted the Church as a relatively unstructured community united by spiritual ties rather than by hierarchy and law, and their opposition to established or institutional Churches has often led them to separate and form new Churches, which in turn tend to develop the features of ecclesiastical organization. Ecclesiasticism also refers to undue concern for the externals of church life and practice as expressed in formalism and ritualism to the neglect of the inner life of love and faith. The term is also used in reference to an emphasis on the role of the Church in salvation and therefore tends to be associated with *sacerdotalism and *sacramentalism; in this sense it is sometimes used in the polemics of low churchmen against high churchmen.

ECCLESIOLOGICAL SIGNIFICANCE of the World Council of Churches, a statement of the Central Committee of the World Council of Churches (WCC), meeting July 9–15, 1950, in Toronto, commended for "study and comment in the churches." This title became the subtitle in the published text of the statement, "The Church, the Churches, and the WCC." Designed to clarify the WCC's view of its own nature and to correct some misinterpretations, it denied that the WCC is a super-church or that it is to be identified with the *Una Sancta*, stating that a member Church is not required to view all conceptions of the Church as equally valid. "Membership does not imply that each Church must regard the other member Churches as Churches in the true and full sense of the word." For the text and discussion concerning it, see *Minutes and Reports of the Third Meeting of the Central Committee.*

ECCLESIOLOGY, the branch of theology that assembles, analyzes, systematically correlates, and proposes what is to be found in the sources of revelation with regard to the Church.

New Testament and Church Fathers. Although ecclesiology did not appear as a distinct branch of theology until the Reformation, reflections on the nature of the Church are to be found in the NT and the earliest patristic traditions. The Pauline doctrine of the mystical body of Christ, e.g., exposes a definite theological insight into the nature of salvation and the communal relationship established thereby. Among the earliest Church Fathers (Clement of Rome, Polycarp, Ignatius of Antioch), the Church was seen as the new Israel, composed of the divinely chosen members of Christ. The distinction between the Church as visible and invisible was not yet used. Irenaeus speaks of the Church as the great body of Christ in which the Spirit works and ensures its key characteristics, esp. its possession of the truth. Clement of Alexandria and Origen stress the universal reality of the Church as the gathering of all the elect ruled by the Word, even those not present in the visible society of believers. Another thought occurs in Cyprian: the Church is an indivisible visible unity, universal but gathered around the local bishop, with whom the believer must maintain dogmatic and eucharistic solidarity. The doctrine of the Eastern Church, esp. after the Council of Nicaea, was contained within its Christology, that union in the life of Christ binds all Christians together. Augustine of Hippo played an important role in the development of ecclesiology. He used the Pauline image of the

Church as the mystical body of Christ and underlined the significance of its unity of belief and charity. Augustine also distinguished between the Church's perfect essence and its imperfect embodiment. It is perfect in essence because constituted by Christ, who establishes its holy people; it is imperfect in embodiment insofar as it is a visible congregation of sinners.

The Scholastic Period. The basic insights of the Fathers continued into the scholastic period, in which the Church was viewed as a union, accomplished through the Spirit's gift of love, between God and man. This union or life of grace, which incorporates itself in the Church, is seen as social, i.e., it establishes a lateral communion among believers as well as a relationship to the Trinity. This lateral communion is so significant that separation from the pope, as the vicar of Christ, is a schismatic separation from Christ himself. However, the medieval canonists (James of Viterbo, Giles of Rome, John of Paris) introduced a considerably different point of view. They stressed the legal and institutional structures of the Church, minimized its communal aspects in favor of the hierarchical, and pressed for a kind of papal theocracy.

Roman Catholic Ecclesiology in the Post-Reformation Period. As a consequence of the Reformation the attention of RC theologians began to focus almost exclusively on the visible aspects of the Church. Robert Bellarmine in particular championed the Church as the kingdom of God on earth—a kingdom, however, which emphasized the qualities of a sovereign state rather than those of the biblical kingdom of God. For the next 3 centuries, this was the dominant ecclesiology. At the time of Vatican I, the majority of bishops refused to call the Church the mystical body because that term was too vague and might appear to favor the notion of an invisible Church. Polemical considerations limited their view of ecclesiology to what was contained in the customary treatises *De ecclesia* and in manuals of apologetics. A new attitude began to emerge during the 19th century. J. A. *Möhler at the Univ. of Tü-

bingen rejected the juridic ecclesiology of an institutionalized Church and affirmed a community of believers brought together in love by the Spirit, a community that all ecclesiastical office was designed to serve. M. Scheeben sought to arrive at an adequate concept of the Church through a synthesis of its juridic and pneumatic aspects. Accordingly, the Church is seen as a mystery in its very being, organization, and activity. It is a work not of man, but of God. The Church is like Christ, whose visible human reality did not totally express the depths of his divine being. This ecclesiological synthesis of the juridic and spiritual, continued into contemporary theology by K. Adam, H. de Lubac, É. Mersch, and S. Tromp. formed the basis for Pius XII's encyclical *Mystici corporis* (1943). The encyclical denies an asocial concept of grace as well as any dichotomy between the visible Roman Catholic Church and the mystical body of Christ on earth. Vatican II's *Dogmatic Constitution on the Church* advances this basic approach and incorporates several other theological developments. The Church is presented as the pilgrim people of God, already established as a community by faith and baptism. The dignity and function of the laity are stressed, as well as the collegial relationship between the pope and the bishops of the world.

Ecclesiology in the Protestant Tradition. Protestantism revolted substantially against the hierarchical, juridical view of the Church that had been developed by the medieval canonists. It saw the Church as an invisible society solely dependent upon Christ, its unique mediator. The concept of hierarchical authority was repudiated and the *priesthood of all believers was affirmed in such a way as to deny any power of *orders beyond that bestowed by baptism. One consequence of this position was that it retarded the development of an ecclesiology properly so called. The insights into Christianity within the Protestant tradition do not contribute to a consideration of the Church apart from the broader issues of soteriology. The refusal to acknowledge any intermediary between God and man predisposes Protestant theology to view church structures and organization as the product of human enterprise, necessary only for good order in preaching the word and distributing the sacrament. The reality of "Church" is, of course, recognized in Protestantism, but the Church is seen as the fellowship in which all the Christians of a place are united in their life and worship. As such, the Church stands in the same relationship to God as redeemed man. Its holiness is that of the pardoned sinner; its glory is derived totally from Christ's saving action. The Church is not an institution, but a brotherhood, not divinely determined to a particular type of polity or episcopal tradition. It is a community of persons seeking the Spirit's guidance to forge those forms through which the word may be effectively proclaimed. This word alone has authority. The cardinal principle of Protestant ecclesiology is, in K. *Barth's terminology, actualism; the worship community is entirely under the influence of an always new action of the Lord, who is not limited to specific sacramental rites. The essential nature of the Church stands in antithesis to all law. (See S. Jàki, *Les Tendances nouvelles de l'ecclésiologie* (1957); H. Küng, *The Church* (tr. R. and R. Ockenden, 1967); G. Weigel, "Catholic Ecclesiology in Our Time," in *Christianity Divided* (ed. D. Callahan et al., 1961).

ECK, JOHANN (1486–1543), German theologian, RC opponent of Luther. He was born Johann Maier at Eck in Swabia, and as a student in 1505 took the surname Eckius, or Eccius. He studied law, philosophy, and theology at Heidelberg, Tübingen, Cologne, and Freiburg and was ordained at Strassburg in 1508. Professor of theology at Ingolstadt (1510–43), he also served as dean, pro-rector, and rector. Friendly at first to Luther, he perceived in the *Ninety-Five Theses the revolutionary character of Luther's position. His annotations on 30 of the theses, which he marked with an obelisk, were circulated (1518) as *Obelischi;* Luther answered with *Asterisci.* The famous *Disputation of Leipzig (1519) began with E. bet-

tering *Karlstadt in debate; when Luther himself became the disputant, E.'s tactics brought out the Reformer's attack on the doctrinal authority of Rome; it was a decisive stage in Luther's break with the old Church. E. went to Rome, where he was charged with publishing in Germany the bull excommunicating Luther, *Exsurge Domine* (1520), which he had helped to draft. He also was a coauthor of the *Confutatio,* the RC reply to the *Augsburg Confession (1530), and was generally regarded as the chief RC spokesman against the doctrine of the Reformers. His more than 100 works, most of them in Latin, include *Enchiridion locorum communium adversus Lutheranos* (1525), which went into 90 editions. See R. Fife, *Revolt of Martin Luther* (1957), 327–394.

ECKHART, MEISTER (*c.*1260–1327 or 1328), Dominican theologian and mystic. A native of Thuringia, E. became a Dominican at Erfurt, was at Paris in 1277 studying the arts, and before 1280 began to study theology at Cologne. At Paris during 1293–94 he commented on the Sentences of Peter Lombard. He held office as prior of Erfurt (1294–*c.*1300), and as vicar provincial of Thuringia (1294–98). At this time he published the ascetical instructions he had given to the young friars at Erfurt as *Reden der Unterscheidung.* He graduated as master of theology and lectured as regent at Paris (1302–03). He served (1303–11) as provincial of the Dominican province of Saxony and was appointed (1307) vicar general of the province of Bohemia. He held (1311–13) a second regency in theology at Paris. His *Quaestiones Parisienses* and commentaries on the Scriptures derive from his two regencies. He lectured (1313–22) in theology at Strassburg, where he became active as a preacher and spiritual director. He also served as vicar of the Dominican nuns in Alsace and Switzerland. At Strassburg he wrote two German works, *Das Buch der göttlichen Tröstung* and *Von dem edeln Menschen* (together called the *Liber benedictus*), and began an encyclopedic *Opus *tripartitum* that would have dealt with a wide range of philosophical, theological, and biblical subjects.

Eckhart ran into serious difficulties about his doctrine when the Abp. of Cologne initiated a process against him, based on two sets of propositions extracted chiefly from his sermons. Eckhart defended himself vigorously, esp. in a "Justificative Report," and contested the jurisdiction of the Cologne tribunal. Submitting in advance to the ultimate decision and protesting his faith, he appealed to the Pope, Jan. 1327. Hoping to defend himself personally, he set out for Avignon, but died before the case was concluded. On Mar. 27, 1328, John XXII condemned 28 of his propositions according to their obvious sense: 17 as heretical or erroneous, and 11 as unobjectionable if properly explained. Eckhart was not a voluntary heretic. His difficulties were caused by the abstruse nature of the matter he dealt with, his not-always-careful phraseology, his use of a developing vernacular, and his clash with the Franciscans and the partisans of Louis of Bavaria. He also suffered from the suspicions directed toward various heterodox groups. The Cologne and Avignon processes can be criticized for not checking propositions taken from Eckhart's sermons against his formal writings. Yet it is hard to defend the condemned propositions, and nearly all of them occur in his writings.

Eckhart drew his teaching from many sources as well as from his own experience. His mysticism, speculative in character, was trinitarian and transcendental. He taught the absolute transcendence and unknowability of God, and total detachment in order to find the unity and image of God. He sought to verbalize the interior spiritual process by which a person, through a radical self-stripping, achieves union with God in the inmost depth of the soul. Though Eckhart's works were seldom copied after his condemnation, his teaching survived indirectly through such writers as John Tauler, Henry Suso, Jan van Ruysbroeck, and others in Germany, Switzerland, and the Low Countries. Editions: *Die deutschen*

und lateinische Werke (ed. Deutsche Forschungsgemeinschaft, 1936); Latin works (ed. J. Koch et al., v.1–4, 1936–61; v.5–6, in progress 1969); German works (ed. J. Quint, v.1, 1936–58; v.5, 1954–63; v. 2–4, in progress 1969); *M. E.: An Introduction to the Study of His Works with an Anthology of His Sermons* (ed. and tr. J. M. Clark, 1957); *M. E., Selected Treatises and Sermons . . . from Latin and German* (ed. and tr. J. M. Clark and J. V. Skinner, 1958); *M. E.: A Modern Translation* (ed. and tr. R. B. Blakney, 1941; pa., 1957). See J. M. Clark, *Great German Mystics* (1949); J. Ancelet-Hustache, *M. E. and the Rhineland Mystics* (tr. H. Graef, pa., 1958).

ECUMENICAL COUNCILS (Gr. *oikoumenē*, the whole inhabited world), councils that represent the whole Church in doctrinal or disciplinary matters of common concern. The dogmatic Constitution on the Church *Lumen Gentium*, issued by Vatican Council II, says, "A council is never ecumenical unless it is confirmed or at least accepted as such by the successor of Peter. It is the prerogative of the Roman Pontiff to convoke these councils, to preside over them, and to confirm them" (Vat II ConstCh 22). Papal confirmation may be *post factum*, because there have been ecumenical councils not convoked by the Pope (e.g., Nicaea) and not presided over by him (e.g., Constance). Although there is no official listing of ecumenical councils, all Churches in the East and West recognize seven: Nicaea (A.D. 325); Constantinople I (381); Ephesus (431); Chalcedon (451); Constantinople II (553); Constantinople III (680–681); and Nicaea II (787). Contemporary RC authors generally list another 14: Constantinople IV (869–870); Lateran I (1123); Lateran II (1139); Lateran III (1179); Lateran IV (1215); Lyons I (1245); Lyons II (1274); Vienne (1311–12); Constance (1414–18); Ferrara-Florence (1438–39); Lateran V (1512–17); Trent (1545–63); Vatican I (1869–70); and Vatican II (1962–66). This list, exclusive of the two Vatican councils, seems to have been popularized by Caesar

*Baronius late in the 16th century. Even RC scholars have serious reservations about the ecumenicity of some: Constantinople IV was first counted as ecumenical by the canonists of Pope Gregory VII (1073–85). The first three Lateran councils (1123, 1139 and 1179) are more properly called "general councils"; they came to be considered ecumenical only in the late Middle Ages, even though their organizers did not recognize them as such.

Historians and canonists have until recently said more about ecumenical councils than theologians. With the modern evolution of ecclesiology, dogmatic questions about the nature of ecumenical councils have attracted attention. According to Hans Küng, the Church itself is an ecumenical council of divine convocation; the historical councils, of human convocation, are representations of the Church. As a corollary, Küng also questions the exclusively episcopal make-up of modern councils. Another view, enunciated by Joseph Ratzinger, Hubert Jedin, and others, holds that the council represents only one particular aspect of the Church. Its structure is determined more by the constitution of the episcopal college than by the membership of the Church. Karl Rahner attempts to synthesize the views of Küng and Ratzinger. In summary—and this holds for Protestant views as well—it seems that any conciliar theory is determined by an ecclesiology. See F. Dvornik, *Ecumenical Councils* (1961); H. Jedin, *Ecumenical Councils of the Catholic Church* (1959); G. Baum, "Nature of Ecumenical Councils," *The Ecumenist* 1 (Oct., 1962), 4–6.

ECUMENICAL CREEDS, *creeds so called because of universal or widespread acceptance or use. The *Nicene, *Athanasian, and *Apostles' Creeds have received this designation. Only the Nicene (Niceno-Constantinopolitan) Creed can be called ecumenical in the full sense, since it has been professed and used liturgically in both East and West. The RC Church has employed the three creeds in teaching and liturgy. The Reformation Churches for the most part have accorded recognition to these creeds, but the Apostles' Creed has had widest use. The Lutheran Churches (in the *Formula of Concord) and the C of E (in the *Thirty-Nine Articles) have explicitly adopted the three as doctrinal standards; the Protestant Episcopal Church omitted the Athanasian Creed from its adaptation of the Articles and the Book of Common Prayer. Those who designate these creeds as ecumenical regard them as a possible basis for Christian unity. The epithet "ecumenical," however, is not acceptable to all, not even to some who acknowledge the creeds in question.

ECUMENICAL MOVEMENT, the process toward a greater expression of unity and cooperation among all Christians. "The 'ecumenical movement' means those activities and enterprises which, according to various needs of the Church and opportune occasions, are started and organized for the fostering of unity among Christians" (Vat II Ecum 4). By extension the phrase is also applied to efforts toward greater understanding and cooperation between Christians and persons of other religions.

Development. The 1910 *Edinburgh Conference is generally taken to mark the beginning of the movement in its modern form. At this conference representatives of 159 missionary societies agreed that the historically rooted denominational divisions of Europe and N America were generally irrelevant to the missionary task and that competitive *denominationalism was harmful. Remote antecedents of the movement include attempts to heal the schism between East and West, as in the Councils of Lyons (1274) and Florence (1439), and various unity efforts following the Reformation. In the 19th cent., prior to Edinburgh, many unity efforts had been made. In 1846 the *Evangelical Alliance was formed in London. Ecumenical cooperation in mission work had existed since the organization of the *London Missionary Society (1795). Some confessional bodies had created worldwide organizations: Lambeth Conference (1867), Alliance of Reformed Churches (1875), World Methodist Council (1891), Baptist World Alliance (1905), and others. Organizations such as the YMCA (1844) provided for ecumenical cooperation in particular projects.

Ecumenical, from the Greek *oikoumenē*, literally has a geographical reference: that which pertains to the whole inhabited world. Thus, church councils regarded as authoritative for the whole world (beginning with Nicaea I in 325) were called ecumenical councils. During World Wars I and II ecumenical leaders emphasized this aspect in the desire to transcend the national divisions of wartime. Also they have emphasized that the ecumenical nature of the Church requires a missionary concern for the whole world. Since, however, Christians of different nations sometimes have such differences that they are not in communion with each other and since Christians within a particular nation are often divided among various denominations, the movement has involved interconfessional as well as international relationships. Following Edinburgh the movement developed along three lines, marked particularly by international conferences. The *Life and Work movement, seeking practical cooperation of the Churches for a stronger witness in the secular order, held the Stockholm (1925) and Oxford (1937) Conferences. The slogan for Life and Work was "doctrine divides, service unites." The expression "ecumenical movement" is thought to have been first used by A. Deissmann in an address concluding the Stockholm Conference. Apb. N. *Söderblom was a key leader in this movement. A second line of development was the *Faith and Order movement, designed to discuss the doctrinal divisions that Life and Work minimized. Faith and Order met at the Lausanne (1927) and Edinburgh (1937) Conferences; Bp. C. H. *Brent was a leader in this movement. Participants in the two movements, often the same persons, came to feel that the two could not properly be separated. At the Oxford and Edinburgh Conferences

(1937) plans were laid that led to merger, and to formation of the World Council of Churches (WCC) at the Amsterdam Assembly (1948). A third line of development was through the *International Missionary Council (IMC), organized in 1921, which sponsored a series of ecumenical conferences on missions: Jerusalem (1928), Madras (1938), Whitby (1947), Willingen (1952), and Accra (1957). In 1961 the IMC merged with the WCC at the New Delhi Assembly, bringing together two major concerns of the ecumenical movement: unity of all Churches of the world and mission to all people of the world. While this development was taking place on the international level, corresponding ecumenical efforts were made on national, regional, and local levels. Biblical and theological scholarship was becoming more ecumenical, and the Christian youth movement was developing along ecumenical lines. Also, members of different confessions were brought together by their common efforts to resist Nazism and to build a better world order.

Roman Catholic Participation. The RC Church did not participate in the ecumenical movement in the beginning, although some of its members worked along similar lines. Catholics in Germany participated in Una Sancta following World War I; the Malines Conversations between Roman Catholics and Anglicans were held (1921–26), and in the U.S. Fr. Paul (Lewis T. Wattson) of the Society of the Atonement founded the Week of Prayer for Christian Unity. After the Stockholm and Lausanne Conferences, however, Pius XI declared in 1928, "The Apostolic See can by no means take part in these assemblies nor is it in any way lawful for Catholics to give such enterprises their encouragement and support. If they did so, they would be giving countenance to a false Christianity quite alien to the one Church of Christ" (*Mortalium Animos*). Catholics were invited to attend the 1948 Amsterdam Assembly, but they were forbidden by the Holy Office (now Congregation for the Doctrine of the Faith) in the Monitum *Cum compertum*, issued June 5, 1948. In 1949, however, the Holy

Office issued the Instruction *Ecclesia Catholica,* which gave recognition to the movement and set guidelines for Catholic participation under certain restricted conditions. The way for greater Catholic participation was opened with the establishment by Fr. J. G. M. Willebrands in 1952 of the Catholic Conference for Ecumenical Problems, and involvement progressed rapidly during the pontificate of John XXIII. When Pope John called for an ecumenical council, he took account of both senses of the term. It was an ecumenical council of the RC Church in that it was constituted by the hierarchy from all parts of the world, but observers from other Churches were invited to attend, giving it also a character to some degree ecumenical in the interconfessional sense, though only Catholics were full participants. Also, under Pope John RC observers first attended a WCC assembly (New Delhi, 1961). Through the efforts of John XXIII and Paul VI and the actions of Vatican II (1962–65) the ecumenical movement received full RC acceptance. The Secretariat for Promoting Christian Unity was established in 1960 and prepared the Decree on Ecumenism adopted by Vatican Council II in 1964. The decree stated, "This sacred Synod, therefore, exhorts all the Catholic faithful to recognize the signs of the times and to participate skillfully in the work of ecumenism" (4). It also acknowledged that divisions between Catholics and non-Catholics have been caused by faults on both sides. While in Rome for the Council, the bps. of the U.S. established a Commission for Ecumenical Affairs, which has its headquarters in Washington, D.C.

Ecumenical Leadership. Leaders of the ecumenical movement have sought to overcome the divisions caused by doctrinal differences without falling into *indifferentism. They have sought doctrinal unity through emphasis on biblical categories and terminology and through *interfaith dialogue to overcome misunderstandings. They have also sought to develop a greater sense of unity through cooperative work in missions, evangelism, and humanitarian service. The ecumenical movement as expressed in the WCC has involved most of the Protestant and Orthodox Churches of the world, though some conservative groups have chosen not to participate. These have feared that participation would result in compromise of doctrinal conviction and that the movement might result in a centralized, authoritarian organization that would endanger freedom. In the U.S. the Southern Baptist Convention, the Lutheran Church—Missouri Synod, and several smaller conservative bodies have refused to participate. Liberal groups, such as Unitarians, have also remained outside the WCC, because they do not meet its membership requirement of belief in Jesus Christ as God and Savior. Among conservatives the movement has found some expression apart from the WCC. These conservatives, while approving ecumenical cooperation, have objected to the WCC because it includes some groups they consider unorthodox and because they object to positions taken by WCC leadership on various social questions. Some conservatives support ecumenical activity that involves closer cooperation with other conservatives but with no goal of organic union. Some favor ecumenical cooperation with all Christians on such limited projects as evangelistic campaigns and Bible distribution. Some conservatives have organized the World Evangelical Fellowship (1951); the *International Council of Christian Churches has been organized (1948) under the leadership of Carl McIntire.

The ecumenical movement has been expressed also in a number of denominational mergers, including the United Church of Canada (1925), the Church of South India (1947), and in the U.S. the United Church of Christ (1957) and the United Methodist Church (1968). In 1960 E. C. Blake, then stated clerk of the United Presbyterian Church and later general secretary of the WCC, proposed a merger of certain of the main Churches of U.S. Protestantism; this proposal led to the *Consultation on Church Union which, if successful, would mean a historic step toward Christian unity.

Motivation. The ecumenical movement has been motivated in part by the increasing difficulties felt by the Churches in witnessing to the modern world. It is believed that a united Church would make a stronger impact, witnessing to the power of Christ to overcome the divisions among men and bringing a unity of effort to bear on the problems involved in preaching the gospel under modern conditions. The movement has given special emphasis to the words of Jesus' prayer: "that they may all be one; even as thou, Father, art in me, and I in thee, that they also may be in us, so that the world may believe that thou hast sent me" (Jn 17.21). The movement has recognized that Christian divisions are caused not only by doctrinal disagreement but also by differences of nationality, race, culture, social class, and institutional loyalty. To overcome these factors it stresses fraternal charity, sometimes called the ecumenical spirit. Leaders of the ecumenical movement have also stressed the importance of Church renewal, of *aggiornamento*. They have taught that the need of the Church is not merely for organizational unity but for an inward renewal of the life of all Churches that would make them more effective in their service of Christ. The goal is for each Church to gain greater unity with Christ and thereby to grow toward greater unity with other Churches.

See G. Baum, *Catholic Quest for Christian Unity* (1965); G. K. Bell, ed., *Documents on Christian Unity* (4v., 1924–58); R. M. Brown, *Ecumenical Revolution* (1967); B. Leeming, *Vatican Council and Christian Unity* (1966); J. Mackay, *Ecumenics* (1964); J. T. McNeill, *Unitive Protestantism* (1930); R. Rouse and S. C. Neill, eds., *History of the Ecumenical Movement* (1967); Reports of WCC Assemblies, W. A. Visser 't Hooft, ed.; Decree on Ecumenism in W. M. Abbott, ed., *Documents of Vatican II* (1966).

ECUMENISM, concern for the realization of greater unity among Christians. By extension the term is sometimes used in reference to closer relationships between Christians and persons of other religions. It is distinguished from *evangelism and *proselytism in which one communion tries to win converts from another. In the 20th cent. the historic interest of Christians in unity has received renewed impetus, as is seen in the ecumenical movement leading to such developments as the World Council of Churches and the unity efforts of Vatican Council II. Ecumenism stresses Jesus' prayer: "that they may all be one; even as thou, Father, art in me, and I in thee, that they also may be in us, so that the world may believe that thou hast sent me" (Jn 17.21), as well as other biblical passages that speak of the unity of Christians in the Church. It holds that unity is given by Christ and therefore is intrinsic to a true expression of the Christian faith; it is also motivated by the desire to bring a more effective witness to the world ("that the world may believe"). The Churches have felt increasing difficulty in reaching the modern world, and it is thought that a united Church would better witness to the power of Christ to overcome divisions among men, and that a pooling of resources would enable Christians to make a greater impact. Opponents of ecumenism, however, warn of the danger of weakening the Christian message through doctrinal compromise.

Some ecumenists have sought unity on the basis of a lowest common denominator of belief, the few beliefs upon which everyone could now agree. The principal leaders of the movement hold that the distinctives of the different Churches should not be disregarded; they do not hold that unity requires uniformity in thought and church life; instead they seek, through cooperative activity and *interfaith dialogue, to develop deeper mutual understanding and to enable each tradition to contribute its distinctive values to the total Christian community. Ecumenism demands not a belief that one system of doctrine or *church order is as valid as another but a willingness on the part of all Churches to recognize that they do not have a monopoly upon truth and virtue, that other Churches are not totally in error and sin. Since divisions among Christians are due not only to doctrinal differences but also to national, cultural, racial, and personal antagonisms, ecumenism calls for the spirit of brotherly love in removing these sources of division.

Ecumenism is generally associated with church renewal, or *aggiornamento.* Organizational unity is considered inadequate unless Christians are united with Christ; conversely it is felt that as Christians draw closer to Christ, they will draw closer to each other. Ecumenism, therefore, is not a search for some scheme upon which all may compromise, but a mutual search for the form of church life which will best express the will of Christ. See bibliog. for Ecumenical Movement.

EDDY, MARY BAKER (1821–1910), founder of the *Church of Christ, Scientist. She was a chronic invalid, unhappily married and separated from her husband, when in 1862 she first became acquainted with the doctrines of Phineas *Quimby, a Maine faith healer. By 1866 she had developed her own faith-healing system and in 1875 published *Science and Health.* She taught that Christian Science is the wisdom of the Eternal Mind, revealed through Jesus Christ, who taught the power of Mind (Truth, God) to overcome illusions of sin, sickness, and death. In 1876 she formed the Christian Science Association, chartered in 1879 as the Church of Christ, Scientist. Her *Journal of Christian Science* (began 1883) contributed to the growth of her following. After 1889 Mrs. Eddy lived in seclusion in Concord, N.H., but continued to direct Christian Science and to revise and enlarge her book. In 1892 she formed the First Church of Christ, Scientist, in Boston, giving the Mother Church authority over the entire movement. Alert to the end, she established the *Christian Science Monitor* in 1906, primarily to meet attacks on her movement in *McClure's Magazine* and other popular journals. Whether wholly original or not, Mrs. Eddy's system brought consolation to many and became a worldwide religion within her lifetime. See E. F. Dakin, *Mrs. Eddy* (1930); N. Beasley, *The Cross and the Crown* (1942).

EDICT OF NANTES, an act of toleration for the French *Huguenots; the best known of the numerous treaties passed during the *Wars of Religion, but not the most remarkable. Issued by Henry IV on April 13, 1598, it was an intricate compendium of older documents; it lacked the clarity of the treaty of Beaulieu ("Peace of Monsieur," 1576). The Edict comprised the Edict proper consisting of 92 articles; 56 secret and private articles; 2 commissions (*brevets*) bearing on guarantees given to the Huguenots; and additional secret articles. It was predominantly concerned with judicial guarantees. It stipulated freedom of conscience but only limited freedom of worship: the Huguenot nobility was allowed to have *Reformed worship, as were the citizens of some 200 towns. It granted civil equality; promised subsidies for the maintenance of Huguenot pastors, schools, and troops; and guaranteed the fair administration of justice (special chambers to include one Huguenot judge each), the maintenance of garrisons for another 8 years, and the right to hold synods and provincial political councils. Although the Edict initiated a period of peace, it did not solve the underlying religious problems: it was a temporary measure that was defective because it was too rigid and failed to accommodate future changes. After the death of Henry IV (1610) the Huguenots were increasingly persecuted; by the Edict of Alais in 1629 they lost all civil rights, although nominally retaining religious freedom. This also was taken away when Louis XIV revoked the Edict of Nantes in 1685. See bibliog. for Huguenots.

EDICT OF RESTITUTION (1629), a decree of the Holy Roman Emperor, Ferdinand II, aimed at strengthening Hapsburg power and restoring Catholic supremacy. At a high point of imperial fortunes during the Thirty Years' War, the Emperor was emboldened to issue this edict without consultation of the Imperial Diet. It called for restitution of all church properties taken over since the Convention of Passau (1552); outlawed all Protestants except Lutherans of the Augsburg Confession and reinstated the principle *cuius regio eius religio*. Relentless enforcement displaced thousands of persons from their homes. The edict was the occasion for the decisive intervention the next year of *Gustavus II Adolphus on the Protestant side.

EDINBURGH CONFERENCES, two meetings held in Edinburgh that had great bearing on the *ecumenical movement: (1) that held in 1910, attended by 1,200 delegates of many denominations, at which the International Missionary Council was formed; (2) the second world conference of the *Faith and Order movement, held at Edinburgh, Aug. 3–18, 1937. The subjects considered were grace, the Church and the word of God, the communion of saints, the ministry of the Church and sacraments, and the unity of the Church in life and worship. Like the Lausanne Conference, this one failed to elicit any agreement on the number of sacraments or on the nature and transmission of the Church's ministry. The communion of saints was defined as representing the Church, the Body of Christ, in heaven and on earth. The conference agreed on a statement on grace (never approved, however, by the Churches represented). Grace was viewed as the expression of the loving-kindness of God toward man, manifested in the Church through the word and the sacraments; justification and sanctification were seen as inseparable aspects of grace, which, however, did not override human responsibility, but required a response by faith. The Conference, coming immediately after the Oxford Conference of the *Life and Work movement, voted a merger of the two movements in a proposed *World Council of Churches. See

L. Hodgson, ed., *Second World Conference on Faith and Order* (1938).

EDWARD VI (1537-53), KING OF ENGLAND from 1547. Son of *Henry VIII and Jane Seymour, the boy was little more than 9 years old when he ascended the throne. His disposition was studious, his learning precocious. His religious feelings were intense, and his persuasions were those of his favorite preacher, Hugh *Latimer. His policies were steered in a Calvinist direction by an Erastian government, at first by Protector Somerset and later by Northumberland, who shrugged off the contention of the Catholic leaders that the royal supremacy should be in abeyance. J. *Knox and continental Reformers, notably M. *Bucer, *Peter Martyr Vermigli, and B. *Ochino, flocked in, and the King was hailed as the English Josiah. During his short reign the progress of the Reformation was marked by the imposition of the first *Book of Common Prayer (1549); a new *Anglican Ordinal (1550); a more Calvinist revision of the BCP (1552); and by the *Forty-Two Articles of Religion (1553). He showed signs of Tudor obstinacy and seemed indifferent to natural affection, laconically assenting to the execution of his uncles and priggishly promoting the persecution of his sister, Mary; yet when he died, of a rapid consumption, his will disclosed how completely he had been manipulated by the ambition of the Dudleys. See J. D. Martin, *Earlier Tudors* (1925); Hughes RE.

EDWARDINE ARTICLES, alternate name for the *Forty-Two Articles promulgated for the Church of England in 1533 during the reign of Edward VI.

EDWARDS, JONATHAN (1703–58), eminent American Congregationalist theologian and preacher in the *Great Awakening. Born at East Windsor, Conn., E. entered Yale in 1716, graduating in 1720. His boyhood interest in matters scientific and spiritual flourished at Yale under the stimulus of reading Isaac Newton and John Locke. E.'s life and thought were dominated by a crucial religious experience by which he came to a "delightful conviction" of the sovereign majesty, power, and beauty of God. He was to rehearse this theme severely in the sermons of the Great Awakening period. In a gentler vein he cast the same conviction into a virtually neoplatonic form in his late treatises. After briefly holding a pastorate in a Presbyterian church in New York (1722), he returned to Yale as a tutor (1724). He married Sarah Pierrepont, of New Haven, in 1727, the year he was called to be the associate pastor of the Northampton, Mass., church with his maternal grandfather, Solomon Stoddard, whom he succeeded 2 years later. His evangelical preaching led to vigorous revivals in his parish and elsewhere in New England. Misunderstandings with his church members concerning the qualifications of those presenting themselves for church membership brought on a bitter controversy that led to his dismissal in 1750. The following year, burdened with a large family and virtually disgraced, he accepted the frontier mission post at Stockbridge, Massachusetts. He remained there until Jan., 1758, when he removed to Princeton to become president of the College of New Jersey (now Princeton University), but he died of a smallpox inoculation on March 22.

As an evangelist E.'s reputation rests on the sermons preached during the Great Awakening, many of which detailed the horrors of divine punishment as well as the glories of salvation. As a philosopher and theologian his fame rests upon a series of treatises written in his Stockbridge days. *Concerning the Religious Affections* (1746) is a discriminating examination of true and false emotions and provides his most sustained defense of the role of genuine religious affections in the Great Awakening. His acute attack upon *Arminianism concerning freedom of the will is contained in his treatise *A Careful and Strict Enquiry into . . . Freedom of Will* (1754), wherein he argues logically against freedom of choice and defends a causality of will exempt from

compulsion. *The Great Christian Doctrine of Original Sin* (1758) propounds the theory that all men unfailingly fall into sin. Both treatises fit well within the framework of Calvinism. Among his posthumous writings, *The Nature of True Virtue* expands his early notes on excellence, where true virtue is interpreted as the cordial and benevolent consent of intelligent beings with Ultimate Being or Being in General. His essentially neoplatonic vision of reality is expressed in *The End for Which God Created the World.* In that work the purpose of divine creation is interpreted as the emanation of the divine being for its own sake. E.'s influence was to continue in the thought of Joseph Bellamy and Samuel Hopkins, who set in motion the theological movement known as the *New England theology. E.'s thought exhibits many contrasts. He consciously defended the *Five Points of Calvinism, yet preached also the need and value of personal religious experience in conversion. He was as biblical as any Puritan, yet steeped in the philosophy of the *Enlightenment. He was an evangelical preacher, but also a profound speculative theologian. The intense study of his writings begun in the 1950s has not yet yielded a complete or definitive evaluation. Modern editions of E.'s works include: P. Ramsey, ed., *Freedom of the Will* (1957); J. E. Smith, ed., *Religious Affections* (1959); E. Williams and E. Parsons, eds., *Works* (10v., 1847; repr. 1968); D. Brainerd, ed., *J. E.: His Life and Diary* (1968). A critical edition from original manuscripts is in process, under the editorship of T. A. Schafer. See D. J. Elwood, *Philosophical Theology of J. E.* (1960); O. E. Winslow, *J. E.* (1941); P. Miller, *J. E.* (1949); C. Cherry, *Theology of J. E.* (1966); S. E. Ahlstrom, ed., *Theology in America* (1967), 149–192.

EFFICACIOUS GRACE, see GRACE, EFFICACIOUS.

EIELSEN SYNOD, the first Norwegian Lutheran synod in the U.S., its constitution was written in 1846 by Elling Eielsen (1804–83), a Norwegian lay-preacher. *EVANGELICAL LUTHERAN CHURCH IN AMERICA (EIELSEN SYNOD).

ELDER, an Eng. tr., in preference to "priest," of the Gr. *presbuteros* and the Lat. equivalent *presbyter* to designate one who holds a certain office in a Church. The elder is esp., but not exclusively, characteristic of Presbyterianism. In the *Reformed Churches generally the ministry includes presbyters who preach and administer the sacraments (teaching elders) and presbyters who assist ministers of the Word in pastoral care and in the government of the Church (ruling elders). For the ruling elder, John *Calvin used the terms *senior, seigneur,* and *ancien;* he distinguished the elder as a second order from the ministers of the word and sacraments, whom he called variously bishops, presbyters, pastors, or ministers. Presbyterian use of elder ordinarily refers to the ruling elder. The elder is a layman, or in many Reformed Churches a laywoman, representing the people in the *church session and the *presbytery. Ordination to the office is by a minister, and for life, although in practice an elder may serve only for a term of years, then retire until reelected. In the Churches of God in North America (General Eldership) the term is used in much the same way. In Methodism the ministry is held to consist of the orders of deacon and elder, the second being the higher. A minister is elected elder by the Annual Conference, and is ordained by a bishop and other elders. The office is still thought to consist essentially in the power to administer the sacraments; while deacons and, in certain cases, lay preachers may exercise this power, only the elder can do so everywhere in the Church. In the Church of Jesus Christ of Latter-day Saints (Mormons) elder is the lowest of the order of the Melkisedek priesthood.

The term elder has also a more general use in Churches that do not accept the idea of a sacred ministry or ordination, and play down any distinction between clergy and laity. Elder or deacon then signifies anyone who officiates at worship or has a function in the governing of a Church. Such is the usage in the Christian Churches (Disciples of Christ).

ELECTION, in general, God's free choice of his creatures for a share in the redemptive graces; it is a biblical as well as a theological term. The OT history of Israel is the narration of its election by God, indicated by God's covenantal action by which he chose Israel from among many nations to be his own peculiar possesion (Dt 14.2). The signal proof of this election was the deliverance from Egypt. The prophets unfailingly preached that it was an election by grace; indeed, throughout the OT the emphasis is that this election is due not to any human merit or excellence but solely to the free love of God (Dt 7.7–10), and in return it calls for an offer of responsible obedience to God. Besides the choice of a nation, there was the election of individuals, e.g., Abraham and David, yet not as a personal prerogative, but to serve God and his people. In the NT the Church becomes the people of God chosen by grace (Rom 11.5), and as a new congregation elected and made holy in Christ, it is to mediate salvation to all men.

Theologically, election is related to *predestination, but both words are not to be taken as synonyms, though some early Fathers of the Church have used them interchangeably. Since the predestination of certain individuals to eternal salvation presupposes that God first wishes their salvation, theological speculation places the divine act of election prior to that of predestination (ThAq ST 1a, 23.4). Hence, election is that sovereign free act of God, prior to predestination, in which he resolves out of his love to offer an individual eternal salvation together with its concomitant graces and the aids requisite to attain this final glory, without doing away with man's personal decision and fidelity in this matter, but rather in granting these. In *Reformed theology, and esp. in Calvin's *Institutes of* the Christian Religion, election plays an eminent role. For Calvin, election is the divine choice—rooted in God's sovereignty —whereby he adopts some to salvation and denies it to others (3.21.1). Calvin conceived election as having two degrees: the first is a general election, as that of a total nation, but one that is not firm and effectual since some individuals within the collectivity may be rejected, e.g., Ishmael and Esau. The second is the firm, effectual, and irrevocable election of individuals whereby God not only offers salvation but by his irresistible grace so assigns it that the certainty of its effect is not in doubt (3.21.6–7). This election flows exclusively from the divine sovereignty, and is not dependent upon the foreknowledge God has of man's good works, or of his faith; man is chosen by God to be holy, he is not chosen because he wills to be holy (3.22.3). See J. Farrelly, *Predestination, Grace and Free Will* (1964); G. C. Berkouwer, *Divine Election* (1960). *PREDESTINATION.

ELIM MISSIONARY ASSEMBLIES, a Pentecostal body organized in 1947; its membership (1968), mostly in Pa. and N.Y., numbers about 4,000. The origins of the denomination include two Bible schools in N.Y., important in the history of Pentecostalism, and a ministerial fellowship that has given the denomination its missionary concentration. The body is fundamentalist in teaching; its polity is congregational. See J. T. Nichol, *Pentecostalism* (1966), 129–130.

ELIOT, JOHN (1604–90), Puritan preacher and "Apostle to the Indians." Born in Hertfordshire, Eng., and educated at Cambridge, in 1631 he migrated to New England, where he was pastor at Roxbury, Mass., for about 60 years. Besides serving as pastor, he was a missionary to Indian tribes of that area. Having learned the Algonquin language, he prepared a grammar, translated the Bible into that tongue, established a school to train native leaders, and organized his converts into 14 segregated Indian

towns. During King Philip's War, the "praying Indians" were scattered, and the number of towns was reduced to four, which gradually disappeared. Eliot was the author of several books, besides those in and about Indian languages: *The Christian Commonwealth* (1659); *Communion of Churches* (1665); and *The Harmony of the Gospels* (1678). With Thomas Weld and Richard Mather, he prepared *The Bay Psalm Book* of 1640. See O. E. Winslow, *J. E., "Apostle to the Indians"* (1968).

ELIZABETH I (1542–1603), QUEEN OF ENGLAND from 1558. This article is confined to the steps whereby E. made final the Church of England's break with Rome. During the reign of her half-sister Mary Tudor (1553–58), E. conformed at least outwardly to the old Catholic faith. Upon her accession, however, she was out of sympathy both with her RC subjects and with the radical Protestants who wished to place greater authority in the hands of the clergy. Her intent was to make the English sovereign and Parliament absolute in matter of doctrine and discipline. This she effected by two enactments of Parliament: the *Act of Supremacy (1559) and the *Act of Uniformity (1559). The former designated her the only "supreme governor . . . as well in all spiritual or ecclesiastical things or causes, as temporal." This title she preferred to that of supreme head of the Church used by Henry VIII, since by it she avoided offending Catholics, who looked on the pope as their chief, and the Puritans, who admitted only Christ as their head. E. moved completely to the side of the Protestants when her cousin Mary Stuart, Queen of Scotland, made herself leader of the Catholics in England and attempted to gain the English throne. As a result, Pius V in the bull *Regnans in excelsis* excommunicated and deposed E. in 1570. This act, however, really strengthened her position at home and abroad. The C of E came to be identified with English nationalism. In 1571 Parliament made it high treason to state that E. was a heretic and should be deposed. In the last decades of the century E. put through further legislation against Catholics. The worst parts of the penal codes were, however, dictated by new causes: the threat of foreign invasion and the remarkable success of missionary priests in England. During E.'s reign the C of E took on a form uniquely English. It retained much of Catholic tradition, though less than the Queen would have wished; but it subjected all things spiritual to the power of the realm. At the end of E.'s life only about 200,000 Catholics remained, along with a smaller number of stanch Puritans. Both groups could claim many martyrs; and succeeding monarchs inherited a host of religious problems. See H. J. Grimm, *Reformation Era* (1965), 464–479.

ELY, RICHARD THEODORE (1854–1943), social economist who influenced the *Social Gospel movement. Most of his professorial career was spent at the Univ. of Wisconsin. By his writings, e.g., *The Labor Movement in America* (1886) and *Social Aspects of Christianity* (1886), and by his association with the Church Social Union and the American Economic Association, E. promoted the theme that in Christian ethical teaching lies the solution to the problems of society. His ideas were accepted by many ministers, among them Washington *Gladden and Lyman *Abbott.

EMANCIPATION, CATHOLIC, see CATHOLIC EMANCIPATION.

EMBURY, PHILIP (1728–73), founder of Wesley Chapel, John Street, New York City, in 1768 (see METHODIST EPISCOPAL CHURCH). His parents were German Lutherans who had emigrated from the Palatinate to Ireland in 1709. He was converted under John *Wesley in 1752, becoming a local preacher, and immigrated to Colonial America in 1760. In 1766, inspired by his cousin Barbara Heck, who asserted that the immigrants, grown careless about religion,

would "all go to Hell together," E. began preaching in his own home. He formed a Methodist *society that was given impetus by an ardent Methodist Thomas *Webb. A carpenter himself, E. supervised the building of Wesley Chapel (now a Methodist Colonial Shrine) and dedicated it Oct. 30, 1768. With other German Methodists he went (1770) to Camden, near Troy, New York. There and at Ashgrove, N.Y., where he is buried, he established Methodist societies. See HistAmMeth 1:76–78; N. Bangs, *History of the Methodist Episcopal Church* (1839); 1:47–48; S. Seaman, *Annals of New York Methodism* (1892), 1–50.

EMERSON, RALPH WALDO (1803–82), American essayist and philosopher. The son of a Unitarian minister, E. studied at Harvard and prepared for the Unitarian ministry at Harvard Divinity School. After receiving approval to preach in 1826, he was ordained at the Second Church in Boston, which he served as minister until 1832. He resigned his ministry because he believed the observance of the Lord's Supper had no valid authority. He did, however, continue to preach. During a trip to Europe in 1833, he met S. T. Coleridge and Thomas Carlyle; he became a close friend of Carlyle. On his return he settled in Concord, Massachusetts. Thereafter he lectured on literature and philosophy, attaining eminence in American life. Among his many notable lectures were "The American Scholar," delivered before the Phi Beta Kappa Society at Cambridge in 1837, and "An Address Delivered before the Senior Class" of Harvard Divinity School in 1838. The latter address significantly modified the future of American Unitarianism through its influence on Theodore *Parker and others. Emerson's philosophy is inseparably related to transcendentalism as a religious idealism combining rationalism and intuitionism. An early work, *Essays* (1841), stressed the concept of the "Oversoul," portraying the immediate presence of God's spirit in nature and in man. Works: complete edition (ed. E. W. Emerson, 12v.,

1903–06); *Journals* (ed. E. W. Emerson and W. E. Forbes, 10v., 1909–14); *Letters* (ed. R. L. Rusk, 6v., 1939). See G. W. Cooke, *Bibliography of R. W. E.* (1900); F. O. Mathiessen, *American Renaissance* (1941); R. L. Rusk, *The Life of R. W. E.* (1949); S. E. Whicher, *Freedom and Fate* (1953); P. Miller, *Transcendentalists* (1950).

EMMANUEL HOLINESS CHURCH, a Pentecostal body organized in 1953 in Whiteville, N.C., by dissenters at the general conference of the Pentecostal Fire-Baptized Holiness Church who objected to certain matters of church discipline. The original group was joined by other dissidents, and by 1955 the body had 1,200 members, in 56 churches.

EMOTIONALISM, here understood as an excessive emphasis upon emotions in religion. With the rise of revivalism in the 18th cent., emotionalism became a controversial factor in mainstream American Protestantism. Earlier Puritans had stressed inward experience as a sign of regeneration, but this experience did not commonly include a loss of emotional control. The *Great Awakening, however, introduced a type of preaching that often induced anxiety, crying aloud, shouting in exultation, etc. Many ministers deplored such displays of feeling; e.g., Charles *Chauncy preached a sermon *Enthusiasm Described and Cautioned Against* (1742). Jonathan *Edwards discouraged visible manifestations of emotions, but in his *Treatise on the Religious Affections* (1746), he defended "feelings" as essential to religion. He asserted that a moving religious experience might cause bodily manifestations but also warned that such phenomena could be delusions of Satan. The early *camp meetings were marked by shouting, weeping, and peculiar physical behavior. The "new measures" of Charles G. *Finney tended to play on the emotions, but Finney disapproved of emotional exhibitions. Later in the 19th cent. the revival meetings of Dwight L. *Moody

and other professional evangelists were less demonstrative. Nevertheless, most revivalists used music, stories, and methods calculated to stir emotions to lead people to conversions. In the 20th cent. Billy *Sunday was criticized for his use of sensational methods; the revivals of Billy *Graham are much more moderate and controlled. Today there is little evidence of emotionalism in most Protestant services, but in *Pentecostalism *glossolalia (tongues-speaking), and other outward manifestations are regarded as evidence of the Holy Spirit's presence. Debates continue over the line between appeals to emotions that are essential to the religious experience of human beings and "emotionalism." See H. S. Smith et al., *American Christianity: A Historical Interpretation with Representative Documents* (2v., 1960–63).

EMS, CONGRESS OF, the meeting held by the deputies of the prince archbishops of Trier, Mainz, Cologne, and Salzburg at Bad Ems from July 25 to Aug. 25, 1786. It culminated a long history of disputes between those German metropolitans and the papacy; the immediate reason for the conference was their fear that the establishment of a nunciature in Munich (1785) would lead to greater papal influence over their suffragans. The Congress agreed on a common program, the *Punctation of Ems* (*Emser Punktation*), which would restrict papal powers regarding faculties, appeals, dispensations, taxes, and decrees. The Punctation revealed the influence of *Febronianism on church polity among German ecclesiastical leaders. The program failed to win imperial or significant episcopal support and was soon abandoned. See H. Holborn, *History of Modern Germany, 1648–1840* (1964).

EMSER, HIERONYMUS (1478–1527), polemicist against Martin *Luther. E. studied at Tübingen and Basel and developed strong interests in church reform according to humanist and Erasmian ideas. From *c.* 1505 he was secretary to George, Duke of Saxony, whom he represented at Rome to plead for the canonization of Benno, Bp. of Meissen. E.'s biography of Benno (1512) is unreliable. Hearing Luther at the *Disputation of Leipzig (1519), E. turned against the Reformer's theology, and the two became literary adversaries. E. was ill-fitted theologically for the task, but the exchange was popular and vitriolic. After Luther's translation of the NT appeared (1522), E. attempted to reply with his own translation; what he produced, however, was largely Luther's translation corrected to match the Vulgate text. The Emser Bible went through numerous editions under RC auspices (16th–18th cent.). E. also engaged in controversy with *Karlstadt over images and with H. *Zwingli on the Mass. See E. Iserloh, LTK 3:855–856; F. Lau, RGG 2:462.

ENCOUNTER, a concept that in contemporary theology is particularly associated with Emil *Brunner (1889–1966), for whom the source of religious truth was God's personal act of meeting with man. Somewhat dependent upon existentialism and upon M. *Buber's *I and Thou* (1923), encounter stresses the personal nature of God and the personal quality of his dealings with men. The divine-human relationship of encounter is contrasted with that view which understands man's knowledge of God as a matter of propositional knowledge, given through objective revelation in the Bible, in creeds or the dogmatic teaching of the Church, or developed through reasoning (as in *natural theology). Those who stress encounter understand the knowledge of God either wholly or in major part as personal relationship rather than objective knowledge. They understand revelation as God's decision to reveal himself as a person, rather than information about himself, speaking to man and demanding a personal response from man. This approach is also in contrast to *subjectivism in which knowledge of God is something man already possesses on the basis of his own nature.

Those who stress this personal encounter also understand the response demanded from man to be personal, a decision to repent and to act in accordance with the command of God. This is in contrast with the view that would understand man's proper response to be primarily the intellectual acceptance of propositional statements, or, by subjectivists, the full realization of his own nature. Belief is understood by those who stress encounter as an attitude that is revealed in personal obedience, rather than in acceptance of doctrinal statements about God and his nature. The emphasis upon encounter is a reaction against both the objectivity of orthodoxy and its emphasis on right belief and against the subjectivity of *Pietism and its emphasis upon inner feelings. Encounter seeks to correlate in the manner of *dialectical theology the objectivity of the word of God and the subjectivity of faith, maintaining the fully personal character of both.

In the views of 20th-cent. theologians who emphasize encounter, doctrine, although not disparaged, is understood as secondary to the divine-human encounter. From the primary relationship of the encounter doctrine emerges as man's attempt to understand and express what has happened, and therefore has an auxiliary role. Scripture and sacraments are also interpreted in this dialectical way, not as objective in the sense that one might impersonally handle and control the truth of God or his grace or as superfluous externals, but as means through which the personal encounter of God with man takes place. See E. Brunner, *Divine-Human Encounter* (1938).

ENDOWMENTS, among Mormons the name for the secret temple rites in which only Mormons in good standing participate. Among these is the celebration of Mormon *celestial marriages.

ENDURA, in *Cathari teaching, sacred suicide, the highest act of virtue, liberating man's spirit from matter.

ENGLAND, CHURCH OF, see CHURCH OF ENGLAND.

ENGLISH CHURCH UNION, founded in 1859 as the Church of England Protection Society to defend and foster *high-church principles. Renamed the year after, it supported priests who were prosecuted for *ritualism, and was for many years under the presidency of Lord *Halifax. In 1934 it became part of the *Church Union.

ENLIGHTENMENT (Ger. *Aufklärung*), the complex cultural movement of 18th-cent. Europe. The relationship of the Enlightenment to religion has been widely misrepresented, largely by a failure to admit fully its claims to distance from the Christian world. It was essentially the use of powerful new ideas to influence a social situation, to reconstruct an entire culture, to provide intellectual justification for the practical efforts of practical men. Yet the *lumières*, as they liked to call themselves, were hardly practical; nor were most of them influential on men of affairs. Hume and Gibbon in Britain, Lessing and Kant in Germany, and the host of philosophes— Voltaire, Rousseau, Helvetius, Holbach, Diderot, d'Alembert, and the rest— mounted an attack that undermined effectively both an obsolete socio-political order and the religious attachments by which the old regime sought to preserve itself and clothe itself with a sacred authority. C. L. Becker's thesis (*The Heavenly City of the Eighteenth Century Philosophers*, 1932) that Enlightenment was a derivative, vulgarized restatement of traditional Christian values, a secularized faith, hope, and charity, is largely discredited as a distortion. Religion, which meant Christianity, was essentially and radically challenged by a vigorous, hostile secularism. Cassirer is surely mistaken in describing Enlightenment as fundamentally religious.

The philosophes, or spokesmen of Enlightenment, claimed that Christians had assimilated and debased pagan virtues while they had incorporated and intensified pagan vices. The rationalist version of Christianity, worked up in the 16th and esp. the 17th cent., were absorbed by the philosophes and employed in the campaign against all organized religion. The men of Enlightenment were the natural heirs of "Christian" stoicism and skepticism, which had undermined the very reasonableness of religion. Deists and later apologists would strive mightily to reestablish this reasonableness, but the gap between reason and religion was exposed as unbridgeable and the philosophes undertook to demonstrate this by every means available.

Among British deists and German *Aufklärer* there was an overt and not unimportant religious component, but most French philosophes, and unbelievers like Gibbon and Hume, had a profoundly anti-Christian animus. The argument began, logically and chronologically, with the deists discarding all that was mysterious and miraculous about Christianity. There is, subsequently, no single strain of Enlightenment antireligious argument, but rather a number of elaborations. By mid-century Christianity was socially vulnerable to secularization. Yet the age of Enlightenment was still a religious age (Enlightenment itself was, then, a countercurrent), even in the midst of a barrage of philosophic propaganda. There took place, rather, a subtle shift of attention in which religious institutions and explanations were slowly displaced from the center to the periphery of life. Europeans in great numbers suffered the opposite attractions of inherited beliefs and a newly fashionable unbelief. The receptive public for philosophic thinking increased year by year as antireligious propaganda became more seductive and plausible. The movement was probably less a response of this specifically anti-Christian campaign than the expression of a grave crisis in religious confidence. Internecine squabbles, between and within religious denominations, were symptomatic of a general spiritual malaise. A bland piety, a self-satisfied reasonableness, the facile conviction that the Churches must, after all, move with the times, all these concessions to worldiness embodied the treason of the clerks. In Britain the Church's pursuit of social acceptability and political advantage pointed in the direction of the drift of the times.

In the German states the religious situation was less parlous but more complicated. Fratricidal war, alternating with a tolerance based on indifference, veiled the real enemy. Religion went on the defensive, dissipating into a vague religiosity or a worldly piety. In France the Church was extremely wealthy and powerful, yet the clergy marched on the way of self-destruction. The progress of philosophy was only a part of a cultural evolution. By the 18th cent. unbelievers and believers alike had lost much of the key to the symbolic language of Christianity, which was still medieval. The loss of religious fervor was widespread. In the face of mounting secularization the higher clergy were largely indifferent, the lower clergy powerless. The absurd state of religion, established yet impotent to stem the advance of godlessness, was ironically underlined by the empty and ostentatious piety of such immoral men as Louis XV. Curiously, the Churches turned modern with a vengeance, appealing constantly to reasonableness and fiercely rejecting *enthusiasm. Apologists prettified the image of God, and preachers emphasized the naturalness and ease of a Christian life accommodated to men's feeling and ambition. By the 1760s, when Enlightenment was everywhere on the offensive and laments about atheism multiplied, a frightened orthodoxy responded in panic. Often the contest between believers and philosophes had the unreal aspect of a contest decided in advance. Christians paid a heavy price for fraternizing with the enemy. The *lumières* appropriated the results of Christian labors, esp. the fruits of historical erudition, for secular and eventually for antireligious purposes. In return, Christians took every measure to suppress and harass the progress of philosophy. Anticlericalism and skepticism became political and on the eve of revolution joined forces with a naturalistic world view. The century of Enlighten-ment ended with religious interests seriously undermined and antireligion proposed as the ultimate remedy for the spiritual malady of the age. See P. Gay, *Enlightenment: An Interpretation* (1966); J. H. Overton and F. Relton, *English Church, 1714–1800* (1906); E. Cassirer, *Philosophy of the Enlightenment* (1960), Ch. 4; R. R. Palmer, *Catholics and Unbelievers in Eighteenth Century France* (1939); F. E. Manuel, ed., *Enlightenment* (pa., 1965).

ENTHUSIASM, a claim to unmediated union with God; also the kind of religious life that tends to result from belief in such union. Enthusiasm has been a primary source of many of the forms, some of them extravagant, that Christianity has taken. The term *entheos*, possessed by a god, was used by the Greeks to refer to divine possession, as by Apollo or Dionysius, and in Plato poetic inspiration is called a kind of enthusiasm. The English word became prominent during the 17th and 18th cents. as a term of reproach applied to those who claimed such direct and individual union with God as to give them an immediate and certain knowledge of their relationship to God and of his will. The term has been applied to such groups as Montanists, Cathari, Fraticelli, Convulsionaries, Quakers, and Methodists. In the Reformation era Luther used the equivalent *Schwämerei* of the Anabaptists. During the *Great Awakening, George *Whitfield was denounced by the president and faculty of Harvard as an enthusiast, as "one that acts either according to Dreams, or some sudden impulses and impressions upon his mind, which he fondly imagines to be from the Spirit of God, perswading and inclining him thereby to such and such actions, tho' he hath no proof that such perswasions or impressions are from the Holy Spirit."

Modern authors use several criteria to classify and criticize manifestations of enthusiasm: the claim to immediate revelations that leads to a disregard for historical revelation as contained in Scripture and tradition; the claim to personal direction by the Spirit of God leading to rebellion against both civil authority and the disciplines of the Church; the claim to certainty of salvation through the direct action of God fostering a disregard for the sacraments and other forms of worship; the presumed direct knowledge of the will of God leading to *antinomianism and pride; and the emphasis upon the felt working of the Spirit resulting in unhealthy emotionalism and contempt for reason. Those charged with enthusiasm, however, reply that the examples of inspiration and unusual workings of the Spirit that are found in the Bible support the validity of such phenomena in the present and that a personal and direct contact with God is essential if Christian faith is to be a living reality.

In general enthusiasm may be considered a reaction to formalistic religion, and is often marked by ecstatic or charismatic emphases, such as *glossolalia. It also often engenders a sense of impending crisis with expectations of the end of the world, i.e., *millenarianism. To some extent it is associated with *revivalism and the crisis experience in which a person has immediate assurance of his conversion and of the forgiveness and salvation that he has surely received. See R. Knox, *Enthusiasm* (1950); E. Troeltsch, *Social Teachings of the Christian Churches* (tr. O. Wyon, 2v., 1956); L. McCann, NCE 5:446–449.

ENTIRE SANCTIFICATION (holiness, second blessing, second work of grace), the form of *perfectionism taught in *Holiness Churches and, with less emphasis, in *Pentecostalism. The doctrine is an interpretation and extension of John *Wesley's idea of *Christian perfection. In *A Plain Account of Christian Perfection*, Wesley, departing from the Reformation adage *homo simul justus et peccator* (man is at once righteous and a sinner), taught a grace of sanctification that is distinct from justification: by justification God saves a person from sins already committed; by sanctification God "extirpates man's sinful nature."

The idea of sanctification, *Arminian in its basis, was prominent in 19th-cent. American *revivalism; C. *Finney taught that the sanctified "habitually live without sin or fall into it at intervals so few and far between that, in strong language, it may be said that they do not sin" (see OBERLIN THEOLOGY). During the revivalistic Holiness Movement, esp. after the Civil War, Wesley's teaching was given an interpretation regarded by Methodist authorities as extreme. Sanctification or perfection came not to mean a gradual process of attainment through the actions of Christian living, but an instantaneous endowment with sinlessness through the power of the Holy Spirit.

This sanctification is called entire because, while justification takes away or covers the guilt of voluntary, sinful actions, sanctification fills man with a holiness that takes away "inbred sin," the roots of sin, and the abiding tendencies left by original sin (see CONCUPISCENCE). Certain Holiness writers seem to explain entire sanctification as the indwelling of Christ in the sanctified. Some Pentecostals have viewed it as prerequisite to the *baptism with the Holy Spirit; Spirit baptism, however, not entire sanctification, is the core of Pentecostalism. This second blessing is achieved without the help of sacraments or of any ecclesial mediation. Although there is no time assigned in man's life to receive it, the general expectation is that it should happen during the revival services of the Churches. Entire sanctification may grow progressively throughout a person's life; although the possibility of loss of this grace is admitted, stress is laid upon its conferring assurance of salvation. One consequence of the teaching is a strict, often puritanical, moral code, the observance of which is viewed as an expression of freedom from interior inclination to what is sinful or frivolous. See Mayer RB 311–314 and bibliog.; N. Bloch-Hoell, *Pentecostal Movement* (1964), 122–129.

ÉON DE L'ÉTOILE (fl. 12th cent.), a fanatic Breton preacher. E. was an uneducated layman who took the first words of the liturgical formula for exorcism, *per eum qui venturus est iudicare vivos et mortuos* (through him who is to come to judge the living and the dead), to be a reference to his own name. He proclaimed therefore that he was the Son of God, commissioned to judge the world. He organized followers, sometimes called Breton Heretics, who lived in the forest, engaging in immoral practices and emerging to pillage homes, monasteries, and churches. E. was cited before a provincial council at Reims in 1148 and was confined to prison as a madman.

EPHRATA COMMUNITY, a communal body founded (1732–34) by Johann Conrad *Beissel, who established the groups in the wilderness of Lancaster Co., Pennsylvania. The community was known as Ephrata, and the village, restored, is now a state historical possession (1968). Practices of Ephrata featured celibacy, Sabbatarianism, and the use of monastic names, apparel, cells, and regimen. Authority for customs, practices, and doctrine were alleged to have been received by Beissel in mystical trances and inspiration. The community was industrious, excelling in farming, milling, printing, and calligraphic art. The worship was mystical, characterized by long sermons, devout prayer vigils, and highly stylized vocal music. The society lasted less than 100 years because of internal dissension and lack of leadership. The *Seventh Day Baptists, however, trace their origins to Beissel's foundation.

EPISCOPACY, a term referring to the office of bishop (Gr., *episcopos*), i.e., the office itself or period of tenure in it (episcopate); a body of bps. in a Church or geographical region; or that form of *polity according to which the Church is governed by episcopal authority. In the last sense episcopacy is in opposition to both the presbyterian and congregational forms of polity. *HISTORIC EPISCOPATE.

EPISCOPAL CHURCH, an alternate, official title for the *Protestant Episcopal Church, approved by the *General Convention of the Church in 1967.

EPISCOPAL CHURCH IN SCOTLAND, an *autocephalous province of the *Anglican Communion with a membership of about 100,000, in 7 dioceses. The *Primus is one of the diocesan bps. elected by his fellows as the Church's presiding officer. Political tensions between the English and Scots were paralleled in ecclesiastical matters long before the Reformation. In the 16th cent. the Lutheran and Reformed elements in continental Protestantism found their way quickly into Scotland. Despite English countermeasures, by 1560 the reformed *Church of Scotland had been firmly grounded, Presbyterian in polity and Calvinist in doctrine. A century of bitter political and ecclesiastical contest followed, but the outcome of that tangled history was the establishment, in 1690, of the (Presbyterian) Church of Scotland as the national Church. The minority who chose to retain *episcopacy following the 1690 settlement continued a fragile and threadbare existence. Suspect because of their Jacobite sympathies, harassed by hostile political forces in England, disendowed, and often penalized for their continuing tradition of Catholic worship and doctrine, the tiny community survived the harsh tests of 18th-cent. Scottish history. In 1764 the Church produced its own liturgy, restoring the oblation and invocation (epiclesis) to the canon. In 1784 the first bishop-elect of the newly free Protestant Episcopal Church in the U.S., Samuel *Seabury, was consecrated by the Scottish bishops in Aberdeen, since it was then legally impossible for the C of E to give episcopal orders to other than its own clergy. In gratitude for the gift of the episcopate, the Episcopal Church of the U.S. agreed to base its eucharistic liturgy on that of the Scottish Church, thus strengthening a significant second liturgical tradition within Anglicanism. See S. Neill, *Anglicanism* (pa., 1958).

EPISCOPALIAN, a member of the *Protestant Episcopal Church; also used inaccurately sometimes as a synonym for Anglican; one who holds that episcopacy is the true form of *polity in the Church.

EPISCOPALISM, a view of the Church that maintains that supreme teaching and governing authority is vested immediately in the body of bps., as successors of the Apostles. RC, Eastern, Anglican, and Old Catholic Churches are agreed in this teaching as it differs from Presbyterianism, Congregationalism, *collegialism, or *territorialism. Episcopalism historically, however, has also meant a denial of the personal primacy of the pope, maintaining that he is simply *primus inter pares* (see CONCILIARISM; FEBRONIANISM; GALLICANISM). By the dogmatic definition of papal infallibility of Vatican Council I the RC Church differs from other Churches in rejecting this sense of episcopalism; Vatican Council II explains RC teaching on the body of bps. in discussing their *collegiality (Vat II ConstCh 18–29).

EPISCOPATE (Gr. *episcopos*, bishop), the office itself or the tenure of a bp.; the body of bps. in a Church or region. The term, however, frequently refers to the office or order of bp. as an institution in the Church, esp. in the phrase, recurrent in ecumenical discussions, *historic episcopate. Many Churches, whether or not they recognize *apostolic succession or the office of bp. as a sacred order, maintain that the episcopate has from NT times been an essential of the Christian Church. Others, esp. in the traditions of Presbyterianism or Congregationalism, disagree. *LAMBETH QUADRILATERAL; *ECUMENISM; *CONSULTATION ON CHURCH UNION.

EPISCOPI VAGANTES (Lat., literally, wandering bishops), in the ancient and early medieval Church, a designation for bps. who were itinerant for various reasons; missionary or otherwise; in modern times, bps. who have secured, but through irregular or fraudulent means, valid episcopal orders, or, having obtained them regularly, have then broken off relations with the body that ordained them and have become more or less unaffiliated. While often assuming grandiose titles and jurisdictions, these bps., not being in communion with any historic Christian ecclesial body, usually have at most only a small, personal following. Two prominent modern *episcopi vagantes* who in turn were the source of a much larger number of other episcopal ordinations in the 20th cent. were Arnold Harris Mathew (d. 1919) and Joseph R. Vilatte (d. 1929). These two, together with Leon Chechemian, an alleged Armenian bp., consecrated a considerable number of other free bps. for such small groups as the American Catholic Church, the African Orthodox Church, the Liberal Catholic Church, and even organizations of theosophical tendencies. Eastern Orthodoxy does not recognize the validity of orders of the numerous prelates claiming affiliation with, or canonical descent from, Orthodox or other Eastern hierarchs. See H. R. T. Brandreth, *Episcopi Vagantes and the Anglican Church* (2d ed., 1961); P. Anson, *Bishops at Large* (1964).

EPISCOPIUS, SIMON (Bishop; 1583–1643), Arminian theologian. E., a native of Amsterdam, studied at the Univ. of Leiden under both J. *Arminius and F. *Gomarus and in 1612 succeeded the latter in the chair of theology. He was the principal spokesman for the the *Remonstrants at the Synod of *Dort, and protested against the prejudgment of their case. He was banished by the Synod and during the time of his exile composed (1622) a *Confessio*, a doctrinal statement of *Arminianism. After the death of the enemy of the Remonstrants, Prince Maurice of Nassau (1625), E. was able to return to Holland and in 1634 became rector and professor at the college of the Remonstrants in Amsterdam. In his *Institutiones theologicae* (4v., 1650–51) E. did what Arminius had not done, namely, presented a systematic exposition and defense of Arminianism. Broad and tolerant in his views, E. minimized the importance of speculative dogmas and insisted rather on the practical aspect of Christianity, stressing man's responsibility to such an extent that he was accused of *Pelagianism. Like most Arminians at the time, he was also, probably without foundation, accused of *Socinianism. See Bihlmeyer-Tüchle 3:202; W. F. Dankbaar, RGG 2:531–532; H. C. Rogge, EncRelKnow 4:159–160.

EPISTOLAE OBSCURORUM VIRORUM (Letters of Obscure Men), a satire against the enemies of J. *Reuchlin. The title plays on that of the *Epistolae clarorum virorum* (Letters of Renowned Men), a short collection of testimonials published by Reuchlin in his own behalf (1514). The *Epistolae obscurorum virorum* contains more than 100 letters; the first series, by Johannes Crotus Rubianus (1486–1540), appeared in 1515; the second series, by Ulrich von Hutten (1488–1523), in 1517. The letters are written to Ortwin *Gratius, humanist of the anti-Reuchlin party, purporting to be from scholastics and clerics, for whom fantastic names were invented. Parodying a barbarous scholastic Latin, the biting shafts of the letters made the personal lives and intellectual aridity of churchmen who were resisting the *New Learning the laughingstock of the humanist world. The *Epistolae* were a sign of a cultural environment favorable to the Reformation. See F. G. Stokes, *Epistolae obscurorum virorum: The Latin Text with an English Rendering, Notes and Historical Introduction* (1909).

EPWORTH LEAGUE, a Methodist youth organization. Various organizations for youth existed in the Methodist Episcopal Church when, May 14–15, 1889, their representatives met in Cleveland to form a single organization, the Epworth League, its name commemorating the birthplace of John Wesley. In 1890 it published its official periodical, the *Epworth Herald*, and in 1892 the *General Conference approved the new organization. It had four departments: Spiritual Work; Mercy and Help; World Evangelism; and Literary and Social. The members pledged to "take some active part" in the Church. It served as a link between the Sunday school and the adult church and as a training ground for church leadership. It was also adopted by the Methodist Episcopal Church, South, and the Methodist Church of Canada. In 1944 the Epworth League was succeeded by the Methodist Youth Fellowship. See HistAmMeth 2:645–646.

EQUALITY EVANGELISTS, the name taken by the preachers from whom the *Christian Nation Church traces its origins.

ERASMUS, DESIDERIUS (1467–1536), greatest of the humanists through his personal and literary influence. Desiderius is a latinization of Erasmus, the name he adopted as the Greek form of Herasmus, his baptismal name. Born at Rotterdam (thus the designation Roterodammensis or Roterodamus), he was probably the son of a priest; during his studies at Deventer with the *Brethren of the Common Life his humanistic interests began. He entered a monastery of Augustinian Canons Regular at Steyn near Gouda in 1486, and was ordained in 1492. Shortly thereafter he received permission to leave the monastery, and he never returned; a papal brief of 1517 terminated his canonical affiliation. At Paris in 1495, repelled by scholastic theology, he cultivated literary interests. He visited England in 1499, where J. *Colet directed his interests to Greek and the New Testament. He returned to France in 1500, made a second visit to England, 1505–06, then spent 3 years, 1506–09, in Italy. While in England again, 1511–1514, he was Lady Margaret Professor of Greek and theology at Cambridge and completed his *Novum instrumentum*, the first published edition (Basel, 1516) of the Greek NT, with Latin translation and notes. The edition was the basis for many vernacular translations of the time and a landmark in scriptural studies. From 1514 to 1521, E. moved from place to place in Belgium and Holland, then settled at Basel with the printer John Froben, until the city accepted the Reformation in 1529. His last residence was at Freiburg, but he died at Basel while on a visit.

Erasmus is the very epitome of the strength and weakness of Renaissance humanism as an active force in the affairs of men. His intellectual inspiration is Roman rather than Greek; among the Fathers his guide was not the philosophical and mystical Augustine but the literary and urbane Jerome (he edited the works of Jerome, 9v., 1516–18, as well as those of Augustine and other Fathers). E. typifies the fatal indifference and hostility of the entire humanist movement to the speculative or scientific imagination. He ridiculed concern with natural science as a distraction from the humane wisdom of life. From the Florentine Platonists he borrowed not their metaphysics but their practical program, a universal and tolerant ethical religion, stripped of theological sophistication and directed solely to conduct. The guiding idea throughout all his subtle but mordant attacks on the religious institutionalism around him is that simple moral teaching is the true lesson of the Gospels and the genuine "philosophy of Christ." He prided himself on being the Christianizer of the Renaissance and the humanizer of Christianity.

Erasmus was distressed by the Church's elaborate theological and sacramental structure, and in his *Enchiridion militis christiani* (1503; tr. J. P. Dolan, *Handbook of the Militant Christian,* 1962) and other works he advocated a simple, humane, and undogmatic Christian religion. He appeals frequently to the Sermon on the Mount and insists that Christ called for a life, not a debate; a transformation rather than a process of reasoning. He could not see the human function of external rites and ceremonies, but he reserved his bitterest barbs for the monastic ideal, its essence and not

merely its perversions and corruptions (esp. in his *Encomium Moriae* 1509; tr. H. H. Hudson, *Praise of Folly,* 1941). His exalted conception of human dignity and worth, man's power and freedom, lacked the philosophical acumen to give it systematic grounding. His most pretentious theoretical essay, a defense of man's freedom under grace, against Luther, reveals a lack of speculative power (*Diatribe de libero arbitrio,* 1524; Luther's reply is the *De servo arbitrio,* 1525; both works in E. F. Winter, tr., *Discourse on Free Will,* 1961). E.'s writings directly contributed to the religious revolution. He himself at first cautiously welcomed the reform attempts of Luther, but he came to be repelled by what he regarded as excesses and intemperate language. Retiring from the battle between defenders of RC orthodoxy and the Protestant Reformers, E. was assailed by both. He continued to employ his rhetorical skill in behalf of a tolerant, humane, cosmopolitan culture. He looked backward, to the Bible and classical antiquity; his spiritual legacy is that of a witty, charming, mediating conservative; but his own program was too vague to achieve the peace and unity he sought. See P. Smith, *Erasmus: A Study of His Life, Ideals, and Place in History* (1923); J. Huizinga, *Erasmus* (1924); M. P. Gilmore, NCE 5:508–511, with bibliog.

ERASTIANISM, control of ecclesiastical affairs by the State. Deriving from Thomas Erastus (1524–83), the term is often applied to situations unrelated to his views. Opposing the introduction of Genevan theocratic discipline, Erastus, a Swiss professor at Heidelberg (1558–80), taught that in a Christian state all coercive power, even excommunication, belongs to civil magistrates. More a type of Church-State relationship than a precise system, Erastianism in many variations has existed in Lutheran states, England, and elsewhere. *Reformed Churches sought to subordinate the State to the Church, but in practice Reformed countries often were Erastian. Thomas Hobbes, in *Leviathan* (1651), developed an

Erastian system in an extreme form. It should be noted that all Churches have tried to exclude certain areas from State domination, but under any Erastian system such distinctions are difficult to maintain. See J. N. Figgis, "Erastus and the Erastians," *Divine Right of Kings* (1914).

ESBJÖRN, LARS PAUL (1808–70), Swedish-American missionary and professor. Educated at Uppsala, E. was ordained in 1832 and served as pastor and teacher in Sweden for 17 years. He left his country in 1849 to minister to Swedish Lutherans who had settled in the United States. At Andover, Ill., he helped organize the Augustana Synod and set up the mother church. He also established a number of preaching stations and new congregations. By personal appeal he obtained four ministers from Sweden to assist him. He was called to Springfield, Ill., in 1858 to teach and became president of the newly founded Augustana Seminary in 1860; but he left the U.S. 3 years later to resume the care of souls in Sweden. See G. E. Lenski, EncLuthCh 1:796.

ESCHATOLOGICAL THEOLOGY, the theology named for its orientation to eschatology, the doctrine concerning the final outcome of the universe and humanity. As a result of the revival of biblical studies, it is one of the emphases that have characterized theology in the first half of the 20th century. The term was widely used by the historians of religion when they spoke of the beliefs of the Egyptians, Babylonians, Persians, Greeks, Romans, etc.; it is also used for the tract *De novissimis*—*novissima* being the Latin equivalent of the Greek *ta eschata*. Among RC eschatologists are L. Bouyer, L. Cerfaux, R. Guardini, J. Daniélou; among Protestants, A. Schweitzer, P. Tillich, R. Niebuhr, D. H. Dodd, and R. Bultmann. Generally speaking, they feel that Christianity is carried along toward the future and the coming of Christ by a powerful dynamism, though some think the future bodes ill for the universe. Others hold that human progress can be turned into good or evil, depending upon the use Christians make of it. See F. Martin and M. E. Williams, NCE 5:524–538; J. Moltmann, *Theology of Hope* (tr. J. W. Leitch, 1967). *INCARNATIONAL THEOLOGY.

ESOTERICISM, restriction of religious doctrine or ritual participation to initiates; also the cultivation of occult doctrines or practices. The word derives from the Gr. *esōterō*, comparative of *esō*, within. Esotericism was first connected with the Greek mysteries, then with a distinction between the teachings given by philosophers to the many and those given to an inner circle. As a religious or quasi-religious phenomenon, it is present in the case of the secret fraternal orders and in such religio-philosophic systems as *theosophy, *spiritualism, and *anthroposophy. Certain esoteric aspects may be seen in early Christianity, with the distinction between the Mass of catechumens, open to all, and the Mass of the faithful, restricted to the baptized. The mysteries of the NT, however, are not items of esoterica, but are proclaimed as the wonders of God's gracious action saving man. Esotericism may be rooted in a primitive fascination with the magical. It does represent an attitude that sacred things are profaned by the presence of unbelievers or that the benefits bestowed by sacred things are rightly restricted to committed disciples.

ESTABLISHED CHURCH, in general any Church the doctrines, worship, and discipline of which are supported by law; but the term has special reference to England. The C of E does not trace its establishment to a specific statute. The Canons of 1603 mention "the Church of England by law established," and thereafter the term appears in Parliamentary Acts, but these references are simply recognition of an already existing condition. The essence of establishment is incorporation of church law in the law of the realm, and such had been the case from

Anglo-Saxon times. Nowhere carefully defined, the nature of the establishment has gradually developed by custom and through a long series of legislative measures, such as the adoption of the *Book of Common Prayer, the *Thirty-Nine Articles, and disciplinary measures. Symbolized in the coronation of the king by the abp. of Canterbury, the relation of Church and State is one of interdependence. In the House of Lords, two abps. and 24 bps. have opportunity to inform that body on ecclesiastical matters and to influence political and social legislation. The sentences of ecclesiastical courts are enforced by the State. Although the State does not provide financial support of the clergy, it shares oversight of endowments and income. As representatives of the Church, clergymen have considerable prestige and influence upon the public mind. Special prayers are offered in behalf of king and Parliament, judicial and executive agencies, and the nation as a whole. A system of parishes includes the entire populace; neither sparsely settled areas nor congested cities are without the ministry of the Church. The influence of the priest pervades every community, as his services are available to all persons in a parish in baptism, confirmation, matrimony, and burial. With its close connection to the State, the C of E has a specific responsibility to inform the consciences of people as to the moral obligation to express justice and love in law and judicial acts.

Benefits that accrue to the established Church also make it vulnerable to a state control adverse to its interests. Appointment of bps. and deans of cathedrals and other church patronage are rights of the Crown, and all clergy declare allegiance to the king and his successors. The Church may not alter its doctrinal formulas or its Book of Common Prayer without Parliament's approval, and a secular court is the highest appellate court in deciding ecclesiastical cases. New dioceses or parishes require the consent of an agency responsible to Parliament. The resources of the Church are also under the administration of the State, largely through the Church Com-

missioners, a body of laymen and clergymen appointed by Parliament. While the Church enjoys a large measure of freedom, there is always potential for conflict of interest and for interference with doctrines and use of endowments, especially since today Parliament is composed largely of non-Anglicans. A serious controversy arose in 1928, when a revision of the *Book of Common Prayer was voted down by the House of Commons. See C. Garbett, *Church and State in England* (1950). *STATE CHURCH; *NATIONAL CHURCH.

ETERNALS, Christians who believed that the present world would not pass away but would continue forever in glory after the final resurrection. Filaster (*Haer.* 80), the only early source, gives them no name; Augustine (*Haer.* 67) repeats Filaster; the *Praedestinatus* ascribes the belief to the Sataunians. The name Eternals (*Éternels*) was coined by the *Dictionnaire des hérésies* (1847), 1:677. See G. Bareille, DTC 5:911–912.

ETHICAL CULTURE MOVEMENT, ethical humanism originating with the founding of the New York Society for Ethical Culture, May 15, 1876, by F. *Adler. Although most of the approximately 100 original members were Jewish, later many of Christian background were added. Societies were organized in other cities, and in 1889 a federation, the American Ethical Union, was formed; it currently includes about 30 societies, with some 7,000 members. A corresponding movement began in England in 1887 under the leadership of S. Coit (1857–1944), an American, and the English Ethical Union was formed in 1896. A Berlin society was organized in 1892, and the first meeting of the International Ethical Movement was held in Germany in 1893. In 1952 the American Ethical Union joined ethical unions and other humanist organizations of several countries to form the International Humanist and Ethical Union, with headquarters in Utrecht. The movement makes no metaphysical or theological affirmations, though it generally holds that the moral law is grounded in objective reality. Societies have weekly meetings, normally on Sundays, without prayer or ritual, but with music, reading, and an address. They also conduct forums, clubs, youth groups, and other programs. The movement has supported a wide variety of liberal social causes and has been influential beyond its numbers because of the high intelligence level of much of its membership. See H. Blackham, *Ethical Movement during Seventy Years* (1946); D. Muzzey, *Ethics as a Religion* (1951).

ETHICS, PROTESTANT CHRISTIAN, see PROTESTANT CHRISTIAN ETHICS.

EUCHARIST, the common meal instituted by Jesus Christ "on the night when he was betrayed" (1 Cor 11.23) and celebrated by Christians as a sign and a means of his presence. Christian devotion and theology have long pondered its meaning, and from their thought has come a great variety of eucharistic doctrines, practices, and emphases. Some of these are so central as to require inclusion in any catalogue of eucharistic teaching, however brief it may be. By the very circumstances of its institution, as recounted in Mt 26.26–28, Mk 14.22–24, Lk 22.17–20, and Cor 11.23–25, the Eucharist necessarily involves an act of remembrance. Stories such as that of the disciples on the way to Emmaus (Lk 24.30–31) suggest that the very repetition of the ritual act of breaking the bread and sharing the cup was a means of calling him to mind and of sustaining the memory of his saving words and deeds. The institution of the Christian Eucharist is set into the framework of the commemoration of the Jewish Passover, where the remembrance and recital of the acts of God in the Exodus from Egypt linked the Israelite of the present with the events by which the covenant between God and Israel was established. Similarly, eating and drinking "in remembrance of me" are a link between the Christian believer and the days of Christ on earth. Although the development of more elaborate forms of Christian ritual has sometimes tended to obscure this, the gestures and actions of the celebration are also intended to serve this memorial purpose. Especially the participation in the bread and in the cup evoke in the Christian memory the life, death, and resurrection of Jesus Christ, permitting Christians to become contemporary to those events, as men "before whose eyes Jesus Christ was publicly portrayed as crucified" (Gal 3.1).

No less prominent in any account of the meaning of the Eucharist is its social character. In many religions—and, for that matter, in the common life of many cultures—eating and drinking together has made men into a community (see the etymology of the word "symposium"). Some forms of Christian piety, both Protestant and Roman Catholic, have tended to obscure this communal nature of the Eucharist by their concentration upon the benefits given to the individual through his private and personal devotion. But the NT, esp. 1 Cor. 10–11, is too explicit in its teaching to permit this individualism to stand. The relation between the Eucharist and Christian community is, however, a bilateral one. On the one hand, there is a degree of unity in faith and doctrine that seems to be presupposed by the Eucharist, such that a lesser degree would make a sharing in the communion impossible for many Christians. On the other hand, the Eucharist not only symbolizes but also effects a unity, including a unity of faith and doctrine. This bilateral relationship makes esp. difficult and painful the problem of *intercommunion between Christians of differing denominational traditions, and the problem has been a prominent issue for discussion in the modern ecumenical movement.

The problem of the nature of the eucharistic presence is, for many traditions, related to the problem of intercommunion; for it is on the doctrine of the presence that many Christians diverge. The first theological controversy over the presence did not come until the 9th cent., and the history of the question before that time does not present a clear line of doctrinal development. But most Christians appear to have believed that Jesus Christ was present in some special sense and in some unique way. He was present in the celebrating community, but he was also present in the Eucharistic elements, which were regularly called the body and blood of Christ. The doctrine of *transubstantiation is the form taken by the doctrine of the *Real Presence in the Latin West; it is intended to be not a speculative doctrine of metaphysics but a dogma of faith in the intention of Christ as expressed in the institution of the Eucharist. The belief in the presence of the body and blood of Christ also forms the basis for the many forms of Eucharistic devotion outside the framework of the community's celebration. If he is present, he may be addressed in prayer.

The doctrine of the Real Presence is also the dogmatic basis for the sacrificial interpretation of the Eucharist. Christians are agreed that Christ, as the eternal High Priest, "entered once for all into the Holy Place, taking not the blood of goats and calves but his own blood, thus securing an eternal redemption" (Heb 11.12), and that therefore the sacrifice of Calvary neither needs to be nor can be repeated. But the idea of Christians offering themselves as a sacrifice at the Eucharist is an ancient one. It is based on the union between the sacrifice of the believer and the sacrifice of Christ on Calvary, in the name of which one comes to the altar. Thus we plead the merits of the one sacrifice of Christ, offering up ourselves to God in union with the body and blood that were sacrificed on the Cross and that are present in the eucharistic celebration. Some theologians, esp. in the later Middle Ages, spoke of the "repetition of Calvary" less carefully than sound theology would have dictated, and various forms of folk devotion have followed this example. But in the public teaching of the Church the absolute uniquess of the sacrifice of Christ has remained uppermost.

This brief list does not exhaust even those eucharistic themes that have been prominent in Christian language. A widespread idea has been the teaching that the Eucharist contained and conveyed a "drug of immortality," which enabled the physical nature of man to participate in the eternal life of God. The symbolic interpretation of the Eucharist has been important even to those theologians who have insisted that it be seen as more than a symbol, and in some forms of Protestant sacramental theology this interpretation has tended to become central. Much of the meaning of the Eucharist in all the traditions has been expressed not in theology, but in the liturgy, to which theology has sought to conform, with greater or lesser success. See A. Vonier, *Key to the Doctrine of the Eucharist* (1960); Y. Brilioth, *Eucharistic Faith and Practice, Evangelical and Catholic* (1934); D. Baillie and J. Marsh, eds., *Intercommunion* (1952).

EUPHEMITES, non-Christian ascetics of Mesopotamia, Epiphanius (*Penar.* 80; cf. Augustine, *Haer.* 57) mentions them along with the Euchites and Messalians. All existed in the same region and had some similar practices, but the Euphemites were pagans. See É. Amann, DTC 10:792–795.

EVANGELICAL (Gr. *euangelion*, gospel), a term whose meaning must be determined by the context. During the Reformation, Protestants distinguished themselves from Catholics by the term "evangelical," believing that they had recovered the gospel in their doctrine of justification by faith. In Prussia the union of Lutheran and *Reformed Churches was called the Evangelical Church, and the Protestant Church of Germany today is known as the Evangelical Church of Germany. In parts of Europe "Evangelical" may signify Lutheran as distinct from Reformed Churches. The 18th-cent. Wesleyan revivals in England were known as the "evangelical revivals," and a *low-church party within the C of E but influenced by the Methodist movement were also called "evangelicals." In the U.S. the term may refer to those who stress *evangelism and personal religious experience, biblical authority, human sinfulness, the atonement of Christ, and the necessity of a new birth (see NEW EVANGELICALISM). It may also simply signify Protestant in contrast to RC or Orthodox. See K. S. Latourette, *History of Christianity* (1953). *EVANGELICALISM.

EVANGELICAL ADVENTISTS, in the history of Adventism, a name adopted by early followers of W. *Miller. Some of them organized the American Millennial Association at Boston, Mass., in 1858 to spread Adventist teachings. This group followed Sunday observance and differed from other Adventists by belief in everlasting punishment and rejection of *conditional immortality and *annihilation. The denomination disappeared in the first quarter of the 20th century.

EVANGELICAL ALLIANCE, an interdenominational organization founded in 1846 to associate and concentrate the strength of enlightened Protestantism against the encroachments of popery and Puseyism (see OXFORD MOVEMENT) and to protect the interests of scriptural Christianity. The organizing meeting in London was attended not only by English but by American and continental churchmen. The question of slavery in the U.S. was an early disruptive factor; German participation was diverted with the formation of the *Evangelische Bund. Nevertheless the Alliance flourished and established an admirable record of aiding persecuted Protestant minorities and of ecumenical activity. The American branch of the Evangelical Alliance was formally organized after the Civil War, predominantly by Presbyterian and *Reformed groups. Doctrinal positions were conservative; the early leader was Philip *Schaff. In the late 19th cent. the *Social Gospel was prominent in the activities of the Alliance. The Alliance was replaced by 1908 by the Federal Council of Churches, for which it had prepared the

way. The World Evangelical Alliance continues to exist, with headquarters in London, but its activities are largely confined to British Protestant interests. See R. Rouse and S. C. Neil, eds., *History of the Ecumenical Movement, 1517–1948* (1967).

EVANGELICAL AND REFORMED CHURCH, since 1959 part of the *United Church of Christ, a denomination formed in 1934 through the merger of the Reformed Church in the United States and the Evangelical Synod of North America. This union reflected the similarities in background and teaching of the participants. Polity in both Churches was along the lines of Presbyterianism. By 1959 the Evangelical and Reformed Church had c.800,000 members and a flourishing program of education (eight colleges, three seminaries) and of home and foreign missions.

The Reformed Church in the U.S. was first a *synod dependent on the Reformed Church in Holland, organized by M. *Schlatter at Philadelphia in 1747. Members were immigrants to Pa. from the *Reformed tradition in Switzerland and the German Palatinate. In 1793 this synod declared itself independent as the German Reformed Church; in 1863 "German" was dropped from the title. Growth was principally in Pa. and Ohio; in 1924 a majority of the Hungarian Reformed united with the Church (see HUNGARIAN REFORMED CHURCH IN AMERICA). The major problem experienced by the Church was the 19th-cent. incursion of *revivalism, which diminished the stature of the *Heidelberg Catechism and in turn the historical confessional identity of the Church. The *Mercersburg theology, an interpretive reemphasis on the Catechism, was a reaction that led to a *high-church vs. *broad-church polarization among members. The Catechism did regain its place as the doctrinal standard and was recognized as having a place in church life. At the same time a liberal attitude toward doctrine and worship and attention to "deeds not creeds" characterized the spirit of the Church. At the time of the 1934 merger there were *c.* 350,000 members in the U.S., and missions in China, Japan, and Iraq. See REFORMED CHURCH IN THE U.S.

The Evangelical Synod of North America had as its background the Evangelical Church proclaimed in Prussia in 1817 as the state Church by King Frederick William III. This Church united Reformed and Lutheran Churches, on the basis of F. *Schleiermacher's theory that confessions of faith were irrelevant. The first organization in the U.S. was at St. Louis in 1840, the German Evangelical Church Union of the West; the present name was adopted in 1877 after other similar German synods in the eastern and midwestern states joined the Missouri group. The Heidelberg and Luther's *Catechisms, as well as the *Augsburg Confession, were accepted as doctrinal standards, but liberty of conscience toward them was proclaimed. Greater stress was put upon purity of life and a practical, social Christianity than upon doctrine. Membership at the time of the merger was about 280,000.

EVANGELICAL ASSOCIATION, translation of Evangelische Gemeinschaft, the name officially adopted in 1816 by the German-speaking denomination organized along Methodist lines by Jacob *Albright. In 1922 it became the Evangelical Church and in 1946 entered the merger forming the *Evangelical United Brethren Church. The latter has been part of the United Methodist Church since 1968.

EVANGELICAL BAPTIST CHURCH, INC., GENERAL CONFERENCE OF THE, see GENERAL CONFERENCE OF THE EVANGELICAL BAPTIST CHURCH, INC.

EVANGELICAL CHURCH IN GERMANY, a federation of Lutheran, Reformed, and United Churches of Germany. Formed in 1918 at Eisenach, the Evangelische Kirche in Deutschland (EKD) supersedes two other attempts at reorganization made after the collapse of the monarchy in 1918: the Deutscher Evangelischer Kirchenbund (1922) and the Deutsche Evangelishe Kirche (1933), which had been rendered powerless by the Nazis. The EKD does not interfere with the confessional affiliation of its members, but it does emphasize their common foundation in the message of Jesus as contained in the Scriptures. The chief agencies are a synod and an executive council. Deliberations are limited to such common interests as missions, social service, ecumenism, and relations with the Federal and East German governments. Of the 27 member Churches, 13 are Lutheran, 12 are United, and 2 are Reformed. See J. Beckmann and G. Wasse, RGG 2:779–785; H. Schussler, NCE 5:647–648.

EVANGELICAL CONGREGATIONAL CHURCH, a body formed when less than 20,000 members of the United Evangelical Church refused to ratify the 1922 reunion with the Evangelical Association, which created the Evangelical Church (see EVANGELICAL UNITED BRETHREN CHURCH). Maintaining a polity and evangelical spirit similar to its parent body, the Evangelical Congregational Church in 1968 had a membership of about 30,000 in 161 congregations. Headquarters are at Reading, Pa.; the Church supports a college and seminary at Myerstown, Pennsylvania.

EVANGELICAL COVENANT CHURCH OF AMERICA, an association organized in Chicago in 1885 as the Swedish Evangelical Mission Covenant of America; present name, 1957. The original organization merged the Swedish Lutheran Mission Synod (1873) and the Ansgarius Synod (1874). Both societies were composed of Swedish immigrants, chiefly in Ill., who had been members of *free Churches in Sweden. Through Pietist and Moravian influences, they were more interested in the experience of the new birth and of Christian community than in the *confessionalism or doctrinal preciseness of the State Lutheran Church. The Church stresses the primacy of God's word, personal faith, a consecrated life, and evangelism. "Covenant" in the title signifies the unity of members in a living faith and in the desire for sanctification. The Lord's Supper and baptism are recognized as sacraments. Ministers are ordained by the congregation; polity is similar to that of Methodism. Headquarters are in Chicago, Ill.; membership in 1968 was 64,950, in 521 churches. Missions are supported in Africa, Alaska, Ecuador, Formosa, Indonesia, and Japan. See Mayer RB 341–342.

EVANGELICAL FREE CHURCH OF AMERICA, a body originally formed at Boone, Iowa (1885), of congregations declining to join what has since become the Evangelical Covenant Church of America. The Evangelical Free Church of America was first called the Swedish Evangelical Free Mission, then the Swedish Evangelical Free Church. The founding congregations wished to remain even freer in doctrine than the Evangelical Covenant Church, with no written articles of religion or confessions of faith. The denomination believes in the Bible as the word of God; ministers are permitted to interpret for themselves such doctrines as the atonement, the Lord's Supper, and baptism. Conversion and a Christian life are the only requirements for membership. In 1950 this Church was joined by the Evangelical (formerly Norwegian and Danish) Free Church Association. Headquarters are in Minneapolis, Minn.; membership in 1968 was 50,312, in 517 churches. The denomination supports three institutions of higher learning and mission centers in Japan, Hong Kong, the Philippines, Congo (Kinshasa), Germany, Singapore, and Venezuela.

EVANGELICAL FRIENDS ALLIANCE, an association of the Ohio, Kans., Ore., and Rocky Mountain Yearly Meetings of the Religious Society of Friends formed in 1965 for the purpose of providing closer fellowship and common action. Belonging to the *Gurneyite tradition, the member yearly *meetings subscribe to the main tenets of evangelical Protestantism (the Bible as the rule of faith, Jesus' vicarious atonement, salvation and forgiveness of sin, the Church as a visible and eschatological reality), but Quaker belief on inward spiritual experience is also preserved. Alliance members are active in evangelism at home and abroad. In 1966 there were about 30,000 members. See E. B. Bronner, ed., *American Quakers Today* (1966).

EVANGELICAL LUTHERAN CHURCH, merger effected in 1917 by several bodies of Norwegian immigrants: the Hauge Norwegian Evangelical Synod, the Synod of the Norwegian Evangelical Lutheran Church in America, and the United Norwegian Lutheran Church. Until 1946 its official title was the Norwegian Lutheran Church in America. Its characteristics are *Pietism, orthodoxy, and a desire for unity. In 1960 its 1,153,000 members united with other Lutheran bodies to form the *American Lutheran Church. See E. C. Nelson, EncLuthCh 1:49–52.

EVANGELICAL LUTHERAN CHURCH IN AMERICA (Eielsen Synod), a small Lutheran denomination formed in Wisconsin in 1846 by Elling Eielsen. He united various groups of Norwegian immigrants who had been gathered into congregations by laymen connected with the revival instituted in Norway by H. N. *Hauge. The American denomination grew slowly because proof of conversion was a prerequisite for church membership. Doctrinal splits occurred in 1848 and in 1858. In 1876 the Church decided to liberalize its stand to the extent of admitting to membership all who would unconditionally accept the Christian faith and lead a moral life. Eielsen and some others opposed this innovation and severed relations with the liberalizers. He and his followers retained the original name of the denomination while the innovators were incorporated as Hauge's Norwegian Evangelical Lutheran Synod, now part of the *American Lutheran Church. In 1968 the Eielsen Synod had about 4,000 members. See EncLuthCh 1:769.

EVANGELICAL LUTHERAN JOINT SYNOD of Wisconsin and Other States, the name from 1918 to 1959 of the *Wisconsin Evangelical Lutheran Synod. At its first organization meeting in 1850 it had been called the First German Lutheran Synod of Wisconsin.

EVANGELICAL LUTHERAN SYNOD, a small Lutheran body founded by a minority group of 13 pastors and their congregations who declined to unite with other Norwegian bodies when the Norwegian Lutheran Church was founded in 1917. The cause of their dispute was largely doctrinal—the tenets of grace and election. In 1920 they were incorporated under the laws of Minnesota and were formally received into the Lutheran Synodical Conference. (They were originally called Minority Synod, Little Synod, or Norwegian Synod.) In 1955 they withdrew from the Synodical Conference. Their present name was adopted in 1958. They are completely congregational in polity. In 1965 their membership was 14,000. See J. G. Anderson, EncLuthCh 1:816–817.

EVANGELICAL LUTHERAN SYNODICAL CONFERENCE, see LUTHERAN SYNODICAL CONFERENCE.

EVANGELICAL MENNONITE BRETHREN, a body organized in 1889 in Neb. and Minn. among Mennonites from Russia as a result of revival movements. Members were also called Defenseless Mennonite Brethren of Christ in North America; the present name was adopted in 1937. Emphasis is upon the need of personal regenera-

tion for membership in the Church and upon strict church discipline. In 1968 there were about 3,500 members, in 36 congregations. Since 1953 the Church has formed a joint conference with the Conference of the Evangelical Mennonite Church. See MennEnc 2:263–264.

EVANGELICAL MENNONITE CHURCH, CONFERENCE OF THE, see CONFERENCE OF THE EVANGELICAL MENNONITE CHURCH.

EVANGELICAL METHODIST CHURCH, a small Methodist denomination organized in Memphis, Tenn., in 1946, when it withdrew from the Methodist Church in protest against modernism and undemocratic ecclesiasticism. The Church is fundamentalist, revivalistic, and *Arminian. Polity is congregational; each local church controls and owns its property and calls its own ministers. The General Conference meets annually rather than quadrennially. Mission work is conducted in Mexico and Colombia. Headquarters are in Wichita, Kansas. In 1968 there were 150 churches, with about 9,000 members. In 1958 members rejected a proposed merger with the Southern Methodist Church.

EVANGELICAL PRESBYTERIAN CHURCH, a Presbyterian body that merged in 1965 with the *Reformed Presbyterian Church, Evangelical Synod. In 1937 a group led by Carl McIntire left the Orthodox Presbyterian Church and formed the Bible Presbyterian Church. A further division in 1955 led to separation into two bodies, each called Bible Presbyterian Church. The one, headed by McIntire, became the Bible Presbyterian Church (Collingwood Synod); the other, the Evangelical Presbyterian Church.

EVANGELICAL SYNOD OF NORTH AMERICA, a Church originally organized in St. Louis, Mo., in 1840, which adopted the above title in 1877, and in 1934 entered the merger forming the *Evangelical and Reformed Church. The latter in 1959 became part of the United Church of Christ.

EVANGELICAL UNION, a group in Scotland, also called Morisonians. James Morison (1816–93), one of the ablest younger ministers of the United Associate Synod was ejected from the Synod in 1841 for departing from the Calvinist doctrine of election and for holding that Christ's death is "sufficient to the salvation of all." With three others who shared his views, Morison formed the Evangelical Union at Kilmarnock in 1843, a movement of independent (i.e., congregationalist) polity, which was significant as representing the first organized protest in 19th-cent. Scotland against the Calvinist orthodoxy of the *Westminster Confession. Most of the Morisonian churches united in 1897 with the Congregational Union of Scotland.

EVANGELICAL UNITED BRETHREN CHURCH, a Church formed in 1946 in Johnstown, Pa., by the union between the Evangelical Church and the Church of the United Brethren in Christ. These two denominations both were American-born, emerging from German-speaking forebears in Pa. and Md.; both were products of the *Second Great Awakening—espousing *Arminianism in theology and emphasizing conversion coupled with an individual sanctification ethic that expressed their *Pietism. Both had adopted a polity patterned after that of American Methodism —with powers delegated from the *General Conference (national) to the local conference (congregational) through the annual conference, which possessed certain presbyterial features. In both denominations pastors were stationed annually by the bishops in conjunction with the annual conference superintendents; both denominations were small. The 441,566 United Brethren and the 263,536 Evangelicals were clustered in the town and country areas of Pa., Ind., Ill., and Ohio.

The Church of the United Brethren in Christ was formed when revivalist preachers of several Protestant denominations began in 1800 to gather annually to promote extension of their Pietism among German settlers in America. Philip W. *Otterbein (1726–1813), a German Reformed pastor in Baltimore and a friend of F. *Asbury, Methodist bp., and Martin *Boehm, a Mennonite lay preacher, were the early leaders. A reluctance to move beyond the nonsectarian, voluntary societal pattern was gradually overcome under the leadership of Christian Newcomer (1749–1830), whose organizational efforts resulted in 1816 in the first General Conference of delegates in Mount Pleasant, Pa., which adopted a *Discipline* containing an elemental confession of faith and rules providing for an itinerant ministry. Further constitutional development in 1841 was preceded by the appearance in 1834 of the *Religious Telescope*, the denominational paper, and followed by the opening of Otterbein College, Westerville, Ohio (1847), the founding of the first missionary society (1853), and opening of the first theological seminary (1871). In 1889 the expanding denomination suffered schism: it revised its Articles of Faith and Constitution, and dissident conservatives who preferred the Constitution of 1841, which prohibited membership in secret societies, withdrew to organize the United Brethren in Christ, Old Constitution. During the 20th cent. the original body manifested a growing unitive spirit, attempting two unsuccessful transconfessional unions, joining the Federal and World Councils of Churches, and cooperating with other denominations on the foreign field in China, Japan, the Philippines, Puerto Rico, Ecuador, and to some extent, Sierra Leone. Home missions were located in N.Mex. and Fla. among Spanish-speaking people.

The Evangelical Church was begun through the evangelistic, itinerant preaching of Jacob *Albright, a Pa. Lutheran farmer whose conversion experience and spiritual concern impelled him to preach.

Albright ministered independently, organizing his first *classes in 1800 and holding the first annual conference of his preachers in 1807. In 1809 a *Discipline* containing Articles of Faith very similar to those of the Methodist Episcopal Church was adopted. At the first General Conference, held in 1816, the name Die Evangelische Gemeinschaft (Evangelical Association) was adopted. The German-language ministry predominated until World War I. Growth was augmented by the appearance of the church papers, *Der Christliche Botschafter* (1836) and the *Evangelical Messenger* (1848); the creation of a missionary society (1839); and the opening of North Central College, Naperville, Ill. (1861), and a theological seminary (1876). An unfortunate division occurred (1891–94) because theological differences over the doctrine of sanctification turned into a personality duel between two bishops. While three-fifths of the membership of the Evangelical Association remained in the continuing body, the remaining two-fifths seceded in 1894 to organize the United Evangelical Church. This rupture was healed in 1922 when, with the exception of several thousand United Evangelicals who preferred to organize the Evangelical Congregational Church, the two groups reunited to create the Evangelical Church. At the time of the union of 1946, this body supported missions in Japan, China, Germany, Switzerland, and Nigeria, and U.S. missions among Wis. Italians and Ky. mountaineers.

Divided into seven episcopal areas, with headquarters in Dayton, Ohio, the Evangelical United Brethren Church supported seven colleges and three seminaries. In 1962 it revised its Confession of Faith. It was a member of the National and World Councils of Churches and also of the *Consultation on Church Union. The long and amiable relationship sustained by its predecessor bodies with the Methodist Church lent considerable logic to its 1968 union with that body, which created the *United Methodist Church. See P. H. Eller, *These Evangelical United Brethren* (1950); R. Albright, *History of the Evangelical United*

Brethren Church (1925); *Book of Ritual of the Evangelical United Brethren Church* (1955).

EVANGELICAL UNITY OF THE CZECH-MORAVIAN BRETHREN in North America, the name until 1959 of the *Unity of the Brethren, a denomination organized in 1903 by Czech immigrants in Granger, Texas.

EVANGELICALISM, a term with a variety of applications. It may be taken as a synonym for Protestantism, in keeping with the Reformers' reference to themselves as *evangelical Christians. In the U.S. evangelicalism sometimes means the *revivalism that became a characteristic of American Protestants in the 19th century. Stressing religious experience and the need for decisive individual conversion, evangelicalism in this sense tended to ignore *confessions of faith, *ecclesiology, and sacramental theology, as well as other aspects of systematic theology, and brought criticism from J. *Nevins (SEE MERCERSBERG THEOLOGY), H. *Bushnell, and others. The term is also used in opposition to liberalism and *modernism to designate conservative Christianity within all denominations. Since the early 1950s many theological conservatives (e.g., H. J. Ockenga, E. J. Carnell, C. F. H. Henry) have expressed dissatisfaction with the lack of social concern, the dearth of scholarship, and the limited scope of interest in theological subject matter of the fundamentalists; they have become known as the New Evangelicals and their movement as New Evangelicalism (see FUNDAMENTALISM). Early associated with Fuller Theological Seminary, Pasadena, Calif., and with the fortnightly *Christianity Today*, New Evangelicals have produced a number of scholarly works and have had a wide influence in American Protestantism. Differences exist within the New Evangelicalism, but it is characterized by stress upon the authority (and inerrancy) of the Bible, *evangelism and the necessity of individual conversion, the need for comprehensive and competent theological scholarship, and some expressions of Christian social concern. Holding to traditional doctrines, it emphasizes the lost condition of sinful men, the efficacy of the atoning death of Christ, and the grace of God, which justifies men who come to him in faith and repentance. See B. L. Shelley, *Evangelicalism in America* (1967); R. H. Nash, *New Evangelicalism* (1967).

EVANGELICALS OF THE AUGSBURG CONFESSION, often used as an official designation for Lutherans in European countries. *AUGSBURG CONFESSION.

EVANGELISCHE BUND (Evangelical League), an organization established at Erfurt in 1886 by W. Beyschlag and others "for the protection of German Protestant interests." The association was at first strongly anti-Catholic, but after 1914 patriotic and ethical motives brought about a change in attitude. With the election in 1935 of the Heidelberg church historian Heinrich Bornkamm as long-term president, theological interests became primary. In 1947 the Bund established an institute for confessional research at Bensheim. It also supports a number of *deaconess motherhouses and charitable institutions and sponsors the Bensheim Circle for evangelical pastors who were formerly Catholic priests. See K. Nitzschke, RGG 789–92; *idem*, EncLuthCh 1:818.

EVANGELISCHE MICHAELSBRUDER-SCHAFT (Lutheran Confraternity of Michael), a German Protestant movement founded in Marburg in 1931 as an outgrowth of the *Berneuchen circle. It aims for renewal of the Protestant Church through the Eucharist and through spirituality and retreats, and has also become prominent through its ecumenical efforts in the *Una Sancta movement. See R. Mumm, LTK 7:402–403; M. J. Taylor, *Protestant Liturgical Renewal* (1963).

EVANGELISM, a term meaning proclaiming the gospel. Although the word "evangelism" does not appear in the NT, *euangelion* (gospel) and related words do, and the idea of proclaiming the gospel and winning converts to the Christian faith is present. Evangelism has been basic to the Church's mission, but methods of evangelizing have varied widely. Person-to-person witnessing by early Christians, debating in synagogues, spontaneous addresses to informal assemblies, winning a tribe by converting its leader, and catechetical instruction for inquirers were among the early forms. Renewed emphasis upon personal religious commitment led to the Methodist revivals in England and the *Great Awakening in the U.S., where *revivalism became the chief means of evangelism for nearly 2 centuries. As the effectiveness of mass evangelism declined and *secularism increased, new methods of reaching those alienated from the Churches have been sought. The World and National Councils of Churches have departments of evangelism, as does nearly every denomination. In 1967, a worldwide meeting in Berlin considered the theology and methodology of evangelism. Considerable controversy has been evoked since mid-20th cent. by the question as to whether ministering to men's material and social needs is an essential part of evangelism or simply an after-effect. According to a widely accepted definition, evangelism is "the presentation of the good news of God in Jesus Christ, so that men are brought, through the power of the Holy Spirit, to put their trust in God; accept Jesus Christ as their Savior from the guilt and power of sin; follow and serve Him as their Lord in the fellowship of the Church and in the vocations of the common life." See C. F. H. Henry and W. S. Mooneyham, eds., *One Race, One Gospel, One Task* (2v., 1967); W. A. Visser 't Hooft, ed., *Report of New Delhi Assembly* (1962).

EVANSTON ASSEMBLY, second general assembly of the World Council of Churches (WCC), Aug. 15–31, 1954, at Evanston, Illinois. It was attended by 502 delegates from 48 countries; its theme was "Christ the Hope of the World." The preliminary report prepared by a board of 32 theologians was debated at length with the European and American approaches to eschatology clearly differing. The more orthodox European view saw the ultimate hope for the unity of the Churches in the second coming of Christ, whereas the more activist American approach emphasized the unity already existing and the good that Christians can do here and now in the world. Though there was never a complete meeting of minds, the major document of this assembly—"The Christian Hope"—did emerge from these discussions. The six subsidiary themes of the assembly were: our oneness in Christ and our disunity as Churches; the mission of the Church to those outside her life; the responsible society in a world perspective; Christians in the struggle for world community; the Church amid racial and ethnic tensions; and the Christian in his vocation. See W. A. Visser't Hooft, ed., *Evanston Report* (1955).

EXCALCEATI (Lat., unshod), a group of superstitious people, classified by Filaster (*Haer.* 81; cf. Augustine *Haer.* 68) as heretics. They went about barefoot because, according to their interpretation of Ex 3.5, Jos 5.16, and Is 20.2, the wearing of shoes was sinful.

EXCLUSIVE BRETHREN, those of the Plymouth Brethren who reject association with non-Brethren. The division into Exclusive and Open Brethren dates from 1848. *PLYMOUTH BRETHREN.

EXISTENTIAL THEOLOGY, the manner of theologizing that uses existentialist philosophy as a hermeneutic, i.e., as a principle of interpretation of revelation. Contemporary existentialism traces its inspiration to S. *Kierkegaard (1813–55). Its best-known religious exponents have been M. *Buber, P. *Tillich, G. Marcel, and R. Bult-mann. It expresses a rejection of a Christianity as a body of doctrines to be understood and explained, and looks to revelation as an answer to the question of human existence whereby the gospel can help man to achieve real selfhood through the active realization of his existence. As wholly transcendent, God cannot become an object of thought or analysis, but is known only as encountered in the personal decision of faith. The gospel speaks of the human existence to be realized. The Scriptures must be demythologized, or stripped of antiquated symbolic categories, so that they may call contemporary man to his proper situation. Since the Scriptures serve only to make known the historical character of man's own existence, it is unnecessary to inquire into the historical truth of the gospel events. Faith in turn is not response but an existential understanding of self in its existence and in its relations to God and the world. The practical expression of faith is obedience, in which man attains his authentic being. The existentialist approach has been criticized principally for ignoring the importance of the historical events for the gospel narratives. The existentialist hermeneutic seems unable to accommodate all the streams of scriptural thought and, by choosing to ignore all but one, seems to distort the gospel. See J. Macquarrie, *Existentialist Theology* (1955).

EXPERIENCE, RELIGION OF, a phrase used to classify the various interpretations of Christianity that make the affective response in the believer, rather than the authority of Bible or Church, to be the *rule of faith. (see ENTHUSIASM). In the history of Protestantism emphasis on experience lies at the origin of such groups as Anabaptists, Quakers, Moravians, and Methodists. *Pietism, *revivalism, the *Holiness movement, and *Pentecostalism all have stressed the experience of the individual believer. None of these forms of Christianity has opposed the authority of the Bible; some have been fundamentalists; some have even acknowledged the authority of *confessions of faith. Each, however, in varying ways, has given primacy to the experienced word of God within the believer, presupposing a correspondence between this experience and the content of the biblical message because of the one divine source. In this sense "religion of experience" has been contrasted with "religion of authority," which is the interpretation of Christianity made by exponents of orthodoxy. The exponents of orthodoxy see faith as authenticated by scriptural texts or by authoritative interpretation of these texts, whether by theologians (e.g., in Lutheran *orthodoxy) or by teaching authority or *magisterium (in the RC Church).

Beginning in the 19th cent. *liberal theology explicitly placed experience as the basis for religious belief. The teaching of F. *Schleiermacher was widely accepted: that all religion, Christianity being its highest form, is based on the feeling of absolute dependence, and religious doctrines are a projection of man's affective states. This approach was strengthened by the development of the psychology of religion; e.g., in William James's *Varieties of Religious Experience* (1902) religious beliefs and practices were examined to determine their basis in the inner life of man. By an appeal to human experience as the basis for belief, liberal theologians sought to make religion compatible with science and philosophy, or at least to make religion immune from attack by turning for vindication to the subjective rather than to biblical text or church dogma. A similar trend was thought to be present in RC *modernism, which met with papal condemnation. From the end of World War I the place of experience in the life of faith has received continuing attention. Karl *Barth led in the reaction to liberal theology and in the rejection of its appeal to human experience, asserting the transcendence of God and his objective saving word. Exponents of orthodoxy have continued to warn against subjectivism and to defend the essential relationship of Christian faith to the historical events of Jesus' life and, in some cases, to the classic Protestant confessions of faith or to RC dogmatic definitions. *Existential theology, *experience theology, *kerygmatic theology, and the demythologizing of the *Bultmann School, however, all may be viewed as renewed assertions of the primacy of personal response. Some RC theologians seek to narrow the separation between authority and experience by pointing out that tradition, or the living understanding of revelation, comes from both the ordinary and the charismatic experience of the whole Christian community, including its head and its members.

In RC teaching the virtue of faith is understood to be a direct, personal response to God; the teaching authority of the Church simply declares what has been revealed and its meaning. The theology of St. Thomas Aquinas, inspired by NT teaching on the Holy Spirit, makes the gifts of the Holy Spirit, which are essentially experiential, indispensable to living faith and to salvation (ThAqSt 1a2ae, 68.1 and 2). The Reformation principle *sola scriptura* was originally understood as an appeal not to a written text but to the word of God made living in the believer by the experience of faith. Often the opposition to religion of authority has been a reaction to an objectification and externalization of faith and grace that have disregarded their essentially personal nature. See J. E. Smith, *Experience and God* (1968).

EXPERIENCE THEOLOGY, a methodological approach originating in the 19th cent. that viewed the theological enterprise as descriptive of religious experience. Its principal exponents, F. *Schleiermacher, R. Otto, and J. W. Oman, held that the data of theology are not revelation but experience of faith, which is a personal awareness of the divine encounter. Statements of dogma are the reflective articulation of the understanding implicit in the variety of religious sentiments. Subjectivism is tempered by the judgment and acceptance by the Christian community of religious attitudes, which becomes current but changeable tradition. Scripture is similarly valued as stimulating and regulating the individual and group experience. Experience theology sought to introduce a vitality into theology by reacting against the contemporary conceptualist orthodoxy and rationalism. Experience theology has been criticized for its practical identification of religious experience with revelation and the resultant inability to evaluate the saving act of God in men. See J. Macquarrie, *Twentieth-Century Religious Thought* (1963), 211–225. *LIBERAL THEOLOGY.

EXSURGE DOMINE, the initial bull of excommunication issued against Martin *Luther by Leo X, June 15, 1520. Luther was given 60 days to make submission; he did not, and sentence of excommunication was rendered in the bull *Decet Romanum Pontificem,* Jan 3, 1521. This culminated the canonical process that had begun in Rome in June 1518 as a result of Luther's *Ninety-Five Theses but had dragged on until the appointment of a commission headed by Cardinal Cajetan and Pietro Accolti in Feb. 1520. The commission prepared, with the aid of J. *Eck, a text of 41 propositions drawn from Luther's writings on indulgences, the efficacy of the sacraments, and the primacy of papal authority. Cajetan had wished a specific condemnatory qualification attached to each proposition, but the commission followed Eck's proposal and condemned the ensemble as "heretical, scandalous, offensive to the faithful, misleading and erring from Catholic truth" (D 1451–92). *Exsurge Domine* incorporated the propositions and the condemnation. As official promulgator of the bull, Eck met with little success. The German bps. thought it inopportune politically, and it ran counter to their own attachment to *conciliarism. Throughout Germany, many regarded Luther as the champion of their grievances against Rome and of their hope for reform of the Church. On Dec. 10, 1520, at Wittenberg, Luther burned the bull together with a copy of the canon law of the Church. See Jedin Trent 1:172–182.

F

FABER, JACOBUS STAPULENSIS, see LE-
FÈVRE D'ETAPLES, JACQUES.

FABER, JOHANNES (Fabri; 1478–1541), German Catholic theologian, bp. of Vienna from 1530. Because of his friendship with *Erasmus, F. at first sympathized with *Melanchthon and *Zwingli in their efforts at reform; however, when he became aware of their doctrinal changes, he actively opposed them. As vicar-general of Constance he debated unsuccessfully with Zwingli in 1523. His sobriquet, "hammer of heretics," was suggested by the title (*Malleus in haeresim Lutheranam*) given to later editions of his tract against Luther (1524). He wrote on such doctrinal subjects as faith and good works, the Mass, and the Eucharist, and published numerous polemical treatises and sermons. He was a zealous pastor and helped prepare for the Council of Trent. See L. Helbling, RGG 2:856.

FAITH, in the classic definition of the Epistle to the Hebrews (11.1), "the assurance of things hoped for, the conviction of things not seen." The brevity of this definition has often tended to obscure the complexity of faith and the difficulty of identifying its place in the total context of the Christian way of life. There is perhaps no better way to describe faith than to make clear what it is not and thus, by exclusion, to make possible some understanding of what it is or at least can be. A concordance study of how the words "faith" and "to believe" are used in the OT and the NT, combined with an examination of their occurrence in Christian theological writers, would lead to classification such as the following. Emphasis on one or another of these aspects of faith has marked the differences between various Christian traditions. Yet most Christians would agree that these are essential to the meaning of faith.

Faith is trustworthiness. Perhaps the root meaning of the word is "reliability." Especially in its adjectival form, the Greek term *pistos* means "deserving of faith," and this meaning is never altogether absent from the biblical use of the term. For, in the last analysis, it is God who is *pistos*, utterly dependable in his promises, reliable in what he swears. "Every one utters lies to his neighbor" (Ps 12.2), but God does not lie. And so "God is faithful, by whom you were called into the fellowship of his Son, Jesus Christ our Lord" (1 Cor 1.9). In ordinary language a person is said to have our faith when he is trustworthy and reliable in his words and deeds. Christian faith, to be sure, means more, but it never means less; and "good faith" in the Roman and legal sense of *bona fides* is never absent from even the most radically biblical discussions of faith, whether it be the faithfulness of God in his dealings with man or the faith of man in response to God.

Faith is obedience. The English word "obedience" does not (unless one hears in it the echoes of the word "audience") show the intimate connection between obeying and hearing, as do the Greek and Latin terms for "obedience." The Epistle to the Romans makes the connection clear in its use of the word "faith." According to the Apostle Paul in Rom 10.17, "faith comes from what is heard, and what is heard comes by the preaching of Christ." Thus faith is a response to the proclamation of the word of God about Christ and his work of redemption. Elsewhere in the same epistle this "hearing of faith" is equated with obedience. In his opening salutation St. Paul declares that through Christ "we have received grace and apostleship to bring about the obedience of faith for the sake of his name among all the nations, including yourselves who are called to belong to Jesus Christ" (Rom 1.5–6). God has issued his call to a participation in Jesus Christ, and he has done so through the apostolic message. Those who hear the message and accept it are in "the obedience of faith." In the concluding peroration of the Epistle to the Romans the same theme recurs. There St. Paul speaks of "my gospel and the preaching of Jesus Christ, according to the revelation of the mystery which was kept secret for long ages but is now disclosed and through the prophetic writings is made known to all the nations, according to the command of the eternal God, to bring about the obedience of faith" (Rom 16.25–26). Here again the definition of faith as obedience is a way of emphasizing its close dependence on the preaching of the gospel, as this is contained in Sacred Scripture and communicated in the apostolic proclamation. At the same time, it is essential to note that when faith is called obedience, this does not refer primarily to the moral life of the believer (sometimes called "the new obedience"; see *Augsburg Confession, Art. 6), without which the faith is dead. It refers, rather, to taking God at his word when he announces his mercy in the proclamation of the gospel.

Faith is assenting knowledge. To cite the most extreme case, the NT ascribes "believing" even to the demons: "You believe that God is one; you do well. Even the demons believe—and shudder" (Jas 2.19). In such a context, presumably, to believe is to know a religious truth and to accept it as true, for the demons do not obey or trust even though they are obliged to acknowledge that monotheism is an accurate theory about the divine. Nor would it be accurate to confine to the demons this aspect of faith as assenting knowledge. Saving faith, too, attaches itself to a specific truth, which has a content. "Whoever would draw near to God," says the Epistle to the Hebrews (11.6), "must believe that he exists and that he rewards those who seek him." The object of this faith is, in the ultimate sense, nothing less than God himself. Nevertheless, it is also valid, on the basis of scriptural usage, to make a proposition of Christian doctrine the object of faith. Thus St. Paul speaks of "confess[ing] with your lips that Jesus is Lord and believ[ing] in your heart that God raised him from the dead" (Rom 10.9). To "believe that" something is so or

that something has happened is to know the content of the dogmatic proposition and to assent to the truth of it. It is much more than this, to be sure, for the proposition deals with the saving will and power of God; but it is not less than this. The recurring tendency, esp. in RC theology, to define faith largely in terms of assenting knowledge has led to an excessive intellectualism, in which "the faith which one believes" (*fides quae creditur*) overshadows "the faith by which one believes" (*fides qua creditur*), with the result that the personal dimension of faith is lost.

Faith is trust. In Luther's formula, which every major Christian theologian would affirm, "a god is that to which we look for all good and in which we find refuge in every time of need. To have a god is nothing else than to trust and believe him with our whole heart." The paradigm for this kind of faith in Scripture is Abraham, who is thus "the father of us all" because "in hope he believed against hope, that he should become the father of many nations" (Rom 4.16, 18). In this trusting faith Abraham "obeyed when he was called to go out to a place which he was to receive as an inheritance; and he went out, not knowing where he was to go" (Heb 11.8). Here the knowledge of faith is clearly subordinated to the obedience of faith and to the trust of faith. He who believes in God is one who has confidence that God can be relied upon even in times and places that are still unknown. Faith is therefore "the assurance of things hoped for, the conviction of things not seen," an assurance that may not know what awaits it but is certain who awaits it. The certainty and confidence of such a faith have been well summarized in the words of 2 Tim 1.12: "I know whom I have believed, and I am sure that he is able to guard until that Day what has been entrusted to me." Sometimes, in reaction to the sort of intellectualism described in the preceding paragraph, theologians, esp. in the Protestant and existentialist traditions, have attempted to restrict faith to trust and to regard other aspects of it, particularly the aspect of assenting knowledge, as alien or at least subordinate. Distorted though such a view is, it does make the valid point that in the Bible trust is central to faith.

Faith is courage. This meaning of the word becomes most evident not in the words that Scripture uses about faith but in the concrete examples of the men of faith whose heroic deeds Scripture recounts. The two portions of Scripture in which this dimension of faith is most visible are Heb 11 and Sir 44–50. The "famous men" praised in the latter, no less than the "men of old" whose faith is catalogued in the former, were men whose valor was not simply a heightened version of the powers that are natural to all mankind but was an affirmation of the power of God. Similar though Samson and Prometheus are, they differ in this fundamental respect as heroes: Samson's courage came from his obedience and trust in God, while the courage of Prometheus consisted in his defiance of the gods. Early Christianity recognized the quality of faith as courage when it began to compose the lives of martyrs and saints. For example, the *Life of Antony*, which was probably written by St. Athanasius, described his many deeds of saintly heroism and quoted him as saying: "We have learned our lessons from the saints and do as they have done and imitate their courage." Bizarre though some of the exploits ascribed to some of the saints may have been, their boldness in the face of their tormentors and in the presence of death is a dominant theme of this literature. And even though fortitude was classified as one of the "cardinal virtues" rather than one of the "theological virtues" (see the next paragraph), faith as courage transcended that distinction.

Faith is a theological virtue. Its place among the virtues, together with its similarities and dissimilarities to hope and love, occupied St. Thomas Aquinas at considerable length. The greatest of the theological virtues, by apostolic authority (1 Cor 13.13), is love, and hope in turn proceeds from faith. In addition, faith pertains to the intellect, while both hope and love pertain to the will. Quoting St. Augustine's defini-tion of faith as "a virtue whereby we believe what we do not see" and St. John Damascene's definition that "faith is an assent without inquiry," St. Thomas made its classification in the virtues dependent upon its nature as a "habit"; for "any habit that is always the principle of a good act may be called a human virtue. Such a habit is formed faith." This view of faith as a theological virtue has enabled theologians to make clear both its relation to the truth of revelation and its basis in the inner life of the believer. All the other definitions of faith listed here may thus be included in this one. See ThAq ST 1a2ae, 62–67; 2a2ae, 1–7; J. H. Newman, *Grammar of Assent* (1870); P. Tillich, *Dynamics of Faith* (1957); *idem, Courage to Be* (1952).

FAITH AND ORDER, a branch of the *ecumenical movement directed to the theological aspects of the search for unity among Christian Churches. Faith and Order took its origin from a 1910 resolution of the General Synod of the Protestant Episcopal Church in the U.S., which, conscious of the scandal of disunity as an obstacle to Christian mission work, called for a conference of Christian Churches throughout the world to work for unity, "that all may be one, so that the world may believe." After several preliminary conferences, the first World Conference on Faith and Order met in Lausanne, Switzerland, in 1927. The conference invited the participation of all Christian Churches on the basis of a common belief in Christ and the gospel. At the second World Conference on Faith and Order (Edinburgh, 1937) it was decided to merge with the *Life and Work movement, a more socially oriented branch of the ecumenical movement. From this merger was born the World Council of Churches (WCC), within which the Faith and Order movement thereafter continued to function semiautonomously. The Constitution of the Faith and Order Commission admits to membership Churches that are not members of the WCC. As the Commission on Faith and Order of the World

Council of Churches, it held its third world conference in Lund, Sweden, in 1952, and its fourth in Montreal in 1963. The reports prepared by these world conferences, and sometimes voted on by the delegates, are without binding power on the Churches represented, which are free to accept or reject them. After each world conference, reports are published and circulated among the Churches and their responses solicited and studied. Regional and other sub-groups meet to discuss issues, and working committees undertake further theological studies, preparing preliminary reports for the next world conference and for the general assemblies of the WCC.

The initial efforts of Faith and Order were devoted largely to defining areas of doctrinal agreement and disagreement among the Churches, in the hope that a deepened understanding of their various positions might remove some of the obstacles to unity. Later studies centered about the Christological concept of the Church as the Body of Christ, united in one baptism and in the Eucharist, and associated tradition with scriptural study. At first tending to reflect doctrinal positions identified with Anglicanism, the world conferences later witnessed a growing prominence of the Lutheran and *Reformed traditions, esp. in relation to the doctrines of grace and justification. Orthodox Churches represented at the world conferences have been influential and uncompromising in their presentation of the Catholic viewpoint. Increasingly, RC theologians have taken part, as authorized observers, in recent world conferences and have contributed to the preparatory theological studies of the working committees, esp. since the creation by the Vatican of its *Secretariat for Promoting Christian Unity and the establishment, by the Secretariat on Faith and Order of the WCC, of a Joint Working Group and a Joint Theological Committee. In 1968 nine of the RC observers at the fourth General Assembly of the WCC at Uppsala, Sweden, were elected to membership on the Faith and Order Commission. Interim reports of the Commission on Faith and Order after the 1963 conference have indicated a new emphasis on a theology of man in the modern world. This emphasis can be expected to be reflected in future world conferences and to draw the Faith and Order movement closer in orientation to those sections of the ecumenical movement concerned esp. with the Christian approach to social problems. See J. E. Skoglund and R. J. Nelson, *Fifty Years of Faith and Order* (1963); L. Vischer, ed., *Documentary History of the Faith and Order Movement 1927-63* (1963); *New Directions in Faith and Order, Bristol 1967* (1968). *EDINBURGH CONFERENCE; *LAUSANNE CONFERENCE; *LUND CONFERENCE; *MONTREAL CONFERENCE; *UPPSALA CONFERENCE; *WORLD COUNCIL OF CHURCHES.

FAITH HEALING, a phrase used in two ways: (1) in its broader usage, any cure of bodily ills that relies on purely religious rather than medical means; (2) in its specific meaning, mental or metaphysical healing by the power of spiritual mind over matter, the evil cause of sin, sickness, and death. *HEALING; *DIVINE HEALING.

FAITH MISSION, a phrase connoting a specific type of missionary endeavor. "Faith" indicates the intention of relying completely on divine providence both for financial support and for the actual direction mission work should take. Thus the faith mission makes no provision for guaranteed sources of income, nor is it affiliated with or directed by a home mission board or organization. One of the primary aims, and accomplishments, of the faith mission is to become completely indigenous in its mission field. The faith mission often is a non-denominational project; the missionaries are bound together simply by the desire to preach the gospel; they are usually evangelicals and fundamentalists. The faith mission concept has been prominent in the growth of Pentecostalism in the U.S., and in the remarkable Pentecostal missionary expansion throughout the world.

FAITH ONLY, see SOLA FIDE, SOLA GRATIA, SOLA SCRIPTURA.

FAMILISTS, a religious body founded by H. *Niclaes, who called it the Family of Love (Familia Caritatis), or the House of Love. The Familists existed in Germany, Holland, and France, but principally in England, where Niclaes visited in 1552 or 1553. Their teaching was that the divine spirit of love within them raised them above Bible, creed, liturgy, or law. They were accused of *antinomianism. In spite of legal repression they survived in England until the end of the 17th cent. when most of them were absorbed into the Society of Friends. See R. Knox, *Enthusiasm* (repr., 1961), 140–141, 171–172; G. Bareille, DTC 5:-2070–72 s.v. "Famille d'amour"; R. M. Jones, *Studies in Mystical Religion* (1923), 428–448.

FANATICISM, unreasoning devotion to a particular form of religious expression, sometimes centering around a set of doctrines, sometimes around a group (e.g., a church or sect), sometimes around an ethical code or other pattern of behavior. Devotion to the object of fanaticism is expressed without regard for rational balance or ordinary standards of prudence. Some observers interpret fanaticism as evidence of repressed doubt, which the personality subconsciously tries to deny by exaggerated devotion. Theologically, fanaticism may be interpreted as a form of idolatry. The fanatic gives to some particular object, person, or code of actions the loyalty that belongs only to God. No distinction is drawn between the being of God and the symbols and acts that relate to him. Examples that are often cited include: *snake handlers; extreme puritanical groups who attempt to make their standards obligatory for the total society; persons whose devotion to particular religious forms and their propagation becomes so consuming that they are unable to maintain normal human relationships; and those whose devotion leads them to persecute others who do not share it as enemies of God.

FAREL, GUILLAUME (1489–1565), French-Swiss Protestant Reformer. F., like John *Calvin, with whom his name is linked in the history of Genevan Protestantism, was born in France and studied in Paris. At first a disciple of the humanist Jacques *Lefèvre d'Étaples and a member of the reform circle of Bp. Guillaume Briçonnet of Meaux, F. was affected by Luther's writings; in 1523 he was forced to leave the country, taking refuge in Switzerland. He settled first at Basel, where his violent zeal brought him into conflict with Erasmus. During this period he came under the influence of J. *Oecolampadius and *Zwingli. Expelled from Basel in 1524, he preached reform in various localities (Montbéliard, Strassburg), finally settling in La Suisse Romande. In this period he wrote the first Protestant treatise published in French, *Sommaire et brève déclaration* (1525), a short, not very profound work. From Berne (1526) and Aigle, he exercised an influence on many in France as well as in Switzerland. He became the Reformer of Neuchâtel in 1530; he went to Geneva in 1532 and 1533 to preach. In July 1536 he persuaded Calvin, who was passing through the city, to remain and join in the attempt to impose that strict discipline for which the city was to become famous. This first effort failed, and both he and Calvin were forced (1538) to leave the city. Calvin, of course, returned in 1541 to become the undisputed master of the godly city, while F. was content to return to Neuchâtel, where he remained pastor until his death. While he preceded Calvin in time, F. became his disciple, overshadowed by the greater man in the history of Protestantism. See J. Olin, NCE 5:835; Léonard HistProt 1:315–317, and *passim.*

FATHER DIVINE PEACE MISSION, a religious movement that began in the U.S. about 1919 and attained its peak in the decade 1935–45. It centered on the person of its leader, Father Divine, born George Baker, also known as Major Morgan J. Devine *(c.*1865–1965). He is said to have spent the first 50 years of his life in and near Savannah, Georgia. He reputedly initiated his own movement at Valdosta, Ga., *c.*1914, after a supposed earlier association with Samuel Morris. In his lifetime, Father Divine denied all of these reports, although the courts ruled that he was George Baker of Savannah. In 1919, as Major M. J. Devine, he purchased a house in Sayville, Long Island, N.Y., after gathering (1915–19) a small following in Brooklyn. At Sayville, his willingness to house and feed his followers and his habit of preaching to them at lengthy meals gained great notoriety. A determined effort to force him and his followers to leave Sayville, including judicial harassment and civil suits, gave his movement considerable publicity. After several months, he moved his headquarters to Harlem. It caught the imagination of many thousands of Negroes, as well as many whites, and within a few years missions, hostels, restaurants, stores, and other businesses conducted by Father Divine were to be found in every major city in the eastern U.S., the Midwest, on the West Coast, and to a lesser extent, in the southern States.

Soon after establishing himself in Harlem, he adopted the name Father Divine and began to call his hostels heavens. Harlem in the 1920s was a "burned-over district" for both religious and social cults, dominated by Marcus Garvey and his Back-to-Africa programs. Father Divine's Peace Mission took strong root in this soil because it was primarily a social protest movement, expressed in the terminology and emotionalism of a religious revival, but completely "this-worldly." Father Divine studiously avoided giving himself the attributes of God, but his followers paid him honor as God and constantly acknowledged him as the deity in his presence. He dwelt among his followers, constantly visiting their banquets to preach to them, and provided for their daily needs. These banquets formed the worship services of the movement. A cult of his presence developed, so that his followers felt that they were blessed by seeing him and attributed cures to his presence, his touch, or even his photograph. In his daily preaching, which was published verbatim in his newspaper the *New Day*, Father Divine stressed personal morality and the ethical side of religion. Members of his sect were forbidden to drink or smoke, gamble, or own life insurance. A strict honesty, which extended to a pin found in the street, was enjoined. Members were to give an honest day's work for a day's wage. They were also encouraged to live evangelically by abstaining from sexual intercourse, even when husbands and wives continued to live together. The reward for this strict morality was immediate and tangible. Members of his sect were invited to live in one of his heavens, or hostels, where they were fed, clothed, and sheltered in considerable comfort throughout the harrowing Depression years, either at a minimal charge or by working in the heaven. The gifts of the members to their local churches made up any deficit. Non-resident members had low-cost restaurants and other services available. In New York and other states, the movement acquired rural property to move slum dwellers to farms, whose produce supplied the urban members' needs. For urban Negroes, who were often turned away by public welfare agencies at this time, Father Divine was a miracle worker.

In addition to his own role in the movement and the personal ethics of his followers, Father Divine made world peace and interracial justice the dominant theme of his movement. He greatly revered the U.S. Bill of Rights and called for its fulfillment in laws that would abolish lynching, segregation in schools and public places, prejudice in hiring for jobs or in leasing or selling houses, and every other vestige of racism. He also called for complete disarmament and interracial and international brotherhood. His movement began to decline after World War II, accelerated perhaps by his marriage to a white woman in 1946 and by judgments secured against him in the courts. Although by the time of his death in

1965 membership had diminished, the Peace Mission continued in existence. See S. Harris and H. Crittenden, *Father Divine: Holy Husband* (1953); R. A. Parker, *Incredible Messiah: The Deification of Father Divine* (1937).

FAUSTUS OF RIEZ (d. *c.*495), Semipelagian author and bp. of Riez in Provence from 458. In 433 F. became abbot at Lérins, the center of opposition to certain extreme interpretations of St. Augustine's teaching on grace. In the years 477–485, he was exiled from his see by the Visigothic King Euric. In answering the extreme predestinarian teachings of one Lucidus, he wrote *De gratia*, urging the necessity of human cooperation with divine grace and the universal salvific will of God. His teaching was approved by the Councils of Arles and Lyons (473, 474) but was later condemned by Council of *Orange II in 529. In addition to *De gratia*, F. wrote two books on the Holy Spirit. Some of his letters and homilies also survive. Works: PL 53:681–890; 58:783–870; crit. ed. A. Engelbrecht, CSEL 21 (1891). See Altaner 566–567.

FEBRONIANISM, the radical ideas concerning *episcopacy and *Church and State proposed by N. Von *Hontheim in *On the State of the Church and the Legitimate Power of the Roman Pontiff* (pub. 1763 under pseud. "Justinus Febronius"). Von Hontheim, then auxiliary bp. of Trier, expressed both his own convictions and the grievances of the German metropolitans against the papacy and esp. the papal nuncio at Cologne. Von Hontheim claimed that the popes had usurped the rightful powers of the bps., who stood in direct succession from the Apostles. The pope was only "first among equals" and lacked jurisdiction within dioceses. A general council had legitimate authority over the pope, and his decrees could be revised by national or provincial synods. Metropolitans should have the power to confirm and depose bishops. Clement XIII put Von Hontheim's work on the Index (1764). He

was protected and honored by his superiors for many years, but his abp., Klemens Wenzeslaus of Trier, finally required him to publish (1778) a qualified disavowal of his earlier views. That he actually changed his beliefs is highly doubtful, though he died (1790) in full communion with the Church. His debt to *Gallicanism was evident from his sources and his insistence that rulers should protect their churches against papal interference.

*Josephinism in Austria derived its theoretical justification from Febronianism. However, Von Hontheim and his patrons really wanted to establish a German national Church on an essentially episcopal basis, and in this the secular rulers did not aid them. On the contrary, the elector of Bavaria welcomed the establishment of a nunciature at Munich (1785), and Emperor Joseph II refused to support a program devised at the Congress of Ems (1786) to curtail papal powers in Germany. Many suffragan bps. were either unenthusiastic or were opposed to a policy that would only increase the authority of the metropolitans. The failure of the Ems program and the contemporary revolutions in France and Belgium (1789–90) led the Rhenish abps. to seek better relations with Rome. The destruction of the ecclesiastical principalities and the closing of the new Univ. of Bonn, founded to promote Febronian ideas, were serious blows to the movement. In 1815 Metternich briefly toyed with the idea of setting up a national Church in Germany, but then dropped it. The reaction against the State–Church systems prevalent in Germany after 1815 produced a new flowering of Ultramontanism in both clerical and lay circles. By mid-19th cent. Febronianism lingered at most only as an attitude of mind. See H. Holborn, *History of Modern Germany, 1648–1840* (1964). *CONCILIARISM; *PISTOIA, SYNOD OF; *CHURCH AND STATE.

FEDERAL COUNCIL OF THE CHURCHES OF CHRIST in America, a body formed in 1908 for interdenominational cooperation among Protestant Churches, predecessor of the *National Council of the Churches of Christ in the U.S.A. The idea for the Federal Council of Churches grew out of earlier cooperative ventures, e.g., the *Evangelical Alliance and the National Federation of Churches and Christian Workers, and was inspired by the *Social Gospel. Emphasis on evangelistic and social ideals rather than on theological dialogue brought together Churches of widely differing traditions. By a merger in 1950 with seven other smaller interdenominational mission boards and administrative agencies, the Federal Council became the National Council of Churches.

FEDERAL THEOLOGY, called also *covenant theology, a designation for the theologies in the *Reformed tradition that have used God's covenants (Lat. *foedera)* with man as a theme. In the 16th cent. the thought of *Zwingli was continued and synthesized by H. *Bullinger in *De foedere et testamento Dei unico et aeterno* (1534), presenting the biblical concept of covenant as the key to the continuity of the OT and NT history of salvation. Calvin in his *Institutes* formulated the idea of one covenant of grace manifested from Adam to Christ. The distinction between the covenant of works before the Fall and the covenant of grace afterwards, was incorporated into the *Westminster Confession (c. 7) and the *Helvetic Consensus Formula (Art. 23–25). There were many variations and elaborations within orthodox Calvinism on the various covenants of God with man, but two adaptations of the covenant theme are esp. important. The biblical theologian J. *Cocceius (1603–69), whose *Summa doctrinae de foedere et testamento Dei* (1648) is regarded as a systematization of federal theology, substituted the covenant idiom for the orthodox, scholastic Calvinist terminology. He interpreted the covenant as God's expression of how to share in the divine love, and traced salvation history through the biblical manifestations of the covenant. His thought provoked resistance

from the strict Calvinist theologians of the Netherlands and had influence on *Pietism as developed at Halle. Covenant theology among the Puritans of England and New England, by employing political and legal terminology to express the covenant with God, mitigated the Calvinist doctrine of absolute decrees of predestination and gave recognition to the meaning of human cooperation within the framework of a reasonable compact of salvation. Karl *Barth, in his theology of reconciliation, gave renewed prominence to God's covenant: the eternal divine covenant, God's gracious election of men in Christ, is the basis for justification and reconciliation.

FEDERATED CHURCHES, a term describing two or more churches of different denominations that combine for worship and work. Each congregation retains its corporate identity and denominational affiliation, but both call the same minister and carry on a common program. Such churches exist usually in rural areas where population is too sparse to make it possible for several churches to be self-sustaining. The first instances of federated churches were in Mass. as early as 1887. In the 1916 U.S. census they were listed as *independent churches, but in 1926 and 1936 they were called federated churches. No reliable statistics are available for this type of church; those reported in the *Yearbook of American Churches* cannot be considered accurate. See R. A. Felton, *Cooperative Churches* (1947); F. S. Mead, *Handbook of Denominations* (4th ed., 1965). *MERGER; *UNION CHURCHES.

FELIX OF URGEL (d. 818), bp. of Urgel in Spain, with *Elipandus a leading proponent of *Adoptionism, the teaching that Jesus as born of the Father is true son of God, but as born of the Virgin Mary is only God's adopted son. The works of F. are lost; his teaching is to be seen only in the texts of his adversaries, Alcuin among them. F. was summoned before Charlemagne (792); he died in the custody of Bp. Agobard of Lyons. He is named in the condemnation of Adoptionism by the Council of Frankfurt (D 615). See L. Ueding, LTK 4:71; bibliog. for Adoptionism.

FELL, MARGARET (1614–1702), "mother of Quakerism." F. was the wife of Thomas Fell, vice-chancellor of the duchy of Lancaster; they made their home, Swarthmoor (Swarthmore) Hall, a haven for itinerant preachers. When G. *Fox stopped there in 1652, she became convinced of his message. Thereafter Swarthmoor Hall became a secure base for Quakers, and F. herself advanced the movement by her counsel, preaching, correspondence, and fund-raising. She also sought mitigation of harsh anti-Quaker measures, writing frequently (1655–57) to Oliver Cromwell, and obtaining from Charles II (1661) the release of 4,000 Quakers from prison. She herself was imprisoned for 4 years, 1664–68. Her husband had died in 1658, and in 1669 she married Fox. See V. Noble, *Man in the Leather Breeches* (1953); I. Ross, *M. F., Mother of Quakerism* (1949).

FELLOWSHIP, a translation of the Greek *koinonia*, signifying varied relationships (e.g., association, partnership, community, participation). *Koinonia* and related words in the NT are used in various ways, but they refer primarily to the unique Christian communion based upon sharing new life in Christ. It sometimes indicates participation in something—e.g., God's grace (Phil 1.7), the Holy Spirit (Phil 2.1), or the body and blood of Christ (1 Cor 10.16–18). Other passages emphasize sharing with Christ (Phil 3.10) and with God (1 Jn 1.3). Still others indicate the communion of Christians with one another (1 Jn 1.3, 7). Recent discussions on the Church have recognized the importance of the concept of fellowship, which indicates that the Church is a divine-human community constituted and sustained by God. Emil *Brunner goes so far as to state: "The Body of Christ is nothing other than a fellowship of persons. . . . The faithful are bound to each other through their common sharing in Christ and in the Holy Ghost" (*Misunderstanding of the Church* [1953], 10–11). Although some would consider this an extreme statement, esp. since it adds that the body of Christ "has nothing to do with an organization," it illustrates the point that modern theologians consider the NT idea of fellowship essential to understanding the nature of the Church. The same viewpoint is evident in RC ecclesiology and liturgical practice esp. since Vatican Council II. In common parlance, the word has taken on more superficial meanings, ranging from a gathering for public worship to mere sociability experienced in eating or recreation. The term also has a specialized, restrictive use, namely, as applied to the place of the *local church stressing a *congregational polity in relation to centralizing organizations. This relationship is described as one of fellowship, to indicate that the local church does not surrender its autonomy; the centralizing organization does not have jurisdiction, but exists to foster mutual interests and assistance. See Kittel TD 3:789–809; J. R. Nelson, *Realm of Redemption* (1951).

FELLOWSHIP OF EVANGELICAL BAPTIST CHURCHES IN CANADA, religious body originating in 1953 from the merger of the Union of Regular Baptist Churches of Ontario and Quebec with the Fellowship of Independent Baptist Churches of Canada. Headquarters are in Toronto, Ontario.

FIDEISM (Lat. *fides*, faith), the tendency to underestimate the powers of reason and overload the burden of faith in getting to philosophical, moral, and religious truths. In an extreme form, fideism is the systematic disparagement of scientific discourse and exclusive reliance on belief and affectivity. It is a perennial position in the history of Christian thought. It was advanced in the Middle Ages by holders of the "double truth theory," represented by the hardheaded thinker *William of Ockham, who taught that only by faith can we be certain about God's existence, the immortality of the soul, and the moral law, and was prominent in the reaction of *traditionalism to 18th-century rationalism, subjectivism, and skepticism. All the same we should proceed with caution. "Fideist, a nonce-word," the *Oxford Dictionary* declares briskly, and justly, for in truth it has been thrown about too freely, thus at such thinkers as S. Kierkegaard (d. 1855), A. Gratry (d. 1872), and A. Bonnetty (d. 1879). It is better to reserve it to controversies in the last decades of the 19th cent. and the first decade of the 20th. There it crops up in French Protestant and Catholic circles, in each case with a different emphasis. E. Ménégoz stressed the necessity of *sola fides,* faith alone, "faith" as going to God himself, not to credal statements, "alone" as being independent of the arguments of liberal Protestantism; A. Sabatier was in agreement with him (see SYMBOLOFIDEISM). Among Catholics part of the modernist controversy was about the strength of the assent that can be given to the objective grounds of rational credibility, the *preambula fidei,* on which Vatican Council I (see D 3008–09, 3026, 3033–34) had taken so firm a stand: the so-called fideists were those accused of reducing the preambles of faith to imperatives from subjective experience or inspiration. See E. Doumergue, *Le Dernier mot du fidéisme* (1907); R. Aubert, *Le Problème de l'acte de foi* (3d ed., 1958).

FIELD PREACHING, a characteristic of early Methodism: preaching out-of-doors, wherever large crowds may easily gather. It was begun by George *Whitefield in 1739, when, finding many of the churches closed to him, he preached to about 200 colliers on Kingswood Hill near Bristol. John *Wesley at first opposed field preaching; but seeing the good results of Whitefield's work and finding a precedent in the life of Jesus, particularly in the Sermon on the Mount, he joined in at Kingswood. Soon he enthusiastically urged field preaching by Methodists everywhere and felt that Methodism would lose its power when it gave up preaching out-of-doors. The *camp meeting was a development in keeping with the tradition of field preaching. See J. Dawson, *John Wesley on Preaching* (1903), 149–162; R. M. Cameron, *Rise of Methodism: A Source Book* (1954).

FIFTH MONARCHY MEN (Quint Monarchy Men), a fanatical sect that, during the Puritan revolution in England, sought to establish a theocracy. They professed a form of *millenarianism, namely, that the fifth monarchy (Dt 2, 44; the other four were the Assyrian, Persian, Greek, and Roman) was at hand; Christ with his saints would come to rule for 1,000 years. When Oliver *Cromwell and then the Restoration disappointed their hopes for rule by the godly (themselves), they rose in armed revolt (1657, 1661). Their leaders were beheaded and the sect was dissolved. See W. C. Braithwaite, *Beginnings of Quakerism* (2d ed., 1955), 18–19; L. F. Brown, *Political Activities of the Baptists and Fifth Monarchy Men in England during the Interregnum* (1912).

FILLMORE, MYRTLE (1845—1931), **and CHARLES** (1854—1948), founders of the *Unity School of Christianity. They were married in 1881. While promoting real estate in Colorado and later in Kansas City, Mo., they took *New Thought courses and were influenced by Emma Curtis Hopkins. In 1889 they began *Modern Thought* magazine, which became *Unity* in 1891. The Unity School of Practical Christianity developed from the magazine, chartered as a local Kansas City association in 1903 and as a denomination in 1914. Charles Fillmore, a prolific writer on religious subjects, published *The Twelve Powers of Man* (1896), *Jesus Christ Heals* (1914), and *Prosperity* (1928), besides editing a half dozen periodicals on Unity. Originally Methodists, the Fillmores combined traditional Christianity with belief in reincarnation, eternal life in the body, the conquest of disease by mind, and other insights drawn from New Thought sources.

FINNEY, CHARLES GRANDISON (1792–1875), evangelist and theologian of the *Oberlin theology. F. was born in Warren, Conn., and grew up in central N.Y. state. After his conversion in 1821, he gave up the practice of law and became a revivalist in upstate N.Y.; later, as his reputation spread, he expanded his efforts to the larger cities of N.Y., New England, and England. His style of evangelism, which was referred to as "new measures" and included the use of the *anxious bench, was successful, but was criticized for its emotional effects. At first a Presbyterian, he later became a Congregationalist and assumed the pastorate of the Broadway Tabernacle in New York City. In 1835 he was called to the Oberlin Collegiate Institute as professor of theology. Although lacking and mistrusting formal theological training, he proved to be a powerful instructor. In 1837 he became pastor of the First Church in Oberlin; he was president of Oberlin College from 1851 to 1866. Influenced by the *New England theology, his views nevertheless reflected the Oberlin theology. He rejected the determination of the will and the imputation of guilt, while holding to human depravity; man (he taught) can freely respond to the claim of the divine will and embrace the aim of moral perfectionism. The will is either completely virtuous, fastening upon the good of Being in General (see ED-WARDS, JONATHAN), or wholly sinful in its actions. F.'s influence as an evangelist and his sympathy for antislavery views won the support of wealthy sponsors for the struggling Oberlin institution. Mainly through his writings he influenced the establishment of the YMCA in London. See C. G. Finney, *Autobiography* (1876); G. F. Wright, *C. G. F.* (1891); W. G. McLoughlin, Jr., *Modern Revivalism* (1959).

FINNISH APOSTOLIC LUTHERAN CHURCH OF AMERICA, name adopted in 1929 by a body of *Laestadians organized in 1871 in Calumet, Michigan. Since 1879 the word "Apostolic" was used to distinguish this Church from the non-Laestadian, or Evangelical Lutheran, bodies among Scandinavian Americans. In 1962 the name was changed to *Apostolic Lutheran Church of America.

FINNISH EVANGELICAL LUTHERAN CHURCH (Suomi Synod), a Church formally organized in 1890, but with its beginnings in the mid-19th cent. among the Finnish immigrants in northern Michigan who were not *Laestadians, or "apostolic," i.e. revivalistic Lutherans. In 1962 the Church became part of the *Lutheran Church in America.

FIRE BAPTIZED HOLINESS CHURCH (Wesleyan), a body formed as the Southeast Kansas Fire Baptized Holiness Association c.1890 by Methodists wishing greater emphasis on the doctrine of *sanctification; the present name was adopted in 1945. The Church retains Methodist polity but considers its main teaching to be a return to John *Wesley's idea of *Christian perfection. While it has only about 1,000 members, the Church conducts a vigorous program of evangelism.

FIRE BAPTIZED HOLINESS CHURCH OF GOD of the Americas, a Pentecostal denomination, established separately by Negroes on racial grounds in 1908; "of God" was added to the name in 1922; "of the Americas," in 1926. The denomination, in its handbook, *Basis of Union*, states full acceptance of *Pentecostalism and strong opposition to the "teaching of the so-called Christian Scientists, Spiritualists, Unitarians, Universalists, and Mormons." The Church is headed by a bishop; headquarters are in Atlanta, Ga. See J. T. Nichol, *Pentecostalism* (1966), 129–130.

FIRST CENTURY CHRISTIAN FELLOWSHIP, a name used by *Moral Re-Armament, on the basis that members unite in a way modeled after the earliest Christian communities.

FIRST CONGREGATIONAL METHOD-IST CHURCH OF U.S.A., a small Methodist body of about 7,500 members, organized at Forsyth, Ga., in 1852; it was incorporated in Ala. in 1937, but now (1969) lists itself as unincorporated. The denomination withdrew in 1852 from the Methodist Episcopal Church, South, on grounds that *episcopacy and *itinerancy were unbiblical and undemocratic. The doctrine of the Church is Methodistic; polity is more nearly congregational. "First" was added to the title in 1968. See HistAmMeth 3:594.

FIRST PRESIDENCY, the supreme governing body of the Church of Jesus Christ of Latter-day Saints. It is composed of the president and two counselors, who are high priests of the priesthood of Melkisedek. "President" was a title adopted by Joseph *Smith.

FIVE-MILE ACT, a *Restoration measure further inhibiting activities of *Dissenters in order to safeguard the established Church of England. During a plague, many Anglican clergy fled, while Dissenters returned to former parishes, caring for the sick, burying the dead, and preaching. Fearing an increase of Dissenters, Parliament (1665) passed the Five-Mile Act. *Nonconformist ministers were to swear that "it is not lawful . . . to take arms against the king" and that they would not seek to alter "government either in Church or State." Those refusing this oath were forbidden to come within five miles of any place where they had served as ministers. They were also prohibited from teaching school. See H. Gee and W. J. Hardy, *Documents Illustrative of English Church History* (1921); G. Clark, *Later Stuarts, 1660–1714* (2d ed., 1955).

FIVE POINTS OF CALVINISM, designation for the basic tenets of strict Calvinism as contained in the canons of the Synod of *Dort (1618–19). The five points can be indicated by the mnemonic t-u-l-i-p: total depravity of man, unconditional predestination and reprobation, limitation of the Redemption to the elect, irresistibility of divine grace, perseverance in grace assured to the elect. See Mayer RB 225–226; bibliog. for Synod of Dort.

FIVE POINTS OF FUNDAMENTALISM, tenets of conservative Protestant faith, also referred to as the five fundamentals: the inerrancy of the Bible, Jesus Christ's divinity, virgin birth, substitutionary atonement, resurrection, and future second coming. They were formulated at the Niagara Bible Conference of 1895. While many denominations described as fundamentalist do adhere to such teachings, the so-called five points cannot be taken as an adequate reflection of *fundamentalism.

FLACIUS ILLYRICUS, MATTHIAS (1520–75), Lutheran theologian, polemicist, and historian. His Croatian name was Vlacic (hence Flacius); he came from the Adriatic coast of ancient Illyria (Illyricus); studied at Basel and Tübingen; and after 1541 became Luther's faithful follower. F. was one of the main editors of the *Magdeburg Centuries, in which he gave better proof of his apologetic gifts than of his objectivity as a historian. There was hardly any controversy in his lifetime in which he was not a protagonist (see ADIAPHORA; SYNERGISTIC CONTROVERSY). He held views more extreme than Luther on human sinfulness, regarding original sin as the "essential substance" in man's nature. This near Manichaeism required a response in the *Formula of Concord (art. I). F. remained for life the great inquisitor of Lutheran orthodoxy. He is also known for his *Clavis scripturae sacrae* (1567), a treatise on biblical interpretation much appreciated by contemporaries, which went into several editions. He also edited the so-called *Missa Illyrica* (1557), wrongly dating it from the 8th century. See R. Seeberg, *Textbook of the History of Doctrines* (1956), 2:364ff.; C. Krauth, *Conservative Reformation and Its Theology* (1875).

FLAGELLANTS, itinerant semi-organized bands of penitents practicing self-flagellation. This practice was an ancient form of penance, practiced in monasteries and by individual ascetics. The flagellants, however, constituted a widespread, largely lay movement, unorthodox in doctrine and subversive of social order. The first major appearance of the flagellants was in Italy at Perugia in 1260, the year when the last age of the Church was to begin according to *Joachim of Fiore (see JOACHIMISM). It was an era of devastating wars and apocalyptic foreboding. The processions of flagellants from town to town and their self-floggings had a great impact on the populace; the movement spread to southern Italy, and throughout northern and central Europe. Flagellants ignored the clergy, absolved each other, and upset the civil peace. They were repressed by ecclesiastical and civil authorities, and the first outbreak faded, although there were isolated recurrences at Strassburg (1296), Bergamo (1334), and Cremona (1346). The coming of the Black Death to Europe revived the phenomenon on a grand scale, except in England, where recruiting failed, and in France, where the flagellants were outlawed by royal decree. The confraternities of this period were more highly organized, with strict entrance requirements, a carefully detailed ritual and rule of life, and a distinctive garb. During this period they came to claim authorization by a letter sent from heaven to Jerusalem in 1348, pardoning the sins of all who scourged themselves. The same antisacramental, antiauthoritarian, and antisocial views developed. The flagellants also engaged in anti-Jewish pogroms and massacres.

Pope Clement VI banned the flagellants in 1349. The third major appearance was in the 15th cent., esp. in Germany and the Low Countries. Conrad Schmid was one of the leaders, claiming to be a reincarnation of Elijah come to judge the world. Denials of Catholic doctrine became more detailed. Flagellation was said to be a second baptism, a baptism of blood that alone availed to salvation; other sacraments were disregarded; the doctrine of indulgences, the veneration of saints, and purgatory were rejected. The movement was violently antiecclesiastical and adopted many of John *Wycliffe's teachings. After condemnation by the Council of Constance (1414), the flagellants were gradually repressed by harsh penalties, such as imprisonment and death. From the 14th to the 16th cent. there were confraternities in Italy, the Disciplinati, under church supervision practicing flagellation. Group flagellation reappeared in some countries in southern Europe as late as the 19th century. In some Latin American countries and in the Archdiocese of Santa Fe, New Mexico, secret groups of *penitentes* survive in spite of ecclesiastical prohibition. See P. Bailly, DSAM 5:392–408; G. Leff, *Heresy in the Later Middle Ages* (1967), 2:485–493; N. Cohn, *Pursuit of the Millennium* (1961), 124–148.

FLETCHER, JOHN WILLIAM (b. de la Fléchère; 1729–85), friend of John *Wesley and the Methodist movement. Born at Nyon, Switz., F. studied at Geneva. He went to England in 1752, was for a time tutor in an English family, then was ordained in the Church of England. He became dedicated to Methodism, and was named by Wesley to succeed to leadership of the movement, but predeceased him. F.'s writings centered mostly upon the Arminian–Calvinist controversies of his day.

FLOATING PARISH, a name coined to describe any group of Christians who choose to form their own worship community apart from the conventional, i.e., territorial parish. The name also connotes the practice frequently followed of varying the place for each gathering of the groups. The floating parish is inspired by the desire to create a more dynamic Christian community than the participants find in the established local church or parish. The group is usually made up of whole families. Liturgical experimentation and spontaneity are prominent features, but an intense concern for social problems is also a mark of such groups. Adoption of the floating parish idea has been particularly widespread among Roman Catholics since Vatican Council II. In 6 of the 154 dioceses in the U.S. such communities operate with the approval of the bishop; elsewhere they form part of the *underground Church.

FOOTWASHING, a practice, based on Jn 13.4–20 and I Tim 5.10, observed as an *ordinance by some Protestant bodies; it is also observed in some Eastern and RC Churches on Holy Thursday. Early Lutherans strongly repudiated the rite as a Roman abomination. The Anabaptists and Mennonites gave prominence to the practice to signify brotherhood and humility; it has been observed by them as equal in significance to the Lord's Supper. American Mennonites still continue the practice. The Moravians (until the 19th cent.), Particular Baptists, some Churches of God, the Evangelical United Brethren, and Seventh-day Adventists have also observed footwashing. There are various reasons for the usage: a return to the practice of the primitive Church; the interpretation that Jesus' command at the Last Supper made it obligatory; an emphasis on brotherly love; a view of the Lord's Supper as equally and simply a symbol of fraternity.

FORBES, ALEXANDER PENROSE (1817–75), Anglican bp. of Brechin, Scotland. As a student at Oxford, he was much influenced by E. B. *Pusey, who secured him the Church of St. Saviour's, Leeds, in 1847. The next year he was elected bp. of Brechin in the Episcopal Church of Scotland. In this position he promoted Anglo-Catholic principles and practices, and in 1860 he was censured by the college of bishops for his doctrine of the Real Presence. Among his writings is a 2-volume commentary on the *Thirty-Nine Articles (1867–68) giving them a Catholic interpretation.

FORENSIC JUSTIFICATION, an understanding of the process of man's being made righteous usually ascribed to Martin Luther and his disciples. "Forensic" here means "by a legal act," i.e., by a declaration; accordingly, righteousness is imputed to man by God without man being thereby inherently affected. This is doubtless the sort of theory against which the Council of Trent formulated canon II of the decree on justification (D 1561). It is questionable, however, whether Luther himself ever took so gross a position. According to his commentary on Galatians, for example, "righteousness *is* our possession, to be sure, since it was given to us by God out of mercy. Nevertheless, it is alien to us, because we have not merited it." Thus Luther stresses the idea of "alien righteousness," and not that sense of justification which for so long was the object of RC polemics. It does appear, however, that in the Lutheran tradition the strong emphasis on righteousness as unmerited has played down the change that takes place within man on the basis of the divine work. It also seems probable that persons formed according to this tradition might neglect the reality of the soul's union with the Lord Jesus, established by faith, and thus live as if the grace of Christ were only being imputed to them forensically. *JUSTIFICATION.

FORM OF PRESBYTERIAL CHURCH GOVERNMENT, a statement of *polity formulated by the *Westminster Assembly (1643–49). With the arrival of the Scottish commissioners at the Assembly, the divines turned from the question of doctrine to that of church government. The Scots had already had experience of Presbyterianism, the majority of divines favored it, the English Parliament had abolished episcopacy (1642), and some provision had to be made for the ordination of ministers. The Presbyterian majority, who for the most part subscribed to the *jure divino* theory of Presbyterian polity, sought to conciliate the minority *Independents, who opposed the claim that Presbyterianism could be found in Scripture. After some delay the Presbyterian system was finally adopted by a nearly unanimous vote, and in Oct. 1645 the Form of Government was submitted for approval to Parliament. It was adopted in Scotland in the same year. The Form of Government represents a triumph for the Presbyterian view of the parity of presbyters and the regulation of the affairs of the Church by the counsel and will of the whole body; it has remained a standard for Presbyterian church government. See bibliog. for Church of Scotland. *WESTMINSTER ASSEMBLY.

FORMAL PRINCIPLE, the source and criterion accepted by a Church for its tenets; correlative of material principle, i.e., the central doctrine or doctrines that are authenticated by this formal principle. The terminology was first used by historians and theologians to analyze what was doctrinally distinctive of the Reformation: the Bible alone was the formal principle; the material principle was the doctrine that man is saved by grace alone through faith. The headings formal principle and material principle are often used also to study or classify the doctrine of the Churches.

FORMULA MISSAE ET COMMUNIONIS, a Latin text prepared under Luther's direction in 1523 for the celebration of the Eucharist. It was the basis for the *German Mass of 1526, which supplanted it, and so of future Lutheran liturgy. The old order of the Mass was kept as far as the Credo; there then followed a silent preparation of the elements, a preface incorporating the words of institution; the elevation took place during the Sanctus and Benedictus. The old canon was rejected; the Pater Noster and Agnus Dei were retained. The *Formula* was issued as a guide, allowing for the celebrant to improvise. Text LW 53:17–40; L. Reed, *Lutheran Liturgy* (1960).

FORMULA OF CONCORD, the last of the Lutheran *confessions of faith, prepared in 1577 and published in the *Book of Concord (1580). The 30 years following the death of Martin Luther on Feb. 18, 1546, saw the division of his followers into theological parties. One group, the disciples of Philipp *Melanchthon, maintained his brand of irenic and humanistic doctrine; the other gave a strict construction to Luther's theology and sought to hold the line against both deviations from within and against other communions (see PHILIPPISM; GNESIOLUTHERANISM). A controversy between M. *Flacius Illyricus and Victorin *Strigel dealt with original sin; Flacius was also involved in a debate about conversion. Other doctrinal conflicts dealt with the relation between *law and gospel, esp. the "third use of the law," and with the relation between justification and sanctification.

The Formula of Concord was the climax of a series of efforts, both theological and political, to restore unity to the Lutheran party in Germany. This it did by reaffirming the validity of Luther's theology and the authority of the *Augsburg Confession. Original sin did indeed render a man incapable of taking the initiative in conversion, but it was Manichaean to call it the "substance" of fallen man, as Flacius had carelessly done (Art. 1). Law and gospel were to be distinguished, and each was to be applied at the appropriate point in preaching (Art. 5, 6). Good works did not cause a man's salvation, but it was wrong to say that they were inimical to it (Art. 4). In addition to these intramural controversies, the differences between Lutheranism and other Protestant bodies were also specified in the Formula. In opposition to Calvinism, the Formula rejected the idea of predestination to damnation (Art. 11); it also reaffirmed Luther's doctrine of the Real Presence in the Eucharist (Art. 7) and the doctrine of the person of Christ that Luther had affirmed in the context of the eucharistic controversies (Art. 8). Against the left wing of the Reformation (see ANABAPTISTS), Article 12 of the Formula of Concord also drew the line of Lutheran orthodoxy.

After its composition and adoption in

1577, the Formula of Concord received widespread endorsement in various Lutheran provinces of Germany. But in other provinces and in portions of Scandinavia it was not adopted, and its place within the corpus of Lutheran confessional writings has continued to be challenged from time to time. See T. G. Tappert, ed., *Book of Concord: The Confessions of the Evangelical Lutheran Church* (1959); E. Schlink, *Theology of the Lutheran Confessions* (tr. P. F. Koehneke and H. J. A. Bowman, 1961).

FORSYTH, PETER TAYLOR (1848–1921), British Congregational minister and theologian. F. was born in Aberdeen, and he graduated from Aberdeen Univ. in 1869. He later studied with A. *Ritschl at Göttingen, and at New College, London. He was ordained in 1876 and held six pastorates. In 1901 he became principal of Hackney College (Congregationalist), London, a post he held until his death. Early in his career F. was militant in his *liberal theology; but, while he remained open to new currents, such as biblical criticism, he turned from the liberal doctrinal dilution of man's need for redemption. Through pastoral work and personal experience he developed a deeper appreciation for the historic doctrines of sin and redemption and new insights into the substitutionary atonement of Christ; he came to center his thinking on the cross. Among the more influential of his 25 books are *The Person and Place of Jesus Christ* (1909) and *The Principle of Authority* (1912). Renewed interest in F.'s theology has developed in recent years. See J. Rodgers, *Theology of P. T. F.* (1965).

FORTY-TWO ARTICLES, a doctrinal standard, called also the Edwardine Articles, for the C of E, completed largely by T. *Cranmer before 1552. Cranmer's original plan, overoptimistic in itself and thwarted by political events, was for a meeting of British and continental Reformers to frame a commonly accepted statement of doctrines. He was able to consult some continental Reformers resident in England, and other divines, John *Knox among them. Under authority of Edward VI the articles were published in 1553, although probably they never were approved by *Convocations. Mary Tudor's accession made them a dead letter, but under Elizabeth I they became the substantial basis of the *Thirty-Nine Articles. See J. Gardiner, *English Church in the Sixteenth Century* (1904), 308–311; Schaff Creeds 1:613–615.

FOSDICK, HARRY EMERSON (1878–   ), liberal preacher and author. F. was a graduate of Union Theological Seminary, N.Y., where he later taught practical theology, 1915–46. During the same period he was pastor first at Park Ave. Baptist Church, then (1930) of the newly built Riverside Church. F. achieved considerable celebrity as a preacher and became a spokesman for the liberal position and a target for fundamentalists. He rejected the divinity of Christ, the virgin birth, and miracles; he affirmed vital faith in God, Jesus as master, man's immortality, and the gospel power to change human life and society. See *Living of These Days: An Autobiography* (1956).

FOUNDERY (Foundry), "mother church of Methodism"; hence a frequent title for Methodist churches. On Nov. 11, 1739, John *Wesley preached in Windmill Street, London, in the ruins of a former foundry for cannon, wrecked by an explosion in 1716. He acquired the property and built a meeting house there. It no longer exists; some of its appointments are preserved in City Road Chapel, London. See F. C. Gill, *In the Steps of John Wesley* (1962), 42–43, 48–50.

FOUR ARTICLES OF PRAGUE, the reform platform (1420) of the *Utraquist party of *Hussites: (1) priests' freedom to preach; (2) *communion under both kinds; (3) public punishment for grave sins of all, even clerics; and (4) renunciation of property and civil office by clerics.

FOUR GALLICAN ARTICLES, see GALLI-
CAN ARTICLES, FOUR.

FOURSQUARE GOSPEL (Fourfold Gospel), the teaching, esp. of *Holiness
Churches and in *Pentecostalism, that the
complete gospel message includes four
themes: *justification; *entire sanctification
through *baptism with the Holy Spirit; *divine healing; and *premillenarianism. Jesus
is Savior, Sanctifier, Healer, and Coming
Lord. See A. B. Simpson, *Fourfold Gospel*
(1925).

FOX, GEORGE (1624–91), founder of the
Religious Society of Friends. F. was born at
Fenny Drayton, Leicestershire, and by
choice received only a rudimentary education. Sensitively religious, he was early de-
pressed by the state of the Church in Puritan England and by its Calvinist teachings.
To quiet his tormented searching, there
gradually dawned in him a deeply mystical
conviction, a belief in the *Inner Light; and
from 1647 F. was an itinerant preacher of
his own individualistic brand of Christianity. In the midlands and north of England he attracted many followers, especially from groups dissatisfied with organized Christianity: Seekers, Familists, Anabaptists, and Ranters. His preaching against
the establishment also brought him
eight jail sentences, totaling 6 years of periodic imprisonment. A vivid, captivating
preacher, undaunted by suffering, F. gave
organizational stability to the Friends, esp.
with his "Rules for the Management of
Meetings" (1668). He also showed himself
to be rather inconsistently authoritarian
(see NAYLOR, JAMES). F. undertook many
journeys to spread his message, one to
America in 1671–72. The last period of his
life he spent in London working for the
*Toleration Act (1689). In an ungrammati-
cal but forceful style, F. set out his teachings in many books and pamphlets, esp. in
his *Journals*, published posthumously in
1694 (modern eds. J. L. Nickall, 1952; H. J.

Cadbury, 1963). See R. Knox, *Enthusiasm*
(1950), 139–175; Mayer RB 409–422, with
bibliog.; V. Noble, *Man in Leather Breeches*
(1953); H. Van Etten, *George Fox and the
Quakers* (tr. E. Kelvin Osborn, 1959); W. C.
Braithwaite, *Beginnings of Quakerism* (2d
ed., H. J. Cadbury, 1955). *RELIGIOUS SO-
CIETY OF FRIENDS.

FOX SISTERS, the women whose "spirit
rappings" at Rochester, N.Y., began the
modern Spiritualist movement. They were
Margaret Fox (b. 1833), Kate Fox (b. 1836),
and their older sister, Leah (Fox) Fish
(later Underhill). Margaret and Kate first
experienced mysterious tapping and rat-
tling sounds in 1847 at Hydesville, N.Y.,
and later at Leah's Rochester home. The
three sisters developed an alphabet to interpret the spirit messages. In 1850 they
created a sensation in New York City, with
the help of Horace Greeley and the New
York *Tribune*. Their lecture tours convinced thousands that the dead could send
messages to the living through a Spiritualist
medium. Among notable converts was
Robert Dale Owen (1801–77), who became
a major publicist of Spiritualism. The Fox
Sisters also lectured in England, where
Kate married and settled permanently.
After her conversion to Catholicism in 1888,
Margaret exposed the "Rochester rappings" as deliberate frauds; later she recanted and continued to lecture on Spiritualism with Leah for several years. The
phenomena described by the Fox Sisters
inspired the development of Spiritualist circles, which drew their ideas largely from
Andrew Jackson *Davis. The three sisters
contributed little to Spiritualist thought or
the organization of the movement they had
inspired. *SPIRITUALISTS.

FOXE'S BOOK OF MARTYRS, classical instance of a book making history, rather
than history the book, first published in
1573, and reaching its seventh edition by
1684. The author, John Foxe (1516–87), had
been a fellow of Magdalen and a refugee in

Germany from Mary Tudor; he had already published the Latin work, begun on the suggestion of Lady Jane Grey, which was the basis of his *Actes and Monuments of these latter and perillous dayes, touching matters of the Church, wherein ar comprehended and described the great persecutions & troubles, that have bene wrought and practised by Romishe Prelates, speciallye in this Realme of England and Scotlande, from the yeare of our Lorde a thousande, unto the tyme now-present.* Its main wealth lies in materials from the 14th to the 16th centuries. It was composed in the household of the Duke of Norfolk and the printing office of John Day. Though quickly riddled by Nicholas Harpsfield, the work, with its passages of coarse ribaldry at the expense of opponents and written from a blazing hatred of Spain and the Inquisition, was a superb journalistic scoop. It met the occasion, and successive editions and abridgments, embellished with woodcuts, did more than anything to fan and maintain the flame of anti-Catholic feeling. A copy was ordered by Convocations (1570) to be placed in every collegiate church, and soon it came next only to the Bible in Protestant reading. One of the charges against W. *Laud was that he had refused to license it. Until 1837–42, when S. R. Maitland exposed the numerous errors in the narrative, a majority accepted it as authentic history. Certainly it contains falsifications and fictions, and common criminals are made into martyrs; generally it adopts the loose notions of literary ethics prevalent in the polemics of the period. But if Foxe was a man who, in the words of Anthony à Wood (1632–95), believed all he was told, the present tendency is to recognize his substantial historical learning and even to attach a socio-psychological importance to his work, though the therapeutic value of its vicarious violence may well be questioned. See W. Haller, *Elect Nation: The Meaning and Relevance of Foxe's Book of Martyrs* (1963).

FRA DOLCINO, see DOLCINO, FRA.

FRANCISCAN SPIRITUALS, see SPIRITUALS, FRANCISCAN.

FRANCK, SEBASTIAN (1499–c.1542), German religious writer and historian. Educated at Ingolstadt and Heidelberg, where he heard Luther and met M. *Bucer, he was ordained priest in 1524, but within a year became a Lutheran. While pastor near Nuremberg he became acquainted with humanist writings, left the ministry (1529), and moved to Strassburg. There he published his *Cronica, Zeitbuch und Geschichtesbibel* (1531), important not as a chronicle but for F.'s spiritualizing views on Christianity. In this and other works he extolled the inner word of God, the experience of Christ within, an invisible, nonsectarian Church, and the primacy of each man's conscience. He rejected creeds, sacraments, any institutional Church, and the use of force against religious adversaries, esp. the Anabaptists. He favored a personal mystical experience of Christ as the true Christian life. Some have regarded him as a forerunner of pure liberalism and subjectivism, but his writings profess belief in the divinity of Christ and in the spirit of the Scriptures. Expelled from Strassburg in 1531, he was finally able to settle at Ulm, where he published the fullest expression of his views in his *Paradoxa* (1534). He died in Basel. See W. Zeller, RGG 2:1012–13; R. M. Jones, *Spiritual Reformers of the 16th and 17th Centuries* (pa., 1959), 46–63.

FRANCKE, AUGUST HERMANN (1633–1729), leading figure in the spread of *Pietism, educator. Born of a devout family in Lübeck, Ger., F. studied theology at Erfurt and Kiel, where he developed a special interest in biblical study and became acquainted with the work of the Pietist P. *Spener. While lecturing at Leipzig (from 1685) he met Spener and was completely converted to the Pietist position. F.'s preaching and devotional exegesis in the Collegia Philobiblica, which he helped to establish, aroused opposition from orthodox Lutherans, and he was obliged to leave Leipzig. Through Spener he eventually received (1692) a professorship in Oriental languages (later in theology) at the newly founded Univ. of Halle and a pastorate at nearby Glaucha. By lecturing, preaching, and catechizing, F. disseminated Pietist ideas: the need for a personal conversion experience; stress on sin, repentance, and grace; the practice of a godly life. To communicate his message, he drew on the witness of his own religious experience. Through him Halle became the center for the inculcation and diffusion of Pietism. He established a complex of schools, which became known as "institutes"; they became centers for training teachers, and besides contributing greatly to the spread of his religious ideas, they are important in the history of pedagogy. An orphanage he established (1697) became the first Protestant center for the formal training of foreign missionaries. He assisted his friend K. H. von Canstein (1667–1719) in the formation (1710) of a pioneer *Bible society. Although F. wrote some popular and practical works, his main influence was exercised through his personal pastoral activity and his work of organization. See bibliog. for Pietism.

FRATICELLI, a name for various factions of Franciscans who separated themselves from their order and from the RC Church in bitter disputes concerning poverty. The same (disparaging) term was also indiscriminately used in chronicles and inquisitorial reports of the 14th and 15th cent. for other groups, such as the *Apostolici and the *Beghards. The first papal use came in the bull *Sancta romana* of John XXII (1317), condemning the *Clareni, who were called contemptuously *Fraticelli de paupere vita.* The following year the same Pope excommunicated a number of Tuscan *Spirituals. The Fraticelli had their origins among the Spirituals, Franciscans who insisted on literal observance of poverty after the manner of St. Francis and his earliest companions. So obstinate was their primitivism that they repudiated as betrayals of

the Franciscan ideals the three papal interpretations of the rule issued during the 13th century, concerning the way poverty was to be observed. Two groups of Italian Spirituals refused to heed John XXII's command to submit to the superiors of the order. They established themselves as independent bodies and declared that they alone were legitimate Friars Minor and constituted the true Church of Christ. After the condemnation mentioned above, both groups fled into southern Italy and Sicily, where they were given protection by Kings Robert of Naples and Frederick of Sicily. They enjoyed a large measure of popular support, being much admired by the common people for their austere way of life. There are records of groups of Fraticelli in southern France, Spain, Germany, and Bohemia; there is, however, no evidence of any historical connection between Fraticelli and the *Hussites. The eventual disappearance of the Fraticelli was brought about by the zeal of inquisitors like SS. John Capistran and James of the March, both appointed in 1428, and by the rise of the Franciscan Observants, offering to those zealous for primitive Franciscan poverty a life within the legitimate Franciscan family.

The Fraticelli pushed the teachings of the Spirituals to extremes. They rejected papal interpretations of Franciscan poverty and the very legitimacy of the popes beginning with Boniface VIII and consequently of all ecclesiastical power of orders or jurisdiction thereafter. They thus set themselves up as the true spiritual Church, with their own bishops, priests, and preachers, including women. Their ecclesiology and eschatology were markedly influenced by *Joachimism. The *Michaelites are sometimes classified as *Fraticelli de opinione,* but they did not go to the same doctrinal extremes as the true Fraticelli. See D. Douie, *Nature and Effects of the Heresy of the Fraticelli* (1932); M. D. Lambert, *Franciscan Poverty: The Doctrine of the Absolute Poverty of Christ and the Apostles in the Franciscan Order, 1210–1323* (1961); C. Schmitt, DSAM 5:1167–88.

FREE CHRISTIAN ZION CHURCH OF CHRIST, a body formed in 1905 at Redemption, Ark., by E. D. Brown, a missionary of the African Methodist Episcopal Zion Church, and a number of Negro ministers of various denominations. Doctrine and polity are substantially those of Methodism, but with certain Pentecostal elements. Relief of the needy and care of the poor are viewed as a Church responsibility and remain characteristic works of this group. Membership in 1966 was 22,260, with 742 churches.

FREE CHURCH OF ENGLAND, a small body of believers of evangelical conviction who separated themselves from the C of E because of their antagonism to the *sacerdotalism that the Tractarian movement had aroused in the established Church. The secession occurred in consequence of a dispute in 1843 between James Shore, a clergyman of Exeter, and his bp., H. Philpotts. T. Thoresby, a London minister of the *Countess of Huntingdon's Connexion, defended Shore, and, with the cooperation of evangelical clergymen and ministers of the Connexion, spent the next years devising a scheme of church polity. The Free Church, which accepted the *Thirty-Nine Articles, was formally organized in 1863. The original *presbyterian pattern gave way to popular demand for legitimate episcopal orders, and the consecration of Benjamin Price as first bp. was obtained in 1873 through the U.S. *Reformed Episcopal Church, with which body the Free Church became formally united in 1927. In 1967 the Free Church was said to have 37 places of worship and 6,514 members.

FREE CHURCH OF GOD IN CHRIST, Pentecostal sect originating at Enid, Okla., in 1915, when 16 Baptists experienced *baptism of the Holy Spirit and formed a congregation under the leadership of E. J. Morris. There was a temporary merger (1921–25) with the Church of God in Christ, to which the Free Church is very similar. It has about 900 members in 20 churches.

FREE CHURCH OF SCOTLAND, Church formed when, in the Disruption of 1843, about one-third of the membership of the Church of Scotland broke away, largely in protest against state intrusion, and to some extent also against patronage. Part of a larger revival of evangelical Christianity in the 19th cent., the Free Church, led by men like Thomas Chalmers (1780–1847), sought to reaffirm the idea of a *national Church while remaining loyal to orthodox Calvinism (which it subsequently modified). Under the influence of Robert Rainy (1826–1906), a union with the United Presbyterian Church was achieved in 1900. The *United Free Church rejoined the Church of Scotland in 1929. See J. R. Fleming, *History of the Church in Scotland, 1843–1925* (2v., 1927).

FREE CHURCHES, a description used primarily in contrast with *state Church; hence, other Churches existing alongside an *established Church. On the Continent it refers especially to Anabaptists and their descendants, but also includes other denominations. In Great Britain, this term superseded *Dissenters and *Nonconformists c.1900. During the 19th cent., Nonconformist denominations augmented their numbers and played an important role in achieving religious and political freedom, as well as social reforms. Their early loose-knit organizations (National Council of Free Churches, 1896; Federal Council of Evangelical Free Churches, 1919) merged in 1941 into the Federal Council of Free Churches. In the U.S. the phrase has less significance; Mead, however, states that it "designates those churches under the system of separation of church and state"(103). It is frequently used, however, to designate Churches that emphasize individual conversion, *believer's baptism, and democratic organization. See G. Westin, *Free Church through the Ages* (tr. V. A. Olson,

1958); E. A. Payne, *Free Church Tradition in the Life of England* (3d ed., 1951); S. Mead, *Lively Experiment* (1963).

FREE METHODIST CHURCH of North America, a strong Methodist denomination of about 100,000 members in over 1,100 churches in its world organization; it was formed in 1860 by Methodist ministers expelled (1859) by the Methodist Episcopal Church. The chief founder was the Rev. B. T. Roberts, who favored abolition, criticized the older Church for neglecting the experience of *entire sanctification, opposed pew renting or pew sales, secret societies, and the use of liquor and tobacco. In 1910 the Genesee Conference of the Methodist Episcopal Church, which had expelled Roberts and others, retracted its action.

Doctrinally the Church stresses Christ's deity, atonement, and resurrection, and the experience of sanctification; it is opposed to evolution as unsupported by any proved fact of science. "Free" in the title stands for free pews, freedom in worship, freedom from sin, and freedom from supervisional domination (bishops are elected for 4 years rather than for life, although they may be re-elected). The Church maintains a missionary program in the Dominican Republic, Mexico, Brazil, Paraguay, Egypt, Africa, India, Japan, Hong Kong, the Philippines, and Formosa, and in 1960 supported 200 missionaries. In 1959 it had merged with the small Holiness Movement Church of Canada. While it is affiliated with the World Methodist Council, the National Holiness Association, and the National Association of Evangelicals, it is not linked with either the National or the World Council of Churches, partly because it does not agree doctrinally with some of the Churches in these two bodies. See C. L. Howland, *Story of Our Church* (1940); HistAmMeth 3:589–592.

FREE WILL BAPTISTS, a group distinguished by belief in man's freedom to accept or reject God's saving grace, and originating in 18th-cent. American revivalism. In Perquimans Co., N. C., they were organized by Paul Palmer (1692–1763); and at New Durham, N.H., by Benjamin Randall (1749–1808), whose *Arminianism was unacceptable to the Regular Baptists. The Free Will Baptists spread through New England, the South, and the West, being reinforced by other Baptists who traced their descent from English *General Baptists. The Free Will Baptists of the North merged with the Northern Baptist Convention in 1911, but the movement in the South and West continues, with about 175,000 members. They remain Arminian, observe baptism by immersion, the Lord's Supper, and *footwashing. See N. A. Baxter, *Free Will Baptists* (1957).

FREEDOM, RELIGIOUS, see RELIGIOUS FREEDOM.

FREEMASONS (Masons), members of those fraternal organizations that follow the principles, usages, and rites known as Freemasonry. Freemasons trace their origins to the medieval stonemasons, who were called free masons because they worked on free stone; these artisans, whose worksheds were called lodges and who had their own guilds, were working or operative masons. In England these fraternities of working masons, which had a religious and moral purpose, gradually admitted nonworking, honorary, or "accepted" members; and when the building of churches stopped after the Reformation, the lodges came to be made up mostly of nonworking Masons and the tools and terms of the trade took on a purely symbolic meaning. The nonworking Masons, esp. after the lodges espoused deism in the 18th cent., are designated speculative Freemasons. Modern Freemasons have their origins in the Grand Lodge of England, formed from four lodges there in 1717. After 1721 the Freemasons attracted many members from the royalty and nobility, and the lodges grew in size;

Grand Lodges were established also in Scotland and in Ireland (the ecclesiastical prohibitions were not promulgated there for many years). From England the organization moved to continental Europe. In France it became anticlerical and occultist; in Belgium and in the Latin countries of Europe and South America it became extremely anticlerical and anti-Catholic. In Germany the Order of *Illuminati infiltrated the Masonic lodges and used them for their subversive program. The various Masonic fraternities in the world are grouped into the lodges of the Anglo-Saxon world, the Grand Orients of Europe and Latin America, Negro Masonic lodges, and splinter lodges, including some that initiate women. Freemasons number about 6 million, of whom 4,200,000 are in the U.S., 550,000 in England, 400,000 in Scotland, 440,000 in Australia and New Zealand, and 200,000 in Canada. Membership is much smaller in the Scandinavian countries, Germany, France, and elsewhere. Communist countries have banned Masonry, as has Spain, Portugal, and the United Arab Republic.

The history of the Freemasons in the U.S. begins shortly after the establishment of the Grand Lodge. Daniel Coxe was appointed Grand Master of N.Y., N.J., and Pa. in 1730. Leading figures in the American Revolution, such as George Washington, Benjamin Franklin, Patrick Henry, and John Paul Jones, were Masons. Besides Washington, eleven U.S. presidents have worn the Masonic apron. The Masonic lodges not only grew enormously in membership, but they became the model for many other fraternal organizations for men of lower social rank or of beliefs incompatible with Freemasonry (see INDEPENDENT ORDER OF ODD FELLOWS). An American Mason begins his Masonic education by receiving the first, or Entered Apprentice, degree in a Blue lodge. He advances to the degrees of Fellow Craft and Master Mason. If he wishes he may elect to receive the degrees of the York rite, which culminates in the Knights Templar, or of the Scottish rite, which confers the 4th to the 32d de-

grees and the honorary 33d degree. Masonic authorities disagree as to what are the essential features, the "landmarks," of the fraternity but are in accord that they include at least the three-degree system of initiation, the methods of recognition, acknowledgment of the Great Architect of the Universe and the immortality of the soul, acceptance of the story of Hiram Abiff, legendary stonemason for the temple of Solomon, the place of the Volume of Sacred Law on the Altar, secrecy in the lodge, and the equality of all Masons in a lodge.

Freemasonry has a religious content. In Anglo-Saxon countries the deism connoted by the designation of God as Great Architect and the general naturalism signify a neutral or nondenominational attitude rather than the hostility to religion prevalent among Freemasons of France and the Latin countries. Anglo-Saxon Freemasons are rather concerned with social and benevolent activities; the anti-Catholicism associated with Masonry was more a part of the religious antipathy between Protestants and Catholics than an essential of Freemasonry. Still, a majority of all Christians belong to denominations that condemn Masonic affiliation; not only for Roman Catholics but for Eastern Orthodox Christians, Lutherans, Quakers, Brethren, Mennonites, Jehovah's Witnesses, Mormons, Christian Reformed, and Seventh-day Adventists membership is forbidden or discouraged. The chief objections of these Christian Churches to Freemasonry have been to an avowed naturalism that ignores the essentials of the gospel, and to the imposition of an oath of secrecy with regard to something frivolous (the secrets of the lodges are not secrets at all but accessible in any public library). RC prohibitions were chiefly prompted by the anti-Christian and anticlerical program of Freemasons in France and the Latin countries. The first condemnation was issued in a bull of Clement XII in 1738; Benedict XIV, Pius VII, Pius IX, and Leo XIII all condemned Freemasonry. According to present legislation (CIC c.2335) a Catholic who joins incurs excommunication reserved in a simple manner to the Holy See; he may not receive the sacraments or Catholic burial. The legislation may be changed; some attempt has been made in the U.S. since Vatican II to have the penalties attached to membership lifted; active fellowship between Masons and the Knights of Columbus has been fostered. See H. S. Box, *Nature of Freemasonry* (1952); W. Hannah, *Darkness Visible* (1952); B. E. Jones, *Freemasons' Guide and Compendium* (1950); W. J. Whalen, *Christianity and American Freemasonry* (1958); *idem, Handbook of Secret Organizations* (1966).

FREETHINKERS, a term brought into universal notoriety and established currency in religious controversy in England by Anthony Collins's *Discourse of Free-Thinking, Occasioned by the Rise and Growth of a Sect Called Free-Thinkers* (1713). In late 17th-cent. France, the concept of freethinking formed part of what was understood by *libertinage,* although the radical heterodoxy of the *libertin* was associated with a more or less serious moral laxity and even depravity. Freethought arose, in both countries, as a conscious reaction against some phases of conventional, traditional doctrine. It embodied a claim to pursue any question, however sacrosanct, with fearless honesty, and, in practice, the undermining of the claims of religious faith and, at times, of conventional morality as well. Both the English word libertine and the French *libertin* were reserved for the sexually vicious when Richardson created his Lovelace and Laclos his Valmont. It was from the first, however, assumed by their theological adversaries that freethinkers logically and inevitably indulged in free-living. By the beginning of the 18th cent., the English expression freethinker replaced libertine and came to stand for one who defied religious orthodoxy in an esp. outrageous and contemptuous fashion and defended the right to unbounded intellectual curiosity. Freethinkers thereafter were identified as religious skeptics, although the

name concealed undoubted differences among them in point of departure, object of chief concern, and degree of unbelief. In the 19th cent., Karl Pearson stressed, paradoxically, the "essentially religious character of freethought," which he identified with science and with an ethic "superior to the Christian." See J. M. Robertson, *Short History of Freethought* (1957); J. S. Spink, *French Freethought from Gassendi to Voltaire* (1960).

FRELINGHUYSEN, THEODORUS JACOBUS (1692–1747?), one of the principal evangelists of the *Great Awakening in America. F. was born in Westphalia, Ger., and early came under the influence of *Pietism. He was ordained by the German Reformed Church in 1717, came to N.J. in 1720, and was made pastor of a group of Reformed Churches in the Raritan Valley. F.'s pastoral and preaching methods at first shocked his parishioners and the clergy and laymen of the Reformed Dutch Church in New York. His emphasis upon personal repentance and a more emotional expression of religion was very different from the formal kind of religion practiced in the area. Many of F.'s parishioners came to accept his revivalistic methods and experienced conversion under the pressure of the new evangelism. F. became noted, also, as a champion of self-government for the Dutch Reformed churches. Candidates for the ministry had to take the dangerous journey to the Netherlands for ordination, and two of F.'s sons died making such a journey. Victory in the fight for autonomy came only at the end of the colonial period. See P. Frelinghuysen, Jr., *T. J. F.* (1938). *REFORMED CHURCH IN AMERICA.

FRERE, WALTER HOWARD (1863–1938), Anglican bp. of Truro and liturgical scholar. He was educated at Cambridge, was ordained in 1887, and joined the Anglican Community of the Resurrection in 1892. He became a bp. in 1923, resigning in 1935. He published numerous studies on the history of the liturgy, esp. a new *History of the Book of Common Prayer*, and was active in the ecumenical movement, being a participant in the *Malines Conversations.

FRIENDS, RELIGIOUS SOCIETY OF, see RELIGIOUS SOCIETY OF FRIENDS.

FRIENDS OF GOD, a term long used to denote holy persons, but applied in a specialized sense in the 14th cent. to certain pious folk of all ranks of society: laymen, diocesan priests, monks, friars, and nuns, esp. in Bavaria, Switzerland, the Rhineland, and the Low Countries. They sought to live lives of devotion, prayer, austerity, and intense union with God. They were held together in loose association by their spiritual interests, their distress at the political and social evils of the day, the exchange of letters, visits, and spiritual writings, and the guidance of experienced leaders, esp. Henry Suso and John Tauler. Notable among them were two Dominican nuns, Margaret and Christine Ebner, and the secular priest Henry of Nördlingen, a friend of Suso and Tauler. His letters exchanged with Margaret Ebner, considered the oldest collection of letters in the German language, are a monument of German spirituality. Also prominent among the Friends was Rulman Merswin (d. 1382), a rich merchant of Strassburg, and composer of pious romances. The Friends of God were completely orthodox in their beliefs and should not be confused with the Brothers and Sisters of the Free Spirit, Waldenses, or the unorthodox Beguines, who concealed their heretical and separatist tendencies by using the same name. See DSAM 1:493–500; J. M. Clark, *Great German Mystics* (1949), 75–97; A. G. Seesholtz, *Friends of God: Practical Mystics of the Fourteenth Century* (1934); R. M. Jones, *Flowering of Mysticism: The Friends of God in the Fourteenth Century* (1939).

FRIENDS OF MAN, see AMIS DE L'HOMME, LES.

FRIENDS OF THE BIBLE, see BIBELFREUNDE.

FRIENDS OF THE TEMPLE (Ger. Tempelgesellschaft), a religious body that originated in Germany for the purpose of bringing about the kingdom of Christ on earth in their autonomous communities. The founder, the Württemberg Pietist Christoph *Hoffmann (1815–85), envisaged the restoration of the Temple and a theocracy at Jerusalem. Together with Georg David Hardegg (d. 1879) and Christian Paulus, he set out to found other Temple communities, first in Germany and then in various places of the Holy Land. Usually good schools and hospitals were connected with each community, and the Friends thus became known for their cultural and social contributions. The Friends of the Temple spread to Russia and North America (1905), where they became closely associated with the Unitarians. The movement was suppressed in Germany during World War II; emigrants founded a Temple community in Australia in 1950. Some adherents still exist in the Württemberg area. Hardegg had separated from the group in 1876 to found the so-called Temple Union (Reichsbruderbund). See C. Kolb, EncRelKnow 4:397–398; H. Hohlwein, RGG 6:688.

FRIENDS UNITED MEETING (before 1965 known as the Five Years Meeting of Friends), the largest and most influential body within the American Religious Society of Friends. It originated in 1902, when eleven yearly meetings loosely confederated. Although this Meeting descends from the *Gurneyite tradition, there was and is considerable variety in the tendencies of the member bodies. The organization seeks to unite the talents and resources of the Friends and to coordinate and strengthen their activities. It meets triennially, includes 14 yearly meetings, and has a membership of 70,673, with 502 churches.

FRIENDS WORLD COMMITTEE FOR CONSULTATION (FWCC), an organization established to promote the purposes of the Religious Society of Friends. The FWCC was first proposed in 1920 by the London World Conference of Friends and was brought into being by the Swarthmore, Pa., World Conference of 1927. There is an American and a European section; an African section is planned. The autonomous Friends yearly meetings freely associate themselves with the FWCC, and 29 of them in the Western Hemisphere belong to the American section. The committee fosters the internal interests of Friends—communication, mutual understanding and assistance, and the establishment of new Friends meetings. The organization also seeks to bring Quaker pacifist and philanthropic concern to the world at large and is recognized at the United Nations as a nongovernmental organization with consultative status. The American section has encouraged conferences on race relations, penology, civil rights, and world peace. See E. B. Bronner, *American Quakers Today* (1966), 105–107; W. R. Williams, *Rich Heritage of Quakerism* (1962), 213–215.

FROHSCHAMMER, JAKOB (1821–93), priest, philosopher, professor at the Univ. of Munich. F. was condemned by Pius IX in the letter *Gravissimas Inter* (Dec. 11, 1862) on two points: that once supernatural truths were revealed, they could be proved by human reasoning; that philosophy is absolutely above all control from authority (see D 2850–61). F. did not submit to the prohibition of his works, was suspended, and remained unreconciled.

FROUDE, RICHARD HURRELL (1803–36), a Devonshire man, fellow of Oriel, where he and J. H. Newman formed a close and affectionate friendship: many pages of the *Apologia* are about him. Already F. detested the Reformation, and was powerfully drawn to the medieval, but not to the primitive, Church. A high Tory of the cavalier stamp, of a classical and historical temper, with no strong bent to theology as such, he became an influential figure in the early *Oxford movement. Symptoms of consumption caused him to go to the Mediterranean to winter, where he was joined for a time by Newman; he was shocked by the degeneracy he thought he saw in the Catholics of Italy. His early death found him at the stage reached by his friend—"a Catholic without popery," he professed himself, "and a Church of England man without Protestantism."

FRY, ELIZABETH (1780–1845), English Quaker, prison reformer, sister to J. *Gurney. She became an approved Quaker minister (1811) and an effective preacher. In 1817 she formed an association to improve the condition of female prisoners at Newgate prison. Her efforts led to the introduction of practices now taken for granted in penology: segregation of the sexes, classification of prisoners, female supervision of women prisoners, and programs of both general and religious training. Her energies, always religiously inspired, were also devoted to other philanthropic causes. See J. P. Whitney, *E. F., Quaker Heroine* (new ed., 1945).

FRY, FRANKLIN CLARK (1900–68), leader in the Lutheran Church in America (LCA) and in the World Council of Churches (WCC). Born in Bethlehem, Pa., F. studied theology at Philadelphia Lutheran Seminary, Mt. Airy, Pa., and was ordained in 1925. For 5 years pastor in Akron, Ohio, he became president of the United Lutheran Church, predecessor of the LCA, 1945–62; then of the LCA, from 1962 until a week before his death. He was also president of Lutheran World Relief (1954–60) and of the Lutheran World Federation (1957–63). He was chairman of the policy and strategy committee of the National Council of Churches, 1954–68; chairman of the Central and Executive Committees of the WCC, 1954–68. F. put his superior executive and organizing ability at the service of his highest goal, the unity of the Christian Churches; he strove to make the WCC an effective channel of ecumenical communication.

FULL GOSPEL, a phrase for the message of *Pentecostalism, used frequently in Pentecostal history and literature. The connotation of the phrase is that the complete teaching of the Gospel includes: (1) justification by faith; (2) premillenarianism; (3) divine healing; (4) baptism with the Holy Spirit and its charismatic effects. *Foursquare gospel has the same meaning.

FULL GOSPEL BUSINESSMEN'S FELLOWSHIP INTERNATIONAL, laymen's association for mutual witness to the experience of *baptism with the Holy Spirit. The organization was Pentecostal in inspiration, and was formed in 1951 in Los Angeles by a businessman, Demos Chakarian, and the evangelist Oral *Roberts. Membership has grown to more than 100,000. The Fellowship has spread the message of spirit baptism and interest in *glossolalia throughout many denominations in the United States. See J. T. Nichol, *Pentecostalism* (1966), 241–242.

FUNDAMENTAL METHODIST CHURCH INC., a small denomination, organized at Ash Grove, Mo., in 1942. The organizers had withdrawn from the Methodist Protestant Church after the 1939 merger with the Methodist Episcopal Church and the Methodist Episcopal Church, South. Originally named the Independent Fundamentalist Methodist Church, the Church assumed its present name in 1956. It stresses the doctrines of *fundamentalism. It has no bps., one district superintendent, and one secretary. There were (1967) about 700 members, and 12 churches. Headquarters are at Springfield, Mo. See HistAmMeth 3:595.

FUNDAMENTALISM, a conservative theological movement in American Protestantism that arose in the 1920s in opposition to *modernism. No adequate interpretation of this movement has yet appeared. There are numerous articles and two books on the subject, some of which furnish valuable data, but most of them suffer from the tendency to explain fundamentalism in socioeconomic or psychological terms, treating the religious aspects as peripheral. While cultural factors were important, the original fundamentalist movement was rooted in genuine theological concerns. Further confusion has arisen from repeated reference to the *five points of fundamentalism, a myth that has scant foundation and provides little help in understanding the movement.

Fundamentalism should be understood primarily as an attempt to protect the essential elements (fundamentals) of the Christian faith from the eroding effects of rationalism and naturalism. It was not a monolithic movement, but had a variety of expressions. Although it emerged as a party in the fundamentalist–modernist controversy after World War I, its roots go back into the 19th cent., when evolution, biblical criticism, and other intellectual currents began to challenge old assumptions concerning the authority of biblical revelation. At the same time, new kinds of ethical problems accompanied the development of an urban-industrial society, appealing to the Christian conscience for social and economic reforms. The so-called "higher criticism" (historical and literary, as distinguished from textual, analysis) of the Bible was introduced into the mainstream of American Protestantism following the Civil War, and by the time of World War I, after overcoming strong resistance, came to be generally accepted in seminaries and colleges. Heated exchanges took place in scholarly journals and public forums, and Baptists dismissed a few professors (C. H. Toy, E. P. Gould), while Presbyterians held heresy trials (C. A. Briggs, A. C. McGiffert). In 1897, warning that "the lines are being drawn, and the party spirit is gaining strength," a prophetic voice forecast an impending conflict between progressives and conservatives.

As more extreme liberals reduced Christianity to a sociological or psychological phenomenon, and as many seminary students and young ministers lost their faith and quit the ministry, the conservative opposition crystallized around leaders who emerged to champion the claims of the Gospel. A considerable preparatory influence was the publication (1910–15), of *The Fundamentals*, which were distributed free to all pastors, seminary students, and many others in the United States. The emphases of these booklets were on the authority of the Scriptures, the deity of Christ, the efficacy of Christ's atoning work, etc. By 1918, the term "fundamentals" had become a common usage, but "fundamentalist" and "fundamentalism" were coined in 1920 by Curtis Lee Laws, Baptist editor of the *Watchman-Examiner*, who proposed that a group within his denomination adopt the name "fundamentalists." Those whom he represented were moderate conservatives, who believed that the modernists in their attempt to come to terms with modern learning were surrendering the "fundamentals" of the Gospel, namely, the sinful nature of man, his inability to save himself without divine grace, the adequacy of Jesus Christ to regenerate individuals and renew society, and the authoritative revelation in the Scriptures of God's redemptive activity. This group, which first applied the name "fundamentalists" to itself, was identified neither with *premillenarianism and *dispensationalism nor with a crusade against evolutionary teaching or an effort to abolish biblical criticism. They asserted repeatedly that they were concerned only about matters central to the Christian faith throughout the centuries. Before long a more militant group split off from this moderate party, calling itself the Baptist Bible Union. Gradually fundamentalism came to be used loosely for all theological conservatism, including extremists, moderates of the Laws type, and those who, like J. G. *Machen, represented a scholarly Presbyterian tradition. Eventually the fundamentalist image became stereotyped as closed-minded, ignorant, belligerent, and separatistic, and many conservatives sought a different appellation to distinguish their brand of conservatism. In the 1950s H. Ockenga renounced the fundamentalist label and proposed that "neo-evangelical" be the name of a conservatism that would be scholarly, balanced, and socially concerned. John Carnell, Carl F. H. Henry, Fuller Theological Seminary, the periodical *Christianity Today*, and other individuals and groups have been identified with the new evangelicalism, which considers itself the heir of the spirit and purpose of the original fundamentalists. See W. Hordern, *Layman's Guide to Protestant Theology* (1957); N. F. Furniss, *Fundamentalist Controversy, 1918–1931* (1954); S. G. Cole, *History of Fundamentalism* (1931); W. S. Hudson, *Religion in America* (1965); E. R. Sandeen, "Toward a Historical Interpretation of the Origins of Fundamentalism," *Church History*, 36 (March 1967); L. Loetscher, *Broadening Church* (1954).

FUNKITES, the first schismatic group of the American Mennonites, named after their leader, Christian Funk (1731–1811), a Mennonite bp. and member of the Franconia Conference of the Mennonite Church in Pennsylvania. For his support of the right of the State to collect war taxes and to demand an oath of allegiance during the American Revolution (a position in direct conflict to the nonresistant Mennonites, who refused to support the war on scriptural principles), Funk was excommunicated (1778). He later rejected attempts of reconciliation with the main body of Mennonites, although many of his followers rejoined. As a separate group the Funkites had disintegrated by 1855. See MennEnc 2:421, 424.

G

GALLICAN ARTICLES, FOUR, a Declaration of the French Clergy in 1682 asserting the freedom of the French Church. The Declaration was issued by an assembly of bishops and lower clergy, convoked by Louis IV, and representing itself as expressing the mind of the entire French clergy. The Articles stated that the king of France was independent of papal authority in temporal matters, that general councils were superior to popes, that the ancient liberties of the French Church could not be violated, and that individual popes could err (i.e., their judgments were not irreformable) though the Church was indefectible because of a reforming process helped along by the remonstrances of the assemblies of the clergy and the king. Behind this declaration was the long history of *Gallicanism, both political—that the French king had no superior within his kingdom—and ecclesiastical—that the French Church and particularly its bishops had broad freedom of action. The immediate issue was the *régale*: the claim of the French king to the income of vacant bishoprics. In line with his policy of increasing royal power and institutional uniformity Louis XIV tried to extend the *régale* to include dioceses incorporated into France since the Concordat of 1516. Pope Innocent XI chose to resist this extension. The Gallican Articles were the result. Difficulties were created on both sides by those who preferred coercion to Louis XIV's proposed negotiations. By the time of Innocent's death in 1689 the excesses on both sides had created a desire for settlement. In 1690, by the constitution *Inter multiplices,* Alexander VIII condemned the Articles. In 1693 Louis XIV had the French bishops officially withdraw those aspects of the Articles derogatory to the papacy. The Pope in return allowed some extension of the *régale.* Despite this compromise the Gallican Articles continued to be accepted by many in France. See J. B. Wolf, *Louis XIV* (1968).

GALLICAN CONFESSION *(Confessio Gallicana, Confession de foi,* French Confession), the confessional standard adopted at Paris (1559) by the First National Synod of the *Reformed Church in France. The original draft in 35 articles was sent from Geneva by John *Calvin, and revised by Antione de la Roche Chandieu (1534–91); it was presented to Charles IX at the Conference of *Poissy (1561). A second revision in 40 articles was made by the 7th national synod of the French Reformed Church at La Rochelle in 1571 under T. *Beza; hence the document is sometimes called the Confession of La Rochelle. These original versions were all written in French. The Gallican Confession ranks as the clearest credal summary of *Calvinism. Throughout its difficult history after the revocation of the Edict of Nantes in 1685, the Reformed Church in France adhered to the Confession. A new declaration of faith was adopted in 1872 and modified in 1936. See Schaff Creeds 1:490–498.

GALLICANISM, a 19th-cent. term for various assertions of the freedom of the French Church *(l'église gallicane)* from papal authority. Exponents of Gallicanism held that the power of the pope in France, particularly in temporal matters but also in matters of doctrine and discipline, should be limited. Though the theory was formulated in the 14th cent., it was claimed to have historical basis in ancient privileges. The most consistent advocate of the doctrine was the Paris Parlement, which after 1418, despite variations by both king and clergy, never relaxed its support. Royal power had developed from the late 10th century. At the same time the papacy asserted its claims to spiritual and temporal sovereignty over kings. Pope Boniface VIII tried to interfere with King Philip IV in the early 14th cent., and in reaction Gallicanism assumed a political aspect, contending that the king had no temporal superior within his kingdom.

In the last years of the 14th and the beginning of the 15th cent. so-called ecclesiastical Gallicanism developed. Appointments to benefices and bishoprics were declared free from papal control in an attempt to end the *Great Western Schism and bring reform to the French Church by restoring election to these positions. In practice these appointments fell into the hands of the king and, to some extent, of the nobles. This procedure was transformed into a theory by the Paris Parlement, accepted by the French clergy through the Pragmatic Sanction of Bourges (1438) and by the Pope through the Concordat of Bologna (1516).

In the late 15th and early 16th cent. the question of the legitimacy of tyrannicide added a new dimension to the problem and led to the strengthening of Gallicanism, as did attempts to introduce the decrees of the Council of Trent, since they would have interfered with the powers granted to the king by the Concordat of 1516. During the Wars of Religion in the second half of the 16th cent. the final theoretical developments took place. Popes Sixtus V and Gregory XIV were trying to prevent Henry IV from becoming king of France because he was a Huguenot. The Popes had the support of the extreme Catholic League, but more and more Frenchmen, sickened by 30 years of civil war, were moving toward support of Henry IV. Though the latter's absolution by the Pope in 1595 ended the practical difficulties, the Gallican theories were greatly strengthened during the 10 years of struggle over the question, particularly through the work of Pierre *Pithou.

By the early 17th cent. the French bishops in their attempts to reform the French Church were becoming ultramontane, but the theories of the Parlement of Paris were maintained by the third estate at the Estates General of 1614. As the power of the king increased during the 17th cent. so did support for Gallicanism. Louis XIV was able to make it the accepted theory in France, and though he was forced to mod-

erate the Four *Gallican Articles of 1682, Gallicanism remained a strong force throughout the *ancien régime*. Many of the partisans of *Jansenism were Gallicans. Examples of Gallicanism in the 18th cent. include the expulsion of the Jesuits in 1764 and the reformation and suppression of a number of religious orders on royal initiative in 1768. The Synod of *Pistoia reasserted Gallican principles. After the Napoleonic era, Gallicanism lingered in France. The discussions and declarations of Vatican Council I clearly marked its incompatibility with RC teaching.

Though the ideological content of Gallicanism varied with time and group, its main points included the following: (1) The pope has no temporal power within France. He cannot prevent the legal heir from ascending the throne, release the French from obedience to the king, interfere with the rights of the crown or the exercise of duties by royal officials, or exercise absolute authority over the French clergy. (2) The king is the only head of the state. He is the protector of the Church, can convoke councils to handle discipline and temporal affairs, can ask the clergy to contribute money for the general needs of the kingdom, can reform or suppress religious communities. His courts have jurisdiction over all cases not exclusively spiritual. (3) In the spiritual realm the king has power to decide whether or not papal pronouncements are in accord with those of former councils already accepted in France. (4) Gallicans also claimed that a general council was superior to the pope, whose judgments are not irreformable; truths of faith are guaranteed by the consent of the faithful. (5) Gallican bishops claimed the right to be judges of doctrine and discipline in their own domains, independent of the Pope. See V. Martin, *Les Origines du Gallicanisme* (2v., 1939); *idem*, *Le Gallicanisme politique et le clergé de France* (1929).

GARDINER, STEPHEN (*c.*1493–1555), bp. of Winchester. He took his degree in civil and canon law, in which fields he attained eminence as secretary of Cardinal Wolsey and later of Henry VIII in attempting to win papal approval of the King's divorce. After some hesitation he supported Henry's claim to be head of the English Church, yet he opposed the Protestant tendencies of Thomas Cromwell and Abp. Cranmer and wrote a vigorous defense of the Real Presence and the Mass. Appointed Lord Chancellor by Mary Tudor, he supported her in restoring Catholicism. His conversion seems to have been sincere, although he was conspicuous throughout life for his skill in double dealing. His treatise *De vera obedientia* is considered the ablest vindication of Henry's claim to supremacy over the Church of England. See J. J. Scarisbrick, NCE 6:287-288; J. A. Muller, *S. G. and the Tudor Reaction* (1926).

GATHERED CHURCH, the theory on the nature and polity of the Church that considers the Church to exist only in the local congregation, limited in membership to committed Christians. "Visible churches," its adherents state, "are made up of visible saints." A credible profession of faith and evidence of Christian character are required for admission, and members covenant together under discipline of the word of God. Such congregations believe they are led by the Holy Spirit and have authority from Christ to choose officers and determine members. The theory is in opposition to the idea of the *parish as simply a local unit of the visible, universal Church; or to the idea of the Church organized into a national or even regional entity. Beginning c.1580 with Robert *Browne at Norwich, the gathered church concept continued as the characteristic of the Congregationalists and the Baptists. Congregational polity was stated in England by the *Savoy Declaration (1658) and in New England by the *Cambridge Platform (1648). See P. Miller, *Orthodoxy in Massachusetts* (1933). *INVISIBLE CHURCH; *COVENANT THEOLOGY; *CHURCH (THEOLOGICAL INTERPRETATIONS); *CONGREGATIONALISM; *BAPTISTS.

GAZIER, AUGUSTIN (1844–1922), French historian of *Jansenism. A professor of literature at the Sorbonne (1880–1914), G. took a keen interest in the religious history of the 17th century. His masterwork was his *Histoire générale du mouvement janséniste depuis ses origines jusqu'à nos jours* (2v., 1922); this was entirely his work, though it appeared after his death. He was staunchly Catholic, but his works provide evidence that theologically he was somewhat imperceptive and that sympathy for *Port Royal led him to classify as Jesuit distortions the doctrines distinctive of Jansenism. Nevertheless, his works led to more precise perspectives in historical research into Jansenism. R. Knox in his *Enthusiasm* (1950) takes frequent issue with G.'s *Histoire.*

GEMEINDE JESU CHRISTI (Congregation of Jesus Christ), a small German Pentecostal group founded (1943) by the German-American Wilhelm August Waltke in Stammheim near Calw, Württemberg.

GENERAL ASSEMBLY (Presbyterian), the chief *court in Presbyterianism, representative of the whole Church. It is responsible for all matters of faith and order; it institutes and supervises agencies for missions at home and overseas, for education, and for relations with other Churches. The general assembly is a conciliar, judicial, and executive body that usually meets annually, or, if necessary, as called, and consists of an equal number of ministers and elders elected by their presbyteries. Its presiding officer is termed moderator, and may be a minister or elder; his office is one of honor, not jurisdiction. The first assembly of the Reformed Church of Scotland met at Edinburgh in 1560, though the functions of the assembly were not defined until 1581, when A. *Melville's *Book of Discipline was inserted into the register of the acts of the assembly. Most Presbyterian Churches today adhere to the general definition of the powers of the assembly contained in the

Book of Discipline. In *Reformed Churches the same court is called a general *synod.

GENERAL ASSOCIATION OF GENERAL BAPTISTS, a body of *General Baptists that derives from the Church established (1823) at what is now Evansville, Ind., by Benoni Stinson. The Association was organized in 1870; it traces its origins to the General Baptists in England, many of whom migrated to the American colonies. The same upsurge of *Calvinism that threatened the *Free Will Baptists for a time eroded the General Baptists in the East; Stinson's foundation was a renewal. The General Association adheres to *Arminianism, practices *open communion, and strives to further cooperative union with other Baptist groups. The 64,498 members in 844 churches (1968) are mainly in the Midwest.

GENERAL ASSOCIATION OF REGULAR BAPTIST CHURCHES, formed by the withdrawal (1933) of 50 churches from the *American Baptist Convention (then the Northern Baptist Convention). These churches were uneasy with the alleged theological liberalism of the Convention and with its denominational structure for the support of mission work. The churches of the General Association subscribe to the *New Hampshire Confession, its last article modified to express *premillenarianism; to the *five points of fundamentalism; and to Satan's authorship of sin, man's creation by God and birth in sin, and the divine institution of civil government. Headquarters are in Des Plaines, Ill.; membership in 1968 was 170,299 in 1,244 churches.

GENERAL BAPTISTS, a designation for those Baptists who believed that Christ's atonement made salvation available to all men. Living in the Netherlands while the controversy over *Arminianism was rife, these early English Baptists rejected the Calvinistic doctrine of *predestination.

John *Smyth, the first pastor, declared that *original sin is "an idle term," and that "God doth not create or predestine any man to destruction." Thus these Arminian Baptists were distinguished from *Particular Baptists by the emphasis they placed upon the power of man's free will either to accept or to reject God's salvation in Christ. See R. G. Torbet, *History of the Baptists* (rev. ed., 1963). *BAPTISTS.

GENERAL CHURCH OF THE NEW JERUSALEM, a Swedenborgian body, formed in 1890 by a division of *Churches of the New Jerusalem in and around Philadelphia from the parent body, *General Convention of the New Jerusalem in the U.S.A. Denominational headquarters and educational and publishing work were located at Bryn Athyn, Pa., with the generous assistance of John Pitcairn, who built a cathedral for the General Church of the New Jerusalem there in 1914. The Church has bishops, who are chosen by the annual general assembly, and it asks for unanimity in the decisions of the assembly and the council of bishops. In 1968 there were 1,496 members in 10 churches.

GENERAL CONFERENCE (Methodist), the highest legislative body of the Methodist Church. *CONFERENCE (METHODIST).

GENERAL CONFERENCE MENNONITE CHURCH, the first *Mennonite body to be organized in the U.S. (1860, at West Point, Iowa). Members trace their origins to Mennonites from W. Prussia, Russia, and Switzerland. The Church follows traditional Mennonite teaching but is open to fellowship with other Christians and does not resist modernization in mode of life and dress. The more than 80,000 members are found chiefly in the western states and provinces of the U.S. and Canada. The Church has headquarters in Newton, Kan., and operates a publishing house there, as well as Bethel College in nearby North

Newton and Bluffton College, in Bluffton, Ohio. See MennEnc 2:469–471.

GENERAL CONFERENCE OF THE EVANGELICAL BAPTIST CHURCH, INC., a group of churches sympathetic with the views of *Free Will Baptists and located in North Carolina. This denomination was known previously as The Church of the Full Gospel, Inc.; the present designation was chosen in 1935. Although the concept of local church independence is preserved, the structure of the General Conference allows for more effective cooperation, both internally and with the Wilmington Conference of Free Will Baptists. In the mid-1960s there were 31 churches, with about 2,200 members.

GENERAL CONVENTION (Philadelphia, 1789), the body that completed the reorganization of what had been the C of E in the colonies into the *Protestant Episcopal Church in the United States. Though established in some provinces, the C of E never had had any general organization in the colonies or any colonial bishops. As a result of the Revolution, it had lost its establishments and the aid it had formerly received from the *Society of the Propagation of the Gospel in Foreign Parts. Following the Revolution, a series of conventions (1784, 1785, and 1786), under the leadership of W. *White and representing principally the middle states, framed a constitution, obtained the consecration in England of two bps. (White of Pa. and S. Provoost of N.Y.), and through a committee recommended a radical revision of the Book of Common Prayer. This revised version came to be known as the Proposed Book, because it never received final approval. In the meantime, the clergy of Conn. had secured the consecration of S. *Seabury by bps. of the Episcopal Church in Scotland. The General Convention at Philadelphia united these two strands of development under a revised constitution that provided for a bicameral general convention (with a house of bishops

and a house of clerical and lay deputies), the body that still governs the Episcopal Church. It also adopted a more conservative revision of the BCP, which remained in force until 1890 (see AMERICAN PRAYER BOOK). Under a rule adopted by the first house of bishops, the bishop senior by consecration became presiding bishop (this office was made elective in 1919). See W. W. Manross, *History of the American Episcopal Church* (3d ed., 1959), 191–201; C. O. Loveland, *Critical Years* (1956), 236–272.

GENERAL CONVENTION (Protestant Episcopal), the legislative body of the Church. The deliberations of the convention, which meets every 3 years, are conducted by the *House of Bishops and the *House of Clerical and Lay Deputies. The convention also functions as the Church's judicial branch, interpreting the constitution (which it alone can amend) and the canons (which it enacts). The convention has provided courts only for the trial of bishops and for review of diocesan trials of other clergy. Historically the convention, through its officers and committees, has served also as the Church's executive branch. A gradual transfer of limited executive authority began in 1919, when the convention began electing the presiding bishop; in 1922 it created an executive council filled largely by vote of the convention. See E. A. White and J. A. Dyckman, *Annotated Constitution and Canons for the Government of the Protestant Episcopal Church in the U.S.A.* (2v., 1954), 4–38.

GENERAL CONVENTION OF THE NEW JERUSALEM in the U.S.A., a Church founded in Philadelphia in 1817, to unite the scattered Swedenborgians into a formally organized church body (see CHURCHES OF THE NEW JERUSALEM). William Glenn first brought the works of E. *Swedenborg to America in 1784, and by 1792 the adherents of the New Jerusalem Church were sufficiently numerous to establish a church in Baltimore. Hetty Barclay of Bedford County, Pa., carried the new faith to the West. By 1817 there were congregations in western Pa., western Va. and eastern Ohio, and also in Baltimore and Philadelphia. Some advances were made in New York and New England, 1820–40, but none in the South. The general convention includes 5,096 members in 62 congregations and supports a theological school and an extensive publishing program, esp. of works of Swedenborg.

GENERAL COUNCIL, a phrase with several ecclesiastical meanings: (1) From the 6th cent., a council or *synod of all the bishops of the Church, in distinction from a particular or provincial council of a diocese or region (see D 447). The papal general councils of the Middle Ages, which evolved from the Roman synods presided over by the popes, legislated for the whole Church. Although "general" is sometimes used as a synonym for "ecumenical," only an *ecumenical council in the strict sense is authoritative for the whole Church. (2) The General Council of the Congregational and Christian Churches was the agency for cooperation formed when the local congregations of these two Churches joined together in 1931 (they became part of the *United Church of Christ in 1957). (3) In Presbyterian Churches the term General Council refers to the administrative agency of any of the church *courts.

GENERAL SIX-PRINCIPLE BAPTISTS, the earliest group of *Arminian Baptists to appear in the colonies, established as a church in R.I. in 1670. The name refers to the six principles in Heb 6.1–2, urged (*c.* 1659) by a group of General Baptists in London, to which the R.I. colonists belonged, as the sole creedal formula: repentance, faith, baptism, laying on of hands, resurrection of the dead, and eternal judgment. This Baptist association has its greatest numerical strength in Rhode Island.

GENERAL SYNOD, in the *polity of Reformed and some Lutheran Churches, the supreme legislative and administrative agency (see SYNOD). Historically, it was the title of the union of the Lutheran bodies in Pa., N.Y., N.C., Md., and Va. formed in 1820, which, because of disagreements in doctrinal points, was gradually weakened and by 1870 had disintegrated.

GENEVA ROBES, the garb worn usually by clergy of the *Reformed Churches. These Churches, following Calvin's directives for Geneva, discarded most of the old vestments, retaining only the outdoor dress of the clergy, which was to be used also in church services. This consisted of cassock, gown, bands (or other neckwear), black velvet cap, and scarf. The Geneva gown is somewhat fuller than the academic gown, which may be worn in its place.

GENEVAN CATECHISMS, two *confessions of faith for the *Reformed Church at Geneva; also called Calvin's Catechisms. (1) The first, entitled *Instruction and Confession of Faith according to the use of the Church of Geneva*, was presented in its printed text to a conference at Lausanne in Feb. 1537. The document was not a *catechism at all but a doctrinal exposition in 58 sections, probably composed by Calvin and based on his *Institutes of the Christian Religion.* His conception of the Church and of the high status of the minister of the word are prominent. A short time later a confession of faith in 21 articles, obligatory for all citizens, was added. (2) The Catechism of 1541 was composed in French by Calvin to implement the section of the *Ecclesiastical Ordinances* on the education of children. It was later (1545) translated into Latin for wider circulation. Using the Apostles' Creed, the Ten Commandments, and the Lord's Prayer as a framework, this catechism, unlike its predecessor, takes the form of questions and answers, beginning with: "What is the chief end of human life?" "That men should know God by whom they are created." The work is heavily theological, and is divided into four parts: Faith, Law, Prayer, Sacraments. To facilitate summarization and memorization, the contents of the French edition were distributed to correspond to the Sundays of the year. For a long time this catechism was used as the basis for instruction in the Reformed Churches of France and Holland; it influenced the formulation of the *Heidelberg and *Westminster Catechisms. See J. K. S. Reid, ed., *Calvin: Theological Treatises* (LibCC 22; 1954); Schaff Creeds 1:467–471; Léonard HistProt 1:325–326.

GEORGE OF PODEBRAD (1420–71), leader of the *Utraquists, King of Bohemia. G. resolved the religio-political impasse between Utraquist and pro-Roman factions by seizing Prague in 1448. He then was accepted by both parties as regent during the minority of King Ladislas. In 1452 he defeated the *Taborites. At Ladislas' death (1458) G. was unanimously elected king. First conciliatory toward Rome, he took a hard Utraquist and anti-Roman line when the conflict of factions was renewed in 1462 with Pius II's annulment of the *Compactata. Paul II excommunicated him, released his subjects from allegiance, and had Bohemia invaded by *Matthias Corvinus, King of Hungary. Before G.'s death Matthias was proclaimed king of Bohemia by the pro-Romanist nobles. G.'s reign was marked by persecution of the *Bohemian Brethren. See F. G. Heymann, *George of Bohemia: King of Heretics* (1965).

GERARD OF BORGO SAN DONNINO (d. *c.*1276), Franciscan *Spiritual. Without authorization, G. published at Paris in 1254 his *Liber introductorius in Evangelium aeternum*, also incorporating the *Concordia, Apocalypsis*, and *Psalterium* of *Joachim of Fiore. The book fostered the agitations of the Spirituals. A commission at Anagni (1255) under Alexander IV denounced 31 errors in G.'s work. The incident led to the resignation of the Franciscan minister general, John of Parma. The latter's successor, St. Bonaventure, imprisoned the obstinate G. for life. See Bihlmeyer-Tüchle 2:303–305, with bibliog. *JOACHIMISM.

GERATI, alternate name for the *Concorezzenses, a group of 13th-cent. Italian *Cathari.

GERHARD, JOHANN (1582–1637), German theologian, important exponent of Lutheran *orthodoxy. After studying medicine at Wittenberg and theology at Marburg and Jena, G. was made superintendent at Heldburg in 1606. In 1615 he became general superintendent in Coburg and prepared a new *church order for Duke John Casimir of Saxe-Coburg-Gotha. In 1616 Elector John George of Saxony prevailed on the Duke to release G. to the Univ. of Jena, where he lectured, despite many invitations elsewhere, until his death. A prodigious worker, G. wrote numerous exegetical treatises, more than 10,000 letters, and the *Loci communes theologici* (9v., 1609–22), which book stands as the classic exposition of Lutheran theology. In his polemical *Confessio catholica* (4v., 1634–37) he endeavored to prove the true Catholicity of Lutheran doctrine against contemporary systematic presentations of Roman Catholicism. He also wrote patristic, exegetical, and devotional works. See A. C. Piepkorn, EncLuthCh 2:905–906, with bibliog.; W. Elert, *Structure of Lutheranism* (1962).

GERMAN BAPTIST BRETHREN, see GERMAN BAPTISTS.

GERMAN BAPTISTS, a name given to the Brethren, who were founded in Schwarzenau, Ger., by A. *Mack. The members were not connected with the Baptists of English origin, but were called Baptists from their practice of *trine immersion. Their doctrinal origins were in German *Pietism. *DUNKERS; *BRETHREN CHURCHES.

GERMAN CATHOLICISM, see DEUTSCH-KATHOLIZISMUS.

GERMAN CHRISTIANS (Deutsche Christen), Protestants under the Hitler regime who attempted to combine Christianity and Nazi ideology. While professing to complete the Reformation begun by Martin Luther, they sought to eliminate confessional differences and to engender total obedience to the *Führer.* They accepted Nazi racist ideas, rejected the OT, and attempted to de-Judaize the NT, wishing even to purge St. Paul. Germany was viewed as the true Holy Land, with Hitler the embodiment of God's law. After gaining ground, by ruse or by force, in various local areas, they demanded at the national assembly of Protestant Churches in 1933 a national Church under a national bishop. With Hitler's assistance they won a majority in the subsequent church elections, and Ludwig Müller, their most influential leader, became *Reichsbischof.* His extreme Aryanizing policies alienated many, and Müller's power was superseded with the appointment of Hans Kerrl as minister for church affairs in 1935. Strong resistance to the German-Christians was found in the *Confessing Church (Bekennende Kirche). The German-Christians declined rapidly after 1935 and in 1945 totally disappeared with the Third Reich. See A. Cochrane, *Church's Confession under Hitler* (1962).

GERMAN MASS, a formulary for divine service *(Deutsche Messe und Ordnung des Gottesdients)* composed by *Luther in 1526. While he had advocated in his writings a vernacular liturgy, Luther first issued a Latin *Formula Missae et Communionis (1523).* Alarmed by innovations introduced by T. *Münzer, and *Karlstadt, he wrote a vernacular text for the "uneducated masses." Simpler than the *Formula Missae,* the *German Mass* omitted many sections of the Roman Mass but kept the words of institution, which were to be sung. Luther also put the text to music, in order to foster

*congregational singing. The formulary was not made obligatory, but was accepted by many churches. Text in LW 53:53-40. See L. Reed, *Lutheran Liturgy* (1960).

GERMAN METHODISTS, the congregations established in Pa. by Jacob *Albright beginning in 1796, so named because, while German-speaking, they followed Methodist doctrine, discipline, and polity. In 1816 they adopted the title Evangelical Association (Evangelische Gemeinde); in 1922, Evangelical Church. Through a merger in 1946, the Evangelical Church became part of the *Evangelical United Brethren Church, which in turn became part of the *United Methodist Church in 1968.

GESS, WOLFGANG FRIEDRICH (1819-91), German Protestant theologian. G. taught at Basel (1864), then was prof. of exegesis and systematic theology at Göttingen (1871-80) and Breslau (1880-85). In his works, such as *Die Lehre von der Person Christi* (1856) and *Christi Person und Werk* (3v., 1870-87), G. proposed an extreme form of kenotic theory: that the abasement of Christ included the transformation of the Logos into Christ's human soul. See EncRelKnow 4:479-480.

GIBBON, EDWARD (1737-94), English historian. G. entered Magdalen College, Oxford, at 15, and within a year converted to Catholicism. His father at once transferred him to Lausanne, where under Calvinist influence he reverted to Protestantism. His chief work is the still authoritative *Decline and Fall of the Roman Empire* (6v., 1776-88), the thesis of which is that Christianity caused the downfall of the Empire; the Middle Ages are "the triumph of barbarism and religion." Everything supernatural G. treated with irony and ridicule, a method more telling than direct attack, which would have alienated many readers. He assigned the rapid spread of Christianity to five causes: the intolerant zeal of

Christians; their belief in a future life; the purity of their morals; the discipline enforced; and the miracles ascribed to Christianity. See *Decline and Fall* (ed. J. C. Bury, 7v., 1904–14); S. T. McCloy, *Gibbon's Antagonism to Christianity* (1933).

GICHTEL, JOHANN GEORG (1638–1710), Bavarian founder of the *Angelic Brethren, who were also called, after him, Gichtelians.

GICHTELIANS, the followers of Johann Georg Gichtel, also called *Angelic Brethren.

GIDEONS, INTERNATIONAL (formal title, Christian Commercial Men's Association of America), a group of laymen dedicated to evangelism, chiefly through distribution of the Bible. The name is an allusion to the Book of Judges, ch. 6–8; Gideon was one of the major judges (i.e., leaders) who by his faith and obedience served God in the liberation of Israel. The account of Judges 7 also explains the emblem, a two-handled pitcher with a torch. The group was founded by two commercial travelers who met in a hotel in Janesville, Wis., in the fall of 1898; they organized the association the following July. The Gideons place Bibles in hotel rooms, hospitals, prisons and public schools. Headquarters are in Chicago, Illinois.

GLAS, JOHN, see GLASITES.

GLASITES (Sandemanians), a small body that separated from the *Church of Scotland under the leadership of John Glas (1695–1773). He was a Presbyterian minister who repudiated the idea of a *state Church in his treatise *The Testimony of the King of Martyrs* (1729). He was deprived of his ministry by the national presbytery in 1734 for his dissent from the *Westminster Confes-

sion. In polity, the Glasites observed *independency; elders were in charge of each congregation, and personal property was at the disposal of the community. They strived to live in strict imitation of the early Christians, especially after Glas's son-in-law, Robert Sandeman (1718–71), took over the leadership (1739). They adopted the practice of footwashing and celebrated the agape (with broth). The designation Sandemanians was used esp. in England and the U.S. The body has not existed since the beginning of the 20th. cent. See J. Ross, *History of Congregational Independency in Scotland* (1900).

GLOSSOLALIA (Gr. *glossa*, tongue; *lalia*, talking), ecstatic speaking in tongues. In *Pentecostalism tongues-speaking is regarded as the manifestation of *baptism with the Holy Spirit. "Over and against all objections the Pentecostal Movement affirms a baptism in the Holy Spirit accompanied, as at the beginning, with scriptural evidences of speaking with tongues as the Spirit gives utterance. . . ." (statement of the World Pentecostal Conference, 1952.) The occurrence of this charismatic gift in the early Church is attested by Acts 2.4–21, 23–32; 8.9–24; 10.46; 1 Cor 12–14. Pentecostal authors point to the recurrence of the phenomenon in the case of some medieval groups and the *Camisards, the Jansenists, American revivalists, and the *Catholic Apostolic Church. In no form of Christianity since apostolic times, however, has glossolalia been stressed to such a degree, or so claimed to be part of the ordinary Christian life, as in Pentecostalism. Tongues-speaking is for Pentecostals "the reason for their separate existence even to the point of divergence with other evangelical churches" (Brumback). It is the landmark of the beginnings of Pentecostalism, and separated it from the *Holiness Churches. Some distinguish between glossolalia as a sign, initial evidence of Spirit baptism, and glossolalia as a more permanent gift of grace to be exercised as witness to the Spirit-filled character of the Pentecostal message. Glossolalia is usually in the form of unintelligible sounds or utterances, although cases of xenoglossy (or xenolalia, ecstatic speaking of a language by a person who had no previous knowledge of that language) have been cited. Consequently, for glossolalia to be profitable to others the gift of interpretation (1 Cor 14.10) is required; often the interpreter restricts himself to conveying a comprehensive meaning of what the tongues-speaker has said. Abuse of glossolalia has caused many Pentecostals to point to the need for control over its use. Some Pentecostal bodies seem to have de-emphasized its importance.

*Neo-Pentecostalism is the term for the growing interest in tongues-speaking within other Churches. In 1968 the General Assembly of the United Presbyterian Church instituted an inquiry into the spread of glossolalia. There has been a manifestation of interest among members of the Protestant Episcopal Church, the American Lutheran Church, the American Baptist Convention, the Reformed Church in America, the Methodist Church, and the Evangelical United Brethren. Interest has been in part attributed to the *Full Gospel Businessmen's Fellowship International (Nichol, 240–244). Even in some RC circles the practice of tongues-speaking has been cultivated in recent years. Neo-Pentecostalism, however, seems to look upon charismatic occurrences as a sign not of Spirit baptism but of the active presence of the Holy Spirit in the Christian community. See C. Brumback, *What Meaneth This?* (1947); M. Kelsey, *Tongue Speaking* (1964); J. P. Nichol, *Pentecostalism* (1966); N. Bloch-Hoell, *Pentecostal Movement* (1964); J. L. Sherrill, *They Speak with Other Tongues* (1964).

GNESIOLUTHERANISM (Gr. *gnesios*, true, genuine), name given c.1700 to the conservative segment of second-generation Lutheranism led by M. *Flacius Illyricus (1520–75), which claimed to be the defender of genuine Lutheranism against anyone who would compromise the Reformation, even among those who called themselves disciples of Luther. The controversies belonged to two principal categories. First, the doctrine of justification had to be defended against the synergists, who tended to compromise with the doctrine of the Church of Rome concerning the necessity of good works for salvation (see SYNERGISTIC CONTROVERSY). Second, the Gnesiolutherans were concerned with the doctrine called *Crypto-Calvinism, concerning the person of Christ and the Lord's Supper.

GODESCALC, see GOTTSCHALK.

GOD'S INVASION ARMY, a home mission force of the *Baptist General Conference, made up of young people who serve for a year as volunteer workers.

GOGARTEN, FRIEDRICH (1887–1967), existentialist theologian, important proponent of theological personalism. He was a Lutheran pastor, then became professor of theology at Jena (1927) and later at Göttingen (1933). With Karl *Barth, he rejected the optimistic, man-centered theology of the 19th cent. in favor of *dialectical theology. Fundamental Lutheran positions on the sovereignty of God, the gratuity of grace, and the crisis in which God's word places man were central to his early thought. He maintained that Christianity is not found in a realm of ideals or universal truths but in the continuing interaction between persons, a Thou-I relationship, in which man is always dependent upon God's initiative. In 1933, G. broke with Barth and moved toward a more existential theology in which traditional doctrine could be rethought in historical rather than metaphysical categories. He strongly supported the biblical demythologizing of R. Bultmann and often confronted the speculative problems raised by liberal NT exegesis. Acceptance of the gospel message should be viewed not as the subjective assent to objective truths but as the affirmation that God's saving action, revealed in the historical Jesus, continues in the present.

After World War II, he recognized secularism as the major issue facing Christianity and tried to indicate man's radical responsibility for the world. Since man is saved by faith alone, he is free to work in the world with true objectivity and is able to avoid any divinization of the historical process. Grace renders man free from the world as a source of justification, yet man remains responsible for the world as his possession. These notions strongly influenced D. *Bonhoeffer, Harvey Cox, and the *death of God theologians. Works in English: *Demythologizing and History* (tr. N. H. Smith, 1955), *Reality of Faith* (tr. C. Michalson, 1959). See L. Shiner, *Secularization of History* (1966).

GOMARITES, a name given the *Contra-Remonstrants, because of the prominence of F. *Gomarus as the opponent of *Arminianism. *DORT, SYNOD OF.

GOMARUS, FRANCISCUS (Gomar; 1563–1641), Dutch Calvinist theologian. After studies at several universities, including Oxford, Cambridge, and Heidelberg, G. became (1587) pastor for the Dutch residents of Frankfurt-am-Main. From 1594 to 1611 he was professor of theology at the Univ. of Leiden. Theologically he was a rigid supralapsarian, and vigorously opposed J. *Arminius; because of his leadership the strict Calvinists, anti-Arminians, were called Gomarites (see CONTRA-REMON-STRANTS). He was one of the five official theologians at the Synod of *Dort (1618–19). From 1618 he was professor at Groningen, and in this period collaborated in the revision of the Dutch version of the OT books. Works: *Opera theologica omnia* (1644). See Bihlmeyer-Tüchle 3:202; W. F. Dankbaar, RGG 2:1691–92; D. Nauta, EncRelKnow-Suppl 1:467; bibliog. for Arminianism.

GOOD WORKS, or simply works, the upright deeds or actions of man. The Chris-

tian Churches in their official teaching reject *Pelagianism, the doctrine that works prompted by man's natural good will win salvation or God's grace. Reliance on good works in this sense is rejected as opposed to the gratuitousness of grace. In Christian practice, however, this opposition has not always been respected; in liberal or rationalist theological trends, man's capacity for good has been exalted to the point of obliterating the specific meaning of grace (see LIBERAL THEOLOGY). In the framework of a recognition of the divine initiative in grace, there are still diverse understandings of good works. According to one understanding they are deeds through which one attempts to fulfill the law and so please God, or appear innocent in his sight (see Rom 3.20). In another understanding good works are synonymous with "fruits of the Spirit" (Gal 5.22), against which "there is no law"; they are the effect of coming under the dominion of the indwelling Spirit. In the Renaissance Church, the two understandings appear not to have been adequately distinguished (see NOMINAL-ISM), and the Reformation may be viewed as an attempt to reestablish the distinction. Even where there is agreement that only the good works which are the fruit of the Spirit have any relation to salvation, there is difference as to what the relation is. On the basis of the Lutheran position that man's righteousness comes from faith alone through grace, Protestants, rejecting the idea of works being meritorious, regard them as necessary only in the sense that they are an inevitable evidence of the presence of the Spirit. According to the Council of Trent good works are at once gifts of the Spirit and meritorious of salvation (D 1582). Contemporary theologians view the opposition between authentic RC and Lutheran teaching as more verbal than real. *JUSTIFI-CATION; *JUSTIFICATION BY FAITH; *LAW AND GOSPEL; *ARMINIANISM; *MAJORISTIC CONTROVERSY.

GOODMAN, GODFREY (1583–1656), Anglican bp. of Gloucester. Educated at Cambridge, C. held various pastoral posts in England until 1616, when the publication of his most noted work, *The Fall of Man*, brought him to the attention of the court. Thereafter, he was rapidly promoted until he was named bp. of Gloucester in 1625. His sympathy with and tendencies toward Rome frequently caused him difficulties, not only with the Puritan faction in Parliament, but also with the high church abp. of Canterbury, William *Laud. During the Civil War (1642–46), he was imprisoned and deprived of his see. After his release, he remained in London, where he died in communion with Rome. See G. Soden, *G. G., Bishop of Gloucester, 1583–1656* (1953); J. Hanlon, NCE 6:629.

GORE, CHARLES (1853–1932), Anglican bp., educated at Harrow and Balliol. G. became fellow of Trinity, Oxford; librarian at Pusey House (1884); canon of Westminster; and bishop, successively, of Worcester (1894–1902), Birmingham (1902), a see he was largely responsible for founding (1905), and Oxford (1911). He resigned in 1919. He was a man of academic distinction, pastoral zeal, radical tastes, and devotion to the cause of social justice. He was a founder of the Community of the Resurrection (the Mirfield Fathers). His was perhaps the chief formative influence in modern *Anglicanism. He fought *modernism, defended *episcopacy, and resisted the Romanizers with much learning and cogency in speech and writing. His mind was open to the conclusions of biblical criticism, and his *Lux Mundi* article "The Holy Spirit and Inspiration" (1889) grieved conservative contemporaries, yet his candor ultimately emphasized his completely committed *Anglo-Catholicism. Among his writings, *The Ministry of the Christian Church* (1888) defended the apostolic origins of *episcopacy in the Church; the *Body of Christ* (1901) was an exposition of an Anglican eucharistic theology of the *Real Presence. His trilogy, the *Reconstruction of Belief* (1926), is a monument to his liberal orthodoxy. See life by G. L. Prestige (1935).

GORTON, SAMUEL (c.1592–1677), founder of the Gortonites. A native of Lancashire in England, G. emigrated to Mass. in 1637 in search of religious freedom. He established a sect at Plymouth, but his views turned the Puritan authorities against him. Together with some of his followers he went to R.I. and there at Shawomet purchased land from the Indians. When harassment from the Mass. government continued, he went to England (1643); after 5 years he finally was able to return to the settlement in R.I. with a letter of protection from the Earl of Warwick. In the settlement, renamed Warwick, he composed several religious treatises during the remainder of his life. Among the doctrinal points that involved him in difficulties was his denial of the Trinity and of the reality of heaven and hell. Gortonites survived as a small sect into the 18th century. See A. Gorton, *Life and Times of S. G.* (1907).

GORTONITES, see GORTON, SAMUEL.

GOSPEL MISSION CORPS, a nondenominational, evangelistic body and home missionary society organized (1962) along military lines in New Jersey. It observes baptism and holy communion and stresses the doctrines and experience of full salvation and practical Christian living.

GOTTSCHALK OF ORBAIS (c.803–c.868), monk, theologian, poet. Committed as a child by his parents to the Abbey of Fulda, G. left the monastery before receiving major orders and was absolved of his monastic obligations by the Synod of Mainz (829). This dispensation was rescinded upon the objection of Rabanus Maurus; and he was obliged to return to the monastic life and take an assignment to the monastery of Orbais, where he devoted himself to theology. He developed a doctrine of extreme predestinationism, holding for a double predestination, one to life, and the other a positive reprobation to death. Hincmar of Reims, charged by the Synod of Mainz (848) with the responsibility of dealing with him, had him imprisoned by the judgment of another synod held at Quiercy-sur-Oise (849). Hincmar also wrote against his doctrine on predestination as well as against his trinitarian theology. G. was mentally deranged toward the end of his life, possibly in consequence of the harsh treatment he had received, and refused to the end to abjure his errors. His few extant poems show him to have been among the leading poets of the Carolingian era. Works: *Oeuvres théologiques et grammaticales de Godescalc d'Orbais*, SSL, 20 (1945); poetry, MGH Poetae 3:707–738; 4:934; 6:86–106. See J. Svövérffy, *Die Annalen der lateinischen Hymnendichtung* (2v., 1964–65), 1:235–244; J. M. O'Donnell, NCE 6:648.

GRACE (*gratia*, Vulg. tr. of Gr. NT word *charis*), understood to mean God's favor, either in the sense of divine gratuitous love for man, or as a gift received in virtue of that love.

Gratuitousness of Grace. In the West, *Pelagianism viewed man's own nature as "grace," with the capacity to achieve eternal life without any special divine assistance. The essential reaction of St. Augustine became a position to which almost all Christian Churches have given common assent, at least in principle. Grace comes from the special divine favor of *predestination; it is absolutely gratuitous; no disposition native to man, nor anything that he can do on his own as a *good work does in fact call down or merit God's favor; the gratuitousness of grace is the greater because of the sinfulness of man's fallen state. In the foremost medieval theological synthesis on grace, St. Thomas Aquinas largely incorporated Augustine's teaching but took a more restrained view of the Fall, precisely distinguished man's natural from his grace-given capacities, and affirmed that grace is inwardly received in man, enabling, transforming, and empowering him for a new life.

*Luther's intuitive reassertion of the gratuitousness of grace was a reaction to what seemed a new Pelagianism, the optimistic exaltation of good works by *nominalism. The Lutheran doctrine is characterized first of all by close association between grace and faith. By faith alone, which is itself a gift of God and not a good work, the believer is made receptive to the graciousness of the merciful God. Grace is utterly beyond merit in any sense, even after justification through faith. The graciousness of God's gift is in contrast with man's utter sinfulness; if not Luther himself, his followers understood the justified man to remain inherently sinful, with righteousness not inherent in, but imputed to, him (see FORENSIC JUSTIFICATION). *Calvinism and the *Reformed Churches use the term "grace" almost exclusively in reference to the divine good pleasure. God's graciousness is emphasized by the characteristic doctrine of *double predestination, according to which God chooses some men to be saved from sin, while reprobating others. The mystical doctrines of some Anabaptists, and the Quakers' *Inner Light teaching, regarded man more optimistically and God's grace as within the believer. But the predominant emphasis in Protestant teaching remained the free grace of God saving ever-sinful man. *Liberal theology made most of this emphasis irrelevant by effacing in effect the distinction between grace and nature and by diluting the meaning of sin and of God's saving interventions in human history.

The Council of *Trent enunciated RC teaching by reaffirming the gratuitousness of grace and its saving, transforming effect on man. The transformation consists in a share in God's own righteousness imparted to the recipient, so that he inwardly has the power to live the life of grace. Man by the free grace of God is given the power to consent in the process of his justification and to work out the progress of his salvation. The good works that proceed from the grace-given life in him are at once a gift, since God is their first source, and are meritorious, since these acts are a real exercise of freedom by man living under grace. RC theology seeks to express this teaching by elaborating the distinction between actual grace (enlightenment, inspiration, influence upon the human will) given in sufficiency to all men according to the foreknowledge of God; and sanctifying grace, an inner, abiding share in God's own righteousness, a source of new life.

Dynamics of Living in Grace. The relationship of grace to human responsibility and freedom has led to controversies, even to the formations of new Churches or new emphases in the Christian life. Against Pelagian exaltation of free will, St. Augustine insisted that fallen human nature is so corrupt that no act of free choice (*liberum arbitrium*) has any effectiveness for salvation. *Irresistible grace alone, the effect of God's predestination, gives the freedom (*libertas*) of the sons of God. Man needs this grace to keep his power of free choice from leading him into personal sin, for which he is responsible. *Semi-Pelagianism gave to human freedom the power to initiate the process of salvation, which grace would perfect. Council of *Orange II (529) taught that the whole process of salvation, which includes man's own willing, is a gift of grace. St. Thomas Aquinas sought to explain human freedom under grace through God's transcendent causality, acting effectively but without coercing the will to bring about man's free choices. The Council of Trent stressed man's free, active cooperation in receiving grace and living in grace. The *Congregatio de auxiliis (1597–1607) centered on the question whether grace became fruitful, either in conversion or subsequently, from its inherent efficacy or from the response of the human will. *Quietism was an extreme interpretation of the passivity of man under grace. *Jansenism, which claimed the authority of St. Augustine, stressed the total sinfulness of human nature and man's need of the irresistible, necessitating power of grace.

To Luther free will and its native activities belonged to the level at which man was a sinner, and from which he was saved by grace; human freedom was irrelevant to the order of grace. The *Synergistic Controversy, however, arose within Lutheranism because of P. *Melanchthon's theories of human cooperation in conversion. Freedom and responsibility were simply not entertained as problems in the Calvinist system, with its roots in the absolute sovereignty of God's predestination of the elect. Historic *Arminianism, however, rejected absolute predestination and irresistible grace, defending the role of human freedom; it gave its name, as well, to an interpretation of salvation and the Christian life stressing human effort. This attitude has been a particularly pronounced feature in American Protestantism, esp. through *revivalism. While many of the Churches retained their adherence to classic Lutheran or Calvinist doctrines, the widespread effect of revivalist preaching put an emphasis upon the believer's power to choose to be saved and to live righteously. In liberal theology human capacity to prepare oneself for grace was simply an irrelevancy. In recent years both RC and Protestant theologians have sought to free their explanations of the mystery of grace from overtones of polemics and controversy; to interpret the essential meaning of historic confessional formulations; and esp. to give a richer, more biblical expression to the nature of grace.

GRACE, EFFICACIOUS, a term used primarily to signify a grace that infallibly moves a man to perform an act leading to salvation while leaving him perfectly free to consent or resist. It is an actual grace, i.e., a help conceived of as an impulse or a movement bestowed on the recipient. An efficacious grace not only gives a man the power to act but unfailingly secures the free use of that power. It is efficacious, therefore, not merely in the event of man's cooperation but from the moment it is given by God, before man's consent is given.

The difficult problem of a grace that efficaciously brings about the will's consent and still leaves the freedom of the will intact has vexed theologians for many centuries. Among the various solutions, two that were defended by the 16th-century Spaniards Domingo Báñez, O.P., and Luis de Molina, S.J., are historically famous. Báñez ascribed the efficaciousness to the grace itself, to the divine movement that directly affects the will itself, and called this movement physical predetermination. Man is unfailingly prompted to perform salutary acts but with freedom; God predetermines him to determine himself freely. Molina conceived of the efficaciousness as something extrinsic to the grace itself. The grace is efficacious, he said, because imparted by God in the light of man's foreknown consent; i.e., by the foreknowledge called *scientia media* God has foreseen that a particular grace, a moral persuasion offered, would be accepted if it were given. Because God has foreseen the effect it will have, the grace is said to be efficacious before it is actually conferred; once given, it cooperates with the act of the will consenting, and the salutary act is performed. The RC Church grants full freedom for the teaching of these and other theories provided two truths are safeguarded: the dominion of God over man's actions and the freedom of the will. See H. Lange, *De gratia* (1929). *CONGREGATIO DE AUXILIIS.

GRACE, SUFFICIENT, a grace that confers on man the capability of a salutary act (that is, one leading to salvation) and moves him to it, but that man refuses to use. The Jansenists denied the existence of such graces. For them all grace is efficacious and cannot be resisted. The Church condemned their error and defined the truth that God sometimes gives a grace that remains without salutary effect because man chooses not to cooperate. Absolutely speaking, the term sufficient grace taken in itself means a sufficiency of power for a supernaturally good action; it prescinds from use or nonuse of the power. Therefore, in strict theological the modifying adverb "merely," or the adverb "purely" is added to bring out the notion of rejection of the grace. So it is that theologically and historically considered, with reference to Jansenism, sufficient

grace is purely, or merely, sufficient. This expression always signifies a grace that God bestows with the intention that it be accepted but at the same time foreseeing and permitting its nonacceptance. The existence of purely sufficient graces is a corollary of some of the words and actions of Jesus himself. For instance he condemned the people of Chorazin and Bethsaida for not believing in him (Mt 11. 21). But they could not have believed without grace. Their sin, therefore, was a refusal to accept the grace of faith, and this grace was what one calls purely sufficient. See H. Lange, *De gratia* (1929).

GRAHAM, WILLIAM FRANKLIN (BILLY) (1918–), foremost contemporary evangelist. G. was born in Charlotte, N. C., was graduated from Wheaton (Ill.) College in 1943, became a lay preacher while still a student at Bob Jones Univ. and Florida Bible Seminary, and was ordained a minister in the Southern Baptist Convention in 1939. His evangelistic work began in 1946 with Youth for Christ International. The first of the many campaigns for which he has become famous was in Los Angeles, Cal., in 1949; since that time he has conducted them in all parts of the world. Through his broadcasts, the *Weekly Hour of Decision*, he has reached millions. His preaching is eloquent, impassioned; he stresses fundamental biblical themes, above all grace, sin, salvation, the need for repentance, and the Second Coming. The objective of his campaigns is to bring about a "decision for Christ," and the return of those converted to their Churches.

GRANT, FREDERICK CLIFTON (1891–), biblical scholar. Born in Wis., educated at the General Theological Seminary (New York) and Western Theological Seminary (Chicago), he was ordained to the priesthood in the Protestant Episcopal Church (1912). After serving as assistant and rector in several parishes (1912–24), he was dean of Bexley Hall at Kenyon College

(1924–26), professor at Berkeley Divinity School (1926–27), president and dean of Seabury-Western Theological Seminary (1927–38), and professor of biblical theology at Union Theological Seminary in New York (1938–59). His scholarly work in various areas, esp. NT studies, is represented by some 30 books and scores of articles. The following are representative: *The Economic Background of the Gospels* (1926), *The Gospels: Their Origin and Their Growth* (1953), *The Earliest Gospel* (1943), *Ancient Judaism and the New Testament* (1959), *Roman Hellenism and the New Testament* (1962), *Introduction to New Testament Thought* (1958), *Nelson's Bible Commentary, New Testament* (1962), and his work as joint editor of *Hastings Dictionary of the Bible, Revised Edition* (1963). He was editor-in-chief of the *Anglican Theological Review* (1924–55). He has been a member of the committee on revision of the American Standard Revised Version since 1937, and was a member of the versions committee of the American Bible Society (1944–54). He was one of three Anglican observers at Vatican Council II.

GRATIUS, ORTWIN (van Graes; *c.*1480–1542), German humanist and theologian. G. studied under the celebrated humanist Alexander Hegius (*c.*1433–98) at Deventer, in Holland (so was also called *Deventianus*); became a member of the arts faculty at Cologne (1507), and at the Quentell publishing house supervised the publication of many Latin classics. In 1514 he became a priest. G.'s academic and personal reputation were tarnished by the *Epistolae obscurorum virorum*, addressed to him for joining the opponents of J. *Reuchlin. His belated replies, *Epistola apologetica* (1518) and *Lamentationes obscurorum virorum* (1518), were rather weak. His principal work, *Fasciculus rerum expetendarum ac fugiendarum* (1535), a collection of historical and legal documents pointing to the need for church reform, was judged to be anticlerical and placed on the Index by Pope Benedict XIV after G.'s death. See G.

Krodel, RGG 2:1831; D. Reichling, *O. G.* (1885); F. G. Stokes, *Epistolae obscurorum virorum: The Latin Text with an English Rendering, Notes and an Historical Introduction* (1909).

GRAU, FRIEDRICH, see NAUSEA, FRIEDRICH.

GREAT AWAKENING, a series of religious revivals that spread throughout the American colonies from approximately 1725 to the early 1760s in reaction to religious indifference and secularism. The opening phases of the movement occurred in N.J. with the vigorous preaching of T. J. *Frelinghuysen of the Dutch Reformed Church. G. *Tennent carried on a similar ministry among the Presbyterians, becoming the most prominent revivalist in the Middle Colonies. Jonathan *Edwards, Congregationalist of Northampton, Mass., began the New England phase of the Awakening by his forceful and logical sermons emphasizing the dangers of punishment in hell for the unrepentant and the hope of heaven for the converted. Into this scene came G. *Whitfield about 1740 with his own itinerant preaching, which was to extend the fervor of the movement throughout all the colonies. His work provided a measure of geographical unity and a uniformity of pattern to the revival. Samuel Davies proved to be the leading figure in introducing the Awakening to the Presbyterians of Va. in its later phases. Less balanced preachers, such as James Davenport, by their extravagant charges against clergy who would not support the revival, and by their histrionics in the pulpit, brought the movement into disrepute. Charles *Chauncy of Boston led the attack upon the movement, sharply criticizing it as encouraging eccentric behavior and irrationality while yielding few, if any, moral effects. Edwards, a careful observer as well as an agent of the revival, defended it as a work of the spirit of God. In *Some Thoughts Concerning the Present Revival* and later in his treatise on the *Religious Affections*, he discriminated between its beneficial and detrimental effects and described in detail the nature and function of the emotions. In New England those who followed Edwards and other defenders of the Great Awakening were known as New Lights, and became proponents of the *New England theology; those who opposed it were known as Old Lights. The Presbyterians also split into New Side and Old Side groups.

The Awakening tended to weaken the authority of the clergy, as laymen claimed to be able to judge for themselves the validity of their spiritual condition. Some Churches were invigorated; many were divided, giving rise to sectarian differences in the same denominations or to shifting memberships from Congregational to Baptist churches. Antagonism toward the Calvinism of the Churches participating in the revival arose among the more liberal-minded members, and many of them later moved into the ranks of the Unitarians and Universalists. Dissenting groups growing from the revival in Va. helped to overthrow the established Anglican Church in that colony. Increased missionary activity among the Indians is also traceable to the movement, as represented by the work of David Brainerd, Eleazar Wheelock, and Samuel Kirkland. Early antislavery sentiment was fostered, as well as increased interest in education, evidenced by the founding of many academies and of Dartmouth, Princeton, Brown, and Rutgers. See M. Gewehr, *Great Awakening in Virginia, 1740–1760* (1936); E. S. Gaustad, *Great Awakening in New England* (1957); Olmstead, 155–191. *REVIVALISM.

GREAT WESTERN SCHISM, the period of divided allegiance (1378–1417) when Western Christendom was torn between two, and at times three, rival claimants to the papacy. The roots of the schism can be traced to the period when the papal curia, under French influence, preferred Avignon to Rome. The actual begining, however, is dated in 1378, shortly after Pope Gregory

XI (1370–78) restored the papacy to the Eternal City. Not until the Council of Constance (1414–17) was the schism healed.

The death of Gregory XI in Rome set the stage for the first papal election in that city in 75 years. The 16 cardinal electors, aware of the popular desire for a Roman or at least an Italian pope, went outside their own numbers for a candidate. They selected Bartholomew Prignani, Abp. of Bari. Taking the name Urban VI (1378–89), and crowned on April 18, he began almost immediately to alienate the cardinals who had elected him. Either Urban's extreme tactlessness or, as modern authors suspect, evidence of his dementia led the cardinals to flee the Papal States. Regrouping at Anagni, they repudiated Urban VI and held a new election. This time their choice was Card. Robert of Geneva who took possession of the papal palace in Avignon as Clement VII (1378–94).

The support given the rival claimants reflected national interests: most of Italy, the Holy Roman Empire, Hungary, England, and Scandinavia supported Urban VI; Naples, Sicily, France, Spain, and Scotland were loyal to Clement. Division, confusion, and scandal were caused by the schism, yet there was no recognized canonical machinery for healing the breach. Each obedience, convinced of its own position, continued the rivalry. Urban's successors in the Roman line were Boniface IX (1389–1404), Innocent VII (1404–06), and Gregory XII (1406; d. 1417). The proposals to end the schism generally fell under one of three headings: (1) the *via cessionis* called for the resignation of both claimants; (2) the *via compromissi* proposed that a tribunal be appointed to judge the rival claims; and (3) the *via concilii* looked to a general council to decide the issues.

When the procrastination of Gregory XII and the intransigence of Benedict XIII further worsened the situation, cardinals from both obediences agreed to solve the crisis *via concilii*. Although both Popes opposed it, a council met at Pisa in 1409 for the express purpose of ending the schism. The end result, however, was further division, since Pisa elected a third claimant to the papacy, Alexander V (1409–10); and upon his death, John XXIII (1410; d. 1419). Finally in 1414 the *via concilii* was tried again at the Council of Constance. More careful planning, better leadership from the "conciliarists," and a prominent role for the Emperor Sigismond, contributed to its success. The Roman Pope Gregory XII gracefully resigned, July 4, 1415. John XXIII had been formally deposed March 29, 1415, and when Benedict XIII was declared deposed on July 26, 1417, the way was open to elect a pope who would be accepted by the entire Western Church. On Nov. 11, 1417, the council ended the schism by electing Martin V (1417–31).

Much of the confusion about the legitimacy of the rival claims of Rome, Avignon, and Pisa still remains. Those who elected Urban VI and Clement VII argued that the Roman mob during the first balloting inspired so much fear that a free election was impossible. Just as the canonical means for resolving the impasse were inadequate in the 14th cent., so today historical and ecclesiological criteria for judging the conflict remain unclear. Certainly, however, the doubt and disputes about the real pope and the real Church deeply affected all levels of Christian life; the schism directly prepared for the destruction of Christian unity a century later in the Reformation. See W. Ullmann, *Origins of the Great Schism* (1948); O. Prerovsky, *L'elezione di Urbano VI e l'insorgere dello scisma d'Occidente* (1960) Hughes HC 3:299–305.

GREBEL, CONRAD (c.1498–1526), leader of the Swiss Anabaptists. The son of a prominent Zurich family, G., as a student and scholar at Basel, Vienna, and Paris, was a humanist with little religious interest. Returning to Zurich (1520) he was converted by H. *Zwingli, but by 1524 broke with him, advocating a religion of inner experience, the rejection of *infant baptism, and the complete separation of Church from State. G.'s followers were known as the Swiss

Brethren. In Jan. 1525 he put into practice *believer's baptism by re-baptizing G. *Blaurock. He suffered persecution until his early death from the plague. See H. S. Bender, *C. G. ca. 1498–1536, The Founder of the Swiss Brethren, Sometimes Called Anabaptists* (1950).

GRELLET, STEPHEN (Étienne de Grellet du Mabillier; 1773–1855), evangelical Quaker preacher. Fleeing Revolutionary France, where he had been reared a Catholic, G. came to Newtown (Queens), N.Y., where he became a Quaker in 1795 and an approved minister in 1798. In his lifetime he traveled 100,000 miles in missionary journeys in North America and Europe. His preaching expressed the evangelical Protestant strain introduced into American Quakerism. The conflict of this point of view with the *Inner Light teaching as interpreted by E. *Hicks, whom G. opposed, led to the orthodox-liberal split of 1827 in Quaker ranks. G.'s memoirs were edited by B. Seebohm (2v., 1860). See W. W. Comfort, *S. G.* (1942); B. Forbush, *Elias Hicks, Quaker Liberal* (1956).

GRISWOLD, ALEXANDER VIETS (1766–1842), bp. of the Protestant Episcopal Church in the Eastern Diocese. Born in Simsbury, Conn., he was ordained priest in 1795. After serving three parishes in Litchfield County, Conn., he became rector of the Episcopal church in Bristol, R.I., in 1804. The Episcopal churches in all of the New England states except Conn. combined in 1811 to form the Eastern Diocese, and Griswold was chosen bishop. During his long episcopate, he built the Church up to such strength that each of the member states was able to support its own bishop. He was a leader in the formation of the Domestic and Foreign Missionary Society in 1820. After the death of Bp. W. *White (1836), G. became presiding bishop of the Episcopal Church. See J. S. Stone, *Memoir of the Life of the Rt. Rev. A. V. G.* (1854).

GUÉRINETS, a name given to a group of illuminists in Picardy in the late 17th cent. by many historians because of their supposed connection with Pierre Guérin (*c.* 1596–1654), a parish priest at Roye. He did found a congregation of nuns, Filles de la Croix, who were popularly called Guérinettes; he was also twice investigated for alleged novelties in doctrine, but was acquitted. Any association with the suspect *Illuminés is questionable.

GUNTHERIANISM, a theory concerning the truths of Christian revelation proposed by Anton Günther (1783–1863). He was a RC priest and theologian who, in Vienna, devoted himself chiefly to private tutoring and writing. He was thoroughly read in the works of contemporary German philosophers, esp. Hegel. In 1857 nine of Günther's works were placed on the Index; he himself submitted, but some of his followers did not (after Vatican Council I, several "Guntherians" became Old Catholics), and in the brief *Eximiam tuam*, June 15, 1857, Pius IX renewed the condemnation of Günther's works. Guntherianism was censured for being rationalistic and for teachings opposed to the consubstantial unity of the three divine persons, the essential union of body and soul in man, and the freedom with which God created the universe (see D 2825–31; 3025).

GURNEY, JOSEPH JOHN (1788–1846), English Quaker, philanthropist, and writer. G. worked with his sister, E. *Fry, for penal reform and the abolition of slavery; he visited Canada and the U.S., 1837–40. His name was given to those orthodox Quakers who in the 1840s stressed evangelical Protestant belief more than the *Inner Light. They were called Gurneyites as distinct from the Wilburites (see WILBUR, J.). Among G.'s works were *Observations on the Distinguishing Views and Practices of the Society of Friends* (1824) and *Essays on the Habitual Exercise of Love to God* (1834).

See E. Bronner, ed., *American Quakers Today* (1966), 20–21. *RELIGIOUS SOCIETY OF FRIENDS.

GURNEYITES, those 19th-cent. Quakers who followed the evangelical emphasis of J. *Gurney; also the Quaker bodies that trace their origins to that movement. *RELIGIOUS SOCIETY OF FRIENDS.

GUSTAVUS II ADOLPHUS, King of Sweden (1594–1632). G. came to the throne (1611) in an era of internal unrest and foreign wars. Aided by the skill of his chancellor, Axel Oxenstierna (1585–1654), he overcame these problems. One of the great captains of history, he has been called the "Protestant Hero" because of his decisive intervention on the Protestant side during the Thirty Years' War. The *Edict of Restitution (1629) issued by the Hapsburg Emperor, Ferdinand II, outlawed all Protestant bodies except Lutherans of the Augsburg Confession. G. entered the war (1630) for motives that were at least in part genuinely religious. He was aided by the support of Cardinal Richelieu, given at first secretly, but later publicly through the treaty of Bärwalde (1631). G. led his army of small, highly mobile units on a march through Germany, defeating the Catholic imperial army under Count Tilly at Breitenfeld (1631), on the Lech (1632), and at Lützen, near Leipzig (1632). In the last battle G. fell in a cavalry charge, mortally wounded. He was not only an innovative military tactician but also a great king, raising Sweden to the status of a great power and enhancing its economic and cultural life. See M. Roberts, *G. A.: A History of Sweden 1611–32* (2v., 1953–58), bibliog.

GUYON, JEANNE MARIE BOUVIER DE LA MOTTE (1648–1717), French controversial spiritual writer. Born at Montargis, at 15 she married Jacques Guyon de Chesnoy, 20 years her senior. He died in 1676, leaving her with three children and a large fortune.

In 1681 she left her family to help found a community of Nouvelles Catholiques, converted Huguenots, near Geneva. The Barnabite priest François La Combe, who was imbued with certain quietist tendencies, became her director, and the two traveled through Italy and southern France expounding ideas on prayer contained in G.'s *Moyen court et très facile de faire oraison* (1685). At Paris in 1687 by order of G.'s half-brother, then Barnabite provincial superior, La Combe was imprisoned in the Bastille, then moved to Lourdes, where, having become insane, he died in 1715. De Harlai, Abp. of Paris, had been encouraged by Louis XIV to quell quietist tendencies in France, and the arrest of La Combe paralleled that of M. *Molinos in Rome in 1685. Mme. Guyon was restrained in a Visitation Convent in Paris from January to August of 1688, when release was secured by Mme. de Maintenon, who initiated Mme. Guyon into the "Court Cenacle" and into St. Cyr, where her *Moyen Court* became influential. In October 1688 she met F. Fénelon, then superior of a Paris community of Nouvelles Catholiques, and the two met occasionally and corresponded until 1693, when a proceeding against possible quietist ideas in Mme. Guyon's writings was begun by J. B. Bossuet; this was later expanded into the famous Issy Conferences of 1694–95, attended by Bossuet, L. de Noailles, Abbé Tronson, and Fénelon. The resultant 34 articles condemning aspects of the *Moyen Court* and *L'Explication du Cantique des Cantiques* were signed by Fénelon and Mme. Guyon, but Bossuet, dissatisfied with the temperateness of the Issy condemnation, angered by G.'s sudden departure from his diocese of Meaux, and aided by a now jealous Mme. de Maintenon, had the State arrest G. on Christmas Eve, 1695. She was imprisoned in Vincennes, then in Vaugirard, and finally in the Bastille until her release in 1703 into the custody of her daughter, who brought her to Blois, where she died. During part of her imprisonment Bossuet and Fénelon carried on the great controversy over mystical prayer and *l'amour pur*, pure or disinterested love of God, in which Fénelon never denied G.'s good faith and intentions, despite the obvious excesses in her writings. Contemporary scholarship, which radically challenges the condemnation of Fénelon by Rome in 1699, would also disagree with those who have too readily labeled G. as a quietist. See M. De La Bedoyere, *Archbishop and the Lady* (1956); H. Brémond, *Apologie pour Fénelon* (1910); L. Tinsley, NCE 6:869–871. *SEMIQUIETISM.

H

HABANISTS, a name (possibly a derivative of Haushaben, a Ger. variant for *Bruderhof) given originally to the *Hutterian Brethren in Slovakia. Later it was applied to those Hutterian Brethren who became Catholic after 1760, but were allowed to continue their communal life. Habanists were known for their craftsmanship in ceramics. They were eventually Slavicized; a few descendants still live in villages in W Slovakia. See MennEnc 2:618–619.

HAGENAU, CONFERENCE OF, an unsuccessful reunion meeting in June 1540 between Catholics and Protestants of Germany, convened by the Emperor Charles V. The conference was poorly attended, became bogged down in procedural matters, and postponed its business until the Disputation of *Worms.

HALF-WAY COVENANT, in 17th-cent. New England Congregationalism, a compromise measure on church membership. Only members of the Church enjoyed citizenship, and in 1643 only 11% of the population enjoyed this privilege. In pure Congregational doctrine there were two ways of joining the Church: (1) by joining through a covenant, living a godly life, submitting to church discipline, and partaking of the Lord's Supper, after testifying to an experience of regeneration; and (2) by being born of parents in covenant relation to the Church and being baptized. Persons joining by the second method, however, were never admitted to the Lord's Supper until they personally claimed regeneration and joined in the covenant relationship. The question then arose as to whether those who were members only because of their birth and baptism and remained "unregenerate" might have their own children baptized.

A ministerial body was appointed by the General Court of Massachusetts in 1657 to study the question and present a decision. Its findings were accepted by the Court in 1662, and became known as the Half-Way Covenant. Its decision was that members by birth who "owned the covenant," lived respectable lives, and promised to support and obey the Church might have their children baptized though they themselves had no conversion experience and could not partake of the communion or participate in ecclesiastical affairs. Many persons of standing and position in New England took advantage of these provisions. By 1665, under pressure from the Crown, the right of franchise had ceased to be restricted to members of the Congregational Churches. In church life itself the principle of the Half-Way Covenant was extended, esp. by Samuel Stoddard, pastor at Northampton, Mass., to admit all baptized of upright lives to communion even though they had not experienced conversion. His son-in-law Jonathan *Edwards, in the *Great Awakening, restored the requirement of the conversion experience. See Olmstead 84; W. Walker, *History of the Congregationalists* (1894), 170–182.

HALIFAX, CHARLES LINDLEY WOOD (1839–1934), Second Viscount Halifax; ecumenist. Pusey, Liddon, and Wilberforce shaped his *high church piety and devotion at Oxford. Closely attached to the Cowley Fathers, he was also a great benefactor of the first Benedictine communities in the C of E. As president of the *English Church Union (1864–1919; 1927–34), he was in the thick of the fights of the period, e.g., the *Public Worship Regulation Act and the *Revised Prayer Book. Together with his friend the Abbé Portal, he opened an ecumenical approach to Rome that ended unhappily with the bull *Apostolicae curae* (cf. H.'s *Leo XIII and Anglican Orders,* 1912; J. J. Hughes, *Absolutely Null and Utterly*

Void, 1968); but with true Yorkshire doggedness he reopened it in the famous *Malines Conversations with Cardinal Mercier. In England the authorities on the Anglican side fought a delaying action and on the RC side opened a counteroffensive; both were looking backward rather than forward. The Conversations themselves, which were conducted in an admirable spirit, set in motion a series of talks that for two decades were private and informal, but that now are official and recognized. See life by J. G. Lockhart (2v. 1935, 1936).

HALL, FRANCIS JOSEPH (1857–1932), Episcopalian priest and theologian. He studied at Racine College as well as at General Theological Seminary in New York City and at Seabury-Western Theological Seminary, Evanston, Illinois. Ordained in 1886, he was professor of dogmatics at Western Theological Seminary and later at General. His *Theological Outlines* (3v., 1892–95; rev. ed., 1933) and his *Dogmatic Theology* (1907) are classics of Anglo-Catholic theology and have had a widespread influence upon many priests of the Protestant Episcopal Church. A foe of *modernism, he wrote *Christianity and Modernism* (1924). He served as a member of the world Conference on *Faith and Order in Lausanne (1927) and wrote *Christian Reunion in Ecumenical Light* (1930).

HAMANN, JOHANN GEORG (1720–88), German Lutheran religious writer. H. studied various disciplines at Königsberg. While in London on business (1756–58) he experienced a sudden conversion and devoted the rest of his life to opposing the *Enlightenment with Christian ideas based on lived experience and intuition. He considered the only reality to be God's giving himself humbly to the world. With deep conviction he championed the views of Luther on sin and redemption. Some of his ideas were taken over by S. *Kierkegaard; others were reflected in the theology of the

irrational proposed by F. E. *Schleiermacher and A. *Ritschl. See I. Ludolphy, EncLuthCh 2:975–976.

HAMILTON, PATRICK (1504–28), a Scot of noble birth who was burned at the stake for preaching reformed doctrine at St. Andrews. While studying on the Continent, he was influenced by Lutheran doctrines; he returned to Scotland to preach his faith, and was summoned on a charge of heresy. He was offered life if he would recant. His courage and steadfastness at his execution (it took 6 hours to burn him) had a far-reaching effect, and his short book *Loci Communes* (*Patrick's Places* or *Patrick's Pleas*) became a cornerstone of Protestant theology. The text is in J. Knox, *History of the Reformation in Scotland* (W. C. Dickinson, ed., 2v., 1949). See P. Lorimer, *Scottish Reformation* (1860); *idem*, *P. H.* (1857); A. R. Macewen, *History of the Church in Scotland* (1913); J. McKinnon, *Luther and the Reformation* (1925).

HAMPTON COURT CONFERENCE, a meeting in Jan. 1604, presided over by James I, between Anglican bps. and Puritan leaders. The latter presented grievances against the liturgy of the *Book of Common Prayer (see MILLENARY PETITION) and the Anglican notion of episcopacy; they received little satisfaction. The conference did, however, lead to the publication of the Authorized Version of the Bible.

HARD SHELL BAPTISTS, derogatory name for *Primitive Baptists, applied to the group because of its ultraconservatism and literalism.

HARDENBERG, ALBERT RIZÄUS (c.1510–74), German Lutheran theologian. Educated at Groningen, H. entered Aduard Monastery c.1527; but after study at Louvain and Mainz he embraced the Reformation in 1539. In 1542 he became a disciple of

Philipp *Melanchthon at Wittenberg and in 1544 helped the abp. of Cologne introduce reforms. He held a pastorate in Kempen and then became cathedral preacher in Bremen; but because of his Crypto-Calvinist doctrine of the Lord's Supper he was forced to leave the city in 1561. He spent 5 years in a monastery near Oldenburg and then accepted invitations to Sengwarden (1565) and Emden (1567). H. is regarded as the founder of the Reformation in Bremen. See C. Bertheau, EncRelKnow 5:145-147; J. Moltmann, RGG 3:74.

HARMANDSZOON, JACOB, see AR-MINIUS, JACOBUS.

HARMONY SOCIETY, a group of separatists and Pietists, also known as Harmonists or Rappites after their founder, the Württemberg farmer Johann Georg Rapp (1757-1847). Rapp immigrated to the U.S. with some followers in 1803 for a freer exercise of belief. After founding the Harmony settlement in Butler County, Pa., the members moved to to establish New Harmony, Ind., in 1814. They sold this property in 1824 to Robert Owen, the socialist reformer and agnostic, who continued his own community there, and Rapp and his followers moved back to Pa. and set up a third colony, named Economy, now the town of Ambridge, NW of Pittsburgh. They recognized no authority save the Bible, denied the Eucharist, advocated celibacy, rejected school attendance of children, led a communal life without individual possessions, and believed that in an imminent regeneration of the world the "harmony" of male and female elements in man would be reestablished. By their simple and strict life they developed prosperous agricultural communities. The Harmonists adopted children and also sought new emigrants from Germany, but neither these measures nor a temporary merger with a similar group, the Bernhardusbrüder, prevented extinction by the end of the 19th century.

See J. S. Duss, *Harmonists* (1943); T. Horgan and R. Brown, "Communal Movements," NCE 4:29-32, esp. 30 and bibliog.; W. H. Larrabee, EncRelKnow 3:187.

HARNACK, ADOLF VON (1851-1930), German church historian, and theologian. Next to F. *Schleiermacher, H. was probably the most influential Protestant thinker of the 19th and the early 20th cents. because of his immense historical scholarship and his contributions to *liberal theology. H. studied at the Univ. of Leipzig and taught there for 5 years. He then became professor of church history at Giessen and at Marburg. In 1889 he was called to Berlin despite the strenuous opposition of the Lutheran Church Senate because of his liberal views. He was also the director of the state library in Berlin. With T. Mommsen he founded the series *Griechische christliche Schriftsteller,* to provide definitive texts of the Fathers of the first 3 centuries. In 1899 he gave a course of lectures stressing the moral side of Christianity, esp. the message of universal brotherhood. These appeared the following year as the epoch-making *Das Wesen des Christentums.* H. traced the infiltration of Greek metaphysics into early Christianity until the emancipation effected through Luther's reform and his ethical approach to the God of goodness. H.'s capacity for work (his bibliography numbers about 1,700 items), clearness of vision, powers of organization, brilliance of style, and ability as a lecturer were matched by his gift both for planning and for scholarly detail. See W. Schneemelcher, RGG 3:77-79; Y. Congar, Catholicisme 5:516-519; F. X. Murphy, NCE 6:929-930.

HARRIS, HOWELL (1714-73), founder of the *Calvinistic Methodists. H. was born at Trevacca, Wales, in 1714 and had a conversion experience in 1735. A student at Oxford in the same year, he became disturbed by the immorality there and returned to Wales, and though not ordained, he began to preach. He became an itinerant evangelist, and separated from the Church of England. In 1743 with George *Whitefield, whom he had met in 1739, and some others, he formed the Welsh Calvinistic Methodist Church. He was also a friend and admirer of John *Wesley. He was persecuted by mobs, and when his health broke, founded a community for needy persons at Trevacca. He was befriended and assisted by Selina, Countess of *Huntingdon. See H. E. Lewis, *H. H.* (1912); W. Williams, *Welsh Calvinistic Methodism* (1872).

HASTINGS, SELINA, see HUNTINGDON, COUNTESS OF.

HATTEMISTS, followers of Pontiaan Van Hattem (1645–1706), a deposed Dutch Reformed preacher who taught a practical piety and passive Christianity. Everyone was to wait passively for Christ to reveal himself inwardly and not to seek him out by interpreting the Scriptures. Thus, regenerated by the Holy Spirit in him, a person no longer would be inclined toward evil. Since the Hattemists rejected the authority of Church and State and since their moral behavior caused scandal, the authorities issued an edict against them in 1733. With the founder's death his followers united with the *Hebrews, but after 1760 there are no further traces of them. See H. Bornkamm, RGG 3:86–87; S. D. van Veen, EncRelKnow 5:168–169.

HAUGE, HANS NIELSEN (1771–1824), Norwegian Lutheran revivalist. The son of a farmer, H. underwent a religious experience in 1796 which convinced him that he was called by God to arouse his countrymen. He preached first in his own neighborhood and then throughout Norway from 1797 to 1804. He was assisted in his work by numerous other lay preachers. Their sacramental teaching was at times unclear, but H. himself was always faithful to Lutheran beliefs. The main points in his program were conversion, the need of personal wit-

ness, and duty to the community. He emphasized obedience and sanctification rather than justification and differed from the Pietists in stressing fidelity to one's earthly calling as service to God. In this connection he assisted in organizing industrial enterprises, thus incurring the hostility of the privileged merchant class. H. was constantly threatened with arrest, since lay preaching was against the law. From 1804 to 1811 and again from 1814 to 1816 he was in prison, and he was also fined for transgression of the Conventicle Act and for offenses against the clergy. He retired a broken man; but his reputation grew, and even church dignitaries visited him at his farm near Oslo. In 1839 his pupil, Elling *Eielsen, brought his ideas to America, where they remained influential among Scandinavian Lutheran immigrants. See E. Molland, EncLuthCh 2:988; D. Carter, RGG 3:88.

HEALING, the cure of bodily ills by religious means, a teaching and practice that appear in various forms among Christian bodies. Beside Jesus' own ministry of healing, the NT attests to the charisma of healing given to the Apostles and to the early Church (Mt 10.1; Acts 3.1–16; 8.7; 9.32–42; 1 Cor 12.9, 28, 30) and to the connection between bodily ills and sin (Jn 9.2–3). The instruction in Jas 5.14–16 was followed in the early Church in both liturgical anointings and prayers for the sick. The RC Church came to regard the anointing of the sick as one of the seven sacraments (D 1696), and its meaning as a sacrament for the sick has been reaffirmed in recent times (Vat II SacLit 73). Beside this sacramental healing, private blessings and prayers for the sick, sometimes involving the use of relics, have continued in RC practice. Other Christian bodies, while not recognizing a sacrament for the sick, still have retained the use of prayers, blessings, laying on of hands, and anointing as profitable for bodily health. The continuance of charismatic healing has been recognized by the RC Church in the miracles performed by saints or attached to places of pilgrimage such as Lourdes as authentication of the Christian message. Through the centuries other groups, e.g., the Waldenses, Moravians, and the Irvingites, have claimed the presence of this charism among them. Particular importance has been attached to it in *revivalism, the *Holiness Churches, and as part of the *foursquare gospel message that healing is an essential part of the Christian message; that as Jesus saves from sin, so also he heals the body from the consequences of sin. In Pentecostalism charismatic, *divine healing is regarded as an essential part of the Christian life, connected with *baptism with the Holy Spirit. *Faith healing has come to mean not just the power of belief to obtain an answer to prayer for health but a specific teaching: mental or metaphysical healing, the power of spiritual mind over matter, which is considered to be evil, the source of sin, sickness, and death. In this sense faith healing is associated with New Thought, Spiritualism, and esp. Christian Science.

HEALING, FAITH, see FAITH HEALING.

HEBREW CHRISTIAN CONGREGATION (Ger. Judenchristliche Gemeinde), a religious body whose members are Jewish converts to Christianity; headquarters are in Israel. Its founder was a Russian journalist, Abram Poljak (b. 1900), who had immigrated to Jerusalem from Germany in 1933. Having been christened by a Baptist minister, he wanted to unite other Jewish converts in a separate union in the new state of Israel. He also wished to keep certain Jewish practices, such as circumcision, observance of the Sabbath, and Bible reading; he taught a form of *adventism, which stressed fulfillment of biblical prophecies by the conversion of Israel. He met with little success and returned to Europe, where he founded in 1952 the Judenchristliche Reichsbruderschaft, since 1954 called Reichsbruderschaft Jesu Christi. Small communities exist in Germany, Switzerland, and England. Works by A. Poljak:

Das Kreuz im Davidstern (1937) and *Die jüdische Kirche* (1945). See F. Majer-Leonhard, LTK 8:1121.

HEBREW CHRISTIANS, a society of Protestant evangelicals of Jewish extraction who promote the Jewish-Christian dialogue. Earlier organizations of Christian Jews had been the Sons of Abraham, founded in 1813 in London, and the Hebrew Christian Alliance, established in 1865. In 1915 a delegation of English and American Hebrew Christians met to plan a society that would unite Hebrew Christians scattered throughout the world. Their efforts resulted in the International Hebrew Christian Alliance, founded in London in 1925. In its fifth international congress (Budapest, 1937), delegates voted not to establish an independent church structure but to remain members of their own Churches. The aims of the Alliance are to promote the spirit of fellowship among members by organizing them into local alliances; to interpret the Jewish spirit to Christians and the Christian spirit to Jews; to aid Jewish candidates for the Protestant ministry; to protest anti-Semitism; and to identify Jewish Christians with their fellow Jews. In 1965 there were 18 national alliances. International headquarters are in London; American headquarters, in Chicago, with branches in 12 cities.

HEBREWS, a Dutch religious group of the late 17th cent., founded by a theology student, Isaak Verschooren. They received their name from their insistence on reading the Bible only in Hebrew. Otherwise their teachings were similar to those of the *Hattemists, with whom they merged in 1706.

HEERBRAND, JAKOB (1521–1600), German Lutheran theologian and professor. After study at Wittenberg (1538–43) H. served at Tübingen until his opposition to the Ausgsburg Interim (1548) resulted in his removal. He was one of the Württemburg theologians sent to the Council of Trent

(1552). Entrusted by Archduke Christoph with many commissions, he helped introduce the Reformation into Baden (1556) while pastor at Pforzheim. In 1557 he began 42 years of teaching at Tübingen, where he was second in influence and honors only to J. *Andreä. H. was outstanding as a preacher and as an exegete of the Pentateuch. His *Compendium theologiae* (1573), which in its 2d edition followed the *Formula of Concord, enjoyed wide distribution. See W. Maurer, RGG 3:113; I. Ludolphy, EncLuthCh 2:999.

HEIDELBERG CATECHISM, a *Reformed *confession of faith published in 1563. While officially approving Calvinism, the elector of the Rhine Palatinate, Frederick III, desired a formula of belief, catechetical in form and temperate in content, to quiet the violence of theological conflict between Lutherans and Calvinists. The exact authors are not certain, but Z. *Ursinus and C. *Olevianus had a principal part in its preparation. The Catechism incorporates Lutheran ideas on man's sinful condition, tones down rigid Calvinist teaching by not mentioning double predestination or limited atonement, and is more concerned with Christian living than theological preciseness. Simple and warm in language, it was translated into Latin at the time of publication. Gradually the Catechism was accepted by the Reformed Churches, not only in Germany but throughout Europe; one of the main concerns of the Synod of *Dort was approval (1619) of this document as a confessional standard. The first English translation appeared in 1572; in English-speaking Reformed Churches the Catechism ranks second in importance after the *Westminster Confession. The three parts of the Catechism, on man's misery in sin, redemption, and the new life, were designed to correspond to the Epistle to the Romans. There are 129 questions divided into 52 lessons for the weeks of the year. The answer to Question 80 (inserted into the 2d and 3d eds., according to some, by Frederick himself; according to others, by Olevianus) is an embarrassingly bitter attack on the Mass, probably as a rejoinder to the Council of Trent. See K. Barth, *Heidelberg Catechism for Today* (tr. S. C. Guthrie, pa., 1964); H. Hoeksema, *Heidelberg Catechism, an Exposition* (1944); W. Hollweg, *Neue Untersuchungen zur Geschichte des Heidelberger Katechismus* (1961); A. Péry, *Heidelberg Catechism* (tr. A. O. Miller, M. B. Koons, 1963); Schaff Creeds 1:535–550.

HELVETIC CONFESSIONS, two Swiss *confessions of faith. (1) The *Confessio helvetica prior,* sometimes called the Second Confession of Basel, was composed there in 1536. The document was prepared by a group of Swiss theologians, headed by H. *Bullinger, for the purpose of a conference with M. *Bucer and W. *Capito. The original was written in German, and a Latin version was immediately made. The 27 articles embodied Zwinglianism, esp. concerning the Holy Eucharist, but also sought for concord with Luther's teaching. (2) The *Confessio helvetica posterior* was written by Bullinger alone in 1562 as a kind of last testimony of his own belief. The desire of the Calvinist elector of the Rhine Palatinate, Frederick III, to defend himself against Lutheran charges of heresy and the need felt by the Swiss *Reformed Churches to have a new confession of faith led to the public adoption of Bullinger's confession at Zurich in 1566. The author himself made the German translation; it was also translated into French. One of the lengthiest of the Reformed confessions (more than 20,000 words), its 30 chapters discourse upon all the main Christian teachings. Continuity of the Reformed Church with the early creeds and patristic witness is emphasized, but the primacy of authority is given to the Scriptures. The influence of both Zwingli and Calvin upon Bullinger is plain in the discussions of the Lord's Supper and predestination; with regard to the latter, the Confession is softer than is Calvin's later thought (see CALVINISM). Dissent from both Lutheran and RC doctrine is expressed. This Confession was accepted or highly regarded in all the Reformed Churches. As a theological document it was unsurpassed; in influence and practical use, it ranked only below the *Heidelberg Catechism and the *Westminster Confession. See E. Routley, *Creeds and Confessions* (1962), 73–86; Schaff Creeds 1:390–420 and 3:237–306 (Lat. text).

HELVETIC CONSENSUS FORMULA, last of the *confessions of faith officially adopted by the *Reformed Church in Switzerland. Composed in 1675 by J. H. Heidegger (1633–98), prof. of Zurich, the Formula, in its preface and 26 canons, was a reaction to the mitigations of Calvinism by the theologians of Saumur, esp. L. *Cappell, M. *Amyraut, and J. de la *Place. The Formula asserted the literal inspiration of Scriptures (even the integrity of the Masoretic Hebrew text); the particular predestination of the elect alone, excluding any hypothetical will of God to save all men; and the imputation of original sin to every man because of a share not simply in the depraved nature but in the sinful act of Adam. The Formula was imposed upon all teachers and preachers; within a generation, however, because its conservatism was divisive, it became a dead letter. See Schaff Creeds 1:477–489.

HELVIDIANS, the followers of *Helvidius. St. Augustine (*Haer.* 83) identifies them with the Antidicomarianites of Arabia. See H. Quillet, DTC 1:1378–82.

HELVIDIUS (4th cent.), an adversary of St. Jerome. He may have been a disciple of Auxentius, the Arian bp. of Milan and predecessor of St. Ambrose. About 380, H. wrote a treatise denying the perpetual virginity of Mary and asserting that she had other children by Joseph (the "brothers of the Lord" in the NT). His principal purpose was to attack the prevailing exaltation of virginity above marriage. Jerome, in reply, wrote *De perpetua Mariae virginitate adver-*

sus Helvidium (PL 23:183–206), stating that these "brothers" were Jesus' cousins.

HELWYS, THOMAS (*c.*1550–*c.*1616), pastor of the first Baptist Church in England and author of the first plea in English for full religious liberty. By 1607 he had become a *Separatist and fled to Holland. In Amsterdam, he was a member of John *Smyth's congregation, which was organized on the basis of *believer's baptism and is regarded as the first Baptist Church. When Smyth made overtures to join the Dutch Mennonites, the Church divided, and H. became pastor of the objecting minority. In 1612, he returned to England, and his Church settled at Spitalfields, near London. Rejecting *limited atonement, his followers were known as *General Baptists. In his *Short Declaration of the Mystery of Iniquity* (1612) he asserted that the king "hath no authority as a king, but in earthly causes" and that since religion is a matter between man and God, the civil government had no right to punish "heretics, Turks, or Jews." Because of this work it is probable that H. died in prison. See W. H. Burgess, *John Smyth the Se-Baptist, T. H. and the First Baptist Church in England* (1911); A. C. Underwood, *History of the English Baptists* (1947).

HEMMINGSEN, NIELS (1513–1600), Danish Protestant theologian. After study in Wittenberg (1537–42) under Philipp *Melanchthon, H. taught Greek, Hebrew, and theology at the Univ. of Copenhagen. Because of his Calvinist leanings he was forced to resign his post in 1579. He spent the remaining years of his life as a canon in Roskilde without, however, losing his international reputation as the teacher of Denmark. He was the first to use the Danish language in writing a text on pastoral theology; and a collection of his sermons was long influential. See A. Otto, LTK 5:228; J. M. Jensen, EncLuthCh 2:1003.

HENRICIANS, followers of *Henry of Lausanne.

HENRY VIII (1491–1547), KING OF ENG-
LAND from 1509. This article is confined to
the steps whereby H. separated the Church
of England from Rome. He was influenced
to some degree by the example of Protestant princes and the writings of men like
William Tyndale; yet he might never have
caused England to separate from Rome had
it not been for his dynastic interests. Since
only a girl survived of his children by Catherine of Aragon and since he feared the
Tudor succession would be disputed, he
wanted to marry again to obtain further issue. Besides, he was in love with Anne Boleyn, lady-in-waiting to the Queen. Accordingly, in 1527 he asked Pope Clement
VII to revoke the dispensation given him 18
years before to marry Catherine, his brother's widow. He reasoned that his failure
to have a male heir was proof of the divine
displeasure that is threatened in Lev
20.21. When it was rejoined that his illicit
relations with Anne's older sister Mary
made him related to Anne in the same degree as to Catherine, he shifted his argument: not all such dispensations were invalid, but his was, for a number of reasons.
A flood of polemical literature followed. To
gain his end, H. asked Cardinal Wolsey to
try the case in his legatine court and only
then to proceed to obtain the Pope's approval. When Wolsey learned that Catherine might appeal his decision, he attempted
to gain the Pope's approval beforehand.
Clement temporized by ordering Wolsey
and Cardinal Campeggio to hear the case in
France but gave the latter secret instructions to persuade H. to drop the suit or
Catherine to enter a convent. By threatening to join the Lutherans, H. forced Wolsey
to open proceedings in May 1529. After
lengthy hearings the court was recessed in
July, to resume in Rome in October. H.
feared a decision given in Rome would be
unfavorable and therefore resolved to try
the case in his own courts. Thomas
Cranmer now advised H. to submit the
question of annulment to university scholars with the proviso that if their verdict
proved unsatisfactory, he declare himself
head of the Church in England and settle

the case in his own courts. H. thereupon
called Parliament and laid the issue before
it. By attacking clerical abuses, he and Parliament intimidated *Convocations, which
acknowledged him as supreme head of the
English Church "as far as the law of Christ
allows."

The next year H. extracted from Convocations the Submission of the Clergy,
whereby it was agreed that ecclesiastical
laws be revised by a committee consisting
of laymen and clerics chosen by the King
and that no new laws be enacted by Convocations without the King's consent. H. also
obtained from Parliament an act depriving
the Pope of his customary annates whenever the King saw fit. When Clement remained unintimidated, H. decided to end
all papal authority in England. He proceeded, Jan. 1533, to marry Anne. Parliament then passed the retroactive Act for
the Restraint of Appeals, which made invalid both Catherine's recourse to Rome
and H.'s original suit. Anne was crowned in
June and on July 11 the Pope excommunicated Henry. At that point Parliament proceeded to legalize the break with Rome. It
stopped all payments to the papacy and by
the Act of Supremacy (1534) made H. the
only supreme head on earth of the Church
of England (*Anglicana Ecclesia*). It also
passed an Act of Succession in favor of
Anne's heirs. The *dissolution of the monasteries took place in 1536 and 1539. While
the views of the continental Reformation
were reflected in the *Ten Articles of 1536,
and in liturgical reforms favoring the vernacular, doctrinally Henry sought to conserve the substance of Catholic belief (see
SIX ARTICLES; KING'S BOOK) during his
reign. See H. J. Grimm, *Reformation Era*
(1965), 289–300; E. Doemberg, *Henry VIII
and Luther* (1961).

HENRY OF LAUSANNE (Henry the Heretic; d. *c.*1145), an apostate monk who began
to preach at Le Mans early in the 12th century. His eloquence and commanding appearance won him many followers, called
Henricians. H. bitterly attacked the world-

liness of the clergy and urged all to practice poverty. He rejected *infant baptism and veneration of the saints, and was finally expelled from Le Mans by Bp. Hildebert of Lavardin. He then moved through S France castigating the official Church and arousing mobs to desecrate churches, assault clerics, and pull down crosses. He was condemned at the Council of Toulouse in 1119, recanted at the Synod of Pisa in 1135, and was again condemned at Lateran Council II in 1139. St. Bernard was sent to preach against him in 1145. The same year H. was imprisoned and died shortly afterward. See H. Daniel-Rops, *Cathedral and Crusade* (1957), 523; E. Delaruelle, Catholicisme 5:622–624; J. Guiraud, *Histoire de l'Inquisition au Moyen-Âge*, I (1935), 3–13.

HERBORN, a Protestant institute of higher studies founded in 1584 by Count John VI of Nassau (therefore also called the "Johannea") to strengthen theological education. Modeled after the Genevan Academy, Herborn flourished under such renowned teachers as Caspar *Olevianus, Johan Piscator, and Wilhelm Zepper, attracting students from many European countries. Under the first academic printer, Christopher Corvinus (Raab) from Switzerland, it became an important publishing center of Reformation literature. The Thirty Years' War and the effects of epidemics brought decline. Herborn survives only as a theological seminary. See H. Graffmann, RGG 3:234.

HERESY (Gr. *hairesis*, what is chosen), originally a particular school or tenet of philosophy, e.g., the Stoics, or a party within Judaism, e.g., the Pharisees or Sadducees. Thus St. Paul refers to himself as having lived "according to the strictest sect of our religion" (Acts 26.5; cf. 5.17 and 15.5). He also denies that the Christian "way" is that of a Nazarene sect (Acts 24.5). When applied by the NT to the Christian body it loses its neutral meaning, and is con-

demned as a division or faction that threatens or destroys unity (1 Cor 2.19; Gal 5.20; Tit 3.10; 2 Pet 2.1). In these passages on the danger to Christian unity, the term heresy is not differentiated from *schism. From the 2d cent. the Fathers begin to draw that distinction; thus Augustine, "Heretics violate the faith by thinking falsely about God, while schismatics break away from fraternal love by their wicked separation, though they believe as we do" (*Fid. et symbol.* 8.21). The Fathers also allowed that not all error was heresy, for it might be based on misapprehension and misunderstanding without intention of setting itself up against church teaching when this had been made clear. The grave wrong lay in obdurate persistence in setting up a sectarian body against the Church. Bad faith was readily suspected, yet Augustine was not alone in holding that "those who have not fathered it but have received it from others, yet who still seek the truth are by no means to be reckoned among the heretics" *(Epist.* 43.1). Catalogues of heresies were drawn up by Justin Martyr, Irenaeus, Hippolytus, Epiphanius, Augustine, and John Chrysostom. The growth of systematic theology in the Middle Ages with its more specific classifications led to a closer and juridically stiffer notion. In practice, however, the term continued to be elastic, and stood comprehensively for all willful separation from the living body of the Church, whether by the rejection of revealed doctrines or opposition to the principles of disciplined life inculcated by authority (see D 902, 906, 1800). Given the strong community sense of Christians, even those of some eccentric and anarchic groups, it was a wickedness too dangerous to be tolerated, and the persecutions and barbarities by orthodox and heterodox alike, which have marked history, reflect and caricature the horror in which heresy was held.

Since the Reformation not only did the RC Church continue in its rejection of heresy, but confessional Churches of the Reformation shared in the same zeal for orthodoxy. The Lutheran and *Reformed *confessions of faith reject as heresy teachings that are contrary to the gospel. In modern times the notion of heresy is often ridiculed. This is in part explained by the minimizing of dogma, rooted in rationalism and in theological liberalism, and in part by the widespread acceptance of the adage "deeds not creeds." Yet many of the Churches continue to recognize the possibility of heresy, the need to resist it, and have juridic processes for those accused of heresy. There is also, however, a healthy contemporary restraint from use of the word "heresy" both by Catholics and Protestants. The term is less frequently used to impugn the genuineness of the belief of fellow Christians. This involves a recognition of past polemical exaggeration, and a hesitancy to accuse others of consciously preferring their own opinions over what is known to be the authentic word of God. Heresy in its strict meaning would be such a choice. See K. Rahner, *On Heresy* (tr. W. O'Hara, 1964); H. E. W. Turner, *Pattern of Christian Truth* (1954).

HERETIC (Lat. *haereticus*, Gr. *hairetikos*), one who professes a *heresy. The history of heretics is a long record of how men may hate one another for the love of God; often savagely persecuted and usually in vain, heretics retorted in kind when they gained the ascendancy. With the decline of dogmatic certainty among Christian bodies, the term is less frequently used in English-speaking countries, and the milder "dissenter," "nonconformist," or "dissident" are preferred. It survives to the extent that fundamentalism survives, and in the RC Church, where it is given a technical and juridical sense. Popularly it has acquired, like a naval swear-word, a jocular and even endearing ring. Official practice, too, has been more generous since Vatican Council II in acknowledging a unity of faith among Christian denominations. Only one who is pertinacious, i.e., who knowingly, willingly, and culpably sets himself up against the Church's divine teaching authority is a "formal" heretic, whereas one who does not recognize this authority, and consequently denies its ruling, is merely a "material" heretic.

HERMAN OF WIED (1477–1552), abp. and elector of Cologne (1515–46). By his own admission H. was more successful as a secular than as an ecclesiastical ruler. Though at first opposed to Martin *Luther, he became friendly to the Reformation through meetings with Lutheran princes and with P. *Melanchthon, *Erasmus, and M. *Bucer. The last worked at Bonn (1542–43) at H.'s invitation; but the cathedral chapter, the university, and civil authorities at Cologne opposed H.'s attempts at reform; when he caused communion to be celebrated according to the evangelical rite, his clergy petitioned the Emperor Charles V to intervene. H. was excommunicated in 1546. He retired to his estates at Wied and died a Lutheran. His removal helped keep northwest Germany Catholic. See J. F. G. Goeters, RGG 3:240–241; A. Franzen, LTK 10:1097–98.

HERMESIANISM, theological and philosophical system taught by Georg Hermes (1775–1831), which sought to use Kantian principles to defend Catholic dogma. Hermes was a priest-professor at Münster in Westfalen (1807) and at Bonn (1820), who enjoyed great respect during his lifetime and was appointed to important offices in the Diocese of Cologne. Since Kantian philosophy was dominant in many universities, Hermes's doctrine won a substantial following in Germany. However, the *semirationalism implicit in the system aroused opposition, and in 1835 the papal brief of Gregory XVI, *Dum acerbissimas*, condemned Hermes's teaching on the nature of faith, revelation, tradition, the magisterium, original sin, grace, proof for the existence and attributes of God, and other points found to be in error (D 2738–40). Hermes's works were placed on the Index of Forbidden Books. The controversy over Hermesianism was heated, but short-lived. When Vatican Council I repeated the condemnation (D 3035-36), Hermesianism already had long been a dead issue. See E. Gratsch, NCE 6:1076.

HERMETISM (Hermeticism), an ancient system of mystical religious teaching combining elements of Platonism, stoicism, neo-Pythagoreanism, and Eastern religions. The Hermetic books, in Greek and Latin, date from *c.*50-300 and are ascribed to Hermes Trismegistus, Hermes the Thrice Greatest. Hermes, the Greek name for the Roman god Mercury, was the name given to the Egyptian god of wisdom and letters, Thoth, who was said to have been the author of the books. The teaching is akin to Gnosticism in that it seeks to show a way of salvation and deification through a special kind of knowledge of God, mixing magic, astrology, philosophy, and theology. Hermetism also has come to mean knowledge concerned with the occult or mysterious. The Hermetic literature includes: *Corpus hermeticum*, composed of 18 writings in Greek, the first of which, *Poimandres*, shows its author's acquaintance with the LXX and contains doctrines on creation similar to those of Genesis and the Fourth Gospel; *Asclepius*, a Latin treatise formerly ascribed to Apuleius and preserved among his works; a collection of 29 writings preserved in the works of Strobaeus; several works found in Coptic translation in Codex VI of the Chenoboskion (Nag Hammâdi) MSS discovered *c.*1945; and miscellaneous other works, including popularizations. See G. Van Moorsel, *Mysteries of Hermes Trismegistus* (1955).

HERRNHUT, a town in Saxony, Ger., established in 1722 as the mother community of the Renewed *Moravian Church. It was founded on the estate of Count *Zinzendorf as an asylum for refugees from Hapsburg lands who sought to keep alive the *Unitas Fratrum of their ancestors. Growing into a flourishing center of *Pietism with worldwide missionary outreach, Herrnhut became a prototype for Moravian communities throughout the world. Its archives contain valuable source material on the Moravian movement. His stay influenced J. *Wesley. See K. G. Hamilton, *History of the Moravian Church* (1967).

HICKS, ELIAS (1748-1830), American liberal Quaker. H. was a Long Island farmer who was active in Friends meetings from *c.* 1765 and became an approved minister in 1778. For 50 years he gave himself to arduous preaching journeys, and in his sermons and correspondence he became a foremost exponent of Quaker liberal mysticism, developing G. *Fox's *Inner Light teaching to the fullest, but advocating a rationalist attitude toward traditional Christian beliefs. He opposed the imposition of evangelical Protestant tenets upon American Quakerism (see GRELLET, S.). When the Quaker separation of 1827 occurred, the evangelical group labeled the liberals "Hicksites," although H. did not have a direct part in the actual process of schism. The schism began in the Philadelphia Yearly Meeting, spread elsewhere, and is still reflected in Quaker divisions. H. wrote a powerful pamphlet against slavery, *Observations on the Slavery of the Africans and Their Descendants* (1811), and his *Journal* was published posthumously (1832). See E. B. Bonner, ed., *American Quakers Today* (1966); R. B. Doherty, *Hicksite Separation* (1967); B. Forbush, *E. H., Quaker Liberal* (1956); R. M. Jones, *Later Period of Quakerism* (2v., 1921).

HICKSITES, a label attached to those Quakers who accepted the interpretation of Quakerism given by Elias *Hicks, and beginning in 1827, separated from the "orthodox" or evangelical Quakers. The name still connotes the lineage of Quaker bodies that originated in that separation. *RELIGIOUS SOCIETY OF FRIENDS.

HIGH CHURCH, a term first used in 17th-cent. England as a descriptive phrase for persons or movements that emphasized the continuity and authority of the C of E and its sacramental life. As with *low church, the phrase has had different connotations during its 2 or 3 centuries of use, sometimes referring to political matters, such as the divine right of kings, and sometimes identifying, very often pejoratively, mere ceremonial usages. Also as with low church, it refers to a school of thought within the Church, not to a separate Church. The terms high church and low church are tending to disappear from common usage.

HISTORIC EPISCOPATE, phrase used in two senses. (1) Understood strictly, it describes the office of bishop as derived from the Apostles through an unbroken series of ordinations. The idea of the historic episcopate has always been central in the Anglican and Episcopal Churches; the specific phrase has been prominent, esp. in ecumenical discussions, since the *Lambeth Quadrilateral (1888). The fourth point of the Quadrilateral declared as essential to Christian unity: "The Historic Episcopate, locally adapted in the methods of its administration to the varying needs of the nations and peoples called of God into the unity of His Church." The *Lambeth Conference of 1930 explained historic episcopate in the sense of historical continuity in ordination. (2) Taken in a wider sense, the historic episcopate means episcopacy as a historically accepted institution or function in the Church. This broader sense of the historic episcopate leaves aside the question of a valid succession of ordinations, and whether the office of bishop is a human or divine institution. In the first sense, the historic episcopate is one aspect of *apostolic succession, as understood by the RC, Eastern, and Old Catholic Churches and by those in the Anglican Communion. In the broader sense, the Constitution of the *Church of South India (1941) accepted the historic episcopate, but without declaring any theory of its meaning. The success of the *Consultation on Church Union may partially depend on the acceptance of historic episcopate in its broader sense, to ac-

commodate those Churches that do not have an episcopal tradition. Yet such an understanding creates an obstacle in the search for church unity for those Churches that regard the historic episcopate in its strict meaning as an essential in the structure of the Church.

HOBART, JOHN HENRY (1775–1830), bp. of the Protestant Episcopal Church in New York. Born in Philadelphia, he graduated from the College of N. J. (now Princeton University) in 1793. From the time of his ordination in 1801, he spent his life at Trinity Parish, New York City. In 1812 he was elected and consecrated as assistant bp. of New York; in 1816 he became the bp. as well as rector of Trinity Parish. He established a society for ministerial studies that developed into the present General Theological Seminary in New York City. In his preaching and writing he emphasized *high-church themes on *apostolic succession and the sacramental-liturgical life of his Church, and was largely responsible for the dominance of a high-church tradition in the Episcopal Church in his era. See M. T. Gardner, *Conquerors of the Continent for Christ and His Church* (1911); *Correspondence of J. H. H.* (6v., 1911–12).

HODGE, CHARLES (1797–1878), American Presbyterian theologian. H. graduated from the College of N.J. (now Princeton Univ.) in 1817 and studied at Princeton Theological Seminary under Archibald *Alexander. He was licensed to preach by the Philadelphia Presbytery in 1819, and in 1822 accepted a call to Princeton Seminary as professor of OT and NT literature. During 1826–28 he studied at Halle and Berlin, where he was influenced by Tholuck, Neander, and the Pietist circle of Ludwig von Gerlach. In 1829 he established the *Biblical Repertory and Princeton Review*, serving as editor until 1868. In 1840 he became professor of systematic theology. H. was the chief theologian of the *Old School Presbyterians, and his theological system was a conservative exposition of the *Westminster

Confession and other *Reformed doctrinal standards. His *Systematic Theology* (3v., 1871–73) was explicitly intended as a bulwark against doctrinal aberration. He personally trained more than 3,000 clergymen, and his influence contributed greatly to the intellectual and doctrinally conservative tradition of *Princeton theology and to the conservative forces both in Presbyterianism and in other Protestant traditions. See Smith-Jamison 1:260–266; A. A. Hodge, *C. H.* (1889); H. T. Kerr, *Sons of the Prophets* (1963).

HODUR, FRANCIS (1866–1953), founder of the *Polish National Catholic Church in America. Born of peasant stock near Cracow, he studied at Cracow Univ. and was ordained a RC priest (1893). He became assistant pastor in Scranton, Pa. (1893), and then (1894) pastor at nearby Nanticoke. Partly inspired by a nationalistic messianism, H. heeded a call (1897) to lead a Scranton Polish parish in a dispute with its bp. over church administration. He vainly brought his cause to Rome, and the bp. excommunicated him (1898). In 1904 H.'s congregation and others formed the Polish National Catholic Church in America; the Synod elected him bishop. Old Catholic bps. consecrated H. in Utrecht (1907). Organizer, theologian, liturgist, and humanitarian, H. was the most influential person in the Church, which he headed until his death. In 1914 he helped establish the Lithuanian National Catholic Church. See T. Andrews, *Polish National Catholic Church* (1953).

HOFFMANITES, a name given to the followers both of C. *Hoffmann and of M. *Hofmann. Members of the *United Christian Church in its early days were also called Hoffmanites, because of the leadership of George W. Hoffman.

HOFFMANN, CHRISTOPH (1815–1885), German founder of the *Friends of the Temple. At an early age H. began to write against the conventional Christianity of his time. In 1848 he established the Evangelischer Verein, consisting of about 450 local branches and a school for lay preachers, to revive *Pietism. He sought to regenerate society by centering God's people on one point, the Temple, thought of partly in a spiritual and partly in a physical sense. He tried to restore a theocracy in Jerusalem, even pressuring the Frankfurt Assembly to prevail on the Sultan to sanction a settlement in Palestine. When his overtures failed, H. undertook to found the new Jerusalem in Germany, near Marbach. He had meanwhile left his Evangelischer Verein and was formally expelled from the national Church in 1859. See C. Kolb, EncRelKnow 4:397–398; G. Lang, RGG 3:413.

HOFMANN, MELCHIOR (Hoffmann; *c.*1500–*c.*1543), Anabaptist preacher. H. was first a Lutheran lay preacher in northern Germany and the Scandinavian countries. Between 1523 and 1533 he wrote more than 35 religious treatises. H. visited Luther in 1525, but by 1527 had lost his initial approval. In 1530 at Strassburg he became an Anabaptist and from 1530 to 1533 propagated his message in Friesland and Holland. Returning to Strassburg he was imprisoned until his death. Along with the usual Anabaptist message of a religion of inner experience, H. strongly accented *millenarianism (1533 was to be the dawn of the new age and he was to be one of the prophets of Rev 11.3) and held Docetist views on Christ's humanity, i.e., that Christ was seemingly, not really, human. B. *Rothmann of Münster was among those strongly influenced by H.'s teachings (see JOHN OF LEIDEN). The followers of H. were called Hoffmanites or Melchiorites; many of them, because of persecution in Holland, fled to England in the 16th century. See MennEnc 2:778–785; bibliog. for Anabaptists.

HOLINESS CHURCH OF GOD, INC., a body established at Madison, N.C., in 1920 and incorporated at Winston-Salem, N.C., in 1928. In 1965 it reported 884 members in 26 churches. *HOLINESS CHURCHES.

HOLINESS CHURCHES, those Christian Churches that emerged from the 19th-cent. *Holiness movement and its emphasis on *entire sanctification. The Church of God (Anderson, Ind.) is one of the oldest; the Church of the Nazarene is the largest. The Holiness Churches are strongly evangelical and fundamentalist; neither the Church nor sacraments are needed for man's sanctification, which is the direct work of the Spirit. They insist on the foursquare gospel—Jesus as Savior, sanctifier, healer and coming Lord (see PREMILLENARIANISM)—and on the reality of a supernatural, experienced sanctification (see BAPTISM WITH THE HOLY SPIRIT). While they have joined other denominations to promote fundamentalism, Holiness bodies have not generally been enthusiastic about the ecumenical movement. In a practical way, however, there are signs of possible rapport with other Christian Churches in fraternal ties and cooperative contacts established in some mission fields. As a classification, Holiness Churches are distinguished from *Pentecostal Churches by a conservative interpretation of entire sanctification. Many of the bodies, e.g., the Christian and Missionary Alliance, refuse to accept the connection, essential for Pentecostals, between sanctification and charismatic gifts, esp. *glossolalia. Many of the Holiness groups still endorse *divine healing, but not as a necessary sequel to conversion and sanctification; they also reject the exuberant emotionalism often found among Pentecostals as a concomitant of Spirit baptism. See Mayer RB 305–323; H. S. Smith et al., *American Christianity* (1963); E. T. Clark, EncRelKnowSuppl 1 1:520–521.

HOLINESS METHODIST CHURCH, a small denomination stressing the doctrines of the *Holiness movement. The Church was organized at Grand Forks, N.Dak., in 1909 as the Constitution Northwestern Holiness Association and took its present name in 1920. It established the Holiness Methodist School in Minneapolis and supports a missionary program in 22 stations in Bolivia. It also maintains camp meeting grounds in Wash., Minn., and N.Dak. for revivals. In 1968 it had about 1,000 members, 23 churches, and 35 ordained clergymen. See HistAmMeth 3:595.

HOLINESS METHODISTS, Methodist bodies or denominations that were originally formed or that broke away from other Methodist bodies because of their belief that the denominations in general, and the Methodist denominations in particular, were not placing sufficient stress in their doctrinal emphasis on personal holiness. Most Holiness Methodists make special claim to fidelity to the true doctrine of *Christian perfection as taught by John *Wesley and as found in the Bible. *HOLINESS MOVEMENT.

HOLINESS MOVEMENT, a post-Civil War emphasis on *entire sanctification that led to the emergence of the Holiness Churches. John *Wesley's doctrine of *Christian perfection was the immediate inspiration of the teaching elaborated during the course of the Holiness movement. Early signs of the movement appeared in Thomas Merritt's *Guide to Christian Perfection* (1839) and in Phoebe Palmer's *Guide to Holiness* (1860). But the Holiness movement proper began, esp. among Methodists, after the Civil War with revivals in which the need of a return to holiness was preached. In 1867 a group of Methodists at Vineland, N.J., formed the National Camp Meeting Association for the Promotion of Holiness; soon similar associations were formed (esp. in Ind.), and the movement became interdenominational; it also spread to England. Some Holiness Churches came into being informally as outgrowths of the Holiness associations; others were separations from the organized Churches, which, as in the case of Methodism, viewed the interpretation of Holiness doctrine as unorthodox. Pentecostalism was a further development of the Holiness movement. See HistAmMeth 2:608–627; H. S. Smith et al., *American Christianity* (1963); J. T. Nichol, *Pentecostalism* (1966), 5–7.

HOLINESS OF THE CHURCH, one of the attributes of the Church professed in the Apostles' and Nicene Creeds. The close attachment of the title "holy" to the Church in both RC conciliar documents and Protestant and Anglican confessions of faith indicates belief that holiness is of the essence or nature of the Church. There is a common belief in the reason for this holiness: the whole Church is not just a body of believers, but Christ the head and those who believe in him. From Christ, the chosen Son of the Father, the body of believers is made holy, set apart as the *People of God. The vital communion of Christ with his members and of the members with one another through Christ is the Church, called for this reason even a communion of saints. Protestants and Roman Catholics differ in their understanding of the implications of this holiness, however, because they differ in their understanding of the Church itself. There are two principal points of divergence. RC theology asserts that the holiness of the Church includes power communicated by Christ to the Church itself to sanctify its members. The essentials of the visible structure and life of the Church, its sacraments, its special priesthood, its hierarchical agencies, are understood as part of the holiness of the Church. Such a mediating role of the Church in the sanctification of its members is denied in principle by Reformation teaching on the *priesthood of all believers and the sacraments. The essential holiness of the Church is the holiness of Christ in himself and as given to the believer. None of the forms or institutions of the Church truly mediate in the sanctification of the believer; in this sense the *visible Church is not holy.

Protestant and Roman Catholics also understand the holiness of the members of the Church differently, although both seek to reconcile the sinfulness in the Church with its essential holiness. RC teaching has refused to accept the notion of the Church as the congregation of the predestined or elect. The Church is holy in its members first because all have the same calling to holiness, to become sanctified. At the same time the Church is a pilgrim Church, never to be completely holy on this earth. The different states of life lived in the Church are meant to reflect the call to holiness and to bring about its fulfillment. The Holy Spirit, the Spirit of Christ, sanctifies the members of the Church individually and corporately (see Vat II ConstCh c. 5–7). In the Reformation the earlier idea of John *Wycliffe and Jan *Hus that the true Church is the congregation of the predestined was repeated in the Lutheran and *Reformed traditions. The contrast between the true, *invisible Church and the external, imperfect visible Church runs through Protestant history. The endeavor to make the visible Church conform to the invisible Church inspired emphasis on church discipline, as well as the *gathered church idea of the Puritans and Congregationalists. While less concerned with the corporate structure of the Church, the spiritualizers, Anabaptists, Mennonites, and Quakers still enforced discipline to keep the brotherhood free of those who were unworthy. Wesleyan and Holiness *perfectionism concentrated on the individual; yet their traditions also imposed strict moral codes in order that the outward conduct of believers might reflect their inward conversion and freedom from sin. See J. Pelikan, *Riddle of Roman Catholicism* (1959).

HOLY CLUB, one of the derisive names given by the students of Oxford Univ. to a religious society formed by Charles and John *Wesley at Oxford in 1729. The original design of the members was to study the classics and works of divinity and to aid one another toward a holy life. Their purpose soon included visiting prisoners in jail, providing help and religious instruction for the poor, and establishing among themselves many of the customs of the early Church, including fasting. Because the lives of the members followed a carefully ordered program of prayer, study, and good works, they were also labeled Methodists. The club was discontinued after 1735, when the Wesleys left Oxford to become missionaries in Georgia. See *Journal of the Rev. John Wesley, A.M.* (ed. N. Curnock, 1938), 1:86–102; L. Tyerman, *Oxford Methodists* (1873).

HOLY COMMUNION, a term used by many Churches for the celebration of the *Eucharist, or *Lord's Supper. It is often called simply communion or the communion service. Although disagreements about the meaning of the rite have been numerous and deep among Christians, they generally agree that one of its meanings is the unity that people of diverse backgrounds have through Christ; they therefore regard the existence of separate Churches not in *intercommunion as an anomaly to be overcome.

HOLY KISS, see KISS, HOLY.

HOLY ORDERS, see ORDERS.

HOLY ROLLERS, a derogatory nickname for religious groups whose meetings are characterized by high emotionalism, manifested by physical agitation. In particular, the name has been attached to Pentecostal groups. The name "Holy Jumpers" has been similarly used. Pentecostals regard the name as offensive, even libelous.

HOMBERGER BRETHREN, a Church similar to the *Plymouth Brethren, existing since 1905 in the area of the Homberg (a mountain) near Thun, Bern, Switz., founded by the evangelists Fritz Widmer and Jakob Städeli. Members are *Open Brethren, admitting others to their communal services.

HOMUNCIONITAE (Melitonii), those teaching that it is the body, not the soul, that makes man the image of God. In his attempt to match a list of heresies to a list of heresiarchs, Filaster probably invented a sect professing such a teaching (*Haer.* 97); Augustine (*Haer.* 76) repeats him. The name Homuncionitae (Lat., *homunculus*, diminutive of *homo*, man) comes from *Praedestinatus* (76); Danaeus, in his edition (1576) of Augustine's *De haeresbius* (PL 12:1209) calls them Melitonii. See G. Bardy, "Le *De haeresibus* et ses sources," *Miscellanea Agostiniana* (1931), 397–416.

HOOGSTRAETEN, JACOB VAN (Hochstraten; 1460–1527), Dominican theologian and polemicist. A native of the Brabant, H. became successively regent of studies at the Dominican house in Cologne (1505) and prior (1508). As prior he was ex officio inquisitor general for Cologne, Mainz, and Trier. He engaged in vigorous controversy, first in defense of the mendicant orders, then against J. *Reuchlin, and finally against Luther. Against Reuchlin, who sought to preserve Hebrew, esp. Talmudic, literature from burning, H. sided with the Jewish convert J. *Pfefferkorn and had Reuchlin's *Augenspiegel* burned (1514). This caused H. to be labeled an enemy of the New Learning, and he was made a target of the biting shafts of the *Epistolae obscurorum virorum* (1515, 1517). H. was himself condemned by the abp. of Speyer (1514) and removed from his office by the Dominican provincial chapter (1517). Leo X, alarmed by events in Germany, reversed both these actions (1520), reinstating H. and silencing Reuchlin. There is no doubt that H. was intemperate in his zeal and wanting in good judgment, but his writings, though lacking conspicuous theological merit, reveal him as something less than the complete fool the *Epistolae* made him out to be.

His three anti-Lutheran works were ed. by F. Pipjer, *Bibliotheca reformatoria Neerlandica* (3v., 1905). See R. Coulon, DTC 7:11–17; F. C. Stokes, *Epistolae obscurorum virorum: The Latin Text with an English Rendering, Notes and an Historical Introduction* (1909).

HOOKER, RICHARD (1553–1600), Anglican theologian and political philosopher. H. studied at Corpus Christi College, Oxford, where he obtained a fellowship (1577). In 1585 he was presented with the mastership of the Temple Church in London. There he came into conflict with Walter Travers, a representative of the Puritan faction, pressing for the polity of Calvin's Geneva as alone suited to the reformation of the Church. In the ensuing controversy H. saw the need of a systematic defense of the Elizabethan ecclesiastical polity; to prepare such a work he had himself appointed to a country rectory (1591), where he wrote his classic of Anglican theology, *Of the Laws of Ecclesiastical Polity*. The first five books of this appeared 1594–97; posthumously, Books 6 and 7 were published in 1648; Book 8, in 1662. Against the Puritan reliance upon the Scriptures alone, he established the necessity of reason and patristic tradition and presented a view of natural law very much like that elaborated by Aristotle and adapted to the context of Christian thought by Thomas Aquinas. Although Aquinas is not cited, H.'s dependence upon his thought is unmistakable. However, where neither reason nor tradition could adequately justify the particular arrangements of the Elizabethan settlement, H., turning from Aquinas, had recourse to the thought of *Marsilius of Padua, who had completely subjected Church to State. H.'s work, in its vindication of episcopacy and the Book of Common Prayer, was the classic apologia for Anglicanism as a middle course, *via media*, between Roman Catholicism and Calvinistic Protestantism. Works: ed. J. Keble (3v., 1836; rev. ed., R. W. Church and E. Paget, 1888); *Of the Laws of Ecclesiastical Polity* (2v., 1954). See P.

Munz, *Place of H. in the History of Thought* (1952); J. Marshall, *H. and the Anglican Tradition* (1964).

HOOKER, THOMAS (1586–1647), English Puritan leader and a founder of the Colony of Connecticut. H. studied at Emmanuel College (then a Puritan center), Cambridge (B.A., 1608; M.A., 1611). For some years he was a fellow of Emmanuel; he received a conversion experience that became a constant theme of his preaching. From 1620 to 1629 he held various parochial positions in Surrey and Essex, but his Puritan preaching was brought to an end by Abp. W. *Laud. In 1630 he fled to Holland and 3 years later, to Massachusetts, where he became pastor of a congregation at Newtown, now Cambridge. Finding the government too autocratic, he led a group of his followers to the Connecticut Valley, where they founded the city of Hartford in 1636. He has been called the father of American democracy because of his insistence that the power to choose public officials lies with the people. He advocated, however, a very limited sort of democracy at most, for the people vested with the power of choice included only those of established social status; the number of these probably did not exceed one-third of the colony's adult males. He did rule out religious tests for citizenship. H. was above all a Puritan preacher; his topics, the experience of conversion and moral duty; his style, the plain and orderly exposition of Scripture. See S. E. Ahlstrom, *Theology in America* (1967), 98–99 (bibliog.), III–114.

HOOPER, JOHN (d. 1555), English Reformer; bp. of Gloucester and later of Worcester; martyred under Mary Tudor. A Cistercian monk, H., upon the *dissolution of the monasteries, went to London and became attached to the ideas of *Zwingli and J. H. *Bullinger. Exiled for his views on the Eucharist, H. lived in Strassburg and Basel until the death of Henry VIII. On his return he received promotion to the episcopacy. He was a powerful preacher, liberal to the poor, but combative and of irksome severity. He stood for the full Protestantizing of the Reformation in England and was highly regarded by the Puritans of the 17th century. Under Mary he was degraded and sent to the stake at Gloucester, enduring his passion with unshaken constancy.

HOPEDALE COMMUNITY, an American communal society founded in 1842 in Worcester, Mass., by Adin Ballou. His intent was to form a Christian utopia whose members would agree to avoid violence, the taking of oaths, and strong drink. No common beliefs were to be required. In 1857 one of the members, Draper by name, bought up the community stock and forced Ballou out. Thereupon the experiment lost momentum. The group was sometimes called the Miniature Christian Republic. See T. Horgan, NCE 4:80.

HOPKINS, SAMUEL (1721–1803), American Congregationalist theologian. H. was born in Waterbury, Conn., graduated from Yale (1741) and studied theology under Jonathan *Edwards. H.'s theological system, inspired by Edwards and known as Hopkinsianism, the *New England theology or (in England) American Theology, is presented in many closely reasoned works, esp. in *A System of Doctrines Contained in Divine Revelation* (1793). He mitigated rigid Calvinist predestinationism and emphasized God's goodness: God wills what is advantageous for the greater number, for this end even permitting sin; and man's duty is to be completely submissive to God's benevolent purposes, even to the extent of a willingness to be damned. From 1770 H. spoke out against the slave trade and urged Negro emancipation. His works, with a biography, were edited by E. A. Park (3v., 1852). See T. H. Foster, *Genetic History of the New England Theology* (1907).

HORTON, DOUGLAS (1891–1968), Congregationalist theologian and ecumenist. H. was born in Brooklyn, N.Y.; graduated from Princeton (1912); studied at Edinburgh, Oxford, and Tübingen; prepared for the ministry at Hartford Theological Seminary; and was ordained in 1915. H. was pastor in Brookline, Mass. (1925–31), and in Hyde Park, Ill. (1931–38). He taught *practical theology at Newton Theological Institute (1930–31) and the Chicago Theological Seminary (1933–38) and Congregational polity at Union Theological Seminary, New York City (1943–55). He was also dean of Harvard Divinity School (1955–59). H. made an impact on theology in the U.S. by his 1928 translation of Karl *Barth's *The Word of God and the Word of Man.* But his chief contribution was to ecumenism. Among other works, he edited an important guideline for the ecumenical movement, *Basic Formula for Church Unity* (1937), and wrote *Toward an Undivided Church* (1967). As minister of the General Council of Congregational Christian Churches (1938–55) he led the discussions that resulted in union (1957) with the Evangelical and Reformed Church, forming the *United Church of Christ. He was prominent in the formation of the National and World Councils of Churches, and for the latter served as chairman of the committee on *Faith and Order (1957–63). As an official observer for the International Congregational Council, he attended Vatican Council II, on which he commented in *Vatican Diary* (4v., 1962–65).

HOUSE OF BISHOPS, one house of the *General Convention of the Protestant Episcopal Church. The original draft of the Church's constitution, following the civil polity of the U.S. under the then-effective Articles of Confederation, provided a unicameral governing body, the House of Clerical and Lay Deputies. The House of Bishops was added to win approval of the Constitution from Bp. Samuel S. *Seabury of Conn. and his followers. Voice and vote in this House are given to all active bishops and to those retired for specified reasons. The House of Bishops acts independently in issuing pastoral letters and in organizing and electing bishops for missionary districts. See E. A. White and J. A. Dyckman, *Annotated Constitution and Canons for the Government of the Protestant Episcopal Church in the U.S.A.* (2v., 1954), 4–38.

HOUSE OF CLERICAL AND LAY DEPUTIES, together with the House of Bishops, the constitutive houses of the *General Convention of the Protestant Episcopal Church. Each diocese is represented in the House of Deputies by four clergymen and four laymen; each missionary district, by one member of each order. The constitution is being amended to permit women to serve as lay deputies, and there is a growing movement to make representation from dioceses more proportionate to diocesan church membership. A "vote by orders" on any measure must be granted when requested. Passage of a measure on such a vote requires both a majority of clerical representatives and a majority of lay representatives from a majority of dioceses. See E. A. White and J. A. Dyckman, *Annotated Constitution and Canons for the Government of the Protestant Episcopal Church in the U.S.A.* (2v., 1954), 4–38.

HOUSE OF DAVID, communal body established by Benjamin Purnell at Benton Harbor, Mich., in 1903. He proclaimed himself to be the last of the seven messengers referred to in Rev 8.6 and 11.15, with the mission of gathering the 144,000 true Israelites to establish the kingdom of God on earth. He was crowned King Benjamin of the House of David. The group is sometimes called the Israelite House of David, since Benton proclaimed the members to be the "ingathering" of the descendants of the 12 lost tribes of Israel. Belief includes acceptance of the doctrine of Jesus Christ, *millenarianism, and *universalism. Members turn over all their property to the community; they are vegetarians; the men must not cut their hair or shave. In the 1920s and 1930s the traveling House of David baseball team and band gave national publicity to the movement. The House of David survived the scandal of Purnell's trials on charges of immorality. A board of directors maintains control over spiritual and temporal affairs; the community supports itself by agriculture and small shops. Membership in 1964 was 350; in 1969 there were 77 members. See W. J. Whalen, *Faiths for the Few* (1963).

HOUSE OF GOD, Which Is the Church of the Living God, the Pillar and Ground of the Truth, Inc., a holiness body formed in 1919 by a group seceding from the Church of the Living God. It has generally retained the structure and teachings of the parent body. According to last available statistics (1956) it had 2,350 members and 107 churches. *HOLINESS CHURCHES.

HOUSE OF THE LORD, a Pentecostal sect founded in 1925 in Detroit, Mich., by W. H. Johnson. It teaches that baptism is confirmed by *glossolalia and that *entire sanctification precludes ownership of property. Various moral precepts regulate private life, and members are forbidden employment that involves liquor, tobacco, or gambling. Its membership is several hundred, with few churches.

HUBMAIER, BALTHASAR (*c.*1485–1528), Anabaptist leader and writer. H. was born at Friedberg near Augsburg, was a student of J. *Eck, became a priest and a celebrated preacher at Regensburg (1516–21). Having become pastor at Waldshut near the Swiss border, he soon embraced Reformation teaching. He formed a bond with *Zwingli, but through C. *Grebel turned to Anabaptist ideas—a religion of inner experience, the rejection of *infant baptism, and the complete freedom of the Church from secular power. H. broke with Zwingli after disagreements on infant baptism at Zurich in 1525. He took part in the *Peasants' War (some attribute the Twelve Articles to him) but opposed the violence preached by T.

*Münzer. Early in 1526, H. was imprisoned at Zurich for his Anabaptist views and temporarily renounced them. He found refuge in Nikolsburg in Moravia, where he engaged in controversy with H. *Hut and wrote a number of Anabaptist tracts. In 1527 he was arrested, brought to Vienna, and burned as a heretic. His works, esp. *Von dem Tauf der Gläubigen* (1525), are a clear exposition of the essential Anabaptist teaching on individual and mystical experience in religion. Works: *B. H. Schriften* (ed. G. Westin and T. Bergsten, 1962). See T. Bergsten, *B. H.* (1961); R. Dollinger, RGG 3:464–465; R. M. Jones, *Studies in Mystical Religion* (1923), 379–383.

HUGHES, HUGH PRICE (1847–1902), Wesleyan Methodist preacher and supporter of social reform and Methodist union. He was born at Carmarthen, Wales, and entered the ministry in 1867, establishing West London Mission in 1887. He emphasized its philanthropic work and conducted a popular preaching service; he founded the *Methodist Times* in 1885, passionately supporting social reform. He worked indefatigably for Methodist union, founding the National Council of the Evangelical Free Churches (1896). He was president of the Wesleyan Methodist Conference in 1898. See D. P. Hughes, *Life of H. P. H.* (1904); M. Edwards, *Methodism and England* (1943), 147–164.

HUGUENOTS, the nickname of French Calvinists—in common use after the Conspiracy of Amboise (1560)—which may derive from the German *Eidgenossen* (confederates, conspirators) or from a legendary King Hugon. The French who favored the Reformation received doctrinal inspiration from Jacques *Lefèvre d'Étaples and Martin Luther, but above all from John Calvin's *Institutes of the Christian Religion*. In organization, both ecclesiastical and political, the Huguenots were influenced by the theocratic state of Geneva —an international center for Protestant

missionaries and a model of authoritarian republicanism and collective parochial living.

The movement grew in France, and with it the opposition of the crown; Francis I (1515–47) initiated persecution and Henry II (1547–59) systematized it by appointing a special commission of the Paris Parlement to try heretics and by codifying the enactments against them. By 1555, however, Paris had its first *Reformed Church and for 70 years the Reformed Church in France played an important political role. The organization of the Church developed gradually; the final structure emerged at the Assembly of Saumur, 1611.

Although the Dukes of Guise intensified persecution of the Huguenots during the short reign of Francis II (1559–60), many of the nobility, such as Admiral de Coligny and the Dukes of Bourbon and Condé, became leaders of the party, which remained mainly aristocratic until the end of the 16th century. By the edict of January 1562, Chancellor M. de l'Hôpital and Catherine de Médicis attempted to ward off war between the religious factions by granting the Huguenots civic status and the right to worship outside the towns; the powerful Guises, however, opposed a policy of conciliation: in the two decades following the massacre of Vassy (March 1, 1562)—which began the *Wars of Religion—there were seven wars and the *St. Bartholomew's Day Massacre (1572).

Soon the Huguenot organization was so strengthened and unified that it resembled a state within a state. Two organizational structures emerged, each with a system of representation: the religious, which included consistories, colloquies, and provincial and national synods; and the political— with its provincial councils, circle assemblies, and general assemblies. Academies were established at Montauban, Montpelier, Nîmes, Sedan, and Saumur—the last being particularly important in the history of Reformed theology (see HELVETIC CONSENSUS FORMULA).

A decline in the power of the Guises, the rise of the Huguenot Henry de Navarre, and the influence of the *politiques*, who were anxious to end hostilities, led to the *Edict of Nantes (1598), a compendium of previous edicts granting some toleration, which remained nominally in effect for 87 years, though it was never applied in its entirety because France was not ready to adopt its principles. The assassination of Henry IV in 1610 removed the sense of comparative security enjoyed by the Huguenots, and the reign of Louis XIII (1610–43) ended their political hopes. Cardinal Richelieu, although he earned a reputation for tolerance, saw a threat to the state in the Huguenot party with its strongholds ("places of surety"). He launched a campaign against the Huguenots, took La Rochelle and Privas, and dictated the terms of the Peace of Alais (June 1629). The Huguenots were made subservient to the state and their party was doomed, but there was no overt persecution. However, Louis XIV (1661–1715), by gradually depriving the Huguenots of their rights, authorizing dragonnades (persecution by troops, 1683–86), and finally by revoking the Edict of Nantes in 1685, probably carried out the Cardinal's real intentions. The revocation caused a massive exodus of from 200,000 to 300,000 Huguenots. French Protestants were granted partial equality of rights by the Edict of Toleration (1787) and full equality by the Napoleonic code. The Reformed Church of France remains the largest French Protestant body; it forms, with other Protestant groups, the Fédération Protestante de France, established in 1907. See W. J. Stankiewicz, NCE 7:201–204, with bibliog.

HUMANISM, in the specific historical sense, the program of learning prevailing during the *Renaissance. Thus the principal humanists were the great Renaissance literary figures. While interpretations of historical humanism are many, its techniques of learning and attitudes toward man's life were significant for religion. Humanism above all consisted in the *studia humanitatis*, the cultivation of the humani-

ties through classical texts. Consequent interest in philology and textual criticism opened a new era in biblical and patristic studies. The humanist program of learning consciously rejected the medieval *scholasticism of the immediate past. Humanist presentation of theological truths sought to be more personal, warm, and direct, in contrast to the scholastic use of logic and philosophy for theological discourse. The celebrated *Epistolae obscurorum virorum* discredited the scholastics before the intellectual world and diminished confidence in traditional theology. Humanism developed in a Christian context; humanists did not assail essential Christian truths; many were eager for the reform of the Church. There was a distinctive interpretation of Christian life, however, in the world view of many humanists. Human values were stressed and the capacity of man to transform self, society, and the Church. The virtues extolled by the ancients were looked upon as a rediscovery of a nobler view of life that the medievals had lost. The humanist interpretation of the Christian life was a highly moralistic one, in which pagan and Christian virtues seemed as one, and the significance of Christ, the Church, and the sacraments were diminished. The humanist program for reform was one of re-education; the ignorance of the clergy came under bitter attack. Optimism and the idealization of the good life made many humanists severe critics of monastic asceticism and institutions. Tolerance in matters of belief, a recurrent theme, suggested a conviction that all religious belief is the expression of the lofty aspirations shared by all men. Extreme exaltation of man contributed to the corruption of the Renaissance papacy; criticism of established institutions created an atmosphere conducive to the breakup of Christianity in the Reformation. The humanist spirit was not compatible with the pessimism of the Reformers toward human nature. But simply as a cultural transition and a concentration upon man, humanism affected the forms and emphasis in both RC and Protestant life. See H. Baker, *Image of Man* (1947); R. R. Bolgan, *Classical Herit-*

age and Its Beneficiaries (1954); E. Cassirer, *Individual and Cosmos in Renaissance Philosophy* (tr. M. Domandi, 1963).

HUMANISM, CHRISTIAN, a description applied to theories that see a positive relationship between purely human values and the life and destiny of man under grace. One such modern form of Christian humanism was given prominence by Jacques Maritain. He saw an integration between nature and grace, so that the capacities for the true and the good inherent in man's nature were fully realizable, not negated or irrelevant, under grace. Teilhard de Chardin's world view, in which the gradual perfection of the universe and its subjection to man will be culminated in Christ the Omega Point, has also been called Christian humanism. The contemporary theory that the living and the pursuit of the Christian message consist precisely in concern for the secular and authentically human is also referred to as Christian humanism. In any of its forms this world view opposes a humanism that would make man absolute to the exclusion of God and his grace and opposes any purely superterresrtrial interpretation of the Christian message that would negate human culture, traditions, and values. Thus incarnationalism in theology can be called a form of Christian humanism. See L. Bouyer, *Christian Humanism* (tr. A. V. Littledale, 1959); J. Maritain, *Integral Humanism* (tr. J. W. Evans, 1968). *SECULARITY.

HUMANISM, SECULAR, a more or less systematic body of thought or action concerned with merely human interests, as opposed to divine, with the implication that it offers a substitute for the service of a being who is altogether out of this world. It tends to be a protest against religion, which it regards as profoundly inhuman. Nevertheless humanism does not itself compose a well-defined creed, code, or cult, nor does it as such either deny or affirm the existence of God. But it insists that humankind must rely on its own resources without looking for outside help or without passive resignation to God's providence to attack misery and bring it to goodness and happiness; all the means at its disposal must be used—science, technology, the communications media, political programs, and the fine arts. The attitude is sober and courageous, and contemporary humanism accordingly exhibits an activist character in contrast to the more contemplative graciousness of historic humanism. It is argued that humanism avoids the great and constant questions of human life and reaches an impasse: man is man's only hope, and human life is the supreme value; life, however, is disclosed as reaching out to beyond. Yet humanism casts out some of the cant that is associated with religion and that has served to impede the progress of the humane decencies. Its challenge is that if only Christianity were eliminated then the ideals of unity and love, originally Christian in inspiration, it is granted, would no longer be a sort of pie in the sky, but could be realized completely in this world. Humanism argues not from the failure of Christians in history but from the intrinsic and irremediable powerlessness of the Christian faith to make real its promises, and from the fact that belief in an "other" world exhausts the believer's energies from doing what is required in this world. See C. Lamont, *Philosophy of Humanism* (5th ed., 1965); J. Huxley, ed., *Humanist Frame* (1962); *idem*, *Essays of a Humanist* (1964); N. Rotenstreich, *Humanism in the Contemporary Era* (1963); R. E. Osborn, *Humanism and Moral Theory* (1959). *SECULARISM.

HUMILIATI, first a lay fraternity, then a religious order for men and women, inspired by the ideal of apostolic poverty and simplicity. Members were also called Berettini from their attire of undyed, grayish wool (It., *beretto*). Their origins are unknown but they existed in Lombardy as early as the mid-12th cent.; they were another manifestation of the desire of laymen of the time to restore the Church to simplicity and to remove the abuses of the clergy (see PATARINES; WALDENSES). The Humiliati sought to live in poverty not by begging but by manual labor; they abhorred lying, refused oaths, practiced fasts, and cared for the poor. Some lived at home, others in community, in double monasteries. The Humiliati began to preach in public for reform in the Church; in 1179 Pope Alexander III ordered them to cease; when they continued, they were excommunicated, together with the Waldenses, by Lucius III in 1184. Many rejoined the Church in 1202, and they became effective counter-agents against groups of similar inspiration who were attacking the Church, especially the *Cathari. Innocent III organized the Humiliati into one order with three parts: regulars, living the religious vows in double monasteries; lay members, living a community life, also in double monasteries; and tertiaries, living at home (these Humiliati were the first to be called tertiaries). The order spread through N Italy and S France and by 1216 had 150 houses. The communities prospered through their interest in the wool industry; by their wealth they were able to become moneylenders. They also began to grow lax, and their numbers decreased sharply; St. Charles Borromeo tried to reform them, and one of them in 1569 attempted to assassinate him. The male houses of the order were suppressed in 1571 by Pius V. In Italy monasteries of nuns, Berettine, still survive. See E. S. Davison, *Forerunners of St. Francis* (1928), 168–200; M. F. Laughlin, NCE 7:234; M. H. Vicaire, Catholicisme 5:1097–98.

HUNGARIAN CONFESSION (Confession of Czenger), a principal *confession of faith of the *Reformed Church in Hungary adopted in 1557 or 1558 at a synod in Czenger (Csenger, NE border of Hungary); it was supplanted (1567) by the Second *Helvetic Confession and the *Heidelberg Catechism. In eleven chapters the Confession expresses Calvinist teaching on salvation (without mention of *double predestination) and the sacraments; it is also a polemic against Unitarianism and Anabaptist teaching on baptism. See Schaff Creeds 1:591–592.

HUNGARIAN REFORMED CHURCH IN AMERICA, a body organized in New York in 1904 in association with the Reformed Church of Hungary. The latter has been one of the stronger *Reformed Churches on the Continent since the Reformation. In 1922 the Church in Hungary sought by the Tiffin (Ohio) Agreement to transfer her American churches to the Reformed Church in the U.S. (see EVANGELICAL AND REFORMED CHURCH). Three congregations preferred to continue as an autonomous American denomination. They formed the Free Magyar Reformed Church in America; in 1958 the group changed its name to the present one. In polity the Church follows a course between *Presbyterianism and *episcopacy; it is organized as a diocese, headed by an elected bishop and a lay curator, and divided into a New York, an Eastern, and a Western *classis. The *Heidelberg Catechism and the Second *Helvetic Confession are *doctrinal standards. There are congregations in 10 states and Canada.

HUNTINGDON, COUNTESS OF (Selina Hastings; 1707–91), foundress of the *Countess of Huntingdon's Connexion. She and her husband, the ninth Earl of Huntingdon, joined the Fetter Lane Methodist *Society in London, 1739. After the Earl's death, she became an active leader in Methodism, the close associate of G. *Whitefield and of John and Charles *Wesley. She built many chapels, with Methodist-trained chaplains, and established a college for preachers at Trevecca, Wales. A strong Calvinist, she broke with J. Wesley over his *Arminianism. Invoking the protection of the *Toleration Act, she established the Connexion as an association of dissenting chapels; there were 64 chapels at the time of her death. See S. Tyler, *Countess of Huntingdon and Her Circle* (1907).

HUNTINGTON, WILLIAM REED (1838–1909), liturgical scholar, author of the Chicago-*Lambeth Quadrilateral. H. was a liberal Episcopalian leader of the House of Deputies of the *General Convention of the Protestant Episcopal Church for 30 years, until his death. As rector, first of All Saints Church, Worcester, Mass. (1862–83), and then of Grace Church, New York City (1883–1909), he led significant movements for the reform of the *Book of Common Prayer and for the organic reunion of the Churches in the United States. Influenced by William White, S. T. Coleridge, and Horace Bushnell, among others, H. continued the search for church unity begun by W. A. *Muhlenberg and in turn contributed to the later ecumenical movement through his influence upon C. H. *Brent and E. L. Parsons. Huntington sought a national Church for the U.S., based on unity by contribution, and at the same time realized the necessity of making the Episcopal Church more "American" in outlook. His major publications were *Church-Idea, An Essay toward Unity* (1870), *Peace of the Church* (1891), *A National Church* (1898), *Theology's Eminent Domain* (1902), *Tract 91* (1907), and *Four Theories of Visible Church Unity* (1909). See W. R. Huntington, *Church-Idea, An Essay toward Unity* (5th ed., 1928); J. F. Woolverton, "W. R. H.: Liturgical Renewal and Church Unity in the 1880s," *Anglican Theological Review* (April 1966).

HUS, JAN (John Huss; c.1369–1415), a Bohemian reformer, executed as a heretic. At the Univ. of Prague, H. began his studies c.1386 and lectured from 1396 onward. As preacher at Bethlehem Chapel from 1402, he decried clerical abuses, urging reform in the Church and in Christian life. He was guided by the ecclesiology of John *Wycliffe. H. ignored the condemnation of 45 Wycliffite statements in 1403 by the predominantly German faculty of the university. When the King revised university voting powers in favor of Bohemians in 1409, the Germans departed and H. was made rector. His troubles with ecclesiastical authorities began the same year, when the abp. decreed that Wycliffe's writings be burned and H. excommunicated. He continued to preach; other measures against him followed, climaxed by a major excommunication in 1412 for leading resistance to an indulgence proclaimed by John XXIII (antipope). H. left Prague and in seclusion wrote his *De ecclesia*, drawing freely from Wycliffe's work of the same title. In 1414, through the urging of Emperor Sigismund, who promised him safe conduct, H. was persuaded to appear before the Council of *Constance. Arriving there in Nov., he was imprisoned until his trial the following June. H. refused to recant the errors extracted from his works, and, in the presence of Sigismund, was condemned as a heretic on July 6 and on the same day was burned at the stake by the town officials. He died bravely and in prayer. At Prague he was proclaimed a martyr and saint.

H. has renown as a Czech patriot; but that he himself conceived his role at Prague as a nationalistic crusade against foreign (German) domination is open to doubt. The Hussites were named for him, but he never taught the practice that became their battle cry, *communion under both kinds (see UTRAQUISTS). He did resist the ecclesiastical authorities, but he could not be called a precursor of the Reformation doctrine of "faith alone" and "Scripture alone." Martin V confirmed (1418) the decree of Constance condemning H.'s errors (D 1201–30; 1250–51). These include a denial of the primacy of Peter, a description of the true Church as the assembly of the predestined, and the judgment that personal holiness alone gives legitimate jurisdiction to pope, bishop, or priest. H. himself disavowed not only Wycliffe's eucharistic teaching, but any share in the heretical sense of Wycliffe's ecclesiology. While condemnatory qualifications are attached to them (D 1251), these propositions are not so startling when viewed in historical context, the age of the *Great Western Schism, and with allowance for H.'s zealous rhetoric. His own intransigence and the doctrinal and political predispositions of his judges did much to bring about his tragic end. See Bihlmeyer-Tüchle 2:438–441; J. Boulier, *J. H.* (1958); M. Spinka, *J. H. and the Czech Reform* (1940); idem, tr., *J. H. at the Council of Constance* (1965); idem, *J. H.'s Concept of the Church* (1966); S. H. Thomson, ed., *Tractatus de Ecclesia* (1956); P. de Vooght, *L'Hérésie de J. H.* (1960).

HUSSITES, adherents of the religious and political movement inspired by Jan *Hus. Antipapal and nationalistic agitation in Bohemia became violent after Hus's execution, and a national Church emerged. The Hussite program far exceeded Hus's teachings; e.g., *communion under both kinds, forbidden by the Council of *Constance (D 1198–99; 1257–58), was not the teaching of Hus but of *Jacobellus. On religious and political grounds the Hussites were divided. The *Utraquists—university people, nobles, and merchants—were moderates. Their religious goals were contained in the Four Articles of Prague (1420): (1) that priests be unhampered in fulfilling Christ's mandate to preach; (2) that communion under both kinds be obligatory; (3) that mortal sins, even of clerics, be punished publicly; (4) that the clergy renounce temporal ownership or office. The *Taborites, mostly artisans and peasants, were far more extreme in doctrine and were violently antipapal; they advocated a communistic society, and the Hussite Wars (1420–33) were marked by the confiscation of ecclesiastical and patrician properties. These wars were a successful resistance, led by the Taborites J. *Žižka and Prokop the Great (d. 1434), against the crusades promoted by Martin V (1420, 1426, 1427) and Eugene IV (1431), and carried out by Emperor Sigismund. The final crushing defeat of the imperial-papal forces came at Taus (Domazlice; 1431). Between the wars there was bloody internal strife among the Hussites. At the invitation of Eugene IV negotiations with Utraquist and Taborite representatives began at the Council of *Basel in 1433, continued at Prague, and resulted eventually in the *Compactata. The only concession to the Four Articles,

and that in a limited sense, was on the point of communion under both kinds. The Taborites rejected the Compactata, and were crushed by the combined Catholic and Utraquist forces at Lipany in 1434. The Compactata were accepted at Iglau (Jihlava) by the Hussites, and Sigismund was proclaimed king of Bohemia (1436). The agreement was approved by Basel (1434) but never received papal approval. In the subsequent religious and political history of Bohemia the Hussites are referred to as Utraquists, and the *Subunists as Catholics, but both considered themselves to be orthodox. The Utraquists, however, were continually in conflict with Rome (see GEORGE OF PODĚBRAD). Internal conflict brought about a split in Utraquist ranks, which eventually led to the establishment of the *Bohemian Brethren (c.1458). At the time of the Reformation, many of the remaining Utraquists went over to Lutheranism, a union expressed in the *Bohemian Confessions of 1535 and 1575; later, however, the *Reformed tradition became dominant. The practice of communion under both kinds was suppressed by the *Edict of Restitution (1629). The Hussite era had important consequences for the evolution of the Reformation and for the rise of nationalism in Europe. See Bihlmeyer-Tüchle, 2:438–444; P. de Vooght, Catholicisme 5:1111–13; F. H. Heymann, *John Žižka and the Hussite Revolution* (1955); J. Macek, *Die Hussite revolutionäre Bewegung* (1958).

HUT, HANS (c.1491–1527), an Anabaptist preacher. H. was a Franconian bookbinder and accountant, who first became a fanatical preacher of revolution under the influence of T. *Münzer. After the *Peasants' War, H. was converted to the Swiss Anabaptist idea of passive *nonresistance by H. *Denk, who rebaptized him at Augsburg in 1527. After a controversy with B. *Hubmaier, H. had to escape from Nikolsburg in Moravia and spent his last years in apocalyptic preaching throughout Austria. He died in prison. See R. M. Jones, *Studies in Mystical Religion* (1923), 390; MennEnc 2:846.

HUTCHINSON, ANNE (*c.*1590–1643), the leader in the Antinomian Controversy in colonial Massachusetts. She migrated from England to Boston in 1634. There her neighborliness and intellectual insights brought her a large following of both laymen and ministers, among them John *Cotton, who later repudiated her teaching. The strife that ensued between her supporters and those who accused her of heresy and sedition affected even the gubernatorial election of 1637. She branded the legalistic discipline of the Massachusetts Puritans as a covenant of works, in contrast with her own conviction, the covenant of grace. Her opponents attached the reproach "antinomian" to her teaching because of her rejection of works of the law, rather than the interior assurance of faith and grace, as the essence of righteousness. She was tried by the civil court and sentenced to banishment; the Boston church excommunicated her. She then joined with others to make the first settlement in R.I., at Portsmouth. See A. H. Newman, EncRelKnow I:200–201; R. P. Bolton, *Woman Misunderstood* (1931). *ANTINOMIANISM.

HUTER, JAKOB (Hutter; d. 1536), founder of the *Hutterian Brethren. After the death of G. *Blaurock, H. was the leader of the Tyrolean Anabaptists. Because of persecution he brought a group of his followers to Austerlitz, Moravia. There, for the practice of their belief, he organized them (1533–35) in an agricultural settlement with a communal form of life (see BRUDERHOF). On a journey to Austria, H. was captured, condemned, and burned at the stake in Innsbruck. See H. Fischer, *J. H.* (1956); MennEnc 2:851ff., 854ff.

HUTTEN, ULRICH VON (1488–1523), German humanist and polemicist. H. was sent to the monastery at Fulda when he was 11, but fled 6 years later and became an itinerant poet and mercenary. After study at Cologne, Erfurt, and Frankfurt he lived for a time in Leipzig, Greifswald, and Rostock. His first meeting with *Erasmus occurred before he went to Rome to study law (1515–17). On his return to Germany H. criticized the Roman Curia in a number of violent tracts. With Crotus Rubeanus he wrote *Epistolae obscurorum virorum*, satire directed against the Cologne scholastics. In 1517 he edited Lorenzo *Valla's *De donatione Constantini*. He published a series of anti-Roman pamphlets in defense of Martin Luther, though the latter disapproved of his threats of force. When H. vainly sought asylum with Erasmus in Basel, *Zwingli gave him refuge and sent him for medical help to the Island of Ufenau in Lake Zurich, where he died. See H. Holborn, *Ulrich von Hutten and the German Reformation* (tr. R. H. Bainton, 1937).

HUTTERIAN BRETHREN, a religious body founded by the Anabaptist J. *Huter. The first of the *Bruderhofs, agricultural settlements following a strictly communal form of life (see Acts 2.44–45), was organized by Huter in Moravia (1533–35). Because of persecution the Brethren migrated first to Russia in 1622 and then to Bon Homme Co., S.Dak., in 1874. There were about 7,600 American members, in 24 groups in S.Dak. and one in Minn. in 1967. Other communities exist in Manitoba and Alberta Provinces, Canada, in England, and in Paraguay. In the substance of their belief and practice the Hutterian Brethren are Mennonites, but their communal form of life is distinctive. See G. Horsch, *Hutterian Brethren, 1528–1931; A Story of Martyrdom and Loyalty* (1931); J. W. Bennett, *Hutterian Brethren* (1967); MennEnc 2:851–865.

I

I AM MOVEMENT, an American religious cult that gained a considerable following in the 1930s and rapidly declined thereafter. Guy W. Ballard and his wife, Edna, organized and promoted the movement; its ideas were drawn exclusively from *Unveiled Mysteries, The Magic Presence,* and other books written by Ballard, under the pen name Godfrey Ray King. In 1934 he published *Unveiled Mysteries,* describing interviews with the Ascended Master St. Germain that began on Mt. Shasta, Calif., in 1930. He and his wife launched the I Am movement with lecture series in Chicago, Philadelphia, New York, Washington, and other American cities; in 1936 they established their headquarters in Los Angeles. The thought of the I Am movement was a maze of borrowings from occult and *New Thought sources. An original veneer of Christianity was dropped, and the Ascended Master St. Germain, who in one of many incarnations had been the 18th-cent. Comte de St. Germain, took the chief place in the pantheon of Ascended Masters. Through successive reincarnations, every member of the movement could become an Ascended Master. Death was impossible, because of the immanence of the Great I Am Presence in every man. By using certain affirmations and incantations, each member could harness the I Am power for health, prosperity, and happiness. The I Am Presence is impersonal, while St. Germain is at once a benevolent demiurge and one of the myriad Ascended Masters. The Ballards were reincarnations of George Washington and Joan of Arc, respectively. I Am study groups were required to purchase Ballard's many publications and to tithe their wealth. They were also obliged to abstain from sexual intercourse, astrology, drugs, garlic and onions, and playing cards. The I Am movement borrowed ideas and members from the Silver Shirt Movement and was characterized by superpatriotism and condemnations of the New Deal, labor unions, and liberals. Ballard's death in 1939 and a series of trials, 1939–47, that culminated in Edna Ballard's imprisonment for mail fraud, made considerable inroads on the I Am membership, and it disappeared altogether in the 1950s.

IARF, see INTERNATIONAL ASSOCIATION FOR LIBERAL CHRISTIANITY AND RELIGIOUS FREEDOM.

ILLUMINATI, ORDER OF, established (1776) in Bavaria, a secret organization first called the Perfectibilists. The founder was Johann Adam Weishaupt (1148–1830), Prof. of Law at the Univ. of Ingolstadt. A system of gradually more elaborate degrees initiated the members into the arcana of the society; they were to achieve progressive illumination through the study of rationalistic philosophy and the humanities. Initiation included an exhaustive life confession and oaths of absolute secrecy and blind obedience to the leaders, whose identity was known only to the highest initiates. The spread of the society throughout Germany and Austria and into France was achieved by infiltration of the lodges of Freemasons. Through revelations by disaffected members, the secrets of the society became known to the civil authorities, and it was outlawed by the elector of Bavaria in 1785. Some historians classify the Illuminati simply as a rationalistic movement, embodying the spirit of the *Enlightenment and mingling itself with the Freemasons. G. Bareille, however, offers evidence that the secrecy and recruitment of the order were aimed by its founder at destroying all authority—domestic, civil, and ecclesiastical. The aim was to retrieve the liberty and equality supposed as a natural primitive human condition suppressed by law and private property. In 1896 a form of the Illuminati was restored in Germany; it went through a reorganization in 1925, but apparently was disbanded under the Nazi proscription of secret societies. See G. Bareille, DTC 7:756–766; R. Le Forestier, *Les Illuminés de Bavière et la Franc-Maçonnerie Allemande* (1950). *ROSICRUCIANS; *ALUMBRADOS.

ILLUMINÉS, also called, with doubtful accuracy, *Guérinets; a group in Picardy in the late 17th cent. affected by religious *illuminism and accused of heresy. They were suppressed by ecclesiastical and civil powers.

ILLUMINISM, RELIGIOUS, a classification for teachings that rely upon a mystical or intuitive divine enlightenment. In this sense it has been applied most regularly to the doctrines of the Gnostics, the *Alumbrados, the *Illuminés of P. Guérin. It has also been used as an equivalent to *enthusiasm, and has been so applied to individuals and movements throughout church history that have deviated from authority or official teaching on the basis of appeal to a higher light. Illuminism has also been used to refer to the exaltation of the clear light of reason characteristic of the *Enlightenment.

ILLYRICUS, MATTHIAS FLACIUS, see FLACIUS ILLYRICUS, MATTHIAS.

IMITATION OF CHRIST, also known as the *Following of Christ,* one of the great classics of Western devotional literature, ranking with **Pilgrim's Progress* as one of the most widely read of religious books, after the Bible. Its purpose is to lead the reader to pattern his life on the model of Christ. Written primarily for the use of religious, it has nevertheless proved useful to ordinary people in opening the way for a deeper inner life. Its language and thought are simple; it avoids the scholastic and intellectual preoccupation that deadens the effect of much ascetical literature, and it emphasizes the affective elements in piety. The work is divided into four books: the first deals with general points useful for the spiritual life; the second, with admonitions conducive to the deepening of the interior life; the third, with interior consolations; and the fourth, with holy communion. The work is regarded as the masterpiece of the piety typical of the *Devotio moderna, and its sources are those most valued by the leaders of that movement: the Bible and the writings of the Fathers, of SS. Bernard of Clairvaux and Bonaventure, and of such Rhineland mystics as J. Tauler and H. Suso.

The book was published anonymously in the early 15th century. In later editions its authorship was ascribed to Thomas à Kempis *(c*.1380–1471). This attribution has been exhaustively controverted since the early 17th century. The debate reached its zenith in the 19th cent. but broke out afresh in the 1920s with the effort of J. van Ginneken, S. J., to credit G. Groote with authorship of the basic text. The question of authorship has not yet been definitively settled, but the greater weight of scholarly opinion favors its ascription to Thomas à Kempis. The book was first written, it would seem, in Latin, but it has been translated into most languages and has appeared in countless editions. It has appealed to Protestants as well as Catholics. In some Protestant editions Book 4, dealing with holy communion, is either omitted or radically revised. The work exercised a considerable influence on John *Wesley, who published a translation of it together with an introduction (*The Christian's Model,* 1735). Despite his high regard for the *Imitation,* Wesley was troubled by a tone of Calvinism he thought discernible in it. The same trait has been noted by some RC critics, who have characterized its point of view as semi-Jansenistic. Others have criticized the work for its absorption in the personal sanctification of the individual to the relative neglect of the more outgoing aspect of the pursuit of holiness.

Among the earlier writers to whom the work has been ascribed are J. Gerson (d. 1429), Giovanni Gersen, an Italian abbot

(Gessen; 13th cent.?), SS. Bernard and Bonaventure, and even Pope Innocent III. The finest English translation of the *Imitation* was made by R. Whitford *(c.*1530). A modernization of this translation by H. C. Gardiner, S.J., published in 1955, has proved very popular. See W. J. Alberts, NCE 7:375–377, esp. for the history of the controversy and for bibliography.

IMMERSION, ALIEN, see ALIEN IMMERSION.

IMMERSION, TRINE, see TRINE IMMERSION.

IMMERSION BAPTISTS, a name connoting baptismal practice. Concerned primarily with *believer's baptism, the earliest Baptists baptized by affusion. They adopted immersion *c.*1640 as the proper mode and have almost universally used it since then. Their main arguments are: (1) the Greek word *baptizein* signifies total submersion; (2) NT examples indicate that candidates were taken into a body of water; (3) the symbolism of baptism as identification with Christ in his death and resurrection requires immersion; and (4) this mode was useful for centuries, as attested by written records and remains of baptistries in ancient Churches. See A. Gilmore, ed., *Christian Baptism* (1959); W. L. Lumpkin, *History of Immersion* (1962).

IMPANATION (Lat. *panis,* bread), a term devised to express or describe certain theories of the *Real Presence. In the 12th cent. this parallel was advanced: as by the Incarnation the Word is personally and substantially united to human nature, so in the Eucharist by impanation Christ is personally and substantially united to bread and wine. The idea was admitted as a tenable alternative to *transubstantiation by John of Paris *(c.*1306) and was espoused by the Lutheran A. *Osiander (d. 1552). In affirming the Real Presence Luther himself rejected any such idea. Nevertheless when C. *Schwenkfeld and others called his sacramental realism impanation (*Einbrödtung*), Luther conceded the designation, for the sake of argument, in his *Confession concerning the Lord's Supper* (1528). RC theologians sometimes described Lutheran eucharistic theory as impanation, but the designation is not apt. *CONSUBSTANTIATION.

INCARNATIONAL THEOLOGY, a type of theology that in major questions draws explanation from the mystery of the God-man. A contemporary RC resurgence of this emphasis reached its apex approximately during the years 1933–55. It stemmed from a rethinking of faith in the incarnation of the Son of God and extended to the Christian involvement in all phases of human activity—economic, political, social, and cultural. M. I. Montuclard, P. Teilhard de Chardin, Y. Congar, H. de Lubac, and G. Thils endeavored to show how the Christian, to be fully human, must assume earthly realities and human values for whatever they are worth so that he can help to build up the Mystical Body of Christ. The need of a theological explanation of the Christian's involvement in the world has given an incarnational direction to both Protestant and RC theology, and explains the appeal of existentialist and phenomenological philosophies to contemporary theologians. There is no total agreement among theologians about the values of the world. The Christian cannot escape in his life the practical question of the continuity and discontinuity between the material and spiritual, sacred and profane, natural and supernatural, worldly achievement and the kingdom of God. Incarnational theology has to be balanced by an eschatological point of view. See N. Sharkey, NCE 7:415–416; B. Besret, *Incarnation ou Eschatologie?* (1964); J. M. Connolly, *Human History and the Word of God: The Christian Meaning in Contemporary Thought* (1965), esp. Ch. 6, "The Catholic Theologies of History." *ESCHATOLOGICAL THEOLOGY.

INDEPENDENCY, that *polity which recognizes local congregations of believers as autonomous under Christ and denies any but ministerial and persuasive authority to any wider fellowship of churches or to any priestly order. In the 17th cent. the word was gradually replaced by the more positive term *Congregationalism. The word and the concept, however, still persist in Wales in the Union of Welsh Independents. In certain parts of England also the term "Independent Chapel" continues to be preferred to Congregational Church. *BROWNE, ROBERT; *INDEPENDENTS.

INDEPENDENT AFRICAN METHODIST EPISCOPAL CHURCH, a Methodist denomination organized in Jacksonville, Fla., in 1897 by eight Negro ministers who withdrew from the African Methodist Episcopal Church after a dispute with the presiding elders of the parent group. Three years later, in Miss., a similar incident occurred. The two denominations, while having the same name, were independent of each other until 1919, when they drew up articles of confederation. Doctrine and polity are like those of the parent body.

INDEPENDENT ASSEMBLIES OF GOD, INTERNATIONAL, an association of Pentecostal ministers that loosely joins autonomous Churches in the U.S. and Canada, esp. for missionary work. The association dates back to 1911, but became more formally organized in St. Paul, Minn., in 1922. It also has been called the Scandinavian Assemblies of God and the Independent Assemblies of God, U.S.A. and Canada. Because of connections in origin and continuing missionary cooperation with the Philadelphia Pentecostal Church in Stockholm, Sweden, Churches of the Assemblies are sometimes called "Philadelphia Churches." Missionary activity is a cooperative effort of the Churches and includes work in the West Indies, Mexico, Argentina, India, New Guinea, Korea, Kenya, South Africa, and Tanzania.

INDEPENDENT BAPTIST CHURCH OF AMERICA, founded at Dassel, Minn., in 1893 by a group of Swedish immigrants. The Church was divided under different names through the years but was reunited in 1927 under the present designation. Admission to fellowship is by the laying on of hands after public confession of faith in repentance and the resurrection, and by baptism by immersion. Pacifism is a distinguishing mark of this community. In 1968 there were 25 members in two churches.

INDEPENDENT CHRISTIAN CHURCHES, designation for a group of Churches fraternally associated but not forming an organization or denomination. They are all Christian Churches, i.e., close in belief to the Disciples of Christ or Churches of Christ, but remain independent esp. for the sake of adherence to a stricter *fundamentalism than they find in those organized bodies. Through their associates these churches support 32 small Bible colleges and hundreds of missionaries; they maintain the Standard Publishing Foundation, Cincinnati, Ohio, for the dissemination of evangelistic literature. There are 3,000 such churches, with perhaps 1 million members.

INDEPENDENT CHURCHES, in England, a synonym for Congregational churches, or those churches that have a congregational polity (see INDEPENDENCY), but in the U.S. a designation for churches having no denominational affiliation. Such churches have proliferated since the fundamentalist-modernist controversy after World War I. This movement had diverse origins, but underlying it was an erosion of the doctrine of the universal Church, to which several influences contributed. *Rationalism, *individualism, and *revivalism fostered a concept of the Church as simply a voluntary association of believers (see VOLUNTARYISM). Plymouth Brethren ideas of the Church, disseminated through the *Scofield Bible, used in many Bible schools, reinforced this tendency. As doctrinal disputes aroused suspicions of major denominations, many churches severed ties with such bodies and existed without relationship to other churches. Independent churches often furnish generous support to missionary and evangelistic causes through numerous independent missionary organizations. There are also *community churches that are independent but that emphasize cooperation on the basis of a comprehensive Christian unity. *INTERDENOMINATIONAL CHURCHES.

INDEPENDENT FUNDAMENTAL CHURCHES OF AMERICA, a nondenominational body organized in 1930 in Cicero, Ill., by representatives of various churches that had severed relations with their denominations because of the inroads of *modernism. While opposing *denominationalism, the group desires to safeguard fundamentalist doctrine and to establish closer fellowship among *independent churches in defense of the Gospel. Membership requires the acceptance of 16 basic articles of faith. Affiliated churches cooperate in maintaining a Bible college, a Bible camp, several Bible institutes, a school, a children's home, and a number of missionary projects. In 1968 this group of churches included 864 congregations, with combined membership of 101,435. Headquarters are in Wheaton, Illinois.

INDEPENDENT FUNDAMENTAL METHODIST CHURCH, INC., the name from 1942 to 1956 of the present *Fundamental Methodist Church.

INDEPENDENTS, an early designation for Congregationalists. The term was in use in England until the 18th cent.; in Wales the Welsh-speaking Congregationalists continue to be called Welsh Independents. The origin of the name is R. *Browne's idea that the local church is itself a full expression of the kingdom of God and thus free of superior authority, civil or ecclesiastical. The Independents were the strongest of the Puritan parties and had a notable influence upon the evolution of the rights of *Nonconformists. There is a second usage of the name among the Disciples of Christ, who call members of their churches engaged in autonomous foreign mission work Independents. See bibliog. for Congregationalism. *GATHERED CHURCH.

INDIFFERENTISM, RELIGIOUS, a term often used in reference to the view and attitude of those who hold that the differences of belief that separate Christians of different denominations, or even adherents of any religion, are of no significance. The term is also applied to the position of those who attach no importance to religious belief of any kind. This article is chiefly concerned with indifferentism in the latter sense.

So understood, indifferentism is the least conspicuous form of irreligion; it is rarely militant and aggressive and rarely given doctrinal expression, because God is totally disregarded. It is often accompanied by indifference to any serious purpose in life and to spiritual values or ideals. As such it is all but closed to religious dialogue or to any exposition of sacred doctrine. Such indifference seems connected, in ways not precisely determined, with certain major characteristics of modern civilization and thinking. Some philosophical and theological conception of religion is undoubtedly involved in the attitude of indifference, but it is hardly worked out in detail by those for whom the things of religion are of little concern. There are degrees of indifference and, in more or less marked forms, it can penetrate the attitude even of believers. The religious problem does not even arise for a person or milieu in the grip of indifference. Whether or not God exists makes no impact on the way things are seen and interpreted or on the way life is lived; everything happens and is understood as if the question of God were totally meaningless. Even for a believer God can be accepted as the ultimate "explanation" of reality but make no significant impression in real life. The line between religious indifference and a kind of lived atheism is much less clear in practice than in theory.

The man of technological civilization is "diverted" (in Pascal's sense) by many immediate attractions. He is, further, distressed by an acute awareness of evil in its individual, cosmic, economic, social, political, and moral dimensions. Religious values must compete with a hypercritical spirit, the pluralist atmosphere, the view taken by exponents of different ideologies that their own values are autonomous, and the alleged existential inefficacy of religion. Religious indifference emerges as a sign of the time and not simply as a personal attitude. Whatever one thinks of God, it is claimed, everything in fact happens as if he did not exist. On the personal level believers seem to be men like others, or at least they are not so different as to make one think that faith has a power to renew and transform. On the social level the great religions, including Christianity, do not seem to have grasped the world's leading problems or contributed to their solution. The most dramatic aspect of the contemporary situation is not so much the rejection of old solutions as the decline of interest in the problems themselves. Indifferentism raises the problem of the authenticity of the image of religion and stresses the need for a profound rethinking of Christianity. See P. H. Simon, "Athéisme, incroyance, indifférence," *Dieu aujourd'hui* (1964); E. Borne, *Atheism* (1959); J. Girardi, "Reflections on Religious Indifference," *Concilium* (v.23), 60–69. *SECULARISM.

INDIVIDUALISM, as a religious term, a tendency to reduce Christianity to the vertical relation between God and the individual person. Beginning with the Renaissance, many influences have contributed to a one-sided emphasis upon individual freedom, competence, and self-reliance, which have affected Christianity. Nowhere has this trend been more apparent than in the United States. The frontier experience fostered self-confidence, the *Enlightenment stressed the competence of the individual's reason and conscience, and *revivalism made individual *conversion the primary focus of concern. The New England circle of *transcendentalists asserted the immediacy of divine guidance, making intuition authoritative in morals and religion, and *liberal theology made "the infinite worth of the individual" a major plank in its platform. Although the Scriptures teach the value of individuals (e.g., Lk 15.7), they also reveal a corresponding acknowledgment of human solidarity, esp. within the Christian community. The Great Commandment (Mk 12.30–31) enjoins both love of God and love of neighbor. Religious individualism has had as consequences: the *subjectivism that makes individual reason and conscience the sole arbiter in faith and morals; the proliferation of sectarian divisions; reduction of the Church to a convenient means by which the individual receives occasional help, but which he may easily ignore; and loss of awareness that the Church of Jesus Christ exists for service and that this ministry is shared by all members.

INDULGENCE CONTROVERSY, the dispute between Martin Luther and J. *Tetzel, regarded as the immediate starting point of the Reformation. Whether the posting of the *Ninety-Five Theses, Oct. 31, 1517, be fact or legend, Luther did challenge the Dominican Tetzel's doctrine on indulgences. Tetzel had been licensed by Albert of Brandenburg, Abp. of Mainz and Magdeburg, to solicit alms for the building of a new St. Peter's in Rome. The indulgence campaign was tied in with sordid and simoniacal financial arrangements. The abp.'s. instruction made no mention of sorrow for sin or confession, but only of the contributions as the condition for gaining an indulgence. Luther protested against Tetzel's doctrine on four points; that an indulgence guarantees salvation; that money given immediately frees a soul from purgatory; that through an indulgence the worst sins were forgiven; and that Tetzel's indulgence freed from all guilt and punishment. Luther mainly protested against the misunderstanding caused in people's minds by the indulgence preaching. But in the storm provoked by his protest, his alienation from Rome, in doctrine and in practical measures of reform, became manifest. In Rome Tetzel's order promoted the canonical process that led to Luther's excommunication. See E. Iserloh, *Theses Were Not Posted* (tr. J. Wicks, 1968); J. P. Dolan, *History of the Reformation* (pa., 1965), 233–238.

INFALLIBILITY, insusceptibility or immunity to error in matters pertaining to divine revelation. It is a corollary of Christian faith that the believer is certain of the object of his faith: "I know whom I have believed and I am sure that he is able to guard until that Day what has been entrusted to me" (2 Tim 1.12). The NT promises that the Holy Spirit "will guide you into all the truth" (Jn 16.13) apply, at least in some sense, to every Christian and not only to the corporate experience of the Church as a whole. From the history of the Church, as well as from the personal experience of every Christian, it is clear that such promises do not exempt the individual from susceptibility to error at every moment in his Christian life, but they do promise the guidance of the Holy Spirit to protect him from a fundamental error in his faith (see ThAq ST 2a2ae, 1.3; 8.4 ad 1 and ad 2). This subjective infallibility must, however, be seen in relation to the infallibility that, as a concomitant of divine inspiration, is predicated of the Bible. Not only is divine revelation itself infallible, but its bearer and medium, Sacred Scripture, is also protected from error by the Holy Spirit. This quality of Scripture is evident from the way the OT is handled in the New, as when Jesus is represented in the Gospel of John as arguing on the basis of the assumption that "scripture cannot be broken" (Jn 10.35). The promise to the Apostles that they will be guided into all the truth would seem to apply with special force to their exercise of their apostolic office, a major component of which was the writing of the NT. Yet it does not necessarily follow that this infallibility of Sacred Scripture implies an absolute scientific accuracy concerning the universe and the laws of nature. Nor does it imply that the writers of the Old and the NT did not make use of literary forms and ideas that were current in the world around them. The chronological data or biological information of the Bible are not on the same level with its message of salvation (see BIBLE, AUTHORITY OF).

The apostolic office is, however, by no means restricted to the composition of the NT. It is an office for the Church and in the Church, and it is to the Church that the promise of divine guidance—and therefore the right to infallibility—is granted. "The church of the living God" is "the pillar and bulwark of the truth" (1 Tim 3.15). In the exercise of this prerogative, the earliest "church council" felt qualified to invoke the formula "It has seemed good to the Holy Spirit and to us" (Acts 15.28). In one way or another, the postapostolic Church has continued to claim this right to speak infallibly as the custodian of divine revelation. Here again it is necessary to note that, from the evidence of history, this right did not prevent the councils and officials of the Church from mistakes of fact and errors of judgment that have been corrected by later generations. Ethical judgments—including, e.g., the prohibition of "what is strangled" in the decree of the apostolic council in Acts 15.29—and dogmatic formulas have been changed, clarified, and even revoked, as the development of the Church and of her teaching office has brought new insights into divine revelation (see Vat II Ecum 6).

It is in the context of the infallibility of the Scriptures and of the Church that the doctrine of the infallibility of the pope is to be understood. *Pastor aeternus* of Vatican Council I (see D 3074) was careful to specify that the pope exercises "that infallibility with which the divine Redeemer willed that His Church be instructed in defining doctrine on faith and morals"; papal infallibility is not separated from the infallibility of the Church. It also identified the infallibility as applying to the pope "when he speaks *ex cathedra,* i.e., in the exercise of his office as pastor and teacher of all Christians"; it is part of this office to be the authoritative interpreter of Sacred Scripture. At the same time Vatican I stated that this infallibility pertained to the pope without "the consent of the Church." The clarification of this combination of statements has continued to engage the attention of theologians. The calling of Vatican Council II would seem to refute any idea that Vatican Council I had vested all authority and all infallibility in the papal office as such (see Vat II ConstCh 25); nevertheless, the decisions of Vatican II were also proclaimed and promulgated by the pope. See B. C. Butler, *The Church and Infallibility* (1954); J. H. Newman, *On the Inspiration of Scripture* (ed. J. D. Holmes and R. Murray, 1967); J. J. Hennesey, *First Council of the Vatican* (1963).

INFANT BAPTISM, the administration of the sacrament of baptism to those who have not yet attained the use of reason, a topic controverted among Christians.

The Case for Infant Baptism. There is no direct evidence in the NT that infants received Christian baptism. However, since male children were initiated into the Jewish religion by the rite of circumcision and since the children of adult converts to Judaism were baptized along with their parents in Jewish proselyte baptism, it is not unlikely that the children of Christian parents were initiated into the Christian religion by baptism. In the earliest detailed rite of baptism, that of Hippolytus (*c.*215), the following rubric occurs: "And they shall baptize the little children first. And if they can answer for themselves, let them answer. But if they cannot, let their parents answer or someone from the family" (*Trad. apost.* 21.-3). According to Augustine, the faith of the child is supplied by the faith of the Church, expressed in the baptismal formula. The Council of Trent anathematized anyone who "denies that infants newly issued from their mother's womb are to be baptized,

though born of baptized parents" (D 1514), and in its Decree on Justification it taught that justification "cannot take place without the laver of regeneration or its desire (*votum*), as has been written: 'Unless a man be born again of water and the Holy Spirit, he cannot enter into the kingdom of God' [Jn 3.5]" (D 1524). RC theologians are generally agreed that infants are incapable of the *votum,* or desire, for baptism. There is, however, a growing number of theologians who suggest that the *votum* need not be the child's, but that as part of the parents and the community into which he is born, the child may participate in their Christian desire that he be baptized.

The Case against Infant Baptism. Those who reject infant baptism do so both on biblical grounds and for theological reasons. Since the NT accounts of baptism make no mention of the baptism of infants, but always indicate that the rite is being administered to persons who have repented and made a profession of faith, the lack of such a precedent furnishes one basis for refusing to adopt the practice. Moreover, many understand baptism to be a human response to God's grace, signifying submission to God's judgment and mercy, identification with Christ in his death and resurrection, and a testimony to others that one has become a Christian; they therefore see no reason for baptizing infants. Furthermore, in the belief that the visible Church should include only those who consciously manifest their faith in Jesus Christ and submit themselves to the disciplines of the Christian community, they contend that baptism should be reserved for those old enough to make a responsible decision. An examination of extra-biblical literature reveals no clear, explicit reference to infant baptism earlier than Origen and Tertullian in the 3d century. Such documents as the *Didache* or the *First Apology* of Justin Martyr imply that the subjects were adults; the former requires the candidate to fast prior to receiving baptism, and the latter says that the recipients are those who "are persuaded and believe" and have been instructed.

Infant baptism appears to have become the usual practice; although some medieval sects, such as the Waldenses, may have renounced it, there was not a strong renewal of emphasis upon *believer's baptism until the Reformation of the 16th century. At that time, Lutherans, Anglicans, and *Reformed, retained the practice of infant baptism, but the *Anabaptists, esp. the *Swiss Brethren of Zurich (and their descendants, *Mennonites, *Hutterites, and others), insisted that baptism was only for those old enough to repent and make a personal profession of faith. Seeking to restore the faith and practice of the primitive Church, they restricted church membership to persons baptized upon a profession of faith. In the 17th cent. English Baptists emerged from congregational Puritanism and became a distinct denomination because of their emphasis upon believer's baptism and a concept of the *visible Church composed only of committed and disciplined Christians. Whether there was any but an indirect connection between the earlier Anabaptist groups and the Baptists is not entirely clear. In 1708 the Church of the Brethren arose in Germany under the leadership of Alexander *Mack, and a few years later moved to America. Several other Brethren Churches in the U.S. also derived from German *Pietism in the 18th century. The Disciples of Christ originated under the leadership of Alexander *Campbell in the U.S. around 1830. All of these groups come within the category of "believers' Churches," admitting to membership only persons baptized after reaching a mature age and having professed their faith in Jesus Christ as Lord and Savior.

Some European theologians have had qualms about infant baptism in recent years. Emil *Brunner was an early critic of infant baptism, declaring in 1937 that the contemporary practice of infant baptism is nothing short of scandalous (*The Divine-Human Encounter* [1937], 132). In 1943 Karl *Barth launched an attack on infant baptism, asserting that such a practice has no biblical basis and that in the NT baptism is in every case the "indispensable answer to an unavoidable question by a man who has come to faith" (*The Teaching of the Church Regarding Baptism* [tr. E. A. Payne, 1948], 41–44). Barth's son, Markus, has written a more thorough book on baptism, in which he rejects the rite of infant baptism (*Die Taufe—Ein Sakrament?*, 1951). Likewise considerable discussion has taken place within the C of E and among some Lutherans concerning the propriety of infant baptism. See D. F. Durnbaugh, *Believers' Church: the History and Character of Radical Protestantism* (1968); A. Gilmore, *Christian Baptism: A Fresh Attempt to Understand the Rite in Terms of Scripture, History, and Theology* (1959); P. Palmer, *Sacraments and Worship* (Sources of Christian Theology 1, 1955).

INFRALAPSARIANISM, equivalent alternative for sublapsarianism or postlapsarianism, the interpretation in Calvinist doctrine that God predestined men to heaven or hell only after the Fall. *SUPRALAPSARIANISM.

INGE, WILLIAM RALPH (1860–1954), English philosopher and religious thinker. Educated at Eton and King's College, Cambridge, he taught at both Oxford and Cambridge before his appointment to the deanship of St. Paul's Cathedral, London (1911); he held that office until his retirement in 1934; the remaining 20 years of his life he spent in scholarly retirement. He was a keen critic of modern civilization and from the pessimistic tone of his epigrammatic comments upon it he was known as the Gloomy Dean. He saw the rationalism of the modern mind as too narrow to reach beyond the world of sense to the world of values and to the supreme value that is God, and hence insisted upon intuition of the mystic as necessary to supplement the defective vision of contemporary rationalism. He was greatly attracted to Plotinus, in whose neoplatonism he saw a blend of true rationalism and mystical insight. Among his works are *Christian Mysticism* (Bampton Lectures, 1899), *The Philosophy of Plotinus* (Gifford Lectures, 2v., 1918), *The Platonic Tradition in English Religious Thought* (1926), and *Mysticism in Religion* (1947). See A. Fox, *Dean Inge* (1960); R. M. Helm, *Gloomy Dean* (1962).

INGHAMITES, an English group formed under the leadership of Benjamin Ingham (1712–72), a Yorkshire evangelist. First closely associated with John and Charles *Wesley, Ingham later became attracted to the Moravian Brethren and founded a number of societies in Yorkshire and Lancashire. In 1753 he and his group formally separated from the Moravians. Ingham's plan to join the Methodists was rejected by John Wesley in 1755. After 1760 Ingham adopted the teachings of the *Glasites; bitter controversy ensued among the Inghamites, and most deserted to the Methodists. See EncRelKnow 5:492.

INITIARII (Lat. *initium*, beginning), those who believed that the Second Person of the Blessed Trinity was co-eternal with the Father but became the Son only by being born at a point in time. Filaster (*Haer.* 127) reports such a belief, and Augustine repeats him (*Haer.* 80); it is mentioned in Tertullian (*Adv. Hermonegenem* 3). Adherents are called Initiarii (or Nativitarii; Lat. *nativitas*, birth) by Danaeus in his edition (1576) of Augustine's *De haeresibus* (PL 12:1254).

INNER LIGHT, the basic and distinctive belief of the *Religious Society of Friends. While others earlier, e.g., among the Anabaptists, had similar ideas, the doctrine of the Inner Light most probably came to G. *Fox, founder of the Quakers, from his own personal religious experience. Neither in Fox's enthusiastic writings nor in R. *Barclay's more formal *Apology of the True Christian Divinity* (1678) was the Inner Light precisely categorized. God is its source and dwells within it; Fox called it the Light of Christ; Barclay at times

seemed to identify it with Christ Himself. While evangelical emphases within Quakerism on the Bible and the historical Christ have sometimes subtly altered its role, the Inner Light has remained for Quakers the essential rule of faith; Scripture or anything else outside the soul is simply confirmatory. Although some moderns, e.g., Edward Grubb (1854–1939), have given it a naturalistic interpretation, for most Quakers the Inner Light is neither conscience nor reason, but a unique religious sense; an immediate revelation, a personally experienced contact with God, it is unerring, self-authenticating and saving. Barclay stressed its being a corporate experience. All men, even those predating or not knowing the historical Christ, have received it; for those who use it rightly it means consciousness of Christ's inner saving presence. The American Quaker Rufus M. Jones (1863–1948) stressed the affinity between the Inner Light and mysticism. Belief in the Inner Light underlies the Quaker deemphasis of dogma, their understanding of sin and redemption, their benevolence toward all men as sharers in the light, and their proper mode of worship. See R. Knox, *Enthusiasm* (1950), 152–171; L. Eeg-Olofsson, *Conception of the Inner Light in Robert Barclay's Theology* (1954); Mayer RB 409–422, with bibliog.

INNER MISSION (Ger. *Innere Mission*), a term first used by J. H. Wichern in 1848 to designate mission work within Christendom as opposed to mission work outside it. It included all charitable, social, and religious endeavors of German Lutherans except parish work. By means of a central committee it endeavored to coordinate such efforts. The movements grew out of *Pietism, the Awakening (a return to the historical and confessional roots of Lutheranism), and industrialization. The chief aims were to reclaim lapsed Christians and to assist the needy of all social classes. The organization soon spread to other European countries. In the U.S., Lutherans promoted it, changing its name after a time to

Christian Social Welfare. In Germany, the Inner Mission merged in 1957 with Hilfswerk, a society that had been set up in 1945 by the *Evangelical Church in Germany (EKD). Even in its early stages Inner Mission was criticized for obscuring the importance of doctrine, ignoring church authority, and overstressing social action. See W. Schütz, RGG 3:756–763.

INQUISITION. The harshness of the old Judaic death penalty for heresy (Dt 13.5–19; 16.21–17.13; 18.20) was opposed by early Christians, who saw religion as a matter of conscience and free will and regarded excommunication as a sufficient punishment.

History. The caesaropapist emperors viewed the protection of religion as their first concern and would have made heresy tantamount to high treason. St. Optatus of Milevis (d. *c.*400), citing the OT, defended the imperial position; but the execution of Priscillian (386) brought strong objections from Siricius, Ambrose, and Martin of Tours, besides the reaction in Spain. By the 11th cent., with the revival of Roman law, the idea of a perfect and sovereign Christian society based upon objective revelation was current enough in Europe for heretics to be hanged by Henry III (1051–52), burned by Robert I (1122), and lynched by several mobs. Why the papacy in 1231 moved to establish a special Inquisition in the hands of the newly founded mendicant orders, the Franciscans and Dominicans, is not clear. It appears that the decision, long in developing, was prompted as a defense against the caesaropapism of Frederick II Hohenstaufen. Neo-Manicheans entered Western Europe from the Balkans *c.*1000 (see BOGO-MILS) and by the late 12th cent. gave alarm to the authorities of Church and State, especially in N Italy, S France, and Germany. England had little heresy, although some 30 heretics were branded under Henry II and turned out to die in the winter of 1166. Peter II expelled heretics from Aragon (1197), but they came back during the Albigensian War; Aragon feared heresy less than the loss of her lands in S France.

In Flanders and N France a fair number of heretics died at the stake.

Ecclesiastical measures began with Lateran Council II (1139), which required civil rulers to prosecute heretics; Alexander III called for prison and confiscation (1163); Lateran Council III (1179), soon after a council of *Cathari met near Toulouse, ordered the use of force. In 1184 Lucius III in *Ad abolendam* initiated the episcopal inquisition, which required aid from secular rulers, denunciations of heretics by the faithful, semiannual diocesan visitations, and strong measures against supporters of heresy. Neither episcopal nor secular aid was forthcoming, and Innocent III put his hopes in the holy life and holy thought of Cistercians working with local parish commissions of inquiry. In 1206 St. Dominic began to work with the Cistercians in S France. When the papal legate was slain in 1208, Innocent excommunicated the Count of Toulouse and gave all Catholics freedom to persecute his person and occupy his lands. The Albigensian War followed, and dynastic and regional rivalries prevailed over religious interests.

While Paris was extending its sway into S France, Frederick II was issuing decrees against heresy (1220, 1224, 1227). Innocent III and Lateran Council IV (1215) had acted to safeguard episcopal authority and to defend heretics against secular judgment, and Innocent disapproved of the death penalty; but Gregory IX in 1227 gave support to the 1224 law of Frederick II, which burned all those convicted by bishops. When Frederick was excommunicated in late 1227, the papacy had to assume direct control. The Council of Toulouse (1229) only confirmed regulations already in use; but the Statutes of the Holy See (1231), sent to all bishops, initiated the Inquisition. The Statutes consisted first of Gregory's constitution, which offered life imprisonment as a penance for abjurers of heresy and restricted secular punishment to those condemned by the Church, and secondly of the statutes of the Roman Senator Annibald, which confiscated heretics' goods, demolished their dwellings, fined or exiled sympathizers, and required future senators to prosecute them. Episcopal zeal was still lacking, and Gregory in 1232 advanced the Dominicans as agents of the new Inquisition. What was peculiar to the new institution was that the jurisdiction over heretics was reserved to a legal system controlled by the papacy. The hunting of heretics, the judicial procedure, and the punishments had existed for years; torture would not be accepted until later.

The first Inquisitors went to the Rhineland, Burgundy, Aragon, and Lombardy. Local bishops and nobles in France and Italy opposed them; Lombard cities, except Bologna, resisted the intrusion of a new judicial authority. Kings supported the Inquisition as long as it was in their interest. By 1255 the new system was established. Areas of jurisdiction varied according to the intensity of heresy but respected ecclesiastical and political boundaries. Only the pope could reverse the judgments of the Inquisitors, who were practically irremovable from office. At first, Inquisitors rode the circuit in pairs, but they soon took up residence in centers where their persons and records were safe; several were slain. In 1254 Innocent IV required episcopal consent in sentences of life imprisonment and death, and this order was confirmed in 1262, 1265, and 1273. Boniface VIII required episcopal approval for all judgments. Everywhere the Inquisition depended on the support of local force.

Some early Inquisitors were quite harsh. Robert le Bougre, a former member of the Cathari, burned 137 people in Champagne (1239); 200 more were burned in Moissac; 200 Perfecti (members of the elite group of the Cathari), at Montségur (1244); and 50 heretics and 18 cadavers at Castelbon in Aragon. From 1227 Conrad of Marburg, a diocesan priest at Mainz, and two associates burned "countless" peasants and then turned against the nobility in a reform of the German Church, and were assassinated.

Inquisition Procedures. The conduct of an Inquisition began with a sermon exhorting aid from the faithful and repentance of heretics within a month's period of grace. Penitents were treated leniently but had to name their associates; the Inquisitors had to prove the guilt of those remaining suspect after a month. Roman and OT law required at least two witnesses for trial, but the Inquisitor could be accuser as well as judge. False witnesses were liable, as in OT, to the same penalty as was the accused; the testimony of heretics and other infamous persons was not accepted until 1261. To prevent retaliation, the accused did not know the witnesses against him until Boniface VIII ruled otherwise; but he could name his enemies, whose testimony would be stricken from the record. Rarely did witnesses appear for the accused and risk incriminating themselves. Eventually, the accused was allowed legal aid, mostly exhortations to confess by lawyers whose orthodoxy was above suspicion. The accused could reject a judge because of prejudice and at any time before sentence could appeal to Rome, which would then render the verdict. Such appeals were not rare, and Inquisitors strove to make their trials irreproachable. A permanent council of judges assisted them, and a jury of *boni viri* reviewed the cases without knowing the names of the accused; they had to decide on the reliability of the witnesses, the nature of the guilt, and the penalty. While advisory, their judgment was usually followed; any modification of their opinion was toward leniency.

Papal bulls based on the acts of provincial councils determined procedure. Inquisitors also composed manuals, the most famous being that of Bernard Gui, Inquisitor of Toulouse (1307–24). Charges were read twice to the accused, who was then asked to swear on the Bible. The list of questions varied according to the heresy. Promises of indulgence and planted informants were used to elicit confessions, which were the goal of the Inquisitor. When a person strongly suspect would not confess, constraint could be employed: prison, chains, fasting, sleeplessness, and (after 1252) torture so long as it did not mutilate or cause danger of death. It could be applied only once for one-half hour, unless new evidence appeared. The grand solemnity of torture sessions was calculated to produce confessions through terror rather than through pain. Confessions obtained through torture had to be repeated voluntarily. Most Inquisitors put little faith in torture, but some abused it. When there was no confession, the testimony of two witnesses in agreement was enough to convict, although more witnesses were usually required. Punishments for repentant heretics, imposed by the Inquisitor, were viewed as salutary penances. Those unconfessed and convicted by the testimony of witnesses were handed over to civil authorities as obstinate heretics for punishment, death at the stake. Penitents beforehand agreed to accept the sentences, from which there was no appeal. Death and life imprisonment entailed confiscation of goods, and so many posthumous trials were held. Sentences were pronounced at a solemn assembly of notables and populace (*sermo generalis*). Lesser penalties were public or private and included scourging, visits to churches, pilgrimages, wearing the cross of infamy, fines, and alms. Commutations and suspensions of penalties were frequent, as were escapes from prisons, which were the unwelcome responsibility of bishops. Ordinary imprisonment was tolerable, but solitary confinement had no regard for health. Relapsed heretics, even though repentant, were liable to death but were often spared. The death penalty was not frequent. Confiscations accrued to the king and great nobles; but unless these personages met the expenses of the Inquisition, which were heavy, a part of the confiscations went for expenses. Houses frequented by heretics were subject to demolition; but because of conflict with other interests, such as confiscation, this penalty was rarely applied.

After 1300 the power of the Inquisition was restricted, mainly because it became depenent upon episcopal approval. It lost importance as the Cathari disappeared, although Waldenses, Franciscan Spirituals, Fraticelli, Beguines, Lollards, crypto-Jews, and witches attracted its attention. Philip IV used it to destroy the Templars (1312).

The 15th-cent. decline in papal prestige caused by the Great Western Schism also hurt the Inquisition, which fell into the hands of the secular rulers. By the 16th cent. the Inquisition was generally inoperative, except in Spain and Portugal; in France it gave way to the king's authority and parliament. The Inquisition did develop objective rules that not rarely operated as protections against popular prejudice. As an institution it cannot be defended but merely explained by that social intolerance of deviations that was general in all communities and continued even long after the Reformation. See Y. Dossat, NCE 7:535–541, bibliog. *INQUISITION, SPANISH.

INQUISITION, SPANISH, the institution in Spain that followed the same procedure as the papal *Inquisition but differed in two respects from the Inquisition elsewhere: (1) royal control played a much more prominent part in it; and (2) it acted mainly against secret adherents to established religions, i.e., to Judaism (the Marranos) and to Islam (the Moriscos), who overtly professed Christianity, rather than against heresies. The medieval Inquisition was of little note in Spain. Several Inquisitors were killed; Nicholas Eymerich, an Inquisitor known for moderation, wrote a manual (1346) based on 44 years of experience. In 1478 Sixtus IV, in the interest of peace, agreed to revive the Inquisition in Spain against crypto-Jews. So strong did crypto-Judaism prove to be in Seville (1481) that the Inquisition quickly extended to Córdoba, Ciudad Real, Segovia, and Aragon. In 1483 Isabella established a tribunal of appeal under the abp. of Seville, without prejudice to Rome, and Tomás de Torquemada (d. 1498) began a 15-year career in which as Inquisitor General he established the machinery of the Spanish Inquisition. His *Instructions* (1485, 1488, 1498) were completed by Cisneros (1516) and issued in definitive text by Valdés (Toledo 1561). The Inquisitor General, an expert in theology or canon law, presided over a supreme council of seven Inquisitors that held nine sessions a week;

eight other officials, several theologians, and clerks assisted them in Madrid. Staffs also assisted particular Inquisitors in 15 Spanish, 3 Portuguese, 2 Italian, and 3 American tribunals. There was also an Inquisition of the Fleet. Until 1647 the supreme council dealt only with appeals from lower tribunals; after 1647 it had to confirm all judgments. There seems to be no way to estimate the number of sentences pronounced at Spanish *autos-da-fé, but they were fewer, it appears, than condemnations for witchcraft in the rest of Europe.

Moriscos, baptized en masse in 1499 and forced to choose between Christianity and exile in 1502, rose against the Inquisition and allied with enemies of Spain in 1568. Expelled by Philip III in 1609, they disappeared. In the era of the *Alumbrados (16th–17th cents.) there were few harsh punishments administered to those guilty of immorality. Some Protestants suffered, but the Inquisition was mainly concerned with preventing circulation of unauthorized Bibles and the works of Luther and Calvin. The Spanish Church consistently opposed ties with Protestant countries. Witchcraft was practically ignored. Under the Inquisition, Spanish authors were quite free in their choice and treatment of topics, and Spanish readers had access to almost all European philosophical and scientific literature. The era was probably the greatest in Spanish literary history.

In 1579 Philip II used the Inquisition against Antonio Pérez, but Aragonese patriots protected him in a defense of their political rights. In 1644 Philip IV prevailed over the Inquisition in the case of a seduced nun. There were few trials in the 18th century. Suppressed by Napoleon (1808) and the Cortés of Cadiz (1813), the Inquisition was restored in theory by Ferdinand VII (1814) and finally suppressed by Maria Cristina (1834).

The Inquisition came to the New World on Columbus's second voyage (1493). From Hispaniola it went to Mexico (1532) and Lima (1539). In 1569 Philip II put the New World Inquisition directly under the supreme council; permanent tribunals were established at Mexico and Lima in 1571 and at Cartagena (Colombia) in 1610. The New World Inquisition sought to control undisciplined clergy and to keep out Protestantism, Judaism, and Islam. It dealt with a few captive English and Dutch pirates but did not concern itself with the Indians. By 1650 there was not much for it to do. See Y. Dossat, NCE 7:540–541; E. Hibbert, *Spanish Inquisition* . . . (3v. in 1, 1967); D. W. Lomax, NCE 14:205, s.v. "Torquemada, Tomás de."

INSPIRATIONISTS, an early name for members of the *Amana Church Society, which was called also the Community of True Inspiration.

INSTALLATION, in its precise sense, the formal seating of a canon in his cathedral stall, symbolizing conferral of his office. The term also is used more broadly for inauguration into any ecclesiastical office: for taking "canonical possession" of a diocese by a RC bp. or of a parish by a pastor; as an Anglican term, enthronement of a bp. or induction of a rector. Lutherans, Presbyterians, Baptists, and others in the U.S. frequently call the public recognition of a new minister or church officer an installation.

INSTITUTES OF THE CHRISTIAN RELIGION, English title of the treatise by John *Calvin, the most important theological exposition of early Protestantism. It was first published in Basel in 1536; the final and definitive edition was published in Geneva in 1559. Calvin called the work "a summary of the principal truths of the Christian religion." He originally composed the treatise shortly after his own conversion to Protestantism as a statement and defense of the beliefs of the French Protestants, and he revised and enlarged it several times during the course of his life. The original version was in Latin (*Christianae religionis institutio*); revised Latin texts appeared in 1539, 1543, 1550, and 1559. Calvin's French translations of these revisions were published in 1541, 1545, 1551, and 1560. The first draft of the *Institutes* was printed by Thomas Platter in Basel, where Calvin had taken refuge after his flight from France. He was then but 26 and on the threshold of his great career. The *Institutes* introduced him to the world as a Reformer and was an immediate success. The first edition consists of six chapters that observe the order of Martin Luther's *Larger Catechism*: (1) the Ten Commandments, (2) the Creed, (3) the Lord's Prayer, (4) the sacraments of baptism and the Eucharist, (5) the other sacraments (rejected by Calvin), and (6) the theme of Christian liberty. The doctrine is largely Lutheran. The second edition was published in Strassburg in 1539, during the time Calvin lived there in temporary exile from Geneva. It is three times larger than the original text and contains, among other new material, an extended statement of the doctrine of *election or *predestination. The formulation of this tenet, so closely associated with Calvin, was greatly influenced by the Strassburg Reformer Martin *Bucer, whose tutelage during these years shaped the development of Calvin's thought. This edition, translated by Calvin into French and published in Geneva in 1541, was an important event in French literature and religious history. The final edition of the *Institutes* appeared in 1559, followed by a French translation in 1560. This definitive edition is five times the length of the 1536 edition and consists of 80 chapters divided into four books, which follow generally the topics: Father, Son, Holy Spirit, and the Church. The organization and additions render it practically a new book, the fullest statement of Calvin's biblical theology and the *Summa* of *Reformed Protestantism. The famous statement on "Eternal Election" is found in Book 3, Chapter 21; Calvin's distinctive exposition of the role of civil government, in Book 4, Chapter 20, concludes the work. The 1559 *Institutes* was soon translated into most of the languages of Europe. A Dutch version appeared in 1560, an English translation in 1561, and a German edition in 1572. The best English

edition is in the *Library of Christian Classics* (v.20–21, ed. J. T. McNeill, tr. F. L. Battles, 1960). See F. Wendel, *Calvin* (tr. P. Mairet, 1963).

INSTITUTIONAL CHURCH, a term used in two senses. (1) A description of any Church as organized with some structural form of authority, pursuing a special mission and accepting set means of sanctification and modes of worship. The Church as institutional for any or all of these reasons is often contrasted unfavorably with the "charismatic Church," i.e., the spiritual assembly or community of those living under the direct guidance and gifts of the Holy Spirit, or is regarded as an impediment to the "desacralization" or secularization required of the Church in the modern world. Disparagement or dismissal of the institutional Church is not acceptable to many of the Protestant Churches that recognize certain objective elements as constitutive of the Church established by Christ. In RC teaching, Vatican Council II taught that the visible and invisible elements are not opposed but are necessarily two aspects of one reality, the Church (Vat II ConstCh 8). (2) An instrument of the *Social Gospel movement. The term was applied to churches that also sought to be agencies for social service on behalf of the urban poor. St. George's Episcopal Church in New York City and Grace Baptist Church in Philadelphia were famous examples.

INTERCOMMUNION, a relationship between Churches in which each accepts members of the others for holy communion and authorizes its own members to receive communion from the other. It is allowed by the RC Church only with regard to Eastern Churches (cf. Vat II EastCath 26–29; Ecum 8); these Churches do not ordinarily practice it. The Anglican Communion has maintained intercommunion with Old Catholic Churches since 1932 (see BONN AGREEMENT); the *Lambeth Conference of 1968 permitted Anglicans to receive communion even in Churches not recognizing the *historic episcopate, admitted non-Anglicans to communion, and encouraged full intercommunion with Churches with which merger discussions are in progress. In Protestant Churches generally there is a wide diversity of practice, depending on the view of what constitutes a valid ministry (see OPEN COMMUNION). In the *ecumenical movement intercommunion receives two interpretations: one, that it is a means of expressing unity despite diversity; the other, that it should be practiced only when the goal of unity has been achieved.

INTERCONFESSIONALISM, movements of thought and action relating Churches that have different *confessions of faith. With the rise of the *ecumenical movement the importance of Christian unity has made it seem necessary for Christians to seek some way of securing a united witness despite their differences of doctrinal expression. This is done not by ignoring differences between the confessions but by searching for greater mutual understanding. It is seen in certain cases of *intercommunion, in ecumenical agencies, e.g., the World Council of Churches, and in interfaith dialogue. See D. Baillie and J. Marsh, eds., *Intercommunion* (1952).

INTERDENOMINATIONAL CHURCHES, a term that may designate two types of churches. (1) The *community church, which may be either federated (two or more congregations, retaining identities but sharing one minister, service, and community program) or union (people of diverse denominational backgrounds united in one congregation upon a broad Christian platform). These are sometimes loosely affiliated through the International Council of Community Churches. (2) This type is exclusive rather than inclusive. Rejecting denominational differences, this group stresses agreement in doctrinal orthodoxy (usually understood as *fundamentalism) and evangelistic interest. While adhering to

*independency, some of these churches have fellowship in the *Independent Fundamentalist Churches of America. See J. R. Howe, "Community Churches," EncRelKnowSuppl 1:278–279; Mayer RB 376–378. ANTIDENOMINATIONALISM.

INTERFAITH DIALOGUE, conversation between representatives of different communions with the aim of developing greater understanding and finding a basis for greater cooperation. It is distinguished from debate, in which representatives try to prove that the position of their communion is right and the others wrong. It proceeds from the conviction that one may learn from his partner in *dialogue, particularly that one will be enriched by mutual sharing with fellow Christians of different background and outlook. Dialogue requires a willingness to listen to representatives of other communions with the intent of gaining greater understanding, and to explain one's own point of view with candor and courtesy. It emphasizes respect for other communions, but insists that participants speak honestly about points of disagreement. Through the process of dialogue it is hoped that misunderstandings may be overcome, that the extent of basic disagreement may be clarified, and that the sense of what is held in common may be deepened. In interfaith dialogue participants speak responsibly as representatives of their communions; therefore they should have thorough knowledge of what their communions teach, and should refuse to sacrifice convictions in the interest of a superficial unity. In the *ecumenical movement various agencies, notably the World Council of Churches, have been established to further interfaith dialogue. It was commended in the Decree on Ecumenism (9) of Vatican Council II. See R. M. Brown and G. Weigel, *American Dialogue* (1960).

INTERFAITH MOVEMENTS, cooperative efforts by members of different religious communions to work for common goals. In the development of the *ecumenical movement many Christians came to desire cooperation with Christians of other Churches. In some cases this cooperation was in regard to a particular project, as in the case of Bible societies organized to promote distribution and use of the Scriptures. In other cases this cooperation was more general. Christian youth work, as in the YMCA and the World Student Christian Federation, developed largely on an interfaith basis. The ecumenical movement itself, with the development of the World Council of Churches and regional ecumenical bodies, may be considered the most important interfaith movement. Interfaith movements are based on the conviction that men who are divided on some things may nonetheless profitably cooperate on matters upon which they agree, and particularly that Christians despite their divisions share a significant body of common conviction and common concern for the welfare of the general society. Critics warn against the dangers of *indifferentism, with participants ignoring the basic distinctive elements of their Churches. *DENOMINATIONALISM; *VOLUNTARYISM.

INTERIMS, three Reformation edicts designed to achieve for the time being (*ad interim*) a religious truce in Germany. (1) Regensburg Interim (1541). Charles V terminated the fruitless reunion Conference of *Regensburg on July 29, 1541. In the document of recess, over the objection of Card. Contarini, papal legate, the Emperor Charles V deferred doctrinal settlement to a national council in Germany. To win the Protestant princes to help him in his war against the Turks, Charles also granted them freedom in the interpretation of disputed doctrines, the right to receive Protestants into their territories from others, and guaranteed to the princes the church property they had secularized.

(2) Augsburg Interim (1548). The formula of this truce, approved by the Diet of Augsburg, was a crucial issue in the Reformation. The document was prepared by Protestant and Catholic theologians. On the main points of justification, the nature of the Church, and the sacraments, it imposed Catholic interpretations. To the Protestants it conceded the points of a married clergy and communion under both kinds. It also guaranteed secularized church property to the Protestant princes. Most of the Protestant princes refused to sign. In Rome, Paul III gave reluctant approval only in Aug. 1549. Since the Interim was to be imposed, many of the Reformation leaders had to flee from their pastorates; the South German cities resisted vigorously; M. *Bucer departed from Strassburg for England. Among the Lutherans, there was strong reaction to the doctrinal implications, esp. by N. *Amsdorf and M. *Flacius Illyricus. P. Melanchthon was blamed for compromising Luther's teaching (see GNESIOLUTHERANISM).

(3) Leipzig Interim (1549). This was an effort to ease the resumption of some RC rites by Protestants. It was drawn up by Maurice of Saxony, Melanchthon, and George II of Anhalt-Dessau. Some RC ceremonies were classified as *adiaphora, neither good nor bad in themselves, and thus permissible. The document led to further bitter controversy (see ADIAPHORISTS). Only in the Duchy of Saxony was there any acceptance. See B. J. Kidd, ed., *Documents Illustrative of the Continental Reformation* (1911), 340–346 (Regensburg) and 359–362 (Augsburg); H. Holborn, *History of Modern Germany* (2v., 1959), v.1, *Reformation*; Léonard HistProt 1:260–262.

INTERNATIONAL ASSOCIATION FOR LIBERAL CHRISTIANITY and Religious Freedom (IARF), an organization founded at Saint-Gall, Switzerland, in 1932 for the purpose of promoting communication and fellowship among liberals of all religious beliefs. The organization in its present form developed from an earlier international council founded by Unitarians in Boston in 1900, which held congresses with delegates from as many as 30 nations, including liberal Moslems and Hindus as well as Jews,

Catholics, and Protestants. The movement declined as the liberalism of the early years of the century passed its peak, but was revitalized by the revival of humanism in the decade preceding World War II. The IARF permanent secretariat, established in The Hague in the 1930s, suspended activity when The Netherlands was overrun by Germany early in the war but resumed afterward, and the first postwar international congress was held in Amsterdam in 1949. The IARF, while maintaining its distinctively humanist approach, reflects the tendencies of European Christian theology, with emphasis on Scripture and on the one Church. The influence of its American heritage is seen in its stress on ethics, brotherhood, and "practical Christianity" as its basic principles. See W. Gaade, *IARF and Its Vision* (1955).

INTERNATIONAL CHURCH OF THE FOURSQUARE GOSPEL, Pentecostal denomination growing out of the evangelistic work of Aimee Semple *McPherson and incorporated in Los Angeles in 1927. The Canadian-born evangelist served as a missionary in Hong Kong and as a tent revivalist before arriving in Los Angeles in 1918. There she built Angelus Temple and founded a Bible college and a radio station. Once widowed and twice divorced, Mrs. McPherson received widespread notoriety in the 1920s and 1930s, most of which she was able to turn to the promotion of her cause. When she died in 1944 her son Rolf assumed leadership of the Church. *Divine healing has been emphasized by the International Church of the Foursquare Gospel, as has the *baptism of the Holy Spirit, Christ's second coming, and speaking in tongues (see GLOSSOLALIA). All members of the Church must subscribe to the fundamentalist Declaration of Faith composed by Mrs. McPherson. Each congregation makes a monthly offering for home and foreign missions. This Church supports 961 missionaries and native pastors in 1,300 mission stations in 27 countries. It also operates 18 day schools, 20 Bible schools, and 3 orphanages. In the U.S. there were in 1968 about 89,000 members in 741 congregations; worldwide membership was about 218,000. Rolf McPherson holds the lifetime position of president of the Church, but other officers are elected by delegates to the annual convention. An eight-member board of directors governs the Church and appoints field supervisors in charge of ten districts. Ministers are trained at the Lighthouse of International Foursquare Evangelism (LIFE) Bible College in Los Angeles, which has graduated more than 5,000 men and women.

INTERNATIONAL CONGREGATIONAL COUNCIL, a world gathering of Congregational representatives. The first such meeting was held in London in 1891. Subsequent meetings were held alternately in the U.S. and Great Britain at intervals of about 10 years. The meetings were essentially for inspiration, the exchange of ideas, and the strengthening of Congregationalism. No permanent organization was established. In 1948, however, a representative organization was formed, a secretary appointed, and an office opened in London. To the initial membership of 15 Churches, others were added later. The total individual membership of the Churches never exceeded 2½ million. After 1948 meetings were held every 5 years. The council never became an authoritative body but worked through studies, exchanges, and publications as well as through meetings. After negotiations covering some years it was decided in 1968 that the council should merge in 1970 with the World Alliance of Reformed Churches.

INTERNATIONAL COUNCIL OF CHRISTIAN CHURCHES (ICCC), an organization founded at Amsterdam, The Netherlands, in August 1948, as a conservative counterpoise to the *World Council of Churches. Carl McIntire, former minister of the Presbyterian Church in the U.S. who was deposed in 1936 after being found guilty of "violation of his ordination vows" and other charges, has been president from the beginning, and was reelected at the Seventh Plenary Congress in 1968. The ICCC reported 61 Protestant evangelical Churches of 29 countries at its founding, and 116 constituent and 60 affiliated members in 1968. The number of persons represented by these Churches is unknown, but none of the larger Churches is included in the Council. ICCC headquarters are in Amsterdam, and an American office is maintained at Collingswood, N.J.; the official publication is the *Reformation Review,* a quarterly. Major emphasis of the ICCC has been opposition to the World Council of Churches, which it has charged with theological error in failing to uphold biblical infallibility and other emphases of *fundamentalism, with communist influence on the part of churchmen from communist countries and some church leaders in the West, and with betrayal of Protestantism through acceptance of Orthodox Churches and cooperation with the RC Church.

INTERNATIONAL COUNCIL OF COMMUNITY CHURCHES, an organization formed at Lake Forest, Ill., in 1950, from two earlier bodies, the National Council and the Biennial Council of Community Churches. The Council does not exercise jurisdiction but provides fellowship and a channel of missionary outreach for *community churches in the United States. Headquarters are at Columbus, Ohio; only about 10% of the community churches in the U.S. are members.

INTERNATIONAL GENERAL ASSEMBLY OF SPIRITUALISTS, an alliance of Spiritualist churches throughout the world, formed in 1936 at Buffalo, N.Y., to foster cooperation among Spiritualist bodies. It was an outgrowth of the General Assembly of Spiritualists in New York. The purpose of the International General Assembly is primarily to see that newly formed churches meet the standards of the Spiritualist movement. Individual congregations

are chartered by the International General Assembly and affiliated with it in a loose alliance. Local churches are congregationally governed and reluctant to surrender their independence to a central body. Since Spiritualist churches are frequently gathered by an individual and disintegrate when their leader dies or moves elsewhere, the International General Assembly provides a continuity and cohesiveness for the movement and a minimum standard for its clergy. In 1968 the International General Assembly reported 84 member churches in the U.S., with an aggregate membership of 16,000; headquarters are in Norfolk, Virginia. It is the largest Spiritualist body in the U.S.

INTERNATIONAL MISSIONARY COUNCIL (IMC; 1921–61), an organization of Protestant national missionary organizations and Christian councils designed to facilitate the presentation of the gospel to non-Christian peoples through the development of coordinated activities, common· study and consultation, and united action. The historical background of the IMC was the rise of Protestant missions in the 19th cent. with the consequent increase in problems of duplicated and splintered efforts on the part of disunited denominations. Six Anglo-American Conferences (1854–1900) called to deal with the situation preceded the 1910 World Missionary Conference held in Edinburgh, which in turn led directly to the formation of the IMC at Mohonk Lake, N.Y., in 1921 (see EDINBURGH CONFERENCES). The IMC, through its creation of a global network of national Christian councils, its stimulation to cooperative activities in the mission field, and its meetings (Jerusalem 1928; Madras 1938; Whitby, Ontario, 1947; Willigen, Ger., 1952; Ghana 1958), substantially prepared the way for the establishment of the World Council of Churches. In 1961 at New Delhi, the IMC formally joined the World Council, becoming the Division of World Mission and Evangelism. See W. R. Hogg, *Ecumenical Foundations* (1952).

INTERNATIONAL PENTECOSTAL AS-SEMBLIES, a body formed in 1936 by the Union of the Association of Pentecostal Assemblies (1921) and the National and International Pentecostal Missionary Union (1914). A teaching distinctive of this body within Pentecostalism is opposition to all war. A strong missionary program is maintained in Kenya and Mexico. Headquarters are in Atlanta, Ga.; membership (1968) was 7,500. See J. T. Nichol, *Pentecostalism* (1966), 143–144.

INTERNATIONAL SOCIETY OF CHRISTIAN ENDEAVOR, see CHRISTIAN ENDEAVOR, INTERNATIONAL SOCIETY OF.

INTINCTION (Lat. *intingere*, dip in), method of administering holy *communion under both kinds simultaneously. Either the consecrated hosts are simply dipped into the chalice, or they are dropped in and a spoon is used to give them to the communicants. The practice is known to have existed in the East from the 7th cent. and became widespread by the 9th; it continues there esp. with the use of the spoon. In the West intinction was practiced from the 7th to the 12th century. There was objection to it, e.g., by the Council of Braga in Spain (689) and by Pope Paschal II (1099–1188), on the grounds that it did not conform to Christ's action at the Last Supper. It seems to have been practiced chiefly in giving communion to the sick. As communion under both kinds ceased in the West, so did intinction. In the modern RC restoration of communion under both kinds, the two are received separately.

INVARIATA (*Confessio Augustana invariata*), the version of the *Augsburg Confession (1530) prepared for the *Book of Concord (1580). It is designated as "Unaltered" in relation to the *Variata, the revision of the Confession prepared by Melanchthon in 1540. This revision included expressions on the *Real Presence conciliatory to the Swiss *Reformed Churches but unacceptable to most Lutherans. The Invariata is the text accepted as the chief Lutheran *confession of faith. This version differs in minor points from the 1530 text of the Confession. See F. Bente, *Historical Introduction to the Book of Concord* (1959), 15–28.

INVASATI, a sect, probably related to the *Turlupians, that arose in Germany and spread into France during the 14th century. Adherents engaged in obscene dances while invoking the demons. For these practices and for their *antinomianism they were condemned by Gregory XI in 1373.

INVISIBLE CHURCH, a description intended to designate the true Church, a spiritual, eschatological community, as a reality distinct from the visible Church, an empirical, imperfect, organized institution. Modern RC rejection of this distinction appears in the theme, repeated in documents from Pius IX's *Syllabus of Errors* to Pius XII's *Mystici corporis*, that the Church is essentially a visible society. The *Constitution on the Church* of Vatican Council II holds that the visible and invisible are two aspects of the one reality, that there is a necessary and objective, not merely a psychological, relationship between spiritual discipleship and visible communion. Accordingly, in the visible structure of the RC Church the true mystical body of Christ achieves its fullest realization on earth; through these structures the body is drawn into closer union with the risen Savior. The Church also insists that visible communion without interior adherence is of no avail; that many elements, interior as well as visible, of its own reality are found in persons and Churches not in communion with it. The Council speaks of a dynamic tendency of all Christians toward a visible unity, the achievement of which, however, may be eschatological (Vat II ConstCh 8, 9, 14, 18, 23;

Ecum 3). John *Wycliffe and Jan *Hus, in their dissatisfaction with the conditions of the contemporary Church, proposed the idea of an invisible Church, known only to God, and rejected the Church as a hierarchical institution. The Reformers believed in the "holy, catholic church" of the creeds but did not equate it with a particular organization. Martin Luther held that the true Church is invisible, known only by faith; not wishing to reduce the Church to a Platonic idea, however, he taught that the invisible aspects of the one Church are hidden in its visible aspects. In keeping with his doctrine on predestination, John Calvin defined the invisible Church as "the true members of Christ sanctified by the Holy Spirit"; this Church of the elect was an indiscernible object of faith. The visible Church was a society of those who accepted the Scriptures, partook of the sacraments, and led godly lives; Calvin's system of discipline was meant to detect some of the more obvious nonelect. The *Thirty-Nine Articles of the C of E made no mention of the invisible Church, but the definition of the visible Church as a "congregation of faithful men" implied the idea of an invisible Church. The miscellaneous Anabaptist groups did not all use the actual terms visible and invisible, but most of them did insist that true Churches must restore the faith and practice of the primitive Church and must restrict membership to professing Christians. Many stressed individual experience and attached little importance to organization.

The Puritans, with rigid logic, sought to make the visible Church correspond in membership to the true, invisible Church. The terms visible and invisible appeared in the Presbyterians' *Westminster Confession the Congregationalists' *Savoy Declaration, the General Baptists' *Orthodox Creed, and the Particular Baptists' *Second London Confession. For Congregationalists and Baptists the distinction was basic to the *gathered church principle. Affirming belief in the "holy, catholic church," they held that it was invisible; the visible Church was a congregation of visible saints.

In the 18th cent. the emphasis of the evangelical revivals upon subjective experience further weakened objective institutional authority. The Church was thought to be the total number of saved people, mingled in many denominations. Since religion was personal, individual, and spiritual, the Churches were simply of instrumental value for winning people to Christ and nurturing them. In the 19th and 20th cents. the tradition of *liberal theology in the U.S. spread the idea of a universal Church, which was made up of those who lived practical Christian lives, but was invisible, not an organization. A consequence of this viewpoint, which was quite general among evangelical Christians in the U.S., has been a certain reluctance, e.g., among Baptists and others related to this tradition, to be interested in any organized ecumenical movement; since spiritual unity is all that is necessary or desirable, they see no point in seeking organic union of Churches. Contemporary theologians generally avoid the terms visible and invisible, but some of them have views that seem similar. For Karl *Barth, e.g., the true Church cannot be seen, but the word of God quickens men in the visible Church, where the word of Scriptures is read and preached. Although Barth emphasized the oneness of the Church, he did not urge all Christians to unite in a single institution. Emil *Brunner did not find the terms visible and invisible useful, but his sharp distinction between the *ecclesia as a fellowship of persons in Christ and the Church as an institution seems an echo of these ideas; the ecclesia, the true Church, can never be identified with any specific Church. Paul *Tillich referred to a "latent" and a "manifest" Church and judged that one can belong to the former without ever being connected with any outward organized Church. See P. Althaus, *Theology of M. Luther* (1966); K. Barth, *Church Dogmatics* (IV/2, 1958); E. Brunner, *Misunderstanding of the Church* (1953); J. Calvin, *Institutes of the Christian Religion* (ed. J. T. NcNeill, tr. F. L. Battles, 1960); R. N. Flew, ed., *Nature of the Church* (1952); F. Littell, *Anabaptist Concept of the*

Church (2d ed., 1958); A. H. Strong, *Systematic Theology* (v.3, 1909); P. Tillich, *Systematic Theology* (v.3, 1963); C. W. Williams, *John Wesley's Theology Today* (1960); H. F. Woodhouse, *Doctrine of the Church in the Anglican Reformers* (1954). *UNITY OF THE CHURCH.

IONA COMMUNITY, a community of clergy and laymen, married and unmarried, established in 1938 by G. MacLeod, a minister of the Church of Scotland, with which the community is associated. It has restored the monastic buildings at Iona, an island famous for its association with St. Columba, and sponsors programs there for visitors. It also maintains a Community House in Glasgow and its headquarters in Edinburgh. Members commit themselves to an economic and devotional discipline and meet periodically at Iona and elsewhere to further their community life. Concerns of the community include world peace, the healing ministry of the Church, and the renewal of church life in industrial areas. It currently has about 150 members and 600 associates. In 1967 MacLeod was succeeded as leader by I. Reid. See T. Morton, *Iona Community Story* (1957).

IRELAND, CHURCH OF, see CHURCH OF IRELAND.

IRENICISM (Irenics; Gr. *eirēnē*, peace), an attitude or approach seeking peaceful or conciliatory resolution of theological differences for the sake of Christian unity; the opposite of polemics or *polemical theology. A false irenicism is tantamount to indifferentism and is generally rejected as ultimately harmful to the ecumenical movement. Genuine irenicism includes more than an emphasis on points of agreement, or on separation of essentials from nonessentials of belief; it also seeks in mutual understanding and charity to discover beyond controversial associations or con-notations the true meaning intended in points of doctrine.*ECUMENISM.

IRISH ARTICLES, a "rule of public doctrine" formulated by the first convocation of Protestant clergy in Ireland (Dublin, 1615). The principal author is thought to have been James Ussher (1581–1656), later (1625) abp. of Armagh. The 104 articles under 19 titles express rigid *Calvinism, and Puritan Sabbatarianism; they do not mention the need for ordination by a bishop. The Articles were supplanted as a *confession of faith when in 1635 the *Thirty-Nine Articles were adopted. The chief interest of the Irish Articles is that they served as a model for the *Westminster Confession. See Schaff Creeds 1:662–665; 3:526–544.

IRRESISTIBLE GRACE, a formula to express the power of divine grace to bring about man's conversion. The idea is found in St. *Augustine, who speaks of grace acting *indeclinabiliter et insuperabiliter*, i.e., as excluding the possibility of man's refusal impeding its effect; such effectiveness is attributed to grace because of fallen man's need to be protected against the defectiveness of his own free choices (*liberum arbitrium*). The actual phrase "irresistible grace" is historically associated with *Calvinism and the teaching that grace has its source in the absolutely sovereign will of God. The Synod of *Dort reaffirmed the irresistibility of grace against *Arminianism. Appealing to St. Augustine, *Jansenism included the view that grace interiorly necessitates man's consent.

IRVING, EDWARD (1792–1834), Scottish Presbyterian minister, whose ideas strongly influenced the beginnings of the *Catholic Apostolic Church. First a student at the Univ. of Edinburgh and then a schoolmaster, I. became a preacher in the Church of Scotland in 1815 and worked among the poor. He received an appointment to a small Presbyterian chapel in London in

1822, became interested in *millenarianism, and published *The Coming of the Messiah in Glory and Majesty* (1827), a translation of a Spanish work. He also was an advocate of *glossolalia, *divine healing, and *baptism with the Holy Spirit, and is regarded by some to have been a forerunner of Pentecostalism. Because of the revivalistic outbursts in his chapel and a book in which he claimed Christ had a sinful nature, I. lost his place in the Presbyterian Church (1832). He had, however, received a welcome in the prayer circle at the home of Henry Drummond (1786–1860), where interest in recapturing the spirit of the primitive Church made the members responsive to I.'s preaching. His ideas on Christ's second coming, the restoration of a college of Twelve Apostles, and a new outpouring of charismatic gifts, led to the formation of the Catholic Apostolic Church. Members were often called Irvingites by outsiders. I. himself, however, never received high rank in the Catholic Apostolic Church. See A. L. Drummond, *E. I. and His Circle* (1937).

IRVINGITES, a name for members of the Catholic Apostolic Church. They disapprove of this name, which was given them because of the prominence of E. *Irving in the establishment of their Church.

ISRAELITE HOUSE OF DAVID, see HOUSE OF DAVID.

ITINERANCY, the system characteristic of early Methodism whereby preachers were frequently transferred from one station to another and never allowed to remain in one *charge for more than a year. The term referred secondarily to the custom of appointing a preacher to serve a group of *societies or *circuit over which he presided by "itinerating," i.e., traveling among them. Itinerancy was in sharp contrast to the system practiced in the C of E, where a priest often served only one parish throughout his lifetime. John *Wesley began the system when he and his colleagues, as missionaries in Georgia, established their headquarters both at Frederica and Savannah, exchanging places with one another at frequent intervals. He continued the practice in England, and he defended it in a letter to Samuel Walker, Vicar of Truro (1756). He stated that should his preachers remain for too great a time in one place, "they will 'ere long grow dead themselves, and so will most of those that hear them. I know, were I myself to preach one whole year in one place, I should preach both myself and most of my congregation asleep. . . . We have found . . . that a frequent change of teachers is best. . . . No one whom I ever yet knew has all the talents which are needful for beginning, continuing and perfecting the work of grace in a whole congregation." The system was also used in early American Methodism. While it is no longer mandatory that a minister transfer from one church to another after a stated time, Methodists still tend to "move" more often than preachers in other denominations. Furthermore, in most Methodist bodies every preacher's assignment is for one year only, although he may be reassigned to the same place year after year. Other Protestants also speak of traveling preachers or evangelists as "itinerating."

IUS CIRCA SACRA, in the terminology of natural-right jurists in Germany (e.g., H. Grotius), the sovereign power of the State over religious organizations. What had previously been regarded as the duty of the Christian prince became a right inherent in the power of the State. Included were church legislation, appointment to ecclesiastical offices, discipline, and administration of church finances. The *ius circa sacra* tended to make civil functionaries of church officers and to subordinate religion to politics. The *ius in sacra* was a contrasting concept. See J. Hachel, "Cura religionis, Ius circa sacra, Ius in sacra," *Festschrift Ulrich Stutz* (1938); A. L. Drummond, *German Protestantism since Luther* (1951).

IUS DEVOLUTUM, a law in the Church of Scotland according to which the *presbytery must take steps to appoint a minister to a vacant charge when the time limit for the congregation to elect its minister (6 months, with extension to 9 at most in exceptional circumstances) has expired.

IUS IN SACRA, the right of the Church over its own affairs. It was first called *ius in ecclesiastica* by 17th-cent. Protestant theologians in Germany (J. Gerhard, D. Pareus) who sought to defend the spiritual autonomy of the Church. The contrasting concept was the *ius circa sacra.*

J

JACOBELLUS (James of Mies; 1372–1429), colleague of Jan *Hus, who from 1414 onward, in teaching and practice, advanced the theory that communion under both kinds is necessary for salvation (see UTRAQUISTS).

JANSEN, CORNELIUS OTTO (Jansenius; 1585–1638), Dutch theologian and bishop, from whom *Jansenism received its name and doctrine. Born at Accoi in Holland, he was aided by benefactors to study at the Univ. of Louvain, winning first honors in 1604. From Jacques Jansson he imbibed the "positivism" of Baius (see BAIANISM), as well as a contempt for scholasticism and for the Jesuits. In France he studied the early Fathers and councils with Jean Duvergier de Hauranne, later the Abbé de *Saint-Cyran. J. was ordained in 1614. He became bachelor of theology in 1609 and doctor in 1619. As professor of exegesis at Louvain and director of Sainte-Pulchérie Seminary (1619–21), he studied St. Augustine's teachings on grace and found Baianist allies in Saint-Cyran and Florent Conry, an Irish Franciscan. J. corresponded with Saint-Cyran in elaborate codes about "Pilmot," their ambitious and mysterious project of radically reforming the Church from laxity and rationalism. At the court and universities of Spain in 1624 and 1626, J. thwarted expansion of Jesuit education in Louvain. As Regius Professor of Scripture after 1630, he stressed literal exegesis and patristic teaching; he also undertook anti-Protestant polemics. Named rector of Louvain in 1635, he developed its library and archives. His pamphlet *Mars gallicus* attacked the policies of the French king and Richelieu, and Protestant alliances. Rewarded as a loyal scribe of his Spanish sovereign, J. was consecrated bp. of Ypres in 1636. Meanwhile his work *Augustinus*, begun in 1627, proceeded with interruptions. Viewing Augustine's doctrine as the last word on nature and grace, J. adopted Baius's interpretations, already condemned by Pius V and Gregory XIII. He completed his revisions in April 1638 and died peacefully on May 6, apparently of plague. His will entrusted publication to friends, who achieved it secretly on July 19, 1640; the papal internuncio Stravius obtained a prohibition from Urban VIII just too late. Louvain's faculty declined to condemn *Augustinus*, and the three ponderous Latin folios sold widely among Catholic and Calvinist clergy. They were reprinted in Paris and Rouen (with Conry's treatise consigning unbaptized infants to hell appended). A long controversy between Jansenists and Jesuits ensued. Dying after 18 months as bp., J. had said, "If the Holy See wishes any change, I am an obedient son of the Church." He was remembered as pious, austere, learned and eloquent, a tireless worker devoted to the Church, rather cold and inflexible but with a lofty sense of duty. See F. Mourret, *History of the Catholic Church* (tr. N. Thompson, 8v., 1931–57), 6:362–389; H. Daniel-Rops, *The Church in the Seventeenth Century* (tr. J. J. Buckingham, 1963), 327–346; E. J. Fortman, ed., *The Theology of Man and Grace* (1966), 271–284; J. Orcibal, *Origines du Jansénisme* (1947); J. Carreyre, DTC 8.1:319–330.

JANSENISM, a religious movement chiefly among 17th- and 18th-cent. French intellectuals, originating with a distinctive doctrine on grace, but developing also into an adherence to *Gallicanism and moral rigorism. It lasted beyond 1800 and is survived by a small schismatic Jansenist Church founded in Holland in 1723 (see LITTLE CHURCH OF UTRECHT). Its name and doctrine derive from Cornelius *Jansen; its organization, from Jean Duvergier de Hauranne, Abbé de *Saint-Cyran. These friends, after studying the Church Fathers, developed an ambitious project to reform the Church from rationalism and laxity. Jansen, as professor of Scripture at Louvain, produced *Augustinus*, a study of St. Augustine's doctrine on grace, posthumously published in 1640. He taught that: (1) divine grace is man's by right; (2) its loss through original sin has mutilated man's very nature; (3) fallen man's will no longer controls his decisions but necessarily obeys the stronger attraction, either of *concupiscence or of grace; (4) all acts of sinners are sins; (5) salvation and damnation depend on God's eternal predestination alone; and (6) Christ died not for all but for the predestined few. Jansen thus systematized *Baianism, which had already been censured in 1567 and 1579 (see D 1901–80); consequently, Urban VIII formally condemned *Augustinus* in the bull *In eminenti*, 1643. Meanwhile Saint-Cyran organized support for Jansen's doctrine, aided by the influential *Arnauld family. Mère Angélique Arnauld was the reforming abbess of *Port-Royal convent near Paris, where Saint-Cyran became director in 1635 and established the center of Jansenism. Suspicious of Port-Royal and resentful of Saint-Cyran's refusal to rebut the anti-Richelieu pamphlet *Mars gallicus* (actually Jansen's work), Richelieu imprisoned Saint-Cyran, 1638–42. Freed at the cardinal's death, Saint-Cyran died in 1643.

Jansenism might have died with him, but Antoine Arnauld became a second founder, defending *Augustinus* and counterattacking with *De la fréquente communion* (1642), in which he teaches that, since no one is worthy to receive Christ, respectful abstention honors him more than frequent communion does. Furthermore, absolution requires perfect contrition and should be withheld pending severe penances. Arnauld's attack on Jesuit casuistry shifted the controversy from grace to morality. But Innocent X convoked a commission of cardinals to study a résumé of doctrine in five questionable propositions attributed to *Augustinus* and condemned all five in *Cum occasione*, 1653. Arnauld devised his famous distinction between *droit* and *fait*, admitting the condemnation of the propositions as heretical but denying

that they in fact reflected Jansen's thought. Alexander VII, however, with *Ad sanctam beati Petri sedem*, 1656, explicitly reaffirmed this fact. Required to accept this censure, the nuns of Port-Royal quibbled and protested, and finally 12 were dispersed to other convents. Blaise *Pascal, brother of one of the nuns, produced in 1656 his classic epistolary series, the *Provincial Letters, which deride Jesuit probabilism. Read everywhere, they were condemned by the Holy Office and ordered burned by Louis XIV, but they popularized Jansenist ideas. The sensational cure of Pascal's niece furthered the movement, and Jesuit rebuttals fell on deaf ears. After the *Peace of the Church under Clement IX in 1669, Jansenist influence grew in the Sorbonne and in the seminaries and spread abroad. The party published Pascal's *Pensées*, a French Bible, numerous impressive textbooks, and a voluminous assault on Jesuit moral doctrine. But as Port-Royal continued loudly recalcitrant, in 1679 a new abp. forbade receiving novices, and thus the community declined. In 1709 Louis XIV dispersed the score of nuns remaining and 2 years later razed the convent. Louis saw the Jansenists as heretics and rebels, hence Arnauld's persistent polemic led to his exile in the Netherlands, where he died in 1694.

Arnauld's companion and successor, Pasquier *Quesnel, reorganized Jansenism, emphasizing Gallicanism and moral austerity. His *Réflexions morales* expounded a Protestant view of the Church, and in 1713 Clement XI in *Unigenitus proscribed 101 propositions verbatim (see D 2400–2502), whereupon nine Jansenist bishops held that the Pope had erred in faith. Rigorist, Gallican Jansenism thrived on the subsequent pamphlet war and won temporary favor from the regent Philip of Orléans after Louis's death. In 1717 four bps. appealed from *Unigenitus* to an ecumenical council; though these *Appellants enlisted a dozen bishops and 3,000 of the 100,000 French clergy, they were excommunicated. Compromise failed and a decade of exiles and imprisonments ensued.

In Paris Abp. Vintimille, successor to

the vacillating Noailles, had *Unigenitus* made law and exacted acceptance by the Sorbonne, Parlement, dioceses, and religious communities. As convinced Appellants died out and no new leaders appeared, moribund Jansenism lapsed further into bigotry and gloom. The journal *Nouvelles ecclésiastiques* sustained its martyr mentality, 1728–1803, recounting marvels such as those claimed by the *convulsionaries of Saint-Médard. Jansenism was dogmatic under Saint-Cyran, moralistic with Arnauld, political after Quesnel, and anti-Jesuit first to last. A moral Puritanism and the infrequent reception of holy communion were effects on RC life that lingered into the 20th century. See N. Abercrombie, *Origins of Jansenism* (1936); J. Orcibal, *Origines du jansénisme* (1947); A. Gazier, *Histoire générale du mouvement janséniste* (1922); R. Knox, *Enthusiasm* (1950); DTC, *Tables générales* 2:2387–2415; L. J. Cognet, NCE 7:820–824. *PISTOIA, SYNOD OF.

JANSENIST CHURCH OF HOLLAND, a commonly used name for the *Little Church of Utrecht (OBC), also called the Old Catholic Church of the Netherlands. In 1889 it became an Old Catholic body, but its beginnings date from the 18th-cent. Schism of Utrecht, a separation from Rome partly over *Jansenism.

JARRATT, DEVEREAUX (1733–1801), first C of E, then Protestant Episcopal, rector of Bath, Va., from 1763 until his death. His parents belonged to the class of small landowners, sometimes called yeomen, who were held to rank socially between the great planters and the landless populace. Though his opportunities for education were limited, J. succeeded in acquiring enough learning to become a schoolmaster and, eventually, to obtain ordination in the Established Church. As the C of E had no bps. in the colonies, he had to go to England for orders. He was ordained deacon and priest by the bp. of London in 1762 and on his return to Va. was chosen rector of

Bath. His religious awakening had occurred under the influence of Presbyterians who had been converted in the *Great Awakening, and his preaching retained a revivalistic flavor. When Methodist preachers appeared in the colony on the eve of the Revolution, he encouraged them but opposed their separation from the Anglican Church. He supported the Revolution, but with well-controlled enthusiasm, for, while he favored separation from the mother country, he disliked the "leveling" tendencies that accompanied it. In addition to his autobiography, *The Life of the Reverend Devereaux Jarratt* (1806), he published *Sermons on Various and Important Subjects in Practical Divinity* (3v., 1795).

JEDNOTA BRATRSKA, Czech name for the *Unitas Fratrum, also known as the *Bohemian Brethren, later to become the Moravian Church.

JEHOVAH'S WITNESSES, religious body that traces its beginning to the *millenarianism of Charles Taze *Russell. Russell was succeeded by Joseph F. *Rutherford, who devised new missionary techniques that have helped this movement to grow from 50,000 in 1938 to worldwide membership of more than 1 million in 1969. Until 1931 adherents of the movement were known as Watch Tower People, Millennial Dawnists, Earnest Bible Students, and Russellites, but Rutherford gave them the name Jehovah's Witnesses. Present head of the legal corporation, the Watch Tower Bible and Tract Society, is Nathan H. Knorr (1905–). As their central doctrine the Witnesses have their own form of millenarianism. The present world is the reign of Satan and his tools—government, business, and organized religion—in conflict against the theocratic rule of Jehovah. All men have mortal souls, but they will be recreated and given a second chance at salvation during the millennium. Those who reject it by wickedness will be annihilated; the just will reign everlastingly in this renewed world. Christ and the 144,000 elect alone have immortal souls, as a reward for their obedience to Jehovah, and reign as spiritual creatures in heaven, not on this earth. The task of the Jehovah's Witnesses is to announce the second coming of Christ, which will be marked by the Battle of Armageddon, in which Satan and his allies will be defeated. Witnesses declare that the doctrine of the Trinity is a pagan addition to Christianity. Their Christology is vague but resembles a crude Arianism. They teach that Jesus did not rise from the dead in his physical body but as a spirit creature subordinate to Jehovah.

All baptized members, including children and women, are considered ordained ministers. An active witness will attend three or four meetings a week at which the Bible and Watch Tower materials are studied. The sect schedules only one communion service a year, on Nisan 14; only those who consider themselves to be among the 144,000 elect may partake of the bread and wine. In 1966 1,971,107 people attended this memorial service, but only 11,179 actually received communion. Witnesses consider themselves to be citizens of a theocracy and therefore refuse to serve in the armed forces of any nation, salute the flag, vote, or hold political office. They are willing, however, to pay taxes. Their refusal to allow blood transfusions, because they are believed to be forbidden by the Bible, have brought them into conflict with the law. Avoidance of the secular world characterizes the committed Witness. He is encouraged to find fellowship in the congregations that meet in Kingdom Halls. Witnesses may not celebrate feasts such as Christmas and Easter. They abstain from active participation in labor unions, lodges, or secular organizations. Smoking, drinking, dancing, and card playing are discouraged but not flatly forbidden. After providing a decent living for themselves and their families, Witnesses are asked to turn over the excess of their income to the Watch Tower Society.

Each member is expected to devote at least 10 hours a month to door-to-door mis-sionary work; some sell copies of the Society's publications on street corners. About 35,000 "pioneers" devote their full time to missionary efforts around the world. There are 1,500 men and women who work at Bethel headquarters in Brooklyn, N.Y., and at other centers. They set type, print, and bind the books and magazines, write, and handle correspondence. The Watch Tower Society has always relied heavily on the printed word. The *Watch Tower* magazine reports a circulation of 4,950,000; and its companion, *Awake!*, 4,550,000. Thus they have the widest circulation among all religious periodicals published in the U.S. The Witnesses also publish books, tracts, and copies of their own New World translation of the Bible. This edition is edited and annotated according to their beliefs.

During the 1930s and 1940s the sect grew as much as 25% a year, but this has leveled off to about 3% a year. About 305,000 Witnesses live in the United States. Large concentrations are also found in West Germany, Canada, Nigeria, the Philippines, Mexico, Zambia, the British Isles, and Brazil. They are banned in Iron Curtain countries. Many thousands attend meetings in Kingdom Halls, read the Society's literature, and attend Bible classes, but have not been baptized and are not recorded on membership rolls. Members have usually come from the lower socioeconomic class, but as the movement has evolved more members have risen to a higher social and educational level. In the U.S. the Witnesses have made a special effort to attract Negroes, Spanish-Americans, and members of other minority groups. Their proselytizing techniques have become noticeably less aggressive in recent years. See R. Pyke, *Jehovah's Witnesses* (1954); W. J. Whalen, *Armageddon around the Corner* (1962); W. C. Stevenson, *Inside Story of Jehovah's Witnesses* (1968).

JEROME OF PRAGUE (1380–1460), friend and lay collaborator of Jan *Hus. At Prague, while a student of Hus, and later at Oxford, J. pursued an interest in the philosophical and theological teachings of John *Wycliffe. He brought Wycliffe's writings back to Prague *(c.*1401) and became a violent proponent of Hus's reform ideas in Prague, Hungary, and Austria. He went to the Council of *Constance to defend Hus, was himself arrested in 1415, and after an initial abjuration of errors, again became suspect. He thereupon renounced his first recantation and was burned at the stake as a relapsed heretic. See Bihlmeyer-Tüchle 2:440.

JESUS ONLY, the slogan and name of a movement within early American Pentecostalism. The first phrase of the movement occurred in 1913 during a Pentecostal camp meeting in Calif.; many of those in attendance claimed a new insight into the power of Jesus' name and, citing Acts 2.38 and Jn 3.5, asserted that baptism must be administered only in the name of Jesus, not of the Father, Son, and Holy Spirit. A further development soon led to the teaching that, in the Godhead of Father, Son, and Holy Spirit, only Jesus is truly a person. The teaching came to be called the New Issue and split Pentecostal ranks, esp. in the Assemblies of God. The Pentecostal Assemblies of the World started as a unitarian, or Jesus Only, group. See J. T. Nichol, *Pentecostalism* (1966), 89–91.

JEWEL, JOHN (1522–71), Anglican apologist and bp. of Salisbury. At Oxford J. achieved some prominence as an intellectual leader in the reforming party. Under Queen Mary he went into exile and became closely associated with *Peter Martyr Vermigli in Strassburg and Zurich. In 1560 Elizabeth appointed him to the See of Salisbury. He was active in the defense of the C of E against Roman Catholics and Puritans. In 1562 he published his *Apologia Ecclesiae Anglicanae,* which led to a long and acrimonious controversy on the papacy with Thomas Harding of Louvain, important for its influence upon the course of subsequent polemics. Works: ed. R. Jelf (8v., 1848);

Eng. tr. of his *Apologia,* ed. J. Booty, *Apology of the Church of England* (1963). See W. Southgate, *J. J. and the Problem of Doctrinal Authority* (1962); J. Booty, *J. J. as Apologist of the Church of England* (1963).

JOACHIM OF FIORE (Flora; 1132?–1202), Cistercian abbot and visionary. Born at Celico, Italy, son of a notary to the Norman Kings of Sicily, J. spent his youth at court. His experiences during a pilgrimage to the Holy Land occasioned his decision to retire from the world. About 1159 he took up the life of a lay preacher, but later chose to enter the Cistercian Order at Sambucina, Sicily. He was ordained in 1168 and elected abbot of Corazzo in 1177. Five years later he resigned this office to devote himself to biblical study and contemplation. In 1191 he obtained permission to found a community of hermits at Fiore (Flora) in Calabria for the more austere observance of the Cistercian Rule. The foundation was given autonomy as the Order of Fiore by Pope Celestine III in 1196.

A fervent monk and dedicated scholar, J. was held in high esteem by popes and nobles. Soon after his death the title of blessed was attached to his name by popular acclaim. The religious ideas of J. centered on biblical prophecy as applied to the future reform of the Church and his speculation displayed a clear tendency toward *illuminism. His three major works, *Liber concordiae novi et veteris testamenti, Expositio in Apocalipsim,* and *Psalterium decem chordarum,* are strongly marked by *apocalypticism (see JOACHIMISM). Toward the end of his life J. submitted his writings to the judgment of the Holy See, instructing his followers to accept whatever decision might be forthcoming. In 1215 Lateran Council IV condemned his teaching on the Trinity but did not censure J. personally as a heretic (D 803–807). Joachim's allegorical interpretation of history created a contagious excitement during the 13th century. Commentators and popularizers produced a host of pseudo-Joachimite treatises containing extreme and heretical interpretations of the abbot's thought (see GERARD OF BORGO SAN DONNINO). This literature was the source of the Joachimism that served as a rationale for such discontented groups in medieval society as the Franciscan *Spirituals. See H. Bett, *J. of F.* (1931); M. W. Bloomfield, "J. of F.: A Critical Study," *Traditio* 13 (1957), 249–311; B. D. Dupuy, *Catholicisme* 6:878–887; E. Jordan, DTC 8:1426–58; M. F. Laughlin, NCE 7:990–991.

JOACHIMISM, a name given to an apocalyptic theology of history and a reform spirit derived from the writings of *Joachim of Fiore, or from Joachimite apocrypha. During his lifetime Joachim's orthodoxy was hardly questioned, but after his death zealous enthusiasts gave his eschatological theories interpretations that inspired a whole spectrum of reformers, ranging from fervid idealists to crass opportunists. Joachim claimed to have acquired through mystical experience a supernatural insight into the true spiritual meaning of history and the inner relationship between the Old and New Testaments. His writings consisted principally of allegorical interpretations of the Scriptures interspersed with prophecies concerning the future of the Church. He was a lyrical rather than a systematic thinker, and the meaning of his highly figurative language is often far from clear. As conceived by Joachim the historical process is dominated by a double pattern of two's and three's corresponding to the OT and the NT and the persons of the Trinity. Time is divided into Three Ages, each lasting about 40 generations and influenced by pairs of historical personages. The First and Second Ages were merely preparatory to, and images of, the Third—the apotheosis of history—which will evolve by a double procession from the First and Second. The First Age, the epoch of the Father (Law), began with creation and terminated with the advent of Christ; the Second, the epoch of the Son (Grace), was to end in the year 1260, when the Final Age of the Holy Spirit (Love) would begin.

With the passing of the Ages the human race would progressively grow to a fuller realization of the meaning of the historical process and would gradually become perfect. Each Age would be announced by a prophet and be brought to fulfillment by a fructifier. In the Third Age Spirit and Love will prevail; *viri spirituales*, members of a new religious order will win all mankind to true faith; liberty, peace, and equality will unite the world in mystic fellowship; structured disciplinary institutions will become obsolete; and a spiritualized Johannine Church will take the place of the carnal Petrine Church of the Second Age.

Both Dominicans and Franciscans saw in themselves the *viri spirituales* of Joachim, and in their foundation his Age of the Spirit. But Joachim's writings and the many spurious works attributed to him provided a rationale esp. for the numerous radical reform groups of the 13th century. One such group was composed of dissident Franciscans known as *Spirituals. This uncompromising minority refused to tolerate the slightest mitigation of poverty, insisting that all friars live after the manner of St. Francis and his earliest companions. When this extreme position was rejected by the Franciscan Order, the Spirituals appealed from man to God, invoked the higher law of heaven, and took refuge in apocalyptic fantasy. Their conviction of persecuted innocence, their feeling of impotent fidelity, and their weak theological background all combined to predispose the Spirituals to find prophetic justification for their cause in Joachimist writings.

In 1254 a sensational book entitled *Liber introductorius in evangelium aeternum* was published in Paris by *Gerard of Borgo San Donnino, an ardent young Spiritual. He applied the prophecies of Joachim in a garbled but provocative manner to the Franciscan Order. Joachim was identified as the prophet of the Third Age, St. Francis as its fructifier, and the Friars Minor as the *viri spirituales*. The Masters of the Univ. of Paris found 31 errors in the *Liber introductorius*. A year after its publication it was censured by Pope Alexander IV. William of

Saint-Amour singled it out as a typical example of mendicant perfidy; John of Parma had to resign as Franciscan Minister General because of his penchant for Joachimite prophecy. The preaching of Gerard *Segarelli, *Fra Dolcino, and the *flagellants of Italy were inspired by Joachimism.

About the beginning of the 14th cent. the hardcore Spirituals in France and Italy became known as *Fraticelli. The writings of their spokesmen, such as *Angelus Clarenus, *Ubertino of Casale, and *Peter John Olivi, were heavily tinged with Joachimism. The effectiveness of such groups was virtually destroyed by the energetic measures taken against them by Boniface VIII and John XXII. Nevertheless, Joachimism did not lose its fascination for the medieval mind, and vestiges of it can be detected in many apocalyptic groups even up to the 16th century. See E. Algerton, *L'Évangile éternel* (1928); E. Antichkof, *Joachim de Flore et les milieux courtois* (1931); M. W. Bloomfield, "Joachim of Flora: A Critical Survey," *Traditio* 13 (1957), 249–311; M. W. Bloomfield and M. E. Reeves, "Penetration of Joachimism into Northern Europe," *Speculum* 29 (1954), 772–793; B. D. Dupuy, *Catholicisme* 6:887–895; F. Russo, *Bibliografia Gioachimita* (1954); D. L. Douie, *Nature and Effect of the Heresy of the Fraticelli* (1932), 22–48; A. S. Turberville, *Medieval Heresy and the Inquisition* (1920, repr. 1964), 34–54.

JOHN OF LEIDEN (Jan Beuckelszoon, Bockelson, Beuckels, Johann Buckholdt; 1505–36), Anabaptist fanatic. A native of Leiden in Holland and a tailor by trade, he became an Anabaptist through M. *Hofmann. With Jan *Matthys and other refugees from persecution in Holland, he was able with the aid of B. *Rothmann to take over Münster in 1534. After Matthys's death, J. claimed new revelations and proclaimed himself king of a new Zion. His theocratic reign was marked by religious extravagance, extreme cruelty, and moral excess, including the practice of polygamy. With the fall of Münster in 1535 to the forces of the bp., F. von Waldeck, J. was

captured and, after months of torture, executed. See bibliog. for Anabaptists.

JOHNSON, SAMUEL (1696–1772), American Anglican rector, philosopher. Born in Guilford, Conn., graduated from Yale in 1716, he was ordained a minister for the Congregational Church. He became convinced of the necessity of ordination by a bishop, however, and embraced Anglicanism, sailing for England to receive orders in 1722. His conversion, along with that of Timothy Cutler, formerly president of Yale, caused a great stir in the New England colonies. J. established the first Anglican parish in Conn. at Stratford in 1724. His influence was responsible for a high-church tradition in the Protestant Episcopal Church well into the 19th century. He helped in the foundation of the Univ. of Pa. and King's College (Columbia Univ.), of which he was first president (1754–63). As a philosopher and as a friend and disciple of Bp. Berkeley, J. sought to establish a union between religion and science. His *Elementa philosophica*, published in 1752 by Benjamin Franklin, was the first philosophical textbook to be published and used in the United States. See EncPhil 4:290, with bibliog.; Olmstead 58–60.

JONAS, JUSTUS (Jodocus Koch, Jobst Koch; 1493–1555), German Reformer. He studied law at Erfurt and Wittenberg, and was ordained in 1516. He became professor of law at Erfurt in 1518, then, encouraged by *Erasmus, studied theology at Wittenberg, where he became the friend and follower of Martin Luther. J.'s contribution to the Reformation started when he accompanied Luther to the Diet of *Worms, 1521. He participated in the Marburg Colloquy with the Zwinglians, 1529 (see MARBURG ARTICLES), and in the preparation of the *Augsburg Confession, 1531. He introduced the Reformation in Halle, prepared several important *church orders for other German cities, and contributed to Lutheran hymnody in his revision of the liturgy. He collaborated in Luther's translation of the

Bible. He himself translated many Reformation documents, among them Luther's *De servo arbitrio* and Melanchthon's theological text, *Loci communes*, into German. He preached at the funeral service held at Eisleben when Luther died there in 1546. See M. E. Lehmann, *J. J., Loyal Reformer* (1963).

JONES, BOB, SR. (1883–1968), evangelist, founder of Bob Jones University. Born Robert Reynolds Jones in Dale Co., Ala., where his father was a farmer, he was licensed to preach at 15 by the *Methodist Episcopal Church, and after attending Southern Univ., Greensboro, Ala., began preaching in evangelistic campaigns. Noted for his *fundamentalism and militant attacks on those he considered modernists, he left the Methodist Church in 1939 in protest against its liberal trends and had no church affiliation during the latter part of his life. To further his principles, he founded his university (originally a junior college) in 1927 near Panama City, Fla., moving it to Cleveland, Tenn., in 1933, and to Greenville, S.C., in 1947, when he was succeeded as president by Bob Jones, Jr. The enrollment in the university was about 3,000 in 1968; it does not have accreditation. One of the foremost American evangelists, J. preached in every state of the U.S. and in many foreign countries; he also conducted a widely broadcast radio program of evangelism.

JONES, CHARLES P. (fl. 1889–1900), a Southern Baptist preacher who was in charge of churches in Selma, Ala. (1889–92), and Jackson, Miss. (1892–94). Influenced by the Holiness movement, then in decline among major religious bodies, J. founded the *Church of Christ (Holiness). He was made its elder in 1898. Little is known about the remainder of his life.

JONES, GRIFFITH (1684–1761), Anglican divine. He was born at Kilredin, Wales, and educated at Carmarthen. Rector of Lland-

dowror (1716), he was an eloquent preacher and revivalist. His greatest work was the founding of the Welsh Free Schools in 1730, in which traveling teachers strove to reduce illiteracy among the poor and provide them with religious instruction. Supported by subscriptions and offerings, the schools numbered 3,000 at J.'s death and included 158,000 scholars. He also induced the *Society for Promoting Christian Knowledge to publish two inexpensive editions of the Welsh Bible for the benefit of the poor. See T. Kelly, *G. J., Llanddowror* (1950).

JORIS, DAVID (Jan Jorisz, Jan Joriszoon, David George; c.1501–56), Flemish visionary, preacher of *millenarianism. As a youth J. accepted the teachings of the Reformation and in 1533 became an Anabaptist. But in 1536 he gathered adherents to his own revelations: he was the new messiah (a third David); he and his followers were so spiritualized as to be beyond sin or the need of moral restraint (see ANTINOMIANISM). Jorists survived until the 17th cent. in Friesland and North Germany. Some allege that J. influenced H. *Niclaes. In 1538 J. was pursued as a heretic and stopped preaching. The bizarre *'t Wonderboeck* (Book of Wonders) belongs to the period of his preaching but was published anonymously in 1542. Many of his more than 200 writings were composed at Basel, where he lived from 1544 under the alias Jan van Brugge, pretending to be a Lutheran. Three years after his death his true identity was detected; the Protestant authorities exhumed his body and burned it, along with his writings. See A. Ingold, DTC 4:152; R. M. Jones, *Studies in Mystical Religion* (1923), 442.

JOSEPHINISM, the name given to the close control exercised by the state over the RC Church in Austria from the late 1760s to the early 1850s; it also implies a liberal policy toward non-Catholic minorities. The system was primarily devised by Wenzel von Kaunitz, chancellor of Empress Maria Theresa. However, her piety and Kaunitz's own judgment set limits to state interference with church life and the ties with Rome. Joseph II (d. 1790) exercised no such restraint, and from him the system takes its name. An apostle of the *Enlightenment and imbued with *Febronianism, he sought to make the Austrian Church autonomous and to create of it an instrument of progressive government. He suppressed purely contemplative orders, severed ties between monasteries and their foreign superiors, subjected church correspondence to government control, and placed seminaries under bureaucratic direction. The pope was largely ignored in the planning and execution of these changes. Josephinism did bring some gains to the Church, since Joseph II built many new parishes; non-Catholics also benefited from his policies. The system itself remained in being until 1850, when Franz Josef I decided that political conditions dictated more respect for the Church's own conception of its mission and rights within the state; the effects of Josephinism, however, lingered for another century. See F. Maass, ed., *Der Josephinismus* . . . (5v., 1951–61); M. C. Goodwin, *Papal Conflict with Josephinism* (1938).

JOSEPHISTS (Josepins), an obscure sect that appeared in parts of France, Germany, and Italy in the late 12th century. "Josepins" were condemned by Lucius III in 1184 (see D 760) and by Gregory IX in 1231, but their distinctive teachings are not known. Because it was alleged that adherents spurned marriage but allowed full indulgence of the passions outside that state, the sect is often listed as a branch of the *Cathari; this relationship, however, has not been established by any historical documentation and is doubted by historians. See É. Amann, DTC 8:1547–48; DE 2:207.

JUDGMENT, PRIVATE, see PRIVATE JUDGMENT.

JUDICATORY, another term for the courts characteristic of Presbyterianism. *CHURCH SESSION; *PRESBYTERY; *SYNOD; *GENERAL ASSEMBLY.

JUDICIAL COUNCIL (Methodist), a kind of supreme court of the Methodist Church since 1939. Members are elected by the *General Conference, which also determines their number, qualifications, terms of office, and method of election. The Council decides the constitutionality of any act of the General, Jurisdictional, or Central Conferences and passes on questions of law raised in the Annual Conference and on the legality of any actions of the boards and agencies of the general Church. Its rulings are decisive and final. See *Doctrines and Discipline of the Methodist Church* (1964); HistAmMeth 3:464.

JUDSON, ADONIRAM (1788–1850), Baptist missionary. While a student at Andover Theological Seminary in Newton, Mass., J. participated in the plan that led to the formation of the *American Board of Commissioners for Foreign Missions. Ordained a Congregationalist minister in 1812, he was sent immediately by the Board to India; on shipboard he, like L. *Rice, came to accept *believers' baptism, and in India, with his wife, he was rebaptized as a Baptist. From 1813 on he spent the rest of his life in Burma as a missionary, suffering adversity and hardship, including 17 months of imprisonment. He published (1840) a Burmese translation of the Bible. See life by C. Anderson (1956).

JULIAN OF ECLANUM (c.385–454), bp. of Eclanum (near Beneventum, Italy) and Pelagian opponent of St. Augustine. He attacked the condemnation pronounced upon *Pelagianism by Pope Zosimus, and was in consequence deposed and driven from Italy. He traveled to the East in search of support and protection from Theodore of Mopsuestia and Nestorius, among others. Instead of helping his cause, his efforts led only to involvement in further trouble. He was condemned by the Council of Ephesus as well as by various local councils. He is said to have died in Sicily. His controversy with Augustine was carried on in the four books to Turbantius and the eight to Florus. These works are lost, but much of what he wrote can be gathered from Augustine's rejoinders, *Contra Iulianum* and the *Opus imperfectum*. J., who also commented extensively on Scripture, was one of the few followers in the West of the school of Antioch. His polemic was bitter and his dialectic skilled in pointing up the weak spots in Augustine's doctrine of grace. But if Augustine can be said to have exaggerated the depravity of human nature, J. certainly erred in the opposite direction. See A. Vaccari, EC 6:744–745; Altaner 442–443; F. Refoulé, "Julien d'Éclane, théologien et philosophe," RechSR 52 (1964), 42–84, 233–247.

JURISDICTIONAL CONFERENCE (Methodist), a large geographical region of the Methodist Church in the U.S., and the administrative agency for that region. *CONFERENCE (METHODIST).

JUSTIFICATION, a term standing for man's passage from sin to justice or righteousness. The common elements of this doctrine, shared by the various Churches, have been greatly underestimated because of the serious controversies that have arisen, esp. from the time of the Reformation. An initial distinction of emphasis can be made, however. Luther affirmed that the doctrine of justification is the *articulus stantis et cadentis ecclesiae* (the article upon which the Church stands or falls). For this reason, the doctrine is at the center of the doctrinal corpus of the Churches of the Reformation, esp. the Churches of the Lutheran confessions. In the RC doctrinal system, however, the doctrine of justification is viewed with what might be called great circumspection. Thus, e.g., in the *Summa theologiae* of St. Thomas Aquinas, it stands in a peculiar but significant place in the treatise on grace (ThAq ST 1a2ae, 113).

The terminology employed by St. Paul is commonly agreed upon to describe the process in virtue of which the sinner is justified: rebirth, regeneration, and becoming an adopted child of God. Justification is also called the sanctification of the inner man, and all hold that the righteousness of the just man is derived from the justice or righteousness of Jesus Christ. The manner in which this derivation takes place, however, is a point upon which there does not seem to be full agreement, even though ambiguities of language make it possible to construct a concordance of Protestant and RC views. In the RC tradition, justification is seen to be the work of God, who because of his mercy and through the merits of Christ declares man to be just. To this declaration, however, there corresponds the free response of man, to which is given the technical name "consent," and which consists in an act of living faith, i.e., faith enlivened by love of God. With this consent righteousness becomes inherent.

The Protestant tradition, which stems directly from the thought of Luther and hardly needs to be distinguished according to particular confessions, puts emphasis upon justification as the work of God. As regards man, the view is that justification consists in his getting a new heart through faith, while God counts him to be just for the sake of Christ. With extreme literalness this may be interpreted to mean that man is not inherently just at the term of the process and that his "justice" is really a fiction. There is no doubt that some Protestants have tended to think of justification in this way. Luther, however, makes the following statement in his lectures on Galatians, which appears to temper the position a good deal and to reduce the point of controversy: "To be outside of us means to be beyond our powers. Righteousness is our possession, to be sure, since it was given to us out of mercy. Nevertheless, it is alien to us, because we have not merited it." See S. Pfürtner, *Luther and Aquinas on Salvation* (tr. E. Quinn, 1964); W. Dantine, *Justification of the Ungodly* (tr. E. W. Gritsch and R. C. Gritsch, 1968).

JUSTIFICATION BY FAITH, to gain one's righteousness from believing in Jesus Christ, not from one's own works. This doctrine corresponds to the demand Jesus Christ made upon his disciples to believe in him but is more immediately derived from Pauline literature, in which the Apostle works out the consequences of this demand (esp. in Galatians and Romans).

Always integral to Christian tradition, this doctrine stands at the very heart of the Reformation controversy. Thus, the RC position was stated in more ample fashion in some of the documents issuing from the Council of *Trent (esp. in the Decree on Justification). The Council clearly taught that faith is the first step in a possibly gradual process of justification in the sense that man is freely moved to believe when faith is conceived from the hearing of the Gospel, so that he believes to be true that which is revealed and promised by God, namely, that God does justify unregenerate man by his grace (D 1526). Furthermore, the "formal" cause of justification is the righteousness of God himself, in virtue of which he makes man to be righteous, i.e., by a righteousness which each man receives, according to the measure of the Spirit and his own peculiar disposition and cooperation (D 1529). This disposition and cooperation can scarcely be understood unless they somehow include faith.

The Lutheran position, as worked out by Luther himself, is stated succinctly in the *Schmalkaldic Articles: "What I hold concerning justification is . . . that through faith, as Peter says [Acts 15.9], we acquire a new and clean heart, and that God, for his part, and for Christ's sake . . . reputes us as just and holy" (Art. 13). Furthermore, Luther held that the faith which justifies man is not a *good work, but rather a laying hold of the merits of Christ. Thus faith is not to be counted among the items in a catalogue of meritorious works. "Faith alone is the means and instrument whereby we lay hold on Christ the Savior, and so in Christ lay hold on that righteousness which is able to stand before the judgment of God" (*Formula of Concord, Art. 3). The *Reformed position on justification by faith is not easy to distinguish from that of the Lutherans. "We receive righteousness, not by any works, but by faith in the mercy of God and in Christ. Thus do we teach with the Apostle that man, the sinner, is justified solely by faith in Christ, not by any works." (Second *Helvetic Confession, Ch. 15; cf. *Westminster Confession, Ch. 11.)

In this controversy (insofar as it is a controversy) the Protestant position tends more to the "justification by faith alone" idea. It would appear that this is based on a reading of St. Paul according to which "law" would stand for any work on man's part by which he intends or attempts to gain God's good pleasure. Protestants generally eschew any tendency in this direction, yet all agree that faith does not remain alone but that the just man does act righteously. See G. W. H. Lampe, ed., *Doctrine of Justification by Faith* (tr. T. Collins et al., 1964).

K

KANSAS CITY STATEMENT, document adopted by the Congregational Churches. The National Council of the Congregational Churches that met in Kansas City in 1913 was outstanding in the many important constitutional changes it effected. The Statement it adopted, setting forth "the things most surely believed among us concerning faith, polity and fellowship," was simple, brief, and forward-looking in its declaration of faith. In polity it emphasized the right of private judgment, the autonomy of the *local church, and "our representative democracy." Mainly, however, it affirmed and promised to cooperate in achieving "the unity and catholicity of the Church of Christ." See Schaff Creeds 3:915–916. *CONGREGATIONALISM.

KARLSTADT, ANDREAS RUDOLF BODENSTEIN VON (*c.*1480–1541), German Reformer. He used the name of his place of birth, Karlstadt, or Carlstadt. After study at Erfurt, Cologne, and Wittenberg, he began to teach Thomistic philosophy at Wittenberg in 1505. Three years later he became canon of the collegiate church and subsequently doctor of theology (1510). It was he who advanced Luther to the rank of doctor of theology in 1512. The same year K. was sent to Rome for a doctorate in canon and civil law, which he acquired in a few months. On his return to Wittenberg he attacked the abuses of the papal court, and scholastic philosophy as well. He was J. *Eck's first opponent at the *Disputation of Leipzig, until the critical intervention of Luther himself (1519). K. was mentioned by name in *Exsurge Domine*, the bull that excommunicated Luther (1520). While Luther was in hiding at the *Wartburg (1521), K. put through many reforms: the marriage of priests, the abolition of private Masses, the discarding of vows. He gave communion under both kinds into the hands of his followers and celebrated the Lord's Supper in secular clothing. His attack upon the externals of worship contributed to the Wittenberg riots of 1521 (see ZWICKAU PROPHETS). Expelled from the city (1524), he wandered for a time in Germany and then received a post at the Univ. of Basel. Mainly through him the Zwinglian doctrine of the *Real Presence was adopted in Switzerland. In the resultant controversies with the Lutherans K. tried vainly to be a conciliator. See E. G. Schwiebert, *Luther and His Times* (1950).

KEBLE, JOHN (1792–1866), poet and divine, leading figure in the *Oxford movement. A Cotswold man, after brilliant studies at Corpus Christi College, Oxford, and receiving an Oriel fellowship at a very early age, K. retired to assist his father, a clergyman of the *high-church school, in a country parish. There he wrote a well-known cycle of poems, *The Christian Year* (1827). Appointed professor of poetry at Oxford in 1831, he retired again and was vicar of Hursley, on the edge of the New Forest, from 1836 until his death; his winning beauty of character continued to exert an influence out of proportion to the diffidence of his personal manners and the modesty of his office. The start of the Oxford movement is counted from his assize sermon on national apostasy (1833), directed against a proposed suppression of 10 Irish bishoprics by a government backed by reforming and liberalizing forces that were regarded as threats to the Establishment. He contributed to *Tracts for the Times* and published a learned edition of the works of Richard *Hooker, and also was an editor of the *Library of the Fathers*, for which he prepared the translation of the works of St. Irenaeus. He remained a firm associate of E. *Pusey after 1845, when, to their sorrow, J. H. Newman had left them. He stressed the Real Presence in his work *On Eucharistic Adoration* (1857). Keble College, Oxford (1870), is his monument, and the Butterfield vigor of its architecture symbolizes how confidently the movement freed itself from the imputation of archeologism and boldly developed from the delicate strength of its progenitor. See G. Battiscombe, *J. K.: A Study in Limitations* (1964).

KEITH, GEORGE (c.1639–1716), early Quaker dissident. Born in Aberdeen, Scotland, K. became a Quaker in 1662 and a colleague of G. *Fox, whom he accompanied, together with R. *Barclay and W. *Penn, to Holland (1671). After immigrating to America (1688), K. expressed a recurrent problem within Quakerism by his resistance to emphasis on the *Inner Light at the expense of traditional Christian beliefs. He called himself and his followers "Christian Quakers" and observed baptism and the Lord's Supper. K. wrote against Penn, *The Deism of William Penn and His Brethren* (1699), and against Barclay, *The Standard of the Quakers Examined* (1702). See E. W. Kirby, *G. K., 1638–1716* (1942), with complete bibliog.

KEMPER, JACKSON (1789–1870), first missionary bp. of the Protestant Episcopal Church. Born near Poughkeepsie, N.Y., after finishing Columbia College (now Univ., 1809), he studied for orders under the bp. of New York. Ordained in 1814, he spent 20 years as assistant to Bp. W. *White at Christ Church, Philadelphia. He made missionary journeys into Pa., Va., Wis., and Ohio. Consecrated as missionary bp. of the Northwest (Mo. and Ind.) in 1835, he found only one Episcopalian priest in his territory. In 1854 Iowa and Wis. came under his care; the same year he became diocesan of Wis., devoting full time to his diocese after 1859. He opened Kemper College, Boonville, Mo., as well as Nashotah House and Racine College, both in Wis., seeing to it that these institutions had a full Anglo-Catholic religious life. See G. White, *Apostle of the Western Church* (1900).

KEN, THOMAS (1637–1711), bp. of Bath and Wells. K. was born in Hertfordshire of Somerset stock and educated at Winchester and New College, Oxford. A friend of Izaak Walton, who married his half-sister, he manifested an equal peacefulness and piety; a Wykehamist, he well exemplified the founder's motto, "Manners makyth man." No timeserver, he disobliged Nell Gwyn (the mistress of Charles II, who referred to him as "the little black fellow that refused his lodging to poor Nelly") and roundly told James II that he had seen enough at Rome to keep him from changing his religion. The two Stuart kings respected him, and he was faithful to them. Though K. was one of the seven bishops who refused to read James II's *Declaration of Indulgence, he was dispossessed of his see as a *nonjuror under William III. He wrote the *Practice of Divine Love* (1685), a classic of Laudian devotion, and died in the C of E "as it stands distinguished from all Papal and Puritan Innovations."

KENTUCKY REVIVAL, a frontier outburst of highly emotional religion that began in 1800 at Gasper River, Ky., N of Nashville, Tenn., and reached its peak at Cane Ridge, Bourbon Co., Ky., in mid-Aug. 1801. Although Kentucky's population was then only 221,000, of whom no more than 10,000 were church members, the crowd that camped at Cane Ridge in Aug. 1801 was estimated at 20,000 to 30,000. The meeting went on for 6 days and nights, until provisions gave out. Called by Presbyterian ministers, 18 of whom attended, the revival also drew active participation from a number of Methodist and Baptist ministers; denominational distinctions were ignored. From stands set up in various parts of the grounds and even from stumps and fallen tree trunks, as many as five or six ministers preached simultaneously to crowds forming, dispersing, and reforming within the camp. Spontaneous singing, praying, shouting, and strange "religious exercises" punctuated day and dark. Preaching, which emphasized the bliss of heaven somewhat less than the terrors of hell, described salvation in strictly individualistic and otherworldly terms. Scores of hearers "under conviction" fell into catatonic trances, jerked in nervous spasms, attempted running flight only to be cast to the ground in trance, danced, sang, and laughed in "holy myrth." It was a kind of excitement suited to the raw and sparsely settled frontier against a background of lawlessness and repressed religiousness. From Cane Ridge the revival spread to N.C., Va., Ohio, Pa., and as far south as Ga., retaining much of its zest into 1803 but waning by 1805. Evidently Methodist camp meetings with their hundreds of campgrounds derived from this origin. *SECOND GREAT AWAKENING.

KERYGMATIC THEOLOGY, a description of theology as receiving its origin, form, and purpose from the preaching of the good news of salvation. In the Gr. of the NT, *kērygma* refers to the proclamation of what God has done in Christ for the salvation of men. *Dialectic theology, or *crisis theology, has been called kerygmatic because of an exclusive concern, chiefly inspired by Karl *Barth, for the proclamation of God's word and self-revelation in Christ, the only saving knowledge for man. This intent includes opposition to any intrinsic function of philosophy within theology. The beginning of RC kerygmatic interest at Innsbruck in the 1930s was partly a reaction to scholastic, or systematic, theology. Kerygmatic theology was first proposed as a distinct discipline, a preaching theology in contrast to an academic or school theology. The point was controversial; ensuing discussions led to agreement by the major theologians that theology is a science, is one, but is both theoretical and at the same time ordained to Christian decision and living. Thus kerygmatic theology denotes the approach and pedagogy necessary to theology as rooted in God's saving word and actions. The kerygmatic emphasis has directed the efforts of RC theologians to a systematization, necessary to theology as science, corresponding to the historic order

in God's saving revelation and a presentation directly related to man's need of salvation. Theology must have kerygmatic aspects that are christocentric, shaped around Christ's life, work, and Church, and stated through biblical themes, rather than philosophical categories. See J. A. Jungmann, *Good News Yesterday and Today* (ed. abr. and tr. W. A. Huesman, 1962); J. MacQuarrie, *Twentieth Century Religious Thought* (1963).

KIERKEGAARD, SØREN AABYE (1813–55), Danish philosopher and religious thinker; first important existentialist. K. reacted against the prevailing Hegelianism of his day, which he saw as a static, unreal system robbing man of his individuality. K.'s alternative was a subjective and passionate Christian faith. He refused to organize his own thought systematically but continually reflected upon the theological themes of faith, sin and forgiveness, ethics and religious commitment, and the nature of the Church. In all of his works, he presents a dialectic of his own experience rather than an abstract philosophy.

K.'s thought was significantly influenced by his personal relationships. His early years were dominated by his father's anxiety-ridden and melancholy piety. In 1835, K. experienced a shattering "earthquake," occasioned by his father's revelation of a childhood curse against God. Thereafter, K. was beset not only by his own melancholy but by a continual awareness of human sinfulness. After obtaining a theological degree from the Univ. of Copenhagen, K. became engaged to Regina Olsen; he broke the engagement after one year, convinced that his inability to react spontaneously and accept the intimacy of marriage would destroy Regina. His love for her remained throughout his life and became the symbol of Abraham's faith in being willing to sacrifice Isaac. In 1846, a disreputable but popular paper, the *Corsair*, launched a vitriolic personal attack upon him. He became even more withdrawn from society and devoted himself to religious writing on specifically Christian themes. The last 2 years of his life were spent in severe criticism of the established Church in Denmark as a mockery of Christianity.

K. argued that a philosophical system, by which he meant that of Hegel, cannot fulfill its promise to explain the human situation. The "system" deals with abstractions and considers individuality as only a passing moment in a necessarily evolving Spirit. But K. refused to reduce the individual as such to any category. The experience of reality and not the concept of it must constitute the basis for reflection. Truth cannot be attained by an objective, logical process. Primacy must be given to subjectivity, i.e., the passionate appropriation of objective uncertainty. It is only when I choose to be related to reality that I reach truth. To be without passion (subjectivity) is not to exist. Hence K.'s notion of faith: a passionate commitment to God in the midst of objective uncertainty. This free choice of faith can alone assure me of authentic existence.

The three stages of life form an important part of K.'s thought. Each stage (aesthetic, ethical, and religious) has its own dynamism and is totally different from the others. Man is faced with a radical choice between God and the world. The aesthetic life is one of pleasure, cultivated humanism, and refusal to limit life's infinite possibilities by permanent choices. In the ethical stage, man chooses duty and responds to general principles of moral conduct. But it is only in the religious stage that the individual through faith makes the ultimate leap beyond despair and dread to a true realization of himself before God. K.'s thought was one of the principal influences that changed the direction, method, and interest of theology in the 20th century. Among K.'s work in English translation are *Either/Or* (v.1, tr. D. F. and L. M. Swenson, 1941; v.2, tr. W. Lowrie, 1944) and *Concept of Dread* (tr. W. Lowrie, 1944). See L. Dupré, *K. as Theologian* (1963), with complete list of K.'s wks.; J. Collins, *Mind of K.* (pa., 1965); W. Lowrie, *Short Life of K.* (1942).

KILHAM, ALEXANDER (1762–98), chief founder of the *Methodist New Connexion. He was born of Methodist parents at Epworth, England. He experienced a conversion at 19 and helped Robert Brackenbury found Methodism in the Channel Islands. An effective evangelist, K. wrote tracts urging Wesleyan Methodists to separate from the C of E. Because of his vehement writing he was expelled in 1796, and with some others founded the Methodist New Connexion (Aug. 9, 1797). See W. J. Townsend et al., eds., *New History of Methodism* (2v., 1909), 1:489–497.

KING'S BOOK, or *A Necessary Doctrine and Erudition for Any Christian Man*, published May 1543, a revision of the *Bishops' Book of 1537 in a more conservative direction following the standard of the *Six Articles of 1539. Prepared by a commission of the two English abps., six bps., and twelve scholars, it received the approval of *Convocation and contained a preface by King Henry VIII. The work was preceded by a survey of the bishops' answers to 17 questions on the nature and number of the sacraments. It remained the official standard of doctrine of the C of E until the death of Henry (1547). The most recent ed. of *The King's Book* is by T. A. Lacey (1932). See *Works of Thomas Cranmer* (1846), 2:115–117.

KING'S CONFESSION, an anti-Roman appendix to the *Scots Confession; sometimes called the Second Scots Confession. It was written by John Craig (d. 1600), a friend of John *Knox, and received its name from the fact that it was signed by King James VI of Scotland. It became part of the *Scottish National Covenant of 1638.

KINGSLEY, CHARLES (1819–75), Anglican novelist and Christian Socialist leader. Ordained in 1842, K. devoted much of his time to writing, producing a number of well-known novels, among which were *Alton Locke* (1850) and *Westward Ho!* (1855). In his earlier life, as a follower of F. D. *Maurice, he became a Christian Socialist in London and served the cause as its leading pamphleteer; but he was disillusioned with it in later life. In his views of church life he tended toward a *broad-church interpretation of Anglicanism. His strong anti-Roman animus led him to publish an incautious statement reflecting unfavorably upon the attitude of the Roman clergy and J. H. *Newman toward the truth. This evoked a shattering rebuttal in Newman's *Apologia pro vita sua.* Works: 19v., 1901–03. See U. Pope-Hennessy, *C. K.* (1948). *CHRISTIAN SOCIALISM.

KIRCHENORDNUNG, German, meaning *church order. The church orders for the *territorial churches are frequently cited sources in Reformation history.

KIRK, mainly Scottish form of the word "church," with which it is used interchangeably in literature and in documents of the Church until the 17th century. It is still used popularly, often to distinguish the Church of Scotland from other religious bodies. The *Westminster Assembly (1645–48) gave official sanction to the title Church (rather than Kirk) of Scotland.

KIRK, KENNETH ESCOTT (1886–1954), born in Sheffield, fellow of Trinity College, Oxford, Regius Professor of moral and pastoral theology, and bp. of Oxford. An Anglo-Catholic in the liberal tradition of Charles *Gore, K. wrote much on traditional Christian spirituality and, at home with the Dominican authors and *Caroline divines, promoted the study of systematic moral theology in the Church of England. His *Bampton Lectures for 1928 produced a work of lasting value, *The Vision of God,* the Christian doctrine of the *summum bonum.* See life and letters, by E. W. Kemp (1959).

KIRK-SESSION, the *church session in the Church of Scotland.

KISS, HOLY (The Kiss), a practice among Mennonites to express Christian love (cf. Rom 16.16; 1 Cor 16.20). Exchange of a kiss by brethren at baptism, at the Lord's Supper, or as a salutation was common among most early Swiss and Dutch Mennonites. Withholding of the kiss from the wayward was part of church discipline. In Europe the practice has almost completely ceased. In N America only the more conservative bodies, such as the Old Order Amish, still observe it. See MennEnc 3:181–186.

KKK, see KU KLUX KLAN.

KNOW-NOTHING PARTY, a secret, political society in the United States. Fear of growing Irish and German immigration led to the formation of the Know-Nothings during the 1850s. It grew out of an oath-bound fraternity, the Order of the Star-Spangled Banner, and other nativist organizations. Initiates were instructed to answer all questions about the movement with "I know nothing," from which it received its popular name. The Know-Nothings opposed "foreign influence, Popery, Jesuitism and Catholicism" and sought to exclude all Roman Catholics and "foreigners" from public office. The party tried to establish a period of 21 years of residence before citizenship, after which such naturalized citizens still could not hold public office. After 1854 the Know-Nothing movement abandoned most of its secret apparatus and called itself the American Party. Its constitution stated: "The object of this organization shall be to resist the insidious policy of the Church of Rome, and other foreign influence against the institutions of our country by placing in all offices in the gift of the people, or by appointment, none but native-born Protestant citizens." A Know-Nothing had to be a native-born citizen, a Protestant born of Protestant parents, reared as a Protestant, and not married to a Roman Catholic. In 1854 the American Party elected governors in Mass. and Del. and gained control of several state legislatures. Former President Millard Fillmore joined the American Party and ran for president on its ticket in 1856. In that election the party won 25% of the popular vote but carried only one state, Maryland. The Know-Nothings entered a disastrous alliance with proslavery Southerners and faded into obscurity in a few years. See A. R. Billington, *Protestant Crusade, 1800–1860* (1938); J. Highman, *Strangers in the Land: Patterns of American Nativism* (1955).

KNOX, JOHN (1515?–72), leader of the Reformation in Scotland. In his *History of the Reformation of Religion within the Realm of Scotland* (modern ed., W. C. Dickinson, ed., 2v., 1949), K. records an epoch in which he was the dominant figure. Born near Haddington and perhaps ordained, he early fell under the influence of George Wishart (d. 1546) and his *Reformed ideas. On Wishart's death K. fled to Saint Andrews, where his work as a Reformer began; but he was captured by the French and deported to France. After his release K. spent 5 years in the service of the C of E, becoming royal chaplain in 1551. Persecution under Mary Tudor drove him to the Continent, where he ministered successively in Frankfurt and Geneva. In 1558 he wrote *The First Blast of the Trumpet against the Monstrous Regiment of Women*, a bitter attack upon women as rulers. On his final return to Scotland in 1559, K. at once took over direction of the reforming cause, and despite Queen Elizabeth's reluctance to aid any who disapproved of feminine rule, the Treaties of Edinburgh and Leith were ratified in Feb. and July 1560, and French forces were withdrawn, though K.'s clash with Mary Stuart was still to come. In Aug. K. and his colleagues produced the *Scots Confession. The first *Book of Discipline, largely the work of K., is an application of his reforming ideas to the whole life of the nation. In 1562 the *Book of Common Order was approved for use by the General Assembly. His one theological work was a *Treatise on Predestination* (1560). Knox represents a sacramental evangelicalism that differs widely from later Scottish Cal-

vinism. A figure who aroused controversy and violent emotion, he was fearless, opinionated, yet deeply sensitive and profoundly influential. See lives by P. H. Brown (2v., 1895) and E. Percy (1965); J. S. McEwen, *Faith of J. K.* (1961).

KNUDSON, ALBERT CORNELIUS (1873–1953), Methodist theologian. K. was professor of OT exegesis (1905–21) and systematic theology (1921–43) at Boston Univ., and through his teaching and writings, which were used in many Methodist seminaries, had widespread influence. His major works in systematic theology were the *Doctrine of God* (1930) and the *Doctrine of Redemption* (1933). K.'s thought was characterized by a liberal and naturalist interpretation of theology, inspired by the personalist idealism of B. P. *Bowne. K. regarded this form of personalism as the only sound basis for theology and believed that thought, the ultimate principle in all reality, is in man the capacity for the reception of grace. The primary Christian doctrine for K. is the Trinity, which he explained as a threefold manifestation of God's being. His ethical theory stressed the absoluteness of human freedom as the condition of all morality and fellowship with God. See HistAmMeth 3:276–280.

KODESH CHURCH OF IMMANUEL, a small, predominantly Negro, Holiness Church. Under F. R. Killingsworth, the Church separated from the African Methodist Episcopal Zion Church, Philadelphia, in 1929; the Christian Tabernacle Union of Pittsburgh, Pa., joined it in 1934. There were in 1968 local congregations in Washington, D. C., and Virginia. The Church teaches *entire sanctification, *baptism with the Holy Spirit, *divine healing, and *premillenarianism. Holiness in conduct through abstention from tobacco, liquor, and worldliness in dress or amusements is enjoined; adultery is the only grounds for divorce. The Church is governed by two annual assemblies, Philadelphia and Washington, and a quadrennial general assembly.

KORNTAL (Kornthal), an evangelical brotherhood founded on an estate close to Stuttgart, Germany. Inspired by earlier Moravian communities, a group led by Gottlieb Wilhelm Hoffmann and Johann Michael Hahn founded the village in 1819 for the purpose of providing a haven for the truly converted and of protecting the Christian faith from the inroads of *rationalism. While independent of the established Lutheran Church, members accepted the *Augsburg Confession with a few modifications. A strong conviction of Christ's immediate second coming characterized the original settlement. Discipline extended to food, clothing, and other matters of daily life. K. became a place of pilgrimage not only for Pietists but for other devout Christians. In 1955 the community numbered 1,200 members. In the now independent city of Korntal it manages hospices, schools on many levels, and a cooperative, Inner Mission work. It has entered also into a community-of-work compact with a congregation of the Lutheran Church organized in K. in 1955. See H. Hohlwein, RGG 4:24–25.

KRAUTH, CHARLES PORTERFIELD (1825–83), Lutheran theologian. Born in Martinsburg, W.Va., K. was educated at Gettysburg College and Seminary. After a succession of pastorates in Md., Va., and Pa., he became (1860) editor of a Philadelphia weekly, *Lutheran and Missionary*. He brought his broad historical and theological knowledge to the service of the paper's interest in Lutheran doctrinal tradition, and labored in opposition to the emergence of a so-called "American Lutheranism" under Samuel Schmucker, which was anticonfessional and influenced by non-Lutheran elements. *The Conservative Reformation and Its Theology* (1871), K.'s masterwork, was a powerful incentive for American Lutherans to study and retain their specific doctrinal identity. The work particularly stressed the need for a return to the positive spirit and confessional documents of the Reformation, and for a strong eucharistic and litur-

gical life in Lutheranism. See A. Spaeth, *C. P. K.* (2v., 1898; 1909); Smith-Jamison 1:275–279.

KRIMMER MENNONITE BRETHREN, a Church formally organized in the Crimea, Russia, in 1869, under the leadership of Jacob A. Wiebe (1839–1921). The members migrated to the U.S. in 1874 and established a settlement near Peabody, Kansas. In 1899 the name Crimean Mennonite Brethren Church was adopted officially, but the popular name continued to be Krimmer Mennonite Brethren. Doctrinal stress was upon experience of conversion; in practice the early Mennonite conservatism in dress and discipline diminished in the 20th century. In 1960 the Krimmer Mennonite Brethren entered a merger with the *Mennonite Brethren Church of North America, which also had its origins in Russia. See MennEnc 3:242–245.

KU KLUX KLAN (KKK), the name of three distinct racist secret societies, the second of which played a major role in American life. All three Klans worked out a similar ritual, employed common symbols and vocabulary, and opposed Negroes, Catholics, Jews, and the foreign-born.

The original KKK was founded by six Confederate veterans in Pulaski, Tenn., in 1865. The name was devised by adding alliterative embellishments to the Greek word *kuklos* (circle). The Klansmen rode about the countryside in white sheets and masks to terrorize the recently freed slaves. In their view they were merely fighting carpetbaggers, radical Republicanism, and the threat to Southern life posed by the emancipation of the Negroes. Gen. Nathan Bedford Forrest lent prestige to the KKK when he became Grand Wizard in 1869, but in the face of ample proof that Klansmen employed lynching, torture, and floggings, the general agreed to direct the dissolution of the KKK, and within 4 years it had disappeared.

An unfrocked Methodist minister and professional fraternalist, William J. Simmons, resurrected the KKK in Atlanta, Ga., in 1915. The glorification of the KKK by T. Dixon's *The Clansman* and by the film *Birth of a Nation* had prepared the way. Two public relations specialists helped Simmons recruit members by the thousands, and in the mid-1920s the KKK had enrolled as many as 5 million men. The Klansmen belonged to local Klaverns, paid Klectokens (dues), followed the ritual presented in the Kloran, and joined in prayers led by the Kludd (chaplain). Between 1921 and 1925 the KKK elected governors in Ind., Maine, and Colorado; controlled legislatures in five states; sent senators and congressmen to Washington; and took over numerous city halls and courthouses. The KKK fought the nomination and election as governor of N.Y. of Alfred E. Smith, a Catholic and anti-prohibitionist. This second KKK claimed to be defending Protestantism from the threat posed by Catholics, Jews, Communists, Negroes, foreigners, and bootleggers. It posed as the expression of 100% Americanism. In fact it was probably more anti-Semitic and anti-Catholic than racist. The conviction for rape and murder of D. C. Stephenson, Grand Dragon of Indiana, and the exposure of the low moral standards of other Klansmen led to a decline of the KKK that was almost as rapid as its rise; by 1930 membership had dwindled to 35,000.

After World War II several groups in southern states took the name of the KKK and enrolled members in a crusade to preserve racial segregation. Taken together, these rival Klans could muster fewer than 40,000 members, most of them in Ga., Ala., and Mississippi. The major Protestant Churches completely repudiate the objectives and methods of the present KKK. It was branded in 1965 by Pres. Lyndon B. Johnson as "a hooded society of bigots." See D. M. Chalmers, *Hooded Americanism: The First Century of the KKK* (1965); W. P. Randel, *KKK: A Century of Infamy* (1965).

KULTURKAMPF (Ger., struggle for civilization), the name given by the pathologist and liberal Rudolf Virchow to the struggle going on between several German states, esp. Prussia, and the RC Church in the 1870s. He first used the term in the Prussian Landtag in Jan. 1873 and then repeatedly, as did his colleagues in the Progressive party, as a campaign slogan in elections. German liberals, moderate and radical alike, believed that Pope Pius IX's *Syllabus of Errors* (1864) and the proclamation of papal infallibility (1870) confirmed their opinion that the RC Church was the foe of free thought and progress; they also attributed to unpatriotic motives RC opposition to German unification under Prussian leadership. Some liberals, Progressives included, rejected the Kulturkampf, but most helped to provide either legislative materials or parliamentary support. The Kulturkampf became a possibility and then a harsh reality when Otto von *Bismarck, Prussian Minister-President and German Chancellor, decided in the early summer of 1871 to align the Prussian state with the anti-Catholic liberals. His motives were political and essentially derived from his fear of the new Catholic Center party, which he thought hostile to the new Reich for combined ecclesiastical and particularist reasons. Three of the Kulturkampf statutes were national in scope: the Pulpit Law ("Misuse of the Pulpit for Political Ends") of Dec. 1871; the "Jesuit Law" of June 1872, which prohibited the maintenance of Jesuit institutions and permitted expulsion of individual Jesuits; and the Civil Marriage Act of Feb. 1875. The major theater of the Kulturkampf was Prussia, where it became intense after the appointment of Adalbert Falk as minister of education and public worship in Jan. 1872. He insisted on state control of all lower and secondary education in the School Inspection Law of March 1872; he then made a massive attack on the bishops' disciplinary and administrative powers in the *May Laws of 1873. Additional legislation a year later provided for severe penalties against churchmen violating the May Laws and for the administration of vacated bishoprics. New laws in May and June of 1875 dissolved numerous religious orders and established communal lay associations to administer church properties. By 1877 eight of the twelve Prussian bishops were either imprisoned or exiled, and about 990 regular parishes were without priests. In the state of Baden, earlier the site of a lesser Kulturkampf, the government tried to impose a state examination on candidates for the priesthood, closed seminaries, introduced interconfessional schools, and insisted on state approval of all clerical appointments. A more moderate government carried on a milder Kulturkampf in Hessen-Darmstadt. By the time Pius IX died in 1878, Bismarck had become weary of a struggle that had stimulated the growth of the Center party, made conservative Protestants wary, and led to the Prussian and Imperial governments' dependence on the liberal parties; he was also concerned about the new socialist movement. After fitful gestures and negotiations throughout the period 1879–86, the Prussian government and the Vatican negotiated a compromise settlement in 1886–87, which led in turn to settlements in several other German states. See E. Eyck, *Bismarck after Fifty Years* (1950).

L

LABADIE, JEAN DE (1610–74), founder of a small communal group called *Labadists. L. entered the Society of Jesus in 1625 and was ordained in 1635. An excellent preacher, but with an unquiet temperament and reforming spirit, he left his order at his own request in 1639 because of illness and stayed for a while with the Fathers of the Oratory. As a diocesan priest in 1644 he founded at Amiens conventicles for prayer, meditation, and Bible study; he stressed the direct inspiration of the Holy Spirit on the believer. Apparently because he distributed *communion under both kinds, he was moved by Card. Mazarin to Southern France. L.'s preaching soon became suspect, and in 1749 he had to ask hospitality of the Carmelites at Bazas to escape arrest. In 1650 he went over to the *Reformed Church. While pastor at Montauban (1652–57), his reforming innovations led to conflict and he moved to Orange in 1657 and to Geneva in 1659. In 1666 he became a pastor in the Netherlands. At first he was well received as a zealous and able preacher. The authorities put a watch on him, however, and when he refused to retract unorthodox statements, the Dutch Synod exiled him. In 1670 he was able to establish his own community at Hereford in Westphalia. He gathered 55 followers, but he was forced to leave Hereford in 1671. He and his disciples went first to Bremen and then to Altona, where he died. L. left 30 treatises, almost all of them written after he had entered the Reformed Church. See G. Frank, EncRelKnow 6:390–392; M. Schmidt, RGG 4:193.

LABADISTS, members of the Reformed sect founded in Hereford, Westphalia, c. 1670 by Jean de *Labadie. They believed that the Bible could be understood only by the immediate inspiration of the Holy Spirit, denied the Real Presence, rarely celebrated the Eucharist, and held that marriage with an unregenerate person was not binding. Their communal life resembled that of the Moravians; in their devotional practices they foreshadowed *Pietism. In 1690 they numbered about 300. Anne Marie Schürmann, who reestablished the group in West Frisia after Labadie's death, looked forward to founding missions in Surinam and along the Hudson River in North America; but the sect dwindled, and after the death of their last preacher in 1732 its remaining members scattered. See B. D. Dupuy, *Catholicisme* 6:1511–12; F. E. Stoeffler, *Rise of Pietism* (1965).

LAESTADIANS, participants in a mid-19th-cent. revival movement inspired by L. L. *Laestadius. The movement began in 1844 with the preaching of Laestadius in Swedish Lapland, and was carried to N Norway and esp. to Finland by lay preachers he commissioned. The Laestadians were Lutheran in basic doctrine, but they rejected baptism and the Eucharist. Their gatherings were marked by ecstatic manifestations and by absolution from sin through the laying on of hands, a practice introduced by J. Raattama (1811–99). Many of the early Laestadians were unlettered people, and some interpreted the message of their election and salvation as a call to take bloody vengeance upon the unconverted. In time three kinds of Laestadians emerged: Old Laestadians, who were antinomian; Newer Laestadians, who accepted both law and gospel; and the Firstborn, a small circle who believed that Christianity only came into being with the preaching of Laestadius. The Laestadian revival continues as a factor in the life of the Church in Finland. In 1866 some Finnish Laestadians immigrated to the U.S. and formed what is now called the Apostolic Lutheran Church of America. See U. Saarnivaara, *History of the Laestadian or Apostolic Lutheran Movement in America* (1947).

LAESTADIUS, LARS LEVI (1800–61), Swedish Lutheran pastor, founder of the *Laestadians. After studying at Uppsala, L. was ordained (1825) and became pastor in Swedish Lapland. He had an interest in botany and became a recognized authority on northern flora. At the death of his infant child and under the inspiration of the simple gospel testimony of a Lapp girl named Maria, L. experienced a religious conversion and became a revivalist preacher. His emotional, vivid sermons stressed justification by faith alone and the need of rescue from sin. He sent out lay preachers to spread his revival. During his latter years he was forced to restrain the violence of some of his unlettered followers. L. published some of his evangelical ideas in Swedish; his sermons were delivered in Finnish (Eng. tr. 1960). The Laestadian revival continues to be a factor in church life in Finland; the Apostolic Lutheran Church in America was established by Laestadian Finnish immigrants. See T. A. Kantonen, EncLuthCh 2:1242–43.

LAICISM, an attitude that passes beyond the reaction of *anticlericalism to a positive and explicit interference into areas regarded as the monopoly of the clergy's influence and competence. Although the term is of fairly recent origin—French Revolution—and has seen its full development in contemporary life, lay intrusion into the doctrinal and sacramental preserves of the clergy is as ancient as the Church's division into the people and their ministers. Such a society in unstable equilibrium is almost bound to result in tensions. *Montanism, e.g., early accorded greater authority to the "charismatic," putting prophet above priest. The Church had hardly emerged from the catacombs when the emperors, esp. Eastern, tried to use their civil power to shape dogmatic definitions and church order; St. Ambrose had to remind Theodosius that the emperor is in, not above, the Church. This was but the beginning of the long struggle, hardly over even now, between lay rulers and church authorities. It reached a peak in the early Middle Ages, a chapter in ecclesiastical history justly named, "the Church in the power of the laity." But the investiture struggle that made the mitre the gift of the crown was but one phase of continuing conflict between an overweening clericalism and a sacristan concern for lay-power even in pulpit and sanctuary. However, it was Luther who, in his *Open Letter to the Christian Nobility* (1520), attacked the very distinction of clergy and laity as over-subtle and hypocritical. Anticlerical feeling had been seething for some time; during the late Middle Ages the quantity of clergy was conspicuously greater than their quality. In his time a St. Bernard took a prophetic stance; and Chaucer indulged in laughing at clerical pretensions. As the *Cathari and *Waldenses gave authority only to the "spiritual," *Wycliffe, and *Hus recognized it only in the predestined. In the era of the Reformation, Erasmus, Rabelais, and St. Thomas More used satire for correction to such an extent that anticlerical literature became almost a genre of its own. One of the key doctrinal position's of Luther was the *priesthood of all believers; Calvin confined NT priesthood to Christ. Protestant secular rulers in large measure ruled the ecclesiastical life. RC rulers also profited from the changed climate, and laicism assumed the shapes of *Febronianism and *Josephinism. A new wave of laicism is observable in the post-Vatican II era; the collegiality of bishops and particularly the emphasis on the Church as the people of God rather than as hierarchical society gives the laicist a strong lever.

All this was within the structures of the Churches; the *Enlightenment and the French Revolution produced what was essentially an anti-Christian laicism; Voltaire may resemble Erasmus in his mockery of clerics, but the underlying motive of his program is not that of a believer. A positive plan for de-Christianization began with the French Revolution, and the laws against religion in Spain, Portugal, and Piedmont of the 19th cent. continued the general attack. France particularly developed a laicist politic that in its most extreme form in the 20th cent. admitted that it was an attempt to destroy the Church and the idea of God. Similarly, Pius XI in the encyclical *Quas primas* (1925) denounced the laicism of totalitarian states as "the plague of our epoch." See B. du Chesnay, NCE 8:323–325.

LAITY, the body of Christian people who have received the sacrament of baptism (and, eventually, confirmation) but not ordination of any kind. The origin of the word is the Greek term *laos tou theou,* "the people of God," a widely used synonym for the Church. As the people of God, the Church has been set apart from the rest of humanity. The fundamental distinction, therefore, is not the one between clergy and laity but the one between the *laos* of God and the world: to be of the laity means to belong to the former rather than to the latter. Yet the NT also distinguishes within the people of God between Apostles and other believers; not every 1st-cent. Christian was an Apostle. After the death of the Apostles, that distinction was carried over into the organized life and developing structures of the Church, and by the 3d cent. there was some such differentiation between clergy and laity.

Whenever the Church has been dominated by some variety of *clericalism, the laity have been thought of as the passive recipients of the grace dispensed by the clergy. Such a conception was prominent in the Middle Ages, as in the bull *Clericis laicos* (1296) of Pope Boniface VIII; this is understandable in the light of social and political conditions, but it has been carried over into other situations as well. The demeaning of the laity ignored both the gratuitous nature of the gifts bestowed upon the clergy and the special form of ministry entrusted particularly to the laity. That ministry is a ministry in the world and to the world. Because the grace given to the Church is not meant as a possession to be hoarded but as a gift to be shared, those Christians whose life is in the world are charged with a special responsibility for proclaiming and carrying out the rule of God beyond the present borders of the Church. Clergy and laity together, each performing its unique ministry, can thus articulate the ministry of Jesus Christ, who at one and the same time was a "layman," being of the tribe of Judah rather than of the priestly tribe of Levi, and a "priest forever, after the order of Melchizedek" (Heb. 5.6). The concept of the laity, far from being negative, can be seen as a special form of Christian existence, with its own privileges, duties, and sacred vocation, as well as its own dignity and promised reward. See Vat II ApostLaity; H. Kraemer, *Theology of the Laity* (1958).

LAKE, KIRSOPP (1872–1946), biblical scholar. Born and educated in England (Lincoln College, Oxford) and ordained to the priesthood in the C of E (1896), L.; after serving two curacies in England, was professor of early Christian literature and exegesis (1904–14) at the Univ. of Leiden, Holland, and professor of history at Harvard Univ. (1914–38). His scholarly work was in textual and historical criticism and in archeology. In the first field he published *The Text of the New Testament* (1900; 6th ed. rev., 1928), *Codex I of the Gospel and Its Allies* (1902) and, with his wife, a photographic facsimile of *Codex Sinaiticus Petropolitanus: The New Testament, the Epistle of Barnabas and the Shepherd of Hermas* (2v., 1911–22). His works of historical criticism include *The Historical Evidence for the Resurrection of Jesus Christ* (1907), *The Earlier Epistles of St. Paul* (1911), and, with F. J. Foakes-Jackson, *The Beginnings of Christianity* (5v., 1920–23), a monumental study of Acts.

LAMBETH ARTICLES, nine propositions affirming a rigid Calvinist doctrine of *predestination, adopted at Lambeth Palace, Nov. 20, 1595. There John Whitgift (c.1539–1604), Abp. of Canterbury, summoned a synod to deal with a minority opposition to unconditional predestination that had arisen at the Univ. of Cambridge. The Articles affirmed God's absolute predestination of the elect, excluding foreseen faith or good works. The Lambeth statement reflected the prevalent Calvinism of the Puritan era, but never was adopted as a doctrinal standard in England. See Schaff Creeds 1:658–661.

LAMBETH CONFERENCES, meetings to which the abp. of Canterbury invites bps. of the *Anglican Communion, and at which he presides. Until 1968, those gatherings, generally held every 10 years, were at his London residence, Lambeth Palace, hence their name. They are informal meetings rather than synods or councils, and their reports and resolutions have no official authority, except as they are implemented by the individual member Churches. However, the influence of the Conferences on the life and witness of the Churches of the *Anglican Communion is substantial, and they play a unique role in expressing the viewpoint of these Churches on contemporary issues. The first Conference was held in 1867, at the request (1865) of the metropolitan and bps. of the ecclesiastical province of Canada, made to the abp. of Canterbury, C. T. Longley (1794–1868). In their request, however, the Canadian bps. were giving voice to a wish widely held in the younger Anglican Churches outside the British Isles—a wish arising from the nature of the Anglican Communion itself. Lacking any central government or single worldwide organization, national Anglican Churches were coming into vigorous existence in every part of the world. The American and New Zealand Churches were already autocephalous; the rest were well started on that road. In consequence of this swift, largely uncoordinated growth, it was becoming clear that the unity expressed in their "full communion" with the C of E required articulation and embodiment in order to develop beyond sentimentality. This need was sharpened by the contemporary political and doctrinal tensions sym-

bolized by the trial for heresy of Bp. Colenso of Natal, in which the judgment of the church court in South Africa had been reversed by the Privy Council in England. The Colenso incident raised vivid questions as to both the Church's doctrine and the freedom of the younger Churches from English domination. The phrase "Anglican Communion" was only then coming into use; the reality that lay behind the phrase needed to be developed, and this development, in turn, depended on the way Anglican unity and diversity were to be reconciled and expressed within some central body.

The hope of the Canadians, and many others, was for a worldwide synod or council of the Anglican Churches. But the possibility of such a supranational authority, which might even override the authority of the established C of E, aroused grave questions within that body itself. Only a minority of English bps. were to attend the first meeting; and the Conference was not permitted to hold official services either in Westminster Abbey or in St. Paul's Cathedral. Abp. Longley, however, recognized the need for such a gathering and accordingly issued an invitation to all the diocesan bps. of the Anglican Communion to attend a 5-day "Conference" at his official headquarters. The use of the word "conference" clearly indicated that the gathering was not conciliar or synodical; and the meetings, during the 100 years since the first, have amply demonstrated their informal, consultative nature. With the growth in the Anglican Communion, the number of bps. attending has steadily increased from the 76 present in 1867. The invitations to the 1968 conference were, for the first time, sent to every bp. in active service, whether diocesan or otherwise; and the number responding was close to 500. Successive Lambeth Conferences (1878, 1888, 1897, 1908, 1920, 1930, 1948, 1958, 1968) have dealt with many of the issues in ecclesiastical life as well as in social and political matters. Notable among the Conferences was that held in 1920, memorable for its concentration on the unity of the Church, chiefly in the "Appeal to All Christian People," which established a new level of responsible Anglican ecumenical concern. The 1958 report on "Family in Contemporary Society" established a broad new Anglican approach to the theology of human sexuality and marriage. Every conference, however, devotes a fair amount of attention to the internal problems of the Anglican Communion and its member Churches as well as to wider issues.

The Tenth Lambeth Conference (July 25–August 25, 1968), called by the Abp. of Canterbury, Dr. Michael Ramsey, opened with a service in Canterbury Cathedral at which he was the preacher and the apostolic delegate to Great Britain was a special guest. At the opening session at Church House, Westminster, London, where, because of the large attendance, the month-long meetings were held, greetings were read from the Pope and the Ecumenical Patriarch. In attendance were 467 of the 740 bps., metropolitans, and primates of the worldwide 47-million-member Anglican Communion. Lambeth '68 was the first Conference to be open to the press and the first to have consultants (25 Anglican specialists in various fields) and some 50 official observers from other denominations, who participated actively in the discussions. The latter included the RC Church, Orthodox and other Eastern Churches, Old Catholic, and all major Protestant bodies, represented by many distinguished religious leaders. The theme was Renewal of the Church, in Faith, Ministry and Unity, with the three sections headed respectively by the primate of Canada, the archbishop of York, and the metropolitan of India. Its 32 subcommittees dealt with subjects ranging from theological questions and social and moral issues to world problems of race, poverty, and war. The most controversial issues were those concerning the ordination of women, and *intercommunion between Anglicans and other baptized Christians, in order to meet special pastoral needs, and between Churches committed to and awaiting full organic union. Such intercommunion involves the Anglican

principle of episcopacy (the fourth point of the *Lambeth Quadrilateral) and the question as to whether intercommunion should be a means to unity or the expression of its fulfillment. Robert Cecil Mortimer, Bp. of Exeter, England, was chief spokesman for the traditional Anglo-Catholic position, and their contention that in some of the current unity schemes under consideration the essentials of Anglicanism are in danger of being lost or compromised.

While the leadership of the Anglican Communion is still predominantly Anglo-Saxon, the native Asiatic and African bps. carried great weight at this conference. Abp. Lakdasa de Mel, Metropolitan of India, pushed through the resolutions endorsing full communion with the *Church of South India and with other uniting Indian Churches upon their inauguration, and the highly controversial Anglican-Methodist unity scheme in England, though not without heated debate and sizable dissent. Lambeth '68 produced a notable statement on prayer, but no radical theology. It proclaimed that the Church of today will be renewed only insofar as it pursues its role as the Servant Church. It stressed the ministry of the laity, encouraged the expansion of the perpetual diaconate and part-time ministries where needed, and recommended that deaconesses be considered to be within the diaconate. The final amended resolution on women and the priesthood stated that arguments on both sides were inconclusive but urged further study by the member Churches and canonical provision for women to preach, baptize, read the Gospel and Epistle, and distribute the elements at the Eucharist.

The bishops authorized the resumption of talks with the Orthodox Church, the continuance of Anglican-Roman conversations, and support for the Anglican Center in Rome; initiation of talks with world Lutheranism; and close cooperation with the World Council of Churches and the establishment of an Anglican Center in Geneva. A total of some 75 resolutions were debated in plenary session and acted upon. One important structural step was the proposed 50-

member Anglican Consultative Council composed of bps., priests, and laity meeting every 2 years, to provide a representative central organization for common action. Another was the Wider Episcopal Fellowship, scheduled to meet in 1969, which will include bps. in full or partial communion with the Anglican Churches. Also proposed was a summit meeting of Christian and non-Christian leaders, to speak in the interest of humanity on behalf of world peace. Other resolutions pressured the governments for relief of social ills; outlawed the use of nuclear and bacteriological weapons; upheld the rights of conscientious objectors; called for the involvement of youth in the Church; denounced racism as a blatant denial of the Christian faith; and reaffirmed the stand of Lambeth '58 that birth control is a matter of individual conscience. At an outdoor Eucharist at London's White City Stadium, 15,000 churchmen received communion, concelebrated by overseas bps. from five continents in thanksgiving for the spread of the gospel. Two other great conference services were held at Westminster Abbey and St. Paul's Cathedral, with consultants and observers present. In addition to its balanced emphasis on spiritual renewal and social action and its prime thrust toward church unity, Lambeth '68 may be chiefly notable for its ecumenical impact.

Increasingly, debate goes on in Anglican circles as to the future place and nature of the Lambeth Conference. As full communion is established by the Anglican Churches with other non-Anglican bodies such as the Old Catholic Churches, and as particular Anglican Churches become more involved in schemes of church unity in their own countries, the concept of unity expressed in the Anglican Communion is more and more sharply tested and questioned. Yet the need for a worldwide expression of the Church's unity remains unsatisfied by anything less than full sacramental communion; and it may be argued that the Lambeth Conference will have a significant part to play in the divided Christian world until fuller and deeper manifes-

tations of unity in the Body of Christ are possible. See A. N. C. Stephenson, *First Lambeth Conference: 1867* (1967).

LAMBETH QUADRILATERAL (Chicago-Lambeth Quadrilateral), a statement of Anglican principles worked out by the American Episcopalian William Reed *Huntington in *The Church-Idea, An Essay toward Unity* (1870). In the Quadrilateral Huntington offered a basis for organic church unity within American *denominationalism; he attempted as well a redefinition of Anglicanism by means of the proposal in the belief that neither the *Thirty-Nine Articles nor the *Act of Uniformity of 1662 was relevant to the American religious scene in the 19th century. The Quadrilateral suggested four points as a basis for the reunion of the Churches: "first, the Holy Scripture as the Word of God, second, the Primitive Creeds as the Rule of Faith, third, the two Sacraments ordained by Christ himself, and fourth, the Episcopate as the key-stone of Government Unity." These points were accepted by the *General Convention of the Protestant Episcopal Church meeting at Chicago in 1886 and by the *Lambeth Conference of 1888. While Huntington's wording (above) underwent changes over the years, the general principles were reiterated by the later Lambeth Conferences of 1920 and 1930 and by the General Conventions of the Episcopal Church of 1949 and 1961. Commentary and interpretation have tended in a catholic direction, particularly with reference to the troublesome fourth point dealing with the *historic episcopate. Claims respecting the *apostolic succession of bishops (*to,* not *of,* the Apostles) were reintroduced however much Episcopalians sought to distinguish between the episcopate as doctrinally understood, as historical fact, or as function. Far from being a source of unity both within and without the *Anglican Communion, the Lambeth Quadrilateral has proved to be something of a focal point for party debate. While Huntington's proposals initiated unity conversations between American Episcopalians and other

Protestant Churches, none of these has resulted in organic union. The Quadrilateral, however, must be seen as an expression of the desire of liberal Christians in the U.S. in the late 19th cent. for reconciliation.

The term "Quadrilateral" comes from the system of fortress-cities in Lombardy comprised of Mantua, Verona, Peschiera, and Legnano, important in the Napoleonic wars and in the Austrian occupation of Italy, 1815–59. Huntington's allusion implied that within such a fortress as his four points the Church might stand secure. See *Documents of Church Unity* (1962); J. A. Hardon, *Spirit and Origins of American Protestantism* (1968), 188–191.

LAMENTABILI, a decree of the Holy Office (approved by Pope Pius X, July 4, 1907) listing 65 condemned propositions without affixing any determined theological censure. While the decree was aimed at the movement later called *modernism (*Pascendi*, Sept. 8, 1907), it mentions no names. Condemned as erroneous are certain views relating to the interpretation, inspiration, and inerrancy of Scripture, the meaning of revelation and of dogmas, certain beliefs about Christ, about the origin of the Church and of the sacraments, and about the immutability of revealed truths. See ASS 40 (1907), 470–478; D 3401–66; V. A. Yzermans, *All Things in Christ* (1954); bibliog. for Modernism.

LANDESKIRCHE, see TERRITORIAL CHURCH.

LANDMARKISM, a Baptist movement that stressed the independence of local churches, denied that the NT refers to a universal Church, and claimed that the Baptist Church is the only true Church. It originated in Nashville, Tenn., in 1850 with James B. Graves and James M. Pendleton. Of significance in understanding the movement is the individualism of the frontier and the fact that in the same period arose Old-School Presbyterians and Baptists, high-church Episcopalians, and German Reformed and Lutheran movements, which sought to counteract the tendency in *revivalism to water down theological distinctions of particular denominations. The movement took its name from Pendleton's *An Old Landmark Reset* (1854). Believing that a succession of properly baptized persons is essential to a true gospel ministry, the Landmarkists maintained that there had been an unbroken succession of Baptist churches, practicing *believer's baptism by immersion, since the time of Christ. Since Baptists alone had such a succession, all baptism by others was held to be invalid; there could be no other gospel Church; and theirs was the only valid ministry. Exchanging pulpits with non-Baptists was condemned, and communion was restricted to the members of each particular congregation (see OPEN COMMUNION). Graves publicly attacked the Methodists in *The Great Iron Wheel* (1856) and the Presbyterians in *The Tri-lemma: or Death by Three Horns* (1860). His comprehensive statement of Landmarkist principles was *Old Landmarkism: What Is It?* (1880). Separately organized in 1905 as the Baptist General Association (since 1924, American Baptist Association), the movement had widespread influence on other Baptists, especially in the South. See R. G. Torbet, "Landmarkism," *Baptist Concepts of the Church* (ed. W. S. Hudson, 1959).

LANGLAND, WILLIAM (c.1322–c.1392), generally held to be the author of all three versions of *Piers Plowman*. L. was born in Ledbury, Herefordshire; he lived in London. He was in minor orders, was married, and earned a meager living singing the Office of the Dead for wealthy patrons. No respecter of persons, L. dressed like a beggar, brooded all his life on man's relationship to God, and kept on writing and rewriting his great poem—the A text in his youth, the B in middle age, and the C when he was 65. See bibliog. for *Piers Plowman*.

LAPSI (Lat., those who have fallen or failed), description applied to Christians who apostatized under the persecution of Decius (249–251). Some offered incense in pagan rites (the *thurificati*), some sacrificed to the Roman gods (the *sacrificati*). The question of reconciling the numerous *lapsi* was the occasion of the *Novatianist schism, which in turn raised the *rebaptism issue. Cyprian of Carthage (d. 258) received the *lapsi* back into communion after due signs of repentance. Novatianists insisted that the *lapsi* be excluded from communion. *LIBELLATICI; *TRADITOR.

LARGE CATECHISM, Martin Luther's *Der Grosser Catechismus*, written in 1529, a Lutheran confessional standard. *CATECHISMS, LUTHER'S.

LARGER CATECHISM, one of the two *Westminster Catechisms, written in 1647; a Presbyterian *doctrinal standard.

LA ROCHELLE, CONFESSION OF, another name for the *Gallican Confession, used because it was revised and adopted in La Rochelle in 1571 at the seventh national synod of the *Reformed Church in France.

LATIMER, HUGH (c.1485–1555), English Reformer. L. was a Leicestershire man of yeoman stock. He became a fellow of Clare Hall, Cambridge, and was early suspected of Lutheranism, which he disowned; he later admitted indiscretions, but not errors, in doctrine. He approved Henry VIII's divorce and marriage to Anne Boleyn, and was favored by Thomas *Cromwell, being appointed bp. of Worcester (1535). He resigned (1539) over the *Six Articles. He applauded the sacrifice of Cardinal Pole's family to the King's vengeance, and was a scoffer at shrines of Our Lady. He continued as a famous court-preacher throughout the reign of Edward VI. Though ill and worn, "as meet to discuss theology as to be captain of Calais," L. was indomitable when, under Mary, he was called to defend himself against charges of heresy. He was condemned to the stake at Oxford, together with Nicholas Ridley. They were allowed to have bags of gunpowder fastened round their necks by friends. Latimer's words still ring: "Be of good cheer, Master Ridley, we shall light such a candle, by God's grace, in England as I trust shall never be put out." See A. G. Chester, *H. L.: Apostle to the English* (1954), with bibliog.

LATIN RITE, one of the 18 canonical rites recognized in the RC Church (the other 17 are Oriental). Canonical rite means not only the liturgical rite but also the canonical discipline and spiritual heritage of a Church. In this canonical sense the Latin rite coincides with the Latin Church. Liturgically, however, there are other Latin rites besides the Roman: the particular rites of religious orders (e.g., Carthusian, Cistercian, Dominican) and the rites of primatial sees, such as those of Lyons (Gallican), of Milan (Ambrosian), and of Toledo (Mozarabic). The obvious characteristic of the Latin rite is the use of Latin in the liturgy and in official church law and communications. Yet, before and after Trent decreed the use of Latin in the Mass (D 1749, 1759), the Slavonic language was used in parts of Croatia and Czechoslovakia. Vatican Council II, while maintaining the principle of Latin for the Latin rite, allows the use of "the mother tongue in the Mass, the administration of the Sacraments, and other parts of the liturgy" (Vat II SacLit 36). The postconciliar period has witnessed a rapid vernacularization of the liturgy the world over. Special features of the Latin rite in canonical sense are the celibacy of priests, use of unleavened bread for the Eucharist, and communion under one kind (this last ruling was modified after Vatican II by special concessions of communion under both kinds on some occasions). See A. Caron, NCE 8:520–521. A. A. King, *Liturgies of Religious Orders* (1955); idem, *Liturgies of Primatial Sees* (1957).

LATITUDINARIANISM, a word used derisively in the latter part of the 17th cent. for a school of thought within the C of E that tended to regard formal expressions of doctrine, worship, or government to be of little importance as compared with man's inner, rational, or mystical experience. England was emerging from a century of sharp and often bitter controversy marked by strong, sectarian loyalties. With the final religious settlement of 1661, the way seemed open to new horizons of scientific and philosophical inquiry and a new spirit of liberty and tolerance. At the least, the nation was weary of ecclesiastical quarrels and theological hairsplitting. More deeply, many needed and sought a recovery of respect for reason and for the deep mystical knowledge of God. One significant group usually identified as latitudinarian was the *Cambridge Platonists, who reacted against formalism and sectarianism and led the way toward a rediscovery of Greek mystical thought. But latitudinarianism as a whole tended toward liberalism without mysticism, even toward the sterile *deism of the 18th cent. (see ENLIGHTENMENT). The movement became identified largely with the rise of Whig politics and finally disappeared in the face of the Evangelical Revival and the *Tractarian movement. The *broad-church adherents of the 19th cent. were in some ways the successors of the latitudinarians, but without the political affiliations of the earlier group.

LATOURETTE, KENNETH SCOTT (1884–1968), ecclesiastical and Oriental historian, missiologist. He was born in Oregon City, Ore., and graduated from Linfield College, McMinnville, Ore., in 1904. At Yale his graduate work was in Oriental languages and history; he received the doctorate in 1909. Through work with the YMCA and the Student Volunteer Movement, he became interested in missions; he went to China in 1910, but ill health forced his return to the U.S. in 1912. He remained devoted to missions, esp. in the Far East, throughout his life. He was ordained a Baptist minister in 1918, but spent his whole active life in the academic world. He was a professor of history at Reed College, Portland, Ore., and Denison Univ., Granville, Ohio, before his appointment as professor of missions at Yale in 1921. He became chairman of the department of religion at Yale in 1938, and from 1946 until his retirement in 1953 was director of graduate studies of the Yale Divinity School. He also served as visiting lecturer at many other universities and at schools of theology. He was president of the American Baptist Convention, 1951–52, a member of the board of several mission organizations, and on the committee for the drafting of a constitution for the World Council of Churches at Utrecht in 1938. Several of his more than 80 books dealt with the political and cultural history of the Far East, esp. China. His works on church history are regarded by many as the foremost 20th-cent. contributions to the field. The two major works are *History of the Expansion of Christianity* (7v., 1937–45) and *Christianity in a Revolutionary Age* (5v., 1958–62); the one-volume *History of Christianity* (1953) is a remarkable accomplishment. His work has been recognized not only for its scholarship but for its freedom from sectarian bias. He exercised as well a wide influence through his own personality, and his dedication to Christian causes, esp. Christian unity.

LATTER-DAY SAINTS, Church of Jesus Christ of, popularly known as the Mormon Church, founded in 1830 in Fayette, N.Y., by Joseph *Smith, Jr. He reported that a heavenly personage, the Angel Moroni, led him to discover a set of golden tables, on which were inscribed characters in Reformed Egyptian, and a set of spectacles, called the Urim and Thummim, to be used for translating the plates. The *Book of Mormon* is the translation; it describes the aboriginal people of the Western Hemisphere and the establishment of a Church in North America by Jesus Christ after his ascension. The book covers a period from 600 B.C. to A.D. 421. Smith declared that all existing Christian Churches were apostate and without authority to preach or baptize. He said that John the Baptist had conferred the powers of the priesthood of Aaron on him and that Peter, James, and John had given him the priesthood of Melchizedek. The Church he founded was to succeed the Christian Churches that had apostatized in the Eastern Hemisphere and died out in the Western.

Smith and his followers built their first temple in Kirtland, Ohio, and then moved to Missouri. Driven out of that state, they purchased land on the banks of the Mississippi and founded the city of Nauvoo, Ill., which grew and prospered so greatly that it aroused the envy of others. Rumors that Smith had introduced polygamy into his Church began to spread, and some of his followers turned against him. An opposition newspaper appeared, but followers of Smith destroyed the printing plant. Smith was arrested on charges of sedition and imprisoned at Carthage, Illinois. A mob stormed the jail and murdered the prophet and his brother Hyrum in 1844. The question of succession caused dissension; some groups broke away from the majority, which followed the leadership of Brigham *Young, senior member of the Council of the Twelve Apostles. Continuing antagonism in Nauvoo culminated in mob violence that compelled the Mormons to leave that city in 1846. Under Young's leadership the first of the Mormons made the difficult journey to the valley of the Great Salt Lake in 1847. In Utah the Mormons established a theocracy and openly practiced polygamy from 1852 to 1890, when the president of the Church declared *plural marriage a suspended doctrine.

The accepted scriptures of the Mormon Church are the Bible, the *Book of Mormon*, *Doctrines and Covenants*, and the *Pearl of Great Price*. The Church also believes in a continuous revelation from God expressed through the president of the Church. In Mormon theology God and Jesus Christ are personages of flesh and bones. God is a polygamist who has countless spirit children. Man has the potential of becoming a god on his own planet with his own spirit children. The Mormon belief is succinctly expressed in the phrase: "What man is now, God once was; what God is now, man may become." The God of this world was once a man himself and is now only one of many gods in the universe. Man has preexisted with God from eternity but is given the opportunity of achieving godhood himself by undergoing the experiences of mortality. Those who wish to reach the highest of the three stages of exaltation in the next life must be Mormons who receive their temple endowments, marry in the temple, obey the priesthood, and lead good lives. Lukewarm Mormons and non-Mormons will enjoy a lower form of bliss, and a small number of men will be condemned as sons of perdition for such sins as adultery and apostasy. *Millenarianism has always been a part of Mormon teaching. Original sin is denied.

Mormons worship in nearly 4,000 local congregations, known as wards. These are grouped in 420 stakes, which correspond to dioceses. Pastors of wards are called bishops and support themselves with secular jobs. Only the top officials of the Church receive salaries. The Sunday sacrament meeting always includes a communion service, at which bread and water are served. Young Mormons are baptized by immersion at the age of 7 or 8. Mormons also believe in *baptism for the dead. Great care is taken to compile genealogies of deceased ancestors, who are baptized by proxy in the dozen Mormon temples. Since 1890 Mormons no longer practice polygamy, although deviationists at times have defied both the State and the Church by taking additional wives. Two qualified Mormons may marry "for time and eternity" in a temple; this is a *celestial marriage. The bonds of such a union are believed to last throughout eternity.

The Church is governed by the *First Presidency (composed of a president, elected for life and known as the Prophet, Seer, and Revelator, and his two counselors) and by the *Council of the Twelve Apostles. Almost every male adult in the

Church holds some rank of priesthood of Aaron or of Melchizedek: deacon, teacher, priest, elder, member of the seventy, or high priest. Negro Mormons may not be ordained or be allowed to enter the temples, because they are thought to have been cursed by God in their previous lives. A Mormon in good standing will tithe his income, observe the Word of Wisdom (no tobacco, liquor, coffee, or tea), attend church regularly, and participate in the secret temple rites known as endowments. The Church promotes education, recreation, a strict sexual code, honesty in personal relations, respect for civil authority, mutual assistance, and large families. The Mormon Church owns many profitable commercial enterprises and it assists any Mormon who is unemployed or sick and maintains warehouses for storing food, clothing, and household goods.

Brigham Young University in Provo, Utah, has become the largest church-related university in the nation, with more than 20,000 students. The Church also staffs colleges in Idaho and Hawaii. Mormons in public schools and state universities receive religious instruction in nearby seminaries and institutes of religion. By 1967 the Church of Jesus Christ of Latter-Day Saints had grown to 2,400,000 members, mostly in the U.S.; Mormons predominate in Utah but make up large communities in Ariz., N.Mex., S Calif., and Idaho. They maintain a corps of about 12,000 young missionaries around the world who devote 2 years to spreading the "restored gospel." See K. J. Hansen, *Quest for Empire* (1967); T. F. O'Dea, *Mormons* (1957); W. J. Whalen, *Latter-Day Saints in the Modern Day World* (1964); R. B. West, Jr., *Kingdom of the Saints: The Story of Brigham Young and the Mormons* (1957). *LATTER DAY SAINTS, REORGANIZED CHURCH OF JESUS CHRIST OF; *CHURCH OF CHRIST (FETTINGITES); *CHURCH OF CHRIST (TEMPLE LOT); *CHURCH OF JESUS CHRIST (BICKERTONITES); *CHURCH OF JESUS CHRIST (CUTLERITES); *LATTER-DAY SAINTS (STRANGITES), CHURCH OF JESUS CHRIST OF.

LATTER DAY SAINTS, Reorganized Church of Jesus Christ of, a Mormon body that considers itself to be the successor of the Church founded in 1830 by Joseph *Smith, Jr. After his murder (1844) thousands of his followers preferred to remain in the Midwest; they rejected the leadership of Brigham *Young, whom they accused of introducing heretical doctrines (see LATTER-DAY SAINTS, CHURCH OF JESUS CHRIST OF). The Reorganized Church was formed in 1852, and in 1860 Joseph Smith (1832–1914), son of the Mormon founder, accepted the presidency. Independence, Mo., became headquarters; total membership (1968) was about 190,000, with 168,355 in 1,000 American congregations. Closer to traditional Protestants in doctrine than the Utah Mormons, members of the Reorganized Church accept the *Book of Mormon* and the Mormon doctrine of continuing revelation but reject polygamy, plurality of gods, and secret temple rites. This Church owns the original Kirtland, Ohio, temple and the manuscript of the *Book of Mormon*, as well as the graves of Joseph, Emma, and Hyrum Smith in Nauvoo, Illinois. Almost all direct descendants of Joseph Smith, Jr., belong to the Reorganized Church. Chief administrative bodies are the first presidency and the quorum of twelve apostles. Unlike the Utah Church, the Reorganized Church admits Negroes to the priesthood. The Church maintains Graceland College in Lamoni, Iowa, and a seminary and a hospital in Independence.

LATTER-DAY SAINTS (STRANGITES), Church of Jesus Christ of, small Mormon Church established by James J. Strang (1813–56). After the murder of the Mormon prophet Joseph *Smith in 1844 several claimants vied for the presidency of the Church. Most Mormons followed Brigham *Young to Utah. A few recognized Strang, who had been a lawyer in Wisconsin and had been baptized while visiting Nauvoo, Ill., in February 1844. Strang attempted to strengthen his position by offering a translation of the unearthed plates of Laban. He first organized dissident Mormons in Voree, Wis., but then led his followers to Beaver Island in Lake Michigan, where he was crowned "king" of the Church. At first violently opposed to polygamy, he eventually married five wives. Strang was shot by two members of the sect, the buildings in the colony were burned, and the 2,500 Strangites dispersed. A remnant of 250 Strangites still accepts his claims, worships on Saturday, practices circumcision, and offers animal sacrifices. See M. M. Quaife, *Kingdom of Saint James* (1930).

LATTER RAIN MOVEMENT, a description used of Pentecostalism, esp. during its early years. Joel 2.23 refers to a former and a latter rain; for Pentecostals the former is the outpouring of gifts on Pentecost and the latter rain is the new outpouring of the same gifts of the Spirit that ushers in a new premillennial dispensation. In 1947 the New Order of the Latter Rain was formed in North Battleford, Saskatchewan, to protest the loss by the organized Pentecostal Churches of the original Pentecostal insights and direction.

LAUD, WILLIAM (1573–1645), Abp. of Canterbury who so dominated pre-Commonwealth Anglicanism that both it and the ideals that survived it are called Laudian. Intransigent in upholding *episcopacy and the sacramental order, he bore severely on those, mainly Puritans, who did not conform. Undergraduate and fellow of St. John's College, Oxford, and later its head, he devoted himself to the restoration of a Catholic liturgy in the C of E and defended the great high road, the *via media,* of its theology against Calvinism; it was the noble period of the *Caroline Divines. Elected bp. of St. Davids (1621), he engaged in controversy with the Jesuit John Percy (a *Relation* of which L. published in 1639), in which he maintained that the RC and Anglican Churches were both parts of one Church Catholic. Translated to Bath and Wells (1626), then London (1628), and appointed chancellor of Oxford Univ. (1629), he was consecrated abp. of Canterbury in 1633. He was a notable patron of learning. Growing hostility and the attempt to enforce his reforms in Scotland led to his impeachment, imprisonment in the Tower of London (1641), a trial conducted with little regard for justice, and his execution (1645) at the block on Tower Hill. He left a remarkable diary of his last years, published among his works in the Library of Anglo-Catholic Theology (7v., 1847–60). See E. C. E. Bourne, *Anglicanism of W. L.* (1947). *ANGLICANISM.

LAURENTIUS ANDREAE, see ANDERSON, LARS.

LAUSANNE CONFERENCE, first world conference of the *Faith and Order movement, held at Lausanne, Switzerland, Aug. 3–21, 1927. Over 100 Protestant and Orthodox Churches were represented. The idea for the meeting came originally from the Protestant Episcopal Church under the influence of Bishop C. H. *Brent. The purpose of the conference was to find bases for doctrinal unity among Christian Churches, starting from their common belief in Christ and the gospel and their deep distress at disunity. The subjects considered were: (1) the call to unity; (2) the Church's message to the world: the gospel; (3) the nature of the Church; (4) the Church's common confession of faith; (5) the Church's ministry; (6) the sacraments; and (7) the unity of Christendom and the relation thereto of the existing Churches. There was wide disagreement on many points, esp. the nature and number of the sacraments and the positions on *episcopacy, *apostolic succession, and *ordination. The statements voted by the conference were therefore largely limited to defining areas of agreement and disagreement. The conference issued a rather general but fervent statement (the only one accepted by the Orthodox) on the gospel as the Church's message to the world and as the "source for social regeneration." See H. N. Bate, ed., *Faith and Order: Proceedings of the World Conference, Lausanne* (1928).

LAW, WILLIAM (1686–1761), Anglican apologist and spiritual writer. L., who was educated and ordained at Cambridge, lost both his ecclesiastical and academic position because he was a *nonjuror (1712). The rest of his life he spent quietly in tutoring, spiritual direction, and writing. His *Three Letters to the Bishop of Bangor* (1717) is a defense of Anglican principles, and his *Case of Reason* (1732) is a skillful reply to M. Tindal, a deist. L.'s most famous work, however, is a *Serious Call to a Devout and Holy Life* (1728; many eds. since). The work, which relied heavily on Catholic spiritual writers (Tauler, Ruysbroeck, Thomas à Kempis) was the most effective Protestant spiritual book in English after *Pilgrim's Progress*, exercising in particular a strong influence upon John *Wesley, and upon evangelical revivalism generally. It stresses the individual ascetical life through the cultivation of the virtues. In his later years L. became interested in J. *Boehme and developed a theory of mysticism similar to that of the *Inner Light, which alienated Wesley. L.'s mystical works are *The Spirit of Prayer* (1749–50) and *The Spirit of Love* (1752 and 1754). See E. W. Baker, *Herald of the Evangelical Revival* (1948); J. B. Green, *John Wesley and W. L.* (1945); S. Hobhouse, *W L. and Eighteenth Century Quakerism* (1927); L. Stephen, DNB 32 (1892), 236–240.

LAW AND GOSPEL, a basic distinction made in many kinds of Christian theology between the two principal modes of God's relation to man. Both the distinction and the close connection between the gift and the command of God are evident as early as the fundamental statement of the Decalogue (Ex 20.2–3): "I am the Lord your God, who brought you out of the land of Egypt, out of the house of bondage. You shall have no other gods before me." The gospel in this declaration is the remembrance that it was God, the Lord of the covenant, who had brought the people of Israel out of captivity. This was the historical basis for any requirement that he would lay upon them. And the requirement was correlative to it, namely, the acknowledgment of his sole claim to deity, together with the refusal to ascribe such deity to anyone or anything less than the Ultimate, who had brought about the Exodus of the people from Egypt. As is evident already in the story of Abraham and in the other patriarchal narratives, the initiative of God in creating a relationship between himself and his chosen ones was always the presupposition for the rule of conduct that he enunciated. The law was grounded in the gospel; the two were inseparable, but they were in a real sense distinct from each other throughout the history of biblical religion, whether in the OT or in the NT.

With the coming of Christianity, however, this distinction took on new meaning. Although Jesus described his mission as one of fulfilling, not of destroying, the law and the prophets, he made clear again what the adherents of the law and the prophets were in danger of forgetting: that the deeds of God, not the works of men, were the foundation for the relation between them. It was esp. in the epistles of the Apostle Paul—and specifically in those to the Romans and to the Galatians—that the distinction between the law and the gospel was developed most fully. God's covenant with Abraham preceded the giving of the law. Therefore "the law, which came four hundred and thirty years afterward, does not annul a covenant previously ratified by God, so as to make the promise void. For if the inheritance is by the law, it is no longer by promise; but God gave it to Abraham by a promise" (Gal 4.17–18). In the gospel of Jesus Christ, therefore, "the righteousness of God has been manifested apart from law . . . the righteousness of God through faith in Christ Jesus for all who believe" (Rom 3.21–22). Other parts of the

NT do not work as explicitly with this distinction, but it is implied wherever the primacy of the divine gift over the divine demand is asserted.

In the 2d cent. Marcion laid such emphasis upon the distinction of law and gospel as to separate rather than merely distinguish them. His opponent, Tertullian, said that "the separation of law and gospel" was "Marcion's special and principal work." But now it was a matter not of differentiating between two modes of God's relation to men, but of differentiating between two Gods: one, the God of the law, the Jewish deity of wrath and punishment portrayed in the OT; the other, the God of the gospel, the Father of our Lord Jesus Christ, revealed in the NT. It is probably correct to see Marcion's teaching as a protest against a tendency already evident in the Church of his time, to depress Christianity into a religion of conduct rather than a message of salvation. But the cure he proposed was no less dangerous than the disease he diagnosed, and the Church was obliged to reject any interpretation of the relation between the law and the gospel that would threaten the unity of God.

Luther, too, protested against the blurring of the distinction between the promises of God and the demands of God, and he made the relation between the law and the gospel a dominant theme of his theology. In his *Lectures on Galatians* (1535) he used this relation as the touchstone by which to identify true and false doctrine in Christianity. Thus, e.g., the Christian doctrine of the sacraments was distorted when they were seen as holy works that we perform in order thereby to become worthy of the favor of God, rather than as means of grace, by which God bestows his gratuitous favor. Lutheran theology since the 16th cent. has continued to lay great emphasis on the proper relation between the law and the gospel. The *Formula of Concord declared this relationship in Art. V, and in Art. VI discussed the "third use of the law," namely, as a reminder to the regenerated of their remaining sinfulness and their need of grace (see ANTINOMIANISM). *Pietism

came to be condemned because it taught that the proper preparation of the heart would make a man ready to receive grace. Various forms of 19th-cent. *liberal theology were interpreted as a relapse into the moralistic distortion of the gospel as a "new law." Many of the debates within the Lutheran theological tradition were, in one way or another, discussions of the proper relation between law and gospel.

The theme of law and gospel is prominent in the *Reformed tradition as well (e.g., *Westminster Confession, ch. 19–20; Second *Helvetic Confession, ch. 12–13). The relationship has a different emphasis, with obedience to law being stressed as a mark of election. The distinction between law and gospel, however, is not a denominational label but an issue to which Christian doctrine in every denomination has been obliged to address itself. See G. Forde, *Law-Gospel Debate* (1969); C. F. W. Walther, *Proper Distinction Between Law and Gospel* (1897); ThAq ST 1a2ae, 106.1 and 2.

LAY PREACHING, public proclamation of the word of God by the nonordained. Acts and the Epistles of Paul attest that lay persons shared in preaching. The charisms of the word, of evangelization, and of prophecy were given to ministers and laymen alike (see Acts 13.1; Rom 12.6–7; 1 Cor 12.10, 28). Preaching was charismatic and not necessarily connected with office or orders. In the patristic era, the period of the organization of church life, lay preaching decreased. As a layman, Origen was invited by the bps. of Caesarea and Jerusalem to preach and explain the Scriptures. Such a practice did not last beyond the 3d century. Lay preaching came to depend on the initiative and control of the bishops. The *Apostolic Constitutions* (4th cent.) still referred to lay teaching; the *Statuta ecclesiae antiquae* (6th cent.) severely restrict teaching by lay persons and women. Pope Leo the Great ruled that preaching belongs to the priestly order. The Middle Ages witnessed a revival of lay preaching in the spiritual movements of the 12th and 13th centuries. *Waldo and companions were allowed by Alexander III to preach "at the request of priests." The *Humiliati of northern Italy, forbidden to preach in 1179 and 1184, were allowed by Innocent III to preach with the bishop's permission, but only the *verbum exhortativum*, i.e., on the Christian life and virtues, and not *de articulis fidei et sacramentis*, i.e., on dogmatic questions. The *Waldenses did not obey such directives; the Humiliati did. In Milan in 1216, 50 communities of these preached in churches and public squares. In the 13th cent. the mendicant orders were given the same faculty for their lay members, and St. Francis of Assisi confirmed it in his rule. Their preaching was to be restricted to exhortation to a Christian life; it was to avoid doctrinal questions.

In 1418, Martin V in the bull *Inter cunctas* repudiated the practice of the followers of John *Wycliffe and Jan *Hus and their contention that lay persons of either sex can freely preach the word of God (see D 1277–78). To Luther's mind, in principle all believers were ministers of the word of God no less than pastors. The enthusiasm of lay preaching, however, led to disorder and the Peasants' War; thus the *Augsburg Confession restricted the right of public preaching to the *rite vocati*, pastors and ministers (Art. 14). The same restrictive policy was followed in the *Reformed Churches (see, e.g., Second *Helvetic Confession, c. 18). Lay preaching was part of the very nature of the Anabaptist and Quaker origins. Mennonite preachers are ordained; but many Quaker bodies do not have an ordained ministry. Methodists have, beside ordained preachers, institutional lay preachers (see LOCAL PREACHERS). The Protestant Churches generally restrict preaching to ordained ministers but make exception for specially qualified laity, theologians, or professors, and for the laity generally at (nonliturgical) Bible services. The question of women preachers still is controverted; but there is wide acceptance of women to the ministry. While most Pentecostal bodies have ordained ministers, the charismatic nature of Pentecostalism essentially includes the testimony and prophecy of all members.

For the RC Church, the Council of Trent ruled that preaching is the function of bishops and priests. The present canon law (CIC *c*.1354) grants the right to preach to priests and deacons and excludes other clerics and laity (even lay religious). Vatican Council II has reopened the question of lay preaching by its teaching on the lay apostolate. The question is: do the right and the duty of the laity to take their part in the apostolic mission of the Church and its prophetic function comprise lay preaching? Vatican II decreed that "the hierarchy may entrust to laymen some functions more closely connected with the pastoral office, e.g., teaching Christian doctrine . . ." (Vat II ApostLaity 24). According to one commentator, F. Klostermann, this extends not only to "catechetical instruction for children but also preaching to adults, preaching in the course of non-liturgical divine services which do not require the presence of a priest, and sometimes the function of preaching in other types of divine service" (Vorgrimler Vat II 382). See Y. Congar, *Jalons pour une théologie du laïcat* (2d ed., 1964), 414–426. *PREACHING.

LAY READER, a title with two principal uses. (1) In the early Church, as Tertullian and the *Apostolic Constitutions* attest, the lector was a minor officer of the Church empowered to read or chant the lessons at Mass. The lectorate has continued in both the Eastern and the RC Churches as a minor order received by clerics in the course of their theological studies. With the liturgical reform instituted by Vatican Council II, the exercise of the office has been revived in such a way that laymen normally read the lesson and lead the congregation in other prayers of the Mass. The Council calls this a "genuine liturgical ministry" (Vat II SacLit 29). (2) Lay reader is a title applied throughout the *Anglican Communion to an unordained person licensed by the bp. to read some public services. The extent of the authorization varies in different jurisdictions, but it usually includes the reading of Scripture, such services of the BCP as are not restricted to priests, and authorized sermons. In some dioceses, lay readers regarded as having sufficient preparation are licensed to preach. Provision for their admission was made in the 1550 Ordinal of Edward VI, and their duties were defined by *Convocations in 1559. Their licensing was discontinued in England in 1775, but resumed in 1866. They performed esp. important work in the expansion of the Anglican Communion in new countries, where there was always a shortage of ordained ministers. See H. B. Restarick, *Lay Readers* (1894); *Regulations for Readers in the Anglican Church* (1915).

LAYING ON OF HANDS, also called the imposition of hands, the placing of the hands by one person on the head of another, a gesture or rite with many Christian uses. In the NT it is a gesture of blessing (Mk 10.16) or of healing (Mt 9.18); it is also used as a sign of the Holy Spirit being received (Acts 8.15–17; Heb 6.2), or of conferring a special mission (Acts 6.1–6; 1 Tim 4.14; 2 Tim 1.6). In the RC Church the laying on of hands by the bp. is an essential part of the sacrament of holy orders to symbolize the reception of the Holy Spirit. Pius XII in 1947 (see D 3860) declared that the "matter," i.e., the essential external action in the ordination of bps., priests, and deacons, is the laying on of hands. It is also included as a subsidiary rite in the exorcism of catechumens before baptism, and as a blessing for healing and pardon in the anointing of the sick. The raising of the confessor's hand before the imparting of absolution is also a trace of the laying on of hands as a symbol of reconciliation. Outside of the ritual of the sacraments, it is part of the blessing of monks, and abbots, and of the consecration of virgins. In the Anglican *Book of Common Prayer, the laying on of hands by the ordaining bp. is essential in the rite of ordination of bps., priests, and deacons. In the Reformation era the laying on of hands was regarded as one of the *adiaphora, acceptable as a sign of blessing, prayer, or conferring a special function in the Church. The most universal Protestant use of the practice has been in the ordination of ministers. But the laying on of hands is also used in invoking the Holy Spirit and in prayers for the sick or those in grave spiritual need. It is an esp. prominent feature in *divine healing, one of the essentials of Pentecostalism.

LAYMEN'S HOME MISSIONARY MOVEMENT, a small body that separated from the *Jehovah's Witnesses in 1920 in opposition to the teachings and leadership of Joseph F. *Rutherford. Headquarters are in Philadelphia, Pennsylvania.

LE COURRAYER, PIERRE FRANÇOIS (1681–1776), French RC defender of Anglican Orders. A native of Rouen, C. became a canon regular at Paris. Beginning with his *Dissertation sur la validité des ordinations des anglais et sur la succession des évêques de l'Église Anglicane,* published anonymously in 1723 at Brussels, he devoted all his efforts to defending the validity of Anglican Orders and episcopal succession. He was welcomed in England when he went there (1732) to spend the rest of his life. In France C.'s work provoked a series of episcopal condemnations. Always protesting his RC orthodoxy, he engaged in literary controversy with those who assailed his thesis. He also published a French translation of Paolo Sarpi's *History of the Council of Trent* (2v., 1736; 3v., 1751), with his own historical and theological notes. This work of C. was itself translated into English, German, and Italian, was explicitly at variance with RC teaching, and provoked further polemical exchanges with his adversaries. See J. Carreyre, DTC 9:112–115; E. Predein, *L'Union des Églises gallicane et anglicane . . .* (1928).

LEE, ANN, founder of the United Society of Believers in Christ's Second Appearing, commonly known as *Shakers. Born in Manchester, Eng., she received no education, but worked as a factory hand and later as a cook. In 1758 she was converted in a revival led by two Quaker tailors, Jane and James Wardley, who had been influenced by some French Prophets or *Camisards then active in England. The Wardley group came to be known as the Shaking Quakers because of a shaking motion, supposedly the result of divine influence, that took place at their meetings. Lee married A. Standerin (sometimes given as Standley or Stanley) in 1762. By 1766 she had borne four children, all of whom died in infancy. Coming to believe that concupiscence was the source of all evil, she began teaching celibacy. Becoming increasingly zealous, she was imprisoned for her religious activities. After her release, she assumed leadership of the Wardley group, who called her "Mother Ann." She claimed to have received a vision of Christ giving her great authority and called herself "Ann of the Word." After another imprisonment, she migrated to America in 1774, accompanied by six men and two women. Sometime thereafter she separated from her husband, and in 1776 established her community at a place near Albany, N.Y., with the Indian name of Niskayuna and the Dutch name of Watervliet. She spent her remaining years in work with the community, and in preaching tours of New England.

LEFÈVRE D'ÉTAPLES, JACQUES (Jacobus Faber Stapulensis; 1455–1536), French humanist, biblical and patristic scholar. He was born at Étaples in Picardy. He was ordained a priest, and became a master of arts at the Univ. of Paris. Visits to Italy led to his first interest, the study of Aristotle. As professor at Paris (1492–1507), he became the center of a circle of men who became eminent scholars. In 1507 St. Germain des Prés, under Abbot Briçonnet, afterwards bp. of Meaux, became his home; there L. lectured and turned his efforts to the study of the Scriptures, the Fathers, and the mystics, esp. Raymond Lull and Jan van Ruys-

broeck. In commentaries on the Psalms (*Quintuplex Psalterium*, 1509), on St. Paul (1512), and on the Gospels (1522) he developed his ideas on justification, the Christian life, and reform of the Church. He participated in the reform movement of Bp. Briçonnet at Meaux, contributing a French translation of the NT (1503) and of the Psalms (1524). The reform at Meaux and L.'s own writings became suspect in the reaction of the Sorbonne and Parlement to the first penetration of Luther's writings into France. L.'s commentary on the Gospels was condemned for doctrinal errors by the Sorbonne faculty in 1523. Called before Parlement to face charges of heresy, he fled to Protestant Strassburg (1525). He was able to return to France in the next year to the post of librarian and tutor for the royal family at Blois. His translation of the whole Bible was published in 1530. The last years of his life were spent at the court of Margaret of Navarre, in writing and editing, esp. works of the Christian mystics, and on mysticism. L. had among his pupils G. *Farel, Calvin's companion in the reform of Geneva; personally or through his writings he influenced Erasmus, Reuchlin, and other humanist Reformers. His ideas on justification and reform of the Church have been regarded as congenial to those of Luther. But L., however, worked for reform within the RC Church and did not break with the old tradition or institution. See E. F. Rice, NCE 8:604–605; Léonard HistProt 1:20–21.

LEGALISM, as a religious attitude, strong reliance on, and strict adherence to, laws. It has been interpreted as "belief that observance of the Ten Commandments or of humanly established laws will gain merit and eternal life" (Mayer RB 566). In this strict sense, it is doubtful that any Christian body can properly be described as legalistic. Mayer applies the term to several Protestant bodies and to Roman Catholics, because of his own views on *law and gospel. None of those to whom he imputes legalism, however, would accept the charge in the sense in which he defines it. To others legalism means excessive emphasis upon conformity to codes of ritual or ethics, and in this sense many groups have a tendency toward legalism. Puritans in England and America were considered legalistic because they opposed recreation or unnecessary work on Sundays (see SABBATARIANS). Many American Protestants have insisted that genuine Christians do not indulge in dancing, card playing, smoking, or drinking. Seventh-day Adventists are often said to be extreme legalists, because of their views of the Sabbath, dietary regulations, advocacy of tithing, and prohibition of drinking and smoking. Denying that they are legalistic, they insist that out of thankfulness to Christ, by whose grace they have been saved through faith, they obey his will as the Scriptures reveal it (see *Seventh-day Adventist Encyclopedia*, 1966). The question of legalism is bound up with the perennial problem of faith and works, which began with Paul's controversy with Judaizers (Galatians and Acts ch. 15). The relationship is a problem that continues to perplex Protestant and RC theologians; many deplore past emphasis on precepts and prohibitions as legalism that neglects the primacy of charity in Christian life. *ANTINOMIANISM.

LEGATE, BARTHOLOMEW (*c.*1575–1612), Seeker, executed as a heretic. L. was a cloth merchant and traveled to Holland, where he was in contact with Mennonites. In England he became a spokesman for Seeker expectation of a new revelation. For his Arian views (because of which Seekers were sometimes called "Legatine Arians") he was arrested (1611), condemned, and became the last person to be burned in London for religious belief. See R. M. Jones, *Studies in Mystical Religion* (1923), 454–455. *SEEKERS.

LEGIO MARIA (Maria Legio; Legion of Mary Church), a Church in western Kenya which, when formed in 1963, was the largest such body ever to have seceded from the RC Church in Africa. Various attempts had been made since 1953 by a Catholic woman of the Nilotic Luo tribe, Mariam Ragot, to form a new religious protest movement *Dini ya Mariam* (Religion of Mary), but on three occasions incipient risings under her leadership were thwarted and suppressed by the colonial administration. By 1963 there was a considerable body of disaffected and lapsed Catholics in the Dioceses of Kisumu and Kisii. At this point a 20-year-old Luo Catholic girl, Gaudencia Aoko, claimed to have had a physical experience similar to death and resurrection followed by a prophetic call from God to form an African Catholic church free from European interference and control. Her magnetic preaching attracted some 60,000 former Catholics; because of the surge of malcontents into the new body, political disturbances broke out, and led to police action and prison sentences for several leaders. Initially almost all adherents were of the Luo tribe, but during the next 5 years membership grew increasingly multitribal and spread also to neighboring Uganda and Tanzania. No RC priests joined the new movement, hence numbers of laymen were ordained; by 1967 some dozen bishops, a cardinal, Carolus Mumbo, and a pope, Simeon Ondeto, known also as *Baba Mtakatifu* (Holy Father), had been designated. After initial troubles with the newly independent Kenya government authorities, the movement asserted its loyalty to the administration and by 1967 had been permitted to register as a legal society claiming 10,000 adult members in East Africa. Early on, Legio Maria made contacts with the 160 Churches of the African independent church movement in Kenya, and joined their militantly antimission federation, the East Africa United Churches and Orthodox Coptic Communion. In 1967 all these Churches abruptly swung in an ecumenical direction by applying for membership to the All Africa Conference of Churches, which is linked with the World Council of Churches.

In doctrine Legio Maria is conservative, stressing orthodox Catholic teaching but inserting a strong element of African culture and world view; the right of Africans to run their Church without European interference is constantly stressed. Practice is conservative and ritualistic; Latin is retained in full as an essential ritual language, and the Mass and sacraments are performed with punctilious ceremonial. Colorful robes based on monastic garb and priestly vestments are worn by all members, with white, black, and mauve especially popular, and members festoon themselves with rosaries, crucifixes, and other Catholic insignia. Services emphasize ex tempore prayer and *glossolalia, mass prayer for the sick, and healing rites. As with many other African independent churches, Legio Maria soon suffered from the recurrent problem of secession. Shortly after its founding in 1963, 300 Luo members in North Mara across the border in Tanzania seceded to form the African Catholic Church under Marcellianus Orongo. In 1967 several small Legio Maria factions in Kenya were discussing further secessions, although the bulk of the movement had settled down as a stable body recognized by a number of other Churches. See D. B. Barrett, *Schism and Renewal in Africa* (1968). *AFRICAN INDEPENDENT CHURCH MOVEMENT; *AFRICAN CHRISTIANITY (CONTEMPORARY).

LEHRERLEUT (Ger., Teacher People), a Hutterite group so called because their founder Jacob Wipf was a teacher, first in Russia, and, after 1877, in South Dakota. Although they had not lived a communal life in Russia, the Lehrerleut founded a *Bruderhof in S.Dak., and 22 more colonies had developed by 1957. Their only (minor) difference from the Hutterites is that they wear buttons on their clothing instead of hooks and eyes. See MennEnc 3:315. *HUTTERITES.

LEIPZIG, DISPUTATION OF, see DISPUTATION OF LEIPZIG.

LEIPZIG INTERIM, see INTERIMS.

LEMAISTRE, ANTOINE AND ISAAC LOUIS, two sons of Catherine Arnault, who became leaders at the Jansenist center, *Port-Royal.

Antoine (1608–58) was a brilliant lawyer, and a counselor of state when he renounced the world (1638) and under the advice of the Abbé de *Saint-Cyran became one of the first *solitaires* of Port-Royal. He collaborated in Isaac Louis' translation of the NT and began his own *Vie des saints.* With skillful eloquence he defended Saint-Cyran against Cardinal Richelieu: *Apologie pour feu M. l'abbé de Saint-Cyran* (1642); *Apologie pour Jean Duvergier de Hauranne* (1645). The *Lettre d'un avocat,* 19th of Pascal's *Provincial Letters, is sometimes ascribed to him.

Isaac Louis (1613–84), better known as Lemaistre de Sacy (anagram of Isaac), was under the spiritual direction of Saint-Cyran when he was ordained (1649). He became director first of the other *solitaires* then of the nuns at Port-Royal. During a period of anti-Jansenist persecution, he was imprisoned in the Bastille (1666–69), where he began an edition of the Bible, *Le sainte Bible en latin et en français* (32v., 1687–1702). His translation of the NT published in 1667, known as the "de Mons" edition, was quite popular, but was condemned (1669) by Clement IX for its Jansenism. He also translated the *Imitation of Christ* (1662), the Psalms, sermons of St. Augustine, as well as Phaedrus's Fables and Terence's comedies. In addition he left many letters of spiritual direction, and *Poème sur l'eucharistie* (1695). His writings helped circulate Jansenist ideas in France. See G. Delassault, *Le Maistre de Sacy et son temps* (1957); bibliog. for Jansenism.

LEPORIUS (5th cent.), priest of Gaul, promoter of a Christological error. John *Cassian in his *De incarnatione Christi* reported that L. maintained Christ to be merely a man who merited divine honor and power by his heroic human life and death. This interpretation of L.'s teaching may have been Cassian's own construction. It actually seems that L., intent on defending the divine transcendence as well as Monophysitism, explained the incarnation as a juxtaposition of the divine and human nature in Jesus, an explanation which destroys true unity of person. L. was condemned by the bps. of southern Gaul. His retractation *Libellus satisfactionis* (PL 31:1221), made for the Gallic bps. and endorsed by African bps., is important as an orthodox Christological statement in the Latin Church anterior to the Nestorian divisions. See É. Amann DTC 9:434–440.

LEVELERS (Levellers), a religious, political party of Puritans. The name, applied from 1647 onward, was intended as a term of derision. The Levelers sought to abolish the monarchy, all class privileges, and any *established Church and to create a democratic republic with complete political and religious equality for all. Their chief strength was drawn from the rank and file of the army; J. *Lilburne was their spokesman and pamphleteer. In 1649 Oliver Cromwell took strong measures against the movement; the Levelers had disappeared by 1660. Their ideas influenced Quaker emphasis on human equality. See J. Frank, *Levellers* (1955).

LEWIS, EDWIN (1881–1959), Methodist theologian. Born in Newbury, Eng., he was educated in Canada, the U.S., and Europe, and in 1916 became a member of the faculty of Drew Theological Seminary, where he taught systematic theology for 35 years. His early publications marked him as a liberal theologian of the personalist-idealist school of B. P. *Bowne, but, influenced by Karl *Barth, he became the champion of *neoorthodoxy through his later articles and books, particularly *A Christian Manifesto* (1934), *A Philosophy of the Christian Revelation* (1940), and *The Creator and the Adversary* (1948). His greatest work was as editor of the *Abingdon Bible Commentary* (1926–29). See D. W. Soper, *Major Voices in American Theology* (1953), 17–36; HistAmMeth 3:284–287; 304–307; 311–315.

LIBELLATICI, a term used to describe those Christians who, during the persecution of Decius (249–251), used a questionable strategy to evade the penalties imposed by the imperial government on those who refused to offer sacrifice or to give other indication of their adherence to the pagan gods and their loyalty to the Emperor. They used bribery to obtain from local officials certificates (*libelli*) falsely testifying that they had offered sacrifice. After the persecution church authorities condemned the subterfuge, but with less severity than the apostasy of those who had offered the required sacrifice (*sacrificati*). The controversy and events connected with the reconciliation of the *libellatici* can be traced in the letters of St. Cyprian and in his treatise *De lapsis*. See Jedin-Baus 222–226.

LIBERAL CATHOLIC CHURCH, a body formed in England by the Old Catholic Bp. J. I. Wedgewood and the theosophist C. W. Leadbeater. According to its *Statement of Principles and Summary of Doctrines*, the Church accepts the principles of *theosophy; high ritualism is also a distinctive mark. Soon after its formation, the Church was disowned by the Old Catholic Church of Utrecht. It claims to be a branch of the one Catholic Church because of *apostolic succession and fidelity to the seven sacraments. Wedgwood was consecrated (1916) as bp. of the Old Catholic Mission in Great Britain in a line that went back to Utrecht through Bp. F. S. Willoughby and Abp. A. H. Mathew (see EPISCOPI VAGANTES). Wedgwood in turn consecrated Leadbeater regionary bp. for Australasia, and by 1918 the two had given the Church its name and distinctive liturgy. Under Presiding Bps. Wedgwood (1916–23) and Leadbeater (1923–34) the Church, with headquarters in London, became worldwide. Membership slowly increased under Presiding Bps. F. W. Pigott (1934–56), A. G. Vreede (1956–64), and Sir Hugh Sykes (1964–), to a total over 10,000, about 2,500 in the United States (1968). Headquarters in the U.S. are in Baltimore, Md., and the present regionary bp. is Newton A. Dahl. (A very small splinter group, which rejects theosophy, broke off in 1947; its headquarters are in Miranda, Calif.; its presiding bp., E. M. Matthews.)

Beliefs include the spiritual presence of the living Christ in the world, his presence in seven sacraments—baptism, confirmation, Holy Eucharist, absolution, anointing of the sick, holy matrimony, holy orders; apostolic succession; and the principles of theosophy, including reincarnation. The Scriptures and Catholic tradition are recognized as rules of faith but not as literally infallible. Vernacular liturgy, including high Mass, stresses devotional and joyous aspiration. Lay members are left free to interpret doctrine and liturgy, since the Church believes that Christ equates religion with love and freedom. Acknowledging diverse paths to truth, the Church practices no aggressive proselytizing. The General Episcopal Synod chooses the hierarchy; the presiding bp. is *primus inter pares*; regionary bps. head provinces; suffragan bps., dioceses; priests, parishes. Bishops and priests are unsalaried; celibacy is optional. Holy orders in the Church include all the other major and minor orders. See E. S. Taylor, *Liberal Catholic Church* (1966); A. W. Cockerham, *Apostolic Succession in the Liberal Catholic Church* (1966).

LIBERAL CHRISTIANS, a designation used by Congregationalist groups or Churches that were turning to Unitarianism in the early 19th cent., before the adoption (1815) of the name Unitarian.

LIBERAL THEOLOGY, a complex theological movement in 19th- and 20th-cent. Europe and the United States. Its features included the view that Christian teaching is simply the expression of natively human religious affectivity; a doctrine of God's immanence in the world; the blending of Jesus' work into the history of human development; optimism in regard to human goodness and social progress; and attention to moral ideals and religious experience rather than doctrine. The remote background for liberal theology, esp. in Germany, was the philosophy of the *Enlightenment, and particularly the idealism of G. Hegel (1770–1831) and his identification of religion with philosophy. F. *Schleiermacher (1768–1834), the father of liberal theology, formulated the viewpoint universal to the movement: religion is a basic human sense of total dependence, and Christianity is simply the highest expression of religion. The liberal attitude was formed, as well, by 19th-cent. biblical higher criticism, the development of evolutionary theory, and the sense of confidence in progress through science.

The center of German liberalism was the Protestant theological faculty at Tübingen. There F. C. Baur (1792–1860) formulated a theology that in a pantheistic interpretation of world history included Christianity as the last state of the "evolving God." Influencing liberal attitudes toward the Bible and the historical Jesus were B. Bauer (1809–92), who denied the historical basis of the NT, and D. F. Strauss (1808–74). Strauss's *Life of Jesus* (1835) represents the NT narratives as "mythical," originating in the poetically inspired reflection of the early Christian community. A. *Ritschl (1822–89) contributed to the movement in the realm of ethics, attempting to relate the gospel to the "secular" aspects of human life. His espousal of the theology of the history of religions, however, called into question the objectively unique character of the Christian religion. In *Das Wesen des Christentums* (*What Is Christianity*, tr. T. Saunders, 2d ed., 1903), A. von *Harnack (1851–1930) defined Christianity as man's consciousness of God's Fatherhood; the dogmas of the Christian Church were a conceptualization (beginning with St. Paul) into Greek thought patterns of this simple consciousness and were a distortion. The *Social Gospel aspect of liberal theology was personified in the bp. of Uppsala, N. *Söderblom (1866–1931), initiator of *Life and Work, the theme of which ("service unites but doctrine divides") reflected the liberal viewpoint.

Horace *Bushnell (1802–76) is called the father of liberalism in the U.S., where the movement came fully into being after the Civil War. The influence of philosophic idealism on religious thought was represented particularly in the "personalistic" idealism of Borden Parker *Bowne (1847–1910). The impact of the higher criticism was fully evident in the *Outline of Christian Theology* (1898) of William Newton *Clarke (1841–1912). The names of Walter *Rauschenbusch (1861–1918) and Washington *Gladden (1836–1918) came to represent the broad influence of the Social Gospel in the United States. Liberal theology had many more exponents and came to dominate numerous theological faculties, esp. in the North. By reason of the so-called fundamentalist–modernist controversy, intra-denominational disputes, and the liberal tendency to minimize any special sacred function of the Church, the movement had its effect on the denominational pattern in the United States.

Liberal theology may be said to linger wherever the reality of the supernatural in interpreting Christianity is set aside as either inconceivable or at best irrelevant to modern technological man. The pervasive influence it had in the first third of the 20th cent. (in spite of strong high church, confessional, and revivalist counteraction) has ceased. *Crisis theology was initiated just after World War I in reaction against liberalism (see BARTH, KARL). In the U.S., the two *Niebuhrs, both of liberal background, by their writings contributed to the move away from liberal theology and to the rise of *neo-orthodoxy. See J. Dillenberger and C. Welch, *Protestant Christianity in the Light of its Development* (1954); Smith-Jamison 1:279–316; D. E. Roberts and H. P. Van Dusen, eds., *Liberal Theology* (1942); K. Cauthen, *Impact of American Religious Liberalism* (1962).

LIBERTINES, a name with a variety of uses in religious history. (1) Antinomian sects have often been called Libertines (see ANTINOMIANISM). (2) In 16th- and 17th-cent. England *Nonconformist, particularly subjectivist, groups (Seekers, Familists, Quakers) were so designated. (3) The term was applied erroneously to the party in Geneva that opposed (1541–1555) Calvin's theocracy. (4) It was used derogatorily of a sect originating in 1525 at Lille. The leaders were a tailor named Quintin (d. 1546) and a priest, Antonin Pocquet (d. c.1560). These Libertines resembled the *Picardians, and are known solely through Calvin's writings against them (esp. *Contre la secte . . . des libertins qui se nomment spirituelz*, 1545). The basis of their teaching was a pantheistic understanding of God's presence and action in men. In consequence they claimed that man was above the law and the Bible and that the only threat to his innocence was any concern over the difference between right and wrong. There is no evidence that this sect was given to immoral excesses. See W. Niesel, RGG 4:356–357. (5) In 17th-cent. France the term *libertin* came to be used in a sense equivalent to *freethinker (e.g., by Pascal in *Apologie de la religion chrétienne*).

LIDGETT, JOHN SCOTT (1854–1953), English Methodist reformer, editor, and advocate of Methodist union. L. became a Wesleyan Methodist minister in 1876. Together with W. F. Moulton, he founded Bermondsey Settlement for the poor in 1891 and was its warden for 58 years. L. was for 11 years editor of the *Methodist Times* and later joint editor of the *Contemporary Review*. He was a leader in, and first president of, the reunion that brought together (1932) all Methodists except the Calvinistic Methodists into the Methodist Church.

LIFE AND ADVENT UNION, a small Adventist body that followed the teachings of John T. Walsh, an early Adventist editor; in 1964 it merged with the Advent Christian

Church. In 1848 Walsh began to teach that there would be no resurrection of the wicked. Those who accepted this position formed the Life and Advent Union in Wilbraham, Mass., in 1863. The Life and Advent Union taught the doctrines common to all 19th-cent. Adventism except for differences concerning the resurrection and the millennium. Rather than picturing the millennium as a period of 1,000 years of peace and happiness in the future, the members of this sect believed that the millennium had already taken place and was a period of religious persecution and suffering. Membership of the Life and Advent Union reached 658 adherents in 13 churches, but by the time of the merger it had dropped to 300 in three congregations. Polity was congregational; a governing council directed publications and missionary work.

LIFE AND WORK, branch of the modern ecumenical movement directed toward achieving unity of action among the Christian Churches in the social, economic, and political spheres, without regard for doctrinal differences; also known as Practical Christianity. The movement owed its origin largely to the Lutheran Abp. Nathan *Söderblom of Uppsala, Sweden, who during World War I became convinced that the Churches must unite to work for peace. The first conferences called to that end, in 1917 in Uppsala and in 1919 in The Netherlands, were unsuccessful; national feelings were still too high in the Churches of the countries that were, or had been, at war. The first truly international conference of the movement met in Stockholm in 1925 for study and discussion of the Church's place in politics, international relations, education, and economics and industry. The reports of the conference were inconclusive, but it established a Permanent Committee on Practical Christianity, which set up commissions to continue studies on social issues, and an International Christian Social Institute.

The worldwide depression that soon followed, and the rise of National Socialism in Germany, with its far-reaching effects on the German Lutheran and other Churches, presented pressing challenges to the movement, and it soon became apparent that the doctrinal bases for Christian social action could not be ignored. The split within the Church in Germany especially focused attention on the nature of the Church, as a starting point for consideration of Church and State relations. By the time the Life and Work movement held its second international conference, in Oxford in 1937, it was moving closer to the *Faith and Order movement, and many members were about to attend the *Edinburgh Conference. At Oxford a merger of the two movements as a first step toward an international ecumenical council was proposed and approved. The Life and Work movement was absorbed into the *World Council of Churches that sprang from this merger, losing its separate identity but not its influence, which has lived on esp. in the Church and Society division of the World Council. See E. Duff, *Social Thought of the World Council of Churches* (1956). *STOCKHOLM CONFERENCE; *OXFORD CONFERENCE.

LILBURNE, JOHN (c.1614-57), English political agitator, pamphleteer for the *Levelers. In 1638 L. was fined for distributing pamphlets against the hierarchy. In *England's Birthright* (1645, often repr. as *An Agreement of the People*) he set forth the program of the Leveler movement, including religious equality; he wrote many other pamphlets urging constitutional reform. He was tried for treason in 1649, but was acquitted; further political agitation led to exile and then confinement until 1655, in which year he became a Quaker. See M. A. Gibb, *J. L., The Leveller; A Christian Democrat* (1948), L. V. Hodgkin, *Shoemaker of Dover* (1943), 44-52.

LIMITED ATONEMENT, the theological position that Christ died only for the elect. The point is implicit in any theology of *predestination that restricts God's will and plan of salvation to include only some, not all, men. In its specific reference limited atonement is one of the five points of Calvinism as defined by the Synod of *Dort (1619) in rejecting *Arminianism. The Arminians taught that Christ died for all men, and that the saving effects of his redemptive act are available to all. The Canons of Dort (Second Head of Doctrine), condemned this position and affirmed that Christ died not for all but only for the elect. One of the propositions ascribed to C. *Jansen's work *Augustinus* and condemned by Pope Innocent X (1653) affirmed a similar teaching (D 2005; cf. D 523).

LINDSEY, THEOPHILUS (1723–1808), English Unitarian. He was educated at St. John's College, Cambridge. As vicar at Catterick from 1763, he began to accept Unitarian views, esp. through his friendship with J. *Priestley. He joined in an appeal to Parliament, the Feathers Tavern petition (1772), against obligatory subscription to the *Thirty-Nine Articles; when the appeal was rejected, he gave up his Anglican ministry and from 1774 preached Unitarianism in London. Among his works was *Historical View of the State of the Unitarian Doctrine and Worship from the Reformation to Our Own Time* (1788). See E. M. Wilbur, *History of Unitarianism* (2v., repr., 1965).

LITERALISM, adherence to the letter of a statement, ignoring in the assessment of its meaning the context of the statement or its use of figures of speech. Such literalism is a feature of *fundamentalism in the interpretation of Scripture. Sometimes it arises from a misunderstanding of the varied types of literature present in the Bible. Genesis 1, e.g., was long interpreted as a descriptive account of the divine work of creation in six days. The Bible itself can succumb to literalism, as is clear from Heb 11.4–7. In these instances literalism may place the Bible in apparent conflict with science, to the detriment of religious faith itself. In other cases the simplistic acceptance of a biblical dictum, e.g., Mt 5.39, may offend against common sense. The antidote to literalism in the interpretation of the Bible is the awareness of literary form, i.e., the particular kind of literary vehicle the inspired author has chosen to convey his thought or reflection. Jesus himself used the traditional rabbinic method of teaching in parables, which, however, were sometimes taken in the early centuries of Christianity as true stories. In the 20th cent. much progress has been made in identifying the various literary forms in the Bible, thus opening the way to a clearer understanding of the true literal meaning of Scripture, i.e., what the inspired writer actually intended to say in his employment of the type of writing current in his time. Literalism may also result from a false principle of biblical interpretation known as *biblicism.

LITTLE CHURCH OF UTRECHT (OBC, Kerk der Oud-Bisschoppelijke Clerezie), the Church originating in the 18th cent. with the *Schism of Utrecht, in 1899 entering into the *Old Catholic communion, and now called the Old Catholic Church of the Netherlands. The Church of Utrecht became formally separated from Rome with the election (1723) of Cornelius Steenoven as abp., and his consecration (1724) by a suspended French missionary bp., Dominique Varlet. The latter also consecrated Steenoven's three successors, the third of whom, P. J. Meindaerts (1739–67), provided for episcopal succession by reviving the Sees of Haarlem (1742) and Deventer (1758). The formal schism was the culmination of protracted disputes with Rome, arising from the Utrecht clergy's defense of the right to elect its ecclesiastical superior (the province was under a vicar apostolic from 1592 because of the disruption of the hierarchy caused by the Reformation) and from accusations of *Jansenism against the Dutch clergy made at Rome, esp. by the Jesuits. These causes were embodied in the case of the deposition in 1704 of the vicar apostolic, Pieter Codde, who had been summoned to Rome (1699) on charges of Jansenism and had refused to sign the anti-Jansenist formula imposed by Alexander VII. The Utrecht Church, which became known also as the Jansenist Church of Holland, refused to accept the pro-vicar apostolic appointed by Rome, Theodorus de Cock, and ultimately chose Steenoven. During the above-mentioned Meindaert's episcopacy a synod held (1763) at Utrecht gave hope of reunion by its rejection of Jansenist teachings; but neither this nor subsequent attempts at reconciliation with Rome in 1823 and 1827 succeeded. By its rejection of the dogmatic definition of the Immaculate Conception (1854) and papal infallibility (1870), and esp. by acceptance of the *Declaration of Utrecht (1889), which rejected the Council of Trent, the OBC became clearly separated in teaching from Rome; in 1950 it also rejected the definition of the Assumption. In discipline, the Church did away with obligatory clerical celibacy in 1923 and imposed a vernacular liturgy. It was from Bp. H. Heykamp of the OBC that the first Old Catholic bp., J. H. Reinkins, received episcopal consecration (1873). In 1889 the *Union of Utrecht bound the OBC in communion with Old Catholic Churches of Germany and Switzerland. In 1968 the OBC had about 7,500 active communicants in three dioceses. The OBC maintains close relations with many Protestant bodies; it is also an active member of the World Council of Churches. Consecration by the abp. of Utrecht has been the source of *apostolic succession for some Churches and is important in the question of the so-called *Episcopi vagantes.*

LITURGICAL BOOKS (Roman Rite), the official books used in liturgical services conducted in accordance with the Roman rite. Such books may be published only by the authority of the Holy See, which in this matter normally acts through the Consilium established by Paul VI in 1964 to implement the liturgical reform prescribed by Vatican Council II, or by competent ter-

ritorial or local authority with the approval of the Consilium. A general revision of these books is in progress. The principal books in use at the present time are: (1) The Roman *Breviary, promulgated in 1568 by Pius V, reformed by Pius X, Pius XII, and John XXIII. The last official edition was 1961. (2) The Roman *Missal, promulgated by Pius V in 1570. The latest official edition of this appeared in 1962, but it has been modified by the *Ordo Missae* and the *Ritus servandus,* which were published separately in the official edition of 1965. Further modification is expected. (3) The Roman Martyrology, published by authority of Gregory XIII in 1584. The last official edition of this was that of Pius X in 1914, and an addition to this was made in 1956. (4) The Roman *Pontifical, published in 1596 by order of Clement VIII. Pius XII and John XXIII made many important changes in it for the revised edition of 1962. (5) The Ceremonial of Bishops, published under Clement VIII in 1600. This contained directions not only for episcopal functions but also for the daily liturgy in cathedrals and collegiate churches. It was supplemented in 1725 with the *Memoriale rituum* for sacred functions in smaller churches, the last official edition of which was in 1920. Both books have been superseded, so far as Holy Week services are concerned, by Pius XII's Ordinal for Holy Week (1956). (6) The Roman *Ritual, published by Paul V in 1614. The last typical edition was in 1952 under Pius XII, and modifications are forthcoming from the Consilium. See L. C. Sheppard, *Liturgical Books* (1962): *idem,* NCE 8:890–892.

LITURGICAL MOVEMENT, the renewed interest in the liturgy, and esp. in the full participation of Christians in the liturgical celebrations. In the 20th cent. the movement has developed in both the Protestant Churches and the RC Church and is closely related to the ecumenical movement.

Protestant Liturgical Movement. Many Protestant Christians are striving to bring about the corporate worship of their respective communities in such a way that there is active, intelligent, and salutary worship by all present. The response of the various Protestant Churches to the liturgical movement depends upon their historical background and theological emphasis. Although the Reformers reacted against the abuses of the Middle Ages, they also accepted some of its presuppositions. One of these presuppositions was the dominant and almost exclusive role played by the minister in the worship service. The liturgical movement therefore has attempted to reinstate the active role of the faithful. The roots of this movement are the historicism and romanticism that developed in the mid-19th century. The Anglican *Oxford movement with its emphasis on the sacraments, Eucharist, ceremony, and chant produced scholars and prayer books. The Lutherans lead by Wilhelm *Löhe (1808–72) and Theodor Kliefoth (1810–95) paved the way for the revision of the Common Service. The *Reformed Churches' recognition of the values of the liturgical movement came through the formation of the Church Service Society (1865) and produced the Book of Common Order (1928), with its subsequent revisions. These standardized liturgies have influenced the prayer forms of the *free Churches. Slowly but surely those with a less structured liturgy have adopted some of the recent structures. The principal agent for the promotion of liturgical reform has been the ecumenical movement, which has had to face the major problems separating Christians. The agreement among biblical theologians and exegetes regarding the meaning of worship in the NT and the Fathers has laid the basis for the introduction of newer communal forms of worship into the Protestant Churches. In many communions the present is a period of liturgical experimentation.

RC Liturgical Movement. In the RC Church there is an organized activity and trend directed toward the awakening of the Christian to his rightful role in liturgical functions and toward their more fruitful celebration. Such a concern has always been present in the Church, but it became more necessary as the liturgy became a work of the clerics. Various individuals attempted to get the people involved in the celebration. Alcuin (9th cent.) demanded that the clergy be instructed in the meaning of the liturgical acts and the people learn to sing the parts proper to them. It was only after Trent (17th–19th cent.), however, that the movement obtained the scholarly tools needed for a profound renovation of liturgical attitudes. The fruition of this scholarship and desire first was evident in the Benedictine Prosper Guéranger (1805–75), who brought liturgy back into esteem and raised the standards for its celebration. At the same time he was limited by his neo-Gothic romanticism and his philosophical traditionalism. Yet the estheticism and juridicism of Guéranger led to the popular liturgical movement of Pius X, as found in *Tra le Sollecitudini* (1903), and the works of L. Beauduin. The primary aim of the modern liturgical movement is the active, intelligent, salvific participation of the people in the liturgy of the Church. It is this aim that has produced the scholarship of such men as Probst, Duchesne, Batifold, Baumstark, Jungman, Leclerc and others. Vatican II's *Constitution on the Liturgy* (1963) and the Consilium for its implementation are the foundations for the movement as it now exists. See K. G. Phifer, *Protestant Case for Liturgical Renewal* (1965); M. H. Shepherd, "The Liturgical Movement in American Protestantism," *Yearbook of Liturgical Studies* 3 (1962), 35–61; M. J. Taylor, *Protestant Liturgical Renewal* (1963); E. B. Koenker, *Liturgical Renaissance in the Roman Catholic Church* (2nd ed., 1966); The Sacerdotal Communities of Saint-Severin of Paris and St. Joseph of Nice, *Liturgical Movement* (tr. L. Sheppard, 1964).

LOCAL CHURCH, a group of Christians who regularly meet for worship, fellowship, and instruction and to plan their corporate activities; distinguished from the universal Church or from a national or regional organization In NT language the term Church often signifies the local church, the community of Christians under their bishop. In the language of Vatican Council II the phrases "local congregation" and "particular churches" are used in this same sense, and the statement is made that "the Church of Christ is truly present in all legitimate congregations of the faithful, which, united with their pastors, are themselves called churches in the New Testament" (Vat II ConstCh 26; see also 27). The phrase may be similarly used of Churches belonging to the *Anglican Communion. In a narrower sense, the local church refers to the congregation or parish, although the latter term strictly implies a connection between residential community and church membership, which the phrase local church does not. As meaning the particular congregation, the local church is esp. important in the *gathered-church theory and in *congregational polity.

LOCAL PREACHER, a layman licensed to preach in a Methodist *quarterly conference. Being so licensed is usually a step preliminary to ordination to the ministry. The use of lay preachers was initiated by John *Wesley. At first he was willing for laymen only to exhort, but not to preach or interpret the gospel. The rapid growth of the Methodist *societies, however, influenced him to change his policy. In 1740, strongly influenced by his mother, he allowed Thomas *Maxfield, who was not ordained, to preach; subsequently Wesley used laymen regularly in his work. He exercised control, however, by granting a license to preach only to one who met requirements he himself prepared. Most of the early Methodist preachers, both in England and in the U.S., were licensed either by Wesley himself or by a recognized Methodist preacher. The survival and early growth of Methodism in the U.S. largely depended on lay preachers. The modern local preacher preaches at the request and direction of the pastor or district superintendent. He is not salaried, or supported by the Church. See R. D. Urlin, *Churchman's Life of Wesley* (n.d.), 137–146; N. B. Harmon,

Understanding the Methodist Church (1961). *LAY PREACHING.

LÖHE, JOHANN KONRAD WILHELM (1808–72), German Lutheran pastor. Except for several vicarates (1831–37), L. spent all of his adult life as pastor in the insignificant village of Neuendettelsau. He sent hundreds of emergency pastors to the U.S. to care for German Lutheran immigrants there. The Missouri Synod, the Franconian colonies in Michigan, and the Iowa Synod all claim him as founder. For the evangelization of Australia and the Americas he organized the Neuendettelsau Foreign Mission Society and established a *deaconess motherhouse for *inner missions. After almost seceding from the Bavarian state Church, he petitioned the general synod to promote strict adherence to the church symbols and to free itself from state control. Chief among his 60 writings are *Drei Bücher von der Kirche* (1845) and a number of prayerbooks. See J. L. Schaaf, *W. L.'s Relation to the American Church* (1962).

LOISY, ALFRED FIRMIN (1857–1940), French priest, theologian, principal proponent of *modernism in France. Born in Ambrières in Lorraine, he studied at the Grande Seminaire of Châlons-sur-Marne, and was ordained in 1879. He served as a parish priest for 2 years before graduate studies under Abbé L. Duchesne at the Institut Catholique in Paris. From 1882 to 1885 he attended the lectures of E. Renan at the Collège de France to learn Renan's position so it could be refuted. Upon completion of his studies at the Institut in 1884 he joined the faculty as professor of Hebrew and OT exegesis, although his doctoral thesis was refused publication because of "relativism" regarding revelation. He was dismissed in 1893 over the question of the inerrancy of the Bible in an article "La Question biblique et l'inspiration des Écritures." The dismissal was bitter and at least partly political, to save Msgr. D'Hulst, the rector, from embarrassment; it resulted in hostility toward ecclesiastical authority on L.'s part. He continued his writing while chaplain to a Dominican convent in Neuilly, 1894–99, even though his faith in Catholicism had disappeared as early as 1886. Five of his works were condemned in the 1903 publication of the Index of Forbidden Books. These were a paper, "La Religion d'Israel," and five books: *L'Évangile et l'église*, *Études évangéliques*, *Autour d'un petit livre*, and *Le Quatrième Évangile*. His reaction was ambiguous and unacceptable to the Holy Office in Rome, and he was formally excommunicated on March 8, 1908. He publicly renounced Christianity and joined the faculty of the Collège de France as professor of church history (1909–30), the position previously held by Renan.

During the period just before his excommunication and after the publication of the encyclical *Pascendi* (1907) L. published extensively. His books included *Simples Réflexions* (1908), on the events leading to his excommunication, and in the same year a major work entitled *Les Évangiles synoptiques*. Later at the Collège de France he published *Les Mystère païens et le mystère chrétien* (1914), *La Religion* (1917), *Les Livres du Nouveau Testament* (1922), the lengthy *Memoires pour servir à l'histoire religieuse de notre temps* (1930–31), and a summary of his final teachings on the NT called *Naissance du christianisme* (1933). Loisy was a man without faith in traditional RC teaching for most of his creative years and was yet dedicated to making the Church modern from within. He was the central figure in French modernism and its principal spokesman. He died without reconciliation with the Church. See A. Vidler, *Modernist Movement in the Roman Catholic Church* (1934); J. Ratté, *Three Modernists* (1967).

LOLLARDS, in England followers of the teaching of John *Wycliffe. In the Low Countries from the early 14th cent. the Alexian Brothers were called by this name (Low Ger. *lullen*, to sing softly), because of their chanting in a muted tone. In England John Wycliffe's "poor priests" and later all his followers in general were called Lollards, the term being used first by the Oxford Cistercian, H. Cromp, in 1382 and in a condemnatory document by the bp. of Worcester in 1387. The name was derisive, having the sense of idler or mumbler. Lollardy in the last 20 years of the 14th cent. was mainly centered at Oxford, among theologians. A document presented to Parliament in 1395, *The Conclusion*, contains the Lollard teaching. Wycliffe's doctrines were pushed to extremes: Lollards rejected the *Real Presence, church authority, auricular confession, and all sacramentals and vows, esp. chastity. They extolled the sufficiency of Scripture and private interpretation. The Lollards also propagated Wycliffe's ideas on lordship and advocated primitive evangelical poverty and a kind of communism. Abuses of ownership by ecclesiastics fostered this sentiment, which is reflected in the creed of *Piers Plowman* (1395). Even after the *De haeretico comburendo* of 1401, the continuance of Lollardy among theologians prompted the repressive measures of the abp. of Oxford, Thomas Arundel, in 1408, and the philosophic apologetics of Reginald Pecock, in 1455. By the early 15th cent. Lollardy was more and more a social movement of the lower classes; a popular rising in 1414 was put down and the Lollard leader, Sir John Oldcastle, was executed in 1417. Thereafter, Lollards gathered in secret, scattered groups, which, however, maintained contact with each other. Periodic legal reprisals continued down through the reign of Henry VIII. The term Lollard came to be applied to all manner of religious dissenters; but the true Lollards were of little significance when the English Reformation came to pass. See J. Gairdner, *Lollardy and the Reformation in England* (4v., 1908–13); R. Hedde, DTC 9:910–925; Hughes RE 1:100, 126–127; J. A. F. Thompson, *Later Lollards 1414–1520* (1966); bibliog. for J. Wycliffe.

LONDON CONFESSION, see SECOND LONDON CONFESSION.

LONDON MISSIONARY SOCIETY (LMS), an agency for foreign missions founded in 1795 by members of many Churches. The distinguishing feature was its evangelical, interdenominational character, its "fundamental principle" being that the Society was committed to spreading the "glorious Gospel of the blessed God" and no particular church form. While still adhering to this principle, it became and has remained an agency of Congregationalism, since its *independency encouraged support of Congregational Churches throughout the British Empire. In 1966 the LMS united with the Commonwealth Missionary Society to become the Congregational Council for World Missions. The first missionaries were sent out to Tahiti in 1796; mission fields have included India, South Africa, China, Madagascar, Central Africa, Papua, S Pacific, and Malaya. The rolls of the Society's missioners include John Williams, David Livingstone, Robert Moffat, Robert Morrison, and James Chalmers. See M. Goodall, *History of the London Missionary Society, 1895–1945* (1954).

LORD'S DAY ALLIANCE of the United States, a group organized as the American Sabbath Union in 1888 and incorporated in New York State under its present name in 1909 to secure Sunday as a day of rest and worship for the working man and to work for legislation to that end. At a time when the 7-day working week was common, the Alliance campaigned to secure Sunday closing, or compensatory time off for necessary Sunday work, esp. for federal and state employees, and fought for laws to curb commercialization of the Sunday by theaters, baseball games, and other amusements. *SABBATARIANS.

LORD'S SUPPER, sacrament of the Eucharist. In 1 Cor 11.20 St. Paul refers to the Lord's Supper. The Reformers, rejecting RC eucharistic teaching and the name "Mass" connoting it, substituted Lord's Supper for the eucharistic celebration; the name appears in all of the main *confessions of faith, continental and English. Along with baptism, the Lord's Supper is recognized by most Protestant bodies as a true sacrament. Although the name still commonly excludes by connotation any sacrificial note from the Eucharist, its positive meaning varies among the Churches (see EUCHARIST; REAL PRESENCE). Recent RC reemphasis on the Eucharist as a meal has taken away the former Protestant flavor of the term Lord's Supper; Vatican Council II refers to the Eucharist as the Lord's Supper in discussing ecumenical dialogue with the Protestant Churches (Vat II Ecum 22).

LOS-VON-ROM MOVEMENT, the concerted attempt made by German nationalist organizations to promote a secession of Austrian Catholics from their Church in the late 19th and early 20th centuries. The expression was first used by a student at a nationalist rally in 1897 and then by Georg von Schönerer, the leader of the Pan-German party, in his manifesto of Nov. 1898, when he called for the conversion of Catholics to the Old Catholic Church or to Protestantism. The movement partly reflected the resentment of German nationalists in Austria against the RC Church for its support of the Hapsburg government, which, after 1892, tried to provide parity for the Czech language in its mixed German-Czech provinces. It was also a reaction to use of Czech RC priests in some German parishes. Nationalist Protestant organizations from the German Reich, e.g., the *Evangelische Bund, provided assistance to the movement. From 75,000 to 85,000 Catholics left the Church between 1897 and 1914. The movement fell far short of its objectives, however, and was not a serious factor in Austrian affairs after World War I. Adolf Hitler, a warm admirer of Schönerer, later wrote in *Mein Kampf* (1925) that the Pan-German leader had made the mistake of waging major campaigns against two foes, the Austrian monarchy and the RC Church, at the same time.

LOTZER, SEBASTIAN (*c.*1490–after 1525), in the German *Peasants' War, author of the *Twelve Articles. L., who was a furrier at Memmingen in Bavaria, was well read in the Bible and the new Reformation literature, as is evident from his five pamphlets on the layman's right to interpret and expound the word of God. In 1525 he put the demands of the peasants into writing, giving the Twelve Articles, the manifesto of the Peasants' War, a strong biblical base. After the peasants' defeat he escaped to St. Gall, and thereafter disappears from history. See bibliog. for Peasants' War.

LOW CHURCH, originating in 18-cent. England, a phrase denoting an attitude tending to minimize the importance within the Church of *episcopacy, priesthood, sacraments, and ceremonial richness as against the more biblical and personal notes of individual conversion, the preaching of the gospel, and salvation by faith. "Low" refers to the slight importance attached to the historical and sacramental claims of the Church. The designation has been applied to proponents of *latitudinarianism, to *Nonconformists generally, and is the opposite of both *high church and *broad church.

LUCIFER OF CAGLIARI (d. *c.*370), anti-Arian bp. of Cagliari, Sardinia. At the Council of Milan (354–355) he steadfastly refused to accede to the wishes of the Emperor Constantius and condemn Athanasius. His vehement resistance to the Emperor led to his banishment to the East, where, in exile, he persisted in his denunciations of Constantius, writing several violent diatribes against him. Taking advantage of an amnesty in 362, he went to Antioch and became embroiled in the conflict raging there in consequence of the efforts of Melitius, the bp., to reconcile repentant Arians. Accusing the bp. of Semi-Arianism, L. consecrated Paulinus, a priest of Antioch, as bp. for those who would not submit to Melitius, thus cooperating in the creation of a schism that lasted many years. He then returned to Sardinia. Reference by Augustine, Ambrose, and Jerome to his followers as Luciferians suggests that L. was excommunicated and the leader of a schismatic group. Writings: PL 13:767–1038. See É. Amman, DTC 9:1032–44; Altaner 429–430.

LUCIFERIANS, a term with two usages: (1) followers of *Lucifer of Cagliari; (2) a name for supposed medieval sects of devil worshipers. Reports of such sects began in the 10th cent. and continued throughout the Middle Ages. The *Cathari did honor to Satan; it is doubtful, however, that there were Luciferians who practiced the blasphemies and obscenities reported in popular tales or in the charges of zealous inquisitors. See É. Amann, DTC 9:1044–56; Bihlmeyer-Tüchle 2:307; R. Knox, *Enthusiasm* (1950), 101.

LUKAS OF PRAGUE (*c.*1460–1528), bishop and outstanding leader of the *Unitas Fratrum. Completing his education at the Univ. of Prague, he left the *Utraquists to join the Brethren. His learning and native gifts soon brought him into prominence as administrator and writer. His catechism, liturgies, and theological works decisively shaped the development of the Brethren from a sect withdrawn from the world to a Church including in its membership a cross section of society and recognizing the need for a learned clergy. The hymnal he edited for his Church in 1501 is looked upon as the first Protestant hymnal. He initiated colloquies with Luther and brought the Brethren into the mainstream of Protestantism. See P. Brock, *Unity of Czech Brethren* (1957).

LUMBER RIVER ANNUAL CONFERENCE of the Holiness Methodist Church, a small denomination, similar in doctrine to, but not joined to, the Holiness Methodist Church. The Church, organized in N.C. in 1900 as the Lumber River Mission Conference of the Holiness Methodist Church, stresses scriptural holiness and the inner witness of the Spirit. Each local church calls its own minister, whose pastorates are not of fixed duration. See HistAmMeth 3:595.

LUND CONFERENCE, the third World Conference on *Faith and Order, held at Lund, Sweden, Aug. 15–28, 1952. The subjects considered were (1) Christ and his Church; (2) continuity and unity; (3) ways of worship; and (4) intercommunion. The Conference marked a change from the *Lausanne and *Edinburgh Conferences, which had endeavored to compare the doctrinal positions of the Christian Churches in the hope that greater understanding of the differences would remove obstacles to unity. At Lund the emphasis on tradition and Scripture as expressed in worship was more effective. Continued efforts were made to define the nature of the Church. In its eschatological aspect the Church was viewed as the "pilgrim People of God," and a strong desire was manifest for greater unity in worship based on an essential unity in faith. At Lund, for the first time, authorized RC observers took part in the discussions, a fact reflecting the RC development of ecumenical theology that followed the 1949 Vatican document *De motione oecumenica.* See O. S. Tomkins, ed., *Third World Conference on Faith and Order* (1953). *WORLD COUNCIL OF CHURCHES; *ECUMENICAL MOVEMENT.

LUNDENSIAN THEOLOGY, a theological school represented by a number of 20th-cent. Lutheran scholars at the Univ. of Lund in Sweden. Their main contribution has been the development of *motif research. To a great extent the Lundensian theology has been the reaction to two previous influences affecting Swedish Lutheran theology: *Pietism, with the revivals of the 19th cent.; and the Kantian metaphysical critique of Christianity. Pioneers were E. *Billing, with his insistence on the centrality of forgiveness in the theology of

Luther, and N. *Söderblom's historical and psychological approach to the Reformer's thought. G. *Aulén found in the eros-agape theory the ground motif to distinguish Christianity from all other religions. A. *Nygren, while accepting Luther's "Copernican Revolution" of a sovereign and gracious God, a concept that had been blurred by the eros motif in medieval scholasticism, denied the right of the school of Lund to regard as the central theme of theology the question, "What is the Christian faith?" when in truth it is "How can the sinner find peace with God?" More recently G. Ljunggren and R. Bring have studied Luther's anthropology; A. Runestam has expressed fear that the Reformer's concept of God's sovereignty might lead to determinism; others have gone to the roots of his dualism. The Lundensian contribution has been outstanding for the contemporary Luther renaissance. See E. Carlson, *Reinterpretation of Luther* (1948); N. Ferré, *Swedish Contribution to Modern Theology* (1938); G. Wingren, *Theology in Conflict* (1958).

LUTHER, MARTIN (1483–1546), Protestant theologian and German Reformer. He was born at Eisleben in Saxony, the son of a miner, Hans Luther, and his wife, Margaret. Despite later legends of extraordinary strictness in his parental home (some of them repeated by Luther himself), his relations with his parents do not appear to have been abnormal. His early education was received in Mansfeld, Magdeburg, and Eisenach; at Magdeburg his teachers belonged to the *Brethren of the Common Life. In 1501 he entered the Univ. of Erfurt, where he became Master of Arts in 1505 and undertook the study of law. These plans were interrupted in July 1505 by a severe personal and religious crisis. The occasion was a thunderstorm, during which L. vowed to St. Anne that he would become a monk. He fulfilled the vow on July 17, entering the Order of Augustinian Hermits at Erfurt. He was ordained in 1507 and during the following years pursued a program of theological study and theological teaching, receiving the degrees of Bachelor in Bible (1509) and of Doctor of Theology (1512). This obligated him to undertake lectures on Scripture, and it was out of these lectures that his historic transformation came. From 1513 to 1515 he occupied himself with the exposition of the Psalms (*Dictata super Psalterium*), which was followed by lectures on Romans, Galatians, and Hebrews. Although it seems impossible to date it with any precision, his "discovery of the gospel" occurred as he struggled with the meaning of the term "righteousness" (*justitia*) in these texts. How could the righteousness of God be revealed in the gospel, as Rom 1.17 declared, if this righteousness was the quality by which God demanded of man that he keep the law? The "new and wondrous definition of righteousness" that enabled him to answer this question—which was above all a personal religious question for him, and only secondly a theological one—was that this righteousness was not what God demanded, but what he conferred as his free gift in Christ. This discovery changed L.'s life—and the history of the Church.

Yet the issue that made him a public figure and precipitated the Reformation was not justification but the practice of indulgences. On Oct. 31, 1517, he issued his *Ninety-Five Theses against the indulgence that had been issued as part of the arrangement between Pope Leo X, Albert of Brandenburg, and the banking house of Fugger. L.'s objections, in which many faithful Catholics concurred, attacked not only the financial corruption of the practice but above all its distortion of the true nature of penance. The notoriety evoked by the Theses brought him into other debates that touched more closely the central concerns of his new theology. Of these, probably the most important in its consequences was the encounter with John *Eck at the *Disputation of Leipzig in July 1519, where L. was moved to voice his opposition to the infallibility of councils and the primacy of the pope. After Leipzig events moved even more swiftly. Various efforts to make the Saxon monk recant failed. On June 15, 1520,

in the bull *Exsurge Domine*, he was ordered to recant in 60 days, under threat of excommunication. He burned the bull. In April 1521 he appeared before the imperial Diet of *Worms and was given another opportunity to recant. He declared instead that here he stood and could not do otherwise.

Now he was both an outlaw before the Empire and an apostate before the Church. Yet none of this kept him from his work as a theologian. To protect him from the consequences of the Diet's action against him, the elector of Saxony spirited him off to the *Wartburg. One fruit of this exile was his translation of the NT into German—his most influential achievement culturally, and perhaps also religiously. But this was also the time when Luther came into conflict with other advocates of reform, who for one or another reason were dissatisfied with either the pace or the scope of the changes. The fierce *Karlstadt wanted the Reformation to move faster toward the abolition of various medieval practices and toward the restoration of the chalice to the laity. The Anabaptists claimed to be drawing the logical consequences of L.'s attack upon the sacramental system when they repudiated *infant baptism. Similarly, J. *Oecolampadius and esp. *Zwingli attacked his retention of the doctrine of the *Real Presence as a remnant of *scholasticism. And Desidierius *Erasmus, whose lampoons against corruption and superstition in the Church had been far more acrid than Luther's, nevertheless could not follow him either in his defiance of authority or in his doctrine of the bondage of the will. The rebellious peasants claimed his support, but he repudiated their revolution (see PEASANTS' WAR).

These developments set the pattern of his thought and of his reformatory movement for the rest of his life. Although, as an outlaw, he himself did not attend the Diet at Augsburg in 1530, the *Augsburg Confession presented there was a faithful, if rather irenically phrased, summary of his doctrine. Most of what his Reformation meant historically had already been determined by this time, and the movement in many ways passed out of his hands. Personally and intellectually, however, he was far from finished. In 1529 he wrote his catechisms, which formed and still form the basis of Lutheran religious instruction (see CATE-CHISMS, LUTHER'S). In 1525 he married Catherine von Bora, thus founding the Protestant manse. His commentary on Galatians (1535) was a mature statement of the central themes of *justification, the distinction between *law and gospel, and the nature of faith. Students from many parts of Europe came to Wittenberg to hear his lectures, and his correspondence extended his influence far and wide. One of the great disappointments of his life was the fragmentation of the reform movement into warring factions. Neither the attempts to reconcile these factions nor the repeated efforts to reopen the dialogue with Roman Catholicism were successful. When he died on Feb. 18, 1546, he had laid the foundations for the history of Protestantism, but had also seen it move in directions that he found dangerous.

These and other disappointments aggravated the profound depressions of spirit that repeatedly came over him throughout his mature years; his German word for them was *Anfechtungen,* "trials." They were compounded of profound reverence, nagging guilt, and persistent doubt. He combined in an unusual measure the self-confidence and self-doubt characteristic of prophetic men in Israel and in the Church. Neither the muckraking of his RC detractors (who have portrayed him as an adulterer, a suicide, a drunkard, a foul-mouthed liar, and a psychopath) nor the idealizing of his Lutheran biographers (who have seen in him the fulfillment of the prophecy in Rev 14.6–7) does justice to the complexity of his character. He was a man of deep contrasts, capable of massive candor about himself and his faults but also given to towering rages and petty grudges. His kindness toward his inferiors was matched by his harshness toward those whom he regarded as deliberate perverters of the word of God. It is characteristic of the man that, in the

20th cent. as in the 16th, almost no one is neutral toward him. From his faith and thought have come some of the most powerful theological insights in Christian history, and he continues to fructify Christian doctrine beyond the borders of the communion that bears his name. See *Luther's Works: The American Edition* (ed. J. Pelikan and H. Lehmann, 1955–   ); R. Bainton, *Here I Stand* (1951); E. G. Rupp, *Luther's Progress to the Diet of Worms* (1951); Enc-LuthCh 2:1356–57, bibliog.; J. M. Todd, *M. L.* (1964); J. McSorley, *L.: Right or Wrong* (1969); J. Wicks, *Man Yearning for Grace* (1968).

LUTHERAN BRETHREN OF AMERICA, see CHURCH OF THE LUTHERAN BRETHREN OF AMERICA.

LUTHERAN CHURCH—MISSOURI SYNOD, a Lutheran church body in North America comprising approximately one-third of the total membership of American Lutheranism. The Lutheran Church—Missouri Synod was formed in 1847 by immigrants from Germany who had begun to arrive in the U.S. in 1839. From its beginnings in such states as Mo., Mich., and Ohio, it has expanded and is now represented in all the states and provinces. Its greatest strength, however, continues to be in the Middle West. Of the three largest *synods—the other two being the *American Lutheran Church and the *Lutheran Church in America—the Missouri Synod has traditionally been the most conservative in doctrine. Although all Lutherans adhere to the doctrines of the *Augsburg Confession of 1530, the Missouri Synod has insisted upon a stricter interpretation of this confessional standard and has added to it a demand for theological orthodoxy also in doctrines not explicitly set forth there. Of special importance has been the doctrine of biblical inspiration and the corollary doctrine of inerrancy, against both the Roman Catholic understanding of *tradition as the authentic interpreter of Scripture and the modern critical approach to Scripture. In church practice also the Missouri Synod has emphasized a strict enforcement of the ban against membership in secret societies and has opposed *unionism, i.e., pulpit and altar fellowship without agreement in doctrine.

The Lutheran Church—Missouri Synod has at the same time accepted and even taken the lead in developing modern techniques for the work and mission of the Church. The Lutheran Hour was the first evangelistic program to be broadcast regularly on a national scale. "This Is the Life" has played a similar role in the field of religious television. Concordia Publishing House in St. Louis, the official press of the Missouri Synod, has been a leading religious publisher, first in German and now in English, since its establishment in 1869. The theological seminaries of the Missouri Synod, both named Concordia, are in St. Louis, Mo., and Springfield, Illinois. The church body also maintains two teachers' colleges (in River Forest, Ill., and Seward, Neb.) to staff its parochial school system, the largest such school system outside Roman Catholicism. The most recent statistics available (1969) place the membership of the Lutheran Church—Missouri Synod at 2,759,308 baptized souls. See E. L. Lueker, EncLuthCh 2:1408–14.

LUTHERAN CHURCH IN AMERICA, the largest of the three Lutheran bodies in North America. The Lutheran Church in America, formed in 1962, united the former *United Lutheran Church, *Augustana Lutheran Church (Swedish), *Finnish Evangelical Lutheran Church (Suomi Synod), and *American Evangelical Lutheran Church (Danish). The United Lutheran Church, by far the largest of these uniting bodies, included those sections of American Lutheranism whose origins go back to colonial days (see MUHLENBERG, H. M.). The ethnic variety suggested by the composition of the bodies which formed it has its counterpart in other aspects of the Lu-

theran Church in America. Thus it combines theological emphases of greater heterogeneity than either of the other two Lutheran groups, the American Lutheran Church and the Lutheran Church—Missouri Synod. It has also taken the lead among American Lutherans in ecumenism, having participated in interdenominational councils and conferences, both national and international, almost since the inception of these ecumenical programs. Significantly, the Churches that formed the Lutheran Church in America were among the earliest Lutheran congregations to make the transition from German or Scandinavian to English and to move from an immigrant status into the mainstream of American Protestantism. The headquarters of the Lutheran Church in America are in New York City. Its theological seminaries are: Hamma School of Theology (part of Wittenberg University), Springfield, Ohio; Lutheran School of Theology at Chicago; Lutheran Theological Seminary at Gettysburg, Pa.; Lutheran Theological Seminary at Philadelphia, Pa.; Lutheran Theological Seminary at Saskatoon, Saskatchewan, Canada; Lutheran Theological Southern Seminary, Columbia, S.C.; Northwestern Lutheran Theological Seminary, Minneapolis, Minn.; Pacific Lutheran Theological Seminary, Berkeley, Calif.; and Waterloo Lutheran Seminary (part of Waterloo Lutheran University), Waterloo, Ontario, Canada. It also operates 19 colleges. In 1969 the Lutheran Church in America numbered 3,157,543 baptized members. See T. G. Tappert et al., EncLuthCh 2:1366–1408.

LUTHERAN COUNCIL IN CANADA, an inter-Lutheran agency in existence since Jan. 1, 1967, to represent the Evangelical Lutheran Church of Canada, the Lutheran Church–Canada (Missouri Synod), the Lutheran Church in America–Canada Section, and the Synod of Evangelical Lutheran Churches—in all, 99.7% of Canada's Lutherans. ". . . The participating bodies are of the conviction that they should and can more effectively carry on their work and further a Lutheran witness by cooperating in matters of common interest and responsibility where cooperation is not at variance with their doctrine and practice" (Preamble, Constitution, 1967). The Council's program is carried on through its departments on: Theological Studies, Canadian Missions, Educational Services, Public Relations, Social Services, Campus Foundation Activity, Service to Military Personnel, and Youth Activities.

LUTHERAN COUNCIL IN THE U.S.A., a cooperative agency, formed in 1966 and active from Jan. 1, 1967. The four component bodies, the American Lutheran Church, the Lutheran Church in America, the Lutheran Church—Missouri Synod, and the Synod of Evangelical Lutheran Churches, represent 95% of the Lutherans in North America. The Council succeeded the National Lutheran Council, which had been organized in 1918 on the basis of the experience of Lutheran cooperation in the National Lutheran Commission for Soldiers' and Sailors' Welfare. The extension of the work of the National Council in coordinating efforts in home and foreign missions, welfare, public relations, and theological and ecumenical discussion was an expression of a continuing desire for Lutheran unity in spite of the differences that have marked Lutheran history in the United States. In the same spirit the National Council began discussions in 1961 with the Lutheran Church—Missouri Synod; these led to formation of the Lutheran Council in the U.S.A., which continued and broadened the functions of the older agency. The Council is also the U.S. committee for the *Lutheran World Federation. See A. R. Wentz, *Basic History of Lutheranism in America* (1955); EncLuthCh 3:1703–09.

LUTHERAN FREE CHURCH, one of the Lutheran bodies that united in 1960 to form the *American Lutheran Church. It was organized in Minneapolis, Minn., in 1897 by various Norwegian Lutheran groups char-

acterized by democratic church polity. See T. O. Burntvedt and J. N. Stensvaag, EncLuthCh 1:52–56.

LUTHERAN SYNODICAL CONFERENCE, a unitive body of strongly confessional Lutheran synods formally established in Milwaukee, Wis., in 1872. The founding members were the Ohio, Missouri, Wisconsin, Minnesota, Illinois, and Norwegian Synods. The original name was Evangelisch-Lutherische Synodal-Conferenz (Evangelical Lutheran Synodical Conference). The history of the Synodical Conference has been marked by a desire to maintain strong doctrinal unity and fellowship only with those Lutherans and non-Lutherans who met the standards of the Conference. The composition of membership, however, has changed constantly, as new bodies joined and others withdrew, usually over doctrinal disagreement. In 1963 both the Evangelical Lutheran Synod and the Wisconsin Evangelical Lutheran Synod withdrew. A close relationship continued between the Lutheran Church—Missouri Synod and the *Synod of Evangelical Lutheran Churches, but the Synodical Conference ceased to exist. See G. T. Mueller, *History of the Synodical Conference* (1948); E. L. Lueker, EncLuthCh 3:2316–17.

LUTHERAN WORLD FEDERATION, a free association of Lutheran Churches throughout the world to act "as their agent in such matters as they assign to it." It was organized at Lund, Sweden, in 1947 to supersede the Lutheran World Convention, which had been in existence for 23 years, seeking not only closer harmony and understanding among Lutheran Churches throughout the world but also cooperation in relief and mission work with special consideration for the weaker Churches, for unity of action and utterance among Lutherans, and for exchange of students, professors, and literature. Lutheran World

Conventions were held at Eisenach in 1923, at Copenhagen in 1929, at Paris in 1935, and at Lund in 1947. At Lund a constitution was adopted that changed the Convention into the Lutheran World Federation. The key figure in the formation of the new organization was S. C. Michelfelder of the American Lutheran Church, who had been sent to Europe in 1945 by the American Section of the Lutheran World Convention for relief and reconstruction work. The functions of the organization are: to further a united witness before the world to the gospel of Jesus Christ as the power of God for salvation; to cultivate unity of faith and confession among the Lutheran Churches of the world; to develop fellowship and cooperation in study among Lutherans; to foster Lutheran interest in, concern for, and participation in, ecumenical movements; to support Lutheran Churches and groups as they endeavor to meet the spiritual needs of other Lutherans and to extend the gospel; and to provide a channel for Lutheran Churches and groups to help meet physical needs. See A. R. Wentz, EncLuthCh 2:1425–30.

LUTHERANISM, the largest of the Protestant bodies in Western Christendom. As its name indicates, Lutheranism traces its historical origin to the work of Martin *Luther. He did not, however, intend to found a new Church; nor was he pleased that the movement that emerged from his work as a reformer was baptized with his name. Before his death there were Lutheran Churches not only in various lands of Germany but in Scandinavia and in eastern Europe. Although these countries still account statistically for the largest part of its membership, Lutheranism has spread to most of the inhabited portions of the earth. Beginning already in the early colonial era, Lutherans immigrated to North America and gained converts there once they had settled, with the result that by the late 1960s the U.S. had almost 10 million Lutherans. In Latin America, Canada, Australia, the Union of Soviet Socialist Republics, Africa, Asia, and the islands of the sea, the combination of various immigrations and several missionary societies planted the Lutheran name.

The international character of Lutheranism and its adaptation to many different cultures are symbolized by its heterogeneity in church organization. There is no Protestant congregationalism more extreme than that of some Lutheran groups, esp. in the U.S.; at the same time, even under the terms of *Apostolicae curae, the *apostolic succession of the Lutheran Church of Sweden may be more nearly valid than that of any except Eastern Orthodox communions. Lutherans themselves are characterized by considerable indifference to questions of *polity; such questions are neither constitutive of the life of the Church nor, in and of themselves, an adequate basis for separation from other Christians. For the first generations of Lutheranism, even the papacy was not such a ground, provided that it could be accepted as *jure humano*. This indifference to polity is combined with a great regard for the office of the ministry. Sociology and theology join in various Lutheran traditions to make the pastor a figure of authority and respect, often to a degree exceeding the regard in which the clergy are held by traditions that, theoretically at least, exalt the office far more.

Lutheran liturgy is no more uniform than Lutheran polity. The "high Mass" of the Church of Sweden has retained some elements of the Western rite that have been discarded by Roman Catholicism, and the liturgical revival of various Lutheran Churches, including those of North America, has involved the recovery of various practices (such as the elevation) lost since the 16th century. Yet within some of the very same Lutheran bodies there are devotional traditions (such as prayer meetings) of an unmistakably Protestant cast. The most distinctive feature of Lutheran worship is its hymnody. The Lutheran chorale, which owes its origins to Luther himself and reached its climax in the work of Paul Gerhardt (d. 1676), epitomizes both the continuity of Lutheranism with the RC tradition (as in the hymn "O Sacred Head Now Wounded," based on the *Salve caput cruentatum*) and its special forms of faith and life (as in Luther's "A Mighty Fortress Is Our God"). It is neither in its polity nor in its liturgy but in its theology that Lutheranism has defined itself most clearly. For Luther himself, the "doctrine of the gospel" was the decisive point on which the Church was not permitted to yield, while on the Christian life it had to recognize the frailty of men and the variations in their capacity. Lutheranism codified this position in its confessional statements, beginning with the *Augsburg Confession (1530) and concluding with the *Book of Concord (1580). Even when, as in *Pietism, Lutheran spokesmen denounced an exclusive preoccupation with doctrine as intellectualism, their very denunciation took theological form. As a consequence, the training of the ministry in the Lutheran tradition has traditionally emphasized the need for a learned clergy. Greek, Hebrew, and Latin, together with church history, exegesis, and dogmatics have made up the curriculum of both the theological faculties in the European universities and the theological seminaries in America. This emphasis upon humanistic erudition in the equipment of the minister has helped to give Lutheranism, esp. German Lutheranism, a dominant position in international theological scholarship, particularly during the 19th century. With its base as much in the university as in the Church, Lutheran theology has frequently manifested a spirit of intense controversy and a tendency toward rapid and radical shifts. Nevertheless, certain common and continuing themes document a unity beyond these fluctuations. Almost without exception, the parties and schools of Lutheran theology have taken the exegetical task with great seriousness, devoting themselves to the biblical text with learning and care. Even in the heyday of Pietism, with its emphasis upon conversion, most Lutheran theologians stressed the primacy of grace over merit and the *monergism of the divine initiative. Thus justification by grace

through faith (a more accurate formulation than the usual *justification by faith) has united Lutheran theologians of diverse positions. On other doctrinal questions unity has been less substantial, esp. in the 19th and 20th centuries. Biblical criticism and the new study of the Gospels have made the formal adherence of confessional Lutheranism to the Christology of Chalcedon quite ambiguous; these and other factors have been responsible for a fundamental recasting of the traditional Lutheran views of such issues as the sacraments, the inspiration of Scripture, the Atonement, and even the Trinity.

These characteristics of the Lutheran Church have shaped its participation in the ecumenical movement, which has included some of the movement's most insp'red leadership (notably Nathan *Söderblom) and some of its sharpest critics. When ecumenism was almost exclusively a Protestant matter, the attitude of various Lutheran groups toward it was determined by their understanding of Lutheran distinctiveness on the questions that set it apart from bodies other than the RC Church, such as the *Real Presence. But with the growth of RC ecumenism in the decades after World War II, Lutheran participation took a different form. Always prominent in ecumenical discussions, Lutherans now began to play a mediatorial role between Roman Catholics and Protestants. Centuries of living in separated communities meant that, in vocabulary and interest, Lutherans and Roman Catholics could not communicate with each other as simply and directly as they had supposed. It is significant that the most effective communication took place in those areas, e.g., portions of Germany and the U.S., where both communities were strongly represented and had at least some theological sophistication.

The distinctive genius of Lutheranism cannot be understood from its confessional statements alone but must be seen in the light of its piety, hymnody, social history, and liturgy; the character and thought of Martin Luther have also continued to be a powerful force in shaping Lutheranism to the present day. As the Lutheran participation in the ecumenical movement makes clear, this legacy determines Lutheran thought also in the 20th century. At the same time, the commitment of Lutheran theology to authorities beyond itself—Scripture, but also the Catholic tradition and, sometimes in tension with this, the implications of an unfettered theological scholarship—has given it the special accent in which it speaks. See T. G. Tappert, ed., *Book of Concord: Confessions of the Evangelical Lutheran Church* (1959); W. Elert, *Structure of Lutheranism* (tr. W. A. Hansen, 1963); C. H. Lytkens et al., eds., *Church in Fellowship* (v.1, 1963; v.2, 1969).

LUTHER'S CATECHISMS, see CATE-CHISMS, LUTHER'S.

LUX MUNDI (1889), a collection of Anglican "Studies on the Religion of the Incarnation," to which H. S. Holland, E. S. Talbot, R. C. Moberly, and F. Paget contributed, under the editorship of Charles *Gore, then principal of Pusey House. Their purpose was "to put Catholic faith into its right relation" to intellectual and moral questions of the time. It was Gore's study, *The Holy Spirit and Inspiration*, that shocked and distressed Anglo-Catholics of the conservative school; he was a freethinker, in the best sense of the term, with a mind open to the new critical problems raised by OT study. In fact his convictions on the fundamental articles of belief were not shaken, and, as his leadership of the Anglo-Catholic party during the next 40 years was to prove, his allegiance was not in doubt.

M

MC CONNELL, FRANCIS JOHN (1871–1953), Methodist bp., social reformer. Born in Trinway, Ohio, and educated at Boston Univ., he became a Methodist minister in 1894. He was made president of De Pauw Univ. in 1909, and elected bp. in 1912. His theological views were influenced by the personalism of Borden Parker *Bowne. In the steel strike of 1919 his work led to the abolition of the 12-hour working day in the industry. His *John Wesley* (1939), a popular biography, was marked by a realistic evaluation of the man, and a critical judgment of Wesley's relationship to Reformation traditions. M. was president of the Federal Council of Churches and active in the programs that led eventually to the formation of the World Council of Churches. See F. J. McConnell, *By the Way: An Autobiography* (1952); HistAmMeth 3.

MACHEN, JOHN GRESHAM (1881–1937), Presbyterian biblical scholar, opponent of *modernism. He completed his studies at Johns Hopkins, Princeton, and Marburg and Göttingen in Germany, and was ordained in 1914. As professor of NT exegesis at Princeton Theological Seminary from 1916, he became known for his conservative views. In the name of fidelity to the *Westminster Confession he opposed the *Auburn Affirmation (1924). His stand led to his resignation from Princeton in 1929; he founded Westminster Theological Seminary and taught there until death. His opposition to liberal policies in the Presbyterian Church in the U.S.A. brought about suspension from the ministry (1933). He helped found (1936) the conservative body later named the *Orthodox Presbyterian Church. M. was not a fundamentalist, but a vigorous conservative apologist, whose clearly expressed writings, esp. *Christianity and Liberalism* (1923), came to the aid of conservatives of many denominations. See E. H. Rian, *Presbyterian Conflict* (1940).

MACINTOSH, DOUGLAS CLYDE (1877–1948), Baptist theologian. Canadian born, M. received his B.A. from McMaster Univ. in Ontario, and his Ph.D. from the Univ. of Chicago; he taught theology at Yale Divinity School, 1909–42. His thought marked a new direction in American *liberal theology. His main theme, as seen in his own work *Theology as an Empirical Science* (1919), and in a collection he edited, *Religious Realism* (1931), was that metaphysics and theology could and must be empirically grounded. He moved away from the subjective idealism of earlier liberalism, towards what he termed "Religious Realism." He held that belief in God must be grounded in the objective experience of a God immanent in the processes of history. He would grant no authority to historical revelation as the basis for belief. He affirmed, as well, that scientific generalizations about the values of Christianity were to be verified through the experiences of the lives of those who will accept the gospel. M.'s last important work was *The Problem of Religious Knowledge* (1940). Already, however, *neo-orthodoxy had begun to supplant liberal theology and "Religious Realism." See K. Cauthen, *Impact of American Liberalism* (1962); Smith-Jamison 1:309–312; 469–470.

MACK, ALEXANDER (1679–1735), founder of the *Brethren Churches. By trade M. was a miller, from Schriesheim near Heidelberg, Germany. Separating from the *Reformed Church, he associated with Pietists who gathered at Schwarzenau in the Palatinate, and led a number of other separatists in search of the apostolic faith, practices, and manner of life. In the summer of 1708 he was chosen leader of a group that covenanted together in forming a new fellowship, which he declared to be "the old Church which Christ instituted through his blood." Because of persecution, M. migrated with his group to Friesland in the Netherlands about 1720, and likewise with them, in 1729, to Germantown, Pennsylvania. There he served the Brethren as minister until his death.

MC PHERSON, AIMEE SEMPLE (1890–1944), evangelist, founder of the *International Church of the Foursquare Gospel. A Canadian by birth, Aimee Kennedy in her public life used the names of the first two of her three husbands. In 1907 she experienced a religious conversion at a revival conducted by Robert Semple, whom she married in 1908. The two worked as missionaries in Hong Kong until his death in 1911. She continued to travel, fulfilling what she regarded as her divine commission to preach. A second marriage, to Harold McPherson, ended in divorce. Her evangelistic campaign carried her to Los Angeles in 1918, and in 1921 she built her Angelus Temple, with a seating capacity of 5,300; she was ordained in a Baptist church in 1922. She organized her Church in 1927, and later established the Lighthouse of International Foursquare Evangelism (LIFE) Bible College and a radio station. Lawsuits, an escapade in which she claimed to have been kidnapped, a third marriage in 1931 to David Hutton, a singer in the Temple choir, which ended in another divorce, brought her great notoriety. Sister Aimee was able to use even this, as well as her pleasing appearance and eloquence, to make herself the foremost woman evangelist in the United States. She preached a pure *fundamentalism and *Pentecostalism. She died leaving 35,000 followers; her son Rolf K. McPherson succeeded her. Her autobiography, *The Story of My Life*, was published posthumously (1951).

MAGDEBURG CENTURIES (*Ecclesiastica historia secundum singulas centurias . . .*), Protestant-inspired, documentary ecclesiastical history. It was a monumental work in 13 volumes, published in Basel, 1559–74. The authors, often called the Centuriators, were seven in number, but the work was planned and supervised by the disputatious M. *Flacius Illyricus (1520–75). The popular title derives from the place of editing and from the division of content by centuries. The work was projected up to the 16th cent., but the last three volumes were not published. This first real Protestant church history, an effort to vindicate the Reformation, is apologetic and partisan. Its thesis is that the Roman Church has progressively corrupted the true gospel. Though based on sources gathered throughout Europe, the work uses them uncritically and with distortions. The myth of Pope Joan is incorporated, and the pope is always designated as anti-Christ, whose empire is the RC Church. Though the *Magdeburg Centuries* represents a break with the often more critical spirit of the Renaissance, it did stimulate historical research as a reaction, beginning with the *Annales ecclesiastici* of C. *Baronius.

MAGISTERIUM, the teaching authority of the Christian Church, held by Roman Catholics to pertain by divine right to the pope and bishops as the successors of the Apostles. This authoritative teaching office in the Church was originally conferred by Jesus himself in a special way on Simon Peter as leader of the twelve Apostles (Lk 22.31; Mt 16.19; Jn 21.15–17) and upon the Apostles themselves (Mt. 18.18; 28.18–20). The Apostle Paul received the same mandate (1 Cor 9.1; Gal 1.15–16). As a group the Twelve were not only personally familiar with Jesus and the events of his ministry, but were also the divinely constituted witnesses to his person and teaching, understood by them in the light of his resurrection (Acts 1.21–22; 10.39–42; 13.31). Thus their teaching authority was exercised on the prophetic level (1 Thes 2.13). Insofar as their authority derived from personal experience of Jesus, and was endowed with a prophetic charism, their apostolic witness was not transferable. But authority to safeguard the content of their witness was transferred by them to the presbyters (elders) and *episkopoi* (overseers), as Luke indicates (Acts 14.23; 20.17–35). This tradition of authoritative teaching authority over apostolic doctrine appears in 1 Tim 6.20 and 2 Tim 1.14, where it is considered to be a key function of the *episkopos*. According to RC theology, the pope and bishops are the legitimate successors of the Twelve, continuing the early tradition of the presbyters and *episkopoi*. They are the chief and authoritative witnesses to the content of faith, i.e., to its meaning and to its implications for conduct ("faith and morals").

In the course of time RC theologians have come to distinguish between the extraordinary magisterium and the ordinary magisterium. The former occurs when the pope alone teaches solemnly, i.e., in a formal, definitive, and public way that addresses itself to the whole Church and declares a precise meaning of God's word as binding in faith upon the Church; and when in the same manner a teaching comes from the bishops together with the pope (as in an *ecumenical council). The ordinary magisterium is exercised when the pope or bishops formulate and express the meaning of God's word in the normal course of the performance of their pastoral teaching responsibility. Both these exercises of the magisterium are authoritative and require religious assent from Roman Catholics. The extraordinary magisterium is believed by Roman Catholics to be infallible, i.e., protected from error by the assistance of the Holy Spirit, since its very aim is to articulate the meaning of God's word in a definitive fashion; thus the extraordinary magisterium shares in the quality of *infallibility characteristic of the divine word. The ordinary magisterium may also be infallible when the pope and bishops teach with moral unanimity, though in practice the fact that such unanimity exists is difficult to ascertain. The teaching of the ordinary magisterium, whether of the pope or bishops, is subject to revision, as the history of papal teaching on such questions as interest-taking, freedom of conscience, and

the relationship of Church and State reveal. See J. R. Lerch, NCE 13:959–965; D. C. Maguire, "Moral Absolutes and the Magisterium," in *Absolutes in Moral Theology* (ed. C. Curran, 1968).

MAJOR, GEORG, see MAJORISTIC CONTROVERSY.

MAJORISTIC CONTROVERSY, the Lutheran dispute over *good works (1552–77), named for Georg Major (Maier; 1502–74) a polemicist and professor of theology who, influenced by Philipp Melanchthon's ideas, advanced the thesis that good works are necessary to salvation, at least in the sense of being required to preserve it. The position was bitterly attacked as in opposition to Luther's *justification by faith alone (see FLACIUS ILLYRICUS, M.; GNESIOLUTHERANISM). N. Amsdorf (1483–1565) went so far as to assert that good works are a danger to salvation. Major sought to defend himself against charges of Pelagianism or Romanism, and refrained from using the expression "necessary for salvation" after 1558, but the controversy continued. The *Formula of Concord (1577) settled the matter (Art. IV), affirming that good works will be done by the regenerate freely and spontaneously in testimony to the presence of the Holy Spirit; they neither cause nor merit salvation or its preservation; nor are they detrimental. *GOOD WORKS.

MAKEMIE, FRANCIS (d. 1708), Presbyterian clergyman and pioneer organizer of the denomination in America. Born in Ireland, M. served in the Barbados as a minister until he moved to Md., where he organized one of the first American Presbyterian congregations in 1684 at Snow Hill. Marriage brought him the status and leisure of a gentleman, and he was able to go about preaching throughout Va. and the Carolinas. He was so successful that with other ministers he was able to organize the first *presbytery in Philadelphia in 1706; he became its moderator. In 1707 he won the sympathy of colonial Dissenters when he was imprisoned for preaching in New York without a proper license; he was acquitted under the 1689 *Toleration Act.

MALINES CONVERSATIONS, a series of discussions between certain prominent Roman Catholics and Anglicans at Malines (Mechelen), Belgium, between 1921 and 1926. The appeal of the *Lambeth Conference of 1920 for efforts toward church unity moved Lord *Halifax to approach his friend F. *Portal, the French Vincentian, with the proposal that they appeal to Cardinal D. J. Mercier to sponsor and be host to a series of Roman Catholic–Anglican meetings. The first of these was held in Dec. 1921, with Halifax, W. H. Frere, and J. A. Robinson representing the Anglican position and Mercier, J. E. van Roey, and Portal, the RC side. After the first meeting the Holy See and the abp. of Canterbury expressed interest and approval, although the private and unofficial character of the meetings was not changed. Further meetings were held in 1923, 1925, and 1926. At the conversations of 1923, C. Gore and B. J. Kidd joined the Anglican representatives and P. Batiffol and M. H. Hemmer the RC participants. The last of the meetings (Oct. 1926) took place without two of the principal participants, Mercier and Portal, both of whom had died earlier that year. The conversations were viewed with suspicion by many evangelically minded members of the C of E and by many English Roman Catholics as well. They were not resumed after 1926. While it must be admitted that they ended without immediate tangible result, their importance as a start in the serious exploration of the possibilities of accord and their contribution to the development of a climate more favorable to ecumenical effort cannot be denied. See J. G. Lockhart, *Charles Lindley Viscount Halifax* (2v., 1935–36); Lord Halifax, *Conversations at Malines, 1921–25* (1930); J. de Bivort de la Saudée, *Anglicans et Catholiques* (2v., 1949).

MANHARTER, also called Hagleitnerianer or Michaelsbrüder, a religious-political group in the Austrian Tyrol during the French occupation of 1809. The Vicar Caspar Hagleitner (1779–1836) and the farmer Sebastian Manzl (owner of the Manhart farm near Brixen) refused to obey those clergy who had taken an oath of loyalty to Emperor Napoleon I. They believed that, since Napoleon had been excommunicated by Pius VII after the invasion of Rome, such an oath of loyalty would automatically excommunicate them, too. They temporarily combined forces with the *Michaelsritter. Eventually Hagleitner and some others returned to the Church, mainly because of the persuasion of Cardinal B. A. Cappellari (later Pope Gregory XVI), and Hagleitner ended his days as pastor at Kalksburg near Vienna. Remnants of the Manharter existed until the end of the 19th century. See W. Schatz, LTK 6:1350–51.

MANUAL OF THE MOTHER CHURCH, also called *Church Manual of the First Church of Christ, Scientist,* the fundamental law of the Church of Christ, Scientist, establishing in minute detail the polity, form of worship, and other particulars of the Christian Science movement. It is composed of a series of bylaws, which cannot be in any way altered or repealed since the death of Mary Baker Eddy and which are binding and normative for all branch Churches of Christ, Scientist. The Christian Science Board of Directors, as Mrs. Eddy's representatives and legal successors, are permitted to act only within the scope of the *Manual,* and its terms are as binding on them as on any other member. The *Manual* was first published in 1895 and was periodically revised until 1906; it has preserved Mrs. Eddy's legislation intact since that time and prevented alteration or dissension within the Christian Science movement.

MANZ, FELIX (1500–27), Swiss Anabaptist martyr. M. was a humanist and at first a close associate of Zwingli, but broke with him and accepted Anabaptist ideas. After the ceremony of rebaptism in Jan. 1525, expressive of Anabaptist belief (see GREBEL, C., and BLAUROCK, G.), and in spite of persecutions and imprisonment, M. won many converts in the N and E of Switzerland. In order to suppress the movement, the city council of Zurich had him drowned in the Limmat River on Jan. 5, 1527. See bibliog. for Anabaptists.

MARBURG ARTICLES, a statement of Reformation doctrine drawn up by Martin *Luther for the Marburg Colloquy, Oct. 1–3, 1529. This conference was summoned by Philip of Hesse with a view to uniting German and Swiss Reformers. Luther was accompanied by P. *Melanchthon; the Swiss side was represented by *Zwingli, M. *Bucer, and J. *Oecolampadius. In 14 of the 15 articles the participants agreed concerning the Trinity, the Person of Christ, faith and justification, good works, confession, infant baptism, and human traditions. The 15th article, however, widened the gap between the two parties, since Zwingli could not accept Luther's doctrine of the *Real Presence. The revision of the Articles made by the Lutheran theologians a few days later, the *Schwabach Articles, formed the basis for the first part of the *Augsburg Confession. See Schaff Creeds 1:212–213. *TETRAPOLITAN CONFESSION.

MARCION (*c.*85–*c.*160), founder of an early separatist sect. A wealthy shipowner of Sinope in Pontus, M. went to Rome *c.*140 and affiliated himself with the Christian community of that city. The claim of Hippolytus and of Epiphanius that he was the son of a bishop excommunicated for violating a virgin vowed to God was probably intended in an allegorical sense. M. developed a system of religious ideas and gathered disciples. When finally expelled from the orthodox community (*c.*144), he established a rival Church of his own, which spread to many places in the empire and continued to exist for several centuries, though many of its communities merged in

time with the Manichaeans. His thought can be described as Gnostic in its dualism, but it is not marked by the mythological tendencies characteristic of Gnosticism. He considered the God of the OT, the creator God or demiurge, to be different entirely from the God revealed by Jesus. The OT God was a God of Law as opposed to the God of Love of the NT; Christ came to liberate men from the tyranny of the Creator God. He insisted that all Judaizing tendencies be resisted and excised from Christianity and esp. from the NT writings. He rejected all the OT and much of the NT as well. He accepted only the Pauline Epistles (except for the Pastoral Epistles and Hebrews) and a revision of the Gospel of St. Luke that omitted all mention of the infancy of Christ. The repudiated sections of the NT were corrupted for him by remnants of Jewish influence. This rejection of sacred writings, by calling attention to the question of canonicity, probably exercised some influence upon the development of the canon of the Scriptures in the Church. Marcion's writings, among which was the *Antitheses,* which stated the Marcionite creed, have been lost except for the fragments cited by his opponents. See Quasten 1:268–272; E. Blackman, *Marcion and His Influence* (1948), A. Stephenson, NCE 9:193–194.

MARIAVITES, since 1906, a separate denomination in Poland, named from the motto, *Mariae vitam imitantes* (imitators of Mary's life). A community of sisters was founded in 1888 at Plock, then Russian Poland, by Felicja Kozlowska (1862–1921); and of priests, by Jan Kowalski in 1892; both groups lived according to the Franciscan rule and were dedicated to the cult of Mary and to the Eucharist. Rome regarded their doctrines and practices, partly based on the visions of Kozlowska, as extravagant, and the two founders were excommunicated in 1906. In the same year the Russian authorities recognized the Mariavites as a separate Church. They were received into communion with the Old Catholic Church in 1909,

Kowalski being consecrated abp. over the approximately 200,000 members. The Old Catholic Church severed the relationship in 1925, esp. because of the cult of Kozlowska as the "Bride of the Lamb" and of Kowalski as a second Michael the Archangel, and because of the mystical marriages between priests and nuns, which were to lead to "immaculate conceptions," children of a new and sinless race. In 1935 a majority rejected Kowalski (he died at Dachau during World War II, and all the Mariavites were severely persecuted by the Nazis). A small group in the Kowalski line remains; the majority of Mariavites, however, numbering about 25,000, with three episcopal sees and about 40 parishes, have entered into cooperative association, but not communion, with the Old Catholic Church. Mariavite teachings agree basically with those of the Old Catholics, esp. in the rejection of papal primacy and infallibility; the practice of auricular confession and the veneration of relics, however, are forbidden. See P. F. Anson, *Bishops at Large* (1965).

MARPRELATE TRACTS, a series of polemical pamphlets published in England (1588–89) under the pseudonym of Martin Marprelate. They were a Puritan attack upon *episcopacy, and their brilliant satire caused alarm among the defenders of the *established Church. However, they appear to have overshot their mark, for their violence inspired renewed adherence to the C of E and brought an increase of suspicion upon the Puritans. Their authorship has never been established beyond doubt, though J. Penry was believed guilty and was hanged in 1593 on the charge of inciting rebellion. A modern edition of the seven pamphlets that survived was published with historical notes by William Pierce in 1911; he also wrote *Historical Introduction to the Marprelate Tracts* (1908). See Hughes RE 3:212–214.

MARRIAGE, see CELESTIAL MARRIAGE; PLURAL MARRIAGE.

MARROW CONTROVERSY, a dispute in the Church of Scotland. The republication in 1718 of an old Puritan work, *The Marrow of Modern Divinity*, originally published in 1646 and recommended for its evangelical doctrines by Thomas Boston and others, marked the beginning of the so-called Marrow controversy. The question of the doctrinal orthodoxy of the *Marrow* increasingly divided the evangelical party from the more accommodating moderates, and in an act condemning the work (1720) the *General Assembly of the Church declared itself against the teachings of the *Marrow* and forbade its ministers to preach or advocate its views. Twelve ministers, including Boston and Ebenezer and Ralph Erskine, signed a representation addressed to the Assembly of 1721 in protest against the condemnation, but the "Marrow men" were themselves rebuked and admonished by the Assembly. The controversy died down, but the bitterness it created was partly responsible for the later secession of the Erskines. *SECEDER TRADITION.

MARSHALL, DANIEL (1706–84), Baptist revivalist. Reared a Congregationalist in Conn., he experienced conversion through the influence of George *Whitefield. About 1752, he went to preach to Indians in western N.Y. and Pennsylvania. By 1754, he had reached Opeckon, Va., where he became a Baptist. In 1755, with his brother-in-law, Shubael *Stearns, he moved to Sandy Creek, N.C., where he was ordained a Baptist minister. His revivalistic preaching led to the establishment of several churches, and he moved to S.C., where he preached for about 10 years. In 1771 he settled in Columbia Co., Ga., where he formed the Kiokee Baptist Church and thus helped to lay the foundations of Baptist work in that state. See J. D. Mosteller, *History of the Kiokee Baptist Church in Georgia* (1952).

MARSILIUS OF PADUA (Marsiglio; *c.* 1275–1342), physician, scholar, and author of the antipapal *Defensor pacis* (1324), his major work, written with some assistance from Jean de Jandun. The *Defensor pacis* had a direct bearing on the contemporary dispute between the Pope and the Emperor, already broadening out into projects for the control of the Church by the State. It was acridly antipapal; when his authorship was discovered (1326), M. had to leave Paris. Siding with Louis of Bavaria, afterward proclaimed emperor in defiance of the Pope, M. was made Imperial Vicar of Rome (1328). Thrown out by a mob after a few months, he remained for the rest of his life at Louis's court in Munich.

The *Defensor pacis* is composed of three books, the third being a brief summary of conclusions. The first is a philosophy of the State in the sober line of the studies on Aristotle's *Politics* initiated by Thomas Aquinas and Peter of Auvergne. The second book is strikingly different. Had it developed the ideals of Dante's *Monarchia* no great dust would have risen nor would odium have been aroused. But it was a theology of the Church that advocated a radical secularism and allowed the spiritual power no coercive jurisdiction of any kind, not even in ecclesiastical affairs, but subjected the Church to civil control. The whole conception of a divinely ordered hierarchical structure, one moreover that was centered in the primacy of Peter, was attacked, and in a temper that far exceeded contemporary anticlericalism. It was for this reason that the work was condemned as heretical in 1327 and 1378. It was studied by Thomas *Cranmer, and translated into English to provide support for the religious policies of Henry VIII. See A. Gerwith, *M. of P., Defender of the Peace* (2v., 1951, 1956).

MARTYRS' MIRROR, a book that possibly exerted a greater and more lasting influence on Mennonites than any other devotional literature. The author was the Dutch Mennonite leader and writer Tieleman Jansz van Braght (1625–64). Published in 1660, it was based on official records and private testimonies of Anabaptist martyrs in the Netherlands, Germany, Switzerland, and Austria. The theme, that truly Christian witness will inevitably bring persecution and possibly martyrdom, is illustrated by OT and NT texts and records of the early Church, as well as by 16th-cent. records dealing with Anabaptists. While not principally a work of critical history, the *Mirror* is recognized as a valuable source. There have been numerous editions of both German and English translations (most recent, 1950). See MennEnc 3:527–529.

MARY TUDOR (1516–58), QUEEN OF ENGLAND from 1553. Daughter of King Henry VIII and Catherine of Aragon, M. was only 12 when her father began divorce proceedings, and she incurred his disfavor by her allegiance to her mother. In 1533 she was pronounced technically illegitimate after Abp. Cranmer declared Henry's marriage to Catherine invalid. Upon the birth of her half-sister, the future Elizabeth I, M. was also denied the title Princess of Wales. In 1536, under compulsion, she signed a statement acknowledging that her deceased mother's marriage had been unlawful and that the pope had no authority. When her half-brother became King, as *Edward VI, in 1547, his advisers attempted to make M. conform to the reformed Church of England, but without complete success. In 1553 they were able to persuade the dying Edward to set aside M.'s right to the throne for fear it would lead to a Catholic restoration. Accordingly, Lady Jane Grey was treasonably proclaimed Queen after Edward's death. Within a fortnight, however, M. marched on London with heavy support and made good her claim to the throne. Her principal adviser, Card. Pole, urged her to overcome schism and heresy at all costs; but she proceeded slowly. In her first year as Queen she induced Parliament to nullify the religious legislation of Edward's reign. In 1554 Henry's legislation was also revoked. She then set out to revitalize Catholicism. Though lenient by nature, she caused 300 persons to be executed for opposition to Catholicism during her reign. Her unhappy marriage to

Philip II of Spain, the loss of Calais, and the Pope's dismissal of Card. Pole saddened her final days. See J. J. O'Connor, NCE 9:391–393, with bibliog.; W. C. Richardson, *Mary Tudor: The White Queen* (1969).

MASON, CHARLES H. (1865–1964), the founder and "Chief Apostle," or bishop, of the *Church of God in Christ. Born near Memphis, Tenn., of slave parents, M. was first a Baptist minister but then established a *Holiness Church (1897) from several congregations in Tenn., Miss., Ark., and Oklahoma. In 1906 he attended the *Azusa Street revival and experienced *baptism with the Holy Spirit, and in 1907 he formally organized his Church as Pentecostal. All through his life he was the guiding spirit and chief administrator of this Church, which has experienced a phenomenal growth. In 1948 he dedicated Mason Tabernacle, Memphis, Tenn., as world headquarters. See J. T. Nichol, *Pentecostalism* (1966), 102–103.

MATERIAL PRINCIPLE, the central doctrine or doctrines of any Church; the correlative of *formal principle, i.e., the source or criterion for doctrines.

MATHER, surname of three Puritan clergymen who were prominent in the civil and ecclesiastical history of colonial New England.

Richard (1596–1669) was born in Lancashire, attended Oxford briefly, and became pastor at Toxteth Park Chapel. In 1635, because of his Puritan leanings, he was suspended from his ministry. He immigrated to Mass. in 1635, became pastor at Dorchester, and remained there until his death. He helped to shape New England's Congregational way, collaborating in preparing the Psalms in meter for the *Bay Psalm Book*, and wrote the original draft of the *Cambridge Platform (1648). He was also one of the men who was responsible for the *Half-Way Covenant, strongly advocating the plan against fierce opposition by those who insisted on the necessity of personal conversion experience.

Increase (1639–1723), son of Richard, born in Dorchester, Mass., he graduated from Harvard in 1656 and from Trinity College, Dublin, 2 years later. He preached in England for 3 years. Returning to Mass. in 1661, he was called to Second Church, Boston, remaining there until his death. While preeminently a pastor, he was involved in politics, served as president of Harvard (1685–1701), and organized a society to discuss scientific matters. He was one of four representatives who persuaded the English government to grant a new charter to Mass. (1691), but had to make some concessions, most important of which were granting suffrage to non-church members and allowing the king to appoint governors. Accused of fomenting the witchcraft troubles at Salem, he was one of those who cautioned against use of "spectral evidence," esp. in his *Cases of Conscience Concerning Evil Spirits* (1692), which influenced Governor Phips to cease carrying out sentences of convicted witches. He was a scholar and the author of numerous political and religious works.

Cotton (1663–1728), son of Increase, also grandson of John *Cotton. He was a precocious youth, entering Harvard at age 12; he graduated in 1678 and received the M.A. in 1681. Ordained at 22 and installed as assistant to his father at Second Church, Boston, he labored there until his death. Primarily a minister, he was active in public affairs, organized numerous humanitarian societies, and was an erudite scholar. Although he was caricatured by later generations as a bigot, such a portrayal does him injustice. While upholding traditional congregational ideals, he was openminded and inquiring. Although sometimes charged with responsibility for the witchcraft affair at Salem, his role in the matter was small. His many learned writings included sermons, theological works, histories, biographies, scientific discourses, and even poetry. Probably his best-known work was the

Magnalia Christi Americana (1702), a collection of miscellaneous works that formed a kind of history of New England. See B. Wendell, *Cotton Mather: The Puritan Priest*, with an introduction by Alan Heimert (new ed., 1963); K. B. Murdoch, *Increase Mather: The Foremost American Puritan* (1925).

MATHEWS, SHAILER (1863–1941), Baptist theologian. A native of Portland, Maine, M. was professor of theology at the Divinity School, Univ. of Chicago (1906–33). Strongly influenced by historical and sociological studies, he held that theology is always the product of social environment. Notions such as the deity, atonement, and resurrection of Jesus Christ are historically conditioned and therefore relative, but also are functional in helping men to adjust to life. His mature views included belief that in the universe are personality-producing forces that men conceptualize as a personal God and that the ideals and life of Jesus inspire men to maintain personal values and to live worthy lives. Despite his liberal, reductionist theology, he remained an active churchman, sharing in the organization of the Northern Baptist Convention (1907) and serving as its president (1916); he was also president of the *Federal Council of Churches (1912–16). He had widespread influence through his teaching and writings, among which were *The Faith of Modernism* (1924), *The Atonement and the Social Process* (1934), *The Growth of the Idea of God* (1931), and *New Faith for Old: An Autobiography* (1936). See K. Cauthen, *Impact of American Religious Liberalism* (1962). *MODERNISM.

MATTHIAS CORVINUS (Mátyás Hunyadi; *c.*1440–90), king of Hungary and of Bohemia. Over the opposition of Emperor Frederick III (d. 1493), M. was elected king of Hungary in 1458. He fought against the Turks, intervened in Bohemia against *George of Poděbrad at the urging of Pius II, and was made king of Bohemia by the pro-Roman faction (1469). Through alliances and through victories over Frederick III, M. extended his rule over most of central Europe. He introduced the Renaissance into Hungary, and at Buda built up a library, the Corvina, celebrated for its illuminated codices. His reign was also one of political stability and justice. See D. Sinor, *History of Hungary* (1959).

MATTHYS, JAN (Matthijsz, Matthyszoon, Matthiessen; d. 1534), Anabaptist fanatic. M., a Dutch baker, was the first ruler during the Anabaptist reign at Münster, 1533–35. On April 5, 1534, picturing himself as a second Gideon, he led a reckless sortie against the siege laid by the bishop, F. von *Waldeck, and was slain. See bibliog. for Anabaptists.

MAURICE, FREDERICK DENISON (1805–72), Anglican social reformer. An East Anglian, reared a Unitarian, M. read law at Trinity Hall, Cambridge, studied at Oxford, and was baptized and ordained in the C of E (1834). He was not personally acquainted with the leading Tractarians, and afterward he stood apart from the high- and the low-church schools; nor was he broad church, for that to him was but a *caput mortuum* that just abandoned disputed doctrines. Like his friend Charles *Kingsley, he was moved by the revolutions of 1848; he was convinced that the Church should enter into, and not merely patronize, social reform; both were among the founders of *Christian Socialism. M. started the Working Men's Colleges (1854), and was appointed Knightsbridge Professor of Moral Philosophy at Cambridge (1866). Gentle and courteous in conversation, he could be sufficiently caustic in controversy. See F. Higham, *F. D. M.* (1948).

MAXFIELD, THOMAS (*c.*1720–84), one of Methodism's first lay preachers. M. was converted by John *Wesley at Bristol, 1739.

Placed in charge of the Methodist *society at the Foundry Meeting House in London, he took it upon himself, though not ordained, to preach. Wesley at first objected, but then relented and in fact thereafter authorized lay preaching extensively. M. was eventually ordained; as one of the chaplains of the Countess of *Huntingdon, he became estranged from Wesley in 1763 over doctrinal differences. See R. D. Urlin, *Churchman's Life of Wesley* (n.d.), 137–146.

MAXIMIANISTS, followers of the Donatist Maximian, who as a deacon was excommunicated by Primian, the Donatist bp. of Carthage, in 392. Maximian received the support and approval of 43 bps. who met at Carthage toward the end of the year. He was further approved by some 50 more bps., dismayed by Primian's misdeeds, at Cebarsussa in June 393. He was consecrated a bp., but then was condemned by a council of 310 Donatist bps. held at Bagai in April 394. He and his 12 coadjutors were excommunicated, and his followers were abused. Throughout his controversy with Primian, Maximian showed himself to be of a much better character than his adversary. See W. H. C. Frend, *Donatist Church* (1952), 213–224. *DONATISTS.

MAY LAWS, four statutes promulgated by the Prussian government against the RC Church in May 1873, aimed at converting the Church into a state institution. They decreed: (1) a special civil court for ecclesiastical appeals; (2) restrictions on episcopal disciplinary powers; (3) state requirements in clerical education and rights of intervention in all clerical appointments; and (4) provision for any citizen, by a simple declaration before a magistrate, to withdraw from the Church in which he was registered and which he had to support by a tax (supposedly to provide relief for Old Catholics). In the peace settlement of 1886–87 the state abandoned the first two statutes but achieved a compromise on

both parts of the third; the original May law on church withdrawals remained intact. *KULTURKAMPF.

MAYFLOWER COMPACT, the agreement made by the Pilgrim Fathers aboard the *Mayflower* off Provincetown, Mass., Nov. 11, 1620. The Compact was an application of the principles of Congregationalism to the civil sphere; the signers sought to form a body politic in the way they held the visible Church to be formed, namely, by the covenant of believers to associate together. *COVENANT THEOLOGY.

MEDICAL MISSIONS, a general term covering the Christian missionary enterprises that seek to bring to the sick in mission lands the benefits of modern medical science. Medical missionary work has received special and increasing emphasis since the latter half of the 19th century. Jesus and his Apostles not only preached the gospel but also healed the sick, and the attempt to mitigate the suffering of those to whom missionaries of later times brought the gospel has never been completely dissociated from the work of evangelizing a non-Christian people. Christian charity and the example of Jesus require a concern for the afflicted; moreover, missionaries have always recognized the importance of the part played by the practical and corporal works of mercy in arousing people to take an interest in the gospel message.

As a specialized form of missionary endeavor, with trained personnel using the best available modern techniques and equipment, medical missionary work began with the establishment of a Medical Mission Association in London, England, in 1878 for the purpose of providing assistance to persons desiring to become medical missionaries. Still in existence and closely associated with many Baptist missionary societies, this organization continues to help students who need special training for the work; it also makes other grants helpful in furthering this aspect of missionary effort. Other denominations have developed comparable programs; hospitals, clinics, and out-station dispensaries are built and operated in missionary areas as frequently as schools and churches. Among Roman Catholics special emphasis on medical work was slower in developing because most RC missionaries were priests or religious or both, to whom their Church granted permission to practice medicine only reluctantly and in exceptional cases. Since the beginning of the 20th cent. the pioneering effort of Dr. Agnes McLaren and Dr. Margaret Lamont—both converts to Catholicism and both experienced in the medical missionary field while still Protestants—much organized effort has gone into the training of personnel and the operation of medical centers in connection with RC missions.

Not all medical missionaries have been associated with particular denominations. Some, like the celebrated Albert Schweitzer, have gone into the work without aid or support of a particular denomination. The development of specialized and skilled assistance to the people of mission lands has gone forward in such other fields as education, social work, and agriculture. All these have as their immediate aim the alleviation of human want and misery, but ultimately they prove an effective and impressive witness to Christian truth and values. They also serve the spreading of the gospel by making it possible for Christian missions to keep some foothold in many places where, were it not for this undeniable contribution to the public good, they would be unable to survive against the emerging spirit of anticolonialism. See J. J. Considine, *Missionary's Role in Socio-Economic Betterment* (1960); M. F. Hoefsmit, *Approach to the Meaning of Medical Missions* (1956); H. Schumacher, "Re-Discovery of the Original Christian Mission Method," *Medical Missionary* II (1937), 98–112; A. Schweitzer, *Out of My Life and Thought* (1933).

MEDIUM, according to the *Spiritualist Manual,* "one whose organism is sensitive to the vibrations from the spirit world, and through whose instrumentality intelligences in that world are able to convey messages and produce the phenomena of Spiritualism." Spiritualists do not maintain that the medium must be the recipient of extraordinary supernatural gifts; their view is rather that the medium acts in accordance with given laws of nature. They also feel that only certain individuals are naturally endowed with the necessary psychic powers and even they must carefully cultivate their sensitivity to spiritual impulses. *SPIRITUALISTS.

MEETING (Friends), a term designating Quaker organizational structure. The monthly meeting is a local congregation that meets weekly for worship and monthly for a business session. The quarterly and yearly meetings are broader geographical and administrative units. The whole corporate unit of some Quaker groups is called a meeting, e.g., the Friends United Meeting and the Ohio Yearly Meeting of Friends Church. The use of the term comes from G. *Fox, who, rejecting the organized Churches and their "steeple houses," designated the gatherings and groupings of his followers as meetings. *RELIGIOUS SOCIETY OF FRIENDS.

MELANCHTHON, PHILIPP (1497–1560), German humanist and close associate of Martin *Luther in the work of the Reformation. Born Philipp Schwarzert, he was something of a child prodigy, receiving the Bachelor of Arts degree at 14 and the Master of Arts at 16; he became Luther's colleague at Wittenberg in August 1518, at the age of 21. He was, however, a member of the philosophical rather than the theological faculty, which he joined as an adjunct member the following year. This joint appointment is representative both of his intellectual interests and of his historical significance. He was a biblical humanist, in the circle of *Erasmus and of his own kinsman,

J. *Reuchlin. Many of M.'s university lectures and published writings dealt with texts of classical authors. He even contemplated the publication of a definitive edition of Aristotle, whom he wanted to rescue from the Thomists. In his work as a theologian, he applied many of the same interpretive methods to biblical texts, the meaning of which he believed to be accessible to sound philological investigation, untrammeled by scholastic apriorism. At the same time, he was more zealous than Luther in his cultivation of the Catholic tradition and in his desire to reconcile the Protestant-humanistic interpretation of the Bible with the teachings of the Fathers.

M.'s place in the history of the Reformation was determined by these factors. Thus his lectures on Romans became the basis for his composition, in 1521, of the first Protestant systematic theology, the *Loci communes*, which he revised several times, changing his theological position (Eng. tr. C. L. Hill, 1944). The controversy between Luther and Erasmus, his two heroes, was a source of personal anguish to him, and he tried unsuccessfully to mediate between them. In 1530 it fell to him to compose the *Augsburg Confession, and in the following year the *Apology of the Augsburg Confession. He was also the author of many textbooks that were used both in secondary schools and in theological instruction. His mediating spirit manifested itself also in his modifications of the Augsburg Confession (see VARIATA AUGUSTANA) to conciliate *Reformed theology, as well as in his repeated efforts to find a common ground with RC theology. After Luther's death in 1546, M. increasingly became a controversial figure, caught between the various parties and no longer able to depend on the support of his colleague-mentor. See *M.: Selected Writings* (ed. E. E. Flack and L. J. Satre, tr. C. L. Hill, 1962); C. L. Manschreck, *M.: The Quiet Reformer* (1958); V. Vajta, ed., *Luther and M. in the History and Theology of the Reformation* (1961). *ADIAPHORISTS; *CRYPTO-CALVINISM; *GNESIOLUTHERANISM; *MAJORISTIC CONTROVERSY; *PHILIPPISM.

MELIORAMENTUM, the *Cathari rite in which the simple believers rendered a kind of worship to the *Perfecti.

MELITONII, see HOMUNCIONITAE.

MELVILLE, ANDREW, (1545–1622), greatest of the Scottish Reformers after John *Knox. M. was born at Baldovy, near Montrose. Educated at St. Andrews, Paris, and Poitiers, he was successively appointed professor of humanity (Latin) in Geneva (1569), principal of Glasgow Univ. (1574), principal of St. Mary's College, St. Andrews (1580), and rector of that Univ. (1590). Through his influence the *General Assembly of the Church of Scotland in 1580 found "the pretended office" of bishop to be unlawful, and in 1581 it ordered M.'s *Book of Discipline, setting forth Presbyterian polity, to be registered in the acts of the *Kirk. M.'s opposition to *episcopacy and royal supremacy brought him exile and imprisonment. On his release from the Tower of London in 1611 he accepted the chair of divinity in France at the Univ. of Sedan, where he remained until his death. Fearless, dogmatic, and even vituperative in his attacks on episcopacy and the Romanists, Melville is one of the stubborn giants of the Scottish Reformation, one of its most humane and distinguished scholars. See *Diary of James Melville* (1842); T. McCrie, *Life of A. M.* (2v., 2d ed., 1824).

MEMBERSHIP IN THE CHURCH. The image of the Church as the body of Christ, into which individuals are incorporated as members, comes from the Pauline Epistles. Most Christians employ this image to describe the Church and recognize some connection between baptism and membership in the Church. Diverse views of church membership arise from differing interpretations of the relationship between the objective work of God and the subjective response of the individual, esp. the relation of grace and baptism to repentance and faith.

Only the classical positions of various traditions in these matters can be outlined, for views as widely divergent as those on the nature of the Church exist within most modern denominations.

Roman Catholic Teaching. The RC Church teaches that one is purged of sin, regenerated, and incorporated into the Church by baptism. The faith of the Church suffices for infants. Those stamped with the indelible character conferred by baptism may obstruct the operation of justifying grace but do not thereby lose the character of objectively belonging to Christ. The Eastern Orthodox Churches also hold that valid baptism is the means of receiving the new birth and illumination, the person being translated from the realm of darkness and evil into the realm of light and abiding divine life. Thus at baptism one is grafted into the Body of Christ, and immediately he receives confirmation and the Eucharist. Modern RC teaching on membership has been understood in close alliance with the necessity of belonging to the Church for salvation. Such membership has two aspects, or connotations: belonging to the mystical body of Christ by incorporation into Christ through grace and belonging to the Church as a visible society. Resisting the Reformation idea of a purely invisible Church, St. Robert Bellarmine (1542–1621) emphasized, almost exclusively, the second aspect. Membership for him consisted in profession of the same faith, participation in the same sacraments, and submission to the authority, esp. of the Pope. In the most important document on the subject prior to Vatican Council II, the encyclical *Mediator Dei* (1943), Pius XII set forth the total Catholic teaching, clearly indicating that through membership in the Church as visible society—teaching, sanctifying, and governing—the incorporation through grace into the mystical body is maintained and intensified. He also repeated the teaching that membership is not destroyed by sin, except the sins of heresy, schism, and apostasy. Those outside the visible body of the Catholic Church through no fault of their own are said "to have a certain relationship" with the mystical body by an unconscious desire and longing. In this way—a relationship to visible membership based on the presence or possibility of grace—the necessity of belonging to the Church was maintained alongside the doctrine of God's will to save all and the fact that most men are not members of the visible body of the RC Church.

The *Constitution on the Church* (14–16) of Vatican Council II expresses the doctrine of belonging to the Church in new language and perspective; it does not speak of members but uses the words "incorporated," "joined," and "related." Incorporation means that "those are fully incorporated into the society of the Church who, possessing the Spirit of Christ, accept her entire system and all the means of salvation given to her and through union with her visible structure are joined to Christ through the Supreme Pontiff and the bishops." Incorporation is accomplished "by the bonds of professed faith, of the sacraments, of ecclesiastical government and communion." Conjunction, or linking, are terms used with reference to "separated brethren"; the Church is *joined* to other Christians because of their union with Christ through baptism, other sacraments, and Christian elements in their lives. In this decree (see 8) and in *Ecumenism* (20–22), the link is acknowledged to be a real, if imperfect, *communion* not only of individuals but of other Churches or ecclesial communities, because of baptism, which is pointed toward full eucharistic and ecclesiastical communion. A *relationship* to the People of God is affirmed of Jews, Mohammedans, and other non-Christians and of all who in some way acknowledge the Creator. The conciliar statements have already had a positive impact on RC ecumenical activities.

Lutheran, Anglican, Reformed and Free Church Traditions. With the Reformation new interpretations of grace, faith, and the sacrament of baptism resulted in varied doctrines of church membership. Luther stressed baptism, considering it the regular means of regeneration and incorporation into the Church. He rejected the idea that baptism effects this new birth simply by its conferral (*ex opere operato*), however, and denied that an indelible character is stamped upon the baptized. Insisting that faith is indispensable for the efficacy of baptism, he did not accept the faith of the Church as sufficient but taught that infants themselves have faith given them by God. Baptism was a sign of God's promise, summoning a person to lifelong repentance and faith and reminding him of God's grace toward sinners. The Anglican Communion regards baptism as the ordinary means by which one is incorporated into the Church of Christ, and prayers at baptism ask that the children be regenerated and incorporated into the Church. Nevertheless, faith and obedience are considered necessary to become a member of the Church in the ultimate sense; the faith of sponsors serves until the child reaches maturity, when he must have a personal faith. Calvin, and the Reformed Churches following him, also thought of baptism as the point at which one became a member of the Church, but baptism was a sign of the covenant of grace by which God had chosen them members of the invisible body of Christ. Incorporation into the Church was not achieved by the rite itself, but by the immediate operation of the Holy Spirit. The child was received into the covenant community in anticipation of his future faith and repentance. While God usually works through the sacrament of baptism, he is not bound to this means, and the unbaptized may be members of the invisible Church without the sacrament. Baptists, Mennonites, Disciples of Christ, and various Brethren groups reject *infant baptism as meaningless and hold that conscious conversion and *believer's baptism initiate one into church membership. Some even interpret baptism as a public testimony that one has already been regenerated by God's grace through faith; i.e., they are already members of the invisible Church and now become members of the visible Church. Congregationalists, although practicing infant baptism, have historically held the *gathered Church idea

and do not regard one as fully a member of the Church until a personal profession of faith has been made. Methodists also put stress upon conversion as the point of the new birth, and, although practicing infant baptism, many of them regard it as primarily a dedication ceremony. The Friends, or Quakers, do not consider baptism either necessary or desirable, holding that membership in Christ's Church depends upon immediate communion with the Spirit of God, which is available to every man. See D. Moody, *Baptism: Foundation for Christian Unity* (1967); R. Dunkerley, ed., *Ministry and the Sacraments* (1937); Vorgrimler Vat II 1:168–185.

MENNO SIMONS (*c.*1496–1561), religious leader from whom the Mennonites are named. Born in Witmarsum, Friesland, the Netherlands, he was called Simons (Simonszoon) from his father's Christian name. Ordained a priest, he began to read the writings of Luther and other Reformers when Anabaptism reached the Low Countries. His evangelical views led him to doubt the sacramental nature of baptism and the Lord's Supper; this led to his conversion to Anabaptism in 1536. He was called by Obbe and Dirk *Philips to gather the Anabaptists through preaching, counseling, and writing (*Foundation Book,* 1539) in the regions of Amsterdam, Danzig, and Cologne. Because of his successful leadership the Anabaptists soon became known as Mennonites. He had numerous debates with both Münster Anabaptists and *Reformed opponents. He had to flee from Witmarsum, and lived in East Friesland and in Wüstenfelde near Oldesloe between Lübeck and Hamburg. He traveled and wrote extensively. His writings have been translated from the Dutch into German and English (*Complete Writings* [tr. L. Verduin, ed. J. C. Wenger, 1956]). See C. Krahn, "M. S. Research," *No Other Foundation* (1962).

MENNONITE BRETHREN CHURCH of North America, a Church established in Russia (1860) and transplanted to the U.S.

and Canada through migrations (1874–80). At the time of its origin stress was laid on evangelistic piety and church discipline. A confession of faith was adopted in 1902 as a summary of what is believed to be the biblical message. Personal conversion is held to be essential to church membership; *nonresistance is stressed; baptism by immersion only, *footwashing, and holy communion are observed. In 1960 this body was joined in a merger with the *Krimmer Mennonite Brethren. English is used for services by American congregations, German continues in use among Canadians. Headquarters are at Hillsboro, Kans., where Tabor College and the Brethren Publishing House are also operated. The Church has about 50,000 members in the U.S. and Canada, and there are churches also in India, the Congo, Brazil, and Paraguay. See MennEnc 3:595–602.

MENNONITE BRETHREN IN CHRIST CHURCH, a body organized in 1883, which in 1947 changed its name to *United Missionary Church, since it had no real Mennonite connections.

MENNONITE CENTRAL COMMITTEE, a joint relief and service agency of North American Mennonites, established in 1920 when the Mennonites of Russia were in need of help. This organization has increased the radius of its constituency and work to a global scale. Originally designed to help suffering fellow Mennonites, it now serves in many countries and aims to provide for any need as far as resources will permit. It aims to do all this work "In the Name of Christ." An example of the outreach is that a constituency of about 300,000 contributed some $8,640,000 between 1947 and 1952. See J. D. Unruh, *In the Name of Christ, 1920–1951* (1952).

MENNONITE CHURCH, the body that traces its origins in the U.S. to the original Mennonite settlement at Germantown, Pa.

(1683). It is the largest Mennonite body in the U.S. (more than 100,000 members). Most members are descendants of Mennonites from Switzerland and S Germany; many Amish Mennonite groups have also become affiliated with this Church over the years. The Church holds to the essentials of Anabaptist, or Mennonite, doctrine, subscribing to the *Dordrecht Confession of Faith and the *Mennonite Confession of 1963. While maintaining the necessity of nonconformity to worldly manners and conduct and of strict church discipline, this Church has been more progressive than some Mennonite bodies. Local congregations are autonomous, but are joined together in regional conferences; there is also a consultative, biennial general conference of the Church. The membership is most numerous in the Eastern part of the United States. Besides operating many charitable institutions and agencies, as well as a strong home and foreign mission program, the Church maintains Goshen College (Goshen, Ind.), Eastern Mennonite College (Harrisonburg, Va.), and the Mennonite Publishing House (Scottsdale, Pa.). See MennEnc 3:611–617.

MENNONITE CONFESSION OF 1963, a confession adopted by the General Conference of the Mennonite Church. Consisting of 20 articles, it is a modern adaptation of the *Dordrecht Confession of Faith. See J. Hardon, *Spirit and Origins of American Protestantism* (1968), 301–312.

MENNONITE WORLD CONFERENCE, international meeting of Mennonites held every 5 years. The first conference (1925), organized by Christian Neff of Weierhof, Germany, commemorated the 400th anniversary of the founding of Anabaptism; the second was devoted to relief efforts for Mennonite refugees from Russia. Since World War II the meetings, increasingly well attended, have been broadly based inspirational and educational sessions.

MENNONITES, a name derived from that of *Menno Simons and applied to all who follow the essential religious teachings of the 16th-cent. Anabaptism. Melchior *Hofmann brought Anabaptism from Strassburg to Emden in 1530; mysticism and humanism created an atmosphere favorable to this teaching in the Low Countries, and the Anabaptists became the first organized Reformation movement there. Some 2,500 were martyred as Charles V sought to exterminate them. While some refugees became leaders in the violent episode of the theocratic kingdom at Münster (see ANABAPTISTS), others were gathered under the leadership of Menno, who stressed the spiritual content of Anabaptist doctrine. After the establishment of the *Reformed Church in Holland, they came to enjoy a degree of freedom in the cities and made notable contributions to industry, social and philanthropic work, and the fine arts. The Mennonites of the Netherlands were the first to organize into conferences, to establish a theological seminary, to open the pulpit to women, and to promote research into their own history and teaching.

In the 16th cent., some Dutch refugees had migrated to W Prussia, then followed the Vistula River into Poland, the Ukraine, and Russia. The first migrations of c.18,000 Mennonites from Russia to the western states and provinces of the U.S. and Canada took place 1870–80, after the Russian introduction of military conscription. The Russian Revolution (1917) and World War II were followed by further migrations to Canada, Brazil (c.21,000), and Paraguay (c.4,000). The approximately 150,000 Mennonites in Russia who survived the persecution of the Stalin era have to a degree been able to reestablish themselves.

Although there is mention of Dutch Mennonites in New York as early as 1643, the first permanent Mennonite establishment was in Germantown, Pa., in 1683. The settlers were descendants of Anabaptists from Switzerland and the Palatinate. Migration from the same source to Pa. continued into the 19th cent., then spread to Ohio, Ind., Ill., Va., and the Province of Ontario. Mennonites and Amish Mennonites from the E Coast to the Mississippi River are mainly of this Swiss and Palatinate lineage. The Mennonites of the prairie states and provinces have spread farther west, and have moved increasingly to urban areas. The conservative Mennonites of Manitoba have sent colonies to Mexico and Paraguay. The adjustment of their environment among the larger Mennonite groups in the U.S. was speeded up during and after World War I, by a process of acculturation away from German customs and language. Their views about *nonconformity to the world and *nonresistance have been altered considerably. Voluntary services for peace and social relief on a global scale sponsored by the *Mennonite Central Committee have awakened and challenged the Mennonites, whose forefathers were driven into isolated areas, but who are themselves now in the midst of a world in need.

Mennonites are not at all united organizationally. The reasons for the main divisions are numerous. From the beginning Anabaptists stressed a truly visible Christian Church, bound together by personal belief and discipleship, not by ecclesiastical structure. Emphasis on separation from the world has also led to numerous divisions (see AMISH MENNONITES). Coming to North America from various places and at different periods, Mennonites had diverse ethnic and linguistic backgrounds. Geographical separation often prevented various groups from becoming acquainted and entering into fellowship with each other. Challenges arising out of their secular environment, and religious influences such as *revivalism have also caused divisions Some of these are disappearing under the influence of common Mennonite efforts to relieve spiritual, social, and economic hardships wherever they are found. The Mennonite World Conference aims to provide a platform on which all common and vital issues may be discussed. There are about 566,000 Mennonites in the world, with more than 350,000 in the United States.

Most Mennonite bodies subscribe to

the *Dordrecht Confession of Faith, but creeds have never been strongly emphasized. The central teaching is still the Anabaptist doctrine of the personally accepted inner experience of Christ. Thus *believer's baptism, usually by pouring, is observed. Personal holiness through living the law of Christ is given greater prominence than traditional Christian trinititarian or soteriological doctrines. In some Mennonite Churches, however, evangelical Protestant influences have been introduced. Church discipline is aimed at making the visible Church, i.e., each congregation, match the invisible Church as a communion of the saints; the *ban and *avoidance of the ungodly have this purpose, but are strictly observed only by conservative groups. The Lord's Supper, footwashing, and the kiss of charity are observed as *ordinances. Mennonites have held steadfastly to nonresistance. They refuse to give service of a directly military nature, and they take no oaths. Local congregations are ordinarily autonomous, though joined in conferences with other congregations within the various Churches. Bishops or elders, ministers, and deacons are the officials and are often nonsalaried. See C. H. Smith, *Story of the Mennonites* (1964). *ANABAPTISTS; *MENNONITE CONFESSION OF 1963.

MERCERSBURG THEOLOGY, a theological position developed at the German Reformed Seminary in Mercersburg, Pa., as a response to the prevailing *revivalism of the early 19th century. It stresses a return to the faith of the Reformers, particularly as enunciated in the *Heidelberg Catechism. John Williamson *Nevin and Philip *Schaff were the leading exponents of this approach, and they made the *Mercersburg Review* its principal organ. In 1844 Nevin published *The Anxious Bench*, the first appeal of the Mercersburg theologians against the revivalist influence. Schaff sounded a similar note in his inaugural address as member of the Mercersburg faculty in 1844; his *Principle of Protestantism* stressed the ancient catholic and Reformation tradition as the dynamic force in Protestantism and explained his theory of doctrinal development. In 1846 Nevin published *The Mystical Presence*, an effort to present the Calvinistic understanding of the Lord's Supper as distinct from the prevailing Zwinglian view of his contemporaries. In 1847 Nevin published studies of the Heidelberg Catechism and of the Church. From the writings and teaching of Schaff and Nevin arose a strong tradition of doctrinal loyalty, liturgical renewal, and ecumenism, which had a marked effect on the Churches of the Reformed and Presbyterian tradition, although Mercersburg theology was never accepted in its entirety and did not lead to the reunion of *Reformed Churches. Its stress on the faith of the Reformers and on the centrality of Christ and his Church preserved an important heritage of Protestantism. In accord with the historical approach of J. A. *Neander, but controlled by a conservative orthodoxy, Schaff and Nevin taught a development of doctrine and polity that has important ecumenical implications. Modification of organization, teaching, and modes of worship are held to be valuable so long as Christ remains the center of the Christian life. In him men are regenerated and united in the spiritual organism of the Church. Sacraments are not mere acts of faith, but seals of God's covenant and channels of grace. Old modes of worship may be set aside, as in the Reformation, but through organic growth in Christ rather than through a series of new births, since there is only one rebirth, when God entered into history in Christ. See J. H. Nichols, *Romanticism in American Theology* (1961); L. Binkley, *Mercersburg Theology* (1952); Smith-Jamison 1:267–271.

MERGER, an ecclesiastical union in which, unlike *federated Churches, the participating bodies lose their separate identities and form a new corporate entity. Two congregations of the same denomination sometimes combine, drawing up new articles of incorporation. Two or more bodies of the same denominational family may merge.

The Methodist Episcopal Church, the Methodist Episcopal Church, South, and the Methodist Protestant Church merged in 1939, to form the *Methodist Church in the United States. This in turn united with the Evangelical United Brethren in 1968 as the *United Methodist Church. In 1869–70, Old and New School Presbyterians formed a merger, and in 1958 the Presbyterian Church, U.S.A., combined with the *United Presbyterian Church. Three German Lutheran synods merged in 1918, forming the United Lutheran Church; a succession of mergers followed so that almost all American Lutherans belong to one of three major bodies, the *American Lutheran Church, the *Lutheran Church in America, the *Lutheran Church—Missouri Synod.

Mergers may also unite churches of different denominations; the United Church of Christ, for example, was constituted in 1957 out of the Evangelical and Reformed Church and the Congregational Christian Churches, each of which in turn had been made up of earlier mergers. One of the most interesting mergers outside the U.S. is the *Church of South India (1947), which combined Churches of Congregational, Presbyterian, and Anglican traditions. Numerous other mergers have been consummated, e.g., *United Church of Canada (1925); others are being contemplated. Most important of the present plans is the *Consultation on Church Union in the United States. See R. Rouse and S. C. Neill, eds., *History of the Ecumenical Movement, 1517–1948* (2d ed., 1967).

MERIT, in Catholic theology, broadly speaking, a good work worthy of reward; strictly speaking, that aspect of a good work by which it is deserving of reward. This is only one of the meanings of the term as it is used in English. The Catholic doctrine on merit, formulated at the Council of Trent (D 1545–49, 1582) against the Protestant rejection of good works as cause of men's justice, only means to express what the Gospel (e.g., Mt 5.1–12; 10.42) and St. Paul (e.g., 2 Tim 4.7–8) taught about the reward awaiting the followers of Christ. The juridical term "merit" is not biblical; "reward," its correlative term, is. The idea of merit was introduced into the Latin tradition by Tertullian (*De paenit.* 2, in which God is presented as debtor); its Greek counterpart, *axia*, is found, e.g., in Justin (*Apol.* 43, *axia tōn praxeōn*). St. Augustine developed the doctrine and explained that there can be no real merit of man before God without grace as its root; when rewarding man's merit, God crowns in man his own gifts (*Epist.* 194.5.19). Trent also explained that God in his love for man wants his own gifts to be man's merits; life eternal is both grace and reward, and so is growth in grace (D 1545, 1576, 1582). The Council likewise stated that before justification there can be no strict merit without grace (D 1532). The object of theological merit of good works in the righteous is growth in grace (and in glory) and life eternal, to be obtained after death in grace (D 1582). Through their meritorious works the just advance toward life eternal; they do so by growing in sanctifying grace. The very increase in grace resulting from these good works constitutes the real expression of their merit of heavenly glory.

The concept of merit, juridical as it is, expresses the personalist aspect of the growth and fulfillment of the life of grace. By their good works the righteous increase their justice and grace, just as evey agent grows in perfection by his proper activity. But the growth in the life of grace is not effected by the good works (as, e.g., knowledge is the fruit of study); it is only merited or striven for as a reward to be rendered by God. This is so because every increase in grace is given or effected by God alone, grace being essentially God's self-gift; it is rendered by God as a reward for the just man's good works. So is the fulfillment of grace in life eternal, viz., God's self-gift to the blessed in the glory of heaven. Thus the personalist aspect of the life of grace (constituted by the personal relationships between God-in-Christ and the just), of its growth and its fulfillment, of necessity entails a place for merit in the doctrine and theology of grace and glory. And because only works done in grace and under the influence of charity or love of God are meritorious in the proper sense, both growth in grace and life eternal, while truly being a reward for merit, are yet grace, or gratuitous gift, grace given for grace. Accordingly, the opposition between the RC doctrine of merit of good works and the Protestant denial of it may well be more verbal than real. It is not the just man's good works by themselves, but only as springing from grace, that have a causal influence in the life of grace. This influence regards, not the beginning of righteousness or of the life of grace, but only its growth and its fulfillment. Only grace, not the nature of man by himself, is the source of merit. The just man's merit springs from Christ's grace and merit, not from man's own power, and so it does not detract from Christ's merit. It rather allows Christ's merit to bear fruit in his members. Nor does the causality of meritorious works impair the relationships between God-in-Christ and the just man. God-in-Christ alone can make the divine self-gift in answer to man's striving for it through works of grace. This self-gift remains grace while being reward for merit. Protestant doctrine too requires good works as the necessary sign and fruit of man's justification. If this can be understood to mean a development of the life of righteousness, then this view approaches the RC doctrine on the merit of the growth and fulfillment of grace. The difference between the two is mainly one of conceptual formulation commanded by a different approach and problematic, e.g., following from different views on sin and justification.

Besides merit in the strict sense, or condign merit, RC theology knows a merit of congruity, in which the claim to a reward is not one of justice but of fittingness. This is insinuated in Trent (D 1532). It regards a gift of grace that has no direct connection with the good act that merits congruously but only a mediate connection, as, e.g., sufficient grace for new good acts needed by growth in grace. The idea of merit of congruity is based on the fittingness that God should bestow certain unpromised re-

wards on those whom he has made his friends by grace. See J. Rivière, DTC 10:574–785; C. S. Sullivan, NCE 9:683–686; *idem, Formulation of the Tridentine Doctrine on Merit* (1959); P. De Letter, *De ratione meriti secundum s. Thomam* (1939); *idem,* "Merit and Prayer in the Life of Grace," *Thomist* 19 (1956), 446–480.

MESSAGE OF THE BRETHREN MINISTRY, a statement of teaching by the ministry of *Brethren Churches. The instrument was adopted by majority vote of attending ministers in annual session of the National Brethren Ministerial Association in 1921. The Brethren Church, being of Protestant free-church tradition, pietistic and non-theological in origin, historically rejected creedal statements. The *Message,* which is regarded as noncreedal, but as containing "essential and constituent elements" for emphasis in preaching and teaching the word, listed nine articles as basic content: (1) pre-existence, deity, and incarnation by virgin birth of Jesus Christ, the Son of God; (2) man's Fall, spiritual death, and utter sinfulness requiring a new birth; (3) vicarious atonement of the Blood of Christ; (4) bodily resurrection and glorification of Jesus Christ at the right hand of God; (5) justification by faith in Christ, obedience to God's will, works of righteousness, resurrection of the dead, judgment of the world and life everlasting; (6) personality and deity of the Holy Spirit; (7) personal and visible return of Jesus Christ as king; (8) nonconformity to the world, esp. by abstention from carnal strife and oaths; and (9) the *ordinances of *believer's baptism by *trine immersion; confirmation; the Lord's Supper; communion of bread and wine; *footwashing; and anointing of the sick with oil.

MESSENGER, a title used by Baptists for a delegate to their *conventions.

MESSIANISM, a term that, besides its proper sense as the biblical hope in the

Messiah, is also used to describe: (1) belief that a person is a reincarnation of Jesus or a new divine emissary to the world; *Éon de l'Étoile, Anna *Lee of the Shakers, and Father Divine are examples of such a claim; (2) any urgent sense of divine mission to save or change the world, esp. through a new revelation or message. In both meanings messianism is associated with *apocalypticism and *millenarianism.

METHODISM, a name that now identifies the doctrines, polity, and discipline of several Protestant denominations tracing their origins to the 18th-cent. revival in England under John and Charles *Wesley, and their friend George *Whitefield. While students at Oxford, these men experienced (c.1725) "awakenings" and, becoming intensely serious, decided to prepare for orders in the Church of England. Three or four other students united with them in their zeal for "inward religion, the religion of the heart," and these members of the *Holy Club, John Wesley wrote, "by the exact regularity of their lives, as well as studies, occasioned a young gentleman of Christ Church to say, 'Here is a new sect of Methodists sprung up,' alluding to some ancient physicians who were so called. The name was new and quaint, so it took immediately and the Methodists were known all over the university."

In 1735 the Wesleys and two of their friends accepted invitations from Gen. James Oglethorpe to cross the Atlantic to the Ga. Colony. On the voyage, and during their ministry in Ga., these "Methodists" became acquainted with some Moravian settlers and were so favorably impressed by them as to accept some of their pietist peculiarities, particularly the felt assurance of justifying faith as the *sine qua non* of the Christian life (see PIETISM). Almost as appealing were the accounts of instantaneous conversions so frequently reported among the Moravians. The effect of these associations on the Oxford missionaries was to intensify their search for "inward holiness" by the expectation of some kind of climac-

tic experience in the achieving of it. Charles Wesley returned to England in Dec. 1736; John, in Feb. 1738. In the following weeks, when asked to preach in Anglican pulpits, John so stressed faith and *Christian perfection in his sermons that several churches banned him. On May 24, 1738, he records the appropriateness of the anthem at St. Pauls', "Out of the depths have I cried unto Thee, O Lord," and in this mood, at a little religious *society in Aldersgate Street, London, that same evening he felt his "heart strangely warmed" and was convinced that he "did trust Christ, Christ alone for salvation." Significantly, he added, "I began to pray with all my might for those who had in a more especial manner despitefully used me and persecuted me." To John Wesley this undoubtedly was the inner witness or impression that he had been urged by his Moravian mentors to seek. Charles Wesley and others reported similar emotional experiences, and this type of religious conversion became a primary characteristic of the Methodist revival.

By 1739 revival excitement was high. Whitefield's emotion-charged sermons were swaying great crowds who came to see the novelty of an Anglican priest preaching in the fields. By 1744 most of the unique features of early Methodist life and organization had been adopted. Required membership in carefully controlled societies harnessed the enthusiasm of the converts. The only requirement for admission was a desire to seek inner holiness and to live a life of prayer, discipline, and fellowship in the Spirit. Large societies were divided into *classes of 10 or 12 members under an appointed class leader who was in charge of their weekly meetings for prayer, examination, and exhortation. *Field preaching, *itinerancy, the annual *conferences, "rooms" and chapels for worship and preachings, printed tracts and hymns, collections and funds—these and many other activities gave strength and order to the movement and, at the same time, encouraged among the Methodists a consciousness of independence. Legal status for the conferences was secured in 1784 by a Deed of Declaration that provided for the continuation of the work after Wesley's death.

Meanwhile, Methodism had spread to Ireland, Scotland, and Wales. In the 1760s lay preachers began to form societies in Md. and N.Y.; Va., N.J., and Philadelphia were at once included in the itinerants' circuits. In answer to their call to Wesley for help, the English Conference sent two local preachers in 1769 and additional pairs almost annually, until the American Revolution made English control impossible. F. *Asbury, who was sent by Wesley in 1771, remained after all the others returned, to become the greatest of the early leaders in America.

In spite of the Wesley brothers' devotion to the traditions and authority of the C of E, the Methodists drifted inevitably toward separation from their Anglican mother Church. A semblance of ecclesiastical dependence lasted as long as the Wesleys (and Asbury) could prevent the societies from having the sacraments and an ordained ministry, but when the situation demanded both of these for America as a practical necessity, John Wesley boldly took what he thought were the proper steps to supply them. On Sept. 1, 1784, believing that the early Church had regarded presbyters and bishops as the same order, he decided to perform an episcopal act himself, and he ordained two of his lay helpers, Richard Whatcoat and Thomas Vasey, as deacons and (on the following day) as elders. At the same time he ordained his fellow presbyter, Dr. Thomas *Coke, as "superintendent" over "the brethren in America." These men were joined by about 60 lay preachers at the *Christmas Conference in 1784. There the *Methodist Episcopal Church was organized; Asbury was ordained; he and Coke were elected "superintendents" (the title was changed to bishop in 1787); and a Ritual, a Sunday Service and Articles of Religion, all abridged by Wesley from the BCP and the *Thirty-Nine Articles, were adopted. No such formal acts of separation were made for English Method-

ists, although Wesley performed more than 20 ordinations for them in Great Britain before he died.

Methodists by tradition enjoy wide freedom in the interpretation of doctrines; at the same time they stress the central Protestant beliefs. This derives from John Wesley's strong dislike of theological controversy and reflects the pietistic *revivalism in which his followers were so prominent. By their larger interests in the Christian life, religious experience, and social issues, they appear to be less concerned with theology. But there has never been among them a theological vacuum. In general they try to maintain a mediating position by the avoidance of extremes. "As to all opinions which do not strike at the root of Christianity," said Wesley, "we think and let think." For doctrinal standards Methodists accept as guides the *Standard Sermons* of John Wesley, his *Notes on the New Testament*, and his *Twenty-Five Articles of Religion*. Their theology is fairly described as *Arminian because they stress an atonement for sin offered for all mankind, and freedom of the human will. A Calvinist minority in the following of Whitefield has been concentrated chiefly in Wales (see CALVINISTIC METHODISTS). The Apostles' Creed is commonly used in worship, but Methodists frequently prefer more modern confessions of faith. Their Social Creed, adopted by the General Conference of the Methodist Episcopal Church in 1908, has since been a model of its kind for many Churches. Heresy trials are almost unknown among Methodists, but several schisms have come from angry disputes over church polity, "worldliness," and social problems, such as slavery and race relations. Abstinence from alcoholic drink, associated with Methodism is based in part on the ideal of a Christian perfection, in part on a tradition of social concern dating from Wesley's own ministry to the victims of the Industrial Revolution. The *Discipline of the Methodist Church was modified in regard to total abstinence in 1968.

Methodist church government, originally episcopal and autocratically controlled by John Wesley through his preachers, has become fully representative through its many conferences. The pastoral charge (which as a *circuit may have more than one church) has its Quarterly Conference, and each church has its Official Board, both composed of laymen. The Annual, District, Jurisdictional, and General Conferences (all regional) have equal lay and ministerial representation. Bishops are the executive and general administrators of the Church's activities in the Annual Conferences assigned to them. They make the pastoral appointments, usually in consultation with the church members, and are elected for life by the Jurisdictional Conferences. Methodists recognize only the orders of deacon and elder; bishops are not a third order, but are elders set apart for administrative work, superintendents over the Church.

The language of the BCP is evident in the sacraments and in the Ritual for ordination, weddings, and funerals. Sunday worship varies, and freedom in forms of prayer is encouraged, although the Methodist Hymnal and Book of Worship are provided. Two sacraments, baptism and the Lord's Supper, are observed; baptism is administered to both infants and adults, usually by sprinkling, but by another form if desired. Membership is on confession of faith or by letter of transfer from other Churches.

There are more than 20 separate Methodist bodies in the United States. Only a few of these, like the Free Methodists and the Fundamental Methodists, claim theological origins by insisting upon a return to Wesleyan standards in doctrine. A union in 1939 brought together the Methodist Protestant Church (which in 1830 opposed episcopacy and demanded lay representation), the Methodist Episcopal Church, South (which in 1845 had separated over slavery and polity), and the Methodist Episcopal Church into the *Methodist Church. In 1968 a union with the Evangelical United Brethren (originally German-Speaking "Methodists") created the *United Methodist Church, numbering more than 11 million members. Other large Methodist denominations are the African Methodist Episcopal (1816), the African Methodist Episcopal, Zion (1820), and the Christian Methodist Episcopal (1870) Churches, all Negro, and together numbering about 2½ million members. The *World Methodist Council, which meets at 5-year intervals, is composed of delegates from 42 countries, representing about 45 million Methodists. The Council meets for fellowship; it is without power to make laws for its constituent members. See N. B. Harmon, *Understanding the Methodist Church* (1955); W. W. Sweet, *Methodists: A Collection of Source Materials* (1946); R. Currie, *Methodism Divided* (1968).

METHODIST CHURCH (Canada), a denomination formed in Canada in 1883 through a series of mergers with other Methodist bodies. Methodist preaching in Canada was started by two Methodist laymen, a Mr. Tuffey of the 44th British Regiment, in 1780, and a Maj. George Teal, in 1786. Preachers from the Methodist Episcopal Church in the U.S. also preached in Canada but returned home during the War of 1812. Canadian Methodists then appealed for preachers to the Wesleyan Methodists in England, who in 1814 sent John Strong and Samuel Leigh. Later the Methodist Episcopal Church in the U.S. again became active in Canada, but in 1833 merged with the Wesleyan Methodists to form the Wesleyan Methodist Church in British North America. A small group who refused to join the merger continued the Methodist Episcopal Church in Canada. By then, other Methodist bodies from England had also become active in Canada, and in 1874 the Methodist Church of Canada was formed by a merger of the Wesleyan Methodist Church in British North America, the Methodist New Connexion, and the Conference of Eastern British America. This Church united 9 years later with the Methodist Episcopal Church in Canada, the Primitive Methodists, and the Bible Christians to form the Methodist Church. In 1925 the Church joined the Presbyterian and Congregational Churches to form the United Church of Canada. See J. F. Hurst, *History of Methodism* (1904), 7:33–89; J. W. Grant, *Canadian Experience of Church Union* (1967).

METHODIST CHURCH (England), a body organized in 1933 with the merger of the Wesleyan Methodist, Primitive Methodist, and United Methodist Churches; 1968 membership was more than 690,000. British Methodists did not become a separate denomination until after the death of John *Wesley. By the Plan of Pacification prepared in 1795 the *Conference permitted *societies to meet during the hours of service of the C of E, to have ministers authorized by the Conference, and to administer the sacraments in Methodist chapels. For years, however, many Wesleyan Methodists considered themselves to be Anglicans; and they still returned to the C of E to receive the sacraments. Final steps for separation were not taken until 1897. The various Methodist bodies prospered in spite of a series of divisive splits. At the beginning of the 20th cent. a change of temper, fostered in part by the Ecumenical Methodist Conferences, directed the Churches toward union. By a series of mergers beginning in 1907 the various bodies united, until by 1933 all but one or two had become part of the one Methodist Church. The doctrinal standards of the Church include the Scriptures as set forth in the historic creeds, Wesley's *Notes on the New Testament* and *Standard Sermons*. In polity, the Church is nonepiscopal and is organized in one Annual Conference. The Church maintains the Methodist traditions in stressing total abstinence, manifesting social concern, opposing war, and promoting ecumenism. With the Methodist Church in the U.S., it forms the core of the *World Methodist Council. On July 8, 1969, a plan for reunion with the C of E, 14 years in preparation, was defeated; the Methodist Church approved it, but because of the issue of the *historic episcopate, the plan failed to win a sufficient majority in the Anglican *Convocations. See R. Currie, *Methodism Divided* (1968).

METHODIST CHURCH (U.S.), the largest Methodist body in the world, organized in 1939 with the merger of the Methodist Episcopal Church, the Methodist Episcopal Church, South, and the Methodist Protestant Church; 1968 membership was 10,300,-000. In the early days of Methodism, followers of John *Wesley, both in England and in the American colonies, considered themselves still to belong to the Church of England. Following the American Revolution, Wesley himself helped to establish American Methodists as a separate denomination. He ordained T. *Coke as superintendent (bishop) of the American work and sent him to the U.S. with two other ministers, whom he had also ordained, with instructions to ordain F. *Asbury also as a superintendent. At the *Christmas Conference (1784) in Baltimore, Md., preachers were elected and ordained, and the Methodist Episcopal Church in America was organized. In the 19th cent., splits occurred among American Methodists over slavery, *episcopacy, and the doctrine of *entire sanctification. The Methodist Church represented a strong reunification; many Methodist bodies, however, continue in separate existence, and some have been born or strengthened in the 20th century. The chief subordinate doctrinal standards of the Methodist Church are the *Twenty-Five Articles of Religion; Wesley's *Notes on the New Testament* and *Standard Sermons* are regarded as guides rather than as actual standards. The Church is an episcopal body but regards *episcopacy as an office, not a distinct order, and makes no claim to *apostolic succession. The organization of church government is through a complex system of *conferences. The Methodist Church has growing missionary enterprises at home and abroad and is a principal member of the *World Methodist Council. American Methodist Churches were powerful forces in the passage of the 18th Amendment to the U.S. Constitution, and continue to favor total abstinence. The Church has strongly favored racial integration, open housing, and equal opportunity. The 1908 Social Creed of the Methodist Church is considered a classic expression for social justice. In the ecumenical movement, American Methodists have played a key role, with G. Bromley *Oxnam and J. R. *Mott prominent in the formation of both the National and World Council of Churches. In recent years the Methodist Church has been a part of the *Consultation on Church Union. The 1968 merger of the Methodist Church with the Evangelical United Brethren Church created the *United Methodist Church.

METHODIST CONNEXION, see CONNEXION.

METHODIST EPISCOPAL CHURCH, the original main body of Methodists in the U.S., formed in 1784. The Church itself was the outgrowth of several Methodist *societies that sprang up in N.Y., Pa., and Md. in the 1760s. In N.Y., Philip *Embury organized a Methodist society in 1766 that later became Wesley Methodist Church. About the same time, or somewhat earlier, Robert Strawbridge began preaching and forming Methodist societies in Frederick Co., Maryland. In 1767 Thomas *Webb, a retired captain of the British Army and a Methodist, first assisted Embury in New York and then traveled to Philadelphia, where he formed a society that later became St. George's Methodist Church. John *Wesley began sending preachers to these societies, among them F. *Asbury. They united the societies under Wesley, and in 1773 the first conference of the American Methodist preachers was held at St. George's. All the Methodist societies of this time, however, were still a part of the C of E, to whom the Methodists turned to receive the sacraments, regarding their Methodism only as a way of fellowship and revivalism. During the Revolution many of the Anglican rec-

tors returned to England, leaving the Methodists without access to the sacraments; many Methodist preachers also returned to England. Asbury, however, remained to carry on the Methodist work with the native Methodist preachers. After the war Asbury wrote to Wesley urging the need for the sacraments in the Methodist societies, and Wesley responded by ordaining T. *Coke, an Anglican clergyman, as a superintendent (bishop) of the American work and two other English preachers, Richard Whatcoat and Thomas Vasey, as ministers. He sent them to America to ordain Asbury also as a superintendent (bishop), with power to ordain those men chosen by the Conference, thus giving them authority to administer the sacraments. Coke and Asbury called the American preachers to the *Christmas Conference at Baltimore in Dec. 1784; there the Methodist Episcopal Church in America was organized and Asbury was ordained as a superintendent. Many critics have challenged Wesley's right to the authority he assumed in ordaining Coke, but the Methodists themselves see in the phenomenal growth of their Church divine approval of Wesley's action. The matter has been endlessly debated. The Church grew rapidly, but also suffered several splits, the most serious being the formation of the Methodist Protestant Church in 1828 and the bisection of the Church in 1844 into the Methodist Episcopal Church and the Methodist Episcopal Church, South. The Church continued to grow with the nation, however, establishing schools, colleges, hospitals, homes, and an extensive foreign and home missionary program. Many attempts were made to reunite the three main American Methodisms, but they were not successful until 1939 when the *Methodist Church was organized. See HistAmMeth 1:75–234; 3:406–478; F. E. Maser, *Dramatic Story of Early American Methodism* (1965). *METHODISM.

METHODIST EPISCOPAL CHURCH, SOUTH, a body formed in 1844 when the Methodist Episcopal Church agreed at its

*General Conference to a bisection of the Church into the Methodist Episcopal Church and the Methodist Episcopal Church, South. The immediate cause of the division, which at the outset was friendly, was the question of slaveholding. The Southern church was formally organized at Louisville, Ky., in 1845. The separation of 1844 later became a serious cleavage when the northern Church tried to repudiate its agreement by judicial action. The Civil War caused a widening of the breach, and the Churches later became rivals both at home and on the mission field. After many unsuccessful attempts, the two Churches and the Methodist Protestant Church finally reunited in 1939 to form the *Methodist Church. See HistAmMeth 2:11–315; 3:406–478.

METHODIST HYMNAL, an official book of the Methodist Church. John and Charles *Wesley published more than 50 different books and tracts of hymns culminating in *A Collection of Hymns for . . . Methodists* (1780). This was the basis for the *Methodist Hymn Book* of 1933 of the British Methodist Church, in which the Methodist Churches in England had united; earlier revisions had been made in 1875 and 1904. The American Methodists used different books of hymns, mostly by the Wesleys, until the organization of the Methodist Episcopal Church (1784). In time, various hymn books were approved, but in 1836 the *General Conference approved a hymn book for Sunday service excluding all others. This was revised in 1849 and in 1878, when it was first called the *Methodist Hymnal*. In 1905 the three branches into which the Methodist Church had split in 1830 and 1844 united in publishing a common hymnal. In 1935 they revised this hymnal, which remained official when they merged into the Methodist Church in 1939. In 1966 another revision was published. Other branches of Methodism have their own hymnals.

The hymnal reveals an evolution in the liturgical and doctrinal emphases of Methodism. From a book of printed hymns it became a hymnal with musical notes, chants, orders of worship, a Psalter, and a large section on the Christian Year. While the first hymn books stressed evangelism and an individual, emotional experience, the later hymnals stressed also corporate worship, creative living, the Church, the social implications of the gospel, and the collective responsibilities of the Christian Church. See HistAmMeth 1:285–286, 2:632–636; B. F. Crawford, *Theological Trends in Methodist Hymnody* (1939).

METHODIST NEW CONNEXION, English Methodist Church, similar in doctrine to the Wesleyan Methodists, organized at Leeds, England, Aug. 9, 1797. The founders were Alexander *Kilham, who had been expelled by the Wesleyan Methodists in 1796, and several other Methodist preachers and laymen who wanted a Church wholly separated from the Church of England. In 1907 they joined with the Bible Christians denomination and the United Methodist Free Churches to form the United Methodist Church. This in turn joined with the Wesleyan Methodist and the Primitive Methodist Churches in 1932 to form the British Methodist Church. See W. J. Townsend et al., eds., *New History of Methodism* (2v., 1909), 1:488–502; W. S. F. Pickering, ed., *Anglican-Methodist Relations* (1961).

METHODIST PROTESTANT CHURCH, a denomination begun in 1828 as the Associated Methodist Churches by persons withdrawing or expelled from the Methodist Episcopal Church. They were motivated by opposition to episcopacy and a desire for lay representation in the *conference. The Church was organized and renamed in 1830, when it had about 5,000 members. In 1939 the merger of its 200,000 members with those of the Methodist Episcopal Church and the Methodist Episcopal Church, South, created the Methodist Church. See HistAmMeth 1:636–638; 2:391–420; 3:406–478.

MICHAELISTS, a small but influential group of Franciscans who supported the minister general of their order, Michael of Cesena (*c.*1270–1342) after he was deposed and excommunicated by John XXII in the course of the *Poverty Controversy. By the bull *Cum inter nonnullos* (1323), the Pope anathematized the opinion that Christ and his Apostles owned no property either personally or in common. The majority of Franciscans reluctantly accepted this pronouncement, but the minister general, together with such prominent friars as William of Ockham, Peter John Olivi, and Bonagratia of Bergamo, refused to assent. In 1328 they fled from Avignon. Later they accepted the protection of Louis of Bavaria and lent him their support in his struggle against the Pope. Michael died in 1342 and Louis in 1347, and the Michaelists ceased to exist. See M. Bihl, "Formulae et Documenta e Concellaria Fr. Michaelis de Cesena," *Archivum Franciscanum Historicum* 32 (1930), 106–171; D. L. Douie, *Nature and the Effects of the Heresy of the Fraticelli* (1932), 153–201; M. D. Lambert, *Franciscan Poverty: The Doctrine of the Absolute Poverty of Christ and the Apostles in the Franciscan Order, 1210–1323* (1960), 208–246.

MICHAELIUS, JONAS (1584–?), the first clergyman of the Reformed Dutch Church in North America. He was a graduate of the Univ. of Leiden and served as a pastor and as a chaplain of the West India Company before coming to New Amsterdam (now New York City) in 1628. The Dutch had practiced their religion there for several years without formal organization. M., in April 1628, summoned them to a convocation and, with about 50 Walloon and Dutch communicants, secured the organization of the Reformed Dutch Church, which worshiped in the Collegiate Church now famous in New York City. He returned to The Netherlands in 1632 and remained there. The *Reformed Church in America traces its American origins to his efforts. See E. Eekhof, *J. M.* (1926).

MICHAELSRITTER (Ger., Knights of Michael), an Austrian religious group founded in 1811 in Carinthia by Agnes Wirsinger, who believed that the Archangel Michael would come to establish a millennium after the Napoleonic wars. The group was briefly associated with the *Manharter, but disappeared with the collapse of Napoleon's empire.

MIGETIUS (fl. 8th. cent.), teacher of unorthodox trinitarian doctrine at Seville about 780; his followers were called Migetians. M. declared a gradual revelation of the Trinity in the persons of David (the Father), Jesus (the Son), and Paul (the Holy Spirit). Synods at Seville (782 and 785) condemned him. The replies of Elipandus, Bp. of Toledo, to M. gave rise to Spanish *adoptionism. See Bihlmeyer-Tüchle 2:81–82.

MILLENARIANISM (Millennialism), a belief that Christ will establish a kingdom on earth for a 1,000-year period (Lat. *mille*, thousand; *annus*, year). Based upon a single passage, Rev. 20.1–10, this concept has given rise to varied speculation and hopes since the 1st century. According to the passage, Satan was to be bound for 1,000 years, and those who had not worshiped the beast or his image "came to life again, and reigned with Christ a thousand years." Since this is an apocalyptic book and filled with imagery, there is need for caution about accepting literally the idea of a 1,000-year reign. Taken in context, the passage probably refers to the time between Christ's resurrection and the end of the world, when Christ raises the dead, judges the world, and creates a new heaven and a new earth. Some early church Fathers (e.g., Justin and Irenaeus) shared the literal belief of a glorious millennial reign of Christ, but it was the *Montanists who not only taught this doctrine but predicted Christ's return at a particular date to establish his kingdom at Pepuza in Phrygia. Opposition of Alexandrian theologians, such as Origen, ended such literal views in the East, but they were preserved longer in the West. Augustine (*City of God*, 20.7–9) helped settle the question by identifying the Church with the kingdom of God on earth. In the Middle Ages some briefly revived millennial hopes, and during and after the Reformation similar literal expectations were aroused. The *Anabaptists at Münster (*c.*1534) expected the return of Christ to establish his kingdom there, and German *Pietism in the 17th and 18th cents. supported such ideas, as did the *Fifth Monarchy Men in 17th-cent. England. The *Plymouth Brethren in England (*c.*1830) were millenarian and developed the basic ideas of *dispensationalism that were systematized and popularized by the *Scofield Reference Bible. Another independent millennial movement began in the U.S. when William *Miller worked out an interpretation of Daniel and Revelation, setting a date for Christ's return in 1843 or 1844. Out of this movement developed the *Seventh-day Adventists. The *Jehovah's Witnesses also hold millennial views but believe that the millennium has already begun. There are many millenarians in the United States. Some espouse premillenarianism, expecting a sudden return of Christ when certain conditions have been fulfilled. Postmillenarianism is the view that Christ's return, after the gospel has gradually permeated the world and after a Christian society has been established, will last 1,000 years, during which the Jews will be converted. Finally there will be an apostasy, a terrible conflict, and Christ will intervene to destroy the world after having raised and judged the dead. There are also amillenarianists, who do not take the idea of a millennium literally. See N. B. Baker, *What Is the World Coming To?* (1965).

MILLENARY PETITION, an appeal, so named because it claimed the support of 1,000 ministers, made by Puritans in April 1603 to James I against ritual and ceremony. The petition led to the *Hampton Court Conference.

MILLENNIAL DAWNISTS, an early name of the Jehovah's Witnesses. *Studies in the Scriptures* (6v., 1886–1904), a work by the founder, Charles Taze Russell, was subtitled *Millennial Dawn*.

MILLENNIUM, a period of 1,000 years. In Rev 20.4–6, a number of martyrs rise with Christ and reign with him 1,000 years until the second resurrection of all the faithful. In the original sense, if taken literally, the author may have looked to an indefinite peaceful reign of Christ after the end of a fierce persecution. If taken symbolically, it could mean that the first resurrection is Christian baptism, or Christ's victory through his death and resurrection. The 1,000 years would be the period of the history of the Church until the second coming, or last judgment. The idea of a millennium is associated with Jewish hopes for the messianic era. Beginning with a number of the Fathers of the Church, various Christian groups have interpreted Revelation as predicting a literal 1,000-year terrestrial reign of Christ. See R. Kuehner and J. P. Dolan, NCE 9:854. *ADVENTISM; *JEHOVAH'S WITNESSES, *MILLENARIANISM.

MILLER, WILLIAM (1782–1849), Baptist lay preacher, founder of modern *Adventism. The Seventh-day Adventists and other Adventist bodies ultimately trace their histories to his preaching and prophecies. M. received a sketchy education, took up farming in upstate New York, and served as a captain in the War of 1812. He became a religious skeptic but underwent a conversion in 1816 and began an intensive study of the Bible, esp. Daniel and Revelation, which led him in 1818 to the conclusion "that in about 25 years from that time all the affairs of our present state would be wound up." In 1831 he began to preach that Christ's second coming would occur in 1843 and was received in many Protestant pulpits. A Boston preacher, Joshua V. Himes (1805–95), became his patron and companion on lecture tours of New England, N.J., and New York. More than 700 Protestant ministers joined the movement and carried its message to western states; as many as 15,000 people attended Adventist rallies to hear M. expound his prophecies. He was licensed as a lay preacher in the Baptist Church, but his Adventist views began to trouble other clergymen, and he urged his followers to leave their Churches for the Adventist movement. When the end of the world did not come in 1843, Miller recalculated and set March 21, 1844, as the new date; he later revised it to Oct. 22, 1844. When that date also passed without incident, his followers became disillusioned. Between 50,000 and 100,000 Americans had expected the end of the world in 1844. Many Millerites returned to their former Churches or abandoned religion; a remnant remained convinced that the end was near. These small groups of Adventists organized the Adventist Churches, which survive and number more than 1,500,000 adherents around the world. M. never gave up belief in Christ's second coming, but ceased to try to fix its date. He took no active part in the new Adventist Churches and died in obscurity. See F. Nichol, *Midnight Cry* (1945).

MILLS, SAMUEL JOHN (1738–1818), one of the founders of the *American Board of Commissioners for Foreign Missions (ABCFM). M., the son of a Congregationalist minister, while at Williams College, experienced a call to the mission during a famous "haystack meeting" in 1807. This experience led to the organization in 1810 of the ABCFM. As a licensed preacher, M. made evangelizing tours of the Mississippi Valley in 1812 and 1815. After ordination (1815) he helped found the *American Bible Society (1816). He also worked for the American Colonization Society, journeying to Africa to help purchase land that eventually became the Republic of Liberia. See P. J. Staudenraus, *African Colonization Movement* (1963).

MILTITZ, KARL VON (1490–1529), German curial diplomat. After study at Mainz, Trier, and Cologne, M. obtained through his uncle the post of papal notary and titular chamberlain c.1514. In 1518 he carried the papal Golden Rose to Frederick the Wise of Saxony, an honor intended at least in part to persuade Frederick to consent to Martin Luther's extradition to Rome for trial. Unsuccessful in this, M. attempted to mediate with Luther at Altenberg; he proposed that Luther undergo trial before the abp. of Trier; but both the Reformer and his supporters mistrusted the offer. Two further conferences with Luther (Liebenwenda, Oct. 1519; Lichtenberg, Oct. 1520) were likewise fruitless. M. held benefices at Mainz and Meissen from 1523 to 1529, dying before his 40th year by accidental drowning. See F. Lau, RGG 4:954; J. P. Dolan, NCE 9:858.

MINISTER, a person performing spiritual offices in the Church. In both RC and Anglican usage, one who administers a sacrament is called a minister; the term is also a general designation for anyone having a function at liturgical ceremonies, e.g., as celebrant, deacon, subdeacon, or acolyte. In *Reformed Churches the term generally means an ordained clergyman, particularly a pastor. The usage follows John Calvin's idea of the minister as one who preaches the word of God, administers the sacraments, and shares in governing the Church. During the Reformation, in the C of E the term minister was preferred to that of priest to designate an ordained clergyman, but many today reverse the preference. The *free Churches use "minister." Luther used both minister and pastor, but modern Lutherans usually prefer the latter. In the U.S., minister is the most widely used designation for an ordained clergyman. Some denominations have lay preachers, but usually only ordained ministers administer baptism and the Lord's Supper. Many American Protestants currently stress the total mission of the Church in which all members share. Thus all members of the Church are ministers, but some are ordained to specialized Christian vocations.

See H. R. Niebuhr et al., *Purpose of the Church and Its Ministry* (1956). *MINISTRY.

MINISTRY, any apostolic or evangelical activity, a body of clergy, or the total mission of the Church; most properly, the threefold office for which ordination is conferred: the conduct of worship and administration of the sacraments, preaching, the care of souls. Biblical scholars differ as to whether the NT provides a clear pattern of ministerial offices, but Protestants generally believe the ministry began as flexible and functional, becoming standardized in the 2d century. The RC Church holds that the threefold ministry is divinely prescribed, and requires the sacrament of orders, received within the line of *apostolic succession. Eastern Orthodox Churches refer rather to a communal succession, i.e., sacramental grace for the ministry is conveyed through the community, the ordaining bp. acting as its representative. For Luther the *priesthood of all believers meant that every baptized person carries out the priestly vocation in his own way, but some by a specialized ministry; the continuity of the Church and the ministry derived not from apostolic succession, but from accord in the apostolic gospel. Luther insisted upon the need for ministerial education. Calvin, whose teaching was adopted with modifications by the *Reformed Churches, held that the NT established a fourfold office in the Church, that of pastor, teacher, elder, and deacon. The pastor's ministry included preaching, the care of souls, and teaching; it required special education. Ordination was by other ministers, but with the civil magistrates and congregation having rights of approval. Some early English Reformers maintained that no particular *church order was indispensable, but that in fact *apostolic succession survived in the English Church. Ordination by a bishop came to be regarded as necessary for the ministry, and holy orders is now regarded by some as a sacrament. For the *free Churches generally, the ministry has been less clearly defined, and ordination has been regarded

more informally. The Anabaptists put emphasis on individual faith and ethical standards; any member was capable of holding pastoral office; choice by lot from the congregation was common; education was lightly regarded. Congregationalists and Baptists also emphasized a spiritual succession, and each congregation had the power to choose its minister. In early Baptist practice, one who ceased to be a pastor ceased to be ordained; ordination now is regarded as permanent, although revocable, and the larger Baptist bodies require special education of ministers. The Friends, or Quakers, in the beginning denied the necessity of an ordained ministry, but in the U.S. some groups have a minister. John Wesley wished to retain the apostolic succession for the Methodists but by force of circumstances had to ordain bishops himself (see METHODISM). In the U.S. the Methodists retained the episcopacy but disregarded apostolic succession. Most Methodists require special education for the ministry. In Protestant Churches generally, women are eligible to participate in the ministry, although they have not received full acceptance by the Churches.

In recent years an increasing emphasis on the ministry of the laity has been evident among Protestants in the United States. Thus the Churches engaged in the *Consultation on Church Union regard the ministry as the total mission to which Christ called the Church, but they agree on the necessity of a ministry that is specialized and representative. Clergy differ from the rest of the people of God functionally, not in status or special grace. Ordination would mean a recognition of qualifications, the conferral of responsibility for the ministry, and a prayer for God's blessing. These Churches would recognize episcopacy as a symbol of continuity, but not as embodying any particular theory of succession. See H. R. Niebuhr and D. D. Williams, *Ministry in Historical Perspective* (1956); E. P. Y. Simpson, *Ordination and Church Unity* (1966); R. Dunkerley, ed., *Ministry and the Sacraments* (1937); *Consultation on Church Union: Principles of Church Union* (1967).

MISSA ILLYRICA, an 11th-cent. text for the order of celebration of Mass, edited (1557) by M. *Flacius Illyricus as a refutation of RC eucharistic teaching. He wrongly dated it *c*.700. The text is of interest to liturgists for its many liturgical apologies, i.e., prayers professing unworthiness.

MISSAL, ROMAN, in the RC Church the liturgical book containing the readings and prayers used in the celebration of the Mass. In the first centuries of Christianity the prayers and readings of the eucharistic liturgy were determined by each bishop for his own church in accordance with its local tradition. Lessons were read directly from the Bible, and much of the prayer of the celebrant was extemporaneous. Gradually fixed forms of prayer, imitating celebrated models, began to be adopted. During the 4th and 5th cents. collections of such prayers were made, from which developed the Sacramentaries. The selection of Bible readings for different occasions also became fixed toward the end of the 5th cent., and special books containing gospel and other texts came into use. The gathering of the readings and prayers into a single volume for convenient use at private Masses dates from the 10th cent.; such a collection was called a Missal. In the Missals used throughout Europe, largely as a consequence of the Carolingian liturgical reform, there was much similarity, but for various reasons there were also many differences. The Roman Missal (*Missale secundum usum Romanae curiae*), known everywhere in Europe through the mendicant friars and traveling officials of the Roman Curia, came into popular use or was closely imitated in many places. Pius V in 1570 published a revised edition and prescribed its use in all dioceses, churches, and religious communities that lacked a Missal of their own in use for at least 200 years. The most recent revision of this Missal appeared in 1961. Further adaptation and revision, in keeping with the liturgical reform proposed by Vatican Council II, is in progress under the direction of the Consilium, established by Pope Paul VI to implement the liturgical reforms decreed by Vatican Council II. See J. A. Jungmann, *Mass of the Roman Rite* (tr. F. A. Brunner, 2v., 1951–55); L. C. Sheppard, NCE 9:897–900.

MISSIOLOGY, the branch of theology dealing with mission work, particularly the principles by which it is conducted. Despite the long history of mission work (see MISSIONS), missiology as a systematic discipline did not develop until recent times. It has its roots in German Protestant theology of the 19th cent., esp. in the work of G. Warneck (1834–1910), who is known as the father of modern missiology. RC missiology is likewise rooted in Germany, notably in the work of R. Streit (1875–1930), and J. Schmidlin (1876–1944). Despite its late development, however, the study has become well established through academic courses offered in most seminaries, the publication of numerous books and periodicals, and important missionary conferences. Twentieth-century popes have given extensive attention to the subject. The encyclical *Maximum illud* by Benedict XV (1919) is regarded as the Magna Charta of modern missions. At Vatican Council II the subject was treated in the *Decree on the Missionary Activity of the Church*.

Early missiology emphasized conversion of individual pagans. The emphasis later shifted to the establishment of the Church in all areas where it did not then exist. Since the Church is now established to some degree in nearly every part of the world, current emphasis is moving toward clarification of the basis of the Church's mission. Greater stress is now laid on its mission to transform society, rather than just win individual converts or establish itself institutionally. Study of the principles of mission work necessarily involves some auxiliary disciplines, particularly the history of missions, and the specialized studies that missionaries will use in their work. In the latter, attention is increasingly given to deeper analysis of the societies where the missionaries will serve and to the social sciences needed for solving the problems of those societies. See R. Hoffman, NCE 9:900–904.

MISSIONARY CHURCH ASSOCIATION, a union of independent evangelical churches, organized in Berne, Ind., 1898, and incorporated 1905. Besides the tenets of *fundamentalism, teaching includes *premillenarianism and the presence of the Holy Spirit to believers for power in daily life and service. While *congregational in polity, the Association has an annual general conference, which examines candidates for the ministry and grants licenses to preach; local churches elect their own ministers. Mission stations are maintained in Hawaii and in the Dominican Republic, Ecuador, Haiti, Jamaica, and Sierra Leone; some Association missionaries serve under the Christian and Missionary Alliance.

MISSIONARY COUNCIL, INTERNATIONAL, see INTERNATIONAL MISSIONARY COUNCIL.

MISSIONS. A mission, as understood here, is the sending or going forth of a person to preach the gospel. From the beginning Christians regarded the gospel message as intended for all mankind and saw it as an important part of their duty to aid in carrying it to every creature (Mt 28.19; Mk 16.15). The Acts of the Apostles is the record of the earliest efforts of the Christian community to fulfill this mandate. In addition to the preaching of the good news by the Apostles and their coworkers, converts from every walk of life whose commercial, military, or other pursuits took them from place to place carried the Christian message abroad. In a remarkably short time there were small cells of Christianity in most of the important cities at the crossroads of the Roman Empire. Their bishops were established as leaders or pastors of the community, the faithful assembled for worship and instruction, and organized forms of a catechumenate developed. As time went on

these pockets of Christianity grew and new ones were formed in other centers. By the time of the Edict of Milan (313), Christians in the Roman Empire already made up a substantial portion of the population—as high as 50% in some provinces. With the end of the persecutions the number of Christians increased greatly and began to include a larger proportion of people of wealth, education, and political importance. Missionary activity, which had in earlier times been chiefly confined to cities and large towns, gradually came to focus more upon the countryside, where zealous bishops and monks labored to drive paganism from its last refuge. In the outlying provinces of the Empire and beyond its limits the transition from paganism to Christianity was complicated by the introduction of a rival missionary thrust in the form of Arianism. Christianity in this form was taught by Ulfilas, apostle of the Goths, to his people along the lower Danube, whence it spread to other German tribes, and when they invaded western Europe and established their kingdoms there, they brought Arianism with them and later took it into Spain, Africa, and Italy. By the time this threat was finally overcome, a new era of evangelization was already under way. Missionary bishops and monks were at work among Germanic and Slavic tribes, often with the support of civil rulers who were interested in consolidating their control and expanding their dominions. The phenomenon of mass conversion was not uncommon; this was in part because of the strong bond existing between chieftains and their people, but, in many instances, because of pressure and compulsion.

After the faith had been well established in Europe, the Western Church turned to mission activity among the Moslems in Spain, North Africa, and the Middle East, but this effort met with small success, except in Spain. In the latter part of the 13th cent. friars moved farther afield, traveling to Persia, Armenia, and Russia, a large part of which was then under Tartar occupation. An embassy under the Franciscan John of Monte Corvino bore letters from the Pope to the Great Mongol Kahn, then at Kahn-balik (Peking), and a missionary archdi-ocese was established at Kahnbalik by Clement V in 1307. But these and other efforts of the 13th and early 14th cents. bore no lasting fruit. In the mid-13th cent. the Black Death swept across Europe, and the spreading power of the Ottoman Turks cut the Western Church off from effective com-munication with either Near or Far East. The hospitality accorded the friars in China by the Mongol dynasty was not continued by the Mings, and troubles and disorders of various kinds in Europe diverted human and material resources from missionary en-terprises. Western missionaries did not re-turn to the East until the 16th century.

Missions of the Eastern Churches. The Church in the East was as vigorous in its missionary activity as it was in the West and accounted for much of the geograph-ical spread of Christianity. By the 6th cent. missionaries had visited far places and there were Christian communities in India and Ceylon. Nestorian Christians pene-trated along trade routes into Mongolia and China as early as the 7th century. From the 8th till the 10th cent. the Byzantine Church labored to evangelize the Slavs, an effort that culminated in the baptism of St. Vladi-mir *c.*988 and led to the conversion of his people. It was chiefly through the Russian Church that the missionary work of the East continued after Byzantium was over-run by Moslems and was no longer able to send out missionaries. The Russians, esp. in their monastic centers, took up the work with zeal. They evangelized their non-Slavic neighbors to the north and east and re-evangelized the portion of their own land held by Mongol and Tartar invaders when these were finally overcome. Later, evangelization followed in the wake of the Siberian conquest and reached to China, Japan, and Alaska.

Roman Catholic Missions. A new period of intense missionary activity fol-lowed upon the voyages of Columbus and other explorers at the close of the 15th and during the 16th century. The first to take up the work were missionaries from Roman Catholic Spain and Portugal. They were the earliest in the field because their countries were the first to become extensively in-volved in colonization and the exploitation of economic opportunities opened up by the new discoveries, and also because there was less internal religious strife in Spain and Portugal to preoccupy the attention of religious leaders. Under the system of royal patronage (*patronato real*) the apostolate was undertaken with great vigor in the West Indies, Mexico, Central and South America, Africa, India, the Malay Penin-sula, and the Philippines. Later, French missionaries in Canada evangelized Indian tribes from the Atlantic to the Great Lakes and Mississippi regions. Much was accom-plished and the hope of greater achieve-ment lay ahead. But a good part of the pro-mise was frustrated by a variety of adverse circumstances. Recurrent war hindered communications and led to the diversion of resources from missionary to military uses. Religious and political developments in the homeland were reflected in shifts in policy regarding the promotion of the missions. There were bitter conflicts between mis-sionary and government officials about the ill-treatment of native populations. There was conflict also between competing mis-sionary orders and serious disagreement concerning the legitimacy of certain adap-tations of Christian thought and practice to the native cultures of those to whom the gospel was being preached. These and other factors were already at work in the 17th cent., when the missionary movement was at its height. Moreover, the defects of the patronage system were even then becoming apparent. The Congregation for the Propa-gation of the Faith was founded, which would provide in time a framework in which the missions could operate indepen-dently of royal patronage. Civil govern-ments, moving under the influence of the Enlightenment in the direction of secular-ism, began to lose interest in the work of the missions and to take an antagonistic view of the missionary activities of the reli-gious orders. Toward the end of the 18th cent. the Jesuits, who were widely involved in mission work, were suppressed. These and other reverses led to varying degrees of decline and stagnation in different mission fields.

Various factors combined to bring about a notable revival of missionary effort in the 19th cent. from the pontificate of Gregory XVI (1829–46) onward. Popular support for the missions was stimulated by the activities of societies established for that purpose, e.g., the Society for the Propagation of the Faith, founded in France in 1822. New religious congregations were formed for missionary work (e.g., the Marists, founded 1836; the Pontifical Institute for Foreign Missions of Milan, 1850; the White Fathers, 1868), and the older orders, long engaged in the work, renewed their commitment. External circumstances also became more favorable. New explorations and discoveries aroused general interest; there was a renewal of colonial competition between European nations. With these developments, governments, however anticlerical at home, saw advantage in encouraging, or at least in not putting obstacles in the way of, missionary activity. In these more encouraging circumstances, the interior of Africa and Oceanica were opened to evangelization, and great gains were made. Nevertheless, much of the evangelical effort could appear too closely allied with colonial interests, and with the rising sense of nationalism in many mission lands it became evident that the work of the missions had to be increasingly dissociated from the politico-economic ambitions of the countries from which the missionaries came. Since the pontificate of Pope Benedict XV (1914–22) stress has been increasingly laid upon the fostering of a native clergy in the different mission fields and on the establishment at the earliest feasible time of local hierarchies with indigenous bishops. The desirability of adapting or accommodating the Christian message to the cultural and social conditions of the people to whom it was brought came to be insisted upon. This principle had suffered from some neglect after the unfavorable stand taken by the Holy See in the matter of the Chinese and Malabar rites, and where missions were too closely coupled with colonial ambitions there had been no strong movement toward its rehabilitation. However, during the 20th cent. the principle has been revived and restored to respectability, and it influenced the thinking of the conciliar fathers at Vatican Council II (see Vat II MissAct 19–22).

Other changing features in contemporary Catholic missionary effort include a new emphasis on education, medical and social work, and the use of lay workers with the specialized skills and training necessary in those fields. Not only does this development provide a practical and impressive example of Christian love, useful in disposing the nonbeliever to take an interest in Christianity, but it also establishes what is often the only basis upon which governments not well disposed toward Christian evangelization are willing to admit missioners and permit them to remain.

Protestant Missions. The Protestant Churches after the Reformation were slower to take up missionary work in the newly discovered regions of the world, chiefly because the countries in which Protestants were strongest were at that time less extensively engaged in colonial expansion and overseas commerce. Moreover, Protestant theological thought during the Reformation period was too preoccupied with other matters to develop the theme of the Christian's responsibility to labor for the spread of the faith. But in the 17th cent. there was already some attempt to evangelize the Indians near the Virginia and New England settlements. John *Eliot in New England translated the Bible into an Indian dialect and preached to the Indians of Massachusetts, and the Quakers also undertook evangelical work among the Indians. The *Society for Promoting Christian Knowledge (SPCK), founded in 1698, had for part of its objective the distribution in foreign places of Bibles and other religious literature, and in 1701 the *Society for the Propagation of the Gospel (SPG) was founded to supplement the SPCK's work in the foreign field. This led to an increase of missionary effort in all the British colonies. Dutch trading settlements in the West Indies in the 17th cent. opened the way for missionaries from The Netherlands. In Germany *Pietism aroused interest in the missions, and the Moravian Church, always conspicuous for its missionary zeal and perhaps esp. well-suited to the work because it did not see itself as a national Church in any sense, sent missionaries to many parts of the world and esp. to British North America. In 1792 the Baptist Missionary Society was established in England, largely through the influence of William *Carey, who himself went (1793) as a missionary to India. Other missionary societies were soon organized— the *London Missionary Society (LMS) for *Nonconformist evangelicals (1795) and the *Church Missionary Society (CMS) for evangelicals within the Anglican Communion (1799). In 1804 the interdenominational *British and Foreign Bible Society was organized with the combined support of both Anglican and Nonconformist groups. Similar organizations were founded in the countries of continental Europe.

In the U.S., the *American Board of Commissioners for Foreign Missions was organized in 1810. It was an interdenominational agency but was principally supported by Congregational bodies. Other societies soon followed: the American Baptist Mission Union (1814), the American Bible Society (1816), the Methodist Board of Foreign Missions (1819), and the Presbyterian Board of Missions (1837). The formation of these organizations evoked by way of reaction an *antimissionary movement that was esp. strong during the years 1820–40. But the tide of missionary enthusiasm was too strong, and the feeling that results could best be achieved through national organization was too general for the opposition to overcome the trend. On the initiative of Robert Wilder, John Forman, and Robert Speer, the Student Volunteer Movement for Foreign Missions became active in 1886 and was formally organized in 1888. Its objective was declared to be "the evangelization of the world in this generation." John R. *Mott was associated with the movement from its beginning and long served as its chairman. The idea was taken up in other countries, and different national groups were linked, principally through the efforts of Mott, in the *World Student Christian Federation (founded 1895). Mott was chairman of the committee that called the first International Missionary Conference (Edinburgh, 1910). A continuation committee carried on the work of the Conference and this led to the establishment in 1921 of the *International Missionary Council, with which the missionary work of most Protestant bodies became associated, although some groups have preferred, mainly for doctrinal reasons, to operate independently of it. In 1961 this council was integrated into the World Council of Churches (WCC) and became the WCC's Commission on World Mission and Evangelism. The effect of the worldwide interdenominational organizations has been to reduce denominational rivalry in the missionary fields, to prevent overlapping of effort, and to develop more effective programs and methods of missionary work. There are many other missionary societies that are national, regional, or local in membership. Most of these are denominational, although they are in great part associated with broader interdenominational societies and ultimately with the WCC's Commission. Some, however, confine their interest to the promotion of their own denomination's missionary work.

Among those bodies that have kept apart from organizational association with other denominations, the Pentecostals are worthy of special mention. By themselves they account for as much as 10% of the total evangelical work being done by Protestants in the various missionary fields. Zeal to bear witness in foreign places has characterized the Pentecostal movement from its inception, and a substantial portion of the growth in membership of these bodies has been won in mission countries.

Through the years new approaches to evangelization have been developed. As hostility toward colonialism gained strength in mission areas during the 20th cent., it became evident that missionary programs would be more effective if they included less direct preaching of the gospel by word and more indirect preaching through service, medical work, agricultural training, and education, with greater emphasis, esp. since World War II, upon helping backward countries to help themselves. More importance has been attached to the preparation of indigenous workers to take over and carry on the work of evangelization. Experience of the past and the realities of the present situation, esp. since the report of the Laymen's Commission, which in 1932 published its findings in a volume entitled *Re-Thinking Missions,* has caused much stress to be laid on the need for the missionary to know the culture, religion, and customs of the people he encounters in foreign lands. See E. L. Murphy, NCE 9:924–928; W. J. Coleman, NCE 9:930–933; B. L. Goddard, ed., *The Encyclopedia of Modern Christian Missions* (1967); K. S. Latourette, NCE 9:938–941; *idem, A History of the Expansion of Christianity* (7v., 1937–45), esp. v.3–7; *idem, Christianity in a Revolutionary Age* (5v., 1958–62).

MODERATOR, in *Presbyterianism the officer presiding over a *church session, *presbytery, *synod, or *general assembly. The moderator of the session is the minister; in the other Presbyterian courts the moderator is elected.

MODERNISM (Roman Catholic), the ideological effort by a number of RC intellectuals to reinterpret the Christian faith in terms of contemporary historical, psychological, and philosophical positions that led to conclusions considered by the Church *magisterium as unorthodox and destructive of faith. The movement may be situated between about 1890 and 1910. Modernism was more a spontaneous orientation than an organized grouping. Three of the chief causes of the modernist crisis were: (1) the backwardness of RC scholarship in its

critical approach to the Bible; (2) the lack of a generally accepted philosophical anthropology and of an epistemology that could handle problems raised by Immanuel Kant; (3) the scholastic rigidity on the part of church officials as they addressed themselves to the newly emerging Catholic thought. Modernism found its chief center in France. M. Hébert in the article "La dernière idole" (1902) attacked the idea of personality in God. God, he held, is the category of the Ideal, immanent but unknowable. Abbé A. *Loisy in 1900 criticized the notion of inspiration as found in the encyclical *Providentissimus Deus* (1893). In 1902 and 1903 he wrote *L'Évangile et L'Église* and *Autour d'un petit livre* as a reply to A. *Harnack's thesis that the essence of the gospel was God and the soul, or the Fatherhood of God, and not a Christology or any other developed dogma. Loisy in rejecting this as an individualism foreign to the gospel insisted on the social aspect of the kingdom of God and the natural inevitability of development of dogma. He claimed, however, that Jesus erred in his teaching about the imminence of the kingdom and wrote: "Jesus announced the Kingdom and it is the Church which came." As a result of subsequent condemnation by the Holy Office, Loisy made an ambiguous retraction of his positions in 1904. In 1902 and 1906 Abbé A. Houtin published a history of biblical criticism that was bitterly critical of RC scholarship. In 1905 E. Le Roy, a layman, asserted that dogma gives the believer a rule for practical conduct or a pragmatic stance rather than intellectual content about God.

In England G. *Tyrrell, who was endeavoring to reinterpret Catholic teaching, was dismissed from the Society of Jesus in 1906 for refusing to retract the ideas in his anonymous *Letter to a Friend, A Professor of Anthropology,* in which he greatly relativized the meaning of dogma. Gradually (especially in *Through Scylla and Charybdis,* 1907) he worked out a theory of revelation in which he emphasized the immanent role of the recipient, accentuated the notion of religious experience in revelation, and gave dogma the secondary and totally relative function of protecting the "prophetic truth" of Scripture. Scripture itself was a record of an experience. The layman F. von Hügel generally supported Tyrrell. While pursuing his own work on mysticism, he made many contacts in Italy, France, and England, and came closest to being an organizer of modernism. However he did not support all the ideas associated with the movement and was chiefly engaged in a crusade to gain for RC scholars the rights to a kind of academic freedom. In Italy the movement had a more social orientation. R. Murri, e.g., pushed for independence from the hierarchy in social and political areas and called for a reform of the Church's institutional structure. S. Minocchi carried on the thought of Loisy and Tyrrell. A. Fogazzaro in his novel *Il Santo* (1905) painted a dark picture of the Church and called for reform of the four evil spirits of untruthfulness, domination, avarice, and immobility. E. Buonaiuti replied to the encyclical *Pascendi dominici gregis* with *Il programma dei modernisti* (1907), in which he demanded that Catholicism be reconciled with scientific findings and attacked scholasticism. In Germany the movement known as *Reformkatholizismus was concerned chiefly with disciplinary questions. It insisted on freedom in scientific religious work, called for the suppression of the Index, and was generally anti-Roman in tone. Out of this only a small modernist group emerged, mostly after *Pascendi*. One of the leaders was J. Schnitzer, who supported Loisy. In the U.S. the most famous modernist was W. L. Sullivan (*Letters to His Holiness Pius X, by a Modernist*, 1910), who left the Paulists and became a Unitarian. The scattered support for the movement in the U.S. was greater than has been generally realized, mainly among seminary professors. However, such tendencies in the U.S. died out rapidly. No one knows the number of Catholics throughout the world with strong modernist tendencies. It seems that it was a moderate-sized group of intellectuals, who did not make a strong impact on the large body of faithful.

On July 3, 1907, the Holy Office in its decree *Lamentabili condemned 65 propositions connected with biblical criticism and dogma. Pius X on Sept. 8, 1907, issued the encyclical *Pascendi dominici gregis*. Probably its chief target was the work of Loisy and Tyrrell. It condemned the theory of error on the part of Christ, theories relativizing dogma, and a biblical criticism in which it found agnostic, pure immanentist, and anti-intellectualist bases. *Pascendi* condemned modernism as "the synthesis of all heresies." However, the encyclical presented a global picture of modernism that was a theoretical construction dictated by contemporary neoscholasticism. It may have described the position of M. Hébert or perhaps even of the later Loisy, but Tyrrell, e.g., could never be described as a pure immanentist. The problems with which many of the modernists were grappling were not handled in all their subtlety. In leveling its attack at *agnosticism and pure immanentism, *Pascendi* finds its permanent value; for many other issues the encyclical seems to have been a premature condemnation without solution. The encyclical set up Committees of Vigilance, which received strong support from simplistic conservative groups, one of which was the *Sodalitium pianum* directed by Monsignor U. Benigni in Italy. Attacks were leveled not only against theologians but against liberal positions in politics and even in literature. The result was a kind of paralysis with regard to broaching questions connected with subjects handled in the encyclical. The *Oath against Modernism (Sept. 1, 1910) sealed this mood upon the Church, a mood that was not totally relieved even by Benedict XV's *Ad beatissimi* in 1914, which was an attempt at checking the campaign of suspicion. Von Hügel alone of the leading characters in the movement escaped official condemnation. However, scholars like Lagrange, Batiffol, Grandmaison, and Rivière were destined to continue their work in an atmosphere of excessive constraint. It was only with *Divino afflante Spiritu* in 1943, which officially approved the use of literary forms as a key to understanding parts of the

Bible, that a change began, a change that culminated in Vatican Council II.

In the overall view, modernism was a challenge to the then prevalent analysis of the notion of official authority in the Church. Some magisterial action no doubt was called for in the face of the excessive challenges thrown out by some modernist writers, or else the result might have been anarchy. Yet the modernist crisis was a tragedy. On the one side there was the large body of the faithful unprepared for the new critical work and church officials who had little sense of the solidity of some of the recent scholarship. On the other side were scholars doing pioneer work who had little respect for the criticism of their often unprepared Catholic colleagues. The result of the condemnation was a temporary pastoral gain for the faithful at large. But the problems that were raised grew into a mountain of difficulties that the Church has had ultimately to face. Positively modernism underlined the relation of revelation to human experience, the immediate orientation of dogma to practical action and prayer, the historically conditioned side of dogma, the need for thoroughly critical work in religious areas, the right to freedom in research, the need to restructure institutions in the Church, and the ultimate limitations to magisterial authority. See A. Vidler, *Modernist Movement in the Roman Church* (1934; rev. ed. in process, 1969); J. Ratté, *Three Modernists: Loisy, Tyrrell and Sullivan* (1967); J. Heaney, *Modernist Crisis: Von Hügel* (1968); J. Rivière, *Le Modernisme dans l'Église* (1929).

MODERNISM (Protestant), a designation for liberal Protestant thought. The term originally applied to a movement within the RC Church (see MODERNISM [ROMAN CATHOLIC]), but it became current in the C of E; then during World War I it came into use in the U.S. and was common during the 1920s in the modernist-fundamentalist controversy, e.g., J. G. *Machen declared that "modern liberalism," which he equated with modernism, was un-Christian, an entirely different religion from Christianity (*Christianity and Liberalism*, 1923). Many liberals, however, accepted it as an appropriate designation, because their aim was to accommodate Christianity to modern knowledge. Shailer *Mathews defined modernism as "the use of the methods of modern science to find, state and use the permanent and central values of inherited orthodoxy in meeting the needs of a modern world" (*The Faith of Modernism*, 1924). Modernism was more a spirit or attitude than a particular system of ideas, and its representatives differed in their approaches to epistemology, metaphysics, traditional Christian affirmations, and attitude toward Christianity in relation to other religions. Despite their variety, modernist theologies all shared certain presuppositions as they faced the cultural changes reflected in philosophy, psychology, historiography, science and technology, and socioeconomic theory. Some of the factors that influenced the development of modernism were: a scientific spirit that considered empirical method the only valid avenue to truth; the complete sufficiency of human reason; naturalism, or a tendency to account for everything in terms of natural causality; historical and literary criticism of the Bible; the authority of individual experience in religion; an emphasis upon practical ethics in religion; and an attempt to isolate the essential in Christianity from the accidental.

To a large extent the basic ideas in this process originated in Europe. In the U.S. they took on a distinctive shape as they were affected by *revivalism, with its stress upon religious experience and depreciation of dogmatic theology; by an emphasis on the practical and an impatience with the theoretical; and by the active spirit of reform that had flourished in American Christianity before the Civil War. Besides common influences, there were also common characteristics in theological content: emphasis upon the immanence of God; an optimistic view of human nature and of moral progress; acceptance of the Bible as a record of man's quest rather than a record of objective revelation; a deemphasizing of sin; an accent on the humanity of Jesus Christ that ignored or denied his deity and pictured him as the teacher and leader par excellence; and the elimination of miracles as superstitious accretions of a prescientific age.

Some modernists might have accepted all of these viewpoints; others held only a few of them. In spite of common influences and tendencies in modernist thought, there were also sharp differences respecting the extent to which they were willing to reinterpret Christianity. Kenneth Cauthen has suggested the categories of "evangelical liberals" and "modernistic liberals" to distinguish two main types of liberal. The former made more effort to maintain continuity with historic Christianity and had a Christocentric emphasis. The latter were less concerned about the uniqueness of Christianity and considered Jesus Christ helpful, but not indispensable, to religious experience. During the 1930s liberalism in the U.S. came under heavy attack from within its own ranks, beginning with such works as Reinhold Niebuhr's *Moral Man and Immoral Society* (1932) and Edwin Lewis's *A Christian Manifesto* (1934). See J. Dillenberger and C. Welch, *Protestant Christianity Interpreted Through Its Development* (1954); H. S. Smith, R. T. Handy, and L. A. Loetscher, *American Christianity: Interpretation and Documents* (v.2, 1963). *FUNDAMENTALISM; *NEO-ORTHODOXY; *LIBERAL THEOLOGY.

MODERNISM, OATH AGAINST, see OATH AGAINST MODERNISM.

MÖHLER, JOHANN ADAM (1796–1838), RC theologian and church historian. Educated at Tübingen, M. was ordained in 1819 and after some experience in the parochial ministry became professor of church history at Tübingen (1828) and later transferred to Munich (1835). He was on friendly terms with Protestant theologians, among whom were F. *Schleiermacher and J. *Ne-

ander, and was strongly influenced, esp. in his earlier work, by the philosophical idealism of F. Schelling. Two of M.'s works in particular, his *Die Einheit in der Kirche* (1825) and his *Symbolik* (1832; Eng. tr. *Symbolism: Or Exposition of Doctrinal Differences between Catholics and Protestants As Evidenced by Their Symbolical Writings*, 1843) entitle him to a prominent place among the precursors of modern ecumenism, and to giving a new direction to *ecclesiology. He has been accused of being a forerunner also of *modernism, but the charge appears to be unjust. See P. Chaillet, ed., *L'Église est une: Hommage à Möhler* (1939); J. R. Geiselmann, *J. A. M.* (1940); R. H. Nienaltowski, *Johann Adam Möhler's Theory of Doctrinal Development* (1959); *idem*, NCE 9:1004–05.

MOLINA, LUIS DE (1535–1600), Spanish Jesuit theologian. He studied the humanities for 4 years at Cuenca, law for a year at Salamanca, and entered the Jesuit novitiate at Coimbra in 1553. After completing his studies he taught philosophy at Coimbra until 1567, and theology at Evora until 1583, when he retired from teaching and thereafter devoted his time to writing. His first published work was *Concordia liberi arbitrii cum gratiae donis* (1588). An *Appendix ad Concordiam* appeared the following year and is bound with some editions of the 1588 *Concordia*. The *Concordia* is M.'s solution to the problem of the reconciliation of free will with efficacious grace, a reconciliation that he based upon *scientia media*, God's foreknowledge, anterior to any divine decree, of free choices that might be made by an individual (the free choices are called futuribles). The *Concordia* was originally written as part of M.'s *Commentaria in primam partem*, but it grew to such length that M. was advised to publish it as a separate work. Some of its contents are still to be found in the *Commentaria*. Although the work precipitated the controversy that culminated in the *Congregatio de auxiliis* (1602–07), the solution it proposed became accepted by a great many theologians. M. also wrote *De justitia et jure*, one of the classic treatises on that subject. Three volumes of it were published during his lifetime, and the rest appeared posthumously—the first complete edition in 1613 (6v.). M. is considered one of the primary authorities on moral probabilism, and a leading authority on the economic questions discussed in his time. Some of M.'s unedited writings were published by F. Stegmüller in *Geschichte des Molinismus* (1935). Text of the *Concordia:* ed. J. Rabeneck (1953). See Somervogel 5:1167–79; J. Rabeneck, "De Ludovici de Molina studiorum philosophiae curriculo," AHSJ 6 (1937), 291–302; *idem*, "De vita et scriptis Ludovici Molinae," AHSJ 19 (1950), 75–145; *idem*, "Antiqua legenda de Molina narrata examinantur," AHSJ 24 (1955), 295–326.

MOLINISM, a system of theological thought based on the teaching of Luis de *Molina in his *Concordia* and further developed by his followers. It is concerned principally with the conciliation of efficacious grace and free will (see GRACE, EFFICACIOUS). The key to the Molinist solution of this problem is *scientia media*. Molinists have also characteristic doctrines on predefinition, predestination, and reprobation. In Molinism *scientia media*, or middle knowledge, is that knowledge by which God infallibly knows, before he makes an absolute decree creating the free creature, what choices it would make in any set of circumstances. This knowledge is called *media* because it is conceived of as partaking partly of the knowledge of simple intelligence, by which God necessarily knows all possible modes of existence, and partly of the knowledge of vision, by which God knows the things he freely ordains to exist.

The object known by *scientia media* is called the free futurible, i.e., a free choice or action that would take place in certain circumstances or conditions. Future events or choices that de facto will occur are known by God in knowledge of vision. The basis of this knowledge is the absolute decree to bestow that grace the acceptance of which was foreseen by *scientia media*.

Theology has always faced the problem of reconciling free will with efficacious grace and its infallible power to obtain human consent before that consent is given. Molinists unanimously teach that this power comes not from the intrinsic nature of efficacious grace but from three extrinsic sources combined. These sources are: first, the objective fact that a man would consent to a grace if it were given; second, from God's foreknowledge of that fact by *scientia media* before he makes any absolute decree about what shall take place; third, from the absolute, benevolent decree to give grace in the light of that foreknowledge. There is no efficacy to grace until this third point is reached. This grace, when given, takes away from man actual dissent, but not the power of consent or dissent, wherein lies freedom of the will.

Molinists, together with all other RC theologians, hold that all good human actions result from an absolute divine decree that a man shall perform a good act. But Molinists differ from other theologians in holding virtual predefinition: God simply wills to give a man grace to which he foresaw man would consent, thereby predefining the resultant good act. But he would give the same grace, even had he foreseen man's resistance, because there was no decree concerning a good action prior to *scientia media*. Molinists also hold that within the divine plan of salvation there is an absolute divine intention to give adults the reward of glory only after, and on account of, their absolutely foreseen future merits. This is the doctrine of virtual predestination. There is no place in the Molinist system for any kind of antecedent reprobation. In the divine plan there is only the positive consequent intention to reprobate the wicked on account of their foreseen death in the state of personal sin. See A. C. Pegis, "Molina and Human Liberty," *Jesuit Thinkers of the Renaissance* (ed. G. Smith, 1939), 75–131; H. Rondet, *Gratia Christi* (1948); G. Smith, *Freedom in Molina* (1966).

MOLINOS, MIGUEL DE (1628–96), Spanish Quietist. After ordination he was sent to Rome to represent a beatification cause. Relieved of this office, he chose to remain in Rome, where he was esteemed as a confessor and spiritual director. In 1675 he published the *Spiritual Guide*, which was widely circulated and translated into several languages. The book soon gave rise to debate. Two Jesuits, Belluomo and Segneri, in defense of meditation, wrote treatises against M.'s doctrine. But M. had influential allies; after several years of debate, the works of Belluomo and Segneri were placed on the Index. In 1685 M. was arrested for reasons not clearly known; historians have conjectured about his moral conduct. The process against him lasted 2 years; seventy witnesses were called in and many letters examined. In 1687 he made a retractation of 68 propositions; he also admitted to certain charges against his morals. He was condemned to penitential imprisonment for the rest of his life. Whether he accepted the penalty because he admitted its justice or as a humiliation sent by God is not clear. The list of M.'s errors contained in the bull *Coelestis pastor* (D. 2201–69) is not taken from his book *Spiritual Guide*. The propositions selected and put in order by the Holy Office reflect a series of concrete applications deduced more or less accurately from principles. The principles in their theoretical formulation do not tend necessarily to lead astray; but the principles were in fact applied to sanction immoral practices in semi-secret gatherings. The *Spiritual Guide* contains chapters with excellent doctrine that recent research has traced to St. John of the Cross. *QUIETISM.

MONASTERIES, DISSOLUTION OF THE, see DISSOLUTION OF THE MONASTERIES.

MONASTIC THEOLOGY, a formula that designates the monastic approach to theology and not the study of the monastic life. It has been in current use since 1953, the 8th centenary of the death of St. Bernard of Clairvaux, but the type of theology it indicates existed long before. During the Middle Ages it was the business of contemplatives within the cloister, generally monks. Though distinct from scholastic theology as studied in the town schools, it was not opposed, but complementary, to it. In the 12th cent. it was exemplified by the writings of Benedictines, Cistercians, and Canons Regular. Because it was in fact the prolongation of the patristic thought of the ancient Church into the mid-13th cent., it may be called medieval patristics. Its value is not to be overestimated, yet it has been acknowledged by historians, including M. D. Chenu. It included the spiritual interpretation of the Bible as exposed by H. De Lubac in *L'exégèse médiéval* (4v., 1959–64) and by F. Vandenbroucke in *La Morale monastique* (1966), as well as in monographs on Aelred of Rievaulx, Bernard of Clairvaux, Bruno of Segni, Geoffrey of Admont, Gilbert of Hoyland, William of St. Thierry, Peter Damian, Peter the Venerable, Rupert of Deutz, and others. It was recommended, at least for monks, by the episcopal synod held at Rome in 1967. The stress it lays on the unity between Bible, patristic thought, and liturgy makes it akin to the theology of the Orthodox Church. Its emphasis on the union that should exist between reflection and spiritual experience gives it some relationship with certain trends of Protestant theology. It thus has ecumenical value. See J. Leclercq, *Love of Learning and the Desire for God* (tr. C. Misrahi, 1961; pa., 1962), ch. 9; P. K. Meagher, NCE 9:1032.

MONASTICISM (Gr. *monos*, unique), an institution establishing and regulating the life of those in the service of the holy, whether in community or in solitude. Monasticism implies a separation from the secular to further an ideal based on celibacy, poverty, and obedience to a spiritual leader. It is a phenomenon observable in all the great religions of the world. Christian monasticism has been marked by distinguished service in education, scholarship, the arts, care of the needy and the sick, and mission work. Monasticism in the West was the instrument that preserved the achievements of Greco-Roman culture and Christianized Europe.

Early Western Monasticism. Organized asceticism began in the West somewhat later than in the East. Individuals who had gone on pilgrimages to the Desert Fathers in Egypt and to monasteries in other parts of the East brought back to the West ideals of abnegation which they followed at home singly or in small groups. An impetus was given to the movement by Athanasius, Bp. of Alexandria, during his numerous exiles at the hands of the Arians. When he came to Rome in 339 to plead his case before a Roman synod, he was accompanied by two Desert Fathers. Marcella, a young Roman of high station, was so impressed by his reports of Egyptian monasticism that she and her companions made her house on the Aventine into a kind of convent. About 356 Athanasius wrote a life of Anthony of Egypt, which he intended as an ideal pattern of the ascetical life. The biography was soon translated into several languages. Augustine (*Confessions*, 8.6) testifies to the influence exerted by the Latin version of Evagrius of Antioch. Martin of Tours founded the first monastery in Gaul—at Ligugé in 361. When he had to leave this retreat upon his election as bishop, he chose a cell near Tours in which to dwell. The influx of numerous disciples gave rise there in 372 to the famous monastery of Marmoutier (the word is a corruption of *maius monasterium*). In 388 Augustine, not yet ordained, founded a monastery at Tagaste. Later at Hippo he lived in common with his clergy under rule, a practice that had already been followed by Ambrose (d. 397) and Eusebius of Vercelli (d. 371), whose community may be regarded as the prototype of the secular canons of the Carolingian reform. This penetration of monastic life into the ranks of the clergy who served the local churches was a characteristic of Western monasticism in contradistinction to the forms it took in the East. At Lérins Honoratus established a monastery combining hermits and ceno-

bites and continued to govern it after he became abp. of Arles, the first of a long line of monk-bishops in that see.

Eastern ideas were freshly introduced into monasticism with the return of John Cassian from years spent studying Eastern institutions. His express purpose was the reform of Gallic monastic life. To this end he founded a double monastery at Marseilles in 415 and composed for his followers two books: *Institutes*, the foundation of many Western rules, and *Conferences*, purported conversations held with prominent Eastern ascetics. The earliest British monasteries date from about 430. At this time Patrick also founded his first community. The greatest of the Western founders was Benedict of Nursia, who drew upon Cassian and other sources to write c.530–540 the first detailed piece of monastic legislation specifically for the West. In his firm outline of the liturgical, administrative, and spiritual life, Benedict provided for the essential autonomy of each house and incorporated a fourth vow of stability. Though the monastery founded at Vivarium by the pious layman Cassiodorus did not long survive his death in 580, his stress on intellectual pursuits gave rise to the tradition of scholarship in religious orders. The copying of manuscripts he fostered was imitated in other monasteries and helped in preserving the classical culture of Europe. The monasteries were important also to the conversion of the barbarians. Augustine of Canterbury, to cite one instance, was sent to England in 596 from a Benedictine monastery which Gregory the Great had founded in Rome. Monks from Gaul developed institutions in Ireland which were destined to bring Christianity and culture back to the Continent. After the arrival of the monk Finnian from Britain, Irish monasteries began to multiply. Finnian trained young monks at Clonard and sent them out to establish independent houses. Prominent among the founder-monks were: Columcille of Derry and Iona, Ciaran of Clonmacnois, Nessan of Mungret, Colman of Cloyne, Finbarr of Cork, Iarlath of Tuam, Ailbe of Emly, Comgall of Bangor, Enda of

Aran, Kevin of Glendalough, and Cronan of Roscrea. Greatest of the founder-nuns were: Brigid of Kildare, Ita of Killeedy, and Monenna of Killeavy.

Of the more than 20 Celtic rules only that of Columban is extant. It is characterized by severe bodily austerity and regards the interior spirit as vastly more important than external organization. For the Irish monks teaching was an important apostolate. In point of fact, the monks replaced the Druids as teachers of the young. Because of the lack of cities as centers of political life, abbots in Ireland became prominent as ecclesiastical rulers; and some bishops who were not monks were subordinate to the administrators of great monasteries. Irish monasticism was established in Luxeuil and Bobbio by Columban. From those centers some 50 other monasteries took their rise.

Later Western Monasticism. The Anglo-Saxon missioners who carried Christianity back to the Continent in the late 7th and the 8th cent. were Benedictines. It was only natural that the new centers they founded should be Benedictine also. In time the Benedictine rule became normative, sometimes with borrowing from older, more austere rules; and the legislation of Charlemagne (817) made it obligatory for all monks and nuns in the Carolingian domain. In Spain and the Celtic lands, however, other rules continued to be used for several centuries. As time passed, extramonastic activity grew. The rise of feudalism made abbeys into fiefs and abbots into feudal lords with accompanying obligations and privileges. Schools and scriptoria claimed much of the monks' time. The first attempt to reduce extramonastic interests was made by Benedict of Aniane. He presided over the monastic Synod of Aachen (817), which decreed the elimination of external work, the lengthening of the Divine Office, and many other changes; but only when Cluny adopted the Synod's legislation (910) did the reform come alive. Up to that time each monastery had been wholly autonomous, the rule being the only link among them. Now all Cluniac houses were made dependent upon a central policy administered by the abbot of Cluny. Reforms occurred also in other places: in southern France and Flanders under John of Gorze; in England under the monk-bishops Dunstan of Canterbury, Ethelwold of Winchester, and Oswald of York; and in Germany, Italy, and Spain. The 10th, 11th, and 12th cents. have come to be called the Benedictine centuries because of the monks who strove as bishops and popes to free the Church from secular control.

Some reforms among the Benedictines emphasized eremetic and contemplative ideals. Romuald inspired the movement that resulted in the Camaldolese (1012); John of Gaulbert, the Vallambrosians (1036); and Bruno of Cologne, the Carthusians (1084). The most important reform of this century was the Cistercian Order (1098), founded by Stephen Harding and Robert of Molesmes and brought to prominence by Bernard of Clairvaux. It was at first purely contemplative, given over to silence, poverty, and manual work. In time, however, the heavy labor was turned over to lay monks who developed the great Cistercian abbey estates. In 1120 at Prémontré, Norbert founded the Canons Regular, using as basis for his regulations the so-called Rule of St. Augustine. His canons are commonly called Premonstratensians or Norbertines. Other reform groups were the Williamites (1157), Sylvestrines (1231), Celestines (1235), and Olivetans (1313). Growths of a different sort also came from the Benedictine root as a result of needs arising during the Crusades: the Hospitallers and various military orders.

The ills attendant on commendation, the *Great Western Schism, wars, and the Black Death so weakened monasticism that Reformation attacks upon it were almost mortal. Yet renewal and reform continued. Two of the most notable reforms were those of the Maurists in 1621 and of the Cistercians at La Trappe in 1664, the origin of the Trappists. A characteristic of the reform movements of more recent centuries is a tendency to group monasteries into congregations with uniform observance and central government. In 1893 a loose federation of all Benedictine congregations was formed with headquarters at Sant'Anselmo in Rome. See J. Décarreaux, *Monks and Civilization* (tr. C. Haldone, 1964); J. Ryan, *Monasticism* (1931). *RELIGIOUS LIFE.

MONERGISM (Gr. *monos*, alone, *ergon*, work), the teaching that God is the sole cause of man's salvation; the opposite of *synergism. The term has been applied esp. to the *Gnesiolutheranism of those who invoked Luther's teaching on justification and the abiding sinfulness of man against P. *Melanchthon in the Synergistic Controversy (1550–77). *Calvinism, particularly as articulated in the Synod of *Dort (1618), may also be classified as monergistic in opposition to *Arminianism.

MONTANISTS, members of a heretical sect founded in the 2d half of the 2d cent. by the Phrygian neophyte *Montanus. The movement spread rapidly and acquired a quasi-universal character. By 177 it had already been preached in Lyons and Rome. The Montanists, who did not entirely disappear until the 9th cent., soon broke up into various factions. Members of the sect came to be known as Phrygians, Cataphrygians, and Pepuzians from their place of origin (Pepuza in Phrygia). In Rome there were Montanists "according to Proclus" and others "according to Aeschines." In N Africa they were known as Artotyrites from their practice of using bread (*artos*) and cheese (*tyros*) in the celebration of the Eucharist.

Montanus and his two female companions, Priscilla (Prisca) and Maximilla, were subject to trances, which they took to be communications from the Holy Spirit. Collections of their prophetic oracles were gathered into "countless books" (Hippolytus, *Philos.* 8.19) and were regarded as being "new Scriptures" (Eusebius, *Hist. eccl.* 6.20.3) of equal authority with the Old and New Testaments. The revelation of the Spirit thus given was believed to be that which Christ had promised to his Disciples at the Last Supper; it announced the imminent end of the world and the dawn of the *millennium at Pepuza. Their millenary expectations induced the Montanists to lead a rigorously ascetical life. Prolonged fasts, virginity, and continence were held in exaggerated esteem. Their general flight from the world even found expression in voluntary martyrdoms. Later leaders, particularly *Tertullian, gave the movement a less charismatic and more dogmatic orientation. In his Montanistic period he taught, e.g., that second marriages were a kind of fornication, that flight from persecution was a form of apostasy, and that there are certain sins that cannot be forgiven by the Church. The emphasis that the Montanists placed upon the guidance of the Spirit caused them to reject episcopal authority. This rejection of the hierarchy and their conviction that the revelations given to the new prophets complemented those of the NT set them apart substantially from the Church.

The religious fanaticism of the Montanists had a powerful influence upon the less stable members of the Christian community. They were opposed by numerous writers, such as Apollinaris of Hierapolis, Miltiades, Melito of Sardis, the Roman priest Gaius, Eusebius, Epiphanius, and St. Jerome. They also attracted the attention of less orthodox Christians, such as Origen and the patripassianist Praxeas. Montanism was condemned by Popes Soter (c.166–175), Eleutherius (c.175–189), and Innocent I (401–417), and by the Emperors Honorius I (407), Justinian I (530), and Leo the Isaurian (722). As the movement gradually lost its formal identity, its members returned to the Church or passed over to other sects, such as the Cathari and the Priscillianists. The last mention of the Montanists in antiquity is a petition of the 9th cent. that the patriarch Nicephorus of Constantinople made to the Emperor to repress the Phrygian heretics.

Montanism has been interpreted as an attempt to recover a primitive religious fervor in the face of a growing secularization. It is perhaps better to understand it as a particularly striking manifestation of a phenomenon that recurs within the Church—a craving for religious experiences to offset the difficulties of a life of faith. The ultimate defeat of Montanism marks the renunciation of the eschatological enthusiasm of the early Church, the affirmation of a hierarchy based upon an apostolic succession, the universality of the Church as opposed to individual propheticism, and the right of the Church to pardon the sins of all its members. See Epiphanius, *Adv. haer.* 2.48; P. de Labriolle, *Le Crise montaniste* (1913); A. Mayer, EC 8:1343–47; H. Bacht, LTK 7:578–580; R. Knox, *Enthusiasm* (1950), 25–49.

MONTANUS (fl. mid-2d cent.), the founder of a widespread apocalyptic movement generally known as Montanism. He may have been a priest of Cybele before his conversion in 156 or 157 (Epiphanius, *Haer.* 48.1), or, much more likely, in 172 or 173 (Eusebius, *Chronic.* II, *Olymp.* 238). Soon after his baptism he began to preach at Ardabau on the boundary between Phrygia and Mysia and later in Pepuza. He claimed to be the organ of the Paraclete that had been promised by Christ and preached the proximate approach of the millennium. Among his first disciples were two ecstatic women, Priscilla (or Prisca) and Maximilla, who left their husbands to proclaim the "new prophecy." All three seem to have died before A.D. 179, but the ideas they had taught spread rapidly from Asia Minor into Syria, Thrace, and even to Lyons, Carthage, and Rome. M. is the prototype of the many apocalyptic preachers in church history. See P. de Labriolle, *Le Crise montaniste* (1913); A. Mayer, EC 8:1343–47; H. Bacht, LTK 7:578–580. *MONTANISTS.

MONTENSES, a name given to the small *Donatist community in Rome. It was composed of immigrants to the city and received Victor of Garba as its first bp. shortly after the origin of the schism in Africa. Since the Donatists had at first no church in Rome where they could assemble, they were forced to meet in a cave in a mountain (*in monte*) outside the city, and from this fact they received their name. Petilian and other Donatists appealed in vain to the existence of this small group as a proof of the universality of their Church. See Augustine, *Ep.* 53.2; A. Pincherle, EC 8:1364.

MONTREAL CONFERENCE, the fourth World Conference on *Faith and Order, held in Montreal, July 13–26, 1963. The topics presented for discussion were: (1) Christ and the Church; (2) tradition and traditions; (3) worship; and (4) institutionalism. The reports of the sections into which the Conference divided for consideration of the various subjects were presented to the participating Churches without a general vote of the Conference. The social implications of the doctrines studied were particularly strong in the reports entitled "The Church in the Purpose of God" and "The Process of Growing Together." The concept that the Churches were component parts of the one Church was rejected in favor of an emphasis on the union of all Christians in the body of Christ, the Church. A new approach to the question of the ministry of the Church was apparent: the ministry was seen as originating in and reflecting the threefold mission of Christ as prophet, as high priest, and as king. Notable at this Conference was the large representation from Eastern Orthodoxy and the participation of more than 20 RC theologians. See P. C. Rodger and L. Vischer, eds., *Fourth World Conference on Faith and Order* (1964).

MOODY, DWIGHT LYMAN (1837–99), American revival preacher who applied business and advertising techniques to evangelism and developed interdenominational revivals to reach urban audiences. M. had only a grammar school education in Northfield, Mass., and left home in 1854 to take a job in a Boston shoe store. The following year he experienced a religious conversion and joined the Congregational Church. Successful as a salesman, he devoted more of his time to religious work. Moving to Chicago in 1856, he formed the North Market Sabbath School in 1858 and was closely associated with the Young Men's Christian Association (YMCA). In 1860 M. became a full-time city missionary, and in 1863 he organized a nondenominational church in Chicago as a center for urban evangelism. The Chicago YMCA made him its president in 1866. He was little known outside Chicago until his 1873 evangelistic crusade in British industrial centers made him world famous. He conducted a series of interdenominational revivals in cities of the U.S. in 1875. His revivals were organized in minute detail and required the active support of all major Protestant Churches in an area. His sermons stressed evangelical "Bible Christianity" and were centered on Christ's redemptive love and call to repent. His preaching was simple, direct, and restrained. With the help of Ira D. *Sankey he succeeded in reaching audiences with simply worded gospel hymns. He toured the British Isles, 1881–84 and 1891–92, preaching in the U.S. and Canada in the intervening years. M.'s hope of reaching unchurched city-dwellers was only partially realized, but he sparked a notable revival among evangelical Protestants. His success among British students led to his founding of the Student Christian Movement. His young converts gave a new impetus to foreign missions and a new direction to campus religious life in the U.S. and in England. His Northfield Conferences for students had a marked influence on the ecumenism of the succeeding decades. The Chicago (now Moody) Bible Institute, which he founded in 1889 to train evangelists, has continued his work to the present day. See W. R. Moody, *D. L. M.* (1930); W. M. Smith, *Annotated Bibliography of D. L. M.* (1948); W. G. McLoughlin, *Modern Revivalism* (1958); R. K. Curtis, *They Called Him Mr. Moody* (1962); J. C. Pollock, *Moody without Sankey* (1963).

MOORE, RICHARD CHANNING (1762–1841), Protestant Episcopal bp. of Va. from 1814. Born in New York, M. became a seaman after studying at King's College (now Columbia Univ.), then a physician before his ordination in 1787. For 20 years he was rector at Grace Church, Rye, N.Y., until his consecration as bishop of Virginia. Alarmed by the progress of the *Oxford movement, which he saw as a revival of the "Romish system," he set a *broad-church, or evangelical, tone, which remains characteristic of the diocese he headed. He gave his support to interdenominational projects, the *American Bible Society among them. He opened the Protestant Episcopal Theological Seminary in Alexandria, Va., in 1823.

MORAL RE-ARMAMENT (MRA), the spiritual revival movement called also First-Century Christian Fellowship and the Oxford Group. The present name was adopted in 1938. Members are often referred to as Buchmanites; MRA's founder was Frank *Buchman, a Lutheran minister, who sought to change the world by changing men. After a career as a youth worker and YMCA college secretary, Buchman experienced a religious conversion in 1908 at Keswick, Eng., and developed his distinctive evangelistic techniques, working with Oxford Univ. people. In the early, Oxford Group period of the movement, concentration was on the moral perfection of the individual; by the time MRA was formally inaugurated, the movement had become a program to save society and the world. During World War II in the U.S. it took on the aspect of a morale-building patriotic organization; since then it has waged a strong anti-Communist campaign. Adherents test their lives by the standards of the Four Absolutes of purity, unselfishness, honesty, and love. The movement prescribes a strict sexual code, promotes racial and religious harmony, and opposes the Communist ideology. Individuals are invited to share their testimonies, to confess their sins publicly, and to change their lives by surrender to the will of Christ, by restitution for any past evil deeds, and by opening themselves to divine guidance. Buchman devised house parties, which resemble a cursillo, or informal retreat, to conduct this program, esp. among students.

Those who belong to MRA undergo no initiation, pay no set dues, and receive no membership card. They simply begin to model their lives after the principles of the movement. Adherents need not withdraw from their own Churches and may, in fact, become more active Protestants and Catholics. The 3,000 men and women who serve as full-time MRA workers receive room, board, and a small personal allowance. MRA is active in 100 nations and publishes literature in 20 languages. Headquarters in the U.S. are at the MRA center at Mackinac Island, Mich.; world headquarters are at Caux, Switzerland. There are also major centers in New York City, London, and Odawara, near Tokyo. The movement uses newspapers and magazines, advertisements, public rallies, television, motion pictures, books, youth organizations, and musical ensembles to spread its message.

Until recently RC authorities have been wary of Moral Re-Armament because they feared it fostered religious *indifferentism and *illuminism. On Aug. 8, 1951, the Holy Office (now Congregation for the Doctrine of the Faith) forbade priests and nuns from participating in MRA meetings and discouraged participation by lay Catholics. Individual national hierarchies and bishops have also banned RC participation, but this attitude has softened since the Vatican Council II. Some Catholics, such as Gabriel Marcel, Karl Adam, and Arnold Lunn, have warmly supported MRA and deny that the movement has the marks of a sect. See W. H. Clark, *Oxford Group: Its History and Significance* (1951); T. Driberg, *Mystery of Moral Re-Armament* (1961); A. Lunn, *Enigma: A Study of Moral Re-Armament* (1957).

MORAVIAN CHURCH, a body first organized in Bohemia as the Unitas Fratrum in 1457 and refounded in Saxony under the impulse of *Pietism in 1722. During its early history the group was also commonly known as the *Bohemian Brethren. The term "Moravian" was first used after its refounding and is largely confined to the English-speaking world. In Germany the Church is better known as Die Brueder Gemeine (Brüdergemeine), or as Herrnhuters. The original name, Unitas Fratrum, is still used throughout the world. Through Count *Zinzendorf (1700–60), a Pietist of means, the virtually extinct Unitas Fratrum began its second phase of history, becoming what Moravians refer to as the Renewed Moravian Church. Refugee Brethren from Moravia and Bohemia founded the village of *Herrnhut on Zinzendorf's estate in E Saxony in 1722. Within a decade it had become a rallying place for Pietists and the center of itinerant evangelism at home and mission work abroad. In 1735 a surviving bishop of the old Church consecrated the first bishop of the renewed Church; this was followed by reestablishment of the threefold ministerial orders: bishop, presbyter, and deacon. Under Zinzendorf the Moravians developed as a Pietist society within state Churches, and at the same time the desire of the refugees to perpetuate their Church prevailed. This gave Moravians in Europe the dual status of being both a denomination and a society, the latter known as the Diaspora. American development has been exclusively denominational.

The Church holds evangelical teachings common to Protestants and does not have a distinctively Moravian creed. Evidencing its Pietism, it emphasizes a life-centered, Christocentric faith. Guiding its members are doctrinal statements in its Book of Order, a catechism, and expressions of faith in its liturgies, esp. the one used at Easter (see EASTER LITANY). It has a liturgical form of worship, following to a modified degree the church year. German chorales have a prominent place in its hymnody. While the theological orientation of the Bohemian Brethren was *Reformed, that of the Church after Zinzendorf tends to be Lutheran. The Moravians pioneered missions and before the *Baptist Missionary Society (1793) had more missionaries than all other Protestants combined. They were indeed the first Protestant body to engage in missionary work unconnected with colonization and undertaken purely on its own account. They have specialized in missions to underprivileged peoples, Negroes, American Indians, and Eskimos. European centers are in Germany, Holland, Switzerland, Czechoslovakia, Denmark, Sweden and England. The Church is divided into 17 geographic provinces with government by *synod and conference. The episcopal office is not administrative, bps. being primarily spiritual leaders whose function is to ordain and to serve the whole Church as pastoral advisors. Former mission fields are moving toward autonomy beside the provinces in the U.S. and Europe. A world synod convenes every 10 years. World membership in 1968 was 350,000 in 1,100 congregations. See G. L. Gollin, *Moravians in the Two Worlds* (1967); K. G. Hamilton, *History of the Moravian Church* (1967); J. R. Weinlick, *Moravian Church through the Ages* (1966).

MORAVIAN CHURCH IN AMERICA, a part of the worldwide Moravian Church, with headquarters in Bethlehem, Pa., and Winston-Salem, North Carolina. The causes that brought Moravians to America were missions to the Indians, Count *Zinzendorf's attempts at church union in Pa., and the threat of suppression in Germany. An unsuccessful settlement in Ga. (1735) was followed by the establishment of Nazareth and Bethlehem in Pa. (1740–41); settlement in N.C. began in 1753. During the colonial period, residence in Moravian communities was restricted to church members. These communities were characterized by religious nurture, music, missionary outreach, handicraft industries, and boarding schools for the education not only of Moravian children but also of those coming from outside the community. Control from Europe stifled growth, and not until the mid-19th cent. did the Church in the

U.S. acquire the autonomy to launch an aggressive home-mission policy resulting in new churches among German immigrants in the East and among Germans and Scandinavians in the upper Midwest. The modern Moravian Church is a representative American Protestant Church with congregations in 18 states and in the Canadian Provinces of Alberta and British Columbia. The transition to the use of English in worship was almost complete by World War II. It is one of the founding members of the National Council of Churches and of the World Council of Churches. The Church has two girls' preparatory schools, a parochial school, a coeducational college, and a theological seminary in Pa. and a girls' preparatory school and a college for women in North Carolina. In 1968, it had 60,000 members in 160 congregations. See K. G. Hamilton, *History of the Moravian Church* (1967).

MORE, HENRY (1614–87), a Lincolnshire poet and theologian. Born in a Calvinistic home, he grew up to make no secret of his attachment to the sacramental life of the C of E at a time when this required courage. A fellow of Christ's College, Cambridge, he refused all preferment "from a pure love of contemplation and solitude, and because he thought he could do the Church of God greater service in a private than in a public office." In character both modest and firm, he was much loved for his ease with his friends and for his corporal works of mercy. Perhaps the foremost of the 17th-cent. band of *Cambridge Platonists, he was kept from pursuing the contemporary vogue for the occult by his piety and conviction that holiness was a way of knowledge. He was a voluminous writer; his best-known work is *Divine Dialogues, Containing Sundry Disquisitions and Instructions concerning the Attributes of God and His Providence in the World* (1668).

MORISONIANS, a group in Scotland organized in 1843 under the leadership of James Morison (1816–93), as the *Evangelical Union, in protest against strict Calvinist teaching on predestination.

MORMON, BOOK OF, see BOOK OF MORMON.

MORMONS, the members of the Church of Jesus Christ of *Latter-Day Saints. The *Book of Mormon is accepted by them as revelation.

MORONI, the name of the angel who, according to Mormon teaching, led Joseph Smith, Jr., to the golden plates, the source of the *Book of Mormon. *LATTER-DAY SAINTS, CHURCH OF JESUS CHRIST OF.

MORTALIUM ANIMOS, an encyclical letter of Pope Pius XI (Jan. 6, 1928) dealing with the *ecumenical movement as interpreted at that time by *Life and Work and *Faith and Order and explaining why Catholics could not take part in the *Lausanne Conference of 1927. The letter pointed out that Christian unity must be based on the acceptance of all revealed truths on the authority of God, that compromise in revealed doctrine is inadmissible, and that the one true Church cannot be composed of independent bodies holding conflicting doctrines. See AAS 20 (1928), 13ff.

MOTHER CHURCH, the First Church of Christ, Scientist, in Boston, Mass., organized by Mary Baker Eddy in 1892. It was established as the Mother Church of Christian Science, and all other churches of the denomination are regarded as branches of the parent vine. The Christian Science *Manual of the Mother Church declared that "In its relation to other Christian Science churches, in its By-laws and self-government, the Mother Church stands alone." Each branch church is regarded as an independent body, even when several are located in the same city, so that later organizations are as directly attached to the parent vine as are any of the earliest foundations, and each congregation depends directly on the Mother Church, rather than on any local or regional association.

MOTIF RESEARCH, a theological method associated esp. with the Swedish Lutheran theologians Gustaf *Aulén (1879–) and Anders *Nygren (1890–). In keeping with 20th-cent. reaction against *liberal theology (see DIALECTICAL THEOLOGY), this approach stresses man's incapacity to initiate a true relationship to God. The task of theology is to discern the motif or distinctive themes in various religious and theological traditions in order to set out the essentials of Christianity. Aulén finds the properly Christian motif in God's spontaneous forgiving love expressed by Christ's atoning death. Through historical study he seeks to show that Luther rediscovered this theme after the scholastics had interpreted Christ's act as a human response to God's justice. Nygren finds the motif in Judaism to be *nomos,* the law; in Greek religion, *eros,* the anthropocentric search for God as fulfilling man's desire; in true Christianity, *agape,* God's gracious, uncaused love reaching out to man. The Reformation reaffirmed *agape* as the sole ground for man's fellowship with God, and for Christian living, after Christianity's misrepresentation in scholasticism and the Renaissance as a religion of *nomos* or *eros.* See G. Aulén, *Christus Victor* (1948); idem, *Faith of the Church* (rev. ed., 1961); A. Nygren, *Agape and Eros* (tr. P. R. Watson, 1953); G. Weigel, *Survey of Protestant Theology in Our Day* (1954).

MOTT, JOHN RALEIGH (1865–1955), Methodist missionary leader and ecumenist. M. was born in Livingston Manor, New York. Educated at Upper Iowa and Cornell Univ., he became (1888) general secretary of student YMCA work and for 21 years was chairman of the Student Volunteer Movement for Foreign Missions. He also was chairman of the First World Missionary Conference at Edinburgh in 1910; this later became the *International Missionary Council, which he headed for many years. Spiritual father of the World Council of Churches, he was elected honorary chairman in 1948 and 1954. His addresses and papers were published (1946–47) in six volumes. Co-winner of the Nobel peace prize in 1946, he also received the Distinguished Service Medal from the U.S., and honors from 15 other countries. See G. M. Fisher, *J. R. M., Architect of Cooperation and Unity* (1952); HistAmMeth 3.

MRA, see MORAL RE-ARMAMENT.

MUGGLETON, LODOWICKE (1609–98), founder of a small millenarian sect, called Muggletonians. A tailor in London, M. was first an ardent Puritan, then he established his own group (1651) on the basis of a personal revelation that he and his cousin John Reeve (1608–58) were the two witnesses of Rev 11.3 and God's last messengers before Christ's second coming. M. was imprisoned for blasphemy (1660 and 1677) because of his denial of the Trinity. With Reeve he wrote down his bizarre revelations in the *Transcendant Spiritual Treatise* (1652). M. was an enemy of the Society of Friends. A few Muggletonians still survived as late as *c.*1870. See W. C. Braithwaite, *Beginnings of Quakerism* (2d ed., H. J. Cadbury, 1955).

MÜHLENBERG, HENRY MELCHIOR (1711–87), commonly designated "Patriarch of the Lutheran Church in America." A native of Eimbeck, Hannover, Ger., M. took up the study of theology in 1735 at the Univ. of Göttingen. After serving as a pastor at Grosshennersdorf, Upper Silesia (1739–41), M. accepted a call to the United Lutheran Congregations in Pennsylvania. He was officially recognized as the duly appointed pastor at Philadelphia in 1742. He traveled extensively through eastern Pa., preaching and administering the sacraments. After establishing and nurturing a large number of congregations, M. orga-

nized (1748) the Pennsylvania Ministerium, the first Lutheran *synod in the United States. In the years following he extended his work also into western Pa., N.J., and N.Y., and in later years visited the Lutheran churches in the South. He exercised a decisive influence on early Lutheranism all along the Atlantic seaboard. See W. J. Mann, *Life and Times of H. M. M.* (1911); T. G. Tappert and J. W. Doberstein, *Journals of H. M. M.* (3v., 1942–58).

MUHLENBERG, WILLIAM AUGUSTUS (1796–1877), priest and leader in the Protestant Episcopal Church. The great grandson of H. M. *Mühlenberg, M. was baptized a Lutheran but brought up as an Episcopalian. Graduating from the Univ. of Pennsylvania in 1815, he was ordained deacon in 1817 and priest in 1820. In his early career he became renowned as an educator through the schools he established on Long Island, New York. In 1846 he became rector of the Church of the Holy Communion, New York City. The parish had its own social agencies and initiated many practices that became general in the Episcopal Church, e.g., daily Offices, weekly Eucharist, emphasis on Holy Week. In 1850 he founded St. Luke's Hospital, and in 1852 a community of deaconesses, Sisters of the Holy Communion, to staff it. On a visit to England M. had come to know Pusey, Newman, and the *Oxford movement. He developed his own ideas of an "Evangelical Catholicism" and his influence was important in lessening tension between *high-church and *broad-church parties within his Church. He presented the so-called "Muhlenberg Memorial" to the *House of Bishops in 1853; although controversial, it did lead to the formation of the Commission on Church Unity and to liturgical reforms. See Olmstead, 318–320; A. Ayres, *Life and Work of W. A. M.* (1894).

MULLINS, EDGAR YOUNG (1860–1928), Baptist clergyman and teacher. After serving pastorates (1885–99), M. became president and professor of systematic theology at Southern Baptist Theological Seminary, Louisville, Ky. His administration was marked by expansion of the school, and his teaching and writings strongly influenced Southern Baptists. Elected president of their Convention (1921–24), he also served as president of the *Baptist World Alliance (1923–28). Presiding over the seminary in an era when theological tensions were mounting in American Protestantism, M. sought to avoid the extremes of rigid conservatism or liberal reductionism. Although retaining a framework of supernaturalism, he was greatly influenced by the personalism of B. P. *Bowne, and he made Christian experience central in his system. The objective facts of Christian revelation in history are corroborated by the Holy Spirit in the individual's experience, giving him a direct knowledge of God. *The Christian Religion in Its Doctrinal Expression* (1920) was the fullest elaboration of his approach. Closely related to his emphasis upon religious experience was an individualistic strain, which is reflected in *The Axioms of Religion* (1908). See W. A. Mueller, *History of Southern Baptist Seminary* (1959); Smith-Jamison 1:303–309.

MÜNZER, THOMAS (c.1489–1525), German radical Reformer. He was well educated and widely read in the mystics. Ordained a RC priest in 1513, he was a chaplain for nuns when he became acquainted with Luther c. 1519. He had already developed his own spiritualistic views of the Christian life, and radical social theories. With Nicholas Storch he was one of the *Zwickau Prophets who caused turmoil at Wittenberg (1521–22) with the message of inner spiritual experience and the establishment of a kingdom of the just by force. Driven out of Wittenberg, he tried to establish a new "Church of the Spirit" at Prague, writing the "Prague Manifesto," his program of reform and social change. His efforts failed; he returned to Germany and served (1523–24) as priest at the small town of Allstedt. There he made a translation of the liturgy into Ger-

man. He also began agitation for violent revolution to establish a new social order. He had to flee from Allstedt, and in Aug. 1524 became a preacher at Mülhausen in Thuringia. Between Feb. and May 1525 he was the chief agitator in the Peasants' War. When the peasants were defeated at Frankenhausen on May 15, he was captured; he was beheaded on May 27. He is said to have reaffirmed the RC faith before his death. M.'s theological position, never clear, is disputed by historians. Anabaptist scholars repudiate the title often given him, "father of Anabaptism." Modern socialists have been interested in his radical theories. See R. Friedman, MennEnc 3:785–789, with complete bibliog.; E. W. Gritsch, *Reformer without a Church* (1969).

MURRAY, JOHN COURTNEY (1904–67), Jesuit theologian, author, ecumenist, and chief architect of the *Declaration on Religious Liberty* (*Dignitatis Humanae*) of Vatican Council II. M. was born in New York City; he entered the Society of Jesus (1920), studied at St. Andrew-on-Hudson, Poughkeepsie, N.Y. (1920–24), at Weston College, Weston, Mass. (1924–27), and at Boston College (1927). He spent 3 years teaching Latin and English literature in the Philippines and returned to Woodstock College, Woodstock, Md., to study theology in 1930. He was ordained in 1933, and pursued further studies at the Gregorian Univ. in Rome (1934–36). He was then assigned to the Jesuit theology faculty in Woodstock, and remained on the faculty until his death. M.'s field of specialization in theology was the Trinity. During his studies, however, he became extremely interested in the problem of *Church and State and made himself an expert in this area. As early as 1945 he engaged in an extensive debate on the issue with two theologians at Catholic University, Joseph C. Fenton and Francis J. Connell. The debate was epoch making in American creative theology but resulted in M.'s receiving direction not to publish further on the Church-State issue without first clearing his writings with his superiors in

Rome. It is recognized, however, that his contribution to the Church-State issue was formative for later theological development and eventually culminated in his recognition as the outstanding American theological expert at Vatican Council II. He was not invited to the first session of the council since he was still somewhat under a cloud for his Church-State theories. However, Cardinal Spellman made him his personal theological expert at the remaining three sessions, and whatever suspicions may have lingered about M.'s orthodoxy were dispelled when he was chosen to be one of the concelebrants with Pope Paul VI of a Mass in the presence of the assembled council fathers.

In addition to his many articles in *Theological Studies*, of which he was the first editor-in-chief, a position he retained until his death, M. wrote several books, including: *We Hold These Truths* (1961); *The Problem of God:Yesterday and Today* (1964); and *The Problem of Religious Freedom* (pa., 1965). He edited *Freedom and Man* (1965) and *Religious Liberty: An End and a Beginning* (1966). For 2 years he was an associate editor of *America*, the weekly Jesuit magazine; he was twice visiting professor of medieval philosophy and culture at Yale. In his personal life, M. was a man of conservative habit who was known as the exemplar of what he liked to call the "tradition of civility." Of the *Declaration on Human Freedom*, M. himself wrote that it promised a new confidence in ecumenical relationships and a new straightforwardness in relationships between the Church and the world. See Thomas Bird, ed., *Modern Theologians: Christians and Jews* (1967), 18–39; T. T. Love, *J. C. M.: Contemporary Church-State Theory* (1965).

MYCONIUS, FRIEDRICH (1490–1546), German Reformer. Born in Upper Franconia, he attended Latin school in Annaberg and entered the Franciscan monastery there in 1510. Ordained in 1516 at Weimar, he was influenced by Luther to adopt Reformation views. In 1524 he became pas-

tor at Gotha, where he helped to order affairs according to evangelical patterns. While pastor at Gotha he took part in church visitations of Thuringia, attended the Marburg Colloquy (1529; see MARBURG ARTICLES), and participated in the *Hagenau Conference (1540). In 1538, he was one of the Lutherans sent to England to effect a rapprochement with leaders of the Reformation there. His chief written contribution was *Historia Reformationis, 1517–1542*.

MYCONIUS, OSWALD (1488–1552), Swiss Reformer. Born at Lucerne, educated at Basel, he became a teacher in Zurich in 1516, where he was influential in having *Zwingli called as pastor. M. soon moved to Lucerne, where he taught until 1522. Teaching briefly at Einsiedeln, he returned to Zurich, where he was an ardent supporter of Zwingli's reform program. In 1531, he became a pastor at Basel, succeeding *Oecolampadius there a year later. Until his death, M. was chief pastor of the city and professor of theology at the university. He finished the First Confession of *Basel begun by Oecolampadius before his death, and was one of the drafters of the First *Helvetic Confession (1536). He was also Zwingli's first biographer.

MYSTICISM, etymologically, from the Gr. verb *muo*, meaning to close the lips for silence and secrecy, in the context of the ancient mystery religions; in Christian tradition, the experience in which the believer arrives at a special kind of union with God. In this sense, Gerson defines mystical theology as a "knowledge of God by experience, arrived at through the embrace of unifying love." The knowledge arrived at in mystical experience has the same object as both natural and dogmatic theology, God. But whereas in "theodicy" the knowledge of God is achieved through the use of normal reasoning powers, and the knowledge of God is achieved in dogmatic theology by applying reasoning to the data of revelation, here the knowledge is more direct and less purely cerebral. Thus, a 13th-cent. commentator, Thomas Gallus, talks of a more profound and superintellectual manner of knowing God. The highest cognitive faculty, he says, is not the intellect; there is one far excelling this, called by him *principalis affectio*, which seems to mean the "high point of the soul" that is rather conative than cognitive. Sense-knowledge, imagination, and simple reasoning are all suspended. The mystic is drawn to God in a way analogous to, though immensely more spiritual than, the way in which a woman is drawn to her lover. Hence the frequency with which the language of human love is employed (e.g., by St. John of the Cross) to describe what is essentially an experience that is both unique and essentially incommunicable.

Non-Christian Mysticism. Although the present article is primarily concerned with Christian mysticism, it is necessary to recognize that there has been mystical experience outside that tradition. Indeed if believing with Augustine that man is made for God, and that his heart is restless until it comes to rest in God, one must expect to find evidence of such Godward striving in any authentic religious tradition. Thus in China an early teaching maintained that man's highest purpose was the quest for *Tao*, which was thought of as Ultimate Reality, source of all that is, pervading and harmonizing all natural phenomena. For man, *Tao* is the exemplar of moral perfection and man can realize himself only by some kind of identification with it. There are interesting parallels between the Chinese and Christian religions as to how this identification is achieved. In the words of Lao Tzu: "Only he who is forever free from earthly passions can apprehend the spiritual essence of *Tao.*" After this purgative phase comes the stage when the achievement of virtue is not a self-conscious, self-regarding effort but rather a connatural condition. Finally, man becomes the unresisting vehicle of *Tao*, so that he can rise above the limitations of matter and is no longer subject to the laws of the physical universe. At the same time in much Chinese speculation there is little

sense of religion as understood today, no sense of a personal relationship with God, or, it would seem, of any obligation to him. In fact the end of the Taoist mystical way seems to be the absorption into some pantheistic being. It is hardly surprising that to all intents Taoism became amalgamated with Buddhism. Of Hinduism it is unnecessary to mention more than the influence that Indian ideas had on the Greek tradition through Pythagoras, and hence on Plato and neoplatonism. Neoplatonic influence on the Christian tradition through Plotinus and Proclus, above all on Pseudo-Dionysius, who was the primary mystical authority for the medievals, is undeniable.

The Role of Grace. Christian writers agree that where genuine mystical experiences occur they are the direct result not of the efforts of the mystics themselves, though they must prepare themselves by purification, but of a special grace, over and above the ordinary graces given to all Christians. The turning away from what is not God in order to arrive at God himself may be the effect of such ordinary graces. Yet, already God's drawing to himself has already begun. Here one of the central problems in the whole discussion is encountered, cooperation between the soul and God. This is, of course, a special example of a larger problem.

Man is utterly dependent on God. This means that the roots of his being at a level deeper than consciousness are to be found in the being of God himself. Yet man's whole conscious life is passed in this space-time world. Moreover, because of original sin, the awareness of God that would seem connatural to man is fitful and obscure. It can be perfected, first by turning away from concentration on the space-time world and allowing the attraction of God to have its full effect. Precisely because so much of our conscious life is bound up with this world of sense-experience, the process of purgation is painful; hence the dark nights of senses and spirit in which the personality is detached from that total absorption in temporal and material reality that has become a permanent distraction from God. Hence the traditional insistence on the necessity for the *via negativa*, the attainment to some indirect knowledge of God by seeing him as the denial of all that is commonly felt or thought of by human beings in their normal cognitive processes. In this "cloud of unknowing" the mystic learns God by unlearning everything that is not God. Moreover, unlike the objects of normal thinking, God is not the passive object of the mystic's contemplative activity. Rather he is the active inspiration, the overwhelming Power to whom the mystic submits, freely and therefore not inertly. Surrender therefore becomes an immense enrichment simply because the knowledge and love of God is the consummation of man's purpose.

The Mystic's Knowledge of God. St. Thomas Aquinas developed what has become accepted as the classical explanation of what may be called the mechanics of the illumination that is an important element of the mystical experience. While human knowledge ordinarily begins with some sense-awareness, the intellect works to abstract from the colored shapes, sounds, feelings, scents, and tastes produced by chemical and physical interaction between an external object and the sense-organ the idea, or "concept," that is the specific object of normal, rational activity. By linking together these abstract ideas, the mind makes judgments; it reasons and infers. St. Thomas suggests that in the state of innocence preceding the Fall there may have been a way of knowing that began with an immediate conceptual activity without a previous stage of sensation and abstraction. Only by special divine help would man be able to abide permanently in such a purely spiritual form of intellection. Having lost that preternatural endowment, he is no longer capable of that direct intellectual awareness of God that, to be adequate,

must clearly be free from the distorting effects of imagery. God is pure spirit and cannot be described in language drawn from sense-experience. But there seems no reason why, in some cases and for special reasons, God should not confer a grace restoring a person temporarily to the state of perfection that man enjoyed before the Fall.

The foregoing remains nothing more than a theory, but it is as far as it goes a coherent explanation and a useful working hypothesis. It helps to understand why the mystic, after his experience, is invariably incapable of describing what has happened. Thus Augustine says: "Thy invisible things, understood by those that are made, I saw indeed but was unable to fix my gaze thereon. My weakness was beaten back and I was reduced to my ordinary experience" (*Conf.* 7.17). Recalling Gerson's definition, "knowledge of God arrived at through the embrace of unifying love," it might be suggested that in the mystic's experience there is complete coordination of will and intellect directed toward God, who is the perfect and adequate end of their activity. Hence it can be seen why the effect of mystical contemplation is not primarily an illumination of the mind but is chiefly a deepening of the whole personality, an enriching of character, a development of virtue.

See W. R. Inger, *Christian Mysticism* (1889); W. James, *Varieties of Religious Experience* (1902); A. F. Poulain, *Graces of Interior Prayer* (tr. L. L. Yorke, 1950); E. Underhill, *Mysticism* (12th ed. rev., pa., 1960); E. C. Butler, *Western Mysticism* (1922); F. von Hügel, *Mystical Element of Religion* (2v., 2d ed., 1923); R. Otto, *Mysticism, East and West* (tr. B. L. Bracey, 1932); D. Knowles, *English Mystical Tradition* (1961); F. C. Happold, *Mysticism: A Study and an Anthology* (1963), excellent bibliog.

N

NANTES, EDICT OF, see EDICT OF NANTES.

NATIONAL ASSEMBLY OF THE CHURCH OF ENGLAND, the formal title of what is ordinarily called the *Church Assembly, the main administrative agency of the Church of England.

NATIONAL ASSOCIATION OF CONGREGATIONAL CHRISTIAN CHURCHES, Churches that declined to participate in the merger that was to form the *United Church of Christ. The proposal to unite the Congregational Christian Churches with the Evangelical and Reformed Church seriously troubled some Congregationalists, who saw in the move a danger to cherished spiritual freedoms. In 1947 an organization called Anti-Merger was formed. Its members united with others in 1949 to create the Committee for the Continuation of Congregational Christian Churches in the U.S.A. In 1955 the committee united with the League to Uphold Congregational Principles to form the National Association of Congregational Christian Churches of the U.S. Formed to protest against and prevent union, the association, once the United Church of Christ had been formed (1957), became a fellowship of continuing Congregational Christian Churches. It did not itself participate in the legal actions taken by some of its member Churches to contest local decisions to enter the United Church. With a simple nonauthoritarian organization, the National Association has no corporate legal existence. It works through an annual meeting to which a number of commissions (Missions, Ministry, Youth, Publications, Women, and Christian Education) are answerable. Its officers, which include one executive secretary, are likewise responsible to the annual meeting. Since its formation the National Association has grown to about 200 member Churches, some being new foundations. It also supports mission work overseas. It has no theological seminary and does not of itself accredit ministers. In 1962 the National Association applied for membership in the *International Congregational Council. The application was denied on the ground that its relationship to the United Church of Christ had not been legally clarified.

NATIONAL ASSOCIATION OF EVANGELICALS, an association of American Protestant evangelistic denominations, Churches, organizations, and individuals united by a commonly accepted creed for the purpose of national identification, fellowship, and service in the field of *evangelism. The term evangelical in this context signifies one who is fundamentalist, conservative, and often Pentecostal in outlook; who holds to *evangelicalism as the necessary doctrine of salvation in Christ; and who practices evangelism as the communication of the gospel by which a person is led to make a commitment to Christ, dedicate himself to a Christian way of life, and become a vital member of a local church. Typical evangelicals are the members of the Assemblies of God, a Pentecostal missionary denomination that grew out of the spiritual revivals of the 1900s. Protesting against what they considered the "liberal," unbiblical, and non-Protestant policies of the *Federal Council of the Churches of Christ (1905–50), approximately 40 denominations and Churches adopted (1943) a constitution forming an association without legislative or executive control but based upon the Bible as the supreme authority in all matters of belief and conduct. Headquarters of the Association are located in Wheaton, Ill., with field offices in seven regions covering the United States. An Office of Public Affairs in Washington, D. C., fulfills the tasks of keeping a watch on federal legislation, of protesting against the infringement of religious liberties, and of advancing the cause of evangelicalism. Other organizations of the Association include: the National Sunday School Association, the Evangelical Foreign Missions Association, and National Religious Broadcasters. A monthly magazine, *United Evangelical Action*, is the official publication. See J. D. Murch, *Cooperation without Compromise* (1956); C. F. H. Henry, *Evangelical Responsibility in Contemporary Theology* (1957).

NATIONAL BAPTIST CONVENTION OF AMERICA, the second largest organization of Negro Baptists (2,668,000) in the U.S., organized in 1916; it withdrew from the National Baptist Convention, U.S.A., Inc., and its early history is that of the original body. The two are referred to as "Incorporated" and "Unincorporated." The schism resulted from a dispute over the National Baptist Publishing Board, which had been established under R. H. Boyd in 1896, separately incorporated in 1898, when it became an independent unit. Attempts to bring the publishing board under control of the Convention led to an unsuccessful lawsuit, and a large group favorable to the board's policies withdrew to constitute the National Baptist Convention of America, electing E. P. Jones president. It is organized with boards for home and foreign missions and for evangelism and education; commissions for benevolence, Christian education, social justice, and chaplaincies; and Junior and Senior Women's Auxiliaries, a National Brotherhood Union, and the Youth Convention. Meeting annually, the Convention comprises messengers from churches, associations, and state conventions who pay the stipulated dues. C. D. Pettaway was elected president in 1957. The Foreign Mission Board has fields in Africa, Haiti, Jamaica, and Panama with about 30 missionaries. The Education Board shares in the support of 10 colleges and seminaries. See R. H. Boyd, *Story of the National Publication Board* (1924); D. C. Woolley, ed., *Baptist Advance* (1964).

NATIONAL BAPTIST CONVENTION, U.S.A., INC., founded in 1895, the oldest and largest Negro Baptist body (5,500,000). Prior to the Civil War a number of Negro Baptist churches were constituted, but their large-scale growth began after that conflict as thousands of freedmen were attracted by the democratic freedom that characterized the Baptist denomination. Interest in missions in Africa gave impetus to the founding of early cooperative organizations. In 1880, by consolidation of numerous regional missionary organizations, W. W. Colley, a missionary to Africa, led in the formation of the Baptist Foreign Missionary Convention of the U.S.A. Next came the American National Baptist Convention in 1886 and the Baptist National Education Convention in 1893. These three organizations merged in 1895 at Atlanta, Ga., as the National Baptist Convention, U.S.A. Its purpose was "to do missionary work in the U.S.A., in Africa, and elsewhere, and to foster the cause of education." Beginning with home and foreign mission boards, in 1896 it added the National Baptist Publishing Board. Strife over control of this board led in 1916 to a schism. The parent body, incorporated in 1915, has been known as the National Baptist Convention, U.S.A., Inc., and its offspring as the *National Baptist Convention of America. The former body has shown strong interest in foreign missions. Its major mission has been in Liberia, where there are about 35 full-time, and several hundred part-time, missionaries; it operates a hospital and several schools. Other mission fields are in the Gold Coast, Sierra Leone, South and East Africa, the Bahama Islands, and Nicaragua. The Convention has also contributed to the work of education, with special interest in Shaw University (N.C.) and other colleges in the South. In 1924, the American Baptist Theological Seminary was established at Nashville, Tenn., offering both liberal arts and theological training. Its Sunday School Publishing Board is a flourishing concern. The Convention has membership in the National and World Councils of Churches and the Baptist World Alliance. The president,

Dr. J. H. Jackson, was admitted as a special observer at Vatican II when the Baptist World Alliance declined to send a representative. In 1961, after failure to effect changes in the Convention's officers, a large number of churches from 14 states withdrew to establish the *Progressive National Baptist Convention, Inc. See E. A. Freeman, "N. B. C., U.S.A., Inc.," *Baptist Advance* (ed. D. C. Woolley, 1964), 190–226; G. W. Lucas, "Negro Baptists Sail Stormy Sea," *Foundations* 4 (1961) 207–215; O. D. Pelt, *Story of the National Baptists* (1960).

NATIONAL BAPTIST EVANGELICAL Life and Soul Saving Assembly of U.S.A., a body of Negro Baptists that separated from the *National Baptist Convention in 1937, after existing as an evangelical agency within the parent organization since 1930. The assembly concerns itself primarily with relief and evangelistic work and states its teaching as "the Bible doctrine as announced by the Founder of the Church, Jesus Christ." General headquarters are in Detroit. The latest available statistics (1951) listed 57,674 members in 264 churches.

NATIONAL CHURCH, a Church officially recognized by a State and independent of control from outside that State. This phenomenon existed in the Eastern Orthodox Churches prior to the modern era, but the rise of national states and the Reformation introduced this system in W Europe. Foreshadowed in the Council of *Constance (1414–18), where representatives voted by nation, the national state idea was far advanced by 1500. Religious uniformity was considered requisite to political unity, and the Reformation offered a choice of religion. Hence there developed the principle of *cuius regio, eius religio*, allowing each prince to decide the religious character of his people. Consequently many national Churches supplanted the one visible Church of an earlier period. Instead of a single Lutheran Church, there were many autonomous Lutheran Churches in German territories and Scandinavian countries; regional *Reformed Churches existed in Switzerland, S Germany, and elsewhere. England had its own Church, as did Scotland. As political theory became more secularized, a spirit of toleration allowed for religious diversity within a particular state. National Churches have continued to be the rule in W Europe, however, although relations between Church and State are generally not as strong as formerly. In a strict sense, the term "national Church" does not apply to the RC Church, since recognition of the primacy of the pope precludes national autonomy. The U.S. was first to experiment without a national Church, and many modern democracies have followed its example.

NATIONAL CONFERENCE OF CHRISTIANS AND JEWS, an organization founded in the U.S. in 1928 to promote understanding, friendship, and cooperation among Jews, Protestants, and Roman Catholics. It grew out of a committee formed by the Federal Council of Churches to counteract the religious prejudice of the 1920s, esp. that of the 1928 presidential campaign. The Conference does not aim at religious *syncretism, nor does it approve of religious *indifferentism. Based on the Judaeo-Christian belief in the equality of all men, it aims at civic cooperation among men of varied religious, ethnic, and social backgrounds. The organization functions through three co-chairmen—one Jew, one Catholic, and one Protestant. Its officers are a president and an executive vice-president, a board of governors, and trustees. In 1966 it staffed 65 regional offices, each having three co-chairmen and a mixed board. The Conference cooperates closely with schools and colleges, labor and management, the police, community leaders, and clergymen. One of its best-known observances is National Brotherhood Week. Prominent among its techniques are workshops, discussions, and clergy dialogues. See J. E. Pitt, *Adventure in Brotherhood* (1955).

NATIONAL COUNCIL OF THE CHURCHES OF CHRIST in the U.S.A. (NCC), an organization of U.S. Churches to facilitate unity in fellowship, witness, and service. Main offices are in New York City. The NCC was established Nov. 29, 1950, in Cleveland, Ohio, as a successor to the *Federal Council of the Churches of Christ (founded 1908). It also incorporates and continues the work of several other organizations that had been established to further ecumenical cooperation in particular causes. The preamble to its constitution declares, "Under the providence of God, communions which confess Jesus Christ as Divine Lord and Savior, in order more fully to manifest oneness in Him, do now create an inclusive cooperative agency of Christian churches of the United States of America to show forth their unity and mission in specific ways and to bring the churches into living contact with one another for fellowship, study, and cooperative action." U. S. Churches were influenced by international developments in the ecumenical movement, and many of their leaders had participated in it. The NCC developed as an independent organization, but in friendly cooperation with the World Council of Churches.

The NCC has 30 member Churches, including all the larger bodies except the Southern Baptist Convention, the Lutheran Church—Missouri Synod, and the RC Church. The work of the NCC is directed by the triennial General Assembly, composed of about 800 delegates from the member Churches, and by the General Board, composed of 250 members elected by the General Assembly and meeting three times each year. The General Assembly elects the officers of the NCC: president, vice-presidents, treasurer, recording secretary, and general secretary. The latter, principal executive officer, directs the work of the full-time staff, which is organized into four divisions (Christian Life and Mission, Christian Education, Overseas Ministries, and Christian Unity) and three staff offices (Planning and Program, Communication, and Administration).

The NCC has received criticism from conservatives because its leadership has included some they regard as too liberal, on both doctrinal and social questions. The NCC and groups under its sponsorship have taken positions on economic, social, and foreign-policy issues that have been opposed by both conservative churchmen, clerical and lay, and by conservative politicians. Some opponents of the NCC who nonetheless favor ecumenical fellowship and interdenominational cooperation have formed the *National Association of Evangelicals (1942). Also, the *American Council of Christian Churches was formed under the leadership of Carl McIntire (1941). Any communion that accepts the nature and purpose of the NCC as set forth in the constitution is eligible for membership. Approval of membership is by two-thirds vote of the General Assembly. Various other organizations have established affiliate relationships with the NCC. The Constitution states, "The Council shall have no authority or administrative control over the churches which constitute its membership. It shall have no authority to prescribe a common creed, form of church government, or form of worship, or to limit the autonomy of the churches cooperating in it" (5.2).

The NCC sponsors conferences for study of various questions of Church and society; carries out projects of humanitarian service, including an extensive overseas ministry; publishes literature of various kinds; and seeks to develop a greater sense of unity and understanding among the Churches. It has adopted statements supporting the United Nations and the UN Universal Declaration of Human Rights, committing itself to "work for a nonsegregated church and a nonsegregated community," and affirming "the right of both employers and employees to organize for collective bargaining." It has pledged support to the public schools and to the separation of Church and State. It supports "the right and duty of the churches . . . to study and comment upon issues of human concern, however controversial." A 1968 policy statement recognizes civil disobedience as a "valid instrument for those who seek justice, consonant with both Christian tradition and the American political and legal heritage." The report to the 1966 General Assembly showed an annual budget of about $15 million, and some 700 employees. See A. W. Barstow, ed., *Christian Faith in Action* (1951); the reports to the triennial assemblies.

NATIONAL COVENANT, see SCOTTISH NATIONAL COVENANT.

NATIONAL DAVID SPIRITUAL TEMPLE OF CHRIST CHURCH UNION (Inc.), U.S.A., Pentecostal body organized in 1932 by a Baptist preacher, David William Short, at Kansas City, Missouri. Short rejected the other Churches because of their racial prejudice and *denominationalism and set up the true spiritual Church of Christ with the gifts, graces, and divisions of ministries indicated in St. Paul's descriptions of the NT Church. As divinely appointed overseer, Abp. Short relied solely upon the guidance of the Holy Spirit in directing the Church. Membership in 1965 was 40,815 in 66 churches; headquarters are in Los Angeles, California. See J. T. Nichol, *Pentecostalism* (1966), 132.

NATIONAL EVANGELICAL LUTHERAN CHURCH, a body that merged in 1964 with the *Lutheran Church—Missouri Synod. The National Evangelical Lutheran Church had been organized formally at Rock Springs, Wyo., in 1898 as the Finnish-American National Evangelical Lutheran Church, a name retained until 1946. The Church was founded mainly by Finnish immigrants. Their strong adherence to the Lutheran confessions was a tradition that prepared for the merger with the Missouri Synod. Membership in 1964 was about 10,000. See J. E. Nopola, EncLuthCh 3:1701–02.

NATIONAL FELLOWSHIP OF BRETHREN CHURCHES, one of the *Brethren Churches formed in 1939 when a large number withdrew from the *Brethren Church (Ashland, Ohio). The Fellowship is often referred to as the Grace Brethren or Grace Group. They hold, in common with other Brethren Churches: historic rites and sacraments of trine immersion, threefold communion of *footwashing, the Lord's Supper, and the Eucharist, and anointing the sick with oil. The Fellowship is strongly Calvinistic, evangelistic, and missionary. Its headquarters are in Winona Lake, Ind., where it maintains a college, a seminary, and publishing interests.

NATIONAL FRATERNAL COUNCIL OF CHURCHES, U.S.A., Inc., an association of predominantly Negro churches in the U.S., organized in 1952 on the model of the *National Council of Churches of Christ in the U.S.A. The African Methodist Episcopal (AME) Church, the African Methodist Episcopal Zion Church, and the Christian Methodist Episcopal Church are the principal members. Bishop Stephen L. Greene of the Second District of the AME Church has been the presiding officer of the National Fraternal Council since 1952. The association's headquarters are in Atlanta, Georgia.

NATIONAL HOLINESS ASSOCIATION, a coordinating agency, founded in 1867, of those religious bodies adhering to Wesleyan-Arminian doctrines. Headquarters are located in Marion, Indiana. *HOLINESS CHURCHES.

NATIONAL LUTHERAN COUNCIL, an organization formed in 1918 for cooperation of several Lutheran bodies in missions, social welfare, and other projects. In 1966 it was succeeded by the *Lutheran Council in the U.S.A., an agency of expanded membership and scope.

NATIONAL PRIMITIVE BAPTIST CON-VENTION, INC., a body of Negro Baptists organized in 1907 at Huntsville, Alabama. In 1968 it reported a membership of 1,225,-000 in 1,876 churches. "Primitive" in the name does not have the same separatistic connotation that it has among other Baptist groups (see PRIMITIVE BAPTISTS); on the contrary, this group is very active in its support of youth work, Christian education, publications, and missions. A radical congregationalism was advocated from the first that reduces the role of the *convention to an exclusively advisory function.

NATIONAL SPIRITUAL ALLIANCE OF THE U.S.A., one of the smaller groups of Spiritualist churches; in 1968 it reported 30 affiliated congregations with an aggregate membership of 3,212. This association was founded in 1913 by G. Tabor Thompson. It acts as a unifying force and as a central agency to ensure that ministers and mediums meet the educational and moral standards of the denomination. Otherwise its member churches are completely autonomous and *congregational in polity. Delegates from the member churches meeting in annual convention select the national officers and determine national policy. The national body directs missionary work and the course of study required of ministerial candidates. Headquarters of the National Spiritual Alliance of the U.S.A. are located at Keene, New Hampshire. Both ministers and mediums must be certified by the national body; mediums are permitted to baptize and conduct services, but only ministers may officiate at marriages or ordinations. Doctrine is the same as in other Spiritualist groups, with a deliberate effort to make creedal statements quite general.

NATIONAL SPIRITUALIST ASSOCIATION OF CHURCHES, oldest and most influential of the Spiritualist groups, founded in 1893 at Chicago. Its purpose is to give a unifying factor to an otherwise loosely organized movement by establishing standards for the ordination of ministers and mediums and by chartering local churches. It maintains the Morris Pratt Institute in Wisconsin for the training of ministers, mainly by correspondence courses, and directs other training courses for its members, lecturers, licentiates, and mediums. It also acts as a central publishing house for the Spiritualist movement, publishing the monthly *National Spiritualist* and other books and pamphlets. It issues *The Spiritualist Manual,* which is widely used in worship services; Spiritualist services usually consist of a reading from the *Manual,* pastoral prayer, sermon, and messages from the spirit world delivered by a medium. While each of its affiliate churches preserves complete autonomy, the tendency of the National Spiritualist Association is to stress the role of Spiritualism as a religious denomination. Many of its affiliates separate contact with the spirits from the regular worship service. They subscribe to a doctrinal statement, embodying belief that God is Infinite Intelligence, that God is in every living thing, that man survives apparent death and can communicate from beyond the grave, that man has moral responsibility and must obey the laws of nature to be happy in this world and the next.

NATIVISM, a recurrent feature of American life that has included an intense dislike and fear of the foreign-born and a particular hostility toward Catholics. By 1850 the RC Church in the U.S. had mushroomed to more than 1½ million, including about 700,-000 immigrants who were the special target of nativist fury. Not infrequently the acrimony of anti-Catholic attacks by revivalistic preachers and nativist magazines, newspapers, pamphlets, and books overflowed into mob violence. Depredations were made against Catholic property and lives, as in the burning (1834) of the Ursuline Convent at Charlestown, Mass., and the riots (1844) in Philadelphia and New York City. Successive waves of popular hysteria swept many sections of the country over domestic issues, such as the Catholic protest against use of the Authorized (King James) Version of the Bible in public schools and the demand for public aid to parochial schools, and foreign developments, such as *Catholic emancipation in Great Britain and the restoration of the English hierarchy.

Nativism found political expression in the *Know-Nothing movement of the 1850s, which became a factor in national politics and enjoyed considerable success in some states and cities. The Civil War temporarily silenced these forces of bigotry, but in the 1880s increased immigration and concern over the growing political strength of Catholics led to a new wave of nativism. The *American Protective Association (APA), founded (1887) at Clinton, Iowa, by Henry F. Bowers and his associates, both fed upon and generated the old fear that Roman Catholicism was part of an international conspiracy to subvert the free institutions of America. Unsuccessful in influencing national politics, the APA gradually withered away after a decade of spreading religious intolerance. Xenophobia, however, continued to thrive in American society, and a revived *Ku Klux Klan grew rapidly, esp. in the South and West, viciously attacking Negroes, Jews, Catholics, and all foreign-born. Its program of terrorism not only spread fear among minorities but also enabled the Klan to gain political control in several states, notably Indiana. Its decline after 1925 was due largely to internal corruption. In 1921 nativist demands for the restriction of immigration were supported by the fear of an alien flood from war-devastated Europe, and Congress responded with a measure radically altering U.S. immigration policy. The quota system that ensued not only reduced immigration to a trickle but also discriminated against aliens from southern and eastern Europe. Thereafter, sporadic attacks by latter-day nativists were directed against internal minority groups, such as Catholics (until after the election of John F. Kennedy in 1960), Negroes, Jews, Communists, and during World War II, Japanese-Americans.

See R. A. Billington, *Protestant Crusade, 1800–1860* (1938); D. L. Kinzer, *Episode in Anti-Catholicism: The American Protective Association* (1964); T. T. McAvoy, *Roman Catholicism and the American Way of Life* (1960).

NATURAL THEOLOGY, a philosophic inquiry leading to conclusions concerning the existence and attributes of God. Called "natural" from its sole reliance on the powers of unaided reason, it differs from theology in the ordinary Christian sense, which is based on revealed truths accepted by the grace of faith. Since the philosopher Gottfried Leibniz (1646–1716), natural theology has also been called "theodicy," i.e., a reasoned defense, or apologia, for the truth of God's existence and providence.

The highest speculations of ancient philosophers, esp. Plato and Aristotle, about a transcendent, divine being are cited as examples of natural theology. In Christian thought the basis for a natural theology was made explicit in the Middle Ages, when clear distinctions were drawn between nature and grace, between truths knowable by the unaided human mind and truths knowable only through divine revelation. St. Thomas Aquinas (c.1225–74) drew these distinctions most precisely, defended the possibility of a conclusive proof of God's existence through reasoned reflection on facts of ordinary experience, and proposed such proofs in his *quinque viae,* or "five ways" (ThAq ST 1a, 2.1–3). While there has been a recurrent skepticism, even among the late medievals, e.g., William of Ockham (c.1300–c.1349), about any natural knowledge of God, there has been a strong RC natural theology tradition, aimed at showing that the findings of reason correspond to Christian belief in one God. In the 19th cent. Vatican Council I proposed as official church teaching, esp. against *fideism, the capacity of the human mind to acquire certitude about God's existence (D 3026). Beginning in the mid-19th cent. there was a renewed attempt at a natural theology based on Aquinas's indications;

there were, however, widely diverse interpretations within Neo-Thomism. Since World War II and the growing abandonment of Thomistic metaphysics, new approaches, based upon contemporary philosophical viewpoints, have been sought.

Reformation teaching, while acknowledging the theoretical possibility of man's having some natural knowledge about God, minimized it and asserted that because of human depravity only the revelation that came through Christ will save man from turning away from all evidence of God (see TOTAL DEPRAVITY). Nevertheless various forms of natural theology were developed by religiously inspired Protestant thinkers. For example, Christian Wolff (1679–1754), adapting the principles of Leibniz, produced a highly rationalistic system of philosophy, a key part of which was a natural theology. The Wolffian system became the target of Immanuel Kant (1724–1804), whose critique was directed against the possibility of any metaphysics and the validity of any reasoned proof that God exists. Kant's attack, and later that of linguistic analysis, led to a loss of confidence by many RC as well as Protestant thinkers in any empirically based knowledge about God. In the 20th cent. natural theology has been attacked most sharply by Karl *Barth (1886–1968) on theological grounds. As a reaction to *liberal theology, which naturalized all theology, Barth reasserted fundamental Reformation teaching. God is knowable and known only through the revelation given in Christ; man, because of his sinfulness, is totally incapable of knowing God by his natural powers. Barth's colleague, E. *Brunner (1889–1966), opposed him in this, holding that a limited place for a natural theology was allowed by both the Bible and Reformation teaching.

Two issues are involved for the Christian in the relevance of any natural theology. Its philosophical validity presupposes the capacity of the mind to know objective truth and to pass from immediate experience to a cause beyond experience. Its value to Christian life is limited; a natural theology may serve to show the reasonableness of theism, but it remains an indirect and inferential knowledge; only grace gives knowledge of God himself and a personal relationship with him. See D. Allen, *Reasonableness of Faith* (1968), with bibliog.; T. C. O'Brien, *Metaphysics and the Existence of God* (1960), with bibliog.

NAUSEA, FRIEDRICH (Grau; 1490–1552), promoter of church reunion, bp. of Vienna. As secretary to the papal legate Card. L. *Campeggio, N. attended the Diet of Nuremberg. In 1525 he became a canon of Frankfurt am Main but was driven out by the Lutherans. Named preacher of the Mainz Cathedral (1526) and court preacher to King Ferdinand (1534), he was appointed coadjutor to the bp. of Vienna (1538) and succeeded him as bp. 3 years later. N. worked actively for the reunion of the Lutherans and Catholics, joined with certain other prelates in petitioning Rome to permit the clergy to marry and the laity to receive *communion under both kinds, and helped in the preparations for the Council of Trent, where his attendance was cut short by death.

NAYLER, JAMES (*c.*1618–60), early Quaker leader. A retired soldier, N. met G. *Fox in 1651, embraced *Inner Light belief, and became Fox's friend and near peer as leader of the Quaker movement. Certain women in London from 1655 began to worship him as a new Jesus, and N. allowed them to stage his "triumphal entry" into Bristol (1656). He was arrested, and in a clamorous trial by Parliament, he was found guilty of blasphemy, sentenced to the cruelest punishments, and imprisoned. Throughout the episode, Fox sternly condemned N. as an enemy of the light; the two were not reconciled until 1660, a year after N.'s release. The affair led Fox to exercise greater control against the recurrence of misguided appeals to the Inner Light. See E. Foegelklou, *J. N., the Rebel Saint* (1931); R. Knox, *Enthusiasm* (1950), 160–166; V. Noble, *Man in Leather Breeches* (1953), 108–143.

NAZARENE, CHURCH OF THE, see CHURCH OF THE NAZARENE.

NAZARENE MANUAL, both a historical document and a handbook for ready reference in all matters pertaining to the life and service of the *Church of the Nazarene. It contains a brief history of the Church, a summary of doctrine, standards of practical ethics, outlines of basic church polity, and detailed procedures of church government. The *Manual* may be amended each 4 years by the General Assembly, which is the supreme lawmaking body of the Church. New editions are regularly published each 4 years, as authorized by succeeding General Assemblies of the Church. The *Manual* is published with the suggestion that "adherence to its regulations will make for cooperative and effective service throughout the church."

NEALE, JOHN MASON (1818–66), author and hymnologist. Scholar of Trinity College, Cambridge, he was an outstanding classicist. He joined the high-church movement in Cambridge and was one of the founders of the Camden Society for the study of ecclesiastical art, an organization important to the 19th-cent. liturgical life of the Church of England. From 1846 he was warden of Sackville College, East Grinstead, the only preferment he ever held; the diocesan exceeded his prerogatives and denounced the chapel ornaments as "fripperies" and "spiritual haberdashery." N. founded (1854) the Sisterhood of St. Margaret, with a rule patterned on those of the Visitation nuns and the Daughters of Charity. A voluminous writer of theology, ecclesiology, and fiction, he won his greatest fame as a liturgiologist. By his contributions, both translations and original compositions, he exerted a lasting influence on Anglican worship. Among his other works were a *Commentary on the Psalms* (4v., 1860–74) and *History of the Holy Eastern Church* (5v., 1847–73), as well as several series of sermons, and devotional writings for children.

NEANDER, JOHANN AUGUST WILHELM (1789–1850), German church historian. Until his conversion to Protestantism from Judaism, he was called David Mendel. His conversion and much of his intellectual formation were influenced by F. *Schleiermacher, whose colleague he became at Berlin in 1813. There he lectured for the remainder of his life on church history and NT exegesis. Besides works on Julian the Apostate (1812), St. Bernard of Clairvaux (1813), Gnosticism (1818), and Tertullian (1824), he published a major work, *Allgemeine Geschichte der christlichen Religion und Kirke* (6v., 1825–52; Eng. tr. J. Torrey, *General History of the Christian Religion and Church*, 5v., 1882). N. conceived of the history of Christianity as evidence of the intervention of the divine into the human, first fully in the life of Christ, then in the lives of individual Christians, which reflected the life of Christ. His portrayal minimizes doctrine and ecclesiastical institutions in favor of a Christianity that has developed as Christ animated the lives of individual Christians. See EncRelKnow 8:95–96.

NEO-CALVINISM, a description sometimes applied to the theological movement led by Karl *Barth. One aspect of this 20th-cent. reaction against *liberal theology was a return to Reformation sources and viewpoints, which in the case of Barth and others of the *Reformed tradition meant a return to John Calvin's thought. The term Neo-Calvinism also suggests that the renewal was not merely a repristination but a new interpretation in the light of the original Reformation insights, esp. regarding the word of God. *NEO-ORTHODOXY; *CRISIS THEOLOGY; *DIALECTICAL THEOLOGY.

NEO-ORTHODOXY, a name given to a Protestant, and dominantly *Reformed, theological movement of the 20th century. Neo-orthodoxy embraces a range of teachings, which have in common the rejection of *liberal theology. The term has a particular reference to the thought of Karl *Barth (see CRISIS THEOLOGY, DIALECTICAL THE-OLOGY), but it is also applied to that of P. *Tillich, R. *Niebuhr, and others. Through translations of the works of Barth and S. *Kierkegaard, much theological effort in the U.S. after 1930 came to be called neo-orthodox. The movement is called "orthodoxy" in the sense that it marks a return to primary themes of the historic Reformation, esp. the impotence of man to attain God, the *total depravity of his nature, and the need for divine grace and pardon. The movement is "new" both in contrast to liberalism and in its reliance on modern thought and discoveries. Neo-orthodox theologians, for example, have not hesitated to employ methods of biblical criticism that were developed in a rationalistic context. See Smith-Jamison 1:309–317; J. Macquarrie, *Twentieth Century Religious Thought* (1963).

NEO-PENTECOSTALISM, the cultivation of the Pentecostal experience outside classical *Pentecostalism, by members of the historic Churches. This interest began among Protestants, c.1955, occurring within Episcopalian, Lutheran, Baptist, Methodist, Reformed, and Presbyterian Churches, and has often met with official disapproval. Pentecostalism among Roman Catholics became widespread and publicized c.1967. Neo-Pentecostalism, unlike classical Pentecostalism, did not begin among the socially and culturally deprived. Its spread is regarded as a sign not simply of an interest in *glossolalia, or even in the charismatic rather than the institutional Church, but of a desire for the immediate experience of the divine promised by the Pentecostal experience. See *FULL GOSPEL BUSINESSMEN'S FELLOWSHIP INTERNATIONAL.

NEO-PROTESTANTISM, a term used particularly by Karl *Barth to describe a type of Protestant thought exemplified by F. *Schleiermacher (1768–1834). In general it may be equated with Protestant liberalism

and is distinguished from Reformation Protestantism and the succeeding *neo-orthodoxy by its shift from objective authority to subjective religious criteria. Barth traced it back to Lutheran and *Reformed theologians from c.1700 and saw its ancestors in *Arminianism and the humanists and radicals of the Reformation period. Later representatives include A. *Ritschl (1822–89) and A. *Harnack (1851–1930). The movement did not give rise to a separate denomination but cut across various Protestant groups. Barth's theology and the movement generally termed neo-orthodox or neo-Reformation theology was a 20th-cent. reaction, opposing Schleiermacher and his divergence from what is considered the authentic Protestantism of Luther and Calvin. Barth particularly opposed liberalism's openness to natural theology, and therefore saw it as standing alongside Roman Catholicism in opposition to the biblical theology of the Reformation. See K. Barth, *Church Dogmatics*, 1.2 (1938). *LIBERAL THEOLOGY.

NETHERLANDS REFORMED CONGREGATIONS, one of the smallest of the *Reformed Churches in the U.S., with 15 churches and about 3,000 members (1965). The original members represented a secession from the *state Church (Reformed) of the Netherlands. A church was formed in South Holland, Ill., in 1865 and one in Grand Rapids, Mich., in 1870. The present body dates from 1907. In addition to the congregations in the U.S., there are nine in Canada. *Doctrinal standards are the *Heidelberg Catechism, the *Belgic Confession, and the canons of the Synod of *Dort. The polity is presbyterian; a synod meets every third year.

NEVIN, JOHN WILLIAMSON (1803–86), American theologian who, with P. *Schaff, developed the *Mercersburg theology. N. was a student of A. *Alexander and C. *Hodge at Princeton Theological Seminary and in 1830 became professor of biblical literature at Western Theological Seminary, Pittsburgh. He resigned in 1840 to accept a call to the German Reformed Seminary at Mercersburg, Pennsylvania. In 1844 N. published *The Anxious Bench*, which, with Schaff's *The Principle of Protestantism*, translated by N. in 1845, marked the beginning of the Mercersburg movement for a return to the true history of the Church and to the Reformation heritage, a reaction against the disregard of confessional traditions that was characteristic of *revivalism. In *The Mystical Presence* (1846) he stressed the central place in the life of the Church that Calvin had given to the Eucharist and that was unappreciated by the American denominations. N. also wrote on the *Heidelberg Catechism and on the nature of the Church. With Schaff in 1849 he founded the *Mercersburg Review*. In 1861 he accepted a professorship at Franklin and Marshall College, Lancaster, Pa.; he became its president in 1866. See T. Appel, *Life and Work of J. W. N.* (1889); J. H. Nichols, *Romanticism in American Theology* (1961).

NEW APOSTOLIC CHURCH, a body established in Germany (1865) as the result of a dispute in the *Catholic Apostolic Church. The death of many original apostles of the parent Church led certain leaders at Hamburg in the 1860s to insist on choosing successors. This was incompatible with Catholic Apostolic teaching; the proponents were excommunicated, and formed the Universal Christian Apostolic Mission in 1865, renamed the New Apostolic Church in 1906. All the basic characteristics of the Catholic Apostolic Church were retained in the articles of belief of the new Church, but RC accretions to these teachings were suppressed. Only three Sacraments, baptism, holy communion, and sealing (confirmation, understood as the reception of assurance of salvation) were recognized. All three could be administered by proxy to the dead (see BAPTISM FOR THE DEAD). Auricular confession was suppressed. The Bible was only one rule of faith; the other was revelation to the Apostles of this Church, esp. the Chief Apostle (*Stammapostel*): Fritz Krebs (d. 1905) originated this office; his successors made it one of absolute authority and indispensable mediatorship with God. One, J. G. Bischoff (d. 1960), solemnly proclaimed in 1951 that he would live until Christ's second coming. The ensuing series of schisms resulting in many splinter Churches has continued since. Another break occurred in 1956 over the rejection by some of the Apostles of sacraments for the dead.

Worship is similar to that of Calvinist bodies, with none of the ceremonies and symbolism of the Catholic Apostolic Church. The New Apostolic Church is highly organized, with Chief Apostle, district apostles, deputy apostles, bishops, district elders, pastors, priests, and subdeacons. About four-fifths of the members live in Germany. The Church was introduced into the U.S. in 1901 by German immigrants, where its official title is the New Apostolic Church of North America; headquarters are in Chicago, Illinois. There were *c.*20,000 members in 176 congregations in 1967. The Church also has communities in Switzerland, Holland, France, England, Canada, Australia, South Africa, and South America; in most of these countries the splinter groups are also represented. See K. Algermissen, *Christian Sects* (1962), 25–34; Gründler 2:947–948.

NEW APOSTOLIC CHURCH OF NORTH AMERICA, the American branch of the *New Apostolic Church, which spread to America from Germany early in its history. In 1967 membership numbered approximately 20,000, in 176 congregations.

NEW CHURCH, a designation for the *Church of the New Jerusalem, often used in the title of its local congregations. The usage stems from the fact that the founder, E. *Swedenborg, was convinced that he was called upon to begin a "New Church."

NEW CONGREGATIONAL METHODIST CHURCH, a small denomination formed by Methodists in Georgia and Florida in 1881. They withdrew from the Methodist Episcopal Church, South, in protest over centralization of polity. Methodist in belief, the Church emphasizes the independence of the local congregation and rejects episcopacy; it also adopted the non-Methodist observance of footwashing. The last reported membership (1958) was 518, in eleven churches. See HistAmMeth 3:594.

NEW DELHI ASSEMBLY, third general assembly of the World Council of Churches (WCC), Nov. 19–Dec. 5, 1961, with 577 delegates representing 181 Churches, plus advisers, staff, observers, and visitors. The theme of the Assembly was "Jesus Christ, the Light of the World." The RC Church was officially represented for the first time at a WCC general assembly, sending five official observers. The membership of the WCC was enlarged with the addition of 23 Churches, including the Patriarchate of Moscow and two Pentecostal Churches of Chile. The doctrinal basis of the WCC was expanded from the *Amsterdam Assembly formula, "churches which accept our Lord Jesus Christ as God and Savior," to "churches which confess the Lord Jesus Christ as God and Savior according to the Scriptures and therefore seek to fulfill together their common calling to the glory of the one God, Father, Son, and Holy Spirit." This change was made to emphasize a more dynamic concept of faith (changing "accept" to "confess"), to evidence deeper roots in the Christian tradition (reference to the Scriptures and the Trinity), and to stress the mission of the Church ("calling"). Essentials to Christian unity were also enunciated. This was the first assembly to meet in the geographical area of the younger Churches, and the WCC became more conscious of their role. The *International Missionary Council merged with the WCC, becoming its Commission on World Mission and Evangelism. See W. A. Visser 't Hooft, ed., *New Delhi Report* (1962).

NEW ENGLAND THEOLOGY, system of modified Calvinistic thought that originated from the works of Jonathan *Edwards, Sr., and flourished among New England *Congregationalists from the mid-18th to the late 19th century. Joseph Bellamy and Samuel Hopkins promoted, with variations, the themes of Edwards's major treatises, as did Jonathan Edwards, Jr. (1745–1801), Nathaniel Emmons (1745–1840), and Nathaniel *Taylor (see NEW HAVEN THEOLOGY). Edward A. Park (1808–1900) of Andover Theological Seminary was its last defender. The New England theology wrestled with the problems of human depravity, the freedom of the will, the nature of virtue, and immortality. The system centered in the sovereignty of God, a doctrine crucial to the senior Edwards's treatises on the freedom of the will, original sin, and true virtue. In denying the freedom of choice but not of action, stressing human depravity, and describing true virtue as the act of cordial consent of beings to Being in General, he had shown the complete dominance of God over all reality. His successors discussed the possibility of moral agents' exercising choice as to their fate in a world governed by, and expressive of, the divine will and attempted to prove that human responsibility remained. They sought to show how sin contributed to the good of the whole, and how benevolence was possible. The New England theology challenged the emerging liberalism of the Unitarians and Universalists. It also influenced the establishment of Andover, Hartford, and Yale Seminaries, and fostered foreign missions, antislavery sentiment, and other social reforms. See G. N. Boardman, *New England Theology* (1899); F. H. Foster, *Genetic History of the New England Theology* (1907).

NEW EVANGELICALISM (Neo-Evangelicalism), movement to strengthen conservative Christianity in the United States. In 1954, H. J. Ockenga (*Bulletin of Fuller Theological Seminary*) pronounced *fundamentalism a failure and asserted that "new evangelicals" would combine traditional orthodoxy with social conscience and scholarship. J. H. Carnell, also of Fuller Seminary, was a proponent of New Evangelicalism. His colleague, C. H. F. Henry, left Fuller Seminary in 1957 to edit the newly founded fortnightly, *Christianity Today*; through this publication, as well as by lectures and books, he became a leading spokesman for *evangelicals (a term more often used than "Neo-" or "New"). Also associated with the movement have been Billy *Graham and numerous preachers, teachers, and business men. Emphasizing basic Christian doctrines, Evangelicals have stressed the authoritative and inerrant Scriptures as the word of God. They have tried to unite evangelicals of many denominations, to promote evangelism, to deal with social issues, to produce scholarly literature, and to deal with a wide range of theological concerns. See M. Erickson, *New Evangelical Theology* (1968); R. H. Nash, *New Evangelicalism* (1968).

NEW HAMPSHIRE CONFESSION OF FAITH, a Baptist confession written in 1832 that soon superseded the *Philadelphia Confession. Originally drafted at the instigation of the New Hampshire Baptist Convention, it was recommended by the board of that body for use in the churches. In 1853, J. Newton Brown, who had helped draft the document, became editorial secretary of the American Baptist Publication Society, and he published the Confession with slight revisions in *Baptist Church Manual,* thus giving it wide circulation. Many Churches adopted it. In length it was a little over one-tenth that of the Philadelphia Confession, and its content reflected the modified Calvinism that was becoming prevalent. In accord with the revivalistic spirit of the Churches, it encouraged "the use of means in the highest degree." Reference to "eternal decrees" was omitted, as were other characteristic emphases of predestinarian theology. Very conspicuous was the absence of any reference to the "Universal Church." Because of this omission, it ap-

pealed to Landmarkists, whose churches and associations made it their standard (see LANDMARKISM). By the 20th cent. Baptists made less use of confessional statements than formerly. The Northern Baptist Convention voted against adoption of the New Hampshire Confession in 1922, claiming the NT as its only creed. The *Southern Baptist Convention (1925) published the Confession in modified form and recommended it to the churches. The *General Association of Regular Baptists, in 1933, adopted it with a premillennial interpretation of its article on eschatology. See W. L. Lumpkin, ed., *Baptist Confessions of Faith* (1959).

NEW HAVEN THEOLOGY, also called the New Divinity, a view that developed at Yale Divinity School principally under N. W. *Taylor, and that modified traditional Calvinism on the crucial points of the *total depravity of human nature and man's freedom of choice. The *Second Great Awakening in Conn. began with a revival at Yale in 1802 and a notable series of chapel sermons delivered by Timothy *Dwight. Under his leadership, Congregationalism moved imperceptibly into the revivalist camp. He had a marked influence on both Lyman *Beecher and N. W. Taylor. As the revival became accepted in New England Congregational circles, preachers sought to provoke a revival by utilizing means calculated to bring their hearers to a decision. The successful use of revivals as a means of bringing reborn Christians into the Church created problems for theologians in the Calvinist tradition and required the rethinking of key issues. In his 1819 sermon on "Salvation Free to the Willing," Taylor wrestled with fundamental problems of the Christian life. His more famous *Concio ad clerum* in 1828 brought a clear statement of Taylor's views on the depravity of human nature. He denied that it was a propensity in human nature, but said it was rather man's own act consisting of a free choice of some object other than God as his chief good. Taylor and his Yale associates believed that they were presenting the true meaning of the Calvinist tradition, but conservatives were scandalized. The New Haven school drew much of its inspiration from the *New England theology of Jonathan *Edwards and Samuel *Hopkins, as did its detractors. The New Divinity exponents sought to make a statement that would save both the fact that the work of regeneration was entirely God's work and the fact that God could not be considered the cause of sin in his creatures. Their ideas were put into practice by Charles G. *Finney, whose *Lectures on Revivals of Religion* was grounded in the New Haven theology. The opposition of conservative Calvinists, esp. C. *Hodge and his Princeton colleagues, to the New Haven teachings was a contributing factor in the breakdown of the Congregational–Presbyterian *Plan of Union in 1837. The stress placed by Taylor and his school on disinterested benevolence as an effect of a true Christian conversion contributed to the growth of charitable, missionary, and social reform movements in 19th-cent. America. See S. E. Mead, *Nathaniel William Taylor* (1942); C. R. Keller, *Second Great Awakening in Connecticut* (1942); W. G. McLoughlin, ed., *Lectures on Revivals of Religion* (1960); Smith-Jamison 1:254–260.

NEW LEARNING, a term sometimes used interchangeably with Renaissance humanism. It is humanism translated into an educational program, as contrasted with the old learning, i.e., *scholasticism. Renaissance humanism begins effectively with Francesco Petrarch (1304–74), but its orientation toward education had its roots in the ancient Roman Quintilian. The Renaissance program of formal education was developed by such humanists as Guarino da Verona (1374–1460) and Vittorino da Feltre (1378–1446). This involved the revival of Cicero's *studia humanitatis*, i.e., the humanities, with a stress upon Greek and Latin literature and grammar, rhetoric, oratory, history, and moral philosophy. It was optimistic and practical, its objective being to train young men for service in Church and State. The New Learning had a profound impact upon education for centuries. See W. W. Woodward, *Vittorino da Feltre and Other Humanist Educators* (1912). *HUMANISM; *RENAISSANCE.

NEW LIGHTS, a designation with two principal uses in church history: (1) In Scotland, among Presbyterians, the *Burghers in 1799 and the *Anti-Burghers in 1806 were both split into Old Light (the Auld Lichts) and New Light factions, the second insisting that the State have no power in church affairs. In the U.S. Presbyterians of Scottish background in the Reformed Presbyterian Church split in 1833 into New Lights, who allowed members to participate in civil affairs, and Old Lights, who refused such participation. (2) In the *Great Awakening, those Baptists and also Congregationalists favoring the methods of revivalism were called New Lights, as against those in opposition, the *Old Lights.

NEW MORALITY, name for a contemporary moral theory that has its roots in at least three major challenges to traditional thought. In metaphysics existentialism has challenged the assumption that human nature is a fixed datum. Contextual or situation ethics has challenged the assumption that certain moral actions are always and everywhere wrong. In moral theology personalism has challenged the assumption that morality is simply a matter of keeping a code. The combination of these three attitudes toward human activity has come to be known as the new morality. Existentialism sees each human being as a starkly given and irreducible complex. No man can generalize in abstraction from his own concrete aspirations and impulses, since from these he is continually fashioning his own nature. Facing a moral decision challenges him to express his own authenticity. His act must be his own in the fullest sense. Situationalism takes its primary guidance from the circumstances in which the individual acts. Shall he tell a lie or tell the truth? Shall he kill or allow life? His answer depends not on recourse to an immutable moral law, but on the situation. Personalism emphasizes the I–Thou dialogue between man and God, man and man. Love is the only norm in the light of which the human person must manage all the moral decisions of his life. A code, whether Jewish, Christian, Hindu, humanist, or whatever, may be acknowledged as a source of counsel, but it cannot be prescriptive. Charity, agape, is the only precept.

One may reject these presuppositions as exclusive yet recognize much that is acceptable in the new morality. Psychology and psychiatry have shown how a man's childhood, his cultural milieu, and many other factors affect his adult decisions. One dare not presume to make sure moral judgments about the activity of any individual, no matter how unusual it may be, without profound personal knowledge of that individual and the influences that shaped him. The unique situation in which a moral action takes place is also crucial; no one acts in isolation; his decisions are shaped by circumstances and above all by people. Love certainly ought to be central. When traditional Christian morality loses that insight and goes over to the external keeping of the law as the critical norm, it needs to be purified and brought back to the clear message of the gospel. The new morality, however, assumes that men do not share in a common human nature, that no recognizably fixed values exist to guide men, that objectively wrong actions do not exist, or that Christian love observes no measure other than itself. Against this assumption it is argued that there are subordinate measures common to all men and expressing perennial values of which the violation is always wrong. Ovid, Dante, and T. S. Eliot display a common human characteristic in interpreting life through creative poetry. The evil men in the Bible and in Shakespeare look very much like those of our day. One can make valid statements applicable to all, recognize constant values and deviations from them and be assured that the way to authenticity is through respect-

ing them. Christ set love as highest and best, but he also cited the other commandments as the way to life (Mk 10.19) and strongly condemned murder and adultery (Mk 7.22) with no hint that possible situations might permit them.

The whole subject of morality is one not open to simplistic statements. The conventional systems of moral theology have received insights from the new school, notably about natural law, historicity, conscience, and love. It would seem that the bridge of reconciliation between the old and the new will be built by a more profound study of the virtue of Christian prudence. It is there the complex elements of a moral decision meet, there that the rule of Christian living is consulted and its immediate and providential environment appreciated, together with all the extenuating, and sometimes excepting, circumstances. See G. H. Outka and P. Ramsey, eds., *Norm and Context in Christian Ethics* (1968); ThAq ST (Eng–Lat), v.18.

NEW SCHOOL (Presbyterians), name for the liberal party in the schisms that split Presbyterian ranks in the 19th cent.; the conservative defenders of orthodoxy were called *Old School.

NEW SIDE (Presbyterians), a name for the *Synod of New York formed in 1745 by Presbyterians favoring *revivalism. During the *Great Awakening Presbyterian ranks became split over the revivalistic tenet that a conversion experience is a more essential qualification for ministry than formal education. In March 1740 Gilbert *Tennent's polemic sermon "The Danger of an Unconverted Ministry" further antagonized the orthodox opponents. At the Synod of 1741 the revivalists withdrew; the Synod of New York was formed by the New Brunswick, New Castle, and New York *Presbyteries, and it became known as the New Side. The Old Side was the orthodox Synod of Philadelphia. During the schism the New Side prospered and the Old Side did not. Tennent contributed to the reunion by his pamphlet "The Peace of Jerusalem." Although the disputed issue remained unresolved, a Plan of Union of 1758 was accepted by both Synods and ended the separation.

NEW THOUGHT, a mental healing movement, embracing a number of religious denominations and organizations and enjoying a wide influence outside of any formal organization. The followers of New Thought believe in spiritual healing, the creative power of thought, and mental and physical strength drawn from an inner source. The movement has strong Gnostic overtones. Inner power is generally available only to those who have been initiated into a new pattern of life. The insights available from New Thought are usually seen as a more perfect understanding of the Christian message than that recognized in the historical Churches. In its various forms and tendencies, New Thought has almost universally stressed the immanence of God and denied or ignored his transcendence. Sin, disease, and other human defects are errors of incorrect thinking, rather than realities. The immediate availability of God and the practical application of the force of spiritual thought to the solution of human problems are emphasized. This philosophical monism is drawn largely from neoplatonic and Oriental thought. The doctrine of immanentism is in most cases avowedly pantheistic. While New Thought generally discusses God in impersonal terms as Life-Principle, it also stresses such personal qualities as his fatherhood and goodness. Although adherents often speak of the unreality of matter, they do not deny the reality of the physical body or other physical objects but maintain that all form is the manifestation of the energy of Mind. Man is regarded as a spiritual being with freedom of choice and with infinite possibilities through the power of constructive thinking in accord with the dictates of the Indwelling Presence in his inner self. While most New Thought groups believe in immortality, and some hold doctrines of reincarna-

tion, the various kinds of New Thought sects are marked by a fundamental this-worldliness. The doctrine of salvation freely given has been transformed to mean assured happiness in the present life for those who are willing to take hold of God's promise. There is no need for repentance, since sin, evil, and suffering are illusory. Jesus Christ becomes simply a symbol of the divine spark in every man. He does not reconcile or redeem but points out that every man is an incarnation of God. His message is an awareness of the consciousness of inner harmony as a source of unlimited blessings. A New Thought group may make considerable use of the Bible, often interpreting its meaning in a secularist or non-Christian sense.

New Thought groups range from the *Unity School of Christianity, whose literature is widely distributed among Christians of different denominations, to such belligerently anti-Christian movements as the *I Am movement and *Psychiana. In origin, New Thought is a secularized *Arminianism. It arose in the U.S. in the decades following the Civil War, when material progress and popularly understood scientific teachings, such as evolution, had unsettled the faith of many Christians. Many of New Thought's most influential prophets, such as Myrtle and Charles *Fillmore, Nona Brooks, and Emma Curtis Hopkins, constructed their eclectic theology as members of the Methodist Church. Others brought to the movement a heritage of mesmerism, spiritualism, or mental healing. Phineas *Quimby, with whom Mary Baker *Eddy was early associated, was a 19th-cent. mental healer who developed some of the ideas later found in Christian Science and New Thought. By the 1880s there were a large number of New Thought groups and associations, some closely allied to Christian Science, others far removed from its teachings. In 1892 an attempt was made to unify these related movements in the International Divine Science Association. The International New Thought Alliance held its first convention at Boston in 1899. Among the many groups in the Alliance have been the Church of Divine Science, the Unity School of Christianity, the Church of the Healing Christ, the Church of Advanced Thought, and the Radiant Life Fellowship. New Thought has always extended beyond any form of organization, and many of its teachings can be found in groups and individuals never formally linked to the International New Thought Alliance.

NEWMAN, JOHN HENRY (1801–90), historian, theologian, leader of the *Oxford movement, cardinal. N. was born into a London middle-class family, attended Trinity College, Oxford (1816), became fellow of Oriel (1822), a deacon in the Anglican Church (1824), priest (1825), and vicar of St. Mary's, the Anglican church at Oxford (1828–41). While vicar at St. Mary's N. became the outstanding preacher at Oxford, and his services were attended by students, faculty, and visitors from various parts of England. His carefully prepared sermons based on Scripture and the Church Fathers were later published in a multivolume work called *Parochial and Plain Sermons*. N.'s first significant exposure to RC institutions was in 1832, when he took a cruise with Hurrell Froude, a close friend and associate from Oriel, and became seriously ill in Sicily. During recovery he made several trips to RC shrines and came to know the customs of the RC Church. Returning from this trip, he wrote the famous "Lead Kindly Light." In England he found a lively debate going on in Parliament regarding the disestablishment of the Anglican Church. N. and his associates undertook the publication of a number of unsigned tracts, eventually 90 in all, of which N. wrote 26, called *Tracts of the Times*. They were designed originally to support the establishment of the Anglican Church and to rebel against what N. saw as growing popery in England. Eventually these tracts took a more ecumenical bent and ceased with the publication of the famous *Tract 90*, which was very pro-Roman Catholic, and was attributed to N. in the popular mind. He became general editor of the *British Critic*, a

magazine published in London (1838–41). He resigned this post when he left St. Mary's as vicar and went to Littlemore with a group of associates to found a small community living according to a religious rule. His departure from St. Mary's was marked by the famous sermon "Parting of Friends." N. became more and more interested in the RC Church, and in 1845 he began preparations for the publication of his *Essay on the Development of Christian Doctrine*.

N. became a RC convert in 1845 and shortly thereafter his *Essay* on development was published. His group moved from Littlemore to the old Oscott College on the invitation of Card. Wiseman. In 1846 N. went to the College of Propaganda in Rome and there for less than a year was exposed to systematic RC theology. He was ordained a RC priest in 1847 and returned to Birmingham to found the first Oratory in England. Frederick W. Faber, a member of his community, later founded the Oratory at London. In 1852, upon the publication of *The Present Position of Catholics in England*, designed to calm the antipapal feeling that had been aroused by the restoration of the Catholic hierarchy (1850), N. was sued by a former Dominican priest, Giacinto Achilli, for libel since he was mentioned in the original publication of this work. N. lost the case and had court costs of approximately $60,000, which were paid by friends. During the years 1852–58 N. was occupied with an effort to establish a Catholic University of Ireland. For reasons partly financial and partly political, this attempt failed and N. returned to Birmingham. He wrote his *Apologia Pro Vita Sua* in a period of 2 months in 1864 and published his *Grammar of Assent* in 1870, during the time of Vatican Council I. N. was invited by Pope Pius IX to attend the council but received permission to stay in Birmingham and care for the problems of the Oratory. N. was not strongly in favor of the definition of papal infallibility at Vatican Council I because he thought it inopportune. After the definition, however, he gave it public support. N. was made a cardinal in 1879 but continued in his quiet life in the Oratory until his death.

N. was a true religious genius who brought to RC theology a psychological and historical dimension that was lacking because of its strong scholastic, systematic orientation. He was an original thinker who produced many books and during the course of his life wrote more than 20,000 letters. His work has been appreciated more fully in Germany and France than in the English-speaking world, although his influence is constantly growing. See *Collected Works* (25v., 1890–1927); C. S. Dessain, ed., *Letters and Diaries of John Henry Newman* (1961–   ); M. Trevor, *Newman: The Pillar of the Cloud* (1962); *idem, Newman: Light in Winter* (1963).

NICENE CREED, most properly the creed formulated by the Council of Nicaea (325), but in ordinary usage a later creed, the one used in the RC Mass and the liturgies of other Churches, called also since the 17th century the Niceno-Constantinopolitan Creed. The convention of designating the first as N and the second as C is followed in this article.

Creed of Nicaea (N). The Council was held to deal with Arianism. The creed is notable for being the first explicitly designed as a test of orthodoxy and for its application to Christ of the nonbiblical term *homoousion* (of one substance with the Father). It is the work of a commission of bishops who added anti-Arian, Nicene phrases to an extant Syro-Palestinian baptismal creed. The theory that N was based on a creed presented by Eusebius of Caesarea is no longer tenable. This creed ends with the simple phrase "And in the Holy Spirit," then anathemas against the Arians are added. N was also formally affirmed by the Councils of Ephesus (431) and Chalcedon (451). With C it is one of the rules of faith acknowledged by all of the Eastern Churches.

Niceno-Constantinopolitan Creed (C). The text of N was not literally the basis for the formulation of C; the two differ too much, not only by the addition in C of articles after that on the Holy Spirit and by the absence of the anathemas of N, but in language and style throughout. Doctrinally C is "Nicene," conformed to the faith of Nicaea, but elaborating the articles on the Son (against the Apollinarians) and on the Holy Spirit (against the Macedonians). It is called Constantinopolitan since the acts of the Council of Chalcedon (451), the primary source of the text, declare that it is the creed of the 150 fathers of the Council of Constantinople I (381). J. F. A. Holt (*Two Dissertations*, 1876) and A. Harnack (see EncRelKnow 3:256–260) denied this origin: the text of C antedated 381, and there is silence before Chalcedon on the promulgation of any symbol by Constantinople. Modern scholarship, however, is more inclined to accept the Chalcedonian tradition, while admitting that the Constantinopolitan fathers adopted C, as supplementing N against current heresies, from some existing baptismal formula (see Kelly; Bihlmeyer-Tüchle 1:258). With acceptance of Constantinople as an ecumenical council, C gained recognition in the East, both as authoritative teaching and as a liturgical formula in baptism and the Eucharist. It remains a primary rule of faith in the Eastern Churches, without, of course, the *filioque*, the affirmation that the Holy Spirit proceeds also from the Son, which was added in the West, where C came to be recognized in the 6th century. The Council of Toledo (589) ordered it sung at Mass. The practice spread from Spain and Gaul, but was not adopted at Rome until 1014. In the RC Church, as the profession of faith made at Mass, and as formally affirmed by the Council of Trent (D 1500), C is of the highest authority. The *Formula of Concord and the *Thirty-Nine Articles of Religion explicitly acknowledge it; the majority of Protestant Churches accept it, although liturgically it is used mainly by Lutherans and Anglicans. Of all creeds C alone is truly an *ecumenical creed accepted by East and West alike. Since the *Lambeth quadrilateral (1886) it holds a central place in modern discussions of Christian unity. See

J. W. D. Kelly, *Early Christian Creeds* (2d ed., 1960); F. X. Murphy, NCE 4:434–437.

NICHOLAS, HENRY, see NICLAES, HENDRIK.

NICLAES, HENDRIK (Henry Nicholas; *c.* 1502–*c.*1580), founder of the *Familists. N. was born in Münster and reared a Catholic, but at age 9 he claimed a revelation of an experiential religion. He established his sect in Amsterdam, at Emden, where he lived, and in England, which he visited in 1552 or 1553. His teaching, influenced according to some by D. *Joris, proclaimed a personal revelation that he was a "begodded man," experiencing a divine spirit of love, which put him above Christ and Moses, as charity is above faith and hope. Those who shared in this inner spirit were divinized, righteous, and raised above dogma, liturgy, or law. N.'s teachings seem to have fostered pantheistic and antinomian excesses among the Familists. Some of N.'s works, such as *The Glass of Righteousness* and the *Evangelium regni*, were translated into English; all were placed on the Index (1570–1582). See R. M. Jones, *Studies in Mystical Religion* (1923), 428–448; R. Knox, *Enthusiasm* (1950), 140–141, 171–172.

NIEBUHR, HELMUT RICHARD (1894–1962), Protestant theologian. The brother of Reinhold *Niebuhr, N. was born in Wright City, Mo.; he was educated at Elmhurst College (Ill.), of which he was later president. After studies at Eden Theological Seminary (Webster Groves, Mo.), N. was ordained in the Evangelical and Reformed Church in 1916. From Yale Univ. he received his Ph.D. in 1924. In 1931 he was appointed professor of Christian Ethics at the Yale Divinity School, where he remained until his death. His intellectual concerns ranged widely in the areas of sociological analysis, value theory, theological ethics, and the purposes of theological education. Although not a prolific author, he exhibited in his major works his interest in the dialogue between Christian faith and culture. His *Social Sources of Denominationalism* (1929) analyzed the secular forces that separate religious bodies in America. From the historical and theological aspect he traced the relation between Christianity and culture in *The Kingdom of God in America* (1937). *The Meaning of Revelation* (1941) set forth revelation as the intelligible event in the internal history of the Christian community, which provided guiding images for a coherent life. His typology of the relations that Christian faith has sustained with culture was expressed in *Christ and Culture* (1951). The theocentrism that ruled his theology was brought face to face with different aspects of modern culture in *Radical Monotheism and Western Culture* (1960), in which he stressed the center of ethics and value theory as residing on the principle of being-itself, the One beyond the many whence all beings derive their being and significance. His posthumous work *The Responsible Self* (1963) provided a truncated version of what might have become his systematic Christian ethics. N. came from a heritage of evangelical Christianity, which was dynamically theocentric yet toughly realistic about social problems. See M. Marty and D. Peerman, eds., *Handbook of Christian Theologians* (1965); P. Ramsey, ed., *Faith and Ethics* (1957).

NIEBUHR, REINHOLD (1892–   ), clergyman and teacher, influential in turning American Protestantism from liberalism toward Reformation and biblical theology. Born at Wright City, Mo., after studying at Elmhurst College (Ill.), Eden Theological Seminary (Webster Groves, Mo.), and Yale (B.D., 1914; M.A., 1915), he was ordained by the Evangelical Synod and was pastor of Bethel Church, Detroit, Mich., until 1928. He then moved to Union Theological Seminary, New York City, where he taught applied Christianity until his retirement in 1960. Having begun his ministry at the high tide of the *Social Gospel movement, he shared much of the optimism that envisioned the kingdom of God on earth. Under his leadership, the small working-class church in Detroit increased in membership, erected a new building, and in addition to public services of worship and its church school program, held Sunday-evening forums to discuss crucial social issues. As he related in *Leaves From the Notebook of a Tamed Cynic* (1929), he became increasingly aware of the plight of the workingman in a depersonalized industrial society. He also became conscious of the illusory hopes of educators and moralists for curing the ills of the world. Basic to his "Christian Realism" has been a conviction that both individuals and groups are prevented from attaining perfection by a deep-rooted egotistic pride. His *Moral Man and Immoral Society* (1932) made a strong impact upon American Protestants, and his analysis of human nature was elaborated in his Gifford Lectures (*Nature and Destiny of Man*, 2v., 1941–43). Reasserting the idea of original sin, he interpreted it as self-centered pride that leads men to absolutize their partial perspectives and to rationalize their own interests, incorporating them into their political, economic, and social structures. His view of human sinfulness was saved from sheer pessimism by his recognition of man's ability to transcend himself and to engage in self-criticism and by his awareness that man has a capacity for good as well as for evil. His provisional pessimism was also tempered by faith in the justifying grace of God, who is both transcendent and immanent. He continued to have a strong ethical concern and was active in reform movements but did not expect to establish a perfect society governed by love. Believing in working for the highest measure of justice possible in a given situation, he sought proximate solutions rather than idealistic ultimate goals. Morover, he believed that group relations are political in nature and as such involve conflicting interests that cannot be resolved except by coercive power. Egoistic impulses of human groups cannot be restrained simply by appeals to reason

and good will. Force must be countered by force, and even war may be necessary, if the alternative is brutal tyranny, such as Nazism under Hitler. Democracy must be preserved, not because men are wise and good, but because it is a safeguard against man's tendency toward injustice. As indicated in *Man's Nature and His Communities* (1965), some of his views underwent modification, but the major themes of his Christian Realism have remained basically unchanged. See C. W. Kegley and R. N. Bretall, eds., *R. N.: His Religious, Social, and Political Thought* (1956); T. A. Kantonen, *Resurgence of the Gospel* (1948); P. A. Carter, *Decline and Revival of the Social Gospel* (1956).

NIEMÖLLER, MARTIN (1892–), German Lutheran pastor. A career officer, he served as a U-boat commander in World War I. In 1919 he entered the seminary at Münster. After his ordination he became executive-secretary for the Westphalian Council for Inner Missions. In 1931 he was called to the pastorate of St. Annen's in Berlin-Dahlem. Although originally a supporter of the National Socialist party, N. opposed at the very outset Hitler's attempt to control the Churches. He founded the Emergency Pastors' League (1933), helped write the *Barmen Declaration, and continued to preach against Nazism until his arrest in July 1937. Nine months later he was convicted on trumped-up charges and sent first to Sachsenhausen and then to Dachau. His wife kept the world press informed about him, and his reputation for resistance became legendary. The U.S. military freed him in 1945 after 8 years of imprisonment, half of it spent in solitary confinement. For 15 years after his release N. traveled throughout the world in the interests of ecumenism and peace. He aroused controversy in 1953 by his letter to Chancellor Adenauer opposing rearmament and again in 1959 by his speech against the atom bomb. On the occasion of the All-German Church Day in Berlin in 1961 he denounced the gathering as "a complete blank in the history of the Evangelical Church." His action caused some former admirers to feel that the Communist regime of East Germany had made use of his prestige to help it sever East German Protestants from their brethren in the West. See C. S. Davidson, *God's Man; The Story of Pastor Niemöller* (1959).

NIHILIANISM, a doctrine expressed in the Christological proposition "Christ as man is nothing" (*Christus secundum quod est homo, non est aliquid*); Christ's humanity has its whole reality from his divine being. The theory, developed out of certain inept passages in Peter Lombard (d. 1160), was taught by some 12th-cent. Parisian theologians and condemned by Pope Alexander III as a denial of the truth that Christ is truly man (D 749–750).

NINETY-FIVE THESES, a series of statements proposed for theological debate by Martin *Luther in 1517. The occasion was the dissemination among the faithful of exaggeration and error through the preaching of a papal indulgence by J. Tetzel. There is a tradition, seriously challenged by E. Iserloh, that Luther on Oct. 31, 1517, nailed his list of theses to the Wittenberg Castle church; the date is therefore marked as the birth date of the Reformation. The theses were made the basis for the canonical process against Luther that began his final break with Rome. Written in Latin and translated into German, they received a wide circulation that transformed the issues that had been personal or academic for Luther into a summons for reform of the Church. Luther challenged the extension of the papal "power of the keys" to the souls in purgatory; more importantly, the theses revealed, esp. in regard to sin, guilt, and forgiveness, that much of what Luther called "my Gospel" had already developed in his mind. Text: LW 31 (1957). See EncLuthCh 3:2388–91; R. Fife, *Revolt of Martin Luther* (1957); E. Iserloh, *Theses Were Not Posted* (tr. J. Wicks, 1968).

NOMINALISM, a term with two meanings, one ontological and the other historical. (1) Ontologically, nominalism is a philosophical doctrine concerning the problem of universals. It holds that only individual things exist. In opposition to Platonism, which explains the similarity of two individuals by saying that they share a common property or nature, i.e., by assuming the existence of a universal, nominalism holds that if individuals similar to one another may be said to share anything at all, this can only be a spoken or written name (Lat. *nomen*) or a mental image, i.e., another individual. In the strict sense nominalism is also opposed to conceptualism, for it rejects universals even as objects of thought. Ontological nominalism has often led to a skeptical attitude concerning the objective value of intellectual knowledge (Hume). The term is therefore frequently used in a loose way, as if it were synonymous with conventionalism, empiricism, positivism. (2) Historically, nominalism is a term applied to certain movements in early and late scholasticism, whose representatives were called *nominales.* Their doctrines included, among others, ontological nominalism in the broad sense, i.e., not excluding conceptualism. The lasting contribution of the early nominalists (Roscelin of Compiègne, Abelard) to scholasticism was that they introduced logic not as a science of disembodied platonist "things" (*res*), but as a formal science of expressions (*voces*), esp. meaningful expressions (*sermones*). They also continued the tradition of earlier dialecticians of applying logical analysis to theological matters, but they were not professional theologians and their formulations were condemned as heretical.

The ontological nominalism of *William of Ockham, the father of the nominalist school, can be interpreted as a reaction against the many subtle distinctions of the Scotists. According to the principle that later became known as Ockham's razor, plurality is never to be posited without necessity, Ockham accepted only real distinctions where each component is real and individual. He defended his ontological viewpoint by revising the logic of the suppositions of terms accordingly. Characteristically his first followers in Paris were censured in 1339 because of their zeal for logical analysis; they had claimed that certain propositions of accepted authorities were "false in virtue of their formulation" (*falsae de virtute sermonis*). But Ockham was not only an eminent logician, he was also a recognized theologian. His ontological nominalism was intimately connected with his view of a free, all-powerful, and all-merciful God. For him, the affirmation of a real distinction implied that God could create one component without the other. In view of God's absolute power (*potentia absoluta*), the coexistence of individuals was entirely contingent; the actual order of nature and grace was necessary only insofar as God had in fact directed his power in this way (*potentia ordinata*). As a consequence, arguments based on man's experience of the *de facto* order of nature could lead only to probable conclusions. Furthermore, observation of regular sequence became the only ground for asserting a causal relation between two natural phenomena. Ockham has therefore been hailed as a forerunner of empirical science. But he himself had shown no particular interest in scientific experiments, and although many 14th-cent. physicists (e.g., Buridan, Oresme) belonged to the nominalist school, they did not follow the physical theories of Ockham but continued rather those of their realist predecessors.

Ockham extended the radical contingency even to the moral order, stressing that commandments were free, even arbitrary, dictates of God's will. Proponents of today's "situation ethics" find this denial of an objective natural law much to their liking, but Ockham did not deny that God had in fact established a particular moral code that all men must obey. Furthermore, it is doubtful that the advocates of situation ethics would follow Ockham's logic to the end and agree that even the first commandment was contingent; that God could also have commanded us to hate him and not to love him. The followers of Ockham formed a

new school, the *via moderna,* in opposition to the old schools of *Scotism and *Thomism the *via antiqua.* It is important to realize that the bitter quarrels that sprang up between these movements took place within theological orthodoxy. It is true that two contemporaries of Ockham, Nicholas of Autrecourt and John of Mirecourt, whose philosophy was similar to Ockham's, were condemned by the Church. But the theology of Ockham himself was never condemned as heretical, despite the fact that he had been personally excommunicated in his quarrel with Pope John XXII (see POVERTY CONTROVERSY).

In the 14th and 15th cents. the leaders of the conciliar movement (Peter of Ailly, Jean Gerson) belonged to the *via moderna,* and, since Ockham's criticism had made philosophical reasonings doubtful, the nominalist theologians (e.g., Gabriel Biel) were especially attracted by the practical Christianity of the *Devotio moderna. The nominalist school has therefore been characterized as "the late medieval ecumenical movement" (H. A. Oberman). The Reformation has to be understood with this background in mind. But it would be wrong to see Protestantism as the direct and necessary outcome of nominalism. Actually Wycliffe, Hus, and Calvin came from the Scotist, and Zwingli from the Thomist school. It is true that Luther was strongly influenced by Biel, but so was his Catholic antagonist J. *Eck, and even some formulations of the Council of Trent go back to Biel. In the important doctrine of justification Luther rejected the Semi-Pelagianism of the nominalists, which said that man could do his very best (*facere quod in se est*) and put himself in the proper disposition for the infusion of grace. See G. Küng, NCE 10:483–485, E. A. Moody, EncPhil 5:533–534; 8:306–317; H. A. Oberman, *Harvest of Medieval Theology* (1963).

NONCONFORMISTS, a term first used to refer to English Puritans who objected to subscription to the *Acts of Uniformity but also declined to leave the C of E; it became interchangeable with *Dissenters during the *Restoration. During the reign of Elizabeth I, Puritanism emerged within the C of E and fragmented into several parties. Some accepted episcopal government but wanted further reforms of ceremonies; others favored a Presbyterian polity for the English Church; another group adopted a *congregational view of the Church and separated from the C of E; but a large number of those who favored congregational principles abhorred schism and remained within the Church. When James I became king, the Presbyterians and nonseparating Congregationalists hoped for his support. The *Millenary Petition was presented to him in 1603, setting forth desired religious reforms, but at the *Hampton Court Conference (1604) he ordered all to conform, or he would harry them out of the land. Supported by the King, Richard Bancroft (1544–1610), abp. of Canterbury, ordered that all clergy accept the Royal Supremacy, vestments, and the Book of Common Prayer. Nonconformity continued to grow, reinforced by those who objected to James's absolutist concept of monarchy. Charles I inherited the religious problem, and in 1628 appointed William *Laud abp. of Canterbury with a mandate to purge the Church's ranks of all who would not accept the Book of Common Prayer. Laud's rigorous policies caused thousands to migrate to Massachusetts Bay and elsewhere. Political and religious opponents of the King combined with parliamentary forces to engage in the civil war that culminated in the beheading of Charles I. Under the Commonwealth and Protectorate of Oliver *Cromwell, a large measure of toleration was granted to Protestants, and new sects (Friends, Diggers, Levelers, Familists, etc.) multiplied. The Restoration began in 1660 with the coronation of Charles II, who in the *Declaration of Breda gave assurances of wider toleration. The Presbyterians hoped for a more comprehensive establishment broad enough to include them, and the Independents, Baptists, and other groups expected freedom of worship. A new Act of Uniformity, in 1662, indicated

the intention to enforce a rigid uniformity of religion, and about 2,000 clergy were ejected from their livings because they could not subscribe. Those who had been in the state Church without conforming to the required rites became Dissenters instead of simply Nonconformists. With ministers squeezed out of the Church by the Act of Uniformity, the people forbidden to worship in private by the *Conventicle Act (1664), and all dissenters eliminated from political and military offices by the *Corporation Act (1661) and *Test Act (1673), great pressure was exerted to compel conformity to the Church of England.

The accession of William and Mary was accompanied by the *Toleration Act (1689), which granted freedom of worship to all Protestants who met certain conditions (an oath of allegiance and acceptance of the *Thirty-Nine Articles, with slight exceptions), but the Test and Corporation Acts and other disabilities remained in force. The main Nonconformist bodies were the Baptists, Presbyterians, and Congregationalists, referred to often as "the three denominations." Greater freedom did not lead to more growth, since the Presbyterians and General Baptists were decimated by Unitarianism and Particular Baptists and Congregationalists were afflicted with a hyper-Calvinism that opposed evangelistic effort. After 1738, the Methodists became an important religious force, but originally they were not classed as Nonconformists or Dissenters, since John *Wesley insisted throughout his life on their remaining within the Church of England. The 19th cent. witnessed a vigorous growth of Baptists, Congregationalists, and Methodists and a revival of the almost defunct Presbyterians. Noted preachers emerged from the Baptists (Charles H. Spurgeon, Robert Hall), the Congregationalists (R. W. Dale, Joseph Parker), and the Methodists (Hugh Price Hughes, John Scott Lidgett). Strong lay leaders were active both in church affairs and in political and social movements. In 1828 the Test and Corporation Acts were abolished; in 1836 marriages were allowed in Nonconformist meeting houses;

in 1880 burial services by Dissenters were permitted in churchyards; in 1868 the payment of church rates was made voluntary; and in 1871 religious tests for Oxford and Cambridge degrees were removed, except for theology. The "Nonconformist conscience" played an important role in effecting social reforms during the century. By the 20th cent. the term Nonconformist was being replaced by *free Churches; these cooperated in various ways. In the 20th cent. all the free Churches have suffered losses of membership and influence along with the C of E, and various proposals for church union have been underway in recent years. See H. W. Clark, *History of English Nonconformity* (2v., 1911–13); H. Davies, *English Free Churches* (1952); R. G. Cowherd, *Politics of English Dissent* (1956).

NONCONFORMITY, aloofness from this world, a major doctrine of the *Mennonites. It is based on Rom 12.2, "Be not conformed to this world," and on other NT passages. Christians in all ages have wrestled with the problem of their relation to the world, to society, and to culture; the term nonconformity particularly denotes the Mennonite response to the problem. Mennonite settlement groups as a rule have had no written regulations for their practices on nonconformity, but where the cultural environment is a threat, specific rules have been adopted by conferences and by ministerial leadership. Every area of life is affected. In business, nonconformity forbids partnership with non-Christians and enforces strict standards of justice and brotherly aid. Some lenders even refuse to accept interest from the needy. In civil life, it rules out standing for office and at times even voting. *Nonresistance and refusal of military service are applications of the rule of nonconformity. In dress, nonconformity means rejection of fashion, sumptuousness, and the use of jewelry and cosmetics. Mustaches are avoided because of their military association, but the men of some Mennonite groups are required to wear beards. Luxury and most forms of recreation—card playing, the theater, and television—are avoided. Prohibition of tobacco and liquor dates only from the late 19th cent., and as the result of outside influences like the temperance movement rather than from Mennonite tradition. Personal demeanor is restrained and quiet. Some conservative Mennonites also cling to the language of their forefathers and to remote rural life, opposing all modern inventions, and industrial work.

Nonconformity is maintained chiefly in three ways: through tradition, indoctrination, and discipline. At times worldliness has been confusedly identified with variations in cultural conventions, and repressive and authoritarian measures have been used to ensure uniformity. The Mennonite ideal seeks to assert the positive aspect of nonconformity, i.e., that it is conformity to God's will and nature, as well as a way of imitating Christ's life. See H. S. Bender et al., MennEnc 3:890–897.

NONJURORS, members of the C of E who, because they had previously taken oaths of loyalty to James II and his lawful heirs, refused to swear allegiance to William and Mary. Holding to a divine-right doctrine of kingship, they denied Parliament's authority to depose the lawful sovereign. Paradoxically, five of the nonjuring bps. had been among those who had helped precipitate the Revolution of 1688 by their disobedience to James's order that his *Declaration of Indulgence be read in all the churches. Their dilemma was that belief in passive obedience to a king conflicted with the conviction that the Church was autonomous in spiritual matters. Among those whose consciences kept them from taking the new oaths was William Sancroft, abp. of Canterbury, who until his death was the spiritual leader of the nonjurors' movement. Seven other bps. and about 400 of the lower clergy also scrupled to take the oaths. Prominent laymen were also nonjurors. Sancroft would not officiate in the coronation of the new sovereigns, but allowed his suffragan to do so. In 1690, he and five bps. were deprived of their offices, two other objectors having already died. When their successors were appointed, they claimed that the choice was unlawful because it was made solely by secular authority; they insisted that although they could not carry out the duties, they were still the rightful incumbents of their offices. Thus they became a schismatic party within the C of E, and after 1694 they began to ordain new bps., although they could assign them to no districts. After 1715, the movement ceased to have real significance, although the schism existed until the death of the last bishop, Boothe, in 1805. See J. H. Overton, *Nonjurors, Their Lives, Principles, and Writings* (1903).

NONRESISTANCE, a doctrine developed by the 16th-cent. Swiss Anabaptists and particularly associated with the Mennonites. Nonresistance is the renunciation of any coercive means, whether employed by individuals or society, to redress wrongs or to achieve objectives; *pacifism and *conscientious objection are allied but not synonymous terms. The *Schleitheim Confession (1529) expressed the doctrinal basis of nonresistance as a religious tenet: "The sword is ordained of God outside the perfection of Christ." The Swiss Anabaptists taught nonparticipation in civil affairs, regarding the civil power as alien to the gospel, a relic of OT law. Unlike the *Zwickau Prophets or the Anabaptists at Münster, they did not seek to establish a theocratic kingdom by the sword but adopted an attitude of passive obedience; nonresistance was part of this. The *Dordrecht Confession of Faith (1632) includes nonresistance in the practice of Christian love, quoting Jesus' teaching to avoid revenge and to love enemies.

Historically, the practice of nonresistance has varied among the Mennonites with regard to military service. Because of persecution in their early history, those who were not martyred fled into isolated settlements in the Swiss Alps, the steppes of Russia, and later to the frontiers of N America. Nonresistance, nonparticipation, and nonconformity developed as characteristics that to this day continue among such conservative Mennonites as the Amish. In W Europe the Mennonites had almost completely given up traditional nonresistance by the time of World War I. Since World War II a revitalization of the peace witness has taken place, particularly in The Netherlands and Germany. In Russia Mennonites served as noncombatants from 1880 to 1930, when it became impossible to claim complete exemption from military service. In N America the first real challenge came to Mennonite nonresistance during World War I. Since that time many traditional Mennonites have served in the armed forces. Nevertheless, the peace witness has been intensified in an effort to express a total Christian way of life in times of strife. Civilian public service, "pax service," and many channels of relief activities are signs of this intensification. Some Mennonites are involved in the struggle for social and racial equality by making use of the legal processes of democracy and even by political involvement. Their isolation belongs to the past. See MennEnc 3:897–907.

NONSECTARIAN, uncommitted to sectarian principles or spirit; or unaffiliated with any denomination. The term may imply a desire to emphasize things on which Christians agree; or it may be used by *independent churches that consider all major denominations as tainted with unorthodoxy and regard denominational distinctions with indifference.

NORMA NORMATA (the rule ruled), a phrase describing confessions of faith esp. in Lutheranism. The *norma normans* (the rule ruling) is Holy Scripture, "the only rule and norm according to which all doctrine and teachers must be appraised and judged" (*Formula of Concord, Epitome). The confessions of faith are held to be genuine rules of faith because they, in fact, conform to the Scriptures; but they are a ruled rule, i.e., subordinate or derived. The Formula of Concord lists as such rules of faith the *Augsburg Confession, the *Apology for the Augsburg Confession, the *Schmalkaldic Articles, and Luther's *Catechisms. Adherence to the confessional principle has varied throughout Lutheran history, and is now strong, esp. with regard to the Augsburg Confession. Other Protestant confessional bodies agree in the principle that all doctrinal standards are rules of faith solely as subordinate to the Bible. See T. E. Schmauk and C. T. Benze, *Confessional Principle* (1911); Mayer RB 142–144.

NORTH AMERICAN BAPTIST ASSOCIATION, a body that separated from the *American Baptist Association in 1950. In opposition to the long-established practice of seating delegates to the national convention who were not members of the local churches that had verified their credentials, the new Association adopted the following principle of cooperation: "Each church in this Association is entitled to three messengers chosen from her own membership, the qualifications of said messengers being determined by the church electing them" (see MESSENGER). In 1968 this denomination reported 200,000 members in 1,500 churches. Old concepts of *Landmarkism and a doctrinal defense of the "eternal security of the believer" are strictly maintained.

NORTH AMERICAN BAPTIST GENERAL CONFERENCE, a body that originated in the Baptist churches organized by 19th-cent. German immigrants. The first such churches, established during the 1840s, became associated in the German Baptist Conference at Philadelphia, 1851, through the work of August Rauschenbusch (father of Walter *Rauschenbusch) and others. New regional conferences emerged with the progress of westward migration; at a meeting of eastern and western conferences in 1865, the present General Conference had its beginnings. There are North American Baptist congregations in 29 states and five of the Canadian provinces. Member churches adhere to characteristic Baptist teachings, acknowledging the *New Hampshire Confession. Their history has been marked by extensive missionary work and contributions to theological education, esp. in association with the Colgate Rochester Divinity School, Rochester, New York. Headquarters are in Forest Park, Ill.; membership in 1968 was 53,742 in 332 churches. The denomination is affiliated with the *Baptist World Alliance.

NORTH AMERICAN OLD ROMAN CATHOLIC CHURCH, the title of two bodies that were one until 1958. The original foundation was made by Prince de Landas Berghes, an Austrian who in 1913 received episcopal consecration in England through the Old Catholic line. He was sent by the Old Catholic Mission in England to become Old Catholic bp. of North America. He consecrated C. H. Carfora, a former RC priest, as bishop, and Carfora became abp. of the North American Old Roman Catholic Church from 1919 to 1958. Doctrine and ritual of the Church were Roman Catholic, with the usual Old Catholic exceptions. Neither this Church nor its divisions, however, became part of the Old Catholic communion. Membership was of English, Italian, Lithuanian, and Polish origin. The division into two bodies came after the death of Abp. Carfora. Leadership was claimed both by Abp. P. A. Marchenna and Abp. H. A. Rogers. Each had his following, and the Church was divided, although both branches retained the same basic doctrines and liturgy. The North American Old Roman Catholic Church of the Marchenna succession has its headquarters in Chicago, Ill., and in 1965 membership was about 18,000. The North American Old Roman Catholic Church (until 1968, called the North American Catholic Church), which Abp. Rogers still headed in 1969, has its headquarters in Brooklyn, N.Y. No membership statistics are available. *OLD CATHOLICS.

NOTES ON THE NEW TESTAMENT (1755), one of John *Wesley's principal works. *Explanatory Notes upon the New Testament* was written to "help serious men, who have not the advantage of learning . . . to understand the New Testament" (from Wesley's introduction). He began it in Jan. 1754, when he was seriously ill, staying at Hot Well, Bristol. He based the *Notes* on *Gnomon Novi Testamenti* by Johann Albrecht Bengel but was indebted also to John Heylyn, John Guyse, and Philip Doddridge. Wesley's brother Charles assisted him, particularly in the third and best edition. The *Notes* are short and manifest Wesley's originality of thought, his evangelical doctrines, and his *Arminianism. The *Notes* have been regarded by some, esp. English Methodist bodies, as a *doctrinal standard. With the *Notes*, Wesley published a new translation of the NT and anticipated modern scholarship by dividing the text into paragraphs. In 1790 he published a pocket edition of the translation without notes but with the analysis of the books and the chapters. He replaced "charity" by "love" in I Cor ch. 13, and "blessed" by "happy" in the Sermon on the Mount. There are about 1,200 departures from the AV; about three-quarters of them have been incorporated into later English versions of the New Testament. See J. S. Simon, *John Wesley and the Advance of Methodism* (1925); F. E. Maser, *Story of John Wesley's New Testament* (1955).

NOVATIAN, ANTIPOPE (d. 258), advocate of a Church made up only of the elect. N. was a prominent Roman priest who wrote to the churches of the world as the spokesman of the Roman clergy during the vacancy after Pope St. Fabian's death (250). Two of his letters to St. Cyprian at Carthage foreshadow N.'s later rigorism toward the *lapsi*, those who had apostatized during the Decian persecution. He was severely disappointed when in 251 Cornelius was chosen pope, and with the support of some of the clergy had himself consecrated bishop and opposed Cornelius, whom he accused of overindulgence toward the *lapsi*. N. gained many adherents to the view that the Church was made up of saints alone and that not only the *lapsi* but all who sinned gravely were excluded. In 251 he was condemned by a synod of 60 bps. in Rome, but Novatianist churches with their own bps. spread, especially in Africa and the East. N. fled from Rome during the imperial persecutions of Gallus and Volusianus; he died, possibly as a martyr or confessor, under the Emperor Valerian. He was the first Roman theologian to write in Latin. His works show him an accomplished stylist and theologian. Of the many works that Jerome mentions, only a few survive. Two, the *De cibis judaicis* and the *De Trinitate*, were preserved among the works of Tertullian; two others, probably N.'s, survived among the works of Cyprian, *De bono pudicitiae* and *De spectaculis*. The *De Trinitate* is the principal work, and except for subordinationist expressions, one of high merit. See Altaner 191–193, with bibliog.; Daniélou-Marrou 194–200; P. H. Weyer, NCE 10:534–535.

NOVATIANISTS, members of a schismatic sect founded by the Roman priest *Novatian, who after the election of Pope Cornelius in March 251, had himself consecrated bishop and proclaimed as a rival pope. To give a theological basis to his schism, he adopted a rigorous attitude toward the *lapsi*, those who had lapsed during time of persecution. He excluded them forever from his Church, and this penalty was later applied to adulterers and murderers as well. Novatian and his followers were excommunicated by a synod of 60 bishops held at Rome in 251. His active proselytizing (Cyprian, *Ep.* 55.24) and the natural attraction his rigorism had for those who had suffered for the faith favored the rapid spread of the schism, particularly in Syria, Asia Minor, and Palestine, where it numbered *Montanists as well as Catholics among its converts. They were opposed by Cyprian of Carthage, Dionysius of Alexandria, Pacian of Barcelona, and Ambrose of Milan. The Council of Nicaea declared the Novatianist priests to be validly ordained. Constantine permitted them to have their own churches and cemeteries, but Honorius and Theodosius included the Novatianists in their legislation repressing heresies. In the East the schism persisted at least until the end of the 6th century. See E. Peterson, EC 8:1976–80; J. Quasten, LTK 7:1062–64.

NUREMBERG DECLARATION, protest of German professors against the decrees of Vatican Council I. J. F. von *Schulte called a meeting at Nuremberg, Aug. 25–26, 1870; 14 professors, including I. von *Döllinger and F. *Reusch, attended. Their manifesto denied the validity of the Council on the grounds that it lacked freedom and moral unanimity; noted that certain chapters of the constitution *Pastor aeternus* lacked conditions necessary for a dogmatic definition; held that the dogma of the pope's immediate ordinary jurisdiction destroyed the divinely appointed nature of episcopacy; declared that papal infallibility would revive papal control of civil affairs and foment boundless discord; affirmed the signatories' solidarity with bps. opposing the conciliar decrees; and demanded a true general council on German soil. Thirty-three faculty members (priests and laymen) from seven universities signed the Declaration, which greatly sparked Old Catholicism. *OLD CATHOLICS; *VATICAN COUNCILS.

NURTURE, CHRISTIAN, see CHRISTIAN NURTURE.

NYGREN, ANDERS (1890–), Lutheran bishop of Lund in Sweden, theologian, and ecumenist. N., prominent in the World Council of Churches, was a delegate to its major conferences, as well as to those, beginning at Lausanne in 1907, that led to its formation. He served (1947–52) as president of the Lutheran World Federation. As a theologian he is chiefly associated with the *motif-research method in theology. Especially in his great work *Agape and Eros* (v.1, 1930; v.2, 1936; rev. Eng. ed., 1961), he presented the distinctive note of Christianity to be *agape*—the unmotivated, completely gracious divine love that alone establishes man's relationship to God and enables him to live in love of neighbor. To N. the glory of the Reformation was the reassertion of this theme after it had been obscured by other motifs dominating Christian theology—*nomos* (law), the characteristic of Judaism, and *eros*, the egocentric human search for God as fulfillment of man, the essence of Greek religious thought. *AULÉN, G.; *LUNDENSIAN THEOLOGY.

O

OATHS, formal affirmations that call upon God or some aspect of divine power as a witness that what one asserts is the truth, or what one pledges will be performed. Oaths have been used in most societies, and they are mentioned, e.g., in the Code of Hammurabi. Among the Jews the custom developed of taking hold of the Scriptures while taking an oath, a practice that has continued in the modern practice of swearing on the Bible. The historian Josephus reports opposition to swearing among the Essenes. In Christian history several groups have opposed all oaths, in literal obedience to the words of Jesus (Mt 5.33–7) and James (5.12). Opposition has come particularly from such groups as Anabaptists and Quakers, who were in tension with the authorities of Church and State that employed oaths. Mennonites have also been noted for their refusal to take oaths, a stand taken by their founder, *Menno Simons, incorporated in their Confession of Waterland (Art. 38), and still maintained in the *Mennonite Confession of 1963 (Art. 17).

The basic point of Jesus' teaching is generally considered to be the necessity for a character of such total honesty that any formal assertion that one is making a true statement would be superfluous. The implication is that the moral demand for truth is absolute, and no distinction can be drawn between ordinary speech and special occasions when an oath is used. Most Christians have regarded Jesus' statement as an example of his use of hyperbole, comparable to such assertions as that a disciple should hate his father and mother (Lk 14.26), and not to be interpreted with absolute literalness. The main authorities of the Churches, therefore, have approved oaths as a necessity for government, both secular and ecclesiastical. Supporters of oaths point out that such OT figures as Abraham swore (Gen 21.24), that Yahweh is said to swear (Is 62.8), and that Paul used oaths (2 Cor 1.23). Although some of the Fathers opposed swearing (see Chrysostom, Homilies 8 and 9 on Acts), St. Thomas Aquinas approved (ThAq ST 2a2ae, 89), and RC canon law regulates the use of oaths (CIC c.1307–21). The main Churches of the Reformation, in contrast to Anabaptists, also supported the use of oaths. The last of the *Thirty-Nine Articles of the Church of England approves oaths, as does c. 22 of the *Westminster Confession.

Most Christians today do not make an issue of taking oaths, though they may agree that ideally they should be unnecessary for Christians. In secular courts, oaths are now primarily a legal tool making prosecution for perjury possible, and alternative forms of affirmation have been devised not only for such groups as object to swearing but also for atheists, whose lack of belief makes traditional oaths meaningless. In general, it may be doubted whether oaths have a significant effect in an increasingly secularized society. See MennEnc 4:2–8.

OATH AGAINST MODERNISM, formula promulgated in the motu proprio *Sacrorum antistitum* of Pope Pius X (Sept. 1, 1910). The oath had to be sworn by clerics before receiving the subdiaconate, and by priests upon appointment to various offices and dignities (CIC cc.1406–08). The oath was a formal affirmation of the principal doctrines proposed by the *magisterium of the Church, esp. with regard to the possibility of human reason's proving the existence of God, the external signs of divine revelation, the establishment of the Church by Christ, the immutability of dogma, and the nature of faith. The oath included a formal, explicit rejection of *modernism. The oath is no longer imposed; on May 31, 1967, the Congregation for the Doctrine of the Faith substituted a very brief, concise affirmation of faith. See D 3537–50; J. J. Heaney, NCE 9:995–996.

OATHS, ENGLISH ECCLESIASTICAL, a series of oaths and subscriptions required of clergymen during the English Reformation in an endeavor to achieve unity in doctrine and practice. After successive alterations in the content and administration of these, the present requirements in the C of E are: an oath of allegiance to the sovereign, a declaration of assent to the doctrines and rites of the C of E, and an oath of canonical obedience. In the Act of Supremacy of 1534, Parliament declared the king to be "the only supreme head in earth of the Church of England" and at the same session made it treasonable to deny the king any of his dignities or titles. In order to receive new commissions from the king, bps. were required in 1535 to repudiate the papacy and to aid in the enforcement of the laws. All except John Fisher, Bp. of Rochester, took the oath and proceeded to bring the clergy of their dioceses to accept the new situation. Fisher was executed for treasonably denying the king's supremacy. In 1550, during the reign of Edward VI, the oath of supremacy was incorporated in the new ordination service, where it remained until 1865, except during the Marian and Cromwellian periods. Declaring the king to be the head of the C of E, it also explicitly repudiated the usurped power and authority of the bp. of Rome. The Act of Supremacy, enacted in 1559, included an oath of supremacy that had to be taken by all persons in ecclesiastical office. It required clerics to swear allegiance to Queen Elizabeth I and her successors and to acknowledge her as the supreme governor of the realm, in matters spiritual as well as temporal. The reference to the usurped power of the bp. of Rome was altered to a renunciation of all foreign jurisdictions, powers, and authorities. William and Mary, in 1689, further modified the form of the oath, in which the ordained swore to "abhor, detest, and abjure . . . that damnable doctrine" that princes excommunicated or deprived by Rome may be deposed or murdered by their subjects, and denied any jurisdiction to foreign powers, ecclesiastical or spiritual. In 1865, a Clerical Subscriptions Act removed the oath from

the ordination service, requiring it to be taken beforehand. The form of the oath was altered in 1868, and at present it is a simple oath of allegiance to the ruling sovereign and his successors, with no mention being made of the king's supremacy.

Other declarations and subscriptions were designed to secure uniformity of doctrine and practice. The adoption of the *Book of Common Prayer, in 1549, was accompanied by an Act of Uniformity. Compliance with its forms was mandatory, and heavy penalties were attached for nonconformity; but no oath was included. The same was true of similar Acts of 1552 and 1559. The Act of Uniformity of 1662, however, required "every Parson, Vicar, or other Minister" to declare before his congregation "unfeigned assent and consent" to the use of everything in the Prayer Book. An oath also had to be taken before the bishop to the same end. With respect to doctrine, the *Forty-Two Articles were published in 1553, and all clerics licensed to preach or instituted to benefices were to subscribe them. They were revised and published in 1563 as the *Thirty-Nine Articles, without any provision concerning subscription. In 1571, however, a Subscription Act was passed, making subscription obligatory upon all clerics. By the Clergy Subscriptions Act of 1865 and subsequent Acts of 1868 and 1871, the required oath and subscription were reduced to a single declaration of assent to the Thirty-Nine Articles and the Prayer Book, and affirming a belief that the doctrine of the C of E is agreeable to the word of God. The declaration is made before the ordination service. The oath of canonical obedience (or due obedience) was originally only for bps. to make in relation to their abps., and it was a part of the Edwardine Ordinal of 1550. Eventually, it was extended to apply to all clerics being licensed to a curacy or instituted to a benefice. It is not a promise of unlimited obedience to a person, but signifies willingness to submit to the administrative authority of bp. or abp. insofar as he officially requires what is in accord with the laws of the Church. See Hughes RE; G. Harford and M. Stevenson, eds., *Prayer Book Dictionary* (1925).

OBERLIN CONFERENCE, the first North American conference on *Faith and Order, held at Oberlin, Ohio, Sept. 3–10, 1957. The general theme, "The Nature of the Unity We Seek," was considered in relation to three main areas: the gospel, the organized structures conducive to unity, and the sociocultural pressures that affect unity. The Conference, attended by RC observers authorized by the local diocese, produced a statement on the Eucharist (not accepted by all the participating Churches) that declared that "this commemoration . . . is more than the mere recollection of a past event . . . [it is] an action in which Christ mediates himself to us in the present moment" and that "in the entire eucharistic action Christ is personally present." In an attempt to define the unity of Christ's Church that was sought, the conference stressed a unity of ministry and members "bound together in a worshipping and sacramental community"—a concept further elaborated in later studies and formulations, notably that of the *New Delhi Assembly (1961). See P. S. Minear, ed., *Nature of the Unity We Seek* (1958).

OBERLIN THEOLOGY, system of Christian thought that flourished in the 19th cent. at Oberlin College in Ohio under the leadership of Asa Mahan (1799–1889), Charles G. *Finney (1792–1875), and James H. Fairchild (1817–1902). The doctrine, first advanced by Mahan and continued by Finney, emphasized Christian *perfectionism and *sanctification. Influenced by the *New England Theology, Finney repudiated the traditional Calvinist doctrines of the determinism of the will and the imputation of Adam's guilt but retained the notion of *total depravity. Especially distinctive of the Oberlin movement was the principle of the simplicity of moral action, a view that maintained each moral choice to be either totally sinful, as self-gratifying, or holy, as surrendered to the general good. Fairchild's *Elements of Theology, Natural and Revealed* (1892) presented similar views in less formal terms. The system proved adaptable to a common-sense view of the Christian life and was a departure from orthodox Calvinism. See G. F. Wright, *Charles Grandison Finney* (1891); F. H. Foster, *Genetic History of the New England Theology* (1907); R. S. Fletcher, *History of Oberlin College* (2v., 1943).

O'BRYAN, WILLIAM (1778–1868), founder of the *Bible Christians in England. Beginning in 1808 he effectively assisted Methodist preachers in Cornwall. In 1810 he was expelled without trial for preaching outside his assigned *circuit. Rejoining in 1814, he was again expelled. A powerful evangelist, he formed his own *society, Oct. 9, 1815, at Shebbear, N. Devon. It grew into the Bible Christian denomination, from which O'Bryan and several hundred separated in 1829, reuniting in 1835. He emigrated to the U.S. and spread Methodism in Canada. See W. J. Townsend et al., eds., *New History of Methodism* (2v., 1909), 1:503–513.

OBSCURANTISM, opposition to enlightenment, scholarship, and intellectual progress, particularly on the grounds of maintaining religious orthodoxy. Use of the term perhaps derives from the *Epistolae obscurorum virorum* (*Letters of Obscure Men*, 1515–17). In the conflicts of religion with contemporary philosophy, historical studies, and science (including scientific criticism of the Bible) obscurantism has been a term of reproach against those who reject the validity of these movements. It is applied esp. to those who reject them without serious study and who try to keep others from having the opportunity to consider them. Obscurantism implies a deliberate refusal to examine evidence or arguments that might lead to a change of outlook. It is associated with such features as censorship of books, dismissal of teachers with liberal views, opposition to an educated clergy, and general indifference to scholarship and other intellectual values.

OCHINO, BERNARDINO (1487–1564), Italian Reformer. A native of Siena, of the 'Oca quarter, whence came his name, O. became first an Observantine Franciscan (*c.*1512), then a Capuchin (1534). He held high office among the Capuchins and until his defection was considered the most powerful preacher in Italy. Through contacts with Juan de *Valdés and *Peter Martyr Vermigli in Naples in 1536, he began to accept Lutheran teachings and to insinuate them into his sermons, e.g., in a series at Venice in 1539. He fled to Geneva in 1542, his departure being a great blow to his order. His life as a Protestant was spent continually moving about; he lived in Geneva, Augsburg, Strassburg, England (1547–55; he was a prebendary at Canterbury), Zurich, and Poland. As a Catholic he published *Dialoghi sette* (1540 and 1542) on Christian perfection and *Prediche nove* (1541), a collection of sermons. His Protestant writings were translated into many languages; two in English were *The Usurped Primacy of the Bishop of Rome* and the *Labyrinth*, in which he opposed Calvinist teaching on predestination. O. derided celibacy and the religious state; but his theories were also considered excessive by the Reformers. He was expelled from Zurich for his *Dialoghi XXX* (1563), which seemed to attack both the Trinity and monogamy. He found brief refuge in Poland, then in Slavkov (Austerlitz), Moravia, where he died in misery. His thought became more and more skeptical with regard to dogma, and he made the individual conscience the supreme norm of morality. See R. H. Bainton, *B. O.* (1940); F. C. Church, *Italian Reformers 1534–1564* (1932).

ODD FELLOWS, INDEPENDENT ORDER OF (IOOF), a secret, fraternal society. The IOOF traces its history to several convivial and mutual benefit societies that started in 18th-cent. England. A re-organization and reform undertaken by the Manchester lodge in 1812 led to a federation of Odd Fellows lodges. Thomas Wildey, a member of an English lodge, came to the U.S. in 1817 and established the first Odd Fellows lodge in Baltimore in 1819; lodges were founded in Boston in 1820, and in Philadelphia in 1821. In 1842 the American lodges declared their independence of the English lodges.

IOOF lodges have four degrees: Initiatory, Friendship, Love, and Truth. A higher Encampment lodge confers three additional degrees: Patriarchal, Golden Rule, and Royal Purple. A uniformed parade unit is known as the Patriarchs Militant. The Odd Fellows ritual has undergone many revisions; the most recent was in 1954. The Ancient Order of Samaritans serves as the "fun" organization for the Odd Fellows; female relatives may join the Rebekah lodge. About 1,400,000 men belong to 22,000 lodges in the U.S., Canada, Australia, Germany, Switzerland, the Netherlands, Mexico, Cuba, and Sweden. Membership has declined since the 1920s, and the lodge has difficulty attracting young men or college graduates. The order maintains a chain of homes for the aged and for orphans. Baltimore, Md. is its headquarters. Negroes are not eligible for initiation; they have organized a separate lodge, the Grand United Order of Odd Fellows in America, which is not recognized by the IOOF. Because of its oaths and naturalistic philosophy the IOOF was condemned by the Holy Office (now Congregation for the Doctrine of the Faith) in 1894. Roman Catholics who join the IOOF are denied the sacraments but are not excommunicated; the religious position of the Odd Fellows was not regarded to be as opposed to Christian teaching as was that of the Freemasons. Individual Catholics may retain passive membership in the lodge for the sake of keeping insurance protection provided there is no danger to faith or scandal to others. Some Lutheran bodies and other Protestant Churches also forbid membership in the lodges. See W. J. Whalen, *Handbook of Secret Organizations* (1966), 117–125.

OECOLAMPADIUS, JOHANNES (Gr. form of his surname, Husschyn or Hussgen; 1482–1531), German humanist and Reformer of Basel. O. studied at Heidelberg and Bologna, was ordained in 1510, and then studied Greek and Hebrew at Tübingen and Stuttgart, where he first met *Melanchthon. In 1515 he helped *Erasmus with his editing of Jerome and of the NT, and began his own lifelong task of editing and translating the Greek Fathers. After serving as cathedral preacher in Basel and Augsburg, he suddenly retired (1520) to the Brigittine monastery of Altomünster to clarify his thinking. There he wrote *Paradoxon,* a treatise on confession. The tension created in the monastery by his views caused him to leave. He returned to Basel, where he was named professor of Scripture. In 1525 he was made pastor at St. Martin's as well. In his dual role as pastor and professor O. guided the church reform of Basel, drafting its *church order (*Ordinances of the City of Basel,* 1529) and its liturgy. His reform measures helped form Calvin's idea of church discipline. O. participated in conferences at Baden (1526), Bern (1528), and Marburg (1529), where he defended the eucharistic teaching of his friend *Zwingli (see MARBURG ARTICLES). See H. R. Guggisberg, RGG 4:1567–68; Léonard HistProt 1:146–151; 155–160.

OHIO YEARLY MEETING OF FRIENDS CHURCH (Evangelical Friends Alliance), a branch of the Religious Society of Friends of the evangelical wing in the *Gurneyite line. In 1965 it joined with the Kansas, Oregon, and Rocky Mountain Yearly Meetings to form the Evangelical Friends Alliance. Membership in the Ohio Yearly Meeting in 1965 was 7,059, with 87 churches.

O'KELLY, JAMES (c.1735–1826), one of the founding fathers of the Christian Churches, which, in 1931, merged with the Congregational Church. A Methodist *lay preacher from c.1775, he was ordained in 1785 and became a presiding elder in southern Va.

(1785–92). During much of this time he contended with Bp. F. *Asbury in opposition to Asbury's episcopal authority. Failing to gain the right of ministerial appeal for appointments in the *general conference of 1792, O'K. and his followers withdrew. They at first formed the Republican Methodist Church (1793), which they renamed the Christian Church at a meeting in Surry Co., Va., in 1794. At the same meeting they took the Bible as their only creed and ruled for a single order of the clergy, Congregational *independency, and government by the laity. O'K. continued as an itinerant preacher through the remainder of his long life. His followers merged with those of Elias Smith and Abner Jones to form the Christian Denomination, later renamed the Christian Churches. They also felt close affinity with Barton W. *Stone, until in 1832 he merged his followers with those of Alexander *Campbell. See C. F. Kilgore, *J. O'K.: Schism in the Methodist Episcopal Church* (1963), with complete bibliog. of original sources.

OLD CATHOLIC CHURCH OF THE NETHERLANDS, the *Little Church of Utrecht (OBC), which entered the *Old Catholic communion in 1889.

OLD CATHOLICS, members of a religious body that arose in the 19th cent. as an organized secession from the RC Church in protest against its teaching on papal primacy and infallibility. They accuse the RC Church of deserting traditional Catholicism in the following instances: the Council of Trent, centralizing power in the papacy; the bull *Unigenitus* (1713), demanding blind obedience to the pope's word; Pius IX's issuing the dogma of the Immaculate Conception (1854) without a council; the *Syllabus of Errors* (1864), manifesting papal despotism; and Vatican Council I, proclaiming under constraint the dogma of the infallibility and universal episcopate of the pope.

Denial of papal supremacy by the celebrated canonist Z. B. van Espen (1646–1728) led to the *Schism of Utrecht inaugurating the independent Little Church of Utrecht (1724), which ultimately became the Old Catholic Church (OCC) of the Netherlands. Van Espen's idea was expanded by J. N. von Hontheim (1701–90), coadjutor bp. of Trier (pseudonym, J. Febronius). He asserted that bps. must govern the Church and that Scripture contained no basis for papal claims to divine right (see FEBRONIANISM). Febronius's ideas were put into practice successfully in the Diocese of Constance by Vicar-General I. H. von Wessenberg (1774–1860), who became the forerunner of the OCC in Central Europe. Vatican Council I aroused German professors including I. von *Döllinger, F. *Reusch, and J. von *Schulte, who issued the *Nuremberg Declaration (1870) that sparked the Old Catholic movement. J. H. Reinkens, elected bp. of the German OCC, was consecrated (1874) by Bp. H. Heykamp of Utrecht. Humanism and rationalism contributed to the birth of the Swiss *Christkatholiken, chiefly a lay movement; Reinkens consecrated the first bp., E. Herzog (1878). The Austrian OCC began in 1872, but the government allowed it no bp. until 1925. Also traceable to the late Hapsburg era and belatedly obtaining a bp. (1924) was the OCC of Czechoslovakia. Disputes with Italy and traditions of independence brought forth the Yugoslav OCC (1923). The Old Catholic Communion, the *Union of Utrecht, dates from 1889. Members are: the Dutch, German, Swiss, Austrian, Czech and Yugoslav (Croatian anti-Kalogjera segment) OCC; the *Polish National Catholic Church in America and Poland (founded by F. *Hodur); the largest, the *Philippine Independent Catholic Church was accepted as a member in 1965. These Churches include about 2,400,000 persons (see MARIAVITES). Several British and European Churches style themselves Old Catholic but are not recognized by the Utrecht Union. This is also true of the following in the U.S.: *American Catholic: Archdiocese of New York, *American Catholic (Syro-Antiochean), *Christ Cath-

olic, and the two *North American Old Roman Catholic Churches. The Liberal Catholic Church traces its apostolic succession through the Dutch OCC. The *Bonn Agreement (1931) established intercommunion between the Utrecht Union and the *Anglican Communion.

The doctrinal standard is the *Declaration of Utrecht. Scripture is the primary rule of faith, and genuine tradition is an authoritative source of teaching. The bishop of Rome is recognized solely as "first among equals." Faith working by love is the means of man's justification. The Declaration accepts the seven sacraments (auricular confession is optional for adults), *apostolic succession, the obligation to hear Mass on Sundays and holy days, and commemoration of the faithful departed. The eucharistic *Real Presence is professed, but not transubstantiation. Divorce is forbidden. Old Catholics reject the treasury of merits of saints; the Immaculate Conception and Assumption of Mary as well as the title "mediatrix of all graces"; compulsory days of fast; indulgences; pilgrimages; processions; veneration of the saints, relics, and images; sacramentals; the Roman Index of Forbidden Books; male religious orders; obligatory reading of the Breviary by priests; and temporal power and privilege for Church and clergy. Clerical marriage, mixed marriages, cremation, and communion under both kinds by *intinction are allowed. The Polish National Catholic Church and the Philippine Independent Catholic Church have minor variations in doctrine and practice.

Church edifices and ornaments are similar to those of the RC Church, but simpler. Liturgy for services and sacraments is based on the Roman rite and uses the vernacular except for the formula "Receive the Holy Ghost," which is said in Latin at a bp.'s consecration. In the Creed the *filioque* is omitted. Rites are recited aloud with the congregation participating. Sunday readings are spread over a 5-year cycle. Each OCC is a national Church; its bp. (abp. in the case of Utrecht) rules as a constitutional monarch. The supreme government is the synod, comprising the bp. and synodal council members (priests and lay representatives of the parishes). Meeting annually, the synod is chaired in Germany by the bp., but in Austria and Switzerland by a layman; it legislates but may not alter or add dogma; by majority vote it elects the bp., who (in Europe) must seek approval by the civil government. The synod chooses members of an executive body, composed of the bp., three priests, and five laymen, which is responsible to the synod. The synod also elects four jurymen of the synodal court; the bp., an ex-officio member, appoints three judges; cases may be appealed to the synod. Each parish elects its own pastor. See V. Conzemius, "Catholicism: Old and Roman," *Journal of Ecumenical Studies* 4 (1967), 426–445; C. B. Moss, *Old Catholic Movement* (1966).

OLD GERMAN BAPTIST BRETHREN (Old Order Dunkers), a dissident group from the Fraternity of German Baptists (name changed to the Church of the Brethren in 1908), named and organized in 1881. Being the ultra-conservatives of the parent Church, they opposed protracted evangelistic meetings, Sabbath schools, prayer meetings and Bible classes, high schools, paid ministry, and modern dress. The continuing fraternity of 4,000 or less consists of frugal, hardworking, plain people adhering to the historical rites of German Baptists. *BRETHREN CHURCHES.

OLD LIGHTS, a designation with two historical uses: (1) In the Church of Scotland, the *Burghers and *Anti-Burghers, the first in 1799, the second in 1806, both were split into *New Light and Old Light factions. The Old Lights allowed the magistrate a limited place in ecclesiastical affairs; the New Lights wished his exclusion. In the U.S., Presbyterians of Scottish background in the *Reformed Presbyterian Church were divided into Old Lights, forbidding members to participate in civil life, and New Lights, allowing such participation.

(2) In the *Great Awakening, Baptists and Congregationalists opposed to revivalism were called Old Lights; those favoring revivals, New Lights.

OLD ORDER AMISH, the most conservative of the *Amish Mennonites. The designation "Old Order" came into use between 1850 and 1870, to connote the resistance of these Amish to modernization either in church life or in manner of living. They continue to wear plain, 18th-cent. dress, live apart, and resist the use of modern machinery and appliances. Because they worship in private homes, they are sometimes called "House Amish," while more progressive Amish Mennonites are called "Church Amish." The Old Amish use German in worship services; in daily life among themselves they use a German dialect, "Pennsylvania Dutch." They object to education above an elementary level. There are settlements in Pa., Ohio, Ind., and Iowa. The main organized body is the Old Amish Mennonite Church; there are some Unaffiliated Conservative and Amish Mennonite Churches. Baptized (i.e., adult) members in the U.S. and Canada number nearly 25,000. See MennEnc 1:43–47.

OLD ORDER AMISH MENNONITE CHURCH, a Church organized c.1865, and having about 2,000 members in 1969. *OLD ORDER AMISH.

OLD ORDER (YORKER) BRETHREN, a Church formed by a division of the Brethren in Christ in 1843. A number of congregations in York Co., Pa., felt that the traditional simplicity and unworldliness of the original Brethren were no longer observed in other districts and separated from the majority. They still worship in barns and private homes and observe the distinctive plain dress of the early Brethren. The Old Order Brethren opposed Sunday schools and foreign missions. In 1963 there were only 7 congregations of Old Order Brethren, served by 5 ministers, with an aggregate membership of 78 persons. All of the Old Order Brethren are in Lancaster and Franklin Counties, Pennsylvania. See A. W. Climenhaga, *History of the Brethren in Christ Church* (1942).

OLD ORDER (WISLER) MENNONITE CHURCH,

a body named for Jacob Wisler (1808–89), who led a separation (1872) from the Mennonite Church in Ind. and Ohio. Other Old Order Mennonites are sometimes also designated as Wislerites. Generally, they are those Mennonites who were motivated by resistance to new elements introduced in part through revivalistic influences. The Old Order Mennonites strongly adhere to conservative Mennonite teaching and practice. The effort to preserve the use of the German language is meeting with failure. There are about 6,000 Old Order Mennonites in the U.S. and Canada. See MennEnc 4:47–49.

OLD SCHOOL (Presbyterians), a party of a schism, which became open in 1837, in the Presbyterian Church in the U.S.A. (see UNITED PRESBYTERIAN CHURCH). Old School Presbyterians objected to the inroad of doctrines from the *New Haven theology of N. *Taylor; the spokesman for orthodox scholastic Calvinism was C. *Hodge (see PRINCETON THEOLOGY). Old School Presbyterians also objected to loosening of church discipline through cooperation with interdenominational agencies. New School Presbyterians were largely members of *synods formed on the frontier as a result of the *Plan of Union of 1801 with Congregationalists. Several New School synods were expelled by the *General Assembly of 1837. Divisions were further complicated by the slavery issue, the New Schoolers being outspoken abolitionists. The two groups became separate denominations, and in the South after formation of the Confederacy the New School party became absorbed into the original Pres-

byterian Church in the U.S.A. The division was healed in 1869–70. See Olmstead 311–315.

OLD SIDE (Presbyterians), name for the Synod of Philadelphia that opposed revivalism in a dispute that divided American Presbyterians, 1741–58. *NEW SIDE.

OLEVIANUS, CASPAR (Olevian; 1536–87), *Reformed theologian. O. was a doctor of law when he became interested in Calvinism. He studied theology at Geneva and Zurich (1557), and became a preacher and teacher at Trier until 1560. At the invitation of the Calvinist Elector Frederick III, O. went to Heidelberg. There as professor, pastor, and church councilor (1560–71), he was one of those principally responsible for the *Heidelberg Catechism (1561), a ritual (1563), and a Genevan type of church discipline (1570). After Frederick's death and the reestablishment of Lutheranism in the Palatinate, O. labored successfully for the Calvinist cause in the Hesse-Nassau region of Germany. His theological writings were an expression of the characteristic teachings of John Calvin and the *covenant theology of J. *Bullinger. See J. F. G. Goeters, RGG 4:1626; J. Ney, EncRelKnow 8:235; bibliog. for Heidelberg Catechism.

OLIVÉTAN, PIERRE ROBERT (c.1506–38), early French Reformer, and translator of the Bible; he signed himself "Louis Olivier." O. was a cousin of John *Calvin and had been won over to the Protestant reforms in the 1520s. Theodore *Beza in his *Life of Calvin* stresses O.'s influence on the young Calvin when the latter was a student at the Univ. of Paris. O. fled France for Strassburg in 1528, where he continued his study of Greek and Hebrew. Later at Neuchâtel, where he was principal of a school, he undertook a French translation of the Bible at the request of the Waldenses of Piedmont. This work, based on the earlier translation of *Lefèvre d'Étaples, was published at Neuchâtel in 1535. Calvin, then a new convert to the Protestant cause, contributed two prefaces to it. O.'s translation, later somewhat revised, was used by French-speaking Protestants well into the 19th century.

OLIVI, PETER JOHN, see PETER JOHN OLIVI.

ONEIDA COMMUNITY, also called Perfectionists, the best-known American communal movement of the 19th cent., established by John Humphrey Noyes (1816–86). He was converted at New Haven, Conn., during the revivals inspired by C. G. *Finney. After association with those perfectionists who believed that Christ's second coming had already occurred, and who carried their idea of *sanctification to the limit of *antinomianism, esp. with regard to sexual matters, Noyes established his community at Putney, Vt. (1845); public outcry forced a move to Oneida, N.Y., 2 years later. The community considered itself the kingdom of God on earth, living in the millennium according to a pattern of life that was communitarian both in its economic organization and in its sexual practice. In the arrangement called "complex marriage," monogamy was repudiated; eugenic theories of Noyes, including the control of the sexual embrace, were also practiced. Because of public opinion, the community life was abandoned in 1880, but a corporation was formed (1881) to carry on its manufacturing enterprises, and remains famous for its silverware. See M. Holloway, *Heavens on Earth: Utopian Communities in America 1630–1880* (1951).

OPEN BIBLE STANDARD CHURCHES, INC., a Pentecostal body formed in 1935 by the union of two older groups. The first was the Bible Standard, Inc., founded in Eugene, Ore., which separated from the Apostolic Faith Mission in 1919. The second was the Open Bible Evangelistic Association of Des Moines, Iowa, which separated from

the International Church of the Foursquare Gospel in 1932. The polity of the Open Bible Standard Churches is *congregational. A strong missionary program with more than 50 missionaries in Africa and Latin America is maintained. Headquarters are in Des Moines, Iowa; membership in 1966 was about 27,000. See J. T. Nichol, *Pentecostalism* (1966), 144–146.

OPEN BRETHREN, those of the Plymouth Brethren who regard as acceptable association with non-Brethren. The division into Open and Exclusive Brethren began in 1848. *PLYMOUTH BRETHREN.

OPEN COMMUNION, term for the practice whereby a Church admits to the Lord's Supper Christians who are not members; the opposite of close, or closed, communion. Although some Catholics have advocated or practiced open communion, RC church law forbids it. Among Protestant Churches open communion has become general. The issue of open vs. closed communion has had particular prominence in Baptist history; the Baptists who accept open communion still distinguish it from open membership, i.e., acceptance as members without rebaptism those who already had been baptized as infants in another Church. *CLOSED COMMUNION; *INTER-COMMUNION.

ORANGE, COUNCILS OF, early synods held at Orange in what is now southern France. The city was an episcopal see from the 4th till the 18th cent.; it is particularly known in the history of theology for two councils, one held in 441, the other in 529. The first, under St. Hilary of Arles, was attended by 16 bps. and enacted 30 canons concerning disciplinary matters, such as the celibacy of deacons. What is historically known as the Second Council of Orange, 529, is of doctrinal importance. It did for the ending of *Semi-Pelagianism what the 15th (16th) Council of Carthage did for Pelagianism. St. Caesarius of Arles, with a view to putting an end to the opposition of the school of Lérins to the teaching of St. Augustine on the need of grace for the beginning of faith and for perseverance in good works, composed what are now known as the *Decrees of the Second Council of Orange*, drawing from a Roman list (or composing himself) the first 8 canons (D 371–378) and adding 17 propositions selected from the *Sententiae Augustini* of Prosper of Aquitaine (D 379–395). He prefaced the document with an introduction of his own and appended a profession of faith (D 370, 396–398). This document was promulgated at Orange, on the occasion of the blessing of a basilica, and signed by 14 bps. and 8 laymen. It apparently had not been submitted to any conciliar discussion. It was sent to Rome for approval and went by the name of *Decrees of the Second Council of Orange*. The following year, at the request of Caesarius, Pope Boniface II confirmed the decrees, particularly the profession of faith (D 398–400). Orange was not included in conciliar collections through several centuries. St. Thomas Aquinas at first apparently did not know of its teaching; but the decrees did influence the Council of Trent (D 1551–53). See C. M. Aherne, NCE 10:712.

ORDERS (Holy Orders), the various grades or ranks of ministry in the Church. In the Catholic tradition the term also refers to the sacrament of holy orders through which a person receives the power of ministry.

Orders of Ministry. In RC, Old Catholic, Eastern, and Anglican teaching there is agreement that diaconate, priesthood, and episcopate are essential orders of ministry in the Church. There are designations of diverse ministries in Acts and in the Epistles of St. Paul (e.g., Acts 11.30, 14.14; 1 Cor 12.28; Eph 4.11; 1 Tim 3.2, 5.17), with mention of *bishops (overseers), *presbyters (elders), and *deacons; in the 3d cent. Eusebius in his *Ecclesiastical History* mentioned other particular offices: subdeacons, acolytes, exorcists, readers, and door-keepers. It was not until the Middle Ages, however, that there was any settled determination of the number of orders, or of the distinction between major orders (priest, deacon, subdeacon) and minor orders (acolyte, exorcist, lector, doorkeeper). Until Vatican Council II RC theologians did not agree on whether the episcopate is an order distinct from priesthood. The Council made the distinction clear. Since the 1550 revision of the Anglican Ordinal made no mention of minor orders, the Anglican Communion does not observe them; in other Churches of a Catholic tradition, there is no uniform practice with regard to minor orders. The term "orders" is not prominent in the purely Protestant traditions. But a distinction and gradation of offices in the ministry of word and sacraments were developed in the Lutheran, *Reformed and *free church traditions on the basis of their varying concepts of the Church and *ministry.

Orders as a Sacrament. In the RC, Old Catholic, and Eastern Churches orders, or holy orders, is numbered among the seven sacraments. The Protestant Churches do not regard orders or the offices of ministry as a sacrament. The Anglican *Thirty-Nine Articles regard orders as one of the five commonly called sacraments but not to be counted a sacrament of the gospel (Art. 25). The sacrament is administered only by a bishop; the essentials of the administration are the *laying on of hands, together with the authorized form of words. Through episcopal administration of orders the line of apostolic succession is maintained by these Churches. Vatican Council II clarified an issue long ambiguous in RC theology. The Council of Trent had declared that the hierarchy in the Church was constituted by bishops, priests, and deacons (D 1776); it did not, however, enumerate episcopacy as a distinct order (D 1765). Vatican II stated that "through episcopal ordination the fullness of the sacrament of orders is conferred" (Vat II ConstCh 21). See B. L. Lambert, *Ecumenism* (1966); G. Weigel, *Churches in North America* (1961); J. C. Wand, *Anglicanism* (1963).

ORDERS, ANGLICAN, see ANGLICAN ORDERS.

ORDERS AND PRAYERS FOR CHURCH WORSHIP, a manual primarily for the use of British Baptist ministers, first published in 1960 (2d ed., 1965). Having no official denominational sanction, the book was prepared by E. A. Payne and S. F. Winward, and its use is purely voluntary. Payne is a church historian and has served as secretary of the Baptist Union of Great Britain and Ireland; he has also been president of the World Council of Churches. Winward is a London pastor and author of *The Reformation of Our Worship* (1964). The manual has been widely used in Great Britain. Baptists usually have had simple, informal services of worship, stressing freedom and spontaneity. The editors of *Orders and Prayers* maintain that freedom does not preclude preparation of prayers and utilization of forms used by other communions. As is explained in the "Introduction," they wished to avoid the extremes of an inflexible, fixed liturgy and the "uninspired disorder" that often results from disregard of traditional forms. Endeavoring to combine freedom and order, they disclaim any intention of offering a Baptist equivalent of the *Book of Common Prayer; they are providing a Book of Common Order. The eight main parts of the book include orders of service; Scripture passages; and prayers for regular public worship, for baptism and the Lord's Supper, and for special occasions. The last section has a lectionary for ordinary and systematic reading of the Scriptures at public services of worship.

ORDINALS, ANGLICAN, see ANGLICAN ORDINALS.

ORDINANCE, a term common among Mennonites, Baptists, and other nonliturgical Churches, used instead of "sacrament." The preference is based on the objection to magical connotations of the latter term (see SACRAMENTALISM). Early Baptists used both terms but preferred ordinances, and later Baptists used it almost exclusively. With reference to baptism and the Lord's Supper, no biblical precedent exists for calling these rites either sacraments or ordinances. The latter, however, is an OT term (e.g., Ex 29.9; Lev 6.18), which was interpreted to mean something divinely instituted and of perpetual validity. See W. R. McNutt, *Polity and Practice in Baptist Churches* (rev. ed., 1959); MennEnc 4:72–73.

ORDINATION, the conferring and receiving of an order or office of ministry in the Church. In Churches of Catholic tradition it is the conferring and receiving of the sacrament of *orders. In the Protestant tradition ordination is the commission or designation of a Christian to exercise a ministry in the Church; it is nonsacramental. A few Protestant bodies do not have an ordained ministry; ministers function either in virtue of a charismatic calling or in virtue of simple designation by the congregation.

In RC and Eastern Churches ordination is always performed by a bishop (see APOSTOLIC SUCCESSION). Ordination to the minor or preparatory orders is nonsacramental but does confer sacred office and function in the Church. Ordination to the subdiaconate is also nonsacramental, although the RC subdiaconate is classified as a major order. The ordinations of deacons, priests, and bishops are sacramental actions. The essentials (matter and form) of these ordinations are the laying on of hands and the pronouncing of the ritual words prescribed for each order; on this point the determination of Pius XII, *Sacramentum ordinis* (1947; D 3857–61), was confirmed by Paul VI in the apostolic constitution *Pontificalis Romani* (1968). Old Catholic Churches have a similar teaching and practice. The Anglican *Thirty-Nine Articles treat of the consecrating of bishops, and the ordering of priests and deacons in Art. 36. Ordination, in accord with Anglican teaching on the *historic episcopate and with apostolic succession, is always by a bishop with the laying on of hands and prayers prescribed by the Ordinal (see ORDINALS, ANGLICAN). Although holy orders is not one of the two sacraments of the gospel, ordination is regarded as an indispensable requisite for the exercise of the sacred ministry necessary to the Church, namely the ministry of absolving, of blessing, and of celebration of the Eucharist.

In Protestant Churches ordination, while not regarded as sacramental, is in most instances held to be essential to ministry. The *Augsburg Confession, reflecting Luther's own teaching, requires that one be "rightly called" before publicly teaching or administering the sacraments (Art. 14). The Second *Helvetic Confession speaks of the necessity of ordination to a ministry divinely established in the Church (c. 18). These basic views of the need of ordination to the ministry have generally perdured. The minister is a layman called by God to exercise the ministry (see PRIESTHOOD OF ALL BELIEVERS); by ordination the Church commissions the minister officially and permanently to fulfill this call. In this sense the minister is set apart from other laymen; he is not, however, considered to be set apart as participating in a special priesthood. Ordination usually includes the laying on of hands, either by a bishop or, in Churches of nonepiscopal polity, by other ministers. See W. J. O'Shea, NCE 10:727–734, s.v. "Roman Rite"; P. Fransen and W. Lohff, LTK 7:1212–24; E. Lohse et al., RGG 4:1671–79; B. Lambert, *Ecumenism* (1967). *MINISTRY.

OREGON YEARLY MEETING OF FRIENDS CHURCH, a branch of the Religious Society of Friends in the evangelical wing of the Gurneyite line. In 1926 it separated from the Five Years Meeting (see FRIENDS UNITED MEETING), fearing the latter's liberal tendencies, and in 1965 joined with the Ohio, Kansas, and Rocky Mountain Yearly Meetings to form the Evangelical Friends Alliance. Oregon Yearly Meeting membership was 6,202, with 62 churches in 1969.

ORIGINAL SIN, in Christian teaching a sinful condition common to every member of the human race. The term "original" denotes a traditional explanation of the community of this condition, namely, that it is derived by reason of origin, and specifically because of carnal descent from Adam. Both RC and Protestant *doctrinal standards have affirmed the fact of original sin in this sense; they have differed on the nature of the sinful condition as it affects each individual. New biblical and theological interpretations are being sought.

Source of Original Sin. The articulation of the universal sinfulness of mankind as a sin through origin from Adam came with St. Augustine. His teaching was reflected in the second canon of the Council held at Carthage in 418 against *Pelagianism (D 223), and in canons 1 and 2 of the Second Council of Orange, held in 529 (D 371–372). These canons were revised and incorporated at the Council of Trent in the decree on original sin, which stands as the normative statement of RC teaching (D 1511–16). The decree speaks of a particular person, Adam, sinning and losing grace and other gifts not only for himself but for all mankind, and of his passing on not only punishment but also sin to his descendants. The sin is described as one in kind because of its one source and as present in each person because of descent from Adam, not because of a personal act imitating his sin. The most recent authoritative comment on this decree is the encyclical of Pius XII, *Humani generis* (1950), which states that it is in no way apparent how the denial of monogenism, the origin of the human race from a single couple, can be reconciled with Tridentine teaching.

The classical Protestant *confessions of faith for the most part simply assumed the explanation of man's sinful condition as a "birth sin." The Lutheran *Augsburg Confession states that all men begotten after the common course of nature are born with sin (Art. II). The *Reformed confessions repeat that original sin is "an hereditary evil" but also introduce the idea of a covenant by which Adam acted for all and his sin was thus imputed to all (*Gallican Confession, Art. X; *Westminster Confession, Ch. VI and VII; *Westminster Catechism, Q. 16). The Westminster Confession is echoed in the *Savoy Declaration of Congregationalism and in the Baptists' *Philadelphia Confession. For Anglicanism the *Thirty-Nine Articles speak of "the fault and corruption of the nature of every man that naturally is engendered of the offspring of Adam" (Art. IX); the *Twenty-Five Articles of Methodism repeat these words (Art. VII).

Pelagianism was a denial of the hereditary sin of mankind. Unitarian rationalism rejected the concept of the Fall and of hereditary guilt. The Anabaptist and Mennonite traditions with their stress on salvation as a personal experience paid little heed to original sin. The *Apology* of R. *Barclay of the Religious Society of Friends recognized no causal connection between Adam's sin and the fallen condition of every man, nor did it recognize any sinful quality in this condition anterior to personal consent. In the preaching of the *Holiness movement original sin is inbred but involuntary and guiltless. Mormons, or Latter-day Saints, simply reject original sin. Even where the Churches officially maintained the traditional acceptance of original sin, actual adherence to the doctrine diminished. Under the influence of the *Enlightenment, rationalism, and higher biblical criticism, Protestants, except for fundamentalists, largely dismissed the doctrine. Liberal theology, with its subjectivism, optimism, and obliteration of the supernatural, had no place for it. In the theology of Karl *Barth and in *neo-orthodoxy, original sin was reasserted basically as a condition of man's creatureliness and egocentricity; there is scant connection with the traditional explanation. Many RC theologians have been directing their efforts to explanations more in keeping with modern biblical exegesis and evolutionary theory and to an understanding of the doctrine that would not make carnal descent from Adam essential in RC teaching on human community in sin. No consensus has been achieved.

Source of Original Sin. The decrees of Trent did not resolve continuing differences between RC theologians as to whether original sin consists essentially simply in the absence of an original righteousness or in *concupiscence. Canon 5 states that all that is of sin, not just its imputation, is taken away by baptism; concupiscence is not sin in a proper sense (D 1515). Canon 2 refers to a loss of sanctity and righteousness, as well as death and other penalties, derived to all men from Adam's sin (D 1512). The moral plight of man, however, does not mean loss of free will (D 1521, 1535, 1941, 1966, 2003); nor does it mean complete incapacity for moral good (1537, 1961, 1962, 1965, 2001, 2401). For Luther original sin is the "capital sin," looming larger than actual sins; it is an abiding condition of blindness, rebellion, and concupiscence besetting human nature; its dominance makes critical the need of grace saving through faith. The Calvinistic tradition speaks of human *total depravity; *Arminianism rejected this idea and extolled man's power to consent to grace. In this vein J. *Wesley accepted the Thirty-Nine Articles' statement that man is "very far gone from original righteousness," but denied that there is true guilt in inbred sin, and proposed the ideal of a sinless *Christian perfection. Holiness teaching on *sanctification also extolls the moral capacities of man; concupiscence is not an insuperable sinfulness. Rationalist or liberalist tendencies in theology, of course, did not recognize any basic deterioration in human nature. The classic "pessimism" of the Reformation was reformulated by Barth and neo-orthodoxy.

ORTHODOX CREED, drafted in 1678 by *General Baptists as "an essay to unite and confirm all true Protestants." It was intended to clear the General Baptists of charges of *Socinianism and to demonstrate their fundamental accord with *Particular Baptists and other *dissenters. Its most notable features were: (1) the preoccupation of its drafters with Christology; the first eight articles of the Creed are devoted to this subject, and the preface states, "We are sure that the denying of baptism is a less evil than to deny the Divinity or Humanity of Christ"; (2) a desire to harmonize differences regarding *Arminianism and *Calvinism among Baptists through the articles on "Predestination and Election," "Original Sin," "Perseverance," "The Invisible Church," and "The Covenants"; (3) the declaration in the article entitled "Of General Councils or Assemblies" that representatives from local churches met in general assembly "make up one church" and that these assemblies have power to deal with heresies or grievances of members of local congregations; (4) the statement of Article 38 that "The three Creeds, viz. Nicene creed, Athanasius' creed, and the Apostles' creed, . . . ought thoroughly to be received, and believed"; this is the only known Baptist confession that includes such a statement. The Orthodox Creed was adhered to by many General Baptist Churches as a *doctrinal standard, but was not as widely accepted as the *Standard Creed of 1660. See W. L. Lumpkin, ed., *Baptist Confessions of Faith* (1959).

ORTHODOX PRESBYTERIAN CHURCH, a denomination organized in 1936 under the title Presbyterian Church of America by dissatisfied members of the Presbyterian Church in the U.S.A. (now the United Presbyterian Church in the U.S.A.) under the leadership of J. Gresham *Machen. The purpose of the new denomination was to defend the orthodoxy of the *Westminster Confession, to provide for theological education, and to support an independent board for Presbyterian foreign missions without interference from the larger body. This Church has firmly maintained many doctrinal positions characteristic of *fundamentalism. Its name was changed in 1939. It has remained a relatively small body, with 124 congregations and about 14,000 members in 1967. Its headquarters are in Philadelphia, and it supports Westminster Theological Seminary (Chestnut Hill, Pa.),

which continues to perpetuate a solid Protestant orthodoxy. *REFORMED PRESBYTERIAN CHURCH, EVANGELICAL SYNOD; *BIBLE PRESBYTERIAN CHURCH (COLLINGSWOOD SYNOD).

ORTHODOXY (Gr. *orthos*, straight, right; *doxa*, opinion), a term with several Christian uses: (1) Adherence to established or traditional belief or practice. Since most Christian Churches profess fidelity to the teachings of Christ, and the Apostles, and many adhere to *confessions of faith or *doctrinal standards, orthodoxy means the claim to doctrinal fidelity, in opposition to heresy or heterodoxy. (2) A body of established beliefs or practices. (3) Conservatism or conformity as opposed to liberalism with regard to doctrine or practice. (4) In Lutheran history, the scholastic systematization of doctrine pursued by Lutheran theologians for a century after Luther's death; *Pietism arose as a reaction. (5) Capitalized, a concrete, collective term for Eastern Churches. Byzantine, Jacobites, Armenian, and Coptic Christians originally classified themselves as Orthodox because of fidelity to the Council of Chalcedon and in opposition to Monophysites and Nestorians. (6) In a cognate abstract sense, conformity to the tradition, thought, practice, etc., of the Eastern or Orthodox Churches.

ORTLIBARII, followers of *Ortlieb of Strassburg.

ORTLIEB OF STRASSBURG (13th cent.), founder of the Ortliebarians. The teaching of O., condemned by Innocent III, was an asceticism that appealed to inner experience against church authority, denied the divinity of Christ, and condemned marriage. His followers, called Ortliebarians, did not survive the 13th century. See Bihlmeyer-Tüchle 2:306–307.

OSIANDER, ANDREAS (1498–1552), controversial German Reformer. O. studied at Leipzig, Altenburg, and Ingolstadt and was ordained in 1520, then taught Hebrew in the Augustinian monastery at Nuremberg. By 1522 he had accepted Lutheran teaching. He worked with Lazarus Spengler, Wenceslaus Linck, and Willibald Pirkheimer to introduce Lutheranism into Nuremberg, and he helped write the Brandenburg-Nuremberg *church order (1533). In 1548 he accepted an appointment as pastor at Königsberg (now Kaliningrad) and chief professor on the theological faculty. His inaugural address gave rise to the controversy sometimes called the Osiandric Controversy on the doctrine of justification. O. rejected *forensic justification and taught that righteousness is the indwelling divine nature of Christ in the believer. He was bitterly opposed by M. *Flacius Illyricus, M. *Chemnitz, P. *Melanchthon, and others. O.'s teaching is dealt with and rejected in the *Formula of Concord (Art. 3). In spite of the opposition O. was able, because of Duke Albert's friendship, to stay on the Königsberg faculty until 1551, when he was made superintendent of Samland. At his death the Duke accorded him a royal funeral. See E. Bizer, RGG 4:1730–31; E. G. Schwiebert, NCE 10:806–807.

OTTERBEIN, PHILIP WILLIAM (1726–1813), founder of the United Brethren in Christ (see EVANGELICAL UNITED BRETHREN CHURCH). Born in Dillenberg, Germany, O. entered the ministry of the Reformed Church. He received a classical education at Herborn, center of *Pietism. Ordained in 1749, he was one of the six young pastors who 3 years later followed Michael Schlatter overseas to mission work among the spiritually needy Pennsylvania Germans. He served pastorates at Lancaster, York, and Reading, Pa., and Frederick, Md., before going to the German Evangelical Reformed Church in Baltimore in 1774, where he served until his death. O.'s Pietism, plus a profound religious experience, led him to react against a prevailingly formalized, confessional churchmanship. In 1767, upon hearing Martin *Boehm, a Mennonite layman, preach, O. embraced him with the words "We are brethren." This incident ultimately gave rise to the creation of the Church of the United Brethren in Christ, with the two as superintendents of this initially nondenominational, revivalistic society that in 1800 began to meet regularly. Just before his death, O. "ordained" three men for this ministry. Combining this Pietism with true ecumenism, he never left the Reformed Church; he led the United Brethren in his day not as a separate Church but as a society given to unity and mission. See A. C. Core, *P. W. O.: Pastor-Ecumenist* (1968).

OXFORD CONFERENCE, a world conference of the *Life and Work movement, held at Oxford, England, July 12–26, 1937, under the title Conference on Church, Community, and State. The ferment initiated by the *Stockholm Conference in 1925 had led to a number of similar international conferences in the early 1930s; and in 1934 the Universal Christian Council for Life and Work, meeting on the Danish island of Fanø, issued a call for a world conference of Churches on social, economic, and political problems. The Oxford Conference itself was only one part of a continuing process of ecumenical thinking that extended over several years. There were intensive studies preparatory to the Conference, and its own reports led to additional works of theologians, economists, sociologists, and statesmen. The stated purpose of the Conference was neither to pronounce authoritatively nor to express a consensus of the Churches, but to provide "as comprehensive and balanced a statement as possible . . . of the present mind of the Church" and to define the points in the contemporary situation at which Christian effort was crucial. The issues were considered under four aspects: Church and community; Church and State; Church, community, and State in relation to education; and the universal Church and the world of nations. The question of the nature of the Church was seen as so central that two comprehensive studies were published for the Conference: *The Church and Its Function in Society* and *Kirche, Staat und Mensch*, the latter representing the Orthodox viewpoint. At the Conference itself, reports drafted by the various sections were submitted to the general session, which studied, discussed, and extensively revised them. The six large collections of papers eventually issued became landmarks of Christian social thought. Not without some dissension, the Oxford Conference approved a proposal for a merger of Life and Work with *Faith and Order, which led eventually to creation of the *World Council of Churches. See J. H. Oldham, ed., *Oxford Conference* (1937).

OXFORD GROUP, the name appropriated by F. *Buchman in 1929 for the religious movement now called *Moral Re-Armament. Many of Buchman's followers were Oxford University people. Others at Oxford tried to prevent this use of the university name, and the movement was sometimes referred to as The Group or as Buchmanism.

OXFORD MOVEMENT (1833–45), an attempt by Anglican clergymen of Oxford Univ. to renew the C of E by a return to 17th-cent. *high-church ideals and ritual. It drew strength from the Catholic roots of the C of E, which had been respected by the Elizabethan settlement, had put forth new growth under the Stuarts, but seemed likely to be killed by the patronage of a latitudinarian state under the Hanoverians. Nevertheless, in 1833 a tradition of Catholic-minded learning and piety persisted, esp. among the country gentry and the clergy, whose social prestige outweighed their political power. Looking forward, the Oxford movement should be seen as opening out into the *Anglo-Catholicism that, in the face of decades of opposition from the bps., the press, and Parliament, has influenced the spirit and focus of Anglican worship. In addition, it has provided the RC Church with many of its most capable recruits, although many mid-Victorian con-

verts were not in direct contact with the movement, e.g., the future Cardinal Manning, who in fact had joined in the general attack on John Newman's *Tract 90 and also had been rebuked by E. *Pusey for attacking the Romanizers.

The history of the movement is taken to start with J. *Keble's not very striking assize sermon on "National Apostasy" (1833), which was part of the high-church flurry produced by the *Catholic Emancipation Act (1829), and by the alliance of Daniel O'Connell with the Whigs, and of dissenters with Benthamites. A more considerable manifestation was the first of the *Tracts for the Times, begun by Newman in 1829; they were pamphlets and treatises to recall the Church to its beginnings, to be faithful to the Christian dogmas, to keep its continuity through *apostolic succession, and to work for a unity transcending national boundaries. They spoke for a band of friends, who included R. I. Wilberforce, C. Marriott, and I. Williams; they were reinforced by the weight of Pusey, later joined by W. G. Ward of Balliol and his circle. All agreed in pulling down the idols of the Reformation; not all agreed in looking to Rome. Keble had no liking for Rome, but Froude, the true spark of the movement, turned Newman's eyes in that direction. Yet it was still the time of the *via media*, between the excess of too much articulation of doctrine and the defect of softening it out of existence. The *Library of the Fathers* was begun in 1836, and the corpus of *Caroline Divines in the *Library of Anglo-Catholic Theology* in 1841, with the purpose of drawing the attention of the Church of England to essentials of its authentic patristic and properly Anglican tradition. Opposition to the Tractarians took the form of honest anger, stupefaction, abuse, and ridicule (the subterfuges typical of vested interests when threatened) and the obscurantism that often goes with liberalism. In 1843 things came to a head with *Tract 90*; only a friendly proctor's *non placet* prevented the imposition of an oath of reprobation. In 1845 Ward's exuberant logic drove him to Rome, and Newman took the step, with more agony. Many followed his example. But Pusey and many more stood firm. It was the parting of friends; the last chapter of a volume, but not the end of a series. See R. W. Church, *Oxford Movement* (1891); E. Fairweather, ed., *Oxford Movement* (1964); M. R. O'Connell, *Oxford Conspirators: A History of the Oxford Movement, 1833–45* (1969). *TRACTARIANISM; *EVANGELICAL ALLIANCE.

OXNAM, GARFIELD BROMLEY (1891–1963), Methodist bp. and ecumenist. His education included studies both in the U.S. and abroad. He was president of De Pauw Univ., Greencastle, Ind. (1928–36), then was elected bishop. He served in Omaha (1936–39), Boston (1939–44), New York (1944–52), and Washington, D.C. (1952–60). He supported the union of the three largest Methodist bodies in the U.S. in 1939 (see METHODIST CHURCH); was president of the *Federal Council of Churches (1944–46); and was a member of the six-man praesidium of the newly organized *World Council of Churches (1948–54). He was a founder (1947) and officer of *Protestants and Other Americans United for Separation of Church and State (POAU). In 1953 he appeared at his own request before the House Un-American Activities Committee to defend liberal clergymen charged with Communist sympathies. His numerous publications centered on preaching, social reform, and international and industrial subjects. See HistAmMeth 3:555–556; 569–571.

P

PACIFIC YEARLY MEETING OF FRIENDS, an unaffiliated group of the Religious Society of Friends established in 1947 at Palo Alto, California. Its membership was about 1,700, with 37 churches in 1967.

PACIFISM, doctrinal and practical dedication to peace. Its positive motivation is a faith that all things worth doing can be done through love; negatively, it is expressed by the refusal to use violence or to feel hatred in accomplishing any end in life. It is older than Christianity, going back to Lao Tse and Buddha in the Orient. Christian pacifism is rooted in the teachings of Jesus on love as a way of life. The early Christian Church was predominantly pacifist until the time of the Emperor Constantine in the 4th century. In the era of the Reformation, the Anabaptists of Switzerland, the Swiss Brethren, taught a form of pacifism perhaps better called *nonresistance. Anabaptists refused to accept public office because it might require the use of force, and many Anabaptist leaders died under persecution without making any effort to defend themselves. Their religious testimony of nonresistance was passed on to their successors, the Mennonites, whose leader *Menno Simons declared: "The regenerated do not go to war. They are the children of peace who have beaten their swords into plowshares and their spears into pruning hooks, and know of no war." Mennonites have continued to maintain this teaching, and the German *Brethren Churches have held to similar belief since their origin. In the 17th cent. in England the founder of the Religious Society of Friends (Quakers), George *Fox, insisted that the Lord told him inwardly that he must live "in the virtue of that life and power that took away the occasion of all war." For more than 3 centuries, Friends have at least officially upheld this religious testimony.

The worldwide humanitarian work of the American Friends Service Committee is based on this conviction, and young Friends have conscientiously objected to military service during every war in which their countries have been involved since the mid-17th century. In recent years, they have been joined by an increasing number of individuals from other Protestant denominations and some from the RC Church. Most of these conscientious objectors have been convinced by their own reflections that the use of force against other human beings is wrong and that what is usually accomplished by violent means can be better accomplished through love.

In World War II the U.S. government set up a program of Civilian Public Service for drafted conscientious objectors; nearly 12,000 men were distributed among large camps, where they did manual labor for such government projects as the Soil Conservation, Forest, and National Park Services. Many went from these camps to mental hospitals or training schools, where they served as attendants, and others performed additional types of "detached service" work. In all, about 25,000 men were willing to be drafted into military service if they were allowed to do noncombatant work; most of these were attached to the Medical Corps. About 5,500 men were much more radical: they either refused to register for the draft under Selective Service or, having been drafted, "walked out" of camps and special service units. Only in war time, when there is conscription, is a man forced to declare himself as a pacifist. In the second half of the 20th cent., with the frightening development of atomic weapons, the number of both religious and secular pacifists and near-pacifist organizations, e.g., the International Fellowship of Reconciliation, the War Resisters' International, and the Women's International League for Peace and Freedom, all reflect this growth. There are many differences of opinion among religious and secular pacifists. The basic one questions whether pacifism is a means or is an end in itself. Is love the best means of achieving any goal, or is it rather a way of life desirable in and of itself, quite apart from its practical effectiveness? Another major difference relates to what the pacifist should do under conscription. Some pacifists will do noncombatant work under the military; others will accept work "of national importance" under civilian auspices; still others will do no form of alternative service under the government and must suffer the legal penalties for following the dictates of their conscience. See L. L. McReavy, NCE 10:855–857, and bibliog.

PAEDOBAPTISM, see INFANT BAPTISM.

PAEDOBAPTISTS (Pedobaptists; Gr. *pais*, child, and *baptizein*, baptize), a term used to designate those who practice *infant baptism. It was coined in the polemic carried on in 17th-cent. England by Presbyterians and Congregationalists against the Baptists.

PAPACY. This article considers the papacy through the careers of some 90 popes; it is based on certain historical presuppositions. In its early history the Roman see resembled the Eastern episcopate, although the bp. of Rome was always *primus inter pares*. Changing political conditions forced the pope to protect Italy when the emperor in Constantinople could not. This responsibility became permanent when the Papal States appeared with Pepin's donation of land in 756. Medieval feudalism affected churchmen: as feudal lords they were responsible for benefices endowed with governmental functions important to their overlords. The papacy struggled thereafter to establish its autonomy. By the 19th cent. the Holy See, though crushed politically, rose to a new spiritual preeminence. This article will suggest how individual popes reveal the politico-ecclesiastical aspects of

the papacy; how historical forces shaped it; what authority is regarded as intrinsic to the papacy; and what is accidental, historical accretion.

Papacy to Gregory I. Whatever the proper setting of Mt 16.16–19, the fact is that Peter after Christ's ascension appears in Acts 1–15 as the undisputed leader of the Church. From these circumstances, the primacy of the Roman see derives: whoever is bp. of Rome is therefore successor to St. Peter and, like him, head of the Church. The early history of the papacy is uncertain; even the listing of the first successors of Peter is disputed. The famous letter of Clement, Bp. of Rome *c*.95, establishes him in that role, but it does not indicate—as earlier attested—that he was acting with special authority over the church of Corinth or that he had been asked to do so. (See H. Dressler, NCE 3:926–927. Hereafter authors cited, unless otherwise noted, are from NCE.) Only a few popes in the 2d cent. are noteworthy: Pius I, brother of Hermas, author of *The Shepherd*, received at Rome men more famous than himself, e.g., Hegesippus, Justin, Polycarp, and Irenaeus (see E. G. Welten, 11:193). Victor I (d. 198?) was deeply involved in controversy over the date of Easter. He was tempted to excommunicate Eastern bishops, but St. Irenaeus, Bp. of Lyons, dissuaded him. The struggle itself is significant as "the first evidence of a move by the Roman Church to influence the internal affairs of Eastern Churches" (Welten, 14:646). Pope Callistus *(c*.217–*c*.222) is important because his election was followed by that of Hippolytus, the first antipope. Historians now doubt that Callistus issued the decree permitting adulterers forgiveness through penance (*exomologesis*) hitherto forbidden them. Of Pope Fabian I (d. 250) Emperor Decius allegedly said that he would lose a legion rather than hear that another bp. of Rome had been elected. Pope Cornelius (251–253) faced a schism headed by Novatian when the Pope permitted *exomologesis* for apostates, a relaxation begun by Cyprian of Carthage. The letter communicating Cornelius's decision to Bp. Fabius of Antioch describes vividly the 3d-cent. Roman Church (J. Chapin, 3:333–334).

Dramatic changes in relations between Church and Empire were introduced by Constantine (306–337). Sylvester I, Constantine's contemporary, was largely overlooked. Constantine's way of handling Donatism and his role at Nicaea (325) seemed to reduce Sylvester to the position of a concerned on-looker. Medieval legends compensated for Sylvester's insignificance, esp. the 5th-cent. *Acts of Blessed Sylvester*, which recount his baptism of Constantine (J. Chapin, 13:857–858). Julius I (337–352) inherited the struggle over Arianism. After Nicaea Arian bishops undermined the key phrase *homooúsion to patrí* (of one substance with the Father), in the creed of Nicaea and deposed the stanchly orthodox Athanasius of Alexandria. Julius vigorously asserted his authority: "Why were we not written to about the Church of the Alexandrians? Are you ignorant that the custom was first to write to us, and then for justice to be determined from here?" At Sardica (354) the assembled bishops witnessed to the Roman primacy, which they said honored the memory of blessed Peter (J. Chapin, 8:51–52). Liberius (352–366), the first pope who described Rome as the Apostolic See, suffered sharp persecution under the Arian Emperor Constantius II. He exiled the Pope to Thrace (355) but recalled him when Liberius agreed to sign a vague creed. Athansius, Jerome, Hilary of Poitiers, all contemporaries, condemned Liberius, who nevertheless continued to teach Catholic doctrine and to oppose Arianism. His successor, Damasus (366–384), was harassed by Arianism until 381, when Emperor Theodosius I outlawed the heresy at Constantinople I. Less happy in the Pope's eyes was the council's elevation of Constantinople as the New Rome to a primacy second only to Old Rome. Innocent I (401–417) asserted his authority on doctrinal matters: "The bishops, our brothers, should refer [them] to Peter, the founder of the episcopate, to provide for the common good of all the Churches" *(Epist.* 30:2; P. Camelot, 7:519–520).

The new problem of Nestorianism beset Celestine I (422–432), who entrusted its solution almost totally to Cyprian of Alexandria. In Celestine's reign, African bishops led by Augustine asserted their independence on the provincial level. Leo I the Great (440–461) fought Monophysitism, convoking (449) the abortive synod of Ephesus; he later designated it, "Not a council but a den of thieves." He agreed to the Council of Chalcedon (451) and its decrees, except canon 28, which transformed Constantinople's primacy of honor into one of jurisdiction. He described his authority as a *plenitudo potestatis*, superior to any bishop's. Leo established the juridical structure on which the primacy has since rested. When Leo's doctrinal statement, the *Tome*, was read at Chalcedon, the bishops cried: "Thus through Leo Peter has spoken," a cry that exactly expressed Leo's own concept of his office (F. X. Murphy, 8:637–639). Gelasius I (492–496), the first pope to be described (495) as "vicar of Christ" (J. Chapin, 6:315–316), addressed a famous letter on the two powers, sacred and secular, to Emperor Anastasius I, whose duty it was "to learn from bishops." Hormisdas (514–523), like his predecessors, fought Monophysitism, officially condemned in 451 but constantly revived. The Formulary of Hormisdas imposed by the Emperor healed the Acacian schism between Rome and Constantinople (484–519) and is "the most strongly pro-Roman and pro-papal statement ever signed by Byzantine bishops" (J. Chapin, 7:148). John I (523–526) journeyed to Constantinople to plead in vain for persecuted Arians. Taken prisoner by Theodoric, Arian king of the Ostrogoths, he died in Ravenna. Pope Vigilius (537–555) also had to face recurring Monophysitism; he succumbed in 554 to unbearable pressures in the complicated Three Chapters controversy (F. X. Murphy, 14:664–667). Pelagius was appointed by the Emperor Justinian to succeed Vigilius as pope—a procedure that horrified the West and set the bad precedent that popes seek imperial approval. Elected pope by popular acclaim, Gregory I the Great

(590–604) already had wide experience as prefect of Rome and later as papal representative (*apocrisiarius*) at the court of Constantinople. He protected Rome, abandoned by Constantinople and Ravenna: Gregory's position as *de facto* ruler aroused Emperor Maurice. Gregory claimed universal jurisdiction over bishops since the Roman see "is set over all the Churches." Though he respected the internal autonomy of dioceses, he objected to the epithet "ecumenical" for the patriarch of Constantinople. His theological, pastoral, and liturgical writings contributed to Gregory's image "as a bridge-builder between the ancient and the medieval world." By 600 the papacy clearly appeared as an institution consciously possessing extensive spiritual, ecclesiastical, and quasi-political powers.

Medieval Papacy. Monophysitism in its variant forms (Monothelitism, Monoenergism) continued to harass the popes. Honorius I (625–638) failed to distinguish adequately the orthodox from the heretical formulation, emphasizing instead the harmony of wills in Christ (H. G. J. Beck, 7:123–125). Martin I (649–653 or 655) in the Lateran Synod also condemned Monophysitism. He was exiled and died for orthodoxy. This synod was the basis of Constantinople III (690), where Monophysitism in all its forms was officially repudiated (C. M. Aherne, 9:300–301). About 730 the popes began a rapprochement to Western rulers, which made them increasingly independent of Constantinople. Gregory II (715–731) threatened Leo III for his iconoclasm, Gregory III (731–741) excommunicated iconoclasts in the Roman synod (731), and both popes asked Charles Martel for help. Pope Zachary (741–752) fostered papal political influence by recognizing Pepin's assumption of the royal title (M. C. McCarthy, 14:1106). Stephen II (752–757), threatened by the Lombards, appealed to Pepin, who defeated them and made over the conquered lands to the Pope (756). Thus were established the Papal States (756–1870). Adrian I (772–795) defended Rome before being forced to appeal to Charlemagne (J. E. Bresnahan, 1:144). Leo III (795–816) was attacked, wounded, and vilified by Adrian's nephews; the Pope cleared himself of their accusations by taking a solemn oath to his own innocence (Dec. 23, 800) for "the first see can be judged by no one." He rejected the addition of *filioque* to the creed as unauthorized (not as untrue). He also crowned Charlemagne emperor. However, Charlemagne objected to the Pope's seizing the initiative in the coronation (R. E. Sullivan, 8:640). Nicholas I the Great (858–867) is noteworthy for daring to censure Lothair II's adultery, for the Pope felt he had a right to judge rulers. Nicholas was deeply involved with Photius, Patriarch of Constantinople (858–867), following Patriarch Ignatius' resignation. Photius sent the Pope letters of introduction seeking recognition. He was at first accepted by papal legates, then repudiated by Nicholas, who disavowed their actions (862, 863), and finally was ordered to Rome for a reexamination of the whole matter (865). In anger Photius summoned a synod (867), which declared Nicholas deposed. Photius showed in this confrontation considerable respect for the papal office. A later pope recognized him (879; see H. G. J. Beck, 10:441; F. Dvornik, *The Photian Schism*, 1946).

The nadir of papal prestige was reached in the 10th and 11th cents., an era ushered in by the tragic reign of Formosus (891–896), involved in the bitter rivalry of two Carolingians, Arnulf and Lambert. After the Pope's death, Lambert tried him, exhuming his corpse, condemning it in the famous "cadaverous trial" to be stripped of papal insignia and thrown into the Tiber. The domination of the papacy for 150 years by Roman nobility began with Sergius III (904–911), who had tried to seize the papacy in 897 and with the aid of Alberic I of Spoleto succeeded in 904; his immediate predecessors, Leo V and antipope Christopher, both had been murdered. Sergius invalidated Formosus' ordinations. He may have been the father of the future John XI by Marozia, a notorious Roman woman. She imprisoned John X and perhaps caused his death. John XII (955–964), son of Alberic II of Spoleto, civil head of Rome, was only 18 when his father forced his election. Even allowing for the virulence of contemporary accounts, John was a most unworthy pope. Otto I's aid against the Pope's enemies resulted in John's crowning him as Holy Roman Emperor (962). Otto tried to become suzerain of the Papal States, but John refused. He died soon after this crisis under scandalous circumstances (S. McKenna, 7:1011). The reign of Sylvester II was a relief from the sordidness of his predecessors. Involved in the power struggle between Carolingians and Capetians, Gerbert (the future pope), supported Hugh Capet. He was censured for accepting a bishopric from Hugh, and fled to the court of Otto III, who appointed him abp. of Ravenna and later pope. As pope he unfortunately fostered the Germanizing policy of Otto among the Slavic peoples but denounced simony, nepotism, and concubinage; he supported provincial councils.

The Church continued to suffer until the unworthy Benedict IX (1033–44) was persuaded to retire by his successor, Gregory VI (1045–46), for an enormous sum of money—a transaction that naturally provoked accusations of simony. Henry III called a synod at Sutri, which persuaded Gregory to resign and then elected—not surprisingly— a German of Henry's choice, Clement II (O. J. Blum, 6:772). Another royal nominee, Leo IX (1048–54), brought the reform movement flowing from Cluny to the papacy itself. He liberated the papacy from the Roman nobility and from the German emperor. But a mission he dispatched to Constantinople to deal with the Patriarch Michael Cerularius contributed to, rather than healed, the breach. His military actions against the Normans in southern Italy failed, although they later became vassals of the pope. Nicholas II (1058–61) further freed the papacy by the electoral law of 1059, which limited the electorate— formerly the people and clergy of Rome— to the cardinal bishops (later expanded to include all the cardinal clergy of Rome), thus freeing the election of political manipulation, at least on the local level.

High and Late Medieval Papacy. The most important medieval pope is Gregory VII (1073–85). A Roman monk, he served Gregory VI, Leo IX, and his successors. His election was obvious, tumultuous, and almost illegal. He considered the papacy as "primarily governmental and as such felt that it presupposed law." The *Dictatus papae*—considered the strongest statement of papal authority ever made—are, Ullmann thinks, chapter headings of a lost collection of canons. His epochal struggle with Henry IV, the German emperor, grew from the latter's blatant violations of Gregory's reforming decrees. His well-timed repentance at Canossa, though of doubtful sincerity, saved him his throne. Henry again "deposed" Gregory in 1084 (as he had in 1076), this time with more success. Gregory fled to the Castle of Sant' Angelo. His Norman vassals rescued him and took him to Salerno, where he died (1085). Henry was in control of Rome in the reigns of Victor III (1087) and Urban II (until 1194). Urban's situation made him a traveling pope, and one conciliatory toward recalcitrant bishops. His reforming activity and growing prestige are evident in the council at Piacenza (April 1095), where envoys from the Eastern Roman Emperor appealed for aid. At Clermont (Nov. 1095) Urban launched the first crusade. Henry IV finally repudiated his own antipopes, but the investiture conflict continued under his son, Henry V (1106–25). Paschal II (1099–1118) offered at Sutri (1111) to surrender the *regalia* attached to all sees in the Empire in return for Henry's surrender of investiture. The bishops objected violently, and Paschal surrendered to Henry. A positive gain was the realization that the *regalia* were not in themselves sacred, a new concept emphasized by Ivo of Chartres. He proposed what in fact underlay the Concordat of Worms (1122), recognition of the mutual rights of Church and State in ecclesiastical feudal estates (D. D. McGarry, 2:1081). Lateran Council I (1123) ratified the concordat.

As desire for reform seized even secular rulers, Innocent II (1130–43) begged for peace and ecclesiastical independence, as did his rival, the antipope Anacletus (J. R. Sommerfeldt, 7:520–521). Eugene III (1145–53), a product of the Cistercian movement and a submissive disciple of Bernard, was a zealous reforming pope. The revolutionary Arnold of Brescia forced the Pope to leave Rome (1146–48). Adrian IV (1154–59) interdicted the rebellious Romans (1155). He had to deal with the incident of Besançon: a papal document used the word *beneficia* (benefits) for papal favors to the Holy Roman Empire. Antipapal churchmen at the imperial court pretended that the Pope was claiming that the Empire was a benefice from the Pope. Adrian, the only English pope, in the bull *Laudabiliter* authorized Henry II of England's expedition to reform Ireland. The struggle between the Emperor, the papacy, and the northern Italian towns organized into the Lombard League benefited Alexander III (1159–81), who supported them. The League triumphed at Legnano (1176), and Frederick I capitulated. Alexander had to deal with Henry II in his conflict with Thomas Becket. Concerned with education in general, he insisted that teachers secure a license to teach. The redoubtable Alexander was succeeded by several aged popes. Celestine III (1191–98) was the last and weakest. Eighty-five at his accession, he was an easy prey of Henry VI, who bullied the Pope into crowning him emperor, invaded Sicily, permitting the capture of the crusader Richard I, and arranged for the murder of a bishop. For the last two crimes he was not even censured by the Pope (W. H. Principle, 3:365).

The ruins of papal prestige lay all around when Innocent III (1198–1216) made "the exercise of papal plenitude of power his hallmark" (W. Ullmann, 7:521–524). The Hohenstaufen problem in Sicily was alleviated by the deaths of Henry VI and, a year later, his wife Constance. She committed her son (the future Frederick II) to the Pope's care, making Innocent regent for Sicily, a task the Pope found impossible to discharge after 1208. The Pope's dream of a crusade materialized in 1202. However, it was diverted into intervention in a civil war

in Constantinople. Crushed by such deviousness, the Pope nevertheless approved the establishment of a western dynasty (Eastern Latin Empire, 1204–61) to heal the Eastern Schism. But relations between the Churches worsened seriously as a result. Innocent was an efficient administrator, establishing sound finances; he worked against heresy and encouraged St. Dominic. Lateran Council IV (1215) brought the medieval Church to the zenith of its influence with a definition of transubstantiation, disciplinary decrees against heresy, and legislation for the Easter duty; it even revived the dream of a new crusade. Innocent III was a statesman: suzerain for about ten medieval kingdoms, including England after 1213, he took his role seriously, e.g., by repudiating Abp. Stephen Langton in favor of John, the Pope's former enemy become his vassal.

Honorius III (1216–27) like Innocent a lawyer, published *Compilatio quinta* (1226), the first official book of canon law (S. Williams, 7:126–127). Both the Dominican and Franciscan Orders were approved by him and were to play a significant role in the subsequent reign of Gregory IX (1227–41). Gregory inaugurated the papal Inquisition (1233), fought Frederick II because he failed his crusader's vow, and dominated northern Italy. Gregory vigorously affirmed the primacy of Rome in negotiations—understandably unsuccessful—for reunion with the Eastern Church. Innocent IV (1243–54) broke the Hohenstaufen power forever—a questionable achievement. His successors continued his policy and supported the worthless Charles of Anjou as ruler of Sicily, for anything was preferable to encirclement by the dreaded German emperors. Urban IV (1261–65) continued to support Charles of Anjou, bestowing on him the "vacant" Sicilian throne against the claims of Manfred, Frederick's illegitimate son. Charles's ambitions were boundless, and included Constantinople itself. His actions alienated the East still more, negating Urban's efforts at reunion (H. Wieruszowski, 14:478). Gregory X (1271–76), after a 3-year delay in his election, established rules to shorten subsequent conclaves. In 1274 he convoked the Council of Lyons II (to which St. Thomas Aquinas was summoned to answer for errors in his writings; luckily he died on route, for 241 errors were discovered!). The Pope's attempts to reunite Eastern and Western Christendom failed. Martin IV (1281–85) continued to support Charles's erratic schemes in the East and in Sicily until 1282, when Charles was expelled from this island and 80,000 Frenchmen residing there were murdered as the Vesper bells were ringing, the infamous Sicilian Vespers.

Charles II of Anjou, with the Orsini and Colonna families, dominated the election of Celestine V (1294), a saintly recluse totally unfit to be pope. After a chaotic reign of 5 months he resigned with strong encouragement from the person who succeeded him as Boniface VIII (J. J. Smith, 3:365–366). Boniface's reign was a disaster. A student of canon law, he was sensitive to the Church's rights and to his own. His chief opponent was Philip IV of France, who was intent upon a policy of greater centralization, financial and political. Boniface wrote a series of letters: *Clericis laicos* (against taxing the clergy), the less demanding *Asculta fili*, then, in 1303, *Unam sanctam*, a very strong papal stance. The redoubtable Philip pursued the humiliated and defeated Pope even to the grave and beyond. For it was Clement V (1305–14) whose agony it was to resist the posthumous condemnation of Boniface only at the price of consenting to the destruction through the Council of Vienne (1311–12) of the Knights Templar. He was responsible also for the move to Avignon (1309) because of dangerous conditions in Italy and out of deference to Philip IV, whom he even absolved from all blame for Boniface's death. The residence of the popes at Avignon (1309–77) was a great scandal. All seven popes were French, as were 113 of 135 cardinals created by them. Accusations of extravagance are true principally of Clement VI. John XXII (1316–34) was involved in a struggle between rival emperors. One of them, Louis of Bavaria, attracted to his court John of Jandun and Marsilius of Padua, author of *Defensor pacis*, a vindication of council over pope. John XXII left a full treasury of 800,000 florins, which was squandered by his successors, esp. Clement VI (D. L. Douie, 3:1014–15). His reign was troubled by a revolution in Rome led by Cola di Rienzi. The English and French kings defeated his attempt to appoint all bishops from Avignon (1344) by seizing benefices held by foreigners. The unsuccessful attempt to return to Rome by Urban V (d. 1370) was realized under Gregory XI (1370–78). However, the anti-French sentiment in Rome made the subsequent papal election difficult. The threatening populace demanded a Roman or at least an Italian. The Abp. of Bari, Bartolomeo Prignani, was elected Urban VI. Although some doubt the validity of this election, others believe that eye-witness accounts definitely validate Urban VI. However, his choleric and unpredictable conduct forced the French cardinals (13 out of 16) to Avignon (1378), where they declared the April election invalid and chose a Frenchman as Clement VII.

Thus began the *Great Western Schism (1378–1415) with its two obediences, two popes, two curias, and two colleges of cardinals. The Council of *Pisa (1409) declared both popes deposed and elected a third, Alexander V. The Council of *Constance, convoked (1415) by Emperor Sigismund, deposed the Pisan pope; Gregory XII (successor in the Roman line) also officially convoked a council and resigned to it, whereupon Martin V (1417–31) was elected. He devoted himself to restoring papal prestige, to reform through periodic councils decreed by Constance (Pavia, 1423; Basel, 1431). Conciliarist himself at Pisa, Martin resisted *conciliarism as pope (K. A. Fink, 9:301–302). His successor, Eugene IV (1431–47), struggled against recalcitrants at Basel and convoked the Council of Ferrara-Florence (1438–45), which perceived that variety in rites could coexist with identity in faith. Statements favorable to Roman doctrines on the *filioque*, purgatory, and papal primacy were accepted by East and West. The Council of Basel, now removed to Lausanne, continued into the reign of Nicholas V (1447–55), who won over the recalcitrant conciliarists. He used the jubilee of 1450 to reestablish papal prestige and devoted himself to Renaissance pursuits (J. Gill, 10:443–445). Constantinople fell to the Ottoman Turks in Nicholas's reign (1453), and he was unable to arouse crusading zeal to rescue her, nor were Pius II and Callistus III successful. Pius (1458–64) was a great humanist before and after his elevation. Renaissance popes of the 15th and 16th cent. (J. G. Rowe, II:393–394) placed themselves at the head of the Renaissance movement in Italy and so identified the Church with it, including its worldliness and corruption. Nepotism and involvement in Italian politics characterized Sixtus IV (1471–84). Through his nephew, Riario, he participated in a scandalous and unsuccessful *coup* to overthrow the Medici family's control of Florence. Innocent VIII (1484–92) and Alexander VI (1492–1503) notoriously exemplified election through simony in the political advancement of their illegitimate children. Innocent VIII made feeble efforts at reform and on his deathbed implored the cardinals to elect a better man. Alexander tried to unite and strengthen the Papal States, trusting too much to his Machiavellian son, Cesare Borgia. He made real contributions to missionary developments in Spanish and Portuguese overseas empires, yet nothing he did could adequately compensate for the iniquity of his politics and his life (M. Battlore, 1:290–292).

The Papacy After 1500. Julius II (1503–13), responsible for the simony of Innocent VIII's election, tried to correct that evil, to reduce nepotism, and to render the papacy financially solvent. Though attached to pomp, he was concerned with reform and convoked Lateran Council V (1512–1517). Supporter of creative arts, in his reign he checked the worst excesses of the Renaissance papacy. His successors, the De' Medici, Leo X (1513–21), and Clement VII (1523–34) reigned disastrously. The former closed Lateran V, urging peace, crusade, and reform. He made a concordat with Francis I unbelievably favoring the mon-

arch. He was incapable of evaluating the impact of Luther at its full strength when he signed the bull excommunicating him (J. G. Gallagher, 8:643–645). The 20-month reign of the Dutchman, Adrian VI (1522–23), last non-Italian pope, was marred by a language barrier and a lack of sympathy with Renaissance culture. Clement VII, as inept as his cousin in handling great affairs, lost England by temporizing over Henry VIII's divorce of Queen Catherine. Complications in Hapsburg-Valois rivalry found Clement again on the losing side.

Paul III (1534–49), considered the first pope of the Catholic reform, appointed several exemplary cardinals (John Fisher, Reginald Pole, Caraffa, later Paul IV), approved the Jesuits (1540) and the Ursulines (1544), revived the Inquisition in Rome (1542), and published an Index (1543). Above all he worked for a council of reform, which finally met at Trent in three extended sessions (1545–1563; C. L. Hohl, Jr., II:13–14). Julius III (1550–55) also championed reform, calling the second session of the Council of Trent (1551–52), appointing good cardinals, and encouraging the Jesuits. Paul IV (1555–59), severe, ascetic, identified the papacy indelibly with reform. He attacked simony and nepotism, abjuring forever his nephews when he discovered they had betrayed papal interests. Pius IV (1559–65) brought Trent to conclusion. His nephew, Charles Borromeo, exemplified its decrees in the archdiocese of Milan. Pius V (1566–72) continued the implementation of Trent, revising the Roman Missal and Breviary and publishing the *Catechism of the Council of Trent* (1566). His international relations were poor, however: he excommunicated Elizabeth I and supported Catherine de Médicis against the Huguenots; on news of the *St. Bartholomew's Day Massacre (1572) he offered a solemn *Te Deum* of thanksgiving. Gregory XIII (1572–85) actualized the aims of the Council of Trent and introduced the Gregorian calendar (D. R. Campbell, 6:779–781). Clement VIII (1592–1605) recognized the *Edict of Nantes (1598), accepting the then-revolutionary principle of religious toleration.

Kiev and the Ruthenian bishops were united to Rome under him (1595; J. C. Willke, 3:933–934).

The Jesuits, one of the principal agents of the Catholic reform, aroused jealousy in other religious orders. Urban VII (1623–44) opened China to all missionaries (1633) rather than to Jesuits only; Benedict XIV (1740–58) suppressed the special rites that Jesuits had requested as expressive of Chinese culture; Clement XIII (1758–69) had to face the hostility of Catholic kings toward Jesuits who were expelled from Portugal (1759), France (1762), and Spain (1767); their worldwide suppression was demanded in 1769. Clement XIV (1769–74) inherited the problem: having promised Charles III of Spain and Louis XV of France, he suppressed the Society (1773) with its 11,000 Jesuits, 266 colleges, 103 seminaries, and 88 residences (E. D. McShane, 3:940–942). The order survived in Prussia and Russia, although Pius VI (1775–99) tried to extinguish it. Weak and indecisive, Pius fatally identified church interests with those of the *ancien régime*, bitterly opposing the French Revolution, which in turn became violently anticlerical. Napoleon Bonaparte protected the Pope, but Pius was taken captive to France and died there during Bonaparte's Egyptian campaign. Papal authority deteriorated rapidly through *Josephinism in Austria, *Febronianism in Germany, and the Tuscan priests' revolt at the Synod of *Pistoia (1786). Pius VII (1800–23), upon Napoleon's return, signed the Concordat of 1801, unfortunately negated by the strongly Gallican Organic Articles. Pius accepted many like humiliations for a measure of spiritual freedom. After Napoleon's fall Pius reestablished control in the Papal States, negotiated with new states in a conciliatory spirit, and most important, reestablished the Society of Jesus (1814; J. Leflon, 11:400–404).

The Church reestablished by Metternich's Congress of Vienna reacted against change under Leo XII (1823–29) by restoring control in the Papal States to clergy and nobles, by anti-Semitic measures in Rome, censorship of press, and an encyclical against Freemasonry and the *Carbonari*, thus striving to check the forces of liberalism and to support the restored monarchy (T. F. Casey, 8:646–647). The ideology of the French Revolution affected all Europe. A circle of French Catholic intellectuals led by Félicité de Lamennais, attempting to reconcile political liberalism with a deep devotion to the Church, denounced the Church's servitude under the *ancien régime*, advocated complete separation of Church and State, and thereby evoked condemnation of Gregory XVI (1831–46), who confused the divine mission of the Church with the status quo both in France and in Italy. This condemnation resulted in Lamennais' defection from the Church. Stop-gap measures of reform were insufficient, and the Pope left a very difficult legacy to his successor, Pius IX.

The Papacy in the Modern World. Pius IX's reign (1846–78) is described as the longest and stormiest in the Church's history (A. Simon, 6:782–788). He manifested an initial liberalism, then a reactionary conservatism after the Revolution of 1848 resulted in the absorption, into the newly established Kingdom of Italy, of Romagna (1860), the Marches (1860), and Rome itself (1870). Rejecting all monetary compensation from the Italian state, Pius became the "prisoner of the Vatican"; the impasse was known as the Roman Question. Pius IX convoked Vatican I (1869–70), which defined papal infallibility, to the bitter displeasure of Protestants, and pronounced on the role of reason in faith. The council was abruptly terminated by the war, which ended the pope's political independence. Pius IX's many dogmatic and doctrinal pronouncements (e.g., Immaculate Conception in 1854), his condemnation of various errors (*Syllabus of Errors*, 1864) are important. Pius was popular: his warmth, humor, even his sufferings endeared him to Catholics (R. Aubert, 11:405–408). The next pope was a great contrast to his predecessor; Leo XIII (1878–1903) urged the Church to become involved, encouraged French Catholics to participate in political life and accepted the term "Christian democracy" (1901).

Intransigent on the Roman Question, he nevertheless favored liberal governments in Belgium, Germany, France, and the U.S. (*Testem benevolentiae*, 1899). An intellectual, he revived the study of Thomistic philosophy (1879) and emphasized biblical studies (1893). His encyclical on labor (*Rerum novarum*, 1891) indicated the Church's concern for the working class, which had been too long ignored.

Pius X (1903–14) was deeply disturbed by doctrinal aberrations, condemning *modernism and thus alienating Catholic scholars (*Lamentabili*, 1907; *Pascendi*, 1907). Noted for personal sanctity and concern for liturgy, he legislated for frequent and early communion (1905, 1910). He was slightly less intransigent on the Roman Question; he also encountered bitterly anticlerical legislation, loss of church property, and secularization of schools in France (C. Ledre, II:408–411). The efforts of Benedict XV (1914–22) to help all victims of World War I and at the same time maintain strict neutrality were alike misconstrued. He contributed to the solution of the Roman Question, published the Code of Canon Law, and established a special congregation for the Oriental Churches. His attempts to mediate for peace (1914, 1917, 1919) were repulsed, but he aided Catholics in some newly established countries. Pius XI (1922–39) faced the bitter aftermath of World War I in the rise of totalitarian regimes in Mexico, Italy, Spain, Nazi Germany, and Eastern Europe. He addressed vigorous encyclicals, notably one on atheistic communism (1937), to the faithful in each country except Russia. He indicated social dimensions of Christianity (*Quadragesimo anno*, 1931) that would be advanced by Pius XII and even more dramatically by John XXIII in *Mater et magistra* (1961). Pius XI succeeded in solving the Roman Question by agreeing to establish Vatican City (109 acres) through the Lateran Treaty of 1929, receiving "a little corner of the earth where I may be master." Thus the Church surrendered the Papal States yet retained political independence. Pius XI's encyclicals on moral questions, *Casti connubii* (1930), *Christian*

Education (1929), and on mass media, *Vigilanti cura* (1936), are important. The reign of Pius XII (1939–58) began with the horrors of World War II (1939–45), which he had tried to prevent. He set up a Vatican Information Center for locating missing persons and worked in behalf of the Jews of Rome and Germany. He laid the intellectual foundations of Vatican Council II. He was the most accessible of popes, meeting more than 10 million persons, making over 3,000 pronouncements in his discourses and encyclicals. His successor, John XXIII (1958–63), can be described as the most popular pope who ever lived. His reign was an extraordinary event marked by two great encyclicals, *Mater et magistra* (1961) and *Pacem in terris* (1963), and by the convoking of Vatican II (1962–65), which restored the Church to the world. His impact was enormous; indeed "He put his arm around the world." By contrast his successor, Paul VI (1963–), has had a hard and painful pontificate. The accelerated pace of change, the problems of *aggiornamento* in a world torn by war, poverty, and racism, have demanded solutions with unprecedented urgency. Internally the Church is anguished by challenges to her authority over birth control, celibacy, obedience, and the right to freedom of inquiry. The prestige of the papacy has suffered a sharp decline; a pilgrim indeed, the Church in the late 20th cent. faces cruel dilemmas: more anguish than certitude, more losses than gains, more hope than happiness.

PARHAM, CHARLES FOX (1873–1937), a chief founder of Pentecostalism. P. was a preacher in the *Holiness movement when he opened Bethel Bible College at Topeka, Kans., in 1900. There early in 1901 he and his students became convinced by their experience that *baptism with the Holy Spirit was essentially connected with, and manifested by, *glossolalia. Efforts to spread the message failed, however, until in 1903 at Galena, Kans., he included *divine healing. The Apostolic Faith movement, as he called it, spread throughout Kans., Mo. and

Tex.; it was not unified, because he opposed any form of ecclesiastical organization. One of P.'s disciples at Houston, Tex., was W. J. Seymour, who later led the *Azusa Street Revival. Because of alleged sexual deviation, P. has sometimes been ignored even by Pentecostal writers, but he must be recognized as a pioneer of modern Pentecostalism. See J. T. Nichol, *Pentecostalism* (1966), 26–32; N. Bloch-Hoell, *Pentecostal Movement* (1964), 18–29.

PARISH, in ecclesiastical usage, a term with several meanings: (1) a subdivision of a diocese, which has its own church building and is under the authority of a rector, parish priest, or pastor responsible for the care of souls (the parish as a civil unit—e.g., in England equivalent to a township, in Louisiana, to a county—corresponds to older ecclesiastical divisions); (2) any local church or congregation and its sphere of activity; (3) a collective word for members of a parish in either of the above senses; (4) the charge of a pastor.

Meanings (1) and (2) have certain ecclesiological connotations. Etymologically the word comes, through the Lat. *paroecia,* or *parochia,* from the Gr. *paroikia,* a word used in early Christian times, like *ekklēsia,* to designate the local Christian community under the care of a bishop. Until the 6th cent. the terms parish and diocese were interchangeable. The roots of differentiation go back to the 2d cent., when multiplication of places of worship served by priests of the bishop's household became necessary; by the 4th cent. the stationing of priests in rural areas began (see ARCHDEACON; ARCHPRIEST). By the 5th cent. the fixing of boundaries started; the bishop's control, however, was always maintained. The territorial principle remained constant as parishes were established where abbeys or feudal lords built churches for the populace. The parish system during the Middle Ages was beset by the abuses of lay investiture and plural benefices. With the Council of Trent reform was initiated that remained the basis of the modern RC parochial system. The parish in its first, territorial meaning, presupposes that all the people in a given area are members of the Church universal as one, visible society; it implies their juridic assignment to the care of a pastor in order to provide for their spiritual needs. That meaning (2) has no such connotations is based ultimately on a different conception of the Church and *membership in the Church. While the territorial parish continued in the Lutheran and English Reformation, in other traditions it did not. The Reformed, or Presbyterian, Congregationalist, Baptist, and Methodist traditions have, in various ways, conceived of the Church as embodied in the local congregation. Members, as it were, make the Church to exist by gathering or covenanting together; they are not thought of as first belonging to the Church universal, then being assigned to a local jurisdiction. (See INVISIBLE CHURCH; GATHERED CHURCH.) The Anabaptists, Mennonites, Quaker, and similar groups also spiritualized the meaning of the Church as the voluntary union of those who share a similar inner Christian experience.

Distinction between the two uses of the term is diminishing, however. The territorial sense of parish is less and less significant in the circumstances of modern mobility and psychology. More importantly, theology has given new prominence to the Church as the assembled community of Christ. The parish is thus thought of as the active, voluntarily gathered community in which the Church is actually expressed and concretely present, esp. as the community actively participates in the Eucharistic celebration. See H. Rahner, ed., *Parish* (tr. R. Kress, 1954); C. Floristan Semanes, *Parish, Eucharistic Community* (tr. J. F. Byrne, 1964).

PARKER, MATTHEW (1504–75), abp. of Canterbury, born at Norwich, and educated at Cambridge. Appointed chaplain to Anne Boleyn in 1535, and to Henry VIII two years later, much of his career was devoted to academic administration as dean of

Stoke-by-Clare College, master of Corpus Christi College at Cambridge, and for a time Vice-Chancellor at Cambridge. While an undergraduate he had imbibed some ideas of reform from Lutheran writings, but he adopted only a few basic Reformation principles. Relatively conservative but broadly tolerant, he was well fitted as Elizabeth I's abp. of Canterbury to lead in the development of a Church representing a *via media*. He helped to fashion Anglican doctrine by sharing in the formulation of the *Thirty-Nine Articles, and he firmly adhered to the *Book of Common Prayer with its required ceremonies and vestments. Although he wrote some books, his chief scholarly contribution was the preservation of hundreds of ancient MSS. His episcopal ordination has been a key issue in the controversies over Anglican Orders. See V. J. K. Brook, *Life of Archbishop Parker* (1962). *ANGLICAN ORDERS.

PARKER, THEODORE (1810–60), American Unitarian minister. After graduating from Harvard Divinity School in 1836, he became a Unitarian minister. Ralph Waldo *Emerson and American transcendentalism exercised lasting, but not determinative, influence on his thought; Kant, Schleiermacher, and H. T. Buckle were also important sources of his philosophical development. His South Boston sermon, "The Transient and the Permanent in Christianity" (1841), and the publication of *A Discourse of Matters Pertaining to Religion* (1842) aroused the hostility of the Boston Unitarian clergy against his rationalistic views of religion. Parker was a scholar, proficient in the use of many languages; a forceful preacher; and a firm advocate of social reform, esp. abolition of slavery. He ranks with William Ellery *Channing as one of the two greatest leaders of American Unitarianism. See *Collected Works of T. P.* (ed. F. Cobbe, 12v., 1863–65); *Works of T. P.* (Centenary edition, 15v., 1907–11); H. S. Commager, *T. P.* (1936); J. E. Dirks, *Critical Theology of T. P.* (1948); W. R. Hutchison, *Transcendentalist Ministers* (1959).

PARMENIAN (d. 391 or 392), Donatist primate, orator, and theologian. He was born in Gaul or Spain, where he came to know Donatus in exile, and was consecrated a bp. in 355. He went to Carthage in 362, where he became Donatus's successor. He brought the Donatist Church through a series of internal crises, and under his rule it reached the height of its power and prosperity. P. wrote one work, consisting of five treatises, on the Donatist view of the Church; and a similar public letter to which Augustine wrote a rebuttal. See W. H. C. Frend, *Donatist Church* (1952), 193–207.

PARSON, an ecclesiastical term, which in English legal terminology means the *rector of a church. Originating from the Latin *persona*, as early as the 12th cent. the word signified the holder of a parochial benefice; the parson was the *persona ecclesiae*, i.e., the representative of the Church in the parish. Strictly speaking, parson signifies only the rector, but in popular usage it came to designate any clergyman. The parson has life tenure in the parsonage, glebe lands, and other rights attached to the benefice. The term came to be applied to *Nonconformist ministers, but in this sense often had a derogatory implication. In the American colonies the word was used esp. by Anglicans; it survives only as a colloquialism.

PARSONS, EDWARD LAMBE (1868–1960), third Protestant Episcopal bishop of California (1924–41), noted liberal theologian, and champion of social justice. He graduated from Yale (1889) and Union Theological Seminary (1892). Following postgraduate study in Berlin, he was ordained in the Episcopal Church in 1894, and served a 2-year curacy at Grace Church, New York. After moving to California, he served as rector of parishes in Menlo Park, San Mateo, and Berkeley until his election as bishop coadjutor (1919). He was a primary leader in the revision of the *American Prayer Book (1913–28), to which he contributed several prayers. A life-long advocate of Christian unity, he served as delegate to the *Faith and Order World Conferences in Lausanne (1927) and Edinburgh (1937), and led the unsuccessful negotiations for unity between Episcopalians and Presbyterians (1937–46). He founded the first community welfare society in the western U.S. and was president of the Church League for Industrial Democracy and a vice-president of the American Civil Liberties Union.

• **PARTICULAR BAPTISTS**, those so named in contrast to *General Baptists, because they believed in a *limited atonement. They held that God had decreed in advance who were to be "elect" and who "reprobate." Since God is infinitely wise, they reasoned, he would not make provision for Christ's atonement to cover persons who could not be saved. Therefore Christ's atoning death was sufficient only for the sins of the particular persons whom God had chosen to save. Arising in England in the 1630s, the Particular Baptists became the main body in Baptist life. See R. G. Torbet, *History of the Baptists* (rev. ed., 1963).

PASCAL, BLAISE (1623–62), mathematician, physicist, and Christian apologist. His father, a mathematician, brought him into early contact with learned circles in Paris. By 1640, several major factors in P.'s life were manifest: a grave malady that plagued him all his life; the influence of his two sisters; and his versatile genius, which began to be recognized in 1639 when he wrote his *Essai pour les coniques.* In 1642 he became famous through the invention of the first known calculating machine. By 1647 he had proved the existence of a vacuum and the weight of air. At Rouen in 1646, P. and his entire family had been converted to *Jansenism by followers of the Abbé de *Saint-Cyran. For P. this step entailed the renunciation of fame, but he continued his research in the field of physics. Aggravation

of his illness then caused him to seek diversion, and he entered upon a brief worldly period. Yet at that time he laid the foundations for the calculus of probabilities, became familiar with Montaigne, and came to center his attention on man himself. In 1648 his younger sister, Jacqueline, became a religious at the Jansenistic monastery of *Port-Royal-des-Champs. P.'s second conversion is marked by the *Memorial* composed after a religious experience in 1654. He became associated with the solitaries of Port-Royal and put his genius at their service in their quarrel with the Jesuits. In 1656–57 he composed, probably with the assistance of Antoine *Arnauld, the pamphleteering masterpiece known as the *Provincial Letters (*Lettres écrites par Louis de Montalte à un provincial*). Their mordant satire of Jesuit casuistry, and their high literary quality made them an effective defense of the Jansenist cause. Soon after publication the Letters were placed on the Index. With a view to the conversion of free-thinking friends, he began to prepare an apologetic, the pieces of which were organized after their writer's death and published under the title *Pensées.* After 1658 P.'s illness became more acute and, while continuing some religious and philosophical work, he retired to the home of his older sister, Gilberte. Without renouncing allegiance to Jansenism, which was not at the time generally recognized as a departure from orthodoxy, he did withdraw from all controversy and died, as he had always thought to live, a devout Catholic. Pascal saw truth, under different aspects, as attainable through two means: (1) geometric reasoning (*esprit de géométrie, raison*) and (2) a certitude of faith, which comes from the heart (*esprit de finesse, coeur*). Reason can do no more than point to those things that surpass it. Corrupted by the Fall, it cannot resolve the difficulties of faith and Christian morality. Only the light of revelation can do this. Reason can, however, grasp the historicity of revelation, and it can realize both the weakness and the greatness of man, who is "a thinking reed." An exploratory hypothesis, based on some facts, has therefore a certain apologetic validity. The *Pensées* were intended not to form a rational demonstration but rather to assist the reader gradually to accept the light of revelation. Pascal opposed any compromise between humanism and Christianity. His profound insight and penetrating style rank him high in the history of literature. Works: *Oeuvres complètes* (ed. L. Brunschvicg and P. L. Boutroux, 14v., 1904–14); *Pensées* (ed. L. Lafuma, 3v., 1951). See J. Mesnard, *Pascal: His Life and Works* (tr. G. S. Fraser, 1952).

PASCENDI DOMINICI GREGIS, an encyclical letter of Pope Pius X (Sept. 10, 1907) analyzing the basic principles and tendencies of *modernism, which it characterizes as "the synthesis of all heresies." It discusses the trend of modernism toward agnosticism, its distortion of religious history, and its teachings about vital immanence, religious sense, and the origin, nature, symbolism, and evolution of dogma. Among the causes of modernism it mentions the arrogance, ignorance, and rashness of its proponents. It concludes with some disciplinary remedies. See ASS 40 (1907), 593–650; D 3475–3500 (Eng. tr. V. A. Yzermans, *All Things in Christ*, 1954); J. J. Heaney, NCE 10:1048.

PASSAGIANI (Passagini), a short-lived Judaizing sect that arose in 12th-cent. Lombardy and was condemned by the Council of Verona in 1184 (D 760). Its principal characteristic was insistence on certain OT practices, especially circumcision, as necessary for salvation. Some Christian beliefs were retained, but like other contemporary reform groups the Passagiani preached against the sacraments and against the authority of the Church. See É. Amann, DTC 11:2206–07; I. da Milano, *L'eresia di U. Speroni nella confutazione del maestro Vacario* (1945), 27–32, 436–444; *idem*, EC 9:907–908; L. I. Newman, *Jewish Influence on Early Christian Reform Movements* (1925), 255–302.

PASTOR, in the U.S. the term commonly used for the priest or minister in charge of a RC or a Protestant parish or congregation; sometimes a designation for any clergyman. In Continental languages the same term or its equivalent is restricted to designate a Protestant minister. Among the gifts of Christ to his Church, according to Eph 4.11, are "pastors and teachers." The imagery involved in the biblical term (Gr. *poimen*; Lat. *pastor*, shepherd) made it natural to apply the word to those in the Church responsible for the care of souls—bishops and elders. In the nomenclature proper to the various Churches, another title is often used to designate the one in charge of a local church (e.g., the Methodist "preacher in charge," the Anglican "rector," the RC Lat. term *parochus*).

PASTORAL BIBLE INSTITUTE, a small body that separated from the *Jehovah's Witnesses in 1916, after the death of Charles Taze *Russell, in opposition to Joseph F. *Rutherford. Headquarters are in Brooklyn, New York.

PASTOUREAUX, CRUSADE OF THE, an uprising of peasants and laborers in France in the mid-13th century. Its leader was a mysterious figure known only as the "Master of Hungary," who claimed to act under instructions of the Virgin Mary. The purpose of the movement was to free King Louis IX from the captivity of the Moslems and to reconquer Jerusalem. The "Master's" motley army moved across France desecrating churches, abusing clerics, and killing Jews as they went. Blanche of Castille, the Queen Regent, finally ordered suppression of the movement. The "Master" was killed at Villeneuve-sur-Cher, several hundred of his followers were hanged, and the remainder dispersed. See J. A. Brundage, NCE 10:1084; J. Delalande, *Les Extraordinaires croisades d'enfants et de pastoureaux au Moyen-Âge* (1962); P. Ferraris, DE 3:104.

PATARINES (Patarenes, Patarelli), members of a movement at Milan (*c.*1050) against the simony and concubinage of the clergy. The quarter of the city where they met, Pataria, is probably the origin of the name. Most of the members were simple laymen, and in their zeal against abuses of the clergy they had the support of Popes Stephen IX and Alexander II. Patarines refused to receive the sacraments from simoniacal bps. or priests; sometimes they used physical force to remove unworthy clergy. In their struggles against the abps. of Milan appointed by the Emperor Henry IV they became opponents of lay investiture. Their leaders SS. Arialdus and Erlembaldus were martyred by agents of the archbishops. The spirit of the movement spread to other parts of Italy and contributed to the Gregorian Reform. By the end of the 11th cent. the Patarines ceased to be active. For uncertain reasons the same name was applied in the 12th cent. to the *Bogomils; Lateran Council IV (1179; D 760) used it as practically synonymous with *Cathari; and in the 13th and 14th cents. it often designated any sort of heretic. See S. Runciman, *Medieval Manichee* (1961), 94–115; C. Violante, *La pataria milanese e la riforma ecclesiastica* I (1955); *idem*, NCE 10:1084–85; E. Werner, *Pauperes Christi* (1956), III–164.

PATERNIANS (Venustians), a sect teaching that the lower parts of the body were created not by God but by the devil. They made this doctrine an excuse for lives of flagrant sexual license. Augustine (*Haer.* 85) says little of their origin, name, or diffusion. Augustine probably derived his information from the Pelagian *Julian of Eclanum, who accused Augustine of a similar teaching on the origin of human sexuality. No doubt the name *Venustiani,* indicating dedication to Venus, was given them because of their excesses. The *Praedestinatus* (1.85) claims that they were condemned by Pope Damasus and that a subsequent civil law made them liable to prosecution on a capital charge. But the *Praedestinatus* is not a reliable source. See É. Amann, DTC 11:2246–47.

PATRISTIC THEOLOGY, that part of Christian theological activity that endeavors to discover, examine, and synthesize the content of revelation by investigating the insights and structuring the analyses and understandings that have been achieved in the period of history from NT times to the close of the 8th cent. (although the limits of the period of patristic witness are not determined). It has its beginning as a discipline separate from biblical, dogmatic, and speculative theology in the 17th century. It is related to patrology, since both study the extensive literature of the Fathers; to the history of dogmas, since both examine the truths of revelation in historical context and seek to discern and explain the development of revelation and show the historical continuity of present Christian forms with the witness found in the doctrinal expositions, biblical commentaries, and sermons of the Fathers. As a theological endeavor it moves from within the community of faith and looks to a true and fuller contemporary apprehension of revelation by enriching current theological understanding with the self-understanding of the early Christian period. This theological concern for faith to some degree limits patristic theology to the writings of the Fathers and ecclesiastical writers, who wrote from the community of faith with the purpose of making known revealed truth and to be witnesses of the Christian faith. To be accepted as such a witness of biblical faith, orthodox doctrine, holiness of life, antiquity, and recognition in some way by the Church provided some criteria for the Church's judgment. See F. X. Murphy, NCE 10:1107–11; H. Musurillo, "New Horizons in Patristic Theology," *Traditio* 14 (1958), 33–61.

PATTON, FRANCIS LANDEY (1843–1932), Presbyterian clergyman and educator. A native of Bermuda, Patton was educated in Toronto and at Princeton Theological Seminary, graduating and being ordained to the ministry in 1865. After serving pastorates and teaching at what is now McCormick

Theological Seminary, Chicago, he was called in 1883 to Princeton Seminary to teach about the relationship of philosophy and science to the Christian religion. In 1888 he became president of the College of New Jersey (now Princeton University), where he was successful as an administrator, an exponent of theism, a teacher of Christian ethics, and an imaginative and witty lecturer. He was involved in the theological controversies of the Presbyterian Church in the U.S.A. in the post-Civil War period. His continued interest in theological matters is indicated by one of his most important books, *Fundamental Christianity* (1926).

PEACE MISSION MOVEMENT, see FA-THER DIVINE'S PEACE MISSION.

PEACE OF AUGSBURG, see AUGSBURG, RELIGIOUS PEACE OF.

PEACE OF THE CHURCH, a phrase that may refer to: (1) the era after the Edict of Milan (313), which had put an end to persecution of Christians; (2) a compromise achieved in the conflicts over *Jansenism, under Pope Clement IX in 1669; also called the Clementine Peace (*Paix de Clément*). The Pope agreed to a qualified acceptance of the bull *Regiminis apostolici* by four bps. who had hitherto flatly rejected it. The decade of comparative suspension of doctrinal and political controversy that ensued is called the Peace of the Church.

PEACE OF WESTPHALIA, see WESTPHALIA, PEACE OF.

PEARL OF GREAT PRICE, Joseph *Smith's translation of the Bible and a doctrinal source for Mormons. The book, first published in 1891, also contains two addi-

tions Smith made to the biblical books, the *Book of Moses* and the *Book of Abraham.* The second contains his advocacy of *plural marriage. *LATTER-DAY SAINTS.

PEASANTS' WAR (Ger. *Bauernkrieg*), armed rebellion (1524–25), against the feudal overlords, which spread through S Germany, Austria, Alsace, and the provinces of the Lower Rhine. There were precedents of peasant militancy against encroachments on their traditional rights; the Peasants' War was connected with the Reformation in that the rule of the gospel was interpreted in support of social demands, esp. by the establishment of an evangelical kingdom that would overthrow existing authority. This is apparent in the extreme teachings of T. *Münzer, one of the leaders, and in the *Twelve Articles of 1525 setting forth peasants' demands. Luther, at first seeking to mediate between princes and peasants, replied to the Twelve Articles, cautioning the peasants against violence; then, unheeded and disturbed by the depradations perpetrated in the name of the gospel, he wrote *Against the Murderous and Thieving Bands* (1525), a pamphlet urging the princes to a course of extermination. This has always been considered a stain on Luther's name, for the Lutheran princes mercilessly put down the revolt; more than 5,000 rebels were slaughtered at Frankenhausen, May 15, 1525. A few remnant forces survived for another year; many survivors joined the Anabaptists. The War solidified the power of the princes and esp. the *territorial church organization that continued in Germany into the 20th century. See H. Green, *Luther and the Reformation* (1964); H. Grimm, *Era of the Reformation* (1959); G. Franz, *Der deutsche Bauernkrieg* (2v., 5th ed., 1958).

PELAGIANISM AND SEMI-PELAGIANISM, teachings on grace, named from Pelagius. His original name is conjectured to have been Morgan (man of the sea); he was a British monk, and little is known about his early life. A harbinger of those remarkable bands who carried back to the Continent the religion and culture they had received from the Celtic coasts, he became an esteemed teacher in Rome, well versed in Scripture and classical literature; his followers were few yet influential. He set himself to fight immorality, excused by the plea of human weakness, by showing that the responsibility was man's own and should not be ascribed to God or the absence of divine grace. His favorite maxim was, "If I ought, I can." With his disciple Celestius, a bolder man and more apt to draw opponents' fire, he crossed to Africa before the sack of Rome by Alaric the Goth (410), and met Augustine, who was to speak of him as a holy man. Shortly afterward he sailed for Palestine, where he found a more congenial religious climate and made his home, at least until 418, when he disappeared from history. In 415 Orosius, a Spanish priest, came from Augustine to warn Jerome about Pelagius's teachings. A synod was convoked at Lydda, a miserable affair, said Jerome—who also was to ridicule Pelagius as "stuffed with Scots porridge"—and the upshot was an acquittal. The fact was resented by the African Church, which appealed to Pope Innocent I. His successor, Pope Zosimus, ratified the Acts of the Council of Carthage (see D 222–231), and, though at first hesitant, drew up a circular inviting all bps. to subscribe to a condemnation of Pelagian opinions. Julian, bp. of Eclanum, a man of birth and sanctity, refused and became the leader of the party, and the target for four works of Augustine, *De nuptiis et concupiscentiis*, *Contra duas epistolas Pelagianorum*, and the two tractates, one incomplete, *Contra Julianum*. Soon Julian and Celestius were disgraced and discredited, and with the condemnation by the Council of Ephesus (431) and with East and West united against it, the cause became hopeless.

Pelagianism can be reconstructed from authentic writings. It was a teaching about divine grace, and it hinged on two principles. First, grace comes from man's own choice, since human free will requires an equipoise before right and wrong, and it is by an act of his own that man takes the initiative in salvation. Second, *infant baptism is useless, since Adam's sin was personal and therefore does not damn others. The massive attack launched by Augustine was directed against the denial or original sin and the gratuitousness of divine grace; the controversy was cleanly conducted without vituperation.

Semi-Pelagianism was an attempt to hold a middle course between the extremes of doctrines that virtually abolished man's intrinsic need for grace and man's freedom. The term Semi-Pelagianism dates from the early 17th cent., and was applied by opponents to *Molinism, a usage forbidden after the *Congregatio de ·auxiliis. Semi-Pelagianism refers properly to a movement that began in the last years of Augustine's life; it is the subject of his *De gratia et libero arbitrio*, *De correptione et gratia*, *De praedestinatione sanctorum*, and *De dono perseverantiae*. Augustine's opposition was continued by Prosper of Aquitaine; Rome from the first favored this opposition but reserved its official endorsement of a predestinarian system. Semi-Pelagianism grew almost as a reaction of Provence to the harsher shores of Africa across the Mediterranean. Men such as John Cassian and Vincent of Lérins disavowed Pelagianism, as well as any doctrine that destroyed human freedom and responsibility. Provoked by the savage damnationism of the priest Lucidus, the learned and holy abbot of Lérins, Faustus of Riez, held that a man takes the first step toward salvation, for which grace is indeed necessary, but which is a recompense for his merits. Under the influence of Caesarius of Arles, abp. there in 503, Rome hardened, and the Semi-Pelagians, called Massilians (from Marseilles), were condemned at the Council of Orange II (529); the condemnation, which was cited at Trent, was given ecumenical authority by the approval of Pope Boniface II (531), and the movement died out.

Pelagianism and Semi-Pelagianism are not, however, simply episodes in Christian history. They represent a perennial human response in the search to express the place of human cooperation with grace. In the controversies of the Reformation, as well as within Protestantism and Roman Catholicism, those who have defended human cooperation have been called Pelagians by their adversaries. In preaching, devotional literature, and in the thought of the ordinary Christian, the naturalness of a Pelagian mentality manifests itself. Those who defend the transcendence and gratuitousness of divine grace regard as a practical Pelagianism the reduction of the gospel of grace and the Christian life to the level of good behavior benignly regarded and vaguely assisted by God. See J. Ferguson, *Pelagius, a Historical and Theological Study* (1957); L. Duchesne, *L'Église au VIième siècle* (1925).

PELAGIUS (354?–418?), monk for whom *Pelagianism is named. His birthplace is variously given as Britain, Ireland, or the East. At Rome *c.*400 he was known as a man of upright life and good education. After the fall of the city (410) he went to Carthage with his disciple *Celestius. He later traveled to Palestine, where Jerome showed antagonism to him because of the warning sent (414) by Augustine's emissary, the priest Orosius. Jerome coined the term Pelagianism for the doctrines P. developed as an answer to Manichaeism. Only some of P.'s treatises survive: *Expositiones XIII epistularum Pauli, Libellus fidei ad Innocentiam I*, and *Epistola ad Demetriadem.* His teaching is fully known from the works of his adversaries, particularly Augustine. In 415 P. was acquitted by the synods of Jerusalem and Diospolis in Caesarea. In 417, however, he and Celestius were both excommunicated by Innocent I, whose successor, Pope Zosimus, was at first favorable to P.; but renewed investigation and the condemnations by the Council of *Carthage XVI (418; see D 222–230) caused him to ratify the council's decrees and to renew his predecessor's excommunication of P. and Celestius in his *Epistola tractoria*, of which fragments survive (see D 231). P.'s history after 418 is unknown. See S. J. McKenna, NCE 11:58–60.

PENANCE, SACRAMENT OF, in RC teaching a true sacrament of the new law, instituted by Christ for the purpose of reconciling the sinner to God as often as he falls into sin after Baptism (see Council of Trent, Session 24; D 911). The rite of penance is made up of the three acts of the penitent—contrition, confession, and satisfaction (the quasi-matter)—and the words of the priest "I absolve you, . . ." (the form). Basic to Catholic teaching on the sacrament of penance is the belief that the ministry of divine pardon was first exercised by Christ in his sacred humanity (see Mt 9.1–8; Mk 2.3–12; Lk 5.18–26), and that it was entrusted by Christ to his Apostles and their successors in the priesthood. Penance is not recognized as a sacrament in Protestantism.

New Testament. Christian tradition appeals to the Gospels of Matthew and John to found the belief that Christ conferred on his Apostles the power of forgiving sins. To Peter Christ promised the power of the keys: "And I will give thee the keys of the kingdom of heaven; and whatever thou shalt bind on earth shall be bound in heaven; and whatever thou shalt loose on earth shall be loosed in heaven" (Mt 16.19). To the Twelve along with Peter Christ again promised the power of binding and loosing, but in the context of a sinner who refuses to hear the Church and who is to be regarded as a heathen and a publican (Mt 18.18). The Fathers of the Church interpret the power of binding as the power of excommunicating the sinner, the first step in the discipline of penance, and the power of loosing as the power of reconciling the sinner to the community, an interpretation that is contextually sound. Thus, whom the Church binds by excommunicating, God binds; whom the Church looses by reconciling, God looses, or reconciles, to himself. Reconciliation with the community is a sign of reconciliation with God. The power promised in Matthew is conferred in John: "As the Father has sent me, I also send you. . . . Receive the Holy Spirit; whose sins you shall forgive, they are forgiven them; and whose sins you shall retain, they are retained" (Jn 20.22–23). Thus the apostolic ministry of forgiveness is regarded as the continuation of Christ's own ministry. Whom the Church in the person of its representatives forgives God forgives—granted, of course, the proper dispositions on the part of the sinner.

Early Discipline. The procedure of penance was normally public; it followed the practice of St. Paul in excommunicating the sinner and ultimately reconciling him (see I Cor 5.5; 2 Cor 2.10). The first step in the discipline was confession, either to the bishop or in more populous churches to the priest-penitentiary. Although penance was public, the confession of sins was usually private. After confession, the sinner was enrolled in the order of penitents, an order corresponding to that of the catechumens. During the period of penance the penitents were excluded from the Prayer of the Faithful and from the eucharistic sacrifice that followed. In private, penitents were obliged to fast, to multiply their prayers, and to contribute alms to the poor. In the Roman Church penitents were reconciled in a solemn ceremony on Holy Thursday. In the East those guilty of more serious crimes usually spent a number of years as mourners, hearers, penitents, and bystanders before qualifying as participants in the Eucharistic Sacrifice. The practice of private penance and of devotional confession for venial sins was probably introduced by the Irish monks and English missionary scholars of the 6th and 7th centuries. On the Continent, however, public penance for those guilty of more public crimes lasted well into the 12th century.

Theological Reflections. The Montanist and Novatianist schisms of the 3d cent. offer indirect proof that Catholics at the time believed that the Church had the power on earth of ministering divine pardon. Again, the sacramental aspect of penance is evidenced by the parallel repeatedly

drawn between baptism and penance. Thus, the author of the Syriac *Didascalia* (*c*.250) likens the final imposition of the hand on the penitents to the effect of baptism: "For whether by the imposition of the hand or by Baptism they receive the communication of the Holy Spirit" (2.41.2). The sacramental nature of the priest's reconciliation as well as its necessity is given eloquent expression by St. Augustine in an exhortation to his clergy to remain at their posts during the Vandal invasion: "How great a crowd of both sexes and all ages is accustomed to gather in the church, some demanding Baptism, others reconciliation, others the discipline of Penance itself, all seeking consolation and the administration of the Sacraments. But if ministers are lacking, how great will be the destruction that follows those who leave this life either unregenerate or bound?" (*Serm.*, 329.3). This early emphasis on the importance of the priest's reconciliation was obscured by early scholastic teaching on the necessity of sorrow motivated by love as the operative element in the sacrament of penance. The absolution of the priest came to be regarded as a simple decaration that the sinner was already reconciled by God through perfect contrition, or as the remission of the temporal punishment due to sin; thus Peter Abelard and Peter Lombard, who had great influence on later scholastic doctors. SS. Bonaventure and Thomas Aquinas also stressed the need of sorrow elicited by the virtue of charity, but they integrated the acts of the penitent and the absolving action of the priest by insisting that the reconciliation of the priest informed and elevated the acts of the penitent as part of the one sacramental sign of penance. Against Luther and the Reformers of the 16th cent. the Council of Trent confirmed the true sacramentality of penance as well as the necessity by divine law of confessing all serious sins committed after baptism.

Recent Trends and Development. Penance is regarded as a sacrament of the new law by the Greek and Russian Orthodox Churches and, since the time of the Oxford movement, by Anglo-Catholics and some Episcopalians. A growing number of Lutherans, particularly in Germany, are reviving the early Lutheran practice of private confession to the minister, or pastor, followed by absolution. In southern France the community of Taizé (a Calvinist foundation) has not only introduced the practice of private confession and absolution, but many of the members regard penance as a sacrament. Among Catholics there is a growing awareness that sin is an offense not only against God but also against the Church and that reconciliation with God ordinarily presupposes reconciliation with the Church. Liturgical expression of this awareness is to be found in the growing practice of introducing some of the more communal and public features of the ancient liturgy of penance. See P. Palmer, *Sacraments and Forgiveness* (Sources of Christian Theology 2, 1960); B. Poschmann, *Penance and the Anointing of the Sick* (tr. F. Courtney, 1964); P. Anciaux, *Sacrament of Penance* (1962).

PENIEL MISSIONS, a name employed by several revivalistic groups, esp. in California, Oregon, and Washington. They concentrate on evangelism, including street preaching. The doctrines of *sanctification, and elements of Pentecostalism are emphasized. The name Peniel (face of God; see Gen 32.30) is an allusion to Jacob's wrestling with God, a symbol of spiritual combat.

PENINGTON, ISAAC (Pennington; 1616–79), prominent early Quaker. P. was the son of the lord mayor of London, Sir Isaac Penington (c.1590–1661).. First an ardent Puritan, P. became a *Seeker, but after meeting G. *Fox, publicly joined the Friends (1658). His prestige, his noble character, and his able writings contributed to the growth of the new movement. After 1661 he suffered loss of property and long imprisonments. His son, Edward Penington (1667–1711), established the family in Pennsylvania. P.'s

collected writings were published posthumously in two parts, 1680 and 1681. See W. C. Braithwaite, *Beginnings of Quakerism* (2d ed., 1955), 13–15; 501–507; DNB 44 (1895), 247–300.

PENN, WILLIAM (1644–1718), Quaker, founder of Pennsylvania. Son of Admiral Sir William Penn (1621–70), at the age of 11 he had an experience of communion with God that gave a religious direction to his whole life. His father tried to discourage the interest in Quakerism that began while P. was at Oxford (1660–61) by sending him to France, but in Ireland in 1665, P. definitively embraced Quaker belief. From 1667 onward he was an approved minister and at London engaged in preaching, controversy, and writing. Twice he was imprisoned (1668 and 1670), the first time for his work *The Sandy Foundation Shaken*, against belief in the Trinity and Christ's atonement. By a grant of Charles II, in payment of a debt due to his father, P. became proprietary governor of Pennsylvania (1680); he formulated a constitution for the new colony, his "holy experiment," and called it the Frame of Government. This incorporated the most enlightened liberal ideas, including religious and political equality even for Catholics. P. resided in Pa. from 1682 to 1684 and again from 1699 to 1701, when he secured final approval of the revised Frame of Government. His life became difficult as political and financial crises multiplied for his colony. He died in England, having suffered a paralyzing stroke in 1712. He wrote many treatises during his Quaker life; *No Cross No Crown* (1669) is a treasured Quaker classic, and his *Fruits of Solitude* (1692) is an esteemed collection of religious reflections. His works were collected and edited after his death by J. Besse (1726). See E. B. Bronner, *W. P.'s Holy Experiment* (1962); V. Buranelli, *King and the Quaker* (1962); W. W. Comfort, *W. P. 1644–1718, a Tricentenary Estimate* (1944); C. O. Peare, *W. P., a Biography*; F. B. Tolles and E. G. Alderfer, eds., *Witness of W. P.* (1957), with selections from P.'s writings.

PENTECOSTAL ASSEMBLIES OF CANADA, the largest organization of Canadian Pentecostals. In the early 1920s the major groups of Pentecostals in eastern and western Canada were joined to the Assemblies of God in the U.S., but the union was shortlived. The Pentecostal Assemblies of Canada grew to include 75,000 members, in 700 churches, and to maintain a strong missionary force. The body adheres to the characteristics doctrines of *Pentecostalism. See G. Kulbeck, *What God Hath Wrought* (1958).

PENTECOSTAL ASSEMBLIES OF THE WORLD, INC., an interracial denomination that separated (1914–16) from the Assemblies of God in support of the *Jesus Only doctrine. Except on this point, the Church does not differ in teaching from other Pentecostal bodies. Polity is connectional like that of Methodism, consisting in conferences (see CONFERENCE). Headquarters are in Indianapolis, Ind.; last available membership (1960) was about 45,000. See J. T. Nichol, *Pentecostalism* (1966), 115–118. *UNITED PENTECOSTAL CHURCH.

PENTECOSTAL CHURCH OF CHRIST, a small body, with headquarters in London, Ohio, originating with the Pentecostal preaching of the Rev. John Stroup during World War I. The Church was formally organized in 1927. See J. T. Nichol, *Pentecostalism* (1966), 127–128.

PENTECOSTAL CHURCH OF GOD OF AMERICA, INC., a body first organized as the Pentecostal Assemblies of the U.S.A. in 1919; the Church adopted its present name in 1922 ("of America" was added in 1933). It was organized out of those bodies resisting, in defense of the autonomy of the *local church, the General Council of Pentecostals at Hot Springs, Ark., which in 1914 formed the Assemblies of God. The Church in its mission work has concentrated on the American Indians. The Church's headquarters are at Joplin, Mo.; membership in 1968 was 115,000 in 975 churches. See J. T. Nichol, *Pentecostalism* (1966), 114–116.

PENTECOSTAL EVANGELICAL Church of God, National and International, Inc., a small denomination organized at Riddle, Ore., in 1960.

PENTECOSTAL FELLOWSHIP OF NORTH AMERICA, an organization founded in 1948 that comprises 15 of the major Pentecostal bodies of the U.S. and Canada. While respecting the full autonomy of the member Churches, it aims to provide unity in witness, fellowship, and coordination of effort, and service facilities in evangelization. Forums and seminars on the national level provide exchange of views on matters of mutual concern, e.g., missions, education, youth programs, and press and radio evengalization. It has also encouraged joint sponsorship of religious rallies on the local level. See J. T. Nichol, *Pentecostalism* (1966), 215–218.

PENTECOSTAL FIRE-BAPTIZED HOLINESS CHURCH, a small denomination in N.C., S.C., Ga., and Tennessee. It separated from the Pentecostal Holiness Church in 1918 in protest against adornment in dress; this body insists on a very rigid code of conduct for its members. Headquarters are in Toccoa, Ga.; membership in 1968 was about 600. See J. T. Nichol, *Pentecostalism* (1966), 124–125.

PENTECOSTAL FREE WILL BAPTIST CHURCH, INC., a denomination formally organized in N.C. in 1959. Before then, it consisted of several loosely associated groups of *Free Will Baptists who early in the 19th cent. had combined Pentecostalism with their Baptist belief. Membership in 1968 was about 10,000. See J. T. Nichol, *Pentecostalism* (1966), 126–127.

PENTECOSTAL HOLINESS CHURCH, INC., a body first organized in 1911, when the Fire Baptized Holiness Church and the Holiness Church joined together at Falcon, North Carolina. Both had been *Holiness Churches that had embraced Pentecostalism under the influence of participants in the *Azusa Street Revival. The Tabernacle Presbyterian Church, which had separated from the South Carolina Synod, joined the Pentecostal Holiness Church in 1915. The Church teaches the characteristic doctrines of Pentecostalism; *divine healing is accepted as the superior way to health, but not as excluding resort to medical science. Members may have their children either dedicated or baptized; the mode of baptism is also a matter of individual choice. Polity is similar to that of Methodism (see CONFERENCE). Headquarters are at Franklin Springs, Ga., where the Church also maintains Emmanuel College; it also operates two theological seminaries. Membership in 1968 was 65,040 in 1,388 churches. See J. T. Nichol, *Pentecostalism* (1966), 104–108.

PENTECOSTAL WORLD CONFERENCE, a triennial worldwide meeting of Pentecostals. There is an advisory committee to prepare for these conferences, but the conference itself does not have a formal membership or constitution. The distrust of Pentecostals toward ecclesiastical organization was partially overcome in the 1920s and 1930s by a desire for some external expression of unity, and several international meetings of fellowship were held. The most significant was a conference on unity in Stockholm, 1939. After World War II efforts were renewed, and the first Pentecostal World Conference was held in Zurich in 1947. The basis for a more effective association of Pentecostals, however, was achieved at the Paris world conference of 1949. Decisions included a triennial meeting and a secretary with advisory committee to serve between conferences; the principle of autonomy of the local churches and Pentecostal bodies was affirmed; fellowship and cooperation of Pentecostals was set as

the objective of the conferences. Subsequent meetings have been held in London (1952), Stockholm (1955), Toronto (1958), Jerusalem (1961), Helsinki (1964), Rio de Janeiro (1967); the 1970 meeting is planned for Dallas, Texas. The meetings have been assemblies for worship and preaching rather than for practical decision making.

PENTECOSTALISM, that form of Christianity teaching the "Pentecostal experience," namely, that *baptism with the Holy Spirit is accompanied and manifested by *glossolalia (tongues speaking) and *divine healing and that the charismatic gifts of the early Church, a continuing Pentecost, should be ordinary occurrences in Christian life (Nichol, xi). Many of the typical elements in Pentecostalism were taught by the 19th-cent. *Catholic Apostolic Church. The actual Pentecostal movement, however, began in the U.S. in the early 1900s, as an outgrowth of the *Holiness movement. Prominent at the origins of 20th-cent. Pentecostalism were the Apostolic Faith movement (1901) of C. P. *Parham in Kans., Mo., and Tex. and the *Azusa Street Revival (1906). Some groups in the East originated as break-offs, over tongues speaking, from the Christian and Missionary Alliance. The intense spirit of evangelism, in the form of *faith mission, spread the movement. There has been traditionally little formal organization in the Pentecostal bodies, and this has often led to internal disputes and divisions. In recent years, however, larger Pentecostal bodies have adopted some set form of church government. The early deliberate downgrading of education has also changed among the larger Pentecostal groups. There are Pentecostal Churches, or, as they are often called, "Assemblies," in all of the states of the U.S. (see major bodies under proper names). Many smaller units of less than a few hundred members exist throughout the country. Certain more extravagant *cults in the South, e.g., *snake-handlers, use the Pentecostal name but are disowned by official Pentecostal bodies. The *Neo-Pentecostalism of recent years refers to the search for the Pentecostal experience by small groups within other Christian Churches; it has no formal connection with Pentecostalism.

Membership. The total number of Pentecostals throughout the world is estimated at more than 10 million; the movement was spread from the U.S. to Europe, by way of Scandinavia, by T. B. Barratt; to S.A. (Brazil and Chile) by W. C. Hoover, L. Francescon, and G. Vingren; and to Asia and Africa by missionaries of the particular Pentecostal bodies. Pentecostalism is widely referred to as a "Third Force" in Christianity alongside the historic Protestant and Catholic Churches. The title has its principal significance because of the missionary impact of the distinctive Pentecostal message; there are more than 5,000 Pentecostal missionaries, laboring on all continents. The 20th-cent. expansion of Pentecostalism in S.A. is one of the most remarkable phenomena in modern Christianity. The highest concentrations of Pentecostals are in Brazil (more than 3 million) and Chile (more than 700,000); there are also large, well-established bodies in Argentina and Colombia. In Africa Pentecostalism in some form is found in all of the sub-Saharan countries, but esp. in S Africa; adherents in Africa number far more than I million (see AFRICAN INDEPENDENT CHURCH MOVEMENT). To a great extent Pentecostal missionary efforts have been aimed not at winning converts from paganism but at bringing over active or nominal members from other Christian Churches. This is considered to be not proselytizing but leading Christians to the acceptance of baptism with the Holy Spirit, without which they cannot be saved. In its missionary endeavor Pentecostalism has to a certain extent achieved what remains a desideratum for other Churches, namely, that members become true apostles to their brethren in the world at large.

Doctrine. Pentecostals agree in their distinctive doctrines, the Pentecostal experience and divine healing and in their *fundamentalism; in other matters there is wide diversity. At times some Pentecostals are accused of diminishing belief in the Trinity (see PENTECOSTAL ASSEMBLIES OF THE WORLD), and of misunderstanding the doctrine of justification by faith. In keeping with their Holiness origins they are *Arminian. Pentecostal *dispensationalism means that these last days are a period for the preaching of charismatic gifts to a morally depraved generation. Baptism and the Lord's Supper are recognized as *ordinances; but the first (water baptism) is seen only as a pledge of regeneration already obtained (see BELIEVER'S BAPTISM), and the second, as a purely symbolic rite. Many Pentecostal groups reject *infant baptism (while practicing at times the dedication of children to the Lord); some observe *footwashing. Pentecostals forbid smoking, drinking, dancing, gambling, and frivolous entertainment. This type of puritanism has been effectively applied against the abuse of alcohol—a widespread vice in more than one nominally Catholic nation—and to cure drug addicts, and has become one of the secrets of their missionary penetration. Ecclesiologically Pentecostals are heirs to the concept of *Pietism, *ecclesiola in ecclesia*; the Church is not an instrument of sanctification but rather a holy club in which the members help each other and thereby sanctify the community itself. They have admirably developed the sense of *koinonia*, mutual brotherhood and friendship. Congregationalism, emphasis on the autonomy of the *local church, has been a traditional ideal for church polity. In practice, with the increase of organization, the governing of many denominations has become more centralized through the adoption of elements from Presbyterian or Methodist polity. Pentecostal authorities often have the power to act in a stern way to enforce church discipline.

Practice. Pentecostals shun elaborate liturgies in order to adhere to the simplicity of the primitive Church. Their religious services are spontaneous, at times even disorderly; the central element is the sermon, long and often delivered in a stylized monotone; it may turn into a dialogue between the preacher and members of the congregation. The topics are biblical, and the emphasis is not on punishment but on the love of God for mankind provided men follow the right path willed by the Lord. Preaching is enthusiastic and geared to create in the listeners a fervent desire for the charismatic gifts of the Spirit. The service may also include testimonies of those who have been healed or have become beneficiaries of divine favors. There are religious services intended almost exclusively to provoke among specially prepared listeners the reception of baptism with the Holy Spirit. In certain European and middle-class American Pentecostal communities, the worship services are losing some of their primitive and spontaneous flavor and becoming more set and sober.

Pentecostals have had little interest in the ecumenical movement; many Pentecostal groups live in utter isolationism. Those that are more open have joined such organizations as the *National Association of Evangelicals, which openly opposes the World Council of Churches. Pentecostalism is trying to achieve greater internal unity, and from 1948 the *Pentecostal World Conference has held conventions on different continents. The admission of two Chilean Pentecostal bodies to the World Council of Churches in 1961 did not end the theological opposition of most Pentecostals to full cooperation with other Christian Churches. Many, however, are establishing useful contacts with other Christian bodies and are tending to establish closer friendship with other followers of Christ. See N. Bloch-Hoell, *Pentecostal Movement* (1962); P. Damboriena, *Tongues As of Fire* (1969); J. T. Nichol, *Pentecostalism* (1966).

PEOPLE OF GOD, an image or metaphor to describe the Church. The phrase was given new prominence by its central use in the *Constitution on the Church* of Vatican Council II. The document refers to the OT passage Jer 31.31–34, and esp. to 1 Pet 2.9–10, "You who in times past were not a people, but are now the people of God." The description of the Church as the People of God epitomizes the view of the Church common to many Christians. The Church is the People of God because it is a community through which God reveals himself as savior. For this purpose he chooses, calls, and gathers his people by his grace (see ECCLESIA). The reference that the phrase has to the OT implies the continuity of the divine plan of salvation beginning with the chosen people, the Jews, then taking a new form through Christ. The image also suggests the biblical themes of God's constituting a community of salvation, not saving men simply as individuals; thus it is connected with the Pauline image of the Church as the body of Christ. People of God does not mean only the laity, but all the members of the Church, through baptism sharing in the priesthood of Christ. The whole People of God as called and gathered are one, holy people; thus the image serves to bring out holiness and unity, essential attributes of the Church as unified and sanctified by Christ. See Vorgrimler Vat II 1:153–168; Kittel TD 4:29–57; Y. Congar *Concilium* 1 (1965), 7–19.

PEPUZIANS, an alternative designation for the *Montanists. The name is derived from Pepuza, a no longer identifiable site in Phrygia, which was the center of Montanism, and where it was believed that Christ would soon come in the parousia to inaugurate his millennial rule.

PERFECTI (the perfect, the pure), those who strictly observed the teaching of the *Cathari and who were their preachers. They were Cathari (Gr. *katharoi*, the pure) par excellence, as distinguished from the ordinary believers or hearers. Initiation into the circle of *perfecti* was through the ceremony called *consolamentum*. Their austere asceticism in contrast to the luxury of many ecclesiastics was one cause of the spread of such Cathari groups as the *Albigenses. A distinction between *perfecti* and believers was also used among the medieval *Waldenses.

PERFECTIBILISTS (Ger. *Perfektibilisten*), the original name of the Illuminati founded by Johann Weishaupt (1748–1830) in 18th-cent. Bavaria. The name alludes to the belief that by a process of initiation the members were to progress to perfection. *IL-LUMINATI, ORDER OF.

PERFECTION, CHRISTIAN, see CHRISTIAN PERFECTION.

PERFECTIONISM. That human perfection can be attained is commonly held by all systems that do not postulate a never-ending evolutionary process, or by cynicisms more or less benign, content to leave men and women just as they find them. The abstract term "perfectionism" was not, however, applied originally to secular movements toward moral, social, or political betterment, but to religious belief in the possibility of perfection in the present life, often negatively described as a condition of sinlessness, and to the consequent methods to bring this about. It appeared in the mid-19th cent.; "perfectionist" a hundred years earlier had been applied to the Methodists, sometimes as a term of disparagement: they are, writes Samuel Richardson in *Clarissa,* "enough to make a better man than myself either run into madness or despair." The evangelical command "Be ye perfect" (Mt 5.48; the word used in Gr. is *teleisi,* end-achievers) was consistently maintained from the beginning by the Christian Church; efforts to restrict membership to the righteous or elect were as consistently resisted (see MONTANISTS). Charity was the bond of perfection (Gal 3.14). Yet this friendship with God and men was a positive and analogical value, which admitted of degrees and growth in intensity. The universal call to holiness finds a classical theological articulation in Thomas Aquinas; nevertheless in practice the note grew uncertain when perfection became specialized to religious life under the vows, the "canonical state of perfection."

Against such professionalism Luther protested. The full Christian has an utter trust in God and confidently asks for what is necessary in his trials and tribulations; he is a justified sinner, yet is still subject to the curse of evil. No more did Calvin's ideal of the man obedient to God's will agree with the Anabaptist picture of the completely blameless man or the *antinomianism that anticipated in this world the perfect state of the blessed requiring no preaching of the law (see LAW AND GOSPEL). Henceforward, it may be noted, Hellenic conceptions of Christian perfection become overcast with the cloud of Reformation and Counter-Reformation writings and their preoccupation with guilt. *Wesley's ideal of the perfect man is the subject of a special article (see CHRISTIAN PERFECTION). He was influenced by the Moravians and also by his father's *Arminianism and by William *Law; the correspondences run deeply between Wesley's insistence on the experience of the great work wrought in us by God in renewing our fallen nature and the teaching of much Catholic spirituality. His own conversion seems to have been "mystical" rather than "evangelical," and he never claimed perfection for himself or the assurance that he was completely free from sin. Methodism has justly been compared with Franciscanism, and the grand division in it between Perfectionists and anti-Perfectionists to that between the *Spirituals and the Conventuals.

A rhetoric at once simpler and more metaphorical, and which preaches *entire sanctification and cleansing from sin, is characteristic of the various *Holiness Churches and of *Pentecostalism. So too the Salvation Army strives that we may be found unblamable and unreprovable before God. The word "perfectionism" was antonomastically applied to the *Oneida Community. All the examples so far indicated agree in committing themselves completely to God in a spirit that is quite non-Pelagian. In our own days, however, "perfectionism," though sometimes used half-admiringly, has come to be recognized almost as a clinical entity in psychological and pastoral treatment, as when we make for ourselves a "pseudo-person" and set up for ourselves a false image of what we think we ought to be, instead of being open and "abandoned" to God. The central tradition in Christianity is wise in looking rather beadily at claims to invulnerability or the preaching of an innocence that may have been once upon a time but never is at present this side of heaven. See M. Piette, *John Wesley in the Evolution of Protestantism* (tr. J. B. Howard, 1937); R. Knox, *Enthusiasm* (1950).

PERTH, ARTICLES OF, five prescriptions designed to conform the worship of the Scottish Church to Anglican usage, but accepted by the General Assembly at Perth, Aug. 25, 1618, only under pressure from the King, James VI (James I of England). The Articles enjoined (1) kneeling at communion; (2) the observance of Christmas, Good Friday, Easter, Ascension, and Pentecost; (3) confirmation at the age of 8 by a bishop; (4) communion of the sick; and (5) private baptism where necessary. The Articles were ratified in 1621 by Parliament, but in 1638 were condemned by the Assembly as contrary to its Confession of Faith.

PETER OF BRUYS (d. *c.*1130), itinerant preacher and reformer in Languedoc and Provence, for whom the *Petrobrusians were named.

PETER OF CHELCIĆ (*c.*1390–*c.*1460), Czech writer and religious leader whose ideas inspired those *Hussites who were dissatisfied with the *Utraquists to found the *Unitas Fratrum in 1457. Though of only limited academic training, P. read *Wycliffe and *Hus and went beyond them in rejecting the authority of the Church, substituting for it the NT, esp. the Sermon on the Mount. He proposed as an ideal a Church divorced from all temporalities. He anticipated the Anabaptists in his pacifism, *nonresistance, and rejection of oaths. The most complete summary of his thought is

Net of Faith, written in 1440 and first printed in 1520. See P. Brock, *Unity of Czech Brethren* (1957).

PETER OF FOSSOMBRONE, see ANGELUS CLARENUS.

PETER JOHN OLIVI (1248–98), Franciscan philosopher and theologian, a leader of the *Spirituals. P. was born at Sérignan in Languedoc. Soon after his entrance into the Friars Minor he became associated with the rigorist party within the order. He studied at Paris from 1267 until 1273, when he was appointed lector at Montpelier. About 1275 he became intellectual leader of the Spirituals of Provence and involved himself in that party's struggle with the *Communitas*. In 1279 he was requested to submit a memorandum on Franciscan poverty for the guidance of a papal commission. While his views on this subject were much less extreme than those of the Italian Spirituals, his polemical writings on the *usus pauper* still led to his being accused of heresy at the general chapter of the order in 1282. The theological commission appointed to examine his writings found 34 propositions worthy of censure, and the minister general ordered his works withdrawn from circulation. But at the chapter of 1287 P.'s orthodoxy was vindicated, and the new general, Matthew of Aquasparta, appointed him lector at Santa Croce in Florence. He was transferred to Montpelier in 1289, where he occupied the same post until 1292, when he was called to the general chapter at Paris to explain his doctrine of the *usus pauper*. He escaped censure by tactical evasion. His last years were spent at Narbonne. P.'s writings played a part in the *poverty controversy even after his death. The Council of Vienne condemned three of his opinions in 1311. The Franciscan general chapter of 1319 forbade circulation of his writings, and in 1326 John XXII condemned his commentary on the Apocalypse. See D. Douie, *Nature and Effects of* the Heresy of the Fraticelli (1932); G. Gál, NCE II:219–220, esp. for bibliog.; M. Lambert, *Franciscan Poverty. The Doctrine of the Absolute Poverty of Christ and the Apostles in the Franciscan Order, 1210–1323* (1961); C. Parte, "Peter John Olivi: Historical and Doctrinal Study," Franciscan Studies 20 (1960), 215–296.

PETER MARTYR VERMIGLI (1500–62), Italian prominent in the English Reformation. P. joined the Augustinians at Fiesole in 1516 and was a superior in Spoleto and Naples as well as a professor. He was influenced by writings of M. *Bucer and H. *Zwingli and accepted reform teachings. He had to flee from Italy and became professor of OT at Strassburg (1542), where he also married. Invited by T. *Cranmer, he went to England with B. *Ochino and became regius professor of theology at Oxford (1548). The 1552 revision of the *Book of Common Prayer reflects his Zwinglian views on the Holy Eucharist; he also collaborated in the reorganization of English canon law. With the accession of Mary Tudor, he was forced to return to Strassburg (1554), and 2 years later he became professor of Hebrew at Zurich. By his correspondence P. continued to influence the English Reformation. His writings included commentaries on Sacred Scripture, on the Nicomachean Ethics, and a *Tractatus de sacramento eucharistiae* (1549); they evidence his power of synthesis and his attempt to reconcile Lutheran and Calvinist teachings. See F. C. Church, *Italian Reformers* (1932); J. C. McLelland, *Visible Words of God, an Exposition of the Sacramental Theory of P. M. V.* (1957), with bibliography.

PETER WALDO, name given to the founder of the *Waldenses. Late in the 14th cent. the Waldenses began to prefix the name Peter to the name of *Waldo as a symbol of his role in the foundation of their Church.

PETITE ÉGLISE, the "Little Church" of those French and Belgian Catholics who refused to accept the Concordat of 1801 between France and the papacy. That agreement completely abolished the existing dioceses, and the pope requested all bps. to resign. In 1801 in London 14 of them, motivated in part by *Gallicanism, but also by their own fidelity during the Napoleonic persecutions of the Church, publicly refused the papal request; 2 years later in London 38 bps. in exile formally protested the Concordat. The exiles had clerical and lay followers in France who comprised the Petite Église. The groups suffered persecution under Napoleon I and the Bourbon Restoration. By 1817 the exiled bps. had been reconciled with Pius VII, except for Bp. de Thémines of Blois; he remained primate of the Petite Église until his death (1829). At its height there were more than 40,000 members of this Church, but it did not proselytize, expecting the imminent collapse of the Concordat. No new bp. was consecrated, nor was any priest ordained. The last priest, Ozouf, died in 1847. In 1869 the two largest congregations petitioned Vatican Council I for recognition of pre-Concordat bishops as the basis for reconciliation, but Rome refused. In the early 20th cent. a French Old Catholic priest and an Anglican clergyman tried unsuccessfully to unite the Petite Église with the Old Catholics. Papal efforts at reconciliation have so far failed, although since 1949 neither retraction nor abjuration of errors is required of any who wish to return. There are nearly 4,000 adherents, most of them peasants. The largest number is in Vendée, where members are called Illuminés; they are known as Louisets in Brittany, Clémentins in Rouergue, Filochois in Toulouse, and Blancs, Burs, Elus, and Fidèles elsewhere in France. In Belgium there are some 400, called Stevenists after the Vicar Capitular C. Stevens of Namur, who led the local opposition to the Concordat of 1801. The Church is not a unit, but the independent congregations have similar practices. A member selected by the community administers baptism, the only sacrament, and officiates at marriages, funerals, and Sunday service. In Vendée divine service is in Latin according to the ancient Paris Breviary; at Lyons it is in French following the ancient Lyons liturgy. Parents teach children the ancient diocesan catechism and prepare them for first (spiritual) communion. The members, pious, austere, and closely knit, observe the festivals abolished by the Concordat. See I. de la Thibauderie, *Églises et évêques Catholiques non Romains* (1962); H. C. Chéry, *L'Offensive des sectes* (1959), 472–473.

PETRARCH, FRANCESCO (1304–74), Italian poet and scholar and one of the first and greatest of the Renaissance humanists. Born in Arezzo, P. was educated at Montpellier and Bologna in law, but his true interest lay in the world of literature and the study of the classics. From 1327 he was deeply affected by his love for a woman called Laura, and neither his assumption of clerical status (1330), nor the fact that his passion was unreciprocated, nor Laura's death (1348) could purge his fantasy of this preoccupation. He wrote poems about her in life and death (*Rime in vita; Rime in morte*). These, together with his other sonnets and *canzoni*, profoundly influenced literary trends throughout Europe. He himself thought less of his vernacular than of his Latin compositions. One of his major Latin works, the *Secretum*, gives an insight into his spiritual life. Besides manifesting the tension Renaissance writers felt between active and contemplative lives, it is an acknowledgment of folly, a recognition of misery, a declaration of repentance, and an expression of hope that he might find God. P.'s Latin writings include collections of letters, a collection of Roman biographies (*De viris illustribus*), and a great epic (*Africa*) on the subject of the war between Rome and Carthage. P.'s humanism (*humanitas*) was a reaction against the cultural sterility of late scholasticism. It stands in contrast not to religious or God-centered values but to the arid subtleties and abstractions with which the schools were then occupied. Far from turning from God and religion, P. proposed rather to seek God in the pursuit of values that can be most effectively set forth concretely and in the round in the manner of the classics. See E. H. Wilkins, *Life of P.* (1961); R. Montano, NCE 11:238–242, esp. for bibliography.

PETROBRUSIANS, a sect named for its founder, Peter of Bruys. A suspended priest, he gained a large following in Languedoc and Provence in the first third of the 12th century. He aroused the people against the clergy and encouraged monks to marry. In matters of doctrine he rejected *infant baptism, the use of church buildings, prayers for the dead, veneration of the cross, hymn singing, the Mass, ecclesiastical authority, and the Bible except for the Gospels. The Council of Toulouse (1119) and Lateran Council II (1139) condemned these teachings. Sometime *c.*1130 the populace of St. Gilles near Nîmes became so enraged when on Good Friday Peter attempted to cook meat over a pile of burning crosses that they put him to death. Many of his followers joined *Henry of Lausanne. Peter the Venerable was active in combating the Petrobrusians. See L. Cristiani, *Heresies and Heretics* (1959), 59; S. Runciman, *Medieval Manichee* (pa., 1961), 118–119.

PFEFFERKORN, JOHANNES (1469–1522 or 23), German Jewish RC convert and polemicist. P. was baptized at Cologne (*c.*1505). He published violently anti-Jewish works, among them *Osternbuch* (1508) and *Judenfeind* (1509), both tr. into Latin by Ortwin *Gratius. P.'s most notorious work, however, was his *Handspiegel*, circulated in 1511 against Johannes *Reuchlin. In the interest of learning, the latter opposed the proposal of P., who knew no Hebrew, that all Hebrew books be burned. P. was supported by the inquisitor Jakob *Hoogstraeten; a long and bitter controversy ensued, during which the *Epistolae obscurorum virorum* appeared, discrediting the supporters of P. before the intelligentsia of Europe.

See F. G. Stokes, *Epistolae Obscurorum Virorum: The Latin Text with an English Rendering, Notes and an Historical Introduction* (1909); R. Coulon, DTC 7:11–17; F. Zoepfl, LTK 8:416.

PHILADELPHIA CONFESSION, a Baptist *confession of faith. The Philadelphia Baptist Association, organized in 1707, adopted the *Second London Confession of 1689 as its standard. The date of adoption is uncertain; in 1742, the association voted that a new edition be printed, but the minutes of 1724 refer to "the Confession of Faith, set forth by the elders and brethren met in London, 1689, and owned by us." No changes were made in the original text, but two new articles were added. One declared that singing praise to God is of divine institution and enjoined churches to sing psalms, hymns, and spiritual songs in their services. The other affirmed that the "laying on of hands (with prayer) upon every baptized believer . . . is an ordinance of Christ." It was the most widely used Baptist confession in America until supplanted by the *New Hampshire Confession. See W. L. Lumpkin, ed., *Baptist Confessions of Faith* (1959).

PHILADELPHIA YEARLY MEETING of the Religious Society of Friends, a group of the Society of Friends comprising since 1955 the former Arch Street Yearly Meeting (Orthodox) and the Race Street Yearly Meeting (Hicksite). It is affiliated with the Friends General Conference.

PHILADELPHIANS, a sect of religious mystics that developed from followers of J. *Boehme who gathered about J. Pordage (1607–81), rector of Bradfield in Berkshire. The most influential of the group was Mrs. Jane Lead (Leade; 1623–1704), who had been a visionary from her youth and who recorded many of her mystical experiences and prophecies in books published between 1681 and 1704. The group was organized in 1670 as the Philadelphia Society for the Advancement of Piety and Divine Philosophy. Although membership in the society was not intended at first to supplant or interfere with existing church affiliation or creedal commitment, the society did eventually put forth its own confession of faith (1703). Its doctrine was inclined to natural pantheism and mystical extravagance as well as to *chiliasm. The translation of one of Mrs. Lead's books into Dutch in 1693 brought her to prominence; through this work and through the influence of F. Lee, a former Oxonian and then a medical student at Leiden, the society gained some Dutch and a few German adherents, whose teachings had some effect upon certain leaders of *Pietism. After Mrs. Lead's death repressive measures taken by the government caused the society in England to dwindle into extinction.

PHILIP OF HESSE (1504–67), Landgrave of Hesse from 1519, promoter of the Reformation. With little formal education, but skilled in politics, he soon established a model government in Hesse. He met Martin Luther at the Diet of *Worms (1521), put down the Peasants' Revolt (1526), and beginning in 1526 established the Reformation in his territory. He founded a university at Marburg (1527) for Protestant theologians. In an attempt, which proved unsuccessful, to reconcile Luther and Zwingli in regard to eucharistic teaching, he called (1529) the Marburg Colloquy (see MARBURG ARTICLES). He also organized the Protestant princes in the Schmalkaldic League (1530), sharing leadership with the Elector of Saxony. The League was hampered by rivalries and by P.'s own alliances with the Emperor, Charles V. His need to placate Charles arose in part from a bigamous marriage (1540), secretly countenanced by Luther. P. did, however, raise an army for the Schmalkalden War (1546–57) against the Emperor; he was captured, imprisoned for 5 years, and upon his release lost interest in politics, but worked for religious reunion. See U. Heinemeger, RGG 5:332–333.

PHILIPPINE INDEPENDENT CHURCH (Iglesia Catolica Filipina Independiente; IFI), a body that separated from the RC Church in 1902; popularly it is known as the Aglipayan Church. Native insurrection about the time of the Spanish-American War included an attack against the friar-bishops, who were identified with Spanish policy. After the failure of political resistance in 1901, the IFI was proclaimed by the nationalist leader, Isabelo de los Reyes, Sr. (1864—1938), and Gregorio *Aglipay (1860–1940), a native secular priest, was acknowledged as supreme bishop. Nationalist feeling initially drew large numbers into the new Church, but the Aglipayans diminished to about 5% of the population in 1966. RC church buildings and property that had been seized earlier were ordered restored by judicial decision in 1906. Initially *apostolic succession was ignored. Doctrinal disputes and strong factionalism developed. One group allied with American Unitarians and split into various parties; another, a trinitarian group, moved toward the Protestant Episcopal Church, from which they received orders in 1948 and with which they were formally united in 1961. The legally recognized IFI is the episcopal and trinitarian body. At the Old Catholic Congress of 1965 the IFI was received as a full member of the *Union of Utrecht. The Church is also in full communion with 12 Churches of the Anglican Communion, and its bishop participated at the Lambeth Conference of 1968. Its supreme bp. is elected by a general assembly for a 4-yr. term. See P. S. de Achútegui and M. A. Bernad, *Religious Revolution in the Philippines: The Life and Church of Gregorio Aglipay, 1860–1940* (2v., 1960–66).

PHILIPPISM, a designation for theological views of Philipp *Melanchthon, as contrasted with pure or *Gnésiolutheranism. Melanchthon's teachings were involved in many of the bitter controversies that beset Lutheranism after Martin Luther's death (see ADIAPHORISTS; · INTERIMS; CRYPTO-CALVINISM; SYNERGISM; MAJORISTIC CON-TROVERSY) and that are reflected in the *Formula of Concord (1577). An important feature in Philippism is *irenicism toward both Calvinist and RC teaching.

PHILIPS, DIRK AND OBBE (Philipsz), sons of a Catholic priest, early leaders of the Anabaptists in the Netherlands.

Dirk (1504–68) had been a Franciscan before joining the Anabaptists in 1533. An associate of *Menno Simons, by his writing and preaching he strengthened the persecuted Mennonites; he eventually left the Netherlands and became founder of the congregation at Danzig. The most learned of the Mennonites of the period, D. wrote an *Enchiridion* (1564) that exerted considerable influence for several centuries, being translated from Dutch into German and English. He stressed the need for the visible Church to be pure, without stain; his strong advocacy of the *ban earned him special regard among Old Order Amish. See MennEnc 2:65–66.

Obbe (*c.*1500–68) first turned away from the Catholic religion to embrace *Sacramentarian views, then became an Anabaptist (1533). His prominence was such that the early Dutch Anabaptists were often called Obbites or Obbenites. He baptized and ordained Menno Simons. His posthumous *Confession* (1584), written in Germany *c.*1560, indicates that he left the Anabaptists, unsure that any visible Church could be the true Church of God. See MennEnc 1:268.

PHILPOT, JOHN (1516–55), English Reformer. After a fellowship at New College, Oxford (1534–41), P. was won over to Reformation doctrine while traveling abroad. Under Edward VI he was made archdeacon of Winchester, but early in the reign of Mary Tudor he was imprisoned for publicly attacking the doctrine of *transubstantiation and was burned at the stake in Dec. 1555. He was the author of numerous works of controversy.

PHRYGIANS, see CATAPHRYGIANS.

PICARDIANS (Picards), a sect of late medieval origin. Interpreting the notion of personal union with God in a pantheistic sense, the Picardians felt themselves free to indulge in community of wives and other immoral practices. They rejected the Bible as revelation, the sacraments, and the hierarchical structure of the Church. They existed from *c.*1406 in parts of France and Belgium. In 1418 some of them, fleeing the Inquisition, went to Bohemia, where they were received among the *Taborites. Soon, however, their ideas were judged pernicious, and many of them were slain. Some Picardians survived in Moravia and Bohemia down to the 19th century.

PIERS PLOWMAN, a Middle English allegory, generally attributed to William Langland; full title, *The Vision of William Concerning Piers the Plowman.* Its subject is the plight of mankind. The poet first invites the reader to see the world as it is. Entering his vision, one sees fine ladies glutting themselves while others are in woeful hovels. Flattery, Liar, and Guile are there and witness a marriage between Lady Meed and Falsehood and watch a friar absolve her "in return for a stained glass window." It is a world in which the poor are neglected and their credulity exploited by a Catholicism that has gone bad and become a religion of amulets, pardons, and bulls. Holy Church has betrayed the trust of men "who would not have held her lore lightly" had she practiced what she preached. The poet then takes the reader off in search of Saint Truth, i.e., of the world as it ought to be. Advice is sought from everyone encountered: from Knowledge, Thought, Study, Clergy, and others until, at long last, Piers Plowman "puts forth his head" and offers to be guide whether one's vocation here is that of Do well (the active life), Do better (the contemplative), or Do best (the episcopal). In the end one comes to Christ on his cross and witnesses in a famous passage his majestic descent into hell to liberate his own.

It is easy to respond to the poet's com-

passion for the poor, his irony, and even his severity expressed in a language full of tang; less easy to grasp is his overall plan. Modern critics insist that he has one and that the work is neither quaint social history nor Wycliffite propaganda but a great religious poem by a poet whom some compare to Dante. There are three versions, the A, B, and C texts, in all of which are references to "Long Will." In 1906 J. M. Manly of Chicago queried their validity and suggested five authors. Modern criticism favors single authorship. Text in translation, J. F. Goodridge, *Piers the Plowman Translated into Modern English with an Introduction* (1959); D. and R. Attwater, *Piers Plowman* (1957). See N. Coghill, *Langland's Piers Plowman* (1964); *idem*, "The Character of Piers Plowman," *Medium Aevum* 2 (1933), 108; H. W. Wells, *Construction of Piers Plowman* (Publications of the Modern Language Association of America 44.1, 1929); G. Kane, *Piers Plowman: The Evidence of Authorship* (1965); for further bibliog. see G. L. O'Grady, NCE 11:351–353.

PIETISM, "the new Reformation" during the 17th and following centuries, which protested against the moral laxity and religious indifference that had befallen the Protestant Churches. In its original inspiration, associated with the names of Philipp Jakob *Spener (1635-1705) and August Hermann *Francke (1663-1727), Pietism claimed to remain loyal to the Lutheran *confessions of faith. It was not the doctrinal substance of the *Book of Concord but the dead orthodoxy based upon it that was a danger to true Christianity. Inevitably, however, the Pietist attack affected the content of orthodox Lutheranism, not only its theological form; and the insistence of the Pietists on deep and genuine conversion came to imply a disparagement both of the conventional Christianity of the Church and of the usual means of grace, baptism, the Eucharist, and the preaching of the word of God.

Pietism was responsible for the development of a number of separate denominations, notably the *Herrnhuters, or Moravians (see MORAVIAN CHURCH), who, under the leadership of Count Nikolaus Ludwig von *Zinzendorf (1700–60), took up the episcopal succession of the Hussite *Unitas Fratrum. Through the Moravians Pietism affected John *Wesley and *Methodism, but the primary importance for church history of the Pietist movement lay in its impact upon the older Protestant communions, the Lutheran and the *Reformed. After the conflicts between Pietism and orthodoxy had subsided, many elements of both combined forces in opposition to *rationalism and the *Enlightenment. Accepting the validity of the Pietist critique but lamenting the emotionalism into which Pietistic religion had often fallen, the defenders of Lutheran confessional orthodoxy during the 19th cent. all showed the effects of the reformation it had wrought.

Perhaps the most visible effect of Pietism within the Churches was the revival of a zeal for the missions. Neither Luther nor the high Lutheran orthodoxy of the 17th cent. had succeeded in organizing a missionary movement—partly because of the paralysis caused by the abolition of the religious orders, partly because of political reasons, but also partly because of failure to accept the demands of the missionary imperative. Pietism corrected this lack in Lutheranism, fostering the formation of missionary societies in the various Lutheran lands and territories. It also took up the task of eliciting vocations to the missions among theological students and clergy. As a result, the evangelical Christianity exported by these missionaries and planted in pagan cultures bore (and often still bears) marks of its Pietist origins: a moral seriousness, a concern for individual conversion, and a stress upon the use of the Bible, esp. upon its private study; but also a tendency to underemphasize the presence and power of God within the structures of nature and of human culture.

From this historical development within Protestantism, specifically Lutheranism, the term "pietism" has acquired a more generic sense. It is often used for a great variety of phenomena within Western Christianity, including Roman Catholicism. Although it is usually meant pejoratively, it does designate certain emphases, particularly in the moral and the devotional spheres, which show analogies to the original Pietist demand for personal religion and good works. Thus total abstinence from alcohol, prayer meetings, opposition to the social mission of the Church, and novenas have all been labeled "pietistic." This usage tends to obscure the original historical meaning of the term and the historical importance of the movement, which is still a factor that one must consider in order to understand Protestant Christianity. See P. J. Spener, *Pia Desideria* (Eng. tr. T. G. Tappert, 1964); F. E. Stoeffler, *Rise of Evangelical Pietism* (1965).

PILGRIM HOLINESS CHURCH, denomination formed by the fusion of a number of *Holiness Churches. In 1897 M. W. Knapp organized the International Apostolic Holiness Union in Cincinnati to encourage the preaching of primitive Wesleyanism. A series of mergers between various Holiness bodies developed, and the present name was adopted in 1917, when the group was joined by former Nazarenes from the Pilgrim Church of California. Doctrines include *entire sanctification, *premillenarianism, *divine healing, and world evangelization. In 1968 it reported 32,814 members, with 952 churches in the U.S. and Canada, and was anticipating a merger with the Wesleyan Methodist Church.

PILGRIM'S PROGRESS, the great epic of Puritanism written by John *Bunyan, probably in 1676, and published in 1678. "Strait is the gate and narrow is the way that leadeth into life" (Mt 7.13) is the text upon which the work is built. It describes the lonely journey of Christian, "a man clothed in rags, a heavy burden on his back," who turns away in anguish from the half-life he has been leading and goes forth to find the road to his salvation. When, with the help of Evangelist, he finds it, it is narrow indeed, and as he presses forward, temptations assail him in the form of monsters with whom he does battle. Violent battles give way to conversations with other pilgrims: with friends such as Hopeful and Faithful; with hypocrites such as Talkative and Worldly Wiseman, subtle tempters who would accommodate religion to a life of cultured ease. These are natural, flowing conversations, in a language homely and racy, with frequent echoes of the Bible. When Christian comes to the cross of Christ, his burden falls from his back, but many are the trials he has yet to endure before he is welcomed to the sound of trumpets into the Celestial City. In Part II, Christian's wife and her friend Mercy set out on a much tamer journey.

Pilgrim's Progress went into innumerable editions, was translated into most languages, and influenced the religious thought of three generations of Englishmen. In the 20th cent., however, the work is seldom read. The modern reader recoils from a religion that permits a man to sin himself completely out of God's mercy and from what seems to be a rejection of the whole secular world as a Vanity Fair. Closer study may convince him that the world rejected by Christian is not "the world whom God so loved as to send his son" but all those forces of the world that, when banded together, conspire to keep him at a lower level and prevent him from becoming his true self. The book has its detractors, those who think that its stern Calvinist theology has done harm to religion, but most critics place it among the classic expressions of Christian imagination. It is more a myth than an allegory. See R. Sharrock, *John Bunyan: The Pilgrim's Progress* (1966); O. E. Winslow, *John Bunyan* (1961); H. Talon, *John Bunyan: The Man and His Works* (tr. B. Wall, 1951); U. M. Kaufmann, *Pilgrim's Progress and Traditions in Puritan Meditation* (1966).

PILLAR OF FIRE, a *Holiness Church, founded in 1901 as the Pentecostal Union; it was incorporated in 1902, and took its pres-

ent name in 1917. Mrs. Alma White (1862–1946) was foundress and first bishop. Wife of a Methodist minister, she began to preach from her husband's pulpit; disputes about this and other matters concerning her teaching and methods led to disapproval by Methodist authorities and to her establishing her own denomination, with headquarters first in Denver, Col., then in Zarephath, N.J. (1908); the Church also moved into England (1908). *Fundamentalism, *premillenarianism, and John Wesley's *Christian perfection, interpreted as *entire sanctification, are taught. Polity resembles that of the Methodist Church. The Church operates several colleges and Bible seminaries; it has an intensive evangelistic program through its several publishing houses and radio stations.

PIONEERS, those Jehovah's Witnesses who devote at least 100 hours per month without compensation to preaching the message of the kingdom. "Special" pioneers are those who devote at least 150 hours or who are foreign missionaries.

PISA, COUNCIL OF, a RC *general council that marked an important phase in the conciliar movement. The council was convened in 1409, when Europe had been divided for 30 years over the claims of rival popes in Avignon and Rome. Instead of healing the *Great Western Schism, the council elected a third claimant to the papal office. At the time of his election in 1394 the Avignonese pope, Benedict XIII, took an oath to do everything in his power to heal the schism. A similar oath was taken by the Roman Gregory XII at his election in 1406. In 1408, when it seemed Gregory would hold on to his disputed office at all costs, his cardinals deserted him. Together with cardinals from Avignon they summoned a council to meet in Pisa the following year. Despite threats of excommunication from both Benedict and Gregory, the meeting was well attended. In the 23 sessions held March 25–Aug. 7, 1409, the council examined the issues; constituted itself a general council representing the universal Church; declared Benedict and Gregory deposed; and elected Alexander V (1409–10). While Pisa did not succeed in ending the schism, it helped nurture the conciliar ideas that were to bear fruit at the Council of *Constance five years later. See E. F. Jacobs, *Essays in the Conciliar Epoch* (rev. ed., 1963); Hughes HC 3:270–282; L. E. Boyle, NCE 11:384–385. *CONCILIARISM.

PISTOIA, SYNOD OF, the diocesan synod held at Pistoia, Sept. 18–28, 1786, which has special interest in the history of *Gallicanism and *Jansenism. It was convoked by Scipione de' Ricci (1741–1810), the reform-minded bishop of Pistoia-Prato, aided and encouraged by the Grand Duke of Tuscany, Peter Leopold. The council fathers were about 250 priests from the diocese, with Pietro Tamburini, the foremost theologian of Italian Jansenism, as promoter of the faith. The Synod met in six formal sessions, passing a number of decrees concerned with pastoral issues. It sought to restore sacramental life to the center of church worship and called for a revision of liturgical texts, use of the vernacular, and better catechetical instruction. Other anti-Roman innovations touched church organization and canon law. Many of the specific reforms suggested at Pistoia have been implemented, though in quite a different spirit, by Vatican II. The acts of Pistoia circulated widely in Europe; in France they became the basis for the *Civil Constitution of the Clergy (1790). In 1794, Pope Pius VI condemned the proceedings of the Synod in the bull *Auctorem fidei,* singling out 85 propositions for specific censure (D 2600–2700). De' Ricci, who was forced by popular resistance to resign in 1791, submitted to Rome in 1805, though with Jansenist afterthoughts. See M. Rosa, "Italian Jansenism and the Synod of Pistoia," *Concilium* 17:34–49.

PITHOU, PIERRE (1539–96), French lawyer and Gallican theorist. He shared an interest with his two brothers in legal codification and theory. P. became a member of the Parlement of Paris in 1560, but lived for a time in Sedan and Basel because he was a Huguenot. He became a Catholic *c.*1573 and gained a position in the French legal bureaucracy. From about 1579 he supported Henry IV and rose in his service. During the controversy over Henry IV's accession to the throne, P. formulated in 83 articles a basic statement of *Gallicanism, *Les Libertés de l'église gallicane* (1594), which in 1682 constituted the basis for the Four *Gallican Articles. After his retirement he edited several volumes of civil and canonical legal codes.

PLACE, JOSUÉ DE LA (Lat. Placeus; 1596–1655 or 1656), Calvinist theologian. A prof. at the theological academy of Saumur from 1633, P. rejected current orthodox Calvinist theory that original sin was imputed to each man as a share in Adam's sinful action. He maintained that Calvin himself recognized only an imputation by reason of the inherited depraved nature. P. published his views in *Disputatio de imputatione primi peccati Adami* (1655). The *Helvetic Consensus Formula repudiated P.'s teaching.

PLAN OF UNION, an agreement made in 1801 for cooperation between Presbyterians and Congregationalists. Evangelical fervor and expansion of settlement into western N.Y. and Ohio led these Churches to cooperate in home missionary work to eliminate unfortunate competition. The Plan of Union made it possible for congregations to be connected with both denominations and to be served by pastors of either. Presbyterian churches might be represented in Congregational associations by elders, while Congregational churches could be represented in presbyteries by committeemen. For a while the Plan worked so well that Presbyterians invited Congregational associations to become integral parts of Presbyterian synods, and Congregationalists formed no separate organizations for clergymen in the West. Unhappiness over "presbygationalists" developed, particularly among Presbyterians who saw a threat to Presbyterian doctrine and church order and who gained enough power to abrogate the Plan in the General Assembly of 1838 and to cut off certain synods that were overly influenced by Congregationalism. See R. H. Nichols, *Presbyterianism in New York State* (1963).

PLURAL MARRIAGE, a designation for the polygamy practiced for a time among the Mormons. In the **Pearl of Great Price* Joseph *Smith maintained that plural marriage was a revealed doctrine. It was not fully and openly put into practice, however, until 1852 in Utah, and was declared a suppressed doctrine in 1890. During the period of its practice Mormon polygamy was an issue of conflict with non-Mormons, esp. with federal authority. Plural marriage was connected in Mormon doctrine with the preexistence of souls, namely, as the means to procreate more bodies for souls to occupy and so undergo mortality as a condition for reaching eternal exaltation. In the Mormon idea of salvation, as well, marriage is essential, esp. for women. Celibacy and the single state are regarded as against the word of God. Only women who are married can reach the highest plane of celestial happiness. Plural marriages could be *celestial marriages, and thus continue in heaven.

PLYMOUTH BRETHREN, a religious body, begun in England and Ireland in the 19th cent., that seeks to imitate the simple Christianity of the apostolic age. The first members called themselves simply Brethren, Christians, or Saints; they were also popularly called *Darbyites (see DARBY, JOHN NELSON); the present name, not an officially adopted title, was given because the largest early center was in Plymouth, England. Dissatisfied both with the formalism of the C of E and with divisions among

*Nonconformists, early members joined together in small groups, united in prayer and in the expectation of Christ's second coming as well as in separation from all non-Brethren. Small assemblies of Brethren were founded in many countries of Europe, in North America, Australia, and New Zealand; they have never had any formal ecclesiastical organization, church buildings, or international unifying agency. In doctrine the Plymouth Brethren adhere to *fundamentalism and *premillenarianism, and in general to the contents of the Apostles' Creed, although rejecting any creedal formula. Their doctrine of salvation is strictly Calvinistic; true believers have *assurance of salvation. The charismatic ministry enjoyed by all believers does away with the need of ordained or salaried ministers. Worship, conducted in a home or small hall, is austere, with the Sunday celebration of the Lord's Supper central; during the week prayer meetings and Bible study are also conducted. Against the division of Christians into sects or denominations, they interpret the Church as the visible congregation of all true believers. This doctrine, however, has been the main source of the many divisions among the Brethren. In 1848 the question of whether to associate with other Christians resulted in the split between Exclusive Brethren and Open Brethren. In the U.S. there are eight distinct divisions, which, because they do not use denominational names, are simply designated by the Roman numerals I through VIII. These groups differ mainly on the points of exclusiveness vs. openness, minor doctrinal emphases, or polity. The eight branches in 1967 numbered about 33,000 members in 665 congregations; Plymouth II was the largest, with a membership of 15,000. See Mayer RB 394–396, bibliog.

PLYMOUTH PEOPLE, the Puritans who landed at Plymouth, Mass. in 1620, arriving there from Holland. With the *Bay People they made the Congregational Church the established Church in Massachusetts.

POAU, see PROTESTANTS AND OTHER AMERICANS UNITED FOR SEPARATION OF CHURCH AND STATE.

POIRET, PIERRE (1646–1719), French Protestant writer on mysticism. A spiritual crisis in 1674, while he was pastor for the French settled in the Palatinate, brought P. to distrust philosophical reasoning and to equate Christianity with mysticism. He lived in Amsterdam with Anne *Bourignon from 1676 until her death in 1680. His *L'Économie divine* (7v., 1687) presented her ideas; he also edited her writings (19v., 1679–84). Through his biographies and editions of Mme. Guyon, J. Olier, P. Bérulle and other earlier writers, P. influenced Gottfried Arnold and Gerhard Tersteegen, and through them, German *Pietism. His masterwork was *Bibliotheca mysticorum selecta* (1708), an extensive collection of authors on mysticism. See R. Knox, *Enthusiasm* (1950), 352, 355, 390, 398.

POISSY, CONFERENCE OF (Disputatio Pussicena), a meeting held in 1561 at Poissy near Paris, between French RC bps. and representatives of French Calvinists. Among the latter were T. *Beza and *Peter Martyr Vermigli. The Conference was summoned by the regent, Queen Catherine de Médicis, in the hope of achieving religious peace. With little communication between the two sides, the meeting had no real success.

POLEMICAL THEOLOGY, theology developed in conscious opposition to doctrinal systems of other Churches. Every theology is to some extent polemical, defending its approach in contrast to others, but polemical theology implies a special interest in defending the tradition of a particular Church and attacking the teachings of other Churches. In the denominational conflicts of past centuries theologians of each Church have been concerned to prove the correctness of their Church's distinctive dogma and the errors of other Churches. As is to some extent the case in the mid-1960s, theologians were considered to be representatives of particular denominations and to have as a part of their professional responsibility defense of their Church's teaching against competing Churches. With the development of the *ecumenical movement in the 20th cent. it has come to be widely felt that greater progress can be made through *interfaith dialogue than through polemics, and agencies such as the *World Council of Churches are designed in large measure to facilitate such dialogue. *FAITH AND ORDER.

POLISH NATIONAL CATHOLIC CHURCH OF AMERICA, an autonomous American foundation, maintaining *intercommunion with the Old Catholic Churches and the Anglican Communion. The Polish National Catholic Church is the largest and most successful secession from the RC Church in the U.S.; separation came as part of a broader upsurge of Polish national sentiment against the power of the predominantly Irish and German RC hierarchy over church property after the Third Plenary Council of Baltimore (1884). A clash occured (1897–1900) at Scranton, Pa., which culminated in the repudiation of RC organization, doctrine, and worship forms by the parishioners of St. Stanislaus Church, led by the pastor, F. *Hodur. By 1905 he was able to give formal organization to the new Church, which had a membership of about 20,000; 2 years later he received episcopal consecration from the Little Church of Utrecht; in 1909 his Church entered communion with the *Union of Utrecht. Two similar Polish separatist bodies joined the Polish National Catholic Church: one from Chicago, Ill. (1907); another from Buffalo, N.Y. (1914). From 1923 a mission, later a separate diocese, was established in Poland. It has suffered both Nazi and Communist persecution; its bp. died in prison (1951), and relations with the Church in the U.S. were severed (1953–59), though some contact has since been resumed. The Lithuanian National Catholic Church, which Bp. Hodur helped found in 1914, became independent in 1923 but merged with the Polish Church in 1964. Latest available figures for the Church (1960) show a membership of about 280,000 in the United States.

The Confession of Faith dates from 1913. Although the Church subscribes to the Declaration of *Utrecht, it does not conform to Old Catholic teaching on all points. Through a theory of *restorationism, it rejects eternal punishment for sin; faith is deemed helpful but not necessary to salvation; confirmation and baptism are parts of the one sacrament, but seven sacraments are kept, since the word of God as preached and heard is a sacrament. Liturgy has been from the beginning in Polish, but English is permissible and is increasingly used. Confession is individual for children, general for adults; clergy may marry. The supreme authority in the Church is the quadrennial General Synod, made up of the bps. and of elected priests and laymen. The bp. of Scranton is prime bp., and with a general council carries on the regular affairs of the Church. See T. Andrews, *Polish National Catholic Church in America and Poland* (1953).

POLITY, in ecclesiastical usage, the form of government of a Church; sometimes extended to refer even to the doctrinal and liturgical position of a Church. In his debate with the Puritans, Richard *Hooker published *Of the Laws of Ecclesiastical Polity* (1593–1597); he preferred to speak of church polity rather than church government, because it "includeth both government and whatsoever besides belongeth to the ordering of the church in public" (Bk. 3.2, 13). A term that includes the laws, offices, nature of authority, and even forms and ceremonies is thus susceptible of a wide variety of combinations. It is often asserted that there are three types of polity: episcopal, synodal (presbyterian), and congregational. Such a

classification, however, is of limited value, for not all episcopal systems are alike, and many *church orders combine elements of all three types. For example, one may characterize the RC, Anglican, Orthodox, and Methodist Churches as episcopal in polity, but the authority, functions, and interpretations of the office of bishop are vastly different in these different communions. Even within a single tradition, there may exist different types of government. In the U.S. most denominations have been influenced to some extent by congregational emphases, favoring the influence of each particular congregation in decision-making and a share by the laity in governing the Church. The C of E considers episcopacy essential to the Church, while American Methodists deny *apostolic succession and regard episcopacy only as one possible convenient form of organization. The source of authority and its theological rationale, the offices and their functions, the liturgical practices, and the processes by which decisions are made and implemented all are necessary for determining the precise polity of any particular Church.

PONTIFICAL, ROMAN, a liturgical book containing the prayers and ceremonies reserved to the bishop for all liturgical acts apart from the Mass. In the early Church there was no special book for the bishop; liturgical books simply assumed that the bishop was officiant. In those services in which a simple priest sometimes took the place of the bishop, he adapted his procedure to that of the bishop in the manner prescribed by local tradition. The modern Roman Pontifical has its remote roots in two sources: the *Hadrianum*, the sacramentary sent by Hadrian I to Charlemagne, whose ecclesiastics supplemented it with Gallican material; and the *Ordines*, or manuals of ceremonial. The Pontifical reached its present form toward the end of the 13th cent. through the work of Bp. Durandus of Mende. Durandus's book attempted to portray the Roman usage but actually was an amalgam of Roman, Gallican, and Germanic practices. This book was generally accepted in Rome in the 15th century. It was first published in 1485 as the typical Roman Pontifical. Recommended by the Council of Trent, it was made obligatory for the whole RC Church by Clement VIII (1596). It is (1969) in process of revision.

POOR CATHOLICS, *Waldenses, led by Durand of Huesca, who were reunited to the Church by Innocent III in 1208. They were suppressed by Gregory IX in 1237. See H. C. Lea, *History of the Inquisition of the Middle Ages* (1888, repr. 1958), 1:246–248.

POOR MEN OF LOMBARDY, a sect of *Waldenses that separated from the *Poor Men of Lyons in 1205. Members were divided into three classes: missionaries, women under vows, and married persons. In 1210 some of them sought reunion with the Church, and Innocent III organized them into an order known as Reconciled Lombards. This group, under their leader, Bernard Prim, rendered useful service in combating the Waldenses and *Cathari, until the mendicant orders were established.

POOR MEN OF LYONS, early name for the Waldenses, members of a movement for evangelical poverty founded c.1175 at Lyons by the merchant *Waldo. Under this name (Pauperes de Lugduno) they were condemned by the Council of Verona (1184) under Pope Lucius III. *WALDENSES.

POPERY, commonly a derisive term for the RC religion, connoting esp. beliefs and practices rejected by the English and Scottish Reformers. Doctrine and ritual that W. *Laud, Abp. of Canterbury, sought to preserve, were impugned by Puritans in England and *Covenanters in Scotland as popery. The term, however, is also used more soberly simply to refer to the polity of the RC Church, in which the pope is the supreme head.

PORT-ROYAL, the Cistercian abbey of nuns founded in 1204, and in the 17th cent. the main center of *Jansenism. The original monastery, about 17 miles from Paris, near Versailles, came to be called Port-Royal des Champs after 1625; in that year the community was transferred to Paris, to a new monastery, Port-Royal de Paris, in the Faubourg Saint-Jacques. In 1665 most of the nuns, having refused to sign a formulary condemning the five Jansenist propositions, were transferred back to Port-Royal des Champs, where they were virtually prisoners for 4 years. With the *Peace of the Church (1669) they enjoyed a decade of quiet. Their continued loyalty to the Jansenist cause, however, was viewed as opposition to his royal power by Louis XIV; in 1679 Port-Royal des Champs was forbidden to receive novices, and its temporalities were severely diminished. In 1706 the aging nuns refused to accept yet another papal condemnation of Jansenism, *Vineam Domini*; 3 years later the abbey was suppressed and the nuns sent to various convents. In 1710 the buildings of Port-Royal des Champs were razed; even the bones in the cemetery were transferred.

The name Port-Royal connotes a whole circle of leading figures in the Jansenist movement. Mère Angélique *Arnauld, named abbess at Port-Royal des Champs at the age of 7, and its reformer at the age of 18, effected the transfer of her flourishing community to Paris. Through her director after 1633, the Abbé de *Saint-Cyran, Port-Royal acquired its spirit of moral rigorism and its loyalty to his friend, Cornelius *Jansen, author of *Augustinus*. Saint-Cyran's disciples, priests and laymen, became Les Messieurs de Port-Royal; solitaries devoted to the spiritual life and scholarship, they lived first near Port-Royal de Paris, then after Saint-Cyran's arrest in 1638, at Port-Royal des Champs. There they established Les Petites-Écoles, important in the history of pedagogy, esp. for the inculcation of moral training and the emphasis on French and Italian letters rather than on Jesuit classical tradition. Among Les Messieurs was Antoine *Arnauld, brother of Mère Angélique. His *De la fréquente communion* (1643) intensified the Saint-Cyranian moral rigorism and shaped the liturgical life of Port-Royal. The Port-Royalists also tenaciously used Arnauld's distinction between the pope's right (*droit*) to condemn the heresy in the five Jansenist propositions, and the fact (*fait*) that the propositions were present in Jansen's *Augustinus*. The name of Blaise *Pascal, author of the Provincial Letters, was also associated with Port-Royal, and his sister Jacqueline was a nun there. See R. Knox, *Enthusiasm* (repr. 1961); L. Cognet, NCE 11:597–598, bibliog.

PORTAL, ÉTIENNE FERNAND (1855–1926), French Vincentian priest and pioneer ecumenist. A chance meeting with the Anglican second Viscount *Halifax in Madeira in Dec. 1889 led to a lifelong friendship and to P.'s principal work: the *rapprochement* of the Churches of Canterbury and Rome. The campaign for Anglo-Roman reunion launched in 1894 by P.'s *Les Ordinations anglicanes* (under the psuedonym F. Dalbus) and skillfully promoted by Halifax in England led to surprising initial success, but then to the condemnation of *Anglican orders by Leo XIII in the bull *Apostolicae curae* (1896). Despite this defeat P. retained both his faith in the cause of *ecumenism and the confidence of his superiors. He broadened his ecumenical interests to include Eastern and esp. Russian Orthodoxy. A scholarly man, P. insisted on history as the necessary basis for dogmatic studies; his principal literary remains are in his pioneering ecumenical periodicals: *Revue Anglo-Romaine* (3v., 1895–96) and *Revue des Églises* (6v., 1904–09). Possessed of a charismatic gift for friendship, P. was able to bring together those with the most varied backgrounds, to communicate his ecumenical enthusiasm to others, and to inspire them to scholarly research, personal contact with Christians of other Churches, and prayer for reunion. P.'s most tangible ecumenical success was the *Malines Conversations (1921–25), which were originated and sustained through his and Lord Halifax's tireless efforts. See lives by H. Hemmer et al. (1947) and A. T. Macmillan (1961); A. Gratieux, *L'Amitié au service de réunion* (1952); J. J. Hughes, *Absolutely Null and Utterly Void* (1968).

POSTLAPSARIANISM, equivalent alternative for infralapsarianism, or sublapsarianism, the interpretation in Calvinist teaching that God predestined men to heaven or hell only after the Fall. *SUPRALAPSARIANISM.

POSTMILLENARIANISM (Postmillennialism), the doctrine that a millennium of righteousness is to come upon earth through the operation of Christian agencies, which will gradually overcome the forces of evil opposed to the gospel until at length its spirit pervades and dominates the entire world. This condition will last 1,000 years, at the close of which there will be a brief apostasy of some, and a final conflict between the saints and the forces of evil. Then Christ will come, the dead will rise to judgment, and the world will be destroyed by fire. Postmillenarianism differs from premillenarianism in holding that the visible advent of Christ follows rather than precedes the millennium. *MILLENARIANISM.

POVERTY CONTROVERSY, a theoretical debate on the nature of evangelical poverty that grew out of a dispute over the practice of poverty in the Franciscan Order. Soon after the death of St. Francis his order requested from the Holy See an official interpretation of certain disputed portions of the rule. Four bulls on this subject were issued between 1230 and 1312. To a group of rigorists known as *Spirituals these pronouncements constituted a betrayal of the founder's ideal of poverty. They sought to separate themselves from the order so that they might live the rule in its primitive severity. Their efforts were stubbornly resisted by the majority party, known as the Communitas, and both Boniface VIII and John XXII took severe measures against them. In 1321 a Dominican inquisitor declared heretical the doctrine of the *paupertas altissima*, according to which Christ and his Apostles owned nothing either personally or in common. This attack on what was considered a basic Franciscan tenet temporarily united the Spirituals and the Communitas. The general chapter of 1322 unanimously affirmed that the doctrine of the *paupertas altissima* was sound Catholic teaching. John XXII answered this challenge by revoking the legal fiction by which the Holy See held proprietorship over the goods used by the Franciscans (*Ad Conditorem*, 1322), and by declaring the doctrine of the *paupertas altissima* heretical (*Cum inter nonnullos*, 1323). Many leading Spirituals and a number of prominent members of the Communitas followed the Minister General, Michael of Cesena, into schism and sought the protection of the Emperor Louis of Bavaria. By 1329 most of these *Michaelists had returned to the order and submitted to the Church. See D. Douie, *Nature and Effects of the Heresy of the Fraticelli* (1932); M. Lambert, *Franciscan Poverty. The Doctrine of the Absolute Poverty of Christ and his Apostles in the Franciscan Order, 1210–1323* (1961).

PRACTICAL THEOLOGY, that division of study, esp. in Protestant seminaries, that relates to carrying out the activities of the Church, as distinguished from such studies as Scripture, church history, dogmatic theology, and philosophy of religion. "When we turn to the fields of homiletics, religious education, and church administration, as well as to liturgy and church music, we come to studies which are often designated "practical" in contrast to "theoretical." . . . What distinguishes these fields is that they have to do with the meaning of Christian faith as it bears upon specific functions of the minister or other religious worker so that work in these fields involves practice as well as instruction" (H. R. Niebuhr, D. D. Williams, and J. M. Gustafson, *The Ad-*

vancement of Theological Education [1957], 102). Pastoral counseling, with its programs of classroom and clinical training, is also included in the practical field. Courses in practical theology have become increasingly numerous in seminary curricula in recent decades. Although critics sometimes assert that too much emphasis is thereby placed upon technique in the training of ministers, the increased role of practical theology seems fairly well established.

PRAEDESTINATUS, a 5th-cent. anonymous treatise written in Italy, possibly at Rome. The title was given by J. Sirmond, who edited the text in 1643. There are three books; the first is a reproduction of St. Augustine's *De haeresibus*, with fanciful additions; the second presents arguments in favor of an extreme theory of predestination, which it falsely attributes to Augustine; the third is a Pelagian refutation of the arguments. See É. Amann, DTC 12:2775–80.

PRAEMUNIRE (Lat., to fortify; confused in medieval Lat. with *praemonere*, to forewarn), a term variously applied in English law: (1) to statutes, 23d Edward III (1353), and 16th Richard II (1393); (2) to the appropriate writs that charged a sheriff, *praemunire facias*, to summon a person accused of prosecuting in a foreign court a suit cognizable by the law of England; (3) to the offense itself; and (4) to the penalty incurred of forfeiture, outlawry, and imprisonment at the king's pleasure. The measures go back to the legislation of Edward I (1206) against papal provisions of benefices, dignities, and their revenues, impositions increasingly resented during the Hundred Years' War and regarded, particularly when the popes were at Avignon, as operating for the comfort of the French enemy. They were not, however, steadily applied until Henry VIII invoked them against asserting or maintaining papal jurisdiction, most famously in his proceedings against

Cardinal Wolsey and in his coercion of the clergy to acknowledge the royal supremacy over the Church.

PRAYER BOOK, AMERICAN, see AMERICAN PRAYER BOOK.

PRAYER BOOK, THE, informal designation for the *Book of Common Prayer.

PREACHING, in its primary Christian meaning, the act of proclaiming God's saving word. The term also denotes the art of pulpit oratory, which has its own history, not considered here. In the first sense, the English term preaching stands for several NT terms: *kērussein*, to herald, proclaim (noun form *kērugma*, proclamation); *euangelizesthai*, to announce the good news (noun form *euangelion*, the good news, the gospel), *marturein*, to witness, is used in the Johannine writings. These are central in the dynamics of Christianity: by preaching Christianity had its beginnings, its growth, and its continuation, whatever the forms it has taken. The fact should not be obscured by exaggerating a contrast between preaching in the RC Church and in the Churches of the Reformation. The Reformation does, however, remain a useful point of division in the history of Christian preaching.

From the NT to the Reformation. NT literature indicates that the one who preaches announces his message with authority; he is commissioned, sent. John the Baptist, for example, was a herald for Jesus, proclaiming the good tidings of the Redemption (Mk 1.38; Lk 4.18). Preaching describes the whole ministry of Jesus and the Apostles (Mk 1.2; 3.14; Jn 1.23; Acts 6.2–4; 1 Cor 1.17; 9.16). When Jesus preached in towns and villages "with him went the twelve" (Lk 8.2), and he commissioned them to proclaim "to the whole world" what he had told them (Mt 24.14; Lk 24.46). They did this, announcing "in season and out of season" (2 Tim 4.2) the word of God received from Jesus (Tit 1.3). No complete record of apostolic sermons remains, but

Acts gives many reports of preaching in which the Apostles' proclamation of the kingdom is revealed (Acts 2.14–40; 3.12–26; 10.28–43). St. Paul preached in connection with the celebration of the Eucharist (Acts 20.7). Preaching is presented as the saving act of God (Mk 1.15; Lk 4.16–21), and its subject matter is the whole work of salvation through Christ (see, e.g., 1 Cor, ch. 1 and 2).

In postapostolic times Justin Martyr mentioned (*c.*150) preaching as part of the regular liturgical service (*Apol.* 1.67). The discourses of Polycarp (d. *c.*116) to his people of Smyrna are referred to by Tertullian (d. *c.*220) and also by Irenaeus (d. *c.*202), whose own sermons, collected in the 4th cent. by Eusebius (*Eccl. hist.* 5.20.6), are no longer extant. Among the earliest surviving preached sermons is a prolix homily on wealth, by Clement of Alexandria (d. *c.*210), based on Mk 10.17–31. By the 4th cent. preaching had become an integral part of Christian worship, as the collected sermons of the great preachers attest. Preachers of East and West were trained rhetoricians, particularly proficient at the exegetical sermon, a running commentary on the Sacred Scripture used in the day's liturgy. Famed in the East were the Cappadocians, SS. Gregory of Nazianzus (d. *c.*390) and Basil the Great (d. 379), together with St. John Chrysostom (d. 407); and in the West SS. Ambrose (d. 397) and Augustine (d. 430). The latter often preached several times a day and composed a work on preaching, Book IV of his *De doctrina christiana.* Gregory the Great (Pope Gregory I, d. 604) wrote series of homilies that were widely read in the following centuries and gave directions for preaching in his *Liber regulae pastoralis,* a guide for parish priests. In the Dark Ages after the barbarian invasions preaching fell into disuse, and the sermon was almost restricted to monastery churches, where homiliaries, collections of patristic sermons, like that of Paul the Deacon (*c.*720–*c.*800), were employed. The Carolingian reforms of the 9th cent. improved both clerical education and preaching, notably by collections of sermons made by Alcuin and Rabanus Maurus, and church councils (at Tours and at Reims, 813; at Mainz, 847) decreed that bishops preach homilies, and in the new vernacular languages. While preaching spread, its quality declined quickly with the invasions of the Moslems and Northmen.

The 12th cent. is marked by the mystical and scriptural preaching of St. Bernard of Clairvaux (1090–1153), which had lasting influence; the era also saw the development, connected with the rise of the universities, of the scholastic sermon. Based on the scholastic method of exposition, this type of sermon was preached at all the university centers by the medieval schoolmen. A desire to fill a need for popular preaching (Lateran Council IV in 1215 complained of the near-illiteracy of most parish priests) led to lay preaching in such reform movements as the *Humiliati and *Waldenses; doctrinal vagaries led to ecclesiastical condemnation. With the coming of the friars in the 13th cent., principally the Dominicans and Franciscans, to whom freedom to preach everywhere was granted (e.g., by the Council of Vienne, 1312), a great rebirth of popular preaching took place throughout the West. Great crowds gathered to hear the friars, and outdoor sermons became a regular practice.

Popular preaching during the centuries preceding the Reformation had several developments. One was the spread of the mystical sermon by Meister Eckhart (1260–1327), Johannes Tauler (c.1266–1367), Henry Suso (c.1295–1366), Jean Gerson (c.1363–1429), and others. Another was the sermon similar to the later parish mission or revival sermon, urging repentance, frequently in apocalyptic terms; SS. Vincent Ferrer (c.1350–1419), Bernardine of Siena (1380–1444), and John Capistran (1386–1456) preached in this style. Preaching was also used as a powerful weapon of reform by John Wycliffe (c.1329–84), who sent out his Lollards and Poor Preachers in England; by Jan Hus (c.1369–1416); and by Girolamo Savonarola (1452–98). The many sermon aids, preachers' manuals, and collections of sermons published throughout these centuries attest to the frequency of preaching; but the strictures of Lateran Council V (1516) indicate that much of it had become devoted to superstition instead of the gospel.

Preaching in the Churches of the Reformation. Protesting against a special sacrificing priesthood, *sacramentalism, and papal teaching authority, the Reformers asserted the primacy of the word of God as present in Scripture, sermon, and sacraments. Early Reformers designated themselves simply "the preachers." Both the *Augsburg Confession (Art. 7) and the *Thirty-Nine Articles (Art. 19) defined the Church as existing where the gospel is rightly preached and the sacraments rightly administered. The preaching of the word was proposed as the instrument through which justification comes about and the Holy Spirit is given (*Formula of Concord, Art. 12; *Westminster Confession, ch. 14). The *Reformed tradition esp. extolled preaching as the primary function of the ministry (Zwingli's Sixty-Seven Articles, Art. 14, 62; First *Helvetic Confession, Art. 20; Second *Helvetic Confession, ch. 14, 18). While Anabaptists—the radicals of the Reformation—and later the Quakers rejected any special ministry, the influence of preaching nevertheless had a paramount influence on their history.

The high value set on preaching as characteristic of the Reformation was exemplified by Luther, Zwingli, and Calvin. A close alliance between the biblical and the preached word was observed through the expository sermon, closely following the scriptural text. The original esteem for preaching the word has never been lost in Protestantism. Conviction that the living word of God is present in the act of preaching inspired the Puritans of England and New England, the evangelists John *Wesley and George *Whitfield, and preachers of *revivalism. Almost every Protestant Church has had its beginning with a great preacher; throughout Protestant history the major figures and the most significant movements are closely connected with preaching.

The content and quality of preaching has naturally reflected theological trends. The original Reformation zeal for the living word of God has sometimes stiffened into a letter-bound *biblicism. Within the century after the Reformation, both Lutheran and Reformed pulpits became platforms for a scholastic orthodoxy, in which emphasis was placed upon correct formulation of doctrine. In reaction, *Pietism developed themes and styles inculcating an individualistic experience of salvation, an emphasis carried on in Wesleyan and revivalistic preaching. The impact of the *Enlightenment and of rationalism turned sermon emphasis away from distinctive Christian dogma in favor of ethical and naturalistic explanations of the gospel. This trend was continued and compounded in the 19th cent. by *liberal theology; preachers sought to present an enlightened view of biblical themes accommodated to evolutionary theory, and stressed the subjective appeal of religious truths. In the *Social Gospel movement the pulpit became a forum for addressing all social questions and for a humanitarian Christianity. Protestants described as *evangelicals resisted both liberals and ritualists (see RITUALISM), and emphasized preaching, relying on a literal understanding of the Bible and minimizing sacraments and ritual (see FUNDAMENTALISM; NEW EVANGELICALISM). In the 20th cent. the rejection of liberal theology in favor of a return to Reformation orthodoxy was led by Karl *Barth, who asserted the primacy of the word of God: the original Word in Christ, the record of that word in the Bible, and the word made present in preaching that depends on the biblical word about Christ. For many Rudolf Bultmann has renewed concern for the preached word; he has sought to show the relevance of the NT to contemporary man by his thesis that the demythologized and dehistoricized kerygma is God's present revelation calling for authentic faith (see BULTMANN SCHOOL). There has also been a return in many Protestant Churches to the relation between word and sacrament, esp. the Lord's Supper, and a strong trend to keep the two together, as conjoined expressions of God's saving action and presence.

RC Preaching since the Reformation. One RC reaction to the Reformation was a strong reaffirmation of church doctrine on the sacraments and the Mass. The Council of Trent also sought to remedy the failure of bishops and priests to preach properly. Early in the Council (Session V, June 17, 1546) preaching was made the topic of a special decree, urging it as the principal function of bishops, legislating that all priests having the care of souls preach on Sundays and great feast days. A reform decree in session 23 (Nov. 11, 1563) reiterated (can. 4) the earlier legislation, recommended special sermons during Advent and Lent, and advised bps. to remind the faithful of the obligation to hear the word of God in their own parishes. The legislation on seminaries earlier in session 23 (July 15, 1563) also was a reform measure that led to a better preparation for preachers. The *Catechism of the Council of Trent* was designed as a doctrinal guide, esp. for preaching. Since Trent there has been a conscientious fulfillment of the preaching ministry, at the parish Sunday Masses, in special sermons, particularly during Lent, and in the development of the parish mission, novenas, and retreats. In these centuries there also have been throughout the Church powerful preachers, sometimes brilliant pulpit orators.

The most significant factor in RC preaching since the reforms of Trent, however, has been a new, or newly stated, evaluation of preaching. The formulation of a RC theology of the word was slow to come. There has been a sense of the obligation to preach; the sermon has been used for doctrinal instruction, moral exhortation, and for polemical or apologetic purposes. Vatican Council II in the *Decree on the Liturgy* recognized the evangelizing, instructional, and exhortatory functions of preaching (Vat II SacLit 9). But the Council described preaching in its fullest significance as "a proclamation of God's wonderful works in the history of salvation, that is, the mystery of Christ, which is ever made present and active within us, especially in the celebration of the liturgy" (35). The one liturgy comprises the "liturgy of the word and the Eucharistic liturgy" (56). The Council recognized the presence of the saving Christ esp. in the liturgy, that Christ is present in sacrifice and sacraments; "he is present as well in his word since it is he himself who speaks when the holy Scriptures are read in the church" (7; see also Vat II MinLifePriests 4). These teachings have led to a richer theology of preaching, to an appreciation of the union between word and sacrament and of preaching as essentially the present celebration of the mystery of salvation. See E. C. Dargan, *History of Preaching* (2v., 1954); NCE 11:684–700, with bibliog.; P. Hitz, *To Preach the Gospel* (tr. R. Sheed, 1963); J. Murphy-O'Connor, *Paul on Preaching* (1964); O. Semmelroth, *Preaching Word* (tr. J. J. Hughes, 1965).

PRECISIANISM, a synonym for historical Puritanism; also the theory or practice of one who is religiously or morally rigid. *PURITANISM.

PRECISIANS, a name used briefly for *Puritans, because of their exactness in religious matters. In a broader sense the term is applied to anyone with similar religious attitudes.

PREDESTINARIANISM, a term to designate any teaching that interprets predestination as the election of some to eternal life and the absolute condemnation of all others to sin and punishment. *PREDESTINATION.

PREDESTINATION (Gr. *proorizo,* decide on in advance), a word that does not occur in the OT and is seldom used in the NT. The chief NT passages (Rom 8.29; Eph 1.5) refer to the divine plan choosing people for a favored position in the external economy of salvation: the chosen people of the OT, the Christians of the NT. This choice is intended to bring them to eschatological salvation; it bears indirectly on it, however, in that men so favored can cast aside the means if they so will, and those not so favored can still be saved (Rom 2.14–16). Nowhere in Scripture is "predestine" used to mean an infrustrable divine arrangement sending a man to eternal happiness (the opposite, reprobation: an infrustrable advance decision sending men to perdition). Still less does Scripture know of such a reprobation decided before consideration of a man's deserts. Rather, it implicitly excludes such meaning in saying (1 Tim 2.4) that God wills all men to be saved. He could not honestly decide this while simultaneously deciding on the perdition of some without even considering their deserts. Nor could he bind himself in the covenant at an infinite price (1 Cor 11.25; 6.20) to offer all graces (Rom 8.32) in favor of each individual man (Gal 2.20) and yet reprobate even Christians without considering their deserts. Rather, he has promised to offer even the critical grace of final perseverance (1 Cor 1.5–8; 1 Th 5.23–24) to all. If an answer to the riddle is implied in Scripture anywhere, it is likely to be in the basic revelation that God is our Father. On the one hand, a father can indeed cast a son out of his house permanently, but not without grave, persistent cause. On the other hand, the basic reason why a father does give his love and care to those who do not rebel is due basically to his goodness, not to any merit on the part of his children.

Early Theology of Predestination. The history of the doctrine of predestination in the Western Church begins properly with St. Augustine, who coined the word *praedestinatio* from the verb *praedestinavit* in the Latin text of Rom 8.29. For Augustine and the whole theological tradition that he inaugurated, the text of Romans dictated the formulation of a doctrine of predestination, even though modern exegesis finds scant support in Scripture for these theological elaborations. Augustine's understanding of predestination evolved from his teaching on the necessity and gratuitousness of grace against *Pelagianism. The Pelagians were intent on defending the reality of free will against the Manichaeans, and in explaining the relationship between free man and God they explained freedom as a total independence, or emancipation, from God and his causal activity. Consequently, by the use of man's free will and his naturally endowed capacities, and without the added aid of God's supernatural grace, man is self-sufficient for the beginning, the process, and the attainment of eternal salvation. The Pelagians did, however, recognize a form of predestination, i.e., God's foreknowledge wherein he knows which men will reach salvation through their own efforts.

Augustine's definition became classic in Western theology; predestination is "the foreknowledge and preparation of those gifts of God whereby they who are liberated are most certainly liberated" (*Persev.* 14.35, PL 45:1014). Both in pre-Pelagian and in anti-Pelagian works he developed this idea that predestination is infallibly effective of itself, anterior to and unconditioned by any foreknowledge of man's actions. The plan to save some men is based on an utterly benevolent or gratuitous divine choice. Concomitantly there is an anteceaent reprobation of those to whom mercy will not be shown; they will be justly left in the "mass of perdition," the condition of original sin. He does not suggest that a divine decree was the cause of the Fall; Augustine's doctrine presupposes the Fall: men are sinners, God freely chooses to save some, the rest are justly left to damnation. As to the working out of the plan of predestination, Augustine describes grace as irresistible, i.e., it necessarily and infallibly accomplishes the salvation of the elect, overcoming the obstacles in the will, bringing about conversion, growth, recovery from sin, perseverance. The irresistible quality of grace is an expression of the gratuitous benevolence of predestination. Some of Augustine's contemporaries and others of the 5th cent. thought Augustine's fundamental principle that the ultimate reason

for the salvation of the elect was God's gratuitous pre-election negated the will to save all men. Their teaching, called since the 17th cent. *Semi-Pelagianism, affirmed the need of divine aid for fallen man to be justified, for with his natural capacities alone he is unable to achieve justification, act meritoriously, and so attain eternal glory. Nevertheless, in many cases at least, it does lie in man's power to make the initial step in seeking God and believing in him. Moreover, since God desires the salvation of all, he does not antecedently to his foreknowledge of men's sins determine their reprobation.

Church teaching gave a measured approval to Augustine's doctrines on the need for grace and on the gratuitousness of grace, but not on irresistible grace. There was, as well, a continued affirmation of human freedom and rejection of predestination to evil. The Council of *Carthage (418) condemned the Pelagian teaching that man could keep the commandments without grace (D 227). Council of *Orange II (529) maintained, against the Semi-Pelagians, the need for grace for the beginning of faith and for final perseverance (D 374–395). With regard to predestination, the conclusion of the council document, by Caesarius of Arles, states that all the baptized having the will to strive faithfully with Christ's help can and must fulfill what pertains to their salvation. The conclusion anathematizes the teaching proposed by Lucidus, a priest of Gaul, that some are predestined to evil (D 397). During the 9th cent. a short-lived predestinarian movement arose under the leadership of the Saxon monk *Gottschalk of Orbais. Claiming a basis in Augustine, he proposed a double predestination, whereby God chooses some for eternal bliss and reprobates others to eternal misery. At the urging of Hincmar of Reims (d. 882), Gottschalk's teaching was condemned at the Councils of Quiercy-sur-Oise (853) and of Valence (855). Both clearly asserted God's will to save all without exception, affirmed predestination to life, and denied predestination to evil (D 621–623; 626–629). Valence declared that God has eternally decreed to punish those whose sins and final impenitence he foresees; their sins are permitted but in no way caused by him (D 626–627).

Medieval Teaching. Thomas Aquinas formulated a definition of predestination as "the plan existing in the divine mind whereby some persons would be directed to eternal salvation" (ThAq ST 1a, 23.2). Predestination is thus distinguished from God's general providence both for all creation and for mankind. In the same context, St. Thomas indicated the elements that became fundamental in later RC theology. Predestination may be considered in its total scope as including the whole series of graces, from conversion through final perseverance, by which men are saved; or in its partial aspect as the plan to confer one or another of these graces. Predestination is affirmed simultaneously with the truth of God's eternal will to save all men. There is no reprobation of some to sin and punishment anterior to the foreknowledge of actual culpability. Predestination in its total scope, however, is antecedent to the prevision of human merit or worthiness; it is not conditioned by man's good actions. Man cannot in any way merit predestination; nor can he positively prepare himself for salvation. The only positive causality is absolutely and entirely rooted in God's benevolence. In the working out of the divine plan, grace so touches the will that man freely responds to the divine initiative.

In the 14th cent. the English theologian Thomas Bradwardine (d. 1349) sought to defend the sovereignty of the divine will against the part in the salvation process attributed to the human will by theologians he called "modern Pelagians." Bradwardine has been classified, perhaps unjustly, by some historians as a determinist, proposing the irresistibility of grace and implying a double predestination. He did have an influence on John *Wycliffe, the Oxford scholar who adopted his theological determinism and espoused Augustinian predestinarianism, developing it in his *Trialogus.* This work not only influenced Jan *Hus, whose predestination teaching was similar to that of Wycliffe, but perhaps Martin Luther as well. The writings of Hus certainly contributed directly to Luther's thought.

The Reformation Era. Luther's position on predestination was explained in his *De servo arbitrio* (1525), a reply to the *De libero arbitrio* of Erasmus, who accepted man's dependence upon God but defended some participation of man's will in the process of salvation. Luther responded with a rigid predestinarianism. From eternity, God chose (prior to any foreknowledge) those whom he would lead to eternal beatitude, and he carries out his will by working everything in them, including their decision to believe and their faith. This is a double predestination, but Luther did not claim that God himself willed and caused the Fall of man and sin itself. Though his teaching is not strictly a form of *supralapsarianism, Luther does use deterministic lines of thought that could easily be construed as supralapsarian if carried to their logical conclusions. His prime concern was to safeguard salvation as due exclusively to the election and grace of God. Later Lutheranism mitigated Luther's teaching with significant limitations. The *Augsburg Confession (1530) does not mention predestination, and Article II of the *Formula of Concord (1577) states that predestination is concerned "only with the pious children of God." It rejects any and all cooperation of the human will in the salvation process and rejects a predestination to damnation. God wills to save all men, so that if anyone is saved, it is exclusively through God's grace; if anyone is lost, he is lost through his own fault.

*Zwingli taught a double predestination in his *Sermo de providentia Dei* (1530). Although predestination holds an eminent place in John Calvin's theology, it is not to be regarded as the cornerstone of his thought. It was his successor in Geneva, Theodore *Beza, who made predestination the basic principle of Calvinist dogmatics. In Calvin's * *Institutes of the Christian Religion* (1536) predestination is defined as "God's eternal decree, by which he compacted with himself what he wills to become of each man . . . eternal life is foreordained for some, eternal damnation for others. Therefore, as any man has been created to one or the other of these ends, we speak of him as predestined to life or to death" (3.21.5). God not only freely wills, but through his irresistible grace he effectually leads the elect to faith, perseverance, and glory. Conversely, God not only wills the damnation of the non-elect, but their very sins have been divinely ordained, just as he had ordained the Fall. While the reprobate are predestined to sin, Calvin claims they still fall by their own fault (3.23.8), and in their predestination to destruction they give glory to God (3.23.6). Predestination and reprobation are God's will, and man ought not inquire into the divine mystery. After Calvin's death, some of his followers adopted a rigid and some a somewhat more flexible understanding of predestination: (1) The supralapsarians, following Calvin, held that divine predestination to glory and reprobation to punishment were antecedent to God's prevision of the Fall; consequently, God did not efficaciously desire the salvation of all men, and Christ's sacrificial death on the cross was a limited atonement. (2) The infralapsarians maintained that the decree of predestination and reprobation came after the prevision of the Fall. In both cases, a double predestination is maintained. *Reformed confessional writings generally reproduce Calvin's predestinarianism, but in the infralapsarian style (e.g., Second *Helvetic Confession, c. 10; *Belgic Confession, Art. 16; *Scots Confession, Art. 8). The *Heidelberg Catechism (1563) makes no mention of it. Article 17 of the Anglican *Thirty-Nine Articles is usually regarded as in the Reformed tradition. The Council of Trent, in addressing itself to the doctrine of the Reformers on justification, implicitly touched on predestination in the following points: (1) According to Scripture Christ died for all men (D 1523). (2) God's grace is needed for every salutary act; grace is utterly gratuitous. (3) God offers grace even to sinners, but it can be rejected (D 1543). (4) All will not receive

the benefits of Christ's death (D 1523). (6) There is no predestination to evil (D 1567). (7) No one can have absolute assurance that he is justified (D 1534) unless he receives a special revelation that he is numbered among the predestined.

Post-Tridentine RC Developments. Not long after Trent the RC Church condemned (1567) an attempt by Michel de Bay (see BAIUS, M.; BAIANISM) to revive rigid Augustinian teaching on grace (D 1901–80). The attempt to reconcile the gratuitousness and efficacy of grace with the freedom of man's will led to the disputes that occasioned the *Congregatio de auxiliis (1598–1607). The theological positions involved, *Báñezianism, and *Molinism, included distinctive explanations of predestination. Bañezians taught a predestination antecedent to any foreknowledge of man's use of grace and based on God's election, and a negative reprobation of the non-elect. Molinists taught a predestination consequent on God's "middle knowledge" (*scientia media*) of how man could cooperate with graces offered. Reprobation is also consequent to the prevision of sin. Other RC explanations were related to one or another of these explanations (see AUGUSTINIANISM). The last important RC decision on predestination was connected with the Jansenist controversies. Cornelius *Jansen, in his *Augustinus*, revived Augustine's doctrine on the irresistibility of grace and taught that Christ died only for the predestined. Both points were contained in the Jansenist propositions condemned in Innocent X's *Cum occasione* (1653; D 2001–07).

Post-Reformation Protestant Developments. Among the Calvinists of Holland, Jacobus *Arminius inaugurated a movement against Calvin's predestinarianism. Arminius and his followers, called Remonstrants, set forth their views in five articles, termed Remonstrances; they championed God's universal salvific will; rejected a limited atonement; admitted that the good deeds of the regenerate are to be ascribed to God but declared that God's grace is not irresistible; and allowed a predestination conditioned by man's free will. At the Synod of *Dort (1618–19) the Reformed Church rejected these articles and excluded the Remonstrants from the Reformed parishes. The Canons of Dort are reflected in Ch. 3 and Ch. 11 of the *Westminster Confession (1648). Arminianism spread with astonishing rapidity. It gave background to the teaching of the *Cambridge Platonists, who sought a proper and truer understanding of human freedom; it found expression in Methodism's emphasis on the moral responsibility of man, and in the whole course of *revivalism; it is discernible in the *New England theology of the late 18th century. In the 19th cent. C. *Hodge and the *Princeton theology sought to reassert the Calvinist orthodoxy of Dort. Revivalism and *liberal theology, however, pushed predestinarian doctrine into practical oblivion. In the 20th cent., the theology of Karl *Barth (d. 1968) has had its admirers and critics. Basically a Calvinist, and responsible for the modern renewal of interest in Calvin, Barth opposed the Reformer's doctrine of double predestination. Man's election to grace can be ascertained only in Christ, in and through whom the Father has elected and predestined man to eternal glory. Christ alone had been chosen for rejection, i.e., through the cross. Barth does not abolish the contingency that some men may be eschatologically rejected by their own doing. His critics, however, seem to find in him a tendency toward universalism, the restoration of all men in Christ. See J. Farrelly, *Predestination, Grace and Free Will* (1964); H. Buis, *Historic Protestantism and Predestination* (1958).

PREGIZERIANS, Lutheran communities in Württemberg, Germany, named after Christian Gottlieb Pregizer (1751–1824), from 1795 pastor of Haiterbach. He tried to influence local pietistic-enthusiastic groups of separatist tendency to remain within the Lutheran Church. Since they did not become a separate religious body, it is hard to define their teaching or to determine their number. They did place extreme emphasis on the effects of justification by faith without works; baptism and the Eucharist put man in a state of bliss and happiness in which he is impervious to sin and sorrow. Because of their joyfulness and the singing of lively songs at their meetings, they sometimes were called Hurrah Christians, or the Merry Ones; because they shook their heads in dissent during sermons in the established Church they were also called Shakers. *Antinomianism apparently was accepted by some extremists. See G. Müller, RGG 5:539–540; C. Kolb, EncRelKnow 9:198–199.

PRELATE, an ecclesiastical official of superior rank. In the RC Church the term is applied to a cleric, whether secular or regular, who has authority over others as determined by law (CIC c. 110). Those having episcopal authority are called major prelates; those who have a quasi-episcopal authority (e.g., abbots, vicars general, vicars and prefects apostolic, and major superiors of exempt religious orders) are called minor prelates. Honorary prelates have no authority; they are either members of the Roman Curia, or clerics receiving the honorary title from the pope. In the Church of England bishops alone are designated as prelates. The term prelacy was used disparagingly from Puritan times of an episcopal polity in the Church, e.g., in the rejection of episcopacy by the *Solemn League and Covenant (1643).

PREMILLENARIANISM (Premillennialism), the belief in a period—a millennium, though not understood by all as a period of 1,000 years—when righteousness will generally prevail throughout the world. This period will be introduced by the visible return of Jesus Christ, who will reign with his saints. Premillenarianism differs from postmillenarianism in its insistence that the millennium is to be ushered in, not terminated, by the visible coming of Christ. *MILLENARIANISM; *ADVENTISM.

PRESBYTER (Elder), a word whose root-meaning in Greek is "elder," but which was also used simply to refer to an old man. In the NT the word is also used collectively and as a plural to indicate leadership. Collectively, the NT usage flows from descriptions of the Sanhedrin, a member of which was designated as belonging to the *presbyteron* (Lk 22.66; Acts 22.5). The plural derives from both Jewish and Gentile designation for leaders and is used of the leaders of the Christian community (e.g., Acts 11.30; 14.23; 15.2; 20.17; 1 Tim 5.17.19). The distinction between *presbyteroi* and *episkopoi* (root-meaning, "overseers") seems small: the former emphasizes dignity; the latter stresses the office itself. In the earliest traditions of the NT, these terms referred to a group who were to "watch over" the flock of Christians in a local community (Acts 20.17, 28). The later tradition of the NT, in the Pastoral Letters, uses the term *episkopos* as a model or type for the *episkopoi*, although there seems to be some indication that an individual was becoming the overseer of a local congregation (1 Tim 3.15; 5.22; Tit 1.5; Rev 1–3). Assuredly by the time of the early Fathers of the Church the leadership involved in the terms *presbyteros* and *episkopos* was resident in a single person in local communities.

The leadership, which the presbyter was to undertake, was found in conserving the apostolic teachings and ruling with apostolic authority in faith and under charity (see esp. Acts 20.17–35). The personal apostolic privileges were, of course, not passed on with the office; it was the office itself and its responsibilities that were transmitted. See H. W. Beyer, Kittel TD 2:608–622, s.v. *episkopos*; J. McKenzie, *Authority in the Church* (1966); J. H. Newman, *Essay on the Development of Christian Doctrine* (1845). *ELDER; *BISHOP; *MINISTRY.

PRESBYTERIAL CHURCH GOVERNMENT, FORM OF, see FORM OF PRESBYTERIAL CHURCH GOVERNMENT.

PRESBYTERIAN, related to the form of church polity in which authority is exercised by the church courts. *Presbyterianism is named from its adherence to this polity, but other Christian bodies also have adopted it. A presbyterian polity is distinguished from both episcopal and congregational forms of church government.

PRESBYTERIAN CHURCH IN CANADA, a religious body which includes those Presbyterian churches that did not merge with the *United Church of Canada when that body was formed in 1925.

PRESBYTERIAN CHURCH IN THE U.S., a Presbyterian denomination that came into separate existence in 1861. The Civil War was the original cause of disruption and separation from the Presbyterian Church in the U.S.A. (see UNITED PRESBYTERIAN CHURCH IN THE U.S.A.); the continued estrangement and an attempt to contribute a particular emphasis to American Presbyterianism has perpetuated the denomination. It accepts the *Westminster Confession and *Westminster Catechisms as doctrinal standards and organizes itself under a series of courts, a *session of the local congregation, a *presbytery, a *synod, and a *general assembly. It recognizes two sacraments —the Lord's Supper and baptism, including the baptism of infants. Since the Civil War the work of the denomination between annual meetings of assemblies and other *judicatories has been carried on by committees. These have become Boards of Education, World Mission, National Missions, and Pensions. Executives of these judicatories and boards have functional, not sacerdotal, status. The denomination has four theological seminaries, as well as other institutions of higher education. Its official periodical is the *Presbyterian Survey*, although its members support several other journals. Among its most influential leaders are James Henley Thornwell (1812–62), Robert Louis Dabney (1820–98), and Ernest Trice Thompson (1894–). Although the denomination is broadly ecumenical (a member of the National Council of Churches, the World Presbyterian Alliance, and the World Council of Churches), it refused to reunite with the parent body in 1954. The plan for a 1970 merger with the *Reformed Church in America, approved by the Presbyterian Church, was voted down in 1969 by the Reformed Church membership. Members of the Presbyterian Church in the U.S. have questioned its distinctive doctrine of the "spirituality of the Church," which was developed during the days of slavery, and the denomination has been more and more progressive in the development of its programs. In 1967 the denomination numbered about 4,000 congregations, 950,000 communing members, and approximately 4,000 clergy. See E. T. Thompson, *Presbyterians in the South* (1963), v.i; T. W. Street, *Story of Southern Presbyterians* (1960).

PRESBYTERIAN CHURCH OF WALES, alternate title for the *Calvinistic Methodist Church.

PRESBYTERIANISM (Gr. *presbuteros,* elder), a form of church government found in the Reformed Churches, i.e., those following John *Calvin in matters of doctrine, worship, polity, and discipline. The name particularly designates Reformed Churches in the British Isles and North America. Calvin's insistence on the divine authority of the Church came to produce a distinctively "presbyterian" type of ministry and congregational life in which preaching, the sacraments, Christian instruction, and pastoral care are integral parts. Though Presbyterian history has at times been darkened by controversy and dogmatism, a characteristic zeal for the glory of God has also given Presbyterianism its passionate theocentrism; its uncompromising criticism of political absolutism; its antipathy toward *popery, prelacy, and *Erastianism; and its desire to regulate the whole of life in accordance with the divine will.

History and Polity. Convinced that the RC Church of the 16th cent. had deformed what John *Knox called "the reverend face of the primitive and apostolic Kirk," the Genevan and Scottish Reformers sought to return to the faith and practice of the early Church. Calvin had returned to Geneva in 1541, and, having secured the collaboration of the city magistrates, he set himself to the task of reordering the life and worship of the Genevan church. Out of this reordering Presbyterianism arose. In the Reformed understanding the Church is *semper reformanda,* i.e., always to be renewed and reformed by the word of God and through obedience to the Holy Spirit. The Church, therefore, can have no final or perfect form. This does not mean that the true Church of God cannot be ascertained, though in the Reformed understanding it certainly cannot be identified exclusively with particular communions or denominations. The *Ecclesiastical Ordinances* (1541) of Geneva and Calvin's *Institutes of the Christian Religion* (1st ed., 1536) both speak of the Church as the community of believers, known by certain signs: the preaching of the gospel of Christ, the administration of the sacraments according to his command, and the exercise of godly discipline. They further teach that the ministry is ordained by God and consists of four offices: pastor, or bishop (who alone may preach and administer the sacraments); doctor, or teacher; *presbyter, or *elder (who is associated with the minister in the exercise of discipline); and *deacon. In Geneva the pastors and elders formed the Consistory, the principal organ of disciplinary oversight and fraternal correction, and the ministers were further required to attend a quarterly assembly called the Venerable Company for mutual admonition and correction. In these two bodies the earliest expressions of Presbyterian polity can be found. The *Scots Confession (1560) and Knox's *Book of Discipline generally follow Calvin's teaching on Church and ministry, though it is only in the second Book of Discipline, written by A. *Melville and officially adopted in 1581, that the developed form of Scottish Presbyterianism appears (see CHURCH OF SCOTLAND).

Presbyterianism has always affirmed the supremacy of the State on secular matters and the independence of the Church in its own affairs. Only in Scotland, however, is the *national Church Presbyterian; yet even there the fundamental principle of spiritual independence has been strongly asserted. Though some Presbyterians have held that Presbyterian polity is *jure divino*, most have taught simply that it is "agreeable to the Word of God," and all have found its origins in the NT itself. Several views of the presbyter or elder have been held within Presbyterianism. The general view is that the NT teaches one order of presbyters, differentiated into ministers of the word and sacraments, and (ruling) elders, assisting in the administration of sacraments, pastoral care, and church government. Occupying an intermediate position between *episcopacy and *Congregationalism, Presbyterianism, though not in the strict sense democratic, provides in its system of graded *courts broadly representative assemblies that legislate on matters of doctrine, government, discipline, and polity. The church session (in Scotland, kirk session), consisting of the minister(s) of a local congregation, together with certain ruling elders, usually elected by the congregation, is charged with maintaining the spiritual government of that church. The presbytery consists of all the ministers and normally one elder from each of the churches within a particular district. The synod consists of a number of presbyteries in a particular region. The highest court in Presbyterianism is the general assembly, which meets at least annually and consists of delegates or commissioners (usually equal numbers of ministers and elders) from every presbytery.

Doctrine. In doctrine the Presbyterian Churches have mainly followed Calvin in holding the word of God given in the OT and NT to be the supreme rule of faith and life. In addition, the creeds of the ancient Church and the confessions of faith and catechisms of the Reformed Churches, tested by the apostolic preaching and teaching, are important subordinate doctrinal standards. The First *Helvetic (1536), *Gallican (1559), Scots (1560), *Belgic (1561), and *Hungarian (1562) Confessions

and *Heidelberg Catechism (1563) have been widely honored and used in the Reformed Churches, though since 1645 almost all English-speaking Presbyterians have adhered to the *Westminster Confession as the chief subordinate standard. This Confession, however, has been substantially modified by some Churches (see DECLARATORY ACTS), and the adoption by the United Presbyterian Church in the U.S.A. of the *Confession of 1967 and of revised formulas for ordination represents a major departure from earlier *confessionalism. In the view of many the Confession of 1967, the fruit of modern biblical and theological studies, is an important restatement of the doctrines held by Presbyterians. While the Calvinism of the *Institutes* has been preserved more or less intact among Presbyterians to the present, certain teachings, notably on predestination, have since been modified, and in the modern period Karl *Barth, who did more than any in his age to illuminate and reinterpret the issues of the Reformation, stated in his preface to the *Church Dogmatics* (II/2) that, though he would have preferred to follow Calvin in his doctrine of *election, he could not do so. Others also have felt themselves driven to reconstruction of other parts of Calvinism.

Worship. In worship the Reformed Churches have never been tied to a fixed liturgy, and though service books have been used, e.g., the Book of Common Order (1940) in the Church of Scotland and the Book of Common Worship, Provisional Services (1966) in the United Presbyterian Church in the U.S.A., their use has been recommended, not mandatory. Worship in the Presbyterian tradition is characterized by an austere simplicity. The sermon occupies a central place, and wide freedom is allowed in the conduct of worship. Though Calvin permitted only metrical psalms to be sung in worship, the use of hymns is now general. Recent liturgical renewal has also encouraged Presbyterian Churches to enter more fully into the liturgical heritage of the whole Church. In the Reformed tradition baptism is the sacrament of incorporation into Christ and initiation into the Christian fellowship. Infant baptism is normal practice, though adult baptism is not uncommon. The Lord's Supper is the supreme act of worship, setting forth the sufficiency of Christ's perfect sacrifice and mediating the mercies of God. From the time of the Reformation it has normally been administered quarterly. In the past this service was preceded by a day of fast and followed by a day of thanksgiving. Today more frequent celebrations are found; Calvin himself advocated a weekly communion. The celebration of the sacrament is a ministerial act, and the bread and wine are usually distributed to the communicants, who remain seated in the pews, though the older custom of approaching the table to communicate standing or seated around it is also found. The bread and the cup are passed from one communicant to another, after being received from the hands of the elders.

Ecumenical Cooperation. In the 20th cent. Presbyterian Churches have participated actively in ecumenical discussions, and there have been several important unions. "No other family of churches has been more consistently favorable to ecumenical cooperation and unity," Dr. John T. McNeill states, and in South India, South Africa, Australia, Canada, England, and Scotland Presbyterians have taken a leading part in movements toward unity, at times across denominational boundaries. In 1958 the United Presbyterian Church of North America and the Presbyterian Church in the U.S.A. united to form the United Presbyterian Church in the U.S.A. (1968 membership, 3,298,583); since 1963 this Church has participated in the *Consultation on Church Union. The Presbyterian Church in the U.S. (the "southern" Presbyterian Church; 1968 membership, 955,402) is also a participant. The *Alliance of Reformed Churches has prepared with the *International Congregational Council proposals, principles, and a draft constitution that, if approved by the respective member Churches, will unite these two confessional bodies, probably in 1970. The existence since 1938 of the *Iona Community, an experimental group in the service of the Church of Scotland, may be regarded as a symbol of a widespread desire among Presbyterian Churches to fulfill their missionary obligations in new and at times radical ways. See J. T. McNeill, *History and Character of Calvinism* (repr., 1968, with rev. bibliog.); G. D. Henderson, *Presbyterianism* (repr., 1956); L. J. Trinterud, *Forming of an American Tradition* (1949). *CALVINISM.

PRESBYTERY, in Presbyterianism, a legislative, executive, and judicial court, presided over by a *moderator, who is elected annually. Quarterly meetings are customary, though the Presbytery may meet as specially called. The Presbytery consists of all the ministers and usually one ruling *elder from each church within a certain district, over which it corporately exercises authority (see CHURCH SESSION). The equal representation of ministers and elders exhibits the parity of presbyters, who share jointly in the government and supervision of the churches they represent. Ministers must hold membership within the Presbytery in which they work, though in some cases (e.g., chaplaincy) permission is given to work beyond the geographical boundaries of the Presbytery. This court is empowered to receive under its care candidates for the ministry, to sanction and approve the call issued by a congregation to a minister, to ordain and install him in his office, and to receive, dismiss, judge, or remove ministers. In this way it exercises a kind of corporate *episcopacy. The Presbytery alone can organize, dissolve, unite, or divide churches. Presbyteries in a particular region constitute the *synod, the next higher court in Presbyterianism.

PRESIDING BISHOP, the head of the Protestant Episcopal Church. He is elected by the *General Convention when the office becomes vacant, and remains in office until the retirement age, set at 68.

PRIEST AND PRIESTHOOD. Christian denominations generally recognize the priesthood of Christ and the common *priesthood of all believers, but not all accept the ordained or ministerial priesthood. All generally hold, in various senses, the threefold function of the priesthood—prophetic, royal, and sacrificial; but they differ greatly in their understanding of the ministerial priesthood, esp. in relation to the Eucharist, the sacrificial character of which is affirmed by Roman Catholics but generally denied by Protestants. Protestants are generally agreed about the priesthood of Christ, who once for all by the sacrifice of the cross brought about man's reconciliation and redemption. Christ is the high priest whose unique and all-sufficient sacrifice has made all other sacrifices superfluous. Protestants also stress the common priesthood of the faithful, who are a royal priesthood meant to offer spiritual sacrifices and to proclaim God's marvelous deeds (see 1 Pet 2.5–9). Luther held that all Christians are truly of the priestly order and that there is no distinction between them except regarding functions. For good order's sake the community entrusts some priestly functions to certain persons. The denial of a ministerial priesthood in Protestantism followed mainly upon the denial of the sacrificial character of the Lord's Supper, or the Eucharist. The pastor or minister has no other priestly functions than such as are common to all believers. The pastoral function of the ordained minister is reduced to preaching and administering baptism and the Lord's Supper. Luther, Calvin, and Zwingli agreed on the nonsacrificial character of the Eucharist. Consequently the clergy are, in their teaching, not priests but ministers or pastors.

In Anglicanism, despite the *Reformed or Calvinistic sense in which eucharistic doctrine is set forth in the BCP and in the Thirty-Nine Articles (a sense always insistently defended by many Anglican divines), there have always been some, and since the *Oxford movement there have been many, who have favored a stronger interpretation of the Lord's Supper that would leave some

room for the notion of sacrifice. This divergence of view has been reflected in a difference of position with regard to the priesthood. Those whose eucharistic thought is in the Reformed tradition see no doctrinal necessity for an ordained priesthood, and they even tend to deny that the common priesthood of the faithful is exercised in the Lord's Supper, which they do not conceive to be an offering in any sense. Their opponents see a place for both the common and the ordained priesthood in the celebration of the Eucharist. For the common priesthood, they see the Eucharist as an offering in which all share, an offering symbolic of the will of the participants to render to God the worship of their whole lives. For the ordained priesthood, because although Christ is the unseen celebrant of every Eucharist, the single mediator between God and man through whom the worship and prayer ascends to the heavenly altar, the observance still requires a visible minister not only to preside at the liturgy on behalf of all but also to act in the name of Christ, esp. in repeating the words and acts of the Lord's Supper. Absolving, blessing, and the eucharistic consecration are seen by these Anglicans as priestly functions, by which the Anglican ministry differs essentially from the Protestant ministry.

RC understanding of priest and priesthood, esp. as proposed by Vatican Council II in the constitutions on the Church and the liturgy and in the decree on priestly ministry and life, gives full recognition to Christ's high priesthood. Once for all he offered the one sacrifice of the new and everlasting covenant, the sacrifice of Calvary, which worked man's redemption. The council describes the Church as the new People of God, commissioned to continue Christ's saving work, not only through the ministry of the hierarchy, but also through the sharing in the Church's ministry by all the faithful. Therefore, Christ's priesthood and mediatorship are shared, and this in two ways. The common priesthood of the faithful enables them not only to offer spiritual sacrifices but also to be co-offerers of the Eucharistic Sacrifice, in which the sacrifice of Calvary is re-presented. The ministerial priesthood is exercised by the ordained priest, who acts in the person of Christ, and through whom the Church offers this re-presentation of the one sacrifice of Christ. Thus in RC teaching the ordained priesthood supposes the sacrificial character of the Eucharist, and the offering of the Eucharistic Sacrifice is the summit of the ordained minister's priestly functions. In this way in the constitutions on the Church and the liturgy Vatican Council II organically unites the priesthood of Christ, that of the faithful, and that of the ordained priest. See P. F. Palmer, NCE 11:768–772; J. Haekel et al., LTK 8:735–748, 756–758; B. Lohse, RGG 5:578–581; K. E. Kirk, *Apostolic Ministry* (1947); B. Lambert, *Ecumenism* (1967).

PRIESTHOOD OF ALL BELIEVERS, the doctrine that by virtue of their union with Jesus Christ, the High Priest, all Christians, through their baptism, participate in his priestly mediation to other believers and to the world. In the NT the word "priest" (Gr. *hiereus*) is never used to refer to the ordained ministers of the Church. It refers either to the Jewish priests, who repeatedly appear in the Gospels, or to the person of Christ himself (esp. in the Epistle to the Hebrews, which is the only NT writing to apply the word "priest" to him), or to believers in Christ. This does not imply, however, that there is any necessary contradiction between the priesthood of all believers and the ordained priesthood of those who have been specially set aside for the service of Christ and of his Church; on the contrary, the two concepts of priesthood are mutually supportive and interdependent, just as both of them are in turn dependent upon their source in the priestly ministration of Christ as "the one mediator between God and men" (1 Tim 2.5).

Nevertheless, the ordained priesthood and the priesthood of all believers were set into opposition during some of the controversies of the Reformation and Counter-Reformation. Martin *Luther, who stressed the universal priesthood of believers, also insisted upon the ministry of word and sacrament. Other Protestant theologians, however, placed the two into disjunction, ascribing to all the members of the Church all the rights and the authority of the priesthood. This position received its ultimate expression in the teaching of the Society of Friends and some other groups of the radical Reformation that have no ordained ministry at all. In opposition not only to this extreme form of the doctrine but also to its more moderate statement in Luther and Calvin, many theologians of the RC Counter-Reformation dismissed the idea of the priesthood of all believers or subordinated it so drastically to the emphasis upon the ordained priesthood as to render it meaningless. Thus the word "priest" in RC usage still tends to refer only to the clergy. The Constitution on the Church and the Constitution on the Liturgy of Vatican Council II may be interpreted as an effort to go beyond this false antithesis to a more balanced and a more scriptural view.

The key text in the NT for the doctrine of the priesthood of all believers is 1 Pet 2.9: "You are a chosen race, a royal priesthood, a holy nation, God's own people, that you may declare the wonderful deeds of him who called you out of darkness into his marvelous light." These words are addressed to all the members of the Church, who, both in their life and in their worship, mediate the wondrous deeds of God to others, an authentically priestly function. Therefore the prayers of the congregation in the liturgy and the work of believers in the world are an extension of the priesthood of Christ. Yet the believers have been constituted as priests by being "called out of darkness." This calling has taken place through baptism and through the teaching of the word of God, which have been mediated to them through the ordained priesthood.

The doctrine of the priesthood of all believers requires, for its full explication and application, a doctrine of vocation by which the life of the Christian in his community, his family, and his daily work is interpreted as a calling from God, where the priest exercises his mediating function in relation to others. It also requires a strong emphasis upon baptism, which is then to be seen as the "ordination" to the universal priesthood of believers. See T. F. Torrance, *Royal Priesthood* (1955); J. E. Rea, *Common Priesthood of the Members of the Mystical Body* (1947).

PRIESTLEY, JOSEPH (1733–1804), English Unitarian. Born at Fieldhead, Yorkshire, P. studied at an academy of *Dissenters at Daventry, where his views changed from a moderate Calvinism and belief in the freedom of the will to Arianism and determinism. After serving pastorates at Needham Market in Suffolk and at Nantwich in Cheshire, he became a tutor at Warrington Academy, where he found the congenial company of other Arians and determinists. He then became pastor of the Mill Hill congregation at Leeds. An acquaintance with Theophilus *Lindsey encouraged his adherence to Unitarianism. The Royal Society awarded Priestley its highest honor, the Copley Medal, for his scientific researches. His discovery of oxygen (1774) and of other gases made him a founder of chemistry. His many theological works include *Institutes of Natural and Revealed Religion* (1772–73), a basic statement of the liberal Dissenters' faith, *Disquisitions Relating to Matter and Spirit* (1777), *A Harmony of the Evangelists* (1777), *History of the Corruptions of Christianity* (1782), and *History of Early Opinions Concerning Jesus Christ* (1786). His ministry at the New Meeting Society in Birmingham, where he preached Unitarianism, ended when a mob burned his church and home because of his defense of the French Revolution, but he escaped to London, where he became pastor of the Gravel Pit Meeting at Hackney. In 1794, he immigrated to America, where he settled in Northumberland, Pennsylvania. Works: J. T. Rutt, ed., *Theological and Miscellaneous Works* (25v., 1817–31). See T. E. Thorpe, *J. P.* (1906); A. Holt, *Life of J. P.* (1931); E. M. Wilbur, *History of*

Unitarianism (2v., repr., 1965); J. G. Gillam, *Crucible* (1954).

PRIMACY OF THE POPE, in RC teaching, a priority among bps. accorded to the pope as bp. of Rome and successor of St. Peter. The pope's primacy is no mere priority in dignity or right to the honor of precedence before other bps. of the Church. He is not simply *primus inter pares* (the first among equals), a prerogative that some who are not Roman Catholics would allow. His primacy means more than a right to impede, as by some sort of veto, the actions or decisions of the episcopal college. Though Vatican Council II emphasized the collegial character of authority in the Church and that the episcopate, which "succeeds the college of the Apostles in the office of teaching and in pastoral direction," is also a "subject of supreme and full power over the universal Church," it also teaches that the college is vested with such power "together with its head, the Roman pontiff, and never without the head"; that this power "cannot be exercised except with the consent of the Roman pontiff," for this college "does not have authority unless it is thought of in union with the Roman pontiff as its head" (Vat II ConstCh 22). In the same section the Council declares that the pope has in the Church "by reason of his office, namely, that of vicar of Christ and pastor of the whole Church, full, supreme, and universal power over the Church, which he can always freely exercise."

The council had already made clear (*ibid.*, 18) that in keeping with the teaching of Vatican I it too held that to secure the unity of the episcopate, Christ "set Peter over the other Apostles and in him instituted a perpetual visible principle and basis for unity of faith and communion," and that it again proposed to the faithful as matter of belief the doctrine enunciated by Vatican I concerning the establishment, perpetuity, nature, and meaning of the primacy and the infallible teaching authority of the Roman pontiff" (see D 3050–75 for the teaching of Vatican I).

If then the authority of the pope is an authority that he shares with the rest of the college of bishops and one that he can exercise in full collegial collaboration with his fellow bps., as occurs most clearly in ecumenical councils, still the pope can so concentrate that authority in himself as head of the college that he can exercise it fully without invoking their actual positive collaboration or consent. As the explanatory note 3-4 (from the acts of the Council, AAS 57 [1965], 74–75) indicates: "It is within the competence of the Pope, to whom the care of the whole flock of Christ has been committed, to decide according to the needs of the Church in what manner this care is to be exercised: by personal action or by collegial action. The Roman pontiff proceeds according to his own discretion and in view of the welfare of the Church in arranging, promoting and approving any exercise of collegiality." Hence "as supreme pastor the Pope can always exercise his authority as he chooses. While the College always exists, it does not for that reason permanently operate through strictly collegial action, as the tradition of the Church shows. In other words it is not always 'in full act'; indeed it operates through collegial action only at intervals, and only with the consent of its head."

In the Catholic mind the difficulties that may be found in the existence of a college and a collegial power that are in some ways unique will be resolved in large measure in the practical order by the unifying Spirit within the whole Church and by living contact and communion among all pastors in the Church. The pope, recognizing that by Christ's will he is the head of a college that shares in his pastorate, will be sensitive and alert to the views, attitudes, and feelings of those who share with him the daily concern for the whole People of God. It was to ensure such constant reciprocal action between the head and the members of the college that the council, in Vat II BpPastOff 5, stated that "bishops from various parts of the world, chosen through procedures established or to be established by the Roman pontiff, will render especially helpful assistance to the supreme pastor of the Church in a council to be known by the name of Synod of Bishops. Since it will be acting in the name of the entire Catholic episcopate, it will at the same time demonstrate that all the bishops in hierarchical communion share in the responsibility for the universal Church." See F. A. Sullivan, NCE 11:779–780; G. Glez, DTC 13.1:247–344; K. Rahner, LTK 8:44–48; K. Rahner and J. Ratzinger, *Episcopate and the Primacy* (tr. K. Barker et al., 1962).

PRIMATE, a title given to certain bps. and abps. in the West. In early usage it was accorded to bps. and abps. with whose sees the office of vicar of the Holy See was annexed; in those times the dignity carried with it certain jurisdictional rights and privileges. The title is retained in modern times, but it is properly accorded only to bps. and abps. of those sees whose occupants were formerly ex officio papal vicars, e.g., Armagh in Ireland and Arles in France. Primates in this modern sense enjoy a precedence of honor but ordinarily no special jurisdiction by reason of their primacy (see CIC c. 271). Sometimes the title is applied in a looser sense to bps. or abps. whose sees are the oldest or most prominent in a particular territory or country. Thus the abp. of Baltimore in the U.S. and the abp. of Westminster in England are sometimes referred to as primates. The *Anglican Communion defines the primate as the first among equals. The abp. of Canterbury is the primate of the entire Anglican Communion. The head of each of the autonomous Churches in the Anglican Communion bears the same title of honor. The Protestant Episcopal Church does not use the title; it elects a *presiding bishop to head the House of Bishops. The title primate is also used in some Old Catholic and other hierarchical Churches.

PRIMIANISTS, followers of Primian, who succeeded Parmenian as Donatist bp. of Carthage in 391 or 392. He antagonized the more solid members of the community by excommunicating the deacon Maximian, readmitting the Claudianists to communion, and indulging in acts of capricious violence. He was deposed by a council of some 50 bps. held at Cebarsussa in June 393 but was vindicated at a more general council held at Bagai in April 394. He took part in the great conference of Carthage held under the presidency of the imperial commissioner Marcellinus in June 411, which brought about the ultimate condemnation of the Donatist schism. See W. H. C. Frend, *Donatist Church* (1952), 213–226. *DONATISTS.

PRIMITIVE ADVENT CHRISTIAN CHURCH, a separation from the *Advent Christian Church. The Primitive Advent Christian Church includes about 600 members, in 12 local churches, all in West Virginia. It seeks to recapture the spirit and doctrine of the early Adventist movement. *ADVENTISM.

PRIMITIVE BAPTISTS, a Baptist denomination that originated in 1835, when the Chemung Association, straddling the border of N.Y. and Pa., demanded a separation from all *associations that participated in missionary activity. The concept of mission appeared to be contrary to a tenet of rigid Calvinism, namely that God elected his own people in Christ before the world was formed. Mission activity, then, is useless at best and could be viewed as contrary to the will of God. Evangelistic preaching is supported as a means of edifying the elect. Support for *Bible societies, church schools, state conventions, colleges, and theological seminaries is totally withheld. Most of the clergy have little or no formal training, the *call being all-important. In the South large numbers of Scotch-Irish immigrants who brought a Calvinistic theological inheritance with them became Primitive Baptists. The 1844 membership of 121,000 in 3,000 churches has decreased to

about 69,000 (1968). *ANTIMISSION BAPTISTS; *ANTIMISSIONARY MOVEMENT.

PRIMITIVE METHODIST CHURCH, U.S.A., a denomination begun in England through a merger of the Camp Meeting Methodists and the *Clowesites, and brought to the U.S. by missionaries in 1829. The first conference was held in 1832, and the first pastors were appointed by the Primitive Methodist Church in England. This Church is now independent of the parent body. In teaching it follows the *Twenty-Five Articles of Religion. In 1968 the denomination had a mission in Guatemala, 86 churches, about 12,000 members, and 60 ordained clergymen. See HistAmMeth 3:586–587.

PRIMUS, in the *Episcopal Church in Scotland, the presiding bishop. The office and its designation date from 1731. The primus does not have the rank of metropolitan; he is elected by his fellow bps. and may be from any of the seven dioceses of the Church.

PRINCETON THEOLOGY, a conservative theological system in the Calvinist tradition, which developed in the 19th cent. at Princeton Theological Seminary. When A. *Alexander became Princeton's first professor of didactic and polemic theology in 1812, he built up a system based solidly on the *Westminster Standards and other *Reformed confessions and the writings of the 17th-cent. Calvinist scholastics, esp. F. *Turretini, who interpreted them. Intelligible explanation, rather than innovation, became the hallmark of Princeton. Alexander's pupil, C. *Hodge, succeeded him in 1840 and further developed a theological tradition characterized by dogmatic rigor and confessional loyalty, fairly meeting the challenges posed by the innovations of N. *Taylor, H. *Bushnell, and the New England liberals. Hodge's *Systematic Theology* (1871–72) was a reasoned, logical approach to traditional Christian doctrine. B. B. *Warfield, who had studied under Hodge, followed him as professor of systematic theology in 1879 and continued until 1921, in the same tradition of loyalty to the historic confessions of the Reformed faith. Hodge, along with Alexander, also developed a clearer understanding of scriptural inerrancy and inspiration to meet the new challenges of modern biblical criticism. Warfield's tradition was broken with the reorganization of Princeton Seminary (1927) and the founding by J. G. *Machen of Westminster Theological Seminary (1929). It has more recently inspired a new generation of *evangelicals at Princeton and elsewhere. See H. T. Kerr, *Sons of the Prophets* (1963); L. Loetscher, *Broadening Church* (1957); Smith-Jamison 1:260–266.

PRISCILLIANISTS, a Christian reform group of the 4th and 5th cents. given to asceticism and called Gnostics and Manichaeans by fellow Christians. They flourished on the Atlantic littoral from Portugal to Aquitaine. Priscillian, a rich and eloquent lay noble, c.375 attracted well-educated people, including women and two bps. to the esoteric movement in Betica, Lusitania, and Galicia. Secret assemblies in out-of-the-way spots; preaching by laymen and women; fasts, abstentions, and contempt of the world beyond Christian custom; unauthorized monastic practices by secular clergy; veiling of virgins before 40 years of age; private handling of the Eucharist; recourse to apocrypha; abuse of the title doctor; communion with excommunicates; and claims to special illumination and prophecy aroused opposition among the bishops. The Council of Saragossa I (380) condemned some Priscillianist practices, if not Priscillian himself; in 382 Emperor Gratian decreed exile for "Manichaeans," as Priscillianists were called, and seized their churches. Priscillian, then bp. of Ávila, moved to Aquitaine and proselytized with success, only to be expelled by Bp. Delphinius of Bordeaux. Failing to get a hearing from either Pope Damasus (a Spaniard) or Ambrose, Priscillian turned to imperial officials, who had the decree annulled. He returned to Spain in triumph. When Emperor Maximus (a Spaniard) replaced Gratian, he recalled the case to Bordeaux (384–385). Priscillian, however, appealed to Maximus, who beheaded him and six followers in Trier for immorality and magic (385).

Priscillian was probably the first Christian to die by the secular arm as a heretic; the decision of the Council of Bordeaux and his own testimony in Trier provided the evidence for his conviction. Martin of Tours, Ambrose, and Pope Siricius were scandalized at the execution, as were some pagans; the reaction in Spain cost Priscillian's enemies their sees as the Priscillianists formed a schismatic Church. Priscillian's relics were returned to Galicia c.396, and he was venerated as a martyr. There is no sure extant textual basis on which to convict Priscillian of heresy. But the general Christian attitude toward him, the refusal of Damasus and Ambrose to receive him, definitely Manichaean developments in Spain a few years later with the barbarian invasions, and the testimony of Sulpicius Severus, Orosius, Augustine, Jerome, and Pope Leo I indicate that Priscillian was hardly a mirror of orthodox asceticism or the victim of an episcopacy that evidently did need reform. Priscillianism, which was contemporary with the rigorist Gregory of Elvira, was put down at the Council of Toledo I in 400; Emperor Honorius condemned Priscillianists by rescript (408–409); the Council of Braga I (561 or 563) condemned 17 errors attributed to Priscillianism, forbidding the use of any hymns but those of the NT. Priscillianist works also contained Trinitarian doctrines that denied the distinctness of the three divine Persons. See J. N. Hillgarth, NCE II:790–791, with bibliog.

PRIVATE JUDGMENT, a phrase suggesting that the believer's understanding of God's word is the rule of faith. The phrase has been used by both historians and polemicists to contrast the Protestant and RC positions on the rule of faith: that through the Reformation principle *sola scriptura* the Protestant believes what his own conscience declares the Bible to mean, not, as in the case of the Catholic, what the Church declares the Bible to mean. Thus Protestantism extols private judgment; Catholicism decries it. The contrast is an over-simplification.

For all Christians the Bible expresses God's word, the content of faith. For Christian theology generally faith is personal, the acceptance and trust in God's word. Faith is first a trusting assent to God himself, and therefore to what his word contains. The essential assent of faith is grace inspired; the Christian believes only because the Holy Spirit prompts and aids him. And because the assent of faith is Spirit-guided it is to the right things, to the true meaning of God's word (see ThAq ST 2a2ae, 1.3). The true RC understanding of the teaching authority of the Church does not and cannot view the Church as supplanting the personal, Spirit-guided assent of faith. Rather it presupposes that the same Spirit which guarantees the assent of the believer also guides the community of believers as a whole and gives special assistance to the church *magisterium, or teaching office. The Reformation was a protest against the teaching Church, authoritatively declaring and proposing the meaning of God's word. The accepted Protestant understanding of the Reformation protest did not mean an arbitrary, purely human interpretation of the Bible. The presupposition is that the one Spirit inspires all believers together to a common understanding of the word of God, to which each believer responds in a personal decision. The principal Protestant traditions, Lutheran and *Reformed, regarded that understanding to be the understanding of the biblical word; the confessions of faith were subordinate rules of faith, as expressions of the true, community understanding of the biblical word. The Anabaptist, Mennonite, and Quaker tradition regarded private judgment to mean the acceptance and understanding of God's

word directly experienced; the experience, though consonant with the Bible, was not mediated through the Bible. There have been, throughout Christian history, manifestations of *enthusiasm and *subjectivism, but these are phenomena apart from the main RC and Protestant traditions and from the overdrawn distinction connoted by the phrase private judgment. See R. McAfee Brown, *Spirit of Protestantism* (pa., 1965), 8–11.

PROBATIONER, a person awaiting ecclesiastical acceptance. For a long time Methodists, following John *Wesley, required a period of probation for a person to prove himself worthy of membership in a *society. Many Methodist bodies refer commonly to one who has been ordained a deacon and plans to become a fully ordained minister as a probationer. In the Church of Scotland, and until modern times among Presbyterians in the U.S., the term was used as a synonym for a candidate for the ministry. Some RC religious communities apply the term to postulants or novices.

PROGRESSIVE DUNKERS, a secondary name for the *Brethren Church. This body split from the *Church of the Brethren in 1882 because of disagreement with the conservatism of the parent body as to methods of witness, polity, and education.

PROGRESSIVE NATIONAL BAPTIST CONVENTION, INC., a group formed by Baptist delegates from 14 states at Cincinnati in November 1961. The preceding September at Kansas City, Mo., the *National Baptist Convention U.S.A., Inc., had refused to adopt a resolution that would have limited the tenure of its officers. The new convention, composed of 521,581 members in 650 churches, was a response to this action and reflected a desire for higher standards of ministerial leadership, more orderly church life, and more effective inter-Baptist and interdenominational cooperation.

PROSELYTIZING (Gr. *proselutos,* one who has come to a place), in a religious reference, the making of converts to a religious belief or ecclesiastical adherence. In the NT "proselyte" is used in the sense of a full-fledged (Acts 2.11) or partial (Acts 10.2) convert to Judaism. Historically in Buddhism, Judaism, Christianity, and Islam proselytizing has been practiced, although to an extent and by methods that have varied considerably by reason of cultural and political influences as well as theological interpretations. Proselytizing is intense where, from a well-defined body of revelation and a strongly developed systematic theology, the conviction arises that the believer has a personal mission to bring to the unbeliever the special redemption, grace, or benefits of the religious message. For Christians the term in itself may simply connote fulfillment of the sense of mission that seems inherent in acceptance of the gospel and is acknowledged by most of the Churches. Proselytizing, however, has often evoked disfavor (Mt 23.15) and is currently used mostly in a pejorative sense to imply unscrupulous methods of persuasion or a divisive competition among the Churches. See *Church for Others* (World Council of Churches Publications; 1967).

PROTESTANT CHRISTIAN ETHICS, as a field of study, in a Protestant context is separate from but not independent of other theological disciplines and is a relatively recent development. As such it does not present a monolithic structure composed of principles or values; rather it must be regarded as a movement still taking shape on the borderline between theology and the social sciences. The diversity of methods, principles, norms, and conceptions of moral authority, as well as the variety of techniques for their practical implementation, are part of the price paid for a freedom of speculation and action that Protestantism has traditionally prized. In the broadest sense the term Protestant Christian ethics may be interpreted as the moment of reflection in the ongoing moral life of the Christian community. It represents an attempt to discover, then systematically and coherently think through, the fundamental norms and principles of action appropriate to human conduct when that conduct is viewed as a response to the divine action and governance known in Scripture, tradition, experience, and preeminently in Jesus Christ.

Areas of Concern. When considered as a discipline in process of formation, Protestant Christian ethics is composed of four areas of study, often merging in the thought of a particular moralist. (1) Historical ethics, including biblical ethics, seeks a descriptive analysis of the ethical positions developed in the traditions of the Christian community as it has faced social and theological problems. Biblical ethics has had especial significance for Protestant moralists, for whom the Bible is the central repository of revelation and the primary source for the development of norms. Traditionally, most attention has been given to the ethical teachings of Jesus and Paul. (2) Theological ethics proper deals with the exposition and defense of norms and values that within a contemporary period most satisfactorily exhibit the claims of Christian faith upon man's moral behavior. In this phase Christian ethics is usually regarded as directly dependent upon the theological position from which it draws its primary insights. Questions as to the relation of justice and love, the role of the Church and biblical revelation, and the connection between duty and love are explored. In some cases, however, Christian ethics is conceived as closely connected with philosophical rather than theological insights, which are taken to be more general in scope than those derivative from theology. (3) Christian metaethics has developed most recently, partially under the impact of analytical philosophy. The concern here is the foundations of the entire Christian ethical enterprise. The nature and meaning of Christian moral discourse, the relations between general ethical and Christian moral discourse, the nature and role of authority in ethics, the question of whether God's will stands superior to or subservient to moral values known independently of revelation, and the manner in which ethical norms are derivative from the divine will are typical issues. (4) Christian social ethics, the fourth area, considers the problem of implementation of ethical norms since ethics is widely understood as leading to, as well as from, action. Here the emphasis is on a critical understanding of methods and tactics by which moral insights may make their weight felt in society. Christian social ethics attempts to bridge political, social, economic, and racial realities and the moral commitments accepted as essential by the Christian community. For this, theological and ethical knowledge is needed, and so are insights from the social sciences. American Protestant ethics has been especially active in this area in recent years.

The Various Styles. No one style of Protestant ethics within the fourfold structure of the field commands exclusive allegiance. Broadly speaking, however, several types may be distinguished by reference to their underlying theological orientations. Conservative Protestant ethics regards obedience to specific commands and duties selectively drawn from Scripture as the sum of religious and moral responsibility. The strong Protestant emphasis on Scripture conceived as embodying the dictates of God is assumed. The form of response is interpreted as the keeping of divinely given rules or laws organized in various hierarchical orders for the sake of salvation and the satisfaction of the Lawgiver. The legalistic motif is characteristic of this type of Christian ethic. Evangelical ethics also clings closely to biblical authority but reduces the legalistic emphasis. Christian ethics here finds its model in Paul's teaching of justification by faith, and the Lutheran development of that doctrine. As with the conservative type, evangelical ethics takes seriously the doctrine of the natural bondage of the human will by sin conceived as pride and self-interest. The beginning of the Christian moral life lies in a total act of faith in the gracious God revealed in Jesus Christ. Ideally, the motivating power of

moral conduct lies less in obedience to law than in an attitude of gratitude, responding to divine command. Morality derives from Christian freedom provided by divine forgiveness and acceptance.

A less traditional form of Protestant ethics may be designated as liberal in character; here Protestant ethical thought shifts from an explicit theological and biblical to a philosophical orientation. The doctrine of sin is either discounted or reinterpreted as an error in moral judgment, and man is regarded as a free moral agent, capable within limits of following the moral example of Jesus, who is regarded less as a divine savior than as a religious and ethical teacher. It is characteristic of liberal Christian ethics to stress the role of moral values recognized either instinctively, rationally, or pragmatically apart from revelation. These values of right or good serve as the criteria of the ethical demands of Scripture or revelation. Usually some form of philosophical idealism or personalistic metaphysic is associated with ethics in this style. Values thereby derived are taken as guides to the fulfillment of human personality, which is often taken to be the goal of the Christian life, with love as the motivating power. In the late 19th and early 20th cents. this movement developed what came to be known as the *Social Gospel. This phase of liberalism arose from a keen awareness of the inadequacy of the characteristic individualistic emphasis in Protestant morality (largely sponsored by revivalism) to deal with the injustices imposed on many by the American economic system.

The Social Gospel attempted to make the Protestant Churches respond effectively to the challenge of a social order in which material benefits were unjustly denied to laboring and poorer classes. It became associated with various forms of socialism and helped to sponsor interest in sociology. As it developed, its concerns included those of man and race, stimulating in some quarters a strong effort to solve racial conflicts in a peaceful and equitable way.

In opposition to Protestant moralists of

a liberal type, theologians like Karl *Barth and Emil *Brunner sought to divorce theology from philosophical speculation and to return to a revelational theology based upon Scripture and the thought of the Reformers. Although they did not return to a doctrine of scriptural inerrancy, these Europeans did find in the Bible the word of God that comes to a man as a crisis of judgment and a hope. In spite of differences among thinkers of this type, the deposit of ethical content offered was one of obedience to God's command, not law, in concrete situations of human life motivated by faith in Christ. Brunner found certain God-given social structures, such as the State and the family, within which moral responsibility was to be enacted. Barth, in a less structured view of man's covenant relation to God, conceived man's moral responsibility as expressed in a faithful witness to Christ enacted in a free and loving concern for others and derived from God's free election of the Christian believer. In both men there was a strong criticism of man's sinful propensity to justify himself by absolutizing himself and his institutions, whereas only God as gracious determiner of destiny is sovereign.

Continental theology and ethics had widespread effects on American Protestant moralists, especially H. Richard *Niebuhr and Reinhold *Niebuhr. Emphasis on divine sovereignty, the prideful pretensions of man, and the need for a faithful integrity of the self in response to God marked their thought, but neither relinquished the Social Gospel concern for social and political awareness. Both Niebuhrs sought to make clear the relation of Christian faith to the relativities of historical existence and brought to the foreground, as liberalism had not, the issue of power in social relations. One of the most recent forms that Protestant ethics has taken is due to the influence of Dietrich *Bonhoeffer. He claimed that Christian morality is not consituted by principles or values, but is based on the form of Christ embodied in the individual self, living and suffering in a secular world as did Christ "the man for others." Ethical response, he argued, comes in the form of faithful obedience to God's commandment, which if it is not "clear, definite to the last detail . . . is not God's commandment." Bonhoeffer's accent on a "world come of age" and "religionless Christianity" and his dismissal of philosophical speculation as determinative of Christian morality have been widely influential in establishing a Christocentric ethic.

The American scene in Protestant ethics finds itself divided between those who take selfless, outgoing love (agape) as the sole motivation and those who find the need as well as the evidence for some directives or principles for moral action, in either tentatively held middle axioms or some form of natural law by which love is guided and implemented in social policy.

Norms Proposed. Some Protestant ethics may be understood as teleological in conception. These have ranged from crudely utilitarian views, in which human happiness is sought in this world and the next by obedience to biblical injunctions and doing good to others for the sake of celestial reward, to self-realization ethics, in which righteousness is conceived as the fulfillment of the human potential. At the other end of the spectrum of goals sought is the glorification of God, best represented in positions associated with Calvinistic or neoplatonic outlooks. Other forms of ethics, influenced by Kant, take duty as basic. Love of God and neighbor is not simply an expression of a changed life but an obligation to be undertaken. Even teleological forms include the factor of duty, since to reach one's happiness or self-fulfillment one ought to love God and one's neighbor. In evangelical and certain other forms of Protestant morality the principle of gratitude and spontaneous loving obedience are offered as motives. However, these positions find it difficult to escape the need for values or principles. The question of the knowledge of the divine will likewise receives a mixed answer. Those who associate Protestant ethics with metaphysics tend to rely on irreducible values immediately interpreted as divine directives or as sanctioned by God. In another form the notion of a natural law imbedded in the self as the image of deity is the source of knowledge. Revelational moralists claim that there is opened to man in Christ both the claim of God and the essential meaning of love of neighbor. However, there is substantial agreement that the need of the neighbor, recognized under the perspective of God's love, is a clear indication of the will of God. This need is not generally conceived in purely individualistic terms. Although division exists as to the degree of involvement with social problems that the Churches should undertake, there is a major constituency that favors concrete expression of Christian concern for social morality. See P. Ramsey, *Christian Ethics* (1950); G. F. Thomas, *Christian Ethics and Moral Philosophy* (1955); F. L. Long, Jr., *Survey of Christian Ethics* (1967).

PROTESTANT CONFERENCE (Lutheran), a group organized in 1927 by ministers suspended from what is now the *Wisconsin Evangelical Lutheran Synod. The title (pronounced Pro-*test*-ant by its members) stems from their protest against the "mistaken dogmas current in the Church . . . and its spirit of self-righteousness and self-sufficiency." The view of the protesters was that Lutheran orthodoxy and dogmatics had been too long dominant and needed to be supplemented by historical and exegetical approach and a continuing self-criticism in the Church. The position is traced to J. P. Koehler (1859–1951), professor at Wauwatosa Seminary in Wisconsin. The denomination in 1968 numbered 1,500 members, served by 14 ministers. See L. Jordahl, EncLuthCh 3:1978–79.

PROTESTANT EPISCOPAL CHURCH (Episcopal Church), that American denomination whose heritage derives from the reformed Church of England established by law in 1559 during the reign of Elizabeth I. The C of E contributed significantly to the political, religious, and economic plans of the Virginia Company in the founding of

Jamestown in 1607. The Church, transplanted with the colonists, reflected the fluid religious situation in the mother country at the time. Largely Puritan in cast, the earliest Church in Virginia was represented by a variety of opinion within that movement. Stricter conformity to Anglican practice after the colony reverted to the crown in 1624 was thwarted by the inability of Charles I and Abp. W. *Laud to send a bp. to America on the eve of the English Civil War (1638). Virginia Anglicans adapted to this lack, and with the Vestry Act of 1641 the Church became lay-controlled and Congregationalist in fact. In the period of the *Restoration the bp. of London sought to exercise control of the Church through a system of commissaries, who contributed to further changes in the colonial Church, ultimately rejecting complete reliance on the State. Commissary James *Blair of Virginia, writing to John Locke in the late 1690s, sharply criticized royal gubernatorial despotism, and Commissary Thomas *Bray of Maryland turned to voluntary means of extending the Church's influence by founding (1701) the *Society for the Propagation of the Gospel in Foreign Parts (SPG). Bray's parochial libraries increased knowledge of the *historic episcopate in the early Church, thereby serving to enhance Anglican assurance and aggressiveness as the Church spread to the Middle Colonies and to the Congregational North. There, converts from Puritanism, such as Samuel *Johnson of Conn., pleaded unsuccessfully for bps. for America. Successive abps. of Canterbury were rendered ineffective on this issue by the powerful Puritan lobby in Parliament. Nevertheless, increased numbers of SPG missionaries, the founding of colleges (William and Mary, 1693; the Univ. of Pennsylvania, 1740), influential churches (e.g., King's Chapel, Boston, 1689; Trinity Church, New York, 1689; Christ Church, Philadelphia, 1695) indicated new strength. This was largely offset by formal ties with the increasingly unpopular British government, by the fact that ministerial candidates had to cross the Atlantic for ordination, by suspicion in New England, by well-organized competition (Lutherans, Presbyterians, Quakers) in the Middle Colonies and by the Church's inability to move beyond aristocratic tidewater areas in the South. Moreover, high churchmen refused to join the triumphant progress of Puritan Calvinism that reached its climax in the *Great Awakening under the aegis of George *Whitefield. Isolation from this first popular movement of the American people resulted in later rejection of such Anglican revivalists as Devereux *Jarratt and John *Wesley's "Methodist" missionaries. After the "Bishops' Controversy" (1760–66), Anglican pamphleteers Charles Inglis, Thomas Bradbury Chandler, Samuel *Seabury, and others sought to justify their Church's needs to an unresponsive Parliament and their "rights" to a religious majority that increasingly chorused for disestablishment in the South.

After the Revolution, remaining Episcopalians were forced to accept denominational *voluntaryism. William *White's *Case of the Episcopal Churches in the United States Considered* (1782) argued for immediate Episcopalian unity, a titular episcopate if necessary, and lay rights by representation. White's Whig constitutionalism and "parochialism" were challenged by high churchmen who, in Conn., elected Samuel Seabury bp., judging that only a "regular" episcopate could serve as initiator of Episcopalian unity. Believing in a nonpolitical episcopate as most nearly reflecting the apostolic Church, Seabury sought consecration abroad. Unable to take the C of E's loyalty oath to the crown, he traveled to Scotland in 1784 to be consecrated by nonjuring bishops (see NONJURORS). Meanwhile White and William Smith of Md. moved ahead on their own, forming local and interstate conventions. These bore fruit; by 1786 White and William Provoost of N.Y. were elected to the episcopate. A special enabling act dispensed with the loyalty oath to the crown, and the two were consecrated at Lambeth in 1787. By 1789 the question of the validity of Seabury's orders (a political issue arising from his loyalist sympathies) was settled by the *General Convention. Unity with Conn. high churchmen assured, the convention went on to adopt a constitution that allowed lay participation in a *House of Deputies. Seabury's request for a separate *House of Bishops was granted. Adoption of canons and a *Book of Common Prayer completed organization (see AMERICAN PRAYER BOOK).

Throughout the 19th cent. Episcopalians debated the nature of their Church vis-à-vis the C of E on the one hand and American *revivalism on the other. Pre-Tractarian high churchmen John Henry *Hobart and Benjamin Moore, along with the faculty of the General Theological Seminary (1817), anticipated the arrival of the *Oxford movement. As a result of the latter, 30 clergy and one bp. (L. S. Ives of N.C.) entered the RC Church. Tractarianism led also to heresy trials within the Church and to debates with similar *high-church movements in other denominations (e.g., Arthur Cleveland Coxe vs. John Williamson Nevin). In the 1870s older high churchmen joined *evangelicals in attempting to suppress the newer Anglo-Catholic movement led first by James DeKoven and later by "Nashotah House" (1841) in Wisconsin (see KEMPER, JACKSON). Despite the "Ritual Canon" of 1873, more elaborate ceremonial and monasticism were accepted, though not before some evangelicals broke from the Church and founded the *Reformed Episcopal Church (1873). Early evangelicals, whose model for their denomination was neither subapostolic nor medieval but late 17th-cent. Calvinistic, were led by Bps. William Meade and Charles McIlvaine and the faculty of the Virginia Theological Seminary (1823). With the abandonment of forensic and penal views of the atonement, evangelicals, some of whom had participated in the *Second Great Awakening, merged into liberalism (see LIBERAL THEOLOGY). Derived from a variety of sources, the so-called *broad-church movement reflected diverse interests. The *Social Gospel, begun in the denomination by Caleb Sprague Henry (1840s), gained momentum with F. D. Huntington's Church Association for the Advancement of the Interests of Labor and the "institutional churches" of Henry C. Potter and William Rainsford; it moved into academic circles with economist Richard T. Ely, socialist W. D. P. Bliss's *New Encyclopedia of Social Reform* (1908), and George Hodges's leadership of the Episcopal Theological School (1867). *Anglo-Catholicism, sanctioned by J. H. Hopkins's *Law of Ritualism* (1866), joined the Social Gospel with James O. S. Huntington and Vida D. Scudder, merging into F. D. Roosevelt's "New Deal" in the persons of Frances Perkins and Henry A. Wallace. Clearly the new Episcopalian social concern marked a dramatic change, for before the Civil War the issue of slavery was never mentioned in the Church, and the "Protestant Episcopal Church in the Confederate States . . ." appeared (1861) and merged again (1865) with the larger body without the slightest difficulty. Liberals related church doctrine to theories of evolution in the writings of Elisha Mulford and William P. *DuBose of the University of the South (1868).

Church unity became an increasingly pressing concern after William A. *Muhlenberg's "Memorial" of 1858. Liberal William Reed Huntington's *Chicago-Lambeth quadrilateral (1886, 1889) was succeeded by Anglo-Catholic Charles Henry *Brent's efforts in arranging for the *Faith and Order Conference at Lausanne, Switzerland (1927). The period prior to World War I, when Episcopalians judged their denomination to be suited for national leadership, came to a gradual close beginning with the debate in the General Convention of 1907 over whether to extend the Social Gospel into the arena of race relations; from this the denomination drew back, the subsequent efforts of such men as William Scarlett and Walter Russell Bowie notwithstanding. Since that time the Episcopal Church has tended to revert to the various types of theological traditionalism seen in the Neo-Anglicanism of Francis Hall and John Macquarrie, Walter Lowrie's introduction of the thought of Søren Kierkegaard to North America, and Norman Pittenger's and A. T. Mollegen's "Anglicized" *neo-orthodoxy. Since 1919 the Church has had a National Council, whose activities

have grown while its authority has remained advisory.

Bishops and priests constitute the ministry, with the order of deacons peripheral and temporary. Organization and authority are maintained in parishes, dioceses, and the General Convention. The denomination maintains that the Holy Scriptures are the ultimate rule of faith. The symbols of doctrine are the Apostles' and Nicene Creed; baptism and the Lord's Supper are considered to be the two sacraments necessary for salvation. Episcopalians use exclusively the Book of Common Prayer (1928) and the Hymnal (1940) in worship. See J. F. Woolverton, "Histories of the Episcopal Church in America: A Survey and Evaluation," *Historical Magazine* (March 1965); W. W. Manross, *History of the American Episcopal Church* (1935); E. Clowes Chorley, *Men and Movements in the American Episcopal Church* (1946).

PROTESTANT PRINCIPLE, the primary Protestant concept of justification by faith, sometimes called the material principle of Protestantism in distinction from the formal principle, the sole and sufficient authority of the Bible. In contemporary theology the concept is associated particularly with P. *Tillich (1886–1965), for whom it made all religious forms relative and therefore subject to criticism in the light of the ultimate. It thus became a principle of protest against idolatries, against absolutizing anything in the human sphere—social, intellectual, or religious. In the light of the Protestant principle no church structure or system of dogma could be considered final. The principle allowed Tillich to accept historical criticism of the Bible and gave him a base for criticizing forms of society that had been traditionally supported by the Churches. Tillich identified the principle with OT prophetism, but not with Protestantism as a historical movement. "The Protestant principle (which is a manifestation of the prophetic Spirit) is not restricted to the churches of the Reformation or to any other church" (*Systematic Theology,* III, 245). According to Tillich the principle is both found in every Church and betrayed by every Church. He correlated the Protestant principle with what he called the Catholic substance, "the concrete embodiment of the Spiritual Presence," and held that both were necessary. See P. Tillich, *Protestant Era* (1948).

PROTESTANT REFORMED CHURCHES OF AMERICA,

a denomination that separated formally from the Christian Reformed Church in 1926. The schism began in 1923, when three *classes of the parent body under the leadership of Herman Hoeksema, of Grand Rapids, Mich., contested the Christian Reformed view of a common grace open to all men. The Church holds to the Reformed confessions —the *Heidelberg Catechism, the *Belgic Confession, and the *Canons of Dort—and defends a doctrine of "particular" grace, i.e., that God's grace is operative for the elect alone. The form of government is *presbyterian, with an annual meeting of a general *synod. A small theological seminary is maintained in Grand Rapids. There are 19 congregations in 8 states, with about 3,000 members.

PROTESTANTISM,

an expression of Christianity emerging from the 16th-cent. Reformation. It has become so diverse that it is difficult to delimit its boundaries or distill its essence. Chillingworth's oft-quoted statement, "The Bible and the Bible only is the religion of the Protestants," is very misleading. Also, the view that "the basic difference" between Catholics and Protestants is "the right of private judgment" (A. C. Knudson, *Protestantism: A Symposium* [ed. W. K. Anderson, 1944], 126) is far wide of the mark. The name "Protestant" originated with the Second Diet of Speyer (1529), when several princes and cities drew up a *protestatio,* objecting to the reversal of a previous decision to allow each prince (or city) to decide between Catholicism and Lutheranism. In support of their stand they affirmed: "In matters which concern the honor of God and the salvation of our souls, every individual must stand alone before God and give his account." The sense of "to protest" is not only negative; it also means "to witness." This positive note can better be seen by reviewing the origins of Protestantism than by surveying its present heterogeneity.

Origins. Although the Reformation has been interpreted in economic, political, psychological, and social terms, there is a growing reaffirmation among Catholic and Protestant scholars that it was primarily a religious movement. The development of Lutheranism was complex, but Luther's personal quest was for a "gracious God," and his insight into the meaning of justification by grace through faith was pivotal for subsequent developments. Misled partly by *nominalism and by exaggerated emphases upon the wrath of God, he found no assurance of divine forgiveness by the usual means. Through study of the Bible, he came to the insight and experience of God's free grace. The Scriptures pointed him to Jesus Christ, in whom God's grace was manifested. Tending to use hyperbole for emphasis, Luther spoke of *sola fide, sola gratia, sola scriptura,* and *solus Christus;* but for him each of these terms symbolized the same pattern, in which a gracious God was central. The Scriptures were "the cradle in which Christ lay," Christ was the fullest disclosure of God's mercy, and the gospel was the good news of free pardon apart from any worthiness of the recipient. One could do nothing to merit salvation but could only repent and trust in God's mercy.

That these concepts were at the heart of Luther's concern is attested not only by Protestant but also by many modern RC scholars (Tavard, Lortz, Küng, Rahner, Adam, Bouyer, and others), who grant that these were part of sound Catholic doctrine (at least as far as they went). Many Catholics are in virtual agreement with the assertion of J. Pelikan that the Reformation was a "tragic necessity" caused by "loyalty of the Reformers to the best and highest in Roman Catholic Christianity" in the face of theological confusion and indifferent leaders (*The Riddle of Roman Catholicism* [1959] 46). J. Lortz wonders whether there would have been a Reformation "if not only Luther and his coreligionists, but all men of the time, had been fully and accurately aware that the doctrines we have mentioned are articles of the Catholic faith" (*The Reformation: A Problem for Today* [1964], 220). There were, of course, other traditions besides the Lutheran that spread over much of Germany and the Scandinavian countries. The *Reformed Churches, stemming from Zwingli, Calvin, and others, became predominant in Switzerland, the Netherlands, and Scotland; and the Puritans were influential in England and in New England. The C of E was another Reformation Church that spread to all subsequent British colonies, although some Anglicans do not wish to be classified as Protestants. A fourth category was that of the Anabaptists, a sect that began at Zurich, and from which Mennonites, Amish, Hutterites, and other groups derived. Finally there was a miscellaneous group of mystics and rationalists, who are sometimes grouped with the Anabaptists as the left-wing of the Reformation. Most of these groups are classified as Protestant, although there are those on the fringes (e.g., mystics and Unitarians on one hand, Anglo-Catholics on the other) whose classification is problematic.

Common Heritage. In spite of many differences, the four main traditions shared Luther's basic convictions about sin, God's grace, the authority of the Bible, the lordship of Jesus Christ over the Church, justification by faith, and the priesthood of all believers. It was not the intention of Luther to found a new Church; all of the Reformers believed that they were simply recovering the pristine gospel that had become obscured by the institutionalism of the RC Church. Nevertheless, in defending his basic insights, Luther progressively questioned the abuse of indulgences, then indulgences themselves, and finally the entire sacrament of penance. Appealing to the pope, he was disappointed and called for a general council; finally he concluded that both popes and councils were subject to error. When the hierarchy seemed indifferent to reforms, he appealed to the German nobility to initiate necessary reforms, con-

tending that they belonged to the priesthood by virtue of their baptism. Ultimately Luther rejected the concept of the Church as a divinely ordained juridical and sacramental institution, headed by a pope who claimed fullness of power over the Church and supremacy over temporal rulers on the basis of a primacy transmitted from Peter through the line of Roman bishops. He defined the Church as the "communion of saints," the congregation of the faithful; and although denying that the Church was invisible, he held that it was hidden except to the eyes of faith. In no sense was the Church a worldwide organization, subject to a single head and having a magisterium that alone could rightly interpret the Bible. The number of sacraments was reduced from seven to two, and these were reinterpreted. Although he retained as much of the older service of the Mass as possible, Luther revised it to eliminate all suggestions of a sacrificial interpretation. He also rejected purgatory, images, veneration of saints, relics, monasticism, etc. Thus, beginning with his understanding of "the just shall live by faith," he had felt impelled to raise one critical question after another until the Church could scarcely avoid excommunicating him.

Protestant Unity. Tensions within original Protestantism have remained difficult to keep in balance: the objective action of God vs. the individual's response to God's grace; the worthlessness of human works vs. recognition of the importance of ethics; the significance of the corporate Christian community vs. the individual conscience; unity vs. diversity; freedom vs. order. These polarizations are already present in the NT, and they opened the way to endless divisions and doctrinal divergence. One must note, however, that nearly 90% of Protestants belong to about six family groups (Lutheran, Reformed and Presbyterian, Anglican, Methodist, Baptist and Disciples, Congregationalist); the 20th cent. has seen a Protestant interest in unity manifested in mergers and in such conciliar movements as the World Council of Churches (WCC) and local and regional church councils. Also, despite differences, the essential characteristics of original Protestantism still constitute a common denominator. While interpretations of the nature of the Bible and its authority vary, there is general recognition that Scripture is the unique witness to God's revelation and that it bears the tradition by which all traditions must be judged. Protestants share Luther's concern for the gospel, although they may not all understand it in the same way. This is the fundamental emphasis of conservative Protestants, of the *Bultmann School's demythologizing and stress on kerygma, of Karl *Barth's stress on Christology as the center of theology, and of P. *Tillich's interest in alienation, ultimate concern, and the new being in Christ. The desire to acknowledge the centrality of Jesus Christ is still prominent in Protestantism, shared by fundamentalists, Christocentric liberals, neo-orthodox, and even exponents of the so-called *radical theology. Thus, despite differences among Protestants, there are still signs of preoccupation with the original interests of the Reformation.

Protestantism and Roman Catholicism. These interests are not foreign to Catholic concerns, although not all Protestant formulations of problems or their answers are acceptable to Catholics. After centuries of hostility, Protestants and Catholics have moved toward a greater degree of understanding, marked by the presence of Protestant observers at Vatican Council II, the appointment of nine Catholics as members of the Faith and Order Commission of the WCC at Uppsala in 1968, and the sharing of classes by many Protestant and Catholic seminarians in the United States. Several factors have contributed to breaking down the barriers between Protestants and Catholics; among these are Catholic recognition of the legitimacy of Luther's original concerns and insights; the conviction that the Protestant doctrine of justification by faith is not essentially different from that of the Council of Trent; Catholic clarification of the Tridentine statement regarding Scripture and tradition and growing Protestant awareness of the importance of tradition; the subordination of juridical

to pastoral concerns; and greater attention to the idea of development in interpreting both doctrine and canon law.

When this greater understanding and mutual appreciation have been gratefully acknowledged, there still remains a question as to whether there is still an insoluble difference that will indefinitely separate Catholics from Protestants. There seems to be an impasse that is related to the doctrine of the Church as a movement and as an institution, and the related points of ministry and Sacraments. It is reflected by G. Tavard when he writes that Luther was interested not only in "purifying his faith . . . , but wished to purge the faith of the church itself" (*Protestantism* [1959], 21). H. Küng says something similar when asserting that "Catholic reform cannot take place in the sphere of the absolute, the essence of Catholicism; it occurs in that of the relative, the working out at the historical level" (*The Council, Reform, and Reunion* [1961], 53). For the Protestant no institution can be exempted from judgment, and the Church itself stands in constant need of correction and reformation. This is what P. Tillich has called the *Protestant principle, i.e., that "every religious and cultural reality, including the religion and culture which calls itself 'Protestant,' " must come under judgment (*The Protestant Era* [1948], 163). Every institution (organizational forms, worship patterns, ethical systems, and doctrinal formulations) that has a human element is subject to the limitations of partial perspectives and self-assertive pride. Of course, God, Christ, and the gospel are not under man's judgment, but human apprehension of revelation develops and changes, and men revise their formulations accordingly.

Hence Protestants generally refuse to accept the possibility of any Church on earth as being exclusively "the" Church of Jesus Christ. They reject the concept of a magisterium that can speak the last irreformable word on any doctrinal question, or a pope (even with the aid of a council) who in speaking *ex cathedra* in faith and morals stands above contradiction or correction. Related to this point is the denial of a special priesthood that receives by ordination special status and power to perform the miracle of *transubstantiation. Indeed, most Protestants regard transubstantiation as alien to the meaning of the Lord's Supper, although some would concede that in the 13th cent. (with its philosophical presuppositions) it might have been an allowable way of stating the reality of Christ's presence in the Eucharist. Protestants understand that the ministry was given by Christ to the whole people of God, but that orderliness requires some specialized ministries representative of the Church as a whole. The specialized minister needs special education, but he differs from the rest of the members only as to function. In case of necessity, an unordained person might do anything that the ordained minister could do. It is difficult to be certain whether an essentially Protestant point of view is irreconcilably opposed to the Catholic meaning of such terms as "irreformable" and "infallible." Perhaps here, as in so many other instances, the difference will ultimately prove to be largely semantic. At present, however, Protestant and Catholic conceptions of Church, ministry, and sacraments seem really opposed. See L. Bouyer, *The Spirit and the Forms of Protestantism* (1957); R. M. Brown, *Spirit of Protestantism* (pa., 1965); D. Callahan et al., eds., *Christianity Divided: Protestant and Roman Catholic Theological Issues* (1961); G. W. Forell, *Protestant Faith* (1960); O. Piper, *Protestantism in an Ecumenical Age: Its Roots, Its Rights, Its Task* (1965); W. Pauck, *Heritage of the Reformation* (rev. ed., 1961); G. H. Tavard, *Catholic Approach to Protestantism* (1955); S. J. Whale, *Protestant Tradition: An Essay in Interpretation* (1955). *CHURCH HISTORY (U.S.).

PROTESTANTS AND OTHER AMERICANS UNITED for Separation of Church and State (POAU), a nonprofit organization formed in 1947 with the stated purpose of maintaining "the separation of Church and State" in accord with the intention of the First Amendment of the U.S. Constitution.

The organization also uses officially the shortened title, Americans United for Separation of Church and State. Headquarters are in Washington, D.C., with local chapters in each state; support is derived from a wide variety of sources. POAU informs people regarding alleged violations of the First Amendment through its monthly *Church and State*, pamphlets, films, and speakers. It sends spokesmen to congressional hearings, seeks the support of members of Congress, and finances litigation in specific cases. The RC Church has been the main target of the POAU. See L. P. Creedon and W. D. Falcon, *United For Separation: An Analysis of POAU Assaults on Catholicism* (1959); S. C. Lowell, *Embattled Wall—Americans United: An Idea and a Man* (1966). *CHURCH AND STATE.

PROVINCIAL LETTERS (Les Provinciales), full title: *Lettres écrites par Louis de Montalte à un Provincial;* a series of 18 letters written in 1656–57 by Blaise *Pascal, probably with the cooperation of Antoine *Arnauld and Pierre Nicole. Meant as a defense of Arnauld, then on trial before the theological faculty of the Sorbonne for his Jansenist views, they satirically attack the Jesuits, characterizing their ideas on moral questions as lax and essentially casuistic (i.e., applying general precepts to a diversity of cases). Letters 5–9 bear the burden of Pascal's ironic attack on Jesuit moral theology; letters 1–3 defend Arnauld; and letters 15–16 protest as unjust the persecution of the Jansenist center at *Port-Royal. The letters were successful from the first because of their topical nature, but they are also a classic of French literature because of the brilliance of Pascal's style and his passionate advocacy of a cause in which he firmly believed. His own deep spirituality was repelled by what he considered mere toying with the divine. The letters were placed on the Index by Roman authorities soon after their publication. See Eng. tr. by A. G. Krailsheimer (pa., 1968); J. Mesnard, *Pascal: His Life and Works* (tr. G. S. Fraser, 1952).

PSYCHIANA, an American religious cult, promoted in the popular press and by direct mail advertising, without any ecclesiastical organization. It was begun in 1929 by Frank B. Robinson of Moscow, Idaho, the son of an English Baptist preacher, who had studied at the Bible Training School in Toronto, Canada. Robinson had very strong prejudices against the Christian Churches and the Christian message itself. He developed a religious system that began with absolute monotheism and totally rejected traditional Christian teachings. Robinson's God was impersonal, being simply Power or Life. The aim of the Psychiana lessons, which Robinson sold to those who answered his advertisements, was to enable every individual to achieve a relationship to or an understanding of the nature of God, which would make the power of God freely available to the individual for his own uses. These lessons consisted primarily of a series of exercises in mental concentration aimed at enabling the reader to correct his own thought processes and to experience the power of God. Robinson regarded himself as a prophet and included dogmatic assertions about the future and rather inane "miracle" stories in his many published writings. As Psychiana was essentially a mail order publishing house, no accurate count of members could be made, but nearly one million sets of lessons were sold between 1929 and 1949. *NEW THOUGHT.

PUBLIC WORSHIP REGULATION ACT, law passed by Parliament (1874) against *ritualism in the Church of England. The measure, drafted by A. C. Tait, Abp. of Canterbury, was hostile to Anglo-Catholics and was amended in Parliament by Lord Shaftesbury, a fervent evangelical who was both a humanitarian and an Erastian. It provided for a special civil judge to try cases involving ritual, allowed for right of appeal to the Privy Council, and at the instance of the primate, for an episcopal veto on proceedings. The imprisonment for contumacy of four respected clergymen brought it into discredit a few years afterward; since then it has remained a dead letter.

PUBLISHERS OF THE KINGDOM, members of *Jehovah's Witnesses, all of whom are expected to be active propagandists.

PURGATORY, in RC belief, the state of purification to which the soul of the just is subjected immediately after death if either unremitted venial sin or temporal punishment for sin is still to be atoned for. The only pertinent scriptural passage to support this belief is 2 Macc 12.39–45: after a battle against Gorgias, Judas found that, contrary to the prescriptions of the law (Dt 7.25), some of the slain Jewish soldiers were wearing amulets. Concluding that their death was a divine punishment, Judas made a collection among the survivors in order to have expiatory sacrifices offered for the dead, that they might be freed from their sins. The inspired author approves of Judas's belief, which embraces both his faith in the resurrection (see, e.g., 2 Macc 7.9, 11, 14) and his conviction that the dead can be helped by the prayers (2 Macc 12.42) and the sacrifices (12.43) of the living. The fallen soldiers are not damned since they expect the final resurrection (12.45), but they still stand in need of purification. This intermediary state is substantially purgatory.

In the NT, 1 Cor 3.10–15 is inconclusive: the fire in question (13, 15) is not purifying but eschatological (13), and, besides, the entire context points in the direction of testing the worthiness of the apostolic work. Other texts sometimes quoted (2 Tm 1.18; Mt 12.32) being equally inconclusive, one may conclude that the scriptural testimony is meager. Nevertheless, this tiny scriptural seed gradually developed through the analysis of faith, the Church's liturgical practice, and a hesitant patristic interpretation, not always free from error. Origen is the first explicit witness to this tradition, but his testimony is a blend of light and darkness. According to him the soul is stained by its union with the body, hence there is a general need for final purification affecting all men. They must all be purified "from the lead that weighs them down and which must be dissolved by fire" (*Hom. in Ex.* 6; PG 12:334). This purification will take place not immediately after death but at the general judgment by means of real fire (see *Cels.* 4.13; PG 11:236). St. Augustine wrote that the final purification does not affect all men (*Civ.* 20.26.1); it takes place immediately after death (*Civ.* 21.13); purgatorial fire is probably metaphorical, not real (*Civ.* 21.4).

Both East and West were joint heirs to this common tradition up to the 13th cent., but at this time the two Churches began to develop distinct though mutually complementary tendencies. In the West, Peter Lombard's distinction between guilt and its temporal punishment is immediately applied to the doctrine of purgatory, and as a consequence the juridical aspect of satisfaction prevails. The sinner has to pay off the debt contracted; his personal guilt is to be fully expiated. The Eastern conception is less juridical and more mystical: purgatory is not a place but a state of "maturation and perfection" (Irenaeus), a final stage of spiritual growth where God's image, blurred by sin, is fully restored. "These two traditions are compatible within the unity of the same ecclesial communion" (Congar). Against this theological background the Council of Florence (1439–45) expounded the doctrine in an eclectic manner. Purgatory is a means of both satisfaction and purification (Latin and Greek conceptions combined); there is no mention of purgatorial fire, but rather of "purgatorial sufferings"; there is no mention of purgatory as a place (see D 1304). This fundamental agreement of the Churches was shaken in 1524 by Luther, who openly rejected purgatory: apart from the lack of scriptural support (he holds even 2 Macc to be a noncanonical book), this "popish" doctrine goes counter to the very core of Lutheran soteriology, in which man is saved exclusively by God alone and therefore any medium of purification after death should be rejected as sheer Pelagianism. The doctrine of Purgatory was rejected in the *Reformed tradition (e.g., Art. 57 of Zwingli's Sixty-Seven Articles; Second *Helvetic Confession, Ch. 26; *Westminster Confession, c.32) and in Anglicanism (*Thirty-Nine Articles, c.32). The Council of Trent in 1563 restated the traditional doctrine but in a very sober manner, which contrasts with certain popular, but only dubiously valuable, descriptions of purgatory. The Council teaches only the existence of purgatory and the possibility of helping souls therein by means of suffrages (see D 1820).

There is a marked tendency among some theologians (P. Fransen, Y. Congar, and L. Boros) to "demythologize" and spiritualize the doctrine: purgatorial fire need not be taken literally as real fire, for the dying person is possessed by the Holy Spirit, who is often associated with fire (Mt 3.11; Lk 3.16; Acts 2.3–4). God's image, which had been imprinted on the soul by the Spirit and obscured by sin, is now restored to its pristine splendor by the same Spirit who "burns" from within. The strange coexistence of joy and suffering in purgatory affects only the psychological level but is rooted in the deeper, ontological coexistence of the Spirit and *concupiscence. The soul rejoices because it possesses the Spirit forever, and yet it suffers on account of its unextinguished concupiscence. Its joy will be unalloyed, without any mixture of suffering, only when it is totally possessed by the Spirit without any trace of concupiscence. The Spirit draws man into himself, scorching and purifying him down to the deepest layers of his personality and making him ready for the Vision. Purgatory is possibly a momentary occurrence, linked to the quality of the decision made at the moment of death. Consequently the duration of purgatory should be measured by the various degrees in the intensity of purifying suffering. The degree to which that "fire" of the Spirit cleanses the soul one tends to express in terms of temporal duration, which would be only an anthropomorphism. This purification is an active loving acceptance of a suffering imposed by Love, before the soul "enters into the joy of the Lord" (Mt 25.21). See Y. Congar, "Le Purgatoire," *Le Mystère de la mort et sa célébration* (Lex Orandi 12; 1956), 279–336; P. Fransen, "The Doctrine of Purgatory," ECQ 13 (1959), 99–112.

PURITANISM, both a religious faction that clearly emerged during the reign of *Elizabeth I and a complex social, political, and theological movement made up largely of middle-class English and American Protestants. At its inception the Puritan party entertained hopes of reforming the established Church on the pattern developed by the Continental Reformers, esp. John *Calvin. The principal points of attack were those most closely associated with Roman Catholicism. Certain liturgical forms, the use of ecclesiastical vestments, and *episcopacy were counted as unscriptural and therefore to be rejected. With the passage of time the movement split into factions. A significant number of Puritans championed Presbyterianism as the form of church government. By the late 16th cent. another group, having surrendered hope of enacting reforms from within the Church, advocated Congregationalism. Puritans of this type were convinced that the Scriptures taught the principle of the *gathered Church as the only valid form of ecclesiastical life. Their emphasis fell upon the need for an autonomous congregation, freed from a nationally comprehensive and coercive Church. These came to be called Separatists. From their numbers grew a variety of sects, including the Baptists, who adopted *believer's baptism as the sign of entry into a regenerate life. The Congregationalists developed a non-Separatist wing that claimed that the essence as distinct from the external structure of the Church was congregational. Strength developed in the total movement by the time James I ascended the throne. From him it was hoped that Puritan reforms would be incorporated into the established Church. At the *Hampton Court Conference (1604), however, Puritan hopes were dashed by James's opposition, the sole benefit of the meeting

being the authorization of the Authorized Version of the Bible. Disappointment of Puritan ambitions drove the movement into opposition to the Stuart rulers. Oppressed under James I and by Abp. *Laud under Charles I, some of the Separatists and non-Separatists fled to Massachusetts in the early 17th century. Puritan political and military power brought about the downfall of Charles I. Conservative Presbyterian forces dominated Parliament, and at the close of the Civil Wars the *Independents, whose strength lay in the army, split with the Parliamentary party, arguing for a religious toleration that was threatened by the Presbyterian dream of a national Church. During the period of Presbyterian predominance (1643–48) the *Westminster Confession and the *Westminster Catechisms were produced. Upon becoming Lord Protector, Oliver *Cromwell, himself an Independent, adopted a policy of religious toleration, exempting only Roman Catholics and Anglicans, mainly for political reasons. Thus the Presbyterian aim of establishing a national Church was again frustrated. On the return of Charles II, Puritanism was made illegal and severely persecuted under the Clarendon Code. Puritans were then designated as Dissenters for their refusal to conform to the practices and government of the re-established Anglican Church.

Although diversity of belief obtained across the entire spectrum of Puritan thought, the main body held strongly to the authority of Scripture as the supreme guide to holiness and as the basis for social, political, and ecclesiastical life. The Calvinistic doctrine of a sovereign God whose majesty and glory were to be worshiped stood as the central focus of the Christian life. The hope of *election by the gift of divine grace, and the necessity of a careful scrutiny of one's daily practice marked the arduous progress of the Puritan's existence. Sin was ever ready to catch the unwary, undisciplined soul on its way through a trouble-beset world. The Puritan was typically self-reliant, frugal, and energetic in fulfilling both his religious and his daily duties. The non-

Separatist Congregationalists who immigrated to Massachusetts Bay did not surrender their belief in the ideal of religious uniformity. Consequently they labored to establish a biblically sanctioned church and political order. However, they denied freedom to those of other religious persuasions, such as Anne *Hutchinson and Roger *Williams, who threatened the regularities they believed themselves to be establishing. Massachusetts Puritans accepted the Westminster Confession as their theological base and in 1648 produced the *Cambridge Platform as the criterion of church order. Eventually the structures of their mode of life were eroded by the coming of immigrants primarily seeking economic opportunity without concern for the ideal of a "Holy Commonwealth." Under a new charter in 1692 the theocratic order was set aside, and although Congregationalism remained the established Church into the early 19th cent., the right to vote was exempted from religious qualifications.

As a common noun puritanism may designate a characteristic recurrent throughout church history: advocacy of a strict moral code as a protest against the mediocrity of a mass Church and as an expression of being an elite. Puritanism in this sense has characterized Montanists, Novatianists, and Donatists in the early Church; the medieval Cathari; the Jansenists; Holiness and Pentecostal groups; and Jehovah's Witnesses. See W. H. Frere and C. E. Douglas, eds., *Puritan Manifestoes* (1954); W. Haller, *Rise of Puritanism* (1938); M. M. Knappen, *Tudor Puritanism* (1939); P. Miller, *New England Mind* (1939); G. B. Cragg, *Puritanism in the Period of Great Persecution* (1957); E. Morgan, *Visible Saints* (1963); A. Simpson, *Puritanism in Old and New England* (1955).

PUSEY, EDWARD BOUVERIE (1800–82), theologian, Oriental scholar, religious leader, Canon of Christ Church, Oxford, and regius professor of Hebrew. He was a Berkshire man, and as a fellow of Oriel was brought into intimacy with Keble and Newman, and set on a course he followed with great courage and steadfastness through "a succession of insulated efforts, bearing indeed upon one great end—the growth of catholic truth and piety among us." Aware that "dead orthodoxism" was not enough, he spent years in Germany preparing for the defense of revealed religion against *rationalism and *latitudinarianism. His students were taught Hebrew in order "to enter more fully into the meaning of God's word, without the dryness of the lower criticism and the precarious assertions of the higher." But it is as leader of the *Oxford movement, after Newman had departed, that he is famous and revered, and still, like Mr. Gladstone, given his prefix, Dr. Pusey, as though he were alive. His books, and above all his sermons—he preached wherever he was asked to go—based on the Fathers and the Anglican divines of the 17th cent., maintained his ideals through many troubles, with the confidence of deep learning and the tranquillity of a life of prayer. For 2 years he was forbidden the university pulpit for his defense of the Real Presence. Suspected of Romanism because he declined to make assertions against the Church of Rome, his first *Eirenicon* was followed by two more; they argued that official doctrines were less the bar to union than unofficial devotions; they were not always received with common courtesy by the authorities to whom they were sent. Himself not given to ceremonies, he formed a rallying-point for the ritualists, or "Puseyites." He is the virtual founder of all Anglican sisterhoods.

PUSEYISM, a contemptuous name, now out of date, for the *Oxford movement, after E. B. *Pusey became the first of the authors of * Tracts for the Times to make his identity known.

Q

QUAKERS, members of the *Religious Society of Friends. G. *Fox states in his *Journal* that the name, which had been used earlier for a small sect in England, was applied to him in scorn by a judge in court. Some associate the name with the tremblings of the early Friends at their meetings. No longer is it used derisively, nor is it offensive to Friends themselves. See OED 8:15.

QUANTA CURA, an encyclical letter of Pius IX (Dec. 8, 1864), which condemns some of the political tendencies of rationalism and liberalism, forcefully insisting that the authority of the Church is supreme because it is received from Christ and therefore completely independent of the authority of the State. It rejects the view that the power of the Church is not distinct from and independent of the civil power and that the legislation of the Church does not bind in conscience unless promulgated by the civil authority. See D 2890–96; J. F. Clarkson et al., *Church Teaches* (1955), 85–86.

QUARTERLY CONFERENCE (Methodist), the governing body of the local church. *CONFERENCE (METHODIST).

QUESNEL, PASQUIER (1634–1719), an Oratorian priest and scholar, who became a Jansenist. He published in 1671 a popular little book, later entitled *Le Nouveau Testament . . . avec des réflexions morales*; suspected of *Jansenism, he left the Oratory, joined his friend Antoine *Arnauld in exile in Brussels in 1685, and succeeded him as Jansenist leader. By 1693 *Réflexions* was four large volumes; it was denounced to the Sorbonne and the Holy Office as a summary of Jansenism. Bossuet recommended corrections that Q. rejected. After much controversy, in 1703 Louis XIV, mistrusting Jansenists, obtained Q.'s arrest; but Q. escaped and won support with his violent pamphleteering. Having read Q.'s confiscated papers, Louis asked Clement XI to condemn the Jansenists and their tracts. The Pope complied with *Vineam Domini*, which was accepted by Parlement and the bps. but not by the nuns of *Port-Royal, who consequently were dispersed. After long examination, *Réflexions* was condemned in 1708; Q. protested and republished it. Upon further study, Clement in 1713 issued the famous bull *Unigenitus*, censuring 101 Quesnellian propositions (see D 2400–2502), esp. for being a repetition of previously condemned Jansenist propositions. The issue at stake in the condemnation and its aftermath was as much *Gallicanism as theological orthodoxy. Eight French bishops objected, 112 fully assented, and a few temporized. In 1717, Q. joined the appeal of four bishops from *Unigenitus* to an ecumenical council (see APPELLANTS). Jansenism, which he developed into a political party including freethinkers in its ranks, gradually deteriorated after Q.'s death. He also published theological and devotional works, notably *Prières chrétiennes* (1687), and an edition of the works of Leo the Great. See J. Carreyre, DTC 13:1460–1535; *Le Jansénisme durant la régence* (1932); J. Tans, *P. Q. et les pays-bas* (1960); Pastor 33:192–313.

QUICUMQUE (*Quicumque vult*), a name for the *Athanasian Creed, a creed composed in Latin and beginning with the words *Quicumque vult salvus esse* (whoever wishes to be saved).

QUIETISM, derived from "quiet," a form of contemplative prayer, a term with two uses. (1) Taken in a general sense, it refers to a recurring phenomenon in the history of the Church. The principles that underly manifestations of quietism down through the ages might be thus summarized: there exist in man two rival tendencies, sensual and spiritual; perfection implies the annihilation (in the moral sense) of the sensual for the benefit of the spiritual; the best means to obtain this is not through the struggle of asceticism but through a total passivity on the sense and intellectual level; only this quiet passivity leads to direct contact with God; in this passivity one is not morally responsible for sensual movements. Typical forms of this quietist passivity are found in certain Manichaean and Gnostic manifestations, in some tendencies of the *Cathari and *Fraticelli, among the *Brethren of the Free Spirit, the *Beghards, the *Beguines, and the *Alumbrados. In a faintly analogous sense, Quaker historians refer to the second generation of Quaker history as the quietist period because of Quaker withdrawal from society.

(2) In its second and more specific sense, Quietism refers to a spiritual movement at a particular time (late 17th cent.) and in a particular environment (Italy and France). In this movement the old principles were applied again. This period of Quietism has been divided by historians into Pre-Quietism, Quietism, and Semi-Quietism, to which they then add Anti-Quietist reaction. Modern investigation has shown that practically none of the Pre-Quietist authors condemned at the moment of the Quietist crisis had presented dangerous innovations in their writings. The Quietist movement in Italy was more popular and widespread; in France it was more confined and aristocratic. The most famous of those accused of spreading Quietism in Italy was Miguel de *Molinos. The worst feature of the Quietist doctrine condemned by the bull *Caelestis pastor* (D 2201–69) is that those in the interior way would disturb their quiet by trying to resist temptation, and that God allows the devil to make some perfect souls do evil. The movement in France may be reduced practically to the events surrounding P. LaCombe and Madame *Guyon. In their writings and ac-

tivities there was more eccentricity and lack of discipline than real error. Rather than on "quiet," they insisted upon "extreme abandon." Late 17th-cent. Quietism was a movement of small proportions, very localized with little effect on the Christian people. The Anti-Quietists, the many writers who attacked Quietism when it was nothing but an unhappy memory, sowed distrust of mysticism. These writers frightened more than one generous spirit when the danger no longer existed. See L. Cognet, *Post-Reformation Spirituality* (tr. P. Hepburne Scott, 1959).

QUIMBY, PHINEAS PARKHURST (1802–66), pioneer in mental healing. He was born in Lebanon, N.H., but lived most of his life in Belfast, Maine. He had little formal schooling and became a clockmaker. In 1838 he began to practice hypnosis as a way of healing but by 1847 developed the idea of healing simply by changing the mental attitudes of patients. Essential in his theory was the denial of the reality of matter. He rejected established forms of Christianity but claimed to have gained the secret of Jesus' way of healing. The "Quimby Manuscripts" expressed his theories, which were developed by followers as the basis of *New Thought. Mary Baker *Eddy was his patient but denied that she owed her theories to him.

QUINQUARTICULAR (Lat. *quinque*, five; *articulus*, article, point), related to the five articles or points summarizing *Arminianism. The disputes culminating in the Synod of *Dort are referred to as the Quinquarticular Controversies. The term is applied to advocates of Arminianism, as quinquarticular theologians. See OED 8:66; Schaff Creeds 1:516–519.

QUINQUECENTENNIAL CONSENSUS, see CONSENSUS QUINQUESAECULARIS.

QUINT MONARCHY MEN, see FIFTH MONARCHY MEN.

R

RACOVIAN CATECHISM, *confession of faith for *Socinianism. On the basis of a draft prepared by F. Sozzini (see SOCINUS), this catechism was written by George Schomann in 1574; it was published in Polish by Valentin Schmalz in 1605 at Raców, and there were versions in German, 1608, and Latin, 1609. In England in 1614 the Latin version and in 1652 an English version by J. *Biddle were burned. The distribution of the contents of the Catechism corresponds to Christ's triple role as prophet, priest, and king. During the 17th cent. it was widely read by rationalist Protestants. An English edition with a historical introduction was published in 1818 by Thomas Rees. See P. Wrzecionko, "Die Theologie des Rakower Katechismus," *Kirche im Osten* 6 (1963), 73–116; bibliog. for Socinianism.

RADICAL THEOLOGY, a recent trend in theology characterized by a rejection of transcendence and traditional structures—intellectual, ethical, and ecclesiastical. Exemplified notably by the *death of God theologians, radical theology attempts to develop an expression of Christian faith that is not religious in traditional terms. Influenced by linguistic philosophy, the movement rejects supernaturalism and metaphysical language about God. It calls for a *new morality of love, as opposed to law, with Jesus as an example, and generally supports a radical social ethic. It is critical of traditional forms of church life and seeks fundamental restructuring or abandonment of the *institutional Church. Associating itself with the prison writings of D. *Bonhoeffer (1906–45), it speaks of a world come of age and sees the contemporary period as one whose secularity makes traditional piety and religious language impossible. To some extent it is reflected in such popular works as Bp. J. Robinson's *Honest to God* (1963), based upon P. Tillich (1886–1965), R. Bultmann, and Bonhoeffer,

and H. Cox's *Secular City* (1965). Radical theology may be taken as an extension of various liberal tendencies found in theology since the *Enlightenment (see LIBERAL THEOLOGY). But whereas liberalism has sought to conserve basic aspects of the Christian tradition while making such adjustments as modern thought seemed to demand, radical theology has minimized any conservative interest, emphasizing relevance to the present and openness to the future. See W. Miller, *New Christianity* (1967).

RANTERS, a pantheistic movement in 17th-cent. England. The Ranters have been called the "dregs of the Seeker movement" (see R. M. Jones, 467). They were mostly unlettered, common people, who pushed the idea of "Christ in men" to the point of claiming identity with the divine, and so rejected the historical Christ, Scripture, Church, and liturgy. They were antinomian, often to a point of gross moral excess, and so were called *Libertines. There were Ranters in the New England Colonies. See R. M. Jones, *Studies in Mystical Religion* (1923), 467–481; R. Knox, *Enthusiasm* (1950), 141, 172–175.

RAPPITES, the followers of Johann Georg Rapp (1757–1847), a German immigrant to the U.S. who organized the communal *Harmony Society.

RATIONALISM, a trend or system that overstresses the role of reason, either in relation to sense observation (philosophical rationalism, opposed to empiricism and positivism), or in relation to faith. Rationalism in this latter sense exalts reason and its autonomy or sufficiency and gives it primacy in religious matters. As a trend rationalism has been confined to no particular period; as a system it is a phenomenon of modern times. Philosophical rationalism manifested itself in the systems of R. Descartes, B. Spinoza, and G. Leibniz in the 17th and 18th centuries. Religious rationalism as a trend underlies systems that reject the spiritual and religious, most conspicuously materialism and naturalism. In patristic times it appeared as one strand in the doctrine of *Pelagianism. In the Middle Ages it was present in Abelard's trinitarian teaching, and later was an element in the theology of *nominalism. Modern rationalistic systems strongly affirm the autonomy of reason and reject revelation and faith, or at least neutralize these by reducing them to the level of human thought. The way was opened to an overt rationalism by the Renaissance, which introduced new modes of thinking and living. The movement toward the emancipation of reason that arose in 15th-cent. Italy spread to other European countries. Rationalists, in fact, were the *libertins* of France who drew the fire of B. *Pascal. In England systematic rationalism took the name and form of *deism, which rejected faith as opposed to the supremacy it attributed to reason. T. Hobbes, M. Tindal, J. Locke, and D. Hume in the 18th cent. advocated a "natural" religion, freed from revelation and incompatible with belief in, worship of, or devotion to the God of faith. In Germany rationalism came to the fore in the *Enlightenment (*Aufklärung*), and Lessing, Goethe, and Schiller were at its service after Reimarus (d. 1768) attacked the whole of revelation. It culminated in Kant's *Religion within the Limits of Reason* (1793).

Among Roman Catholics the same trend led to the rise of the Order of *Illuminati in Bavaria (1776). To meet the onslaught of rationalism, RC theologians G. Hermes (d. 1831) and A. Günther (d. 1863) undertook to show that Christian dogmas known from revelation are open to rational proof, an effort later condemned as *semirationalism (D 2738, 2829, 3035-56). In France the leaders of rationalism were Voltaire (d. 1778) and J. J. Rousseau (d. 1778) and the men of the *Encyclopédie*, whose ideas also exercised a strong influence in Germany. In the 20th cent. rationalism was one of the diverse elements discernible in the heterogeneous body of thought in RC *modernism; it has also been an active force in Protestant modernism and *liberal theology. In the second half of the 20th cent. the current rationalism has little use for a "natural religion." At the root of atheistic, existentialist and materialist systems is a debased rationalism in which reason not only refuses to leave room for faith but also denies its own powers to construct a valid metaphysics. Thus the only option left is simply between God and no God. In the rethinking of dogma and the life of the Church after Vatican Council II there is a noticeable rationalistic trend on the part of some Roman Catholics in the sense of a denial of the supernatural and the mysterious. This appears to be associated with a general trend toward secularism. See A. W. Benn, *History of English Rationalism in the Nineteenth Century* (2v., 1962); J. D. Collins, *God in Modern Philosophy* (1959); E. Cassirer, *Philosophy of the Enlightenment* (tr. F. Koelln and J. Pettegrove, 1951).

RATISBON, CONFERENCE OF, see RE-GENSBURG, CONFERENCE OF.

RAUSCHENBUSCH, WALTER (1861–1918), American Baptist theologian and architect of the *Social Gospel. He came from a family of German clergymen and prepared for the Baptist ministry at Rochester Theological Seminary, after studies in Germany and at the Univ. of Rochester. As a pastor in New York City (1886–97) he became deeply concerned with urban problems and joined with Christian Socialists and social reformers. R. accepted a call to the faculty of Rochester Theological Seminary in 1897 and taught there until his death. The publication of *Christianity and the Social Crisis* in 1907 established him as the recognized leader of the Social Gospel movement. Deeply and sincerely religious in its tone, the book pointed out the interest of the

Hebrew prophets in the social and political life of their nation and the condition of the poor and oppressed. He saw Jesus as the founder of a new society embracing all human needs, powers, and relations and contrasted the social impotence of the contemporary Church with the social power of Christianity in the apostolic age. *Christianizing the Social Order* (1912) insisted upon social justice and economic democracy as minimum requirements for building a Christian social order. More than 20,000 copies of his short manual, *The Social Principles of Jesus*, were distributed by the YMCA alone during 1916. His lectures at Yale Divinity School, *A Theology for the Social Gospel* (1917), discussed the social implications of sin and salvation and had the kingdom of God as its central theme. He saw the kingdom as a collective conception involving the whole social life of man. The solidarity of human society, whose progressive perfection would realize the divine kingdom of righteousness, was predicated on the indwelling of God in his world. The process of Christianizing society required the strengthening of its fraternal and cooperative elements and the rejection of its unchristian elements, e.g., competition, monopoly, the concentration of economic power, and the profit motive. See C. H. Hopkins, *Rise of the Social Gospel in American Protestantism* (1967).

REAL PRESENCE, expression denoting an actual and literally true presence of Christ's body and blood in the bread and wine of the Eucharist or Lord's Supper. The RC Council of Trent asserts that Christ's body and blood are really, truly, and substantially contained in the sacrament, and rejects a merely symbolic presence (see ZWINGLIANISM) or the *virtualism of John Calvin (D 883). The *Augsburg Confession (Art. X) of Lutheranism teaches that the body and blood of Christ are truly present and communicated to the recipients; the *Formula of Concord rejects the *Sacramentarians' interpretation of true presence as that of the Spirit or power of the absent

body of Christ, and affirms a "true and substantial presence" (Art. VII). Article XXVIII of the *Thirty-Nine Articles has received in the C of E and the *Anglican Communion both a symbolic and a realist interpretation. Not only the *Reformed Churches but all other non-Lutheran Protestant bodies reject the Real Presence. Those that recognize the Lord's Supper affirm a sacramental presence of Christ that is true, but either virtual or in some way figurative. The opposition to other teaching underlined by the word "real", then, is between the presence of the natural body of Christ and the presence of what is effected or symbolized by his body; or between a presence in and under the bread and wine of the sacrament and a presence evoked in the believer through faith and the sacramental symbolism.

The manner in which Christ's body and blood become really present is called in RC teaching *transubstantiation; this implies an abiding Real Presence (see TRANSIGNIFICATION). Lutherans, rejecting transubstantiation, assign the sacramental union itself as the reason for the Real Presence; and this presence is verified only in the actual celebration of the Lord's Supper (see CONSUBSTANTIATION). One Anglican form of expressing the manner of the Real Presence is called *receptionism.

REBAPTISM, the practice of repeating baptism; the subject of controversy (255–257) between St. Cyprian of Carthage and Pope Stephen I and again in the Reformation era. Cyprian's view, endorsed by three synods of African bishops, was that heretics or schismatics could not validly administer the sacraments of the Church. Accordingly, those who had received Novatianist baptism had to be rebaptized in order to be received into the Church. The Pope insisted that the practice of the Roman Church recognized baptism by heretics or schismatics as valid (see D 110). Cyprian accused Stephen of subverting church unity. The actual controversy remained unresolved, but the Roman view prevailed in practice and became universal. The controversy has often been an issue in discussions of the primacy of the pope. Rebaptism also is connected with the view of the *Anabaptists (re-baptizers). They did not consider *believer's baptism to be a repetition, however. Their view was that infant baptism is meaningless; baptism can only be received by one who has personally experienced faith and conversion; the baptism is simply and exclusively the outward profession of the inner experience. They were called rebaptizers because those who became Anabaptists and received believer's baptism had already received "water baptism." *INFANT BAPTISM.

RECEPTIONISM, a term invented for the theory of certain 19th-cent. Anglican theologians that in the Holy Eucharist the communicant really receives the body and blood of the Lord along with the bread and wine, which remain unchanged. The teaching of M. *Bucer in the 16th cent., an attempt to mediate between Lutheran and Zwinglian doctrine, was similar. *REAL PRESENCE; *TRANSUBSTANTIATION.

RECTOR (Lat. *regere*, to rule), applied in the Middle Ages to a priest appointed head of a church or university. It is used today in the C of E and the Protestant Episcopal Church to designate the chief pastor, who is responsible for control of worship and spiritual jurisdiction of the parish and has authority over any curate or other person on the parish staff. In continental Europe it is still a common title for the heads of universities, but in England only two colleges at Oxford have rectors. In Scottish universities rectors are elected officials. In RC usage the term refers to priests in charge of nonparochial churches, the heads of seminaries and of some universities, and the heads of the houses of certain orders, e.g., the Society of Jesus. In the U.S. a priest who actually administers a cathedral church, which is properly the bishop's church, is often called the rector.

RECUSANTS ("refusers"), a term that in its principal use in English law was applied to those, esp. but not exclusively papists, who refused to attend divine worship in the established Church. Recusancy laws were in effect from the reign of Elizabeth I until that of George III. Their frankly terroristic intent was to force the people to embrace the English Church, and to reduce to beggary, or drive from the country, or kill those who would not. Their effectiveness was enhanced by a ruling of a committee of theologians at the Council of Trent, among whom was D. Lainez, condemning the casuistry used at first by many Catholics to justify attendance. The harsh penalties for nonattendance included a fine ruinous to all but the very wealthy, various disabilities, and a prohibition of travel beyond 5 miles from one's home. One convicted had either to submit and renounce belief in papal supremacy or, if required by judges, to abjure the realm, i.e., to swear to leave the country and never return without permission of the crown. To fail to depart or to return without leave was a capital felony. The recusancy laws were not always and everywhere enforced with equal rigor. The number of recusants was greater in the North of England, especially in Lancashire, and in certain parts of Wales. See J. R. Roberts, *Critical Anthology of English Recusant Devotional Prose* (1966); J. A. Williams, NCE 12:135.

REFORM AND THE CHURCH. Both historically and from the nature of the Church the process of betterment and of renewal is a fact of church life. Reform, the taking of a new form, refers to the past, regaining the pristine form of life in the apostolic Church; it refers also to the future, to the eschatological ideal placed always before the Church: the building up of the body of Christ to perfect manhood, to the mature fullness of Christ (see Eph 4.13). Both ideals have motivated the many efforts at reform in church history. The desire to recreate the Church of the NT or to come close to the perfect sanctity that is the goal of the

Church have been primary factors in the emergence of almost all new church bodies in the history of Christianity. For example, a return to apostolic simplicity was the motivation not only of the monastic and mendicant orders but also of many lay evangelical movements of the Middle Ages. One of the key themes of the *Humiliati, *Waldenses, and *Lollards was that of evangelical poverty. The spectacle of wealth in the Church, the unworthiness of rich churchmen, was decried as perverting the true image of the Church, betraying the apostolic tradition, and stifling the gospel. Most often the lay evangelical movements led to an attack upon the institutional Church of worldly clerics, and the priesthood and sacraments came to be regarded as part of the institution. An eschatological motivation has usually characterized the apocalyptic or millenarian movements that have proclaimed the millennium, a kingdom of the just that with Christ as leader would prevail over all institutions of the wicked, including the institutional Church.

Reform in the Church. Both the lay evangelical and the apocalyptic types of reform have largely existed on the fringes of the RC and the Protestant Churches. In the major historical Churches there has been a belief that there is something in the essential being of the Church that cannot be reformed. The Church is holy, it is the spouse of Christ "without spot or wrinkle or any such thing" (Eph 5.27). Defects that exist arise from the weakness and sinfulness of members. Thus part of the process of renewal throughout church history has been understood as disciplinary reform, i.e., the correction of abuses by laws on church discipline, and by use of excommunication. Novatianists and the Donatists attempted to keep the Church holy by disciplinary rigorism. The centralization of authority and the codification of law in the medieval Church were reforms of ecclesiastical abuses. The first reaction to the evils in the Renaissance Church was also to seek disciplinary reform. The Council of *Trent gave much of its attention to the reform

decrees concerning ecclesiastical discipline. In the Churches of the Reformation and in their confessional documents church discipline was held out as one of the signs of the true, reformed Church (e.g., Belgic Confession, Art. 29; Scots Confession, Art. 18).

Reform of the Church. Disciplinary reform is described as reform *in* the Church, needed because of the weakness of the faithful. Reform *of* the Church, a purging, a remaking of its very being, is said to be the *Protestant principle, inadmissible in RC theology. *Ecclesia reformata, sed semper reformanda* (the Church reformed, but always in need of reform) has been regarded as central to the Protestant, but alien to the RC, teaching on the Church. The reason for the opposition of views is that the Reformation regarded the holiness of the Church to be the holiness of Christ its head; the Church as an institution, like the justified man, remained sinful; its forms, or visible structures, do not share intrinsically in the holiness of Christ; they are always reformable. RC teaching, however, regards many of the visible elements of the Church as essentials, as unalterable, and not in need of reform. Such essentials are viewed as instituted by Christ; the power to teach, to sanctify, and to govern in the Church are part of the communication by which he makes the Church inherently holy. These elements are not subject to reform.

Theological reflection in the 20th cent. has regarded this opposition as oversimplified. A deepened Protestant appreciation for the mystery of the Church has led to a sense of the need that the Church be faithful to its past. There are new evaluations of ministry, of tradition, of sacraments and liturgy, which recognize that these are essentials in the Church; that the holy Church is not exclusively the invisible Church. From the documents of Vatican II it is clear that there is no longer a refusal of Roman Catholics to speak of reform of the Church: "Christ summons the Church, as she goes her pilgrim way, to that continual reformation of which she always has need, insofar as she is an institution of men here on earth. Therefore, if the influence of events or of the times has led to deficiencies in conduct, in Church discipline, or even in the formulation of doctrine (which must be carefully distinguished from the deposit itself of faith), these should be rectified at the proper moment" (Vat II Ecum 6). The council speaks of renewal in every phase of the Church's life as having ecumenical importance. Protestants and Catholics share in a sense of the simultaneous holiness and sinfulness of the Church. They agree in the urgency of reform whereby the Church adapts itself as a servant Church to the needs of a world to be saved. The diversity of Protestant and Catholic belief in the nature of the Church does mean different acceptances of reform. But the shared desire for church unity is itself a part of Church renewal, of a desire to regain the ideal of the Church in its original design, and so to press on toward an ideal of holiness to be reached. See Y. Congar, *Vraie et fausse reforme dans l'Église* (1950). H. Küng, *The Council, Reform and Reunion* (tr. C. Hastings, 1963); R. E. McNally, *Reform of the Church* (1962); W. B. Blakemore, ed., *Renewal of the Church* (3v., 1963).

REFORMATIO LEGUM ECCLESIAS-TICARUM (*Reform of the Ecclesiastical Laws*), a book first published by J. Foxe in 1571, containing a system of order and discipline projected for the C of E to replace Roman canon law. An act of 1549 had empowered Edward VI to appoint a wide commission to compile a corpus; the work was taken in hand by a cabal, and presented to Parliament in 1553 a few months before the death of the King. In view of its Calvinism the assertion that it would have been sanctioned but for the accession of Mary Tudor is open to question.

REFORMATION, the religious changes occurring in the 16th and 17th cents. on the Continent and in the British Isles. The term itself did not come into general acceptance until the 19th cent.; the Reformers preferred to consider their efforts a renewal or restoration of the primitive purity of Christianity.

CONTINENTAL REFORMATION

The beginning of the Protestant Reformation is usually dated from 1517, with Martin Luther's *Ninety-Five Theses. Basically a religious movement, it was reinforced by complex cultural currents. Long before Luther, there had been persistent demands for reform to deal with incompetence and worldliness of clergy, pluralism of benefices, and a multiplicity of financial abuses. J. *Hus and J. Wycliffe had criticized the Church, questioned papal claims, and challenged commonly accepted doctrine on the sacraments and other theological issues, but their influence was localized and limited. By the 16th cent. new factors were present that were favorable to protest and reform: (1) the rise of national states; (2) a weakening of papal authority by the *Babylonian Captivity at Avignon, the *Great Western Schism, and the conciliar movement (see CONCILIARISM); (3) German resentment of domination by Pope and Emperor; (4) *humanism, which ridiculed *scholasticism and superstition, stressed biblical study in the original language, encouraged Bible translation into the vernacular, and accented NT standards of ethics; (5) the presence of a piety in Germany fostered by practical Christian mystics and such movements as *Devotio moderna; and (6) the invention of the printing press.

Martin Luther. Luther had no desire to divide the Church and at first had no quarrel with fundamental RC teachings. Conferences with papal representatives, written exchanges, the *Disputation of Leipzig, and threats of excommunication pushed him to further examination of the implications of his understanding of the gospel. By 1521, his views had changed radically. He asserted that both popes and councils had erred. He reinterpreted the sacraments, limiting them to two (or possibly three), denying that the Mass was a sacrifice, and disagreeing with the doctrine of *transubstantiation. He affirmed that every Christian is made a priest at baptism, and that the minister has no special power or status that sets him apart from the laity (see PRIESTHOOD OF ALL BELIEVERS). Basic to all of his conclusions was the concept of *justification by faith alone, which came by preaching the gospel of Jesus Christ; the Holy Scriptures that witnessed to Christ were for him the final authority in matters of doctrine. At the Diet of Worms (1521), he refused to recant any of his writings, and therefore was placed under the ban of the Empire and then excommunicated from the Church. Excluded from the RC Church, Luther believed that he and his followers still stood in continuity with the Catholic Church, which had been corrupted in the Middle Ages and was now being reformed. In reforming the liturgy, Luther retained much from the past; but the central elements of the Mass were omitted, and prominent place was given to reading Scriptures, preaching, and congregational singing. Catechisms were prepared for instructing children and adults, and public education was encouraged to enable people to read the Bible. Without the former episcopal structure, he had to devise an administrative system for the churches. Apostolic succession was rejected, and ministers were ordained without the aid of bishops. The "godly prince," as a member of the Church, was considered a suitable leader in reform, and the concept of the prince as *summus episcopus* became general, being reinforced by the principle *cuius regio, eius religio*, firmly established by the Peace of Augsburg (1555). Luther's attitude in the Peasants' War, his dispute with *Erasmus, and his loss of support from the German knights alienated many former sympathizers. Lutheranism spread, however, to Finland and the Scandinavian countries; and Luther's teachings permeated other lands (see LUTHERANISM).

Ulrich Zwingli. The Reformation in Switzerland began with Ulrich *Zwingli at Zurich. In Jan. 1519, he began his ministry there. Stricken by plague in 1520, he had a long period of convalescence, during which he committed himself more fully to emphasize justification by faith and the authority of the Scriptures. Gradually these emphases led him to oppose many Catholic practices, papal authority, the sacerdotal ministry, and finally the Mass as a sacrifice. After two public disputations in 1523, the magistrates voted that Zurich should be an evangelical city, images should be removed from churches, and the Mass should be abolished. Although Zwingli denied any dependence, he was familiar with Luther's writings, and his evangelical development probably owed something to them. At many points he differed from Luther, as in his interpretation of the Lord's Supper, his attitude toward the use of music in worship, and his view of the Church's role in society. Zwingli's work was continued by Henry *Bullinger, and their followers eventually merged with the other Reformed Churches of Switzerland.

John Calvin. The Reformer who did most to give form and substance to the *Reformed Church tradition was John *Calvin. At Basel, he published the first edition of the *Institutes of the Christian Religion* (1536), the monumental exposition of his distinctive teaching on predestination and election (see CALVINISM). Invited by *Farel to assist in reforming Geneva, Calvin soon won recognition by his learning and ability, and took the lead in drafting plans for a new *church order. Agreeing with Luther regarding the authority of Scriptures and the doctrine of justification by faith, as well as many other points. Calvin, perhaps because of his humanistic training, was more rationalistic and more systematic in formulating his theology and his conception of worship. A significant difference from Luther is his understanding of the Church's active role in ordering and changing society. Calvin sought to establish Geneva as a city where everyone assented to orthodox doctrine and observed Christian ethical standards, and where civil magistrates governed in conformity with the word of God. Calvin's views on worship were similar to those of Zwingli; unlike Luther, he did not regard liturgical forms as subject to human opinions. Where Luther held that absence of specific biblical instruction left a question to be decided by the Churches, Calvin held that only what the Bible directly commanded was permissible in the service of worship. His order of service included reading of the Scriptures, prayers, singing, and a lengthy sermon. Instrumental music and pictures were eschewed as distractions, and singing was restricted to Psalms or other biblical passages. Great emphasis was placed upon learned ministers having command of the Greek and Hebrew tongues so that they could expound the Scriptures. Public education was provided, and children were thoroughly instructed in the catechism and in direct teaching from Scripture. The Reformed Church in Switzerland was consolidated when Geneva and Zurich resolved differences over the Lord's Supper, stating their agreement in the *Zurich Consensus (Consensus Tigurinus) in 1549. The influence of Calvin was probably more widespread than that of Luther, partly because of his systematized theology in the *Institutes,* which went through five revisions and were translated into French, Latin, and English. His advice was sought by Protestants in many other countries, and he directly influenced the establishment of Reformed Churches in France, the Netherlands, and Scotland and the rise of the Puritans in England.

The Anabaptists. A third branch of Protestantism was the Anabaptist movement. This term has often been used to include all of the religious parties and individuals who could not be classified as Reformed, Lutheran, or Anglican. Only in recent years has careful research sorted out the tangled skeins of miscellaneous religious dissidents in the movement. There were such mystics as Caspar *Schwenkfeld; rationalistic anti-Trinitarians like Servetus and the Sozzini; and the Anabaptists proper, who called themselves Swiss Brethren. Originating at Zurich, these people believed that Luther, Zwingli, and Calvin had stopped the Reformation at a halfway point. Their early leaders, *Grebel, *Manz,

*Blaurock, and others, were university-educated and friends of Zwingli. They parted company with him over two points, *believer's baptism and freedom of the Church from control by civil magistrates. The essential emphasis of the Swiss Brethren was upon Churches made up only of baptized believers, freedom of the Church from the State, and an ethic of love. Believing *infant baptism not to be a genuine baptism, they baptized only those who had reached a responsible age; and only such belonged to the Church. Following literally the commands of Scripture, they refused to take oaths. Believing that the Bible forbade killing, they would not undertake military service. Since they believed that the duties of a civil official might require him to act contrary to Christian principles, they opposed office-holding in civil government. Considered a threat to public order, these people were fiercely persecuted; thousands of them died by drowning, burning, and hanging. Despite opposition, their numbers increased, and they found refuge in Poland, Moravia, and a few other localities. Today their ideas survive with the Mennonites and Hutterites. See H. J. Grimm, *Reformation Era* (1954); T. Lindsay, *History of the Reformation* (2v., 1906–07); J. T. McNeill, *History and Character of Calvinism* (1954); E. G. Schwiebert, *Luther and His Times* (1950); G. H. Williams, *Radical Reformation* (1962).

In the British Isles

At its inception, the English Reformation was prompted more by personal than by religious considerations, but other factors combined to produce genuine religious reforms. Most of the forces that contributed to a desire for reform on the Continent were present in England. Besides abuses that needed correction, there were the influence of such Christian humanists as John *Colet and Thomas More, renewed study of the Greek NT, vestiges of the *Lollard movement, and acquaintance with Luther's writings. It was Henry VIII's desire for an annulment of his marriage, however, that precipitated the break with

Rome. Supported by the laity in Parliament, Henry proceeded to reduce the clergy to submission. In 1531, Convocations acknowledged that he was "as far as the law of Christ allows, even the supreme head" of the Church in England. One year later, the clergy agreed not to approve any more canons without his consent. Thomas *Cranmer was consecrated abp. of Canterbury in 1533, and a few months later he declared Henry's marriage null and void. In 1534, Parliament passed the *Act of Uniformity, declaring Henry the "supreme head on earth of the Church of England." Denying that this step broke the continuity of Christ's Church, Henry maintained that he was simply restoring an original power of jurisdiction that had been usurped by the papacy. No alterations in doctrine or ceremonies were contemplated, but he suppressed monasteries and confiscated their properties, encouraged Bible reading, and sought to eliminate superstitious practices. Most of the clergy acquiesced in his renunciation of papal authority, but John Fisher, Bp. of Rochester, was put to death for denying the King's supremacy, as were some Carthusians and Thomas More. Among the bps. were Cranmer and Hugh *Latimer who had been influenced by Lutheran teachings and wished to inaugurate further reforms; but few of the clergy favored doctrinal innovations. To secure unity of religious belief, several doctrinal statements were issued during Henry's reign. The *Ten Articles (1536) dealt with three sacraments (baptism, penance, and the Eucharist), teaching the doctrine of the Real Presence, but not mentioning transubstantiation; emphasized the need to teach the Bible and the creeds to the people; declared that justification is by faith, confession, absolution, and amendment of life; and, while not disapproving Masses for the dead, invocation of saints, and the use of images, warned against excesses in these matters. One year later, the *Institution of a Christian Man* (*Bishops' Book) was issued as a handbook on Christian Faith for the ordinary man. Containing an exposition of the Apostles' Creed, the seven sacraments, the Ten Command-

ments, and the Lord's Prayer, it incorporated a statement on justification by faith and another that denied purgatory. In 1543 this work was revised and published as *A Necessary Doctrine and Erudition for Any Christian Man* (*King's Book). It explicitly affirmed transubstantiation and strongly emphasized celibacy of the clergy. An English translation of the Bible was authorized by the King, and a copy was ordered (1536) to be placed in every church. Thinking that he might need an alliance with the Schmalkaldic League, Henry briefly allowed a theological conference of English and Lutheran divines; but he abruptly ended their proceedings in 1539 by the *Six Articles Act. This "whip of six strings" asserted belief in transubstantiation, imposing a death penalty for denying it. Other articles forbade clerical marriage, denied the necessity of communion in both kinds for the laity, and approved the binding power of vows of chastity, auricular confession, and private Masses.

Impetus to additional reforms came during the reign of Edward VI. He was too young to assume personal rule, but the regencies of Somerset and Northumberland advocated Protestant doctrines. The presence of refugees from the Continent, such as Martin *Bucer, *Peter Martyr Vermigli, and Bernardino *Ochino, had considerable influence during this period. The major developments between 1547 and 1553 were: permission of clerical marriage, issuance of the *Book of Common Prayer, and publication of the *Forty-Two Articles. The Prayer Book was largely the work of Cranmer. The first Prayer Book (1549) changed the Mass into the Lord's Supper, allowed communion in both kinds, and was in the vernacular. Some phrases were ambiguous, making possible an interpretation of transubstantiation. This book was unsatisfactory to many, and a revision appeared in 1552. By this time, Cranmer had rejected the doctrine of the Real Presence, and everything suggesting it was omitted. The communicant received bread and wine with the words, "eat [drink] this in remembrance." References to purgatory and prayers for the dead were also left out, as was the rubric requiring the minister to wear alb and cope. The threefold ministry was retained, including apostolic succession, but the term "minister" replaced "priest" in many places. The altar was called a "table" and was placed in the body of the church.

In 1553, Mary Tudor succeeded Edward. Daugher of Catherine of Aragon, she was a staunch Roman Catholic and resented all Reformers. At her instigation, Parliament revoked all laws by which religious changes had been instituted, except that monastic properties could not be retrieved. The Act of Supremacy was revoked, the Book of Common Prayer discontinued, and the Mass restored. Cardinal Pole was put in charge of restoring the former order; other exiled priests were recalled; papal supremacy was again recognized; and old laws against heresy were revived. Abp. Cranmer and Bps. Latimer, Ridley, and Hooper were among the nearly 300 persons executed during Mary's reign. Many ministers fled to the Continent, where they became more thoroughly imbued with Reformed doctrines. Although her subjects accepted the restoration of Catholicism, many became alienated by her burning so many enemies. Moreover, her marriage to Philip II was unpopular, and her joining him in a war against France resulted in the loss of Calais, England's last possession on the Continent.

Elizabeth I sought a religious settlement acceptable to most of her subjects. A new Act of Supremacy was passed in 1559, declaring Elizabeth the "supreme governor of the realm" in both ecclesiastical and temporal affairs. At the same time, an Act of Uniformity adopted the Prayer Book of 1552, with some modifications. Most of the Marian bishops were replaced by new ones, but only about 200 of the lower clergy refused to comply with the new requirements. The *Thirty-Nine Articles were published in 1563, and subscription by the clergy was required by an act of 1571. With this act the direction of Elizabeth's settlement was clear. She wished a Church that was clearly Protestant in its main tenets,

but which retained as much of the ritual as possible and allowed some breadth of interpretation.

Elizabeth's policies were a blow to Catholic hopes, and they also disappointed many Protestants. Catholics continued to seek restoration of England to their faith, hoping for aid from France and Spain. Elizabeth was excommunicated by Pius V in 1570, a series of anti-Catholic laws was passed, and intrigues formed around the imprisoned Mary Stuart until exposure of the Babington Plot led to her execution in 1587. The defeat of Philip's Armada in 1588 brought an end to the fear of invasion, but strong anti-Catholic feelings had been engendered that were to become a legacy of Anglo-Saxon Protestantism for generations. Still, many Protestants considered the Elizabethan settlement a compromise. Opposition flared up around 1565–66 in the Vestiarian Controversy, as Abp. Parker tried to enforce the wearing of clerical vestments in public worship. Those who opposed wearing of alb and cope also objected to making the sign of the cross on a child's head at baptism and kneeling during communion. Many objected to the Book of Common Prayer in its entirety. This party, made up largely of Marian exiles enamored of the doctrine and practice of the Reformed Churches, was variously dubbed "Precisians," "Disciplinarians," and "Puritans." By 1570, some Puritans tried to make the national Church Presbyterian, sending two "Admonitions" to Parliament in 1572, objecting to the existing system, and giving reasons why their proposal was in accord with the Word of God. Although they were unsuccessful in obtaining their desire, a quasi-Presbyterian system was carried on within the C of E in the next few years. By 1580, a Separatist wing of Puritanism had emerged, adopting the *gathered-church idea and forming congregations independent of the C of E. Robert *Browne and Robert Harrison were early leaders in this movement, and it was continued by others to become the Independents or Congregationalists. The Baptists were an offshoot from them in 1609.

In Scotland, the Reformation took a different course. Similar factors contributing to the English Reformation were present, but it was complicated by pro-French and pro-English parties and by political rivalries among the Scottish nobility. Lutheran writings had been disseminated there in the 1520s, and the first martyr was Patrick *Hamilton in 1528. Efforts to stamp out heresy were unavailing, however, and a strong Protestant party developed. After George Wishart, its leading spirit, was burned at the stake in 1546, his friends retaliated by murdering Card. Beaton, Abp. of St. Andrews. Wishart's mantle fell upon John *Knox, who was taken prisoner by the French and served 19 months as a galley slave. Released in 1549, he went to England, but fled to the Continent at the accession of Mary and was greatly influenced during his exile by Calvin and Bullinger. Back in Scotland for a few months in 1555 and 1556, he won support for reform, which resulted in the covenanting of some nobles to establish a Church in accord with the Word of God. At the invitation of these "Lords of the Congregation," he returned to Scotland in 1559 and assumed leadership of the Reformation. With military aid from England, French control of Scotland was broken. In 1660, the Scottish Parliament adopted the *Scottish Confession prepared by Knox, and proceeded to reject the authority of the pope, outlaw the Mass, and revoke all laws not consonant with the new Confession. The first Book of *Discipline outlined a plan of church government generally patterned after Calvin's system, but providing for superintendents who had many former functions of bps. and of lay readers. The *Geneva Catechism was ordered to be used for instructing children. A *Book of Common Order was adopted in 1564, which showed the influence of Calvin and was approved by him. Mary Stuart returned to Scotland in 1561, after the death of her husband, Francis II of France. Refusing to assent to the new laws, she was determined to restore the RC faith. Marrying her cousin Darnley, she was suspected of complicity in his murder and was forced to renounce the throne. Escaping from prison, she fled to England, where Elizabeth held her prisoner until her execution in 1587. The work of Knox was continued by Andrew *Melville, who was instrumental in formulating the second Book of Discipline and the subsequent transfer of administrative powers of superintendents to presbyteries (see PRESBYTERY), thereby giving finished form to Scottish Presbyterianism. Scottish worship followed the Reformed pattern, with singing being confined to paraphrases of the Psalms; the first Psalter was issued in 1564.

In Wales, the course of the Reformation largely followed that in England; but attempts to impose the doctrines and ceremonies of the C of E upon Ireland were unsuccessful except around Dublin and in northern Ireland, where Scottish colonization was undertaken by James I. See Hughes RE; G. Donaldson, *Scottish Reformation* (1960); A. G. Dickens, *English Reformation* (1964).

REFORMED, as a proper adjective, Protestant in the Calvinist tradition, distinct esp. from Protestant in the Lutheran tradition. Within the Calvinist tradition itself, the term Reformed suggests continental origins, while the term Presbyterian denotes origins in England and Scotland. Reformed also connotes a designation on the basis of doctrine; Presbyterian, on the basis of polity. As a common adjective, reformed may simply refer to Churches originating in the Reformation. *REFORMED CHURCHES.

REFORMED CHURCH IN AMERICA, the oldest Protestant denomination with a continuous history in the United States. The probable date of organization is April 10, 1628, at New Amsterdam (Manhattan Island), under the direction of Jonas *Michaelius. The Dutch Reformed churches of N.Y. and N.J. remained under the ecclesiastical control of the Reformed Church of the Netherlands throughout the colonial period. Until 1763 the Dutch language alone was used. When autonomy was granted in

1772, the denomination had 100 churches and 40 clergymen. The first church constitution was adopted in 1792, an adaptation of the articles on *church order of the Synod of *Dort (1618–19). The liturgy framed by the same synod, one derived from earlier sources in the Reformation, was also adopted, with the Nicene and Athanasian Creeds appended. The forms for the sacraments were required to be used; other forms were given optional usage. The *Heidelberg Catechism, the *Belgic Confession, and the Canons of the Synod of Dort were made authoritative *doctrinal standards.

Although the Reformed Church in America did not share in the large growth experienced by the Protestant denominations that moved with the American frontier in the 19th cent., significant growth came in mid-century with a new Dutch immigration to the Midwest. The 20th cent. found a somewhat even balance between the eastern and western branches of the Church. While a gradual growth in number of churches came in a few southern states, the Reformed Church remains for the most part a northern Church. The larger number of its churches are located in rural and semirural areas. Domestic missions are carried on among Indians in the West, among Negroes in Ala. and in inner-city efforts, in schools and churches in Ky., and in a province of Mexico. Dutch immigration to Canada in the past quarter-century added 30 new churches. Foreign missions begun early in the 19th cent. are continuing in a number of countries. The Church has operated or been associated with four colleges, including Rutgers, founded under Reformed Church auspices in 1766. Two theological seminaries, in New Brunswick, N.J., and in Holland, Mich., are operated by the denomination. The *Church Herald* is the official periodical. In 1968 the Reformed Church numbered 902 churches, with an inclusive membership of 378,000.

Theology remains that of a moderate Calvinism. Extreme points of view are avoided. In eucharistic teaching, and in the stronger emphasis given preaching than the sacrament, the Church holds positions closer to those of *Zwingli than of Calvin. In polity the model of *presbyterian government is followed. The denomination has participated freely in the ecumenical movement since its inception. Attempts at merger in 1970 with the Presbyterian Church in the U.S., however, were defeated in 1969 because of grass-roots opposition in the Reformed Church itself. See E. Eenigenburg, *Brief History of the Reformed Church in America* (1958).

REFORMED CHURCH IN THE UNITED STATES, a title used by two *Reformed denominations: (1) A body organized in Philadelphia in 1747, which adopted the name German Reformed Church in 1793 and from 1863 used the title Reformed Church in the United States. The Church joined in the merger forming the *Evangelical and Reformed Church in 1934, which since 1959 has been part of the *United Church of Christ. (2) The former Eureka Classis of the original Reformed Church in the U.S., organized in S.Dak. in 1910, which remained out of the 1934 merger. It continues to use the name Reformed Church in the U.S. The Church follows the doctrine of the *Heidelberg Catechism and is governed by an annual *classis meeting. In 1968 membership was 2,500, in 20 congregation.

REFORMED CHURCHES, those bodies that share a religious and theological heritage derived mainly from the circle of Protestant Reformers having John *Calvin (1509–64) as its chief spokesman; they include both Reformed and Presbyterian denominations. The term "Reformed" was used in an informal and unofficial way in the 16th cent. by the various branches of the Protestant movement. The tense controversy on the Eucharist between the successors of Luther and Calvin near the end of that century did much to compel the upholders of the *Formula of Concord (1577) to adopt the title "Lutheran" in a symbolical and official sense. Calvin's followers became known as "Reformed." The distinction slowly became accepted in the various countries in which the Reformation movement was strong. Followers of Ulrich *Zwingli (1484–1531) also had a claim upon the name "Reformed," but they became attached finally to the developing Calvinistic Church, which, unlike the Zwinglian movement, became international. The Reformed Churches spread in the Reformation period from Calvin's Geneva to France (see HUGUENOTS), the Netherlands, Germany, eastern Europe (Poland, Bohemia, Hungary, Transylvania), Scotland (see CHURCH OF SCOTLAND), England, Ireland, and North America. In some instances, as in the Netherlands and Scotland, the Reformation functioned as the religious phase of movements for political independence and imparted much of the power of these movements; political and religious motivations were thoroughly intermingled. English and American Puritanism, often mistakenly regarded as rather pure forms of Calvinism, and hence Reformed, represent instead an admixture of various Reformation sources, among which the Reformed component is significant but not controlling. Most American Puritans adopted a congregational polity. The complete Reformed tradition was maintained in N.A. by the Presbyterian Churches of English and Scottish origin and by the Reformed Churches established by Dutch immigrants. Contemporary Reformed Churches are associated internationally in the *Alliance of the Reformed Churches; the Alliance includes most of the Presbyterian and Reformed denominations.

The Reformed theological tradition is characterized by a considerable number of variations on theological themes originally proposed by Calvin (see CALVINISM). Rather than unanimity on the meaning of such topics as God's sovereignty, divine *predestination, the manner of Christ's presence in the Eucharist (see REAL PRESENCE), and the ethical task of the Christian man, there is a kind of general agreement as to the proper accent and point of view. In one manner or another the Reformed Churches have been distinguished by their emphasis upon the duty of Christians to do the will of a sovereign God at all costs. Every area of human experience, personal and social, is included in the field of effort. Religious activism has thus typified many of the Reformed Churches and their members. There have also been advocates of mystical piety, which frequently has provided the inspiration and direction for church action. The old Reformed accent upon God's choice of certain persons for salvation, and his repudiation of others (divine election and reprobation), is scarcely heard in any of the Reformed Churches today, though in earlier centuries various views on the subject were a main topic of debate and conversation (see ARMINIANISM; DORT, SYNOD OF). Most Reformed Churches today appear to be more Zwinglian than Calvinistic in their understanding of how Christ is present in the sacrament of the Eucharist. Calvin himself held to the Real Presence "in a spiritual manner." Today most observances lean toward the notion of Zwingli, that the Eucharist is simply a memorial of what Christ did for us long ago in his death. For the most part the Reformed tradition has placed emphasis upon the past, present, and future aspects of the Eucharist.

The Reformed Churches follow a middle-of-the-road attitude in worship procedures. Avoiding, on the one hand, the highly liturgical emphases of RC, Anglican, and other Churches, and, on the other, the casual, informal worship practices of some Protestant bodies, most Reformed Churches have been semi-liturgical. Liturgical forms are used in moderation, mainly in connection with the celebration of the sacraments. Free prayers esp. have marked Reformed worship services. The Reformed Churches employ the presbyterian form of church government, the main principles of which are the following: (1) the Church of Christ is a living communion of the one people of God with the one Christ as their head; (2) Jesus Christ is the only head of his Church; (3) all authority in the Church is received from Christ; (4) representative governing bodies, called *courts, function on several levels; (5) the Church is governed by *elders (clergymen and elected laymen); and (6) the local churches, clergymen, elders, and deacons all on their own level are equal. See J. T. McNeill, *History and Character of Calvinism* (1954).

REFORMED CHURCHES, ALLIANCE OF THE, see ALLIANCE OF THE REFORMED CHURCHES.

REFORMED EPISCOPAL CHURCH, a Church founded in New York City in 1873 by Bp. G. D. *Cummins, and a small group of other members of the Protestant Episcopal Church who felt that tendencies toward Catholic doctrine and ritual were too strong to be resisted within the Anglican Communion. Their movement had gained cohesion from the formation of the Society to Promote Evangelical Religion in 1868 and from the organization of an American branch of the *Evangelical Alliance the previous year. Bp. Cummins's wholehearted participation in the meeting of the Evangelical Alliance at New York in 1873 and his demand for *intercommunion and exchange of pulpits between the Protestant Episcopal Church and evangelical Protestant Churches occasioned the split. No exodus of low churchmen materialized, however, and Cummins's group remained essentially a minority faction. By the consecration of Bp. C. E. Cheney in 1873, the new Church secured episcopal succession. Bp. Cheney was followed as presiding bishop by Bp. Samuel Fallows in 1889. The Reformed Episcopal Church then had 15 clergymen and about 1,200 members and had itself been torn by dissension and schism. Bp. Fallows brought about a reunion with the Reformed Church of England (Canada) in 1894 and commenced the foreign mission work of the Church with a station in India in 1899. In Puerto Rico shortly afterward the Reformed Episcopal Church supported Manuel Ferrando and raised him to the episcopate of an independent Church of Jesus. Additional overseas missions were developed in the 20th cent. in South Africa and the Sudan. In 1927 the Church united with the *Free Church of England. In 1963 there were 64 churches and some 7,000 members of the Reformed Episcopal Church.

As a conservative protest against the influence of the *Oxford movement, the Church adopted a revision of the *Thirty-Nine Articles and the American Book of Common Prayer of 1785 as doctrinal standards. This provisional version of the Prayer Book differed in some details from that adopted in 1789, which, with revisions, has remained the standard of the parent Church. (See AMERICAN PRAYER BOOK.) Both the ordination ritual and the communion service in the 1785 version are so worded as to rule out any interpretation of the ministry as a sacramental priesthood or of the holy communion as anything but a symbolic sharing in the Lord's Supper. In its polity, the Reformed Episcopal Church has been equally conservative, keeping the forms of the Protestant Episcopal Church, but with a virtual autonomy for local congregations. *Episcopacy is retained, not as being of divine right, but simply as an ancient, desirable form of polity.

REFORMED MENNONITE CHURCH, a small, conservative body established by John Herr (1782–1850) at Strasburg, Pa., in 1812. The foundation was the culmination of a movement, begun by Herr's father, Francis, away from the established Mennonite Church in order to return to the primitive form of Mennonite doctrine and practice. See MennEnc 4:267–270.

REFORMED METHODIST CHURCH, a separation from the Methodist Episcopal Church, organized at Readsborough, Vt., in 1814. While retaining Methodist *conferences, the new Church rejected *episcopacy and held strongly to the autonomy of the local congregation. Doctrines included *entire sanctification, *healing, and *pacifism; the Church was strongly antislavery.

In the 19th cent. it reached a membership of approximately 5,000, principally in northern New England and New York. There were, however, only a few hundred members when the Church in 1942 became the North Eastern District of the Churches of Christ in Christian Union. See HistAmMeth 1:622–624; E. T. Clark, *Small Sects in America* (rev. ed., 1949), 60.

REFORMED METHODIST UNION EPISCOPAL CHURCH, a Methodist body of about 16,000 members. It was organized in 1885 at Charleston, S.C., by a group who had withdrawn from the African Methodist Episcopal Church because of a disagreement centering in an election of the ministerial delegates to the *General Conference. Beginning as a nonepiscopal denomination, the Church in 1896 adopted *episcopacy, a bishop of the Reformed Episcopal Church consecrating the first bishop. In 1916 the denomination embraced the polity and doctrines of the Methodist Episcopal Church. See HistAmMeth 3:595.

REFORMED NEW CONGREGATIONAL METHODIST CHURCH, a small denomination organized in 1916 by J. A. Sander of the Independence Mission, and Earl Wilcoxen, an evangelist of the Congregational Methodist Church. While retaining Methodist doctrine, the Church has an independent rather than a *connectional polity (see INDEPENDENCY). It particularly opposes the use of jewelry and personal adornment, secret societies, and divorce for any reason. There were in 1968 about 500 members, in eight churches. See I. L. Holt and E. T. Clark, *World Methodist Movement* (1956), 130.

REFORMED PRESBYTERIAN CHURCH, Evangelical Synod, formed in 1965 by the older Scottish body, the Reformed Presbyterian Church in North America, and the Evangelical Presbyterian Church. (See BIBLE PRESBYTERIAN CHURCH, COLLINGS-WOOD SYNOD). This body attempts to be biblically centered in its faith and life, subscribes to the *Westminster Confession and *Westminster Catechisms, and has attempted in the past to have recognition in the U.S. constitution that God is the supreme power, that Christ is the ruler of nations, and that the Scriptures should be recognized as the source of all faith and life. The denomination sings psalms and observes *closed communion. In 1968 there were about 110 congregations, with about 10,000 members. The body holds an annual synod and publishes the *Reformed Presbyterian Reporter.*

REFORMED PRESBYTERIAN CHURCH of North America, see REFORMED PRESBYTERIAN CHURCH, EVANGELICAL SYNOD.

REFORMED ZION UNION APOSTOLIC CHURCH, a small Methodist body, organized as the Zion Union Apostolic Church in 1869 at Boydton, Va., by J. R. Howell of the African Methodist Episcopal Church. He was first elected president, but in 1874, by a change in the constitution, he was elected bishop for life. Later, disputes completely disrupted the Church. It was reorganized in 1882 by J. M. Bishop under its present name. See HistAmMeth 3:595.

REFORMKATHOLIZISMUS, a term first used in 1898 by Joseph Müller (1855–1942), a German priest-editor and literary critic, to describe the work of prominent Catholic intellectuals trying to reform and renew the Church. These intellectuals came from several countries but were preponderantly German; and while some were still active after World War I or even after World War II, their collective achievement was greatest in the two decades before 1914. The so-called "Reform Catholics" did not constitute a group of even loosely united personalities with the same specific aims; at most they were agreed on trying to make Catholicism more contemporary and effective spiritually and intellectually. Among them were Franz Xavier Kraus, noted art historian and long an opponent of Catholic political activity; Herman Schell, professor of apologetics at Würzburg, who wrote against Catholic exclusiveness and in favor of understanding with other communions; Albert Ehrhard, professor of church history at Freiburg, who stressed the Catholic need to accept science; and Carl Muth, publisher of *Hochland*, who called for a Catholic acceptance of realism and of the secular contribution in German literature. Still other less well known Catholic scholars attempted to organize an anti-Index movement (1907). In the heated debates that occurred among different Catholic groups just before World War I, "Reform Catholics" were often erroneously identified as modernists. See W. Spael, *Das katholische Deutschland im 20. Jahrhundert* (1964).

REGENSBURG, CONFERENCE OF, the meeting on reunion in 1541 between German Protestants and Catholics. It was the high point in attempts at reconciliation sponsored by the Emperor Charles V. The earlier Conference of *Hagenau (June 1540) and the Disputation of *Worms (Nov. 1540–Jan. 1541) had not succeeded but had created an atmosphere of dialogue. In spite of suspicion at the imperial attempts, Pope Paul III sent Card. Gasparo Contarini (1483–1542) as his legate to Regensburg. The Conference opened on April 5, 1541. The Protestant spokesmen were: P. *Melanchthon, M. *Bucer, Pistorius (d. 1583), and Caspar Cruciger (Creutzinger; 1504–48). John *Calvin was also present. The Catholics were J. *Eck, Julius von Pflug (1499–1564), and Johann Gropper (1503–59). The basis of discussion was a 23-article statement drawn up mainly by Bucer and Gropper, and later called the *Regensburg Book*. By May 2, 1541, the discussions had reached a statement of agreement not only on *original sin and *total depravity but also on the crucial issue of justification. The influence on Contarini of G. *Seripando's *double-justice theory seems to have helped the

Catholic party accept a formula on justification agreeable to the Protestants, while they in turn agreed to the place of good works. The Conference came to an impasse, however, on the subject of the nature of the Church, the teaching authority of the Pope, and the Eucharist. In addition there was suspicion on the part of both Rome and Martin Luther that the essential doctrinal opposition did not admit of compromise or concession. The Emperor ended the Conference July 29, 1541, with the *Interim of Regensburg, pending a general council. When at Trent in 1547 the Regensburg formula on justification was examined, it was rejected. See Jedin Trent 1:377–389; Léonard HistProt 1:242–245.

REGIMINIS APOSTOLICI, a bull of Alexander VII dated Feb. 15, 1665, which imposed on four recalcitrant French bishops —Caulet, Buzenval, Pavillon, and Henri Arnauld—the admission that five propositions previously condemned were heretical and were in fact taught by Cornelius *Jansen in his work *Augustinus*. The bishops demurred: the Church can censure but cannot impute authorship infallibly (Antoine *Arnauld's famous distinction between *droit* and *fait*). The bishops bade their people accept the formulary "as to law but not fact." Alexander VII condemned this directive and planned a trial but died in 1667. Clement IX proved conciliatory and accepted from the bishops a modified formulary (see PEACE OF THE CHURCH). His nuncio Bargellini remarked, quite prematurely, "Jansenism is dead." See F. Mourret, *History of the Catholic Church* (tr. N. Thompson), 6:412–415; DTC 1:728.

REGIUM DONUM (royal gift), an annual grant of money to *Nonconformist ministers in England, Scotland, and Ireland. The custom was started by Charles II, who, after the *Declaration of Indulgence of 1672, ordered 600 pounds distributed among Presbyterian ministers throughout Ulster; from 1690 to 1869 Presbyterian ministers in Ireland received financial aid. In England and Scotland the custom was not firmly established until 1723, when George I provided an allowance for needy widows of Nonconformist clergymen. By 1827 the gift had been extended to include Presbyterians, Baptists, and Congregationalists; but in 1851 it was discontinued, in part because of the wishes of the recipients themselves.

REGNANS IN EXCELSIS, the bull of Pius V, issued Feb. 25, 1570, excommunicating Queen *Elizabeth I of England. The document refers to her as the "servant of iniquity," the "pretended queen of England." It blames her for claiming "the place of the supreme head of the Church throughout all England," and lists her heresies and changes of Catholic doctrine and practice. She is therefore formally declared a heretic, and is excommunicated; her claim to the throne is nullified, and her subjects absolved of all allegiance and loyalty. The bull resulted from a formal trial held in Rome against Elizabeth. Its issuance marked the final severance of England from Rome and the beginning of harsher penal laws against Catholic *recusants. See Hughes RE 3:418–420.

REGULAR BAPTIST CHURCHES, GENERAL ASSOCIATION OF, see GENERAL ASSOCIATION OF REGULAR BAPTIST CHURCHES.

REGULAR BAPTISTS, a name that distinguished Particular from Separate Baptists during the *Great Awakening. The term had its chief significance in the South, where Shubael *Stearns and Daniel *Marshall, Separate Baptists from New England, labored as revivalists. The Separates were characterized by emotional preaching, prejudice against educated ministers, and reluctance to accept the *Philadelphia Confession. The Separates and Regulars united in N.C. (1777) and Va. (1787). A group called Regular Baptists exists today

and claims continuity with the original English Baptists. This body is not listed in the *Yearbook of American Churches.* See W. L. Lumpkin, *Baptist Foundations in the South* (1961). *BAPTISTS.

REICHSBRUDERSCHAFT JESU CHRISTI, since 1954 the name of the Judenchristliche Reichsbruderschaft, founded in 1952 by the Polish journalist Abram Poljak. *HEBREW CHRISTIAN CONGREGATION.

RELIEF CHURCH, a body formed by secession from the Church of Scotland, and organized in 1761, in defense of the rights of the congregation in the appointment of ministers. The leader of the protest "for the relief of Christians oppressed in their Christian privileges" was Thomas Gillespie (1708–74). The Relief Church and the United Secession Church merged to form the *United Presbyterian Church in 1847. *UNITED FREE CHURCH.

RELIGION, PSYCHOLOGY OF, a field of psychological inquiry concerned with the phenomena of religious belief and practice. As a special discipline it has taken several forms that differ from one another in the sources of data and in methods of investigation. Theological psychology of religion seeks to resolve theological data into terms meaningful from the viewpoint of psychology; philosophical psychology of religion aims at the philosophical analysis of the operations of the psyche involved in religious belief and practice; and analytical, or psychoanalytical, psychology of religion begins with clinical data and speculates on the role and function of religion in the integration of the human psyche. More especially the name is given to the discipline that employs the methods of a positive science to study the manifestations of religion in individuals and groups. This discipline collects, arranges, and classifies its observations; it seeks to determine the causal factors operative in the arousal and development of religious attitudes, convictions, and forms of behavior. As understood in this sense, it appeared as a special discipline only in the latter part of the 19th century. It is not yet fully organized as a science; nor has it completely shaken itself free of a preoccupation with extraordinary events and psychopathological manifestations, a focusing of attention that has retarded its development. Important advances have been made, however, and the valuable research being conducted in the field is reflected in the number and quality of the reviews and periodicals devoted to the subject. The discipline is closely associated with the study of comparative religion, the sociology of religion, and cultural anthropology. The competence of the discipline does not extend to the evaluation of religious experience in terms of objective validity, a judgment that belongs properly to theology, although the theologian finds the psychology of religion a valuable ancillary discipline in reaching his conclusions. In the field of pastoral theology particularly, in matters such as counseling, vocational guidance, catechetics, the formation of moral judgment, preaching, and liturgical activity, studies undertaken by the psychology of religion have proved most useful. For an excellent select bibliography of the field, see A. Godin, NCE 12:258–261.

RELIGION, SOCIOLOGY OF, the study of religions in their sociocultural context. This point of view regards religion either as an institution emerging with other institutions from the conditions of the larger society or as a unique subculture or set of subcultures interacting with other subcultures in cooperation or conflict. The discipline has gone through several stages. First some classical social theorists in the early 20th cent. took religion as one major institution to be integrated into their great social schemes. Max Weber (1864–1920) first coined the name and is often referred to as its founder. His interest in the sociological analysis of religion was shared by Émile Durkheim (1858–1917), as well as by his friend and collaborator Ernst *Troeltsch (1865–1923). After

World War II, esp. in the U.S., the sociology of religion entered another stage, in which it received increasing academic interest. This revival developed two distinct approaches: one can be considered a technical branch of academic sociology; the other, of broader scope, stems from what is called *Religionswissenschaft,* a term that has acquired a meaning equivalent to "history of religions."

Academic Sociology of Religion. The first is represented by Thomas O'Dea, who treats substantive issues under two heads: functionalist and developmental theories. The functionalist treatment, leaning heavily on Durkheim, looks at religion as having an important role in the maintenance of general society or culture—most often that of providing meaning in the face of life's uncertainties and the inevitabilities of sickness and death. Developmental theory, stemming from Weber and popularized in the U.S. by Talcott Parsons, concentrates on aspects otherwise neglected: the role of religion in social change, its conflict with other elements in the social system, and typical developmental sequences in the growth of particular religions. This approach lists types of generalizations arrived at through the empirical study of religion: the likely sequence of development, the functional significance of religion to social stability, the role of religion in innovation and change, the relationship between historical developments and religious ideas, and the possible options open to religious movements and their probable consequences. Ordinarily these generalizations, although based on historical and other empirical findings, belong to theoretical sociology. Increasingly, however, such generalizations are either supported or challenged by strictly empirical surveys and studies. The two outstanding research centers are at the Univ. of Chicago and the Univ. of California at Berkeley.

Religionswissenschaft Approach. Under the influence of Joachim Wach (1898–1955), whose *Sociology of Religion* (1947) is already something of a classic in the field, the principal center for this approach became the Univ. of Chicago. Max Müller first used *Religionswissenschaft* in 1867 to describe the search for the "universal essence" of religion, but the "history of religions" approach has become much broader. Mircea Eliade suggested that the attempt to grasp the essence of the phenomena of religion by physiology, psychology, sociology, economics, linguistics, art, or any other study is false if it misses the unique and irreducible element in it—the element of the sacred. Nevertheless, assuming such irreducibility of religious phenomena, the approach does make use of all disciplines in conjunction with detailed historical studies of particular religions. One of Eliade's collaborators, Joseph Kitagawa, divides this approach into historical and systematic subdivisions. Under the first come the general history of religion and the histories of specific religions; under the second come phenomenological, comparative, sociological, and psychological studies of religion. Kitagawa suggests that the crucial problem is the development of coordination and cooperation with historians who are competent in auxiliary disciplines as well as scholars in related subjects.

Relation to Other Disciplines. An accurate historical account of the cultural conditions and development of particular religions is obviously presupposed in the *Religionswissenschaft* approach; it is also the groundwork for such theoretical systems as those of Durkheim and Weber. Disciplines whose relationships need to be clarified include the philosophy and the psychology of religion, as well as academic sociology and *Religionswissenschaft* themselves. To clarify them, the three elements common to most religions should be distinguished: the conceptual-philosophical, the personal-mystical, and the sociohistorical. The purpose of the philosophy of religion should be the philosophical analysis of the conceptual element in given religions; that it is not always such is partly a lack of clarity about the nature of the discipline throughout the history of the philosophy of religion. Psychology of religion, a study of the personal-mystical elements, should be

considered with psychological studies of religious men, whether contemporary or historical; in fact, much contemporary psychology of religion concerns itself with conversion, atheism, and myths, and with the relation between religion and psychiatry. In relating *Religionswissenschaft* to general history and sociology, the latter can be taken as an attempt to study man in society, to investigate the conditions and consequences of living in one or another type of society. Sociology thus views religion either as a function of society or as related to the conditions of society. *Religionswissenschaft*, however, while its point of view is generally social as well as historical, insists on treating religious phenomena as irreducible even while relating them to psychological or sociological factors. It may also be worthwhile to relate the sociology of religion to the sociology of knowledge, an important but relatively uncultivated field that goes back to Karl Mannheim's *Ideology and Utopia* (1929). Sociology of knowledge turns the instruments of social analysis inward, reflecting on the work of communities of knowers. This has been done mostly with respect to sciences other than social, but a number of social scientists recognize the need for subjecting their own community to this analysis. What this suggests for the sociology of religion is that its practitioners should subject their work to critical self-evaluation.

Importance for Theology. The sociology of religion supplies material for theological, conceptual analysis, which in turn supplies criteria for evaluating religious experience. Beyond this obvious relationship sociology of religion can supply for theology: (1) a cultural background against which theological statements become meaningful in a way they often are not in the abstract; (2) the related possibility of understanding historical dogmatic statements when external controls are not available (as with the literary genre approach in biblical studies); (3) a ground for the comparison of theologies in an ecumenical spirit; and (4) concrete, dynamic details on how religion is actually lived—something that can safeguard theological conceptualization from excessive idealism. See E. Durkheim, *Elementary Forms of the Religious Life: A Study in Religious Sociology* (Fr. original, 1912; Eng. tr. J. Swain, 1947); M. Weber, *Sociology of Religion* (Ger. original, 1922; Eng. tr. E. Fischoff, 1963); M. Eliade and J. Kitagawa, eds., *History of Religions: Essays in Methodology* (1959); M. Berkowitz and J. Johnson, *Social Scientific Studies of Religion: A Bibliography* (1967); R. McDermott, "Religion as an Academic Discipline," *Cross Currents* 18 (1968), 11–33.

RELIGION, VIRTUE OF. Cicero derived the Latin word *religio* from *relegere,* to read again, to deepen one's knowledge of. Lactantius and Augustine derived it from *religare,* to connect, to join. It is this latter etymology that has prevailed in Christian theology. The word has come to mean the relationship between God and man, a very wide and indeterminate concept. This article discusses only part of this concept: its use in Christian moral theology.

The Bible. The word "religion" is seldom used in Scripture. The biblical expressions corresponding to what theologians call religion are fear and piety (*pietas*).

Fear. Man's immediate reaction to the Godhead is one of anguish. The sacral is acknowledged first as *tremendum* (Ex 20.18). God is the all powerful and all holy, and man is utterly unable to face him (Is 6.5). Man is impressed by the awesomeness of God. The acknowledgment through faith of the fact that this almighty God loves us introduces a new situation inviting respect and devotion and is the NT concept of the fear of God (Acts 10.35).

Pietas. In the Sapiential Books the fear of the Lord is identified with *pietas* (Sir 1.11–20), a much wider concept in biblical language than in ours. The word originally denoted the bond between family, friends, and servants (e.g., filial piety). According to the Covenant it is used to express the relationship between God and his people. Piety then finds its expression in worship, but

also in obedience and dutifulness, in justice and righteousness. Piety toward God is inseparable from a correct relationship with our fellow men (Is 1.10–17). Christ is its perfect expression (Acts 2.27; 1 Tim 3.16) because he gives perfect worship (Heb 10.5–10) and fulfills his Father's will (Jn 8.29). The new man who practices Christ's meekness and takes part in God's worship practices the true religion (Heb 12.28), which is pleasing to God.

Moral Theology. The word "religion" is used in modern theology almost without exception in a psychological, sociological, or religio-historical sense. Modern moral theology is concerned either with the idea of the divine common to all religions or with the psychological factors that characterize man's relationship to God, but hardly at all with religion as a moral virtue. Medieval scholasticism, however, systematized biblical teaching in making it precise but also in limiting it. Thomas Aquinas treats of religion in the second part of the *Summa theologiae* on morals, and makes it a subdivision of justice (ThAq ST 2a2ae, 81–100). Even though religion has God's worship as an object, it does not come under the theological virtues since it belongs to all men and is not specifically Christian. And as God is other than man, religion comes under justice, the cardinal virtue that regulates man's relations with others. What is the right relationship between two people who are unequal—one of whom is unable to give as much as he receives from the other? This unequal relationship—parent to child, government to citizen—brings with it the double duty of respect and service from the side of the inferior. The same is true for man's relationship with God: both in his inner life and in public. St. Thomas limits religion to the direct God to man relationship: respect is expressed through worship, and service, through the liturgy. But the NT notion of service is a much wider one (Jas 1.27); Jesus' words on the two equal commandments (Mt 27.39) widen the field of religion very considerably. On this point the Thomist synthesis belongs more to moral philosophy than to NT theology.

This classical moral theology was the basis for the spirituality of Cardinal de Bérulle (1575–1629). It was a theocentric reaction to the anthropocentric character acquired by Western Catholic spirituality through the *Devotio moderna. Bérulle insisted that worship is the chief duty of man, and that Jesus is the religious man par excellence since he is first and foremost the Father's worshiper.

Protestant theology has not regarded religion as a virtue. The Romantics, F. *Schleiermacher (1768–1824) in particular (who defined religion as the feeling of absolute dependence), used religion as an apologetic; but modern Protestant theology, under the influence of Karl *Barth, has definitely dissociated itself from any form of combination of the gospel and religion, regarding them as two quite different elements.

A standpoint such as that adopted by Thomistic theology will, incidentally, be entirely foreign to a Protestant theology for which the human side of God's relationship is subordinate. One notices less intransigence, where religion is concerned, among those Protestant theologians who are occupied more with pastoral than dogmatic problems, but this has very little to do with the virtue of religion in the ordinary RC use of the term. See A. I. Mennessier, "Virtue of Religion," TL 4:393–444; A. Vonier, *New and Eternal Covenant* (1930); C. M. Magsam, *Inner Life of Worship* (1958).

RELIGIOUS FREEDOM, the human right to accept, reject, or change beliefs, to worship, and to live in accordance with beliefs without external constraint or coercion. As a right, it calls for positive recognition, not mere *toleration.

History. Early Christians experienced persecution because of their claim that they alne worshiped the only true God. With the Edict of Milan (313), Christianity was legally tolerated. The Church soon began to receive special privileges, and by the end of the 4th cent. was the only religion allowed. Having become the state religion, Chris-

tianity became intolerant. Gratian and Theodosius (380) forbade pagan worship and took strong measures against heretics. Even Augustine, who inclined toward toleration, finally decided that coercion was necessary to deal with the *Donatists. Throughout the Middle Ages, the concept of *Christendom prevailed in western Europe, and heretics were severely treated, while Jews were discriminated against but permitted to exist. The Reformation brought little change in the situation, for religious uniformity supported by civil government was a general presupposition of Lutherans, Calvinists, and Anglicans. Only the Anabaptists raised their voices in defense of freedom of conscience.

The Thirty Years' War brought widespread revulsion against religious intolerance, and conciliatory figures (e.g., G. Calixt, H. Grotius, J. Comenius) proposed bases for mutual acceptance among Protestants. In France, the *Edict of Nantes (1598) granted considerable freedom to the *Huguenots, but it was revoked in 1685. English Baptists (J. Smyth, T. Helwys) appealed for complete freedom of conscience, and during the Civil Wars (1642–49) Milton's *Areopagitica* and Roger *Williams' *Bloody Tenent* were published. Williams contended that God wills "a permission of the most Paganish, Jewish, Turkish, or anti-Christian consciences and worships, be granted to all men in all nations and countries; and they are only to be fought against with . . . the Sword of God's Spirit." The English struggle to enforce religious uniformity during the Restoration (1660–88) ended with the *Toleration Act (1689), granting freedom to Protestant *Dissenters. Not until the 19th cent., however, did complete religious freedom even for Roman Catholics come in England.

The U.S. has been the land of the first complete experiment in religious freedom; notwithstanding religious restrictions in early state constitutions, there was a general separation of functions of *Church and State.

Current Status. Progressively the U.S. has achieved a degree of religious freedom that has pointed the way for others. On the Continent, religious liberty had been extended considerably by the 20th cent., but its achievement was due to economic, political, and religious changes that made tolerance more conducive to the public weal. Where communism prevails, religious freedom seldom amounts to more than a toleration of worship. Italy, Spain, and Latin America have been slow to acknowledge the rights of religious dissenters, but the degree of toleration varies greatly in those lands. In non-Christian countries also there are discriminatory religious laws (e.g., in Burma, Israel, and Muslim countries in the Near East). The United Nations, in its Universal Declaration of Human Rights (1948), proclaimed "the right to freedom of thought, conscience, and religion," and a special subcommission drew up a more specific "Code on Religious Liberty" in 1960, but not all nations have subscribed to it. The World Council of Churches (WCC) issued a Declaration on Religious Liberty at Amsterdam (1948) and another at New Delhi (1961). RC Church theologians also have effected a change in the historic attitude of their Church, with John C. *Murray making a great contribution to this development in the United States. Of historic significance was the promulgation (1965) by Vatican Council II of the Decree on Religious Freedom (*Dignitatis humanae*). Declaring that human beings, as individuals or groups, have the right to freedom of conscience, it acknowledged that a man is not to be forced to act contrary to his conscience or restrained from acting in accord with conscience in religious matters. Although some at the Council wished further clarification of ambiguities, the document has met with general approval by Protestants. The Commission on Religious Liberty of the WCC drew up a list of the "fundamental agreements" between the conciliar decree and the WCC declarations on the subject and drafted a project of common Christian insights concerning religious liberty. Thus, although in large areas of the world religious liberty, or even toleration, is minimal, considerable progress has been made in recent years. Significant agreements in principle have been reached, although interpretations of such matters as *proselytism, care of children's religious nurture, and the protection of society remain thorny questions in some nations. See M. Searle-Bates, *Religious Liberty: An Enquiry* (1945); N. Edelby and T. Jiménez-Urresti, eds., *Religious Freedom* (Concilium, v.18, 1966); S. Meade, *Lively Experiment* (1963); J. C. Murray, ed., *Religious Liberty: An End and a Beginning* (1966).

RELIGIOUS LIFE, as understood in the RC Church today, the institutionalized form, sanctioned by the authority of the Church, of the life of the evangelical counsels of poverty, chastity, and obedience. Three canonical types of this life are recognized: religious life properly so-called (entailing the three vows plus community life); societies of common life (entailing no public vows); and secular institutes (entailing no common life). The teaching and decrees of Vatican Council II have made it clear that, although Christ, from whom the evangelical counsels stem, did not establish religious institutes for living a life according to the counsels, such institutes are nevertheless necessary to the life of the Church in its present situation. They are an expression of its charismatic life, each institute taking its origin in a charism given to its founder. Religious life is thus a divine gift to the Church itself, and not simply a grace given to certain of its members.

In history, the first steps toward religious life were the practice and recognition of a special way of life followed by virgins and widows (2d cent.). The 3d cent. saw the beginning of a life of special asceticism practiced by fathers of the desert in Egypt and Syria; groups of anchorites gathered around a master, such as St. Anthony. St. Pachomius developed this into cenobitism, and St. Basil promoted this form of life. In the West St. Augustine drew up his rule for the common life of clerics. St. Benedict organized monastic life for both clerics and laymen, men and women. Medieval reform movements, such as those of Cluny and Ci-teaux, reinvigorated Benedictine monasti-cism, and new forms of it sprang up with the Carthusians and the Orders of Canons Regular and the Premonstratensians. The 13th cent. saw the rise of the mendicant orders—first the Franciscans and Domini-cans, who were freed from the monastic obligation of stable residence in the interest of apostolic activity—and later the Carmel-ites and others. About the time of the Council of Trent a new development ap-peared with orders of clerics regular, who were freed from the obligation of choral office. Among these were the Jesuits and Theatines. Further evolution came with the appearance of congregations whose mem-bers took simple rather than solemn vows, and of congregations whose members took no vows, for educational, nursing, and mis-sionary purposes. In the 17th cent. St. John Baptist de la Salle initiated the nonclerical congregations of teaching brothers. Secular institutes began in the 19th cent. and were sanctioned as a canonical form of the life of the counsels by Pope Pius XII in 1947. The same Pope fostered and centralized the movement for renewal and modernization of religious life. Vatican Council II recog-nized the vitality of the various forms of the religious life, active and contemplative, monastic and conventual, and the secular institutes, and while it encouraged renewal and adaptation to the circumstances of con-temporary life, it also urged a continuous return to the sources of Christian life and to the original inspiration that brought them into being (Vat II RenRelLife 2).

The revival of religious life in Protes-tantism is a phenomenon worthy of atten-tion. Despite the opposition of Luther and Calvin to monastic vows, and despite the rejection of monasticism by the Reformers generally, there have been survivals and revivals of something like organized reli-gious life in Protestantism from its early years; e.g., the Moravian Brethren (18th cent.), the diaconies of Germany, Switzer-land, and France (19th cent.), the Protes-tant Sisters of Charity. The recent cenobitic revival in the *Taizé community is well known, and there are many other witnesses to the vitality of the ideal represented by this way of life. An ecumenical orientation marks several of the new communities. In the C of E the religious orders were sup-pressed, but within a century there were attempts at restoring some form of religious life and these continued in the 17th and 18th centuries. Since 1845 communities of men and women have been growing in number. In 1935 an Advisory Council was estab-lished to look after the welfare of Anglican Religious communities. At the present time there are in the British Isles 11 communities of men, the oldest of which, the Cowley Fathers, dates from 1866; for women there are some 60 communities. The U.S. and Canada also have similar religious com-munities for those who wish to take up this mode of life within the Anglican Commu-nion. See R. F. Smith, NCE 12:287-294; S. Mayer et al., LTK 7:1192-1204; F. Biot, *Communautés protestantes* (1960); P. An-son, *Call of the Cloister* (1955).

RELIGIOUS SOCIETY OF FRIENDS, often called Quakers, the corporate title for those whose distinctive belief is the *Inner Light as preached by G. *Fox. Turning against the "steeple houses" and "hireling ministry" of the organized Churches, Fox began to preach the doctrine of the Inner Light: that the source of all religious truth and life is the voice of God experienced within each person. In the north and mid-lands of England, he attracted Familists, Seekers, and others dissatisfied with the C of E and the *Nonconformist Churches. He and his followers called themselves the "Children of Light," "Friends of Truth," and later the Society of Friends; by 1652 he had given them a sound plan of organiza-tion. Their resistance to laws of religion, military service, oaths, and certain marks of civil deference, made them the target of ferocious legal and popular oppression until the *Toleration Act (1689). Many migrated to the American colonies; Pa. was estab-lished as a refuge under William *Penn, but elsewhere they suffered. The post-persecution era is called the "quietist" phase in Quaker history; they became a "peculiar people," separated, plain in dress, using biblical forms of speech, avoiding all worldly frivolity.

The source of the beliefs and norms for living characteristic of the Friends is the Inner Light. Hence they have a traditional unwillingness to adopt an ecclesiastical structure, creeds, a liturgical or sacramental system, or a teaching authority residing either in Church or Scriptures. All such elements presuppose a mediate revelation of doctrine or a mediate bestowal of sanctity. The immediacy of the Inner Light has led to preoccupation with mysticism and meditation, as well as a high regard for the individual person. Since all men can or do share equally in the Inner Light, in the name of this human equality and dignity Quakers have promoted education, prison reform, and social equality and they have opposed slavery, warfare, and conscription.

Fox and the other early Friends preached the Inner Light within a setting of traditional Christianity. But as the immediacy of the God–man relationship through the Inner Light was stressed, some came to question dependence upon the historical Jesus as Redeemer. Such a line taken by Elias *Hicks (1748–1830) occasioned a schism in American Quakerism; during 1827–28, the meetings in Philadelphia and elsewhere split into "Hicksites" and "Orthodox," i.e., adherents of orthodox Protestant tenets; the schism continued until 1955. In the mid-19th cent. a further schism occurred within the Orthodox group because of the preaching of Joseph J. *Gurney (1788–1846), which stressed traditional evangelical themes and combined the Inner Light doctrine with the teaching that Jesus is the one mediator between God and man. The Gurneyites, who continued to call themselves Orthodox, were resisted by the Wilburites (John *Wilbur, 1774–1856), who were "Conservatives," standing for the sole sufficiency of the Inner Light. The Gurneyite and Wilburite groups in New England terminated this schism in 1945. In the rest of the eastern U.S. most of

the Quakers are Hicksites or Wilburites. In the middle and far West, Quakers are mostly Gurneyites.

Forms of worship reflect varying interpretations of the Inner Light in relationship to the person of Jesus. Those in the Gurneyite line have tended to develop a mode of worship similar to that of the Baptists or Congregationalists. The minister is usually a person who has had theological training; meetings are marked by programmed worship (sermon, organ music, singing, etc.). Quakers of the Wilburite line have emphasized the silent unprogrammed meeting, in which each is free to speak as the Inner Light prompts.

Since Fox's own times, the basic organization of the Friends has been the meeting. The "monthly" meeting is the local unit, gathering weekly for worship, and monthly for business; "quarterly" and "yearly" meetings embrace wider geographical regions. In the U.S., where 60% of the Friends' worldwide membership (approx. 200,000) is found, the various yearly meetings are either unaffiliated or affiliated to the Friends United Meeting, the Friends General Conference, the Evangelical Friends Alliance, or the Conservative Friends. There has been continuing effort toward greater unity among Friends; the *Friends World Committee for Consultation seeks to promote the interests and association of Friends throughout the world. The American Friends Service Committee operates as an effective agency for the betterment of society and for peace in the world. See W. C. Braithwaite, *Beginnings of Quakerism* (2d ed., 1955); R. M. Jones, *Later Periods of Quakerism* (2v., 1921); E. B. Bronner, ed., *American Quakers Today* (1966).

RELIGIOUS SOCIETY OF FRIENDS (Conservative), a group of *Wilburite Quakers comprising the Yearly Meetings of Iowa, North Carolina, and Ohio, who seek to maintain the primitive teachings of the Religious Society of Friends. Membership in 1961 was 1,696, with 21 churches.

RELIGIOUS SOCIETY OF FRIENDS (General Conference), an association of eight yearly *meetings of the Religious Society of Friends, formed in 1900 when seven *Hicksite yearly meetings came together for the advancement of Quakerism, for religious education, and for implementing the social testimonies of the Friends. In 1967 it had 31,670 members, with 292 churches.

RELIGIOUS SOCIETY OF FRIENDS (Kansas Yearly Meeting), a branch of the Society of Friends in the evangelical wing of the Gurneyite line. In 1937 it separated from the Five Years Meeting (see FRIENDS UNITED MEETING), fearing the latter's liberal tendencies, and in 1965 joined with the Ohio, Oregon, and Rocky Mountain Yearly Meetings to form the Evangelical Friends Alliance. Kansas Yearly Meeting membership in 1965 was 8,227, with 89 churches.

REMONSTRANTS, the name given after 1610 to the followers of J. *Arminius. The name comes from the *Remonstrance*, a five-point statement of *Arminianism drawn up after the death of Arminius by S. *Episcopius and H. Grotius, and addressed to the states of Holland and W. Friesland. The opponents of the Remonstrants, sometimes called Contra-Remonstrants, were led by F. *Gomarus. The controversy was on *predestination, but also involved political issues. At the Synod of *Dort (1618–19) the Remonstrants were condemned, and many were persecuted or banished. After the death of Prince Maurice of Nassau (1625), protector of the Gomarites, the Remonstrants were allowed to return and in 1633 were granted religious freedom. The Society of Remonstrants in Holland (Remonstrantse Broederschap) in 1967 had 27 congregations, with about 20,000 members. They have a *congregational polity, the synod having no authority over the local church. In the last century the Remonstrants embraced modernism. See Schaff

Creeds 1:516–519; W. H. van de Pol, *World Protestantism* (1964), 269–271; bibliog. for Arminianism.

RENAISSANCE, the complex era of transition between medieval and modern times. It enjoys no fixed dates. Some have preferred to speak of it as the 15th cent., plus several decades at either end. A more recent view is to enlarge its chronological frontiers to 1300–1600. The problem is compounded by the necessity of differentiating between Italy and the transalpine countries. The Italian Renaissance can be said to have begun 1300–50; the northern Renaissance, c.1450. Most scholars would see the Renaissance as superseded by the Reformation in the 3d or 4th decade of the 16th century.

Personalities and Spirit. Among the key personalities of the Renaissance are Dante (1265–1321), whose *Divine Comedy* is a lyrical synthesis of the Middle Ages, but who in some respects points to the Renaissance; Francesco Petrarch (1304–74), sometimes called the father of Renaissance *humanism, whose attitudes comprise something of the Renaissance in miniature; Giovanni Boccaccio (1313–75), whose *Decameron* and life suggest the moral ambivalence of humanism; Vittorino da Feltre (1378–1446), an educator who played a role in transforming humanism from an enthusiasm to a program; Lorenzo Valla (1405–57), who shows the philological or scientific side of humanism; Marsiglio Ficino (1433–99), neoplatonist philosopher and theologian of the Platonic Academy of Florence; Giovanni Pico della Mirandola (1463–94), the great eclecticist and boundless spirit of this Academy; and Niccolò Machiavelli (1469–1527), whose controversial work *The Prince* suggests a climax of the Italian Renaissance. In the North the key figures are Erasmus of Rotterdam (1469?–1536), prince of Christian humanists, who represents a conjunction of the older *Devotio moderna and Italian humanism; Jacques Lefèvre d'Étaples (1455?–1536), the great French proponent of a moderate religious reform;

Thomas More (1478–1535), English humanist, statesman, martyr, and saint; Ximénez de Cisneros (1436–1517), Spanish cardinal, biblical humanist, educational patron, and religious reformer; and Johann Reuchlin (1455–1522), celebrated Hebraist.

As an era of transition the Renaissance possesses no single character or spirit. It was a highly unstable period between two relatively stable and definable world orders. It contains both medieval and modern features and is a rather ambiguous period of history. C. S. Lewis wrote of it as "a complex of heterogeneous events." This view qualifies or counters the 19th cent. formulation of the Renaissance by the French historian J. Michelet and the Swiss German historian J. Burckhardt. Their view, which became tradition, stressed the revolutionary character of the Renaissance as "the discovery of the world and of man," with a corresponding depreciation of the Middle Ages. Though the Michelet–Burckhardt thesis still has popular adherents, few scholars hold it today without qualification. If one stresses the this-worldly rationality of the period, it can be pointed out that it was a great period of the occult, on the one hand, and a golden age of mysticism, on the other. If it be stated simplistically that the Renaissance was a revival of ancient learning, it can be replied that Aristotle was revived in the 13th cent. with scholasticism and the universities. And if it be urged that the Renaissance was an age of neopaganism, it can be pointed out that it produced great saints, such as Catherine of Siena and Thomas More, and it is today acknowledged an open question whether Machiavelli was more characteristic of the age than More.

Yet there are positive generalizations that can be made about the period. It emerged out of the late Middle Ages, first in Italy and then across the Alps. Its culture was less clerical and feudal than the Middle Ages, more laic and urban. Humanism set the dominant cultural tone. This was not so much a revival of learning pure and simple as it was a continuation of an earlier revival of learning, now accelerated and transferred to the field of arts and letters, with a stress upon the ancient languages, and particularly upon fine Latinity. To contrast it with the Middle Ages, the trend was from philosophy to philology, and within philosophy, from metaphysics to moral philosophy, logic to literature, and to some extent, from the more scientific Aristotle to the more poetic Plato. Finally, the Renaissance was a great period of productivity in the fine arts. The arts have been seen as the form of the Renaissance and the artist as the model of the period. This "cultural explosion," as E. Garin has styled it, was probably related to medieval and Byzantine precedents, to the revival of antiquity, and perhaps to a peculiar Italian genius of the time. One might say that the arts were to the Renaissance what philosophy was to the Middle Ages. And both were more often than not in the service of religion.

The Renaissance and Religion. While humanism fostered a certain eclecticism, breadth, tolerance, and indulgence, it is almost uniformly held today that Renaissance society was basically Christian. There was very little theoretical paganism and virtually no atheism. Morals are another thing, and there probably was a decline in morality, and certainly a decline in the moral authority of the institutional Church. In the late Middle Ages the papacy suffered a long chain of severe shocks that left it in a condition of disequilibrium and disarray, more reactive than dynamic. The medieval papacy probably reached its height under Innocent III (1198–1216), overextended itself in the subsequent wars with Emperor Frederick II (1215–50) and his children, and suffered retribution under Boniface VIII (1294–1303). His struggle with Philip IV of France (1285–1314) issued in humiliation and abuse at Anagni in 1302, the first shock to the late medieval papacy. There followed the Avignonese papacy (1309–77), which compromised the international prestige of the popes. The disputed papal election of 1378 led to the chaos of the *Great Western Schism (1378–1417). This led in turn to *conciliarism, which thereafter ruled discussion of institutional reform, and which the popes resisted as a cure worse than the illness. Moreover, the foregoing dislocations seem to have created a defense psychology in the Roman curia, the cardinals regarding a solidified Papal State as the indispensable guarantor of papal independence, and accordingly electing popes on the basis not of spiritual qualities but of political and financial expertise. This new attitude helps account for the election of the scandalous Alexander VI (1492–1503), the martial Julius II (1503–13), and the statesman and patron Leo X (1513–21). With the election of this last son of Lorenzo the Magnificent, the center of Renaissance humanism was effectively transferred from Florence to Rome. The consequent inattention to spiritual affairs was hardly justified by the lavish patronage of the arts by the papacy. The classics, which involve attitudes like individualism, a lust for fame and glory, and a relaxed attitude toward sexuality, may have had a corrosive effect upon morality in general. The effects of the spectacle in Rome were various. Its example could be paralleled elsewhere. Simony, nepotism, pluralism, absenteeism, and concubinage were widespread. Such conditions engendered the reformist but orthodox protest of the tragic Savonarola (1452–98). In would-be-Catholic countries, it inspired or reinforced anticlericalism and antipapalism. Elsewhere it compromised the very credibility of the papacy, underscoring a Protestant thesis that the papacy was a mere historical growth lacking biblical foundation.

Yet the redeeming and salutary aspects of the Renaissance were felt in the subsequent RC reform movement, as well as in the Protestant Reformation. First, humanism from its origins had a strong didactic and reformist strain. Petrarch sought to wed Christianity with eloquence, in contradistinction to the earlier synthesis of reason and revelation. Second, humanist education, while not theological in the scholastic sense, fostered religious training. Vittorino da Feltre, a model of Renaissance educators, was a saintly man. Third, the philological side of humanism could and did turn from the pagan classics to the Christian classic, the Bible, beginning with Lorenzo *Valla's Annotations on the New Testament*. A more accurate text of the Scriptures was to be a major goal of later humanism. Fourth, reform was a major interest of the Platonic Academy of Florence. The *Theologica platonica* of Ficino breathes much of the same spirit as the *Imitation of Christ* of Thomas à Kempis, and Ficino's influence upon Renaissance religion and art is incalculable. But *Erasmus was probably the foremost influence in Renaissance religion. Some earlier studies of the man have been a caricature of him. He was neither a coward nor a forerunner of Voltaire; and it is now acknowledged that he was a deeply committed and dedicated Christian. He spent the greater part of his life in biblical studies, patristics, ethical concerns, and in trying to effect a system of education that would remedy the evils of his times. His *Philosophia Christi*, with its Christocentric, biblical, personalist, and pacifist stress, had a momentous effect in the 16th century. There were similar humanist figures all over Europe. It was no accident that RC reform began with the Christian humanists and later, under the pontificate of Paul III (1534–49), infiltrated the papacy. Thus, if humanism had some role in the deterioration of the Church, it made its recompense.

The Protestant relation to the Renaissance also reveals ambivalence. In some respects the Reformation continued the Renaissance, as can be seen in the Renaissance revival of the study of Paul and Augustine. It is apparent also in the Renaissance return to the Bible and in a certain though not uniform penchant for an exegesis that was philological and grammatical rather than philosophical and allegorical. The continuity is present in the Reformers' common disdain for the subtleties of late scholasticism, their critique of clerical immorality and ignorance, their pronounced ethical bent, and their indifference or aversion to the fossilized formalism of late medieval piety. Likewise, Protestant educators like Philipp Melanchthon (1497–

1560) continued the humanist curriculum, which became traditional.

In some other respects the Renaissance contrasts sharply with the Reformation. The two inclined to represent different assessments of human potentialities. The stress of classical Protestantism upon *total depravity was incompatible with the humanist emphasis upon the dignity of man. The great confrontation of these principles was the polemic between Luther and Erasmus on free will, 1524–25. It is pertinent that so many of the Italian Reformers, who were almost all of a humanist cast, side-stepped or modified the doctrine of *double predestination. Again, the Protestant reading of the Decalogue's proscription of images made the Reformation generally uncongenial to the arts. Finally, the Christian humanists of the Renaissance envisioned a reform within the context of the Church: they generally considered Christendom inviolable. This judgment is reinforced by the correspondence between humanism and ecumenism throughout the 16th century. In general, both the Reformation and the Counter-Reformation preserved the forms of Renaissance humanism but repudiated much of its spirit. It was truly a question of the letter and the spirit. See W. K. Ferguson, *Renaissance in Historical Thought* (1948), with review of bibliog. from the Renaissance to present; *idem, Europe in Transition: 1300–1520* (1962); M. P. Gilmore, *World of Humanism* (1952), excellent bibliog.; D. Bush, *Renaissance and English Humanism* (1939); M. Bataillon, *Erasme et l'Espagne* (1937); L. W. Spitz, *Religious Renaissance of the German Humanists* (1963); Pastor v.1–7.

REORGANIZED CHURCH OF JESUS CHRIST OF LATTER DAY SAINTS, see LATTER DAY SAINTS, REORGANIZED CHURCH OF JESUS CHRIST OF.

REPROBATION, the divine plan and decree regarding those who do not attain salvation; the opposite of *predestination.

Theologians have classified reprobation as positive and negative; antecedent and consequent. Positive reprobation means the divine decree to condemn or inflict punishment; negative reprobation means a divine decree of non-election to glory, or exclusion from glory. Antecedent reprobation precedes the foreknowledge of an individual's sinfulness; consequent reprobation is subsequent to such foreknowledge. Classical Calvinism included the teaching of a positive antecedent reprobation (see DOUBLE PREDESTINATION). The Council of Trent repeated earlier conciliar rejections of this teaching. *Arminianism also mitigated the Calvinist doctrine. The only positive reprobation accepted in RC theology is consequent. *Báñezianism proposed a negative reprobation that was antecedent; *Molinism, one that was consequent.

RESTITUTION, EDICT OF, see EDICT OF RESTITUTION.

RESTORATION, the term used in English history for the reestablishment of the monarchy with the accession of Charles II (1660) after the collapse of the Protectorate government. In religion the Restoration brought victory to the C of E over the Puritans and made secure the episcopal as opposed to the presbyterian form of church government.

RESTORATION MOVEMENT, a term applied to groups originating in early 19th-cent. U.S. that committed themselves to the dual goals of Christian unity and the reestablishment of simple NT Christianity. Specifically, it refers to the Disciples of Christ led by Thomas and Alexander *Campbell, and to the "Christian" movements that emerged in New England, Va., and Ky. at about the same time. Most of the followers of Barton *Stone who called themselves simply "Christians," merged with the Disciples, but the others continued separately and merged with the Congregational Churches in 1931 (see UNITED CHURCH OF CHRIST). The idea of reforming or purifying the Church by restoring the early Church has been a recurrent theme in church history. Distinctive of the American groups was the combination of concern for restoration with an equally strong concern for Christian unity. Adherents of the movement rejected creeds and ecclesiastical organization, calling their churches simply "Christian Churches." They believed that Christians had become separated into denominations as a result of creedal, organizational, and sacramental developments that occurred after the first cent., and that unity could be realized by a return to pristine faith and practices. Yet this movement aiming to unify Christians has itself experienced division; the Churches of Christ gradually separated from the Disciples of Christ, claiming to be truer to the original intent of restoration than the Disciples. *CHRISTIAN CHURCHES; *CHRISTIAN CHURCHES (DISCIPLES OF CHRIST), INTERNATIONAL CONVENTION.

RESTORATIONISM, a term denoting the subject of a controversy in American Universalism that arose about 1817. In opposition to the beliefs of Hosea *Ballou (1771–1852), some Universalists believed in a future state of punishment that would precede the final restoration of all sinners to a state of holiness and happiness. In 1831 the "Massachusetts Association of Universal Restorationists" seceded from the Universalist General Conventions; in 1841 the separatist organization was dissolved. The Universalist ministers of Boston issued a statement in 1878 that signalized the end of the controversy. See R. Eddy, *Universalism in America* (2 v., 1884–86). *UNIVERSALISM.

REUCHLIN, JOHANNES (1455–1522), German philologist and humanist. By extensive study and travel, especially in Italy, R. perfected himself in the classical languages, Hebrew, and the literature of the Cabala. He published many works reflecting these interests; his *De rudimentis hebraicis* (1506) was an epoch-making introduction of the use of Hebrew in Christian scriptural exegesis. *Erasmus held R. in the highest esteem and wrote an *Apotheosis* at his death. In the last decade of his life, R. opposed the Jewish convert J. Pfefferkorn, who sought to have all Hebrew books burned as a danger to Christian faith. Pfefferkorn circulated his violent *Handspiegel* (1511) against R., who replied in kind with *Augenspiegel* (1511). This work was publicly burned (1514) by the inquisitor J. Hoogstraeten. The controversy was marked by the *Epistolae obscurorum virorum,* written against R.'s enemies. In 1519 R. won an initial victory, being vindicated by the apb. of Spire, but ultimately the *Augenspiegel* was condemned by Leo X (1520), and R. was made to pay the costs of the litigations. He remained a loyal Catholic to the last and even endeavored to win back his nephew Philipp *Melanchthon. See L. Geiger, *J. R.* (1871); K. Hannemann, LTK 8:1260–61, with extensive bibliog.; F. G. Stokes, *Epistolae Obscurorum Virorum: The Latin Text with an English Rendering, Notes and an Historical Introduction* (1909).

REUNION OF THE CHURCHES. The basic rationale of the reunion of Christian Churches is stated by the *Decree on Ecumenism of Vatican Council II. Christ founded one Church, but many Christian communions present themselves to man as the true inheritors of Jesus Christ. Such division "openly contradicts the will of Christ, scandalizes the world, and damages that most holy cause, the preaching of the Gospel to every creature" (Vat II Ecum 1). However, in recent times Christians have been inspired with remorse over their divisions. Many Churches and ecclesial communities that invoke the triune God and confess Jesus as Lord and Savior strive, in an ecumenical movement fostered by the Holy Spirit, for the restoration of unity among all Christians. Their goal is "the one visible church of God, a church truly universal and sent forth to the whole world that the world may be converted to the Gospel and so be saved, to the glory of God" (Vat II ConstCh 1).

Church union negotiations and mergers among Protestant and Anglican Churches have taken place in increasing numbers as the ecumenical movement has grown in strength. In April 1967, the *Faith and Order Commission organized the Consultation on Church Union Negotiations at Bossey, Switzerland. Forty-five participants from 26 countries, representing 27 different union conversations in 8 confessional families, exchanged information, heard about new approaches, and received recommendations for the formation of covenants to make *intercommunion possible and for programs of education for union. A survey of church union negotiations has been regularly carried in the *Ecumenical Review* (April 1954, Oct. 1955, April 1957, Jan. 1960, April 1962, July 1964, July 1966, July 1968). In the various schemes of union under development, a general agreement is emerging that an episcopally ordered ministry in continuity with the *historic episcopate is to be sought in the united Churches, an element echoing the distinctive feature of the *Lambeth Quadrilateral (1888). Other factors also emerging are a common desire for flexibility in church structure, a view that the Church should truly serve in the world as a reconciling force, and a concern over the tension between the necessarily local nature of the Church and its universality. Among the unions already consummated, the *Church of South India and the *United Church of Christ in the U.S., because they involve different concepts of *polity and different traditions of ministry, are most significant. Among those pending, the union of the Church of England and the Methodist Church, and the *Consultation on Church Union involving nine denominations in the U.S. are of major importance. Vatican Council II, by its doctrine of *collegiality, its acceptance of limited worship in common (*communicatio in sacris; see Vat II EastCathCh 26–29), and its praise of authentic theological traditions in the Eastern Church, together with Pope Paul VI's

visits with Patriarch Athenagoras and other friendly gestures, has done much to prepare for eventual reunion of the Orthodox and RC Churches.

No complete theology of church reunion exists, but as developed by the World Council of Churches (WCC) several points are pivotal. The *Amsterdam Assembly (1948) of the WCC declared that although the Christian Churches are divided as Churches, they are one in Jesus Christ, acknowledging him as Lord and Savior. The relationship of the member Churches with each other and with the WCC was not made clear, however. To clarify these relationships the Central Committee of the WCC received a report at its Toronto meeting (1950) on the *Ecclesiological Significance of the WCC. The statement declared that the WCC cannot be based on any one particular concept of the Church, nor does membership in the WCC imply that a Church treats its own conception of the Church as relative or that a specific doctrine about the nature of church unity has to be accepted. The meaning of the unity was further refined at the *New Delhi Assembly (1961).

The *Constitution on the Church* and the *Decree on Ecumenism* of Vatican II present RC theology on reunion. The Church is Christ's presence through his Spirit among the People of God. As such the Church of Christ "subsists" in the RC Church while transcending it (Vat II ConstCh 8). Other Christians are incorporated in the Church of Christ, and Christian Churches are institutions whose ecclesial gifts and sacred actions are capable of admitting their members into the life of grace and the community of salvation. In the teaching of the Council, only the RC Church perfectly embodies the Church of Christ, but this does not prevent the partial realization of the Church of Christ elsewhere. The reunion of Christian Churches is the goal of the movement to which Protestant and Orthodox members of the WCC are committed. Since Vatican Council II, the RC Church has also been committed to the ecumenical movement and is cooperating more and more with the WCC and with other Christian Churches in common action. Yet, as Paul VI stated to the WCC at Geneva, June 10, 1969, many obstacles—theological, pastoral, cultural, and educational—remain. See R. Rouse and S. C. Neill, eds., *History of the Ecumenical Movement 1517–1948* (1954); Official Reports of the WCC Assemblies; L. Vischer, ed., *Documentary History of the Faith and Order Movement 1927–1963* (1963); A. Bea, *Unity of Christians* (ed. B. Leeming, 1963).

REUSCH, FRANZ HEINRICH (1825–1900), ecclesiastical historian and leader of German *Old Catholics. Born in Westphalia, R. attended Bonn, Tübingen, and Munich Univ., and became a RC priest in 1849. At Bonn (1854), he taught and wrote on OT exegesis. Excommunication (1872) followed his condemnation of papal infallibility. Active in international Old Catholic congresses, he ran second in an episcopal election (1873) and became vicar general and a parish priest in Bonn. He was prominent in the *Bonn Reunion Conferences (1874–75). Although conducting occasional services, R. resigned church offices because of Old Catholic abolition of clerical celibacy (1878). Among his works were a magisterial study on the Index of Forbidden Books (*Index der verbotenen Bücher*, 2v., 1883–85) and a historical treatise on the varying schools in RC moral theology, written with I. *Döllinger (*Geschichte der Moralstreitigkeiten in der römisch-katholischen Kirche seit dem 16. Jahrhundert*, 2v., 1889).

REVELATION, the self-disclosure of God and the communication of the truth about his nature and will. Because so much of the Christian doctrine of revelation has been formulated in discussions of its relation to other themes and issues, an examination of several of these relationships may serve as a useful basis for a definition and description of the doctrine itself.

Revelation and event. At the center of the biblical view of revelation, both in the OT and in the NT, is the conviction that God makes himself known through happenings. Above all, it was in the Exodus from Egypt that the OT believer saw a special manifestation of God's relation to the people of Israel; here it was that the covenant between the Lord and Israel had been established, the Law had been given to Moses, and the promises sworn to Abraham about the land had been fulfilled. In the NT the revelation of God reached its consummation and climax when "the Word became flesh and dwelt among us, full of grace and truth; we have beheld his glory, glory as of the only Son from the Father" (Jn 1.14). The biblical theology of the 19th and 20th cents., both Protestant and Roman Catholic, has rediscovered this emphasis upon the deeds of God in human history as the bearers of his communication of himself to men. When God speaks, he speaks by his mighty acts.

Revelation and truth. Earlier generations of theologians often tended to define revelation in the category of truth rather than in the category of event. Revelation is the disclosure of what is supernaturally true about God. For the very events that serve as bearers of revelation become this by virtue of the word of God that is spoken in them and to them. Other nations have emigrated from the captivity of their oppressors; what made the Exodus of Israel from Egypt a revelation was the truth about God that was spoken by him through his servant Moses in the Torah. The revelation in Christ was not simply an event, but "grace and truth came through Jesus Christ" (Jn 1.17). Because this truth has taken the form of doctrines, revelation has often been interpreted as the delivery of accurate and reliable information, stated in the propositions and dogmas of faith.

Revelation and Scripture. Whether as event or as truth, the revelation of God is recorded in the Bible; on this all Christians agree. Where they disagree is on the question whether all revelation is contained in Scripture. Protestants have generally maintained that Scripture, and Scripture alone, records the word and will of God for men. Roman Catholics have assigned to the tradition of the Church a role in the proper interpretation of divine revelation; some have asserted that all revelation is contained in Scripture, at least implicitly, and needs tradition to give it authoritative expression; others have treated tradition as in fact a "second source" of revelation. In practice these differences have often been less sharp than they are in theory; for Protestant theology has continued to confess such dogmas as the Trinity, which are not stated in so many words in the Bible; and Roman Catholics have striven to find biblical warrant even for such dogmas as the Immaculate Conception and the Assumption, despite the acknowledgment that Scripture does not teach them in so many words. (See TRADITION.)

Revelation and religion. From the earliest days of the Church, the Christian claim to be in possession of divine revelation has had to take account of the rival claims of other faiths. Although some theologians have found it possible to dismiss the problem by denying to other religions any true knowledge of God, most interpreters of the question have distinguished between those truths that have been known outside the historical revelation of God—be it through remnants of primitive revelation or through reason or through other means—and those that can be known only through the supernatural act of God's self-disclosure. In its missionary work, too, the Church has proceeded on the assumption that the grasp of the divine already present among non-Christians did not need to be unlearned, but needed to be corrected and completed by the Christian message.

Revelation and reason. A related question is the relation of revelation to what can be discovered by the unaided human reason. Theologians and Christian philosophers have debated the scope and the limits of the truth to which reason can attain. A special case in this debate has been the demonstrability of the existence of God. Most Christian theologians have taught that reason can prove that God is, but *what* God is,

they have taught, is largely the exclusive concern of revelation (see NATURAL THEOLOGY). Much of the work of traditional apologetics has dealt with such issues. Sometimes this has resulted in a theory of revelation that saw it as different from reason only quantitatively, but as similar to it in the way of knowing. But the consensus of theological thought would be that revelation is distinctive not only in its content but also in its form. See J. Baillie, *Idea of Revelation* (1956); J. Baillie et al., *Revelation* (1927); E. Gilson, *Reason and Revelation in the Middle Ages* (1938); H. R. Niebuhr, *Meaning of Revelation* (1946).

REVISED PRAYER BOOK (1928), full title *Book of Common Prayer with the Additions and Deviations Proposed in 1928*, the result of an unsuccessful effort to revise the official liturgy of the Book of Common Prayer (BCP) of 1662. Its background lay in controversies and litigation over ritual and ceremonial deviations developing in the latter half of the 19th century. A Royal Commission Report of 1906 recommended a "reasonable elasticity" in public worship to enforce obedience to the BCP by all parties in the Church. The first stage of this revision was done by *Convocations (1906–20), which was then broadened to include the *Church Assembly, established in 1919, with lay participation. Intense discussion marked the years 1920–27, with publication of several unofficial proposals of revision ("The Green Book," "The Grey Book," "The Orange Book"). A final draft ("The Deposited Book") was approved by Convocations and the Church Assembly in 1927 by large majorities. But the House of Commons rejected it (238 to 205) in Dec. 1927, and again (in a revised form) in June 1928 (266 to 220). The failure of this revision to receive legal sanction was due to partisan strife—neither Evangelicals nor Anglo-Catholics liked the Book; to the attempt to tie disciplinary aims to the law of public worship; and to the prejudice of many members of Parliament to "Catholic" additions to a "Protestant" liturgy—notably the provisions for reservation of the Sacrament. The 1928 Book has, however, been widely used, and has greatly influenced other revisions of the BCP in the *Anglican Communion—notably in Scotland, South Africa, and the United States. See W. K. Lowther Clarke, *Prayer Book of 1928 Reconsidered* (1943); R. Currie, "Power and Principle: The Anglican Prayer Book Controversy, 1927–1930," *Church History* 33 (1964), 192–205. *BOOK OF COMMON PRAYER.

REVIVALISM, a form of evangelism intensely emotional in style, with sin and salvation as its dominant themes and a dramatic conversion-experience as its aim. While applicable to any strongly emotional movement for Christian renewal, the term revivalism has a specific historical connotation, particularly in American Protestantism. A primary cause in its development was *Pietism, with its emphasis on experience religion (see EXPERIENCE, RELIGION OF). Historical revivalism began with Methodist evangelizing, led by John *Wesley, in 18th-cent. England, Ireland, and Wales. Revivalism in the U.S. had its most significant impact on the shaping of Protestantism between c.1725 and the Civil War. The revivalistic history of that era includes the *Great Awakening (see FRELINGHUYSEN, T.; TENNENT, G.; WHITEFIELD, G.; EDWARDS, J.); the *Second Great Awakening (see DWIGHT, T.; STONE, B.) after the Revolution, when the *camp meeting evolved on the frontier; and beginning c.1825 the "new measures" of Charles G. *Finney (see OBERLIN THEOLOGY). After the Civil War, Dwight L. *Moody set the pattern of the so-called professional revivalist, with business-like organization and skillful use of music and theatrical tecnniques in the campaigns. Most famous of the numberless evangelists continuing the tradition into the 20th cent. were Billy *Sunday and Billy *Graham. But revivals are a part of the regular church life of many denominations, and the practice of an annual revivalistic renewal begun in the 19th cent. continues; revivalism is at the origin and remains an essential part of the life of the Holiness and Pentecostal Churches. While essentially a Protestant phenomenon, the revival was paralleled by the parish mission in RC churches during the 19th and early 20th centuries.

The emotional extremes of preachers and the physical extravagances of the converted (paroxysms, the "jerks," barking, tremors) form but part of the picture of revivalism. It also achieved a moral and social betterment of the populace. Its value as genuine evangelism, however, has always been questioned (see CHAUNCY, C.), particularly with regard to the once-for-all conversion experience and neglect of *Christian nurture (see BUSHNELL, H.). Theologically, emphasis on a personal, felt conversion replaced Calvinism by an almost universal *Arminianism stressing free cooperation in salvation. The revivalist approach to doctrine has been simplistic, suited to the audience and the objective; *confessions of faith and doctrinal orthodoxy have been minimized. Revivalism is a nonintellectual approach to faith, and its prevalence impoverished American Protestant theology; some of the most serious orthodox theological efforts in the 19th cent. were reactions (see PRINCETON THEOLOGY; MERCERSBURG THEOLOGY). Yet revivalism was a key element in the survival and growth of the Churches in the American denominational pattern. At the time of colonial revivals, 90% of the population were not church members. The campaign against "infidelity," i.e., *deism and *rationalism, succeeded as a recruitment program for the Churches. The diminution of doctrinal differences created an atmosphere favorable to the experiment of religious freedom in the context of separation of Church and State. Revivalism proved that *voluntaryism works, that without an established Church and the coercion of law, persuasion could create church membership. See W. W. Sweet, *Revivalism in America* (1949); W. G. McLoughlin, *Modern Revivalism* (1959); S. E. Mead, *Lively Experiment* (1963), 120–127; Smith-Jamison 1:322–368.

REVOLUTION OF 1688, the "Glorious Revolution," which settled fundamental issues of government and religion in England. With the *Restoration, the constitutional struggle between Parliament and the early Stuarts, Charles II (1660–85) avoided open conflict with Parliament but worked secretly to reestablish unlimited prerogatives of the monarch. James II (1685–88), less sensitive to the temper of the times, made a host of enemies by arbitrary exercise of power in defiance of Parliament. His religious policies contributed largely to his downfall. Decreeing freedom of worship to all subjects and ignoring the *Test Act, he appointed Catholics to prominent posts. When he ordered his second *Declaration of Indulgence to be read in all churches, the abp. of Canterbury and six other bps. refused to obey and were tried for seditious libel. In 1688, when the birth of a male heir made likely the succession of other Catholic sovereigns, Whig and Tory representatives invited William of Orange to bring troops to England. Deserted by former supporters, James fled from England; Parliament offered the vacant throne to William and Mary. By a bloodless revolution, Parliament had deposed a king and appointed his successor, settling once for all the principle of limited monarchy. The rights of Englishmen were guaranteed by a *Declaration of Rights in 1689, and the *Toleration Act published the same year granted freedom of worship to dissenting Protestants but denied the same to Catholics. See M. Ashley, *Glorious Revolution of 1688* (1967).

RICE, LUTHER (1783–1836), promoter of Baptist missions. Born in Northborough, Mass., he was one of the first seven appointees of the American Board of Commissioners for Foreign Missions and in 1812 was sent to India. Rice, like Adoniram and Anne *Judson, became a Baptist soon after his arrival, and he felt obliged to return to America to arouse Baptist interest in supporting foreign missionaries. He remained in the U.S. to promote the foreign missions. To provide an educated ministry, he was the main founder of Columbian College (now George Washington Univ.) at Washington, D.C. His travels, preaching, and writing helped bind Baptist churches together, but he encountered opposition from Baptists who were suspicious of educated ministers and missionary organizations. See E. W. Thompson, *L. R.: Believer in Tomorrow* (1967).

RICHER, EDMOND (1559–1631), French cleric, canonist, and theorist of *Gallicanism. Son of a poor peasant, he became a doctor of the Sorbonne in 1592, rector of the Collège du Cardinal Lemoine in 1595, and syndic of the Sorbonne in 1602. In this latter position he was called upon to defend the Sorbonne against the religious orders, its traditional enemies, who competed with it for students and jurisdiction. The free education of the Jesuits was the greatest problem, and his attacks on them led R. to develop a radical statement of Gallicanism in opposition to their ultramontanism in his work *De ecclesiastica et politica potestate* (1611; Fr. tr., 1612). This book was condemned through the intervention of the papal nuncio, Cardinal Ubaldini, and the ultramontanist abp. of Sens, Cardinal du Perron; and R. lost his position as syndic in 1612. He continued to defend himself through a number of pamphlets until forced by Card. Richelieu to issue a partial retraction in 1629. R. supported the superiority of a general council over the pope, the competence of all the faithful to preserve divine revelation, episcopal freedom from papal jurisdiction, and the absolute independence of a king within his own domain. His ideas were adopted in a modified form by adherents of *Jansenism in the 18th cent. and had an influence on the lower clergy in the second half of that century. See E. Puyol, *Edmond Richer* (2v., 1876); Pastor v.26.

RIGHTEOUSNESS, the translation of the AV and RSV for the Greek word *dikaiosúnē* (Lat. *justitia*), translated as "justice" in the Douay and Confraternity versions of the Bible. It is a keyword in the doctrine on justification, i.e., that man becomes just or right through the justice or righteousness of God. The biblical connotations, esp. that of St. Paul in Romans, are not the legal senses of the word justice. The term "righteousness" has the advantage of avoiding such connotations. The emphasis on God's saving justice was one aspect of Luther's insight into the gospel of grace. The doctrine of justification means that, through the righteousness by which God himself is absolutely holy, he saves man, making him right or just before God. The righteousness of man, his justice, is not an ethical or legal purity, but the rightness given to him by God in Christ. In English use righteousness has long had a Protestant association; a better Protestant-Catholic understanding of each other's doctrine of justification has taken away some of the reason for this exclusive association. *JUSTIFICATION.

RINGATU, a religious group of the Maoris, the Polynesian natives of New Zealand. Little is known about them except that they broke off from the C of E in New Zealand.

RITSCHL, ALBRECHT (1822–89), German theologian. R. studied at Bonn, Halle, Heidelberg and Tübingen, then taught (1846) NT and patristics at Bonn. The major part of his career was as professor of theology at Göttingen, beginning in 1864. R.'s theology, which centered on the primacy of moral value, had a broad influence that extended into the 20th century. His position sought a middle ground between an ontological or metaphysical articulation of Christian truths, and a theology conformed merely with a subjective piety. Significantly he was the first major theologian to rely on the critical philosophy of Kant. Part of the appeal of R.'s thought was its liberation of theology from a reliance on metaphysics or from any relation to empirical scientific studies. At the same time he sought a theological synthesis that derived its objectivity

and consistency from its assertion of the primacy of moral value in revelation. Jesus Christ is the revelation that God intends man's moral perfection. The kingdom of God is temporal, and consists in the social diffusion of moral perfection. Justification is not juridic nor merely the taking away of sin, but a true reconciliation, a reestablished harmony of the sinner with God. The community of the justified manifests the kingdom of God by their acts of love for each other. The community has priority in R.'s thought. The Church is the expression of the community's striving for ethical redemption. R.'s influence was such that a Ritschlian school of theology developed. But more extensively his socio-ethical and historical view of theology was a main element in liberal theology's estimate of the nature of theology, its interpretation of revelation, gospel, and the development of the *Social Gospel movement. In particular A. von Harnack, E. Troeltsch, K. Barth and R. Bultmann were all in some way conditioned by R.'s theology. His main works were: *Die christliche Lehre von der Rechtfertigung und Verschnung* (3v., 1870–74; Eng. tr. *Critical History of the Christian Doctrine of Justification and Reconciliation*, 3v., 1872–1900); and a history of Pietism (*Geschichte des Pietismus*, 1880–86). See D. Ritschl, NCE 12:523; R. Anchor, EncPhil 7:202–203; K. Barth, *Protestant Thought: From Rousseau to Ritschl* (tr. B. Cozens, 1959), 390–399.

RITUAL (Methodist), the fixed forms and offices of worship prescribed by the *General Conference. Included are: baptism, confirmation and reception into the Church; holy communion; marriage; burial service; ordination of deacons and of elders; and consecration of bishops. These rituals are set forth in the *Discipline. Additional, optional offices for other occasions are found in the Book of Worship. The Ritual is not one of the doctrinal standards of the Church and may be altered by the General Conference. The first Ritual for American Methodism (since revised) was provided in 1784 by John *Wesley, who abridged the *Book of Common Prayer. See N. B. Harmon, *Rites and Ritual of Episcopal Methodism* (1926); R. J. Cooke, *Ritual of the Methodist Episcopal Church* (1900).

RITUAL, ROMAN, a liturgical book of the Roman rite containing the sacramental and extrasacramental rites performed by the priest. The evolution of the Roman *Pontifical for the use of bishops, was supplemented by a parallel development of manuals of ritual for the use of priests. From the 11th cent. on, collections of ritual formulas were gathered by monks. Most formulas were composed with a view to the monastic rather than the pastoral ministry and for that reason tended to be long. After the 12th cent. books of ritual were in common use among the clergy, and with the invention of printing they became indispensable guides in the administration of the sacraments and the execution of the priest's pastoral duties. The rituals of Castellani (1523) and Samarino (1579), both very popular during the 16th cent., provided a basis for the Roman Ritual promulgated by Paul V (1614). That ritual was strongly recommended to bishops and parish priests but it was never obligatory. Its promulgation did not preclude the use of other rituals, and in many dioceses and religious orders special rituals have been approved and employed, esp. for particular formulas. Some of these formulas have been incorporated into the Roman Ritual in an appendix. The Roman Ritual has been revised many times; the last typical edition appeared in 1952. An English translation with introductions and commentary was prepared by P. T. Weller and published in 1965. It incorporates the significant additions and revisions made by the Sacred Congregation of Rites since the last typical edition, as well as the changes introduced by the *Instruction* of Sept. 26, 1964, published by the Liturgy Commission. A complete revision of the Ritual is foreseen in view of the work of Consilium, the council formed in 1964 by Paul VI to implement Vatican Council II's Constitution on the Sacred Liturgy.

RITUALISM, an advocacy or practice of liturgical ceremony regarded as excessive; a word much used in the second half of the 19th cent., and often in disparagement. "Ritualist" originally meant one versed in liturgical rites and ceremonies, then afterwards one who advocated or performed them to an extent regarded as excessive. Together with the more hissing phrase "ritualistic practices," it was applied not to the participants of the *Oxford movement but to the Romanizers in worship and discipline of the *high-church party. In the C of E the implementation of the *Six Points— altar lights, eucharistic vestments, eastward position of the priest at the altar, wafer bread, the mixing in the chalice, and incense—meant falling foul of the average Anglican bishop of the day, the chance of prosecution in the courts, brawls in church, and the jibes of Punch. The matter, featured in Victorian literature, e.g., Ouida's character "who was very religious and strongly ritualistic," was the subject for a Royal Commission set up in 1867; its hostile recommendations proved a dead letter. The ritualists succeeded the earlier evangelicals in promoting the social gospel of the Church; it was not a question of dressing up for the sake of it, but of bringing light and color to the slums. They were better symbolized by the East End parson than by the Pale Curate with a penchant for frills. "I am told," wrote an observer, "they give short and practical sermons." Ritualism has now settled down to respectability in the Church of England. The post-Edwardian style, if less romantic and daring, is more stately and sumptuous than the Victorian. When it comes to pageantry Lambeth can hold its own with anything that can be put on by the Earl Marshal, the Brigade of Guards, or the Papal Master of Ceremonies. *PUBLIC WORSHIP REGULATION ACT.

RIVER BRETHREN, see BRETHREN IN CHRIST.

ROBERTS, ORAL (1918–   ), evangelist and healer. Born in Pontococ Co., Okla., R. was for many years an ordained minister of the Pentecostal Holiness Church; in 1968 he received Methodist ordination. He is second in fame and influence as an evangelist only to Billy *Graham. His evangelistic campaigns, which began in 1947 in Tulsa, Okla., have become worldwide. The organizational center is the Oral Roberts Evangelistic Association, Tulsa, where Oral Roberts Univ. was established with the goal of sending into his crusades 1,000 trained ministers each year. R. preaches the essential message of *Pentecostalism: *baptism with the Holy Spirit, *glossolalia, and *divine healing. He is most popularly known as a healer, and many cures are claimed during each crusade.

ROGATISTS, members of an obscure and conservative sect of *Donatists founded by Rogatus, Bp. of Cartenna in Mauretania Caesariensis *c*.365. He and nine colleagues broke away from the main body of Donatists and established a community based on the principle of nonviolence and specifically opposed to the drunken orgies and cruelty of the *Circumcellions. See Augustine, *Ep.* 93.11, 21, 49; W. H. C. Frend, *Donatist Church* (1952), 197–199.

ROGERS, JOHN (*c*.1500–55), first Protestant martyr of the Marian persecution. R. graduated at Pembroke Hall, Cambridge, and became chaplain to the English merchants at Antwerp. There he became the associate of William Tyndale, turned to Protestantism, and was married. Under the alias "Thomas Matthew" he prepared Matthew's Bible, and his valuable marginal notes constituted the first scriptural commentary in English. He returned to London, where his patron was Bishop Ridley, and to his credit he denounced the greed of the chief courtiers around Edward VI. Arrested in 1554 under Mary Tudor, he and other prisoners drew up a confession of faith that includes extreme Calvinistic doctrines. He endured ill-treatment with great cheerfulness; "there was never a little fellow," remarked Hooper, "that would better stick to a man than he." Before the faggots were kindled at Smithfield, he refused a pardon conditional on recantation. "He died," said Noailles, the ambassador of France, "in a manner as if he had been led to a wedding." See life by J. L. Chester (1861).

ROMAN CATECHISM, the *Catechism of the Council of Trent*, published at Rome in 1566 under the auspices of Pius V, commonly referred to as the *Catechismus Romanus*.

ROMAN CATHOLIC, a term used as an adjective to indicate the association of something with the Church whose visible head is the pope, and as a noun for a member of that Church. The term is not much used by Roman Catholics themselves, for whom "Catholic" needs no qualification to indicate the sense in which they understand it. Often, however, esp. in ecumenical discussion, the qualification is a useful means of obviating possible ambiguity. The term first appeared in the 16th cent. and was used disparagingly by Anglican divines who took offense at the way in which those who remained in communion with Rome appropriated to themselves the description of Catholic. Later the term was useful to those who propounded a *branch theory of the Catholic Church, for its apparent suggestion that "Roman" was a specific form of the genus "Catholic," other forms being Eastern Orthodox and Anglican. The odious connotation of the original use has been forgotten. Even the originally more invidious "Romish," "popish," or "papist" are now likely to sound quaintly humorous rather than acrimonious. The designation is now generally accepted as a noncontroversial and sometimes useful mode of identification. See H. Thurston, CE 13:121–123.

ROMAN CATHOLICISM, the teaching and practice of the Roman Catholic Church. Distinctive of the Church in relation to other Churches of the West is its understanding of itself and of its teaching authority. The Church teaches that its visible structure and the invisible spiritual life of the community of believers are two aspects of the one reality. That one reality is the Church, in historical and doctrinal continuity with the Church as Christ founded it. Full historical and doctrinal continuity is guaranteed for members of the Church through communion with the bishop of Rome as successor of Peter (see MEMBERSHIP IN THE CHURCH). The primacy of the pope is the main connotation of the term Roman in the title of the Church. As to its teaching authority, the Church maintains that the *rule of faith is divine revelation as contained in Scripture; the authentic understanding and the declaration of that revelation belong to the church *magisterium. In this context the meaning of *tradition as a rule of faith is to be understood in RC teaching. Tradition is not understood as an addition (as opposed to *sola scriptura*), rather it is the living understanding of what God's revelation does in fact contain. The acceptance or recognition of Scripture itself is safeguarded or authenticated by the living understanding of the magisterium. Nor is the teaching authority or tradition opposed to the personal direction of the Holy Spirit in the individual Christian. The Church does believe that this guidance for the community is guaranteed in a special way to the community as a whole. That guarantee of corporate fidelity to God's word is given to those who are the ordained teachers and pastors in the Church. Vatican Council II stressed this in its declaration on the *collegiality of the bishops. At the head of the college of bishops is the bishop of Rome. He is the supreme teacher (see PRIMACY). The doctrine of papal *infallibility fits in with this pattern of belief in the teaching authority of the Church as the rule of faith.

RC belief affirms the Trinity and Unity of God, and the redemptive incarnation of the Son of God, Jesus Christ. The special veneration of Mary rests on the belief that she is the mother of Jesus Christ, the Son of God, and for that reason was immaculately conceived and perpetually a virgin. Sacraments are accepted as signs of Christ's continually present, saving grace, and as therefore having the power to produce grace in recipients who believe in Christ. The sacraments are seven: baptism, confirmation, the Eucharist, penance, anointing of the sick, holy orders, and matrimony. Baptism, the sacrament of Christian rebirth, is administered to infants on the basis of the faith of the Christian community, and in the belief that original sin, besetting every human being, must be removed. The Eucharist is celebrated as a sign of Christian love, and of the continuous presence of Christ's sacrificial death in the Church. Penance, the sacrament of reconciliation, includes the need of auricular *confession. The celebration of the sacraments combined with the proclamation of the word of God constitutes the liturgy of the Church. Grace is believed to transform man inwardly, empowering him to work out the way of salvation, in dependence on the freely given promise of grace in his life. Those whose lives have reflected in a heroic degree the working of Christ's grace are venerated as saints, their prayers and intercession as friends of God are sought. Those whose charity is defective in minor degree at the time of death are believed to have need of purgation before being admitted to heaven; their purification can be hastened by the prayers of their living brethren in Christ. Belief is maintained in hell as an everlasting state of punishment for the impenitent sinner.

The polity of the RC Church basically depends on the belief that the teaching and pastoral authority in the Church is a sacred power. The structure is hierarchical. The supreme authority is that of the pope as head of the college of bishops. Through holy orders the bishops are teachers and pastors in the Church. (See COLLEGIALITY.) This, the Church believes, is in accord with Christ's institution.

ROMAN CREED, the ancient creed used at Rome, basis for the *Apostles' Creed in its present form. In the early Church, creedal formulas were committed orally to catechumens, to be repeated at their baptism, as Hippolytus (*c.*170–*c.*236) attests in his *Apostolic Tradition* with regard to the Roman Creed. In substance this was formulated before 190, and from the 4th cent. was referred to as *Symbolum Apostolorum*. The text is found substantially in Hippolytus's work; a Greek version presented at a synod in Rome, 340, by Marcellus of Ancyra closely conforms to the Latin text in *Commentary on the Apostles Creed*, written, 404, by Rufinus of Aquileia. See D 10–36.

ROMAN MISSAL, see MISSAL, ROMAN.

ROMAN RITUAL, see RITUAL, ROMAN.

ROMANTICISM (Religious Aspects), an interpretation of the universe that made man's interests central in the cosmos. Reality is symbolized as "God," "Providence," some "friend who cares," behind appearances. Man's ideals are safe because the Power behind Nature, never precisely defined, is also devoted to them. For the great majority, during the Romantic reaction to *Enlightenment, the failure of "rational religion" was reflected in the revivals of traditional religious faiths. This meant German Pietism, English evangelicalism, and a great resurgence of Catholicism on the Continent. Some Romantics were mere apologists for these faiths, men such as J. G. Hamann (1730–88) and F. Jacobi (1743–1819) or the French traditionalists J. de Maistre (1753–1821) and L. de Bonald (1754–1840). But many were not satisfied to turn to the past for inspiration, and even the prophets of the older faiths were influenced in countless ways by specifically Romantic values and attitudes. Their new interpretations of religion excluded identifying it with a set of pseudoscientific propositions that could not be maintained in the light of scientific reason. Religion was not to be identified with knowledge of what religion is. The influence of J. J. Rousseau (1712–78) on both the traditionalists and the reconstructors in Romanticism was of paramount importance. Rousseau emphasized intuition rather than analytic or discursive reasoning; he stimulated the urge to subjectivity and introspection, encouraged *emotionalism, and strengthened *individualism. His "Confession of Faith of a Savoyard Vicar," from *Émile* (1762), illustrates each of these perspectives on religion.

The Romantics offered three major interpretations of the nature and function of religion. First, religion is a form of knowledge, a philosophical explanation of the universe that uses symbols, whereas pure philosophy uses only concepts. The content and aim of both religion and pure philosophy are therefore equivalent. This view is best presented by G. Hegel (1770–1831) and his followers, but Hegelian idealism is least typical of Romantic concepts of religion. A second interpretation is that religion is not a form of knowledge but a form of art and aesthetic experience. It is a certain organized life of the feelings, a matter of emotion, and not, or only secondarily, of explanation or understanding. Theology furnishes symbols, not for the explanatory concepts of science and philosophy, but for the evocation and expression of man's deepest feelings. This view was worked out by J. Herder (1744–1803) and, more fully, by F. *Schleiermacher (1768–1834). A third interpretation is that religion is a form neither of knowledge nor of feeling but rather a form of action, of man's behavior. The religious life is a moral striving, to realize human and social goals. Matthew Arnold spoke of "morality touched with emotion," making "the will of God prevail." Its greatest 19th-cent. formulator was A. *Ritschl (1822–89), and it had a profound influence even into the 20th cent., through the *Social Gospel movement. See P. E. More, *Drift of Romanticism* (1955); M. Peckham, *Beyond the Tragic Vision* (1962); A. O. Lovejoy, "On the Discrimination of Romanticism," in *Essays in the History of Ideas* (pa., 1960).

RONGE, JOHANN (1813–87), founder of the German Catholic movement (*Deutschkatholizismus). As a Breslau priest he was in repeated difficulties with church authorities, and was suspended and later degraded from the priesthood in 1844 after writing a public letter severely attacking Bp. Wilhelm Arnoldi of Trier for fostering veneration of the relic of the Holy Coat. He thereafter organized a schismatic Church, which shortly abandoned its Catholic foundations, veering toward the contemporary rationalism that R. favored. He was more an agitator than a religious reformer. After a few years of notoriety, he spent the remainder of his life in oblivion.

RONSDORF SECT (Ronsdorf Zionites), a German enthusiastic group founded by Elias Eller (1690–1750) after 1726. He was married to Anna von Buchel, the visionary daughter of a baker, and he and his followers settled at Ronsdorf. He called himself "Father of Zion," Anna "Mother of Zion," and their son "Messiah." Their excesses in religious belief and moral practices caused the pastor of Ronsdorf, the paternal grandfather of F. Schleiermacher, to leave the group. After Eller's death the remaining adherents became (1768) a congregation of the *Reformed Church. See Gründler 2:1196–97; E. Beyreuther, RGG 5:1181; G. H. Klippel, EncRelKnow 10:90–91.

ROSICRUCIANS, a name adopted by certain societies or fraternities claiming hidden knowledge. The symbolism of the rose and cross, from which the word is derived, is uncertain. Rosicrucianism has had two periods of florescence. Its origins in its earlier form are obscure, allegedly because of deliberate efforts to veil the history from outsiders. Stories of obviously fabulous character have been advanced to substantiate claims to antiquity. Some Rosicrucians have held that their order can be traced back to the time of Pharaoh Thutmose III. Others claim that the movement began with the foundation of the Society of the Rose and Cross by Christian Rosencreuz, a German scholar, in 1413 in order to share with others the advanced knowledge of medicine, philosophy, and science he had gathered from Muslim sages on his extensive travels in the East. Authorship of a book that appeared in the 17th cent., an allegorical work of occult science called *Die Chymische Hochzeit*, was attributed to Rosencreuz. However, the earliest appearance of Rosicrucianism of which we can be reasonably sure was in the circle of Paracelsus (d. 1541), the Swiss alchemist and physician. Possibly it was founded by Paracelsus himself, or if not, by one of his disciples. Johann Valentine Andreä published the *Fama fraternitatis* in 1614–15; in 1616 the *Die Chymische Hochzeit* appeared. Andreä gave out the story of Rosencreuz in great detail, claiming that his writings had been buried with him and had only recently been discovered in his tomb. Later, however, Andreä declared that his account of the early history and of the documents supposedly left by Rosencreuz had been a hoax. After Andreä's *Fama fraternitatis* had aroused interest, other treatises on Rosicrucianism appeared in swift succession. The English Rosicrucian Henry Fludd (d. 1637) published two treatises on the subject on the Continent; the manuscript of a third, addressed to King James I, was found among his papers. Like many 17th-cent. philosophers, Fludd was steeped in neoplatonism and his thought was markedly pantheistic. Extant correspondence between Continental Rosicrucians and Fludd indicates that groups of scholars in Germany and elsewhere were organized as members of the Fraternity of the Rosy Cross and that they rejected both Catholic and Lutheran teachings in their pursuit of wisdom. Little is known of the nature of this movement and still less of its formal organization. Its members made use of the language of alchemy, medicine, and the occult to transmit their philosophic speculations.

Kenelm Digby (d. 1665) is thought to have been a Rosicrucian. Thomas Ashmole (d. 1692) is said to have organized a lodge of the fraternity at London in 1646. A translation of *Die Chymische Hochzeit* was published in English in 1690 under the title *The Chemical Wedding*. The later history of both Continental and English Rosicrucianism is as obscure as its origins. It does not seem to have survived the 18th cent. in any recognizable form, except for possible influences on Freemasonry.

A modern Rosicrucian revival began in 1868 with the publication of *The General Statutes of the Order of Knights of the Rose Cross* by R. W. Little. As reorganized by Little, this form of the movement was a branch of Freemasonry. William Wynn Westcott succeeded Little as leader of the *Societas Rosicruciana in Anglia* and published a history of the Rosicrucians in 1885. Little's society was primarily a fraternal organization closely allied to Freemasonry. Local units (colleges) were established in various parts of the English-speaking world and elsewhere after 1875. An American branch was established with headquarters in New York City (*Societas Rosicruciana in America*), and a Rosicrucian Brotherhood was founded at Quakertown, Pa.; Reuben Swinburne Clymer, a prolific writer on religious and occult subjects, reorganized this brotherhood in 1902. The Ancient Mystical Order Rosae Crucis (AMORC) was founded by H. Spencer Lewis in 1915 with headquarters at San Jose, California. AMORC is strongly missionary, advertises extensively, and distributes more than 6 million pieces of literature a year. Both the Rosicrucian Brotherhood and AMORC can be classified as religious movements, although AMORC insists that it is simply a fraternal organization. Both promise their members the power to utilize cosmic forces by discovering the secret wisdom of the ages. Clymer's theology is a mystical Gnosticism based on a progressive divinization of the initiate. Man is created with a spark of the divine in him and, by recognizing and bringing it to consciousness through the secret laws of nature known to the initiated, it becomes an inexhaustible source of wisdom and power. This theme is at the heart of religious Rosicrucianism and can be found in the AMORC literature as well. A fourth branch of the movement, the Rosicrucian Fellowship, founded by Max Heindel at Oceanside, Calif., is also religious in its orientation, with considerable emphasis on astrology. See R. K. MacMaster, NCE 12:676–677; A. C. Jones, Hastings ERE 10:856–858.

ROTHMANN, BERNHARDT (Bernt; b. c.1495), Anabaptist leader at Münster. While parish priest at St. Mauritz in Münster, R. first began to preach Lutheranism (1531), but soon embraced the teaching of M. *Hofmann. When the Anabaptists captured Münster in 1534, R. joined them; in the Münster kingdom, he was court preacher and shared in the practice of polygamy by taking nine wives. He published a manifesto of Anabaptist teaching, *Von rechter und gesunder christlicher Lehre, Glauben und Leben* (1533–35; ed. R. Stupperich, 1964). At the fall of the Münster kingdom, R. probably escaped; the date of his death is unknown. See H. Börsting, LTK 9:67–68; R. Stupperich, *Die Schreiben der Münster: Täufer und ihrer Gegner* (v.1, 1964); bibliog. for Anabaptists.

ROYAL DECLARATION, a solemn affirmation concerning religion made by every monarch of England from William III (1689) to Edward VII (1901). The declaration was imposed by Parliament in 1689 to secure Protestant succession to the throne (SEE DECLARATION OF RIGHTS). At coronation or at the opening of his first Parliament, the king was required to declare his rejection of *transubstantiation, the Mass, and invocation of Mary or the saints. By the end of the 19th cent., long after Catholic emancipation (1829), a movement began to soften the language, which was offensively anti-Roman. Under George V, such a modification was passed by Parliament and approved by the King (1910). The new monarch simply professes that he is a Protestant and will uphold the law of Protestant succession to the throne.

RULE OF FAITH, the criterion or norm that guarantees the truth of what is believed. Christian theology regards faith as an immediate contact with God; the word of God revealing is the motive for the believer's acceptance; and it is the primary guarantee that what is believed is true. But theology has used the phrase "rule of faith" in a more determinate sense. The object or content of faith is a body of truths, the content of God's word. The rule of faith is a norm by which the believer has assurance that what he believes is indeed conformed to what God reveals. Christians generally have agreed that such a rule of faith is the Bible. The Bible is accepted as containing God's revelation, and therefore the believer's understanding must be conformed to the Bible (see BIBLE, AUTHORITY OF). Exceptions throughout Christian history, however, have been the various manifestations of *enthusiasm, religious *illuminism, or *subjectivism, which have replaced the Bible with some direct intuition or experience as the rule of faith.

Sola scriptura, the Bible alone, is a phrase intended to express the division between Roman Catholics and Protestants over the rule of faith since the Reformation. RC teaching was reasserted, but also significantly clarified, by Vatican Council II: "The office of authentically interpreting the word of God, whether written or handed down, has been entrusted exclusively to the living teaching office of the Church, whose authority is exercised in the name of Jesus Christ." However, this "teaching office is not above the word of God but ministers to it, teaching only what has been handed on . . . it draws on the deposit of faith everything it proposes for belief as divinely revealed" (Vat II DivRev 10). The rule of faith according to RC teaching is the Bible as the written word of God; tradition, apostolic or ecclesial, i.e., the living understanding and transmission in the Church of God's revelation (which includes and is not extraneous to the Bible); and the teaching authority, or *magisterium. These three "are so linked together that one cannot stand without the others" (*ibid.*). *Sola scrip-*

tura has an exclusive sense: the rejection of both tradition and the mediation of the magisterium as rules of faith. But the exclusiveness can be oversimplified. Protestant appeal to the sole sufficiency of Scripture has not in fact been only to a book or to the written word. Reliance is upon the Scripture become the living word through the Holy Spirit evoking the response of the believer. In the left-wing Reformation and in the Quaker doctrine of *Inner Light this experience was made more central than the Bible itself. Nor did the Bible exclude the formulation of confessions of faith as subordinate rules of faith (see NORMA NORMATA). The many anticreedal movements in Protestantism are a negative indication that such formulations assumed a major significance for determining orthodoxy. The major 20th cent. theological trends in Protestantism have been a search to reaffirm the meaning of Scripture as rule of faith, to reassert the primacy of God's word.

A real and substantive difference separates Christians in their explanation of the rule of faith. The root of the difference is in diverse concepts of the Church. Yet the mutual enrichment and dialogue of RC and Protestant theologians on the meaning of the mission of the Church, tradition, and the primacy of Scriptures are hopeful signs of progress toward unity.

RUNCARII, the name by which members of one group of *Cathari were known in Germany during the 13th century. Derivation of the term is uncertain, but it was probably a geographic reference. See S. Runciman, *Medieval Manichee* (pa., 1961), 185; H. C. Lea, *History of the Inquisition of the Middle Ages.* (1888; repr., 1958), 1:88.

RUSSELL, CHARLES TAZE (1852–1916), founder of the Watch Tower Bible and Tract Society (see JEHOVAH'S WITNESSES). As a young haberdasher in Allegheny, Pa., R. undertook a study of the Bible and was much influenced by Adventist doctrines. He founded a religious organization (1872) whose members were called Russellites, Earnest Bible Students, Watch Tower People, or Millennial Dawnists until J. F. *Rutherford gave them the name Jehovah's Witnesses in 1931. R. denied the existence of hell, preached that the final battle of Armageddon and Christ's second coming were imminent, and rejected the orthodox doctrine of the Trinity. Pastor Russell, as he called himself, organized Bible study groups throughout the U.S. and began publication of the *Watch Tower and Herald of Christ's Presence* in 1879. He completed a 6-volume Bible commentary called *Studies in the Scriptures*, or *Millennial Dawn* (v.6, 1886–1904). R.'s wife sought a legal separation in 1903, and he was involved in several suits over support payments. In 1908 he moved the headquarters of his movement from Pittsburgh, Pa., to Brooklyn, New York. His marital difficulties and unfulfilled prediction that the world would end in 1914 lost him some followers in his last years.

RUSSELLITES, until *Jehovah's Witnesses was adopted as the official title in 1931, one of the many names by which that group, founded by Charles Taze *Russell, was known.

RUTHERFORD, JOSEPH FRANKLIN (1869–1942), second president of the Watch Tower Bible and Tract Society, now known as *Jehovah's Witnesses. After the death of Charles Taze *Russell in 1916, R. was elected president of the society. Once a small-town lawyer in Missouri, he had become the society's legal adviser. During World War I he served a year in Atlanta penitentiary for excessive defense of conscientious objection. Known to his followers as Judge Rutherford, he supervised the growth of the organization for 25 years. During this time, the membership grew from a few thousand to 106,000, and societies were established in many foreign countries. He wrote a book almost every year, as well as many tracts, pamphlets, and articles; *Harp of God* (1921) summarized his

teachings. R. was particularly critical of Catholicism, although he opposed all organized religion. In 1931 he chose the name Jehovah's Witnesses to identify those who supported the Watch Tower Society.

RUYSBROECK, JAN VAN, BL. (Rusbroek, Ruisbroeck, Russbroec; 1293–1381), Flemish mystic. R. was reared by a saintly uncle, a canon of St. Gudule's in Brussels. After ordination in 1317 he continued to live with his uncle and another canon, F. van Coudenberg. In 1343, the three men withdrew to a hermitage at Groenendael, where they were soon joined by disciples. The group adopted the rule of the Canons of Saint-Victor in 1349, with Van Coudenberg as provost and R. as prior. The society they formed appears to be a link between the *Friends of God and the *Brethren of the Common Life. R. was influenced by Meister Eckhart and was in touch with Gurt de Groote and Johann Tauler. He corrected the error and excess into which the attempts of simple persons to become like God had fallen: that God asks of exalted souls that they become indistinguishable from him. R. preached a true *deificatio*: that the self is not fused in God but preserves its identity, rising to Christian perfection by three stages: the active life, the inward life, and the contemplative life. This he expounded in his earliest extant work, which is also his masterpiece: *The Spiritual Espousals* (c.1330). Other treatises among the 13 ascribed to him are *The Kingdom of Lovers* and *The Tabernacle*; when a copy of the latter was pirated and given to the Carthusians at Herne, they asked R. for an explanation of parts that disturbed them. Their request gave rise to his *Little Book of Enlightenment*, the best defense against the charges, esp. of quietism, that have been made against him. R. has been represented as an untutored man, miraculously inspired; but his writings show that he was a master of theology. Feast, Dec. 2. See L. Reypens, LTK 9:127–128; RGG 3:529–530; R. Wautier d'Aygalliers, *Ruysbroeck the Admirable* (1969).

S

SABATIER, AUGUSTE (1839–1901), Protestant theologian, leader of the "Paris School" in the 19th century. Professor at the Paris Protestant faculty of theology from 1877, S. based his thought esp. on that of F. *Schleiermacher (see LIBERAL THEOLOGY). He regarded the essence of religion as the feeling of dependence experienced by the soul in distress from consciousness of its lofty aspirations and inability to achieve them. Revelation is the progressive presence of God to the soul and the soul to God through this conscious and willed feeling of dependence. All dogma is simply the expression, the objectification as symbol, of subjective religious experience. It is essentially and interminably evolving, to match the feelings it represents. The thought of S., called *symbolofideism, or critical symbolism, influenced the development of *modernism. S.'s works included *The Apostle Paul* (1891), *Outlines of a Philosophy of Religion* (1897), and the posthumous *Religion of Authority and Religion of the Spirit* (1904).

SABBATARIAN BAPTISTS, another name, esp. in England, for Seventh Day Baptists.

SABBATARIANS, a name applied either to those who keep Saturday as the Lord's Day, or to those who are rigid in their interpretation of Sunday observance. (1) Those Jews who are strict in keeping the OT Sabbath are called Sabbatarians. The term is also a classification applicable to those Christian bodies that adopted the OT observance. These include: a group of Anabaptists, followers of Oswald Glait, in Silesia, c.1528, against whose practice Luther protested; an adventist body in 16th-cent. Finland; certain Unitarians in Transylvania who by the 19th cent. had converted to Judaism; a sect in Russia suppressed in 1825; the Southcottians in 19th-cent. England; Seventh-day Adventists; and Seventh Day Baptists. (2) Those who adhere to Sabbatarianism teaching that Sunday observance means abstention from all work, recreation, and amusement (see SUNDAY OBSERVANCE). The insistence upon these prohibitions has been a distinctive feature of post-Reformation Churches of England, Scotland, and Wales. The rigid Sabbatarianism of the Puritans was expressed in Nicholas Bound's *True Doctrine of the Sabbath* (1595); during the *Commonwealth, severe Sabbatarian laws were passed. Every form of recreation, even walking for pleasure, was forbidden. Even more stringent were the laws enforced by the Scottish Presbyterians. Strict Sunday observance was part of life in the New England colonies, and the Blue Laws remaining in some places are vestiges of this stringency. In the 18th and 19th cents., both in England and in North America, Baptists, Methodists, and Presbyterians were zealous Sabbatarians. While there were no RC ecclesiastical laws curtailing Sunday recreation, some Catholics, esp. in the eastern U.S., shared in Sabbatarian attitudes. The secularism of the 20th cent. has not completely overcome Sabbatarian influence in regard to surviving laws or legal decisions concerning Sunday observance. In England there is a Lord's Day Observance Society, and in the U.S., a Lord's Day Alliance, both promoting Sabbatarian objectives.

SABBATIANS, a group of *Novatianists at Constantinople founded by the Jewish convert, and later bp., Sabbatios (d. c.410), who celebrated Easter according to the Jewish calendar and advocated an even greater rigorism than the rest of the Novatianist community. Sabbatios was exiled for life to the island of Rhodes as punishment for having been consecrated a Novatian bishop. His grave was venerated by his followers; the group disappeared by the 6th century.

SACERDOTALISM (Lat. *sacerdos*, priest), a term usually used disparagingly of the claim to special power or its exercise by the clergy. (1) In its specific sense sacerdotalism refers unfavorably to the system of a special priesthood, in which the ordained priest is regarded as possessing sacred power to offer sacrifice, to consecrate, to absolve from sin, to bless. The term sacerdotalism disparages such a system as being opposed to the *priesthood of all believers and as an intrusion of human mediation between the believer and God's communication of grace through Christ. (2) The term is used more generally to connote domination of church life by clergy to the exclusion or downgrading of the laity. *SACRAMENTALISM; *ECCLESIASTICISM, *CLERICALISM.

SACRAMENT, as defined by St. Thomas Aquinas, "a sign of a sacred reality insofar as this reality sanctifies men." Sacraments are sacred actions used in the Church and authorized by the institution of Christ in which physical, external means are made to serve both as signs and as channels of sanctifying grace. This notion is the result of centuries of theological evolution. The word "sacrament" and its Greek equivalent "mystery" have been used in many different ways and for many different actions, some of which do not qualify as sacraments under the current definition. Since any such definition is, in the last analysis, arbitrary, it is necessary in reading any author to ascertain how he uses the word and not to draw conclusions from any such usage about the correctness of his theology. Even in the sacramental system, moreover, some elements in the definition as given apply more easily to some of the sacraments than to others; thus, for example, most theologians today would agree that it is difficult or impossible to find biblical evidence for the direct institution of confirmation by Jesus Christ.

The component elements of the definition should be specified with some care, for each serves to clarify and to limit the meaning of the others. Sacraments must be not only signs of grace but also channels of grace. The use of the sign of the cross, whose ancient provenance in Christian practice may be evidence for an origin in apostolic times and therefore for "institution" by Christ, is not ordinarily interpreted by Christian theologians as a channel of grace. The external, physical means required for an action to be a sacrament would seem to rule out the preaching of the gospel from the category of sacrament, even though it may claim institution by Christ himself and is "the power of God for salvation" (Rom 1.16). Recent RC theologians, however, have been careful to make clear that "institution by Christ" does not necessarily mean an explicit act of the historical person, Jesus Christ, establishing and commanding a sacramental action. As the one who founded his Church and who built it "upon the foundation of the apostles and prophets, Christ Jesus himself being the cornerstone" (Eph 2.20), Jesus also provided it with the instruments by which it would be able to carry out its saving mission. In the development of the sacramental life of the Church, therefore, the risen Christ has continued to exercise his lordship and in this sense to "institute" those actions by which the Church has faithfully carried out its mission.

Above all, then, the sacraments are means and channels of the grace of God. In this understanding of their function and nature, two historic misunderstandings must be avoided. The communication of divine grace through the sacraments is not to be thought of in a mechanical or an automatic sense, as though grace were a measure of sacred stuff distributed in so many doses through sacraments. As the gift and favor of a personal God, grace cannot be reduced to magic or to material; nor can the connection between sacrament and grace be made arbitrary or accidental, as though the recipient of the sacrament could not depend upon the presence of grace in it, but had to wonder each time whether it was in fact being proffered there. The scholastic formula "God is bound by the sacraments but not to the sacraments" seeks to ensure both that the personal relationship to God is not degraded into magic and that the objective availability of divine grace in the sacrament is not jeopardized. As means and channels of grace, the sacraments convey to those who rightly receive them the benefits of the death and resurrection of Christ, uniting them to his work. Although it is more explicit in the case of baptism than in that of other sacraments, this union with the saving work of Christ in his death and resurrection characterizes the sacraments: "We were buried therefore with him by baptism into death, so that as Christ was raised from the dead by the glory of the Father, we too might walk in newness of life" (Rom 6.4).

As means of grace, the sacraments are more than symbols or signs, but they are never less. Their very nature as actions that point beyond their intrinsic meaning to an ultimate significance is bound up with their being "signs." The laying on of hands that takes place in confirmation or in holy orders is an ancient rite by no means confined to Christianity; in Gen 48.14 it was part of the patriarchal blessing. But within the context of the Christian sacraments this ceremony becomes a sign of the grace being conferred in and through the sacramental transaction. Similarly, there have been ceremonial washings and sacred meals in many religions, so that Christian baptism and the Christian Eucharist may attach themselves to a widespread, if not indeed universal, phenomenon of religious experience. Yet they are special "signs" because they point not only to some timeless truth about the cosmos but to the events in the life of Jesus by which the salvation of the human race was achieved. Locked as he is into a world of sense-experience, man cannot look beyond this world without signposts that, appearing within the empirical realm, nevertheless show the way to another realm. The sacraments have a special role among such signposts, and the rituals surrounding their celebration have sought to enhance their importance as signs, their *significance.*

It belongs to the nature of sacraments

that they are properly carried on within the Church. As the body of Christ, who is himself the fundamental mystery (or sacrament) of salvation, the Church participates in his sacramental character and dispenses his sacramental gifts. Thus there have been many writers, both in the scholastic period and again in the modern, who have not hesitated to designate both Christ and the Church as "sacraments." Without becoming involved in dogmatic nomenclature, one may nevertheless see in this a recognition that the sacraments, to be effective, are simultaneously grounded in the person and work of Christ and set into the context of the Church. This emphasis protects them from an individualistic (and often magical) distortion. *Infant baptism, for example, is not a magical incantation over an individual child but the responsible action of the Christian community and of the parents of the child, assuming the responsibilities of *Christian nurture of which baptism is the first and most important step. As the dispenser of the sacraments, the Church through them invites and welcomes men to participation in the life of God himself; as the "sign" of the incarnation and of the redemption, the Church employs the other "signs" instituted by its Lord.

The sacraments are also, in the pregnant phrase of St. Augustine, "the visible words of God." In many definitions of what constitutes a sacrament, the word of God is identified as an indispensable factor. "Let the word come to the elements, and a sacrament comes to be," was St. Augustine's formula. Therefore it is also necessary to consider the sacraments in their relation to the spoken and the written word of God. St. Paul says of the Eucharist: "As often as you eat this bread and drink this cup, you proclaim the Lord's death until he comes" (1 Cor 11.26). Sharing in the sacramental action is evidently a form of that proclamation which is normally carried on by word of mouth. In some forms of Protestant theology, this function of the sacraments as "visible words" has tended to predominate, to such an extent that the sacraments have been thought to confer nothing other than is conferred by the word. But even where this extreme subordination of sacrament to word has not been present, it has been recognized that a co-ordination of the two is beneficial to an understanding of both; and it is no exaggeration when some theologians, esp. within Protestantism but also within Roman Catholicism, have spoken of "the sacramentality of the word" as a corollary of the idea that the sacraments are the visible words of God.

From what has already been said it will be evident that the question of the specific number of the sacraments, about which so much of the polemic between Protestant and RC theology has argued, is not the central issue it has sometimes appeared to be. Theologians of impeccable orthodoxy have maintained, on the basis of a particular definition, that there are more than seven (e.g., fourteen) or fewer than seven (e.g., two or three) sacraments. The seven traditionally identified as sacraments are: baptism, confirmation, the Eucharist, penance, the anointing of the sick (also called extreme unction), holy orders, and matrimony. Protestants have usually restricted the number to baptism and the Eucharist; Luther was willing to call absolution a sacrament as well. Both the problem of a proper definition and the question of a biblically validated institution by Christ have played a part in the debates about the number of the sacraments. See O. C. Quick, *Christian Sacraments* (1917); B. Leeming, *Principles of Sacramental Theology* (1956); J. de Ghellinck, *Pour l'histoire du mot "Sacramentum"* (1924).

SACRAMENTALISM, emphasis on the sacraments as central to the Christian life; often a pejorative term applied to a value allegedly set on sacraments as external acts apart from faith and inward appreciation of their meaning (see SACRAMENTS). The term is particularly used to discredit the theory that sacraments confer grace *ex opere operato*, and suggests that this implies a devotion to sacraments that neglects God, who acts through them, and turns from

faith in Christ himself to dependence on the performance of the signs of his action. Those who affirm the objective effectiveness of sacraments, however, mean that it is God's action that causes this effectiveness, and that the sacraments bring Christ's presence; they agree that actual reception of this effectiveness and presence is in proportion to the faith of the recipient.

SACRAMENTARIANS, a term used in two senses. (1) The primary use was that originated by Martin Luther, opposing the eucharistic teaching of *Zwingli, *Oecolampadius, and others who understood the sacramental presence of Christ in the Eucharist to mean a metaphorical presence, as opposed to a *Real Presence (see *Formula of Concord, Art. VII). Throughout the 16th cent. the term became a designation for anyone denying the Real Presence. (See MARBURG ARTICLES; WITTENBERG CONCORD; UBIQUITARIANISM.) (2) Less commonly, those who teach the objective power of the sacraments to confer grace have been disparagingly called sacramentarians.

SADOLETO, JACOPO (1477–1547), cardinal and bishop of Carpentras. Born in Modena and reared to become a public servant in Ferrara under the Este, he elected to pursue his studies of the classics and went to Rome in 1498. Upon completion of his education, he was recognized as a minor poet and fine Latinist. In 1511 he was ordained; in 1527 he became bishop of Carpentras and in 1536, cardinal. During those years he gained a reputation as a reformer. Although unwilling to compromise with the Protestants on religious doctrine, S. was in favor of implementing reform measures in the Church and participated in a famous reform commission under Paul III. During the years 1527–38 he produced his chief works; the most famous are *De Laudibus philosophiae* (1538), a humanistic work, and *In Pauli epistolam ad Romanos commentariorum libri tres* (1535), a controversial theological work. S. was respected by Protestants, and in 1539 he addressed a letter to Geneva, attempting to win the city back to Catholicism. John Calvin's letter in reply (1539) is a famous *apologia* for the Reformation; the exchange is contained in J. Calvin and J. Sadoleto, *Reformation Debate* (ed. J. C. Olin, 1966). As both a humanist and an advocate of church reform, S. represented the trend from Renaissance to reform in the Roman Church. See R. Douglas, *J. S. (1477–1547), Humanist and Reformer* (1959).

ST. BARTHOLOMEW'S DAY MASSACRE,

the most widely known of several slaughters of the *Huguenots in France; it began in Paris, Aug. 24, 1572. It was probably not premeditated but an expedient adopted on the spur of the moment by Catherine de Médicis. After the third of the *Wars of Religion, Catherine, following her new policy of conciliation, allowed the Huguenot leader Gaspard de Coligny to hold an influential position at the court and to plan with King Charles IX a campaign against Spain in support of William of Orange. Coligny favored an all-out campaign; Catherine was against a major war. She decided to liquidate the Huguenot leader, whose increasing influence over the King displeased her. At her instigation an incident occurred on Aug. 22 in which Coligny was wounded by two shots from an arquebus. Fearing that the ensuing royal inquiry might reveal her own role in the event, Catherine extracted the King's consent to a mass slaughter as a countermeasure against an alleged Huguenot antiroyalist conspiracy. The massacre, in which Coligny was the first murdered, lasted several days and spread to the provinces. No reliable statistics of the number of victims are available; the figures quoted vary from 3,000 to 10,000. The immediate result of the massacre was the fourth of the Wars of Religion. See W. J. Stankiewicz, NCE 7:201–204, s.v. "Huguenots," with bibliog.; P. Erlanger, *St. Bartholomew's Night* (tr. P. O'Brian, 1962); H. Noguères, *Massacre of Saint Bartholomew* (tr. C. E. Engel, 1962).

SAINT-CYRAN, ABBÉ DE (Jean Duvergier de Hauranne; 1581–1643), theologian and spiritual adviser whose writings and activities were very influential in 17th-cent. France, esp. in connection with *Jansenism. Born in Bayonne of a rising merchant family, he studied theology at the Jesuit college in Louvain. There he met Cornelius *Jansen; in seclusion (1611–16) the two made a diligent study of the Scriptures and the Fathers, esp. St. Augustine. (There is no reason to suppose, however, that Saint-Cyran collaborated on Jansen's later *Augustinus.*) Ordained priest (1618), later made abbot *in commendam* of Saint-Cyran (1620), a title by which he was generally known, he lived in Paris, where he became an intimate friend of the founder of the Oratory, Bérulle. He gained fame under the name of Petrus Aurelius by defending the vicar apostolic of England, Richard Smith, against the Jesuits, thus giving wide publicity to Oratorian ideas on the priesthood and the superiority of the secular over the religious clergy. He made further enemies by defending the *Chapelet du Saint Sacrement* of Agnès *Arnauld (1627). But it was his open stand against Richelieu and the extreme position of some of his spiritual direction demanding perfect contrition for absolution that finally led to his imprisonment at Vincennes (1638). At the trial St. Vincent de Paul paid tribute to his zeal for souls and for the Church. During his nearly 5 years of imprisonment he maintained his influence as a spiritual director both by letter and by the visits of a circle of influential clients. His influence on the Jansenist movement was chiefly by his direction of the members of the Arnauld family, esp. Mère Angélique, and Antoine, whom he encouraged to write *De la fréquente communion.* Saint-Cyran's spiritual doctrine, resembling that of St. Francis de Sales, reveals him as a devout man; some of his ideas on the priesthood, obedience to a spiritual director, and reliance on grace, became standard themes in French devotional literature. Jansenist interpretation of predestination and the Jansenist penchant for intrigue are also suggested in his letters and spiritual treatises. His influence extended beyond the RC Church: John *Wesley translated many of his letters and was thoroughly familiar with his doctrine, although he naturally adapted it to his own audience. See J. Orcibal, *Saint-Cyran et le Jansénisme* (1961); bibliography for Jansenism.

SALVATION, the deliverance of man from sin and death through the work of Jesus Christ. The term is variously employed in the Bible and in theological parlance; at least three of its meanings deserve to be noted.

Salvation means atonement. Jesus Christ is called Savior in Christian language because he achieved salvation by his life, death, and resurrection. Western Christian theology has frequently defined this salvation in the language of vicarious satisfaction, as this was formulated in the *Cur deus homo* (c.1097) of St. Anselm. By his death on the cross Christ satisfied the injured justice of God and thus made atonement for human sin. In Greek theology the emphasis has been on the resurrection of Christ as not only the declaration of salvation but its means as well. Christ triumphed over the spiritual enemies of man—sin, death, and the devil—and grants salvation as *Christus Victor*. These emphases are by no means mutually exclusive, but they do stress different aspects of the saving work of Christ. This definition of salvation underlies such biblical statements as Tit 2.11, 13–14: "The grace of God has appeared for the salvation of all men . . . our blessed hope, the appearing of the glory of our great God and Savior Jesus Christ, who gave himself for us to redeem us from all iniquity."

Salvation means conversion. Thus Christians of the *evangelical traditions speak of "the day I was saved" as the day when, through an experience of repentance and conversion, they became Christian believers. The etymological meaning of salvation is "health," and in the NT being saved means being restored to spiritual health and living a healthy life. In this sense, salvation is a state of being, brought about by the saving work of Christ and conferred upon the individual through the gifts of the Holy Spirit. As a new life in Christ, it is also a following in his steps. The joy and courage that are components of salvation in this sense of the word are described not only in the NT but also and esp. in the Old, as in Ps 27.1, 4: "The Lord is my light and my salvation; whom shall I fear? One thing have I asked of the Lord, that will I seek after; that I may dwell in the house of the Lord all the days of my life, to behold the beauty of the Lord, and to inquire in his temple" (see CONVERSION; JUSTIFICATON; JUSTIFICATION BY FAITH).

Salvation means immortality. In some Christian traditions, this understanding of salvation as the life that will commence only after death has largely overshadowed the other meanings of the word, esp. the second. There is good NT warrant for interpreting salvation as immortality—though not for restricting it to this meaning. When St. Paul says that "salvation is nearer to us now than when we first believed" (Rom 13.11), salvation is being used for the eschatological hope of the return of Christ at the second coming and the beginning of life in heaven. But the same Apostle, quoting the Book of Isaiah, could declare: "For he says, 'At the acceptable time I have listened to you, and helped you on the day of salvation.' Behold, now is the acceptable time; behold, now is the day of salvation" (2 Cor 6.2). The solution to this apparent contradiction is to be found in the biblical use of such terms as "eternal life," which refers to an existence that begins here and now within human history but reaches its consummation and perfection only at the end of history. For it is only there that the enemies of salvation are completely abolished and their power taken away. See G. Aulén, *Christus Victor* (tr. A. G. Herbert, rev. ed., 1969); A. Gelin et al., *Son and Savior* (tr. A. Wheaton, rev. ed., 1962).

SALVATION, ASSURANCE OF, see ASSURANCE OF SALVATION.

SALVATION ARMY (SA), a religious body founded and organized on military lines by William *Booth at London in 1865. Booth had been a Methodist evangelist, but he organized the Christian Revival Association as a nondenominational Holiness mission to work exclusively in the slums of London. With slight modifications his organization became the Christian Mission, operating throughout the British Isles, and finally the worldwide Salvation Army. Booth made effective use of recent converts to evangelize others in a language familiar to them, and every enrolled Salvationist was licensed to preach. Booth retained control of every detail of the movement, and when the Christian Mission was reorganized as the SA, ownership of all its property and authority over all its members were vested in him. He issued the *Orders and Regulations for the Salvation Army* in October 1878, prescribing in minute detail the quasi-military organization, dress, and daily occupations of his followers. Expansion in Great Britain followed rapidly. While the Christian Mission operated 30 stations in 1878, the SA maintained 51 stations with 127 full-time evangelists by January 1879. Work began in the U.S. in 1880 and in Canada in 1881. The SA's first station in India was established in 1882. Difficulties came with rapid growth, notably over efforts made by Thomas E. Moore to incorporate the SA as a religious body in the U.S. in 1884, which produced a division now represented by the *American Rescue Workers. A second effort to secure greater autonomy for American Salvationists led to the secession of Ballington Booth and the formation of the *Volunteers of America in 1896. The persistent problem of too much centralization was not solved until 1929, when the newly created High Council, composed of senior territorial officers, received power to elect and depose a commander-in-chief.

Early struggles to combat alcoholism and prostitution in English slums have expanded into the SA's respected and many-faceted social welfare program. In inspiration and purpose the SA is evangelis-

tic, and while Booth did not intend to found another denomination, the SA is in fact a Church, with its own doctrinal and ritual systems. While accepting the primacy of the Bible, Salvationists also emphasize the immediacy of the Holy Spirit's inspiration of the believer. The central doctrines of sin and redemption are understood in an Arminian sense; *entire sanctification as a second blessing is a prominent theme. The traditional Christian sacraments of baptism and the Lord's Supper are disregarded; there is a ritual for the dedication of children, and the Army's own military rituals are considered to be part of the process of salvation. There are about 300,000 Salvationists in the U.S., and about 30,000 officers in evangelizing work throughout the world. See H. A. Wisbey, Jr., *Soldiers without Swords: A History of the Salvation Army in the U.S.* (1956).

SANCTIFICATION, a second work of grace, distinct from *justification and bringing deliverance from sinfulness, or inbred sin. *CHRISTIAN PERFECTION; *ENTIRE SANCTIFICATION; *PERFECTIONISM.

SANDEMANIANS, designation for the *Glasites after R. Sandeman (1718–71) became their leader in 1739.

SANDOMIERZ, CONSENSUS OF, see CONSENSUS OF SANDOMIERZ.

SANKEY, IRA DAVID (1840–1908), gospel singer and hymn writer. S. was born in Edinburgh, Pa., where he became choir master in a Methodist church. From 1870 his name was inseparable from that of Dwight L. *Moody, the great revivalist. For the campaigns they conducted in the U.S. and Great Britain, S. wrote the music for hymns and was soloist and leader of the congregational singing. His style set the musical standard for revivalist meetings. The collections of *Gospel Hymns* that he published beginning in 1875 sold millions of copies and provided funds for evangelistic education.

SATTLER, MICHAEL *(c.*1490–1527), early Anabaptist leader. Born at Freiburg, Ger., he became a Benedictine at the monastery of St. Peter, where for a time he held office as prior. Attracted to Reformation ideas as more in conformity to his study of St. Paul, he left the monastery, married, and went to Zurich. There in 1525 he joined the Anabaptist Swiss Brethren. In the same year he was expelled by the Zwinglian authorities, and fled to Strassburg. He engaged in friendly discussion of their differing views with the Reformers M. *Bucer, and W. *Capito. He left the city, however, fearing that the authorities would prosecute him for his doctrine, and became a preacher around Rottenburg, where he won many followers. He presided at the Conference at which the German and Swiss Anabaptists adopted the *Schleitheim Confession; he probably was its author. Shortly afterward, he and his wife were arrested. They were tried, condemned, and executed at Rottenberg (May 1527); he was burned; she was drowned. See MennEnc 4:427–434.

SAVOY DECLARATION, a *doctrinal standard and statement of *polity for Congregationalism. In 1658 an assembly was held at the Savoy Palace, London. Attending the meeting were 200 ministers and laymen representing 120 independent, or Congregational, churches in England. The statement it prepared was accepted without dispute. The assembly expressed its joy in the fact that the churches, though separate and independent, had preserved through troubled times so close a uniformity of faith and practice. The doctrinal part—the Declaration of Faith in 32 articles—was almost word for word a reproduction of the *Westminster Confession of 1647. It was made plain, however, that it was not to be imposed upon any. Appended to the Declaration of Faith were 30 propositions: "Of the Institution of Churches and the Order appointed in them by Jesus Christ." This is a compact presentation of the principles of Congregationalism (see GATHERED CHURCH) agreed on after almost a century of experiment and experience. The principles were: the headship of Christ only; the constitution of the local church by the union of believers; its complete autonomy; its right to choose and ordain the officers appointed by Christ; the necessity of a call from a church to confer ministerial standing; the consent of the brethren as essential to all admissions and censures; and synods and councils for advice but without judicial authority. In England the Savoy Declaration, as it came to be called, was soon largely lost in events, but it was adopted in Mass. (1680) and in Conn. was incorporated into the *Saybrook Platform (1708). See A. G. Mathews, *Savoy Declaration of Faith and Order* (1959); Schaff Creeds 1:822–833; 3:707–729.

SAXON CONFESSION, a Lutheran *confession of faith prepared by P. *Melanchthon in 1551. Melanchthon wrote it more to fulfill the Emperor's request for a document to be presented at the Council of *Trent than out of conviction that any rapprochement with Rome could be reached. The Saxon Confession was entitled in the original MS, *Repetitio confessionis Augustanae;* it did follow the plan of the *Augsburg Confession, but was more explicit in its rejection of Roman teaching. The delegation to Trent was fruitless. The Saxon Confession was not included in the *Book of Concord. See Schaff Creeds 1:340–343. *WÜRTTEMBERG CONFESSION.

SAYBROOK PLATFORM, a declaration of faith and polity approved by a synod of Congregationalists at Saybrook, Conn., in Sept. 1708. The document was approved by the general assembly of the colony in October and published in 1710. The confession of faith was the adaptation of the *Westminster Confession contained in the *Savoy Declaration (1658). Fifteen articles on polity created agencies to oversee the local churches, a departure toward a presbyterian form of government.

SCHAFF, PHILIP (1819–93), *Reformed theologian and church historian. Born in poverty at Chur, Switzerland, S. won scholarships to finance his education. He studied at Tübingen, Halle, and Berlin and became a *Privatdocent* at the Univ. of Berlin in 1843. At Berlin, J. A. W. Neander influenced his theories of history and of the development of the Christian Church. S. became a professor at the Reformed Seminary, Mercersburg, Pa., in 1844, where with J. W. *Nevin he was instrumental in developing the *Mercersburg theology. In 1870 he became a professor at Union Theological Seminary, New York City. S. wrote widely on church history and ecumenical subjects; his *Creeds of Christendom* (3v., first pub. 1877; repr., 1968) remains an important reference work. He organized the American Society of Church History and served as the editor of a series of denominational histories and of the *Schaff-Herzog Encyclopedia of Religious Knowledge* (1891), based on the German work *Realencyklopädie für protestantische Theologie und Kirche*. See D. S. Schaff, *Life of P. S.* (1897); J. H. Nichols, *Romanticism in American Theology* (1961).

SCHERESCHEWSKY, SAMUEL ISAAC JOSEPH (1831–1906), missionary bp. and Bible translator. Born in Tauroggen, Lithuania, of Jewish parents, educated for the rabbinate, S. was converted to Christianity about the time of his immigration to America in 1854. After being ordained in the Protestant Episcopal Church, deacon in 1859, priest in 1860, he went as missionary to China and began an intensive, lifelong study of the Chinese language. The first edition of his translation of the OT into Mandarin was published in 1874. He was consecrated bp. of Shanghai (1877); his main achievement in that position was the founding of St. John's University in 1880. In 1881 he was partially incapacitated by a stroke and had to resign. He resumed his translation work, revising the Mandarin version and translating the whole Bible into modern, or "easy" Wenli, the prevailing literary language. See J. A. Muller, *Apostle of China* (1937).

SCHISM (Gr., split, crack), a division within the Christian community, local, national or universal, resulting in separated communities or Churches that generally profess the same faith but are not in communion with one another. The term was used by St. Paul to designate the factions in the church at Corinth that threatened its unity (1 Cor 1.10; 11.18; 12.25). The Fathers speak of schism as any sinful splitting off of a group from the Catholic Church without the added element of heterodoxy. Yet most of them felt that error was somehow connected with schism, so they do not always clearly distinguish between schism and heresy. In arguing against the Donatists, St. Augustine held that some sort of error is at the root of schism. In the East St. Basil distinguished between (1) heretics, who have left the faith itself and are completely lost to the Church, (2) schismatics, who because of ecclesiastical causes or problems separate from one another in a way that does not preclude reunion, and (3) dissident groups, such as disgruntled clergy who refuse to obey the bishop without necessarily forming a rival Church (PG 32, 665). The malice of schism, according to the Fathers, consists in defying the one Spirit by leaving the one Body of Christ and setting up a rival altar and a rival Eucharist. St. Thomas Aquinas stressed schism as a violation of the fraternal grace by which the members of the Church are united (ST 2a2ae, 14.2 ad 4), and as the formation of a counter Church challenging the unique role of the RC Church (ThAq *In 4 sent.* 13.2.1). Schism was originally discussed in the context of a *local church and was described as the separation from the bishop, the center of unity. In the medieval West schism was seen more in the framework of the universal Church, with particular reference to the pope, and gradually came to be defined as disobedience to the Holy See, as it is in Latin canon law (CIC c. 1325.2). The Orthodox Churches, however, still generally look upon schism as internal to the local or national church and tend to speak of Roman Catholics as heretics rather than as schismatics. Although surprisingly little theological reflection has been given to the nature of schism, it may perhaps best be defined as a breaking away from the unity of love that is symbolized and effected by the communal sharing of the Eucharist. Contemporary theology is correctly stressing the distinction between the sin of schism and the state of schism, which may or may not be culpable. See Y. Congar, DTC 14.2: 1286–1312.

SCHISM, EAST-WEST, the breaking off of communion between the Eastern and the Western Churches, represented chiefly by the see of Constantinople and of Rome, and the resultant state of separation, or *schism, which still exists between the Orthodox and the RC Churches. Its extremely complex origins involve so many factors that one cannot assign a precise date to its beginning or fix upon any one cause, much less try to determine the blame for it. Perhaps more than any other event, this schism has caused the most serious harm to the Christian Church, in both East and West.

In theory the disruption of ecclesiastical communion was signified by removing a prelate's name from the diptychs, but because of poor communications and other factors several popes were not commemorated in Constantinople. By itself then, removing the name did not constitute schism. A more accurate criterion is the existence of rival patriarchs, Greek and Latin, although this occurred at different times and under different circumstances in the various patriarchates. The schism really began only when the heads and members of both Churches believed that they were no longer in communion with one another.

Religious and political conflicts had occasioned several schisms between Rome and Constantinople, but each time unity had been restored. In the 11th cent. political problems in S Italy apparently caused the removal of the pope's name from the diptychs of Constantinople. About the middle of that century the Byzantine patriarch Michael Cerularius tried to undermine a papal-imperial entente by launching an attack on Roman usages. This provoked the reform-minded Card. Humbert to retaliate with an equally absurd list of trivial accusations against the Greeks. The farce ended with Humbert dramatically excommunicating the Patriarch on July 16, 1054, and being himself excommunicated by a Byzantine synod shortly thereafter. Scarcely noticed by contemporaries, this unworthy episode was not the beginning of the schism as has usually been claimed. In 1089 Emperor Alexius I Comnenus insisted on the pope's name being replaced in the diptychs, since the Byzantine clergy did not know why it had been erased. Certainly at the time of the First Crusade schism did not exist. Early in the 12th cent., though, both Latin and Greek patriarchs laid claim to the sees of Jerusalem and Antioch. Relations between the Latins in the East and the Greeks gradually deteriorated so that by the end of the century the Byzantine canon lawyer, Theodore Balsamon, asserted that the Western Church was clearly in schism. But it was popular animosity erupting in violence and culminating in the Latin capture of Constantinople in 1204 that made the rupture irreparable. Probably the establishment and papal recognition of a Latin patriarch in Constantinople marks the final step in the schism. The Greco-Latin council of Nymphaeum in 1234 was clearly a meeting between representatives of two separated Churches. In 1245 Pope Innocent IV spoke of the schism having occurred "in our own time, only a few years ago." About the same time the other Eastern Churches seem to have aligned themselves with the Byzantine Churches. Subsequent attempts at reunion have been unsuccessful or have been concerned only with small groups.

Differences in language, culture, liturgy, political circumstances, tradition, and customs facilitated the schism and have helped to maintain it, but they were not its causes. Divergence on such dogmas as the procession of the Holy Spirit and purgatory was not, as has sometimes been stated, the principal cause of the schism. Although filling volumes of controversy and polemics, the Eastern and Western viewpoints on these matters are certainly reconcilable. Studies on the schism have often hopelessly jumbled theological and nontheological factors, yet a basic theological issue underlies the whole situation. East and West gradually developed varying attitudes toward the nature and structure of the Church. Unfortunately this difference was never seriously discussed; in both East and West the study of *ecclesiology is a comparatively recent development. The Byzantine theology of the Church was merged in that of its union with the empire, and such matters as relations between bishops came to be regarded as mere administrative problems. As a result bishops seemed unaware of the dogmatic implications of the Roman primatial claims or else replied with ambiguous rhetoric. Eventually the Western concept of the primacy became more definite, universal and absolute, while the Byzantine Church thought only of its autonomy within the imperial framework. There developed, then, two decidedly different views of the structure of the Church. After the fall of Byzantium these attitudes remained fixed both in the West and in the several autocephalous Orthodox Churches in the East. That these two attitudes are not irreconcilable is evidenced by current endeavors to reexamine the notions of primacy and collegiality. Participation of many of the Eastern Churches in the World Council of Churches, dialogue with Rome and with the Anglican Communion have marked the path of progress toward unity between East and West. See S. Runciman, *Eastern Schism* (1955); Y. Congar, *After Nine Hundred Years* (1959); F. Dvornik, *Byzantium and the Roman Primacy* (tr. E. A. Quain, 1966).

SCHISM, GREAT WESTERN, see GREAT WESTERN SCHISM.

SCHISM OF UTRECHT, the separation of 1723–24 of the Church of Utrecht, Holland, from Rome. *LITTLE CHURCH OF UTRECHT.

SCHLEIERMACHER, FRIEDRICH DANIEL ERNST (1768–1834), German theologian. Son of a Lutheran minister who became a Moravian, S. in 1787 entered Halle, the most rationalistic university in Germany. He wrote later, "Religion remained with me when God and immortality vanished before my doubting eyes." In place of Kant's rigorous ethical rationalism, S. posed a certain ideal sense of life and declared that he sensed the divine presence more in Spinoza than in Kant. His fundamental problem was to find a world view that did justice to human personality without slighting the infinite universe to which man lies open. In Berlin Schlegel urged him to publish his *On Religion: Speeches Addressed to Its Cultured Despisers* (1799), which was followed by *Soliloquies* (1800). S. taught theology (1816–34) at the new Univ. of Berlin, of which he became the first head. He produced a most fully elaborated interpretation of religion as an organized life of the feelings and emotions, as primarily an aesthetic experience. Aesthetic openness to the universe *is* religion, a form of "cosmic consciousness." Its seat is the feelings, a sense of the All, a wholly individual matter. Religious experience is consciousness of man's oneness with the world. Religion is an independent sphere, neither that of morals nor that of dogma. The divine is wholly immanent so that the concept of the supernatural is meaningless. Central to S.'s doctrine is a monism and an emphasis on religion as feeling.

The *Soliloquies* were surpassed by *The Christian Faith* (1821), his greatest theological work, the first to make central the categories of religious and Christian "experience" rather than God. Theology is a description, not a speculative science; its data are chiefly men's feelings. The Bible and creeds are records of Christian experience and as such are valuable but have no universal or prescriptive validity. Rational demonstration is absolutely excluded from the sphere of religion. The traditional divine attributes do not represent God in himself but only in respect to men and the world. The sense of the power of Christian love and of the living Christ is what is specifically Christian in S.'s religion. From the works of Christ we conclude to his divinity, not the other way round, as in the 18th century. Christianity is the best religion because in it the religious consciousness is most highly developed. The Church is necessary to foster men's experience of oneness with nature and with each other and to enjoy fellowship in Christ. There are, however, varieties of religious experience, an irreducible plurality.

S.'s influence on subsequent Protestant theology was enormous, in particular his insistence that religion has its seat in the feelings and is the *Bewusstsein* (consciousness) of the All. Christian theology must be drawn from experience and not from authority or speculation. See G. Cross, *Theology of S.* (1911); W. B. Selbie, *S.: A Critical and Historical Study* (1913); R. R. Niebuhr, *S. on Christ and Religion* (1964).

SCHLEITHEIM CONFESSION, a *confession of faith adopted by the Anabaptists at a conference in the Swiss canton of Schaffhausen in 1527. The principal author was Michael *Sattler. The seven articles dealt with baptism, the Lord's Supper, church discipline, the ministry, *nonresistance, and *nonconformity. See MennEnc 1:447–448, s.v. "Brüderliche Vereinigung"; 4:428–429.

SCHMALKALDIC ARTICLES (*Articuli Smalcaldici*), a *confession of faith prepared by Martin Luther in Dec. 1536 and incorporated into the *Book of Concord (1580). The document was intended to pres-

ent Reformation beliefs at the council summoned to meet at Mantua in May 1537; it was inspired by the desire to indicate to the council points both of unity and of unalterable opposition. The proposed council did not materialize until 1545 at Trent. The Articles received their name from the town of Schmalkalden in Thuringia, where the Schmalkaldic League met in Feb. 1537. The representatives at the gathering never did consider or approve the Articles, but most of the theologians present endorsed them, and they were quickly included in the *corpora doctrinae* of the various territorial churches (see CORPUS DOCTRINAE). Philipp *Melanchthon's *Treatise on the Power and Primacy of the Pope*, included in the Book of Concord with the Schmalkaldic Articles, for a long time was erroneously thought to be an appendix. The Articles are arranged in three sections. The first is on points of agreement: the Godhead, the Incarnation, and the Apostles' and Athanasian Creeds. The second section is on points on which the Reformers must remain unyielding; justifying faith and the rejection of the Mass, monasticism, and papacy. The last section includes articles on sin, repentance, baptism, the Lord's Supper, and other points open to discussion with *Reformed or RC theologians. See T. G. Tappert, tr., *Book of Concord: The Confessions of the Evangelical Lutheran Church* (1959).

SCHMALKALDIC LEAGUE, a politico-military alliance formed in Feb. 1531 by Protestant princes of north and central Germany at Schmalkalden in Thuringia. Led by Philip of Hesse and John Frederick I, Elector of Saxony, the League resisted the attempts of Charles V to control the political and religious situation in Germany. It blocked Protestant participation in the Council of Trent and strengthened the formation of *territorial Churches. The coalition dissolved after a military defeat by imperial forces at Mülhausen in 1547. See Jedin Trent 1, index; Léonard HistProt 1:78–180.

SCHMUCKER, SAMUEL SIMON (1799–1873), American Lutheran pastor and seminary professor. S. served for 6 years as pastor in New Market, Va., and then persuaded the General Synod to establish a theological school at Gettysburg, Pa., the first Lutheran seminary in the U.S. (1826). He became its first professor and president, and he lectured on systematic theology until retiring in 1864. S. actively promoted an American Lutheranism that favored fellowship with other American Protestant Churches, but at the cost of departure from the *Augsburg Confession. The controversy over the issue led to a breakup of the General Synod in 1867, and to a reassertion of Lutheran confessional traditions in reaction to S.'s views.

SCHOLASTICISM, originally used derogatorily by 16th-cent. humanists about their predecessors, the medieval schoolmen (*scholastici*); later a commodious term for a movement of thought that prevailed in the Christian West for 4 centuries, lingered for another 4 and almost died, was revived under the aegis of Leo XIII (1879) and after an energetic and influential half-century of work, is no longer in vogue. Once again, "scholastic" tends to become a pejorative term, nevertheless it stands for a character as perennial as "rationalist" or "liberal," and it refuses to lie down. Drawing a distinction between scholasticism in theology and in philosophy will be convenient so long as it is not solidified into an exclusion, for the main interest of most of the schoolmen, even the most protractedly and, it must be confessed, boringly profane, was sacred theology. The first, which manifests a tighter unity than the second, seeks to implement the phrase, "faith seeking understanding" and to render the data of divine revelation into the communicable terms of human reasoning; the resulting meanings are developed, their harmonies displayed, and in various degrees of assurance and scepticism, according to the philosophy adopted, they are related to the data of secular experience. As such scholasticism is generically the same as systematic theology, and so may be contrasted with biblical, positive, or historical theology. More specifically it is that systematic theology which works with the apparatus of Aristotle's *Posterior Analytics*.

In philosophy scholasticism appears at once as more heterogeneous and difficult to fix, for it covers convictions as diverse as those of neoplatonists, of Aristotelians, and of nominalists. Indeed the strains of illuminism from the Ideas, of abstractionism from empirical facts, of positivism in linguistic analysis persist throughout its history and remain largely unreconciled. All the same it is possible, despite the variety, to establish a certain community. This consists mainly in an agreement on the vocabulary and grammar of thought: technical terms abound, many coined to convey the precision of Greek into Low Latin, which serve the purpose of keeping to the point without, however, sustaining the imagination; the terms are highly polished, but their total effect is gritty. Analytic exposition of a text followed by debate is the underlying method. All the parties lived in the same city of thought and conducted a civil conversation in the old sense of the phrase, for in controversy manners were often acrimonious and splenetic to the modern temper. An occupational disease was an arid verbalism within a system closed against historical learning and *litterae humaniores*.

By and large, then, philosophical scholasticism is to be identified less as a system of thought than as a heading in the history of thought. An outline of the movement may treat it in its medieval, middle, and modern periods. There were precursors during the Carolingian renaissance, yet its true originators were Anselm and Abelard in the 11th and 12th centuries, and it flowered early in the humanism of the school of Chartres and the mystical science of the Victorines and Cistercians. Thenceforward its history is that of the rise of the European universities. Augustinian and Platonist, curious about this world though set on the next, a phase worthily represented by Alexander of Hales and Robert Kilwardby, it was convulsed by the reception of Aristotle in the West, at first in Arabic versions. The prospect opened out of a world of reason apparently independent of the world of faith. Following the debates on the "double-truth theory" the various schools emerged; the old Augustinianism was renewed by Bonaventure; Aristotelianism was incorporated by Albert and Thomas Aquinas; the stream of Averroism and Avicennism in Duns Scotus continued to run strong. The main metaphysical debate in the late medieval schools lay between Thomists and Scotists, yet high questions of philosophy were being displaced by formal and material logic, and a widespread *nominalism marks the end of medieval scholasticism. Yet modern research in the history of science has done much to upset the old picture of men who spent their time refining on their quiddities and droning in a vacuum.

The middle period was inaugurated in the 16th cent. by Sylvester Ferrariensis and Cardinal Cajetan, heirs of the Italian Renaissance and powerful philosophical thinkers; but the great names are those of the Spanish divines, Francisco de Vitoria, Domingo Báñez, Francisco de Suarez, and John of St. Thomas. Scholasticism drew aside from the main current of European thought, its glory was that of Spain, and so was its decline. However it was not altogether remote; for it humanized policies in the Indies and so earned the noble tribute of Dr. Johnson to the Univ. of Salamanca; and mixed with elements from Descartes, Leibniz, and Wolff, it survived in the text books for theological training, even in Anglican and Protestant schools.

The modern Leonine revival—neoscholasticism as it is called—began as a reaction against German philosophies of romanticism and by the end of the 19th cent. had grown in a pre-Bergsonian climate into the official party-line for RC clerics; its juridical enforcement did not enhance it from a philosophical point of view. Yet a distinguished band of thinkers, notably at the Univ. of Louvain, and later at Münster and Munich, and from the French Dominicans and Jesuits, have confidently taken its spirit into the social and philosophical sciences. See J. Pieper, *Scholasicism* (1960); E. Gilson, *History of Christian Philosophy in the Middle Ages* (1955); I. C. Brady, J. E. Gurr, J. A. Weisheipl, NCE 12:1153–70, with bibliog.

SCHULTE, JOHANN FRIEDRICH VON (1827–1914), historian of canon law, chief organizer of German *Old Catholics. A native of Westphalia, S., a layman, became professor of canon law at Prague (1854) and adviser to the archbishop. Relinquishing these offices because of his opposition to Vatican Council I, he organized and chaired the first three Old Catholic congresses (1871–72) and obtained Bismarck's permission for an episcopal election. S. secured Old Catholic title to many RC churches in Germany and won Old Catholicism legal status in Austria. Professor at Bonn 1873–1906, he served in the Reichstag 1874–79, defending the *Kulturkampf. His historical studies are of high merit. See C. B. Moss, *Old Catholic Movement* (1966).

SCHWABACH ARTICLES, a Lutheran statement of belief prepared in 1529; the basis for the first part (Art. 1–21) of the *Augsburg Confession. They were 17 in number, and were a revision of the *Marburg Articles, made by Martin Luther assisted by P. *Melanchthon, J. *Jonas, J. Brenz, and others. The articles took sharp issue with the eucharistic doctrine of *Zwingli. Presented at Schwabach, Oct. 16, 1529, they were intended as a statement of creedal unity by the Lutheran princes. See Schaff Creeds 1:-228–229.

SCHWENKFELD, CASPAR (Schwenkfeld von Ossig; 1489–1561), German Reformer, exponent of a spiritualized Christianity. A Silesian nobleman, university educated, S. turned to Lutheran reform ideas *c.*1520. He had early misgivings, however, that Luther's teaching would be interpreted to make justification purely outward, without moral transformation of the Christian. S.'s own central idea was that salvation, a continuous inner experience, is deliverance from sin through Christ, the Divine Word made flesh, who communicates himself to the soul. The place of Bible, Church, and sacraments depends upon this primary inner spiritual experience. S. fell out with Luther in 1527 specifically over the interpretation of the Lord's Supper. He was denounced and persecuted by Lutherans; his doctrines were condemned in Art. 12 of the *Formula of Concord. The *Schwenkfelder Church descends from those "quiet spirituals" who treasured S.'s writings. The ideas of S. anticipated the *Inner Light doctrine of the Quakers and the emphasis on experience in Pietism and Methodism. An edition of his works has been published in the U.S. (v.1–29, 1907–61). See R. M. Jones, *Spiritual Reformers in the 16th and 17th Centuries* (pa., 1959); P. I. Maier, *C. S. on the Person and Work of Christ* (1959).

SCHWENKFELDER CHURCH, a group inspired by the teachings of C. *Schwenkfeld, and owing its origins in the U.S. to a band of 184 religious exiles from Austrian Silesia who came to Pa. in 1734. Led by Christopher Schultz, these Schwenkfelders formed schools (1764) and a charity fund (1774) before formally organizing their Church in 1782 and did not erect a house of worship until 1790. Their five congregations, with about 2,300 members, are all in eastern Pennsylvania. The Schwenkfelder faith is built on experiential religion, like the later Pietism and Methodism, shunning the external for the internal. Faith is needed for a Christocentric life. External baptism cannot wash away sins. One who has heard or read the external word of the Bible without also hearing the inner word of Jesus Christ speaking to his heart has not heard the gospel of grace. Without faith one receives only the bread and wine and not the body and blood of Christ. Essentially a group of born-again Christians, Schwenkfelders have little formal organization, a

congregational polity, and simple Protestant worship. To be baptized, members must profess Christ themselves. There is no proselytizing, although an extensive publication program of books by and about Schwenkfeld is supported, as well as missionary work in Angola and Rhodesia. See S. G. Schultz, *History of the Schwenkfelder Religious Movement* (1959).

SCIENCE AND HEALTH, with a Key to the Scriptures, the principal work of Mary Baker *Eddy and the fundamental doctrinal statement of the *Church of Christ, Scientist. First published in 1875 as *Science and Health*, it was subsequently revised many times by the author. In 1883, the 6th ed., one of the most extensive revisions, added *A Key to the Scriptures* with much other new material. The final revision was made in the 91st edition in 1907. In all Christian Science services, readings from the Bible and from *Science and Health* alternate, and they are received as of equal weight, the latter interpreting the former.

SCOFIELD REFERENCE BIBLE, an edition of the Bible edited by Cyrus I. Scofield (1841–1923), with a dispensational framework for intepreting the Scriptures (see DISPENSATIONALISM). A lawyer without theological training, converted in 1879, Scofield became a pastor and popular Bible Conference speaker. Drawing heavily upon the works of J. N. *Darby and other *Plymouth Brethen, he developed his Reference Bible with the aid of several consulting editors. First published in 1909 (rev., 1917), this Bible with its convenient divisions and explanatory introductions and footnotes offered a simplified and appealing system of Bible study. Adopted by many *Bible schools, the edition spread dispensational teachings across the northern states. In 1967 a revised edition was issued; the basic system was left unchanged, but some archaisms in the biblical text (the AV) were replaced, Ussher's chronology was abandoned, and some ambiguities were cleared

up. See H. Lindsell, "Changes in the Scofield Bible," *Christianity Today* 11 (1967),
711–712; C. N. Kraus, *Dispensationalism in
America: Its Rise and Development* (1958).

SCOTISM, a major scholastic synthesis,
Augustinian in its theological antecedents,
Aristotelian in its philosophical ones. It derives from the development and application
of the teachings of John Duns Scotus, the
"Subtle Doctor." In his own lifetime (1265
or 1266–1308) he attempted to synthesize
the traditional Augustinian theology of the
Franciscans (as in Alexander of Hales and
Bonaventure) with the emergent Aristotelianism of the schools. His followers were to
do battle with those who preferred either
the older way, or the new, nominalistic
Aristotelianism of *William of Ockham.
Scotism achieved the height of its influence
in the 17th century. Identified chiefly with
Franciscans, it also had a wide influence on
thinkers of other orders and even on some
outside the Roman Church, e.g., Christian
Wolff, C. S. Peirce. The philosophical positions of Scotism are different from those of
*Thomism, some markedly so. The proper
object of the human mind is the concept of
being as being, not the essences of material
things. Being is a unique metaphysical concept, and God and creatures are seen as two
modes of being, infinite and finite. Metaphysics is presupposed to all particular
sciences. In *natural theology God's existence is provable from contingence and
from his unique attribute of infinity. God's
freedom and love are paramount. In moral
philosophy man's happiness and freedom
derive from his love of God, for will is the
superior power in man. Man knows the
concrete singular directly and not by recourse to the internal sensible representation. In natural philosophy primary matter
is not purely potential but has an act of its
own, a plurality of forms is asserted, and
essence and existence are not really distinct. The most notable positions in theology are: (1) God's love for man as the
primary motive of the incarnation; (2) the
congruous merit accruing to natural human

acts by reason of God's infinite love for
man and the predestination of man for eternal happiness; (3) the doctrine of Mary's
Immaculate Conception and her intimate
role in man's salvation.

Duns Scotus died at age 42 with the
synthesis he had envisioned unachieved,
but his influence was immediate and began
to spread. The new generation at Oxford
accepted sympathetically his positions on
grace and divine foreknowledge. A number
of disciples appeared at Paris, where Francis of Meyronnes may be noted as the
source of Scotism in its further development. Here two of the hallmarks, the univo-
cal concept of being and the distinction
"actual formal *a parte rei,*" received particular attention. John of Bassolis (d. 1347) expounded the chief points of Scotism, esp.
the objective nature of genera and species.
In the theological controversies of the century, Peter of Aquila (d. 1361) was so faithful
to the master that he acquired the nickname Scotellus. He published a compendium of Scotus's doctrine. The 15th cent.
saw the publication of Scotistic commentaries on Peter Lombard's *Sentences,* works
on the "formalities" of being, and many
works on the Immaculate Conception.
After 1500 several editions of Scotus's
works were printed and commentaries on
them proliferated. The Franciscans in Italy,
esp. Maurice O'Fihely, Antonio Trombetta
(the foe of Cajetan), and Francesco Li-
cheto, spearheaded the new Scotism. Theological and philosophical lexicons and
manuals multiplied. By 1593 Scotus's works
had replaced the *Sentences* as the textbook
in Franciscan houses of study. Interest was
not confined to the Franciscans. At the
close of the 16th and beginning of the 17th
cent. Scotistic chairs were established at
the universities of Salamanca, Alcalá,
Coimbra, Rome, Padua, Paris, Louvain,
Budapest, Cracow, and Kiev. The Franciscan general chapter of Toledo in 1633 made
Scotism the official teaching of the order,
directing that a philosophical manual be
written and that a new edition of Scotus's
works be printed. This was done by Luke
Wadding, an Irish Franciscan. The direc-

tive gave new impetus; over the next 100 years many manuals and commentaries were published in Rome, Paris, Louvain, Spain, and Portugal. Other philosophers were influenced by this trend. The Scotistic concept of being and of the role of metaphysics in philosophy can be noted in the work of Leibniz and Christian Wolff.

The 18th and the early 19th century brought the French Revolution, the supression of religious houses, the Napoleonic wars, and decline for all scholastic systems, Scotism not excepted. But historical studies in the later 19th cent., chiefly non-Franciscan, renewed interest in Scotus. He suffered in obscurity to some extent, for major work was centered on Thomas and Bonaventure, while every philosophical and theological error that had arisen since his time was laid at his door. Recent scholarship (from 1903) has corrected this imbalance. A critical edition of S.'s works is in preparation and should make for an even more accurate judgment on his work. Scotism has generally been viewed in comparison with Thomism; they must be seen as two scholastic systems, both compatible with RC doctrine. From differing philosophical viewpoints (Avicenna for Scotus, Aristotle for Thomas), each strives for a deeper understanding of revelation. See B. M. Bonansea, EncPhil 7:344–345; C. Balic and J. A. Weisheipl, NCE 12:1226–29.

liament on Aug. 17. Grounded on "God's holy Word," it contains 25 articles or chapters, 12 of which set forth the doctrines of the ancient creeds; the influence of Luther and Calvin is also evident in the teaching on justification and good works, preaching, and the sacraments. Article 16, "Of the Kirk," is of particular importance: the Kirk is defined as Catholic, "a company and multitude of men and women chosen of God," outside of which there is neither life nor eternal felicity. This visible Church is also ascertainable, and in Art. 18 the notes of the true Kirk are defined as neither "Antiquitie, Title usurpit, lineal Descence, Place appointed, nor multitude of men approving ane error," but rather the true preaching of the word of God, the right administration of the sacraments, and ecclesiastical discipline uprightly ministered. The powers of the State (Art. 24) are ordained by God "for the singular profite and commoditie of mankind," magistrates are "Lieu-tennents of God," and have therefore both civic and religious powers. The confession is marked by a freshness of expression, enthusiasm, and humility. In 1647 it was superseded by the *Westminster Confession, a creed of severer logic and theological exactness. See J. A. Duke, *History of the Church of Scotland to the Reformation* (1937), 247, 249–255; Schaff Creeds 1:680–685; 3:437–478.

SCOTLAND, CHURCH OF, see CHURCH OF SCOTLAND.

SCOTS CONFESSION (Scottish Confession), the document presented to the Estates of Scotland in 1560 as a summary of the doctrines held by the new Reformed Kirk. It is sometimes known as the First, as distinguished from the Second Confession, the latter, sometimes called the Scottish National or Negative Covenant of 1581, being an anti-Roman appendix to the former. The 1560 confession, written in 4 days by John *Knox and five colleagues, was approved and engrossed in the register of Par-

SCOTT, WALTER (1796–1861), one of four pioneers of the Christian Church (Disciples of Christ). Born and educated in Scotland, he migrated to the U.S. in 1818. His chief contribution was in evangelism. He rejected emotional revivalism with its subjective "signs" of conversion and sought an objective pattern consistent with the rationalism of John Locke and Francis Bacon. This he found in his analysis of "the ancient gospel" from Acts. It involved six steps: three for man (faith, repentance, and baptism by immersion) and three for God, assured on rational grounds and scriptural promise (remission of sins, gift of the Holy Spirit, and life eternal). By combining the

last two steps into one, the five were graphically taught as a five-finger exercise and were widely used for three generations. Scott was the first president of Bacon College at Georgetown, Ky., the Disciples' first college. Chief of seven books S. wrote is *The Gospel Restored*, 1836. See lives by W. Baxter (1874) and D. E. Stevenson (1946).

SCOTTISH NATIONAL COVENANT, a document of 1638, renewing the old Scottish custom of subscribing a band or covenant for mutual defense or in a religious cause. Petitioners against the ecclesiastical arrangements of Charles I appointed Alexander Henderson (*c.*1583–1646) and Archibald Johnston of Warriston (1611–63) to draw up a National Covenant. This incorporated the Negative Covenant (1581), or *King's Confession, that James VI himself had signed, a summary of Acts of Parliament condemning popery and favoring the Reformed Church, and a covenant to resist the evils threatening the *Reformed religion and to uphold the King's honor and the public peace. The Covenant was signed by thousands in Greyfriars Kirk, Feb. 28, 1638, with a zeal that aroused most of the country. The declaration in 1662 that the Covenant was unlawful and in 1685 that it was treasonable produced the trials of the later covenanting period. See Schaff Creeds 1:686–687. *COVENANTERS.

SEABURY, SAMUEL (1729–96), first Protestant Episcopal bp. in the U.S., a native of Conn., and a graduate of Yale (1748), S. studied medicine in Edinburgh but changed to theology and was ordained (1753). After returning to the Colonies, he served various churches in N.J. and N.Y. (1754–75). Loyal to the British during the Revolution, he wrote, under a pseudonym, a series of pamphlets for the British cause and was imprisoned for a time because his authorship was suspected. Released for lack of evidence, he escaped behind the British lines and served as military chaplain. He was chosen bp. by the Episcopalian clergy of Conn. (1783) and

was sent to England for consecration. The English bps. refused to cooperate because S., now an American citizen, could not take the oath of allegiance. He reluctantly turned to the *nonjuror Episcopalian bps. of Scotland, who consecrated him in 1784. He served as bp. of Conn. until his death. See E. Pennington, *From Canterbury to Connecticut* (1941).

SEALING, a ritual term with two usages. (1) In the Catholic Apostolic and New Apostolic Churches, it is a sacrament, also called baptism with fire, conferred by the laying on of hands to bestow the gifts of the Holy Spirit, citizenship in the heavenly Jerusalem, and a share in Christ's rule during the millennium. (2) Among the Latter-day Saints (Mormons), it is one of the temple ceremonies by which a temporal marriage may become a *celestial marriage, or by which families are solemnly joined for eternal association.

SE-BAPTISM (Lat. *se,* self), baptism of oneself, such as that performed by J. *Smyth when he established the first congregation of Baptists in Amsterdam in the 17th cent.; his followers were sometimes referred to as "Se-Baptists." The reason for Smyth's act was his acceptance of *believer's baptism.

SECEDER TRADITION, a protest movement against the Church of Scotland. The secession of 1740 was occasioned by what the Marrow Men—defenders of a warm-hearted evangelical tradition (see MARROW CONTROVERSY)—judged to be a prevailing disparagement of the gospel, and by abuses in the patronage system of the Church of Scotland. In a sermon preached in 1732 Ebenezer Erskine (1680–1754) attacked the Assembly for its moderatism and *Erastianism. Censured by that *court, Erskine and three supporters shortly afterward established an "Associate Presbytery" at Gairney Bridge, Fifeshire, and issued their "Testimony." Though holding that they were seceding only from the dominant patronage party, the Seceders began to act increasingly like an organized Church, conservative, Presbyterian, and national in character. In 1740 Erskine and his associates were expelled by the Assembly. The Seceder tradition was marked in Scotland by frequent internal division. In the U.S. the *Associate Reformed Presbyterian Church of North America is of Seceder lineage. See bibliog. for Church of Scotland.

SECOND BAPTISM, a name sometimes used by Pentecostals for *baptism with the Holy Spirit.

SECOND BLESSING, a description of *entire sanctification. In the teaching of *Holiness Churches, the salvation brought by Christ is twofold: the first blessing is justification; the second blessing, sanctification, which is called a second definite work of grace, and brings deliverance of the believer from domination by sinful inclinations.

SECOND COMING, the visible return of Jesus Christ to earth. The term itself is not used in the NT, but the idea is expressed frequently. Three words often associated with the concept of a return of Christ in visible form are *parousia* (arrival, presence), *apocalypse* (revelation), and *epiphany* (appearing). In Paul's statement of the tradition concerning the Lord's Supper, he said: "For as often as you eat this bread and drink this cup, you proclaim the Lord's death until he comes" (1 Cor 11.26). The Apostles' Creed affirms that "he will come again to judge the quick and the dead." Jesus spoke of the "Son of man coming in clouds with great power and glory" (Mk 13.26). At the Ascension, the disciples were told: "This Jesus, who was taken up from you into heaven, will come in the same way as you saw him go into heaven" (Acts 1.11). Many references in the NT indicate that the early Christian community expected such a second coming of Christ in glory. Belief in Christ's second coming is common to most Christians. The imminence of that coming, with supportive interpretations of the signs of the times, has given rise to the periodic manifestations of *apocalypticism and *millenarianism throughout history (see ADVENTISM; JEHOVAH'S WITNESSES). An emphasis on the literal truth of Christ's second coming is characteristic of fundamentalist Churches (see DISPENSATIONALISM).

SECOND CONFESSION OF BASEL, a name sometimes given to the first of the *Helvetic Confessions, because it was composed at Basel in 1536.

SECOND CUMBERLAND PRESBYTERIAN CHURCH IN U.S., formerly the Colored Cumberland Presbyterian Church, a denomination that came into existence after the Civil War. At that time most Protestant denominations were rethinking race relations within the Church; in 1866 the *Cumberland Presbyterian Church appointed a special committee to study the question, and the *General Assembly decided on the basis of the report that the Negro members of the denomination should organize their own General Assembly. This organization was effected by 46 ministers and 3,000 members, because of white racism and the recognition that the older ecclesiastical paternalism was no longer satisfactory for the Negro. The existence of this denomination has been precarious from the very beginning, although it is difficult to trace its history. Its educational institutions have been weak. After 1906, when part of the Cumberland Presbyterian Church united with the larger *Presbyterian Church in the U.S.A., some of the black congregations did the same. Others were lost through the continual emigration of Negroes from the South to the cities of the North. Latest published statistics (1959) recorded a membership of 30,000, in 121 churches.

SECOND GREAT AWAKENING, a nation-wide revival (1797–1805) among the Churches in America, spreading also to the unchurched. It began in Connecticut among the Congregationalists, where Timothy *Dwight, the president of Yale, was its leading figure. Concerned over the impact of French *deism and naturalism on American life, and a general religious torpor, he had countered with a theology and a preaching that grew into the Second Great Awakening. For the Methodists and the Baptists the Awakening centered in revivals in what was then the West—Kentucky, the Carolinas, and Tennessee. In New England and a large part of the country, among Congregationalists and Presbyterians the Second Great Awakening was unlike the earlier *Great Awakening, inasmuch as it was not accompanied by physical manifestations. Serious interest in the Churches and religion became universal, this time on a severely intellectual rather than an emotional basis. On the western frontier, however, the Second Great Awakening brought with it not only religious renewal but two phenomena, camp-meetings and the jerks.

Camp-meetings were tremendous outdoor gatherings where people came together for several weeks at a time, camping in the woods adjacent to the meeting places. Usually a large shed with benches was erected, sometimes for as many as 5,000 persons, with a large stand at one end for the preacher. The largest and most famous was the Cane Ridge Camp Meeting started by the Presbyterians (1801). According to reports, 25,000 persons gathered, and stands for preaching were strategically placed so that six or seven preachers could speak at one time. Francis *Asbury strongly favored camp-meetings and thought them divinely ordained to bring the gospel to the frontier and the backwoods. Methodists, Baptists, and Presbyterians often united for the services. Later, however, many Presbyterians turned against the revivalist movement. The revival at the frontier lacked the intellectual basis characteristic of the Second

Great Awakening in New England and elsewhere and expressed itself in an emotionalism similar to the days of George *Whitefield. The jerks, a new physical phenomenon, was an uncontrollable and convulsive jerking that overcame a person, sometimes causing him to fall to the ground or to reach for a small tree to grasp as he sought to overcome the jerking of his body. Peter *Cartwright spoke of seeing at one meeting 500 persons with the jerks. Even persons of good education, recognized social standing, and keen intellect were seized by the inexplicable convulsions. Cartwright characteristically described the phenomenon as the judgment of God on sinners who, once they repented of their sins, were released. He also said that a person should not fight the seizure but should relax in prayer and singing and that the spasm would then abate.

The Second Great Awakening brought great good to the country. In spite of the extravagances that marked it on the frontier, the renewal manifested itself in greater church attendance, larger church membership, the beginning of home and foreign missionary work, and a renewed interest in theological education and religious journalism. See C. R. Keller, *Second Great Awakening in Connecticut* (1942); HistAmMeth I:507–524; *Autobiography of Peter Cartwright* (ed. W. P. Strickland, 1857), ch.5; Olmstead 256–263.

SECOND HELVETIC CONFESSION, see HELVETIC CONFESSIONS.

SECOND LONDON CONFESSION, an early Baptist *confession of faith, drawn up in 1677 as a more detailed statement than the First London Confession of 1644. Anxious to manifest doctrinal unity with other *Dissenters during persecution, the *Particular Baptists issued this confession after the Restoration. Like the Independents' *Savoy Declaration (1658), it was an adaptation of the *Westminster Confession, repeating the themes of Calvinism verbatim but omitting chapters connected with Presbyterian polity and modifying the statements on the Church with Baptist teaching on *believer's baptism, the *gathered church, the ministry, and Church-State relations. Adopted by the Philadelphia Baptist Association in 1707 (see PHILADELPHIA CONFESSION), the document was widely accepted as a doctrinal standard until superseded by the *New Hampshire Confession (1832). See W. L. Lumpkin, ed., *Baptist Confessions of Faith* (1959).

SECOND WORK OF GRACE, a reference to *Christian perfection or *entire sanctification as these are distinct from and subsequent to justification, which delivers the sinner from the guilt of personal sin; a second work of grace frees him from all tendency to sin.

SECRETARIAT FOR PROMOTING CHRISTIAN UNITY (SPCU), a Vatican office created by Pope John XXIII with the immediate aim of facilitating fruitful participation of the Orthodox and other Christian Churches in Vatican Council II, and with the broader aim of working with those Churches toward unity. Under Cardinal Augustine *Bea as president, the SPCU arranged for participation of representatives of the Churches in the council as observers and supplied guidance to the council on matters bearing on Christian unity. In 1967 the SPCU issued a *Directory on Ecumenism* for implementation of the council's decisions on ecumenical matters. Since the conclusion of the council the SPCU has been the official voice of the Vatican in the growing ecumenical dialogue. Its new approach to the Churches, not as adversaries but as separated brethren seeking unity in Christ, has resulted in a broad range of active consultations, joint sponsorship of programs and conferences, joint publishing ventures, and collaboration in service programs. A Joint Working Group has been established with the World Council of Churches to consider subjects of mutual concern in the quest for unity; and specialized agencies, such as the Joint Theological Commission on Catholicity and Apostolicity, the Pontifical Council on the Laity, and the Pontifical Commission on Justice and Peace, have been set up to channel joint action in various areas. The SPCU issues a quarterly information bulletin in French and English.

SECT (Lat. *secta*, from the root *sequi*, to follow), meaning first a task, a mode of conduct, later a doctrine or those accepting a certain doctrine, and finally those separating themselves in doctrine from an established religious body. From the last sense, the etymology is sometimes traced to *secare*, to cut. The word has been used in a variety of senses in modern languages. Often it has been applied in a disparaging sense by Catholics to other religious bodies or by Protestants in an established or historical Church to newly emerging religious groups. The term has received more precise definition in the sociology of religion. To account for diverse patterns of religious expression, Ernst *Troeltsch developed a now classic typology: "church," "sect," and "mysticism." The sect-type is characterized by emphasis upon individual religious experience, voluntary membership, radical obedience to a Christian ethic, opposition to political interference in religion, suspicion of professional theologians, and appeal to the authority of the NT and the primitive Church. This contrasts with the church-type, which is more institutionalized, stresses the objective authority of ministry, creed, and sacrament, and seeks to dominate society by close relationship with the State. It differs also from mysticism, which is radically spiritual and individualistic, minimizes doctrine, and does not usually develop permanent organizations.

Although these classifications have been useful for sociological analysis, the dual categories of church and sect do not adequately take account of the variations of organized religion in the United States.

J. M. Yinger uses a six-fold system of classification: the Universal Church, the Ecclesia, the Denomination, the Established Sect, the Sect, and the Cult. Denominations, according to this scheme, exhibit diversities but are predominantly conventional, middle-class in composition, and have compromised with their society, although not so extensively as have the "Churches." The sect is defined essentially in Troeltsch's terms, but it is further subdivided into those that: stress individual faith and moral standards without manifesting hostility to society; seek radical reform of society by means of the individual influence of Christians; or withdraw from the world, accepting the inequities of life and projecting their hopes into the hereafter. The established sect maintains its identity by retention of old emphases, but its members have moved into a more favorable socioeconomic position. Both of these are distinguished from the cult, which is more short-lived and more dependent upon a particular charismatic leader. Sects usually develop among "the disinherited," whose personal needs are not met by the more formal religious bodies, which they regard as compromises with the world. Today, sects flourish particularly among recent migrants to U.S. cities. The type of religious association that will appeal to underprivileged people is affected by the extent to which they feel an identity with the predominant culture and whether they are optimistic or pessimistic regarding their prospects of climbing up the socioeconomic ladder. There is a tendency for sects to become denominations as their adherents gain a better social status. Denominations and Churches, as well as sects and cults, are shaped in part by nontheological factors, and there are fairly clear correlations between the status of American denominations and their social, educational, and economic attainments. See J. M. Yinger, *Religion, Society, and the Individual* (1957); H. Richard Niebuhr, *Social Sources of Denominationalism* (1929); E. Troeltsch, *Social Teachings of the Christian Churches* (tr. O. Wyon, 2v., 1931).

SECTARIANISM, in ordinary usage either the narrow exclusiveness characteristic of a religious body classified as a *sect, or any excessive, even intolerant, attachment to a religious body and its teachings. The term may also be given more benign, historical meaning based on the 17th-cent. application of "sectarian" or "sectary" to Independents or Nonconformists in England; then sectarianism signifies simply *denominationalism.

SECTARY, in 17th-cent. England a term applied by Presbyterians to *Independents. With the proliferation of new movements during Cromwell's Protectorate (Levellers, Diggers, Quakers, Ranters, Familists, etc.), it came to mean an adherent of a schismatic or heretical sect. Today the word connotes a zealous, or even bigoted, member of any religious group.

SECULARISM, the view that holds the separation of God from his creation and denies his presence in the world, if not his existence. The secular city is the world of men and things moving on without him, doing without religion. This secularism as a world view and way of life denies the immanence of God or his existence and man's religious nature. Secularism denies as well the hidden presence and action of God or the cosmic role of Christ. This is a desacralization that denies two basic truths of the Christian faith: creation and Incarnation. See T. F. McMahon, NCE 13:36–38; J. Collins, "Marxist and Secular Humanism," *Social Order* 3 (1953), 207–232. *SECULARITY.

SECULARITY, a mentality regarding the historical process of the secularization of human life as a source of many benefits for man and society. This outlook, characteristic of modern science and generally of this-worldly concerns, is almost universal in civilized countries. Religious secularity considers such an outlook to be compatible with faith in God, and Christian secularity finds it favorable to the message of the gospel. Since the theology of secularity is still developing, its terminology has not yet been settled. Nevertheless contemporary theologians generally use the term secularity as radically distinct from secularism, the ideology that looks upon religion as irrelevant to man's self-fulfillment in the world. Secularism of this type is opposed to religious and Christian secularity.

Secularization is "the historical process by which human culture, temporal society and its institutions, the arts and sciences, etc., have achieved a certain relative autonomy from religion, Christianity in its institutional form and sacral character, and have thereby attained a new and distinctive value in and for themselves" (Clarke). There are various opinions concerning the sources of this process within Western society. Some—Friedrich Gogarten, Arend van Leeuwen, and Harvey Cox—attribute its beginning to the biblical revelation and Christian faith itself. Others are more inclined to trace its real roots to the influence of Greco-Roman culture upon Christendom, and more esp. upon such medieval movements as the departure of St. Thomas Aquinas from *Augustinianism. Still others see the Gregorian Reform of the 11th cent. or the Renaissance and the Reformation as its origin. Whatever contribution these sources may have made to the process of secularization, the complete breakdown of the political and ecclesiastical unities within Christendom took place only with the *Enlightenment at the end of the religious wars between the confessional states. This set the historical stage for the French Revolution, probably the single most significant political event for the process of secularization.

A secularist state, inimical to religion, emerged from the Revolution. Unfortunately, from the viewpoint of secularity, secularization has come to be identified with the ideology of secularism. During the past 150 years Catholicism has been particularly on the defensive against the continually wider separation between the religious and the secular spheres. All too often modern political, social, and economic revolutions have meant the restriction or total suppression of religious freedom for Catholics; thus Catholics have traditionally seemed opposed to progress and human freedom because of their allegiance to religious values. Vatican Council II esp. directed the faithful to a more positive attitude toward the world: "If by the autonomy of earthly affairs we mean that created things and societies enjoy their own laws and values which must be gradually deciphered, put to use, and regulated by men, then it is entirely right to demand that autonomy. Such is not merely required by modern man, but harmonizes also with the will of the Creator" (Vat II ChModWorld 36).

Religious secularity sees the secular order as relatively autonomous, that is, having a meaning and value of its own. Unlike secularism, however, it does not consider temporal realities to be absolutely independent of God. Although the secular order prescinds from man's relationship to his creator, it by no means denies divine presence in the world. The inherent value of all that is directed toward the total welfare of man in this life should be enhanced by his religious convictions concerning the dignity and destiny of creation.

Christian secularity views the secularized society as most genuinely open to the message of the gospel. It favors a free, truly personal commitment of faith. In such a milieu a person's reasons for believing in Christ and the Church are not likely to be more sociopolitical than religious. Faith seems more easily purified of superstition; religious liberty is fostered in a society in which one set of ultimate values is not imposed upon the community, and a valid pluralism provides a culture of mutual enrichment for its members. The clearer differentiation between the religious and secular dimensions of human life contributes to forming Christianity into a worldwide Church. It helps to bring the realization that the cultural patterns of Western civilization are not essential to the message of salvation; there is a greater sense of mission and openness to other cultures and traditions in the work of religious renewal. In the ecumenical movement the religious and theological differences between the Churches can be identified with greater clarity when religion and the ambient culture are adequately distinguished. The effects of secularization may also help liberate the civilizations of Africa and the East from taboos that have blocked the path of progress.

Those who adopt the attitude of religious or Christian secularity are aware of some involved problems. The extremes of sacralism may be avoided only to fall into the pit of secularism. A suggestion pointing toward general solution may be in the vocation of the laity to sanctify without consecrating the secular, i.e., to bring the holiness of ultimate meaning to the world without distorting the world's own meaning. See T. E. Clarke, "What is Christian Secularity?" *Proceedings of the Catholic Theological Society of America*, 21 (1966), 201–221; J. Macquarrie, *God and Secularity* (1967); M. J. Taylor, ed., *The Sacred and the Secular* (1968).

SECULARIZATION, the process by which religious influences on political and social institutions are replaced by a nonreligious orientation. Since the Peace of Westphalia (1648) the term has been used more specifically with reference to the seizure of church property by the State, as was done by many revolutionary governments of the 19th cent. following the pattern established by the French Revolution. It very often signified a radical *anticlericalism, but in some cases it was the only way to secure a more equitable distribution of wealth. See R. H. Potvin and D. Herlihy, NCE 13:38–43.

SEEKERS (Waiters), participants in a religious movement in 17th-cent. England. The name was first used in 1617, but the Seekers appeared earlier, not as an organized sect, but as groups within many Puritan bodies.

Their ideas derived from D. V. *Coornheert, S. *Franck, and C. *Schwenckfeld. They were "seeking" a true Church; convinced that this did not exist in any established form of Christianity, they were content to wait in silence for a new outpouring of the Spirit and a new apostolic age. B. *Legate, a prominent spokesman, was burned for Arian views in 1612. Seekers did gather together and hold meetings in silent prayer. There were many of them in the north of England, who by c.1625 had joined the Quakers. Other Seekers went to extremes and became *Ranters. There were Seeker groups and ideas among the early American colonists. See W. C. Braithwaite, *Beginnings of Quakerism* (2d ed., H. J. Cadbury, 1955), 25–28; R. A. Knox, *Enthusiasm* (1950), 94–142, 173–174; R. M. Jones, *Studies in Mystical Religion* (1923), 449–467.

SEGARELLI, GERARD (Segalelli; d. 1300), founder of a medieval lay group known as the *Apostolici. He was uneducated, given to religious fantasy, and affected by *Joachimism. At Parma in 1260 he determined to embrace the evangelical life in a spirit of true gospel freedom. He and his followers dressed poorly, lived on alms, and preached penance without rule or vows. Their unstructured organization was loosely held together by what S. called interior, spiritual obedience. His harangues against the hierarchical Church, which he described as polluted and carnal, resulted in his temporary imprisonment by the bp. of Parma. His doctrines were condemned by Honorius IV and Nicholas IV; in 1300 he was retried as a relapsed heretic, found guilty, and delivered to the secular authorities for execution.

SEMI-PELAGIANISM, name applied in the 17th cent. to an earlier teaching, mediating between predestinarianism and Pelagianism, condemned at the Council of *Orange II (520). *PELAGIANISM AND SEMI-PELAGIANISM.

SEMI-QUIETISM, a term used in reference to the 17th-cent. debate in France between Bossuet and Fénelon on pure love and contemplation. This debate resulted from their opposing positions at the Conferences of Issy (1694–95), in which the doctrine of Madame *Guyon was examined. The 34 Articles of Issy were due mainly to Bossuet, but since Fénelon was able to take part in the final deliberations, some concessions were made to mysticism. In 1695 Bossuet used the Articles of Issy to condemn Madame Guyon. Fénelon refused to do the same in his diocese, and in correspondence and writings imposed his own interpretation on them. In 1696 Fénelon wrote his *Explanations of the Maxims of the Saints on the Interior Life*, in which he declares his theory of mysticism built on the idea of pure love. He exaggerated the importance of the problem of indifference to salvation. Bossuet began to stir up opinion against Fénelon and a month after the appearance of the *Maxims* published his *Instruction on the States of Prayer*. In his work Bossuet confines the mystical life to a small number of miraculous cases. Fénelon, afraid of being condemned by the Assembly of the Clergy in France, appealed to Rome. Moving his debate with Fénelon to the level of personalities, Bossuet wrote a pamphlet in 1698 entitled *Relation on Quietism*. He made use of confidences Madame Guyon wrote for her director under the seal of secrecy, and published a private letter to her from Fénelon. The pamphlet put both Madame Guyon and Fénelon in a bad light. Innocent XII was sympathetic toward Fénelon, who had been more favorable to the Holy See than Bossuet. The theologians of the commission charged with examining the *Maxims* were also divided. But the publication in Rome of Bossuet's *Relation on Quietism* hurt Fénelon's cause. The intervention of Louis XIV, favorable to Bossuet, put pressure on the Roman Curia and led the cardinals to pronounce against the *Maxims*. Innocent XII gave in, and with the brief *Cum alias*, March 12, 1699, condemned 23 propositions taken from the *Maxims* (D 2351–74). Fénelon submitted to this sentence. Later the Pope made Fénelon a cardinal.

The points of debate between Bossuet and Fénelon may be summarized as follows: Bossuet held that the passive state exists only during the time of prayer. Fénelon taught that it may exist both during the time of prayer and outside of it. Bossuet insisted that perfection is to be found in the practice of the virtues, since the passivity of the mystics is an extraordinary grace, and that the love that presides over the virtues cannot be pure love since such a love cannot be reached in this life. Fénelon held that perfection is found in the pure love that is attained in the passivity of the mystics. Bossuet taught that the ligature of the faculties is absolute; Fénelon, that it is relative, for it is freely accepted. Thus Bossuet was for the active way, Fénelon for the passive way. Each conceded to the other as little as possible. Fénelon overstressed the passive; Bossuet overstressed the active. In comparing the two, scholars today find Fénelon closer to the doctrine of recognized authorities on mysticism than Bossuet. The unfortunate aspect about the condemnation of the 23 propositions taken from the *Maxims* was that it amounted in popular opinion to a kind of attack on mysticism, and this opinion, as Innocent XII feared, was ultimately harmful to the Church. Deprived of the living source of inner experience, the literature of devotion gradually dried up and any mention of mysticism was made with the greatest caution and fear. See L. Cognet, *Post-Reformation Spirituality* (tr. P. Hepburne Scott, 1959). *QUIE-TISM.

SEMIRATIONALISM, designation, esp. in RC theology, for certain 19th-cent. theories that gave rationalistic explanations of dogma. *Hermesianism, the theory developed by Georg Hermes (1775–1831), a German professor of theology, by proposing positive doubt as the basis for theological methodology, made human reason rather than faith the ultimate criterion and unique means for attaining knowledge of supernatural truths (see D 2738). *Guntherianism, named for Anton Günther (1783–1863), a priest in Vienna, was condemned for obscuring the distinction between faith and reason and for teachings opposed to the consubstantiality of the three Persons and God's freedom in creating (see D 2828–31). Jakob Frohschammer (1821–93) affirmed a supernatural order of truths and man's need for revelation, yet negated both by insisting that reason is absolutely free and that its probative power establishes the objective value of revelation (D 2852). Vatican Council I also condemned these theories (D 3015–20; 3041).

SEMLER, JOHANN SALOMO (1725–91), German church historian and biblicist. His early background was in *Pietism, but he adopted a rationalistic theological position that he referred to as *liberalis theologia.* His education and the major part of his professional career (1752–79) were at Halle. His main importance in church history is his study of the historical development of dogma, esp. in a 4-v. study of the biblical canon (1771–76). He evaluated dogma and theology as evolving, inadequate attempts to grasp religious truths. No confession or system should be considered definitive. He was a pioneer in the application of the historical and critical method to the study of the Bible. While maintaining the supremacy of reason and strictly personal character of religion, he also felt that public religious conformity should be secured by the State. See C. Mirbt, EncRelKnow 10:354–355.

SEPARATE BAPTISTS, those who separated from the established Congregational Church in New England during the *Great Awakening and became Baptists. Shubael *Stearns formed an *association of Separate Baptists at Sandy Creek, N.C., in 1758; many other associations grew up in Va. and Kentucky. Most of these eventually united with the *Regular Baptists; those who did not, constitute the present-day Separate Baptists in Christ. See R. G. Torbet, *History of the Baptists* (1950).

SEPARATE BAPTISTS IN CHRIST, the *Separate Baptists who did not unite with *Regular Baptists in the late 18th and early 19th century. Approximately 6,500 members belong to Separate Baptist churches in Ky., Md., Tenn., and Illinois. Their teaching is fundamentalist and *Arminian; three *ordinances, baptism, the Lord's Supper, and *footwashing, are observed.

SEPARATISTS, a term applied in England, esp. in the 16th and 17th cents., to those who separated themselves from the C of E, and first used with reference to the followers of Robert *Browne, who later developed into the Congregationalists or *Independents. *NONCONFORMISTS; *DISSENTERS.

SERIPANDO, GIROLAMO (1492–1563), Augustinian theologian, cardinal legate at the Council of Trent. Seripando entered the Augustinians in 1507, was named vicar general in 1538, and was elected general the following year. While general, he conducted extensive visitations in an effort to offset the Lutheran influence within the order, which he sought to reform by a program of spirituality based upon Sacred Scripture and the teachings of St. Augustine. Challenges posed by the Lutheran theology, as well as by the evangelical and spiritualistic movements in Italy itself, occasioned an important change in Seripando's outlook. His earlier interest in humanism and in Renaissance Platonism began to wane, although he regarded Platonic philosophy as a natural preparation for the study of Pauline theology. Since he now viewed the new theology as a direct attack upon St. Augustine, he undertook an exhaustive study of the saint's writings, from which he elaborated his own theological positions against those advanced by Reformers. He attended the Council of Trent, where, successively as prior general, cardinal president, and papal legate, he espoused the teachings of his school on original sin and the nature of justification. Although these were not accepted by the council, he nevertheless exercised an important constructive influence upon the final formulation of these doctrines. His advocacy of the *double-justice theory, the culminating point in his theology of justification, has its roots in the notion of concupiscence as understood by the Augustinian theologians of the period. For these, concupiscence remains in the baptized, not merely· as the penal consequence of sin, but as a persistent and dynamic source of personal sin. And, because it hinders man's full observance of God's law, it is displeasing in God's sight and therefore somehow sinful. Consequently, unless the justice of Christ is also applied to the members of his Mystical Body, man's personal justice remains insufficient to merit eternal life. See H. Jedin, *Papal Legate at the Council of Trent: Cardinal Seripando* (tr. F. C. Eckhoff, 1947); A. Balducci, *Girolamo Seripando, Arcivescovo di Salerno* (1963).

SERVANTS OF YAH, a small group that separated from the *Jehovah's Witnesses. Headquarters are in Brooklyn, New York.

SERVETUS, MICHAEL (1511–53), physician and antitrinitarian. Born in Villanueva, Spain, he studied at the Univ. of Toulouse. Biblical studies led him to oppose the doctrine of the Trinity, and in 1531 he published *De Trinitatis erroribus libri VII,* in which he distinguished between the eternal Word and the Son, who was not eternal; moreover, he denied that the Holy Spirit was a distinct being. Violent opposition to this work led him to publish *Dialogorum de Trinitate libri duo* (1532), a work that did not significantly change his position. He worked in Lyons as an editor, studied medicine at the Univ. of Paris, and discerned and wrote of the pulmonary circulation of the blood. His correspondence with John *Calvin disclosed serious theological differ-

ences. In 1553 he anonymously published his major work, *Christianismi restitutio.* The work continued earlier antitrinitarianism but also stressed an emanationist view of God and certain Anabaptist themes. He was arrested by the Inquisition in Lyons and imprisoned, but escaped to Geneva. There Calvin also had him arrested; S. was tried and executed at the stake as a heretic, Oct. 27, 1553. See E. M. Wilbur, tr., *Two Treatises of Servetus on the Trinity,* Harvard Theological Studies, XVI (1932); E. Wolf, '*Deus Omniformis, Bemerkungen zur Christologie des Michael Servet,*" *Theologische Aufsätze, Karl Barth zum 50. Geburtstag* (1936); R. Bainton, *Hunted Heretic* (1953); B. Becker, ed., *Autour de Michel Servet et de Sebastien Castellion* (1953); G. H. Williams, *Radical Reformation* (1962).

SERVICE BOOK AND HYMNAL (Lutheran), the name given to a common liturgy and hymnal produced cooperatively by Lutherans of many diverse cultural and linguistic backgrounds in the U.S. and Canada. It was noted in the 1940s that one of the serious divisive factors among North American Lutherans was the diversity of liturgical practice and of hymnody. Many of the various linguistic groups were still conducting worship services in their own German or Scandinavian languages. It was recognized that a common liturgy and hymnal could serve as a unifying force. In 1944 a resolution was passed at the convention of the United Lutheran Church in America (ULCA), authorizing publication of a new revision of its own hymnal, and including a clause instructing the committee "to seek the fullest possible cooperation with other Lutheran bodies in the hope of producing, as nearly as proves feasible, a common Lutheran hymnal in America" (ULCA Minutes, 1944, 436). The Common Service Book Committee of the ULCA, under the leadership of its chairman, Dr. Luther D. Reed, began by extending invitations to the presidents of the various Lutheran Churches to join in the common venture. The Lutheran Church—Missouri Synod was excluded since that synod had recently produced its own new hymnal. The task was monumental in view of the number of individual synods involved, but through discussion and compromise difficulties were overcome, and the work was published in 1958. See L. D. Reed, *Lutheran Liturgy* (1959), 205–227.

SERVICES AND PRAYERS, BOOK OF, see BOOK OF SERVICES AND PRAYERS.

SESSION, see CHURCH SESSION.

SEVENTH-DAY ADVENTISTS, the largest of those Churches that have their origin in the *Adventism of W. *Miller. There are more than 1.5 million Seventh-day Adventists in the world. Among those who remained faithful even after Miller's prediction of Christ's second coming went unfulfilled were Joseph Bates, James White, and his wife, Ellen G. *White. On the basis of Miller's teaching and the observance of Saturday as the day of worship, they formed and organized the Seventh-day Adventists; the first conference of the Church was held at Battle Creek, Mich., in 1863. Mrs. White has always been considered a prophetess by this Church. Her views settled many points of doctrinal interpretation, and her writings are still standard doctrinal works, believed by the Church to be inspired. The Seventh-day Adventists follow a literalist *fundamentalism in accepting the Bible as the sole rule of faith; they also affirm the gift of prophecy not only of Mrs. White but as ever present in the Church. From her they received their primary doctrinal emphasis, the observance of the Sabbath law; it is the mark of those sealed by God and accepting his salvation through Christ. Their attitude toward the Sabbath as strictly enjoined is the basis of their strict observance of OT tithing and dietary laws, their abstinence from all stimulants and from worldly dress or amusements, and their attacks on the pope and the Roman Church for introducing Sunday observance. The second main teaching of the Church is the second coming of Christ; they do not, however, attempt to set a time for this. In accord with a vision of Mrs. White, they believe that Christ began the cleansing of the sanctuary, i.e., a judgment on all men, in 1844; the judgment still goes on in preparation for his coming, which the Adventists are to proclaim. In the meantime souls are asleep. Adventists teach a *conditional immortality: man has a mortal soul and immortality is solely the gift of Christ to the just. At the second coming Christ's 1,000-year reign will begin (see PREMILLENARIANISM); he will take the just, both living and resurrected dead, into the heavens. After 1,000 years the wicked will be raised, judged, and after being led in a mighty battle by Satan, with him they will all be annihilated; there is no everlasting hell. The earth will be renewed and the just will reign upon it in glory. Adventists stress health and healing as adjuncts of the gospel teaching; dietary laws are strict, and many Adventists are vegetarians.

Local churches belong to state conferences, but each is autonomous, congregational in polity. The General Conference, which represents the whole Church, meets every 4 years. National headquarters were moved from Battle Creek to Takoma Park, Md., near Washington, D.C., in 1903. There are members or missionaries in 195 countries. The Church employs all mass media to win converts. One out of every 19 adult members is employed by the Church as a teacher, physician, pastor, missionary, dentist, nurse, printer, or administrator. Membership in the U.S. rose from 26,799 in 1906 to 364,666 in 1967. In keeping with their belief, Seventh-day Adventists have encouraged health reform and medical care; the Church operates a medical and dental school in Calif. and a network of hospitals, sanitariums, and clinics in the U.S. and around the world. Its parochial school system is 3d largest in the U.S.; worldwide, the Church supports 4,460 grade schools, as well as 570 high schools and 64 colleges. A large percentage of Adventists attends college. See E. T. Clark, *Small Sects in America* (1949), 25–45; L. E. Froom, *Prophetic Faith of Our Fathers* (4v., 1946–54); A. A. Hoekema, *Four Major Cults* (1963), 89–169; B. Herndon, *Seventh Day* (1960); Mayer RB 439–448; A. W. Spalding, *Captains of the Host* (1949).

SEVENTH DAY BAPTIST GENERAL CONFERENCE, a Sabbatarian body founded in 1671. Baptists as a group were early and persistent advocates of primitive Christian ecclesiology, but some went further by accepting the Hebrew practice of Sabbath observance as normative for Christians. Sabbatarian practice among certain Baptists was current in the Colonies, but it was not till Stephen Mumford left the Newport, R.I., church of John Clarke that the first official Seventh Day Baptist Church was established. Rigid as to the proper day for worship, this denomination requires no creedal test for membership, allows for *open communion, and has an increasingly progressive policy in education and interfaith cooperation. With headquarters at Plainfield, N.J., the denomination in 1967 numbered approximately 5,700 members, in 64 churches.

SEVENTH DAY BAPTISTS (German, 1728), a Church that has its origins in the *Ephrata Community of John Conrad *Beissel in Pennsylvania. Their teaching and practice are essentially the same as those of the *Brethren Churches. Latest (1951) statistics recorded 150 members, in three congregations.

SHAKERS (United Society of Believers in Christ's Second Appearing; Millennial Church), largest and most permanent of the 19th-cent. religious communal movements in the U.S.; the name was used because Shakers regarded physical trembling as a manifestation of inner spiritual experience. The phenomenon, which arose among the *Camisards of 17th-cent. France, was carried to England, where Quaker converts were called Shaking Quakers, or simply Shakers. In 1774 eight Shakers under the spiritual guidance of Mother Ann *Lee immigrated to New York and established a community at Watervliet in 1776. Although Shaker dogma drew heavily on Pietist thought, i.e., it was millennial, spiritualistic, and literal in its interpretation of the Bible, Mother Ann's teaching led the sect to its distinctive practice of celibacy. She taught that God was of a sexual nature, that the masculine had become manifest in Christ, and that a feminine spirit would continue the work of Christ. Presumably she identified herself as this feminine savior, but this view was later modified. Before the American Civil War, 18 Shaker communities had a total membership of about 6,000. Since Shaker law forbade marriage, enrollment was kept up both by conversion and by adoption of orphans. The Shakers not only maintained economic autonomy but also developed many articles for commercial distribution. Their interior furnishings, simple of line, became famous, and have been widely copied. In 1968, in communities at Sabbathday Lake, Me., and Canterbury, N.H., there were 15 Shakers. See A. F. Tyler, *Freedom's Ferment* (1944), ch. 7; E. D. Andrews, *People Called Shakers* (1958).

SHORTER CATECHISM, one of the two *Westminster Catechisms, written in 1647; a Presbyterian *doctrinal standard.

SHUNNING, in Mennonite usage another term for the penalty of *avoidance, a consequence of excommunication.

SIMEON, CHARLES (1759–1836), leader of the *evangelicals of the Church of England. Educated at King's College, Cambridge, he spent his life as vicar of Holy Trinity Church in Cambridge. He was one of the founders of the *Church Missionary Society (1799) and active in the *British and

Foreign Bible Society. Not only did he spread *low-church influence in the C of E by his evangelical preaching, but he was able to place other evangelicals as parish vicars by securing the right of *advowson. See P. Smyth, *Simeon and Church Order* (1940).

SIMONS, MENNO, see MENNO SIMONS.

SIMULTANEUM, a legal term in German ecclesiastical history, short for *simultaneum exercitium religionis*. In its first use in the 16th cent. the Latin phrase referred to the right of simultaneous practice of two or more faiths in the same territory (see TERRITORIAL CHURCH). *Simultaneum* came more often to refer to a right to the use of the same buildings (called therefore "simultaneous churches") by congregations of different faiths. Such a right to use RC churches was conceded to *Old Catholics in Prussia after 1870, but was resisted by Rome. See EncRelKnow 10:431–432.

SIN, an act or state that violates the will of God for communion between himself and man. As it is usually understood, both in the language of the Bible and in common parlance, sin is often taken as an ethical category. To sin is to do something contrary to the divinely legislated code for proper conduct. "Whosoever committeth sin transgresseth also the law; for sin is the transgression of the law" (1 Jn 3.4). The OT, with its manifold legislation about the ritual and moral conduct of the Israelite, often identifies sin with transgression of this legislation. Yet biblical religion does not make this definition of sin decisive of itself, for the law whose transgression makes an act sinful is not first of all a written code (even though it is also a code and is eventually written), but the revealed will of the creator. Breaking the law, therefore, means acting deliberately in disobedience to him and in rebellion against his intention for his creatures. This rebellion, not the overtly immoral "living in sin," is what makes sin such a serious business in biblical and in Christian theology. The law, e.g., the Decalogue, is intended as a means of discovering that the will of God has been violated, for "through the law comes knowledge of sin" (Rom 3.20); but it is a moralistic distortion to define sin exclusively in the terms of law, even of divine law.

The deepest insight of Christian faith into the nature of sin has been the recognition that sin is an act of severing, or at least of jeopardizing, the intimate relation between creator and creature. As the positive form of that relation is never simply one of conformity to the prescriptions of a book of rules but is always one of fellowship with God himself, so the negation of that relation is inevitably defined in personal terms. A vivid metaphor for the violation, esp. prominent in the prophecy of Hosea but audible in large parts of the OT, is that of the unfaithful wife who has, by a deliberate and wanton act, cut herself off from her loving husband. This personal dimension of sin attends even the expressions of guilt brought on by the remembrance of a moral wrong. Thus Ps 51.4, attributed to David after his adultery with Bathsheba, makes clear that the sin has violated a relation with God: "Against thee, thee only have I sinned." Conversely, the forgiveness of sins is not merely the removal of moral guilt, but the restoration, by God himself as the injured party, of this personal relationship. The liturgical and penitential practice of the Church has aimed to emphasize this dimension of sin in the language it has used for confession and in its pleas for mercy.

In their discussions of sin theologians have introduced several distinctions aimed at clarifying its nature. The most basic is the distinction between *original sin and actual sin: actual sin is the term for those deeds in which a man disobeys the will of God; original sin describes a state brought on by the Fall of man in which man has lost his original sanctifying grace. Theology has distinguished between mortal sin and venial sin (see 1 Jn 5.16–17): mortal sin is so designated because it kills the soul by bringing about the loss of grace; venial sin, though by no means a trifle, does not cause such a loss of grace. The distinction made by theologians between sins of commission and sins of omission is based upon their relation to the law: a sin of commission is a transgression against an express prohibition of the law of God; a sin of omission is a failure to fulfill what that law demands. In all of these distinctions, too, the understanding of sin as the violation of a personal bond with God, not only as a wicked deed, is an essential component.

The central elements of this doctrine of sin are the common property of most Christian denominations, but differences both of emphasis and of content have arisen between Eastern and Western theology and among various schools of Protestant thought. The prominence of St. Augustine in the doctrinal history of the West has been visible in the language about sin used not only by St. Thomas Aquinas but by Martin Luther and John Calvin. In Eastern Orthodoxy the Augustinian emphasis upon inherited sin is often absent, but there is a strong sense of sin as dominance by the demonic. Modern Western theology, both Roman Catholic and Protestant, has subjected the traditional Western view of original sin to critical scrutiny. See R. Niebuhr, *Nature and Destiny of Man* (1941–43); E. Brunner, *Man in Revolt* (1939).

SIN, ORIGINAL, see ORIGINAL SIN.

SIX ARTICLES, "An Act abolishing diversity of opinions," passed by Parliament in 1539 under leadership of the Duke of Norfolk and lay peers, in reaction to recent liberal tendencies of the King's reforming churchmen (see TEN ARTICLES). It affirmed, with heavy penalties for opinions to the contrary, *transubstantiation, communion in one kind, clerical celibacy, vows of chastity, private Masses, and auricular confession. Its opponents called it "the whip with six strings." Because of it, two bps., Latimer and Shaxton, resigned, and Abp. *Cranmer

had to send his wife back to Germany for a time. See H. Gee and W. J. Hardy, *Documents Illustrative of English Church History* (1896), 303–319; J. Ridley, *Thomas Cranmer* (1962), 178–198.

SIX POINTS, the liturgical usages advocated in the 19th cent. by the ritualists, a wing of the *high-church party in the Church of England: altar lights, eucharistic vestments, eastward position of the priest at the altar, wafer bread, mixing water with wine in the chalice, and incense. The points were proposed and approved in 1875 at the annual meeting of the Church Union, even though many of them had been declared contrary to English law in 1871. *RITUALISM.

SKEVIKARE, an originally Danish Pietist group that immigrated to Sweden in 1734, settling at Skevik, a farm on an island near Stockholm. Refusing sacraments and any outward sign of worship, they were guided solely by the inspiration of individual members. Proscribed by Swedish anticonventicle laws, the group soon disappeared.

SLEIDANUS, JOHANNES (Sleidan; 1506–56), the first historian of the Reformation. Born at Schleiden near Aachen, educated in classics and law, he became a Calvinist. In 1544 through M. *Bucer's influence he was appointed by Philip of Hesse to be annalist of the Reformation. His work *Commentarii de statu religionis et rei publicae Carolo V Caesare* (2v., 1555) is regarded as distinctive for its impartiality; it is also valuable as a chronicle of Reformation documents and events beginning in 1517; both religious and political elements are carefully recorded. S. spent some time in England in 1551 under the auspices of T. *Cranmer. He also represented some of the South German cities at the Council of Trent (1551–52), and ended his career as professor of law at Strassburg (1554–56). See Léonard HistProt I:242, bibliog.

SLOVAK EVANGELICAL LUTHERAN CHURCH, a body formally organized among Slovakian Lutheran immigrants in 1902, and since 1959 named the *Synod of Evangelical Lutheran Churches.

SMALCALD, see SCHMALKALDIC.

SMALL CATECHISM, Martin Luther's *Enchiridion,* or *Der Kleine Catechismus,* written in 1529 for the instruction of the laity; a Lutheran confessional standard. *CATECHISMS, LUTHER'S.

SMITH, JOSEPH (1805–44), founder of the Church of Jesus Christ of Latter-day Saints. S. was born in Vermont and brought up on small farms near Palmyra and Manchester, N.Y., where his parents scratched out a marginal living. Writing his own story in 1838, he claimed that two personages identified as God the Father and Jesus Christ appeared to him as a young man in 1820, and that several years later an angel called Moroni visited him and disclosed the existence of a set of plates inscribed with writing in Reformed Egyptian characters, and the Urim and Thummim, crystal spectacles for deciphering the writing. S. reported that he was allowed to dig up the plates in 1827 from the Hill Cumorah, where they were buried. The translation of the plates revealed the history of the extinct original inhabitants of the Americas and the establishment of a Church by Jesus Christ in the Western Hemisphere after his resurrection. This work was published (1830) as the *Book of Mormon.* S. later composed *Doctrines and Covenants* and the *Pearl of Great Price,* which became standards of doctrine in the Mormon Church. S. organized a Church in 1830 that eventually took the name Church of Jesus Christ of Latter-day Saints, often called simply the Mormon Church. He declared that all other Christian Churches had apostatized and lacked authority to baptize or teach. Claiming that he had received the restored priesthood in 1829 from John the Baptist and from Peter, James, and John, S. assumed the title of president of the Church, and also the titles Prophet, Seer, and Revelator. Headquarters of the new Church were moved from Fayette, N.Y., to Kirtland, Ohio, in 1831, to Missouri in 1838, and to Nauvoo, Ill., in 1840. In Nauvoo, S. started construction of a temple, elaborated a secret ritual drawn mainly from Masonic sources, headed a private army called the Nauvoo Legion, in which he held the rank of lieutenant general, and declared his candidacy for the U.S. presidency. Nauvoo became the largest city in Ill., and converts arrived from many places, including some from England and the Scandinavian countries. S. had married Emma Hale in 1827; rumors that he had introduced polygamy into the Church encouraged critics to start a newspaper in Nauvoo to oppose him. S. destroyed their press and was arrested and taken to a jail in nearby Carthage. A mob attacked the jail and murdered him and his brother Hyrum. Most of the Mormons accepted the leadership of Brigham *Young and went west to establish the Church in the valley of the Great Salt Lake. See F. M. Brodie, *No Man Knows My History, the Life of J. S., Mormon Prophet* (1935); E. C. McGavin, *How We Got the Book of Mormon* (1961).

SMYTH, JOHN (Smith; c.1544–1612), regarded as a founder of the Baptists. Educated at Christ's College, Cambridge, and ordained in the C of E (1594), he soon came under the influence of the *Independents and in 1602 became pastor of a *Separatist church, Congregationalist in organization, at Gainsborough. To escape persecution, S. led a group of followers to Holland, probably in 1607, and there found Mennonite teaching congenial to his religious feelings and accepted the need of rebaptism (see BELIEVER'S BAPTISM). To establish his "Brethren of the Separation of the Second English Church at Amsterdam," he first baptized himself—hence he is called the "Se-Baptist" (self-baptizer)—then Thomas *Helwys and other followers. Before his death, S. was of a mind to join his group to the Mennonite Church; Helwys and others, however, returned to England and established the first Baptist Church there. S.'s writings put the rule of inner religious experience above Scripture and the outward Church, insist on the individual's freedom to choose salvation (see ARMINIANISM), and thus reject original sin and Christ's atonement. His works have been published (ed. W. T. Whitley, with biog., 2v., 1915). See W. H. Burgess, *J. S. the Se-Baptist* (1911); R. M. Jones, *Studies in Mystical Religion* (1923), 407–411; bibliog. for Baptists.

SNAKE HANDLERS, cultists in the southern U.S. who, taking Mk 16.17–18 literally, pick up rattlesnakes as part of their religious services. The practice was begun (1909) by George Went Hensley in Tennessee. It was outlawed there, and also in Ky. and Va., after several fatal incidents; but the practice still continues and another fatality occured in Va. in 1969. Snake Handlers also follow the teaching of *Pentecostalism, but they are repudiated by Pentecostals. See J. T. Nichol, *Pentecostalism* (1966), 151–157.

SOCIAL BRETHREN, an *evangelical body, organized in Ill. in 1867 by persons disagreeing with their own various Churches on points of doctrine and discipline. They drew up a confession of faith in 13 articles and a code of conduct. The confession includes an affirmation of the sole sufficiency of Scripture as a rule of faith, and the doctrine of *sanctification. Polity combines Baptist and Methodist elements; there are three annual regional associations and a biennial general assembly. Ministers are enjoined from using the pulpit for political speeches. In 1967 there were in Ill., Mich., and Ind. approximately 2,000 members, in 31 churches.

SOCIAL CREED OF THE CHURCHES, a statement adopted in 1912 by the *Federal Council of the Churches of Christ in America, inspired by doctrines of the *Social Gospel and modeled on the Social Creed of the Methodist Episcopal Church (1908). The document esp. opposed the capitalistic exploitation of the working class and advocated many of the reforms adopted in later American social legislation. The adherence of many of the Churches to the Social Creed directly contributed to the progress of such legislation.

SOCIAL GOSPEL, an attempt to apply the teachings of the Christian faith to problems created by industrial capitalism. The Social Gospel permeated much of American Protestantism in the beginning of the 20th cent., modifying traditional concepts and developing a distinctive theology of social action. In its widest significance, the Social Gospel was a rejection of earlier emphasis on individual salvation and a renewed appreciation of the corporate nature of the Christian commitment. Social Gospel writers stressed the immanence of God, working out his purposes in the world of men. They emphasized the brotherhood of men as children of God and saw a just social order as a preparation for the coming of his kingdom on earth. For many exponents, notably W. *Rauschenbusch, the doctrine of the kingdom of God was a dominant motif in formulating an approach to social problems. The coming of the kingdom implied an ethical ideal in terms of society as a whole, and the Social Gospel proposed a new view of sin in terms of the implications of a solidaristic understanding of society. In approaching social evils, the Social Gospel was fundamentally optimistic, believing firmly in a progressive development of social justice that was, in fact, the working out of God's providence. Its sources were many. The *liberal theology of Horace *Bushnell prepared the way for men like Washington *Gladden who followed up the implication of Bushnell's rejection of Protestant individualism. Others drew their inspiration from the Anglican tradition and particularly the social theology of F. D. *Maurice.

The Social Gospel movement rose largely in response to the rapid urbanization and industrialization that threatened to isolate Protestantism from the working class. The *institutional church, settlement houses operated by church groups, and city mission work attempted to bring the Church to the urban poor. Personal experience of the evils of the changing city stimulated the formulation of the Social Gospel. For this reason it was often clearer in its critique of capitalism than in its blueprint for the Christian social order. In *Applied Christianity* (1886) Gladden found the injustice of employers one of the main reasons for the drift of working men from the Churches. George Herron's "Message of Jesus to Men of Wealth" (1890) indicted a society based on greed for rejecting the doctrine of *stewardship. The failure of capitalism to provide a just social order led others, such as W. D. P. Bliss, to stress the NT basis for a cooperative society in formulating their *Christian Socialism. The need for fraternal cooperation to replace divisive competition as a basis for a Christian social order was also a keynote in the writings of Rauschenbusch. Sin was seen more in its social aspect, as the ultimate barrier to cooperation. In *Social Religion* (1913) Scott Nearing argued that the majority of men would be virtuous if given the opportunity to lead decent lives, and he called on the Churches to help provide that opportunity. The Social Gospel inspired Christians to take an active role in promoting reform movements of various kinds, supporting social welfare projects, and advocating industrial democracy. In some cases, the Social Gospel provided a bridge between rich and poor Christians and between Christians of different denominations for cooperative ventures (these contributed to the rise of the ecumenical movement). In others, it provided a religious statement of prevailing evolutionary views of society, which avoided the harsher alternatives of Social Darwinism. See C. H. Hopkins, *Rise of the Social Gospel in American Protestantism* (1967); S. E. Mead, *Lively Experiment* (1963), 177–183.

SOCIETY (Methodist), John *Wesley's designation for a group of persons desiring "to flee from the wrath to come." He laid down rules governing its members. Individual societies later became the Churches in the various Methodist denominations in the U.S., as well as in England. Religious societies had existed in the C of E before Wesley's time. See J. S. Simon, *John Wesley and the Religious Societies* (1921).

SOCIETY FOR PROMOTING CHRISTIAN KNOWLEDGE (SPCK), an organization founded in England in 1698 by Thomas *Bray with the help of four Anglican laymen. Its purpose was to encourage the establishment of charity schools in England and Wales and to promote Christian knowledge in England and abroad by the distribution of Bibles and religious tracts. In 1701 the *Society for the Propagation of the Gospel (SPG) took over its foreign missionary involvement, leaving SPCK to concentrate upon the education of poor children at home and the publication of religious literature. The Society maintains a publishing house that has served with distinction, esp. in the field of religious publishing.

SOCIETY FOR THE PROPAGATION OF THE GOSPEL (SPG), Anglican missionary organization, founded in 1701 largely through the efforts of Thomas *Bray, Commissary of the Bp. of London for Md., with the active support of the abp. of Canterbury (T. Tenison) and the bp. of London (H. Compton). Bray had previously organized (1698) the *Society for Promoting Christian Knowledge (SPCK), and this body aided in the organization of the new society, which was originally named the Society for the Propagation of the Gospel in Foreign Parts. In 1703, the SPG sent a former Quaker, George *Keith, on an exploratory mission to the British plantations in America. After visiting most of the colonies, he made an extended report. The chaplain of the ship on which he sailed, John Talbot, joined him in his travels and later became the Society's first settled missionary at Burlington, New Jersey. Throughout the colonial period, the SPG aided in the support of ministers in colonies where the C of E was not established, and in some where it was but where the legal stipends were insufficient. As its original charter restricted its operations to "His Majesty's dominions," it was obliged to cease work in the U.S. after the Revolution. It continued work in Canada and the West Indies and, with the growth of the British Empire, extended its efforts to India and Africa. After an amendment of the charter, it entered China, Japan, and other countries, developing a worldwide mission. In 1965, it merged with the Universities Mission to Central Africa to become the United Society for the Propagation of the Gospel. See H. P. Thompson, *Into All Lands* (1951).

SOCIETY OF BROTHERS (Bruderhof), intentional Christian communities. Drawn together in 1920 by Eberhard *Arnold, who had been the scholarly executive of the Student Christian Movement in Germany, the Society set out to be a fellowship based on the Sermon on the Mount: mutual love, pacifism, hospitality to all, no use of money among members, frequent worship, equal value of all work. The pattern was influenced by Christoph F. Blumhardt (1842–1919), whom Arnold esteemed highly, and by Hutterite principles; he briefly joined the *Hutterian Brethren in the Dakotas in the early 1930s. First at Sannerz, Ger., then on a large farm in the Rhoen hills, the Bruderhof flourished. Under Nazi pressure the Bruderhof moved to Devonshire, Eng., then because of wartime anti-German unpopularity, to the Primavera Peninsula in Paraguay. There, after Mennonite colonies helped the pioneering venture, three groups in Paraguay and one in Uruguay gathered some 1,000 members. Later most of these moved to the U.S., after a schism in the early 1960s caused many of the members to withdraw. In 1969 there were about 800 members, all in three communes: Norfolk, Conn., Rifton, N.Y., and Farmington, Pennsylvania. Firm economic roots were put down as the Bruderhof began to manufacture "community playthings," expensive, very well-constructed wooden items for schools and playgrounds. A provision that all young members spend a trial period in "the world," and choose whether to return afterward has resulted in some attrition, even among descendants of the earliest members, but there is continuing dynamism in the common industrial production task, the serious tradition of corporate worship and chorale singing, and the witness to peace and simplicity. See E. Arnold, *Salt and Light* (1967); *idem, Torches Together* (1964).

SOCIETY OF FRIENDS, see RELIGIOUS SOCIETY OF FRIENDS.

SOCINIANISM , Unitarian doctrine partly rationalistic, partly evangelical, developed in the 16th and 17th centuries. Through the theological leadership exercised after 1579 by F. Sozzini (see SOCINUS), Socinianism became the doctrine of the Minor Reformed Church, which had existed in Poland from 1556. The Socinian center was Racôw, near Kraków, where there were a school and a press to diffuse Sozzini's ideas. Among the aristocracy, there were other small congregations and schools. RC reaction led to the closing of the Gymnasium at Racôw (1638) and to the proscription of the Socinians (1658). Thereafter, apart from a few scattered communities (e.g., in Transylvania and East Prussia), Socinianism existed only in its individual representatives scattered throughout Europe. Especially in Holland (the *Bibliotheca Fratrum Polonorum* was published in Amsterdam in 1688) its adherents freely circulated their liberal and rationalist ideas. As a result, Socinianism spread to England and America, where it was absorbed into *Unitarianism, and in Europe it served as a preparation for the *Enlightenment.

The distinctive tenets of Socinianism

(as in the *Racovian Catechism), though not imposed on adherents, were evangelical and rationalistic. The NT was the sole rule of faith and the only source for knowing God; but reason was autonomous in judging the meaning of revelation. Socinianism was a rejection of the Trinity, the Fall, the incarnation, the expiatory redemption, the resurrection of the body, and the natural immortality of the soul (see CONDITIONAL IMMORTALITY). Christ was held to be essentially a man, divine only in the sense of sharing in the power of the Father. The two sacraments, baptism and the Lord's Supper, were mere symbols to show a desire to imitate Christ's obedience in death. Socinians shared the Lutheran and Calvinist concept of the Church's nature and organization but held the Church to be independent of the State. There was no civil power to coerce heretics; neither, however, was civil oppression to be resisted; tolerance was supreme. See L. Cristiani, DTC 14:2326–34; S. Kot, *Socinianism in Poland* (tr. E. M. Wilbur, 1957); G. Pioli, *Fausto Sozzini* (1953); F. Socinus, *Opera* (2v., 1964); E. M. Wilbur, *History of Unitarianism* (2v., rev. ed., 1965), v.I, *Socinianism and its Antecedents*.

SOCINUS, from which the name *Socinianism is derived, the Latinization of the patronymic of Lelio and Fausto Sozzini. (1) Lelio Francesco Maria Sozzini (1525–62), Italian antitrinitarian, uncle of Fausto, was a rationalist in his biblical and theological views. After 1544 he resided in Germany and Switzerland and was in contact with *Bullinger, *Calvin, and *Melanchthon. Visiting Italy (1552), he made a strong impression upon his nephew. He prepared the way in Poland (1556–59) for Fausto's future coming and bequeathed to him his own theological papers. Lelio's biography (*Vita L. S.*, 1814) was written by C. F. Ilgen. (2) Fausto Paolo Sozzini (1539–1604), nephew of Lelio, was the theologian of Socinianism in Poland. A jurisconsult in the family tradition, S.'s predilection was for religious studies. He adhered early to his uncle's views, left Italy (1559) for Lyons, and went

to Zurich (1562) to claim Lelio's papers. His *Explicatio primae partis primi capitis evangelii Ioannis* (1562), like most of his works published anonymously, already expressed his antitrinitarian thought. A letter of 1563 defended *conditional immortality. Outwardly a Catholic, he served at Francesco de' Medici's court in Florence (1563–74), then devoted himself to study at Basel (1574–78). His *De Jesu Christo servatore*, denying Christ's divine nature, was completed in 1578, but published only in 1594. S. went to Poland in 1579 and, after initial difficulties, won acceptance by the Polish Brethren (or Brethren of Christ). Fusing his own ideas with their Anabaptist views, he became a kind of theologian for these antitrinitarian groups among the Polish aristocracy around Kraków. He composed the first draft of the *Racovian Catechism. Though RC reaction under King Stephen Bathory forced S. to leave Kraków (1583) and led to a public burning of his books and manuscripts there (1598), he was otherwise left to spend the rest of his life quietly in the neighboring village of Luclawice. See F. S., *Opera* (2v., 1964); G. Pioli, *F. S.* (1953); bibliog. for Socinianism.

SÖDERBLOM, NATHAN (1866–1931), Lutheran abp. and ecumenical theologian. Born at Trönö, Sweden, he studied at Uppsala Univ., and received the doctorate in theology at the Univ. of Paris in 1901. After a Paris student pastorate among Swedish Lutherans, he became professor of comparative religion at Uppsala (1901–14), then at the Univ. of Leipzig (1912–14). As abp. of Uppsala and thus primate of Sweden (1914–31), and as confidant of the royal family, he prompted a revival of Sweden's church life, while becoming one of the several key leaders of the movement that led to formation of the World Council of Churches in 1948. He called the first universal conference on *Life and Work (Stockholm, 1925) and guided the *Faith and Order conference at Lausanne (1927). At the beginning of World War I, he drafted a message signed by leading Western churchmen urging Christian solidarity against war. He was given the Nobel Peace Prize in 1925. Two of his books, *The Living God* (Gifford Lectures, 1933) and *The Nature of Revelation* (1933), received wide international circulation. Combining profound scholarship in comparative religion, expertness as churchman and preacher, and a passion for Christian unity, he earned the title "prophet of ecumenism." See H. G. G. Herklots, *N. S., Apostle of Christian Unity* (1948).

SOLA FIDE, SOLA GRATIA, SOLA SCRIPTURA, three phrases suggesting essentials of Reformation teaching and its critique of the Renaissance Church. Each phrase points to an emphasis upon the exclusiveness of the factors that the men of the Reformation saw as crucial for the renewal of the Church and Christian life. *Sola fide* refers immediately to the Pauline thesis stated in Rom 1.17: "The just man will live by faith alone." Thus runs Luther's translation, which he defends as authentic in the context of Paul's thought. He sees the phrase to mean, therefore, that by faith alone is man saved, to the exclusion of "works of the law" or *good works done with a view toward man's pleasing God on his own. *Sola gratia* points to man's absolute need of having God take the initiative to save him. The phrase is used with less discomfort by Roman Catholics since it is echoed in the description of man's situation by the Council of Trent. *Sola Scriptura* is originally identified more with the *Reformed branch of the Reformation. In recent times, however, it can be labeled simply as "Protestant" insofar as it bespeaks the notion that the exclusive source and criterion of knowledge about God is the Bible. The phrase rejects as rules of faith esp. what Roman Catholics ordinarily call *tradition or the *magisterium of the Church. See R. McAfee Brown, *Spirit of Protestantism* (pa., 1965), 57, 214–216.

SOLEMN LEAGUE AND COVENANT, a document on church reform in the British

Isles. Overtures made by Parliament in the Civil War of 1642 encouraged the Scottish *Covenanters to hope that the English would reciprocate for the aid they wanted by the acceptance of reformation on the Presbyterian model. The Solemn League and Covenant, drafted by Alexander Henderson and approved by the Scottish Assembly and Convention, was accepted in England in Aug. 1643 by Parliament and by the *Westminster Assembly in September. Those who subscribed it pledged themselves to extirpate *episcopacy from England and popery from Ireland and bring the Churches of the three kingdoms "to the nearest conjunction and uniformity in Religion." In part a defensive bond, in part the seal of an aggressive Presbyterianism, the Covenant proved more divisive than unifying. See Schaff Creeds 1:689–694; bibliog. for Church of Scotland.

SOLIFIDIANISM, the doctrine of *justification by faith alone (*sola fide*). The term is applied esp. to this doctrine as proposed by Martin Luther.

SOUL OF THE CHURCH, a phrase used in several senses. (1) Primarily it refers to the Holy Spirit. In keeping with the theme that the Church is the mystical body of Christ, the Holy Spirit, who is the Spirit of Christ, is described in this image as vivifying and sanctifying the members of Christ's body by grace and charisms. The expression in modern times was taken up by Leo XIII in *Divinum illud munus* (1897), developed at length by Pius XII in *Mystici corporis* (1943), and incorporated into the ecclesiology of Vatican Council II, which pointed out patristic use of the phrase (Vat II ConstCh 7, and note 17). Sanctifying the Church is seen as a primary work of the Holy Spirit, and a question currently discussed by RC theologians is whether this work is a personal mission of "the Lord and giver of life." (2) Some theologians, notably C. Journet in *L'Église du Verbe Incarné* (1951), 2:522ff., have distinguished the uncreated soul, the Holy Spirit, from the created soul of the Church, charity. Charity is received from Christ and is the source of conformity with Christ, i.e., it is derived from the sacraments of Christ and is directed toward the fullness of ecclesial unity. (3) After Vatican Council I some theologians spoke of those who lived in grace and charity but outside visible membership in the Church as belonging to the soul of the Church. This usage ceased after *Mystici corporis.* *MEMBERSHIP IN THE CHURCH.

SOUTH INDIA, CHURCH OF, see CHURCH OF SOUTH INDIA.

SOUTHERN BAPTIST CONVENTION, largest Baptist body in the U.S., organized in 1845. Prior to 1755, Baptists in the South were few, but after the arrival of Shubael *Stearns, a New England *Separate Baptist, revivalistic measures multiplied their numbers to many thousands by 1800. Their organization was limited to local *associations until 1814, when they combined with Northern Baptists to form the Triennial Convention for the support of foreign missions (see AMERICAN BAPTIST CONVENTION). Disputes over slavery and church *polity resulted in the formation of the separate Southern Baptist Convention in 1845. Southern Baptists adopted a plan for a *convention that would incorporate home and foreign mission boards, thus laying foundations for a more unified denomination. Influenced by the hardening sectional spirit of the Reconstruction era, Southern Baptists persisted in remaining separate from those of the North after the Civil War. Devastated by the war, their churches struggled to sustain their missionary activities, and by 1890 had overcome most of the obstacles. In 1968, they reported nearly 11,000,000 members. The Convention recommends the *New Hampshire Confession to its churches; it has had a tradition of conservative theology.

Interest in education began with the founding of Furman University, Greenville, S.C., in 1827; today there are more than 30 Southern Baptist colleges and about 20 junior colleges, most of which are owned by state conventions. The Southern Baptist Theological Seminary was founded in 1859 at Greenville, S.C., but was removed to Louisville, Ky., after the war. There are five other seminaries today, each directly under the control of the convention. From Southern Baptists have come notable preachers (G. W. Truett, R. G. Lee), biblical scholars (J. T. Sampey, A. T. Robertson), and theologians (E. Y. *Mullins, W. T. Conner). In 1965, the Foreign Mission Board reported work in 60 countries, with a staff of 1,769 missionaries. The Home Mission Board engages in diverse types of ministries, employing more than 2,500 missionaries, and having an annual budget of about $8,000,000. The Sunday School Board and the Broadman Press do a multimillion dollar business each year. The Christian Life Commission seeks to inform the consciences of constituents on social issues. State conventions operate hospitals, children's homes, and homes for the aged. During World War II, as southerners migrated to industrial centers of the North, Southern Baptists demanded churches of their own kind, and today they exist in all 50 states. Because the South has retained a more homogeneous population, predominantly agrarian, revivalistic methods have continued to be successful. Between 1940 and 1965, Southern Baptists almost doubled their membership. Although cooperating with other Christians in some endeavors, they have resisted membership in the National and World Councils of Churches. See W. W. Barnes, *Southern Baptist Convention, 1845-1953* (1954); R. G. Torbet and S. H. Hill, Jr., *Baptists—North and South* (1964); D. C. Woolley, ed., *Baptist Advance* (1964).

SOUTHERN METHODIST CHURCH, a small denomination organized in 1939 by a group of laymen who refused to accept the merger of the Methodist Episcopal Church, the Methodist Episcopal Church, South, and the Methodist Protestant Church. They believed that there was infidelity and apostasy in the Methodist Episcopal Church. The Southern Methodist Church claims to be a continuation of the old Methodist Episcopal Church, South, although the courts have overruled this contention in regard to property rights and name. The Church defends segregation. It has no bps. but does have a quadrennial *general conference; churches are owned by the local congregations. In 1968 the denomination had 52 churches, about 4,000 members, and 21 ordained clergy. See L. Corbett, *What, Why, How?—History, Organization, and Doctrinal Belief of the Southern Methodist Church* (1956); HistAmMeth 3:592–593.

SOZZINI, see SOCINUS.

SPALATIN, GEORG (Burkhardt; 1484–1545), German Reformer, one of Martin Luther's first disciples. He was born in Bavaria, at Spalt (thus the name he assumed), and developed an interest in law and humanist studies at Erfurt and Wittenberg. After teaching for a time at Georgenthal, he was ordained, and became (1509) tutor, librarian, and from 1516 adviser and chaplain to Frederick III, Elector of Saxony, whom he strongly influenced in favor of Luther. S. participated as visitator in the introduction of the Reformation throughout Saxony. Luther wrote frequently to him. S. was one of the theologians who assisted P. *Melanchthon in drafting the *Augsburg Confession (1530). He died as pastor at Altenbert.

SPANISH INQUISITION, see INQUISITION, SPANISH.

SPCK, see SOCIETY FOR PROMOTING CHRISTIAN KNOWLEDGE.

SPEER, ROBERT ELLIOTT (1867–1947), Presbyterian layman, secretary (1891–1937)

of the Board of Foreign Missions of the Presbyterian Church in the U.S.A. (now United Presbyterian Church in the U.S.A.). He participated in the organization of the *International Missionary Council and in the conferences that led to the organization of the World Council of Churches. In 1927 he was elected *moderator of his denomination, and played a role as reconciler in the fundamentalist–modernist controversy. He was the author of numerous articles and more than 60 volumes, including *The Finality of Jesus Christ* (1933).

SPENER, PHILIPP JAKOB (1635–1705), German Lutheran theologian, father of *Pietism. S. studied at Strassburg and was profoundly influenced by the doctrines of M. *Bucer and John *Calvin. He became superintendent of Strassburg in 1663 and of Frankfurt in 1666. In the latter city he introduced new practices, such as confirmation and catechetical instruction. Following an idea of Bucer, he gathered a group of parishioners who held devotional meetings twice weekly in his home. These *collegia pietatis* were the origin of the name and ideas of Pietism. His *Pia desideria* (1675; Eng. tr. T. G. Tappert, 1964) called for thorough bible study; awareness of the priesthood of all believers; prayer and exemplary conduct; moral, religious, and practical guidance of seminarians; edifying rather than learned sermons; and study of the mystics. Because his clergy objected to his activities, he was happy to accept a post in Dresden in 1686 as chief court chaplain. In 1691 he went to Berlin as provost and consistorial councilor of St. Nicholas Church. He was influential in the founding of the Univ. of Halle, which soon became the center of Pietism. About 7 years before his death S. withdrew from the controversies provoked by Pietist deemphasis of dogma and devoted himself to purely pastoral work.

SPEYER, DIETS OF, three meetings of the imperial Diet convoked by Charles V at

Speyer, in W Germany, important to Reformation history. (1) The Diet of June 1526 helped the growth of the Reformation by setting aside enforcement of the Edict of Worms (1521; see WORMS, DIET OF) and allowing rulers to control religious affairs in their territories according to their own consciences. (2) The Diet of Feb. 1529 marked the beginning of the use of the name "Protestant," as a minority entered a "protest" against majority legislation revoking toleration to Lutherans in Catholic territories. (3) The Diet of Jan. 1544 made concessions to the Schmalkaldic League and a promise that religious questions would in future be solved not in Rome but in a "free Christian council of the German nation." Pope Paul III severely criticized this last provision. See G. R. Elton, *Reformation in Europe 1517–1559* (pa., 1966); Jedin Trent 1:247–248, 494–499.

SPG, see SOCIETY FOR THE PROPAGATION OF THE GOSPEL.

SPIRIT BAPTISM, see BAPTISM WITH THE HOLY SPIRIT.

SPIRITUALISTS, adherents of a religious movement based on the fundamental belief that communication between the natural world and the spirit world is possible. It began in 1848 with the spirit manifestations reported by the *Fox sisters at Hydesville and Rochester, N.Y., and the publicity resulting from their lecture tours. The ideas and terminology of Spiritualist thought owe their origin to the writings of Andrew Jackson *Davis, particularly his book *The Principles of Nature, Her Divine Revelations, and A Voice to Mankind,* published at New York in 1847. The fame of the "Rochester rappings" and the demonstrations of psychic phenomena by the Fox Sisters gained numerous converts, who then turned to the pages of *Nature's Divine Revelations* for a better understanding of their faith. Horace Greeley opened the columns of the New York *Tribune* to spiritism and Robert Dale Owen, the noted reformer, lectured on spirit phenomena. Seances and discussions of Spiritualism became commonplace in the U.S. and England in the 1850s. Materialism and scientific-technological developments had shaken the faith of many in traditional religious beliefs. Spiritualism had a strong appeal to these individuals by grounding its belief in the afterlife and the supernatural in verifiable experiments, rather than in simple faith.

Davis made the first move to organize Spiritualism as a religious sect when he established a progressive lyceum, or Spiritualist Sunday school, at Buffalo, N.Y. in 1863. Spiritualism has tended to remain a somewhat amorphous movement as the influence of the individual medium is decisive in gathering or dispersing an individual congregation. The Davis association lasted only until 1872. A more permanent effort to unite the Spiritualist movement began in 1893 with the formation of the National Spiritualist Association, now known as the National Spiritualist Association of Churches. It has aimed at establishing minimum standards for the licensing of churches and ministers and prepared the *Spiritualist Manual* as an aid to worship services. It has represented the more churchly, orthodox wing of the movement. The National Spiritual Alliance of the U.S.A., founded in 1913, and the International General Assembly of Spiritualists, formed in 1936, have similar aims and activities. Many Spiritualists are outside these major national groups, and many have harmonized their beliefs with those of other religious bodies. There were an estimated 24,174 members of Spiritualist churches in 1968.

The beliefs of Spiritualists center on the possibility of contact between the world of the spirits and the world we know. Spiritualists believe in Infinite Intelligence and that both physical and spiritual reality are expressions of Infinite Intelligence. They also believe that personal identity and individual existence survive the apparent death of the body. In his writings, Andrew J.

Davis posited a rather elaborate cosmology of the world of the spirits. In his view, man is composed of a mortal physical body, an immortal spirit, and a soul, which is the form of the spirit and clothes it with a quasi-immaterial body recapitulating the physical body. After the death of the physical body, spirit and soul pass into the "Summer-land" of the after-life, progressing through a series of concentric spheres from the lower level of the Summer-land to the Philosopher's Sphere, the Love Sphere, and the Christ Sphere. The beginning point for each one is determined by his previous life, but progress is constant toward a universal redemption. Other writers have adopted slightly different views, and a minority of Spiritualists teach rebirth, but the teachings of Davis are generally accepted. Spiritualist understanding of traditional Christian beliefs may also vary considerably. Their doctrine of God as Infinite Intelligence leaves the individual free to accept or reject much of Christian theology, and they do not emphasize the atonement by Jesus Christ or the Bible as the word of God. Some Spiritualists may profess the doctrines of traditional Christianity, but there is no compulsion to do so, and they often reinterpret these doctrines in their own sense, seeing Jesus Christ as a *medium and the gospel as an account of spirit phenomena. Spiritualist worship services often include scriptural readings and a sermon, as well as congregational hymn singing and pastoral prayer, but the messages from the spirit world delivered by a medium are of paramount interest.

SPIRITUALITY, the form or manner of living the Christian life in such a way as to advance in Christian perfection, and mainly through the practice of prayer. The term itself is used esp. in RC literature, where reference is made to Benedictine, Carmelite, Dominican, Ignatian, Sulpician, and other types of spirituality. The idea, however, is broader than this use of the term. Christian theology generally recognizes the life of grace as a call to live according to the spirit and not according to the flesh (Gal 3.3–6; Rom 8.4–13). The means by which such a call can be fulfilled constitute spirituality. It has taken on a generic meaning because of varying emphases: some forms of RC spirituality stress the pursuit of simple, even mystical, contemplation, others stress the ascetical practice of active virtues in the works of the apostolate; some have developed systematic methods of prayer, others prefer more simple ways of prayer. The Reformation repudiation of good works, monasticism, and many RC devotional practices suggests also the repudiation of spirituality. Yet Luther's own life and writings are deeply concerned with means of living the Christian life (see Wicks). The discipline designed by Calvin was also a spirituality, a quest for conformity to the sovereign will of God. Simply by their concern with perfection, personal experience, and the means to a devout life, however, Pietism and Methodism more obviously are forms of spirituality. There is also a rich spiritual doctrine in the writings of the *Caroline Divines, esp. those of Lancelot *Andrewes. The ideals of the Christian life proposed by groups directly or indirectly belonging to the so-called left wing of the Reformation also may be viewed as forms of spirituality. Great emphasis was put on inner experience, even *mysticism, the practice of meditation, and quiet prayer. The practice of *nonconformity and a nonworldly regulated form of life were meant as a means to deepen the inner life. See L. Bouyer, *History of Catholic Spirituality* (1963); R. Garrigou-Lagrange, *Christian Perfection and Contemplation* (1937); R. N. Jones, *Spiritual Reformers in the 16th and 17th Centuries* (pa., 1959); J. Wicks, *Man Yearning for Grace* (1968).

SPIRITUALS, FRANCISCAN, ideological descendants of the Zelanti, a faction within the Franciscan Order that was in the process of formation even during the lifetime of St. Francis. They believed that the order's first function was to perpetuate the way of life exemplified by the founder and his earliest companions. Every attempt to adapt the life of the friars to the realities of organized existence was to this group of primitivists a betrayal of the Franciscan ideal. They were particularly unyielding in the matter of poverty, holding that the order and all its members were bound to the *usus pauper*, the use of only absolutely necessary things. In an attempt to preserve peace and union within the order, the popes of the 13th cent. issued a series of bulls in which they attempted to clarify disputed sections of the rule. Efforts to enforce these papal pronouncements only served to harden the zealots' resistance. Bl. John of Parma, who sympathized with their aims, was forced to resign as minister general in 1257 because of his involvement in *Joachimism, a form of *apocalypticism to which the persecuted rigorists were strongly attracted. The Zelanti began to be known as Spirituals during the generalate of St. Bonaventure (1257–74). He sought to steer a middle course by opposing both the intolerance of the rigorists and the abuses of the laxists, but his efforts to establish equilibrium and proportion had no appeal for the Spirituals, who began to demand the right to separate themselves from the main body of the order so that they could observe the rule in its primitive severity. Between 1274 and 1317 a bitter battle raged between the Spirituals and the Communitas, as the moderate majority was called. Each side was guilty of excesses in its attacks upon the other. In 1312 there was a papal condemnation of some of the Spirituals' doctrines; the petition for separate, autonomous existence was denied.

Three geographically separated groups of Spirituals functioned independently. Each was headed by a talented and determined leader: *Peter John Olivi in Provence, *Ubertino of Casale in Tuscany, and *Angelus Clarenus in the March of Ancona. In 1317 John XXII launched a determined program to suppress the Spirituals. Many of them returned to the order, some were imprisoned, and a few were burned as heretics. The hard core became *Fraticelli.

By 1325 the Spirituals ceased to be a faction of any significance. See D. Douie, *Nature and Effects of the Heresy of the Fraticelli* (1932), with extensive bibliog.; *idem*, NCE 13:610–611, with selected bibliog.; L. von Auw, *Angelo Clareno et les Spirituels franciscains* (1952); T. MacVicar, *Doctrine of the Franciscan Spirituals* (1963); D. Mussey, *Spiritual Franciscans* (1907); M. Lambert, *Franciscan Poverty: The Doctrine of the Absolute Poverty of Christ and the Apostles in the Franciscan Order, 1210–1323* (1961). *POVERTY CONTROVERSY.

SPORTS, BOOK OF, see BOOK OF SPORTS.

STAKE, in Mormon usage, the name for a regional division of the Church. There were in 1968 approximately 420 stakes in the Church of Jesus Christ of Latter-day Saints.

STANDARD CONFESSION, a *confession of faith of *General Baptists in London, drafted in 1660. The confession was prompted by a desire to present a statement of Christian orthodoxy to Charles II at the time of the *Restoration, since Baptists had been active in the *Commonwealth army, and were accused of being subversive. The name Standard Confession dates from 1663, when the 1660 statement was revised and reconfirmed by a general assembly of the General Baptists. This confession was a source of Baptist unity during the oppression of *Dissenters. See W. L. Lumpkin, ed., *Baptist Confessions of Faith* (1959).

STATE CHURCH, commonly a synonym for *national Church or *established Church, but more precisely any Church that is legally recognized as the official religion of a particular state. As such the term applies to Roman Catholic, Protestant, or Orthodox Churches, where these have such recognition. The term is also used in another sense to signify a Church that exists in direct subordination to the State (see ERASTIANISM). By this meaning a contrast is suggested with a church–state, i.e., a church–state partnership in which the former is dominant, as in a theocracy.

STATED CLERK, an official of governing bodies in Churches of Presbyterian polity. Although the *session (governing unit) of each local congregation elects a clerk, the term "stated clerk" is generally used only in larger administrative units—*presbytery, *synods, and *general assembly. It involves responsibility for maintaining records and is normally not a full-time position for bodies other than the general assembly. The stated clerk of the general assembly, however, is a full-time official in the major Presbyterian Churches. He gives general supervision to the administrative work determined by the general assembly, and in some ways is regarded as the leader of the denomination. Authority, however, rests with the general assembly, over which an elected moderator presides.

STATEMENT OF FAITH (United Church of Christ), a testimony, in broad areas of Christian teaching, of the belief of this Church. It is not a *doctrinal standard, nor can it be imposed on local churches or used as a test for members or ministers. The preparation of a brief statement of faith was the first task of the Church after its formation in 1957. An appointed committee of members in equal numbers from the uniting denominations prepared the text, and it was accepted substantially by the Second General Synod in 1959. Written in modern language, descriptive rather than definitive, lyrical rather than theological, the statement was designed for liturgical use in worship services and has had wide acceptance for this purpose. The affirmations are so phrased and arranged as to accommodate even a non-Trinitarian understanding of Christian teaching.

STATISTICS OF RELIGIOUS BODIES, numerical reports for Churches and other religious organizations on such items as membership, number of congregations, and financial contributions. Such reports are difficult to secure for the total world picture and present special problems of interpretation. Many religious bodies have a loose organizational structure, with no personnel employed to gather accurate statistics. Particularly in the emerging nations of the world, religious bodies may not have the resources or the training, or sometimes may be lacking the interest, needed to keep complete and detailed records. Further difficulties result from a lack of uniformity among the various bodies in methods of gathering statistics and defining terms. Some Churches include children who have been baptized but not confirmed, while others do not. Still others do not baptize infants, and that must be considered in comparing their numerical strength with other groups. Statistics on Jews generally include all who are Jewish by birth. Few religious bodies attempt to distinguish between nominal and active membership. Statistical reports, therefore, do not indicate whether significant percentages of the reported membership may have ceased to participate in worship and other expressions of religious life. Enthusiastic devotees, sometimes unconsciously, may exaggerate the following of their group. Occasionally such figures can be corrected by the studies of more objective, outside institutions, such as government agencies or polls by private organizations. Since some people object to governmental questioning of citizens about their religion, however, government agencies often remain aloof from that area. In the U.S. no government census of religious preference has been taken since 1936. By and large, therefore, those who gather statistics on religious bodies are dependent on the reports given by those bodies.

A further difficulty is estimating the number of people who identify with a particular religious group although they do not have formal affiliation. People may be in general agreement with the teachings of the group and participate to a considerable extent in its community life without becoming formally identified. In mission areas such adherents may compromise a significant number, particularly if the missionaries require thorough preparation prior to baptism. Warnings against undue emphasis on statistics are frequently given; nonetheless, some consideration of statistics seems essential for church planning, finances, and representation in ecumenical bodies. Statistical trends of growth or decline are subject to varying interpretations and cannot be automatically equated with the growth or decline of religion's influence on society. See, for general compilations of statistics, along with some discussion of the difficulty of securing them, H. W. Coxill and K. Grubb, eds., *World Christian Handbook* (1968) and L. B. Whitman, ed., *Yearbook of American Churches* (annual).

STAUPITZ, JOHANN VON *(c.1468–1524)*, German Augustinian, theologian, counselor of the young Martin Luther. S. entered the Augustinian Order in 1490; became a doctor in Scripture in 1500. Invited by the Elector Frederick III of Saxony to reorganize the Univ. of Wittenberg, he became first dean of its theology faculty (1503–12). Elected vicar-general of his order in 1503, he became Luther's spiritual adviser and appointed Luther his successor in the chair of Scripture at Wittenberg. Luther gave credit to S. for aiding him in his torments of conscience by turning his thoughts to Christ's love; in his last letter Luther (1523) told S. that he had led him to the light of the gospel. After Luther's attack on indulgences, however, S. drew apart from the controversies, and would not renounce his own loyalty to Rome. He resigned as vicar-general in 1520 and accepted an invitation to be court chaplain at Salzburg. There in 1532 he joined the Benedictines, dying as abbot of St. Peter's. See E. Wolf, RGG 6:243–343; R. Weijenbourg, LTK 9:1026.

STEARNS, SHUBAEL (1706–71), Baptist revivalist. Reared a Congregationalist in Boston, Mass., S. was influenced by the preaching of George *Whitefield c.1745. In 1751 he became a Baptist and was ordained

a minister. His preaching was highly emotional and proved effective among the frontier inhabitants of N.C., where he and Daniel *Marshall organized the Sandy Creek Church in 1755. By 1758, several other congregations had been constituted, and the Sandy Creek Association was begun. The type of revivalistic preaching represented by Stearns, Marshall, and other *Separate Baptists from New England was not readily accepted by the older Baptist churches of the South, but it led to rapid Baptist expansion and laid the foundations for their subsequent predominance in that section. See W. L. Lumpkin, *Baptist Foundations in the South* (1961).

STEDINGERS, peasants living by the River Weser in Friesland who refused to pay tithes to the abp. of Bremen (1229). An army was sent against them, and they defeated it. Branded as heretics (1230), the Stedingers were the target of a crusade authorized by Gregory IX and were scattered in a battle near Altenesch in 1234. In the polemics against them they were labeled *Luciferians. See K. Algermissen, LTK 9:1027–28; É. Amann, DTC 9:1049; Bihlmeyer-Tüchle 2:307.

STEINER, RUDOLF (1861–1925), founder of the Anthroposophical Society. Born in Karlovic, Hungary, he received a scientific education, studying at the Technical University in Vienna, but his interests lay in philosophy. In 1886 he published *Goethe's Theory of Cognition,* and during the years 1890–97 he helped edit the Weimar edition of Goethe's works. He became interested in Christianity and in *Theosophy and in 1902 founded the German Theosophical Society. Ten years later he established the Anthroposophical Society for the study of human evolution in the light of the Christ-Event. In 1913, due to Steiner's opposition to the Hinduism of Annie *Besant and the Adyar Theosophists, the German Theosophical Society was expelled and its members were absorbed into the Anthroposophical Society. In the same year at Dornach, Switzerland, Steiner built the Gotheanum, a center of his own architectural design, for his followers. He developed Anthroposophy as a system of thought and way of life whereby man could spiritualize his existence; S.'s doctrine did not include theism. His later years were devoted to writings on the social order and to fostering experimental theater and music. His writings are extensive on theosophic and philosophic subjects. See A. P. Shepherd, *Science of the Invisible* (1954). *ANTHROPOSOPHY.

STERCORANISTS (Lat. *stercus,* dung), a word invented in the 11th or 12th cent. suggesting that some theologians taught that the body of Christ became subject to the whole digestive cycle of the recipient of holy communion. There is no sufficient evidence to show that anyone taught this, but only that there was a want of precise formulation in the eucharistic theology of the era. See A. Gaudel, DTC 14:2590–2611.

STEWARDSHIP, the concept, based on such NT passages as 1 Cor 4.1–2, 9.17, that man must live as the faithful trustee of what he has received from God and must render an account. The term, most often used by Protestants, is sometimes given as the theological basis for *tithing, but stewardship of time and of talents is also recognized. Stewardship has been invoked as a justification for great material possessions, which, however, also beget humanitarian obligations. The term was prominent in the *Social Gospel movement; its most recent application has been to describe the Christian's vocation to concern for the world, for the "secular city." See V. Ely, *Stewardship* (1962); T. Kantonen, *Theology of Christian Stewardship* (1964); F. J. McConnell, *Christian Materialism* (1936); H. Cox, *Secular City* (1965).

STOCKHOLM CONFERENCE, the first international conference of the *Life and Work movement, held at Stockholm, Sweden, Aug. 19–30, 1925. The conference found a working model in an earlier conference at Birmingham, Eng., on the application of Christian principles to politics, economics, and citizenship (the so-called COPEC meeting). The Stockholm Conference considered the Church's obligation in view of God's purpose for the world; the Church and economic and industrial problems; the Church and social and moral problems; the Church and international relations; the Church and Christian education; and methods of cooperative and federative efforts by the Christian communions. Under these general headings the delegates studied housing, crime, alcoholism, youth, sex, education, family life, war, race problems, and international law. The reports were not voted on, and the "message" issued by the conference was general in tone, stressing the pressing need for Christian education in social and economic problems and calling for a united effort to build the kingdom of God on earth by working for social justice. See G. K. A. Bell, ed., *Stockholm Conference 1925* (1926).

STODDARD, SOLOMON (1643–1729), Congregationalist; grandfather of Jonathan *Edwards. S. served as pastor at Northampton, Mass., from 1669 until his death. After the New England Congregationalists, under the *Half-way Covenant, began to baptize the children of baptized but noncommuning members of the Church, S. developed the theory ("Stoddardeanism") that the Lord's Supper was instituted as a means of regeneration and that persons could and should come to it even though they knew themselves to be in an unregenerate state. He opened the Supper to all and, by attempting to use it as an *ordinance for conversion, became, according to some interpreters, the first American revivalist.

STONE, BARTON WARREN (1772–1844), one of the four founding fathers of the

Christian Churches (Disciples of Christ). A lifelong frontiersman, S. was a pioneer in Christian union. Educated in David Caldwell's log college at Guilford, N.C., and licensed as a Presbyterian minister, he migrated to Bourbon Co., Ky. (1796). By his agency the *Kentucky Revival reached its climax on the grounds of his Cane Ridge church in Aug. 1801. A feature of this *camp meeting was the subordination of doctrinal disputes to the spirit of cooperation among Methodists, Presbyterians, and Baptists. He withdrew from the Presbyterian Church in 1804, determined to own "no name but Christian," to acknowledge "no creed but the Bible," and to pursue Christian union. He did not accept the doctrine of the Trinity, or of Christ's vicarious atonement. Churches under his persuasion called themselves Christian Churches. They spread throughout Ky., Mo., Ind., Ill., and Ohio. With Christian union as his polar star for life, his greatest success was the merging of his followers with "the Reformers" (Disciples) of Alexander *Campbell in 1832. See autobiog. (1847); lives by C. Ware (1932) and W. G. West (1954).

STONE, DARWELL (1859–1941), prominent theologian of Anglo-Catholicism. Born in Denbighshire, educated at Owens College, Manchester, and Merton College, Oxford, librarian and principal of Pusey House, he wrote many books upholding Catholic teaching, which include the massive *History of the Doctrine of the Holy Eucharist* (2v., 1909). His responsibilities prevailing over his natural reserve, he was drawn into an unequalled position of influence merited by both his knowledge and abilities. More guarded than other Anglo-Catholics in his admiration for the *Caroline Divines and for the specific difference of Anglicanism, he thought that the Anglican Church should be understood only as a fragment of the Church universal. With his venerable beard and his measured and exact mode of speech, he was a familiar Oxford character, the subject of many anecdotes, and was loved and revered for the manifest devotion

of his religious faith, his disregard for personal ambition, and his fairness in controversy. See life by F. L. Cross (1943).

STORCH, NICHOLAS (d. 1530), radical Reformer and agitator. S., a weaver, was one of the *Zwickau Prophets. He was a fanatic, possibly deranged. He preached a doctrine of individual inspiration, and also the establishment of a new kingdom of God by violent revolution. After expulsion from Wittenberg in 1522, he became a wandering preacher in Poland and Bavaria. He is sometimes classified as an Anabaptist because he rejected *infant baptism and argued for rebaptism.

STRANGITES, a Mormon body founded by James J. Strang (1813–56). *LATTER-DAY SAINTS (STRANGITES), CHURCH OF JESUS CHRIST OF.

STRAWBRIDGE, ROBERT (d. 1781), Methodist lay preacher who is thought to have organized the first Methodist *society on the Wesleyan plan in North America, probably in 1764. An emigrant from Ireland, he settled on Sam's Creek, Frederick Co., Md., using his house as a preaching center. He itinerated through the Eastern Shore of Md., Del., parts of Pa., and Va., establishing societies and licensing local preachers. See HistAmMeth 1:75–76; F. E. Maser, "R. S., Founder of Methodism in Maryland," *Methodist History* (Jan. 1966), 3–21.

STRIGEL, VICTORINUS (1524–69), theologian prominent in the doctrinal controversies of second-generation Lutheranism. He studied under Melanchthon at Wittenberg. In the *Synergistic Controversy, he maintained that original sin did not destroy man's power for good and that in conversion there is some human cooperation with grace. His teaching was rejected in the *Formula of Concord (Art. 1). From 1563 he lectured at Leipzig, but was forced to leave because of his Calvinistic interpretation of the Lord's Supper. In 1567 he openly adopted Calvinism and became professor of ethics at Heidelberg. See G. Kawerau, Enc-RelKnow II:113–114.

STUMPF, JOHANNES (1500–78), Swiss Protestant theologian and historian. S. studied at Heidelberg and Strassburg and entered the Order of St. John in 1521. The following year he became prior of his order and people's priest in Bubikon. The date of his conversion to Lutheranism is not known; but he continued as Protestant pastor at Bubikon until 1543, when he took a church in Stammheim. Though usually conciliatory, S. resolutely defended Zwingli's view of the Eucharist. He wrote numerous historical, geographical, and theological works, and his Swiss chronicle (1548) remained authoritative into the 18th century. Another of his treatises, *Reformationschronik*, contains the first biography of Zwingli.

SUBJECTIVISM, as a religious attitude, a tendency to place individual reason and personal experience above objective, external authorities. Luther and Calvin have been blamed for teaching the right of *private judgment but both in fact believed in an objective authority. It was the 18th cent. that brought about a crisis in epistemology that undermined old authorities. After Hume had cast doubt upon the causal nexus, Kant announced in his *Critique of Pure Reason* that one cannot know reality-in-itself, but only appearances. Therefore religion must rest upon man's inner sense of right and wrong, from which God's existence and human immortality may be deduced. F. *Schleiermacher located the essence of religion in "a feeling of absolute dependence upon God." *Liberal theology, deprived of an infallible Bible, grounded authority in God-consciousness, the conscience, or other forms of religious experience. Without intending to do so, *Pietism, *revivalism, and *evangelicalism rein-

forced the tendency toward subjectivism by stressing the "conversion experience" above creeds, Church, ministry, and sacraments. Scientific method, depth psychology, and sociology further contributed to a relativism that permeated every area, including religion. The *Bultmann School's existentialist approach to the NT (see EXISTENTIAL THEOLOGY) and the neo-orthodox separation of the Jesus of history from the Christ of faith are evidences of the lack of confidence in external authorities. In ethics, older systems were supplanted by situational (or contextual) ethics (see NEW MORALITY) . Thus the growing tendency toward subjectivism has made modern man tend to be antidogmatic, skeptical of authority, and reliant upon his own religious and ethical judgments.

SUBLAPSARIANISM, the doctrine, held by some Calvinists and affirmed by the Synod of *Dort (1618–19), that God after the creation and Fall of man decreed the salvation of the elect and the reprobation of the wicked according to his inscrutable will. *CALVINISM; *SUPRALAPSARIANISM; *PREDESTINATION.

SUBUNISTS, the Catholics opposed to the *Utraquists in 15th-cent. Bohemia. The Subunists defended holy communion under one species (*sub una specie*); they were also called Unists. *HUSSITES.

SUNDAY, BILLY, (1863–1935), American revival preacher. Born in Ames, Iowa, of German parents, originally named Sontag, S. had a successful career as a major league baseball player, 1883–91. Converted in 1887 after hearing an itinerant evangelist, he left baseball and took a full-time position in the YMCA in Chicago. His career as an evangelist began in 1895. He received ordination to the Presbyterian ministry in 1903. He was famous for his emotional appeals and his use of baseball terminology to describe the struggles of the soul to accept the grace of conversion. He fully developed D. L. *Moody's use of business techniques to advertise and conduct revivals. A Presbyterian himself, S. relied on the financial support of all local denominations to mount his crusades. His opposition to liquor made him a valuable ally of prohibition advocates. He reached the peak of his influence in 1908–10. Many criticized his methods as theatrical and sensational and disparaged the conversions he elicited as ephemeral. An expensive failure in New York City made his work more difficult, and after World War I he was less influential. See W. G. McLoughlin, *Modern Revivalism* (1958); *idem, Billy Sunday Was His Real Name* (1955).

SUNDAY, the name of the first day of the week. The nominal association of this day with the sun is of pagan origin and was introduced in Rome, along with the observance of the Egyptian week, during the 1st and 2d cents. A.D. Among Christians, esp. for liturgical purposes, the day has been called the Lord's Day (*dies dominica*), possibly with scriptural warrant (Rev 1.10). Sunday began in apostolic times to replace the Jewish Sabbath as the day of worship, although it is erroneous to speak of a transfer of the obligation to worship from the Sabbath to Sunday, since the Jewish law was primarily concerned not with public assembly for worship but with rest (see Gen 2.1–3), whereas the Christian Sunday is primarily dedicated to public worship and only in a secondary and accessory way to rest. The obligation of the Sabbath has been regarded by all but a few Christians as abrogated under the new law (see Col 2.16). There is, however, mention of eucharistic celebration on the first day of the week (Acts 20.7; possibly also in 1 Cor 16.1). The writings of the early Fathers put it beyond reasonable doubt that from the 1st cent. onward an assembly for worship was commonly held on the first day of the week; by the 4th cent., attendance at this service was generally thought to be part of a Christian's duty, although the earliest explicit church

legislation prescribing such attendance is from the first years of the 6th century. The association of the day with rest began with the purpose of providing opportunity for worship. In justification of the common Christian choice of Sunday as the day devoted above others to public worship, it is usual to point to Christ's resurrection and the descent of the Holy Spirit as having taken place on the first day of the week. In the liturgy, the association of the day with the resurrection is esp. important. Liturgically, Sunday is regarded as a little Easter, standing in relation to the week as Easter itself does to the year as a whole.

In common usage one Sunday is distinguished from another by its order in relation to certain seasons (Lent, Advent) or to the Epiphany, Easter, and Pentecost. Some Sundays also have popular names derived from the first word of the entrance hymn, or introit, of the Latin liturgy (thus Gaudete, Rorate, and Laetare Sundays), or from the topic of the Gospel of the day, or from some practice observed (Dominica in albis), event commemorated (Palm and Easter Sunday), or mystery celebrated (Trinity Sunday) on that day. See W. J. Sherzer, NCE 13:797–798; M. Herron, NCE 13:799–802.

SUNDAY OBSERVANCE, the law or custom found in most Christian Churches urging or obliging the faithful to participate in worship and to abstain from servile work and certain public affairs on Sunday. The Christian observance of Sunday was strongly influenced by the Jewish observance of Saturday, or the Sabbath, as a day consecrated to God. The third commandment made this explicit: "Keep holy the Sabbath" (Ex. 20.8). The sanctification of this day involved abstention from work, and participation in religious instruction and special worship. The early Christians clearly knew they were not obligated by these Jewish practices, but the abrogation of the Sabbath observance left a void in the week that very soon came to be filled by Sunday. The development of the two elements of Sunday observance, worship and rest, occurred at different times. During apostolic times Sunday was regarded as particularly sacred because it was the day on which Christ's resurrection took place, and it was very soon known as the Lord's Day (Gr. *kyriakē hēmera*; Lat. *dies dominica*). The Christian assemblies generally seem to have celebrated their Eucharist on Sunday, and it is probable that they met for instruction and worship every Sunday. Certainly the practice of the Sunday Eucharist was firmly established early in the 2d cent., but it was only very gradually that attendance at the Sunday liturgy came to be looked on as obligatory. In the 4th cent. the Council of Elvira enforced attendance under pain of excommunication. Thereafter ecclesiastical legislation became more and more strict, and by the mid-12th cent. it had become part of the law of the Roman Church. The Eastern Church has never considered such attendance as obligatory, although some groups in union with Rome may do so. Observance of Sunday as a day of rest was a later development. As more insistence was laid on attendance at church, and as the services grew longer, it became more desirable to have the day set aside for rest from ordinary work. As early as 321 Constantine had decreed a weekly holiday on Sunday. There also seems to have been a general feeling that the rest on the Jewish Sabbath had been transferred to Sunday. After having been enjoined by many local councils, the Sunday abstinence from work was made binding in the Western Church by Pope Gregory IX in 1234.

The same general trend may be observed among the Protestant Churches. In several Protestant societies, particularly Calvinistic and Puritanical ones, attendance at Sunday worship was stressed and sometimes enforced by the secular authority. In a number of churches not only has abstinence from work been obligatory, but a rigorist prohibition against recreational activities on Sunday has been prominent, the remnants of which still exist in the "Blue Laws" found in several states. In general, however, most Protestant Churches

encourage attendance at worship and abstinence from work on Sunday but do not regard it as binding in conscience. Many RC theologians now give a broader interpretation of the Sunday obligation. Vatican Council II stresses the ideal of Sunday as the day for Christ's faithful to come together and, by hearing the word of God and participating in the Eucharist, call to mind the passion, resurrection, and glorification of the Lord. Sunday should be observed as a day of joy and freedom from work (Vat II SacLit 106). Greater freedom has been given to the faithful in some regions to fulfill the obligations to hear Mass on a day other than Sunday. See H. Dumaine, DACL 4.1:858–994; M. Herron, NCE 13:799–802. *SABBATARIANS.

SUNDAY SCHOOLS, the principal institutional agency developed by Protestants to provide general religious education, esp. for the young. Although there is record of earlier examples of local attempts to operate schools for religious instruction, the Sunday school movement began with Robert Raikes (1735–1811) of Gloucester, England, who in 1780 opened a school to teach poor and neglected children the Bible and elementary school subjects as well. Classes were held on Sundays and also on week days. His efforts met opposition: some feared that the education of the poor might lead to revolution; others objected to the violation of the Sabbath. But his effort was successful. Hannah More (d. 1833) and others became interested in the work and established similar schools elsewhere. News of these developments soon reached the U.S., and by 1791 projects of a like kind were undertaken in New York City, Boston, and Philadelphia. In 1816 two important societies were founded in New York City to promote Sunday schools and a third in Philadelphia in the following year. The Philadelphia society—the Sunday and Adult School Union—soon overshadowed the New York City societies in importance, and the latter associated themselves in an auxiliary capacity with the Philadelphia

Union, which thereupon took the name American Sunday School Union. For the next 40 years the American Union was the dominant influence in the Sunday school movement. Under its leadership there was an enormous expansion in the number of Sunday schools in the U.S. and in their enrollment. The Union published a great number of books for use in the schools, as well as periodicals for children and teachers. Eventually mounting denominational opposition—the establishment of denominational organizations to promote strictly denominational schools and provide denominational literature for use in them—weakened the position of the Union. Leadership in the field as a whole passed from the Union to national (later, international) Sunday school conventions, beginning in 1859. From 1875 until 1914 these conventions were held every 3 years, and after 1914, every 4 years. After 1905 effective leadership passed into the hands of permanent boards or councils of officials who, generally speaking, have been people of notable professional competence, with more clearly defined educational objectives and sound ideas about how they should be achieved.

Objectives and methods of the Sunday schools have developed during these different periods. Before the formation of the Union the schools aimed at providing general rudimentary as well as specifically religious education, and their sessions therefore tended to take up from 5 to 8 hours of the day. The schools at this time sought primarily to impart doctrinal instruction in religious matters, and the method was usually catechetical. Under the Union, the development of secular schools freed the Sunday schools from the need to provide other than religious instruction, and it was possible to reduce the ordinary Sunday session to a much shorter period of time. It also became feasible to concentrate less effort upon the poor and to extend the program to include children from all social classes. Doctrinal instruction and catechetical recitation gave way to the memorizing of passages from Scripture. At first these passages were chosen somewhat haphazardly; in time the Union's *Select Passages* put a measure of order and comprehensiveness in the coverage of biblical material, although memorization continued to be used as the test of mastery. Under the Conventions, effective steps began to be taken toward the training of teachers. Institutes were established in various places from 1861, notable among them the Chatauqua Sunday School Assembly for Teachers (1874; see CHATAUQUA MOVEMENT). With better-trained teachers available, memorizing of biblical texts began to fall from favor. The teachers were given more scope to explain and apply the scriptural texts. A uniform system for the study of the same texts on given Sundays over a fixed period of time was adopted, but with rather more stress on specific content than was later considered desirable. Under the later leadership of boards and committees, and esp. with the programming in the hands of professionally oriented educators, there has been a shift of emphasis from a content-centered to a pupil-centered curriculum: the overall aim has moved away from the communication of specific information and has come to focus more directly upon evoking in the pupil a religious response to the gospel message that will find expression in actual Christian living.

The contribution of Sunday schools to the religious vitality of Protestant denominations has been enormous. They have been established everywhere in the U.S. and have been remarkably well attended. Through the missionary work of the Churches they have spread to other lands, where they also enjoy a splendid record of accomplishment. The involvement of the laity in the work is a circumstance that speeds the development of independent, self-sufficient Churches in mission areas, staffed by indigenous leaders and teachers. With the recognition of the importance of the work of the Sunday school, and the development of its aims and methods, the institutional distinction between Church and Sunday school is less clearly drawn than in former times. In recent years with the general secularization of society, attendance has decreased somewhat in U.S. Sunday schools. This has been a matter of concern to those who see the importance of the work of the Sunday school for the continuing vigor of Christian Churches. The system has been subjected to close scrutiny in the hope of strengthening it to the better performance of its work. Among the criticisms leveled against the schools in the present situation are the following: (1) the lack of adequately trained teachers and leaders; (2) the brevity of the sessions, which generally last no longer than an hour on a Sunday morning; (3) an over-emphasis on teaching older adults with a consequent loss of interest among teenagers and young adults; (4) inadequate and outdated curriculum materials, although writers and planners are seeking to move forward with the times and are striving to make use of the best modern educational methods; (5) generally poor discipline and order, a situation that tends to discourage serious study and faithful attendance. See K. B. Cully, ed., *Westminster Dictionary of Christian Education* (1963); E. W. Rice, *Sunday School Movement, 1780–1917* (1917); J. M. Price et al., *Survey of Religious Education* (1959); G. P. Albaugh, *Encyclopedia of Religion* (ed. V. Ferm, 1945), 744–749.

SUOMI SYNOD, see FINNISH EVANGELICAL LUTHERAN CHURCH (SUOMI SYNOD).

SUPERINTENDENT (Lutheran), a church official in continental Lutheranism. The Reformation, esp. in Hesse and Saxony, was put into practice by superintendents who conducted visitations of, and often prepared church orders for, the *local churches. In the Reformation of Denmark and Norway J. *Burgenhagen substituted superintendents for bishops and ended any continuation of *apostolic succession. In Germany the office of superintendent as an administrator and pastoral official in a region and territory has continued, but increasingly under control of the *synod.

SUPERINTENDENT (Methodist), the original title given to the leaders of the Methodist Episcopal Church in the U.S., Francis *Asbury and Thomas *Coke, who were elected at the *Christmas Conference (1784). The title was soon changed to "bishop," but the *district superintendent remains an important official in Methodist polity.

SUPRALAPSARIANISM, in contrast to *sublapsarianism, the doctrine held by some Calvinists that the decree of *election and the decree of *reprobation are antecedent to the Fall of man. The Fall is merely the means by which the previous decrees are carried out, the elect saved, and the reprobate left to perish. Though this doctrine was repudiated at the Synod of *Dort (1618–19), it was often and widely held in later Calvinism.

SUPREMACY, ACT OF, see ACT OF SUPREMACY.

SUTTON, CHRISTOPHER (c.1565–1629), devotional writer. Canon of Westminster and Lincoln, S. wrote in the tone of Jeremy *Taylor and Thomas *Ken, and his books were well loved in their day. His *Godly Meditations upon the Most Holy Sacrament of the Lord's Supper* (1613) takes a position midway between that of Trent and that of *Zwingli, and together with *Learne to Die* (1600) and *Learne to Live* (1608) was reissued by the Tractarians, with prefaces signed by J. H. N. (i.e., *Newman). *TRACTARIANISM.

SWEDENBORG, EMANUEL (1688–1772), Swedish scientist and religious thinker. Born in Stockholm, the son of a Lutheran bishop, he was graduated from the Univ. of Uppsala in 1709 and studied Newtonian physics and natural sciences during a prolonged stay in England. He was appointed to the Swedish Royal Board of Mines in

1716 and held other scientific posts, while writing extensively on science. His major scientific works include his *Principia* (1734) and *The Economy of the Animal Kingdom* (1740). He grew more interested in religious mysticism, and in 1745 he published *The Worship and Love of God*. In 1756 the eight volumes of *Arcana Coelestia* appeared, followed in 1758 by *The New Jerusalem and Its Heavenly Doctrine*. His many published works on mathematics, geology, anatomy, and cosmology gave him a considerable reputation as a theoretical scientist. His religious writings claim to represent revelations made to Swedenborg in frequent visits by spiritual beings and visions of heaven and hell that he personally experienced. He was the unique channel for this revelation and, through his writings, was to provide the basis for the teachings of a new Christian Church. He did not personally found the *Church of the New Jerusalem, but is regarded by its members as a divinely illuminated seer. His sense of the correspondence of the spirit world with the natural world enabled him to develop a personal religion that he felt consistent with science and reason. See S. Toksvig, *E. S., Scientist and Mystic* (1948); C. O. Sigstedt, *The Swedenborg Epic* (1952).

SWEDENBORGIANS, members of the *Churches of the New Jerusalem, which follow the teachings of Emmanuel *Swedenborg.

SWISS BRETHREN, a name designating the Swiss Anabaptists, followers of C. *Grebel, G. *Blaurock, and F. *Manz. They called themselves simply "Brethren." See J. H. Yoder, *Täufertum und Reformation in der Schweiz* (1962); bibliog. for Anabaptists.

SYLLABUS OF ERRORS, a compilation of 80 propositions issued by Pius IX with the encyclical *Quanta cura*, Dec. 8, 1864. He had previously condemned these proposi-

tions in allocutions, encyclicals, and apostolic letters dealing with pantheism, naturalism, rationalism, religious indifference, socialism, communism, certain secret, biblical, and clerical-liberal societies, rights of the Church, civil society, relations of Church and State, natural and Christian ethics, Christian marriage, temporal power of the popes, and liberalism. The manner in which each proposition is censured can be gathered from the document in which the error had first been condemned. See D 2901–80; W. F. Hogan, NCE 13:854–856.

SYMBOL OF FAITH, a summary formula of the truths of Christian faith. The Gr. *symbolon* (sign) was used for a token of identity such as a signet ring or legal bond. This source of the term was given by some of the Fathers, since the symbol of faith was the mark by which the catechumen was recognized as acceptable for baptism, and was also a sign of uniformity of faith among Christians. The term was applied to early creedal formulas at least from the 3d cent. (e.g., by St. Cyprian, d. 259). The formulas themselves were developed in conjunction with the baptismal ritual, one of the most ancient being the *Apostles' Creed (*Symbolum Apostolorum*). Generally the terms symbol and creed are accepted as synonymous and, although some disagree with the usage, are applied not only to the so-called *ecumenical creeds but also to later RC professions of faith, e.g., that of the Council of Trent, and to the Protestant *confessions of faith. The theological discipline concerned with the study of such documents is called comparative symbolics.

SYMBOLICS, also called Symbolic Theology and *Comparative Symbolics, a study of the *confessions of faith or *doctrinal standards of Churches. *SYMBOL OF FAITH.

SYMBOLOFIDEISM (symbolic fideism; critical symbolism), the theory that all dogmatic and theological formulations are symbols or reflection of subjective religious experience; that, like religious experience itself, dogma is essentially and interminably evolving. The view is associated particularly with a school of Protestant theologians at Paris in the 19th cent., led by A. *Sabatier. It rested upon basic themes of *liberal theology and had its influence upon *modernism among Roman Catholics. *FIDEISM.

SYMMACHIANS, a small Judeo-Christian sect existing until the 5th cent. and considered a Western branch of the Ebionites. Augustine and other Latin authors mention their existence in Africa and Italy. The connection of their name with the Bible translator Symmachus the Ebionite is obscure. See J. Schmidt, LTK 9:1217; F. J. Bacchus, CE 14:378–379, s.v. "Symmachus the Ebionite"; EncRelKnow 11:212.

SYNCRETISM, a term applied disparagingly by A. *Calov to G. *Calixt's proposals for Christian reunion. Calixt sought to overcome doctrinal differences by reducing *credenda* (fundamental articles of faith) to a minimum based on the *consensus quinquesaecularis*. Calov and others insisted that this was a dilution of orthodoxy, an extreme *irenicism that disregarded truth and the criterion of the *confessions of faith as in accord with biblical revelation. Syncretism is used contemporarily in ecumenical discussions to indicate any similar attempt at unity through a disregard or diminution of doctrines or confessions distinctive of the Churches. Such a position is not generally considered a sound principle of ecumenism.

SYNERGISM (Gr. *syn*, together, *ergon*, work; *synergos*, working with; see 1 Cor 3.9), a term historically applied to a theory that the human will actively cooperates with grace in the act of conversion; its opposite is *monergism. Primarily it was used in the *Synergistic Controversy (1550–77)

regarding the doctrine of Philipp *Melanchthon; it has also been applied to one aspect of RC teaching on *justification, and to *Arminianism (see DORT, SYNOD OF). Melanchthon first completely accepted the ideas of Luther on unconditional predestination and the abiding sinfulness and impotence of fallen nature (see *Augsburg Confession, Art. 18). Successive revisions of his theological text, *Loci communes,* manifested a change, and that of 1548 stated that the causes of conversion are the Holy Spirit, the word, and the will of man "not wholly inactive in its own weakness." Melanchthon did not regard the cooperation of the will, however, as a coordinate, equal cause; human consent was itself caused by the Holy Spirit and the word. In the ensuing Synergistic Controversy other Lutherans censured synergism as a betrayal of justification by faith alone, in favor of a revived *Semi-Pelagianism, or of a crypto-Catholicism (see GNESIOLUTHERANISM; FLACIUS ILLYRICIUS, M.). The *Formula of Concord (Art. 2) is addressed to this controversy; it accepts only two causes in man's conversion, the Holy Spirit and the Word, but affirms that the regenerated will. "cooperates in the works which follow."

In RC teaching, the decree of Trent on justification affirms that man's cooperation with grace is necessary and real. Grace invites free cooperation and makes it possible and effective. But God and man are not equal partners; human cooperation is itself a gift of grace, since grace brings about free consent. (D 1551–55). Thus RC synergism is not in basic opposition to the *sola gratia* of Luther.

SYNERGISTIC CONTROVERSY, a doctrinal dispute among Lutherans from c.1550, settled in Art. 2 of the *Formula of Concord. Influenced by the teaching of P. *Melanchthon, such synergists as G. *Major and V. *Strigel defended fallen man's power to cooperate in a limited degree in his conversion. They were opposed by N. *Amsdorf, M. *Flacius Illyricus, and others, who maintained that Martin Luther taught that fallen man is utterly helpless and is a merely passive recipient of grace. The Formula of Concord seeks to express a mediate position. *SYNERGISM.

SYNOD (Gr. *sunodos*, a coming together), in general historical usage, an assembly of bishops. The terms "synod" and "council" were used interchangeably until the time of Nicaea (325). Then council came to be used for the ecumenical council, and synod for regional meetings of bishops. The term "synod," however, in the RC Church still is sometimes used as an alternate term in conciliar documents of ecumenical councils (see GENERAL COUNCIL). In the Eastern Churches, the synod exercises supreme and decisive authority. In the RC Church, synod is used more specifically for the diocesan synod, which is composed of priests under the presidency of the bishop. Its competence is limited to matters of diocesan discipline, and it has only a consultative function (CIC c. 352-356). Vatican Council II urged greater use of the synod by the bishops of the Church (Vat II BpPastOff 36). The following articles deal with other specific uses of the term.

SYNOD (Lutheran), a term used in several senses in Lutheran polity. (1) In Germany it is a body for doctrinal as well as administrative supervision. In Luther's idea the synods of pastors were to safeguard discipline and fidelity to the Scriptures. The synod in its modern sense developed in the 19th cent. with the abandonment of the idea that the civil ruler was also the head of the Church (*summus episcopus*). Church synods are composed of clerical and lay representatives of the local congregations, as well as of delegates from theology and law faculties. (2) In the U.S. the term was first used to designate a whole group of Lutheran congregations organically united. This is the sense of the term in the title, Lutheran Church—Missouri Synod. Many American Lutheran bodies, however, have dropped this use of the term, but the synod as a

regional unit within the general church body is retained. (3) An administrative body for a whole Lutheran body, or for one of its districts. The synod represents the local congregations in matters of common concern with regard to ministerial training, educational, social works, and finances. Members are clerical and lay representatives of the local churches.

SYNOD (Moravian), the highest governing body of the *Moravian Church. It is a legislative assembly of clergy and laity meeting at intervals that vary in different regions from 3 to 5 years. Each of the 17 provinces of the Church has its own synod for the election of executives and bishops and for the enactment of legislation to be carried out by the congregations during the intersynodal periods. Executives and administrators of the Church's institutions are responsible to the synod. A worldwide synod, meeting every 10 years, is authoritative in matters of doctrine and coordinates international mission efforts. See W. H. Allen, *Who Are the Moravians?* (1966); *Book of Order, Moravian Church in America* (1954).

SYNOD (Old Catholic), legislative body for the Church. The Synod governs each national Old Catholic Church; the bishop is chairman of the Synod; members include both priests and laymen representing the parishes. The Synod is empowered to elect the bishop by majority vote. The scope of its rule extends only to administrative affairs of the Church, not to matters of doctrine. Meetings are held annually; an executive council is chosen for the interim, and is composed of the bishop, three priests, and five laymen.

SYNOD (Presbyterian), an ecclesiastical governing body in Churches of presbyterian polity. The term is applied both to governing bodies in particular geographical districts in some *Reformed Churches (hence called particular synods in the *Reformed Church in America), and to the corresponding bodies in Presbyterian Churches (called sometimes regional synods). Membership in the regional synod consists of representative clergymen and *elders from the district. It ranks in authority above the *consistory court or *church session of the local congregation and the *classis or *presbytery, and below the general synod (Reformed) or *general assembly (Presbyterian). The presiding officer, who may be an elder, is usually elected annually and is designated the moderator. The synod meets annually; in practice it is often considerably less important than most classes or presbyteries. This framework of presbyterian government originated in the Calvinist churches during the 16th century. The basic principle is that of representative government at each of the four levels. While the general synod or assembly possesses supreme authority in ecclesiastical matters, its authority rises from the local congregations, passes through the classis or presbytery and the regional synod, and is settled finally in the national body. This principle is best illustrated by the fact that the laws the national body passes must receive the approval of the classis or presbytery. Both the regional and general synod exercise a judicial function, receiving and handling appeals from classes or presbyteries. Their other main function is legislative. Both types of synod also administer missionary, evangelistic, and other kinds of Christian activity. The general synod has the additional task of administering the ecumenical relationships of the national body.

SYNOD (Protestant Episcopal Church), the governing body for the provinces of the Church. There are eight such provinces, into which the dioceses and missionary regions are grouped. These elect as members of the synod one bishop, four priests, and four laymen.

SYNOD OF EVANGELICAL LUTHERAN CHURCHES, a small American Lutheran body organized in Pennsylvania in 1902 as the Slovak Evangelical Lutheran Church. Slovak Lutherans migrated to the U.S. in the latter part of the 19th cent. and shortly after their arrival began to form congregations, the first being in Illinois, Pennsylvania, and Minnesota. Neglected by the mother Church in Europe, they grew but slowly. In 1894, however, preliminary steps were taken to unite the various congregations in the United States. The Synod declared its adherence to the confessions and doctrines of the Lutheran Church and its full agreement in doctrine and practice with the Lutheran Church—Missouri Synod. It joined the *Lutheran Synodical Conference of the Evangelical Lutheran Church in 1908, but it is not a member of the *Lutheran World Federation. It continues to work closely with the Lutheran Church—Missouri Synod, through which it distributes its missionary funds, although it has a mission board of its own. Its teachers and pastors are educated in the colleges and seminaries of the Missouri Synod. For administrative purposes the Synod of Evangelical Lutheran Churches is divided into three general districts. Synodical meetings are held every 2 years. The denomination's periodical is the *Lutheran Beacon*. See J. Daniel, EncLuthCh 3:2317–18.

SYNODICAL CONFERENCE, see LUTHERAN SYNODICAL CONFERENCE.

T

TABORITES, a sect of Hussite extremists. The name comes from the theocratic hill town near Prague where they settled. The teaching of the Taborites went far beyond the *Utraquists, for they advocated a communistic society, denied the *Real Presence, and rejected all the sacraments except baptism and the Lord's Supper (see D 1259). Among them also, there were undercurrents of *Adamite and *Picardian doctrine. The Taborites were crushed and scattered by the combined Utraquist and Catholic forces in 1434; but adherents and ideas of the sect influenced the beginnings of the Bohemian Brethren. See Bihlmeyer-Tüchle 2:442–443; F. G. Heymann, *John Žižka and the Hussite Revolution* (1955). *HUSSITES.

TAIZÉ COMMUNITY, Protestant monastic community founded by Roger Schutz in 1944. In 1939, while studying theology at Lauzanne, Schutz organized study clubs from which sprang the Taizé idea. In August 1940 he moved into a house in the village of Taizé, close to Cluny, in Burgundy, France. Here he devoted himself to prayer, meditation, and community action. After an absence of 2 years in Switzerland, Schutz, accompanied by several companions, returned to Taizé in 1944. On Easter Sunday, 1949, seven men made their profession, agreeing to live in celibacy, to hold property in common, and to submit to authority. By 1968 there were close to 70 members, drawn for the most part from Western Europe, and of the Lutheran and *Reformed Churches. *The Rule of Taizé* was edited by Roger Schutz in 1952–53 and was developed further in 1960. The Rule describes community activities, spiritual discipline, commitments (celibacy, etc.), the duties of the prior, and the work of mission brothers. After a novitiate of 2 or 3 years devoted to the study of the Bible, church history, and sociology, the candidates make their profession, donning a silver ring, the only outward distinguishing mark of their membership in the community. Members of the community reside either in Taizé or are "on mission" in the U.S., France, Germany, Uruguay, North Africa, or the Middle East. Those on mission return annually to Taizé for retreats. The brothers work as physicians, architects, ministers in churches, in the arts, in factories, and on community projects. Seminars are conducted on sociological topics in an effort to bring the community into close touch with current problems. The spirit of ecumenism pervades Taizé, a spirit nurtured by Schutz, who made retreats in RC monasteries, visited Anglican religious communities, kept in close touch with RC parish priests and worker-priests, attended the sessions of Vatican Council II, and did his licentiate dissertation on *The Monastic Ideal until Saint Benedict and its Conformity with the Gospel*. Taizé is best described as a contemplative community working in the world. See J. Heijke, *Ecumenical Light on the Renewal of Religious Community Life: Taizé* (1967); R. Schutz, *Living Today for God* (1961).

TAULER, JOHN (*c.*1300–61), preacher and mystic. He entered the Dominican Order in his native city of Strassburg at the age of 13 and did his early ecclesiastical studies there. He completed them at Cologne *c.*1325–29. In both places he was probably under the tutelage of Meister *Eckhart. Following his studies, Tauler returned to Strassburg, remaining there until the local authorities exiled the Dominicans (who went to Basel) for obeying the papal interdict of 1326 in defiance of Louis of Bavaria. Tauler returned to Strassburg from Basel in 1347. In both cities Tauler carried on a vigorous preaching apostolate and became renowned as a spiritual director and a leader of the *Friends of God. Rulman Merswin, a wealthy merchant of Strassburg and a writer of spiritual treatises, was one of his penitents. Among his friends were the Dominicans Henry Suso, Margaret Ebner of Maria Medingin monastery, Christiana Ebner of the monastery of Engeltal, the secular priest Henry of Nördlingen, and probably the Flemish mystic Jan van Ruysbroeck. Tauler probably corresponded with the Italian Dominican mystic Venturino of Bergamo. His only authentic surviving letter was sent to Margaret Ebner. Most of his 83 extant sermons were preached to nuns and were taken down by his hearers. His warm personality was marked by deep thought, moderation, and humility. His vivid, picturesque sermons were illustrated by examples from everyday life. His spiritual doctrine was influenced by the themes of Eckhart, but Tauler was more practical, plain, direct, and marked by lack of hyperbole. Though advocating resignation to the will of God and stripping of personal interests and desires, Tauler insisted on an active, laborious, and virtuous life. His pretended conversion by the legendary "Friend of God" of the Oberland is a fiction. See F. Vetter, *Die Predigten Taulers* (Deutsche Texte des Mittelalters II, 1910); an English anthology with introduction by Eric Colledge and Sr. M. Jane, *J. T., Spiritual Conferences* (1961); E. Filthaut, ed., *J. T., ein deutscher Mystiker. Gedenkschrift zum 600 Todestage* (1961).

TAUSEN, HANS (1494–1561), the first preacher of the Reformation in Denmark. T. entered the Order of St. John of Jerusalem at Antvorskov and subsequently studied at Rostock, Copenhagen, Louvain, and Wittenberg, where in 1523 he adopted Luther's teaching. When he returned to Antvorskov and announced his conversion, he was sent away to Viborg. There he so favorably impressed his abbot that he was at first permitted to preach the new doctrine. Soon, however, he was expelled from his convent. At this juncture King Frederick I gave him a letter of protection, and the citizens of Viborg opened their largest church

to him. In 1526 equal rights were given to Catholics and Lutherans, and the King called T. to preach in Copenhagen. T. helped draft the 43 articles presented to the Diet at Copenhagen (1530). In the changes of fortune that the two religions continued to experience he showed himself tolerant and even magnanimous. His translation of the Pentateuch appeared in 1535. After the death of the King, T. entered into a compromise with the bp. of Roskilde that harmed his reputation among Lutherans. As a consequence, he was passed over when evangelical superintendents were being named to replace the Catholic bishops in 1536 at the formal establishment of the Reformation. In 1538 he became professor of theology in Roskilde, and in 1542 he was made bp. of Ribe. See J. M. Jensen, EncLuthCh 3:2324.

TAYLOR, JEREMY (1613–67), Anglican bp. and spiritual writer. Born and educated at Cambridge, T. was ordained in 1633. His charm and eloquence attracted the attention of Abp. W. *Laud, through whose favor he received rapid preferment, becoming chaplain to Charles I c.1635. He served as chaplain in the Royalist army and lived out the Commonwealth in Wales as chaplain to the earl of Carbery. After the Restoration he was made bp. of Down and Connor in Ireland (1660) and administrator of Dromore (1661), the Irish rather than an English appointment being due to some suspicion of his orthodoxy stemming from his attack upon Calvinist doctrine in his *Unum necessarium* (1655), and also from his friendship with C. *Davenport, the Franciscan. Of his theological works the best known are his *Liberty of Prophesying* (1647), a plea for tolerance for all whose religious views were not subversive to the state, and his *Ductor dubitantium* (1660), intended as a manual for confessors, the first complete work on casuistry in the English language. His fame chiefly rests upon his spiritual writings, esp. his *Rule and Exercise of Holy Living* (1650), and his *Rule and Exercise of Holy Dying* (1651). These are spiritual and literary classics, putting forth practical religious wisdom in ornate prose, rich with beautiful cadences and delicately wrought images. The abundance of detail and argument, which is a defect in his theological works, proves well suited to the reflective reading of devotion. He urges moderation, cheerfulness, contentment, and hopeful dependence on the goodness of God, and draws often from the Greek and Latin moralists of antiquity. Another spiritual work, *The Golden Grove* (1655), is a manual of instruction and prayers. Works: *Whole Works*, ed. R. Heber, rev. C. P. Eden (10v., 1847–54). See C. J. Stranks, *Life and Writings of J. T.* (1952).

TAYLOR, NATHANIEL WILLIAM (1786–1858), American Congregationalist theologian, professor at Yale Divinity School. After graduation from Yale, T. studied theology under T. *Dwight and was ordained in 1812 as pastor of the First Congregational Church, New Haven. He encouraged *revivalism in his church and was a founder of the *American Bible Society. His liberal Calvinism, termed the New Divinity or *New Haven theology, was foreshadowed by his 1819 sermon on "Salvation Free to the Willing." His more famous *Concio ad clerum*, a sermon preached at Yale in 1828, explained *total depravity to mean not man's nature but his own act, consisting of a free choice of some object rather than God as his chief good. T. was involved in controversy with both Unitarians and the conservatives in his own denomination and wrote voluminously on the disputed questions of predestination and freedom of the will. His classroom *Lectures on the Moral Government of God* (2v., 1859), defending a moral system created by God in which free agents are able to sin, became his major published work. "Taylorism" greatly contributed to the revivalism dominant in pre-Civil War American Protestantism. See S. E. Mead, *N. W. T.* (1942); R. H. Bainton, *Yale and the Ministry* (1957); S. E. Ahlstrom, ed., *Theology in America* (1967), 211–249.

TEMPELGESELLSCHAFT, see FRIENDS OF THE TEMPLE.

TEMPERANCE MOVEMENT, the organized crusade against use of alcoholic beverages that began in the early 19th cent. as one of many expressions of the religious and humanitarian impulses of that period. In an era when many tended to concentrate upon one reform as the panacea for all human ills, abstention from intoxicants was frequently thought of as the remedy for poverty, vice, ill-health, marital discord, etc. The first organized groups were limited to families or segments of congregations, but a national movement to combat intemperance was initiated (1812) by the preaching of Lyman *Beecher (1775–1863). The American Society for the Promotion of Temperance, founded (1826) at Boston, Mass., sponsored reform publications and revivalistic-type meetings across the U.S. and was the model for a similar organization in Canada. As the cause gained in popularity, local societies sprang up; an effort at coordination was made with the creation (1833) of the U.S. Temperance Union, later the American Temperance Union. The first World Temperance Convention was held in London, Eng. (1846), and was attended by American delegates Beecher and William Lloyd Garrison, abolitionist leader. RC interest in temperance grew also, and independent groups were founded in Boston and elsewhere, encouraged by the approval of the bps. at the Provincial Council of Baltimore (1840). Converts to the cause of total abstinence increased as a result of the Catholic–Protestant-sponsored American tour (1849) of the Irish Capuchin preacher Theobald Mathew. However, the national controversy over slavery, Civil War, and the problems of the Reconstruction era brought about a temporary decline in public interest in the temperance movement.

The organization of the *Woman's Christian Temperance Union (1874) revived the cause, and emphasis shifted from temperance to total abstinence and a full-scale attack upon the saloon. The major thrust, however, was initiated by the formation of the Anti-Saloon League of America (1895), an agency manned by socially progressive Protestant churchmen and assisted by a number of liberal Catholics. The revivalistic doctrines of *Christian perfection and *sanctification, as well as commitment to the *Social Gospel for the betterment of the working man, inspired the crusade. By 1900, five of the forty-five states had adopted laws banning the manufacture and sale of intoxicating beverages, while others had made provision for local option. Meanwhile, general RC interest in total abstinence had revived and many RC societies had been founded, including the Catholic Total Abstinence Union of America (1872), a moderate, nonprohibitionist organization that generally avoided politics and confined its activities to moral suasion. However, the drive to suppress the liquor traffic had strong support, and it eventually became a great crusade of many Protestant, and esp. Methodist, Churches. By April 1917, more than 25 states had gone "dry," and before the end of the year a constitutional amendment prohibiting the manufacture, transportation, and sale of alcoholic beverages had been passed by Congress and submitted to the states for ratification. The 18th Amendment became effective in Jan. 1920, but the enforcement procedures established were widely disregarded; a general disrespect for law ensued, with an increase in organized crime. The 21st Amendment (1933) repealed the 18th, ending the unsuccessful national experiment in prohibition. Subsequently, temperance groups devoted themselves to promoting their cause through educational programs and state legislation. Some, like Alcoholics Anonymous (1935), relied heavily on religious motivation and the fellowship of other victims. See J. Bland, *Hibernian Crusade: The Story of the Catholic Total Abstinence Union of America* (1951); J. R. Gusfield, *Symbolic Crusade: Status Politics and the American Temperance Movement* (1963); J. H. Timberlake, *Prohibition and the Progressive Movement, 1900–1920* (1963); A.

Sinclair, *Prohibition, the Era of Excess* (1962); HistAmMeth 3:329–343.

TEMPLE, WILLIAM (1881–1944), Abp. of Canterbury. The son of F. Temple (1821–1902), bp. of Exeter and afterward abp. of Canterbury, he was a Balliol man, president of the Oxford Union, and later a fellow of Queen's. Nominated bp. of Manchester (1920), he became abp. of York (1929) and then of Canterbury (1942). Through the *Faith and Order and *Life and Work movements he became a strong advocate of social and national righteousness. Yet though he entered into and respected the proper medium of reform, to such an extent that he was commonly regarded as a socialist, he always believed that the cause was secondary to the fundamental truths of the gospel. He was the chosen leader of the Life and Liberty movement to secure independence for the C of E, if need be by *disestablishment. He also was a pioneer in the ecumenical movement, acting in concert with the cardinal of Westminster and the moderator of the Church of Scotland. In public he was a formidable leader, not given to caution; in private he was loved for his kindliness and candid humor. It was said of him that he was too much of a theologian for philosophers and too much of a philosopher for theologians. His philosophy moved away from the neo-Hegelianism he had learned from E. Caird; his theology was objectively Christ-centered and stressed the incarnation rather than the redemption. The Gifford Lectures for 1934, *Nature, Man, and God*, if not the most widely read, form probably the most enduring of his writings. See Life and Letters, by F. A. Iremonger (1948).

TEN ARTICLES, a doctrinal formulary issued in July 1536 by King Henry VIII of England, with the consent of *Convocations, "to establish Christian quietness and unity," with statements on the creeds, the Sacrament of the Altar, baptism, penance, justification, images, the saints and their invocation, ceremonies (holy water, lights, ashes, etc.), and purgatory. They were ambiguously composed to defend traditional beliefs and practices while placating Lutheran sentiment. The King was probably assisted in drafting them by Edward Fox, Bp. of Hereford, who had recently returned from an embassy to the German Lutheran princes. The articles were taken up and expanded in the *Bishops' Book of 1537. See C. Lloyd, *Formularies of Faith Put Forth by Authority during the Reign of Henry VIII* (1856 ed.); C. H. Williams, ed., *English Historical Documents 1485–1558* (1967), 795–805.

TENNENT, GILBERT (1703–64), Presbyterian clergyman of Irish origin. While a pastor at New Brunswick, N.J., he fell under the influence of Theodore *Frelinghuysen, who has been credited with beginning the *Great Awakening in the Middle Colonies. A friend of Jonathan *Edwards and Jonathan *Dickinson, and a great admirer of George *Whitefield, T. soon became one of the most ardent preachers of the Awakening. In his polemical sermon "The Danger of an Unconverted Ministry" (1740) he attacked the hypocrisy of ministers who resisted the spiritual ferment of the times; the discourse helped cause the Old Side and *New Side division within American Presbyterianism (1741–58). His pamphlet "The Peace of Jerusalem" also contributed to the restoration of unity. His ecumenical spirit is suggested in one of his chief tracts, *Irenicum ecclesiasticum* (1749).

TERRITORIAL CHURCH (Ger. *Landeskirche*), a term applied to the German Churches that developed during the Reformation. Since no unified German state then existed, it was impossible to establish a single, united Lutheran Church. Therefore each of the nearly 300 political entities established its own autonomous Lutheran Church. The *Augsburg Confession and Luther's Small Catechism (see CATECHISMS, LUTHER'S) furnished a common doctrinal character, but each territorial Church was independent of any power outside its own political boundaries. Having to provide some means of administration to assume functions formerly exercised by bps., Luther advised that civil rulers temporarily take on these duties. Although Luther was not entirely satisfied with such an arrangement, the system became permanent, especially with the establishment of the principle *cuius regio, eius religio* (Peace of Augsburg, 1555). The territorial prince in each domain considered himself the *summus episcopus*, having broad powers of jurisdiction but without the right of preaching the word or administering the sacraments. So long as princes were devout members of the Church, some of the worst features of this form of *Erastianism were avoided. As the concept of the State became more secularized, losing its character as one of God's created orders, the Church became increasingly subordinated to political interests. See A. L. Drummond, *German Protestantism since Luther* (1951).

TERRITORIALISM, a concept of Church-State relationship, based on the natural-right theories of H. Grotius (1583–1645) and C. Thomasius (1655–1725). In practice it is the equivalent of *cuius regio eius religio*. The theory itself, however, rests on the conception that the State originates in the members' natural right to form a society, which includes their ecclesiastical association. Thus the State (or its head) as reflecting this will has power over the Church. *Collegialism puts the origin of the Church in a will of the members to associate, distinct from the will that originates the State. The two theories agree, however, in rooting authority of both Church and State in the will of the members to form a society. See EncRelKnow II:303.

TERTULLIAN (*c.*160–*c.*240), ecclesiastical writer, controversialist, and the most important theologian in the West before Augustine. The son of a *centurio proconsularis*, T. was educated at Carthage, and lived for a time in Rome. His knowledge of history, archeology, medicine, Aristotelian philosophy, oratory, and jurisprudence, combined with his literary talents, forceful personality, and theological interests, made him one of the leading apologists of the early Church. He was converted to Christianity *c.*195, won over it seems by the sight of the constancy of the Christian martyrs. According to St. Jerome he became a priest even though he was married, but this has been questioned by a number of scholars. After his conversion, he dedicated himself to the defense of Christianity against pagans, Jews, and heretics, combining great skill in argumentation and brilliant aphorisms with bitter sarcasm and relentless attack. Because of his choleric and impetuous nature, he became disaffected with the Church *c.*206 and left it to become a *Montanist. T. was a prolific writer, but most of his works are fairly short. They are of an apologetic, polemical, and practical nature. In the first he defends the Church against the attacks of the pagans; in the second he refutes the arguments of heretics and expounds the truths of faith; and in the third he gives rules and exhortations for living a Christian life. In general his apologetic and polemical works belong to his Catholic period and his practical works to his Montanist period. There are 31 authentic treatises still extant; at least 12 others have been lost. Among the most important are the following.

Apologetic Works. In the *Ad nationes* (early 197), Tertullian reproaches the pagans for their culpable ignorance of Christianity and their unjust treatment of the Christians. In the *Apologeticum* (end of 197), addressed to the provincial governors, he repeats many of the arguments of his earlier work but with renewed vigor and in greater detail. This passionate defense of Christianity, despite its vehemence, is without doubt one of the classics of ancient Christian literature. The *De testimonio animae*, written shortly after the *Apologeticum*, argues somewhat paradoxically that, since the pagans believe in the unity of God, the survival of the soul, and the exist-

ence of evil spirits, the "soul is naturally Christian" (see *Apologeticum* 17). The *De pallio* (*c.*210) is a personal apology for his adopting the pallium of a philosopher in place of the more common toga. The *Ad Scapulam* (211 or 213) is a brief letter to the proconsul of Africa describing the sufferings endured by the Christians. It defends their right to profess their faith and threatens the governor with divine vengeance for his treatment of the Christians. The *Adversus Judaeos* (*c.*207) shows how the law of Moses has been replaced by that of Christ.

Dogmatic and Polemical Writings. These are longer and more detailed than his apologetic works, and they firmly establish him as an original thinker and able theologian. In the *De praescriptione haereticorum* (*c.*200), Tertullian applies to heretics the *praescriptio,* a technical device in Roman law to disqualify an opponent before he can even bring his case to trial. Since the Scriptures belong to the Church and have belonged to it from the beginning, delivered to it by the Apostles, heretics have no right to argue from Scripture. The *Adversus Hermogenem* (*c.*201) defends the doctrine of creation against the teachings of a Gnostic painter of Carthage. The *Adversus Marcionem* (3d rev., 207) is by far Tertullian's longest work. It treats of the unity of God, the messianic mission of Christ, and the continuity of the OT and NT. The *Adversus Valentinianos* (*c.*208) is an attack on Gnosticism. The *Scorpiace* (211 or 213) is "a remedy against the sting of the scorpion" of Gnostic heresy, which denied the value of martyrdom. The *Adversus Praxeam* (213 or 217) was directed against the patripassian Praxeas and presents the clearest teaching in the Church on the doctrine of the Trinity before the Council of Nicaea. In another series of antiheretical works, Tertullian attacked particular doctrines. The *De baptismo* (*c.*200) upholds the necessity of this sacrament and discusses its symbolism, minister, matter, and form. The *De carne Christi* and *De resurrectione carnis* (both 210 or 212) refute the Docetists who denied the resurrection of the body. The *De anima* (*c.*210) is the first Christian psychology. It treats of the nature, origin, and functions of the soul even when separated from the body.

Practical Questions. The *Ad martyres* (197) is an ardent exhortation to the confessors to persevere. The *De spectaculis* (197 or 200) gives numerous reasons why it is not lawful for Christians to attend the circuses and games. The *De oratione* (198 or 200) is an instruction for catechumens on prayer and gives an explanation of the Our Father. The *De patientia* (200 or 203) sets forth the meekness of the Savior as an example to be followed and as a preparation for martyrdom. The *De paenitentia* (203) discusses two types of conversion, that of baptism, and that of canonical penance, which is permitted only once after baptism. The *De cultu feminarum* (197–201) condemns female luxury and the use of cosmetics. In his *Ad uxorem* (c.203) he asks his wife to remain a widow after his death or at least marry a Catholic so that there will be a community of faith and affection. The *De exhortatione castitatis* (before 207) and the *De monogamia* (c.217) oppose second marriages. The *De virginibus velandis* (c.207) is an exhortation to a life of virginity and demands the wearing of a veil by virgins in church and in public. The *De corona* (211) proscribes military service for Christians. The *De idolatria* (c.212) forbids any contact with pagans that might give an appearance of idolatry. The *De fuga in persecutione* (c.212) describes flight in time of persecution as a kind of apostasy. The *De ieiunio adversus psychicos* (c.217) is a defense of rigorous fasts against the more lenient practices of the Catholics. The *De pudicitia* (c. 220) denies the power of the Church to forgive serious sins. It may have been directed in part against an edict of Pope Callistus I (217–222).

Doctrine. Tertullian is the founder of the theology of the West. He gave to it not only its language but also its special character. In contrast to the contemporary Eastern theologians, Tertullian was not a philosopher. Though he had some harsh things to say about this science, he accepted it insofar as it agreed with Christian truth. He maintains, for example, that the existence of God and the immortality of the soul can be proved from natural reason. His training as a lawyer enabled him to give a precise definition to his theological speculations. In his exposition of the Trinity he formulated the classical definition: *"Trinitas unius divinitatis, Pater, Filius et Spiritus Sanctus"* (*De pudic.* 21). He affirms the duality of natures in the one person of Christ in terms later adopted by Leo the Great and eventually incorporated into the definitions of the Council of Chalcedon. He makes specific mention of baptism, confirmation, and the Eucharist. Despite departures e.g., his belief in a coming millennium, his teaching on traducianism, his rejection of the virginity of Mary *post partum*, and his ultimate apostasy, Tertullian is without doubt one of the greatest figures of the early Church. Among the later writers he influenced was St. Cyprian, who read something from Tertullian every day and frequently said to his secretary, " 'Give me the master!' meaning Tertullian" (Jerome, *De vir. ill.* 53). See A. d'Alès, *La théologie de Tertullien* (1905); G. Bardy, DTC 15:130–171; M. Pellegrino, EC 11:2025–33; W. Le Saint, NCE 13:1019–22; J. Morgan, *Importance of T. in the Development of Christian Dogma* (1928).

TERTULLIANISTS, members of a sect founded in the early 3d cent. in Carthage by *Tertullian upon Montanistic principles. After brilliantly serving the Church with his pen, Tertullian became disaffected with what he considered to be its laxity. He openly broke with it c.207 and became a Montanist. While retaining the ethical rigorism of this Phrygian heresy, he purged it of its local and provincial character and gave it a more definitive theology. He never mentions Pepuza (see PEPUZIANS), which was to have been the site of the parousia; he rarely refers to Montanus himself; and he excludes women entirely from the office of preaching and teaching. The sect that he thus founded persisted down to the time of St. Augustine, when the few surviving Tertullianists at Carthage returned to the Church and handed over their famous basilica to the Catholics. See St. Augustine, *De haeres.* 86; A. Mayer, EC 8:1345–46. *MONTANISTS.

TEST ACT, an English law of 1673 enacted to prevent "dangers . . . from popish recusants." The Act deprived Catholics and *Nonconformists of rights. It came in the wake of the *Declaration of Indulgence (1672), which had produced anti-Catholic fear instead of more toleration. Suspecting that the King expected eventually to make England Catholic again, and that the Declaration was a first step, Protestants of many parties united to oppose it. Parliament also objected to it because the Declaration was an attempt to set aside laws by royal proclamation. Besides taking oaths of allegiance and supremacy, persons holding civil and military offices were to deny belief in *transubstantiation. Among those excluded from office by this act was Charles's brother James, who had been Lord High Admiral of the Fleet. The Act was abrogated by the Catholic Relief Act of 1829. See H. Gee and W. J. Hardy, *Documents Illustrative of English Church History* (1921); H. W. Clark, *History of English Nonconformity* (2v., 1911–13), v.2.

TESTEM BENEVOLENTIAE, an apostolic letter of Pope Leo XIII to Cardinal James Gibbons (Jan. 22, 1899) disapproving *Americanism, in the sense that the Church should accommodate itself, its teachings, and its discipline to the spirit of the age by recasting certain traditional formulas of faith and glossing over unpopular doctrines. The Pope insisted that Catholic doctrine is a sacred deposit of divinely revealed teachings that must be faithfully safeguarded in their entirety. See J. J. Wynne, ed., *Great Encyclical Letters* (1903), 441–453; D 3340–46; T. T. McAvoy, *Great Crisis in American Catholic History 1895–1900* (1957); *idem*, NCE 1:443–444; W. F. Hogan, NCE 13:1022–23.

TETRAPOLITAN CONFESSION (*Confessio tetrapolitana*, Confession of the Four Cities), a Reformation *confession of faith, composed in 1530 and published in 1531. The document presents the Zwinglian beliefs of the S German cities Strassburg, Constance, Memmingen, and Lindau. M. *Bucer and W. *Capito composed it during the sessions of the Diet of Augsburg (1530), at which the four cities were not represented. The 23 chapters correspond generally in subject matter to the *Augsburg Confession. Chapter 18 on the Lord's Supper attempts a compromise between Zwinglian and Lutheran doctrine. The Confession was never widely accepted or used. See Schaff Creeds 1:526–529.

TETZEL, JOHANN (1465–1519), German Dominican, opponent of Luther in the *indulgence controversy. T. served as prior at Glogau and was inquisitor for Poland in 1509. From 1504, he was an indulgence preacher; in 1516 he was made subcommissioner in Meissen for the indulgence available to those who contributed money for the rebuilding of St. Peter's in Rome. T. preached the erroneous belief that indulgences can be gained for the dead independently of the spiritual dispositions of the person gaining them and can be applied absolutely to a specific soul in purgatory. Luther replied with the "Ninety-Five Theses" (1517). T. answered him with 122 antitheses, drafted by K. Wimpina, and also printed a refutation of Luther's position in 1518. T. was boastful, flamboyant, and not learned, but the charges that he begot illegitimate children were fabrications of polemicists. Luther wrote kindly words to him during T.'s last illness. See J. P. Dolan, *History of the Reformation* (1965), 234–237.

THEOCRACY (Calvinism). Though the political organization of Geneva in the period of *Calvin is commonly termed a theocracy, Calvin himself rejected the idea that the political organization of the Jewish people could be repeated in Geneva, or that the

Church is ever to be equated with the whole of society. The Church for Calvin is witness to the reign of God and to the restoration of man's humanness in Christ; the political order has been created by God with external constraints that maintain a relative order and morality. Calvin assumed that ecclesiastical and secular authorities collaborate in the government of the State and that both alike have a balanced responsibility to implement the will of God in the life of the people. Rulers are responsible to God to do his business and are answerable to him; they are also responsible to their subjects, whom they are to defend against the injuries of the wicked (*Commentary on Romans*, 13.4). The political doctrines of Calvin find expression beyond Geneva particularly in Oliver *Cromwell's *Commonwealth and in Scotland after the Reformation. See R. E. Davies, *Problem of Authority in the Continental Reformers* (1946); W. A. Mueller, *Church and State in Luther and Calvin* (1954).

THEOLOGIA CRUCIS (theology of the Cross), a theme in Martin Luther's reform of theology. Beginning with the Disputation at Heidelberg in 1518 Luther opposed this theme to the *theologia gloriae* of the scholastics. He rejected their concentration on the reasonable ascent to knowledge of God through his works in nature. Luther wished to turn theology away from speculation to the Bible, and to the search for God in the hiddenness, suffering, and powerlessness revealed in Christ and the Cross. The theologian in his quest for knowledge of God must be imbued with a sense of the Cross's contradiction to natural and human values, even as the believer must not seek righteousness in good works. See U. Saarnivaara, *Luther Discovers the Gospel* (1951).

THEOLOGIA GERMANICA (*Theologia deutsch*), a German ascetical and mystical treatise written *c.*1400. Its author, whose name is unknown, was a *Friend of God, a priest, guardian of a house of Teutonic Knights near Frankfurt-on-Main. The earliest known MS, discovered in the 19th cent., is dated 1497 (ed. F. Pfeiffer, 1900). Luther supervised the first printed edition (1516 and 1518); he was interested in the work because of the support it appeared to give to his doctrine on good works. Later the Pietists valued it highly. Although a Latin translation by S. *Castellio (d. 1563) was put on the Index in 1612, the *Theologia Germanica* is Catholic in content and inspiration. Against the *Brothers and Sisters of the Free Spirit, it seeks to define the true Friend of God. The work reflects the mysticism of Meister *Eckhart and J. *Tauler. The experience of God in nonconceptual vision is placed as a goal to be attained by detachment from all creatures, esp. from self-will. The work is pious rather than speculative; its language is simple and often imprecise. Union with God in being is confused with union with God in knowledge and love. Descriptions of obedience and resignation are somewhat quietistic. Text: Eng. tr. of Pfeiffer's crit. ed., S. Winkworth, rev. J. Bernhart (1949). See J. Paquier, *Un Mystique allemand au XIV siècle* (1922).

THEOLOGY, etymologically, doctrine, theory, or science about God. The term has a wide variety of Christian uses. (1) In a general way it is used to signify the doctrinal position of a Church, a group, or a person. (2) More strictly, it is an organized body of knowledge developed by rational reflection on divine revelation. In this sense it is distinguished from *natural theology, a purely philosophical or natural investigation of truths about God. Theology is also different from *faith. Faith is a knowledge of God as a simple assent to God's word in revelation; theology is discursive, it organizes, it correlates, it speculates. There is, however, no universally applicable description of theology in its relationship to the word of God, to faith, and to the resources and methods of human reason. Theologies, therefore, differ on many bases: on the acceptance or rejection of the value of human discourse concerning divine revelation (see

SCHOLASTICISM; THEOLOGIA CRUCIS); on the kind of philosophical categories and methodology appropriated by theology to its work (see THOMISM; SCOTISM; LIBERAL THEOLOGY; DIALECTICAL THEOLOGY); on whether theological inquiry is developed as an intellectual discipline or as an affective commitment of the theologian (see EXPERIENCE THEOLOGY; KERYGMATIC THEOLOGY). (3) Theology may be further qualified by its special method of concentration, distinctive principles of organization, or particular emphasis. Thus theology with a strong philosophical organization is called systematic, as distinguished from a historical or a biblical theology. The concentration on truths concerning God himself and the incarnation is called dogmatic theology; moral or practical theology is concerned with man's relationship to God. (See COVENANT THEOLOGY; NEW ENGLAND THEOLOGY; OBERLIN THEOLOGY; PRINCETON THEOLOGY; MERCERSBURG THEOLOGY). See M. D. Chenu, *Is Theology a Science* (tr. A. H. N. Green-Armytage, 1959); Y. Congar, *History of Theology* (ed. H. Guthrie, 1968); R. W. Bertram, ed., *Theology in the Life of the Church* (1963).

THEOLOGY OF THE CROSS, see THEOLOGIA CRUCIS.

THEOSOPHY, a doctrine that attempts a synthesis of religious, philosophic, and scientific insights drawn from many traditions, but primarily from Hindu philosophy and occult science. In 1875 at New York City the Theosophical Society was founded by Helena Petrovna *Blavatsky, Henry Steele Olcott, and William Q. Judge "to collect and diffuse a knowledge of the laws which govern the universe." This secret lodge of occultists sought to explore "secret laws of nature familiar to the Chaldeans and Egyptians." The theosophical movement early divided into several independent groups, but there has been a general unanimity on doctrinal points. Theosophy does not accept the idea of a personal God.

It is pantheistic in its starting point; God is held to be wholly immanent in the world. He does not create in the traditional Christian sense, but is a part of his creation, which emanates from him. God is the Absolute Principle of Hindu pantheism, impersonal and unknowable. The Logos, who is three in one, in the forms of creator (Brahma), preserver (Vishnu), and destroyer (Shiva), is described as the Supreme Beings who sustain the solar system and are the fount of authority of an extensive occult hierarchy. This hierarchy includes Jesus and other great thinkers who have passed through the cycle of rebirths and attained the state of divinity. Reincarnation is a central teaching, as is the evolution of the soul, for salvation comes by evolution and there is no need for an atonement. Evolution is thought of as a process of self-realization carried on by the cosmic life through repeated incarnations. All matter is held to contain consciousness that is evolving in accord with the divine plan in a twofold movement involving descent into matter and ascent into spirit. The adept can speed up or direct their own courses by observing the hidden rules of nature known to theosophy. Death brings rebirth, liberating the human spirit from its physical body to enjoy the life of the astral world. The astral world is not the true heaven, except for grosser men. Only after repeated incarnations can the true heaven or mental world be reached. Evolution, reincarnation, and karma thus create the rhythm of the universe.

In 1878 the Theosophical Society transferred its headquarters to Adyar, near Madras, India; in 1880 it began publishing *The Theosophist* at Madras. In 1888 Mme. Blavatsky went to London, where she issued *The Secret Doctrine* and formed an Esoteric Section of the Theosophical Society devoted to occult lore. Following her death in 1891, Annie *Besant succeeded her as leader of the Adyar Theosophical Society and greatly increased the role of Hindu thought in Theosophy as well as the occult sciences. William Q. Judge, one of the three founders of Theosophy and president of the American branch, became involved in controversy with the Adyar leadership in 1892 and in 1895 established the fully independent Theosophical Society in America. It made its headquarters first at Chicago, later at Altadena, California. Those loyal to Annie Besant formed the Theosophical Society of New York. Other independent groups include the Temple of the People, founded at Syracuse, N.Y., in 1899, now at Halcyon, Calif., and the Universal Brotherhood, an outgrowth of the Judge group, with its headquarters at Point Loma, California. Opposition to Annie Besant in Germany led to the separation of the Anthroposophical Society formed by Rudolf *Steiner in 1912. In several books, Mrs. Besant advanced the theory that Jesus was an incarnation of the Buddha. In 1908–11 she created further stir by revealing that the Christ was alive and would reappear. She identified a Hindu youth, Jeddu Krishnamurti, as the reincarnate Jesus/Buddha. The formation of the Order of the Star in the East (1911) and the *Liberal Catholic Church (1915–16) was closely connected with the new avatar.

In a more general sense, theosophy may refer to any esoteric explanation of the universe based on mystical, usually pantheistic intuition, reserved to initiates. See C. J. Ryan, *What is Theosophy?* (1944); L. W. Rogers, *Elementary Theosophy* (1950).

THIRTEEN ARTICLES, a document prepared in 1538 as a *confession of faith of the Church of England. While never adopted formally, the Thirteen Articles influenced the later *Forty-Two Articles and the *Thirty-Nine Articles. The 1538 statement was drawn up during the discussions (1535–38) between Anglican and Lutheran theologians. The Articles followed the order of the first 13 articles of the *Augsburg Confession, and adopted some of its language. See Schaff Creeds I:612–613, 623–627.

THIRTY-NINE ARTICLES, in the C of E a counterpart of the Continental *confessions of faith. This has been questioned within the Anglican Communion, but the contemporary writings of the framers, the subtitle of the Articles, and the requirement of some form of assent by the clergy down to the present, make it clear that officially the C of E is a confessional Church. The first version of the Articles was agreed upon by *Convocations in 1562; the accepted form in which they now appear in the Book of Common Prayer was not achieved until 1571 (see TEN ARTICLES; BISHOPS' BOOK; SIX ARTICLES; KING'S BOOK; FORTY-TWO ARTICLES). They are characterized by brevity, dealing only with fundamentals of faith and with points disputed at the time; by clarity, in their positive doctrinal statements and rejection of heresy; by *comprehensiveness, admitting within limits differing interpretations as allowed by Scripture.

Historically three theological streams contributed to the Articles: the pre-Tridentine tradition of the West; the Lutheran tradition, and the Reformed or Calvinistic tradition. Articles 1–5 and 8 evidence the Trinitarian and Christological doctrines of the West and the *ecumenical creeds. The Reformation *formal principle or doctrinal norm, the primacy of Scripture, is established in the C of E by Articles 6 and 7. Lutheran doctrine on justification, the Church, and the distinction between ecclesiastical and temporal power is reflected in Articles 9–24, 31–34, 36–39. The Calvinistic influence is more decisive in the infralapsarian doctrine of *predestination in Article 17; and Articles 25–30 reject RC, Lutheran, and Zwinglian views in favor of a Reformed doctrine on the sacraments (although Article 28 on the Lord's Supper has also been interpreted as allowing for the *Real Presence).

The *Lambeth Conference of 1968 examined the status of the Articles, since throughout the Anglican Communion there are major parties that do not conform to them. It is doubtful, e.g., whether current preoccupation with the *historic episcopate as essential to the Church of Christ is compatible with their letter and spirit; yet radical theological views are clearly excluded. In the Protestant Episcopal Church of the

U.S., while they are largely neglected by clergy and laity alike, the Articles still have an official confessional-liturgical status. Even though specific subscription to them is not necessary, the Constitution of the Church (Article X) requires their use; ordinands solemnly engage to conform to the doctrine of the Church; and the ordination vows of the Book of Common Prayer are all based on the doctrine of the Articles. See J. C. Ryle, *Knots Untied* (1964), ch. 4; E. J. Bicknell, *Theological Introduction to the Thirty-Nine Articles of the Church of England* (1924); H. E. W. Turner, *Articles of the Church of England* (1964).

THOMISM, a blanket term for a body of philosophical and theological convictions set forth by Thomas Aquinas in the 13th cent. and since developed and variously stressed by numerous disciples. The whole is represented: sometimes as a fixed system, deductively complete, virtually closed, and requiring only explicitation in the light of fresh factual information; sometimes as an assemblage of conclusions most of which are acceptable within their frame of reference; sometimes as an organic unity open to further syntheses and homogeneous evolution. Hence the division between juridical, eclectic, and true-blue Thomists. Further subdivision is possible; thus the first include those who repeat their master rabbinically, who treat him as dwelling in a world of essences, ontological, aloof, and intricately divisible, who are devoted to him as a subject in medieval history or archeology, or who use his teachings mainly for administrative needs; the second applaud a prodigious pioneer effort, but in greater or lesser degree replace elements of his construction from elsewhere; the third include cerebral metaphysicians of a Spanish temper, semineoplatonists, and existentialists more in sympathy with the contemporary flux. These interests can be disentangled only rather tentatively, for the living history of Thomism is that of their intertwining. Curiously only the first and second treat their cause as a system; the third are uncomfortable under the name, and paradoxically it is on them that this article concentrates.

Their thought does not develop geometrically but follows the analogies implied by the singleness in variety of being and supplied by exuberant human experience. It is accepted without shrug or apology that the half-real is real, the not wholly perfect sufficiently perfect—jejune phrases that suggest a rare quality for a metaphysician, not, of course, for one who comes to terms with the world on a lower level. The notion of "being potential" is taken to a height and depth only faintly prophesied by Aristotle. God alone is the purely actual; the inference is not drawn, however, that he is the all and only; instead it is because of his infinite transcendence that he can produce other real beings. Creatures are things in themselves, though not from or for themselves. The metaphysics of creation, which lies at the heart of Thomism and is its greatest contribution to Christian thought, is explicated by the distinction between essence and existence, and ramifies into all its characteristic teachings: the reality of matter, of individual things, and of secondary principal causes. Univocation is not possible for discourse about pluralism at this depth, and metaphor is not enough, unless it be sublimated in philosophical analogy. And so this becomes the central method and explains the constant burdens in Thomism, of distinguishing in order the reunite, of being chary about an "either-or" and preferring the "both-and."

Thomism is primarily a theology, though this cannot be understood without its philosophy. It is possible, however, to perform an excision, and to take the philosophy without the theology; in fact this has been accepted by many thinkers who have not shared the beliefs of Roman Catholics or even Christians. Such a philosophy stands as complete as any purely rationalist or humanist account of the world can be expected to be. Accordingly we indicate: first, some of the philosophical principles in Thomism; second, some consequences when they are lifted up into theology. The customary apparatus used is the logic of Aristotle. By induction (which here means an abstractive insight rather than an inductive argument) from sense experience, reasoning proceeds deductively from effect to cause, and vice versa. Physical substances are essentially composed of matter and form, but this hylomorphism is not applied to spiritual substances. Man is a psycho-physical unity, and the embarrassments for the doctrine of the immortality of soul that it is the single substantial form of the body are candidly faced. Moral philosophy is eudaemonistic, directed toward human happiness. The epistemology is one of direct realism, free from the correspondence theory of Descartes.

The development is continuous from philosophy into a theology that is rooted in this world but open to and vivified by the word of God. It observes a tidal movement of ebb and flow from creatures and the creator. Yet though the world shows forth his glory, and Thomism is committed to a demonstrable theism, carefully steering its course by the aid of analogy between anthropomorphism and agnosticism, or even the old *theologia negativa*, its theology is set above all on God for himself, not as the integrator of the universe. His grace is a sheer gift beyond the rights of human nature, yet offers no violence to it. The harmony of grace and nature, faith and reason—and, it may be added, of *agape* and inborn appetites—is a major theme: it was composed under the stresses of the double truth controversy from which Thomism was born. A supplementary theme is the intrinsic efficaciousness of divine grace: the phrase dates from the great debates on predestination in the century following the Reformation (see CONGREGATIO DE AUXILIIS). Free will is seen as operating within God's universal causality with respect to all existence and action from beginning to end, and as contributing nothing that is entirely the creature's own except sin. Thomists were called Jansenists, yet with as little truth they might have been called Pelagians. It is noteworthy how unanxious was

the spirituality that fed on their doctrine of grace, and how full of a joyous abandon to the will of God. Their moral theology remained comparatively immune from the legalisms that dominated the age of casuistry; to be happy rather than to be dutiful is man's final purpose, and duty itself is more a matter of equity than of a code.

The whole is very ordered and strangely open, and the tightening of Thomism into a closely-knit school occurred only a century or more after the master's death; once again it is now loosening out, and with no real loss of continuity and identity. Its history may be outlined under four periods, high medieval, late medieval, Renaissance and Baroque, and post-Vatican I: each era with its catalogue of noble names. Three years to the day after his death in 1274 Thomas was condemned by ecclesiastical authority, in effect for making the human spirit too soil-bound. His old master, Albert the Great, rallied to his support, and he was followed by young Dominicans, notably in England and France. Though they secured the backing of the order, got the condemnation quashed and Thomas himself canonized by the first quarter of the 14th cent., they were too independent, too engaged in forming their own minds, and too close to him to treat him as an oracle and form a school in the narrow sense of the word. But they were men who knew where their intellectual loyalties lay and were fighting for the same cause. In fact in those early years the name of Albert was as potent as that of Thomas, and in Germany the stream of neoplatonism ran strong, where, as in Meister Eckhart, the movement might well be called Albertino-Thomism.

After the Black Death the medieval universities became more stiff and sectarian in their ways, and Thomism became but one of several schools in the same league, each staffed by members of the same religious order, the Franciscans being the most versatile, since they could be Augustinians, Scotists, or Ockamists. A more classical glow came with the opening of the 16th cent.; it moved from the Italy of Cardinal Cajetan to the Rhineland, and Louvain, and settled in Spain. Teachers such as Francisco de Vitoria, Domingo de Soto, Domingo Báñez, and John of St. Thomas are part of the imperial glory of that country. In an earlier age Francisco de Suarez would have been called a Thomist, but not then, when even Thomism was sometimes called *Báñezianism. With the decline of the Spanish Empire it lingered like an elderly don in a cloister, and was all but destroyed at the French Revolution. But it formed the core for the revival of scholasticism under Leo XIII in the later half of the 19th cent. and grew to become the quasi-official philosophy and theology for ecclesiastical power, so much so indeed that there were times when a Thomist who was a yogi rather than a commissar could have wished that the *Summa* might be put on the Index in order that its thought might be freed from such bureaucracy. Fortunately times have changed; Thomism has survived both the patronage and the manuals of instruction that accompanied it, and is now weathering the storms partly occasioned by them both. See E. Gilson, *Christian Philosophy of St. Thomas Aquinas* (tr. L. K. Shook, 1956); *idem*, *Spirit of Thomism* (1964); J. A. Weisheipl, NCE 14:126–135, with bibliog.

THOMPSON, WILLIAM (1733–99), first President of the Wesleyan Methodists of England after the death of John *Wesley (1791). T. was born at Fermanagh, Ireland, and became a Methodist preacher in 1756. A sound administrator, in 1795 he drew up the Plan of Pacification, which settled the question of the relationship between the Methodists and the Church of England.

THORN, COLLOQUY OF, a conference held in Thorn, W Prussia, in 1545, under the auspices of King Vladislav IV of Poland and aimed at religious peace (*colloquium caritativum*). RC, Lutheran, and *Reformed theologians participated, but factions and divisions made the meeting a failure. It is notable for contributing to the syncretistic controversy, esp. because of the opposition between the Lutherans A. *Calov and G. *Calixt (see SYNCRETISM), and for a Reformed declaration of faith drawn up by the Reformed theologians and later adopted by some Reformed Churches. This declaration strongly asserts agreement in faith with the early creeds and councils. See Schaff Creeds 1:560–563.

TILLICH, PAUL JOHANNES (1886–1965), Protestant theologian. T. was born in Starzeddel, a village in the German province of Brandenburg, where his father was a Prussian territorial church minister. T. received his Ph.D. from Breslau in 1911, and a licentiate in theology from Halle in 1912. He was ordained in 1912 by the Evangelical Lutheran Church, served 2 years as a pastor, and then spent the war years as an army chaplain. Following World War I, T. began his academic career as *Privatdozent* of theology at Berlin (1919–24), later teaching at Marburg (1924–25), Dresden (1925–29), and Leipzig (1928–29). He was professor of philosophy at Frankfurt from 1929 until 1933, when he was dismissed because of his criticism of Nazism. Through the efforts of Reinhold *Niebuhr he came to the U.S. and taught philosophical theology at Union Seminary, New York (1933–55). From 1955 to 1962 he taught at Harvard, and from 1962 until his death, at Chicago.

Prior to his emigration T. published numerous works in German, including *Die religiöse Lage der Gegenwart* (1926), which appeared in the U.S. in 1932 as *The Religious Situation* with translation and introduction by H. Richard *Niebuhr, making available T.'s thought to American readers. Among his later books were *The Courage to Be* (1952), *Love, Power, and Justice* (1954), *Dynamics of Faith* (1957), and *Christianity and the Encounter of the World Religions* (1963). His most substantial work was his *Systematic Theology* (3v., 1951, 1957, 1963). He took as the norm of his theology "New Being in Jesus as the Christ," and used the method of analyzing the questions involved in human existence and correlating them with the answers given by theology. He saw his theology as apologetic, in contrast with the *kerygmatic theology of K. *Barth.

T. was deeply influenced by the German philosophical tradition, particularly Schelling. Through contact with Heidegger he developed an existential approach to theology, though he did not accept existentialism as a philosophy. He combined a conservative appreciation for the history of Christian thought with a desire sometimes to reformulate it radically in modern terms. He emphasized the *Protestant principle, which he interpreted as the criticism of all expressions of religion, including Protestant Christianity, its dogmas, and its forms of church life, in the light of the ultimate. He accepted biblical criticism and held that the foundations of faith, which he defined as "ultimate concern," were beyond the reach of historical criticism. T. worked to relate theology to cultural and political questions. In Germany he was an active supporter of religious socialism. He was also interested in modern painting, and in psychotherapy stemming from Freud. Toward the end of his life he developed a special interest in comparative religions, which he saw as the basis for future developments in theology. See C. W. Kegley and R. W. Bretall, eds., *Theology of P. T.* (1952); D. H. Hopper, *Tillich: A Theological Portrait* (1968).

TILLOTSON, JOHN (1630–94), Abp. of Canterbury, preacher, polemicist. T. was the son of Puritan parents, educated at Clare Hall, Cambridge, and ordained in 1661. He participated in the *Savoy Conference on the *Nonconformist side. As a preacher of practical, moral sermons, he not only won renown, but was also imitated by many. He was dean of Canterbury (1670), later canon (1675) and dean (1689) of St. Paul's, London. In 1691 he agreed, with reluctance, to accept election as abp. of Canterbury. His polemics were directed against Roman Catholicism (e.g., in his *Rule of Faith*, 1666) and "atheism" (i.e., rationalism). He sought unsuccessfully to broaden membership in the C of E to include all Nonconformists except Unitarians. See J. Moffatt, ed., *Golden Book of Tillotson* (1926).

TIME SETTING, calculation and determination of the day of Christ's second coming. It has usually been a feature of *adventism in its various forms. From the "signs of the times," as well as from complex, often numerological interpretations of Scripture, time setters seek to discover and predict the moment of an impending disaster that will mark the destruction of the wicked and the beginning of the millennial reign of Christ and the just. *MILLENARIANISM; *DISPENSATIONALISM; *JEHOVAH'S WITNESSES.

TITHES, the tenth (or other) part of one's produce or other income due, according to custom or law, to a Church for its support and the maintenance of its liturgical, educational, and charitable activities. Some form of tithing is known to have been practiced by certain pagan religions. The law of the OT insisted upon the payment of tithes, and after some centuries of its existence the Christian Church adopted the practice, but more generally in the West than in the East. In earlier times the Church was supported by voluntary offerings, but when these became insufficient for the Church's need, synods made the payment of tithes obligatory, and in time civil legislation enforced their payment. The support of the practice by civil law began on the Continent under Charlemagne and in England with the beginning of the 10th century. Earlier exactions of a portion of the produce of the land (praedial tithes) were enlarged to include portions of certain other kinds of income. After the Reformation the evangelical state Churches retained tithes in Germany, but they were gradually repealed with the change of economic, social, and religious conditions, generally with some compensating indemnity, or they were converted into other forms of taxation. In England some tithing was retained down to 1936. For the RC Church the Council of Trent insisted on the payment of tithes, but civil enforcement of the obligation ended in most places in Europe with the French Revolution, after which the ecclesiastical legislation was modified by custom. The RC Church in the U.S. never required the payment of tithes, although the practice was observed in the Mississippi Valley when that area was under French and British control. The Code of Canon Law now in force prescribes the payment of tithes in those places in which they are still sanctioned by existing law and custom. Among Protestant Churches, the payment of tithes is considered obligatory in some bodies marked by a legalistic tendency and a bias in favor of OT observances. Thus it is required in certain Adventist Churches and by the Mormons. The value of a voluntary form of tithing has been given some emphasis in the theology of *stewardship (see, e.g., R. P. Roth, "Tithing as an Essential Act of Stewardship," in R. G. Burnbull, ed., *Baker's Dictionary of Practical Theology* [1967], 334–338). Similarly there has been an effort made in certain RC dioceses in the U.S. to induce the faithful to accept voluntarily a program of tithing. See P. K. Meagher, NCE 14:174–175; H. Thurston, CE 12:466–472; J. A. MacCulloch, Hastings ERE 12:347–350; E. Sehling, EncRelKnow 11:453–456.

TOLERANCE, a permissive attitude toward persons who affirm beliefs different from one's own. It is used to refer both to the attitude of an individual and to the policy of a state. Christians generally consider it required of them to be intolerant of error, and because the Christian faith is held to be the true faith it is impossible to look upon all beliefs as equally true, the error of *indifferentism. In past centuries when the Church held a stronger position in the State, this intolerant attitude was often translated into a policy of legal repression. In modern times the power of the Church to persecute heretics by use of the authority of the State has largely been lost. But churchmen have also come to distinguish between tolerance of opinions and tolerance of persons. It is now recognized that one can be intellectually intolerant of all error while yet accepting the full rights of all persons to hold whatever views appear true to them. The old phrase "error has no rights" is thereby balanced with the affirmation of the rights of persons. The tolerance practiced by most modern governments in the field of religion is generally considered to be the historical result, first, of the division of Christians into many competing groups, with the consequent impossibility of enforcing the beliefs of any one of them; and second, of the influence of the *Renaissance and the *Enlightenment, which reduced the overall influence of the Church in society. Important steps in this development are the *Toleration Act (1689) in England, and the Bill of Rights in the U.S. Constitution. Some consider the concept of tolerance inadequate, as implying the reluctant concession of a privilege rather than the recognition of a right, and prefer to emphasize the more positive concept of *religious freedom.

TOLERATION ACT, in England, an act of Parliament in 1689 granting a degree of *religious freedom. Toleration was granted to *Dissenters, provided they believed in the Trinity, but not to RC *recusants. The penalties prescribed by the Conventicle Act of 1670 were rescinded, on the condition that Dissenters make a declaration rejecting transubstantiation and swear oaths of allegiance and supremacy (Quakers were permitted to make a simple affirmation). The Toleration Act left in force the *Test Act (1673) barring Dissenters from civil office. For freedom in their ministry, dissenting ministers were required to subscribe to the *Thirty-Nine Articles, except the two on *infant baptism. While the granting of limited toleration was prompted by a desire to unite all Protestants politically in the loyalty to the King, William III, the Act did represent progress in the cause of religious liberty and brought relief from the persecutions long suffered by English Baptists, Quakers, and others. The Act also brought greater religious freedom to minority groups in the American colonies.

TONGUES SPEAKING, a phrase commonly used as an equivalent for *glossolalia, the charismatic gift of speaking in strange languages, which is emphasized esp. in *Pentecostalism.

TORGAU ARTICLES, the basis for the second part (Art. 22–28) of the *Augsburg Confession, dealing with matters of worship and discipline. The Articles were drawn up in March 1530, on instructions of John Frederick I, Elector of Saxony, in preparation for the Diet of Augsburg, by Luther, P. *Melanchthon, J. *Jonas, J. *Bugenhagen. They are named for the place where they were presented to the elector. See Schaff Creeds 1:229. *SCHWABACH ARTICLES.

TOTAL DEPRAVITY, a description of the sinful condition of man caused by the Fall. The particular historical association of the phrase is to the Calvinism taught by the Synod of *Dort (1619) against *Arminianism (see FIVE POINTS OF CALVINISM). The Canons of Dort, like other Protestant *confessions of faith (e.g., *Augsburg Confession, Art. XVIII; Second *Helvetic Confession, c. IX; *Westminster Confession, c. VI), acknowledged that human nature and its own power for truth and goodness are not destroyed by original sin. "Depraved nature" means rather a concrete incapacity actually either to live an upright ethical life or, more importantly, to cooperate in the process of salvation. Arminianism took the position that man can and does cooperate in his conversion; Arminian optimism became a characteristic of the teaching of John *Wesley and of American *revivalism. Human depravity was affirmed by Dort (3d and 4th Heads of Doctrine, Art. III–IV, X–XII), denying such cooperation.

It is not simply a denial that anything positive can come from man's powers by which he prepares himself for salvation. Rather, the process of salvation is so described that grace and the Holy Spirit supply the operation of the will in conversion. The powers of man are not in their inherent nature really salvaged by grace; they remain corrupt. This position contrasts with RC teaching: under grace man does consent and cooperate in his own conversion; i.e., grace heals, and elevates the power for good inherent in man's natural powers even after sin so that the act of conversion does come vitally from them. When a doctrine of total depravity is attributed to the Reformation generally, it is because salvation by faith and grace alone was presented as excluding human cooperation even under grace in the process of salvation. The acts of man are in themselves, at worst, as Luther claimed, continuously sinful or, at best, irrelevant to salvation.

TRACT 90, the last of J. H. *Newman's *Tracts for the Times*, published Feb. 27, 1841. In *Tract 90* Newman applied a historical method of interpretation to certain passages in the *Thirty-Nine Articles and showed that they could be subscribed to in a Catholic sense since they did not condemn the Council of Trent and were directed less against the formal teaching of the Holy See than against the abuses of popular religion. A Protestant clamor arose questioning his honesty; he refused to withdraw his assertion and retired into lay communion with the Church of England.

TRACTARIANISM, the *Oxford movement; more precisely the tenets and practices set forth in *Tracts for the Times, by Members of the University of Oxford*, started by J. H. *Newman in 1833 and brought to a close by him in 1841, with the controversial *Tract 90* on the *Thirty-Nine Articles. The tracts comprised brief pamphlets and also extended treatises, such as that by E. B. *Pusey on baptism. The

Tractarians, an extreme wing of the *high-church party, stood for a conservative return to ancient doctrine and discipline, and operated within the larger setting of the Oxford movement and certainly of *Anglo-Catholicism, which soon displayed, like contemporary Romanism, a vitality of its own in adapting itself to new environments. Tractarianism, less formally and courteously called Puseyism (which term, now out of date, suggested the extravagances of *ritualism to 19th-cent. Protestant sentiment), still lingers to mean a learned, mellow, and historically minded devotion to patristic and conciliar orthodoxy and traditional *church order.

TRACTS FOR THE TIMES, a series of pamphlets and books—E. *Pusey's contribution on baptism was an elaborate treatise —launched by Newman and his friends, hence Tractarians, to recall the C of E to its Catholic witness, apostolic descent, and *via media*. The first three appeared Sept. 9, 1833; the last was the famous *Tract 90* (1841), catastrophic in its effect. They were greeted with surprise, dismay, ridicule, and abuse from Protestants and bps. of the C of E, but met with eager sympathy from many, and were so sought after that printers could not meet the demand.

TRADITION, in the religious sense, the body of Christian teaching and practice handed down whether in oral or written form, separately from, but not independently of, Sacred Scripture. Practically all Christian theologians acknowledge tradition as operative in all Christian denominations, but they do not explain its significance in the same way. In RC doctrine and theology, tradition constitutes a source and *rule of faith, i.e., it contains in a real sense divine revelation. The Council of Trent (1546) affirmed both the Bible and tradition as divine sources of Christian doctrine but left unclear the relationship between them. Vatican II in Ch. 2 of its *Dogmatic Consti-*

tution on Divine Revelation (Dei Verbum) declared that Scripture and tradition form a unity in the transmission of divine revelation; they are not, therefore, two independent sources of revelation. Further, the council conceived tradition in a dynamic fashion as "growth in the understanding of the realities and words which have been handed down." This concept of tradition as dynamic rather than static accounts for the undeniable development of doctrine in Christian thought, while it allows at the same time for the setting aside of past tradition that later understanding perceives not to have been adequate (see MAGISTERIUM). Within Protestantism the view of tradition most widely held conforms to the position of the *Thirty-Nine Articles of the Church of England, where tradition is presented as essential to the Christian faith, but only insofar as it is judged to be in explicit accord with the Bible. Thus for Protestantism generally doctrine such as the RC teaching on the Immaculate Conception and the Assumption of the Virgin Mary does not pertain to divine revelation and is not of faith, since it is not unmistakably identifiable in Scripture.

Each of these positions on tradition has manifested its own inherent dangers: within Roman Catholicism the tendency, largely dissipated by Vatican II, was to depreciate the role of Scripture in Catholic thought and practice; within Protestantism the trend was to overly restrict divine revelation to the Bible. Under the impulsion of Vatican II Christian theologians have begun to listen to one another undeterred by denominational barriers; their dialogue can bear nothing but good fruit for growth in the understanding of the relationship between the Bible and tradition. See G. Moran, *Scripture and Tradition* (1963); J. P. Mackey, *Modern Theology of Tradition* (1960); C. Hanson, *Tradition in the Early Church* (1962).

TRADITIONALISM, the 19th-cent. theory developed by some RC philosophers and theologians that the human mind cannot acquire knowledge of natural truths, whether metaphysical or moral, without divine revelation, passed on by oral instruction or tradition. It was a reaction to the uncertainties caused by rationalism and to the upheavals of the French Revolution. Principal exponents were Louis de Bonald (1754–1840), A. Bonnetty (1798–1879), F. de Lamennais (1782–1854), and J. de Maistre (1753?–1821). Two encyclicals of Pius IX *Mirari vos* (1832) and *Singulari nos* (1834), were directed against Lamennais's political and traditionalist doctrines. Vatican Council I condemned the position that unaided human reason could not attain knowledge about God (see D 3004, 3026).

TRADITOR, a term having a technical sense in the time of the Donatist schism in N Africa. During the persecution under Diocletian it was possible for a Christian to save himself from death by handing over copies of the Scriptures in his possession to the authorities to be burned. Those who did so were called *traditores,* and the term was extended to cover those who handed over sacred vessels, or their brethren. The Donatists maintained that *traditores* by their crime lost their power of orders, so that bps. who had been *traditores* could not validly consecrate others. See R. A. Knox, *Enthusiasm* (1950), 54–57. *DONATISTS.

TRANSCENDENTALISTS, in the U.S., those participating in the movement arising (1830s) in New England as a revolt against the rationalistic philosophy of the *Enlightenment and the rigor of conventional Protestantism. The tenets of the American Transcendentalists are indirectly traceable to German idealism—the view that ultimate reality transcends phenomena and is apprehended by intuition—and certain mystical elements of *Romanticism, but more immediately to the influence of Thomas Carlyle and Samuel T. Coleridge. Associated with the movement at one time or another were most of the literary, religious, and social-reform leaders of New England, including such prominent figures

as Ralph Waldo Emerson (1803–82), George Ripley (1802–80), Orestes Brownson (1803–76), Bronson Alcott (1799–1888), and Henry David Thoreau (1817–62). Basically eclectic, the Transcendentalists held widely differing views but were bound together by their belief in an "order of truths that transcends the sphere of the external senses." And since "the truth of religion does not depend on tradition, nor historical facts, but has an unerring witness in the soul," they rejected all external authority. For a short period they organized a community of their own at *Brook Farm. See W. R. Hutchinson, *Transcendentalist Ministers* (1959); P. Miller, ed., *Transcendentalists: An Anthology* (1960).

TRANSIGNIFICATION, a term some contemporary RC theologians have substituted for *transubstantiation; transfinalization is similarly used. For some theologians the change in terminology implies a denial of any ontological or real change in the bread and the wine in the Eucharist. For the more traditionally rooted theologians, however, the new terms avoid belaboring the philosophical aspects of the dogma and simply bring out the long-neglected sign value or significance of the Eucharist. To paraphrase Irenaeus of Lyons, writing in the 2d cent., the Church's gift of bread and wine, the fruits of the earth, are not rejected, they are transformed, changed in their signification and in their reality (see PG 7:1125–27). Transignification intends to express that the meaning of bread and wine as physical nourishment is transformed as they become spiritual nourishment. See Encyclical of Paul VI, *Mysterium fidei,* AAS (1965), 753–774; J. Powers, *Eucharistic Theology* (1967); E. Schillebeeckx, *Eucharist* (1968).

TRANSUBSTANTIATION, in RC teaching the technical term for the eucharistic change. Reflecting Aristotelian philosophy, the term affirms a change of the substance of bread and wine into the substance of Christ's body and blood, without any change, however, in the accidents, or appearances, of bread and wine. The fathers of the Council of Trent adopted the word "transubstantiation" as "apt" to describe the reality of such a change, without canonizing the philosophical system that helped to coin the expression. The substantive issues with which Trent was concerned were two: (1) the meaning of Christ's words, "This is my body," is that "this" is no longer bread but is my body; (2) if this be so, the "no longer bread" is verifiable only in the ontological order, known to faith, and not in the empirical order, or the order of appearances (see D 1642).

In the Ante-Nicene Church, Ignatius of Antioch, Justin Martyr, Irenaeus of Lyons, Hippolytus of Rome, and Cyprian of Carthage are all witnesses to the belief that the bread is the body of Christ, that the bread becomes, or is made, the body of Christ. To cite Justin: ". . . just as, through the word of God, our Savior Jesus Christ became incarnate and took upon himself flesh and blood for our salvation, so we have been taught, the food which has been made the Eucharist by the prayer of his word . . . is both the flesh and blood of that Jesus who was made flesh" (*1 Apol.* 66). After Nicaea (325) further precision was introduced by reference to the change, or transformation, of the elements of bread and wine into the body and blood of the Lord. It might have been argued that bread and wine are made, or become, the body and blood of Christ without ceasing to be bread and wine, just as in the incarnation the Word was made flesh, without ceasing to be the Word. The possibility is removed by the word "change." Thus, Cyril of Jerusalem states the essentials of the doctrine of transubstantiation in language free of all technicality: "Of old in Cana of Galilee, he changed water into wine of his own will. Is he less worthy of credence when he changes wine into blood . . .? Therefore, look not upon the bread and wine as bare elements, for they happen to be, according to the Lord's assurance, the body and blood of Christ; for even though the senses suggest this to you, let faith make you certain and steadfast. Do not judge the matter by taste, but by faith rest assured without any misgivings that you have been deemed worthy of the body and blood of Christ" (*On the Mysteries* 4.-2.6). In the medieval period Lanfranc in his reply to Berengarius can use the words "substance" and "appearances" in the non-technical sense that "the earthly substances . . . are transformed . . . into the essence of the Lord's body, the appearances (*species*) of these same remaining along with certain other qualities" (PL 150:430). "Substance" and "appearances" are essential words in the traditional nomenclature of the East and the West and as such are in no sense to be confused with the Aristotelian categories of substance and accidents. The actual term "transubstantiation" came into use in the West in the 12th cent.; in the 13th it was used officially by Lateran Council IV (D 802) and the Council of Lyons II (D 860), and by all theologians. In the 14th cent. John Wycliffe, and in the 16th cent. all the Reformers rejected transubstantiation. See P. F. Palmer, *Sacraments and Worship* (1955); J. M. Powers, *Eucharistic Theology* (1967); E. Schillebeeckx, "Transubstantiation, Transfinalization, Transfiguration," *Worship* 40 (1966), 324–338; C. Vollert, NCE 14:259–261. *REAL PRESENCE; *CONSUBSTANTIATION; *VIRTUALISM.

TRAVELING PREACHER, a layman licensed to preach in a Methodist *annual conference. Admission to the office by the annual conference amounts to a 2-year "admission on trial" under the supervision of a bishop. At the end of the probation the candidate is examined according to norms established by John *Wesley for his preachers. If approved, he is admitted fully to the ministry. Ordination is conferred only on those approved as preachers. See N. B. Harmon, *Understanding the Methodist Church* (rev. ed., 1955).

TREATISE CONCERNING THE POWER AND PRIMACY OF THE POPE (*Tractatus de potestate et primatu papae*), a confessional document written by P. *Melanchthon in 1537. The *Treatise* was incorporated in the *Book of Concord because it was thought to be an appendix to the *Schmalkaldic Articles; in fact it had been written as a supplement to the *Augsburg Confession, which had no article on the papacy. The assembly of the Schmalkaldic League at Schmalkalden in Feb. 1537 had as its purpose a statement of Lutheran doctrine in view of the general council summoned by Pope Paul III to meet at Mantua in May. The Schmalkaldic Articles prepared by Luther were not approved as a confessional document; Melanchthon's treatise was. In signing the articles, he had attached a conciliatory statement in regard to the papacy. The *Treatise*, however, reflecting the view of the assembly, was adamantly antipapal. The first part considers the pope; the second, the bishops. Papal primacy by divine right over the Church and secular princes is rejected, as is the necessity to accept the primacy in faith and obedience. The power exercised by bishops is condemned as a usurpation, and the *Treatise* teaches that episcopacy is not essential to the nature of the Church. See G. Gieschen, EncLuthCh 3:2183–89; T. G. Tappert, ed., *Book of Concord* (1959), 319–335; R. Stupperich, *Melanchthon* (pa., 1965).

TRENT, COUNCIL OF. The imperial city of Trent situated in the Alps near the southern end of Brenner Pass was the scene for the most important assembly of Catholic prelates in modern times. It came as a tardy response to Luther's demand for a "free Christian council on German soil." In *Laetare Jerusalem*, the bull announcing the Council, Pope Paul III directed it toward three goals: (1) to heal the schism; (2) to reform the Church; and (3) to take precautions against the Ottoman Turks. Despite its limited success in these tasks, Trent emerged as a dominant influence on church history over the past 4 centuries. The history of the Council, written over a period of 18 years, has three distinct chapters: Dec. 13, 1545 to Feb. 16, 1548; May 1, 1551 to April 25, 1552; and Jan. 18, 1562 to Dec. 4, 1563. In all, 25 solemn sessions were held.

Sessions 1–10 (1545–48). After several delays due to poor attendance and political upheaval, the Council opened on a note of controversy. The papal forces wanted to begin with the doctrinal issues, whereas the Emperor Charles V's supporters insisted that church reform be the first order of business. Three sessions were spent on this and other procedural questions before a compromise was reached. It was finally decided that questions of doctrine and reform were to be considered side by side in separate commissions and reported out alternately in the plenary sessions. The fact remains, however, that the early discussions on reform were inconclusive, and the important declarations in this phase of the Council were primarily doctrinal. One decree issued (April 8, 1546) at the fourth session was the Catholic answer to the Protestant *sola scriptura*. It enumerated the books of the OT and NT canon; endorsed the Latin Vulgate; and insisted on reverence for tradition (D 1501–08). The Catholic position regarding various aspects of *original sin was defined in session 5 (June 17, 1546; D 1510–16). The sixth session came at the end of months of debate (Jan. 13, 1547). It addressed the critical issue of *justification, which had become the touchstone of Luther's doctrinal position. The conciliar decree sought to repudiate Reformation teaching on the subject without at the same time condemning any of the divergent opinions held by Thomists, Scotists, and Augustinians (D 1520–83). The notion and nature of the seven sacraments were clarified in the seventh session (March 3, 1547; D 1600–30). On March 11, 1547, at the eighth session, the papal supporters seized upon an outbreak of typhus as a reason for transferring the council to Bologna. The move further antagonized Charles V, who was already bitter over the direction of the Council. After two solemn sessions in Bologna, at which no important decrees were issued, Paul II suspended the Council.

Sessions 11–16 (1551–52). Soon after he was elected in 1550, Pope Julius III sum moned the Council back to Trent the following year. New overtures were made to the Lutherans, who conditioned their participation in the Council on three points: (1) questions of doctrine that had already been considered were to be discussed anew; (2) Lutheran representatives were to have equal voice and vote with the Catholic prelates; and (3) the pope's legates should no longer preside over the proceedings. The council fathers extended safe-conduct to a delegation of the German princes, but were unable to meet their other demands. The most important contribution of this second phase was the Council's doctrinal statement on the Eucharist. In the 13th session (Oct. 11, 1551) it defined the Real Presence in terms of transubstantiation (D 1635–61). Catholic teaching on the sacraments of penance and extreme unction was clarified in the 14th (Nov. 25, 1551; D 1667–1719). War in Germany forced another suspension of the Council in the spring of 1552. More than 10 years elapsed before it met again.

Sessions 17–25 (1562–63). When convoking the Council in 1560, Paul IV was purposely silent on the question whether it was to be a continuation of the previous sessions or a new Council. The council fathers gave their answer by voting to take up the deliberations from where they had left off in 1552. Sessions 21 and 22 were devoted to eucharistic doctrine and practice: the first (July 16, 1562) dealt with holy communion, giving the rationale for denying the chalice to the laity (D 1725–34); the second (Sept. 17, 1562) explained the sense in which the Mass is a sacrifice (D 1738–59). In discussing the sacrament of orders the 23d session (July 15, 1563) brought to a head the debate over the episcopacy. Already in 1546 the Council had discussed the obligation of bishops to be resident in their sees; in 1563 the debate turned on the source and, by inference, the seriousness of the obligation. Though Trent's decree on holy orders did not settle all questions, it contradicted the Protestants on several points by declaring the priesthood to be truly a sacrament (D 1763–78). It also directed bishops to establish seminaries for the training of priests.

The crucial issue of reform continued to divide the Council. The papal forces were pushing to end the Council, but the Spanish, French, and imperial bishops were unwilling to adjourn before some substantive reform was legislated. The non-Italians suspected that the Roman Curia would be satisfied with token measures. Their fears were in large part allayed by Cardinal Morone, the papal legate newly appointed to preside over the Council. In the summer of 1563, he drafted a comprehensive program of reform that took cognizance of the complaints submitted by the Spaniards, the French, and the Emperor. Morone's proposals served as the basis for discussion. After extensive revision it was passed by the Council in sessions 24 (Nov. 11, 1563) and 25 (Dec. 3 and 4, 1563). Despite the juridical nature of the reform decrees, they were prompted by pastoral concerns. They established qualifications for cardinals, bishops, and all the clergy; the manner of life, duties, and procedures for appointing them to office were spelled out. Bishops were directed to conduct visitation of their sees; diocesan and provincial synods were to be held regularly. Some of the exemptions from episcopal jurisdiction enjoyed by religious orders in pastoral matters were curtailed. General norms were set down regarding the admission of candidates to religious orders. Stringent laws governing the cloister had lasting effect on orders of women. The important decree *Tametsi* reforming marriage legislation was also passed at the 24th session. It prohibited clandestine weddings and laid down certain forms and procedures required for the validity of a marriage (D 1813–16). The concluding session lasted 2 days (December 3–4, 1563). In addition to the work it did on reform, it approved committee reports on indulgences, purgatory, and the veneration of images; and finally it made arrangements to take care of unfinished business. The Council called upon the Pope to commission new editions of the Index of Prohibited Books, the breviary, the Roman Missal, the catechism, and the Latin Vulgate. Although the Sixto-Clementine edition of the Vulgate appeared only in

1592, the other works were published within a decade after the Council ended. Together with the decrees of the Council itself these works became the principal instruments of "the Tridentine reform." The *Catechism of the Council of Trent* (1566) proved to have an extraordinary effect in disseminating Catholic doctrine as defined by Trent. It was not a catechism in the usual sense of the word, but rather a manual of instruction for pastoral clergy.

Pius IV gave formal approval to Trent in the bull *Benedictus Deus* (Jan. 26, 1564; D 1847–50). The Pope did not alter the canons and decrees, but he maintained that the Apostolic See alone has the right to interpret them. In Aug. 1564 Pius created a special commission to safeguard and explain the decrees of Trent. It was continued with expanded responsibilities under his successors as the Congregation of the Council. Initially the success of the Council depended upon acceptance of the reform measures by the Catholic governments. Italy, Portugal, and Poland accepted them immediately. Ferdinand I approved them for his hereditary possessions, but the decrees were never published for the empire as a whole. Nor were they ever promulgated officially in France. In Spain they were published with the saving clause, "without prejudice to royal authority." The Catholic powers were willing to accept the doctrinal teaching of Trent, but when its reform measures ran contrary to national law or privilege, they were reserved.

Historical Perspective. In terms of the mandate given to it in *Laetare Jerusalem*, the Council of Trent was only a limited success. It set the stage for reform within that segment of Western Christendom that remained in communion with Rome, but it did not bridge the gap between Catholics and Protestants. Before a final appraisal of Trent can be made in ecumenical terms, another question must be answered: to what extent was it responsible for the ensuing polemics and controversies? Historical evidence suggests that the spirit at Trent itself was more irenic than the post-Tridentine spirit. The council fathers made an effort to get a first-hand knowledge of the Protestant confessions; unlike earlier councils, it condemned errors, but not persons; and in making room for the divergent opinions within Catholicism itself, it did not present the Church as a monolithic structure. From a historical perspective, it is now recognized that Trent was handicapped by the small number of representatives it attracted and that no one seems to have seen the problem whole. Despite the fact that a principal occupation of both papal and theological writings in the 14th and 15th cents. was ecclesiology and that the chief underlying concern of Protestant Reformers in the 16th cent. was the nature and mission of the Church, Trent never confronted this issue directly. It said a great deal about the teachings of the Church, but nothing on the Church itself; much on the sacraments, but nothing on the Church as the great sacrament. Nor was the Council well served by its critics, for they too had a limited vision. Despite the piecemeal approach, however, the Council became the focal point and symbol of post-Reformation Catholicism. Both its apologists and critics are one in admitting Trent's importance in shaping church history in the West. See G. Alberigo, ed., *Conciliorum oecumenicorum decreta* (1962), 633–775, a critical edition of the official text of canons and decrees first published in Rome in 1564; H. Jedin, NCE 14:271–278, with bibliog.; Jedin Trent; H. J. Schroeder, *Disciplinary Decrees of the Council of Trent* (1937).

TRIDENTINE, the adjectival form of reference to the Council of Trent (from *Tridentum*, the town of Trent in northern Italy); e.g., the Tridentine Catechism is the *Catechism of the Council of Trent*; the Tridentine reform is that instituted by the decrees of Trent.

TRIFORMIANS, those who taught that God is of three "forms," or parts: Father, Son, and Holy Spirit are partial beings; the three together make up the perfection of the Trinity. The belief was described by Filaster (*Haer.* 93) and Augustine (*Haer.* 74). The name *Triformii*, or *Triformiani*, was invented by Danaeus in his edition (1576) of Augustine's *De haeresibus* (PL 12:1205).

TRINE IMMERSION (Triune Immersion), a ritual for baptism in which the recipient kneels in water and is immersed three times, in the name of the three Persons of the Trinity. This method of baptizing is esp. characteristic of the *Brethren Churches.

TRINITARIANISM, the belief or the theology affirming that the one God is three Persons, Father, Son and Holy Spirit. The term is frequently used in opposition to Unitarianism.

TRITHEISM, any teaching that sees in the Trinity, besides a distinction of persons, also one of natures or substances. Thus there would not be one God, but three Gods. Historically tritheism has not been a heresy taught explicitly, but rather an implication of the philosophical expressions used by certain theologians in discussing the Trinity. In this sense the following are classified as tritheists: John Philoponus (fl. 6th cent.), because he identified nature and person; Roscellin (d. *c.*1125), by teaching that there could be no nature common to many persons; Gilbert de la Porrée (1076–1154), by asserting that the common nature was a fourth distinct reality in the Trinity (D 745); Joachim of Fiore (*c.*1132–1202), by teaching that the three Persons had a collective nature (D 803–806). A. Günther (1783–1863), employing Hegelian language, taught that the three divine Persons were distinct substances, the one divine consciousness being the only bond of unity (D 2828).

TRIUMPH THE CHURCH AND KINGDOM OF GOD IN CHRIST, a Holiness body founded in 1902, on the claim of a special revelation to E. D. Smith. It stresses *entire sanctification, Christ's second coming, and *baptism with the Holy Spirit. Government is by quarterly and annual conferences; the principal official in the Church is called the Chief Bishop. In 1967 it reported membership of 45,000, with 420 churches. Headquarters are in Atlanta, Georgia.

TROELTSCH, ERNST (1865–1923), German theologian and religious sociologist. After studies at Erlangen, Göttingen, and Berlin, he was for 3 years a Lutheran pastor in Munich. His professional career was spent mainly at Heidelberg, as professor of systematic theology (1894–1915); and at Berlin, as professor of philosophy (1915–23). His major work, *Die Soziallehren der christlichen Kirchen und Gruppen* (1912; Eng. tr. O. Wyon, *The Social Teaching of the Christian Churches*, 2 v., 1931), became a classic, esp. in its interpretation of the forms of Christianity under the classifications church, sect, and mysticism. The work is a comprehensive historical presentation of the relation of the Churches to the process of social change, and the development of Christian social teaching. T. was also concerned with the claim that Christianity is an absolute and unique doctrinal and moral teaching. Influenced by the thought of A. *Ritschl and Kant, his own terms of inquiry led him to a relativism: claims to absolute value are a reflection of aprioristic thought patterns; the forms and ideas of Christianity were to be accounted for by their historical and environmental source. See I. Ludolphy, EncLuthCh 3:241–247; H. Benkert, RGG 6:1043–48.

TUNKERS (Ger. *tunken*, to dip, immerse) once a nickname for the German Brethren, also called Dunkers or Dunkards. The name refers to their practice of baptism by *trine immersion. *BRETHREN CHURCHES.

TURLUPIANS, a minor medieval sect, probably related to the *Brothers and Sisters of the Free Spirit. Their origin and the derivation of their name are uncertain, but their prophetess Jeanne Debanton was burned at Paris in 1372. The following year Gregory XI condemned their teaching, which included antisacramental, antinomian, and pantheistic elements, and doctrines similar to those of the later quietists. J. Gerson claimed their ritual included nudism and obscene practices but offered no proof for the accusation. The Turlupians did not survive the severe persecution directed against them by Charles V of France. See E. W. McDonnell, *Beguines and Beghards in Medieval Culture* (1954); H. C. Lea, *History of the Inquisition of the Middle Ages* (1888; repr., 1958), 1:126; N. Cohn, *Pursuit of the Millennium* (1957), 176–177.

TURRETINI, three *Reformed theologians at Geneva, originally from Lucca in Italy. (1) Benedetto (1588–1631), professor from 1612, wrote a defense of the Bible translations made at Geneva. (2) Francesco (1623–87), son of Benedetto, was the best known in the U.S., where the family name is usually given as Turretine. His scholastic exposition of strictly orthodox Calvinism, *Institutio theologiae elencticae* (3v., 1679–85), became the standard text at Princeton Theological Seminary under A. *Alexander. (SEE HODGE, C.; PRINCETON THEOLOGY.) (3) Giovanni Alfonso (1671–1737), son of Francesco, brought about a moderation of adherence to the rigid Calvinism of the Synod of *Dort and the *Helvetic Consensus Formula and strove for union between the Reformed and Lutheran Churches. See EncRelKnow 12:42–44.

TWELVE ARTICLES, *Claims of the Whole Peasantry*, a declaration of their demands made by the peasants of Swabia for religious and social reform (Feb. 1525). The Twelve Articles were composed by S. *Lotzer, although they have also been attributed to B. *Hubmaier. The document, which became the manifesto of the *Peasants' War, claimed as divine rights, sanctioned by Scripture, the election and

dismissal of pastors, as well as freedom from serfdom and taxes on water, forests, and pasture lands. In April 1525 Luther replied in *Appeal for Peace, Touching the Twelve Articles of the Swabian Peasants.*, warning against the use of violence by the peasants. See Bihlmeyer-Tüchle 3:30–31; Léonard HistProt 1:104-105; bibliog. for Peasants' War.

TWENTY-FIVE ARTICLES OF RELIGION, a *doctrinal standard prepared by John *Wesley for U.S. Methodists. At the *Christmas Conference (1784) T. *Coke presented the Articles. Along with Wesley's *Notes on the New Testament* and the *Standard Sermons*, they were adopted for the newly organized Methodist Episcopal Church. The Conference added one Article to the 24 prepared by Wesley, numbering it the 23d ("Of the Rulers of the U.S.A.") and renumbering the original. Wesley's document was an adaptation of the *Thirty-Nine Articles of the C of E; his deletions and modifications were designed to remove any Calvinistic, RC, or ritualistic elements. The Articles have continued unaltered throughout the history of the Methodist Episcopal Church and the Methodist Church. See H. Wheeler, *History and Exposition of the Twenty-Five Articles of Religion of the Methodist Episcopal Church* (1908), bibliog. and parallel textual comparison with the Thirty-Nine Articles; N. B. Harmon, *Understanding the Methodist Church* (rev. ed., 1955), 25–79, text with commentary.

TWENTY PRINCIPLES OF RELIGION, a Congregational statement of faith, which constituted an important part of the Declaration of Faith and Order agreed upon in 1833 by the Congregational Union of England and Wales. It was the first statement of faith formulated by English Congregationalism since the *Savoy Declaration (1658). The statement, which was not authoritative, was without great merit in form or substance. Mainly it signifies a drift from traditional Calvinism, manifested more in a weakening of the original conviction than by an assertion of any alternative. This is particularly true with regard to its pronouncements about the sacraments.

TWO-SEED-IN-THE-SPIRIT PREDESTINARIAN BAPTISTS, a Baptist group originating in the second half of the 18th cent. as a result of Daniel Parker's protests against *Arminianism. They believe that in the Garden of Eden two seeds entered the life stream of humanity, a good seed implanted in the spirit by God, and an evil seed implanted in the spirit by the devil. Each person is born with one seed or the other and therefore is absolutely predestined. They oppose missions, have no paid ministry, and follow congregational polity. They have all but disappeared in the 20th century.

TYRRELL, GEORGE (1861–1909), English Jesuit theologian, the apostle of *modernism in the English-speaking world. He was born in Dublin, of Anglican parents, and was influenced by a Calvinist aunt; he studied at Trinity College, Dublin, became devoted to the *high-church movement, and later became a Roman Catholic (1879). A year later he entered the Jesuits, was ordained in 1891, and taught moral theology at Stonyhurst until 1896, when he went to the Jesuit Church of Farm Street in London as a curate. He published three popular books of devotion, *Nova et Vetera* (1897), *Hard Sayings* (1898), and *On External Religion* (1899). His thought then took on immanentist qualities because of the influence of F. von Hügel and his reading of Loisy, Blondel, Bergson, and other 19th-cent. French writers. His rebellion against scholasticism and the exterior formalism of Catholicism appeared in his article "The Relation of Theology and Devotion," and one month later in "A Perverted Devotion" in the *Weekly Register* (1899). He had the former article reprinted in 1907 and insisted it was the matrix of his thought. It was concerned with keeping the immanent apprehension of the divinity from being overwhelmed by the structure of belief and external forms. These articles led to his removal from Farm Street and to retirement. He wrote *Oil and Wine* (1900), but it was held up by his superiors for 2 years before it was published. His *The Faith of Millions* appeared in 1901 and the *Lex Orandi* in 1903. He published *A Much Abused Letter* (1906), which resulted in his being suspended by the Jesuits, but he continued to write. *Lex Credendi* appeared in 1906, *Through Scylla and Charybdis* in 1907, and two letters of protest against the encyclical *Pascendi*, which resulted in his excommunication in 1907. His two last works were *Medievalism* (1908), an attack on the neo-Thomist revival, and *Christianity at the Cross-Roads*, published posthumously in 1909. Tyrrell was a brilliant speaker and writer with a large following. He was devoted to Christian spirituality but his belief in the immanentist philosophies of 19th-cent. France put him outside the structure of traditional Catholicism. He felt finally that Christianity was the beginning of a major world religion but did not of itself contain all that was necessary to be universal. He died with the last rites of the RC Church, but Henri Bremond, the French spiritual writer, was suspended for conducting T.'s funeral (Ratté, 167). See A. Vidler, *Modernist Movement in the Roman Catholic Church* (1934); J. Ratté, *Three Modernists* (1967).

U

UBERTINO OF CASALE (1259–*c*.1330), a leader of the Franciscan *Spirituals. U. was born at Casale in the Diocese of Vercelli and entered the Franciscan Order in 1272. After 9 years of study and lecturing at Paris, he returned to Italy and engaged in an effective preaching apostolate, during which he came in contact with John of Parma, Peter John Olivi, and other ardent Spirituals. He espoused their cause and became leader of the movement in Tuscany. His most important writing, *Arbor vitae crucifixae* (1305), mercilessly castigated high-living prelates and lax friars. Its argumentative style and *Joachimism caused U. to be accused of spreading heresy and promoting schism within the order. He took a prominent part in the acrimonious debate on Franciscan poverty between 1309 and 1322. Because of U.'s intransigence, John XXII ordered him to transfer to the Benedictines. When another charge of heresy was lodged against him in 1325, he fled Avignon. The remainder of his life is shrouded in mystery. See D. Douie, *Nature and Effects of the Heresy of the Fraticelli* (1932); E. G. Salter, "Ubertino da Casale," *Franciscan Essays* I (ed. A. G. Little, 1912), 108–123. *POVERTY CONTROVERSY.

UBIQUITARIANISM (Lat. *ubique*, everywhere), a designation for the teaching that the body of Christ shares in the divine omnipresence. Such a position was held earlier, e.g., by John Scotus Erigena, Amalric of Bène, William of Ockam, but it is particularly associated with early Lutheranism. Martin Luther taught such a doctrine in refutation of *Sacramentarian denial of the possibility of the *Real Presence (*Confession Concerning the Lord's Supper*, 1528). The *Formula of Concord makes the same point (Art. VII). Luther did not, however, base his affirmation of the Real Presence on the ubiquity or omnipresence of Christ. Johann Brenz (1499–1570), who espoused an absolute omnipresence, was opposed by Martin Chemnitz (1522–86), who held for a simple multipresence of Christ, effected by his will, as in the Eucharist. In some form, ubiquitarianism remained a part of Lutheran orthodoxy up to the 18th century.

ULTRAMONTANES (Lat. *ultra*, beyond, *montes*, mountains), advocates of strong papal authority. The term reflects the location of Rome as viewed from France, Germany, and England. Ultramontanes were those who opposed *Gallicanism, *Febronianism, *Josephinism, and also who defended the pope against 19th-cent. attacks in Italy on the temporal power of the papacy. The term was frequently used in reference to champions of papal infallibility at *Vatican Council I.

UNA SANCTA MOVEMENT, name given to the ecumenical efforts of reconciliation in Germany of both Roman Catholics and Lutherans. These efforts began after World War I, but were based on earlier attempts since the Reformation times. The term was taken from the Nicene Creed (*"Credo in . . . unam sanctam . . . ecclesiam"*) to indicate the desire for reunification. Pioneering attempts began in 1918 with the founding of the Protestant high-church movement (*Hochkirchliche Vereinigung*) by the Berlin pastors Friedrich Heiler and F. Seigmund-Schultze. But it was Max Joseph Metzger (1887–1944) who in his Una Sancta Brotherhood (1928) unified scattered Catholic-Protestant study groups concerned with reunion. Dialogues spread to similar movements, such as the *Berneuchen Circle and the Michaelsbruderschaft. Suppressed by the Nazis (who executed Metzger), the movement reflourished after World War II, gaining popularity under the leadership of Matthias Laros, a Catholic pastor from the Rhineland. After his death (1965) the Benedictine Abbey of Niederaltaich became the center; there its journal *Una Sancta* (formerly *Rundbriefe*, founded 1946) had been edited (1953–63) by Thomas Sartory and A. Ahlbrecht (1963–   ). The forces inspiring the movement are a new appraisal of Luther research both by Protestants and Catholics (e.g., Josef Lortz, *Die Reformation in Deutschland*, 1939–40), the liturgical movement, a scriptural renaissance, and increasing lay participation in the RC Church; the Nazi persecution of all Christians and the effects of the war, which uprooted people and brought them into closer physical contact, strengthened the movement. Una Sancta has found expression in various forms of dialogue, study groups, theological institutes, conferences, and printed media. The Una Sancta efforts were not always viewed favorably by the RC Church, e.g., the encyclical *Mortalium animos, 1928, and there were periods of restrictions and mistrust until the 1950s, when official sponsorship by Lorenz Jäger, Abp. of Paderborn, and the participation of prominent theologians (Hugo Rahner, Heinrich Fries, Otto Karrer, and the Lutheran Hans Asmussen) brought it new momentum, later increased by the ecumenical sentiments of Vatican Council II. See S. J. T. Miller, NCE 14:381–382; J. Höfer, LTK 10:463–466; J. Lell, RGG 6:1117–19; L. J. Swidler, *Ecumenical Vanguard: The History of the Una Sancta Movement* (1966).

UNDERGROUND CHURCH, a movement to create a new form of ecclesial community in place of the *institutional Church. The term "underground," to which some participants object, connotes that the views and practices of groups involved in the movement are at odds with established structures, laws, conventions, and that, consequently, the existence and meetings of such groups are kept secret from ecclesiastical authorities. Participants share generally in the conviction that only by revolution, not simple, gradual adaptation within existing patterns, can there be a Church genuinely relevant to actual human

conditions. Among Roman Catholics the underground movement appeared first as the expression of a desire for free liturgical experimentation. While spontaneous liturgical celebration, often at variance with church law, continues to be a mark of underground groups, their objectives have widened into an intense social concern, a desire to discard the parish system, and to change or bypass the basic authority structure of the Church. Among Protestants the underground movement is equally strong and has similar goals. Protestant underground groups have often been motivated by ecumenical and social interests contrary to policies of their denominations. There is in fact little reason to differentiate sectors of the underground movement on any denominational basis. Participants are united in an essential humanism and minimize doctrinal differences separating Christian from Christian, or even Christian from atheist. See M. Boyd, ed., *Underground Church* (1968). *FLOATING PARISH.

UNIFORMITY, ACTS OF, see ACTS OF UNIFORMITY.

UNIGENITUS, a bull (Sept. 8, 1713), elicited from Clement XI on the insistence of Louis XIV, after thorough examination renewing the condemnation of P. *Quesnel's *Réflexions morales*, which had already been placed on the Index in 1708. The *Unigenitus* cited as errors 101 propositions quoted verbatim (D 2400–2502). Quesnel taught that: (1) man's will necessarily obeys whichever attracts more strongly, concupiscence or grace; (2) all acts not motivated by pure charity are evil; and (3) the Church errs in condemning *Jansenism. Almost all French bishops accepted *Unigenitus*; a few refused or hedged. The Sorbonne and Parlement submitted; the Jansenists replied with contention and intrigue. Ensuing controversies split the French Church, fostered irreligion, and engendered revolution. See J. Carreyre, DTC 15.2:2061–2162; J. Thomas, *La Querelle de l'Unigenitus* (1949).

UNION AMERICAN METHODIST EPIS-COPAL CHURCH, a body with origins in one of the earliest independent U.S. Negro Methodist denominations. The Union Church of Africans was organized by Peter Spencer in 1813 at Wilmington, Del., as the culmination of a split (begun in 1805) from the predominantly white Asbury Methodist Episcopal Church. Members of the Negro Church desirous of an episcopal polity formed the Union American Methodist Episcopal Church in 1850; other members formed what is now the African Union First Colored Methodist Protestant Church, Inc. See HistAmMeth 3:595.

UNION CHURCH, a type of *community Church that begins with the merging of two (or more) existing congregations or with the organizing of a new Church on a non-denominational basis. It usually has no other affiliations and is strictly independent. Made up of people from diverse religious backgrounds, union Churches vary widely with respect to liturgy, theological complexion, and type of ministry. This kind of Church is common, but it is almost impossible to obtain statistics regarding the number of Churches and their members. When they are listed or discussed, they are usually subsumed under the categories "community" or "independent." *INDEPENDENT CHURCHES.

UNION OF UTRECHT, the alliance of Old Catholic Churches adhering to the Convention of Utrecht. Abp. Heykamp of Utrecht summoned and chaired the Utrecht conference of 1889. It included the Old Catholic bps. and theologians from Holland, Germany, and Switzerland. Reaching complete harmony, the conference issued the Convention (Agreement) of Utrecht to effect a union of Old Catholic Churches, according to this plan: First, an assembly of bps. was established for mutual consultation, the abp. of Utrecht being chairman as *primus inter pares*; each Church is independent and regulates its own affairs according to its need; no bp. may consecrate anyone without the consent of all the bps. and without acceptance of the Convention of Utrecht by the candidate. Second, an International Old Catholic Congress was scheduled every 2 years. Third, the bps. issued the Declaration of *Utrecht containing doctrinal principles binding on Old Catholic bps. and priests; an Old Catholic is one who accepts this declaration. The conference's decisions were later accepted by the Old Catholic Church in Austria. The union was joined (1897) by Bp. A. S. Kozlowski's short-lived Polish Old Catholic Church (in the U.S.) and later by the Polish National Catholic Church. In 1908 the Old Catholic Mission in Great Britain entered, but it soon was expelled by the assembly of bps. because Bp. Mathew broke the Convention of Utrecht. The Union admitted the *Mariavites of Poland (1909) but dropped them (1925) because of the abp.'s views. Other members are the Old Catholic Church of Czechoslovakia, the Old Catholic Church of Yugoslavia, and the Polish National Catholic Church of Poland, all of which have suffered adversity since World War II. At the Old Catholic Congress in 1965 the Philippine Independent Church was accepted by other member Churches into membership in the Union of Utrecht. See U. Küry, *Die Altkatholische Kirche* (1966); C. B. Moss, *Old Catholic Movement* (1966).

UNION OF WELSH INDEPENDENTS, a fellowship of some 800 Welsh-speaking Congregational Churches with about 100,-000 members. The first Church was formed in 1639. County groupings were gradually formed, and meetings were held. The Union was not formed until 1871. It has remained a very loose federation with a minimal central organization and only one full-time official. There is, however, a strong sense of national unity. Proposals toward union with other Churches in Wales were entertained recently, but independence is strongly cherished. English-speaking Welsh Congregational Churches belong to the Congregational Church in England and Wales.

UNIONISM, in its religious usage a disparaging term with several applications. (1) The amalgamation of Lutheran and *Reformed Churches first decreed in 1817 by Friedrich Wilhelm I, King of Prussia, but not accomplished until 1833. In this policy he was advised by F. *Schleiermacher. The stanchly confessional Lutherans termed the policy unionism, criticizing its adulteration of historic confessionalism. (2) The attempt in the 19th cent. to develop an "American Lutheranism," led by S. *Schmucker and aimed at closer fellowship with the Protestants, but at the expense of fidelity to the *Augsburg Confession, was denounced by opponents as unionism. As a consequence Lutheran Churches in the U.S. increasingly emphasized their proper confessional heritage. (3) In a more general sense, unionism has been used to criticize attempts at interdenominational and ecumenical cooperative efforts that disregard or dismiss doctrinal differences. *IRENICISM; *SYNCRETISM; *ECUMENISM.

UNISTS, an alternate name for the Subunists, i.e., those in 15th-cent. Bohemia defending the practice of communion under one kind, in opposition to the *Utraquists, who insisted on communion under both kinds. *HUSSITES.

UNITARIAN UNIVERSALIST ASSOCIATION, a religious denomination of liberal persuasion, with churches in the U.S. and Canada. The denomination is the result of a merger, in 1961, of the American Unitarian Association (founded in 1825; incorporated in 1847) and the Universalist Church of America (initial organizational form, 1779; incorporated in 1866). The two denominations shared common concerns during the 19th cent., yet they remained separate. They drew closer together during the first half of the 20th cent., and the formation, in 1953, of a Council of Liberal Churches (Unitarian Universalist) enlarged departmental cooperation during the decade when full merger was being considered. The merged denomination continues significant traditions that were held in common by the parent movements, such as congregational polity; a programmatic creedlessness; strong social and ethical concerns; the cherishing of freedom of religious belief in a disciplined quest for truth; a deep respect for human dignity (expressed in an early rejection of the doctrine of *total depravity); a strictly humanitarian Christology; acceptance of theists, religious humanists, and agnostics in religious fellowship; and a striving for a worldwide, interfaith, religious community. The creedless character of the denomination distinguishes it from many other religious movements. Individual churches or fellowships may have covenants or bonds of union, as long as these statements are not used as creedal tests. The association of autonomous churches and fellowships is governed by a president, a board of trustees, and a general assembly. The constituency, which contains a high proportion of members who have come from other denominations, included, in 1968, a total of 274,325 persons affiliated, 892 ministers in fellowship, 686 churches, and 449 fellowships. The Unitarian Universalist Association is a member of the *International Association for Liberal Christianity and Religious Freedom (IARF); it is a member of neither the National, nor the World, Council of Churches. *UNITARIANISM; *UNIVERSALISM.

UNITARIANISM, as a theological classification, any belief that affirms the one God but rejects the Trinity of persons. Historically, Unitarians have, on biblical and rational grounds, rejected the doctrines of the Trinity, the divinity of Christ, and the *total depravity of man. Unitarianism does not have a creed. In mid-20th cent., it embraces such differing views as Christian liberalism, naturalistic theism, existentialism, and a concern for the development of a scientific theology. Contemporary Unitarians cherish as prime religious responsibilities the critical examination of religious beliefs and the relevant expression of these beliefs in areas of social responsibility.

In the Reformation era, Juan de *Valdés (*c.*1500–41), Bernardino *Ochino (1487–1564), and Michael *Servetus (1511–53) influenced the rise of historic Unitarianism. It developed indigenously in Poland, Transylvania, England, and the United States. The movement no longer exists in Poland, but it has had a continuing history in each of the other three countries. In Poland, an incipient division in the *Reformed Church was furthered by Italian evangelical rationalists, who came to Poland via Switzerland. After the failure of a conference to reconcile the division, those who were excluded because of their antitrinitarian views formed the Minor Reformed Church of Poland in 1565. Faustus *Socinus (1539–1604) came to Poland in 1579 and was thereafter recognized as the leader of the movement; the Polish and Lithuanian antitrinitarians adopted the name Socinians. After his death, Socinus's followers published the influential *Racovian Catechism (Polish ed., 1605; Latin ed., 1609). Mounting RC opposition to the movement led to the destruction of the Socinian school and printing press at Raków in 1638 and the complete expulsion of Socinianism from Poland by 1660 (see SOCINIANISM). Transylvanian Unitarianism also arose as a division within the Reformed Church when Francis *Dávid (1510–79) began questioning the biblical bases of the doctrine of the Trinity. *The True and False Knowledge of God*, published by Dávid and Giorgio *Blandrata, showed the influence of Servetus's writings in Transylvania. The decree of the Diet of Torda (1568) ensured religious toleration for the Unitarians, and King John Sigismund granted them legal recognition in 1571. Dávid's increasing rejection of the invocation of Christ in prayer, however, threatened to introduce an illegal "innovation," which could have caused the Unitarian movement to be deprived of legal recognition. Hence, Dávid was sentenced and died in prison. After centuries of severe persecution, Unitarianism still exists in Hungary and Romania. The four hundredth anniversary was celebrated in 1968 in Koloszvár (Cluj) and in Budapest.

Unitarianism was first maintained in England by John *Biddle (1615–62) in *XII Arguments Drawn out of the Scripture* (1647) and *A Twofold Catechism* (1654). Unitarians were excluded from the provisions of the *Toleration Act (1689) and were subject to legal penalties until 1813. Samuel *Clarke (1675–1729) and William Whiston (1667–1752) advocated an "Arian" view of Christ as a subordinate being. Theophilus *Lindsey (1723–1808) left the Anglican ministry to affirm a belief in the strict humanity of Christ. He established the first Unitarian chapel in London in 1774. The influence of Joseph *Priestley (1733–1804) and the leadership of Thomas Belsham (1750–1829) marked the ascendancy of a stress on Christ's strict humanity. The British and Foreign Unitarian Association was organized in 1825. James Martineau (1805–1900) was probably the most creative English Unitarian theologian of the 19th century. In 1926, the British and Foreign Unitarian Association merged into the General Assembly of Unitarian and Free Christian Churches.

American Unitarianism arose within New England Congregationalism as a result of the influences of *Arminianism and *antitrinitarianism. Sharp controversy developed in 1805, when Henry Ware, a liberal, became Hollis Professor of Divinity at Harvard. William Ellery *Channing (1780–1842) defended the liberals in 1815 and gave them a clear theological platform in his famous "Baltimore Sermon" of 1819. The American Unitarian Association was founded in 1825. Ralph Waldo *Emerson (1803–82) and Theodore *Parker (1810–60) introduced insights from *transcendentalists into Unitarianism and, by this influence, ensured that Unitarianism, while including a Christian orientation, cannot be limited to that alone. In the 20th cent. the rise of religious humanism has significantly modified the movement. After a period of decline, the American Unitarian Association grew under the presidencies of Frederick May Eliot and Dana McLean Greeley. A "Council of Liberal Churches (Unitarian Universalist)" was formed in 1953 to enlarge departmental cooperation between Unitarians and Universalists. A merger in 1961 resulted in the *Unitarian Universalist Association. See *Bibliotheca Fratrum Polonorum qui Unitarii Appellantur...* (8v., 1656); E. M. Wilbur, *History of Unitarianism* (2v., repr., 1965); *idem, Our Unitarian Heritage* (1953); G. H. Williams, *Radical Reformation* (1962); C. Wright, *Beginnings of Unitarianism in America* (1955); *Transactions of the Unitarian Historical Society* (1916–); *Proceedings of the Unitarian Historical Society* (1925–).

UNITAS ASSOCIATION, an international organization formed in Rome in 1945, under RC auspices, to promote spiritual unity among Christians. The organization was founded by Charles Boyer, a French Jesuit, who became its first president. In spirit the Association is related to the earlier spiritual ecumenism of Abbé Couturier in France and Lewis Thomas *Wattson of the Atonement Friars in the U.S., the two men whose separate apostolates led to the establishment of the annual *Church Unity Octave, or *Week of Prayer for Christian Unity. The Association, which has affiliated groups in European countries and in Canada, sees its work as threefold: promotion of prayer for Christian unity; fostering of fraternal rapprochement between Christians of the East and the West; and exposition of the meaning of Catholicism to Protestants. Through its quarterly review, *Unitas*, published in English, French, and Italian editions, it circulates information about all aspects of the ecumenical movement.

UNITAS FRATRUM (Unity of Brethren), original name of the Bohemian Brethren, organized in 1457. Before formal organization, members used the name Fratres Legis Christi (Brethren of the Law of Christ), but to avoid being thought of as a new monastic order they changed it to simply Brethren. When organization had finally been effected, they assumed the name Unitas

Fratrum, or in Czech, Jednota Bratrská. When the almost extinct Brethren became the Moravian Church through its renewal under Count *Zinzendorf, the name Unitas Fratrum was retained; it continues as the official designation of the denomination. See E. de Schweinitz, *History of the Unitas Fratrum* (1885). *MORAVIAN CHURCH.

UNITATIS REDINTEGRATIO, see DECREE ON ECUMENISM.

UNITED BAPTISTS, a body originating in cooperative meetings between *Regular Baptists and *Separate Baptists of Ky. and Va. that began in 1787. Organized as a separate denomination (Va., 1794; Ky., 1804), the larger portion of the membership merged with the northern and southern conventions of Baptists; the minority constitutes the United Baptists, in 32 *associations. Some teach *Arminianism, others *Calvinism; some practice open, others *closed, communion; most observe baptism, the Lord's Supper, and *footwashing as *ordinances.

UNITED BIBLE SOCIETIES (UBS), an international association established at a meeting in Elfinsward, Eng., in 1946, for cooperation among the more than 20 major national *Bible societies. Earlier coordination of work by such agencies as the *American Bible Society and the *British and Foreign Bible Society led naturally to its formation. Offices are in London and Geneva.

UNITED BRETHREN IN CHRIST, a denomination that came into existence at York, Pa., in 1889 as a result of a secession from the parent Church of the United Brethren in Christ, when the latter's General Conference approved a new and enlarged confession of faith and constitution. The dissident minority protested the replacement of the constitution of 1841, which had condemned membership in secret societies, and designates itself "Old Constitution." In 1968 the Church comprised 304 congregations; headquarters are in Huntington, Indiana. *EVANGELICAL UNITED BRETHREN CHURCH.

UNITED CHRISTIAN CHURCH, a body consisting of 600 members located in 12 congregations served by 8 pastors, organized at Campbelltown, Pa., in 1878 as a result of an earlier secession from the Church of the United Brethren in Christ (see EVANGELICAL UNITED BRETHREN CHURCH). In recent years this denomination, centered in Lebanon Co., Pa., has continued the customs of *footwashing and wearing of the prayer-veil by women.

UNITED CHURCH OF CANADA (UCC), Church formed by the union (1925) of the Congregational, Methodist, and Presbyterian Churches. The history of the Church chronicles a continual effort to reverse the process of fragmentation besetting the Christian community. Each of its founding communions was itself a product of reunion. The early Presbyterianism of British North America consisted of more than a dozen independent groupings, divided by national origin into Scottish, Irish, and Dutch, by differences in *polity into *free Churches and national Churches, and by a basically political dispute into *Burghers and *Anti-Burghers. To all this was added the natural divisions of geography. Canadian Methodism was likewise greatly fragmented, the major cause being the cleavage between those congregations founded by the American *Methodist Episcopal Church and those which gave their allegiance to the nonepiscopal, Wesleyan fellowships in England. By and large the divisions within Canadian Congregationalism were geographical. The challenge to achieve effective ministry in a vast new land succeeded in reducing this multitude to essentially three major groupings through the formation of the Presbyterian Church in Canada (1875), the Methodist

Church (1884), and the Congregational Union of Canada (1906).

A desire for yet greater unity had resulted in sporadic calls for interconfessional union as early as 1874, but official negotiations did not actually begin until 30 years later. By 1908, however, a Basis of Union had been agreed upon, setting forth the doctrine and polity of the proposed Church. That very year, individual congregations of the three communions, particularly in western Canada, began to effect local amalgamations on this Basis of Union and in anticipation of the united Church to come. Some 3,000 such local unions preceded the formal merging of the mother Churches. The final consummation was delayed by the outbreak of World War I and was not achieved until June 1925. Although a substantial number of Presbyterians remain separated, the merger nevertheless represented the first major union of differing traditions within Protestantism and, as such, was a significant event in the ecumenical movement. Since 1925 several additional Protestant communions have joined the UCC, the Evangelical United Brethren being the latest (1968). Intensive negotiations aimed at a 1970 completion of a plan of union are underway with the Anglican Church of Canada.

The thought and life of the UCC reflect its history with its fundamental doctrine (as set forth in the 20 articles of the Basis of Union) presenting the essence of a faith common to all Reformation communions. The Bible is acknowledged as the supreme authority, but tradition is also recognized, specifically in the "great creeds of the ancient Church" and in the confessions of the *Reformed Churches. A careful balance is observed between the Presbyterians' Calvinist heritage and the *Arminianism of John *Wesley. Moreover, the Presbyterian emphasis upon loyalty to the doctrine of the Church is united with the Congregational insistence upon the individual's freedom in matters of faith. Candidates for ordination are required only to be "in essential agreement" with the stated doctrine.

Worship in the UCC is marked by the Reformation emphasis on the reading and exposition of the word of God. The regular service is composed of hymns, prayer, Scripture, and a meditation but does not routinely involve the celebration of the Lord's Supper. A deepening interest in liturgy is apparent, yet there still remains the Protestant concern for simplicity in worship. Although freedom in prayer and in the selection of Scripture is still the custom, the *Book of Common Order, adopted by the Church in 1932 as a guide for the conduct of worship, usually sets the pattern in most congregations. It is closely followed for the sacraments and special services of the Church.

The UCC recognizes only two sacraments, baptism and the Lord's Supper, or holy communion. *Infant baptism is the normal practice and is usually administered as a congregational rite at the regular Sunday morning service. The sacrament of holy communion is dispensed a minimum of four times per year and is understood more as a eucharistic and fellowship meal than as a sacrifice, although the latter theme is also expressed in the liturgy. Marriage, confirmation, and ordination are recognized as rites of the Church but, in keeping with Reformation theology, are not regarded as sacraments.

The polity of the UCC is a synthesis of elements from its threefold heritage. Authority, as in each of the founding communions, is invested in a hierarchy of *courts rather than a hierarchy of persons. (All ministers have the same rank and differ only in office.) From Congregationalism comes the recognition of the whole congregation as the supreme local authority rather than the *session or *elders as in Presbyterianism. This authority is also greater in relation to the higher courts than in the Calvinist tradition. The next court, the *presbytery, consists of some 25 to 50 pastoral charges and is responsible for the general supervision of church life. The *Conference, composed of perhaps 10 presbyteries, comes from the Methodist tradition. It meets annually and is responsible

for the placement of ministers and for the examination and ordination of candidates for the ministry. Its exercise of the former function again reflects its complex heritage. Congregations retain the right to call a minister, as in Congregational and Presbyterian practice, but the authority to confirm such appointments rests with the "settlement" committee of the Conference, thereby continuing the tradition of the Methodist "stationing" committee. The settlement committee is charged, wherever possible, to respect the wishes of ministers and congregations. The supreme court of the Church is the General Council, presided over by a moderator, who acts as titular head of the Church for the 2-year period between sessions of the Council. It alone has the authority to legislate on matters of faith and discipline. All courts, other than the congregation, have equal numbers of clergy and laity. Laymen may assume any office in the Church with the exception of Conference president, since the latter serves as the ordaining officer of the Conference. All offices of the Church, including the ministry, are open to women as well as men. The UCC is a member of the World Council of Churches and of the World Methodist Council, the Alliance of Reformed Churches, and the International Congregational Council. See G. C. Pidgeon, *United Church of Canada* (1949); G. W. Mason, *Legislative Struggle for Church Union* (1956); J. W. Grant, *Canadian Experience of Union* (1967).

UNITED CHURCH OF CHRIST, denomination formed in June 1957, through the union between the General Council of Congregational Christian Churches and the *Evangelical and Reformed Churches. The United Church of Christ (UCC) has significance in the ecumenical movement in that it combines two forms of polity: *Congregationalism and *Presbyterianism. It also reflects the noncreedal position that was part of the history of the two merging bodies. First steps toward union were taken in 1941; by 1944 a Basis of Union had been prepared. After the plan had been circulated within each body and independently accepted (with some resistance), a joint meeting in Cleveland, Ohio, in 1957 accomplished the union. In 1959 a *Statement of Faith was formulated at Oberlin, Ohio. Agreement was still needed on a constitution; this was reached at Philadelphia, Pa., 1961, when permanent officials also were elected. Membership in 1968 was 2,063,481, in 6,945 churches. The UCC is a member of the World and National Council of Churches, as well as the International Congregational Council and the World Alliance of Reformed Churches. Unity efforts of the Church continue by participation in the *Consultation on Church Union and through discussions with the Christian Churches (Disciples of Christ) and the *Community Churches.

The Statement of Faith represents an affirmation of agreement in broad areas of Christian teaching; it cannot be imposed as a *doctrinal standard or for subscription by local congregations or individuals. Its standing in the Church conforms to the noncreedal tradition of the Congregational, Christian, and Evangelical and Reformed Churches. Baptism and the Lord's Supper are accepted as sacraments; ordination is the setting aside by prayer and the laying on of hands for ministry in the whole Church. The autonomy of the *local church stands as a cardinal and inviolable principle. Doctrine, worship, and participation in the connectional life of the whole Church rest with the local congregation. This connectional life is maintained through associations of local churches in a region; through conferences uniting associations; and through a general synod of the whole Church, meeting biennially. The general synod, presided over by a moderator, establishes what are called "instrumentalities" of the Church, i.e., agencies for foreign and home missions, education, welfare, social action, and ecumenism. There is an executive council appointed by the general synod for current affairs of the Church. See D. Horton, *United Church of Christ: Its Origins, Organization and Role in the World Today* (1962). *CONGREGATIONAL CHRISTIAN CHURCHES, NATIONAL ASSOCIATION OF.

UNITED EVANGELICAL LUTHERAN CHURCH, one of the American Lutheran bodies that merged in 1960 to form the *American Lutheran Church. Before 1946 it had been called the United Danish Evangelical Lutheran Church; it had been organized at Minneapolis, Minn., in 1896 by the merger of several churches made up of Danish immigrants in the Midwest subscribing to the same confessions as the Lutheran Church of Denmark. The Church went through a process of Americanization, esp. after World War I; most of the members were of Danish descent. Growth was mainly in Wisconsin, Iowa, and California. At the time of the 1960 merger there were about 70,000 members in 182 congregations. See P. Nyholm, EncLuthCh 1:56–59.

UNITED FREE CHURCH, in Scotland the union of 1900 between the United Presbyterian Church and the Free Church, which, though not acceptable to a dissident minority (the "Wee Frees"), brought together the two largest Presbyterian bodies in Scotland outside the established Church. The new United Free Church was marked by its stress on the independence and exclusive jurisdiction of the Church in its own affairs, and its freedom to change or modify its constitution and subordinate standards. In October 1929 this Church was united with the Church of Scotland to make a *national Church, Presbyterian in government and broadly representative of the Christian faith of the Scottish people. See bibliog. for Church of Scotland.

UNITED FREE WILL BAPTIST CHURCH, a Negro fellowship of *Free Will Baptists, organized officially in 1901. With a membership of some 75,000 in 350 churches, these Baptists are to be found in greatest number in N.C., Ga., Fla., Miss., La., and Texas. Congregational polity is maintained, but emphasis is given to the decisions of the national body.

UNITED HOLY CHURCH OF AMERICA, INC.,

a Negro Pentecostal body, originating in 1886 as the Holy Church of North Carolina; its present organization and name were adopted in 1918. Headquarters are in Goldsboro, N.C., and membership in 1960 was 28,980.

UNITED HOUSE OF PRAYER FOR ALL PEOPLE,

a Pentecostal cult organized by Bp. Charles Emmanuel Grace (Marcelino Manoel da Graça?) at West Wareham, Mass., in 1919. Until his death in 1960, "Sweet Daddy" Grace was the undisputed head and object of worship for a membership claimed to number 3 million in 14 states. Appealing mostly to unlettered, culturally deprived Negroes, the House of Prayer stresses charismatic elements of Pentecostalism; its meetings are highly emotional services. Grace was succeeded as bishop by Walter McCollough.

UNITED LUTHERAN CHURCH IN AMERICA,

largest of the four church bodies entering the merger that formed the *Lutheran Church in America in 1963. The United Lutheran Church (ULC) had been organized in 1918 by a merger of Lutheran synods (General Synod of the Evangelical Lutheran Church in the U.S.A. [1820], General Council of the Evangelical Lutheran Church in N.A. [1867], and United Synod of the Evangelical Lutheran Church in the South [1886]) that gave it a lineage back to the beginnings of Lutheran synodical organization in the U.S. under H. M. *Mühlenberg in 1748. The formation of the ULC in 1918 came after unity efforts culminated during the 400th anniversary of the Reformation. The ULC had a vital doctrinal and theological tradition and a dedication to ecumenism and to missions. Constituent synods were spread throughout the U.S.,

and there were a Carribean and an Icelandic Synod. At the time of the 1963 merger the ULC membership was nearly 2½ million. Franklin Clark *Fry, Lutheran and ecumenical leader, was its second president (1944–62). See D. A. Flesner, EncLuthCh 2:1375–79.

UNITED METHODIST CHURCH (England),

English Methodist body formed in 1907 by a union of the Methodist New Connexion, the Bible Christians, and the United Methodist Free Churches. In 1932 the denomination united with the Wesleyan Methodist Church and the Primitive Methodist Church to form the British Methodist Church. See W. J. Townsend, et al., *New History of Methodism* (1909), 1:485–552.

UNITED METHODIST CHURCH (U.S.),

the 1968 union of the Evangelical Brethren Church and the Methodist Church; it involved about eleven million members. Its basic ecclesiology is catholic, evangelical, and ecumenical: "The church is a community of all true believers under the Lordship of Christ. It is the redeemed and redeeming fellowship in which the Word of God is preached by men divinely called, and the Sacraments are duly administered according to Christ's own appointment. . . . The Church of Jesus Christ exists in and for the world" (*Constitution*, "Preamble"). Creedally the Church accepts the cardinal doctrines of historic Christianity, emphasizing the universality of the atonement and the freedom of every person through faith to enter the way of salvation. Its polity provides for connectional structures and an ordered ministry. Organization for mission is expressed through *conferences: general, jurisdictional, central, annual, and charge. Bishops, elders elected by jurisdictional and/or central conferences and consecrated to administer such structures, preside over annual, jurisdictional, central, and general conferences (*Plan of Union*, #51). Order for ministry is held to be derived from the ministry of Christ: "All Christians are called to ministry and theirs is a ministry of the people of God within the community of faith and in the world" (#301). But "there are persons, within the ministry of the baptized, who are called of God and set apart by the church for the specialized ministry of Word, Sacrament, and Order" (#302)—namely, deacons and elders (#307). The act of ordination includes prayers and the laying on of hands (#310); deacons are ordained by a bp., elders by a bp. assisted by other elders in the laying on of hands. Appointment of ministers to charges is done by the bp. after consultation with district superintendents (#59).

Christian practice stems from the tradition of an earnest and patient attempt to embody "the life of Christ" on earth. Understanding itself to be a part of the Church universal, the United Methodist Church has determined to implement the conviction that "all persons, without regard to race, color, national origin, or economic condition, shall be eligible to attend its worship services, to participate in its programs, and, when they take the appropriate vows, to be admitted to its membership in any local church in the connection. . . . No conference, or other organizational unit of the church shall be structured so as to exclude any member or any constituent body of the church because of race, color, national origin, or economic condition" (#4). To this same end the Church has amplified the Methodist Social Creed of 1908, which was a prophetic landmark in the enunciation of Christian conviction on economic issues, into a generous and sensitized concern for the material, as well as the spiritual, welfare of all people. Thus the teaching on ministry is ordered to mean practical servanthood in every phase of human life. See *Plan of Union of the Methodist Church and the Evangelical United Brethren Church* (1967); *Book of Discipline of the United Methodist Church* (1968).

UNITED METHODIST FREE CHURCHES, English Methodist denomination, formed at Exeter Hall, London, May 14, 1857, when the Wesleyan Methodist Association united with a group of reformers who had been expelled from the Wesleyan Methodist Church. Their expulsion was due to their active attempts to secure connectional and constitutional reform and greater lay participation in the Church. In 1907 the denomination joined with the Methodist New Connexion and the Bible Christians to form the United Methodist Church, and in 1932 this Church joined with the Wesleyan Methodist Church and the Primitive Methodist Church to form the British Methodist Church. See W. J. Townsend et al., *New History of Methodism* (1909).

UNITED MISSIONARY CHURCH, a body formally organized in 1883 as the Mennonite Brethren in Christ Church, by older Mennonite groups from Ohio, Ind., Pa., and Ontario. The present name was adopted in 1947, because early in its history the Church had adopted the doctrines of the *Holiness movement, and a Methodist form of polity, and had gradually ceased to be Mennonite in teaching or government, although *nonresistance and *nonconformity are continued. The beliefs emphasized are *entire sanctification, *divine healing, and *millenarianism. Annual *camp meetings are held. From the beginnings evangelistic and missionary work have been intense; there are missions in Africa, Asia, and Latin America. Membership in 1968 was 11,733, in 216 churches; headquarters are in Elkhart, Indiana. In 1947 the Pennsylvania Conference did not accept the new name or reorganization and withdrew, continuing as the Mennonite Brethen in Christ Church. See MennEnc 4:774–776.

UNITED PENTECOSTAL CHURCH, INC., the largest *Jesus Only (unitarian) Pentecostal body in the United States. This Church is a merger (1945) between the Pentecostal Assemblies of Jesus Christ and the Pentecostal Church, Inc., white Churches that had separated from the interracial Pentecostal Assemblies of the World, Inc. The United Pentecostal Church has a highly centralized system of government and is notably rigid regarding avoidance of amusement and worldly manners in dress. Headquarters are in St. Louis, Mo., with a membership in 1968 of more than 200,000. See J. T. Nichol, *Pentecostalism* (1966), 118–119.

UNITED PRESBYTERIAN CHURCH (Scotland), a Church formed in Scotland in 1847, when the Relief Church, a broadly evangelical body opposed to the practice of *covenanting and favoring *open communion, united with the larger United Secession Church, which remained loyal to the *Seceder Tradition and was more rigid in discipline. The new Church, predominantly urban, was almost as large and influential as the Free Church. By its *voluntaryism and general opposition to the establishment principle, the United Presbyterian Church brought into the 1900 union with the Free Church (see UNITED FREE CHURCH) a tradition of loyalty to civil and religious liberty, open communion, evangelical preaching, and missionary concern. See bibliog. for Church of Scotland.

UNITED PRESBYTERIAN CHURCH IN THE U.S.A., a denomination formed as a result of a union between the United Presbyterian Church of North America and the Presbyterian Church in the U.S.A. in 1958. The first, the smaller of the two bodies, was formed in 1858 by a union of two types of Scottish Presbyterianism, the Covenanters and the Free Church of Scotland, members of which had immigrated to America. While this denomination attempted to preserve such practices as *closed communion and Psalm singing, its Presbyterianism gradually became more and more American, making union with the larger body possible.

The older and larger body of Presbyterians, with predominantly English, Scottish, and Irish roots, along with some continen-

tal influence, was organized in its first *presbytery in 1706, its first synod in 1716, and in its *general assembly in 1789. The denomination has accepted under various subscription formulas the *Westminster Confession and Westminster Catechisms as *doctrinal standards, a Presbyterian form of government involving government by elders in representative *judicatories (beginning with the session of the local congregation), and the two sacraments of the Lord's Supper and baptism, including the baptism of infants. In worship, the denomination was influenced in the past by the Puritan and revivalistic traditions. By the mid-19th cent. the Church began to draw upon the richness of the *Reformed liturgical tradition, and since 1906 it has used a *Book of Common Worship. The work of the denomination between meetings of judicatories has been done by boards, which are now four in number and are known as the Board of Christian Education, the Board of Home Missions, the Commission on Ecumenical Mission and Relations, and the Board of Pensions. The executives of the denomination, including the *moderators and *stated clerks of the various judicatories, have a functional, not sacerdotal, status.

The Church is committed in its ecclesiology to the ecumenical movement. Its own history has been marked by division and then often by reunion, e.g., the "New Side" and "Old Side" (1741–58), the "New School" and "Old School" (1838–69), and the Cumberland division, partially healed in 1906. The "North" and "South" division of 1861 has not been healed (see PRESBYTERIAN CHURCH IN THE U.S.A.). The denomination has been a strong supporter of and a participant in the World Alliance of Reformed Churches, the International Missionary Council, the World Council of Churches, the Federal Council of Churches, and the National Council of Churches. In recent years it has engaged in conversations with Lutherans and Roman Catholics, and has been one of the leading promoters of the *Consultation on Church Union.

The United Presbyterian Church has been concerned with problems of the social order. Its members were deeply involved, e.g., in the movement for American independence, the antislavery cause, and the *Social Gospel, although Presbyterians have also been a strong conservative force in American life. Recently the denomination has stimulated discussion of Church-State relations, civil rights, the Vietnam war, and international affairs involving rich nations and poor nations of the world. After the union of the two denominations (1958), Presbyterians adopted a new confessional position in a Book of Confessions that still included the Westminster Confession and the *Confession of 1967. This new confession emphasizes God's reconciling work, man's ministry of reconciliation, and the fulfillment of reconciliation. In this Confession the Church deals with the implications of reconciliation for the problems of war, race, poverty, and sex in modern life. The most aggressive Presbyterian body in America, the United Presbyterian Church numbers about 9,000 congregations, 7,800 clergy with charges, and about 3,300,000 communing members. See L. Trinterud, *Forming of an American Tradition* (1949); L. Loetscher, *Broadening Church* (1954).

UNITED PRESBYTERIAN CHURCH IN THE U.S.A., CONFESSION OF 1967 OF, see CONFESSION OF 1967 (UNITED PRESBYTERIAN CHURCH IN THE U.S.A.

UNITED SECESSION CHURCH, in Scotland, a body formally organized in 1820, but which dated back to the Associate Presbytery, a secession in 1733 from the Church of Scotland in defense of the right of the congregation to appoint ministers. The United Secession Church and the Relief Church formed the *United Presbyterian Church in 1847. *SECEDER TRADITION.

UNITED SEVENTH DAY BRETHREN, a merger of two small *independent Churches in 1947. The Church teaches *premillenarianism and worships on Saturday. Membership (1968) was about 125 in four churches in Okla. and Nebraska.

UNITED SOCIETY FOR THE PROPAGATION OF THE GOSPEL, the name taken in 1965 when the *Society for the Propagation of the Gospel (SPG) united with the Universities' Mission to Central Africa.

UNITED SOCIETY OF BELIEVERS in Christ's Second Appearing, the official name adopted by the *Shakers.

UNITED STATES CONFERENCE FOR THE WORLD COUNCIL OF CHURCHES, see WORLD COUNCIL OF CHURCHES, UNITED STATES CONFERENCE FOR THE.

UNITED WESLEYAN METHODIST CHURCH OF AMERICA, a small Methodist denomination in the United States. It began as a single church organized in Brooklyn, N.Y., in 1905 for Methodists coming from the West Indies who wanted to continue the polity and customs of British Methodism. Several other churches were formed, and in 1927 the denomination was organized in New York City with four churches. In 1968 there were five churches, with about 500 members. Following the tradition of British Methodism, it is a nonepiscopal body, the chief officer being an elected president.

UNITED ZION CHURCH, originally known as United Zion's Children, formed as a Church in 1855 from a division in the Brethren in Christ Church. Matthias Brinser (1795–1889), a schoolmaster and preacher in the Brethren in Christ congregations in Dauphin Co., Pa., was the leader of a group who wanted to erect church buildings and in other ways be more like other Protestant Churches. A conflict resulted between Brinser's congregation and the rest of the Brethren in 1853–55 and led to the ouster of the "Brinsers," who then formed their own network of congregations in south-central Pennsylvania. The Church has not attempted to spread beyond its original centers, and the number of congregations in 1906 and 1963 was the same. In 1968 there were 17 churches, with 880 members. See A. W. Climenhaga, *History of the Brethren in Christ Church* (1942).

UNITY OCTAVE, ordinary way of referring to what is formally entitled the *Chair of Unity Octave, an annual period of prayer for Christian unity, Jan. 18–25, inaugurated by Lewis Thomas *Wattson. *WEEK OF PRAYER FOR CHRISTIAN UNITY.

UNITY OF THE BRETHREN, a denomination of some 30 congregations and 6,000 members, organized at Granger, Tex., in 1903 by Czech immigrants whose ancestors had belonged to the *Unitas Fratrum. In Europe the same people had more recently belonged to Lutheran and *Reformed Churches. Originally called the Evangelical Unity of Czech-Moravian Brethren of North America, the Church adopted the shorter name in 1959. The group tends to identify with the Presbyterian tradition, but because of a common *Hussite heritage is also in close fraternal relations with the *Moravian Church. Most of its ministers have studied either at Austin Presbyterian Theological Seminary or at Moravian Theological Seminary. See J. Barton, *Texas Brethren* (1949).

UNITY OF THE CHURCH, together with holiness, catholicity, and apostolicity, one of the attributes predicated of the Church in the Nicene Creed: "I believe in one holy catholic and apostolic Church." The Church is one because Christ is one. Therefore, she is "eager to maintain the unity of

the Spirit in the bond of peace. There is one body and one Spirit, just as you were called to the one hope that belongs to your call, one Lord, one faith, one baptism, one God and Father of us all, who is above all and through all and in all" (Eph 4.3–6). The threat of division or *schism in the Church is therefore countered with the rhetorical question "Is Christ divided?" (1 Cor 1.13.) If he is not, then neither should his Church be. Christ is not only the sign and the model of the unity of the Church; he is also its foundation and its source. Whatever other factors may be at work in the establishment and preservation of church unity, it is the common bond of allegiance to his lordship that is, in the Holy Spirit, the tie that binds Christians together within the fellowship of the Church. Yet the NT makes it clear that this allegiance is no simple emotion of personal loyalty but an obedience to a common body of truth as revealed in Christ. Both the narratives in the Acts of the Apostles and the exhortations in the epistles describe the unity of the Church as a unity in doctrine. The most nearly complete statement of Christian doctrine in the NT, the Epistle to the Romans, warns in its concluding paragraphs (Rom 16.17): "I appeal to you, brethren, to take note of those who create dissensions and difficulties, in opposition to the doctrine which you have been taught; avoid them." Unity in Christ is therefore unity in teaching. The term *heresy is used in the NT primarily for the party-spirit that creates divisions within the Church, but its specific application by the Fathers to the false teaching that has this effect is a logical development of this usage.

Unity in doctrine has as its corollary a unity in church life and structure. Christians of various traditions are not in agreement about the necessity and the proper form of such unity. Roman Catholicism maintains that the unity of the Church is both expressed and achieved through unity with the See of Peter, while both Eastern Orthodox and Protestant theologians assert that the Church is one even if it does not owe fealty to a single visible head. In some forms of Protestant ecclesiology this assertion has taken the form of the doctrine of the Church as essentially invisible; the evident disunity, error, and infidelity of the visible empirical Church do not vitiate the true unity, which can be seen only by faith (see INVISIBLE CHURCH). Even the RC position, moreover, is less monolithic than it appears to be; for it also postulates the existence of those who, while not externally affiliated with the Roman Catholic Church, are already one with it in faith, hope, and love. Thus the full scope of the Church's unity is, through baptism, wider than its institutional boundaries (see Vat II ConstCh 13–15). As the reference to baptism suggests, the sacraments occupy a special place in the theological understanding of unity. Baptism is the rite of initiation into the Church; therefore, it is also the source and the sign of its unity: "one Lord, one faith, one baptism." But it is esp. the Eucharist that functions as a force to unite believers. In the exposition of its meaning in 1 Cor, ch. 10–12, the Eucharist is seen as the most intimate and meaningful articulation of oneness in Christ. The relation of the Eucharist to church unity is, however, two-directional. For while it is theologically sound to describe the Eucharist as an activity that fosters true unity, there is also a measure of unity that must be present before Christians share in the Eucharist. The necessity of this is the reason for the anomalous situation arising esp. in ecumenical relations, that Christians may find themselves united in everything except the sacrament that is intended to unite them, which thus becomes a divisive force (see INTERCOMMUNION).

Counterbalancing this emphasis upon unity in doctrine and in structure is the recognition of the inevitable variety that is evident throughout the Church. From the very beginning there have been differences in forms of worship between various regions, due in part to linguistic peculiarities. Church structure likewise manifests both development and diversity, even when the unity of visible Christendom has been preserved. Nor is the area of doctrine a place where unity is tantamount to uniformity; already in the NT it is possible to speak of a Pauline theology or a Johannine theology, beneath and beyond the unity in the doctrine of the gospel. The relation between the unity of the Church and such diversities has become esp. important since the growth of the *ecumenical movement, which has compelled the Churches and their theologians to ask all the ecclesiological questions in a new way and with a new urgency. See A. C. Outler, *Christian Tradition and the Unity We Seek* (1957); R. Rouse and S. C. Neill, eds., *History of the Ecumenical Movement 1517–1948* (2d. ed., 1967); J. Pelikan, *Riddle of Roman Catholicism* (1959).

UNITY SCHOOL OF CHRISTIANITY, one of the largest and most influential of the *New Thought groups. It was founded by Charles and Myrtle (Page) *Fillmore in 1887 at Kansas City, Mo., although the Unity School of Practical Christianity, the local Kansas City center, was not chartered until 1903 and the Unity School of Christianity was incorporated only in 1914. During a residence in Pueblo, Colo., the Fillmores had come to know Emma Curtis Hopkins, who was also instrumental in the development of the *Church of Divine Science. They had long been building up an eclectic theology and had taken more than 40 courses from different New Thought centers. In 1889 the Fillmores began the magazine *Modern Thought,* which became *Unity* in 1891 and gave its name to their movement. Originally Unity teachings were offered to members of any or no denomination, without any effort to develop a membership or denominational organization. Its earliest function, Silent Unity, is a worldwide prayer movement, to which those in need may send a request for prayer. Through Silent Unity, a counseling service is also available to anyone who writes for help. Silent Unity has been particularly devoted to requests for healing. Unity has many close affinities to both Christian Science and the wider New Thought movement.

While accepting many of the doctrines

of traditional Christianity, Unity interprets them in its own way, harmonizing them with its commitment to reincarnation and the regeneration of the body by successive rebirths. God is thought of as impersonal Life, Mind, and Spirit. In the attribute of Mind is the meeting ground of God and man. God is immanent and is dwelling within his creatures. Unity teaches the doctrine of the Trinity, however, and the divinity of Jesus Christ, but also sees earlier incarnations of Jesus in the prophets and lawgivers of the OT. The significance of the Cross is the overcoming of mortal beliefs that hold us thrall to disease, sin, and death; salvation consists in the recognition of our sinlessness and incorruptibility. The promise of eternal life is seen as literal immortality. Both are attained by breaking out of the cycle of births and reaching the level where the true spiritual body replaces the physical body and man puts on Jesus Christ in a new life. Unity stresses the Bible and encourages its reading but often understands the text in an allegorical sense. As in Christian Science, health is considered the natural state of man, and healing is by affirming health in the body. Affirmation, rather than belief, is the means of developing Christ-consciousness in the individual, who is also counseled to strive for absolute sinlessness and to turn away from carnality. While not demanding compliance of its followers, Unity definitely discourages sexual intercourse, allowing the use of sex only for procreation, if at all, and urges abstention from meat, tobacco, drugs, and intoxicants as well. The emphasis in Unity is not negative, but on the positive influence of religion as a constant factor in daily life. The adoption of a creedal statement in 1921 and the opening of Unity Training School for ministers in 1930 indicated the beginning of Unity's development as a separate denomination, but its influence is much wider than its own local Unity Centers or their membership.

UNIVERSALISM, the doctrine affirming the ultimate salvation of all men (see APOCATASTASIS). This view has traditionally been grounded on a doctrine of God that stresses divine love and divine desire to bring all men to holiness and happiness. Modern Universalism, however, includes both theistic and nontheistic views. Clement of Alexandria, Origen, and John Scotus Erigena were earlier advocates of universalist doctrines. Universalism developed greater influence in the modern era. Gerrard *Winstanley, Samuel Richardson, and Jane Lead were early influential English writers. Both English and American Universalists were strongly influenced by John William Petersen, George Klein-Nicolai (pseudonym, Paul Siegvolck), John David Schaeffer, Christopher Schuetz, and Ferdinand Oliver Petitpierre. James Relly (1720–78) left George *Whitefield in 1750 to proclaim Universalism. Relly's treatise, *Union* (1759), argued thus: since all souls (not only the elect) were in an indissoluble union with Christ, Christ was thereby guilty of the sins of the race; Christ was punished, therefore there is no more punishment. John Murray (1741–1815), Relly's disciple, brought this theology from England to America in 1770. He became the pastor of a Universalist congregation in Gloucester, Mass., which dedicated its church in 1780. George de Benneville (1703–93) came in 1741 from Germany to Pa., where he gave personal leadership to a variety of groups that espoused universalist doctrines (e.g., Schwenkfelders, Quakers, mystics). Many persons in these groups had been influenced by Klein-Nicolai's *Everlasting Gospel,* Schuetz's *Golden Rose,* and Schaeffers's *Everlasting Gospel.* Charles *Chauncy, pastor of the First Congregationalist Church in Boston, published his influential *The Salvation of All Men* in 1784. Elhanan Winchester (1751–97) asserted the finite, future punishment of sinners and the eventual salvation of the race in his *Dialogues on the Universal Restoration* (1788). Hosea *Ballou became the most important leader of early American Universalism, primarily through his *A Treatise on Atonement* (1805), in which he asserted that the atonement was moral, not legal, in nature. As a determinist, Ballou denied that man can resist God's loving will to save all men. He explicitly rejected the doctrine of future punishments. In his treatise, Ballou also asserted that Christ was human, and not divine.

The early organizational pattern of American Universalism was the development of state or regional conventions. In 1803, the New England ministers met at Winchester, N.H., to adopt a general statement of agreement, the *Winchester Profession of Belief. The New England Convention went through several changes before it became the Universalist General Convention in 1866. In the interim some believers in future punishment temporarily seceded (1831–41) to form the Massachusetts Association of Universal Restorationists. In 1942 the name of the national movement was changed to the Universalist Church of America, which merged with the American Unitarian Association in 1961 to form the *Unitarian Universalist Association. Clarence Skinner (1881–1949) was the leading Universalist theologian in the 20th century. See R. Eddy, *Universalism in America* (2v., 1884–86); J. H. Allen and R. Eddy, *History of the Unitarians and Universalists in the United States* (American Church History Series, v.10, 1894).

UNIVERSALIST CHURCH OF AMERICA, see UNITARIAN UNIVERSALIST ASSOCIATION; UNIVERSALISM.

UPPSALA ASSEMBLY, fourth general assembly of the World Council of Churches (WCC), July 4–20, 1968, at Uppsala, Sweden. Its theme was "Behold, I make all things new"; in attendance were 701 delegates from 238 Churches. At this assembly, the emergence of a new emphasis on secularity and relevance brought conflict between the more theologically oriented conservatives and those who emphasized social ethics and Christian involvement in the strategies of economic development and revolution. The report of section I, "The Holy Spirit and the catholicity of the Church," was more conservative, but put emphasis on the quest for the unity of mankind. Such questions of current interest as the war in Vietnam and the population explosion occupied the delegates. The shift in interest from theology to secularity was indicated by several features: the slogan that the Church should let the world's agenda be its own; the presence of President Kaunda of Zambia, Negro novelist James Baldwin, and economist Barbara Ward as speakers, and the increasing importance of the youth delegates. RC participation became more pronounced as Roberto Tucci delivered a major address on relations between the RC Church and the WCC. Several RC theologians were accepted as full members of the Commission on Faith and Order.

URBAN CHURCH HISTORY, study of the impact that cities have made on the Christian Church and the influence the Church has had on cities. A highly specialized branch of the general field of urban history, it is of current interest because of the changing character of Western civilization. Whereas in 1800 approximately 5% of the population of Europe and the U.S. lived in cities, recent U.S. census figures indicate that 75% of Americans live in urban areas. If the present trend continues, it appears that by the year 2000 approximately 95% of the people of the Western world will live in cities.

Urban historians point out that the Church began as a movement among the people of the Roman cities and that it was an urban institution when it became the Empire's official religion. In subsequent centuries, however, the strongly rural character of western Europe left its mark on the Church, which, however, did not lose all urban characteristics. The rise of cities, the Renaissance, and much of the Reformation were urban influences. The Industrial Revolution found the Church still a predominantly rural institution, and much of the writing of urban church historians deals with its adjustment to an urbanized society. In the U.S. the pioneering work on urban church history is C. H. Hopkins, *The Rise of the Social Gospel in American Protestantism, 1865–1915* (1940). This was followed by A. I. Abell, *The Urban Impact on American Protestantism* (1943), and H. F. May, *Protestant Churches and Industrial America* (1949). Numerous publications in the general field of urban history touch on this subject, but a great deal of research is still needed on the specific question of the Church and the city.

URSINUS, ZACHARIAS (1543–85), Protestant theologian, a principal author of the *Heidelberg Catechism. He studied at Breslau and at Wittenberg (1550–57), where he formed close ties with P. *Melanchthon. After visiting Zurich and Geneva, where he met John *Calvin, he adopted Calvinist theology, esp. with regard to the Lord's Supper. In 1561 he was placed in charge of the Collegium Sapientiae at Heidelberg by the Elector of the Palatinate, Frederick III; and in 1562 he was given the chair of theology. At this time U. composed a *Summa theologiae* and a *Catechismus minor*, which served as preparations for his collaboration with C. *Olevianus on the Heidelberg Catechism. Against his own temperament, U. was continually drawn into controversy at Heidelberg; he had to defend both the Catechism and the *Reformed teaching officially adopted in the Palatinate, against the Lutherans. His proposals in *Monitum Ursini* (1568) for church discipline similar to that of Geneva earned him many enemies among his colleagues. After the death of Frederick and the closing of the Collegium Sapientiae (1577), U. taught at Neustadt-on-Hard (near Worms) in the Collegium Casimirianum. Here he wrote *De Libro concordiae, admonitio christiana* (1581), a Calvinist critique of the *Formula of Concord and *Book of Concord.

USAGERS, a party among *Nonjurors in the 18th-cent. C of E, which preferred certain "usages" from the first *Book of Common Prayer (1549) and other sources to the more Protestant BCP of 1552. Jeremy Collier (1650–1726) began a spirited series of tracts on the topic in 1717. The Usagers were accused of holding Romish views; among the usages in celebrating the Eucharist were the mixing of water with the sacramental wine; prayers of oblation; prayers for the dead; and prayers for the descent of the Holy Spirit upon the elements (Epiclesis).

UTRAQUISTS, the moderate party of the *Hussites. The name denotes their position that all must receive holy communion under the species of both bread and wine (Lat. *sub utraque specie*). The Utraquists were also called Calixtines (Lat. *calix*, chalice). They were not as anti-Roman doctrinally, or as extreme politically, as the *Taborites. The Utraquist practice was sanctioned by the *Compactata (1433) but was suppressed by the Edict of *Restitution (1629). See Bihlmeyer-Tüchle 2:441–444; bibliog. for Hussites.

UTRECHT, DECLARATION OF, see DECLARATION OF UTRECHT.

UTRECHT, SCHISM OF, see SCHISM OF UTRECHT.

UTRECHT, UNION OF, see UNION OF UTRECHT.

V

VALDÉS, JUAN DE (*c.*1495–1541), Spanish humanist and religious writer. Born in Castile, he studied at Alcalá. During his early years, the influence of Erasmus on him was strong, but his mature religious thought derived more from an indigenous Spanish Catholic piety. His *Dialogue on Christian Doctrine* (1529) and two works by his brother Alfonso incurred the hostility of the Spanish Inquisition because of their Erasmian tendencies, and he went to Italy. From 1531 until his death Juan remained there, first as chamberlain to Pope Clement VII, and after 1534 employed by Cardinal Ercole Gonzaga at Naples. During the latter period he wrote *The Christian Alphabet* as a spiritual guide for Giulia Gonzaga. In these last years he also wrote *One Hundred and Ten Considerations* and commentaries on the Psalms, Romans, Corinthians, and Matthew. While he never repudiated the RC Church or the seven sacraments, he did subordinate ceremony and forms to personal experience of sin and guilt, faith and repentance, and works of love as the fruits of the indwelling Holy Spirit. Through direct contacts V. exerted a profound influence on many prominent persons, and his fame became more widespread after the posthumous publication of his works. Most studies of V. are in languages other than English. An exception is E. Boehmer, *The Lives of Alfonso and Juan de Valdés* (1882). Easily accessible is an introduction to his life and thought, along with excerpts from three important works, in A. M. Mergal, ed., "Evangelical Catholicism as Represented by Juan de Valdés," *Spiritual and Anabaptist Writers* (ed. G. H. Williams, v.25, LibCC, 1957). See F. C. Church, *Italian Reformers, 1534–1564* (1932), 50–54.

VALLA, LORENZO (1407–57), Italian humanist. Educated in Rome and ordained in 1431, he taught eloquence at the Univ. of Pavia (1429–33), became secretary to King Alfonso V of Aragon and Sicily (1437), and eventually was made apostolic secretary to Pope Nicholas V (1448). He first achieved fame through two works: *De voluptate* (1431) and *Elegantiarum linguae latinae libri sex* (1444). The former, a set of three dialogues presenting Stoic, Epicurean, and Christian ethical values, often construed as representing Renaissance paganism, was an attempt to show that the true Christian life is pointed toward pleasure and happiness. The latter treatise reveals his interest in philology and linguistics and expresses the stock humanist disgust with the Latin of the Middle Ages. V. also attacked scholasticism, but rather ineptly. He launched Renaissance biblical scholarship with his *Adnotationes in Novum Testamentum* (edited by Erasmus, 1526), wherein he applied to the sacred texts the methods used for pagan authors. The *De libero arbitrio* (1493) was esteemed by Martin Luther. His famous *De falso credita et ementita Constantini donatione declamatio* (1440), begun under the auspices of King Alfonso, was a decisive attack on the validity of the document known as the Donation of Constantine, on which the Church largely based her claim to temporal power. This work also has been cited by historians as evidence of V.'s skepticism and his critical spirit. The work, which also challenged papal temporal power, was in reality an attempt to help Alfonso secure Naples. V. soon found himself before a tribunal composed of his enemies and was able to escape punishment only through his protector's intervention. While visiting Rome in 1446 he was again surrounded by enemies and forced to flee for his life. When Pope Nicholas V was elected, he forgave V. and made him apostolic secretary. V. has been regarded as a forerunner of the Reformation or even as a pure skeptic. RC scholars, however, regard his attempt at a synthesis of antiquity and Christianity, of theology and philology, as intended to serve the Catholic faith. See J.

Leuschner, RGG 6:1227–28; R. Montano, NCE 14:522–523, with bibliog.

VALOR ECCLESIASTICUS, the appraisal of all church properties and revenues in England made by royal commissioners in 1535. The legislation by which Henry VIII became (1534) supreme head of the Church in England made him recipient of a large portion of ecclesiastical and monastic revenues. The evaluation made proved a prelude to the *dissolution of the monasteries. These records, sometimes called the "King's Books," provided a survey of the ecclesiastical establishment of the time, which is valuable to the historian. They were published in 6 volumes, 1810–34, by the Records' Commissioners in England. See Hughes RE 1:282–283.

VAN RAALTE, ALBERTUS CHRISTIANUS (1811–76), principal founder and developer of the Dutch immigrant colony at Holland, Mich. in the mid-19th century. He joined others in 1834 in revolt against the repressive policies of the Netherlands government in its enforcement of a *state Church. Ordained in 1836 by the Free Reformed Church, in 1846 he led many to the U.S. as a haven from persecution. In 1850 V. represented the immigrant group in securing union with the Reformed Dutch Church of the eastern United States. His labors furnished a foundation for the whole western section of the *Reformed Church in America, largely through the establishment of Hope College (1851) and Western Theological Seminary (1866), both in Holland, Michigan. See life by A. Hyma (1947).

VARIATA, the edition of the *Augsburg Confession prepared by Philipp *Melanchthon in 1540. Because of differences from the earlier editions (1530 and 1531), this came to be disparaged by Lutherans as the Altered Augsburg Confession, and was disowned by the *Formula of Concord in distinction from the *Invariata, the unaltered. The *Variata* reflects Melanchthon's *synergism, and particularly in art. 10, a toning down of the Lutheran doctrine of the Real Presence in an attempt at concord with Zwinglian and Calvinistic eucharistic teaching. The *Invariata* is the edition accepted by Lutherans as their primary *confession of faith. *CRYPTO-CALVINISM; *GNESIOLUTHERANISM.

VATICAN COUNCILS. The great Renaissance edifice, St. Peter's basilica in Vatican City, was the theater for two modern councils of exceptional importance. Although they were nearly a century apart, there were certain similarities between them: both were called to address problems arising from a changed intellectual and social milieu in which the Church found itself; the number of conciliar fathers far surpassed the attendance at any previous council; Vatican Councils I and II were catholic in the sense that they drew a large proportion of their representatives from non-European countries; and each in its own way was primarily concerned with ecclesiological issues.

   Vatican Council I (1869–70). Between the solemn opening on Dec. 8, 1869, and the suspension of its activities on Sept. 1, 1870, the Council met in three other solemn sessions and 89 general congregations. Taking part in it were 774 prelates, from five continents. Two short doctrinal constitutions were promulgated, and much business was left undone. Pope Pius IX first proposed an ecumenical council to a closed meeting of cardinals on Dec. 6, 1864. He announced it publicly at the end of June 1867, and a year later issued the bull *Aeterni Patris*, formally convoking it. The bull of convocation was addressed to bishops, abbot-presidents, and generals of religious orders. In September 1868 papal briefs were sent to the patriarchs of the Orthodox, Armenian, Jacobite, and Coptic Churches inviting them to attend; but, displeased by the wording of the invitations, they refused. Pius's public appeal "to Protestants and all non-Catholics" to return to the true fold was also rebuffed and widely resented.

In the spring of 1867 the Pope appointed a steering committee, the "Central Commission," which in turn appointed five subcommittees to prepare materials for the Council. These subcommittees, taking into consideration proposals and suggestions sent in by the bishops, drafted 51 schemata. Shortly before the Council opened Pius IX issued an apostolic letter, *Multiplices inter* (Nov. 27, 1869), governing the Council's procedures. Based on an important memorandum drafted by Bp. Hefele, it established four deputations, elected by the Council, to prepare final drafts on faith, ecclesiastical discipline, Eastern Churches, and religious orders. Though every conciliar father enjoyed the right to speak in the general meetings, only the pope, as head of the Council, could introduce topics to the agenda. Later, in an effort to speed up the work of the Council, the procedures were somewhat modified by another rescript, *Apostolicis litteris* (Feb. 20, 1870). The Central Commission spent much time weighing the possibility of a definition of papal *infallibility. The spectrum of Catholic opinion ranged from those who strongly opposed a definition to those who would set no limits to it whatever. When the showdown came, the Council itself seemed to be divided between the "infallibilists" who, with varying degrees of enthusiasm, favored the definition, and the "inopportunists" who, for one reason or another, thought the definition inadvisable. The eventual outcome of the debate was predictable because the infallibilists led by Abp. Manning of Westminster, among others, succeeded in electing to the deputation on faith only those known to favor a definition of papal infallibility. Moreover, the infallibilists had the backing of Pius IX. Although 51 schemata were drafted by the preparatory committees, only six were discussed in the general congregations. The two dogmatic constitutions ultimately passed by the Council, *Dei filius* and *Pastor aeternus*, represented modified versions of the original proposals. *Dei filius*, approved in the third solemn session (April 24, 1870), is a dogmatic statement, divided into four chapters treating: (1) God the

creator of the universe; (2) the possibility for man to know God and the need for divine revelation; (3) the nature of faith; and (4) the twofold order of knowledge found in faith and reason (see D 3000–45). *Dei filius* is a revision and abridgment of only the first part of the original schema on the Catholic faith, *Apostolici muneris*.

The issue of papal infallibility, which overshadowed the proceedings of the Council from the very beginning, was after much debate resolved in the dogmatic constitution *Pastor aeternus* (D 3050–75). In the form finally approved in the fourth session (July 18, 1870), it consists of a prologue and four chapters: (1) the institution of papal primacy; (2) its continuation; (3) its extent; and (4) the solemn definition of papal infallibility. The original schema on the Church, *Supremi pastoris*, distributed to the fathers on Jan. 21, 1870, consisted of 15 chapters; it made no mention of infallibility. *Pastor aeternus* represents a recasting of chapters 11 and 12 of *Supremi pastoris*, together with a distillation of many amendments proposed by the fathers of the Council. The outbreak of the Franco-Prussian War in July and the Italian occupation of the Papal States in September brought the Council to an abrupt standstill. On Oct. 20, 1870, Pius IX formally suspended it *sine die*, but the seed sown by the Council did not wither and die. The encyclicals of Leo XIII on ecclesiological questions and on relations of Church and State drew heavily on the archives of Vatican I. Though the Council promulgated no disciplinary decrees, changes in church law proposed by the preparatory committees made their way into the reform legislation of Pope Pius X and the Code of Canon Law (1918).

Vatican Council II (1962–65). Over a period of 4 years, the Council met in 168 general congregations and 10 public sessions. Present at the opening on Oct. 11, 1962, were 2,540 prelates, and the attendance held well above 2,000 throughout. In addition, the number of delegate-observers from Orthodox and Protestant Churches reached 93 in the last year of the Council. Vatican II issued 16 formal statements and was the occasion for uncounted volumes of study documents and published speeches. On Jan. 23, 1959, 3 months after his election, Pope John XXIII announced his intention of calling an ecumenical council. On Pentecost (May 17) he appointed a planning committee to consult with bishops, the curia, and faculties of theology and canon law with an eye toward organizing an agenda. A year later (June 5, 1960), Pope John issued a motu proprio, *Superno Dei nutu,* establishing a Central Committee, 10 preparatory commissions, and two secretariats to draft schemata; in all, 73 documents were prepared in advance of the Council. The formal convocation came with the bull *Humanae salutis* on Christmas, 1961. The motu proprio *Appropinquante concilio* (Aug. 6, 1962) gave guidelines for the organization and procedures of the Council. It established an international steering committee of 10 cardinals, who also took turns presiding over the general congregations. Ten commissions, roughly corresponding to the preparatory commissions, were set up for: (1) the doctrine of faith and morals; (2) bishops and government of dioceses; (3) the discipline of the clergy and Christian people; (4) religious; (5) the discipline of the sacraments; (6) the liturgy; (7) studies and seminaries; (8) the Oriental Churches; (9) the missions; and (10) the lay apostolate, communications media, and entertainment. Each commission was to have a chairman, 8 members were to be appointed by the pope, and 16 were to be elected. A parliamentary maneuver by Cardinal Lienart of Lille in the very first general congregation wrested the initiative from the curialists and made it possible to elect truly representative commissions. (Pope John appointed nine members instead of the prescribed eight, and Pope Paul VI later increased the size of the commissions to 30.)

Another crucial move in the early days of the Council was Pope John's decision to make the *Secretariat for Promoting Christian Unity under Cardinal Bea equal in status to the ten commissions. The secretariat had arranged for several Orthodox and Protestant communions to send delegate-observers. Although they were not permitted to speak or vote in the general congregations, the delegate-observers were able to make their views known to the conciliar commissions through Bea's secretariat. Although Pope John died after the first period of the Council, Oct. 11–Dec. 8, 1962, his influence was felt throughout. In an address on opening day John expressed the pastoral concern and the hope for unity among all men that were to dominate all the subsequent discussions and proceedings. The first public statement of his successor, Paul VI, announced the continuation of the Council. Before it reconvened Pope Paul revised some of the procedural rules and invited laymen, representing Catholic agencies in various parts of the world, to attend. Later, lay and religious women were welcomed into the Council as auditors. Under Paul Vatican II met over 3 years. While the work of the commissions was continuous, the full Council met only in the fall: Sept. 29–Dec. 4, 1963; Sept. 14–Nov. 21, 1964; Sept. 14–Dec. 8, 1965. By the time the Council adjourned in December 1965 it had issued four constitutions, nine decrees, and three declarations, totaling more than 100,000 words. The tone of the conciliar statements is positive and the style straightforward. The Council made a conscious effort to avoid rigid definitions and condemnatory anathemas and, wherever possible, to couch its teaching in biblical language rather than scholastic or juridical terms. The constitutions, even the ones labelled "pastoral," are primarily doctrinal statements expressing the common faith of the Church about itself. The decrees have more immediate practical significance and deal with particular aspects of church life. The declarations express general principles and guidelines normative for the Church in its relations with other societies.

The Council's statements with their official Latin titles and the dates of promulgation are as follows:

Constitution on the Sacred Liturgy (*Sacrosanctum concilium*). Dec. 4, 1963.

Dogmatic Constitution on the Church (*Lumen gentium*). Nov. 21, 1964.

Dogmatic Constitution on Divine Revelation (*Dei Verbum*). Nov. 18, 1965.

Pastoral Constitution on the Church in the Modern World (*Gaudium et spes*). Dec. 7, 1965.

Decree on the Instruments of Social Communication (*Inter mirifica*). Dec. 4, 1963.

Decree on Ecumenism (*Unitatis redintegratio*). Nov. 21, 1964.

Decree on Eastern Catholic Churches (*Orientalium ecclesiarum*). Nov. 21, 1964.

Decree on the Bishops' Pastoral Office in the Church (*Christus Dominus*). Oct. 28, 1965.

Decree on Priestly Formation (*Optatum totius*). Oct. 28, 1965.

Decree on the Appropriate Renewal of the Religious Life (*Perfectae caritatis*). Oct. 28, 1965.

Decree on the Apostolate of the Laity (*Apostolicam actuositatem*). Oct. 28, 1965.

Decree on the Ministry and Life of Priests (*Presbyterorum ordinis*). Dec. 7, 1965.

Decree on the Church's Missionary Activity (*Ad gentes*). Dec. 7, 1965.

Declaration on Christian Education (*Gravissimum educationis*). Oct. 28, 1965.

Declaration on the Relationship of the Church to Non-Christian Religions (*Nostra aetate*). Oct. 28, 1965.

Declaration on Religious Freedom (*Dignitatis humanae*). Dec. 7, 1965.

Even before Vatican II ended Pope Paul took steps to ensure implementation of the conciliar directives. By a series of motu proprios, he set up the administrative structures to carry on the work of reform and renewal called for by the Council: *Sacram liturgiam* (Jan. 25, 1964) instituted a commission to implement the Constitution on the Sacred Liturgy; *In fructibus multis* (April 2, 1964) established a commission for the communications media; *Integrae servandae* (Dec. 7, 1965) reorganized the Holy Office into the Congregation for the Doctrine of the Faith; *Finis concilii* (Jan. 11, 1966) created five more postconciliar com-missions, a new Central Committee to coordinate their work, and gave permanent status to the Secretariats for Promoting Christian Unity, for Non-Christian Religions, and for Non-Believers. The five postconciliar commissions corresponded to the commissions of the Council itself, for (1) bishops and the government of dioceses; (2) religious; (3) the missions; (4) Christian education; and (5) the apostolate of the laity.

Historical Perspective. The century bracketed by the two Vatican Councils was a period of revolutionary upheaval. Empires fell and national borders were redrawn, and in that 100 years men became aware that every frontier of human experience—social, cultural, economic, political and scientific, emotional, psychological and intellectual—had changed. The Councils illustrate the difference. Pope Pius IX announced Vatican I on Dec. 6, 1864, 2 days before he published the encyclical *Quanta cura*; he intended the Council to address itself to the issues outlined in the *Syllabus of Errors*. When Vatican II took up the problems of the Church in the modern world a century later, there was an entirely different life-style. The questions were new, and the style of the answers seemed as important as the content to men of the 20th century. Vatican II became a symbol of many important changes, but most importantly it seemed to symbolize the Church's willingness to accept change. In the face of the unknown future, the openness of Vatican II won the sympathy of all honest searchers after truth. The concern to reestablish unity within the Christian community proved inspirational to all believers in Christ. The catholicity of the Council, bringing men together from all over the world, gave it truly ecumenical appeal. See for Vatican I, C. Butler, *Vatican Council* (2v., 1930; abr. ed., 1962); H. Jedin, *Ecumenical Councils of the Catholic Church* (1961), 143–180; J. J. Hennesey, NCE 14:559–563; idem, *First Council of the Vatican: The American Experience* (1963); see for Vatican II, R. F. Trisco, NCE 14:563–572; W. M. Abbot, ed., *Documents of Vatican II* (1966);

H. Vorgrimler, *Commentary on the Documents of Vatican II* (5v., 1967–69); F. Anderson, ed., *Council Daybook: Vatican II* (3v., 1965–66); Xavier Rynne, *Vatican Council Two* (1968); V. A. Yzermans, ed., *American Participation in the Second Vatican Council* (1967); J. Deretz and A. Nocent, eds., *Dictionary of the Council* (1968); H. Küng et al., eds., *Council Speeches of Vatican Two* (1964).

VAUDOIS, an alternate name for the *Waldenses. Vaudois is derived through French from the name of the founder, Waldo or Valdo.

VEDANTA SOCIETY, a religious body cultivating the Vedas, sacred writings of Hinduism. The society was established in the U.S. in 1898 by the Swami Vivekananda (1863–1902), who had introduced his ideas at the World's Parliament of Religion held in Chicago in 1893. He stressed esp. the idea, derived from Ramakrishna-Paramahansa (1834–86), that all religions are in essence one, expressions of many ways for man to achieve full self-realization. The Vedanta teachings and methods of achieving wisdom are a form of *theosophy. The headquarters of the society are in Calcutta, India; there were 11 centers in the U.S. in 1968, each largely independent; combined membership was c.1000. The principal center is the Vedanta Society of New York.

VERGER (Lat. *virga,* rod), a term with two main meanings: (1) one who carries a mace (verge) or other symbol of authority before dignitaries as they enter a cathedral, church, or university gathering; and (2) a person who has responsibility for caring for the interior of the church, combining the functions of usher and sexton.

VERMIGLI, PIETRO MARTIRE, see PETER MARTYR VERMIGLI.

VESTIARIAN CONTROVERSY, in 16th-cent. England a dispute over Puritan resistance to the use of vestments. The first manifestation was during the reign of Edward VI, when John Hooper refused (1550) to wear surplice and rochet for his consecration as bp. of Gloucester, feeling that they were remnants of popery. The matter was settled by compromise, with Hooper agreeing to the vestments for his induction and for his first sermon before the King. The controversy arose again after the Act of Uniformity (1559) of Elizabeth I; Puritans, many of them under the influence of Geneva from their exile there during Mary Tudor's reign, again objected to the prescribed use of vestments. The *Book of Advertisements (1566) sought to enforce uniformity and met with bitter opposition. The issue became secondary in the broader program of Puritan reform of the Church throughout the 17th century.

VESTRY, in Anglican usage, a group of persons responsible for parish business; also one of their meetings. The name comes from the fact that meetings were held in the vestry, the church room for vestments and vesting. In the C of E the vestry became less important with the formation (1921) of parochial councils; it still administers poor relief. In the U.S., parishes of the Protestant Episcopal Church have vestries consisting of *rector, *churchwardens, and vestrymen. The number of vestrymen, their duties, and methods of election vary in different dioceses, but in general they serve as trustees representing the religious corporation in matters of property and in relations between parish members and clergy, esp. regarding the appointment of a rector. See D. Stevick, *Canon Law: A Handbook* (1965).

VICAR, in general, one who is the official representative of another. In England the term was originally applied to the cleric who exercised the functions of a parish priest as the delegate of the proper rector or of the religious community to whom the church was entrusted. In such a case the tithes, or a major portion of them, went to the rector or the religious community represented by the vicar. In later usage the term has been applied to the incumbent of any church whose tithes are impropriated or appropriated. The vicar in this sense enjoys all the spiritual jurisdiction that would be his if he were a rector in the full sense of the term. *RECTOR; *CURATE.

VILATTE, JOSEPH RÉNÉ (1854–1929), a bishop numbered among the *episcopi vagantes. Born in Paris, V. came to North America, where he took part in the religious services of various denominations in Canada and the U.S., settling finally in Wisconsin. Ordained deacon and priest in 1885 by Dr. Herzog, Old Catholic bp. in Switzerland, he worked for a while among Belgian immigrants in the Green Bay area. After making various inquiries of Episcopalian and Orthodox authorities in the hope of receiving episcopal orders, he finally journed to Ceylon, where he was consecrated bp. in May 1892 by Abp. Alvares of the "Independent Catholic Church of Goa and Ceylon," a prelate of dubious standing in the Jacobite Church. This consecration was allegedly performed on the authority of a bull of Patriarch Ignatius Peter III of Antioch. Because of doubts surrounding this action, both Indian Jacobite and American Episcopalian authorities have denied the validity of the consecration. V., however, continued to ordain and consecrate others. In 1898, he sought to be reconciled to Rome, but he was formally excommunicated in 1900 after consecrating an Italian priest for the "Italian Episcopal Church." He continued his activities in the U.S. until retirement in 1920. He was succeeded by Bp. Frederick Lloyd, whom he had consecrated in 1915, the date of the official incorporation of his followers as the "American Catholic Church." After being reconciled to Rome in 1925, he died in France in 1929. See H. R. T. Brandreth, *Episcopi Vagantes and the Anglican Church* (2d ed., 1961), 47–54; P. Anson, *Bishops at Large* (1964).

VINCENT OF LÉRINS, ST. (d. c.445), a monk of Lérins in Gaul, formulator of the so-called Vincentian canon. His fame rests on his two *Commonitoria*, written c.434, only one of which has survived. The work is celebrated for its enunciation of the canon or criterion of orthodoxy *quod ubique, quod semper, quod ab omnibus creditum est*: the orthodoxy of a doctrine is to be judged on the basis of its geographical and historical universality; that is Catholic truth which has been held always, everywhere, and by all the faithful. Many see in V.'s work an attack upon Augustine's anti-Pelagian writings, or at least upon an extreme interpretation of them, and consider V. to have been a Semi-Pelagian. V. has had some veneration as a saint, but there is evidence to show that his cult is not an ancient one. Works: critical edition, A. Juelicher (2d ed., 1925); translations, R. Morris, FathCh 7 (1949), 255–332, and G. McCracken, LibCC 9 (1957), 23–89. See Butler 2:382–383.

VIRTUALISM, the teaching of John Calvin and the *Reformed Churches that in the Holy Eucharist the life-giving power (Lat. *virtus*) of Christ's glorified humanity becomes present to one receiving with faith. The position avoids RC and Lutheran affirmations of the actual presence of Christ's body and blood in the Eucharistic elements, as well as the Zwinglian reduction to a simply symbolic presence. Virtualism proposes a dynamic presence of Christ, in the communication of the saving effectiveness of his flesh and blood. *REAL PRESENCE; *TRANSUBSTANTIATION.

VISIBLE CHURCH, an expression contrasting the Church as an empirical, imperfect, organized institution, with the invisible Church, the true Church as spiritual community. Such a distinction, made by many Reformers, is still maintained by some Protestant bodies; it has always been rejected in RC teaching, which regards the Church as a single reality with visible and invisible aspects. *INVISIBLE CHURCH.

VOCATION, a term used in two principal ways: (1) God's summons to men to salvation (see CALL); (2) a particular office or state in the Christian life. In RC ecclesiastical usage the term is applied esp. to the priesthood and the religious life.

VOLUNTARYISM (voluntarism; voluntary principle), the theory and practice according to which church membership or support is a matter of personal choice, free of civil or even ecclesiastical coercion. Voluntaryism is closely associated with *denominationalism; it stands opposed to any form of *established Church, of *Erastianism, or even of authoritarian ecclesiastical system. The idea clearly emerged in 17th-cent. England in the *gathered Church theory (see INDEPENDENCY; NONCONFORMISTS). Dropping the original qualifying emphasis upon God's initiative in the gathering process, John Locke defined the Church as a purely voluntary organization: "A church then I take to be a voluntary society of men, joining themselves together on their own accord, in order to the public worshiping of God" (*First Letter concerning Toleration*). As a principle of church life voluntaryism clearly emerged in the *Great Awakening in the U.S., and "the voluntary principle in religion has been the great tradition of the American churches" (W. S. Hudson, *The Great Tradition of the American Churches* [1953], 19). The full development of the principle was made possible by the incorporation of religious freedom and separation of Church and State into law in the U.S.; the voluntary principle allowed for the proliferation of sects and denominations; these in turn strengthened the force of voluntaryism in American Christianity. Without an established Church each denomination had to win adherents, raise financial support,

and find means of influencing society. *Revivalism proved to be a natural concomitant of voluntaryism as the Churches sought aggressive approaches to win multitudes of churchless people. The success of the Churches in winning converts is apparent from statistics of church membership, attendance, budgets, buildings, and the like.

Voluntaryism affected the dynamics of church life in the form of "voluntary societies." While Americans resolved to separate the spheres of religion and civil government, they did not intend to separate religion from the rest of life. In the early 19th cent., numerous local, state, and national voluntary societies, or associations, were organized to propagate the Christian faith and to reform society. Among the better known were: American Bible Society (1816), American Colonization Society (1817), American Sunday School Union (1824), American Tract Society (1825), American Temperance Society (1826), American Education Society (1827), American Peace Society (1828), and the American Anti-Slavery Society (1833). Promoters of revival were often linked with reform movements, and many individuals held membership in several societies, forming a network that came to be known as the "Benevolent Empire." Although many members belonged to Churches, they were not official representatives. Thus through informal interdenominational cooperation, the fabric of American political and social life was permeated. Struck by the vitality of religious life in America, many European visitors commented on the good and bad effects of the voluntary principle. Philip *Schaff, after a dozen years in the U.S., explained the benefits of the "so-called voluntary principle" to former compatriots in Germany, pointing out also its limitations. The voluntary principle was not without its critics, who complained that it fostered excessive *individualism and *subjectivism, weakened objective standards of authority and denominational loyalties, and stressed personality traits above theological competence as qualifications for the ministry. See C. I. Foster, *Errand of Mercy: The Evangelical United Front, 1790–1837* (1960); M. Powell, ed., *Voluntary Church: American Religious Life (1740–1865) Seen through the Eyes of European Visitors* (1967); F. H. Littell, *From State Church to Pluralism* (1926); S. E. Mead, *Lively Experiment* (1963).

VOLUNTEERS OF AMERICA (VA), an organization founded in 1896 by Ballington *Booth, son of *Salvation Army founder William Booth, as the result of an effort to make the Salvation Army (SA) more democratic. The VA is similar in most respects to the parent body. Ballington Booth and his wife, Maud Charlesworth Booth, were appointed joint commanders of the American forces of the SA in 1887. They resigned in 1896 when recalled to England, after a long struggle to convince the elder Booth of the need for greater local autonomy, but discouraged any secession from Salvation Army ranks. They founded the VA as a new organization but drew heavily on the experience and methods of the Salvation Army. Officers are chosen democratically, and all with the rank of major or higher form the Grand Field Council, which has direction of the Volunteers under a commander-in-chief whom it elects for a 5-year term. The VA has the same fundamentalist beliefs and evangelistic, nonliturgical worship as the SA, but it has adopted its own forms for the administration of baptism, the Lord's Supper, and marriage. The VA directs a variety of evangelistic and social work projects, including a special ministry to inmates of prisons, the Volunteer Prison League. There were 45 stations with 40 evangelists and 5,500 members in 1968.

W

WAITERS, another name for the *Seekers, a 17th-cent. group of English Puritans who protested against the organized Church and waited for the realization of the true spiritual Church.

WALDECK, FRANZ VON (1491–1553), count and bp. who favored the Reformation. W. sought to establish a duchy out of the three sees that he held simultaneously, Minden (from 1531), Münster, and Osnabrück (from 1532). To this end he openly favored the Reformers but was thwarted by the cathedral chapters, and the dioceses remained Catholic. During the Anabaptist uprisings at Münster (1533–35), W. besieged and eventually recaptured the city. See H. Börsting, LTK 10:933; bibliog. for Anabaptists.

WALDENSES, a body of Christians with origins in southern France in the 12th century. Historians disregard the claim that the Waldenses go back to apostolic times. They were founded by *Waldo, a merchant of Lyons, who *c.*1170 gave his wealth to his relatives and began a life of evangelical poverty. His followers, who were also called Poor Men of Lyons, *Pauperes Christi, Leonistae, Pauperes spiritu,* and *Insabbatati,* observed strict poverty and preached against the wealth and laxity of the clergy. They were approved in 1179 by Pope Alexander III with the proviso that they obtain authorization from local clergy before preaching. For not complying with this condition they were condemned (1184) by Pope Lucius III and later (1215) by Lateran Council IV. In 1211 more than 80 of them were burned as heretics at Strassburg. Waldensian teaching was similar to that of other medieval lay dissenters. Clerics have no special right to speak in God's name. All Christians can preach since each is a depositary of the Holy Spirit. Only Wal-

denses preserve the ideals of primitive Christianity, and the Church is the community of Satan. The efficacy of the sacraments depends on the sanctity of the ministers; and the practice of poverty empowers a person to administer all sacraments. Purgatory, indulgences, fasting, and the cult of the saints are to be rejected. Each Holy Thursday the Waldenses celebrated the Lord's Supper in a simple rite, but they did not believe in the Real Presence. Worship services consisted of scriptural readings, sermons, and the Lord's Prayer. Some of their beliefs and practices were borrowed from the *Cathari. Like the Cathari, they were divided into Perfecti and simple believers. The former were celibates who eschewed manual labor and went about as mendicant preachers. The believers were married, and worked to provide for the material needs of the Perfecti. The ministers (*barbes,* uncles) came from the ranks of the Perfecti. At times to avoid persecution Waldenses remained outwardly faithful to the Church. Their modest way of life made them liked by the common people, but their popularity waned with the founding of the Franciscan and Dominican Orders in the 13th century. In spite of repressive measures against them, the Waldenses survived through the centuries, esp. in remote places. In 1532 they subscribed to some Protestant doctrines; and with the passing of time most adopted Calvinistic theology. In the 17th cent. they were persecuted in RC territories. Napoleon granted them toleration; and in 1848 the Duke of Savoy, in whose domain most of them then lived, gave them full political and religious liberty. The modern Waldenses number about 30,000, almost all of them in Italy. Since the 19th cent. they have conducted a vigorous program of evangelization in Italy, and have established a theological school in Rome. See L. Cristiani, EC 12:966–970; Y. Dossat, NCE 14:-770–771 with bibliog.

WALDO (Valdes, Valdesius; d. *c.*1215), wealthy Lyonnaise merchant, founder of the Poor Men of Lyons, or *Waldenses. Little is known about his personal life. Partly as a result of his study of the Gospels, which he had had translated into Provençal, he experienced a spiritual conversion in 1176. In imitation of St. Alexis he left his family, gave his goods to the poor, and took a vow of poverty. As an itinerant preacher he waged a vigorous campaign against worldliness in the Church. His way of life was approved by Alexander III in 1179, but he was forbidden to preach. He ignored this prohibition and was condemned as a heretic by Lucius III in 1184. Nothing is known of his life after that event. From 1368 he was referred to as Peter Waldo by the Waldenses. See L. Cristiani, EC 12:966–970; F. Hayward, *Inquisition* (1965), 29–31; H. Daniel-Rops, *Cathedral and Crusade* (1957), 524–527.

WALES, CHURCH IN, see CHURCH IN WALES.

WALTER, JOHANN (Walther, b. Blankenmueller; 1496–1570), German Lutheran composer and musical adviser to Martin Luther. Nothing is known of W.'s schooling or musical preparation except that he attended a Latin school. In 1517 he obtained a place in the Hofkapelle of Frederick I of Saxony through the good offices of its conductor. He spent 3 weeks in Luther's home in 1524, working with Luther and K. Rupsch (Rupff) on the music of the Lutheran Church. His first work, *Geystlich Gesangk Buchleyn* (1524), was destined to become the model for almost all Lutheran hymnals. Twenty-three of the 30 hymns, as well as the Preface, were by Luther. The hymnbook was entirely independent of the three other songbooks that appeared the same year, and it was the first to have systematic arrangement. W.'s songs were intended for church, school, and home use; but they did not lend themselves easily to congregational singing. He was the first to set to music Luther's translations of the Bible. See W. E. Buszin, EncLuthCh 3:2455–56.

WALTHER, CARL FERDINAND WILHELM (1811–87), conservative Lutheran theologian. A native of Germany, W. began the study of theology at the Univ. of Leipzig in 1829, graduated in 1833, and was ordained in 1837. Because of his convictions about pure doctrine and a vital personal faith, he could not accept the growing rationalism in the state Church. With a large body of like-minded people from Saxony, he migrated (1839) to St. Louis, Mo., and became a pastor in Perry Co., Mo.; there he helped form, and taught in a log-cabin college that developed into Concordia Seminary. In 1841 he accepted the pastorate at Trinity Church in St. Louis; after the transfer of Concordia to St. Louis, he was also professor of theology (1850–87). In 1844 he began publishing *Der Lutheraner*, a periodical directed at bringing together Lutheran conservatives; in 1855 he founded the quarterly *Lehre und Wehre*, in which most of his theological writings appeared. He played a leading role in the formation in 1847 of what is now the Lutheran Church—Missouri Synod, which he served as president, 1847–50 and 1864–78. W. communicated to the Missouri Synod an insistence on doctrinal orthodoxy as the first basis of unity in the Church. Although estrangement between the Missouri Synod and other synods resulted from it, W. strongly defended, against *revivalism and *liberal theology alike, man's unconditional dependence upon grace for salvation. See C. F. W. Walther, *Proper Distinction between Law and Gospel* (tr. W. Dau, 1929); W. G. Polack, *Story of C. F. W. W.* (1947); L. Spitz, *Life of Dr. C. F. W. W.* (1962); Smith-Jamison 1:272–275.

WARD, in Mormon nomenclature, the local congregation of the Church.

WARDEN, see CHURCHWARDEN.

WARFIELD, BENJAMIN BRECKIN-
RIDGE (1851–1921), Presbyterian theologian. Born near Lexington, Ky., W. studied
at the College of New Jersey (now Princeton Univ.), Princeton Theological Seminary, and the Univ. of Leipzig. After
ordination (1879) he taught at Western Theological Seminary (now Pittsburgh Theological Seminary) until he was called (1887)
to teach theology at Princeton Seminary.
He engaged in intense study of many fields,
including biblical criticism, patristics, theology, and church history. He defended the
orthodox Calvinism of C. *Hodge in highly
rationalistic terms and supported what he
called evangelical religion (see PRINCETON
THEOLOGY). W. helped to define the doctrine of biblical inerrancy as the basis upon
which the Presbyterian Church in the
United States of America and other sympathetic Christians defined the authority of
Scripture. He was chief editor of the *Presbyterian and Reformed Review* (1890–1903),
to which he made many contributions, and
his posthumous works include, among
many others, *Revelation and Inspiration*
(1927), *Calvin and Calvinism* (1931), and *The
Westminster Assembly and Its Work*
(1931).

WARS OF RELIGION, primarily eight
French civil wars involving the *Huguenots
and Catholics between 1562 and 1598, but
the whole period of religious wars did not
end until 1629. The first war (1562–63) began
after the Massacre of Vassy (March 1, 1562)
and was terminated by the Peace of Amboise (March 19, 1563), which granted the
Huguenots liberty of conscience but restricted freedom of worship. An anti-
Huguenot "little" League was formed. The
second war (1567–68) was equally inconclusive: the Peace of Longjumeau reestablished the terms of the previous settlement.
The third war (1568–70) broke out as a result of Catherine de Médicis' plans to seize
the Huguenot leaders Condé and Gaspard
de Coligny. The Huguenots were defeated
at Jarnac (March 1569) and Moncontour
(October 1569); their losses were heavy but

the Peace of Saint-Germain (Aug. 8, 1570)
was favorable, permitting them to garrison
four strongholds. In the fourth war (1572–
73), which followed the *St. Bartholomew's
Day Massacre (Aug. 24, 1572), in which Coligny was murdered, royal forces besieged
the Huguenots in their strongholds. The
treaty of La Rochelle (July 8, 1573) restricted their freedom of worship to three
towns. During the fifth war (1574–76) Francis, Duke of Alençon, brother of King
Henry III, joined the revolt with Henry of
Navarre; after the defeat of the Huguenots
by Henry of Guise at Dormans, the treaty
of Beaulieu ("Peace of Monsieur," May 6,
1576) established religious and civil equality
and authorized six additional strongholds;
this caused considerable resentment and
led in 1576 to the formation of the Catholic
League. The sixth war (1577) and the seventh war (1580) were local. The eighth war
(1586–89) was provoked by the League,
which prevailed on Henry III to issue the
Treaty of Nemours (July 1585), canceling all
previous concessions and in effect banning
Calvinism. In this "War of the Three Hen-
ries," Henry of Navarre won a victory at
Coutras (Oct. 20, 1587), and Henry of Guise
and Henry III were murdered. Henry of
Navarre then became King Henry IV and
reconquered the country. He was recon-
verted to Catholicism and fought a victorious war against Spain; the war was brought
to a close by the Treaty of Vervins (May 2,
1598), which was also the political end of the
Wars of Religion. The *Edict of Nantes
(April 13, 1598) gave the Huguenots freedom of conscience and civil equality but
restricted their freedom to worship. The
ensuing period of religious truce was
broken by several Huguenot revolts (1615,
1620, and 1625) and by the siege of their
stronghold, La Rochelle (1627–28), conducted by Cardinal Richelieu, who destroyed the power of the Huguenot party by
imposing, in June 1629, the Peace of Alais.
This deprived Huguenots of civil and political rights, and the religious freedom
granted by the Edict of Nantes was not
honored. See W. J. Stankiewicz, NCE
7:201–204, s.v. "Huguenots," with bibliog.

WARTBURG, the castle near Eisenach in Thuringia, where Martin Luther, disguised as "Knight George," took refuge in 1521 after the Diet of *Worms. The name also connotes the "Patmos" period in the Reformer's life (May 1521–March 1522), during which he translated the NT into German and wrote many pamphlets and treatises. Disorders aroused by the radical innovations of *Karlstadt and the *Zwickau Prophets, which he had tried to control by incognito excursions, led to his return to Wittenberg. See K. Wessel, *Luther und der Wartburg* (1955); M. Reu, *Luther's German Bible* (1934); M. Gravier, *Luther et l'opinion publique* (1942).

WATCH NIGHT, a gathering for prayer, praise, and exhortation, begun in 1742 by Methodist colliers in Kingswood, England, who before their conversion had spent Saturday nights drinking. John *Wesley encouraged the watch night and introduced it himself in London, April 9, 1742, choosing the Friday night nearest a full moon. Wesley likened it to the vigils of the primitive Church and those mentioned in the Book of Common Prayer. The custom continues in various denominations only on New Year's Eve.

WATCH TOWER BIBLE AND TRACT SOCIETY, the name of the legal corporation of the *Jehovah's Witnesses. The president is Nathan H. Knorr; headquarters are in Brooklyn, New York.

WATERLAND, DANIEL (1683–1740), a Lincolnshire man, fellow and master of Magdalene College, Cambridge, and canon of Windsor. He maintained the traditional Christian position against *deism and did more than any other divine to halt the spread of *latitudinarianism in the C of E. Wary of mysticism, he rested his case on external evidence; his deep and accurate learning, and his wiry and perspicuous style made him a redoubtable opponent. His publications include considerations of Arianism, vindications of the divinity of Christ, and a critical history of the *Athanasian Creed, which has been many times reprinted. In the C of E his moderate eucharistic theology won wide approval.

WATTSON, PAUL JAMES FRANCIS (1863–1940), ecumenist, founder of the Society of the Atonement. Born Lewis Thomas in Millington, Md., he studied theology at General Theological Seminary, New York City, and after ordination in the Episcopal Church (1886) worked toward unity between his Church and Rome. He founded (1898) at Graymoor, N.Y., in conjunction with Mother Lurana White, an Episcopal nun, the Society of the Atonement, a group of Franciscan friars and sisters whose prayer and activities were designed to further Christian unity. When he had passed a year in the novitiate of the Anglican Fathers of the Holy Cross, he received the habit of his order, taking the name Paul James. In 1903 he began publication of *The Lamp* and in 1909 inaugurated the period of prayer called the Church Unity Octave. This became the *Chair of Unity Octave and was observed by other Christian Churches as the Universal Week of Prayer for Christian Unity. The Graymoor community was received corporately into the RC Church in 1909, and W. was re-ordained a priest in 1910. He also founded at Graymoor a refuge for homeless men and organized the Graymoor Press and the "Ave Maria Hour" on radio. See D. Gannon, NCE 14:828; T. Cranny, *Father Paul, Apostle of Unity* (1955).

WEBB, THOMAS (c.1724–96), layman, prominent in the establishment of Methodism in the United States. He was a captain in the British Army who assisted P. *Embury in N.Y., founded St. George's Methodist Church in Philadelphia (1767), and strengthened Methodist *societies in Del., Md., N.J., and on Long Island. See HistAmMeth 1.

WEE FREES, in Scotland a nickname for the minority who resisted the 1900 union that formed the *United Free Church.

WEEK OF PRAYER FOR CHRISTIAN UNITY, organized by Abbé Paul Couturier (1881–1953), an annual period of prayer for Christian unity in which all Christians are invited to pray that unity may come as Christ wills and by the means he wills. In 1932 Couturier visited the Benedictine community at Amay, Belgium, where he learned about the *Chair of Unity Octave. He introduced the octave in Lyons, his native city, in 1933, but decided that the basis direction of the octave should be changed. In accordance with the theology of the times, the octave then advocated submission and conversion of non-Catholics to the RC Church for the attainment of Christian unity. The Abbé realized that such views did not allow non-Catholic Christians to pray with sincerity because of their contrary beliefs. Holding spiritual ecumenism to be the heart of the ecumenical movement, Couturier substituted a new formula of prayer for unity so that each person could pray according to his own conscience. The World Council of Churches adopted the Couturier formula, and a Joint Working Group of the World Council and the RC *Secretariat for Promoting Christian Unity now yearly develop a common service for the Week of Prayer, Jan. 18–25, for use according to local circumstances throughout the Christian world. See M. Villain, *Abbé Paul Couturier* (1959).

WEIGEL, GUSTAVE (1906–64), American Jesuit theologian, ecumenist. He entered the Society of Jesus in 1922, was ordained in 1933, and completed his theological studies with a doctoral course, 1935–37, at the Gregorian Univ., Rome (S.T.D., 1938). The first phase of his professorial career was as professor of dogmatic theology at the Catholic Univ. in Santiago, Chile, 1937–48. He was appointed dean of the theological faculty in 1942; published *El Cristianismo*

oriental (1945) and *La Psicología de la religión* (1946). From 1948 until his death he was professor of theology at Woodstock College, Woodstock, Maryland. He entered into contact and dialogue with many Protestant theologians, including Paul *Tillich. With his colleague and friend John Courtney *Murray he collaborated in studies of the Church-State problem. He published two philosophical works: *Knowledge: Its Values and Limits* (1961) and *Religion and Knowledge of God* (1961).

From 1954 onward, after a period of serious illness, W. stood with Murray at the forefront of the movement toward renewal in the RC Church in the United States. He became the most prominent American RC theologian in the ecumenical movement, and as participant or observer attended the national and international meetings of the World Council of Churches. His ecumenical concentration was reflected in his works: *Catholic Primer of the Ecumenical Movement* (1957); *Faith and Understanding in America* (1959); *American Dialogue* (1960); *Churches in North America* (1961); *Catholic Theology in Dialogue* (1961); and *The Modern God* (1963). As a culmination to this work he was called to Rome to help prepare Vatican Council II's *Decree on Ecumenism. During the Council he acted as a liaison and interpreter for the observers from other Churches. His diary of the beginnings of the Council is preserved in the archives of Woodstock. See *Woodstock Letters* (v.97, 1968), n.4; W. J. Burghardt, NCE 14:843–44.

WEIGEL, VALENTIN (1533–88), German religious writer. W. was Lutheran pastor at Zschopau. He became well known only after his death when his works were first published (Halle, 1609). He was a precursor of *Romanticism whose influence is seen in J. *Arndt and J. *Boehme. W. believed that man possesses a divine spark, which if developed will eventually supplant Scripture, the means of grace, the ministry, the science of theology, and all historical elements of religion. He felt that the knowledge of God is personal and autonomous, derived more from interior prayer than from the Bible and the sacraments. See I. Ludolphy, EncLuthCh 3:2464; R. H. Grützmacher, EncRelKnow 12:285–287.

WEISMANN, CHRISTIAN EBERHARD (1677–1747), German Lutheran mystical theologian. Educated at Tübingen, W. became deacon at Calw (1701–04); he was next made court chaplain at Stuttgart (1704–07), where he also taught church history and philosophy in the local gymnasium (1707–21). He was called to be professor of theology at Tübingen in 1721 and served after 1729 as provost of St. George's as well. W. was a distinguished preacher and a popular author of hymns. Nourished by Meister *Eckhard, J. *Tauler, and P. J. *Spener, he showed marked sympathy for *Pietism and opposed the *Enlightenment. His theology-centered church history avoids the one-sidedness of the *Magdeburg Centuries. See D. Scheib, LTK 10:1006–07; E. Beyreuther, RGG 6:1581.

WESLEY, CHARLES (1707–88), younger brother of John *Wesley; Anglican priest and hymn writer. The brothers were born at Epworth, Lincolnshire, where the father was rector of the parish. In 1716 Charles entered Westminster School, London, and in 1726, Christ Church, Oxford. There, in 1729, he became part of the *holy club of students, who in ridicule were dubbed "methodists." He was ordained in 1735, and for the next year served as Gen. Oglethorpe's private secretary in the Ga. colony. Ill and disillusioned over his Ga. mission, W. was back in England in Dec. 1736. Like his brother he had a conversion experience the following Whitsunday, which satisfied the longing, inspired by contact with Moravians in Ga., for a personal saving faith in Christ. He voiced his mood of exaltation in his famous hymn, "Where Shall My Wondering Soul Begin?" and became an enthusiastic preacher-evangelist of the Methodist revival, itinerating

(see ITINERANCY) until 1756, and thereafter preaching regularly at Bristol and at London. He was always a loyal partner and champion of his brother, who was the more prominent authority in the movement. The brothers, however, differed at some points; Charles strongly disapproved of John's 1784 ordinations (see ASBURY, F.; COKE, T.) and generally showed a fiercer, though not stronger, devotion to the established Church. He wrote more than 6,000 hymns as effective means of evangelizing; they made the Methodists a singing people, and enriched the hymnody of other Churches. More than 500 are of excellent lyrical quality; many are still useful and almost universally known, e.g., "Jesus, Lover of My Soul," and "Hark! the Herald Angels Sing." See C. W. Flint, *C. W.* (1957); J. E. Rattenbury, *Evangelical Doctrines of C. W.'s Hymns* (1941); E. Routley, *Musical Wesleys* (1968).

WESLEY, JOHN (1703–91), founder of *Methodism. Older brother of Charles, W. was born at Epworth in Lincolnshire. His father, Samuel, was a devout and studious parish priest; his mother, Susanna (Annesley), a woman of remarkably independent spirit and high mental gifts. Their legacy to the children was a devotion to the Church, the Bible, and the Book of Common Prayer, a Puritan morality, and esp. a disciplined way of life. In 1709 W. was saved from a fire in the parsonage, and afterward thought of himself as a "brand plucked from the burning," the recipient of miraculous divine intervention for a purpose largely fulfilled by the Methodist revival. He entered Christ Church, Oxford, in 1720, where from c.1725 his reading of books by W. *Law, J. *Taylor, and Thomas à Kempis gave him "a settled conviction to become a real Christian." This "alteration of his temper" was accompanied by the decision to take holy orders; accordingly he was ordained deacon in 1725 and priest in 1728. Periodically he served as his father's curate, and upon returning to Oxford in 1729 became leader of a *holy club, a group of serious students who had united with Charles to seek "inward holiness." Strict regularity of life earned them the jeering name "methodists" from other students, but they were soon widely known for their good works and their unusual devotion to the Church and the sacraments. In the Ga. colony (1735–38) his parishioners rejected his ministry; the Indians were unreceptive to the Gospel; and the young girl he loved married another man. But his religious desires were deepened by association with some Moravian settlers, who proclaimed the felt assurance of faith to be the very essence of scriptural Christianity.

Back in England he "preached faith" with such enthusiasm that he was barred from several pulpits. On May 24, 1738, at a little *society in Aldersgate Street in London, he felt his "heart strangely warmed," and he was given the faith in Christ he had been seeking so long. After a summer's visit among the Moravians at *Herrnhut in Germany, W. returned to England and gave himself to the revival then in progress, preaching, organizing societies and *classes, and directing all related activities. He adopted the *field preaching introduced by G. *Whitefield, appointed local and traveling lay preachers, opened houses of worship (see FOUNDRY), and raised funds for the preachers and benevolent causes. As editor and author he prepared grammars (Hebrew, Greek, French, Latin, and English), sermons, poems, hymns, letters, abridgements of classics, *A Christian Library, Rules, Advices,* and *Instructions,* and treatises in theology, politics, science, and medicine. For 52 years W. so dominated the Methodist movement that for the most part it became the creation of his mind and spirit. Many journeys to Scotland, Ireland, and Wales spread his influence more widely. Because of his love for the C of E, W. hoped the Methodists would never leave it, but many practical steps he took, particularly the ordinations he himself performed beginning in 1784 (see ASBURY, F.; COKE, T.), broke ecclesiastical law and forced a separation; his lay preachers, appeal to *Nonconformists, and distrust of the parish system (see ITINERANCY) also

contributed. In time active opposition to the Methodists gradually lessened, and mob violence, so common earlier, disappeared; in his last years he was honored as "England's grand old man." He died, an Anglican priest to the last, and was buried behind the Methodist City Road Chapel, London.

The spread and organization of the Wesleyan revival combated 18th cent. *deism and rationalism. Although he distrusted extremes both of mysticism and enthusiasm, he encouraged emotionalism and passionately insisted on the primacy of a personal experience of faith and of God's love. His central doctrine, *Christian perfection, which drew away from Luther's view of sinful human nature, inspired *revivalism and the *Holiness movement. His *Arminianism, as opposed to Calvinistic predestination, stressed the universal availability of grace and an optimistic view of every form of human goodness. The minutely disciplined Christian life that he taught against Moravian *antinomianism had a widespread effect on moral standards, both personal and social. Emphasis on the gospel message as communitarian fostered Christian social consciousness. The possibility of a personal experience of sanctification widely affected attitudes toward the mediating role of Church or sacraments. Through such ideas W. has had an impact on Christian thought and life next only to that of Luther and Calvin. See J. W., *Journal* (ed. N. Curnock, 8v., 1909–16); R. W. Burtner and R. E. Chiles, eds., *Compend of W.'s Theology* (1958); V. H. H. Green, *J. W.* (1965); Mayer RB 284–294; R. C. Monk, *J. W.: His Puritan Heritage* (1966); M. Piette, *J. W. and the Evolution of Protestantism* (tr. J. B. Howard, 1937); J. M. Todd, *J. W. and the Catholic Church* (1958); M. Schmidt, *J. W.: A Theological Biography* (v.1, tr. N. P. Goldhawk, 1962); C. Williams, *J. W.'s Theology Today* (1960).

WESLEY REFORM UNION, an English Methodist body organized at Sheffield in 1859 by a group who had been unfairly expelled from the Wesleyan Methodist Church, not on moral grounds but because of their active interest in connexional and constitutional reform and their dedicated support of teetotalism. Later, many of their churches joined with the United Methodist Free Churches. The denomination, however, stood out from union and is still a small separate Methodist body in England with about 6,000 members. See W. J. Townsend et al., *New History of Methodism* (1909), 1:539, 2:359.

WESLEYAN METHODIST CHURCH OF AMERICA, a Methodist denomination organized in 1833 by a group withdrawing from the Methodist Episcopal Church to protest its indifference to slavery. The new Church was originally called the Wesleyan Methodist Connexion of America, the present name becoming official in 1947. The Church adheres to Wesleyan doctrines, stresses holiness, the inerrancy of the Scriptures, and Christ's second coming. It rejects evolution, looking upon man as an "immediate creative act of God." It opposes secret societies, divorce, and the use of tobacco and intoxicants. Headquarters are in Marion, Indiana. The Church maintains mission work in about 14 countries and home mission projects among American Indians, Mexicans, and mountaineers. In 1966 there were more than 49,000 members in the U.S., in 1,171 churches. See HistAmMeth 3:587–589; I. F. McLeister, *History of the Wesleyan Methodist Church of America* (rev. ed., R. S. Nicholson, 1959).

WESTERN SCHISM, see GREAT WESTERN SCHISM.

WESTMINSTER ASSEMBLY, a synod appointed by the Long Parliament in June 1643, for the purpose of remaking the C of E in accordance with the demands of the Puritans, who claimed that the Church had not yet been purified of errors. Among the 151 members of the Assembly were 30 laymen and 120 theologians. Convinced advocates of *episcopacy did not attend, and the field was left to the larger group of Presbyterian sympathizers. The Assembly began by considering revisions of the *Thirty-Nine Articles, but under the influence of the *Solemn League and Covenant, it framed a completely new document, the *Westminster Confession. Under increasing Presbyterian domination, the Assembly was joined by eight commissioners from Scotland. The *Westminster Directory for Public Worship, which for a time replaced the *Book of Common Prayer (1645–61), and the two *Westminster Catechisms were also issued. The Assembly met intermittently until 1653 and was never officially dissolved. The Westminster Standards, the documents produced by the Assembly, were in effect only briefly in England, but they are still recognized by the *Church of Scotland and by Presbyterians generally. See W. Beveridge, *Short History of the Westminster Assembly* (1904); S. W. Carruthers, *Everyday Work of the Westminster Assembly* (1943).

WESTMINSTER CATECHISMS, the Larger and Shorter Catechisms, approved in 1648 by the *Westminster Assembly and intended to be, together with the *Westminster Confession, the doctrinal standard of the Presbyterian Churches. The Larger Catechism is based on earlier catechisms, e.g., Luther's *Catechisms and Calvin's *Genevan Catechisms, and more directly on the *Irish Articles (1615) and James Ussher's *Body of Divinity* (1645). Written mainly by Anthony Tuckney (1599–1670) of Emmanuel College, Cambridge, it tends to be philosophical rather than biblical in its definition of God and departs from the evangelical character of the older Calvinist tradition by implying a doctrine of *limited atonement. The Shorter Catechism, also written mainly by Tuckney, is a notable example of later Calvinism at its best in its pedagogical method, its unity of thought, and terseness of expression. Intended "for such as are of a weaker capacity," i.e., for children who found the Larger Catechism too detailed for memorizing, the Shorter Catechism is divided into two main sections, totaling 107 questions and answers: first, doctrines to be believed and, second, duties to be performed. Though the Catechisms are no longer in general use, their influence in and beyond Presbyterianism has been immense. See Schaff Creeds 1:783–787; 3:676–704.

WESTMINSTER CONFESSION, the primary *confession of faith for Presbyterianism, and a major *Reformed document. Toward the close of 1640 a document written probably by Alexander Henderson (c.1583–1646) was presented from Scotland to the English Lords of the Treaty at London, declaring that it was desirable "that there were one Confession of Faith, one form of Catechism, one Directory for all the parts of the public worship of God . . . in all the Churches of his majesty's dominions." In 1642 the English Parliament affirmed its desire for "a most firm and stable union between the two kingdoms of England and Scotland." The General Assembly of the Scottish Church expressed its own desire to agree upon a common Confession of Faith, Catechism, and Directory for worship, and in Aug. 1643 elected commissioners to attend the *Westminster Assembly for this purpose. Drafted in 1646, the confession was published in 1648 with the approval of both Houses of Parliament, but it was never sanctioned in its entirety in England. In Scotland its acceptance was more immediate, the *General Assembly having already in 1647 expressed its approval, "judging it to be most orthodox and grounded on the Word of God."

The Confession contains 33 chapters dealing with Scripture, God, the eternal decrees, creation and providence, the Fall, sin, the covenant, Christ the mediator, free will, effectual calling, justification, sanctification, faith, repentance, good works, perseverance of the saints, grace, the law of God, Christian liberty, worship, the magistrate, Church and sacraments, censures, synods and councils, and death and judgment. As used by Presbyterians in the U.S., ch. 23 (magistrates) and ch. 31 (synods and councils) have been altered. Hendry lists four characteristics of the Confession: its approach is excessively legalistic; it assumes that every question has a right or wrong answer; it sees everything in terms of black and white; it is individualistic and does not express the social significance of redemption. Yet ch. 1 on Scripture is an excellent statement of the Calvinist position. The "awful decree" of *double predestination is discussed in ch. 3, though few Presbyterian Churches now hold to the doctrine as here expressed. The Confession departs from earlier Calvinism, however, by speaking of two covenants (works and grace); when it discusses the sacraments (ch. 27), not so much as seals of the word of the gospel as seals of our faith in the gospel, it tends to restrict the evangelical character of the covenant of grace.

In Scotland commitment to the Confession became increasingly rigid. From 1690 university teachers and from 1711 *probationers and ordinands were required to subscribe to it as "founded upon the Word of God" and to acknowledge it as the confession of their own faith. The Confession, though held to be subordinate to Scripture, of which it was a summary and guide for interpretation, came to be regarded as the touchstone of Calvinist orthodoxy. There were, nevertheless, remarkably few dissentients, and only in the 19th cent. were certain of its major doctrines seriously questioned. The *Articles Declaratory of the Church of Scotland (1926) distinguished between fundamental doctrines of the Christian faith and those on which liberty of opinion was permitted, and the formula of subscription to the Confession has been considerably modified in most Presbyterian Churches. See Schaff Creeds 1:753–782; 3:598–673 (text); G. S. Hendry, *Westminster Confession for Today* (1960); E. A. Dowey, Jr., *Commentary on the Confession of 1967 and an Introduction to the "Book of Confessions"* (1968). *AUBURN AFFIRMATION; *CONFESSION OF 1967.

WESTMINSTER DIRECTORY FOR WORSHIP, the *Directory for the Public Worship of God*, produced by the *Westminster Assembly and imposed by Parliament in 1645 as a replacement for the Book of Common Prayer (BCP) to bring about in worship the uniformity of practice advocated in the *Solemn League and Covenant. The framers of the Directory were mainly English churchmen of Puritan or Presbyterian inclinations. The influence of the BCP and the *Book of Common Order is evident, and though its use was never widespread in England, the Directory remained a standard of worship in the Church of Scotland until the 1860s, when reforms in worship began to be introduced. In the 1890s similar developments began in American Presbyterianism. The Sunday morning service in the Directory is one of solemn simplicity and strongly scriptural content, with all responses and the Apostles' Creed omitted. The sections on the sacraments, drafted by the Scottish Commissioners at the assembly, preserve the older Scottish tradition. The celebration of communion ("frequently to be celebrated") consists in a warning against unworthy reception and the narrative of institution from 1 Cor 11; the outlines of a prayer of consecration are indicated. For text and commentary see T. Leishman, *Westminster Directory* (1901).

WESTMINSTER STANDARDS, a collective reference to the Confession, Catechisms, and Directory for Worship formulated by the *Westminster Assembly.

WESTPHALIA, PEACE OF, the name for two treaties simultaneously concluded on Oct. 24, 1648, ending the Thirty Years' War. The Treaty of Münster was between the Holy Roman Empire and France; that of Osnabrück, between the Empire and the Protestant Estates as well as Sweden. By the political and territorial determinations, Sweden and France were both greatly strengthened, the independence of Switzerland and the Netherlands was recognized, and the Empire was reduced to a shadow of its former prestige and power. The principle *cuius regio eius religio* was extended to the *Reformed Churches. Protestant and Catholic states were to be equals in the Empire. The *Edict of Restitution (1629) was set aside, and the situation prevailing on Jan. 1, 1624 as to ecclesiastical lands was ratified. Religious questions in the Diet of the Empire were to be settled amicably rather than by coercion, and Protestant administrators of church lands were to be seated. A prince who changed his religion was to forfeit his lands. The influence of the papacy on German ecclesiastical affairs was greatly restricted (Pope Innocent X protested against the treaties in the bull *Zelo domus Dei*, Nov. 16, 1648). By the Peace of Westphalia Protestantism gained strength and official recognition. See C. V. Wedgwood, *Thirty Years' War* (1939).

WHICHCOTE, BENJAMIN (1609–83), a Shropshire man, fellow and tutor of Emmanuel College, Cambridge. His sermons strove to turn men's minds from the form of words to the "inwards of things." Appointed provost of King's College under the *Commonwealth (1644), he was ejected, protesting, at the *Restoration. One of the leading *Cambridge Platonists, he was averse to the pessimism of stiff Puritan doctrine and advanced a freer and more rational spirit in men's converse with God. He was, in consequence, charged at various times with *latitudinarianism, *Arminianism, and *Socinianism. See F. J. Powicke, *Cambridge Platonists* (1926).

WHITE, ELLEN GOULD (1827–1915), cofounder and prophetess of the *Seventh-day Adventists. As a young girl she joined the Methodist Church but embraced *Adventism after hearing W. *Miller preach. The year after her baptism as a Methodist she was disfellowshiped for her Adventist views. She married James White, an Adventist preacher, in 1846. Along with Joseph Bates they are considered the founders of the Seventh-day Adventists. In 1855 the Whites moved to Battle Creek, Mich., where the first church conference was held in 1863. After her husband died (1881), W. traveled and lectured in Europe (1885–87) and in Australia (1891–1900). At the time of her death the Seventh-day Adventists had 136,879 members. Although never ordained a minister or elected to any church office, W. has been the most influential figure in the history of her Church. Adventists consider her to have possessed the gift of prophecy; her numerous visions were decisive in resolving many problems of doctrine and practice. Her first vision took place in 1844; in it the tiny band of Adventists were described as the remnant of true believers. When in a trance state, W. appeared to suspend breathing, her muscles became rigid, and sometimes she remained deprived of sight for 3 hours. One vision depicted the commandment "Remember that thou keep holy the Sabbath day" surrounded by a halo of light. Although her formal education ended at the age of 9 because of a head injury, during her lifetime she wrote 24 books, 4,600 articles, and numerous tracts, pamphlets, and unpublished manuscripts. Her total literary output exceeded 25 million words. Her works include the *Conflict of the Ages* series (5v., 1888–1911) and *Testimonies for the Church* (9v., 1855–1909). In Seventh-day Adventist seminaries and colleges her writings are still studied as inspired. See F. D. Nichol, *E. G. W. and Her Critics* (1951); D. M. Canright, *Life of E. G. W.* (1919).

WHITE, WILLIAM (1748–1836), bishop, leader in the formation of the *Protestant Episcopal Church. Graduated from Franklin's College (now the Univ. of Pa.) in 1765, he was ordained in the Anglican Church (deacon in 1770, priest in 1772). As assistant rector and later rector of Christ Church, Philadelphia, W. was prominent among his fellow churchmen who were Whigs during the Revolution; he was chaplain of Congress (1777–1800), and after the war worked to moderate popular antipathy toward his Church. In the reorganization that led to the Protestant Episcopal Church, he helped draw up a constitution that emphasized lay control and the equality of all Churches in a free nation. Consecrated bp. of Philadelphia (1787), he became first president of the *General Convention in 1789, and in 1795, presiding bishop of the Episcopal Church. His primary contribution to American religion was the application of John Locke's political theories to the polity of the Episcopal Church. See W. W., *Case of the Episcopal Churches in the United States Considered* (ed. R. G. Salomon, 1954); W. H. Stowe, *Life and Letters of Bishop W. W.* (1937); W. H. Manross, *W. W.* (1934).

WHITEFIELD, GEORGE (1714–70), one of the greatest pulpit orators of the 18th century. W. was born in Gloucester, England; he left school for a year to assist his widowed mother, but continued reading, esp. the Bible and the *Imitation of Christ*, which deeply impressed him. In 1732 he entered Pembroke College, Oxford, as a servitor, working for his education. In 1734 he met Charles *Wesley, who invited him to join the *holy club, and he began a life of severe asceticism. This brought him no satisfaction, but in 1735 he found peace through faith in Christ. He was ordained a deacon at Gloucester, June 20, 1736, and became a popular preacher around London. At the invitation of John *Wesley he went to Ga., where he conducted a successful ministry. Returning to London, he discovered that the strong language in his published *Journal* had hurt his popularity, and some church doors were closed against him. He was ordained priest in the C of E in 1739, and the same year preached in the open fields (see FIELD PREACHING) to large crowds of colliers at Kingswood. At his request John Wesley assisted him, and outdoor preaching became important to the growth of Methodism. Back in the American colonies, 1739–40, he was one of the leading figures in the *Great Awakening and preached effectively along the entire Seaboard. In 1743 in Wales he assisted Howell *Harris in organizing the *Calvinistic Methodists. He split with the Wesleys, favoring the Calvinist doctrine of election against the Arminian doctrine of free will (see ARMINIANISM). He was chaplain for Selina, Countess of *Huntingdon, preaching in her home and chapels to her friends. In all he made seven American preaching tours. The impact of his preaching came not from its content but from his personality. He is not considered a founder of Methodism in America; he disregarded denominational lines. While differing from the Wesleys, he remained their friend and requested that John Wesley preached his funeral sermon. He died, however, in Newburyport, Mass., and is buried there. See S. C. Henry, *G. W.: Wayfaring Witness* (1957); *G. W.'s Journals* (introd. I. Murray, 1960); HistAmMeth 1:69–73.

WHITGIFT, JOHN (c.1530–1604), abp. of Canterbury; resister of Puritan influence. W. turned to Reformation doctrine even before becoming a student at Cambridge. Having received his M.A. in 1557, he was ordained in 1560 in one of the first ordinations of Elizabeth I's reign. At Cambridge he was made Lady Margaret Professor of Divinity in 1563, and in 1567 master of Trinity College and Regius Professor of Divinity. In 1577 Elizabeth made him bp. of Worcester, and in 1583 abp. of Canterbury. Opposition to the Puritans began when W., while master of Trinity and vice-chancellor of the university, had T. *Cartwright deprived of his professorship (1570) for attacking *episcopacy in the Church of England. The abp. sought to enforce ritual uniformity, dealt severely with the circulators of the *Marprelate Tracts, and thwarted Puritan efforts in 1584–85 to abolish episcopacy in the Church. The *Lambeth Articles issued under his sponsorship in 1595, however, attest to W.'s acceptance of the Calvinistic doctrine on absolute predestination of the elect and reprobation of all others. See V. J. K. Brook, *W. and the English Church* (1957); Hughes RE, 3:167–174, 193–201, 206, 228.

WHOLE DUTY OF MAN, the title of a devotional manual widely used in England. Published c.1658 under the *Commonwealth, when high Anglicanism had gone underground, it is composed of 17 moral discourses, "one whereof being read every Lord's Day, the whole may be read over thrice a year." It was probably composed by Richard Allestree, the preface is by Henry Hammond, and John Fell seems to have been associated with its production; all three were Oxford men who inherited and transmitted the noble spirituality of the *Caroline Divines and combined ideals that were exacting with lessons that were practicable.

WILBUR, JOHN (1774–1856), American Quaker. Born in Hopkinton, R.I., he became the leader of those orthodox Friends who, in the 1840s, gave more emphasis to the traditional Quaker belief in *Inner Light than to evangelical Protestant tenets (see HICKS, E.; GRELLET, S.). These Friends were called Wilburites or Conservatives, as against Gurneyites (see GURNEY, J.) or Evangelicals. See E. Bronner, ed., *American Quakers Today* (1966), 20–31; bibliog. for Friends.

WILBURITES, the 19th-cent. Quakers who followed J. *Wilbur's emphasis on *Inner Light; also the Quaker bodies tracing their separate origin to Wilbur's interpretation of Quaker teaching.

WILLIAM OF OCKHAM (Occam; c.1285–1347), as representative of "the modern way" (*via moderna*), one of the most influential philosophical and politico-theological figures of the 14th century. He was born in Surrey, Eng., became a Franciscan, and studied and taught at Oxford. A robust and prolific controversialist and a complex but unified thinker, his work may be considered under the three heads of logic and epistemology, of scholastic theology, and of Church-State relations. Under the first, he is a seminal force in the history of *nominalism; his close and exact analysis of the grammar of scientific discourse, in which he anticipated theorems of modern logic, and his severe economy about the multiplication of entities—"Ockham's razor"—set up a terminism that reduced universals to conceptual modes applied to unique and irreducible things. It was opposed to the critical realism of the Thomist, Scotist, and Augustinian schools, and became prevalent in the universities, notably Paris, Oxford, Heidelberg, Vienna, Erfurt, and Leipzig.

His skepticism about the validity of metaphysics entered into theology; this was marked by a sort of retreat from reason to faith, which, however, was never headlong and brought off its rational baggage intact. The freedom of omnipotence was stressed against the alleged necessitarianism of divine ideas; the universe was conceived as an expression of God's will rather than of his mind. Hence the paradoxes that God could create "impossibilities" and could contradict what men consider to be his moral law. Constant recourse was made to the distinction between the ordinate power (*potentia ordinata*) and the absolute power (*potentia absoluta*) of God. He looms largest, however, in religious history as a leading figure in the fight between the twin establishments of secular and sacred power, and between the last and the poverty ideals of the Franciscan *Spirituals. O. was summoned from Oxford to Avignon by John XXII, no mean antagonist; though many of his propositions were judged open to censure, he was not condemned, perhaps because an assessor, the Dominican Durand of Saint-Pourçain, was himself a stormy petrel. O. threw himself into the support of his minister general, Michael of Cesena, attacked the Pope, and fled to the side of the Emperor, Louis of Bavaria, at Munich. There he conducted a vigorous polemic, giving as much as he took, against papal jurisdiction in temporalities. He was, of course, excommunicated, but those were

the days when harsh words broke no bones and ecclesiastics could not be closely and effectively regimented. He was much respected, his title was the *venerabilis inceptor*; he was elected general by the brethren of his party, and died professing his obedience to legitimate authority. His position in the genealogy of Lutheranism, of Pietism, and of positivism calls for very cautious and qualified attribution. See P. Boehner, *Ockham, Philosophical Writings* (1957); G. de Lagarde, *La naissance de l'espirit laïque* (1956–63), v.4. and 5.

WILLIAMITES, a designation applied to a number of religious groups, from the name of their founders. Among the more important of these are: (1) the Benedictine congregation founded by St. William of Vercelli (d. 1142); (2) the Hermits of St. William organized by disciples of St. William of Maleval (d. 1157); and (3) a short-lived heterodox sect headed by Wilhelmina of Milan (d. 1282). See M. Habig, NCE 14:942.

WILLIAMS, GEORGE (1821–1905), founder of the *Young Men's Christian Association (YMCA). He was a young clerk in London when, with 12 fellow workers, he formed the YMCA to assist urban workers to live a good Christian life. From 1886 until his death he was president of the association, which spread throughout the world. During the 50th anniversary of the London YMCA, W. received knighthood from Queen Victoria. He was also active in the *British and Foreign Bible Society, the *Church Missionary Society and other organizations devoted to temperance and mission work.

WILLIAMS, ROGER (c.1603–83), champion of religious liberty. Born in England and educated at Cambridge, W. was ordained in the C of E but early became a *Separatist and went to Massachusetts Bay in 1631. He alienated pastors and magistrates by his extreme Separatist views, his insistence that only purchase, not royal grants, conferred title to land, and his denial that civil magistrates had any authority in strictly religious matters. Banished from Mass. in 1636, he obtained land from Indians to establish with other associates Providence Plantations, the Rhode Island colony, granting complete religious freedom to all inhabitants. At Providence, W. helped to organize the first Baptist church in America, but he remained a Baptist for only a few weeks. The rest of his life he was a *Seeker. Believing that direct *apostolic succession is necessary to a true Church, and that no such ministry had existed since the early centuries, he concluded that there is no true Church on earth. In *The Hireling Ministry None of Christ's* (1652), he published his opinions on this subject. During a visit to England in 1644 he published *The Bloudy Tenent, of Persecution for Cause of Conscience.* After a rebuttal by John *Cotton, he wrote *The Bloody Tenent Yet More Bloody* (1652). Williams's writings were revived by Isaac *Backus during his struggle for religious liberty in Massachusetts. Modern historians have portrayed W. as a liberal democrat and an agnostic, who was far in advance of his time. They failed to recognize that his views differed radically from the natural-rights philosophers. In his theology, W. was a Puritan of the Puritans, and his doctrine of religious liberty derived from his Calvinist views on God's absolute sovereignty and predestination and from a typological interpretation of the OT. He held that church membership must be restricted to the regenerate and could not include a whole civic community. An established Church could only be maintained by coercion, which has no place in matters of conscience. Church and State must be kept totally separated. Often acclaimed as the pioneer Baptist in America, his brief relationship with that denomination had little influence upon its development. Baptists honor him, however, because he so well symbolizes their concern for religious freedom. His works are contained in *Complete Writings of R. W.* (ed. P. Miller, 7v., 1963). See P. Miller, *R. W.* (1953); L. A. Moore, "R. W. and the Historians," *Church History* 32 (1963), 432–451; B. E. Winslow, *Master R. W.* (1957).

WIMPFELING, JAKOB (1450–1528), German humanist. In his early schooling he came under the influence of the tradition of the *Brethren of the Common Life, and he went on to study at Freiburg, Erfurt, and Heidelberg (where he served for a time as rector). He was cathedral preacher at Speyer, 1484–98. He was actively interested in the revival of classical literature and was leader of a circle of humanists at Strassburg (1501–15). In his two educational treatises, *Isidoneus* and *Adolescentia,* he stressed the value of grammar, literature, and ethical formation in the spirit of the Devotio moderna. Despite his fundamental conservatism, W. sympathized with much of Luther's criticism of the Church. He attacked monastic orders, charging them with decadence; urged the strict observance of priestly celibacy; and called for an end to simoniacal practices. Yet he remained loyal to the papacy and was saddened toward the end of his life to see scholars whom he had helped to educate turning to the Reformation. See L. W. Spitz, *Religious Renaissance of the German Humanists* (1963), 41–60; *idem,* NCE 14:954.

WINCHESTER PROFESSION OF BELIEF, a statement of faith adopted by the New England Convention of Universalist Churches meeting at Winchester, N.H., in 1803. The Profession contains three articles: that Scripture contains a revelation on "the character of God" and on human destiny; that God is one, and is love revealed in Jesus by the Holy Spirit of Grace, and that there will be a final restoration of all mankind (see APOCATASTASIS); that happiness and holiness are inseparably connected.

The document was intended to allow both Trinitarian and Unitarian views, and various interpretations of Universalism (e.g., those of John Murray, Elhanan Winchester, Caleb Rich, Hosea Ballou, Abel Sarjent). The Profession was a statement of principles for all who accepted Universalism and was not a formula to be imposed as a condition for membership. See R. Eddy, *Universalism in America* (2v., 1884–86); Schaff Creeds 1:933–934. *UNIVERSALISM.

WINEBRENNER, JOHN (1797–1860), founder of the Churches of God in North America (General Eldership). Born in Frederick Co., Md., he attended Dickinson College, Carlisle, Pa., and was ordained in 1820 as pastor of Salem German Reformed Church, Harrisburg, Pennsylvania. W. wholeheartedly accepted *camp meetings and *revivalism. His prayer meetings and fellowship with Methodists led to his expulsion from the *Reformed ministry in 1825. He formed "a church on the New Testament plan" with others, taking the Bible as the only rule of faith. His evangelism throughout central Pa. developed a movement among German-speaking Christians similar to that led by Alexander *Campbell. W. published *A Brief View of the Formation, Government and Discipline of the Churches of God* in 1829 and reluctantly accepted denominational leadership as general elder in 1830. He was an active champion of temperance and the abolition of slavery and served as pastor of the Harrisburg congregation until his death.

WINSTANLEY, GERRARD (1609–c.1660), *Leveler, religious and social writer. W. began to write first of his mystical experience of the divine light within man, in his *New Law of Righteousness* (1648); Thomas Coomber, Dean of Durham, writing in 1678, mistakenly called him the founder of the Quakers (see INNER LIGHT). W. next advocated a classless society without private property, e.g., in *The Law of Freedom in a Platform* (1652); he became the leader of the short-lived *Digger movement; his thought turned to materialism and pantheism, and he came to view religion simply as a means for fostering social justice. See L. D. Hamilton, ed., *G. W., Selections from His Works* (1944); R. M. Jones, *Studies in Mystical Religion* (1923), 493–500.

WISCONSIN EVANGELICAL LUTHERAN SYNOD, Lutheran denomination organized in 1849 as the First German Evangelical Lutheran Synod of Wisconsin. Its constitution was adopted by five ministers, who represented 18 congregations. Early growth was rapid, the young synod being greatly aided by the Langenberg and Berlin Mission Societies and by the Home Mission Society of Pennsylvania. By 1881 the Church had penetrated into Nebraska, Washington, Oregon, Idaho, and Montana. In 1892 it joined with the Michigan Synod and with the Minnesota Synod, which had been organized by a group of pastors from Philadelphia and Pittsburgh Synods at work in Minnesota. The merger was called the Joint Evangelical Lutheran Synod of Wisconsin, Minnesota, and Michigan. The three synods formed a closer union in 1917 under the name of the Evangelical Lutheran Joint Synod of Wisconsin and Other States. In 1958 their title was changed again, this time to the Wisconsin Evangelical Lutheran Synod. Doctrinally, the Synod accepts "the Confession of the Evangelical Lutheran Church embodied in the Book of Concord of 1580, not insofar as, but because, they are a correct presentation and exposition of the pure doctrine of the Word of God." The Church had 853 congregations and 182 mission stations in 1965, and its membership was 354,840. See E. C. Kiessling, EncLuthCh 3:2480–83.

WITHERSPOON, JOHN (1722–94), Presbyterian clergyman, educator, and statesman. After graduation from the Univ. of Edinburgh, near his birthplace, W. served pastorates in Scotland. He stood with the evangelicals against the moderates, whom he satirized in *Ecclesiastical Characteristics* (1753), a work that brought him considerable attention. In 1768 he assumed the presidency of the College of New Jersey (now Princeton), where he served with distinction, lecturing on theology, moral philosophy, and rhetoric, and where he encouraged the study of Hebrew, French, and science. He was the only clergyman to sign the Declaration of Independence (1776). Through him the Scottish Common Sense Realists were an influence on the *Princeton theology of A. *Alexander and C. *Hodge. See V. L. Collins, *President Witherspoon* (2v., 1925).

WITNESS, personal testimony. In secular and biblical literature, the Greek term *martys* signifies the attestation of a person. Personal testimony may express itself in a confession, preaching, prayer, teaching, or martyrdom, but it always conveys, unless it is false, a personal commitment to a fact or truth. In the Bible witness has both legal (Dt 19.15; 2 Cor 13.1; 1 Tim 5.19) and theological significance. Jesus himself is a witness to the Father (Jn 3.11; 5.36; 8.14, 26; 18.37). The Apostles in turn are to testify to him (Lk 24.48; Acts 1.8; Jn 15.27), to his resurrection as well as to his earthly life (Acts 1.22; 4.33; 5, 32; 10.42; 13.31; 22.15; 26, 16). This role of witness to faith in Jesus was taken up by the entire Christian community and was manifested in martyrdom (Acts 22.20); it helped to characterize the age of the Church Fathers. The historicity of the biblical witness has been so debated, almost throughout the Christian era, as to have occasioned methodological questions about history and faith, the Jesus of history and the Christ of faith, factual testimony and the testimony to truth. The outcome of the debate is not yet in sight, but a solution lies in linking fact with significance. The purpose of Christian witness is twofold: to bring the believer to the full realization of his faith, his unique relationship to God, and to win others to Christ (2 Th 1.10). See EDB 2591–94.

WITTENBERG, CONCORD OF, an effort to harmonize Lutheran and Zwinglian teaching on the Eucharist, at a meeting held in Wittenberg in 1536. Martin Luther himself was there; Philipp *Melanchthon presented a document setting forth Lutheran teaching on the *Real Presence. Martin *Bucer, who represented the Zwinglian side and whose efforts at conciliation since the failure of the *Marburg Articles (1529) had brought about the meeting, gave assurance that the doctrine as stated could be accepted by the Churches of S Germany and Switzerland. The hopes of Wittenberg were dashed, however, when the Swiss Churches rejected the agreement.

WOMEN'S CHRISTIAN TEMPERANCE UNION (WCTU), a society for the encouragement of personal total abstinence based on Christian principles, and for the abolition of the liquor traffic. The idea for such a society came at a *Chatauqua meeting; organization was completed in Cleveland, Ohio, in 1874. Frances E. Willard (1839–98), who was first corresponding secretary, then president (1879–98), established branches throughout the U.S., and in 1883 formed the World's WCTU. She was a Methodist, and the organization received the strong support of the Methodist and other Protestant Churches. The WCTU, in spite of the setback represented by the repeal of the 18th Amendment, continues to work for its objectives. There are units in all the states and organizations for all age groups. Headquarters are in Evanston, Ill., where the Frances E. Willard Memorial Library for Alcoholic Research is also located. See M. Earhart, *Frances Willard: From Progress to Politics* (1944). *TEMPERANCE MOVEMENT.

WORLD ALLIANCE OF REFORMED CHURCHES, a shorter alternate title for the *Alliance of the Reformed Churches throughout the World Holding the Presbyterian Order; it is also named the World Presbyterian Alliance.

WORLD CONVENTION OF CHURCHES OF CHRIST, an agency formed in 1930 for communication and fellowship for the Christian Churches (Disciples of Christ) throughout the world. Membership of the churches served by the World Convention was over 2,500,000, in 33 countries, in 1968. The organization also serves the aim of unity with other Christians on a NT basis. Assemblies of the World Convention are held every 5 years; headquarters are in New York City.

WORLD COUNCIL OF CHRISTIAN ED-UCATION (WCCE), a service agency founded in 1907 to link together the Christian church bodies of all countries dealing with religious education. With 71 member units and 5 associated regional organizations, WCCE is devoted to the development of more effective educational programs and competent leadership by the provision of educational aids and training materials, by educational consultations and studies, and by international educational institutes. Its program revolves esp. around improved biblical studies and the encouragement of interdenominational cooperation toward Christian unity. In 1967 it presented to the Bristol meeting of the World Council of Churches' *Faith and Order Commission a detailed program for ecumenical commitment in Christian education.

WORLD COUNCIL OF CHURCHES (WCC), an international, interconfessional organization of Christian Churches designed to facilitate unity in fellowship, service, and mission. Headquarters are in Geneva, Switzerland. The WCC at its beginning defined itself as "a fellowship of Churches which accept our Lord Jesus Christ as God and Savior." In 1961 at the *New Delhi Assembly this was expanded to "a fellowship of Churches which confess the Lord Jesus Christ as God and Savior according to the Scriptures and therefore

seek to fulfill together their common calling to the glory of the one God, Father, Son, and Holy Spirit." The WCC was formally constituted Aug. 23, 1948, at the *Amsterdam Assembly. Groundwork for the organization had been laid at a 1938 meeting in Utrecht, but World War II intervened, and until the Amsterdam Assembly the letterhead of the organization carried the line "in process of formation." At Utrecht, Abp. W. *Temple (1881–1944) was elected chairman of the Provisional Committee, and W. A. Visser 't Hooft, secretary; in 1948 the latter became the first general secretary of the WCC. The WCC represented the union of two lines of ecumenical development, *Life and Work and *Faith and Order. Life and Work, led initially by Abp. N. *Söderblom, sponsored the *Stockholm (1925) and *Oxford (1937) Conferences, which sought a unity of Christian efforts, despite doctrinal differences, toward the solution of various problems of society. Faith and Order, led initially by Bp. C. H. *Brent (1862–1929), sponsored the Lausanne (1927) and Edinburgh (1937) Conferences, which sought to deal with doctrinal differences. At the Oxford and Edinburgh Conferences both groups, which included many of the same individuals, decided that the two aspects of the ecumenical movement could not properly be separated, so plans were laid that led to the organization of the WCC; the name was suggested by S. M. Cavert, an American ecumenist. At the New Delhi Assembly a third line of ecumenical development, represented by the *International Missionary Council (IMC), merged with the WCC, becoming the Division of World Mission and Evangelism.

The highest authority of the WCC is the General Assembly, which normally meets every 7th year. Between assemblies the WCC is guided by a central committee of 100 members, normally meeting once a year, and a smaller executive committee, which normally meets twice a year. The WCC has a presidium composed of six presidents, who are chosen to give broad representation, geographically and confessionally. The full-time executive staff is headed by the general secretary. Eugene Carson Blake, former Stated Clerk of the United Presbyterian Church, succeeded Visser 't Hooft as general secretary in 1966. The WCC is not itself a Church; nor does it exercise the authority of a Church. Membership in the WCC does not require that a Church recognize other member communions as Churches in the full sense, that it accept the full validity of their ministries, or that it practice *intercommunion with them. The WCC is an organizational means for the members to work together in service projects, to meet together for deeper fellowship and mutual understanding, and to present a more united witness in preaching the gospel. The WCC continues the work of those lines of ecumenical development that it incorporates, sponsors such projects as the Christian Student Movement and Church World Service, and maintains the Ecumenical Institute at Chateau de Bôssey, near Geneva. Statements on various subjects issued by the WCC are not binding on the member bodies.

The membership of the WCC currently embraces most of the Christian Churches of the world, about 225 in 1968, including most of the Eastern Orthodox Churches. Some conservative groups have chosen not to seek membership, fearing that it would mean compromise of doctrinal conviction and that the WCC might become a centralized, authoritarian organization that would endanger freedom. In the U.S. the Southern Baptist Convention, the Lutheran Church —Missouri Synod, and several smaller conservative bodies have remained outside. Liberal groups, such as the Unitarians, are prevented from belonging because they do not meet the WCC requirement of belief in Jesus Christ as God and Savior. Some conservatives, although they favor ecumenical cooperation, oppose the WCC because its leadership includes some whom they consider too liberal in doctrine, and because they object to positions taken by WCC leadership on contemporary social issues (see WORLD EVANGELICAL FELLOWSHIP; INTERNATIONAL COUNCIL OF CHRISTIAN CHURCHES).

Roman Catholics, although invited to attend the Amsterdam Assembly, were forbidden to do so by a *monitum* of the Holy Office. In 1928 after the Stockholm and Lausanne Conferences, Pius XI declared, "The Apostolic See can by no means take part in these assemblies nor is it in any way lawful for Catholics to give such enterprises their encouragement and support. If they did so, they would be giving countenance to a false Christianity quite alien to the one Church of Christ." With the coming of Vatican II, however, and the change of atmosphere associated with John XXIII, official RC observers were sent to the New Delhi Assembly, and WCC observers were invited to, and attended, Vatican II. In 1965 Paul VI and the WCC established a joint continuing committee to work on a regular basis for dialogue and cooperation. Nine of the official RC observers at the Uppsala Assembly (1968) were elected to membership on the Faith and Order Commission. On a visit to WCC headquarters at Geneva on June 10, 1969, Paul VI stated that the question of RC membership in the WCC was not yet mature. See official reports of the Assemblies ed. by W. A. Visser 't Hooft; G. K. A. Bell, *Kingship of Christ* (1954).

WORLD COUNCIL OF CHURCHES, United States Conference for the, an organization of the Churches in the U.S. that are members of the *World Council of Churches (WCC). It is a continuation of the American Committee for the WCC established in 1938, when plans were first laid for the formation of the WCC. When the WCC was formally constituted at the 1948 *Amsterdam Assembly, the Committee was renamed the Conference of U.S.A. Member Churches of the WCC, and the name was later changed to its present form. The Conference meets annually and is composed of the delegates and alternates from the U.S. Churches to the preceding general assembly of the WCC. Normally one of the presidents of the WCC is an American, and he serves as chairman of the Conference. The Conference employs a full-time staff—the only regional conference of the WCC to do so—and its offices are at 475 Riverside Drive, New York City. The Conference promotes the work of the WCC in the U.S. and works to raise the U.S. portion of the WCC budget (currently about $600,000 annually, more than half the total), as well as its own budget of about $100,000. The Conference serves as the coordinating link between WCC headquarters in Geneva and the U.S. member Churches. It is to be distinguished from the *National Council of Churches, which cooperates with the WCC and has generally the same membership but is an independent organization.

WORLD EVANGELICAL FELLOWSHIP, an association formed at Woudschoten, Holland, in 1951. The Fellowship regards the *World Council of Churches as too liberal, and the *International Council of Churches as reactionary. Headquarters in 1968 were maintained in Don Mills, Ont., Canada, with an editorial office in London. Among the affiliates are the *Evangelical Alliance and the *National Association of Evangelicals.

WORLD METHODIST COUNCIL, a federation of Methodist bodies for promoting ecumenical, evangelistic, educational, and historical emphases among autonomous Methodist bodies in 86 different countries. The functions of this agency are fraternal and cooperative, and it has no legislative powers. Named the World Methodist Council in 1951, it is the successor to the Ecumenical Methodist Conference, which convened at 10-year intervals from 1881. Permanent secretaries were established in 1951, one in England and one in the U.S., and a slate of officers and representatives was chosen as a World Executive Committee to sponsor a World Methodist Conference every 5 years and to carry on the work of the organization in the interim. Headquarters were established at Lake Junaluska, N.C., in 1953. Among its activities the

Council has helped sponsor a series of publications, including a *Who's Who in Methodism* (1952), and is currently (1968) preparing an *Encyclopedia of Methodism.* The Council supervises ministerial exchanges among Methodists of different countries, and has established the Oxford Theological Institute, a quadrennial meeting of 100 selected Methodist theologians at Lincoln College, Oxford. The Council named the Methodist observers to Vatican Council II and planned (1968) to open an office at the Ecumenical Center in Geneva to replace the office in London. Its official periodical is *World Parish.* See Hist-AmMeth 3:578, 579; I. L. Holt and E. T. Clark, *World Methodist Movement* (1956), 89–120.

WORLD PRESBYTERIAN ALLIANCE, shortened title of the *Alliance of the Reformed Churches throughout the World Holding the Presbyterian Order.

WORLD STUDENT CHRISTIAN FEDERATION, a union of national student Christian movements organized at Vadstena, Sweden, in 1895 to aid in building and strengthening a multiracial, ecumenical witnessing community of Christians in institutions of higher learning throughout the world. With headquarters in Geneva, Switzerland, it now embraces student organizations in more than 75 countries. It is affiliated with the international YMCA and YWCA, as well as with the World Council of Christian Education and the World Council of Churches; it maintains relations with other international student groups, such as Pax Romana and the World Union of Jewish Students, and enjoys consultative status in the United Nations' Educational, Scientific, and Cultural Organization (UNESCO).

WORLD'S CHRISTIAN ENDEAVOR UNION, an agency formed in 1895 to coordinate the activities and interests of the member organizations of the Christian Endeavor movement throughout the world. *CHRISTIAN ENDEAVOR, INTERNATIONAL SOCIETY OF.

WORMS, DIET OF, in Reformation history the sessions of the Imperial Diet, Jan. 27–May 25, 1521, before which Martin Luther was summoned to defend his teaching. That this civil body sat in judgment on doctrinal issues was not in accord with papal views or wishes, but it served the national interest to solve the problems raised by Luther in Germany. The papal legate at Worms, Aleander, urged the implementation of the excommunication of Luther already given at Rome (see EXSURGE DOMINE). Luther appeared in the presence of Emperor Charles V, on April 17–18. On the first day, before a small committee of the Diet, he requested more time to deliberate about his own subscription to what he had written, esp. against the sacraments and the primacy of the pope. On the second, before the whole assembly, he made his refusal to recant in a statement that tradition quotes in the words, "Here I stand. I can do no other," rejecting popes and councils and appealing to his conscience, captive to the word of God. On May 25 the Edict of Worms was signed by the Emperor, making Luther liable to punishment by burning for subverting the established order. But before that Luther had been given refuge in the *Wartburg.

WORMS, DISPUTATION OF, conference on reunion held at the Diet of Worms between Catholics and Protestants, begun in Nov. 1540 and terminated in Jan. 1541. Most of the time was spent on procedural matters. Finally, with J. *Eck the spokesman for the Catholics and P. *Melanchthon for the Protestants, a discussion based on the *Augsburg Confession was conducted. A formula of agreement on *original sin was reached, but the Emperor Charles V transferred the discussion to the Conference of *Regensburg. See Jedin Trent 1:374–377.

WORSHIP, the exhibition to God by some act of mind or body, or both, of the honor and reverence due to him by reason of his supreme dominion. Such acts may be private or public and communal. Different forms of worship include, with varying emphasis, confession and repentance for sin, praise, petition, and thanksgiving. Among Roman Catholics the term has been applied not only to the cultic acts due to God alone (*latria*), but also to those rendered to his saints because of their special relationship to him (*dulia*). In later usage, however, the term is more commonly restricted to the kind of reverence shown only to God, and, to avoid misleading ambiguity, the honor exhibited to the saints is generally spoken of as veneration. Among Protestants the word is sometimes used to distinguish one form of service from another, e.g., a worship, as distinguished from a preaching, service; in Catholic practice the specific forms of service are generally designated by their proper names.

WORSHIP, BOOK OF, see BOOK OF WORSHIP (METHODIST).

WÜRTTEMBERG CONFESSION, a Lutheran *confession of faith, prepared in 1551 by Johannes Brenz (1499–1570) for presentation at the Council of *Trent. Like the *Saxon Confession, it was prepared to satisfy the wish of the Emperor and Duke Christopher of Württemberg for representation of Lutheran teaching at Trent. The delegation presenting the document, Jan. 24, 1552, had no success. The Württemberg Confession follows closely the *Augsburg Confession, but it was not incorporated into the *Book of Concord. It was consulted in the preparation of the *Thirty-Nine Articles of the Church of England. See Schaff Creeds 1:343–344, 627–628.

WYCLIFFE, JOHN (Wiclif, Wyclif, etc.; *c.*1320–84), English reformer. A native of Wycliffe-on-Tees in Yorkshire, W. received appointments as parish priest of Fillingham (1361), Ludgerhall (1368), and Lutterworth (1374). His life, however, was passed mainly in the academic world of Oxford, where he developed those teachings that were later condemned as heretical by the Council of *Constance (1415; see D 1151–95). His title "Morning Star of the Reformation" rests primarily upon his denial of *transubstantiation and upon his *ecclesiology. W. was not a profound philosopher or theologian; no philosophical position except that of extreme realism in regard to universals shaped his religious thinking. His denial of transubstantiation was a purely speculative consequence. The substance of bread and wine could not be changed, much less annihilated as the Scotists taught, because, like everything that exists, these substances were participations in the eternal, necessary, and real universals existing in the divine mind. Transubstantiation would mean God's negating himself. However obscure his own explanation of the Real Presence, W. did not anticipate later Zwinglian, Calvinistic, or Lutheran teaching; nor did he deny the sacrifice of the Mass.

A theological determinism derived from Thomas Bradwardine (*c*.1290–1349) enabled W. to look at the Church the way he looked at the world of universals; it was the *universitas praedestinatorum*, neatly determined through the infallible workings of faith in the predestined. They were surely guided interiorly to interpret the gospel, which was the sole and sufficient rule of faith; and they had no insuperable need for a sanctifying ministry. It was, then, no problem for W. to do away with the teaching and sanctifying ministry of the Church. This he did through his theory of *dominium*, lordship, in *De dominio divino* (1375) and *De civili dominio* (1376). These are the first two of the collection of treatises called his *Summa theologiae* (written 1374–84; of its other treatises, the *De ecclesia* [1378], *De potestate papae* [1379], and the *Trialogus* [1382] were much used by Jan *Hus). He was also a popular preacher and pamphleteer; instituted his "poor priests,"

itinerant and unlicensed lay preachers (see LOLLARDS); and the Wycliffe Bible was a part of this campaign of popular instruction. W.'s theory and applications on lordship must also be taken against the background of his political and reform activities. From 1374 onward he several times favored the civil over the ecclesiastical powers in conflicts on provisions, papal tithes, and the law of sanctuary. The theory itself was derived from Richard Fitzralph, and fitted W.'s practical resistance to ecclesiastical jurisdiction. Lordship meant feudal suzerainty; it belonged properly to God alone, was shared through grace by all the predestined, and by them only, and was lost by mortal sin. He extended the notion to include the teaching and sanctifying power of the Church, and, esp. after the *Great Western Schism (1379), rejected the papacy outright as a diabolical usurpation. W. also inveighed against the religious orders (he called them "sects"), but this seemed to have been a reprisal for their opposition to his Eucharistic doctrine.

In 1377 Gregory XI condemned a series of W.'s propositions (D 1121–39) and called for an inquiry, which never took place. A synod held at Blackfriars, London (1382) censured 24 propositions from W.'s writings; W., however, was supported by the Univ. of Oxford and suffered little inconvenience. The instruction of Constance that his bones be exhumed and scattered was finally carried out in 1428. W.'s chief impact was not upon the English, but upon the Continental Reformation, through Hus and the *Hussites (see JEROME OF PRAGUE). See Bihlmeyer-Tüchle 2:435–437; J. Dahmus, NCE 14:1050–52; Gilson HCP 771–772; M. Spinka, *Advocates of Reform from Wyclif to Erasmus* (1953); S. P. H. Thomson, EncPhil 8:351–352; H. B. Workman, *J. W.* (2v., 1926).

WYCLIFFE BIBLE TRANSLATORS, INC., a society for translating the Scriptures into all languages now in use. It had its beginning in a Summer Institute of Linguistics organized in Sulphur Springs, Ark., in 1934 by William Cameron Townsend and L. L. Letgers. In 1935 the first translation team was sent to Mexico. In 1942 the Institute was moved to the campus of the Univ. of Oklahoma. There are now three such institutes in the U.S. and four in other countries. More than 1,500 workers are involved in translating the Bible into 330 languages. The Wycliffe Bible Translators cooperate with other *Bible societies and with all Christian Churches. In 1947 it established a Jungle Aviation and Radio Service, Inc., a department to service its linguists in remote areas. This division also renders valuable aid to natives, esp. in emergencies. The doctrinal views of the organization, as contained in the articles of incorporation, include belief in the divine inspiration of the Scriptures; the Trinity; man's Fall and redemption by Christ; justification by faith; the resurrection of the body; and eternal reward or punishment.

WYCLIFFITES (Wyclifites), a term used, esp. in late medieval ecclesiastical documents, to designate not only *Lollards but anyone accepting the teachings of John *Wycliffe or similar doctrines. See D 1151–95; 1247–79.

X-Y-Z

XENOGLOSSY (Xenolalia), the ecstatic utterance of a strange language (Gr. *xeno*, strange, foreign; *glossa*, tongue; *lalia*, talking) by a person who had no previous knowledge of that language. Among Pentecostals *glossolalia usually occurs as sounds, inarticulate or articulate, that are not identifiable as a language. Cases of xenoglossy, however, have also been reported. See N. Bloch-Hoell, *Pentecostal Movement* (1964), 141–145.

YORKER BRETHREN, see OLD ORDER (YORKER) BRETHREN.

YOUNG, BRIGHAM (1801–77), Mormon leader and colonizer. Although he had only 11 days of formal schooling, Y. became one of America's great colonizers and religious leaders. Born in Whitingham, Vt., he worked as a carpenter and glazier as a young man. He joined the Methodist Church at 21 but read the *Book of Mormon, accepted its authenticity, and was baptized in the Mormon Church in 1832. Y. joined the Mormon prophet Joseph *Smith and the infant Church in Kirtland, Ohio, and rose to the rank of apostle. He accompanied the Mormons to Missouri and to Nauvoo, Ill.; in 1840 he left Nauvoo for a mission assignment in England. When Smith was murdered in 1844, Y. was seeking converts in the eastern states. He hurried back to the Mormon city and assumed leadership of most of the stricken Mormons. He directed the epic march to the valley of the Great Salt Lake and established the Mormon theocracy in Utah. He was appointed governor of the Utah territory in 1850, but aroused the hostility of the federal government and many non-Mormons when he openly preached the doctrine of *plural marriage after 1852. Federal troops threatened to occupy Salt Lake City (1857–58), but Y. countered by making plans to burn the city and the military action was abandoned. Y.'s superb administrative abilities enabled the Mormons to survive and prosper in their western sanctuary. He married 27 wives, who bore him 56 children. His 27th wife filed suit for divorce and toured the nation denouncing polygamy. Y.'s theological views are elaborated in the 26 volumes of his *Journal of Discourses.* Contemporary Mormons venerate him as a prophet but may not share all his views on polygamy, plurality of gods, blood atonement, and other doctrines. See M. R. Werner, *B. Y.* (1925); R. B. West, Jr., *Kingdom of the Saints: The Story of B. Y. and the Mormons* (1957).

YOUNG MEN'S CHRISTIAN ASSOCIATION (YMCA), an interdenominational Protestant group, whose aim is to provide an opportunity for spiritual, physical, and educational development in a wholesome atmosphere. It was founded in London in 1844 by George Williams (1821–1905), then a 22-year-old clerk, in order to provide a center for young working men to hold Bible study classes and prayer meetings. The movement grew rapidly and spread to different parts of the British Empire. In 1850 the first North American branch was organized at Montreal. The following year the YMCA movement reached the U.S. with the formation of a branch at Boston by T. J. Sullivan. In 1852 other branches were established at Washington, D.C., New York City, Philadelphia, and other cities; the movement had also spread in continental Europe. In 1855 an international meeting at Paris unified the previously amorphous movement into a single worldwide organization.

One practical effect of the revival movement that spread through urban America, 1857–59, was a remarkable growth in the YMCA movement and the strong support for religious centers for city workers. Several outstanding young businessmen became full-time YMCA workers; among them were Dwight L. *Moody, who became secretary of the Chicago YMCA, John Wanamaker, secretary of the Philadelphia YMCA, and Robert R. McBurney, secretary of the New York City YMCA. James Mercer Garnett formed the first campus unit of the YMCA at the Univ. of Virginia in 1858. By 1868 there were more than 500 separate YMCA branches in the United States. R. R. McBurney is generally credited with the development in the 1860s and 1870s of the characteristic YMCA programs of gymnasiums, swimming pools, and athletic events. In the later 19th cent. the YMCA also became a center for courses in practical and academic subjects. Acceleration of this trend in the first quarter of the 20th cent. led to the founding of several institutions of higher learning that eventually broke off from the parent YMCA. Another longtime YMCA program has been the providing of inexpensive living and dining facilities for young men in urban centers.

Fundamental to the YMCA has been its religious program. The Association Press has been an important adjunct of this effort by publishing religious books of many types. As a non-denominational religious body, the YMCA has been a valuable auxiliary for Protestant missions in Africa, Asia, and Latin America. Only active members of an evangelical Protestant Church were eligible for YMCA membership under the rules adopted at Paris in 1855 and reaffirmed in 1914, but this rule was relaxed in the 1920s. Under the leadership of John R. *Mott, the YMCA Student Department of the U.S.A. played an important part in ecumenical concerns, particularly through the Student Christian Movement (see WORLD STUDENT CHRISTIAN FEDERATION). The ecumenical spirit of the YMCA contributed to the foundation of the World Council of Churches. In 1955 the YMCA had more than 4,000,000 members in all parts of the world. In 1968 there were some 5,200,000 members in the U.S., and 1,800 local branches. Local Ys are independent,

but in 34 nations they are associated in national councils; the movement worldwide is represented by a service agency, the World Alliance of the YMCA, with headquarters at Geneva, Switzerland. See C. H. Hopkins, *History of the YMCA in North America* (1951).

YOUNG WOMEN'S CHRISTIAN ASSOCIATION (YWCA), a nondenominational Protestant group, intended to provide a means for young Christian women and girls to develop a healthy spiritual, physical and moral outlook. It was formed, on the model of the *Young Men's Christian Association, in London in 1855 under the patronage of Lady Mary Kinnaird. In 1858 the movement spread to the U.S. with the formation of the first American YWCA in New York City by Mrs. Marshall O. Roberts, the wife of a steamship magnate. The earliest efforts of the YWCA closely followed the YMCA pattern, chiefly providing wholesome places of residence and recreation for young women working in urban centers. In 1894 the World's Young Women's Christian Association was formed to unite the movement internationally. It repeated the YMCA commitment to evangelical Protestantism and reiterated the same fundamental stance in its 1913 reorganization. It has worked closely with Protestant missionary efforts in many lands. In 1911 Frances Gage and Anna Welles, two Americans, developed a YWCA movement in the Ottoman Empire and the Balkan countries. The YWCA was also active in war relief and refugee efforts during both World Wars. In 1928 there was a serious division in the international movement on the question of admitting Roman Catholics to membership. Finland and South Africa withdrew their YWCAs at this juncture. In 1951 the YWCA made a complete commitment to ecumenism. The American and Latin American branches have been open to Catholics for 40 years, while a vigorous movement began in Italy and eastern Europe between the World Wars. In Scandinavia and Germany the YWCA is usually organized on a parish basis and works closely with the Churches. In 1968 there were some 4,000,000 members around the world and an estimated 2,200,000 in the U.S. See M. S. Sims, *YWCA: An Unfolding Purpose* (rev. ed., 1965).

ZINZENDORF, NICHOLAS LUDWIG VON (1700–60), Pietist leader and founder of the Renewed *Moravian Church. Count Zinzendorf, born into nobility at Dresden, was, by his father's early death, brought under the care of his maternal grandmother, a prominent Pietist. His precocious piety was deepened by 6 years at A. *Francke's preparatory school at Halle. Yielding to family pressure, he spent 3 years studying law at Wittenberg and in 1721 entered state service. His own choice would have been a career in the Church. Married to a woman who shared his religious interests, he opened his Dresden home to Pietist meetings. With inherited money he purchased an estate, including the village of Berthelsdorf, with a Lutheran church, near the home of his grandmother, and proceeded to build a manor house. His intention of making this estate a religious center was quickened by the arrival of refugees from Moravia seeking freedom to worship in the manner of their forefathers, the *Bohemian Brethren. They established their village of *Herrnhut in 1722, a mile from the village church. Attending the church for preaching services and the sacraments, they also held their own religious meetings at Herrnhut under the direction of the Count. Within a decade Herrnhut was a flourishing Pietist center with missionaries throughout the world and diaspora evangelists in the churches at home. Z. kept a tight rein on this development and soon left state service (1727). He was ordained a Lutheran clergyman in 1734 and received episcopal consecration from a Moravian bp. in 1737. During the years 1736–47 he was banished from Saxony for unorthodox religious activities. His travels extended his influence, and in that period he spent 14 months in America, where he took part in the Moravian settlement of Bethlehem, Pa., in 1741. Though he was free to return home in 1747, work in England, Holland, Switzerland, and W Germany kept him away. Only during the last 4 years of his life did he direct the Church from Herrnhut. He lived long enough to see as the fruit of his activities new life in state Churches all over Europe; Moravian Churches on the Continent, in England, and in America; and converts on the mission field from Greenland to Africa. It had been Z.'s intention that his society remain as a vivifying influence within the Lutheran Church; circumstances, esp. missionary development, led to the emergence of the separate Moravian Church. The Christ-centered theology of his many writings emphasize a deeply felt faith in the creator, savior, and preserver of all. This *Herzensreligion*, a religion of warmth and experience, influenced church life in Germany and, through its effect on F. *Schleiermacher, the subsequent course of theology. As an 18th-cent. hymn writer, Z. was second only to Charles *Wesley in the number of hymns composed. See J. R. Weinlick, *Count Z.* (1956).

ŽIŽKA, JOHN (*c.*1376–1404), Bohemian patriot, leader of the *Taborites. Z. was the military leader in the victories of the people of Prague during the first Hussite wars (1420–23) against the Emperor Sigismund and the crusades authorized by Pope Martin V. He was also one of the heads of the Taborite community and during 1423 successfully led it in the civil wars against *Utraquists and Catholics. See Bihlmeyer-Tüchle 2:442.

ZURICH CONSENSUS (*Consensus Tigurinus*), a document of agreement between Zwinglian and Calvinistic parties of the Reformed Church. Luther, who insisted that the body and blood of Christ were actually present in the bread and wine (see CONSUBSTANTIATION), condemned *Zwingli's doctrine of Christ's spiritual presence in the

Eucharist. Calvin tried to mediate between these positions with his concept of Christ's real spiritual presence for the elect who received the elements in faith. In 1549 he and G. *Farel worked out with H. *Bullinger a harmonizing statement in the *Consensus Tigurinus.* It maintains that in the Lord's Supper the body and blood of Christ are not received carnally, but that by the power of the Holy Spirit the elect receive Christ spiritually. See Schaff Creeds I:471–473.

ZWICKAU PROPHETS, agitators, esp. T. *Münzer and N. *Storch, who at Zwickau in Saxony preached a religion of inner inspiration and a chiliastic kingdom of God to be established by force. Expelled from Zwickau, they had some success in Wittenberg (1521–22), impressing Philipp *Melanchthon and converting *Karlstadt. The latter, along with the Prophets, had to flee before Luther's wrath when he returned to Wittenberg in March 1522.

ZWINGLI, HULDRYCH (Ulrich; 1484–1531), Swiss Reformer and patriot. Following humanistic studies at the Univ. of Basel, he was ordained at Constance in 1506 and sent to serve in the parish of Glarus. At that time he was affected by the three forces that formulated his theological thinking and his career: a series of sermons by Thomas Wyttenbach, who impressed him with the supremacy of the Scriptures in the life of the Christian; a chaplaincy with the Glarus mercenaries at Rome, where he became disillusioned with Roman liturgy as well as the mercenary system (he experienced the defeat of the Swiss at the Battle of Marignano in 1515); and an enlivened interest in the *New Learning, leading to his friendship with *Erasmus. He was removed from Glarus to a retreat in the monastery of Einsiedeln (1516) because of his strong opposition to sending Swiss mercenaries abroad. There he studied the Greek NT, the Fathers, and the *Enchiridion* of Erasmus. In 1518 he was chosen people's priest for the Great Minster at Zurich through the influence of his friend Oswald *Myconius, and

against the stern resistance of some who found fault with his love of music and with his life, which he admitted to be unchaste. His preaching was lauded, and in 1522 he published the *Archeteles* and the *Sixty-Seven Conclusions,* attacking church ceremonies and proposing radical reforms. In 1524 images were removed and the Mass abolished. In this year he announced his marriage to the widow, Anna Reinhard, to whom he had been secretly married for 2 years. In April 1525 the first celebration of the Lord's Supper according to Zwinglian principles was held in the cathedral. He brought about (1525) persecution of the Swiss Anabaptists who resented his alliance with the civil magistrates (see GREBEL, C.; MANZ, F.). In the intense civil warfare between Zurich and the Catholic cantons Zwingli was slain in the Battle of Kappel. Although in Switzerland the Reformation gradually become Calvinistic, Z. had great influence on Reformation theology. His theory of the Eucharist esp. continues to be accepted by many Churches.

In accord with the theological trend of the Reformers, Z.'s thought was basically bibliocentric, setting Scripture as the sole guide of belief. Thus he dismissed the need for an authoritative interpretation of the Bible outside individual religious experience. He taught further that faith was an internal implant, placed in the Christian by Christ and only indirectly stimulated by the external words of revelation. His own tendency to interpret the Scriptures rhetorically furthered the importance of subjective response. His theology was also primitivist in character, rejecting scholasticism and the elaborate liturgy that grew from the Middle Ages and reaching back to the simpler practices of the primitive Church, as indicated in the testimony of the Fathers. This interest in the Fathers was in part influenced by his contact with Erasmus and his writings. The religious belief of Zwingli in summary form was a revolt against the hierarchical structure of the Church and the preeminence of the bishop of Rome. To Z. the Church was a body both visible, embracing all members signed with baptism, and invisible, incorporating the elect of God. Its visible design, though admitting no hierarchy, did call for pastors, who were not only teachers of the word, but recipients of inspiration and charism. Its polity was congregational but with a strong reliance upon the lay authority (Council of the Canton) for cooperation in religious policies and for the enforcement of penalties for transgressions, including those meriting removal from the church community.

Z. acknowledged only baptism and the Eucharist as sacraments instituted by Christ. These, moreover, were not productive of grace when rightly performed and under conditions of proper intention but were mere tokens (*signa nuda*) of divine favor, like the rites of circumcision and the Passover ceremonies of the OT. His stand on the symbolic presence of Christ in the species of bread and wine became a promi-

nent theory in the sincere but fruitless attempts at doctrinal compromise among the Reformers. While Luther denied the Mass but affirmed a Real Presence in the Eucharist, Zwingli denied both, and Luther vehemently opposed this view (see MARBURG ARTICLES). Zwingli's theory of divine providence and predestination was fatalistic to an extreme. Man, since Adam's fall, is helpless to will what is good and, as the victim of sin, is completely at God's pity. God thus becomes an inexorable deity who has fixed the fate of men, foreordaining them to election or damnation. In this divine plan God is glorified in his goodness by the chosen, and in his justice by the reprobated. See G. W. Bromiley, ed., *Z. and Bullinger* (1953), a compilation including Z.'s *Exposition of the Faith*; J. V. Pollet, *H. Z. et la Réforme en Suisse* (1963); O. Farner, *Z. the Reformer* (tr. D. G. Sear, 1952).